3ds max™ 4

In Depth

Jon McFarland

Rob Polevoi

Publisher
Steve Sayre

Acquisitions Editor
Beth Kohler

Development Editor
Michelle Stroup

Product Marketing Manager
Patricia Davenport

Project Editor
Sally M. Scott

Technical Reviewer
John Evansco

Production Coordinator
Meg E. Turecek

Cover Designer
Jesse Dunn

Layout Designer
April E. Nielsen

CD-ROM Developer
Chris Nusbaum

3ds max™ 4 In Depth

The Coriolis Group, LLC
14455 N. Hayden Road
Suite 220
Scottsdale, Arizona 85260

(480)483-0192
FAX (480)483-0193
www.coriolis.com

Library of Congress Cataloging-In-Publication Data
McFarland, Jon.
3ds max 4 in depth / by Jon McFarland and Rob Polevoi.
p. cm
Includes index.
ISBN 1-57610-869-4
1. Computer animation. 2. Computer graphics. 3. 3ds Max 4 (Computer file) I. Polevoi, Rob.

TR897.7 .M39 2001
006.6'96--dc21 2001028384
CIP

Printed in the United States of America
10 9 8 7 6 5 4 3 2 1

A Note from Coriolis

Thank you for choosing this book from The Coriolis Group. Our graphics team strives to meet the needs of creative professionals such as yourself with our three distinctive series: *Visual Insight*, *f/x and Design*, and *In Depth*. We'd love to hear how we're doing in our quest to provide you with information on the latest and most innovative technologies in graphic design, 3D animation, and Web design. Do our books teach you what you want to know? Are the examples illustrative enough? Are there other topics you'd like to see us address?

Please contact us at the address below with your thoughts on this or any of our other books. Should you have any technical questions or concerns about this book, you can contact the Coriolis support team at **techsupport@coriolis.com**; be sure to include this book's title and ISBN, as well as your name, email address, or phone number.

Thank you for your interest in Coriolis books. We look forward to hearing from you.

Coriolis Creative Professionals Press
The Coriolis Group
14455 N. Hayden Road, Suite 220
Scottsdale, AZ 85260

Email: **cpp@coriolis.com**

Phone: (480) 483-0192
Toll free: (800) 410-0192

Visit our Web site at **creative.coriolis.com** *to find the latest information about our current and upcoming graphics books.*

Other Titles for the Creative Professional

Canoma Visual Insight
By Richard Schrand

Poser® 4 Pro Pack f/x and Design
By Richard Schrand

Bryce® 4 f/x and Design
By R. Shamms Mortier

Softimage®|XSI Character Animation f/x and Design
By Chris Maraffi

Character Animation with LightWave™[6]
By Doug Kelly

Digital Compositing In Depth
By Doug Kelly

To my sons, Zachary and Jacob.
—Jon McFarland

❧

About the Authors

Jon McFarland is the manager of the CAD department for Forest City Enterprises, a national developer/owner/manager of retail, office, residential, and entertainment complexes based in Cleveland, Ohio. His department's responsibilities include the creation of computer graphic stills and animations depicting proposed facilities and the incorporation of 3D models into photographs and videos. In addition, Jon teaches 3ds max to graphic arts students at The Virginia Marti College of Fashion and Art, a small accredited college in Lakewood, Ohio.

After high school, Jon spent seven years "blowin' stuff up" as a paratrooper in the U.S. Army. This naturally led to a career in computer graphics and animation. Jon has a degree in mechanical engineering technology, but he focuses his energy in the architectural visualization and animation fields.

He is committed to his family as well as to his work, educating his students and expanding his own capabilities in the computer-graphics realm.

Jon lives in Sheffield Lake, Ohio, and coaches baseball, soccer, and wrestling for his sons, Zachary and Jacob. He can be reached at any time at **jonmc@centurytel.net** with any questions, concerns, comments, or ideas.

Rob Polevoi is Director of Developer Relations, Education and Support at Eyematic Interfaces, Inc. Prior to his current position, he was a fulltime professor at Cogswell College in Sunnyvale (Silicon Valley), California, teaching 3D modeling and animation.

Rob has long covered the 3D graphics world in his 3D Animation Workshop web site at **www.webreference.com**. He was the author of *3D Studio MAX R3: In Depth* (Coriolis, 1999), and his most recent book is *Interactive Web Graphics with Shout3D* (2000).

Rob lives with his wife Andrea, and daughter, Hannah, in Oakland, California.

Acknowledgments

In the constantly evolving field of computer graphics, nothing drives invention as much as need. For that reason, I must voice my appreciation to my employer, Forest City Enterprises, for constantly feeding me challenges to overcome and for pushing my abilities to new extents. Without FCE, I wouldn't be where I am today. I would also like to thank the staff and students at The Virginia Marti College of Fashion and Art for the opportunity to teach and, at the same time, to learn.

At The Coriolis Group, I would like to thank Beth Kohler, my acquisitions editor, for giving me the opportunity to write the book; and Sally Scott, my project editor, for keeping me on track during the hectic production schedule. I'd also like to thank Meg Turecek, Michelle Stroup, Patti Davenport, Laura Wellander, April Nielsen, Chris Nusbaum, and Jesse Dunn.

Finally, in order, but not in precedence, I would like to thank my family for their support during the last few months. And especially to my sons, Zachary and Jacob, whose entrance into a room is all it takes to remind me of what is truly important.

—Jon McFarland

Contents at a Glance

Table of Contents

Introduction

3D graphics and animation is an exciting field that is populated by some of the most creative people around. It has made inroads into the fields of motion pictures, advertising, art, architectural visualization, prototyping, dynamics simulations, and game design and creation. New uses for 3D animation are continually being found, and the discipline is ever expanding—as is the need for qualified and competent 3D artists and modelers.

We had a single objective in mind when creating this book: To cover the required subjects in a clear and concise manner, thus providing a tool that would enable its readers to unleash their creativity and skills into a 3D environment. Necessarily, some topics are addressed in greater detail than others, which reflects the authors' desire to document those skills that provide the greatest benefit to the creation process. For example, much attention is focused on animation using function curves within the Track View panel; once you understand this process, it will help to bring your animations to life. On the other hand, considerably less is written here about the powerful but much-less-often-used method of creating mathematical expressions to control animation. To sum up, this book gives the greatest attention to the topics that will best add to the reader's arsenal of MAX knowledge. This book is designed to teach the skills required to work in the 3D environment and is not intended as a "cookbook" of effects to be created but not understood.

Who This Book Is For

This book is targeted at a wide range of 3ds max 4 users. Those who are teaching themselves the program are introduced to the topics that make MAX the best-selling 3D modeling and animation package. With teachers in mind, *3ds max 4 In Depth* has been laid out in a logical order, with concepts and tools clearly explained; this makes it an outstanding textbook. For experienced MAX users, those upgrading from 3D Studio MAX 3, and individuals migrating to MAX from other 3D programs, this book provides insight and background into MAX's capabilities, workflow, and toolset.

What Is "In Depth" about This Book

3ds max 4 is, necessarily, a deep and complex program providing its users with the tools required to create and output incredible 3D scenes. No single book can cover all the possible uses of every distinct tool and parameter available. The "Depth" of this text is in the approach to the important tools and concepts discussed within its pages. This book explains concepts, examines tools, and gives free reign to creativity in order to exploit the knowledge gained while completing the exercises. Computer graphics is an ever-evolving field, and, with every new release of major software and hardware products, the potential for even greater work is unrestricted. To remain competitive, 3D artists must take an "In Depth" approach to learning and developing their skills and understanding the related concepts.

How to Use This Book

This book is filled with exercises that teach the concepts and principles necessary to create outstanding static images and animations effectively. Many of the tools found in MAX have similar tools and parameters; when applicable, they are covered in the first instance only. A few exercises (the head model created with spline cages in Chapter 9 comes to mind) contain too many individual steps for each one to be described in detail. Doing so would also rob readers of the opportunity to exercise their creative input in completing the projects. In these occurrences, the foundation and framework is explained, and readers are free to complete the model to fit their specific tastes.

The book is designed to be a tool that teaches MAX from start to finish, and following the chapters in order will provide the clearest understanding of the program. Several concepts and tools introduced in early chapters are used in later chapters. If, however, you want to jump right into a specific topic, it is recommended that you at least complete the first four chapters in order to understand the very basics of how MAX works and how to navigate through the viewports.

3ds max 4 In Depth uses a common, logical convention to designate the path to a specific command or rollout. The instruction to "Create|Geometry|Standard Primitives|Box" indicates that the reader is to activate the Create tab of the Command panel, click on the Geometry button, ensure that Standard Primitives is the current choice in the drop-down list, and then click on the Box button. This may seem a bit cryptic at first, but MAX is laid out well, and this procedure will be second nature after just a few uses.

What's in the Book

3ds max 4 In Depth presents MAX in a logical order that follows the workflow and procedures used by modelers and animators every day. It teaches the fundamentals of the program, and it then moves on to cover more complex concepts. Each chapter lays the groundwork for a subject and then examines the nuances of related toolsets or procedures. This book is intended to provide information so that readers can grasp and understand the methods of creating, editing, adding materials to, rendering, and adding effects to simple and complex 3ds max scenes.

Here's a short synopsis of the contents:

Part I: The Big Picture

Chapter 1, "Introducing 3ds max 4," provides a brief history of MAX and the requirements needed to run the program. The concept of the parametric object and the 3ds max 4 interface is covered before the chapter jumps right into the heart of MAX by stepping through the basics of a typical project's workflow, from creation to rendering.

Chapter 2, "Using Primitives and Splines," focuses on the creation and editing of the standard and extended 3D and 2D parametric objects that are the building blocks of many modeling projects.

Part II: Working in MAX

Chapter 3, "Selection and Transform Tools," explains the many tools available to select, transform, and control the objects in a scene. This chapter presents a thorough knowledge of, and comfortable approach to the use of, the toolsets that allow for the movement, relocation, and scaling of a scene's objects, groups, and selection sets.

Chapter 4, "Managing the Display," provides the basic knowledge for controlling the display of individual objects in a MAX scene as well as the scene as a whole. Topics include the new manipulation capabilities of the 3ds max 4 viewports, hiding and freezing objects, viewport selection, and navigation and layout options.

Chapter 5, "Working Smart," focuses on the tools that allow for a faster and more efficient workflow by eliminating redundant steps is the modeling process. Topics include clones, mirroring and aligning objects, and using MAX's indispensable snap tools. Also covered are the Tape and Protractor helper objects, keyboard shortcuts, and the new wiring capability in which the parameters of one object can be linked to those of another object.

Part III: Modeling

Chapter 6, "Modeling with Modifiers," concentrates on the many modifiers provided with MAX that are applicable to the modeling process. These include the basic modifiers that alter an object along a specific axis, modifiers that add randomness to an object, and modifiers that add control over the polygon count and density of an object.

Chapter 7, "Mesh-Level Modeling," limits its focus to the manipulation of the individual components (vertices, edges, faces, polygons, and elements) of mesh, or nonparametric, objects. Special consideration is given to the use of mesh-level modeling in the creation of low polygon models suitable for game design.

Chapter 8, "Compound Objects," examines the creation of single, complex objects through the compositing of two or more simpler objects. Of note are the use of Boolean operations to union or subtract the components of splines or mesh objects, and the use of splines to create impressive lofted objects.

Chapter 9, "Patch Modeling," walks the reader through exercises showcasing the use of MAX's exciting patch-modeling toolset and the use of spline cages to build impressive, organic models. The tools discussed in this chapter are especially well suited to the field of character modeling.

Chapter 10, "NURBS Modeling," introduces one of the more sophisticated elements of the 3ds max 4 toolset. Included are explanations of how to create and adjust surfaces from Non-Uniform Rational B-Splines (NURBS) as well as extracting the splines from the NURBS surfaces.

Part IV: Materials and Textures

Chapter 11, "Materials and the Materials Editor," explains the concept of a material in 3D graphics and the adjustable parameters that are used to determine a Material's appearance in MAX and, therefore, the appearance of the surfaces to which the Material is applied. Several exercises are provided to work through many of the elements that make MAX's Material Editor a very powerful tool.

Chapter 12, "Maps and Mapping," covers the use of image files as components to Materials. Included are the topics of assigning and adjusting an object's mapping coordinates, procedural materials, applying multiple materials to a single object and achieving true reflections through the use of a Flat Mirror map.

Part V: Lights, Camera, Render!

Chapter 13, "Lights," explains the differences found between the lighting of a physical scene and the lighting of a computer-generated scene. This chapter includes exercises that demonstrate the methods of lighting a scene effectively, setting the parameters for the five possible light types, adjusting attenuation, selecting objects for exclusion from the light source, and selecting applicable shadow types.

Chapter 14, "Cameras," examines the use of the Camera objects and their use in viewing the elements of a scene. Addressed are the parameters that adjust the field-of-view, clipping plane, and Camera viewport specific navigation tools. Exercises are provided that cover matching a virtual camera to the camera that took a specific photograph, as well as the new Motion Blur and Field Of View tools that are now available.

Chapter 15, "Rendering Tools," covers the necessary tools for rendering MAX scenes into static images and animation files. Covered are the Virtual Frame Buffer, use of Production and Draft renderers, and the new ActiveShade tool. Exercises demonstrate the new Render Elements capabilities that allow the rendering of shadows and other scene information as separate image files.

Chapter 16, "Environment and Render Effects," showcases MAX's tools that add pleasing visual effects to a scene using means other than the manipulation of geometry. The Render Effects toolset allows for Glow, Star, Fire Effect, and other post-processing features to be added to a MAX scene. Atmospheric effects including Fog, Volumetric Fog, Volumetric Lights, and Fire Effects are also discussed.

Part VI: Animation

Chapter 17, "Animation Essentials," introduces the basic concepts of animation in 3ds max 4, including creating and editing animation keys and the use of the Track Bar. The chapter focuses special attention on the Track View and the use of function curves to determine an object's animation.

Chapter 18, "Animating the Transforms," covers the subjects that are at the heart of animation. Exercises are provided that demonstrate the application of different animation controllers and the use of Inverse Kinematics to control the components of a complex, jointed model.

Chapter 19, "Deforming the Geometry," focuses on the fundamental tools for character animation, which are included in the standard 3ds max 4 toolset. The Morpher modifier and path and surface deformation are covered, with special attention focused on the skinning and bending of a leg based on the movement of the assigned Bone structure.

Chapter 20, "Special Animation Topics," is a chapter that covers the animation features that do not fit into the other animation chapters. This chapter provides exercises on particle systems, space warps, dynamics simulations, and the use of mathematical expressions to control the animation of objects.

Chapter 21, "Using Video Post," introduces the Video Post capabilities in some of its more useful applications. The chapter also discusses the concept of the Video Post Queue and its use for editing animated sequences together, adding filter effects, and adding fades and dissolves to terminate sequences and cuts between cameras.

The CD-ROM

The CD-ROM contains all of the files necessary to complete the exercises, as well as selected projects in progress and final states.

Other Resources

The Internet has opened a wide array of sources for information about 3ds max; some are better than others. The following are a few sites that are indispensable in learning more about the program. The home page for Discreet, and the starting point for information relating to any of their existing products, is **http://www2.discreet.com/**. The site containing the 3ds max discussion forums, **http://support.discreet.com:8080/~max/login**, is where you can ask, or answer, questions related to the program. The home of 3D Café, **http://www.3dcafe.com**, is a site dedicated to all facets of 3D modeling. 3ds max 4 is a program with many tools and capabilities, but users will always need additional power and project-specific techniques and abilities. The Discreet-preferred distributor for plug ins—programs that add to MAX's functionality—is Digimation; they can be reached at **www.digimation.com**.

Part I

The Big Picture

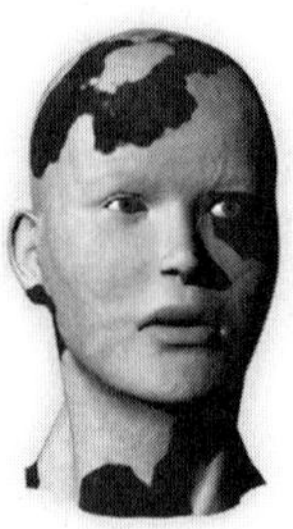

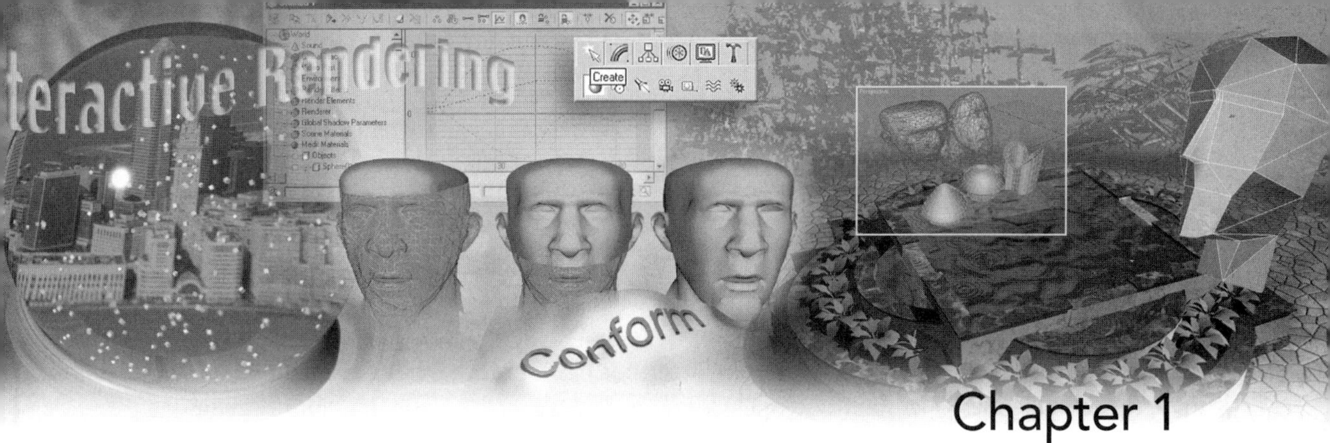

Chapter 1

Introducing 3ds max 4

3ds max 4 is a computer modeling and graphics package that can be used to create outstanding images and animations. Its toolset and workflow are powerful and unique, yet easy to learn and, with time and practice, to master.

MAX, as the program is referred to, requires you to think your project through before beginning it, in order to exploit the toolset to its fullest potential. When you understand the principles behind how MAX operates, and the tools available to you, you'll be able to craft your workflow to maximize the potential of the program. MAX is a program with an incredible amount of depth, but it is put together logically; thus, the learning process is easier than you might expect.

How MAX Developed

Although this is 3ds max 4, it is the eighth major release of the program. Developed by the Autodesk Multimedia Group, the program, initially called 3D Studio, was one of the last strong DOS applications. It consisted of five modules: the 3D Editor, Shaper, Lofter, Material Editor, and Key Framer. Each had its own thinly defined responsibilities and tools, and only one could be active at a time. Rudimentary by today's standards, 3D Studio put computer modeling on desktops; its functionality rivaled that of software used in major production houses (which sometimes cost hundreds of thousands of dollars), and it opened the industry to the masses. There were four releases of 3D Studio.

With the Windows environment quickly becoming the standard, 3D Studio held its ground as a DOS program. Developers felt that the standard Windows, with its own resource requirements and 16-bit programming, could not adequately handle the tasks MAX would require. The

Autodesk Multimedia Group was spun off as a separate company called Kinetix. Seeing the shift to the Windows operating system as inevitable, Kinetix made the jump to the Windows NT environment—its 32-bit programming, multitasking capability, and multiple processor support were more able to handle MAX's requirements. The program, now named 3D Studio MAX, had an entirely new interface. Gone were the restrictive modules; they were replaced by an environment in which all the tools were accessible at all times. Although it required most users to change their operating system, it was a major advance in capabilities and workflow and well worth the switch. Eventually, MAX added the capability of running under Windows 95, but this version suffered from a somewhat significant performance and reliability decline. There were three major releases of 3D Studio MAX.

In early 2000, Kinetix purchased Discreet, a Canadian company that produces high-end video editing and compositing packages, and took the Discreet name as its own. With the company's name change came a name change for Kinetix's flagship program: 3D Studio MAX became 3ds max 4. It is one of the most popular modeling and animation packages available.

System Requirements

MAX is a large program capable of performing many tasks unheard of just a few years ago; yet the system requirements to run it are well below those found in off-the-shelf computers. Be advised, though, that the requirements listed are the minimums needed to run the program—very large or complex scenes may require additional resources to enable you to manipulate them effectively:

- *Operating system*—MAX is designed to run optimally under Windows 2000. Windows 98 is also supported. Although Windows NT is not supported, MAX will also run under it; this capability is more for compatibility with existing systems than performance, however. A 300MB Windows swap file is required, but the swap file should generally be three times the size of the available RAM.
- *Processor and RAM*—You will need a 300MHz Intel (or compatible) processor. Windows 2000 and NT allow the use of multiple processors, and MAX will take advantage of them if present. 128MB RAM is the minimum, but, as with the processor, more is always better. If you must decide where to dedicate the funds for a system, your performance will benefit most by addressing the processor(s) and RAM.
- *Display and hard drive*—A resolution of 1024×768 running in High Color is acceptable, but 1280×1024 running in True Color is recommended. The hard drive space required varies, depending on the components installed, but you can expect to use about 400MB of space. This book uses the core components of MAX; therefore, the Software Development Kit (SDK) is not required. The 3ds max tutorials are also not required for this book, but they do offer an excellent source for MAX instruction.
- *Network*—To take advantage of MAX's network rendering capabilities (Windows 2000 and NT only), a TCP/IP network is required.

- *Internet Explorer and QuickTime*—To authorize MAX online and to access the online help, Internet Explorer 5 (or later) is required. To run the QuickTime plug-in, QuickTime 4.1.2 must be installed. Both Internet Explorer and QuickTime are available on the 3ds max 4 program CD-ROM.
- *Other requirements*—Most of the remaining requirements are standard on today's systems: a sound card and speakers if audio is added to a scene, a CD-ROM to install the software and access files not initially installed, and a Windows-compatible pointing device. 3ds max 4 is optimized to take advantage of the Windows Intellimouse, and, in some situations, a pad and stylus are preferable.

Objects and Parametrics

The basic element in MAX is the object. An *object* is any single element in a scene. It can be a 2D object, 3D object, Helper object, Light, Camera, or anything else that can be created in MAX. Once an object is created, it becomes a member of the current *scene*.

Below the object level, most objects are composed of subobjects. 3D objects are compositions of vertices, edges, faces, polygons, and, sometimes, elements. 2D objects can be broken down to their vertices, segments, and splines. These subobjects are, themselves, editable to change the appearance or functionality of the object.

In computer modeling terminology, a basic, common object that an application can create is called a *primitive*. In MAX, primitives can be either 3D (Boxes, Cones, Spheres, and so on) or 2D (Rectangles, Lines, Circles, and so on) and, in most cases, the primitives are *parametric*. A parametric object is one whose parameters (that is, defining information) are adjustable without the need to adjust the location of its subobjects manually. For example: What information is necessary to define a box-shaped object? In the real world, you'd need its length, width, and height. This holds true for MAX's Box primitive as well, with the additional parameters that control its *segmentation* (number of cross sections it is broken down into in any one direction). The color or Material assigned to the Box is also parametric (color can be broken down and adjusted at its red, green, and blue [RGB] component level), as are any modifiers that are applied to the Box. To change a non-parametric box-shaped object from 2 units to 5 units in height, you would need to move the top two vertices 3 units away from the base. For a parametric Box object, you would only need to enter "5" in the Height parameter field to see the effect reflected in the object. The parametric characteristic of most primitives is a core feature in all 3D applications and a fantastic time-saver. Imagine trying to change the radius of a Sphere by manually relocating the individual vertices.

Getting Started

3ds max 4 is a large program that provides its users with tools that allow them to create outstanding images and animations. Surprisingly, the interface, workflow, and toolset are easy to learn, as you'll see in the following sections.

The Interface

The default MAX interface, shown in Figure 1.1, consists of several specific elements used to access the features in MAX.

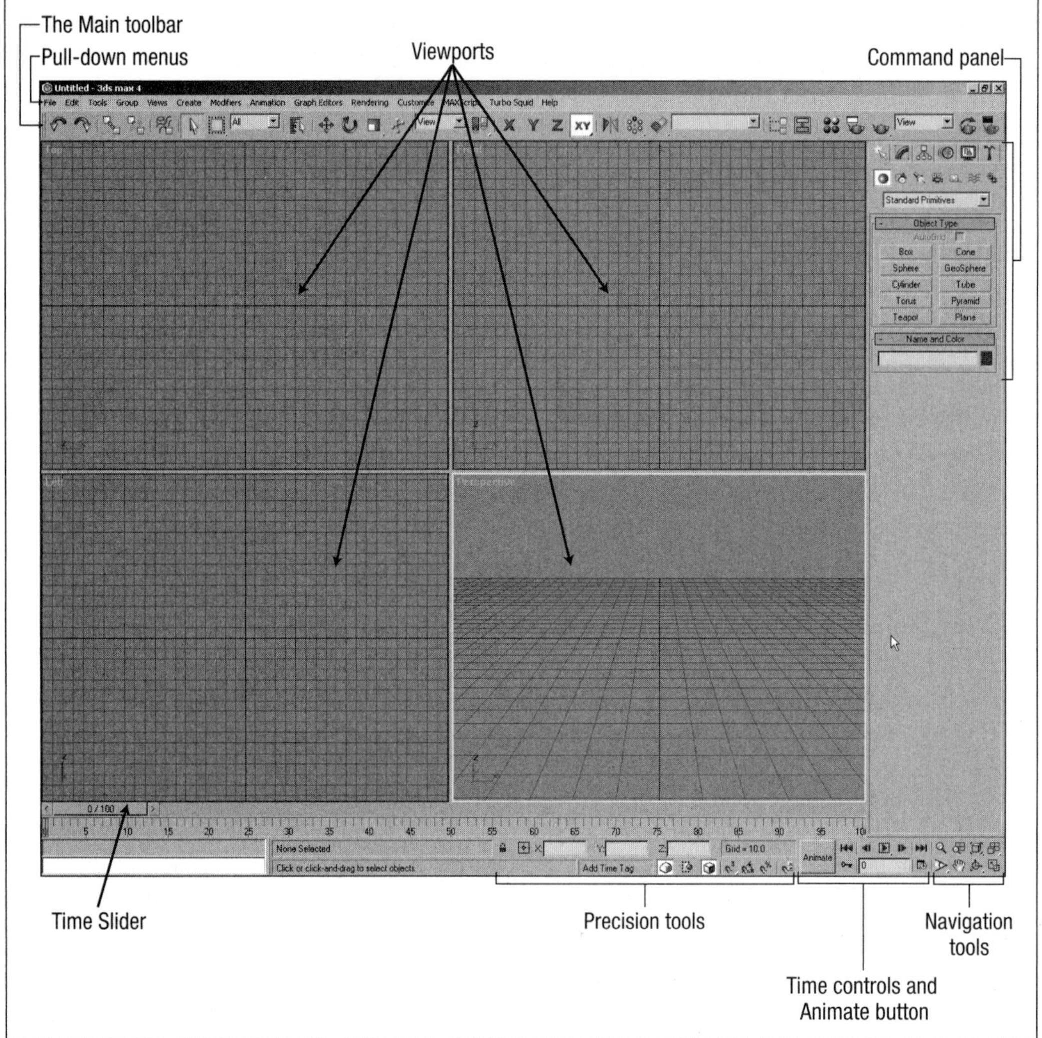

Figure 1.1
The default 3ds max 4 interface.

The Pull-Down Menus

Across the top of the window, just below the title bar, are the pull-down menus—also referred to as drop-down menus. In most cases, MAX provides several ways to access its commands or features, allowing users to customize their workflow practices; the pull-down menu is one of these ways. As in any standard Windows program, clicking on a menu name expands the menu into the workspace. Menu items that lead to additional menus are indicated by a triangular arrow, as shown in Figure 1.2. Items that open dialog boxes are indicated by an ellipsis (three dots) and, if they exist, predefined keyboard shortcuts are listed to the right.

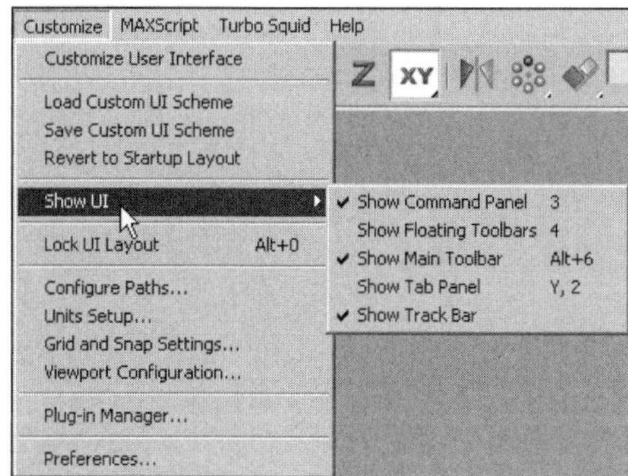

Figure 1.2
The expanded Customize pull-down menu shows the features of MAX's pull-down menus.

The Main Toolbar

Directly below the pull-down menus is the Main toolbar. Each group of icons is separated by a short, vertical line to indicate the logical division of features. Pause your cursor over any of the icons and a flyout appears, indicating the icon's name. Pull-down lists are available to specify parameters for the tools around them. Many of the features used in this book will be accessed from the Main toolbar.

The Command Panel

To the right of the MAX window is the Command panel; this is where this book will indicate the locations for access to most of MAX's tools. The top row of icons refers to the tabs that define, like everything else in the Command panel, the items below them. From left to right, the tabs are Create, Modify, Hierarchy, Motion, Display, and Utilities; their purposes are self-explanatory. Figure 1.3 shows the Common panel with the default Create tab selected.

The Create tab is different from the others in that it determines future objects, whereas the rest alter existing ones. Below the Create tab is a row of icons that determines the family of object to be created; below that, a drop-down list further defines that family. Beneath the drop-down list is the field that contains vertical menus, called *rollouts*, that are the heart of the MAX interface. You open or close a rollout by clicking on its name. Many panels have extensive rollouts, so it's prohibitive to keep them in a constantly expanded state. In Figure 1.3 only two rollouts—Object Type and Name And Color—are present, so you don't need to expand or contract them.

Viewports

The heart of the MAX interface is the viewport area. By default, four equal viewports are present, but as few as one can be displayed at a time. The name of each viewport is displayed in the viewport's upper-right corner; right-clicking on this name opens a viewport control

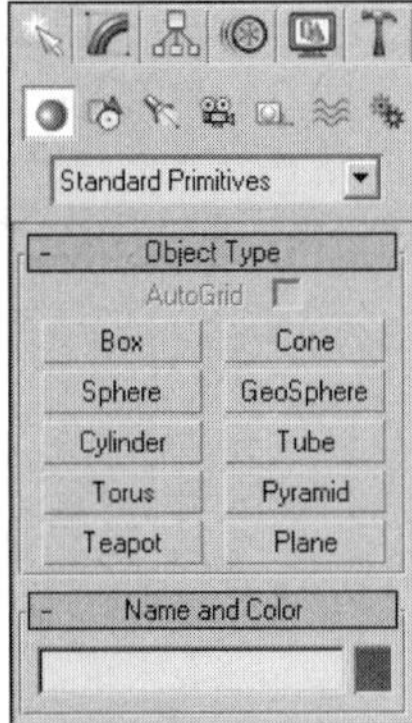

Figure 1.3
The default appearance for the Create tab of the Command panel.

menu. 3ds max 4 has greatly increased users' ability to customize the size and shape of the viewports over the program's previous version.

Navigation Tools

Figure 1.4 shows the eight viewport navigation tools found at the bottom-right corner of the MAX window. These tools, which are used with orthographic viewports, customize themselves to the type of viewport that is active.

Figure 1.4
The viewport navigation tools.

Time Controls and Animate Button

Figure 1.5 shows, to the right, the scene's time controls. Here, animations are played and stepped through, and the scene's time parameters (length, frames per second, and so on) are determined.

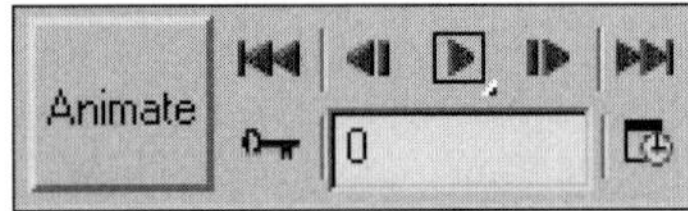

Figure 1.5
The time controls and Animate button.

To the left of the time controls is the Animate button, which controls when an action in the MAX interface is static or relative to a prior condition.

Snaps and Transform Type-Ins

Figure 1.6 shows several of MAX's precision tools. The fields in the top row are the Transform Type-Ins where you can enter specific or relative object locations, rotations, and scales, rather than adjusting them in the viewports.

Figure 1.6
Several of the precision tools found in MAX.

The lower row shows, to the right, the *snaps* (features that allow adjustment relative to existing scene elements) and, to the left, tools that control the use of shortcuts, selection methods, and snap use.

The Tab Panels

3D Studio MAX 3 introduced the Tab panels, a row of icon-driven tab menus for accessing MAX's tools. In 3ds max 4, these panels are no longer the default, and this book does not use them; however, you can display them by choosing Customize|Show UI|Show Tab Panel from the pull-down menu.

Creating Primitive Objects

Creating and adjusting objects in MAX is one of the basic tasks that is easy to learn and quick to master. The steps here will be addressed in greater detail in future chapters. Follow these steps to create a simple scene consisting of 3D primitive objects:

1. In the Command panel, make sure that the Create tab is active. The Geometry button, in the row of tools below the tabs, should be active as well, and Standard Primitives should appear in the drop-down list.

2. In the Object Type rollout, click on the Sphere button. It turns yellow to indicate that it is active, and it will remain active until another object or action is selected.

3. In the Top viewport, click and hold the mouse button (whenever a specific mouse button is not indicated, assume it to be the left button) and drag to change the Sphere's radius. Release the mouse to set the radius. Your Perspective viewport should look similar to Figure 1.7.

4. Three additional rollouts have been added to the Create panel. The bottom rollout, Parameters, determines the settings for the Sphere that was just created. To change the Sphere's radius to a specific value, type a new value in the Radius field of the Parameters rollout. To change the radius without a specific target value, click, click and hold, or click and drag on the up or down spinner button to the right of the Radius value. Try at least one of these methods. Be aware that clicking in the viewports will begin the creation process for a second Sphere.

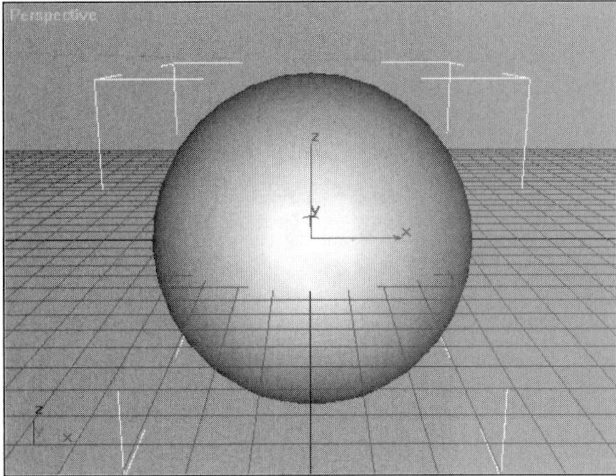

Figure 1.7
The Perspective viewport after creating a Sphere primitive.

5. Expand the drop-down list and choose Extended Primitives. In the new Object Type rollout, choose Capsule.

6. In the Top viewport, click-drag-release above the Sphere to set the Capsule's radius (just as you did with the Sphere). Move the cursor upward and click to set the Capsule's height.

7. In the Main toolbar, click on the Select Object button (sixth from the left) and then click on any blank space in the viewport to deselect the Capsule. This action clears the Create panel of the rollout that controlled the Capsule's parameters. To access that rollout once more, use the Select Object tool to click on the Capsule, which turns white to indicate its selected status.

8. With the Capsule selected, click on the Modify tab of the Command panel to reveal the Parameters rollout. Increase the number of Height Segments from 1 to 10 and watch as the number of cross sections between the curved ends increases.

9. To get a better look at the Capsule, click on the Select And Move button in the Main toolbar and position the cursor over the Capsule in the Top viewport. Click and hold the mouse and drag the Capsule to relocate it to the right of the Sphere. Right-click in the Perspective viewport (right-clicking allows you to change viewports without deselecting objects). A yellow border around the Perspective viewport indicates that it is now active. To fit the objects within the boundaries of the viewport, choose Zoom Extents from the top row of navigation tools. Pause your cursor over the icons until you find the appropriate one. Crisply click and release to initiate the command; holding down the button will cause additional options to appear. Your Perspective viewport should look similar to Figure 1.8.

10. MAX maintains a history of the modifications made to the scene in the current session. To relocate the Capsule to its former location, click once on the Undo button in the Main toolbar. To move it back to the location next to the Sphere, click once on the Redo button. To move further back in the scene's history, right-click on the Undo button to open a

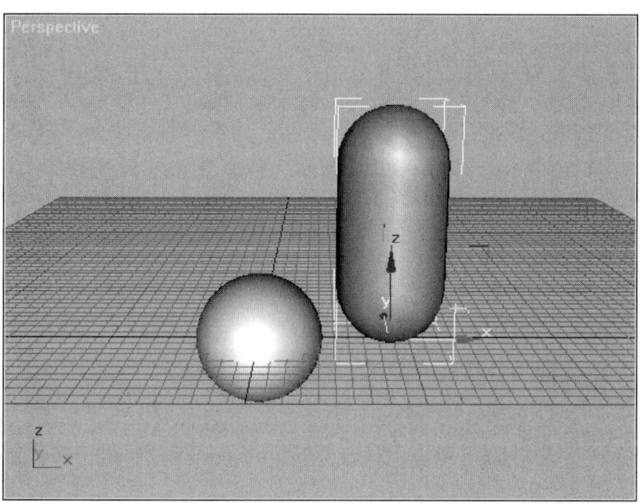

Figure 1.8
The Perspective viewport showing the Sphere and Capsule that have been created.

history list; then click on the action at the point you want to return to. For this exercise, leave the Capsule next to the Sphere.

Adding a Modifier

Primitive objects are often altered through the use of modifiers, as shown in this continuation of the exercise. Follow these steps:

1. With the Capsule still selected and the Modify panel open, click on the downward-pointing arrow to expand the Modifier List. In the Parametric Modifiers area, choose Bend.
2. A Parameters rollout is present in the Modify panel, but it is different from the previous one. This is the Parameters rollout for the Bend modifier, not for the Capsule itself. Enter "–90" in the Angle field and press the Enter key to add a 90-degree bend, from right to left, along the height of the Capsule. Your scene should look like Figure 1.9.
3. Like most other features in MAX, the Modifiers are parametric and can be adjusted as required. Experiment with the other settings in the Parameters rollout; then, return them to their current state.
4. To copy the Capsule, hold down the Shift key and move it to the left of the Sphere. The shift key causes a copy (or *clone*, as MAX calls it) to be created. Release the mouse when an acceptable location is reached. Click on OK to accept the default settings in the resulting dialog box.
5. With the new Capsule selected, click once on the Mirror Selected Objects button near the middle of the Main toolbar. Again, click on OK to accept the defaults. Perform a Zoom Extents to fit the new configuration into the Perspective viewport. Your scene should look like Figure 1.10.

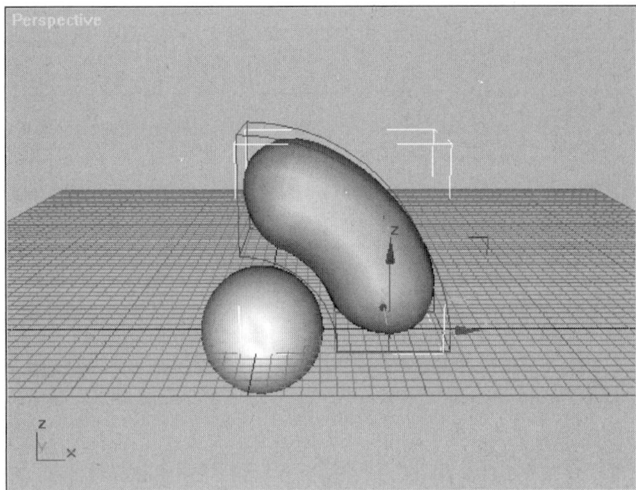

Figure 1.9
The same as Figure 1.8, with a Bend modifier applied to the Capsule.

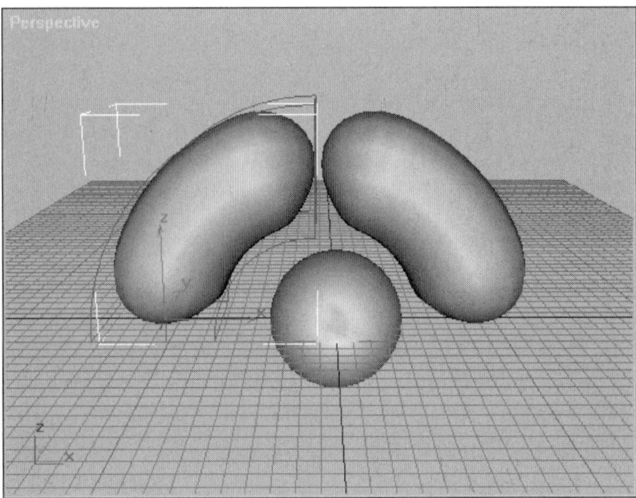

Figure 1.10
The scene from Figure 1.9, after the Capsule has been cloned and mirrored.

Adding Materials

The scene thus far is very plain. The objects have color to distinguish them from one another and the background and to give definition to the shapes, but they have no real material that would make them look realistic or pleasing. Continue with the exercise to add materials to the objects that you've created:

1. From the right side of the Main toolbar, click on the Material Editor button to open the Material Editor shown in Figure 1.11. Select the upper-left sample slot by clicking on the sphere inside it to make it active. Any changes to the material will be reflected in this slot.

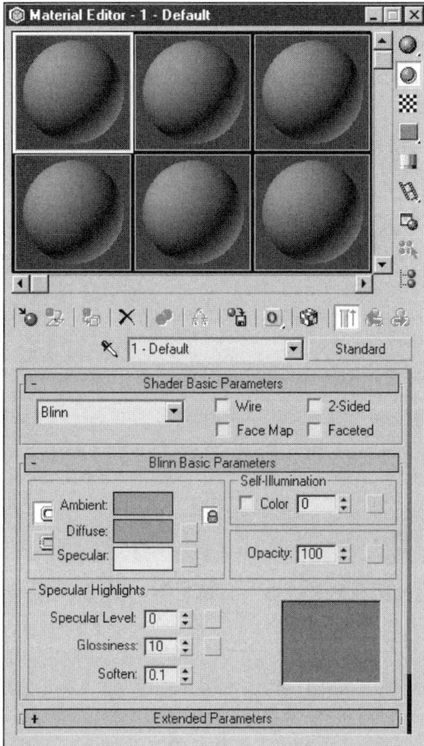

Figure 1.11
The Material Editor with its default settings.

2. From the row of icons below the six Material slots, choose the left-most icon labeled Get Material to open the Material/Map Browser dialog box shown in Figure 1.12. This is where you determine the type of Material to be created. In the Browse From section, select Mtl Library. Scroll down the list of Materials that appears in the field to the right until you see the entry Bricks_Bricks_1 (Standard). Click on it one time to see a sample in the preview window. Double-click on the list entry to copy the Material from the material library to the active slot in the Material Editor.

3. In a viewport, make sure the second Capsule is selected. In the Material Editor, click on the Assign Material To Selected button from the row of icons. The object in the shaded Perspective viewport takes on the appearance of the Material assigned to it.

4. Activate the second slot in the Material Editor and place the Metal_Rust (Standard) Material into it. Assign this Material to the Sphere.

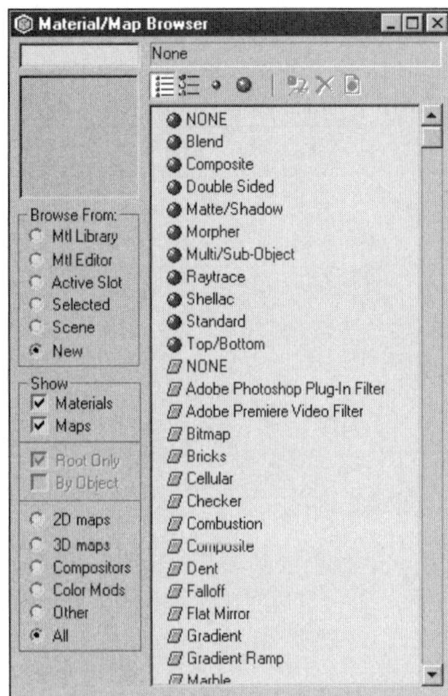

Figure 1.12
The Material/Map Browser dialog box.

5. Activate the third slot in the Material Editor. In the Blinn Basic Parameters rollout, click on the gray color swatch next to the word Diffuse to open the Color Selector shown in Figure 1.13. Enter "200", "30", and "180" in the Red, Green, and Blue fields, respectively, to make a dark magenta color. Close the Color Selector and assign the Material to the first Capsule.

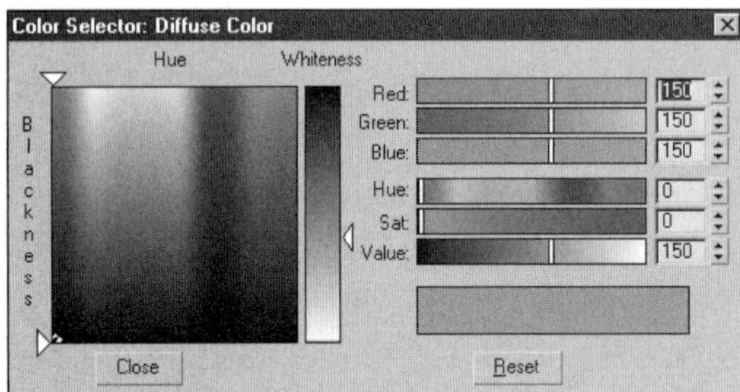

Figure 1.13
The Color Selector found in many locations throughout MAX.

Animating the Scene

Static scenes are fine and have many useful applications, but animation is one of the most powerful features of 3ds max. Nearly every object or parameter found in the program can be adjusted over time. Whenever you look into a viewport, you are looking at the scene at a specific point in time. Altering the conditions over time is the fundamental concept of computer animation. To see some of the basic steps in animation, continue the exercise by following these steps:

1. Below the viewports is the Time Slider, which controls which frame is the current frame displayed in the viewports. Click and drag to move the Time Slider to the right until it reads 50/100, indicating that the current frame is number 50 out of a total of 100 frames.
2. Select the Capsule to the left and click on the Modify tab to edit the parameters of the Capsule's Bend modifier. Simply changing the values at this point will not result in the values being animated. You must first activate the large Animate button at the bottom of the screen. Click on the Animate button; it, as well as exposed areas of the Time Slider, turn red to indicate the animation status. Change the Angle value from –90 to 90.
3. Select the Sphere and change its radius to about half its current value. Change the Hemisphere value to 0.5. Move the Sphere toward the bottom of the Perspective viewport.
4. Open the Material Editor and notice the red border around the active slot containing the magenta Material assigned to the right Capsule. In the Blinn Basic Parameters rollout, change the Opacity value from 100 to 50 and note that the color swatch appears to darken as the black background now shows through the 50 percent opaque Material. Close the Material Editor.
5. Turn off the Animate button. Your scene should look like Figure 1.14.

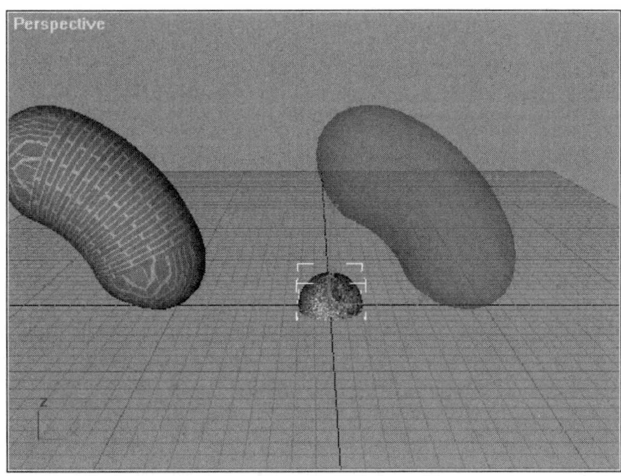

Figure 1.14
The scene at Frame 50 after several of the objects' parameters have been animated.

6. Click on the Play Animation button in the time controls area. For a moment, it appears that nothing has happened. This is the case because the animation is being played from Frame 51 to 100 first, where no parameters have been altered, before cycling through Frames 0 to 50. Click on the Play Animation button again to stop the animation.

7. Let's adjust the animation a bit. From the right side of the Main toolbar, click on the Open Track View button. The Track View panel, as shown in Figure 1.15, displays a linear representation of every animatable parameter in a scene. The black bars that begin and end at Frames 0 and 50 indicate the range of the animation in the scene.

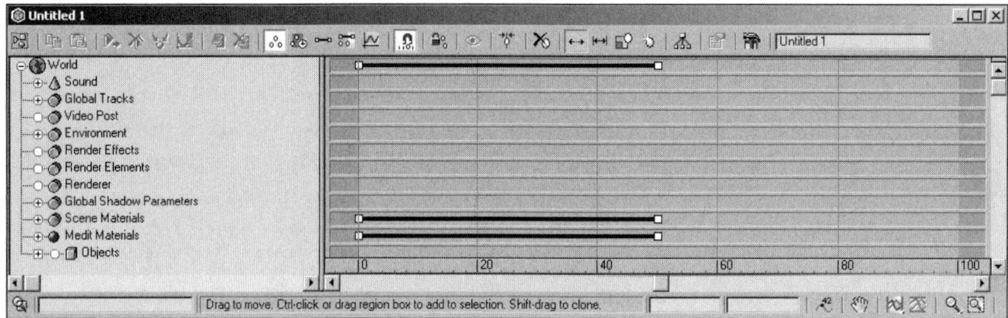

Figure 1.15
The Track View panel showing the animation range for the scene shown in Figure 1.14.

8. In the left side of the Track View panel, click on the plus symbol next to the Objects entry to expand it and to see a list of the objects in the scene. Click to expand the Capsule02 entry, and then its Modified Object and Bend tracks. Select the Angle track (the word, not the green arrow) to select and highlight the track. Your Track View panel should look like Figure 1.16.

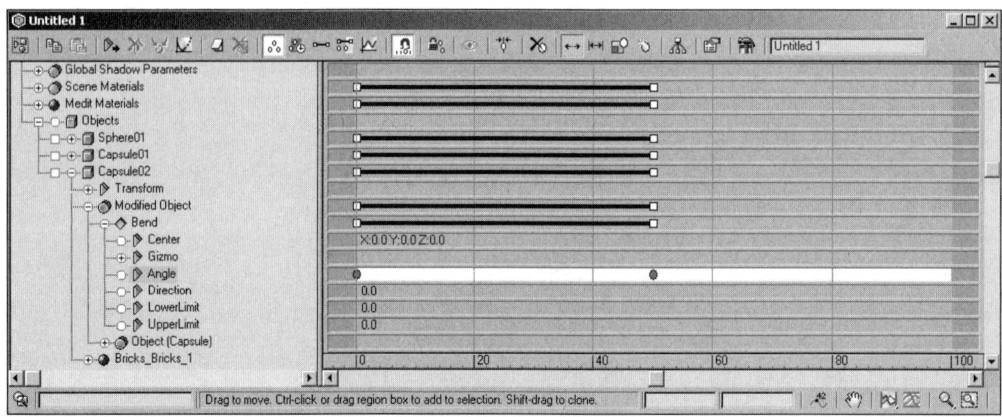

Figure 1.16
The Track View panel with several of the tracks expanded and the Capsule02 object's Angle track highlighted.

9. The gray circles represent the frames where the animation has been defined. Frame 0 is the starting point, when the Bend modifier's Angle value is set to –90, and the animation terminates at Frame 50 (Angle = 90). This may be easier to understand in a graph type of view rather than a linear one. From the middle of the Track View's upper toolbar, choose Function Curves. The Track View panel changes to look like Figure 1.17.

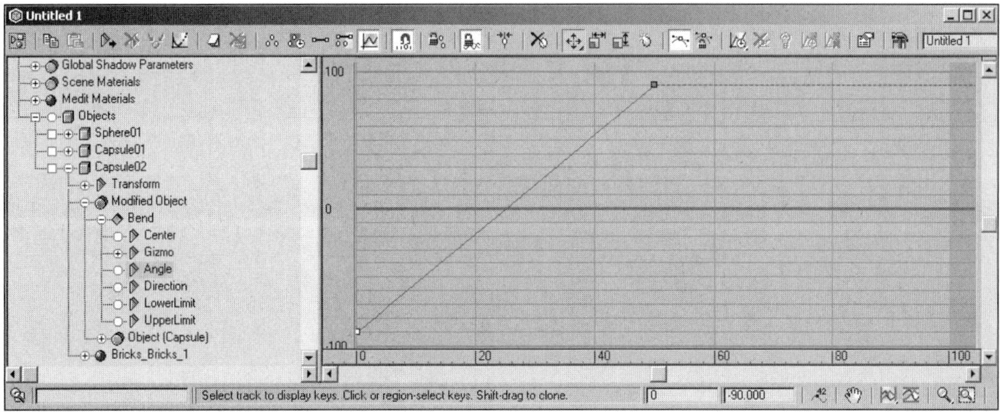

Figure 1.17
The Track View panel from Figure 1.16 using a Function Curves view.

10. Don't be intimidated by the graph; it's actually quite straightforward. The numbers along the bottom of the right panel indicate the frames, and the numbers along the left side indicate the highlighted parameter's value. This graph shows a key at Frame 0 with a value of –90 and a key at Frame 50 with a value of 90. The straight line between the keys shows that the transition from –90 to 90 is constant. Click on the Move Keys button in the Track View toolbar, and then click and drag the key at Frame 50 to Frame 100 as shown in Figure 1.18. Play the animation and you'll see that the Capsule now takes the full 100 frames to transition between the keys.

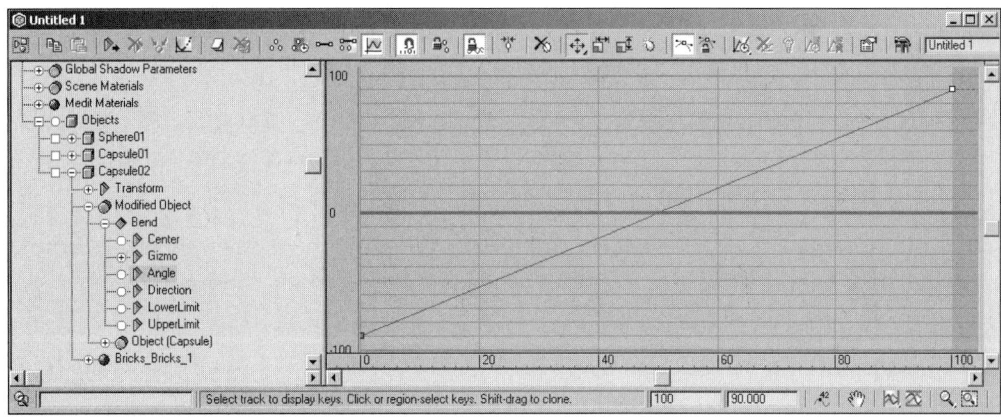

Figure 1.18
The Track View panel from Figure 1.17 with the second key moved to Frame 100.

11. To alter the shape of the curve, and, therefore, the rate of change in the animation, click on the Add Keys button and then click on the diagonal animation line at about Frame 60 to add a key at that point. Use the Move Keys tool to move the new key up until it is even with the horizontal line, indicating a value of 90. Your Track View should look like Figure 1.19.

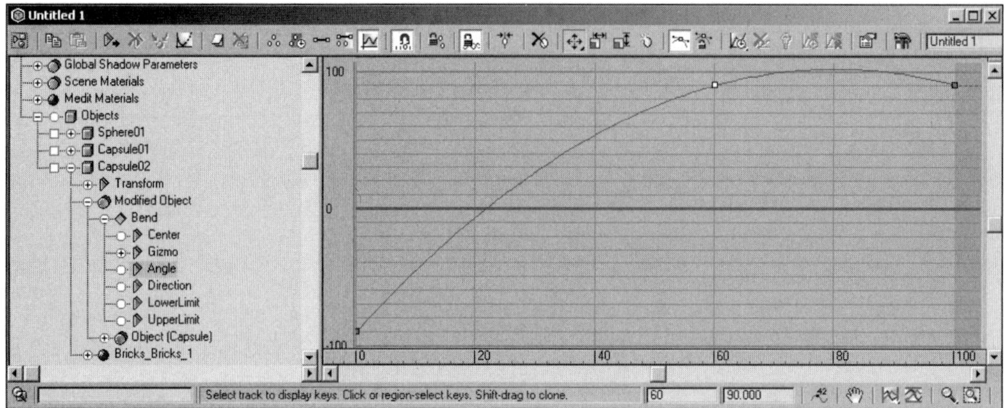

Figure 1.19
The Track View panel from Figure 1.18 with a third key added at Frame 60 and moved to a value of 90.

12. Before you play the animation, think about how the action of the second Capsule should react. At Frame 0, the angle is set to –90. By Frame 60, it has increased to 90 degrees; it climbs to about 101 degrees at Frame 80. At Frame 100, the angle has backed down to 90 degrees. Play the animation and watch both the viewport and the Track View panel to understand how the animation of the Bend modifier's Angle parameter is applied.

Rendering

Seeing images and animations in the viewports is fine for the purpose of creating the scene, but the goal is always to render the scene out to an image or animation file. Continue with the exercise to see how this is done:

1. Close the Track View panel. Make sure the Perspective viewport is active and click on the Render Scene button in the Main toolbar (the fourth button from the right). Doing so opens the Render Scene dialog box. Click and drag the bottom edge of the dialog box until it is expanded to show the Render Output area, as shown in Figure 1.20.

2. Move the Time Slider to Frame 0. Click on the Render button and a new window, called the Virtual Frame Buffer, shows a high-quality rendering of your scene, similar to the image shown in Figure 1.21.

3. With the Virtual Frame buffer still open, click on the Save Bitmap button in its toolbar to open the Browse Images For Output dialog box, similar to the one shown in Figure 1.22. Enter a name in the File Name field and set the file type as .jpg in the Save As Type drop-down list.

4. The scenes can be viewed as animations as well as still images. In the Render Scene dialog box, select the Active Time Segment radio button in the Time Output area. Doing so causes all the frames to be rendered rather than just the current one. In the Render Output area, click on the Files button to open the Render Output File dialog box, which is similar

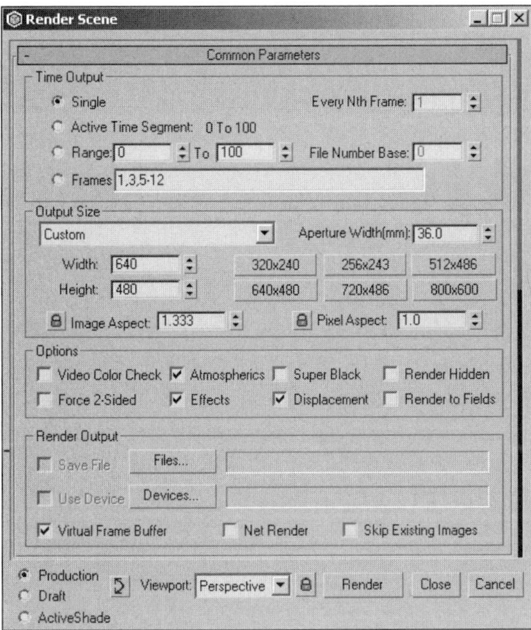

Figure 1.20
The Render Scene dialog box.

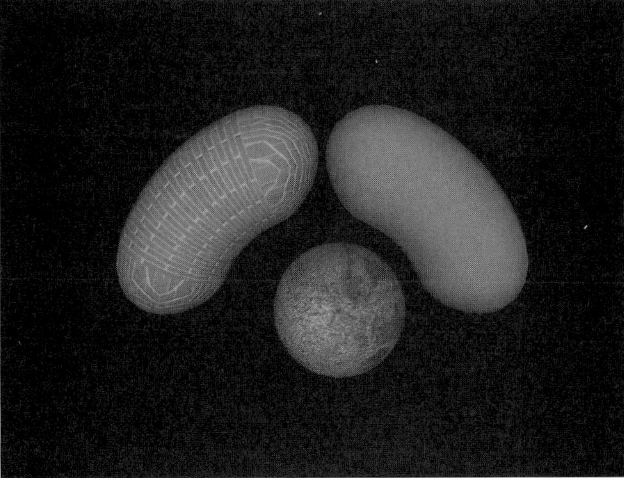

Figure 1.21
A rendering of the current scene at Frame 0.

to the Browse Images For Output dialog box from the previous step. Name the animation (choosing .avi as the file type) and click on OK in the subsequent dialog box. Click on OK to close the Render Output File dialog box. Click on the Render button in the Render Scene dialog box to start the rendering process.

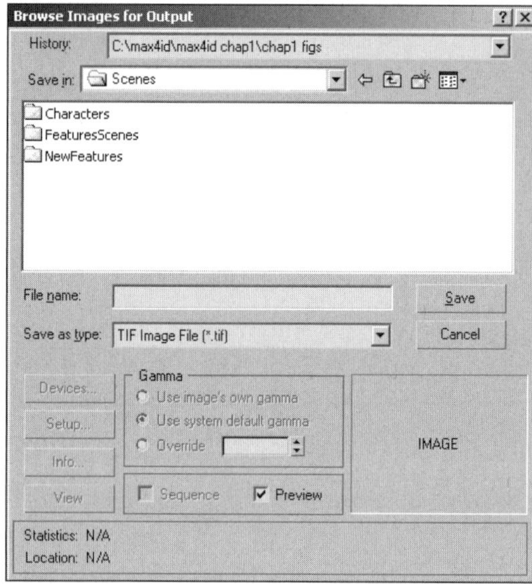

Figure 1.22
The Browse Images For Output dialog box where you enter the name and output path for the rendered scenes.

5. To view the files that you've created, choose View Image File from the File drop-down list. In the View File dialog box, navigate to one of the files and double-click on it to open the program on your system associated with that type of file. In most cases, that program will be Explorer or Photoshop for the still image and Windows Media Player for the animation.

Moving On

This chapter began by giving a brief history of MAX through the release of 3ds max 4, and then it followed with a description of the program's system requirements. An explanation of the basics of parametric objects and the layout of the 3ds max 4 interface were also discussed. Finally, the exercises at the end of the chapter introduced you to many of the core skills and procedures used to create, modify, apply materials to, animate, and render objects in a scene.

The next chapter jumps right into the heart of MAX, creating and adjusting many 3D and 2D primitives found in the program.

Chapter 2

Using Primitives and Splines

When you're using 3ds max, several approaches exist for creating objects. Whether you decide on a Non-Uniform Rational B-Splines (NURBS), Patch Modeling, or Boolean approach, your starting point will—more often than not—be the use of 3D and 2D primitive objects. *Primitives* are basic 3D or 2D objects created through the Create|Geometry tab of the Command panel. Although their uses are extensive, only minimal effort is required to create them, and you can easily modify their parameters. When creating a scene, you may need to use several modeling techniques and incorporate many of the primitive objects included with the MAX program.

To get an idea of what is being described, look around the room you're in. Try to identify the basic three-dimensional shapes that make up the objects you see. Generally speaking, the walls, floor, and ceiling are boxes. The door is also a box, as is the opening (the doorway) that it occupies. The desk, table, or countertop on which you're working may be a box or cylinder with chamfered edges, whereas its supports are boxes, cylinders, cones, tubes, or other shapes that have been extruded (given depth and surfaces) perpendicular to floor. Also look at the individual components of complex objects. For example, a lamp may have a cylinder for a base, a tube for a body, a tube or half sphere for a shade, and a combination sphere and cone for an incandescent bulb (fluorescent bulbs are simply cylinders or tubes). Even the CD with which you installed MAX is just a very short tube with a relatively small inner radius.

Splines are two-dimensional objects that can be introduced into a scene. They consist of curved line segments, beginning and ending with vertices or nodes. The type and configuration of the vertices determine the curve of the segments on either side. It is important to note that, mathematically, even straight segments are considered to be curved, with the curve value set to zero.

Why would you need 2D objects in a 3D program? Once in place, splines can serve many functions in modeling and animation techniques. A spline can be used as a cross-section that is extruded or revolved around an axis to create depth and surfaces. (We'll discuss this technique in greater depth in Chapter 7.) For example, a box is a rectangular spline that has been extruded. A spline can be a cross-section that is maintained along an irregular path (lofted), where the path is a second spline (more on this in Chapter 8). Or, the path that an object, light, or camera moves along during the course of an animation can be a spline (this procedure is covered in Chapter 18). Splines are the basis for adding text to a scene. They can even be rendered as they are, without any modification.

This chapter will not discuss every setting of every primitive; most settings apply to several different objects. Instead, you can get a feel for MAX's workflow by creating each object as it is being explained and by experimenting with the many available settings. An object as simple as a sphere can take on many looks if you just change its parameters.

3D Primitives

The controls for 3D primitives are located under the Create tab of the Command panel. Select the Geometry option and be sure Standard Primitives appears in the drop-down list. Figure 2.1 shows the Command panel with the Box button selected in the Object Type rollout and all other rollouts expanded.

Creating a primitive follows one of two conventions: Click to set the starting point and then drag to set the parameters, or enter the location and parameters in the Keyboard Entry rollout and click on the Create button. Begin a new session of MAX, or Reset (File|Reset) the current one; we will look at both methods in the sections that follow.

Box

A Box, like the other primitives, is easy to create. First, examine the click-and-drag method:

1. Make sure you are using the Create|Geometry|Standard Primitives Command panel. In the Object Type rollout, click on the Box button. It will become highlighted, and additional rollouts will become visible.

2. Make sure the Box radio button is selected in the Creation Method rollout, and then click and drag in the Top viewport. Doing so will set the footprint of the Box.

3. When the desired size is reached, release the mouse and drag and click to set the height. Look in the other three viewports—or pause the mouse and look at the Length, Width, and Height spinners in the Parameters rollout—to gauge the distance you want to move. Note that dragging up (towards the top of the screen) produces a positive height, and dragging down produces a negative height. Be careful to click only once, or you will begin to make another Box. (Using the Cube creation method would have resulted in the first pick determining the center of the bottom face, and the following drag setting would equal all three size parameters.)

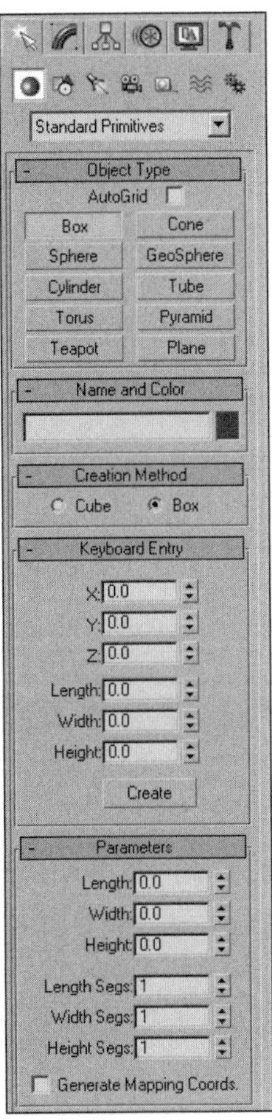

Figure 2.1
The Command panel with the Create|Geometry|Standard Primitives option chosen. Box is selected from the Object Type rollout, and all other rollouts have been expanded.

To create a Box with the Keyboard Entry method, enter the X, Y, and Z coordinates of the pivot point (the center of the first face created) and the size values in the Keyboard Entry rollout. Then, click on the Create button.

In the shaded Perspective viewport, the Box you created is now framed in a white cornered *bounding box* to indicate that it is the currently selected object. With the Box selected, you can adjust its parameters in the Parameters rollout.

Box Parameters

In the Parameters rollout, the Length, Width, and Height are self-explanatory; the Segments values determine how many times the cross-section is divided along any one axis. When a modification, such as a bend or twist, is applied to an object, it is applied evenly across the segments; a greater number of segments results in a smoother transition of the shape. If the

Box becomes unselected, you can access the same Parameters rollout by choosing the Select Object tool from the top toolbar and clicking once on any of the Box's edges; then, go into the Modify tab in the Command panel.

The viewport in which the Box (or any other linear primitive) is created is important when you're deciding how to relate the Length, Height, and Width values. Length and Width are determined by the first two picks, and Height is determined with the third pick. Therefore, a 1×1×10 Box created in the Top viewport is a tall, thin post, whereas the same Box created in the Left or Front viewport is a long, thin rail. Figure 2.2 illustrates how the results differ depending on the viewport used when the Box is created.

The Name And Color rollout shows the Box's name as Box01. You should get in the habit of highlighting the assigned name with the cursor and typing in a short, descriptive name. Several weeks into a project, or if you collaborate on a project with others, you may not remember what Box256 is.

The color swatch shows the Box's randomly assigned color. To change the color of an object, click in the color swatch to bring up the Object Color dialog box (shown in Figure 2.3), choose the palette of colors to use, and select a color swatch. If you need a more precise color, click on Add Custom Colors to bring up the Color Selector dialog box shown in Figure 2.4.

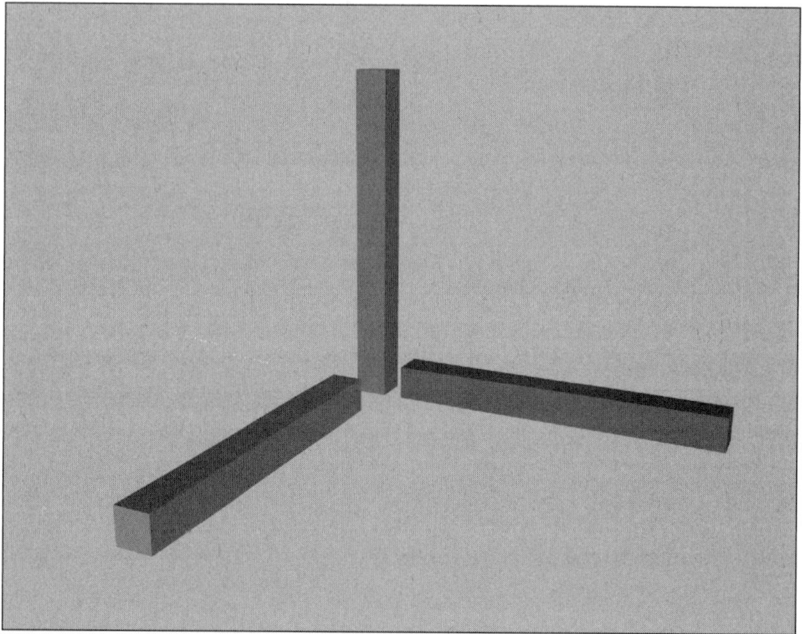

Figure 2.2
Three 1×1×10 Box primitives. The Box on the left was created in the Left viewport, the middle Box was created in the Top viewport, and the Box on the right was created in the Front viewport.

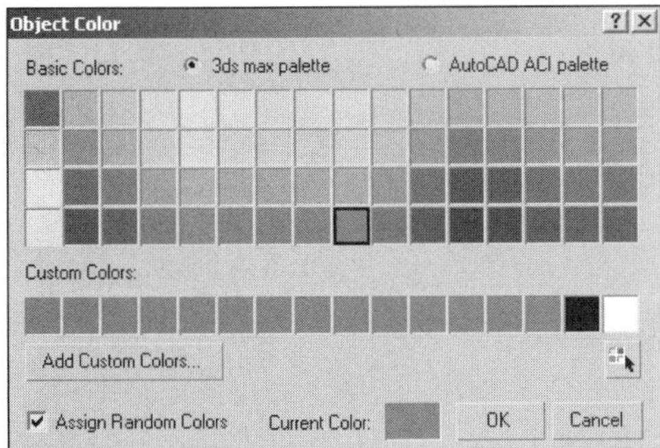

Figure 2.3
The Object Color dialog box.

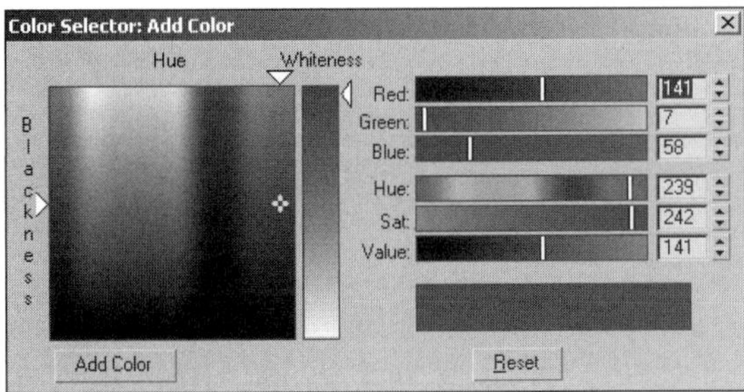

Figure 2.4
The Color Selector dialog box.

***Note:** If all new objects are being assigned the same color, then the Assign Random Colors checkbox in the Object Color dialog box has become deselected.*

At the bottom of the Parameters rollout is a Generate Mapping Coords checkbox. This checkbox tells the program how to apply a bitmap image to the surfaces of the primitive. (This subject is addressed in Chapter 12.)

Most of the remaining primitives have similar features, settings, and procedures; the rest of this chapter will address only those that differ significantly.

Sphere and Geosphere

The Sphere and Geosphere primitives are both spherical objects, but each puts the geometry together in a different way. Create one of each in the Top viewport by clicking to set the center point and drag-releasing to set the radius. Figure 2.5 shows how each is constructed. The Sphere, on the left, is made up of bands of quad (four-sided) patches in a longitudinal and latitudinal pattern. The Geosphere, on the right, is composed of triangular patches, each at a slightly different angle than the three with which it shares edges. The Geosphere is a more efficient shape, resulting in a smoother spherical object with fewer faces; the Sphere, on the other hand, has slightly more control over its shape.

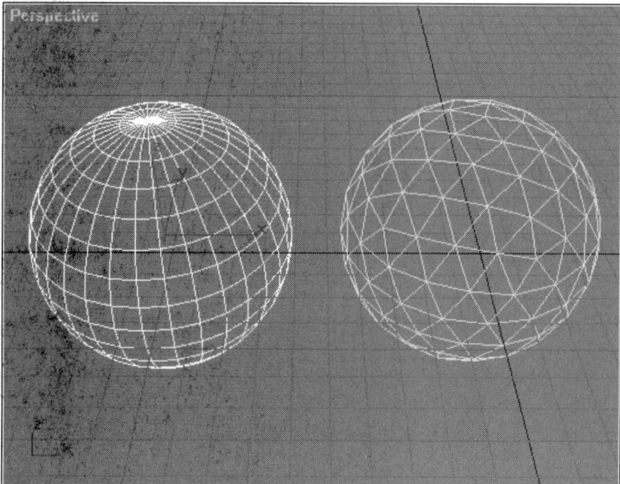

Figure 2.5
The Sphere *(left)* is constructed from bands of quad patches, whereas the Geosphere *(right)* is composed of triangles.

Sphere Parameters

Each Sphere has parameters that let you set the radius and number of segments; it also has a Smooth checkbox. Both spherical objects are composed of flat surfaces, and, in most cases, you want them to appear curved. The Smooth checkbox instructs the Renderer or rendered viewport to show the transitions between non-coplanar faces as blended rather than faceted. Figure 2.6 shows the difference when the Smooth checkbox is unchecked.

The Sphere has an additional Hemisphere control that allows a bottom portion of it to become flattened. The Squash option maintains the number of latitudinal bands, whereas Chop reduces the number relative to the Hemisphere setting. The Hemisphere option is also available for a Geosphere, but its only option is to cut the object in half at the equator. By checking the Slice On box and entering Slice From and Slice To values, you can remove longitudinal sections of the Sphere. The Base To Pivot checkbox moves the pivot point of the Sphere from the center to the center of the base.

Cylinder, Tube, and Cone

A Cylinder primitive is simply two equally sized circles, one directly above the other, connected with sides. A Tube is similar to a Cylinder, but a cylinder of material is removed from its center. A Cone is also similar to a Cylinder, but the top and bottom radii may be different. Figure 2.7 shows Cylinders, Tubes, and Cones with various parameter settings. Their creation methods are all similar: Click and drag to set the base point and initial radius, and then perform a series of drags (depending on the primitive) to set the other parameters.

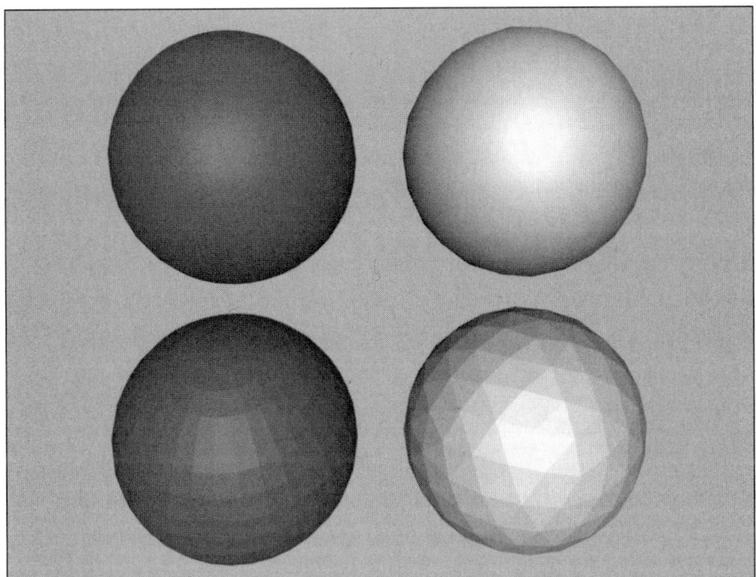

Figure 2.6
The Sphere and Geosphere on top have the Smooth checkbox checked; the objects on the bottom do not.

Figure 2.7
Cylinders, Tubes, and Cones, with various parameter settings.

Pyramid, Plane, Torus, and Teapot

The Pyramid primitive has a square base and four triangular sides that join at a point directly over the center of the base. Unlike a Cone, a Pyramid cannot have a flat plane at its top.

A Plane primitive appears to be a simple, flat quad patch, but it has greater significance than that. The Scale and Density values in the Render Multipliers section of the Parameters rollout control how the Plane reacts when being rendered. These values are multiplied by their related numbers above them in the rollout to allow a small, inconspicuous plane to play a larger role in a scene without being overbearing in a viewport. The number of total faces may seem to be twice as many as you would expect, but MAX considers faces to be triangular—it subdivides the quads you see.

The Torus primitive is shaped like a doughnut. Radius 1 is the distance from the center point of the object to the center of the circular ring surrounding it, and Radius 2 is the distance from the center of the ring to the outer edge of the shape. The Rotation option moves the vertices around the outside of a circular cross-section, causing them to move from the inside of the Torus to the outside without losing their radial position. The Twist option moves the vertices along the cross-section in a slanted pattern. When you apply a twist to an unsliced Torus, you should do so in 360-degree increments to avoid an unwanted "pinching" of the vertices at the beginning point of the Torus ring. Turning Slice on and leaving both Slice values set to zero may avoid the pinch and will allow the ends to be misaligned.

A Teapot primitive doesn't appear primitive at all. This primitive was used in the early releases to show the power of 3D Studio. Teapots are interesting, but you should use them sparingly—they are easy to make, and they appear in far too many scenes.

Extended Primitives

The Extended Primitives available in MAX offer additional parametric objects. Some are more useful than others, and all are accessed by expanding the drop-down list in the Create|Geometry Command panel and choosing Extended Primitives. Figure 2.8 shows the available Extended Primitives.

ChamferBox and ChamferCyl

The ChamferBox primitive creates surfaces along the edges of a box, whereas the ChamferCyl primitive creates a face between the sides of a Cylinder and the end caps. In the real world, it's rare to see two faces of an object come together at a precise 90-degree angle without a smooth or flat transition. Chamfered corners also help to reflect light and add a level of clarity to a scene.

The Fillet and Fillet Segs parameters set these primitives apart from their cousins. Fillet is the distance (created on screen with a final upward drag of the mouse) on any one side that is lost to the chamfer. Fillet Segs determines how many times the chamfered edge is subdivided. The greater the number of fillet segments, the rounder the transition will be.

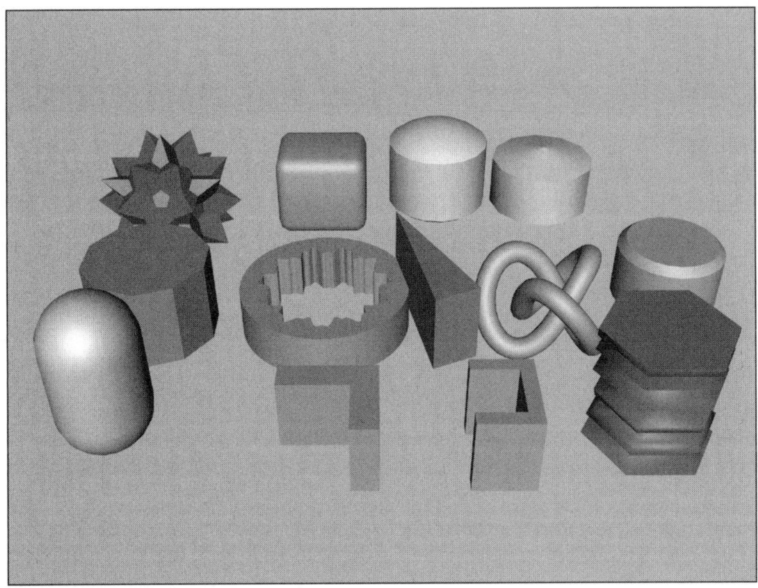

Figure 2.8
The 13 available Extended Primitives. Back row: Hedra, ChamferBox, OilTank, and Spindle. Middle row: Gengon, RingWave, Prism, Torus Knot, and ChamferCyl. Front row: Capsule, L-Ext, C-Ext, and Hose.

Gengon, OilTank, Spindle, and Capsule

A Gengon primitive is basically an extrusion of a polygon. The number of sides can be specified, as well as a fillet radius. Whereas the fillet of a ChamferCyl primitive is between the sides and end caps, the fillets of the Gengon occur between the sides only.

OilTank, Spindle, and Capsule primitives are all circular extrusions with different treatments applied to the end caps; these treatments range from curves to points to half-spheres. These primitives are surprisingly useful for anything from spaceship and robot elements to mechanical or architectural items.

Hedra, Torus Knot, Prism, L-Ext, C-Ext, and RingWave

The Hedra and Torus Knot Extended Primitives both seem to be exercises in mathematics, but you can find uses for each. After creating a Hedra, cycle through the five types in the Family group of the Parameters rollout to see the different styles (Tetrahedral, Octahedral, etc.).

The best use for a Torus Knot is to create a soft-sided tube, as follows:

1. Drag out a Torus Knot in the Top viewport.
2. In the Base Curve group of the Parameters rollout, click on the Circle radio button to change the knot type. (This type of Torus is more functional than that in the Standard Primitives family.) Set the Radius value to 30; in the Cross-Section group, set the Radius value to 20. The result should look like the left object in Figure 2.9.

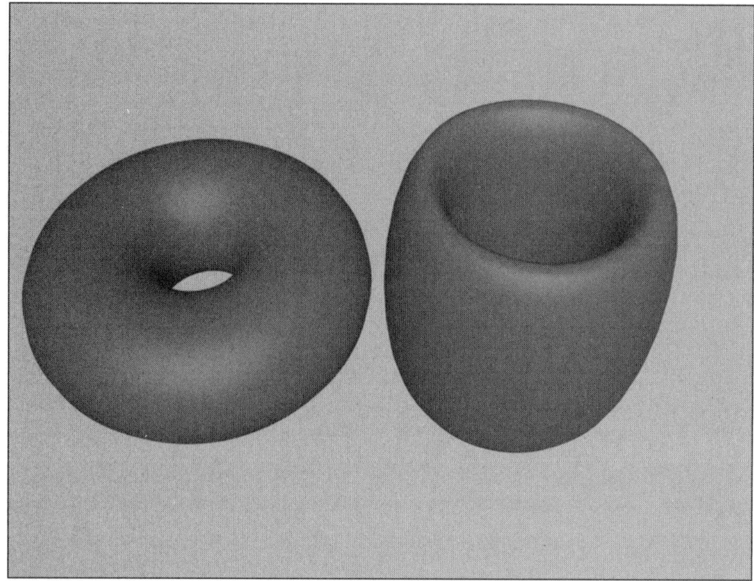

Figure 2.9
The Torus Knot Extended Primitive can be used to create soft-sided tube shapes. The only thing different between these two shapes is the Eccentricity value.

3. In the Cross-Section group, set the Eccentricity value to 0.5 to stretch out the sides. The result will look like the object on the right in Figure 2.9.

You should experiment further with the Warp and Lump settings to see the many forms the Torus Knot can take.

A Prism primitive is an extruded triangle that gives you precise control over the individual side lengths and side segmentation. The options found in the Creation Method rollout determine if the triangular base is Isosceles, Obtuse, or Scalene.

The L-Ext and C-Ext primitives are L-shaped or C-shaped extrusions with rectangular cross-sections. Holding down the Ctrl button when dragging the side lengths restricts them to equal lengths.

A RingWave primitive appears to be just a tube with a rough inner radius, but it is really much more. It is designed to be an animated object that flows from one size to another; the rough inner surface breaks up the transition to represent a radial shock wave. Without getting too far into animation (which is covered in Part VI), let's examine the basic setup of a RingWave:

1. Reset MAX. Select RingWave from the Extended Primitives menu. In the Top viewport, click and drag to set the outer radius.
2. Release, and then drag and click to set the inner radius or ring width to about one-third of the radius.

3. In the RingWave Timing group of the Parameters rollout, select Grow and Stay. The Start Time is the first frame in which the object appears at a scale of zero. Grow Time specifies when the object will reach the size at which it was created.

4. At lower right, click on the Play Animation button (the single right-arrow) and observe the Top viewport. The RingWave should grow from frames 0 through 60 and then continue to move until frame 100.

5. To stop the animation, click on the same button you used to start it (the button now displays two short, vertical lines).

Hose

New to the list of Extended Primitives in 3ds max 4 is the Hose; like the Teapot, it seems far from primitive. It represents a flexible, corrugated tube or conduit that can be freestanding as well as fixed to two objects. In a fixed mode, it will adjust itself, as required, when the associated objects are relocated. Be aware that there is no self-collision protection—if adjusted improperly, the Hose section's geometry can cross itself in a way that would not be physically possible.

To form an example Hose, follow these steps:

1. From the Chapter 2 Files directory on the CD-ROM, open the file Chap2_Hose.max.Two identical Boxes have been placed in this scene; one is higher than the other and offset in the positive X direction. Figure 2.10 shows the scene as displayed in the Perspective viewport.

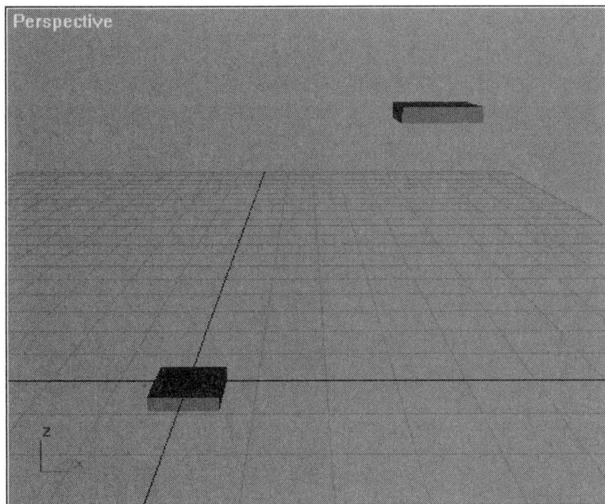

Figure 2.10
The initial scene for this exercise, composed of two offset Boxes, as shown in the Perspective viewport.

2. Choose Create|Geometry|Extended Primitives|Hose. In the Top viewport, click near the center of the left Box and drag the radius of the Hose to slightly less than the size of the Box. Release to set the radius. Move the mouse toward the top of the screen to set the height—a specific height is not required for this exercise.

3. In the End Point Method group of the Hose Parameters rollout, choose Bound To Object Pivots.

4. Right-click in the Perspective viewport to change viewports while maintaining the Hose as the selected object.

5. In the Binding Objects group, click on the Pick Top Object button; then, move the cursor over the upper Box. When the cursor changes from an arrow to a cross (indicating it is over a valid object), click to select the Box. Click on the Pick Bottom Object button, and then select the bottom Box. The Hose will adjust itself to fit the parameters set. Your scene should look like Figure 2.11.

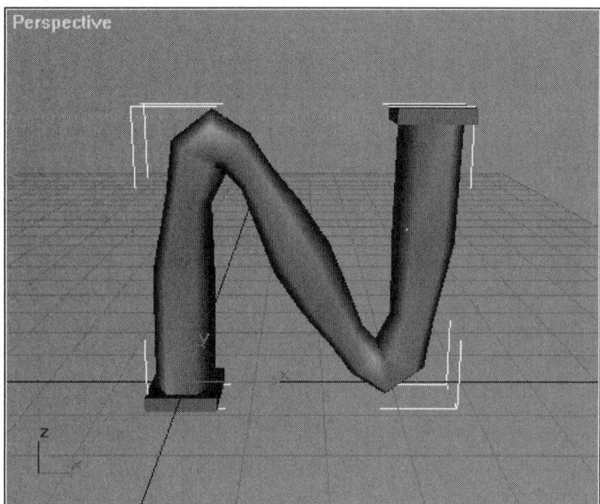

Figure 2.11
The Hose has been created and bound to the two Boxes.

6. The Hose is too long for the exercise, but the Height parameter is available only when the Hose is not bound. Adjust the length by changing the Tension values under the Pick Top Object and Pick Bottom Object buttons. A value of about 60 works well in this instance.

7. In the Common Hose Parameters group, two settings—Cycles and Segments—control the number of corrugations in the flexible section of the Hose: Cycles sets the quantity of corrugations. Segments sets the number of cross-sections, allowing for a smooth transition from one corrugation to the next. Set Cycles to 25 and increase Segments to about 90, until the Hose looks good.

8. The Starts value determines the percentage of the total Hose length, at the beginning, that is straight. The Ends value sets the straight section's length at the end. Diameter is the relative size of the minor diameter of the flexible section compared to the major diameter. Leave these settings at their defaults.

9. The Hose Shape group gives you additional control over the Hose's cross-section shape. Experiment with the different types, and then return to the default Round Hose. Your scene should look like Figure 2.12.

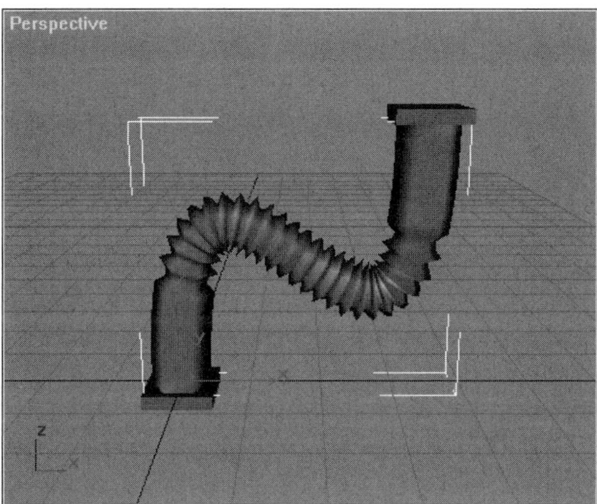

Figure 2.12
The finished Hose primitive.

2D Primitives

In computer graphics terminology, a *spline* is a two-dimensional object composed of vertices with one or two segments attached to each vertex. The splines used in MAX are Bezier (pronounced beh-zee-AY). These curves' shapes are defined by the *location* and *type* of the vertices and the *weight* assigned to each vertex. As far as splines are concerned, a square and a circle are quite similar—each contains four vertices and four segments. For the circle, the segments have a curved appearance; the segments of the square take a more direct route. Splines can be open or closed, and all segments do not have to be contiguous (as you will see with the Donut primitive). Although they have no faces, splines can be rendered and viewed as an entity in a scene—but this is not a common practice.

MAX comes with 11 spline primitives in the Create|Shapes|Splines Command panel. All except the Line and the result of the Section are parametric objects. The Line is a freeform method of drawing a spline, and the Section is a method of extracting a spline from an existing mesh object. In the following sections, we'll examine the various types of spline primitives.

Rectangle

Creating a Rectangle is as simple as it gets:

1. Go to Create|Shapes|Splines|Rectangle and, in the Top viewport, click-drag and release to set the opposite corners. Holding down the Ctrl key will restrict the shape to a square.

2. In the Parameters rollout, set the Length and Width values to 125 and the Radius value to 15. Doing so sets your shape as a square with rounded corners.

3. 2D objects, which inherently have no faces, can nonetheless be rendered by first expanding the Rendering rollout and checking the Renderable box. Set the Thickness value to 20, leave the Sides and Angle values at their defaults, and, in the Main toolbar, click on the Quick Render button. Doing so renders your Rectangle with a round cross-section 10 units in diameter (see Figure 2.13). Select the Display Render Mesh checkbox to see the result in the viewports.

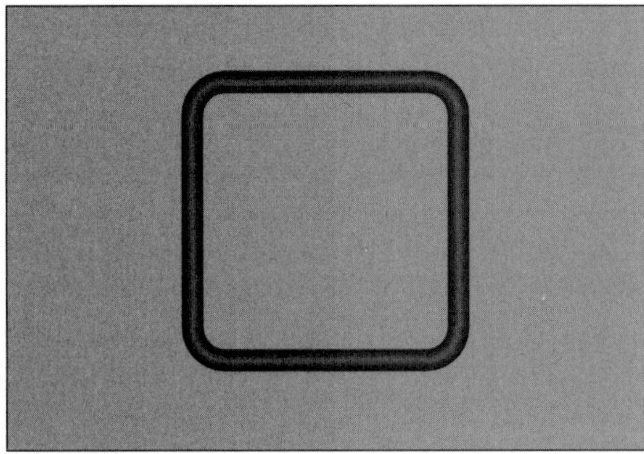

Figure 2.13
A radius-cornered Rectangle rendered with a 10-unit thickness.

4. Expand the Interpolation rollout. The Steps setting controls the number of subdivisions in each segment. Currently, the Rectangle has eight segments: four straight sides and four corners. You can reduce the number of cross-sections by selecting the Optimize checkbox, thus enabling the straight sections to contain a single cross-section for the entire length while maintaining the number of cross-sections in the curved segments. Selecting the Adaptive checkbox will reduce the number of cross-sections in the straight sections and increase the number in the curved sections.

Circle, Ellipse, Donut, and NGon

Circle and Ellipse primitives are simple pick-and-drag entities; you pick the center point and drag out the radius. The vertical location of the cursor determines the shape of the Ellipse. If you create either one and then change the Steps value in the Interpolation rollout to zero, all curvature between the vertices is lost—you're left with a diamond shape. A larger number of steps results in a smoother spline, but it will also result in a greater number of faces if the spline is extruded or revolved around an axis. If the spline is used as an animation path, the object associated with it will move as if the path were infinitely smooth.

A Donut is an example of a shape with noncontiguous segments. Two radii are set for the object (either radius can be the inner one) to create a shape with two concentric circles, eight vertices, and two splines.

An NGon primitive is similar to the Gengon 3D primitive: It is a multisided object based on a circular radius. The Inscribed and Circumscribed radio buttons determine whether the NGon is created based on being inside or outside the Radius value. The number of sides can be as few as three. Selecting the Circular checkbox will curve the sides appropriately to force the NGon into a circular shape. The Corner Radius value specifies the amount of curvature applied between the straight segments. Figure 2.14 shows some of the effects that can be achieved by altering the NGon parameters.

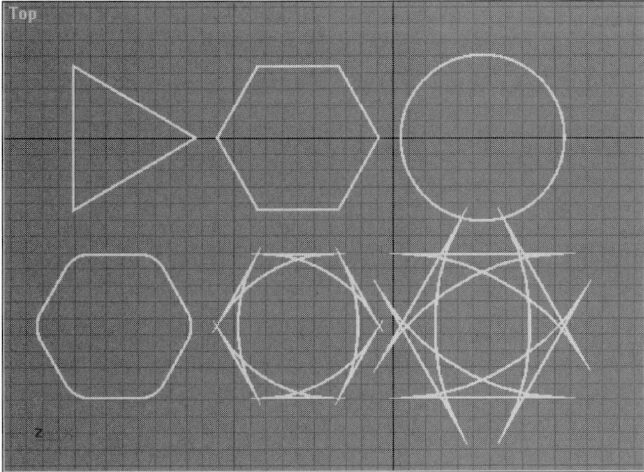

Figure 2.14
All NGon primitives are inscribed with a radius of 50. Top row: The first has a total of three sides, and the second and third have six sides. For the third NGon, the Circular checkbox is selected. Bottom row: Three different Corner Radius values (15, 90, and 125) have been used.

Arc, Star, and Helix

When you're creating an Arc using the default End-End-Middle method, you click-drag-release to set the end points and then move the mouse and click to set the shape of the arc. In the Parameters rollout, the From and To values set the beginning and ending points of the arc. With the X-axis running through the center point of the arc, 3 o'clock corresponds to 0 degrees and 6 o'clock to 180 degrees. The Pie Slice option closes the Arc by creating segments from the end points to the center point. From and To values that differ by less than 180 degrees create a pie slice shape; values that differ by more than 180 degrees create a pie shape with a slice missing.

Note: *Before setting the shape, notice that one of the end vertices is surrounded by a small square. This square identifies the first vertex and the direction in which objects following the spline will go. After creating the Arc, selecting the Reverse checkbox will set the opposite endpoint as the first vertex.*

A Star is a fun shape to experiment with. It has only six parameters, yet you can achieve an extensive number of looks. Here's how to create the Stars shown in Figure 2.15:

1. Drag a Star in the Top viewport and set the Radius 1 value to 100, the Radius 2 value to 25, the Points value to 6, and the remaining three values to 0. The result should look like Star 1 in Figure 2.15.

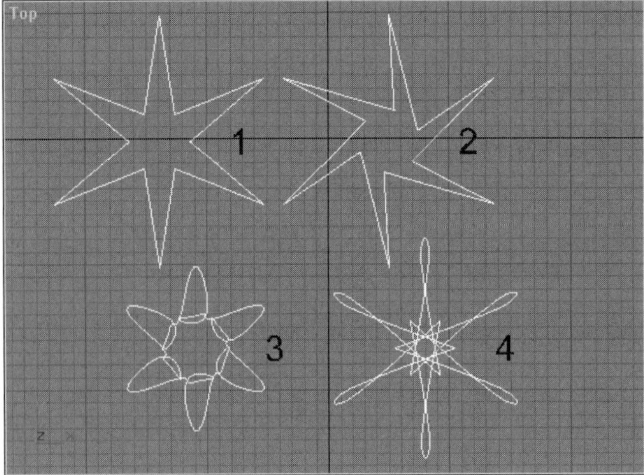

Figure 2.15
Many results can be achieved by modifying the parameters of a Star primitive.

2. Set the Distortion to –40 to get the "throwing star" look of Star 2.
3. Create the flower shape of Star 3 by setting the Distortion value to 40, the Fillet Radius 1 value to 60, and the Fillet Radius 2 value to 10.
4. The geometric pattern of Star 4 is achieved by setting the Distortion value to –180, the Fillet Radius 1 value to 22, and the Fillet Radius 2 value to 0.

A Helix is the only parametric 2D primitive that is not inherently created on a flat plane. To make a Helix, follow these steps:

1. Click-drag-release to set the radius at the beginning of the helix.
2. Drag-click to set the shape's height.
3. Drag-click to set the radius at the end. By default, one full turn is completed, but this value can be adjusted in the Parameters rollout. The Bias value forces the turns to be weighted to one end of the helix or the other. You can choose the direction using the CW (clockwise) or CCW (counterclockwise) radio button at the bottom of the rollout.

Text

Text is used to add verbal rather than visual information to the scene. It can be scrolled under the action in a sequence or provide information before starting a sequence, and it is often the basis for corporate logos.

To add text to a scene, follow these steps:

1. Click on the Text button. Click in the viewport to place the text and drag to reposition it. The default *MAX Text* is created.

2. In the Text field of the Parameters rollout, type three lines of text. Unless the Manual Update checkbox is selected, the text on the screen is updated as you type. Text can also be pasted from the Clipboard using the Ctrl+V key combination; however, be aware that MAX does not support word wrapping, and you must press Enter to force the end of a line.

3. To change the font, select a font from the drop-down list. Alternately, you can expand the drop-down list and then use the up and down arrows on the keyboard to cycle through the available fonts. The text on screen will update to reflect the currently selected font; complicated fonts may take a few seconds to appear.

4. The I and U buttons control whether the text is italicized or underscored. The four buttons to the right control the text justification.

5. The Size option is self-explanatory. The Kerning value adjusts the space between characters, and the Leading value adjusts the space between lines.

All fonts installed in Windows and Type 1 PostScript fonts can be used with Text primitives. To enter a special Windows character, hold down the Alt key and enter the character's numeric value on your keyboard's *numeric keypad.* To find the numeric value of a special character, open the Windows Character Map, choose a font, and then select any character. Use the four directional keys to navigate through the characters, watching the bottom-right corner of the Windows Character Map window. If a special character is available, its numeric value will appear. For example, you can add the ® symbol by pressing the Alt+0174 key combination.

Note: *In order for MAX to find Type 1 PostScript fonts that are not located in the default Windows Fonts folder, the fonts must be in the folder identified in the Fonts path in the Configure Paths|General tab of the Customize drop-down menu.*

Section

The Section primitive is a tool used to extract a shape from an existing 3D object by placing a cutting plane through it and determining the cross-section. To use Section, follow these steps:

1. From the Chapter2 directory of the CD-ROM, open the file Chap2_Section.max. This file consists of a Cone primitive rotated at an angle, as shown in Figure 2.16.

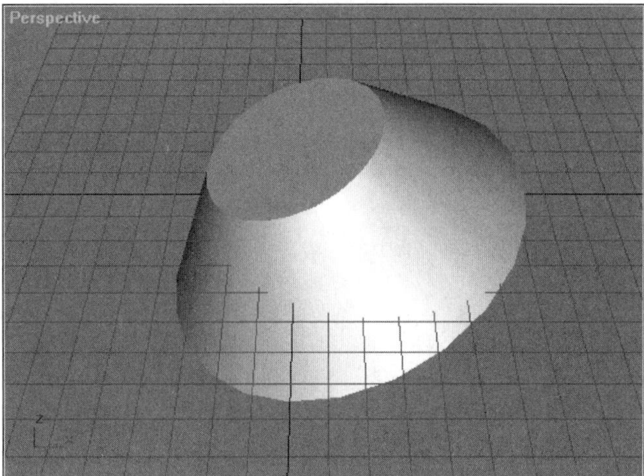

Figure 2.16
The Perspective view from the Chap2_Section file on the CD-ROM.

2. Click on the Section button. In the Front viewport, pick near the center of the Cone and drag out a rectangular plane that is slightly larger than the Cone. A yellow shape will appear, following the perimeter of the cross-section where the Cone crosses the plane. With the Infinite radio button selected in the Section Extents group, cross-sections will be extracted for all objects in the scene that are in line with the section plane. The Section Boundary option limits the effect to within the confines of the plane; Off disables the effect altogether.

3. Right-click in the Front viewport and move the Section vertically. Notice in the Front viewport how the highlighted cross-section updates to reflect the plane's position.

4. When you are happy with the section's location, click on the Create Shape button. Give the shape a name in the resulting dialog box.

5. Move the Cone and Section to see the shape you created clearly. This shape is an editable spline and is not parametric.

Line

The final 2D primitive we will cover is the Line—the only primitive that is not parametric. Each vertex of a line can be one of four types: Bezier Corner, Bezier, Corner, or Smooth. Each type gives a different look to the segments on either side of it.

Follow these steps to see two types of vertices:

1. Click on the Line button. Click to set the four corners of a square, being sure not to drag the cursor when the mouse button is down. After creating the fourth corner, click on the first point, and then click on Yes in response to the Close Spline prompt to complete the square. This action *welds* the vertices and ensures that no gap occurs between the start and end points. Your scene should look similar to Figure 2.17.

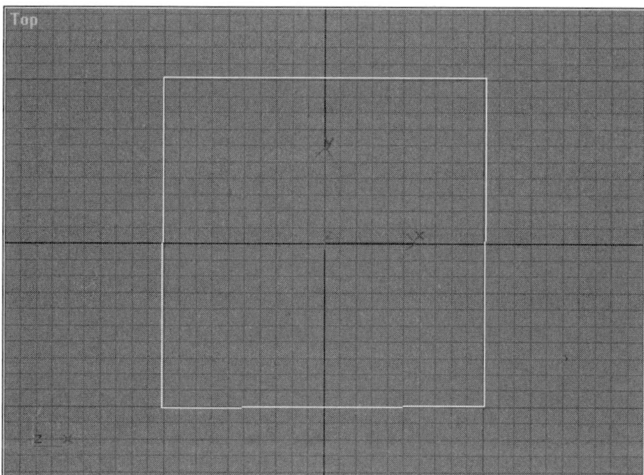

Figure 2.17
A square created by clicking to set the vertices.

2. Delete the square and draw it again, this time dragging the cursor a little after the corner points are set. This time, your scene should look similar to Figure 2.18. In Step 1, the simple click set the type of vertex as a Corner, with no curvature. The click-drag of Step 2 created Bezier vertices. The type of corner achieved with a click-drag is determined by the selection in the Drag Type group in the Creation Method rollout. Notice that the first vertex picked is a corner as specified in the Initial Type group.

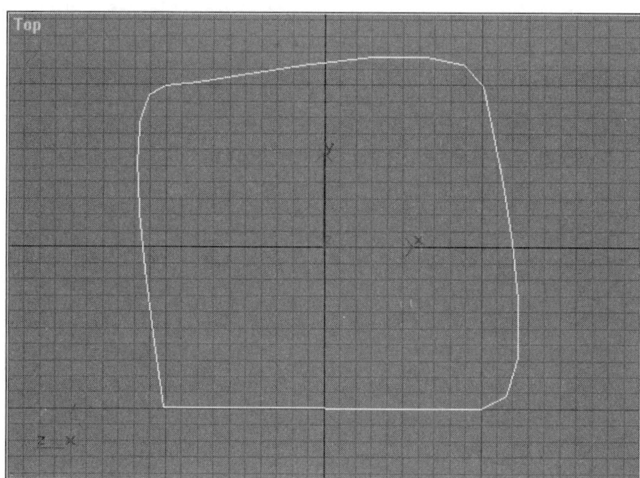

Figure 2.18
A somewhat square shape created by clicking and dragging to set the vertices.

The vertex type can be changed or its effect altered in the Modify panel. Although doing so is more in the realm of modifying objects in a scene (which is covered in full in Chapter 6) than primitives (the focus of this chapter), it is difficult to believe that you can draw a Line exactly as you want it on the first try. Let's work through another example. Begin by opening the file Chap2_Line.max from the CD-ROM. It consists of a Box primitive with a company's logo (Joes) applied to it as a material. The low-resolution image (which could have been scanned from a menu) looks like Figure 2.19. Your task is to re-create the logo as splines:

Figure 2.19
The Joes logo as it appears in the file Chap2_Line.max.

Note: *To see the images applied to the Box, the image files must be in the same location as the MAX file, or their location must be listed in the Bitmaps tab of the Customize|Configure Paths dialog box.*

1. Activate the Line command. Then click and drag the vertices around the *J*. Experiment with the relationship between the cursor location and the shape of the curve it creates. An overly large number of picks is not required and may make the spline harder to manage. One possible solution is the pick location and order shown in Figure 2.20.

2. With the spline selected, click on the Modify tab at the top of the Command panel. The rollouts in the panel are the same as those brought up by applying an Edit Spline modifier to any of the other 2D primitives. Click on the top-left button in the Selection rollout, which looks like two pairs of offset points; this button lets you manipulate the individual vertices in the spline. The button becomes highlighted in yellow to indicated that it is active and that no other object in the scene can be selected until it is deactivated.

3. Make sure the Select Object tool is active in the Main toolbar. Click on the first vertex (the one with a square around it) to select it. It will turn red, and an axis Tripod will appear at its center point. A new feature in 3ds max 4 is the Quad menu system that lets you edit an object's parameters without having to navigate to a specific menu. Right-click on the selected vertex to bring up its Quad menu, as shown in Figure 2.21. In the upper-left quadrant, a checkmark indicates that the current vertex type is Corner; change it to Bezier.

Figure 2.20
The Line and its vertex pick order and location around the *J*.

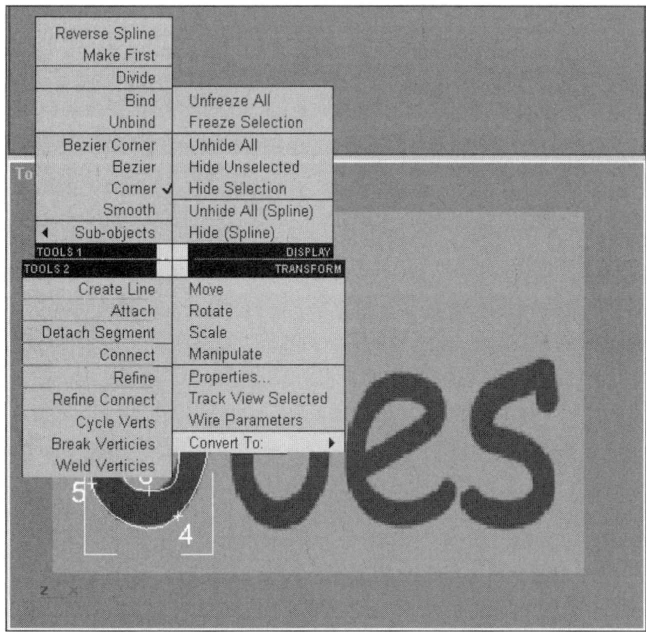

Figure 2.21
The Quad menu for the selected vertex is displayed by selecting it and then right-clicking.

4. Two control handles have appeared on either side of the vertex. These handles are used to adjust the curve as it enters and exits, and they affect only the segments on either side of the vertex. Use the Select And Move tool to relocate the vertices themselves, to pull the handles closer for a rounded curve, to pull the handles farther away for a sharper curve, or

to change the direction of the curve laterally. If the direction in which the vertices or handles can be moved is limited to one axis, make sure the Restrict To XY Plane button is selected in the main toolbar. Switch between the first and second vertices until the curve at the top of the *J* looks right; then continue around, fitting the spline to the pattern until it looks similar to Figure 2.22.

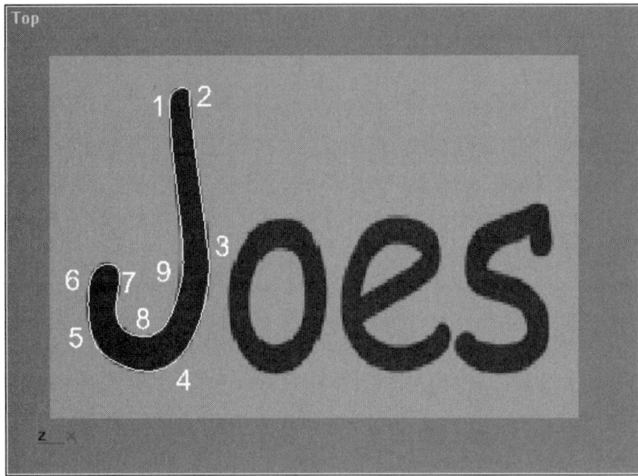

Figure 2.22
The completed spline around the *J*.

5. Drag a Circle primitive at the center of the *o* to fit around the outside radius. Right-click on the Circle; then, scroll down to the bottom of the Transform quad to expand the Convert To menu. Choose Convert To Editable Spline to eliminate the parametric abilities of the Circle and bring up the now-familiar Edit Spline rollouts. Enter Vertex mode by clicking on the + symbol next to the words *Editable Spline* near the top of the Command panel and choosing Vertex. Adjust the vertices and handles until they match the outside radius of the *o*.

6. Switch from the Vertex subobject mode to the Spline subobject mode, and the entire spline will turn red. Scroll down the Modify panel to find the Outline button in the Geometry rollout. Click on the button to activate it, and then click and hold over the up or down spinner button. Move the mouse up or down to change the value until an offset spline is about the size of the inside radius of the *o* (the value will be about 16 in this case). Adjust the vertices until they are aligned with the logo. Then, use the Line tool to create the *e* and *s*. Figure 2.23 shows the completed splines, with an apostrophe added to correct the grammar.

Note: *Clicking the spinner buttons is not an option with the Outline command, because doing so will create an offset spline one unit away from the selected spline; multiple clicks create identical splines stacked on top of one another. Instead, you must scroll to the value or type it in.*

Figure 2.23
The completed splines around all four letters, plus an apostrophe. For clarity, all entities have been assigned a white color, and the box in the background has been hidden.

7. Currently, the scene has up to seven separate splines, depending on how they were created. You need to combine them into one spline with seven noncontiguous pieces. Select the J spline and, in the Modify panel, go to the Spline level. Scroll down to the Geometry rollout and either click on the Attach button and pick each spline (the cursor will change when it is over a valid object) or click on the Attach Multiple button to pick the splines from a list. Whichever method you choose will result in a single spline representing the logo for Joe's. Save your file.

Moving On

Primitive shapes exist throughout the real world, and many 3D and 2D primitives can be easily created and modified in 3ds max. This chapter discussed the fact that most of these primitives are parametric. It also outlined how you can modify their parameters—a simple object can yield an exceptional result through the creative use of parameters.

The Bezier splines created in MAX are both powerful and flexible, and such splines will be revisited many more times in this book. To use them fully, you must have a thorough understanding of the vertex types and how to manipulate the tangent handles.

The next chapter will focus on the many ways you can select and transform the objects that exist in a scene. It will also address placing objects in Groups or Named selection sets, as well as constraining transforms to specific axes and using the Transform Type-Ins.

Part II

Working in MAX

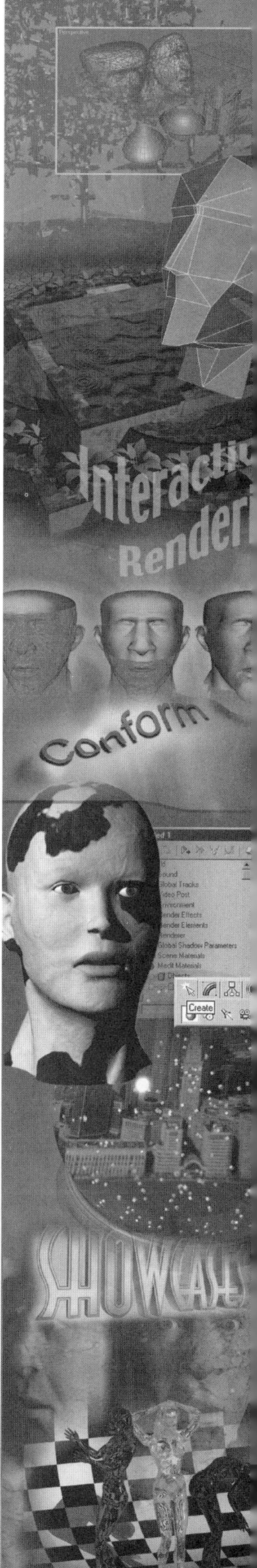

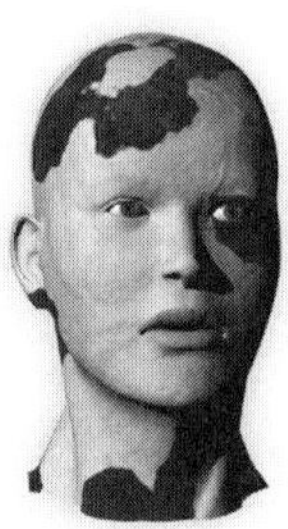

Chapter 3

Selection and Transform Tools

Computer graphics and animation are exciting and constantly growing fields. The cutting-edge technology and state-of-the-art hardware enable artists to do more amazing things every year. But no matter how easy it becomes to create objects, all objects and their components must be painstakingly selected, transformed (moved, rotated, scaled, or manipulated), and adjusted. In this chapter, you will learn many ways to select and transform the objects and subobjects in a scene.

Selection Methods

We briefly discussed the Select Object tool in Chapter 1, and we will revisit it here. An object must be selected before you can transform it, apply a modifier, assign a material, or even adjust its parameters.

Direct Methods

The easiest way to select an object is to click on the Select Object button and then click on any of the object's visible edges. As you move the cursor over an object, the cursor will change from an arrow to a cross, and a flyout displaying the object's name will appear. You can also drag a boundary to identify a perimeter within which all objects should be selected.

Let's look at an example of how to select and deselect objects:

1. Open the file Chap3_Select1.max on the CD-ROM. It contains 65 GeoSpheres, arranged as shown in Figure 3.1.
2. Activate the Select Object tool in the Main toolbar. Pause the cursor over the GeoSphere in the lower-left corner; its flyout should read GeoSphere01. Click to select it. The object will

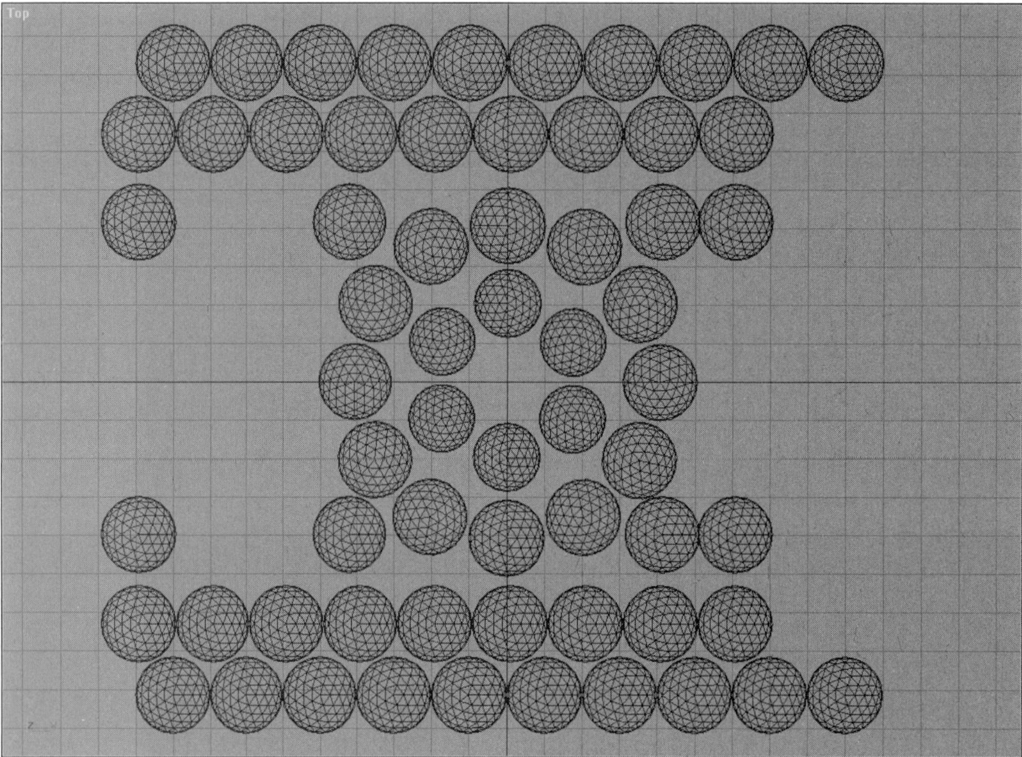

Figure 3.1
A series of GeoSpheres that will be used to examine the different selection methods.

turn white, and a red axis tripod will appear at its pivot point. If the viewport was in a Smooth+Rendered mode (the default for the Perspective viewport), the selected objects would be surrounded by a box with white corners.

3. Hold down the Ctrl key and continue to select the GeoSpheres along the bottom row. When objects are selected, they become part of a *selection set*; notice that as each object is added, the axis tripod centers itself within the selection set.

4. After all the GeoSpheres in the bottom row are selected, you should deselect every other one. The Ctrl key acts as a toggle; hold it down and pick a second time on an object to change its selection status from selected to deselected and back. Holding down the Alt key while picking an object, however, simply deselects a selected object, but you should use this technique only in congested scenes to avoid unnecessarily selecting additional entities. Either method yields the same result.

5. To deselect all the objects in the scene, you must clear the selection set. The quickest way to do this is to click on a point in the viewport that is void of any objects.

Selecting Multiple Objects

As mentioned earlier, multiple objects can be selected or deselected simultaneously by dragging a boundary to define a window around them. At the bottom of the MAX window, the second button from the left is the Selection Type toggle, which controls how the window affects the objects it surrounds. When this toggle is set to Window Selection mode, only objects that are completely within the boundary of the window are added to the selection set. When the toggle is set to Crossing Selection, all objects within the window and all objects that cross the dashed window line are selected.

To see how you can select multiple objects, follow these steps:

1. Make sure the selection set is cleared and that Crossing Selection mode is active. Click to the right of the upper-right GeoSphere and drag a window down and to the left, crossing the four objects in the third row but not the top object in the circular pattern. Your window should look like Figure 3.2.

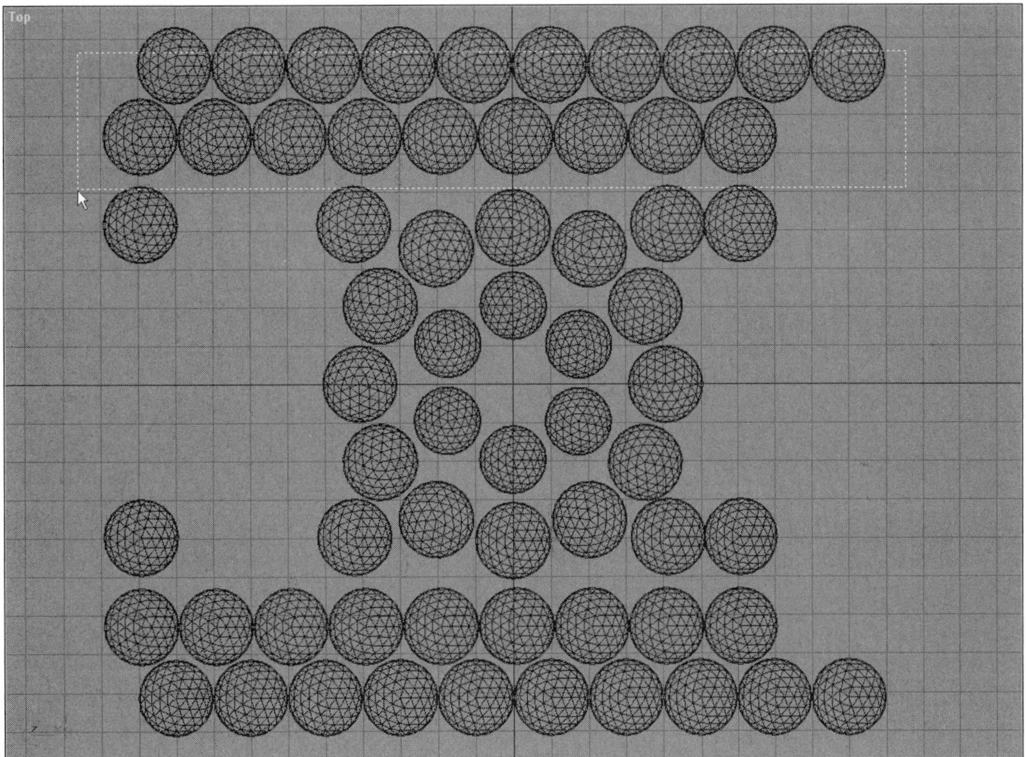

Figure 3.2
The top three rows are selected with a crossing window.

2. Deselect the second row by holding down the Alt key and dragging a narrow window that crosses through that row only. The cursor will display a small minus symbol to indicate that selected objects will be removed from the selection set.

***Note:** If you make a mistake when selecting or deselecting objects, use the Undo button or press Ctrl+Z to return the scene to the state it was in before the error was made.*

3. Toggle to Window Selection mode, hold down the Ctrl key (the cursor will display a plus symbol), and drag a window that completely encompasses the five GeoSpheres farthest to the left in the bottom three rows. Your scene should look like Figure 3.3.

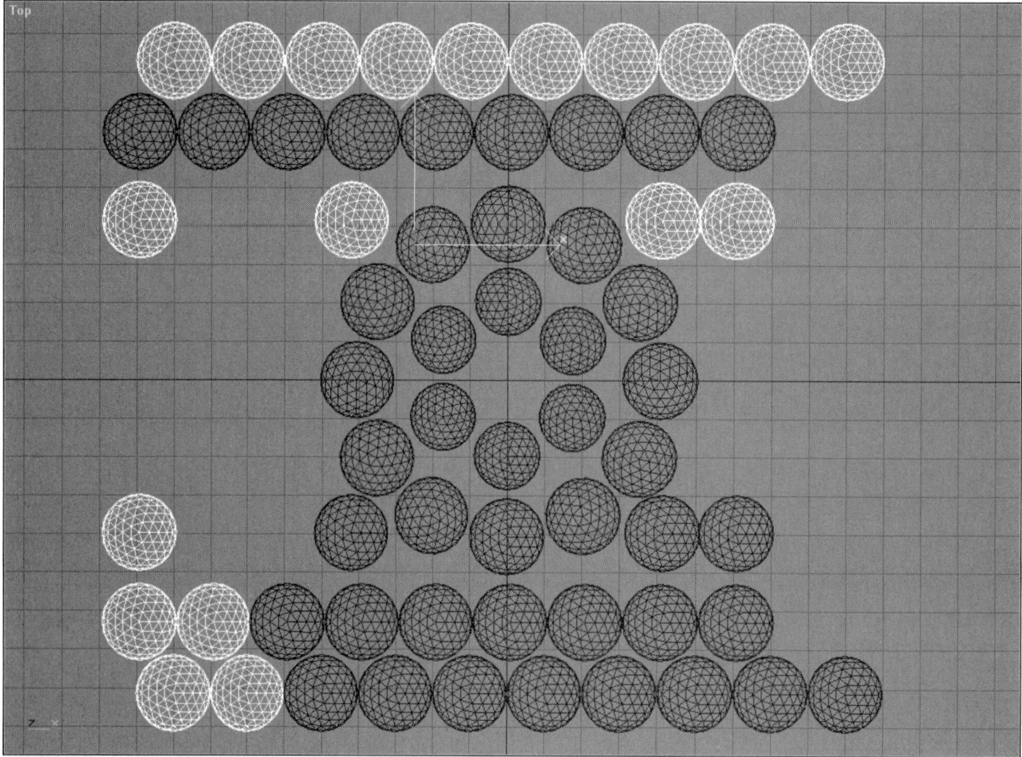

Figure 3.3
The current selection set after deselecting the second row from the top and adding the five objects at lower left.

4. The selection window is not restricted to a rectangular shape. Click and hold the Selection Region button to the right of the Select Object tool to show the other options available. Scroll down to the circular icon and release the mouse button to enter Circular Selection Region mode.

5. Toggle to Crossing Selection mode, hold down the Ctrl key, pick near the origin, and drag a circle that crosses the outer ring of GeoSpheres. Hold down the Alt key and drag a circular region to deselect the inner ring. The GeoSpheres composing the central rings should look like those selected in the central ring in Figure 3.4.

6. Click and hold the Selection Region button, and choose the Fence Selection Region option. This option allows you to draw a polygonal shape to specify the selection area. Hold down

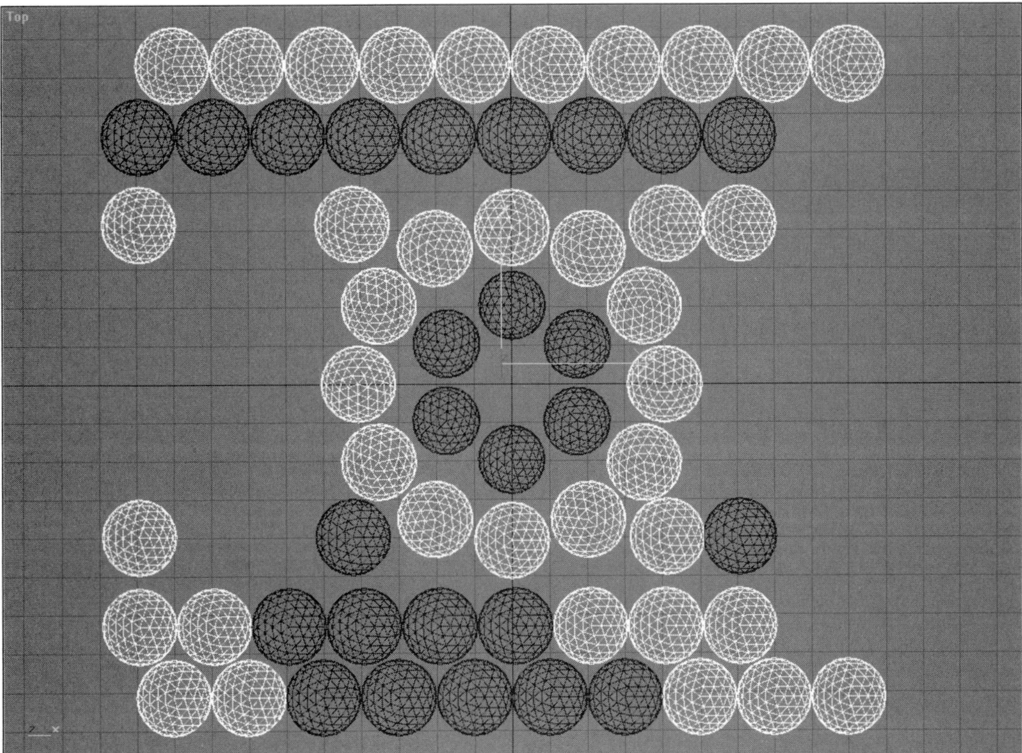

Figure 3.4
The final selection set for this exercise.

the Ctrl key and pick to the right of the bottom-right GeoSphere. Drag into the third object from the right. Continue picking points until the three objects farthest to the right in the bottom two rows and the second object from the right in the third row are crossed. To complete the polygon, move the cursor back to the starting point (it will change to a crosshair shape) and click. Your selection set should look like Figure 3.4.

You can use the Filter Selection drop-down list to limit the types of objects affected by a pick or by a selection window. This list appears to the right of the Selection Region button. Using the default All option selects all types of objects, whereas choosing Geometry or Shapes will allow only those types of objects to be selected. You can also specify Combinations of types to be filtered using the Filter Combinations dialog box accessible from the Filter Selection drop-down list.

The Select Objects Dialog Box

Each object in a scene has a unique name. As a result, it can be selected from a list in the Select Objects dialog box. When a scene is congested, you may prefer to select objects this way instead of (or in conjunction with) selecting them manually.

To open the Select Objects dialog box, either choose Select By Name from the Main toolbar or press the H hotkey. If the list of objects is long, you can jump to any entity by typing the beginning of its name in the top entry field. To select multiple objects, hold down the Ctrl key and click on the entries. (Holding down Ctrl while picking again removes entries from the list.) To select a block of objects, pick the top object in the block, hold down the Shift key, and pick the bottom object in the block.

Note: *Hotkeys, or shortcuts, can speed and simplify your workflow. For example, in addition to opening the Select Objects dialog box, the H hotkey brings up a list of appropriate objects whenever a function in MAX requires a selection. A complete list of MAX shortcuts appears in the Appendix.*

Let's walk through an example of how you can select objects in this dialog box:

1. Open the file Chap3_Select2.max from the CD-ROM. It contains a collection of 21 2D and 3D primitives, arranged in a way that makes it difficult to select only the proper objects using manual selection methods alone.
2. Press the H key to open the Select Objects dialog box, shown in Figure 3.5. As you can see, it's important to give your objects descriptive names, to make them easier to find in list form.

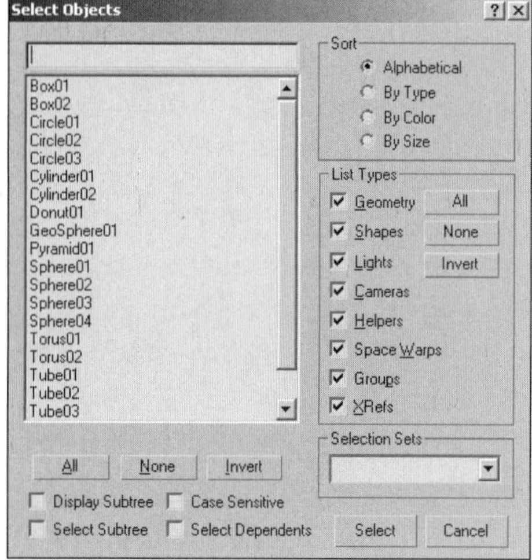

Figure 3.5
The Select Objects dialog box shows all the objects in the Chap3_Select2.max file.

3. Select all the Spheres and Tubes. To do this, select Sphere01, hold down the Shift key, and select Tube05. Deselect the two Tori by picking them while holding down the Ctrl key. Click on Select to close the dialog box and return to the scene. The status bar near the bottom of the MAX window indicates that nine objects are selected.

4. Return to the Select Object dialog box. To select everything except the Donut, select Donut01, and then click on the lower Invert button to toggle the selection status of all objects in the list. (The All and None buttons select and deselect all objects on the list, respectively.)

5. The Sort group arranges entities in the list alphabetically or by type, color, or size, where size is determined by the number of faces an object has. Select the By Type option to arrange the objects first by geometry and then alphabetically.

6. The List Types group filters the objects that appear in the list. Deselect Geometry and click on the second Invert button to display only 3D objects in the list.

7. The Selection Sets group and the four checkboxes at lower left apply to named selection sets and groups (covered next in this chapter). Click on Select or Cancel to return to the scene. Clear the selection set.

Named Selection Sets

Named selection sets allow you to specify a name for an assortment of objects, so you can select them all with one pick from a list. Using this function, similar or geographically close objects can be selected in a fraction of the time required to select them individually. Named selection sets are commonly used to access all the elements of a room, all interior or exterior objects, characters, or objects with the same material. Any time a series of objects must be selected redundantly, but transformed independently, named selection sets are the way to go.

Let's walk through an example. If it isn't already open, open the file Chap3_Select2.max from the CD-ROM. Now, follow these steps:

1. Select the four Spheres and the GeoSphere. The Main toolbar contains four drop-down lists; the second from the right is the Named Selection Sets drop-down list. Expand it to see that it is empty.

2. Click in the field and type "Spheres". Press Enter to assign the current selection set to that name.

3. Clear the selection set. Expand the Named Selection Sets drop-down list and pick Spheres to select the fives objects assigned to that name.

4. Make a named selection set using all the 2D shapes; name this set Shapes. Make another selection set named Rounds that contains the GeoSphere and the Donut. Notice that objects can belong to more than one named selection set.

5. To select both the Shapes and Spheres sets, pick one name from the list, hold down the Ctrl key, and pick the other name.

6. Clear the selection set and open the Select Objects dialog box. The Selection Sets group contains the same drop-down list that is accessible from the Main toolbar.

Editing Named Selection Sets

The objects contained in named selection sets are not fixed; the sets can be easily edited. Lists can be merged or deleted, objects contained in multiple sets can be extracted into sets of their own, and the list of objects contained in a set can be modified. Here are some examples:

1. Clear the selection set. From the Edit menu in the Main toolbar, choose Edit Named Selections to bring up the Edit Named Selections dialog box. Click on the Shapes entry to display its list of objects, as shown in Figure 3.6.

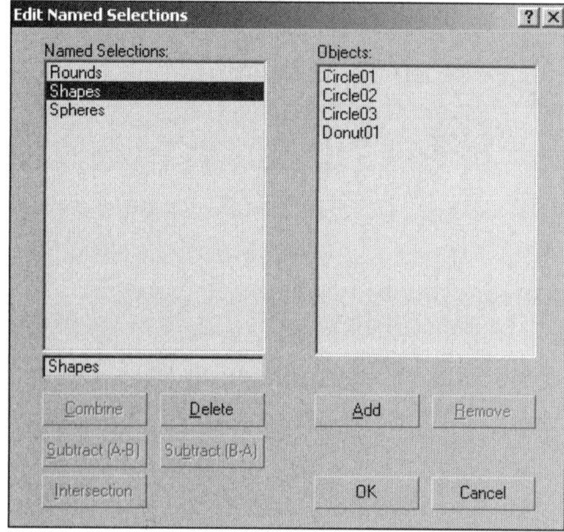

Figure 3.6
The Edit Named Selections dialog box with the Shapes entry selected.

2. Select all three entries in the Named Selections field. Click on the Combine button to create a fourth named selection set containing all the objects listed in the first three sets. In the resulting Merge Names Selections dialog box, enter the name "Combo" for the new, merged set.

3. Back in the Edit Named Selections dialog box, cycle through the four named selection sets and compare them to see that all objects listed in the first three sets are contained in the new Combo selection set. Select the Combo set and then the Rounds set, and click on the Subtract (A-B) button. Doing so removes entities found in Rounds (set B) from Combo (set A). The Subtract (B-A) option performs the reverse operation: Entities found in Combo would be removed from Rounds, leaving the Rounds selection set empty. The Intersection option forms a new set containing only objects found in both selection sets.

4. Select the Combo set. In the Objects field, select Sphere01 and Sphere02. Click on Remove to delete them from the selection set.

5. With Combo still selected, click on Add to open the Add To Named Selection dialog box shown in Figure 3.7. It's nearly identical to the Select Objects dialog box; the Select button is replaced with an Add button, and the list contains only the objects *not* already contained in Combo.

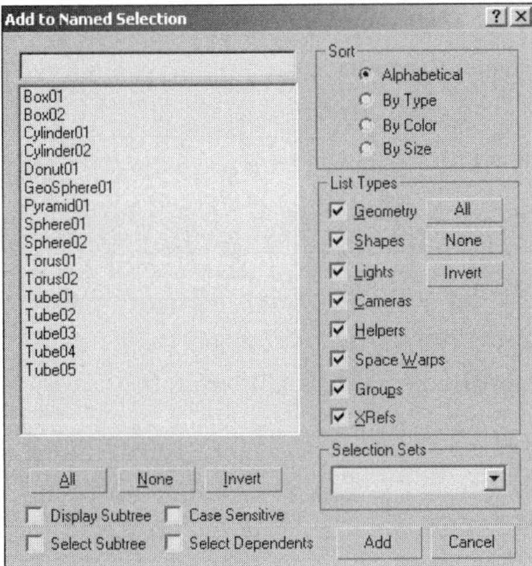

Figure 3.7
The Add To Named Selection dialog box shows the list of scene objects eligible to be added to the Combo selection set.

6. Select Sphere01 and Sphere02 and add them back into the Combo selection set. Click on Add to accept the changes made or Cancel to reject them and return to the scene. Be aware that the Undo button doesn't work inside the Edit Named Selections dialog box.

Using Subobject Named Selection Sets

Named selection sets also work with the components of an object and are indispensable when working on facial animation. Imagine trying to reselect the exact same series of vertices on a complicated head model time after time. For now, draw a Line in the Top viewport, to the left of the objects, as shown in Figure 3.8. Then, follow these steps:

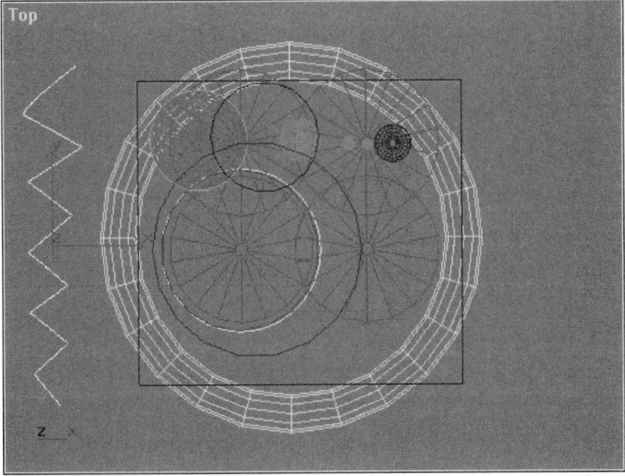

Figure 3.8
The Line drawn to the left of the objects will be used to make subobject selection sets.

1. With the Line still selected, enter the Modify tab of the Command panel and go to its Vertex level.
2. Select all the vertices to the left of the zigzag.
3. In the Named Selection Sets field, type "Line-Left" and press Enter.
4. Leave the Vertex level or deselect the Line and expand the Named Selection Sets drop-down list. The named selection set consisting of the vertices will not appear on the list unless the object to which the vertices belong is selected and at the appropriate subobject level. As a result, many subobject-named selection sets can be available without cluttering the list.

Groups

Although named selection sets let you quickly select individual objects, grouping objects together forces all the members of a group to act like a single entity. Groups are far from static or permanent; in fact, they're very flexible. Once a group is formed, objects can still be added, or objects can be released from the group's control. A group can be temporarily opened to manipulate individual objects, or it can be permanently disbanded.

Groups can contain any variety of objects, including other groups (this technique is called *nesting groups*). In a typical scene, the elements of a table or desk (top, legs, base, drawers, etc.) may be one group, the objects found on top of the desk may be a second group, the two groups may be elements of a third group, and so on.

Here's an example:

1. Continue with the scene you worked on in the named selection sets exercise, or open the file Chap3_Group.max from the CD-ROM.
2. Select the five Tube primitives.
3. From the Group menu in the Main toolbar, choose Group. Give the group a short, descriptive name, such as Tubes. You don't have to include the word *group* in the name, because group names are displayed within brackets in all lists.
4. Place the two Boxes in a group called Flats and the two Tori and the GeoSphere in a group named Tori Plus.
5. Using the Select Object tool, click on one of the Tubes. Notice that all the objects in the Tubes group are selected.
6. Open the Select Objects dialog box. The top three entries on the list, which appear within brackets, are the groups you created. The groups' members (the Tubes, Tori, Boxes, and GeoSphere) are absent from the list. Select the Tori Plus group and return to the scene.

Note: *If groups do not appear in the Select Objects dialog box, make sure that the Groups option has been checked in the List Types area of the dialog box.*

7. To manipulate the individual members of a group, the group must be in an opened state. From the Group menu, select Open. Notice that the group's members are no longer selected, and a pink bounding box (visible in all viewports) identifies the extents of the group's members.

8. Pause the cursor over the large, yellow Torus. Notice that the flyout shows both the object's name and its group affiliation.

9. Use the Select And Move tool to reposition the Torus down and to the left, as shown in Figure 3.9. The bounding box will adjust to meet its new requirement.

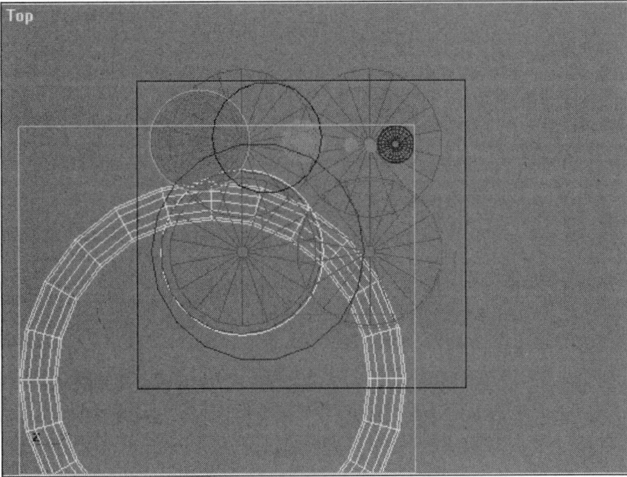

Figure 3.9
The relocated Torus and bounding box from the opened Tori Plus group.

10. Open the Select Objects dialog box. Both the Tori Plus group and its members are listed; they will remain listed until the group is closed. Select the GeoSphere (or any other group member) from the list, return to the scene, and select Group|Close to close the Tori Plus group.

11. To add the Pyramid to the Flats group, select Pyramid01, choose Group|Attach, and select any existing member in the group.

12. To remove the Pyramid from the Flats group, open the group, select the Pyramid, and choose Group|Detach. Then close the Flats group.

Be Careful when Using both Named Selection Sets and Groups

Using named selection sets essentially replaces manually picking objects from the screen. However, a selection set treats objects just as if they were manually selected. You must consider this behavior when using both selection sets and groups. From the Named Selection Sets drop-down list, choose Rounds (the set that contains the Donut and the GeoSphere). Because the GeoSphere is a member of the Tori Plus group—and picking its selection set is the same as picking it on screen—all the members of the Tori Plus group are also selected.

---

13. Select all the objects and groups. Form a comprehensive group named All that contains the 3 groups and 11 free objects.
14. Move a member of the Tubes group by opening the All group, selecting and opening the Tubes group, and then moving the member.
15. To close all groups quickly (including open, nested groups), select all objects in the scene that are group members, or simply select all objects in the scene, and choose Group|Close. Use this procedure to close all open groups in the MAX scene.

The two final group options to consider are Ungroup and Explode. Ungroup disbands a group into its individual members, retaining the integrity of any nested groups it contains. Explode, on the other hand, disbands the group and any nested groups into individual objects.

Groups are essential to a clear and concise workflow. They can greatly reduce the number of entities listed and allow you to select many objects with a single pick.

Transform Tools

The most basic way to manipulate an object is to use one of the transforms. Each transform alters an object in a different way relative to a fixed coordinate system. It's difficult to imagine any object being created without using one or more of the following transforms:

- *Move*—Relocates an object without changing its orientation.
- *Rotate*—Changes the orientation of an object without moving it.
- *Scale*—Resizes an object along one or more axes without moving or rotating it.
- *Manipulate*—Alters an object based on the values of an associated Manipulator helper or associated Manipulator parameters. (This subject will be covered in Chapter 5.)

Especially when you're using Rotate and Scale, it's important to understand that an object's location actually means the location of the object's pivot point. If the pivot point is not centered on an object, and that object is rotated or scaled, the action will occur relative to the pivot point's location. For example, if the pivot point is located in the corner of a Box, and the Scale transform is applied, the Box will appear to expand from or contract toward that corner. Pivot points will be covered later in this chapter.

Understanding Coordinate Space

At the root of 3D space is the *World coordinate system*. This is a framework of planes, each of which expands infinitely in two of the three directions: X and Y, Y and Z, or Z and X. Each of these planes is perpendicular to one of the other two, and the point at which they all intersect is called the *origin*. The viewports display the grids and indicate the locations at which the planes cross with heavier, darker grid lines.

To help understand how objects are transformed in 3D space, you must remember two *right-hand rules*. Begin by imagining that this book is an object in 3D space, with the origin located in the lower-left corner where the book meets the desktop. The left-to-right configuration of the letters runs in the X direction, one sentence moves to the next in the Y direction, and the pages are stacked in the Z direction. Each direction is further defined as positive or negative relative to the current location or orientation.

The first right-hand rule applies to an object's location:

1. Using your right hand, form an L shape with your thumb and forefinger. Extend the remaining fingers perpendicular to the palm.
2. Keeping this configuration, place your hand, palm up, next to the book. Unless you're a contortionist, your hand will be to the right of the book and on the opposite side from the spine.
3. The first rule states: "If your thumb is pointing in the positive X direction and your forefinger is pointing in the positive Y direction, your remaining fingers will be pointing in the positive Z direction." This rule indicates that the letters in the sentences run in the positive X direction, the sentences themselves run in the negative Y direction, and this page has a positive Z location relative to the desktop.
4. Moving the book to the left (negative X) or dropping it to the floor (negative Z) will not change world space, only the book's location within it.

The second right-hand rule applies to an object's orientation. When an object is selected in MAX, an axis tripod appears at its pivot point with arrows identifying the positive X, Y, and Z directions, as shown in Figure 3.10. Examine this figure briefly.

Figure 3.10
This quick book model (with a total creation time under one minute) shows the procedures for using the second right-hand rule.

Now continue with the following steps:

1. Again using your right hand, extend your thumb and curl your fingers as if you were hitchhiking.
2. With the pivot point centered on the book, the Z arrow of the axis protrudes up through the center of the page, the X direction extends through the right side, and the Y direction runs through the top.
3. The second right-hand rule states: "If your thumb is pointing in the axis's positive direction, your fingers are pointing in the positive rotation direction."
4. To stand this book up on the desk, it must be rotated about the X-axis and moved in the Z direction. "Grab" the X arrow (your palm must be up for the thumb to point in the positive direction), and your fingers will indicate that a positive rotation is required.
5. If this were actually a 3D environment, rotating about the X-axis of the pivot point would drop almost half the book below the top of the desk. A positive Z movement would be required to bring it up.

Constraining the Transforms

Transforming objects arbitrarily is easy, but moving them with precision takes a bit of practice. One method of precise transformation is to constrain the axes in which a transform is applied. To continue with this section, you must understand the default View coordinate system used in the orthographic viewports (Top, Bottom, Front, Back, Right, and Left).

When you're working in the Perspective viewport, the World coordinate system is used; but the default coordinate system for the orthographic views is named View. As a result, the transforms used in these viewports can all be treated the same way, with right-left as the X direction and up-down as the Y direction. To move an object in the positive Z direction, change to the Left or Front viewport and move the object in the positive Y direction—think of the first right-hand rule. The axis tripod for the selected object(s) will adjust itself to keep the positive X direction to the right, and the multicolored axis in the lower-left corner of each viewport always reflects the positive directions in World space.

In the Main toolbar are four Axis Constraint buttons labeled X, Y, Z, and XY. These buttons identify the axis or, in the case of XY, the plane to which they will restrict a transform. For the Move and Scale transforms, the default is XY, allowing objects to move or scale freely along the plane used with the View coordinate system. For example, objects can be moved right or left, or up or down, but they cannot be moved closer or farther from the viewer. When you're using Rotate, the default axis is Z, allowing familiar clockwise/counterclockwise movement.

The Axis Color Choice

The three colors used for the World axis tripods found in the viewports were not arbitrary selections. As is common in most 3D packages, the three base colors of a monitor—red, green, and blue (RGB)—were assigned correspondingly to the three axis directions (XYZ).

Although this subject may seem confusing at first, the exercise that follows should clarify the use of transform constraints. Follow these steps:

1. Open MAX if it is closed, or choose Reset from the File menu. Reset empties the scene and restores the default views and settings.
2. In the Top viewport, create a Teapot near the origin with a radius of 35. Create a Box, also centered near the origin, with Length, Width, and Height values set to 250, 350, and –5, respectively. The Top and Front viewports should look similar to Figure 3.11.

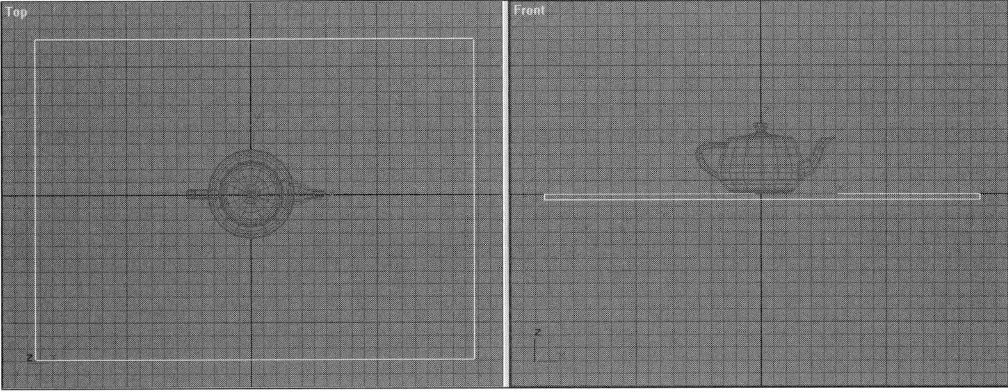

Figure 3.11
A Box and a Teapot have been created near the origin. The Box has a negative height, dropping it below the XY plane.

3. Still in the Top viewport, select the Teapot and apply the Move transform. At the Teapot's pivot point, the axis tripod changes to the Transform Gizmo, a device designed to limit the axes in which a transform can be used. (The arrowheads follow the same RGB=XYZ color convention mentioned earlier, whereas the unselected axes' letters and lines remain yellow. For clarity, an axis direction is not shown if it points directly along the viewport's Z-axis when using the Move or Scale transforms.)

Entering a Transform Mode

There are three ways to place an object into a transform mode:

- Select the object (manually or from a list) and click on the Select and [*name of Transform*] button on the Main toolbar.
- Use the Select and [*name of Transform*] buttons to both select the object and transform it. This method is recommended only if the transform is intended to be applied without any significant level of precision. Minor mouse movements during the selection stage of this process can result in minor, unwanted transformations of the object that may go unnoticed until much later in the project.
- The third method is new to 3ds max 4 and, in our opinion, is the best. Select the object and then right-click on it to bring up the Quad menu. In the Transform quad, select the desired transform.

4. Move the cursor over the Teapot, avoiding the axes of the Transform Gizmo. Click and hold and move the cursor in a circular motion to make the Teapot move in the same manner.

5. Click on the Restrict To X Axis Constraint button on the Main toolbar. Again avoiding the axes of the Transform Gizmo, move the Teapot with the same mouse motions. This time, only the mouse's right and left movements are reflected in the location of the Teapot. To remove a transform's axis constraint, click on the Restrict To XY Plane button. With a little practice, the axis constraints can be used in the Perspective viewport. Holding down the Restrict To XY Plane button reveals the two other planes to which an object can be restricted; they're fully useful only in a nonorthographic viewport.

6. Click on the Undo button until the Teapot is in its original state. Move the cursor over the X-axis of the Transform Gizmo and notice that the Y-axis line and letter turn green. Click and hold, and move the mouse in a circular motion. To know exactly how far the object is being moved along any axis, watch the Transform Type-In fields at the bottom of the MAX window.

7. The Transform Gizmo has a similar effect using the Y-axis. However, be aware that once an axis of the Transform Gizmo is used for a transform action, that constraint is fixed for that transform—you can choose another axis, but you can no longer move the object freely. To allow free movement once again, click on the XY button or other appropriate plane restriction button in the Main toolbar.

Working with the Transform Gizmo

Controls are available that allow you to customize the Transform Gizmo. To change its size or appearance, or to turn it off or on, choose Customize|Preferences to open the Preference Settings dialog box. Select the Viewports tab and go to the Transform Gizmo group.

After using the Transform Gizmo to transform an object along a specific axis, the constraints for that transform are fixed to that axis until set otherwise. This is intended as a time-saving step, but it may not work well with your particular workflow methods. To set up MAX so that the Transform Gizmo does not fix the transform into a restrictive mode, you can make a quick modification to the 3dsmax.ini file. Shut down the program and open the 3dsmax.ini file in Notepad. (It's always a good idea to make a copy of any program file before changing it.) Look for the lines that read:

```
[Performance]
TransformGizmoRestoreAxis=0
```

In the second line, change the 0 to a 1. Then, restart MAX. Your system will stay in the new mode unless this line is altered or replaced.

---

8. To move the Teapot above the Box, right-click in the Front or Left viewport to make it current without losing the Teapot selection. Move the Teapot in the positive Y direction.

9. Click on Undo to return the Teapot to the surface of the Box.

10. Change to the Rotate transform and, if necessary, the Front viewport.

11. Place the cursor over the blue Z-axis arrowhead pointing directly at you, and rotate the Teapot –90 degrees. Your Perspective viewport should look like Figure 3.12.

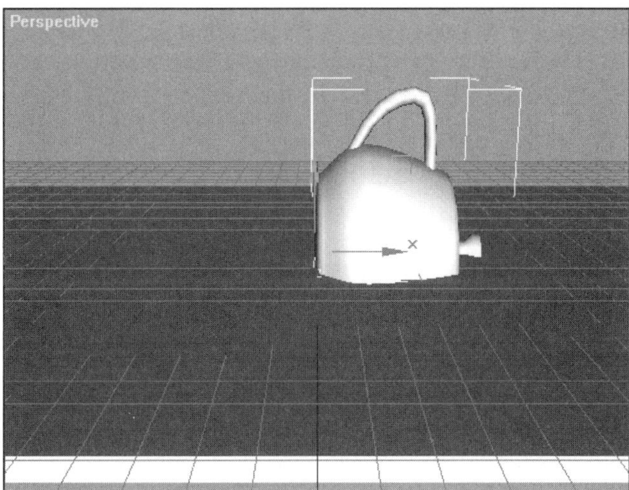

Figure 3.12
The Teapot after being rotated –90 degrees about the Z-axis in the Front viewport.

12. Rotate the Teapot back to its original orientation and change to the Uniform Scale transform mode. This is the first of three types of Scale transforms that scale the object equally in all three directions.

13. Click on the Teapot and drag the mouse down until the object is about one half its original size. Picking on a Transform Gizmo axis has no constraining effect in this scale mode.

14. Select the Modify tab in the Command panel and examine the Radius parameter of the Teapot. Even though the Teapot is half its original size, its radius is still 35. This is an important concept to understand. When you applied the transform, none of the parameters were affected: The entire object was altered, and its history was stored with it. Scaling the object has resulted in a Teapot with a radius of 35 and a 50 percent scale factor, rather than a Teapot with a radius of 17.5. This notion is analogous to looking at a blue body of water through a yellow filter. Although the water appears green, the light rays have just been altered before reaching your eyes. In the next section, you'll learn how to revert back to an object's original scale (or rotation or location).

15. Click and hold the Scale tool and choose the Select And Non-uniform Scale option. The resulting warning box informs you that this method may be too restrictive to be practical and suggests the use of the XForm modifier. Click on Yes to dismiss the box and continue.

16. Drag the cursor over any Transform Gizmo arrow to restrict the scale to a single direction.

17. Choose the Scale tool's Squash option, click on Yes in the warning box, and then click and drag the mouse over the Teapot. Squash, which is also unaffected by the axis constraints, scales in all threes axes simultaneously while maintaining the object's constant volume.

The Transform Gizmo debuted in 3D Studio MAX 3 and is the predominant way to constrain the affects of the transforms. The original method is still valid and useful, and it consists of choosing the axis to constrain to with the Restrict To [Axis] or Restrict To [Plane] button in the Main toolbar. With a transform selected, pick one of the Restrict To buttons to constrain the transform to a single axis or plane.

Using the Transform Type-Ins

Scene objects can be moved manually, as shown, or their transform values can be entered in the Transform Type-Ins. To access the transform type-in fields, select a transform and then right-click to bring up the appropriate Transform Type-In dialog box. Or, select a transform and use the Transform Type-In fields located near the bottom of the MAX screen. Figure 3.13 shows the Move Transform Type-In dialog box moved to the vicinity of the Transform Type-In fields.

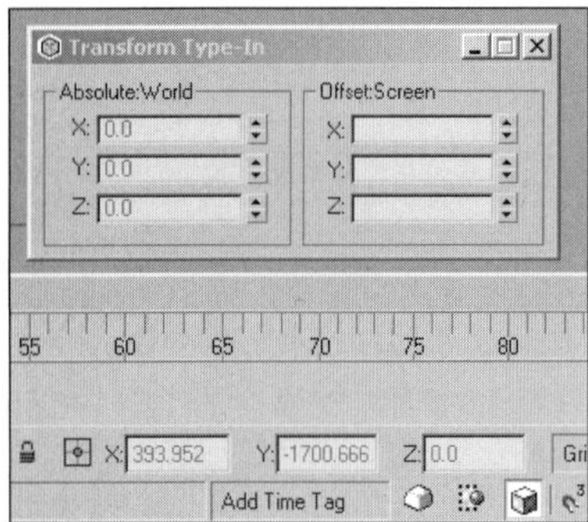

Figure 3.13
The Move Transform Type-In dialog box and the Transform Type-In fields.

Two types of data coordinates can be entered in the fields: Absolute and Offset. Absolute values relate to the World coordinate system for the Move and Rotate transforms and to the Local coordinate system for the Scale transform. Offset values are relative to the object's location, rotation, or scale on screen. When you're using the Transform Type-In dialog boxes, you enter Absolute values in the left column and Offset values in the right column. When you're using the Transform Type-In fields, the mode is selected using the toggle button to the left of the X field.

With practice, you'll find that the Transform Type-In fields are the faster method to use; to learn the underlying concept, however, we will use the dialog boxes in our example. Follow these steps:

1. Continue working with the same file or open the file Chap3_Transform.max from the CD-ROM.

2. Select the Teapot, enter the Select And Uniform Scale transform mode, and then right-click on the Scale button to bring up the Scale Transform Type-In dialog box. It should look similar to Figure 3.14.

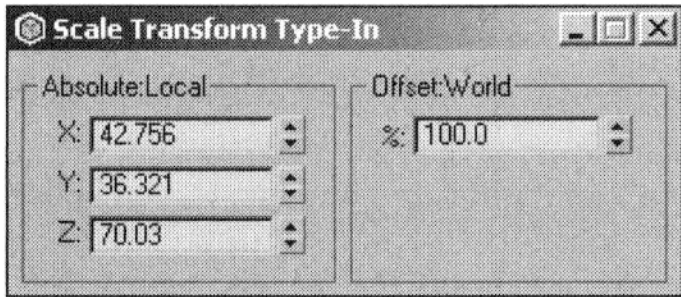

Figure 3.14
The Scale Transform Type-In dialog box for the Teapot.

3. The Absolute values show the percentage of the object's size, as determined by its parameters, that exists in each of the axes. In this case, the Teapot's size in the Z direction is about 70 percent of what it would be if the Scale transform were not applied. Type "100" in each of the fields to return the Teapot to its correct size.

Changing Field Values Quickly

If you need to change multiple fields in a dialog box or rollout, here is a time-saving procedure. Highlight the current value in the top field and type in the new value. Rather than pressing Enter, press the Tab key: Doing so will keep the value you typed and highlight the next field down, readying it for a new value. If the current value is acceptable, press the Tab key again (or press Shift+Tab to move backward). You can use this technique to cycle through all the fields without touching the mouse a second time.

4. In the Offset field, type "50" and click on Enter. The Teapot is now half its original size. The Absolute values reflect this change, and the Offset value—because it is always relative to the object's current size—has been reset to 100.

5. Select the Rotate tool, and the dialog box will change to the Rotate Transform Type-In. All values are set to zero because the rotation values you've applied have been followed by the Undo command.

6. In the Top viewport, you'll rotate the Teapot 90 degrees so that its spout points toward the top of the screen. Using the second right-hand rule, "grab" the blue Z-axis with your thumb pointing straight back at you. The shortest way to rotate the object is counterclockwise, and your fingers are curled counterclockwise; therefore, the Teapot must be rotated positive 90 degrees about the Z-axis. Enter this value in the appropriate Absolute field.

7. To rotate the Teapot to point to the 9 o'clock position, enter either "180" in the Absolute Z field or "90" in the Offset Z field.

8. Select both the Teapot and Box and open the Move Transform Type-In dialog box. As you'd expect, the Offset values are set to zero (see Figure 3.15). The Absolute values are blank,

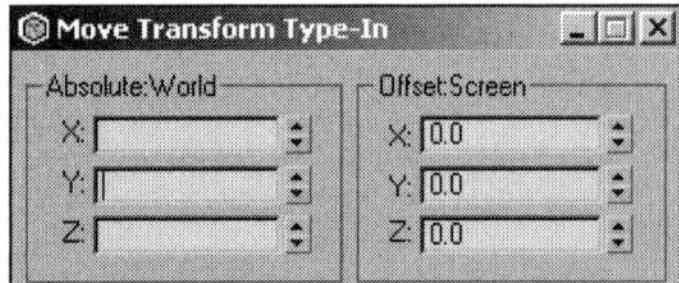

Figure 3.15
The Move Transform Type-In dialog box with multiple objects selected. The Absolute values remain blank.

because the pivot points for the two objects are not located at the same coordinates when more than object is selected. Enter "0" in the three blank fields to move both objects to the origin.

Every object in your scenes will be transformed one way or another—most of them multiple times. Become familiar with the transforms and the ways to constrain or manipulate them with precision, and your workflow and production will reap the rewards.

Choosing a Coordinate System

When applying transforms, MAX users can choose from no less than seven different coordinate systems: View, Screen, World, Local, Pick, Grids, and Parent. Each coordinate system has a different result on the creation and transform processes. Understanding and taking advantage of their individual properties are key steps in maintaining a smooth workflow and creating outstanding animations. Coordinate systems are global; they affect all objects in a scene, and given objects do not have the option to override the coordinate system. Once set, the chosen coordinate system applies to the current transform; each transform can have a different coordinate system.

The Main toolbar has four drop-down lists, and, just to make things interesting, two of them display the default value View. The Reference Coordinate System drop-down is the second from the left, nestled between the transform and axis constraint groups of buttons.

The rest of this section will examine the seven coordinate systems.

View

The View coordinate system was discussed earlier. It consists of the positive X direction to the right, the positive Y direction to the top, and the positive Z direction toward the user. This coordinate system applies to the orthographic views only; when it is selected, transforms are subjected to the World coordinate system in a Perspective or other nonorthographic view. View is the coordinate system that you will use most frequently.

Screen

The Screen coordinate system is similar to View, but it carries the orthographic view convention into the remaining view types. This coordinate system is useful when you're viewing a scene through a nonorthographic viewport but you want an element, such as text, to move in a straight line parallel to the screen's borders. To see how this works, follow these steps:

1. Reset MAX. In the Top viewport, create a Teapot near the origin, leaving plenty of room for it to move around.
2. Switch to the Perspective viewport. With the View coordinate system still active, move the Teapot along the Y-axis and see that it moves to the front and back.
3. Note the orientation of the Transform Gizmo. Expand the Reference Coordinate System drop-down list and choose Screen.
4. The Transform Gizmo is now reoriented with X to the right, Y to the top, and Z pointing directly at you. No matter what point of view the viewport reflects, the coordinate system will reorient to this condition.

World and Local

The World coordinate system is the only one that remains a constant; it's always there, as evidenced by the axis tripod visible in the lower-left corner of the viewports. If a scene becomes congested or your viewpoint in relation to the scene becomes confusing, you can use World to regain perspective on the objects' relationships with each other.

When an object is created, it possesses a Local coordinate system that is solely its own. This coordinate system is based on the object's relationship to the World coordinate system or to the active grid when it was created, but it is altered when the object is transformed. To see how World and Local differ, begin by moving the Teapot used in the previous exercise back to the origin and then creating a similar one next to it, as shown in Figure 3.16.

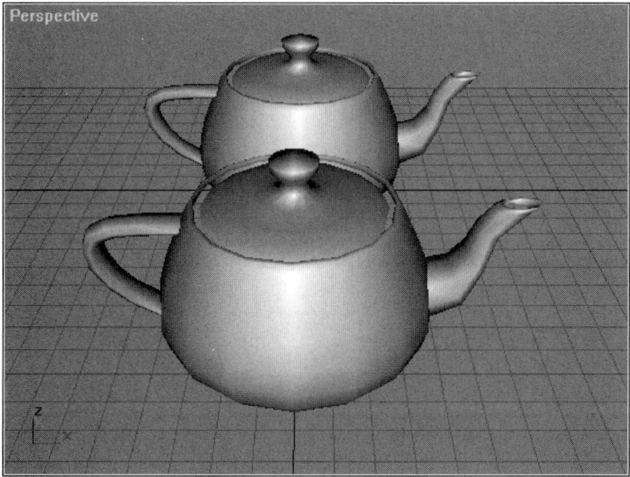

Figure 3.16
The Teapot from the previous exercise, along with another Teapot, as seen in the Perspective viewport.

Note: *From time to time, you may notice that you can see through parts of some objects, such as the tip of the Teapot's spout or the perimeter where the lid meets the body. In these situations, the object's creation method caused a surface that was intended to point outward to point inward, instead. This occurrence is somewhat common, and we'll present a variety of methods to correct it throughout the book.*

Now, follow these steps:

1. With World as the current coordinate system, select the second Teapot and choose the Rotate tool. In the Transform Type-In fields at the bottom of the screen, enter "–25", "–35", and "45" as the X, Y, and Z values, respectively. Figure 3.17 shows the new orientation of the objects; the Transform Gizmo remains oriented to the World coordinate system.

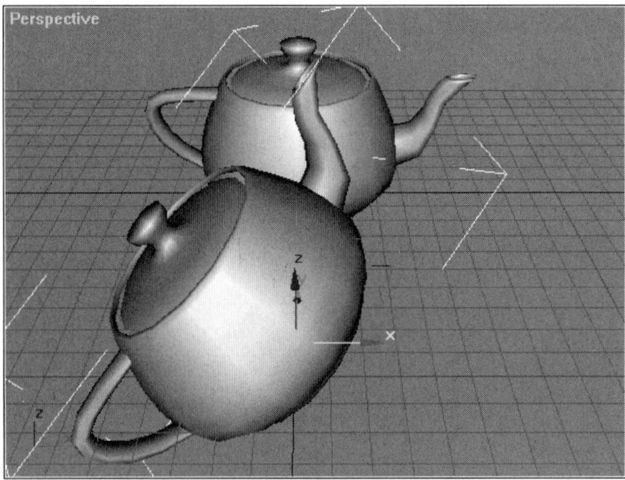

Figure 3.17
The two Teapots after one is reoriented using the Transform Type-In fields.

2. You want to rotate one of the Teapots about the same axis in which its spout points, regardless of the object's current orientation. With the first Teapot selected, switch to the Perspective viewport and select the Rotate tool.

3. Using the Transform Gizmo, click on the X-axis and drag up or down. The Teapot rotates along the same axis as the spout, but only because this is the default orientation when a Teapot is created.

4. Follow the procedure from Step 3 with the second Teapot. It rotates about the World X-axis, disregarding the orientation of the object.

5. Switch from the World to the Local coordinate system and watch the Transform Gizmo reorient itself to match the Teapot. Its location (the bottom-center of the Teapot) hasn't changed—just the direction the axes themselves are pointing.

6. Rotate the Teapot along the X-axis again. It will rotate about the Local X-axis, pointing in the same direction as the spout.

It's rare that objects in a scene remain oriented precisely to the World coordinate system axes; most will be transformed in some way. If that transformation must be relative to an object's current orientation, Local is the way to go. Take a few moments to experiment with the Local coordinate system using the Move and Scale transforms.

Pick

The Pick coordinate system sets up one object's transforms in relation to another object's Local coordinate system. To look at an example, begin by opening the file Chap3_Pick.max; as shown in Figure 3.18, it consists of a ChamferCyl primitive at the base of a Box oriented as a ramp. To move the object up the ramp, its coordinate system must be oriented to the ramp's Local coordinate system. Follow these steps:

1. Select the ChamferCyl primitive.
2. Expand the Reference Coordinate System drop-down list and choose Pick.
3. Select the Box as the source object for the ChamferCyl primitive's new coordinate system. (In a congested scene, you can use the H key to bring up the Select Object dialog box, in which you can pick the target object.)
4. The axis tripod is now oriented with the positive X direction pointing up the ramp. The name of the source object appears in the Reference Coordinate System drop-down list, where it will remain for the duration of the current MAX session. Move the ChamferCyl primitive, constraining to the X-axis, and it will stay on the surface plane of the Box.

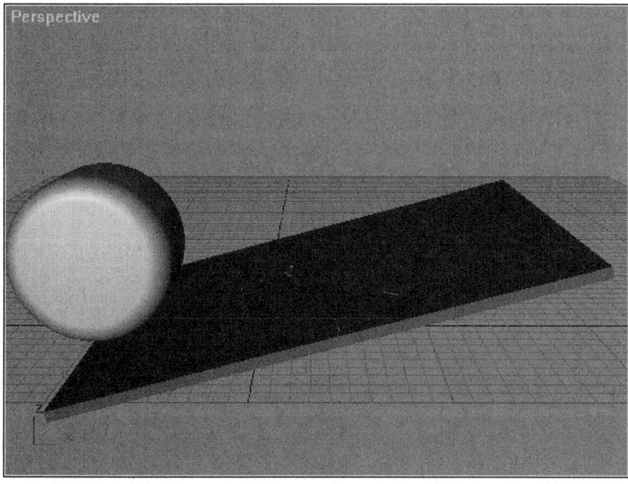

Figure 3.18
A ChamferCyl primitive and a Box primitive, with the Box oriented as a ramp.

Grids, the Grid Coordinate System, and AutoGrid

When you're looking at the MAX viewports, the visible grids—called the *Home grids*—reflect the three planes (XY, YZ, and ZX) of the World coordinate system. Each grid exists at the zero value of the axis to which it is perpendicular. For example, in the Top viewport, the visible grid exists in the XY plane, and anything created on it is created at a Z value (or *elevation*) of zero.

If you need to create objects with an orientation that is not standard, you can make a Grid, activate it, and assign its coordinate system to the transforms you apply. For example, this technique is applicable when you create or move objects along the panels of a ship's hull, or if you need to create objects at an elevation other than zero. To create a Grid and choose its coordinate system, reset MAX and follow these steps:

1. Under Create in the Command panel, click on the Helpers button. (*Helpers* are objects that add functionality to a scene but do not render.) When Standard appears in the drop-down list, six choices are available in the Object Type rollout.

2. Choose Grid from the rollout. Drag out the two opposite corners of a rectangle in the Top viewport. Although the Spacing value (the distance between grid lines) in the Parameters rollout is 10, the Grid is divided into four quadrants. To help keep the scene as clean as possible, the grid lines set by the Spacing value are only visible when the Grid is active.

3. At this point, the Grid is like any other object and is subject to the same transforms. Select it and rotate it 5, 35, and –60 degrees about the X-, Y-, and Z-axes, respectively.

4. To activate the Grid, expand the Views menu in the Main toolbar and select Grids|Activate Grid Object. The grid lines appear on the new Grid but they disappear on the Home grid, except where they pass through the origin.

5. Create a few primitives in the scene and notice that they are all oriented to the new Grid—even objects that are not created directly on it. Try the transforms and constraints to see that they now respect the new Grid.

6. From the Views menu, choose Grids|Activate Home Grid to return the Home grid to an active state. To transform any of the objects created on the new Grid, choose the Local coordinate system. To transform objects as if they were created on that Grid, however, expand the Reference Coordinate System drop-down list and choose Grid.

AutoGrid

If one object must be created on the surface of another, the MAX AutoGrid option can greatly reduce production time. AutoGrid creates a temporary coordinate system based on the orientation of any particular face of an object, with positive Z pointing away from the selected face. This option is found at the top of every Object Type rollout for all panels accessible by clicking on the Create button. You can select the option whenever a button beneath it is activated.

How hard is it to create a Cone with its point touching a face of a Sphere, while maintaining a perpendicular orientation to that face? With AutoGrid, it's not difficult at all; just follow these steps:

1. Create a Sphere near the origin.
2. Click on the Cone button and select the AutoGrid checkbox.
3. Without clicking, move the cursor over the surface of the Sphere and observe how the axis continually adapts itself to maintain a Z-axis perpendicular to the current face. When the cursor leaves the vicinity of a valid object, it matches the World coordinate system axes.

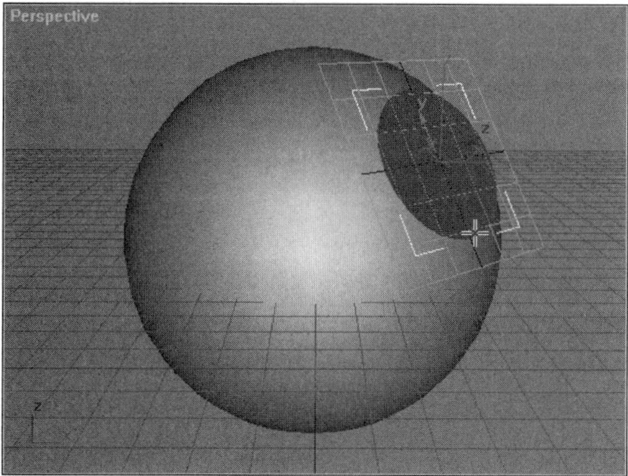

Figure 3.19
When using the AutoGrid feature, a temporary grid is created with the Z-axis perpendicular to the selected face.

4. Click and drag Radius 1 of the Cone. As shown in Figure 3.19, a temporary grid is created, by which the orientation of the Cone will be determined. Once you finish creating the Cone, the temporary grid is eliminated.
5. In the Parameters rollout, set the Radius 1 value to 0 and the Radius 2 value to any larger value to point the Cone back toward the sphere.

Parent

The final, and least used, coordinate system choice is Parent. Generally, one object is linked to another (as discussed later in this chapter) in order to make the transforms applied to the parent apply, in a relative fashion, to the child. Similar to Pick, using Parent aligns the selected object's coordinate system to that of another object—in this case, the parent. If the parent's coordinate system changes to World, Screen, Local, or another system, the child's will change to match it. The only use for the Parent coordinate system that comes to mind is the case of a flock of linked objects that are oriented differently and that need to roll or pivot independently of the parent, but along the same axis.

Pivot Points

As stated earlier, when you consider where an object is located, you are really considering where its pivot point is located. The transforms are also based on the location and orientation of the pivot point; to achieve the desired result, the pivot point often must be moved or rotated.

MAX uses two types of pivot point: true and temporary. An object's true pivot point is initially determined when the object is created. The true pivot point's relative location varies from object to object. This pivot point can be relocated at will to modify the effects of the transforms. It's important to remember that when you're animating the transforms, the true pivot must be used. Temporary pivot points allow the transforms to be applied to a short list of designated center points through the use of the Use Center flyout button that appears to the right of the Reference Coordinate System drop-down list. Thus far, you have been using one of these options without even knowing it. Let's look at some examples of how you use the two other types of pivot point.

Temporary Pivot Points

To see the result of using temporary pivot points, reset the scene and create a Box primitive, a Teapot primitive, and a Sphere primitive in the Top viewport, near the origin. The Box and Teapot have a true pivot point at the center of their base; the Sphere's is at its actual center. Your Perspective viewport should look similar to Figure 3.20. Now, follow these steps:

1. Select the Teapot and activate the Rotate transform. The Transform Gizmo appears at the true pivot point. Move the cursor over the Use Center button to read the flyout indicating that the default temporary pivot point option is Use Pivot Point Center. This option uses the true pivot point as the actual pivot point.

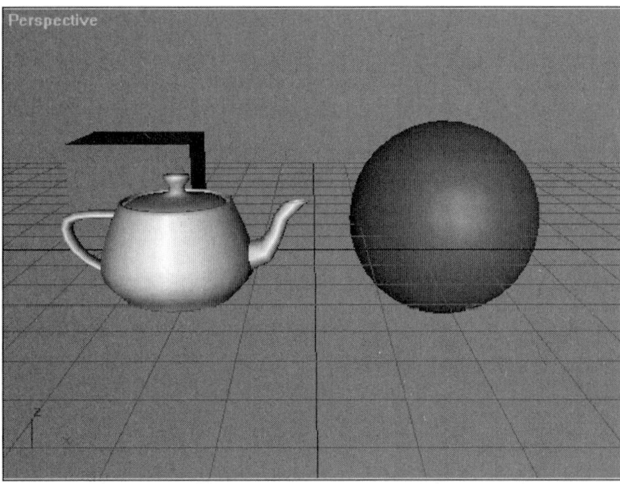

Figure 3.20
A Box primitive, a Teapot primitive, and a Sphere primitive, all near the origin.

2. Expand the options of the Use Center button and choose the Use Selection Center option. The pivot point relocates itself to the geometric center of the Teapot; now, any transforms applied will occur using this point as the basis for the operation. Rotate the object to see the effect of using this center; then, Undo the operation.

Note: *It's somewhat confusing that when a flyout button is expanded, the flyout portion appears directly beneath and in line with the button. The current option appears in both the Main toolbar and the flyout options. For example, when the Use Center flyout is exposed, it appears that there are four options to choose from; in fact, there are only three. The current option appearing in the toolbar also appears in the flyout. To help clarify this situation, a small triangle appears in the bottom-right corner of the current option in the flyout, just as it does on the button in the Main toolbar.*

3. Switch to the Use Transform Coordinate Center choice in the Use Center flyout. This option relocates the temporary pivot point to the origin of the current coordinate system.

4. Change the transform to Scale, and the pivot point will switch to the Use Pivot Point Center option. The temporary pivot points are transform dependent, and each transform can maintain any of the options.

5. Switch back to Rotate and select all the objects in the scene. Watch as the temporary pivot point relocates to the center of the selection set, as seen in Figure 3.21. When multiple objects are selected, the Use Selection Center option is automatically activated; the pivot point is determined by calculating the average center point for all objects in the selection set. Rotate the objects to get a feel for how this option works.

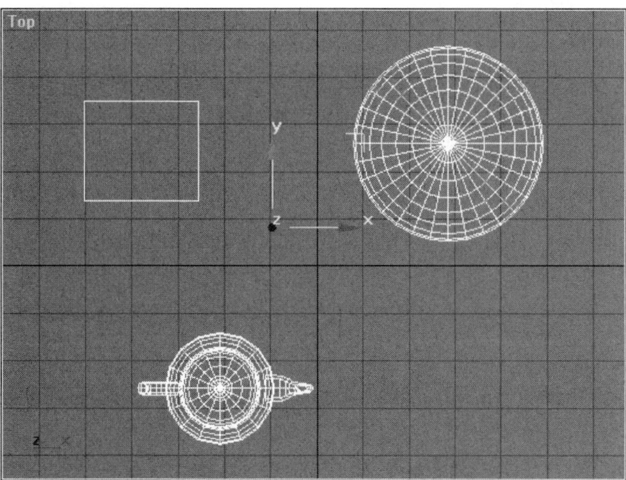

Figure 3.21
With multiple objects selected and the Use Selection Center option active, the temporary pivot point is located at the geometric center of the objects.

6. Select the Use Pivot Point Center option. Each object now maintains its own pivot point for transform, as shown in Figure 3.22. Using the Rotate tool rotates each object about its own pivot point.

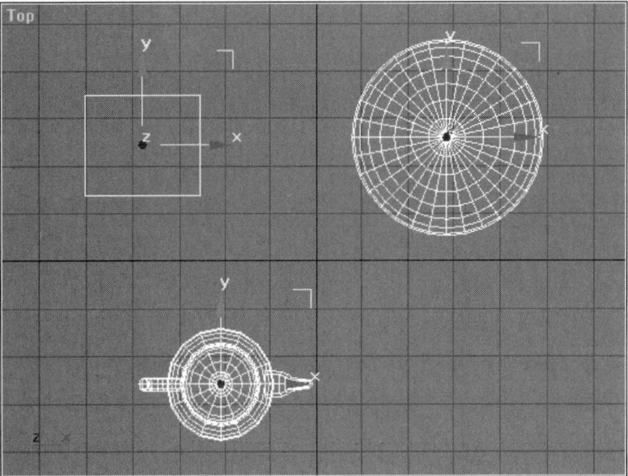

Figure 3.22
With multiple objects selected and the Use Pivot Point Center option active, the temporary pivot point is located at each object's true pivot point.

Pivot Points and Groups

Because groups of objects react like a single object, they maintain a single pivot point for transforms. The temporary pivot points can be used, but their effect will apply to the group as a whole rather than to its members. For example, if the objects in a group must be scaled from their individual pivot points, the group must be opened and the objects themselves selected and scaled with the Use Pivot Point Center option active.

Temporary Pivot Points and Subobjects

Subobjects (the components of 2D and 3D entities) can also be transformed, and the transform constraints and temporary pivot points will still be valid. In this exercise, assume that the letter *D* with the word *MAX* in the void area is your company's logo, and that the letter's center space is very tall and narrow. No font contains an appropriate example, but Times New Roman is a good place to start. By manipulating the spline and vertex subobjects, you can achieve the desired result. Follow these steps:

1. Reset MAX. In the Top viewport, create a Text primitive consisting of the letters *DMAX*, as shown in Figure 3.23, using the standard Windows font Times New Roman. Name this object DMAX Logo.

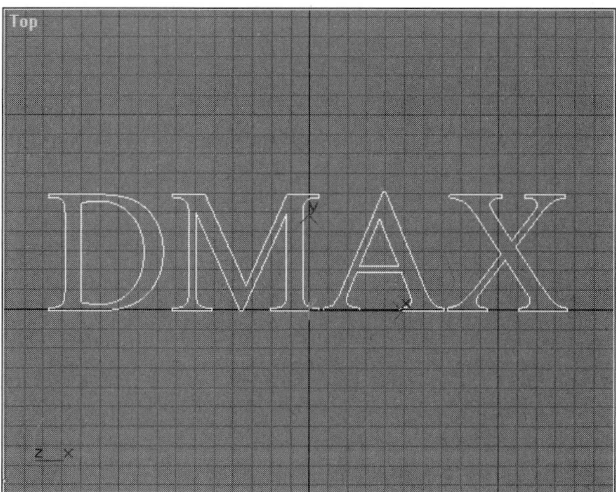

Figure 3.23
The DMAX Logo text uses the Times New Roman font.

2. Go to the Modify tab and highlight the entity type—Text—in the third field from the top. Right-clicking on this entry opens a pop-up menu that allows you to convert an object's type to one of up to five other types, as you can see in Figure 3.24. A parametric object can be converted to a mesh or spline, but the reverse is not true.

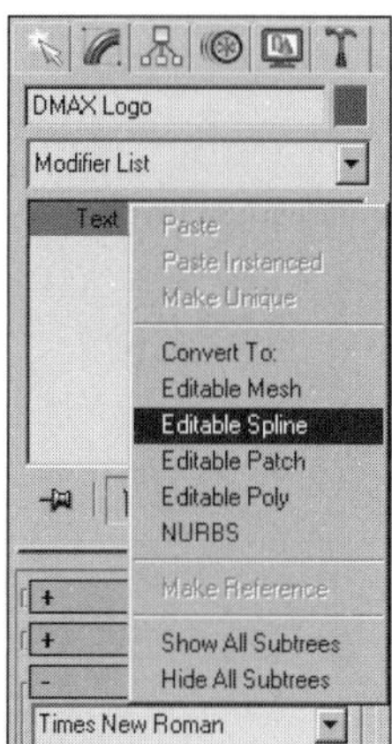

Figure 3.24
Right-clicking on an object's type opens a pop-up menu that gives you control over the object's type.

3. From the Convert To list on the pop-up menu, choose Editable Spline. This option removes any parametric capabilities of the Text primitive but will allow control over the object's vertices, segments, and component splines.

Note: *You can also gain control over a parametric spline's subobjects by applying an Editable Spline modifier (modifiers are covered in Chapter 6). Although this method retains the spline's parametric capabilities, stepping back and altering the parameters may not yield the desired result. For example, suppose you created a 10-pointed Star shape and then deleted all the vertices on the right side, leaving a half-star facing to the left. What would be the result if you changed the number of points in the Parameters rollout to 4? If you guessed two uneven points, oriented downward with the smaller leg to the right, you're either lucky or gifted.*

4. Use the Min/Max toggle in the bottom-right corner of the MAX window to expand the Top viewport to the entire width of the viewport area. Go to the Spline subobject level and select the letters *M*, *A*, and *X* with a crossing window. The letters will turn red to indicate that they are selected.

5. Choose the Scale transform, make sure that Use Selection Center is active, and apply a uniform scale to the subobjects until they are small enough to fit inside the *D*.

6. Rotate the letters 90 degrees about the Z-axis, again using the center of the selection set as the temporary pivot point.

7. Finally, move the *M*, *A*, and *X* inside the D and apply uniform or non-uniform Scale transforms to adjust the look of the letters. Exit the Spline subobject mode. Your quick logo, consisting of a single spline, should look similar to Figure 3.25.

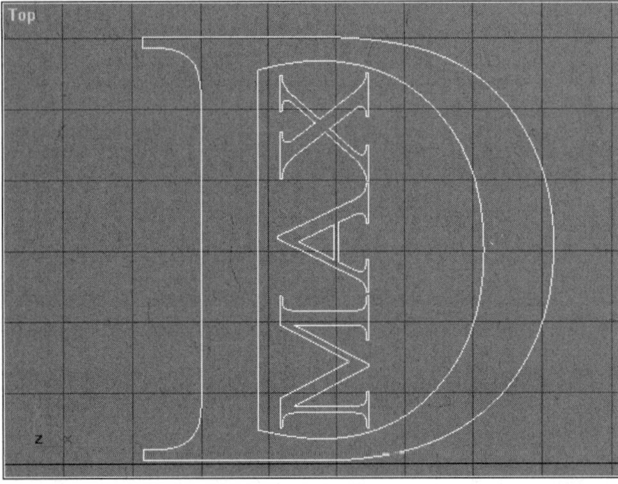

Figure 3.25
The final DMAX logo, created with one spline using the transform tools and temporary pivot points.

True Pivot Points

Each object's true pivot point (used with the Use Pivot Point Center option) can be relocated and reoriented to change the effects of the transforms. The controls for adjusting the pivot point are found under the Hierarchy tab of the Command panel. The options in the Move/Rotate/Scale group of the Adjust Pivot rollout determine how the pivot point is relocated in relation to the object. If you choose the Affect Pivot Only option, the object is stable while the pivot point is altered. The Affect Object Only option keeps the pivot stable while the object is altered. When objects are linked, the Affect Hierarchy Only option scales or rotates the position of the pivot point, but not the pivot point itself.

Let's work through an example of relocating an object's pivot point. Create a rectangular Box primitive, ensure that Use Pivot Point Center is active, and follow these steps:

1. Apply a Scale transform to the Box and watch as it appears to grow from, and shrink toward, the center of the bottom face.
2. Go to the Hierarchy tab of the Command panel and make sure the Pivot option is active in the top row of buttons. Choose Affect Pivot Only in the Adjust Pivot rollout. A bolder version of the axis tripod will appear at the pivot point.
3. Use the Move tool to relocate the pivot point to one of the Box's corners. Your scene should look similar to Figure 3.26.

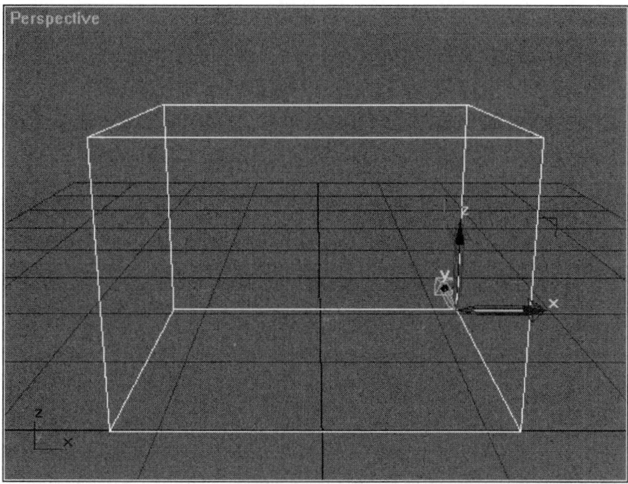

Figure 3.26
The pivot point has been relocated to one of the corners using the Affect Pivot Only option. The Perspective viewport is shown in a wireframe mode for clarity.

4. Turn off Affect Pivot Only mode (this step is often overlooked, and the transforms or commands are applied to the pivot point rather than the object itself) and apply the Scale transform. This time, the object scales from the corner where the pivot point is located.
5. Click on the Reset Pivot button in the Pivot Group to relocate and reorient the pivot to its default state.

6. You want to rotate the Box about its center point and across its corners. To do this, you manipulate the pivot point. Choose Affect Pivot Only and, in the Alignment group, pick Center To Object to move the pivot point to the geometric center of the Box.

7. Pick the Rotate tool and, in the Transform Type-In fields, enter "45" for the Z rotation. Turn off the Affect Pivot Only option.

8. To rotate the Box about any of the new axes' orientations, you must use the Local coordinate system. Choose Local and then rotate the box about its X- or Y-axis; it will tumble, as intended.

Linking Objects

When you're working in a MAX scene, often the transforms of one object must relatively affect the position, rotation, or scale of other objects. This effect is especially important when you're working in character animation. For example, suppose you have an arm bent at the elbow. If you rotate the shoulder, the angle at the elbow (and the locations of the hand and fingers) should remain the same, relative to the shoulder's new rotation. MAX makes this possible through a procedure known as *linking*.

Linking, which is sometimes called *parenting* in other applications, is the act of attaching one object (the child) to another object (the parent). It differs from grouping in a significant way: Linking creates a hierarchy of objects, with the child subjugated to the parent. If a transform is applied to a parent, it will also have an effect on the children; if a transform is applied to a child, the parent is unaffected.

Using the Link and Unlink Buttons

Located on the left side of the Main toolbar are the Select And Link and Select And Unlink buttons, which are used to set up hierarchies. It is important to note that child objects always pick the parents, and not the other way around—therefore, the first step in the linking process is to select the child.

To see how linking works, open the file Chap3_Link.max. It consists of seven Box primitives and two Spheres, as shown in Figure 3.27. Follow these steps:

1. Click on the Select And Link button and click-hold-drag the Sphere on the left. A dashed white line will appear between the object and the cursor, and the cursor will change shape when it is over an edge of another object.

2. Position the cursor over the far-left Box and release the mouse button. The Box will flash white briefly to indicate that the linking operation was successful.

3. Select the Box. Its pivot point has been moved to the far-left side. Rotate it about the Y-axis and notice that the Sphere rotates with it; however, its *relative* location, with respect to the Box, is unchanged.

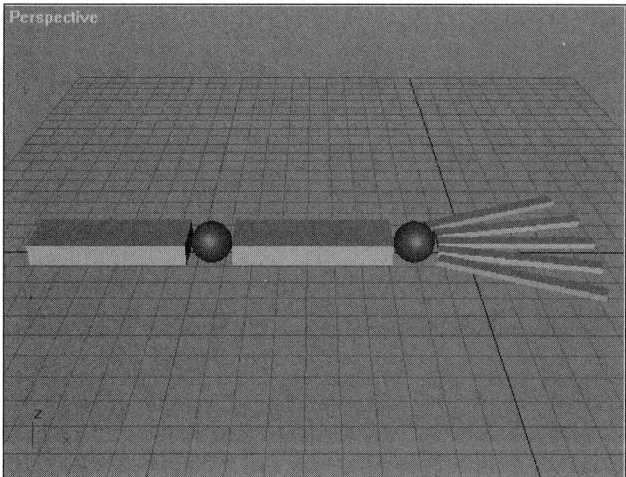

Figure 3.27
The initial layout of the Chap3_Link.max file, as seen in the Perspective viewport.

4. Undo the rotation. Link the middle Box to the left Sphere, and the right Sphere to the middle Box. Take a moment to experiment with the hierarchy to make sure it functions properly.
5. Continuing to use the Select And Link button, select all five unlinked Boxes and, in one step, drag the cursor to see a dashed line going from each Box to the cursor. Link these Boxes to the left Sphere.

You now have a hierarchy consisting of all the objects in the scene. You can arrange the objects in configurations that would be difficult and time consuming to achieve by transforming each object independently. Make sure you are using the Local coordinate system to allow proper rotation along the axis of the object, and experiment with the limitless possibilities available when applying transforms to the individual parent objects.

On occasion, you may need to transform a parent object temporarily, without altering its child. To do so, follow these steps in the scene from the previous example:

1. Select the left Sphere. Enter the Hierarchy tab in the Command panel and, in the Adjust Transform rollout, click on the Don't Affect Children button. Move the Sphere away from its current location—its children do not move with it.
2. Turn off the Don't Affect Children option. Rotate the Sphere, and the children will rotate about its new location. If the relationship between the parent and the child is to be permanently broken, use the Select And Unlink option and pick the child.
3. Open the Select Objects dialog box. The Display Subtree and Select Subtree options apply to hierarchical situations. Select the Display Subtree checkbox and observe that the child objects become indented under their parent object, as seen in Figure 3.28. The Select Subtree checkbox causes all child objects to be selected when the parent is selected.

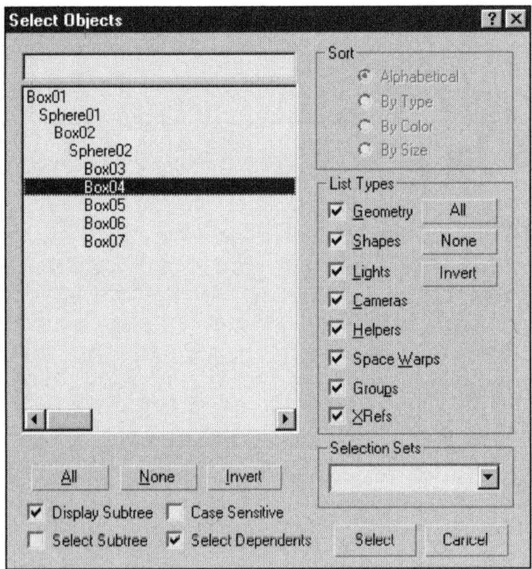

Figure 3.28
The Select Objects dialog box, showing how the hierarchy appears when the Display Subtree checkbox is selected.

Leaving the Link Mode

The Link and Unlink buttons, the transforms, and several other buttons place you in a mode that you must leave in order to continue operating in MAX. The quickest way to do this is to click on Select Object; doing so places you in the mode that has the least direct impact if inadvertently used in a scene.

Linking to Dummy Objects

A Dummy is a helper object in MAX that has an axis and Local coordinate system but that does not render. Dummies are used when a hierarchy is required but one or more of the objects should not be visible, or when the objects must be rotated along more than one axis at a time. MAX has two types of Dummy objects to choose from: Dummies and Points. These options appear under Create|Helpers in the Command panel. Both have identical capabilities. The Point is shaped like a cross, and the Dummy is a Box; the Dummy is generally easier to see.

We'll use the Dummy in the following exercise, which is designed to animate the rotation of a logo around two axes simultaneously. This operation is impossible using the Rotate transforms of a single object.

1. Open the Chap3_Dummy.max file from the CD-ROM. It contains an extruded version of the DMAX logo that has been rotated about its X-axis. The pivot point is centered on the object, and the logo is located at the origin.

2. Activate the Dummy option, and then create a Dummy about the same size of the logo by picking the center point and dragging out a cube. The exact size is irrelevant.

3. Use the Transform Type-In fields to move the Dummy to the origin. Doing so centers it on the logo.
4. Link the logo to the Dummy and test the link.
5. Slide the Time Slider to frame 100 and click on the Animate button. The button will turn red to indicate that MAX is in an animation mode.
6. Ensure that the Dummy is selected. Rotate it –90 degrees about the Local Z-axis.
7. Select the logo and rotate it –90 degrees about its X-axis. The Transform Type-Ins should read 0.0, 0.0, and –90.0, from left to right. The logo should be lying flat, as shown in Figure 3.29.

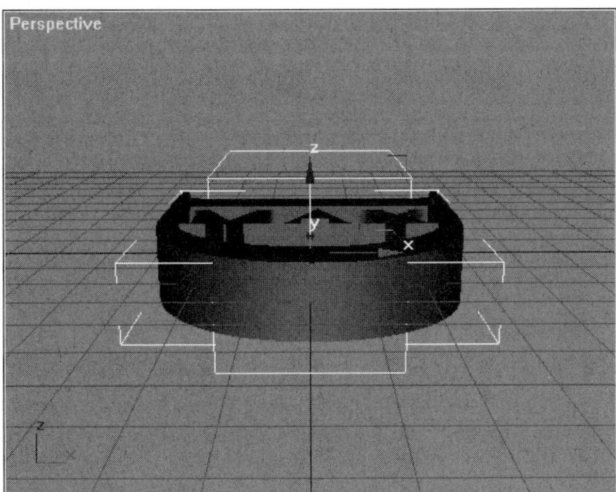

Figure 3.29
The extruded DMAX logo after applying rotation transforms to it and to its parent Dummy.

8. Click on the Animate button to exit the animation mode, switch to the Perspective viewport if necessary, and click on the Play Animation button in the Time Controls area. As expected, the logo smoothly rotates about two axes to lie down in the XY plane.

Dummy and Point objects are indispensable in setting up objects and particularly in animating the objects in a scene. You will find yourself using them in many of the scenes you create.

Moving On

This long chapter addressed many of the basic elements of manipulating a scene. Using and understanding the concepts and interactions of coordinate systems, pivot points, linking, and Dummy objects are not easy tasks, but they are requirements if a scene is to be put together and animated properly and efficiently. The bright side is that you will use these operations all the time, and they will soon become second nature to you.

The next chapter will address the many commands and controls that are available to manage the MAX viewports and the appearance and visibility of objects in those viewports. Different tasks require different ways of viewing and manipulating the current scene, and MAX gives you the tools to do this efficiently.

Chapter 4

Managing the Display

When you look at the viewports in the MAX window, you see a representation of a virtual world that you have created. The special relationship between objects is governed by their parameters and the transforms applied to them, as well as their locations in the World coordinate system. To allow you to manipulate these objects more easily, MAX provides tools to change the viewpoint from which you see the scene, to hide or reveal objects, to control the appearance of objects, and to "freeze" objects so they are seen but cannot be altered. This chapter will discuss both the tools you can use to control the display of objects in the viewports and the controls that alter the viewports themselves.

The Viewports

MAX scenes can be configured to display up to four distinct viewports, each showing the scene from a different point of view. Viewports can show orthographic or perspective projections, or arbitrary User views; none of these views has a distinct relationship with anything created in the scene. Viewports can also show the scene from the point of view of a virtual camera or from several different types of light. The following sections examine the various types of MAX viewports.

Perspective and Orthographic Viewports

When scenes or events are depicted on a flat medium, such as paper, canvas, or a computer screen, two styles of view are generally used: perspective and orthographic. A person's eyes see a *perspective view*, as does a camera or other type of lens. In perspective, a cone-shaped field of view is determined, either naturally or through the use of lenses, and all light is channeled to the cone's apex—the eye. Because objects farther from the eye take up a smaller angular portion of the cone, they appear smaller than objects closer to the eye. When objects transition from near to far, like the railroad tracks in Figure 4.1, they appear to converge at a vanishing point on the horizon.

Orthographic views are most commonly used in technical layouts. This type of view differs from a perspective view in that all light rays travel perpendicular to each other and project onto a plane, rather than converging at an apex. (In computer graphics, the plane is the computer screen or a particular viewport.) As a result, all objects appear the same size, regardless of their distance from the projection plane; no convergence-related distortion occurs.

To see examples of both types of view, open the file Chap4_Ortho_Pers.max from the Chapter 4 section of the CD-ROM. The scene consists of 20 identical Cylinders in a row extending in the World Y direction. The Top and Left viewports (both orthographic) show the row with no distortion, whereas the Perspective viewport shows a distinct difference in the Cylinders' visible height from the front to the back of the row. If the Left viewport was a similar perspective view (with the apex of the field-of-view cone even with the middle of the row), the end Cylinders would be slightly smaller than those in the middle because the linear distances between them would be slightly greater. Figure 4.2 shows the Left and Perspective viewports. The grid lines adhere to

Figure 4.1
In the photograph, the railroad tracks converge at a vanishing point at the horizon. This is an example of the convergence inherent to perspective views.

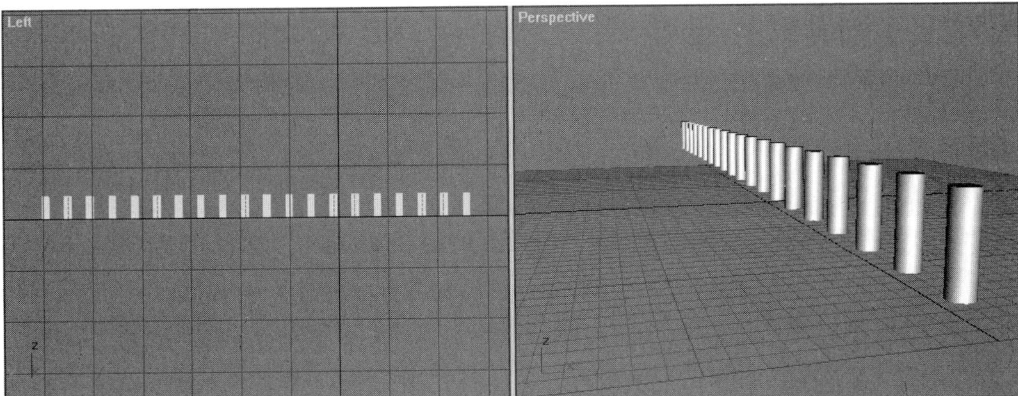

Figure 4.2
In the Left (orthographic) viewport, the Cylinders all appear the same size and the grid lines are parallel to each other. In the Perspective viewport, the Cylinders shrink with distance and the grid lines converge.

the orthographic and perspective rules—those in the Left viewport run parallel to each other, and those in the Perspective viewport converge as the distance from the viewpoint increases.

The Front viewport is the most descriptive orthographic view. It shows all the Cylinders; because they are identical and appear the same size in an orthographic viewport, however, their edges line up perfectly. Thus, the first Cylinder blocks the rest from view.

Top, Front, and Left are the most commonly used orthographic views, but Bottom, Back, and Right are also available. See the section "Viewing and Layout Options" for the methods of changing views.

The Field-Of-View Tool

The Perspective viewport relies on the field-of-view concept (similar to the viewable area, seen through a camera lens, that is determined by the focal length) to determine its appearance. Watch the viewport navigation tools in the bottom-right corner of the MAX window as you switch between an orthographic and the Perspective viewport. In the Perspective viewport, one of the icons changes to a pie-slice shape, indicating that it is now the Field-Of-View tool; this tool alters the viewable angle available in the viewport.

To see the Field-Of-View tool in action, make the Perspective viewport current. Activate the Field-Of-View tool, and the cursor will change to look like the icon. Click in the viewport and drag up and down to see the effect as the viewpoint remains constant while the angle viewed increases or decreases. The larger field-of-view angles have the greater perspective distortion effect.

Note: *Because nothing in the scene has been transformed or modified, you can't undo changes to the field-of-view angle or viewpoint; nor can you undo any other alterations, such as zooming or panning, in a viewport. If the change does not yield the desired result, you must reissue the command until the view is satisfactory.*

With a viewport active, you can enter an exact angle manually by right-clicking on any of the viewport navigation tools to bring up the Viewport Configuration dialog box shown in Figure 4.3. In the Perspective User View group of the Rendering Method tab, enter the desired angle in the Field Of View box (this option is disabled in orthographic views); click on OK to apply it and return to the scene. Any angle from 1 to 180 is valid, but extreme values are rarely of any use because of the excessive distortion or minute visual angles they provide. Figure 4.4 shows the Chap4_Ortho_Pers.max file with a 90-degree field-of-view angle on the left and a 30-degree field-

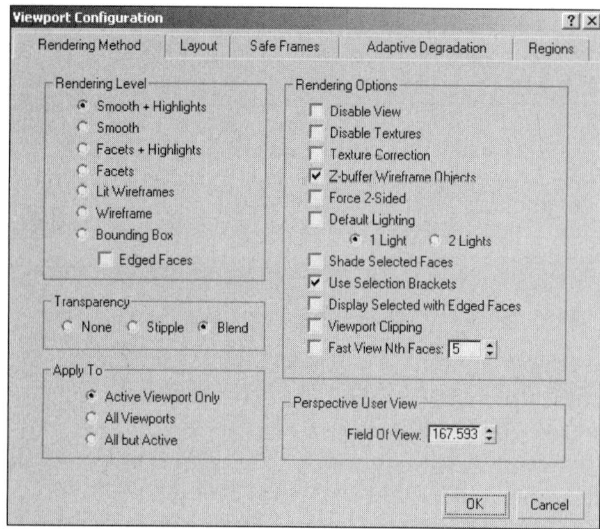

Figure 4.3
You can enter an exact Field Of View value in the Viewport Configuration dialog box.

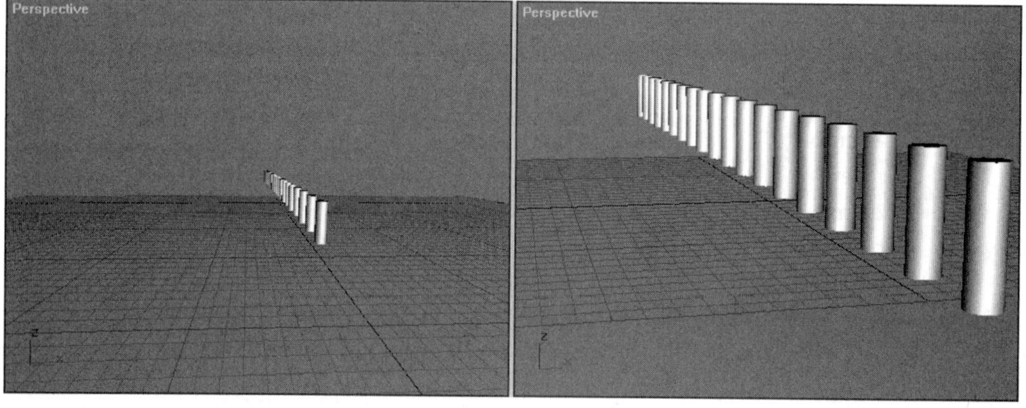

Figure 4.4
The Cylinders are shown with a 90-degree field-of-view angle on the left and a 30-degree field-of-view angle on the right.

of-view angle on the right. Be aware of the perspective distortion; especially in indoor scenes, this distortion can be more evident and detrimental, because of the close quarters and parallel walls.

User View

A User view is a blend of the orthographic and perspective views that has traits of both. The true orthographic views are square to the World coordinate system; their viewpoint looks straight along one of the axes. The perspective views are not square to the World coordinate system; their viewpoint can be at any location. User views maintain an arbitrary parallel projection of the scene from any location without encountering any perspective distortion. You use the Arc Rotate tool to create and modify User views, as explained in the next section.

Viewport Navigation Tools

A smooth and efficient workflow requires that you be able to view the object or objects you are currently working on quickly and easily. Mastering the tools that let you modify the way a viewport displays the virtual world is essential and surprisingly easy.

The viewport navigation tools are the eight icons located in the bottom-right corner of the MAX window. As you've seen with the Field-Of-View icon, different tools are available when different types of viewports are used. (Additional tools are available when the viewports display the scene through a light or camera; these tools will be discussed in Chapters 13 and 14.) The tools that remain constant for various types of viewports often have different effects, depending on the type of viewport in which they are implemented. Open the file Uhg.max from the Chapter 4 section of the CD-ROM (Uhg is the character's name—it's pronounced like the sound you make when a six-year-old unexpectedly punches you in the stomach) and, as you read through the tools' descriptions, experiment with them in the viewports.

The Zoom and Zoom All Tools

When you're in an orthographic viewport, the Zoom and Zoom All tools let you move the viewpoint closer or farther from the scene by clicking and dragging up or down. The Zoom tool affects only the current viewport, whereas the Zoom All tool affects all orthographic, perspective, and User viewports equally. The Zoom, Zoom All, and many other viewport navigation tools are *modal*, meaning they stay active once you use them; you must exit them by switching to another tool or right-clicking when they are no longer needed.

In contrast to the Field-Of-View tool, the Zoom and Zoom All tools change the distance from the scene to the viewpoint in a Perspective viewport without changing the field-of-view angle.

If you're using a mouse that has a wheel (this type of mouse is highly recommended), the wheel can be used in lieu of the Zoom tool. By rolling the wheel, you can zoom the viewport without leaving the current command.

Zooming about the Mouse Point

You may have noticed that as you use the Zoom tool, the objects in the scene appear to move closer to the cursor as well as to the viewpoint. This feature allows you to zoom to a relatively small object in a large scene simply by placing your cursor on it when using the Zoom tool and dragging upward. To turn off this feature, so no lateral change in the viewpoint occurs during a zoom, choose Preferences from the Customize drop-down menu and then click on the Viewports tab of the Preference Settings dialog box. In the Mouse Control area, select those checkboxes that determine in what type of viewport zooming about the mouse should occur.

The Zoom Extents and Zoom Extents All Tools

Clicking on the Zoom Extents tool expands the current viewport as required to show all objects present in the scene. Holding down the button reveals a second option, Zoom Extents Selected. This option expands the viewport to show all objects that are part of the current selection set.

The Zoom Extents All tool and its expanded option, Zoom Extents All Selected, perform the same operations as their counterparts—but in all orthographic, perspective, and User viewports. None of the four zoom options covered here affect Camera or Light viewports; those viewports have separate controls that determine their views.

The Region Zoom Tool

The Region Zoom tool collapses a viewport to fit everything within a rectangle that you draw within the viewport. New to 3ds max 4 is a feature that allows this tool to be also available in perspective views; just click and hold the Field-Of-View button.

The Pan Tool

The Pan tool changes the viewpoint laterally without changing the distance to the objects. You can also implement it by holding down the middle button roller (or wheel) on a wheeled mouse and dragging. If you need to pan through a very linear scene, holding down the I key while dragging accelerates the movement.

The Min/Max Toggle

The Min/Max toggle simply expands the current viewport to fill the space occupied by all viewports on screen; or, if only one viewport is displayed, it toggles all others into view. Of all the viewport navigation tools, this one is probably used most frequently, because it allows the biggest possible view.

The Arc Rotate Tool

The Arc Rotate tool creates a User view by changing the point of view while maintaining an orthographic projection. The following exercise will show you the basics of using the Arc Rotate tool, but doing so will become second nature only with practice and time. Follow these steps:

1. Perform a Zoom Extents All to fill all the viewports with the Uhg model.

2. Make the Front viewport active and click on the Arc Rotate icon. A light-colored "trackball" circle appears centered in the viewport, with crosses and boxes at each quadrant, as shown in Figure 4.5. This circle helps control the viewpoint's movements by allowing you to restrict the planes being moved about by dragging directly on the quadrants. When you drag, having selected Arc Rotate, the center of the viewport is used as the center point for viewpoint movements.

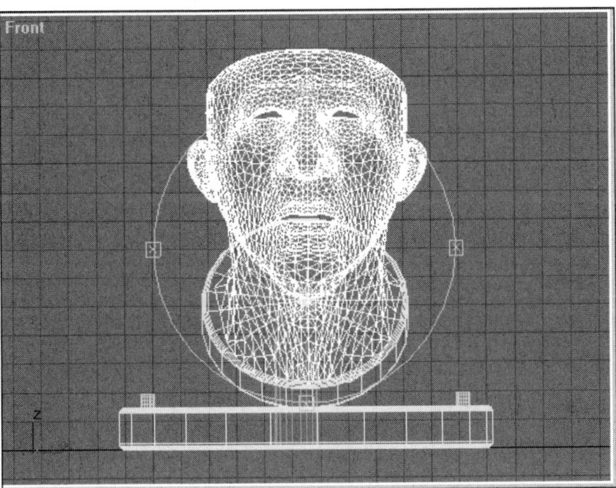

Figure 4.5
The Arc Rotate tool creates a temporary circular icon to help control the viewpoint's movements.

Changing Viewports

It's easy to lose control of your location using the Arc Rotate tool—when you first try to use it, you may need to start over. To change a viewport from its current state to an orthographic, perspective, user, camera, or light view, right-click directly on the name in the upper-left corner of any viewport. In the resulting pop-up menu, scroll down to the Views option to see an expanded list of all available views. Select the one you want, and it will replace the current viewport.

---

3. Select one of the side quadrants and drag right and left, using short movements; watch as your point of view pivots around the center of the viewport. Try the same movements using the top or bottom icons, but be aware that it is possible to rotate the view so that the objects are beyond the boundaries of the viewport.
4. Change the viewport (now named User) back to a Front view and select the head. Click and hold the Arc Rotate tool and choose the middle Arc Rotate Selected option from the flyout. With this option, the current selection is used as the center point when you drag the quadrants. The Arc Rotate subobject option uses a subobject selection as the center point rather than the entire selected object.

With practice, the Arc Rotate tool will become an invaluable way to display and navigate through your scenes.

Viewing and Layout Options

You have nearly total control of the quantity (up to four at a time) and configuration of the viewports in MAX. Many default configurations are available, and each can be customized to fit a particular work style. The following sections discuss the methods for adjusting the shape and quantity of the viewports as well as surrendering viewport spaces to accommodate expanded Command panels.

Viewport Configurations

To see the available viewport configurations, right-click on any viewport configuration tool and select the Layout tab in the Viewport Configuration dialog box, as shown in Figure 4.6. Across the top are 14 possible viewport configurations; an enlarged view of the current configuration appears in the center of the dialog box.

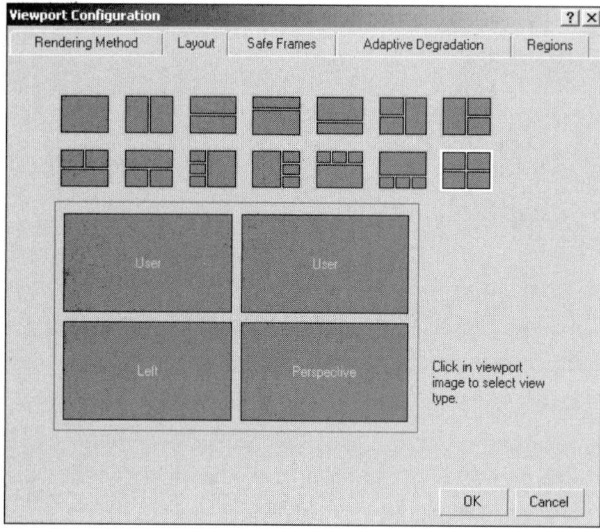

Figure 4.6
The Layout tab of the Viewport Configuration dialog box allows you to configure the type and layout of the viewports.

Clicking in any of the enlarged viewports brings up a menu identical to the one that appears when you right-click on a viewport name to change the viewport type.

Each viewport can maintain a different level of detail. While still in the Viewport Configuration dialog box, switch to the Rendering Method tab. The Rendering Level group contains all the available ways a viewport can display the objects in a scene. The highest quality option, Smooth + Highlights, shows the clearest view of the objects. The Bounding Box option replaces all the geometry in the display with the smallest possible boxes in which the geometry will fit. The options between Smooth + Highlights and Bounding Box are on a sliding scale of display quality. The tradeoff between the highest quality and lowest quality are speed and functionality. A large scene may take several seconds to execute a zoom or pan command if it must calculate the Smooth + Highlights display; on the other hand, a Bounding Box view is extremely fast but not very practical. A common compromise is to use Smooth + Highlights in Perspective or Camera viewports and to use the Wireframe option (where only the edges of objects show) in other viewports. The rendering level controls are also available by right-clicking on the viewport names.

New to 3ds max 4 is the ability to configure the viewports manually to any rectilinear size. To do so, place the cursor at the intersection of the four viewports, click, and then drag the intersection to anywhere within the viewport windows. Placing the cursor between any two viewports will let you resize them in a similar way, but you're constrained to a single axis.

Multiple Columns

Often, the Command panels are so long that you must scroll down to see the required commands. Another new feature in 3ds max 4 is the ability to make long Command panels appear as multiple columns. To do so, place the cursor between the far-right viewports and the Command panel and then drag to the left. Figure 4.7 shows the Uhg.max file with the viewports in a custom configuration and the Command panel expanded so it's three columns wide.

Displaying the Scene

The Display tab in the Command panel contains the controls that determine what is displayed in the viewports. The options in the rollouts determine how objects appear globally. Objects can be hidden from view—frozen so that they cannot be modified—or they can be displayed in a variety of ways, as shown in the following sections.

The Display Floater and Quad Menu

Many of the tools discussed here are also available in the modeless Display Floater dialog box or Quad menu. Select Tools|Display Floater or bring up the Quad menu by selecting and then right-clicking on an object.

Hide By Category and Hide

Sometimes you need to hide objects that can't be deleted, in order to clean up a scene and allow a better workflow. The Hide By Category rollout determines which types of objects are *not* displayed in the viewports. For example, if the Lights checkbox is selected, all lights are hidden from view, although their effect is still evident.

The Hide rollout contains controls that determine whether a specific object—rather than an entire category—is viewed. Most of the six Hide and Unhide buttons are self-explanatory. The two By Name buttons bring up a now-familiar dialog box, and the Hide By Hit button activates a mode in which objects to be hidden are picked directly from the screen.

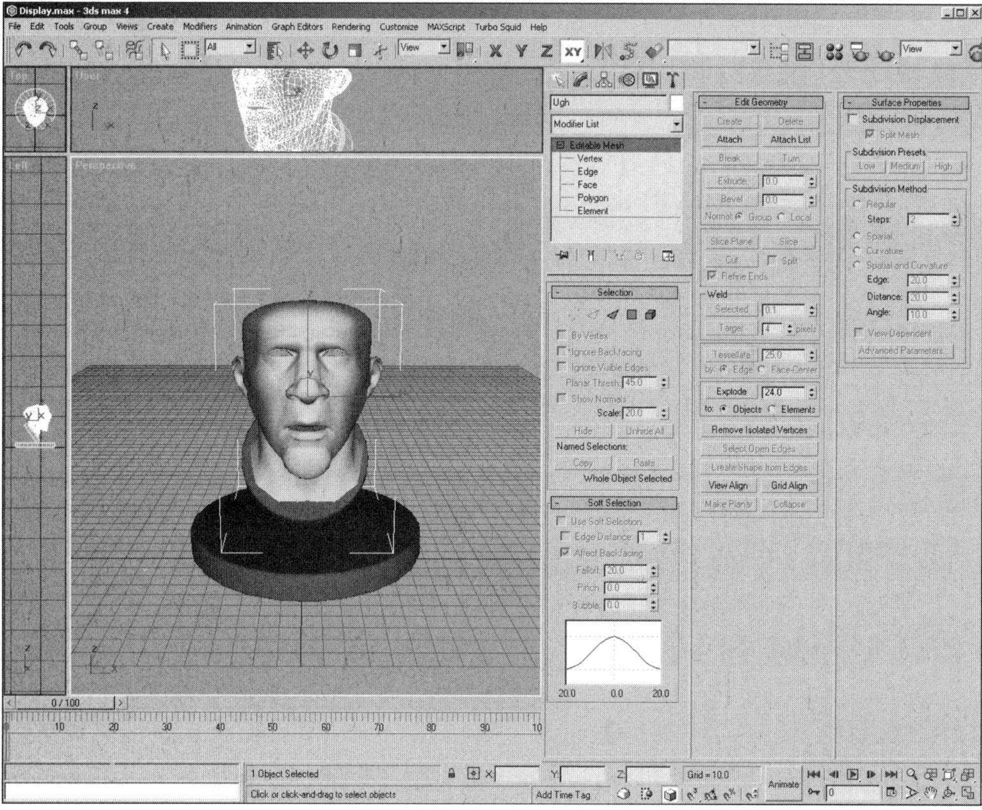

Figure 4.7
The Uhg.max file with a custom viewport configuration and expanded Command panel.

Freeze

Freezing an object makes it nonselectable but maintains its visibility. Once an object is frozen, it is displayed by default in a dark gray color, but you can retain its original color by deselecting the Show Frozen In Gray option in the Display Properties rollout. The downside to this option is that frozen objects are now undistinguishable from unfrozen ones. You can't do anything to the object—including select it—until it is unfrozen. Use this tool when an object must remain exactly as it is, and when hiding it is not a feasible option.

Display Properties

The Display Properties rollout determines how objects are displayed in the viewports only; these options are disregarded when the scene is rendered. Many of the commands have limited uses and are covered in other sections of this book; to help you understand those that are discussed here, however, let's look at an example:

1. Continue to use the Uhg.max file. Toggle the Perspective viewport to a full screen, change it to a Wireframe view, and perform a Zoom All. The viewport should look similar to Figure 4.8.

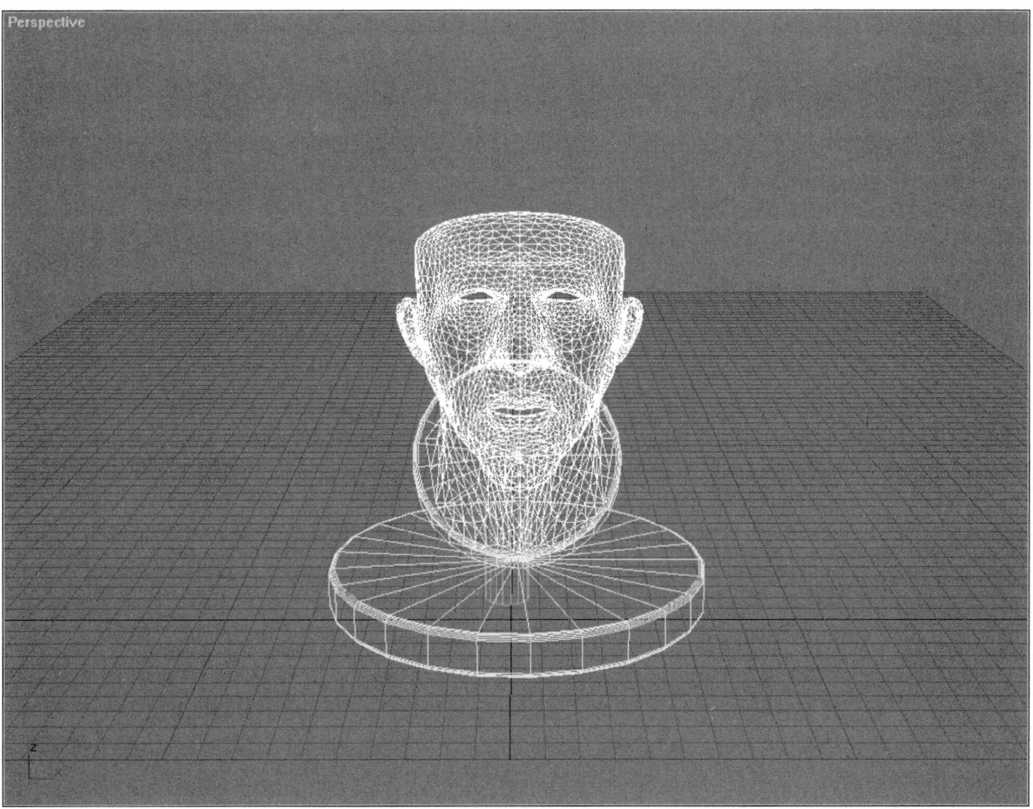

Figure 4.8
The Uhg.max file in a Wireframe mode with the Perspective viewport maximized.

2. Select the Base object. Notice that the edges that wrap around the back of the object are *culled*, or disregarded. To make these edges visible (often making the object's shape easier to understand), deselect the Backface Cull checkbox in the Display Properties rollout.

3. Change the Perspective viewport back to Smooth + Highlights view and select the head. To help identify one object's relationship to another, MAX gives you the ability to display an object as semi-transparent. Select the See-Through box in the Display Properties rollout; you can now see the platform on which the head is sitting.

The Isolate Tool

When you're working on a relatively small object, several steps may be required to bring only that object into a close-up view. You may need to hide many objects and zoom in on the desired object; then, after the work is done, you must perform these steps in reverse order to reset the view to its previous state. The Isolate tool takes care of all these tasks.

For example, to isolate the post that holds up the platform in the Uhg.max file, follow these steps:

1. Select the Post object.
2. Press and hold the Ctrl key and right-click on the post to bring up a modified Quad menu.
3. Choose Isolate Tool from the menu's Display section, and click on it to open the Isolated dialog box. MAX hides all other objects and zooms the post to fit the current viewport. After making any necessary modifications, click on the Exit Isolation button in the Isolated dialog box to return to the original scene.

Changing Colors

To further customize the way MAX displays entities on the screen, you can change the color of nearly everything imaginable. To change the default colors of MAX's many entities, choose Customize|Customize User Interface to open the Customize User Interface dialog box. Click on the Colors tab, as shown in Figure 4.9.

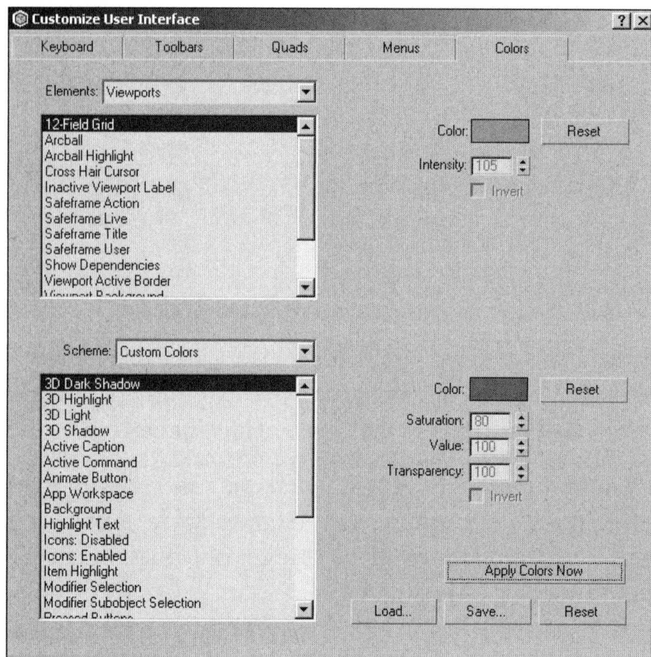

Figure 4.9
The Colors tab of the Customize User Interface dialog box.

As an example, follow these steps to change the viewport's background color:

1. Choose Viewports from the Elements drop-down list. All of the viewport-related entities appear in the field below the list.

2. In that field, select Viewport Background.
3. Click in the Color swatch to bring up the Color Selector dialog box. Pick the new background color and then click on Close to return to the Customize User Interface dialog box.
4. Click on Apply Colors Now and close the dialog box.

Adding a Background Image

It's very common to display an image in the background of a viewport. Doing so relieves you of the responsibility of creating an entire virtual world and adds a great deal of realism to the scene. The uses of background images vary from simple skies that appear over intricate environments to complex images to which the MAX scene must be matched.

The following procedure places a background image in the viewport only; a separate step (identified in Chapter 14) is required to place the image in the scene during a render. To place a viewport background image, follow these steps:

1. Switch to the viewport in which the image is to appear. Choose Viewport Background from the Views drop-down list.
2. In the Background Source group, click on Files and navigate to the appropriate image file. If an image is already designated for use as a background for rendering, the Use Environment Background checkbox is available to match the viewport background to the rendering background.
3. Make sure the Display Background checkbox is activated, and click on OK to leave the dialog box. The viewport now displays the selected file as a background image.

MAX has the additional ability to treat viewports as virtual viewports, allowing you to zoom in on the background as well as on the objects in front. Virtual viewports are used when objects in the scene must be placed precisely in regards to the background elements. To do this, the video driver used must be an OpenGL type; it can be set and configured in the Display Drivers group of the Customize|Preferences|Viewports tab. With the viewport containing the background of the current one, reopen the Viewport Background dialog box. Activate Match Bitmap in the Aspect Ratio group, select the Lock Zoom/Pan option, and then click on OK. Perform a zoom in the viewport, and the background zooms in also.

Moving On

This chapter covered the many tools available for managing and customizing the viewports and objects in MAX. Learning and practicing with these tools until they are second nature to you will result in a workflow that is smooth and consistent. Time is money, and the less time you spend adjusting the view of an object, the more time you'll spend modeling and perfecting the scene.

The next chapter covers many of the MAX features and tools that save you time by streamlining the creation process and adding precision to your scenes. Some of the topics discussed include features such as cloning to create independent copies or copies that retain relationships with one another, creating arrays to generate multiple copies in an organized pattern, and using the Snapshot tool to create copies along an object's animated lifespan.

Chapter 5
Working Smart

Over the course of its existence, MAX has been upgraded constantly to enhance its ability to be used as a high output, highly accurate modeling and animation package. Repetitive tasks have been streamlined, shortcuts have been implemented, and the precision tools have been made easier to use. This chapter concentrates on the powerful and indispensable tools that make working in MAX easier so that its creative uses can flourish.

Cloning (Duplicating) Objects

MAX refers to the process of duplicating objects as *cloning*. You can create three types of clones:

- *Copy*—A *copy* is a completely new object that has no affiliation with the object from which it was cloned. Modifying an object has no effect on its clone, and modifying a clone has no effect on the original object.
- *Instance*—An *instance* is a clone of an object in a capacity where both objects share the same modifier stack and parameters. If any instanced object is modified or its parameters are adjusted, the changes will be immediately visible in all the instances of that object. In addition to letting you modify many objects simultaneously (imagine needing to change the radius of 200 fence posts if they were not instanced clones), using instances reduces the file size. Rather than having to define each object separately, the program needs to define only one; it then identifies the location and orientation of all the others. The transforms (Move, Rotate, Scale, and Manipulate) do not apply to the instances, so instances can be positioned and oriented independently.

- *Reference*—A *reference* is a blend of a copy and an instance. When an object is referenced, it shares the modifier stack with the original, up to the point that it was created. Additional modifiers applied to the reference clone do not apply to the original.

When you're creating clones, the choice of the clone type is important. If you are certain that the object must remain independent of all others, choose Copy. If the slightest possibility exists that the object will need to remain identical to the original, choose Instance. If the instanced relationship needs to be broken at some point, you can select the object and click on the Make Unique button in the Modify panel. The selected object will then become a simple copy of the original object. References are used under specific circumstances, so choosing this clone type depends on the type of project. The referenced relationship can also be broken at any time with the Make Unique button.

MAX has several tools you can use to make single and multiple duplicates of objects. They range from simple copies to multidimensional arrays that change the location, rotation, and scale of the original. We'll discuss basic cloning, arrays, snapshots, and mirroring in the following sections.

Cloning Basics

The simplest way to clone an object is to select it and then choose Clone from the Edit drop-down menu. The Clone Options dialog box appears, as shown in Figure 5.1.

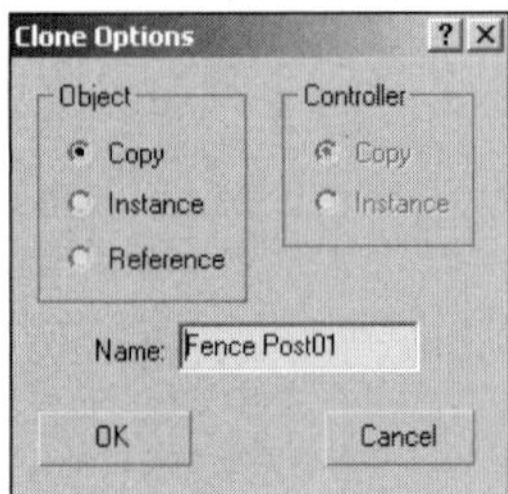

Figure 5.1
The Clone Options dialog box, opened from the Edit menu.

In the Object group, you specify the type of clone to be made. The Controller group will be grayed out if an object rather than an animation controller is selected. By default, the Name field shows the original object's name with an incrementally higher number for each clone; you can override this value simply by typing in a new name. When you click on OK, the duplicate is created in the same location and orientation as the original—you must move it in order to see it.

***Note:** When you're using any of the cloning methods addressed in this book, remember that after the cloning operation is completed, the last object created—not the original—is now the selected object.*

The more common method of cloning objects is to hold down the Shift key while using any of the transforms. This method lets you make multiple copies at incremental locations, rotations, or scales, and leaves the original object in place. The following exercise will demonstrate this method, as well as show the effect of using the Copy, Instance, and Reference clone types. Follow these steps:

1. Open the file Chap5_Clone.max from the CD-ROM. It shows a tall, thin Box with a Bend modifier applied to it.
2. Select the Box in the Top viewport and hold down the Shift key. Move the Box approximately 20 units to the right, using the Transform Type-In fields as a guide.
3. The resulting Clone Options dialog box is different from that shown in Figure 5.1; it has an additional Number Of Copies field. Enter "7" in this field and make sure Copy is selected in the Object group. The dialog box should look like Figure 5.2. Click on OK.

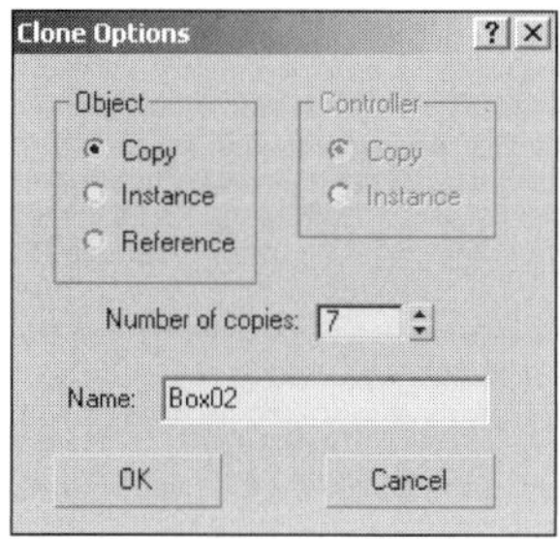

Figure 5.2
The Clone Options dialog box just prior to making multiple copies of the Box.

4. The scene now contains eight objects (seven copies plus the original), and the eighth Box is selected. Go to the Modify tab of the Command panel, which shows the parameters for the Bend modifier applied to the original Box (and also to the clones), as shown in Figure 5.3. Use the spinner buttons to change the Angle value. The selected Box bends, but the others remain stable—the clone type is Copy, so each is an independent object. Undo the scene until only the original Box remains; or, if necessary, delete the seven Box copies and then select the original.

Rapidly Changing Spinner Values

Clicking the up or down spinner button often has only a small impact on the associated value. To make rapid changes to the value, click and hold a spinner button and drag the mouse up or down.

5. Repeat Steps 2 and 3, choosing Instance as the clone type. Change the Angle value of the last Box; this time, all the Boxes reflect the change. Select any of the other Boxes and change the Angle value; the result is the same.
6. Select the last Box and make one more clone to the right, this time choosing Reference as the clone type.

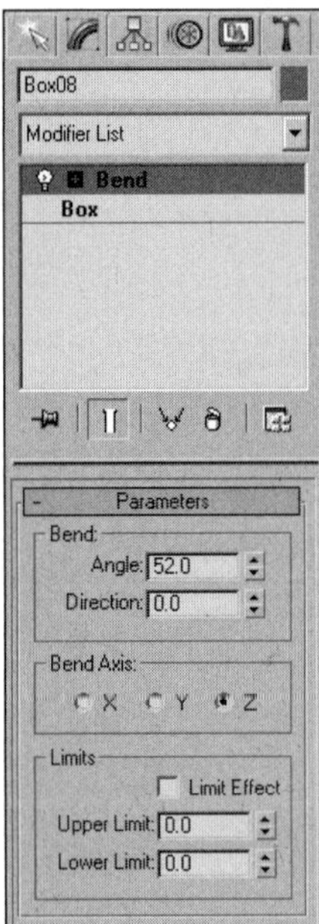

Figure 5.3
The Modify panel for the Box clones showing the parameters for the Bend modifier.

7. The Modify tab shows a gray bar above the Bend modifier to signify that the Box is now a reference. Open the Modifier List drop-down list, scroll down to the Parametric Modifiers area, and choose Twist.

8. In the Parameters rollout (that is, the Twist Parameters, not the Bend Parameters), change the angle. This time only the last Box is affected, because the Twist modifier was applied after the reference copy was made.

9. Select any of the other Boxes and change the Bend angle. All of the Boxes—even the last reference clone—are affected, because the Bend modifier was applied before the reference clone was made. If you need additional clones that follow the settings of the final Box you created, simply make instanced clones of it.

Using the transforms is a simple and common way to create many identical objects, each of which may or may not have additional modifiers applied. As another exercise, try making the spokes of a wagon wheel by holding down the Shift key while rotating a cylinder and making several instances.

The Array Tool

An *array* is a regular grouping or arrangement of objects. You've been creating a simple array by using the Move tool to create multiple clones in an organized pattern. MAX provides the Array tool, shown in Figure 5.4, to help you create multidimensional arrays that can use all three transforms at the same time. The top controls fall into two categories. The left side, Incremental,

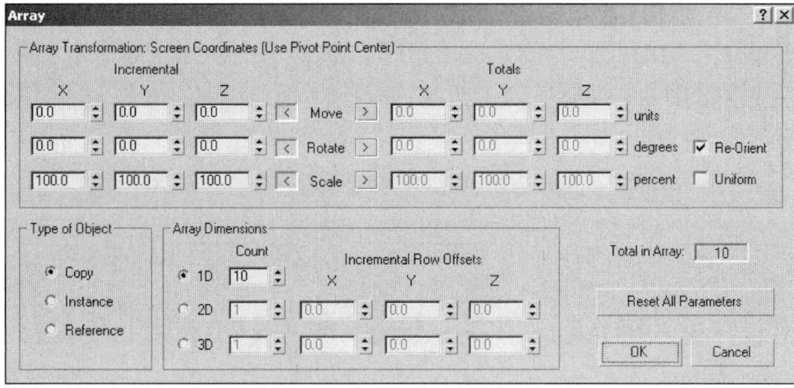

Figure 5.4
The Array dialog box with its default settings.

contains fields in which you enter the amounts the transforms change between objects. The right side, Totals, contains fields in which you enter the sums of the amounts the transforms change between objects. You can use either set of controls by clicking on the arrows next to the transform names. For consistency in our examples, we'll use the Incremental controls exclusively. At the bottom of the Array tool, the Type Of Object group determines the type of clone to make, and the Array Dimensions group determines the complexity of the array.

A one-dimensional array in MAX applies the transforms to each object as directed, whereas a two-dimensional array creates linear copies of a one-dimensional array. A three-dimensional array creates linear copies of all the objects in a two-dimensional array. This description may seem confusing, and the Array dialog box can be a bit intimidating; however, the next few exercises will help familiarize you with these techniques.

A One-Dimensional Array

You'll begin by creating a simple one-dimensional array. Follow these steps:

1. Open the Chap5_Uhg_Array.max file from the Chapter 5 section of the CD-ROM. This is the same Uhg model used in Chapter 4, but without the Base, Post, and Platform objects. The model has also been optimized to reduce the total number of faces and vertices, to make the scene easier to manage, and to speed up refreshes.

2. In the Top viewport, select the head. Click on the Array icon in the Main toolbar to open the Array dialog box.

3. Enter "100" in the Incremental X Move field, change the Type Of Object setting to Instance, and set the Count value to 5. These values will create a row of 5 instanced heads 100 units apart (center to center). (Notice that a Count value of 5 results in a Total In Array value of 5, whereas using the transforms and setting the Number Of Copies value to 5 in the Clone dialog box would result in six models total.) Click on the OK button to create the array, and then perform a Zoom Extents All to see it properly.

4. You could have created this array easily with the Move tool. To see the true power of the Array tool, undo the array, making sure the head remains selected. Open the Array dialog box and be sure it displays the values you entered in Step 3.

5. Enter "100" in both the X and Y Move fields and "45" in the Z Rotate field. Your dialog box should look like Figure 5.5. Click on OK; your Perspective viewport should look like Figure 5.6. Take a moment to understand how the Array tools work. Each value from each field is applied to the second object in relation to the first; then, the same values are applied to the third object in relation to the second. Look at the Top viewport to see that each head is rotated 45 degrees more than the one before it; the last head is rotated 180 degrees from the first.

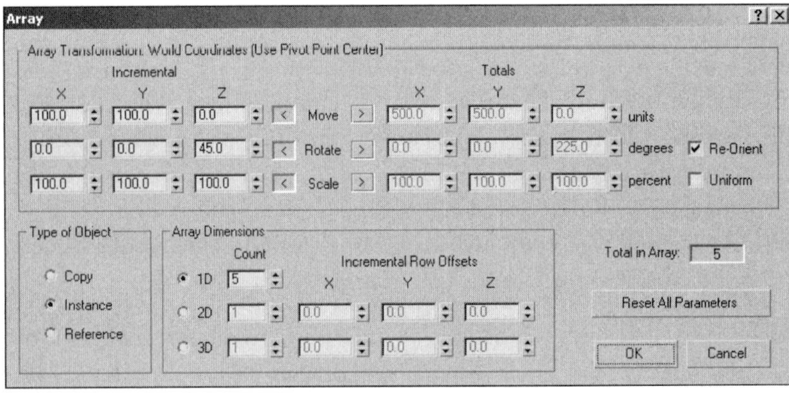

Figure 5.5
The Array dialog box with the settings for Step 5.

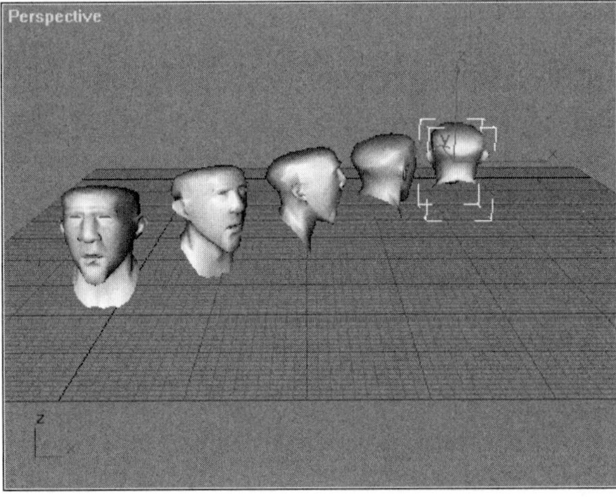

Figure 5.6
The array that results from using the settings in Step 5.

Adding a Second Dimension

Follow these steps to add a second dimension to an array:

1. Undo the steps from the previous section until only the original selected head remains. Activate the Array tool and enter "100" in the X Move field (clear the Y Move field), "45" in the Z Rotate field, and "90" in the X Scale field. Select the Uniform checkbox to apply the scale factor to all three dimensions. Click on OK to create an array in which each object is 100 units away from, is rotated 45 degrees more than, and is 90 percent the size of the previous object.

2. Click on the Undo button. Reopen the Array dialog box, retaining values from Step 1. (It's easiest to build multidimensional arrays in steps.) In the Array Dimensions group, select 2D to create a two-dimensional array. Enter a Count value of 5, and notice that the Total In Array field now shows a value of 25. Enter "100" in the Y field under Incremental Row Offsets. These settings take all the objects created in the one-dimensional array and copy them four times (five arrays total), 100 units apart in the Y direction. The Array dialog box should look like Figure 5.7. The Perspective viewport of the two-dimensional array should be similar to Figure 5.8.

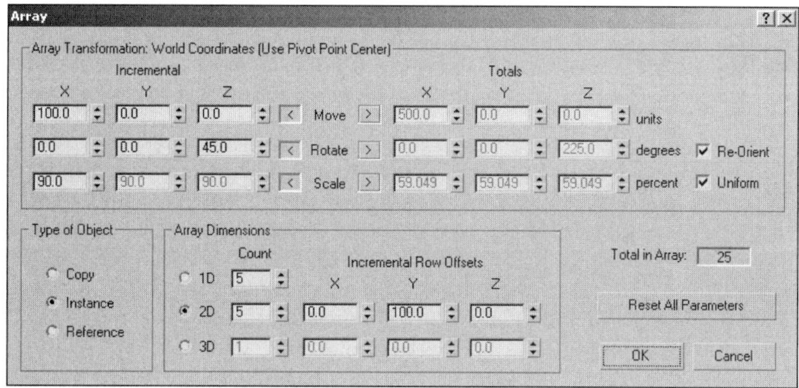

Figure 5.7
The Array dialog box with the settings for the two-dimensional array.

Adding a Third Dimension

Adding a third dimension copies the two-dimensional array in up to three directions. The result of a multidimensional array should be apparent at this point. Follow these steps:

1. Undo the previous steps until only the original head remains. Make sure that it is selected.

2. Open the Array dialog box and leave the existing one-dimensional and two-dimensional values as they are. Select 3D under Array Dimensions, change the 3D Count to 5 (resulting in a Total In Array value of 125), and enter "100" in both the Y and Z Incremental Row Offsets fields. Click on OK. The three-dimensional array should look similar to Figure 5.9.

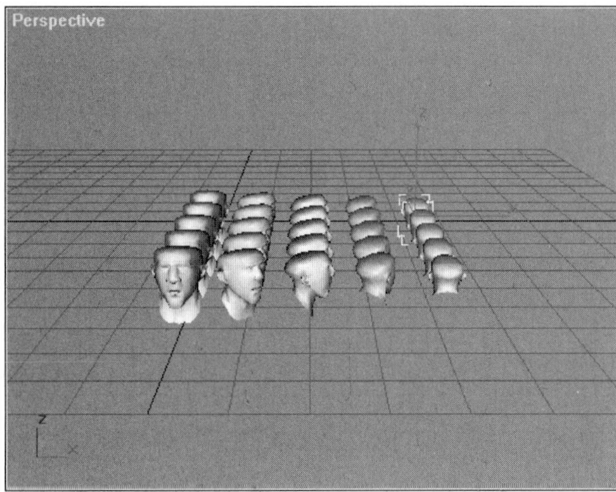

Figure 5.8
The result of the two-dimensional array.

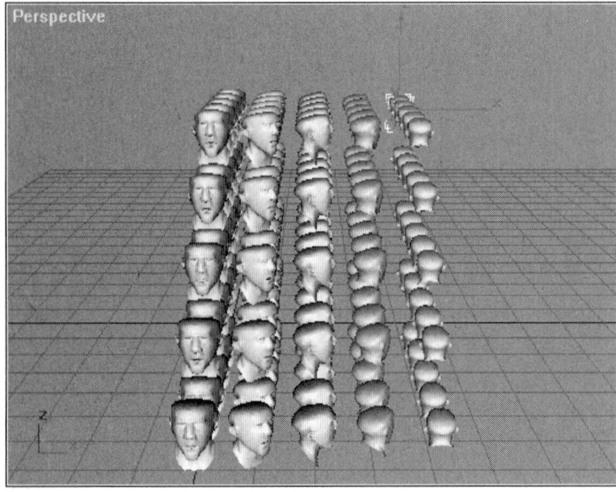

Figure 5.9
The result of the three-dimensional array.

Using Circular Arrays

Circular arrays are constructed by moving the pivot point away from an object that is rotated. They can also be used as the basis for a multidimensional array. Work through this exercise to make an interesting column of heads:

1. Undo the scene until only the original, selected head remains; or, reopen the Chap5_Uhg_Array.max file. The Top view should be the current viewport.

2. Go to the Hierarchy tab in the Command panel and click on the Affect Pivot Only button.

3. At the bottom of the MAX screen, toggle the Transform Type-In fields to Offset Mode. Activate the Move transform and then enter "100" in the Y field to move the object's pivot point 100 units away from its original location in the Y direction.

4. Turn off Affect Pivot Only and test the pivot point relocation by rotating the object. Undo the rotate operation when you are satisfied that it worked.

5. Open the Array dialog box and click on the Reset All Parameters button to clear all the previous values and return the dialog box to its default state.

6. In the Z Rotate field, enter "30"; change the Type Of Object value to Instance; and set the Count to 12. Click on OK to create a circular array of heads, all facing outward, as seen in Figure 5.10.

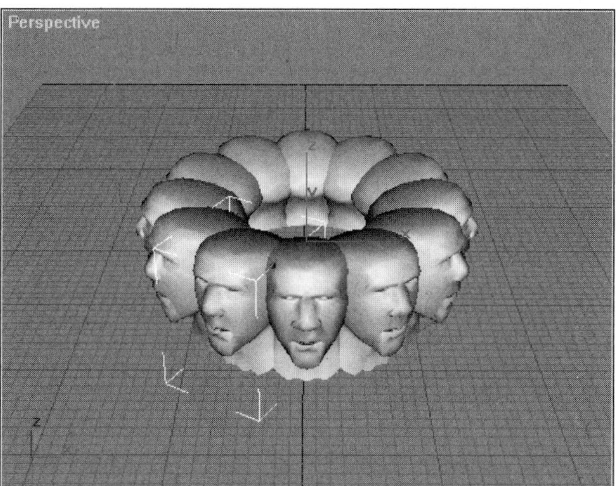

Figure 5.10
You can create a circular array of heads, all facing outward, by moving the pivot point of the object before implementing the Array command.

Using the Transform Center

If the exact location of the circular array is unimportant (or the array will be relocated after it's created), then, rather than moving the pivot point, you can move the object near the origin and use the Transform Center.

---

7. To make this array into a column of heads, click on Undo until only the original head remains. Undo the array and then open the Array dialog box. Change the Array Dimension to 2D and the 2D Count to 6; enter 90 in the 2D Incremental Row Offsets' Z field. The result should look similar to Figure 5.11.

You could easily fill a dungeon scene with such columns in a matter of minutes, with only a minor increase in file size. The original Chap5_Uhg_Array file is 168KB; the completed column,

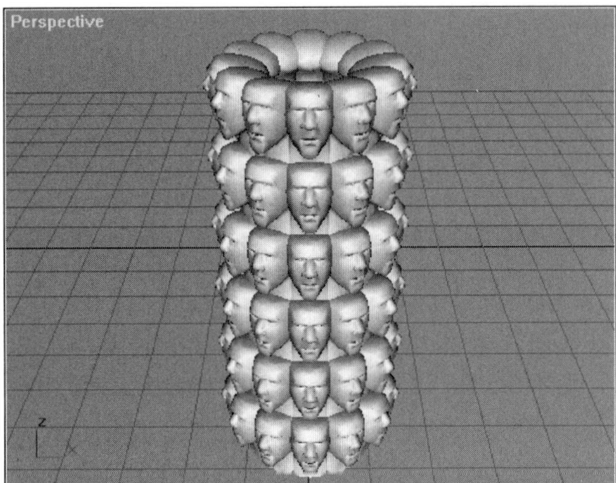

Figure 5.11
The column of heads created with a multidimensional array.

consisting of 72 instances of the model, requires only 207KB—a relatively minor increase in size for a substantial increase in objects.

The Array tool is powerful and surprisingly useful for setting up scenes. It can be used to make anything that consists of a regimented pattern of objects, from a series of soldier ant formations marching in a column, to several squadrons of fighters flying in staggered V formations, to ornamentation or architectural elements throughout a structure. Even objects as common as a set of stairs or a series of lights or tables can quickly be created with an array—the possibilities are enormous. Whenever a pattern of objects repeats itself, consider using the Array tool to complete the task.

The Snapshot Tool

The Snapshot tool creates clones of an animated object at various equal time increments. It's similar to the Shift+transform method of making multiple copies, but the transforms and/or modifiers are already applied to the object. Animation will be covered in several later chapters, so the animation has already been assigned to the object in the following exercise. To try out the Snapshot tool, follow these steps:

1. Open the file Chap5_Snapshot.max from the CD-ROM. It consists of a single picket that varies in height over time and is assigned to a path to control its motion. During the course of the animation (160 frames), the picket follows the entire path and cycles between full height and two-thirds' height 10 times.

2. Click on the Play Animation button and switch between the viewports to familiarize yourself with how the picket moves and changes over time.

3. Stop the animation and select the picket. Click and hold the Array tool icon until the other options appear; choose the middle option, which has a serpentine icon. The Snapshot dialog box will appear, as shown in Figure 5.12.

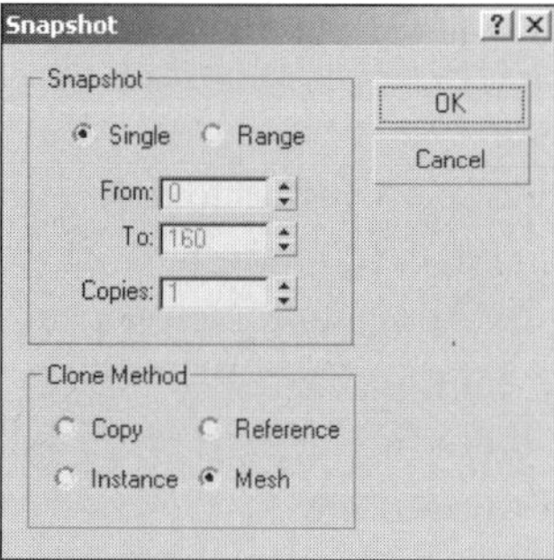

Figure 5.12
The Snapshot dialog box.

4. The Snapshot group controls the quantity of copies and the time range from which they are to be taken. Select the Range option, enter "160" for the number of copies, and select Instance in the Clone Method group. Click on OK. The Perspective viewport should look like Figure 5.13.

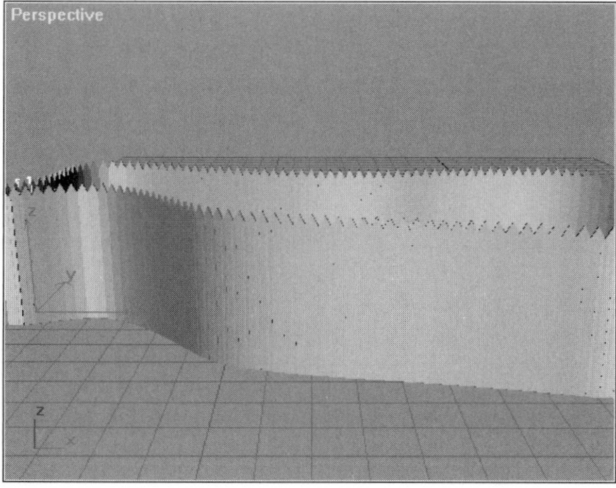

Figure 5.13
The result of the Snapshot operation, using the settings in Step 4.

Using the Mesh Clone Type

One of the Clone Method options for the Snapshot tool is Mesh. This option converts objects to basic, non-parametric faces, edges, and vertices. This conversion can be useful when you create objects with plug-ins and then need to transfer the objects to a MAX machine that does not possess that particular plug-in, assuming further modification above the Mesh level is not needed. Check with the plug-in's documentation to be sure this usage does not violate the user license.

---

5. This isn't the expected result. The pickets are too close together, and they don't vary in height as they did in the original animation. Manually move the Time Slider near the bottom of the MAX window and watch all the instances change, as the original does during its travels along the path. Because Instance was chosen as the clone type, the clones respect the original's current state rather than the state it was in when the clones were made. Undo until only the single selected picket remains.

6. Select the Snapshot tool and notice that, like the Array tool, it retains its values to make adjustments easier. Change the Copies value to 90 and the Clone Method to Mesh. Click on OK to achieve the result shown in Figure 5.14: a pattern of pickets following a path, with each picket varying in height in a smooth and continuous rhythm.

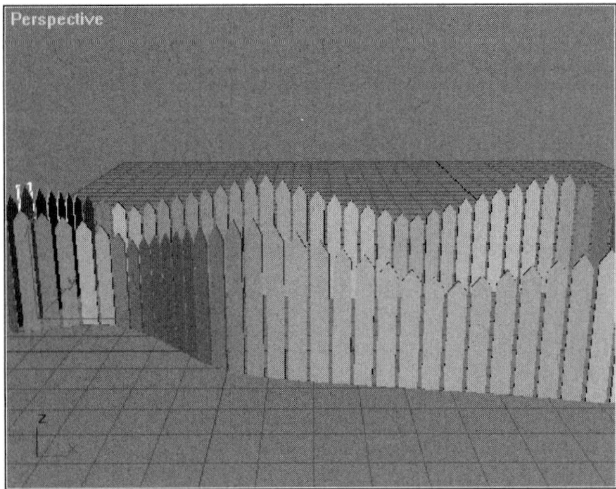

Figure 5.14
The result of the Snapshot operation after revising the settings.

Mirroring Objects

When objects are mirrored, they are flipped across a plane and, in most cases, cloned at the same time. When you're modeling a head or many other symmetrical objects, you'll usually create one half of the object and mirror the other half. The mirrored object does not have to be dependant on the original, and it can maintain its own modifiers to allow nonsymmetrical imperfections to be incorporated into the model. Even nonorganic objects that are symmetrical (for example, cars, spacecraft, robots, and buildings) can be created using mirrored objects.

Note: *Non-Uniform Rational B-Splines (NURBS) have their own mirroring tools within their toolset to augment the main Mirror tool.*

Mirrored objects are used throughout the modeling process. The following exercise focuses on the methods of mirroring:

1. Open the Chap5_Mirror.max file from the CD-ROM. It consists of the word *Mirror*, which has been extruded and beveled.

2. Select the object in the Top viewport and switch to the Local coordinate system. The Local coordinate system is most often used when mirroring, because objects rarely remain perpendicular to the axes of the World or View coordinate system. Using the Local coordinate system allows them to be mirrored in the planes specific to them.

3. Click on the Mirror button in the Main toolbar to open the Mirror dialog box shown in Figure 5.15. Notice that the object displays a preview of the Mirror operation according to the default settings in the dialog box; the current coordinate system is displayed in the dialog box's title area.

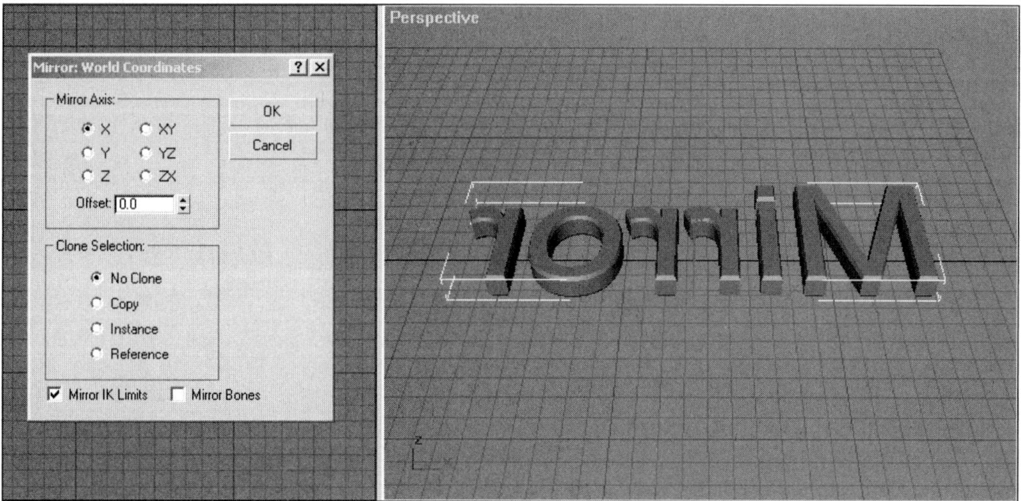

Figure 5.15
The Mirror dialog box and the mirrored object, showing a preview of the operation.

4. The Mirror Axis group determines the axis or axes that the object will be mirrored along—this is the opposite of the axis concept used when rotating objects. To achieve the same result on screen (mirroring along the X-axis) using the Rotate transform, the object would have to be rotated *about* the Y-axis. The reason MAX departs from this standard is unclear, but both procedures are easy to learn. Mirroring along the Z-axis may seem to have no effect, because the extruded text is symmetrical in that plane. Experiment with the dual-plane mirroring to see the result of mirroring along one axis and then along a second in one step.

5. Select the Y Mirror Axis and choose Instance as the clone type in the Clone Selection group. Your Perspective viewport should look like Figure 5.16.

Figure 5.16
The result of mirroring the text along the Y-axis and simultaneously creating an instanced clone.

6. The object is mirrored about its pivot point (in this case, the base of the text), so no gap appears between it and the clone. The Offset field contains the distance the clone object should move in the direction of the Mirror Axis. Enter a value of –10 to create a small space between the objects. Click on OK to complete the Mirror operation.
7. Select both objects and mirror and clone them so that they appear similar to the objects seen in Figure 5.17.

Figure 5.17
The original object and the mirrored clone are both mirrored again to make the beginning of an interesting matrix of objects.

As you can see in Figure 5.18, it is not difficult to create an extensive pattern of objects that clearly flow from one to another using the Mirror tool. This tool can be used to create a series of elements when an array is not practical, and it can even be used to duplicate flocks of birds or crowds of people.

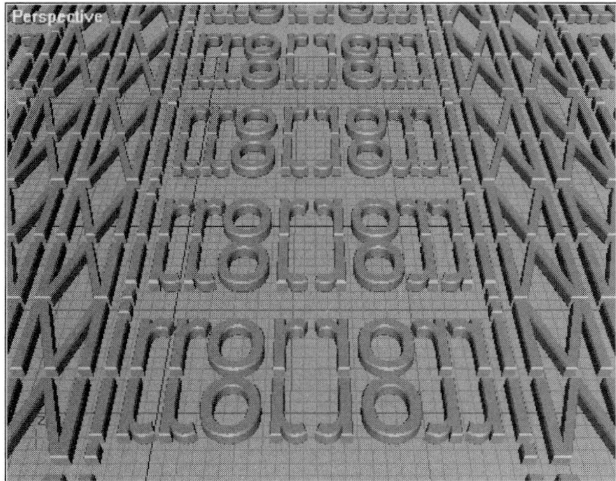

Figure 5.18
A continuation of the mirrored pattern to fill the base of the scene with instances of the original object.

Precision Tools

MAX puts at your disposal many tools that add precision to the objects in your scenes. These tools ensure that objects are moved, rotated, or scaled exactly as desired, and they speed up the creation process. In this section, we'll discuss snaps and alignment tools.

Snaps

Like a magnet, the snap tools draw the cursor to designated features in the scene. Controlled by the four magnet icons at the bottom of the MAX window, the snaps can control the incremental angle that rotations use, the percentage jump when scaling, and much more.

The following exercises will demonstrate the many uses of MAX's snap controls. Follow these steps:

1. Create a Box with Length, Width, and Height values all set to 10. Also create an inverted Cone, similar to that shown in Figure 5.19.
2. Right-click on any of the three magnet icons to the left (not the one on the far right) to open the Grid And Snap Settings dialog box. Right-clicking on each of these buttons brings up a different tab; click on the Snaps tab, and the dialog box should look like Figure 5.20. This is a modal dialog box, so it can remain open in order to make adjustments to the snap settings easier while you're using other MAX tools.

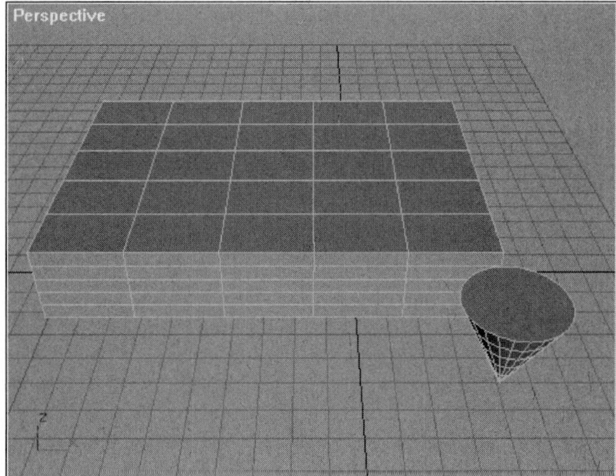

Figure 5.19
The Box and Cone that will be used to demonstrate the snap controls available in MAX. To better display the geometry of the objects, right-click on the viewport's name and select Edged Faces.

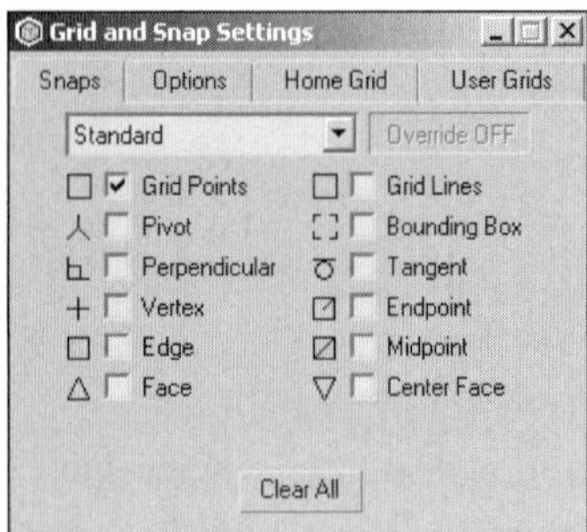

Figure 5.20
The Snaps tab of the Grid And Snap Settings dialog box.

3. The 12 checkboxes toggle the cursor to "snap" to each of the different types of conditions. The icon to the left of each checkbox represents the icon that will appear on screen when the mouse passes over that particular condition. Any or all of these checkboxes can be selected at one time, but be cautious of selecting too many—doing so may make selecting the desired condition on screen difficult. Select Grid Points and Vertex. Close the dialog box by clicking on the X button in the upper-right corner.

4. The options are active, but the snaps are not toggled on. Click on the 3D Snap Toggle button, activate one of the transforms, and move the cursor around in the viewport. Whenever the cursor moves near a grid point (the intersection of two grid lines), a light blue box with crosshairs appears, indicating that any transforms will originate from that point. When the cursor crosses over a vertex on the Box, a small cross shape appears at the vertex. You may have noticed that the Grid Points icon appears when the cursor is over the

Box; this occurs when the cursor is not near enough to a vertex to trigger the snap and, secondarily, chooses the grid point on the grid beyond the Box.

Note: *The 3D Snap Toggle has two other options available: 2D and 2.5D. Using the 2D option allows you to select only snap options that are on the construction grid. When in 2.5D mode, all the features of the objects can be snapped to, but the snap point is projected to the grid, parallel to the direction of the view.*

5. The task now is to move the Cone to one of the Box's top corners and then copy it to the other three corners. Activate the Move tool, place the cursor at the apex of the Cone, and drag it to one of the Box's upper corners. It will snap to that location, as shown in Figure 5.21.

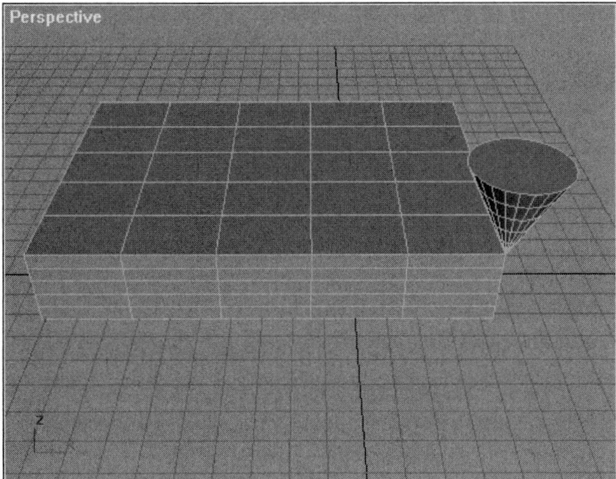

Figure 5.21
The apex of the Cone has been moved precisely to the vertex at the corner of the Box.

6. With the Cone still selected, hold down the Shift key and use the snaps to copy it to the other four corners.

Setting the Snap Strength and Marker Options

The cursor is pulled to a designated snap feature (Vertex, Edge, etc.) when it is a specific distance, in pixels, from that feature. To modify this setting, open the Grid And Snap Settings dialog box and click on the Options tab. The Snap Strength field controls the cursor-to-feature distance required to initiate the snap.

The colored snaps represented in the viewports help identify which type of snap is being used. If you're comfortable using snaps without seeing them, you can specify whether they're displayed, as well as their color and size, in the Marker group of the Options tab.

---

7. Select all five objects and group them.

8. Turn on the Angle Snap Toggle and activate the Rotate transform. In the Top viewport, move the cursor over any vertex and rotate the group about that point, noting that the Transform Gizmo has temporarily relocated to that spot. Watch the Transform Type-In fields; you'll see that the rotation is occurring at exact five-degree increments. To change the increment, enter a new value in the Angle (deg) field in the Options tab of the Grid And Snap Settings dialog box shown in Figure 5.22. In this case, the Angle Snap was used in conjunction with the 3D Snap; however, each of the snap tools can be used independently, using the pivot point as the base point for transforms.

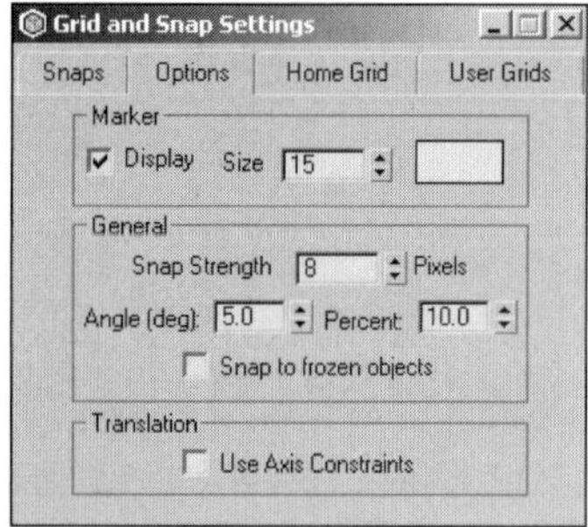

Figure 5.22
Snap options are determined in the Options tab of the Grid And Snap Settings dialog box.

9. Turn on the Percent Snap and activate the Scale transform. In the Options tab of the Grid And Snap Settings dialog box, change the Percent field to 5 to set the incremental amount by which the Scale transform will alter the object.

10. Activate the Scale transform and scale the object to see the effect of the Percent Snap.

11. The last snap tool available is the Spinner Snap, which overrides the default settings for the spinner buttons in the Command panel. Right-click on the Spinner Snap Toggle button to open the General tab of the Preference Settings dialog box, as shown in Figure 5.23. In the Spinners group, reset Precision to 4 and Snap to 3, and leave the Use Snap checkbox deselected.

12. Open the group and select the Box. Go to the Modify tab of the Command panel and, with the Spinner Snap off, click on the up arrow for the Length Segments field. Note that the segment count rises, one number at a time. Turn on the Spinner Snap and repeat the procedure; the count rises three at a time. Click the down arrow for the Length field; notice that the number decreases by three with each click, and that the precision has increased to four decimal places. The Spinner Snap essentially allows you to have two default snap increments that are selectable with a toggle.

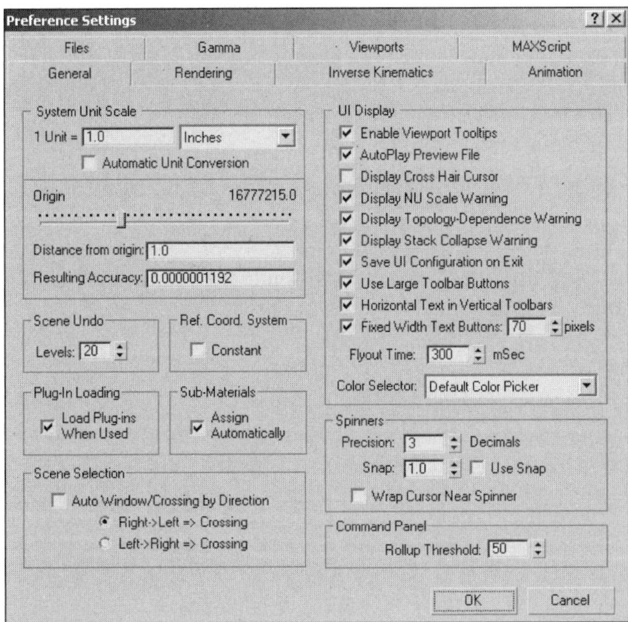

Figure 5.23
The General tab of the Preference Settings dialog box. Selecting Preferences from the Customize menu also opens this dialog box.

Alignment Tools

Several choices are available when you click and hold the Align button in the Main toolbar. All these options affect one object in relation to another. The default Align tool is used most often; it moves one object into a specific relationship to another.

The Align Tool

As seen when an object is selected or a group is opened, the extents of any object can be defined by a bounding box that is the minimum size required to envelope the object or group of objects. In many cases, one object may need to be placed precisely on top of, next to, or centered on another; the bounding box determines where the side or top of the object is. The Align tool can be used to place a picture on a wall, a place setting on a table, or a character's shoes on the road without having to "eyeball" the move or relying on burying one object in another to prevent light from leaking between them.

The following exercise demonstrates how the Align tool can complete these tasks. Note that, by default, the Align tool uses the View coordinate system in the orthographic viewports and World coordinate system in the Perspective viewport. Therefore, you constantly need to be aware of which viewport and coordinate system are current. For this exercise, all operations will be executed from the Top viewport. Reset the MAX scene and follow these steps:

1. In the Top viewport, create a Box with a Length and Width of 66 and a Height of 20. Also create a Pyramid with a Width of 35, a Depth of 15, and a Height of 30. Select the Box, go

to the Display tab of the Command panel, and select See-Through in the Display Properties rollout to help see the results of this exercise.

2. Remain in the Top viewport. Select the Pyramid (the current object) and click on the Align button. The cursor changes to look like the Align icon, and a crosshair is added whenever the cursor moves over a target object. Nearly every object in MAX can be an Align target, including members of groups (the group doesn't need to be open).

3. Move the cursor over an edge of the Box (the target object) and select it to bring up the Align Selection dialog box, as shown in Figure 5.24.

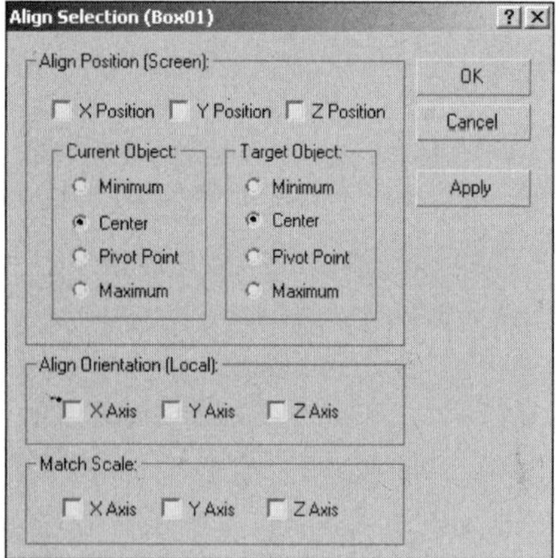

Figure 5.24
The default settings for the Align Selection dialog box.

Note: *The Align Position group's title line shows that the Screen coordinate system is being used. By changing the coordinate system prior to initiating the Align command, you can change the coordinate system used within it.*

4. The three checkboxes in the Align Position group allow you to determine the axes in which the Align tool will move the current object. Move the dialog box out of the way, if necessary, and select the X Position checkbox. The Pyramid moves to be even with the Box (from right to left), as if both objects are straddling the same Y-axis line. The Align command has not actually completed the task yet; this is only a preview of the action that will occur when it is complete.

Note: *Take a moment to look at the dialog box and examine how its settings defined the result. The relevant feature selected in both the Current Object (Pyramid) group and the Target Object (Box) group is Center. The X Position checkbox is selected, indicating that the Pyramid will be moved in the X direction until its center is aligned with the center of the Box. It's important to understand that the center being referred to is the point equidistant from either side of the bounding box—not the geometric* *center of the object. For example, the center of the bounding box for a teardrop-shaped object would be midway between the leading edge and the tail, whereas the geometric center would be skewed toward the more voluminous lead section.*

5. Select the Y Position checkbox, leaving X Position selected, as well. The Pyramid centers itself on the Box, as seen in the Top view. The Pyramid has been moved to align its center with the center of the Box. Your Perspective viewport should look similar to Figure 5.25.

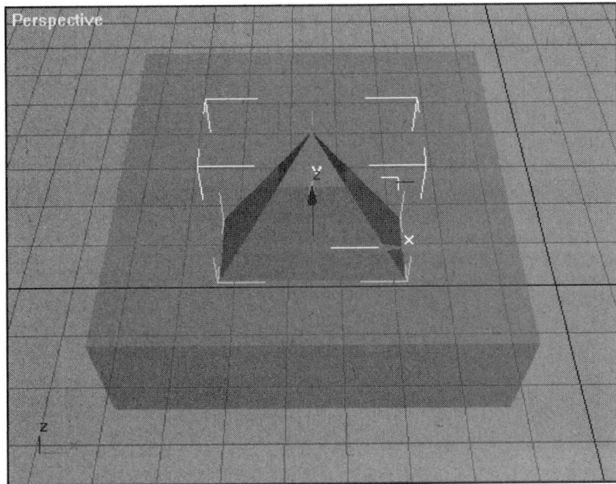

Figure 5.25
The center of the Pyramid is aligned with the center of the Box in both the X and Y directions.

6. Select the Z Position checkbox. The Pyramid drops to align the centers of both objects along the Z-axis. For this exercise, however, you want to center the Pyramid on the Box in the X and Y directions but place the bottom of the Pyramid on the top of the Box.

7. Deselect the Z Position checkbox. Two buttons in the Align Selection dialog box control the execution of the designated settings: OK and Apply. OK executes the settings and closes the dialog box, whereas Apply executes the settings, clears the Position checkboxes, and leaves the dialog box open to accept additional alignment operations for the current and target objects. Click on the Apply button.

8. The scene should again look like Figure 5.25 in the Perspective view. The Top viewport is current, and the Align Selection dialog box is still open with the Position checkboxes all deselected. To set the Pyramid on top of the Box, select the Z Position checkbox and select Minimum under Current Object to align the minimum Z location of the Pyramid (the base) with the center of the Box. Complete the move by selecting Maximum under Target Object to align the minimum Z location of the Pyramid with the maximum Z location of the Box. Click on OK.

Avoiding the Z-Axis

Many people are uncomfortable moving objects in the Z-axis. If you're one of them, you can avoid this by aligning the objects in the X and Y directions in the Top viewport, reissuing the Align command in the Front or Left viewport, and aligning the objects in the Y direction.

Multiple objects can be aligned with one another in a single move, to reduce the redundancy of similar operations. To see how, follow these steps:

1. Create a Sphere with a radius of 6 and four Spheres that each have a radius of 3. In the Top viewport, select the large Sphere. Use the Align tool to balance it on the peak of the Pyramid, following the procedure from the previous example. Your Perspective view should look like Figure 5.26.

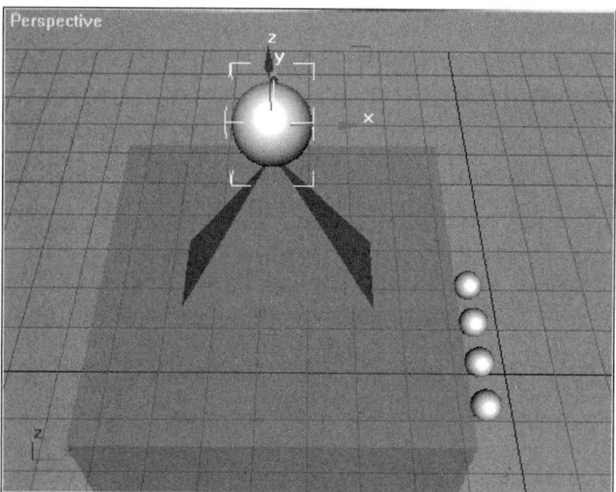

Figure 5.26
The large Sphere is balanced on the apex of the Pyramid, and the four smaller Spheres are waiting to be aligned.

2. Select all four small Spheres, activate the Align tool, and select the large Sphere as the target object. When the Align Selection dialog box opens, select all three Position checkboxes and select Center for both the Current and Target objects. Click on OK; all the small Spheres become centered on the larger one.

3. Zoom in on the Spheres, if necessary, and use the H key to select only one of the small Spheres. Activate the Align tool and align the left side of the small Sphere with the right side of the large one (X Position selected, Current Object set to Minimum, Target Object set to Maximum).

4. Align the remaining small Spheres around the larger one until your scene looks like Figure 5.27.

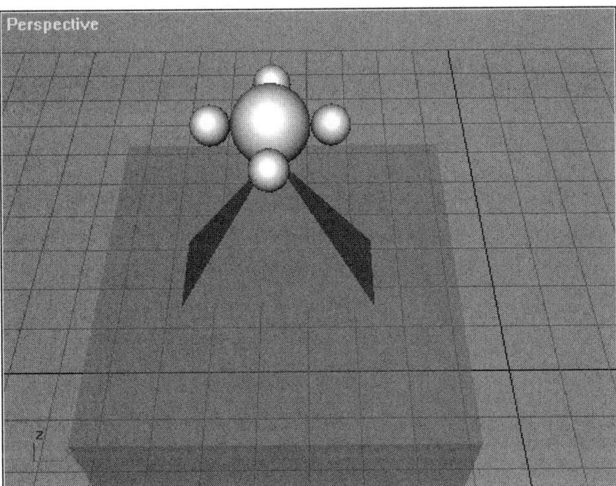

Figure 5.27
The four small Spheres are aligned to the quadrants of the larger Sphere.

The Normal Align Tool

Every face in a MAX object has a *normal* direction, usually pointing outward in a mesh object and perpendicular to the surface. If each face were considered to have its own local coordinate system, the normal would point in the direction of the local Z-axis. The Normal Align tool, found under the main Align tool, reorients and moves the current object so that a specific face aligns with a specific face on the target object. To see how this tool works, follow these steps:

1. Continue with the previous exercise or open the file Chap5_Align.max from the CD-ROM.
2. In the Front viewport, create a small Tube. Switch to the Perspective viewport and activate the Normal Align tool.
3. Click and drag the cursor over the surface of the Tube. Notice the blue arrow that projects from the face at the location of the cursor. The point where the blue arrow meets the face is where the Tube (current object) will meet the reciprocal point on the target. Release the mouse button on a face near the middle of the Tube. Click and drag on the Pyramid using the green arrow as a guide. Release the mouse; the Tube moves and orients to align the two designated faces, and the Normal Align dialog box opens.

The settings in the Normal Align dialog box determine the offset, in local coordinates, by which the two alignment points miss connecting. A positive value in the Z field creates a gap between the objects, as shown in Figure 5.28. Entering a value in the Angle field rotates the object about its local Z-axis. The Flip Normal option rotates the object so that the two normals face the same direction.

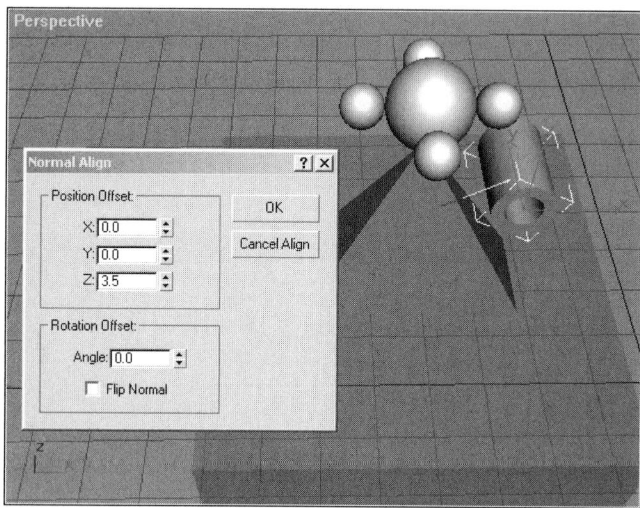

Figure 5.28
The Normal Align dialog box is used to create a gap between the normals of the two designated faces.

The Place Highlight, Align Camera, and Align To View Tools

The remaining alignment tools are used much less often than Align and Normal Align. The Place Highlight tool moves and rotates a light so that it creates a highlight centered on a selected normal point. Align Camera positions a camera so that its view is perpendicular to the selected surface. Align To View rotates the selected object so that one of its local axes, determined by the dialog box shown in Figure 5.29, is oriented parallel to the current viewport.

Figure 5.29
The Align To View dialog box is used to orient an object's axes parallel to the viewport.

Tape and Protractor

The Tape and Protractor are nonrendering helper objects that measure distances or angles between objects or specific object features. Consider the two Star1-type Hedras in the Chap5_Tape_Pro.max file on the CD-ROM, shown in Figure 5.30. To determine the width of the largest object that can fit between them, follow these steps:

1. From the Create|Helpers|Standard Command panel, choose Tape. Click-drag-release in the Top viewport. Two objects are created: a Tape and its target. The distance between them is reflected in the Length field of the Parameters rollout.

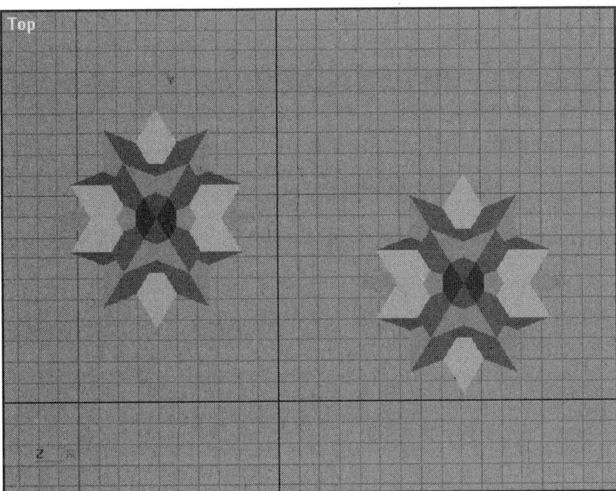

Figure 5.30
Two Star1-type Hedras used to explore the functionality of the Tape and Protractor helpers.

2. Open the Grid And Snap Settings dialog box and clear all options in the Snaps tab except Vertex and Pivot. Turn on the 3D Snap Toggle.
3. Activate the Move transform. Use it to select the Tape object (snapping to its pivot point); then, drag the Tape to the vertex at the end of the right Hedra that is closest to the left Hedra, until it snaps in place.
4. Repeat the procedure, this time dragging the Tape target to the end vertex of the left Hedra that is closest to the right Hedra.
5. Reselect the Target Object and look at the Length field. To answer the initial question, the width of the largest object that can fit between the two Hedras is slightly smaller than 56.1973 units.

Using the Pivot snap only or the Align tool in conjunction with the Tape helper can determine the distance from center to center of the Hedras. You can select the Specify Length checkbox and enter a value to create a Tape with a fixed length.

The Protractor helper measures the angle between two objects from a third point:

1. Place a Protractor in the Top viewport and use the Move transform and the Transform Type-In fields to place it exactly at the origin.
2. Switch to the Modify panel. Click on the Pick Object 1 button and one Hedra; then click on the Pick Object 2 button and select the other Hedra. The value in the Angle field is the angle from pivot point to pivot point. The Protractor tool ignores snaps; therefore, to determine the angle between the two nearest points, you would have to create Dummies centered on those points and use them as Object 1 and Object 2.

Keyboard Shortcuts

Keyboard shortcuts, or *hotkeys*, are fantastic timesavers in any application, and MAX uses them extensively. For example, you can change the current viewport to a Top view either by pressing the T key or by right-clicking on the menu title, scrolling down, expanding the view's submenu, and then choosing Top.

MAX makes it easy to determine or modify the existing set of hotkeys or to make an entire new set to your own preferences. A complete list of the default keyboard shortcuts is included in the Appendix. Review the existing hotkey settings by examining the Customize|Customize User Interface|Keyboard tab, as shown in Figure 5.31, and stepping through the different Groups and Categories available through their respective drop-down lists.

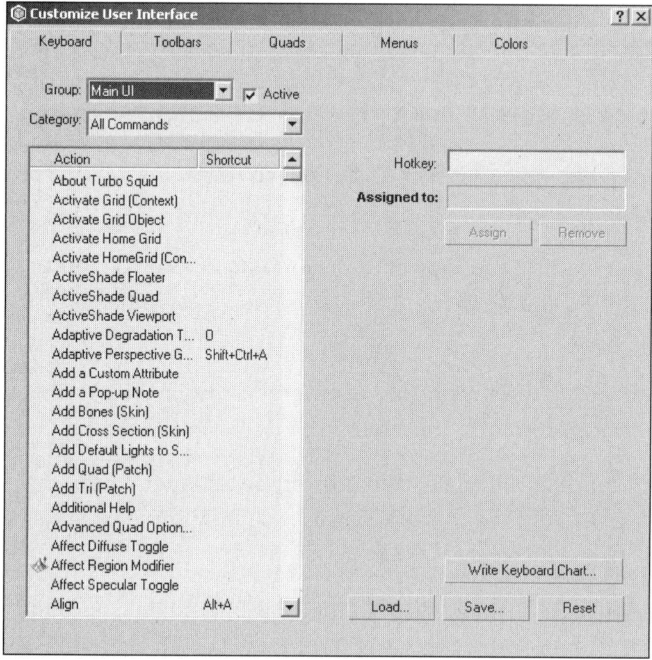

Figure 5.31
The Keyboard tab of the Customize User Interface dialog box, where keyboard shortcuts (hotkeys) are set.

To create a new shortcut, press and hold down the key plus any special keys (Shift, Ctrl, or Alt). They will appear in the Hotkey field. If the combination is already assigned, the associated command will appear in the Assigned To field. However, you can modify assigned hotkeys by selecting a command in the Action column and clicking on the Assign button. If the key combination is free (all single keys are already taken), <Not Assigned> appears in the Assigned To field.

Once you've created a customized set of hotkeys, click on the Save button to create a KBD file. It's recommended that you create an entirely new file, rather than overwriting the default

MaxKeys.kdb file. That way, if you reinstall MAX, the file is not overlooked and overwritten. In addition, if you need to work on a machine that is not yours, you can transfer the file without overwriting someone else's standards.

Scene and Object Properties

Knowing what is in a scene and what properties an object possesses is helpful when you're determining where and how a scene can be trimmed or how an object can be altered to suit the scene better. Several tools are available to access that information and to manipulate the properties, including the Summary Info dialog box and the Object Properties dialog box.

Summary Info

Open or create a scene that has several objects in it. Especially at render time, the number of faces present, also called the *face count*, is important: The higher the number is, the longer the scene will take to render, and the larger the MAX file will be. To see the properties of the scene, choose Summary Info from the File menu. The Summary Info dialog box will appear, as shown in Figure 5.32.

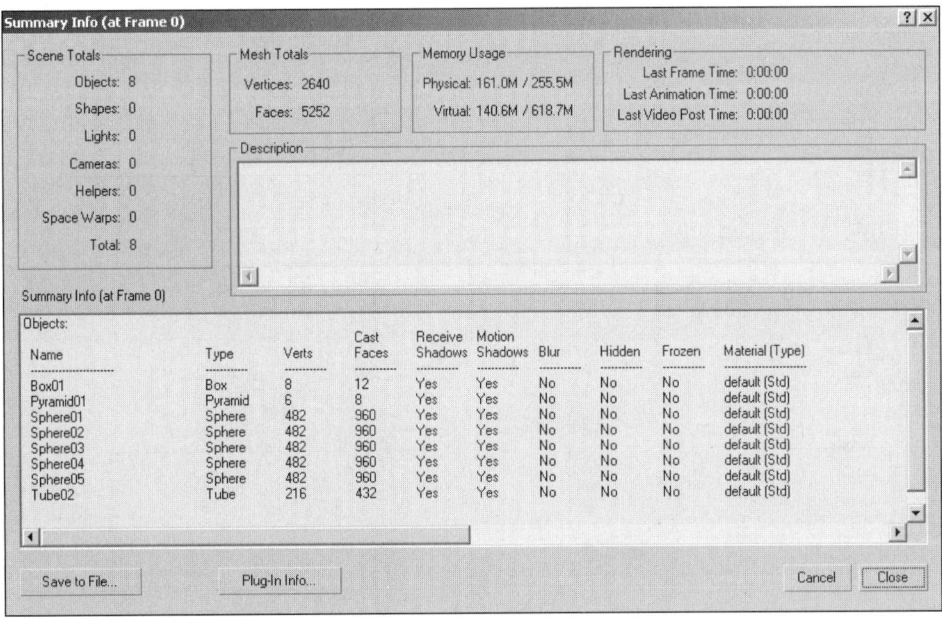

Figure 5.32
The Summary Info dialog box, which presents information about the entire scene.

The data you will be most interested in appears in the Mesh Totals group; this group lists the number of vertices and faces. If a scene is rendering more slowly than expected, check here to see if the face count is higher than estimated; this situation can be caused by just a few objects being modeled improperly or inefficiently. For example, a Teapot primitive created with the default values consists of 1,024 faces, whereas the same Teapot with the MeshSmooth modifier applied with four iterations increases to an incredible 258,048 faces, with little improvement to its appearance. This problem is multiplied further if the object is cloned within the scene.

To determine if a certain offending object is present, scroll through the Objects list in the Summary Info field, keeping an eye on the Cast Faces column. This field describes all the objects in the scene, as well as shapes, cameras, helpers, and so forth.

Object Properties

You'll often need to find out or alter the properties of a specific object. To do so, select an object, and then right-click on it; in the Transform section of the Quad menu, choose Properties to open the Object Properties dialog box shown in Figure 5.33.

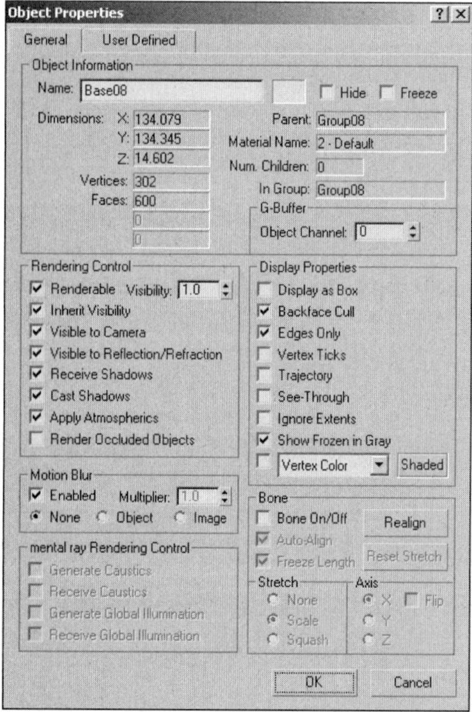

Figure 5.33
The Object Properties dialog box, in which information about an object can be accessed or manipulated.

This dialog box consolidates several functions and data fields found in other locations in MAX, as well as having some specific functionality. The functions in the Display Properties group are also found in the Display tab of the Command panel, as are the Hide and Freeze checkboxes. The Rendering Control group is used to determine whether the object renders with the default settings (all checkboxes selected except Render Occluded Objects) or by its own standards. The other commonly used areas of the Object Properties dialog box are the Motion Blur group, which sets the value for distorting a moving object's rendered appearance, and the G-Buffer Object Channel, which determines whether an object accepts Video Post Filter effects. These last two functions will be covered elsewhere in this book.

XRefs and Proxy Objects

Scenes' face counts have a tendency to become very large, and, as a result, the performance of the computer will suffer. Of particular note is the speed at which the viewports can redraw the screen during zooms, pans, and Min/Max toggling. In addition, multiple people in a shop may need to work on separate areas of the same project. External References (*XRefs*) can alleviate these problems through the use of referenced and proxy objects.

To XRef an object (or an entire scene, for that matter) means to take an object from another MAX file and to bring it in to the current scene. The object is still a member of its original scene, and it cannot be edited below the level at which it was inserted; but it is subject to having additional modifiers and transforms applied to it. XRefs work similarly to referenced clones, in that modifiers applied to them do not affect the original object. (In the case of XRefs, these objects reside in a completely different file.) When using XRefs, one person can be working on the original file while another works on the file in which the XRef appears.

Proxy objects typically are low-resolution representations of external objects that act as stand-ins for their high-resolution counterparts. For example, if you take an object as complicated as a spacecraft and multiply it into an entire armada, the number of faces soon becomes prohibitive to work with. By using XRefs and proxy objects, you can work in the scene much more easily and quickly; you can then substitute the originals back at render time.

The following exercises will demonstrate the power and ease of use of XRefs and proxy objects. Your first goal is to XRef a high-resolution model into the scene. Follow these steps:

1. Open the file Chap5_Xref.max from the CD-ROM. It consists of nine of the pedestals used to hold the Uhg head model.
2. From the File menu, choose XRef Objects to open the XRef Objects dialog box shown in Figure 5.34.
3. Click on the Add button and, in the Open File dialog box, navigate to and select the Chap5_Uhg_HiRes.max file. Click on the Open button to open the XRef Merge dialog box, shown in Figure 5.35.
4. The XRef Merge dialog box is similar to the Select Objects dialog box. In it, you select the specific objects to be referenced. In this case, the scene contains only one object: the Uhg model. Highlight it in the list and click on OK to return to the XRef Objects dialog box. The externally referenced scene is listed in the upper field, and the object is listed in the lower field. The Uhg head has also appeared in the viewports. Close the dialog box.

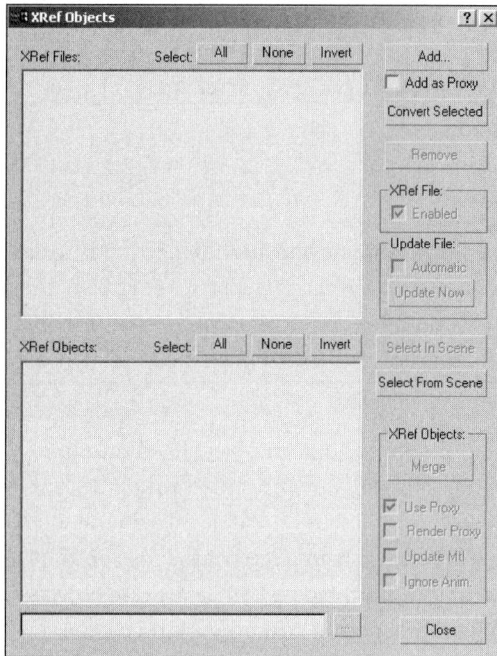

Figure 5.34
The XRef Objects dialog box is used to link objects in external files to the current scene.

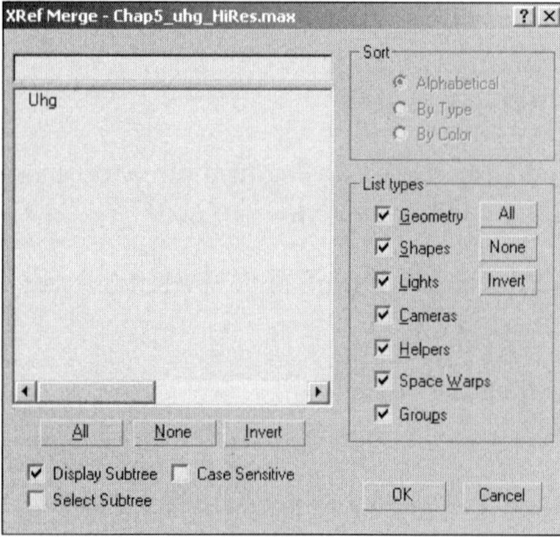

Figure 5.35
The XRef Merge dialog box is used to select the objects to be referenced.

5. Instance clone the head to all the pedestals. Notice if your system suffers a performance hit as it deals with 318,600 faces in four viewports simultaneously. The Perspective viewport should look similar to Figure 5.36. Experiment with the objects by applying the different transforms, including Non-Uniform Scale and Squash.

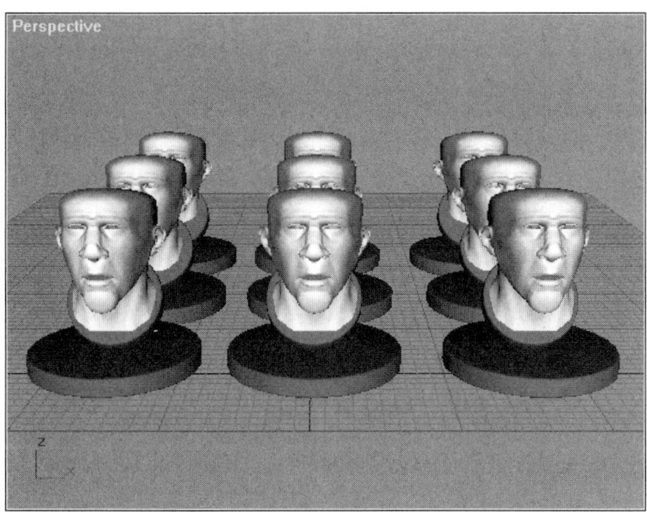

Figure 5.36
The Perspective viewport after the XRef'd object has been instance cloned and a clone has been placed on each pedestal.

6. When you're satisfied, save the file and open Chap5_Uhg_HiRes.max.

7. Select the object. In the Modify panel, click on the Vertex button in the Selection rollout (the icon in the top row is composed of three dots). All vertices in the object turn blue. Using a region selection, select all the vertices of the left ear, keeping in mind that precision is not important; this exercise is just to show you how XRefs work. Move the selected vertices a short distance to the right, making the ear protrude unnaturally from the head.

8. Save and close the file and reopen Chap5_xref.max. All the XRef'd heads now have the protruding left ear.

To quicken the pace at which the viewports redraw themselves, it is easy to replace the current heads with low-resolution proxy substitutes. Follow these steps:

1. Reopen the XRef Objects dialog box (File|XRef Objects) and highlight the referenced file in the upper field.

2. In the lower field, highlight the Uhg object. Select the Set Proxy checkbox and click on the Set button.

3. In the File Open dialog box, maneuver to and choose the file Chap5_Uhg_LoRes.max. In the Merge dialog box, select the Uhg object and click on OK. All the Objects in the scene are replaced with low-resolution copies; your Perspective viewport should look similar to Figure 5.37. Note that two files are now listed in the upper field of the XRef Objects dialog box: one for the original and one for the proxy. Your scene now consists of a total of 16,416 faces, and it should react more quickly to viewport-related commands. Close the dialog box and return to the scene.

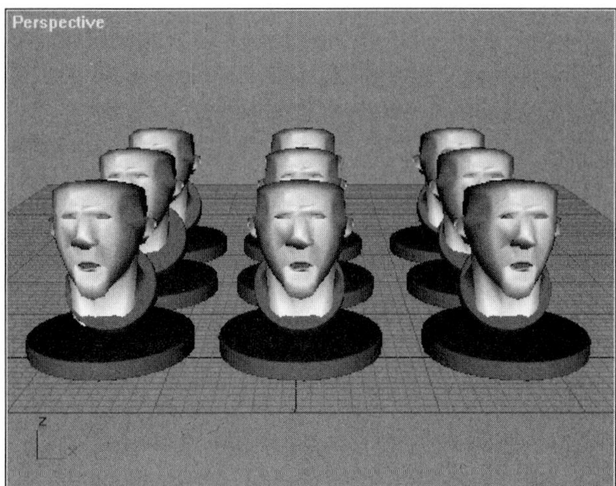

Figure 5.37
The Perspective viewport after the XRef'd objects have been replaced by low-resolution proxy objects.

Note: *The proxy object was created by saving a copy of the original head as a separate file and then applying the MultiRes modifier (covered in Chapter 6) until its face count was about 10 percent of the original's.*

4. In the Main toolbar, click on the Quick Render button to render the scene without opening a dialog box. The scene renders using the higher-resolution XRef object rather than the lower-resolution proxy that appears only in the viewports. If you want the proxy rendered in lieu of the true object (to accelerate the render time for a non-final render), select the Render Proxy checkbox in the XRef Objects group of the XRef Objects dialog box.

Binding and Extruding XRefs

To change an XRef into a scene object, select the object in the XRef Objects dialog box and then choose Merge in the XRef Objects group. When this conversion is complete, the object and its modifier stack can be manipulated.

To change an existing object into an XRef, select the object in the scene and then open the XRef Objects dialog box. Choose Convert Selected and, in the Save File As dialog box, choose the new file name and destination for the object.

Wiring and Manipulators

3ds max 4 has two new features that you may soon find indispensable. The first is the ability to link, or *wire,* the parameters of one object to those of another. The second is to link parameters to Manipulator transforms that are visible in the viewports at all times. We will discuss both new features here.

Wiring

Unlike an instanced clone, the objects being wired do not have to be of the same type. The direction of control can be either from one object to another or bi-directional. Other variables can be added to control the result of the wiring operation. This powerful tool lets you maintain control of and adjust the parameters of several objects at a time. Wiring can be used in a similar manner to linking, in that transforms can be wired between objects with the added ability to limit the transforms used in an operation.

Let's work through an exercise on wiring. The goal is to make three Tubes adjust themselves and maintain a consistent wall thickness, while allowing a Sphere to fit through the smallest Tube. Open the file Chap5_Wire.max from the CD-ROM; it consists of three centered Tubes in a stack and a Sphere, as shown in Figure 5.38. Now, follow these steps:

1. Select the Sphere (named Sphere_Wire) and right-click to bring up the Quad menu.

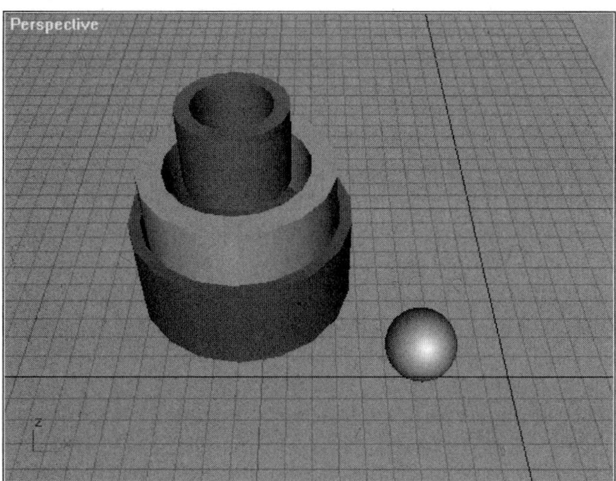

Figure 5.38
The Perspective viewport for the Chap5_Wire.max file used to experiment with the wiring ability in MAX.

2. In the Transform area, choose Wire Parameters. Doing so brings up a small, modeless menu that gives you the choice of wiring the Sphere's transforms or its Object parameters; the object type appears in parentheses. Choose Object (Sphere) and Radius from the expanded menu, as shown in Figure 5.39.
3. A dashed white line now follows the cursor. Move the cursor over the smallest Tube (Tube_Small) and click to bring up the same small, modeless menu. Choose Object (Tube) and Radius 2 to open the Parameter Wiring dialog box shown in Figure 5.40. Wiring is performed in this dialog box. (You can reach the dialog box directly by choosing Animation|Wire Parameters|Parameter Wire Dialog from the drop-down menus. Going directly to the dialog box requires both objects and their parameters to be selected from all scene objects in a list.)

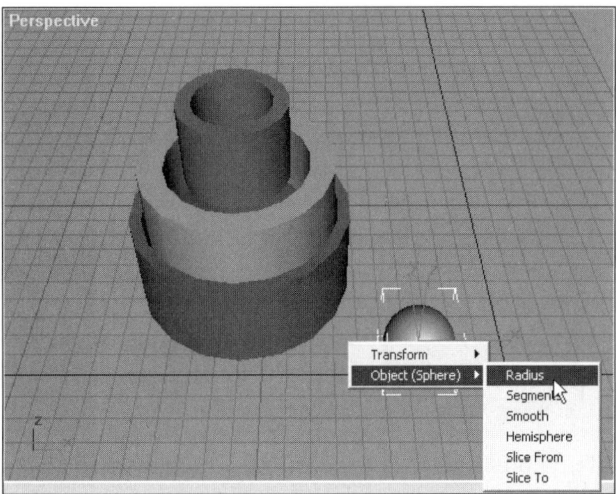

Figure 5.39
Select the Sphere's Radius parameter for wiring.

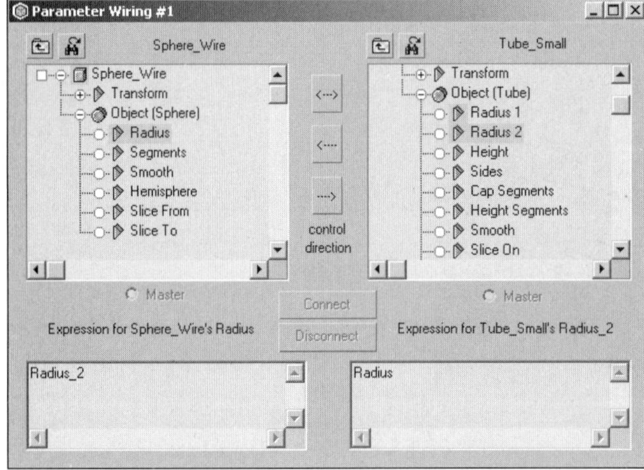

Figure 5.40
The Parameter Wiring dialog box, set to wire the two selected parameters.

4. The dialog box is set up with Sphere_Wire on the left, Tube_Small on the right, and the selected parameters highlighted for each. Between the two windows are the controls that determine which parameter of one object (if either) controls the parameter of the other. Choose the bottom arrow, which lets the Radius value of Sphere_Wire control the Radius 2 value of Tube_Small. Click on the Connect button to complete the wiring. Close the dialog box.

5. Go to the Sphere's Modify panel and note the Radius value. Then, look at the Radius 2 value for the wired Tube. It's the same as the Sphere's Radius value—grayed out and not adjustable. Switch back to the Sphere and change its Radius value; watch as both the Sphere

and the Tube change. One evident problem is that the Radius 2 of the Tube can become larger than the Radius 1, causing an odd transition point and making the Tube vary from the stated objective for the exercise.

6. To solve this problem, you can wire the other Radius value to the Sphere but account for the wall thickness. From the Sphere's quad menu, choose Wire Parameters|Object (Sphere)| Radius and wire it to Tube_Small's Radius 1 parameter (Object (Tube)|Radius 1). The fields at the bottom of the Parameter Wiring dialog box contain the expressions that define the associated variables. If you were to connect them now, the Radius 1 value of the Tube would be set equal to the Radius of the Sphere just as it was for Radius 2, creating a Tube with no sidewall measurement. Instead, the expression to define the Tube's Radius 1 should read "Radius+2", ensuring that the outer radius will remain two units larger than the Sphere and therefore two units larger than the inner radius. The dialog box with the proper settings is shown in Figure 5.41. Select the bottom control direction (right panel controls left), click on the Connect button, and close the dialog box. Select the Sphere and change its Radius value; both Radius values for the Tube will compensate, so that the inner radius matches the Sphere and the outer value maintains a two-unit separation from the inner radius.

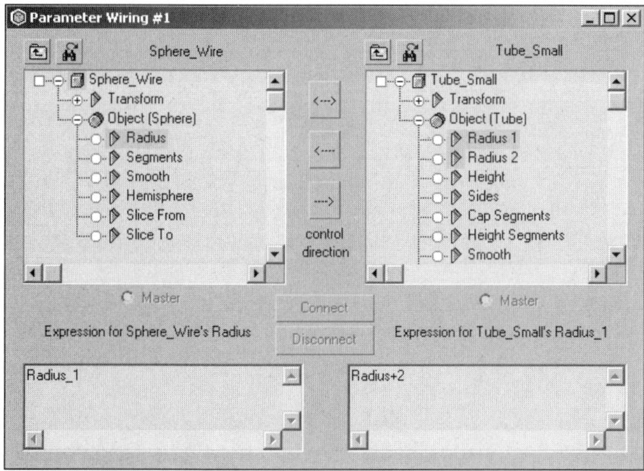

Figure 5.41
The Parameter Wiring dialog box with the settings to keep the Tube's outer radius two units larger than its inner radius.

Note: *An* expression *is a mathematical evaluation of variables and operations. Your first geometry lesson probably taught the Pythagorean theorem:* $A^2 + B^2 = C^2$. *This equation is used to find the length of the unknown side of a triangle when two sides are known. By rearranging the equation as* $C = \sqrt{(A^2 + B^2)}$, *the variable C is defined by the expression on the right of the equal sign. If you know A and B, you can plug them into the equation and evaluate it, and the result is equal to C. In MAX, the variables used in the expressions are the object's parameters; the results can also be set as the values of other parameters.*

7. Wire the Radius 1 value of Tube_Med to two units greater than the radius of the Sphere (the same as the Radius 2 of Tube_Small) and wire the Radius 2 value to four units greater. Wire the two radii of Tube_Large to the Radius value of the Sphere, maintaining an inner radius the same as Tube_Med and an outer radius two units larger. Adjust the radius of the Sphere, and all the radii for the Tubes will compensate for the adjustment. Your scene should look like Figure 5.42. (If necessary, the project at this point is available on the CD-ROM as Chap5_Wire_Final.max.)

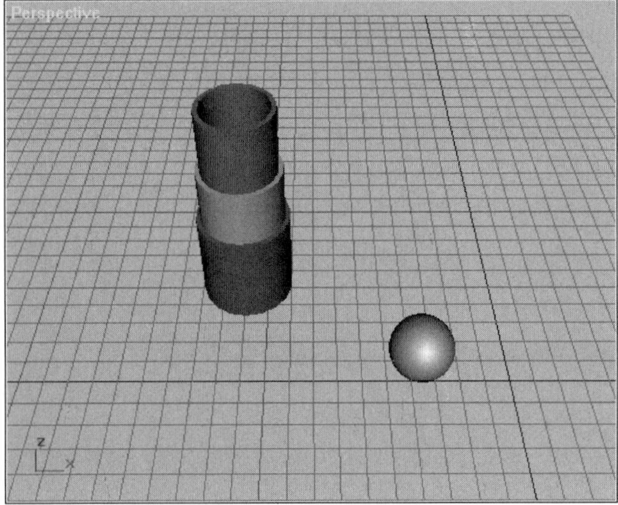

Figure 5.42
The scene after the objects are wired together.

Further wiring is possible to tie the number of segments between objects or the height and location of the Tubes; the list of possibilities is enormous.

Manipulators

Manipulators are helper objects that can give you visual feedback when used as wiring objects. Three different *flavors* of manipulators are available: Cone Angle, Plane Angle, and Slider. They accomplish the same tasks with different visual appearances. For the following exercise, you'll be using the Slider manipulator, which gives the most control. Follow these steps:

1. Continue with the previous exercise or open the file Chap5_Wire_Final.max from the CD-ROM.

2. From the Create|Helpers menu, expand the drop-down list and choose Manipulators. Select Slider and click once in the Perspective viewport.

3. Switch viewports. The Slider appears in the current viewport only and maintains a consistent size regardless of the zoom factor. Return to the Perspective viewport.
4. Select the Sphere and wire its Hemisphere value to the Value property of the slider. When the Parameter Wiring dialog box appears, choose the middle Connect option. Letting the Slider control the Sphere, click on Connect. Close the dialog box.
5. In the Main toolbar, activate the Manipulate transform button. The Manipulator has many parts, and the transform must be active in order to adjust any of them. The small box to the Slider's left controls its movement (the Move transform has no effect), and the plus symbol controls the helper's visibility. The diamond shape controls the length of the Slider line, and the triangular marker determines the value reflected in the numeric indicator above the line. Move the Slider to the right as you observe the Sphere. Any value greater than 1 causes the Sphere to disappear, because the valid values for the Hemisphere setting are between 0 and 1. The Slider must be adjusted to contain only valid values.
6. Set the Slider value to 0, turn off the Manipulate transform, select the Slider, and open the Modify panel. In the Name field, enter "Hemisphere" to make a descriptive name appear above the Slider bar. This name helps you keep track of the Slider's wiring purpose—it does not change the name of the Slider object. Leave the Minimum value at 0 and change the Maximum to 1. Activate the Manipulate transform again and move the marker.

As you can see, the new Manipulator helper object can give you quick and customizable adjustment tools to add to your scenes. If any object needs frequent adjustment, use Sliders to relieve the need to select the object or an object within a group, and then search for the parameter in the Modify panel.

Schematic View

The Schematic View tool provides a graphical view of a scene, similar to a flow chart. Groups appear at the top of the chart, and the flow of all objects and their modifiers can be traced down. You can rename objects and rearrange, expand, or contract the chart elements to provide the information you need.

Choosing Schematic view from the Main toolbar opens a window similar to Figure 5.43. Any items with a red down-arrow can be expanded to reveal further information. The top toolbar in the Schematic View window provides adjustment and visibility tools; the bottom toolbar provides tools for zooming into and out of the window.

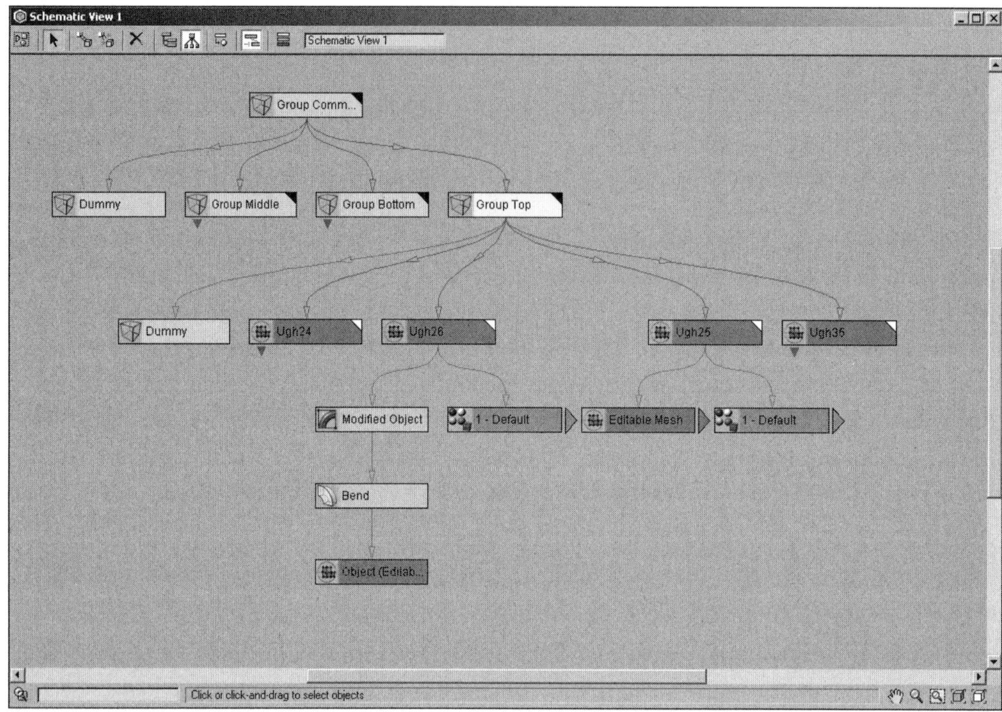

Figure 5.43
A Schematic View window of a scene, with nested groups and modifiers. The objects to the left and right of the expanded objects have been closed for clarity.

Moving On

This chapter covered a substantial amount of information about working smarter to accomplish more in MAX, and it showed the many ways you can clone objects and the different types of clones from which to choose. You learned how to use the alignment and precision tools to place objects in a scene accurately, and you learned how to replace current objects with XRefs and proxies. You were exposed to the new wiring capabilities of 3ds max 4 as well as the Schematic View tool.

In the next chapter, you will experiment with the many modifiers available in MAX. Modifiers adjust, alter, or even create geometry and splines, and we will experiment with the ways they can impact the modeling process.

Part III

Modeling

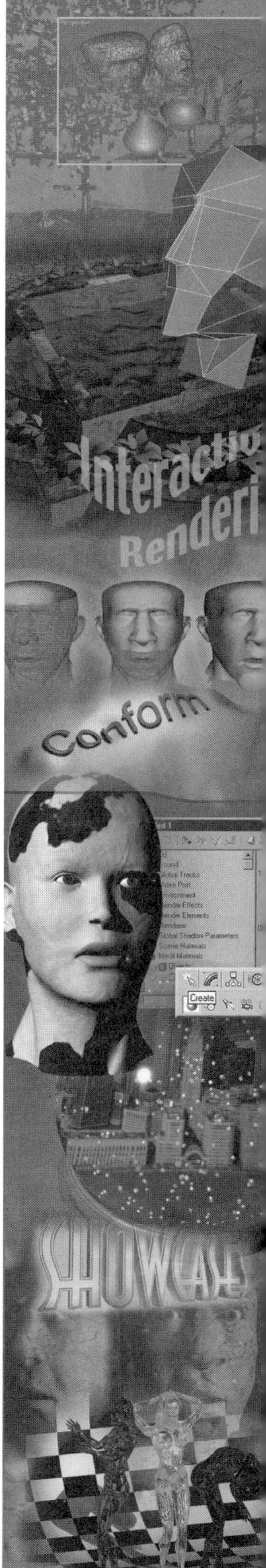

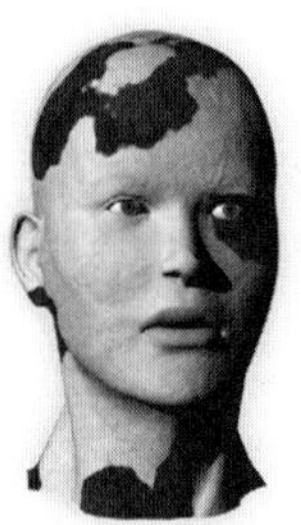

Chapter 6

Modeling with Modifiers

So far, we've covered the methods of creating basic geometry or primitives in MAX. Although it's true that, even in their most basic form, these objects are all around us, they are often the basis for more complex geometric models. Of course, you aren't limited to using modifiers only with primitives; you can use them at any level of the modeling process. Many modifiers are limited to a specific task, whereas others cover a wide range of possible functions. Some of them alter the geometry of objects, and some actually create the geometry. This chapter covers those modifiers that apply to meshes and splines; we'll discuss the rest of the modifiers in chapters whose goals are in line with their focus.

Modifiers and the Modifier Stack

"MAX remembers everything." Understanding that phrase is the most important step in learning how to use MAX's modifiers properly to change the appearance of the objects in your scene. When MAX debuted, it introduced a unique approach to editing geometry through the centralized use of deformation tools rather than direct editing of a mesh's elements. These tools can be applied one after another, with the first modifier building on the object, the second building on the result of the first, the third building on the result of the second, and so on. This approach, called a *modifier stack*, lets you enter the stack at any level and change the parameters or settings; those changes are then reflected in every higher level in the stack. Because MAX remembers everything, objects do not need to be modeled perfectly at each level before you move to the next level—you can always perfect objects later or update them as requirements change. (Objects can also be *collapsed* and reduced to basic meshes; only at this point does MAX disregard an object's modification history.)

Through MAX's open architecture approach to programming, many modifiers in addition to those that come with MAX are available as plug-ins. Several modifiers that are now included in the core package were once external features.

The traditional methods of mesh-level modeling, as well as some new techniques, are available and widely used; these will be covered in Chapter 7. These methods are still bound by the modifier stack theory, but they sometimes bring with them inherent problems with regard to modifying prior stack levels.

***Note:** Modeling with modifiers was once considered a practice restricted to use with inorganic mechanical or architectural elements. This is no longer the case: The list of available modifiers contains many that soften or smoothly manipulate objects to give them an organic look.*

Basic Axial Modifiers

Some of the most important modifiers deform an object along a specific axis. They're easy to learn and, with a little creativity and practice, can greatly enhance your scenes with minimal effort.

The axial deformers generally follow the same panel convention. The Parameters rollout consists of three groups: The first defines the amount of the effect, the second defines the axis, and the third determines whether the modifier's effects are applied to the entire object or only to a specified area. In this section, we'll discuss the Bend, Taper, Twist, Stretch, Squeeze, Push, Mirror, and Skew modifiers and how they can affect the scene's geometry.

Bend

The Bend modifier deforms an object by curving it along the designated axis. It's one of the easiest modifiers to learn. A flower stem, an industrial conduit, or a spaceship's exhaust tube may start as a linear object to which the Bend modifier is later applied. The exercises in this section will demonstrate how to use the Bend modifier specifically, as well as the features that are consistent across the other axial deformers.

Angle, Direction, and Axis

Before you begin this exercise, right-click on the Perspective viewport's name and choose Edged Faces from the pop-up menu. Doing so will let you see the segmentation of the objects in the Smooth + Highlights rendered Perspective viewport. Now, follow these steps:

1. Create a Box primitive on the ground plane with Length and Width values of 10 and a Height of 50. Leave all Segments values set at 1.

2. Go to the Modify tab and expand the Modifier List, as shown in Figure 6.1. This list is specific to the type of object selected—it does not contain modifiers that cannot apply to the object, such as modifiers that edit splines exclusively. Scroll down to the Parametric Modifiers area and select Bend.

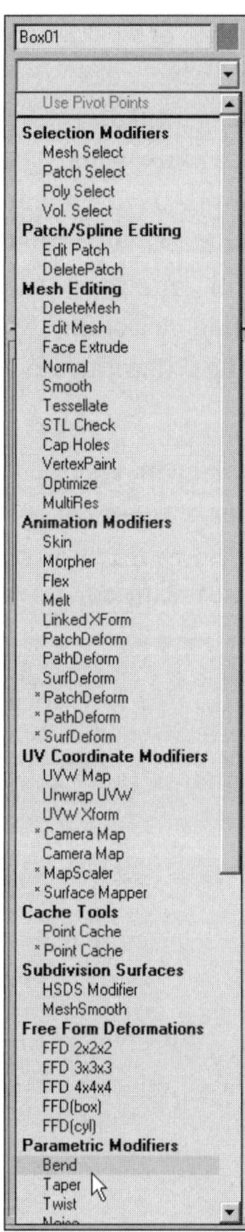

Figure 6.1
The expanded Modifier List for the selected Box primitive contains no less than 70 possible modifiers for this type of object.

3. Nothing appears to have happened to the Box, other than an orange bounding box enveloping it. This box is the Bend Gizmo, which identifies the optimum possible curve based on the current parameter settings. Enter a value of 90 in the Angle field and observe the reaction in your geometry. The top and bottom faces of the Box are 90 degrees apart, but the sides are canted rather than curved because the modifier is applied incrementally to each segment along the axis specified in the Bend Axis group. In this case, the default Z-axis has only one segment assigned.

4. To increase the curvature, you must add segments to the Box. Look at the list of stack entries in the field between the Modifier List field and the short toolbar. This is the Stack View window, also known simply as the Stack View, where the modifier stack is viewed and adjusted. You begin with this list, which contains the modifier history of the Box, when making changes to events in the stack. The last modifier applied (Bend) appears at the top of the stack, and, in this case, a light bulb icon and a plus symbol appear to the left of the modifier. The light bulb indicates whether the effect of the icon is turned on, and the plus symbol indicates that the modifier has subobjects available for modification. Select the Box level to make the Bend Gizmo disappear from the viewport and the Box's Parameters rollout appear in the Command panel.

5. Begin to increase the Height Segments value. The Box becomes more curved with each additional segment, as it tries to conform to the Bend Gizmo. Choose 15 as the number of height segments, and then return to the Bend level of the modifier stack. Figure 6.2 shows three Box primitives with identical Bend modifiers applied. The number of height segments for each Box, from left to right, is 2, 15, and 30.

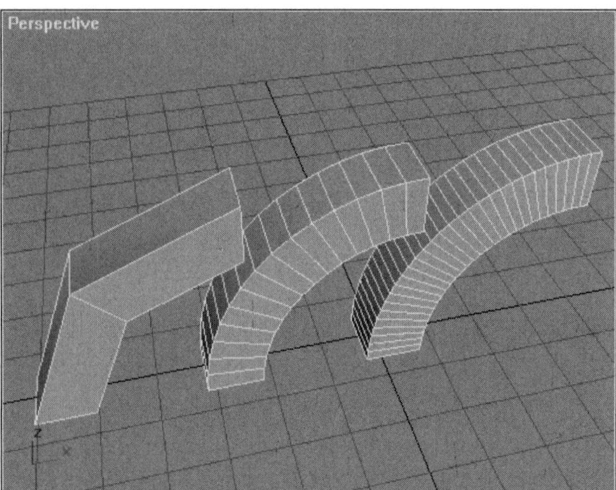

Figure 6.2
Three Box primitives, after applying a Bend modifier.

Setting the Level of Segmentation

As a general practice, you should get into the habit of setting the segmentation of an object to the lowest possible value that achieves the desired result. When MAX renders a scene, it must consider the color of every face separately—which takes time. If a Box remains as a primitive, with no modifiers applied, you gain no advantage by increasing the segmentation and thus increasing the rendering time. If an object is only a small background feature on screen (say, a vase on a distant table), the segmentation can be less than that of a similar feature in the foreground, thereby reducing the rendering and screen-redraw times without adversely affecting the scene's quality. For the Box in this exercise, you'll see little improvement between 15 and 30 height segments.

6. In addition to choosing the correct bend angle, you also need to choose the bend direction. Zero degrees runs in the positive World X direction; the direction increases in a counterclockwise direction. Figure 6.3 shows the Boxes from Figure 6.2 at 0, 90, and 270 degrees, respectively.

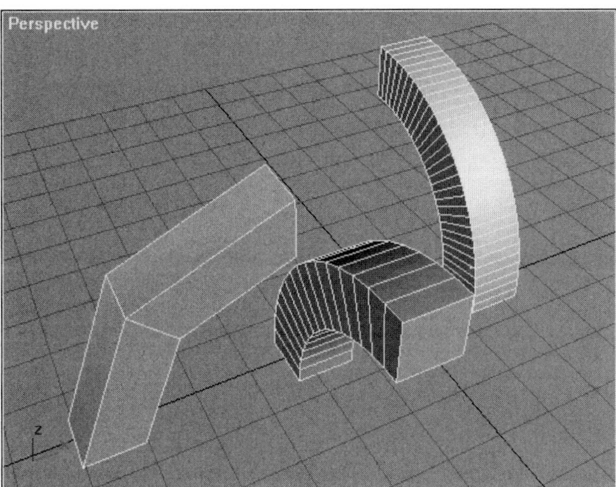

Figure 6.3
From left to right, the Boxes are at 0, 90, and 270 degrees.

7. The Bend Axis group determines the Local axis to which the modifier applies. Experiment with the options on the current Box. Create a Box in the Front or Left viewport and cycle through the same options.

Using Limits

Limits are methods of concentrating a modifier only over a specific portion of the object. Continuing with the Box from the previous exercise, follow these steps:

1. With the Box well segmented, set the Angle to 90, the Direction to 0, and the Bend Axis to Z. Select the Limit Effect checkbox. The object lies down with its bottom face tapered. This happens because the default Upper and Lower Limit values are both set to 0, restricting the effect to the base of the object.

2. Using the spinner buttons, increase the Upper Limit value. Watch as the orange marker rises along the Box; everything before the marker is bent, whereas everything after it is straight. A setting that projects the marker beyond the Box seems to have the same effect as no upper limit, and thus seems like a wasted effort—but remember, you can always go back to the Box's parameters and increase (or animate) the Height value to surpass the marker's location. Set the Upper Limit value to 20.

3. The Lower Limit value is somewhat less useful than the Upper Limit. It works with negative values and initially moves its marker out of the boundaries of the Box; this apparently causes the effect of the Bend modifier to lessen. Set the Lower Limit value to 0.

Note: *It is important to understand that the Limit values are measured in units rather than percentages; thus, a very large object, such as a skyscraper, may require an enormous value to achieve the desired result.*

The Modifier's Subobjects

The Bend modifier has two subobjects—Gizmo and Center—that control exactly how the modifier is applied to an object. Transforming a modifier's Gizmo or Center changes how the modifier affects the object. This effect is a projection of the Gizmo, because its location relates to the location of the object.

Continuing with the Box from the previous exercise, follow these steps:

1. Expand the Bend modifier entry in the Stack View panel by clicking on the plus symbol next to it. You'll see two choices: Gizmo and Center. Select Gizmo, and a yellow box will surround the Box between the Upper and Lower Limit values. Move the Gizmo up and down along the Z-axis and watch as the Box adjusts, and even relocates, to conform to the new Gizmo location. Moving the Gizmo above the Box removes the effect of the modifier, because no Lower Limit value was set; moving it below the Box causes the Box to move to the location it would occupy if it was projected from the end of the Gizmo's location. Move the Gizmo about half way up the Box and a small amount in the positive X direction. (See the second Box in Figure 6.4 to see the effect of the Gizmo centered along its height.)

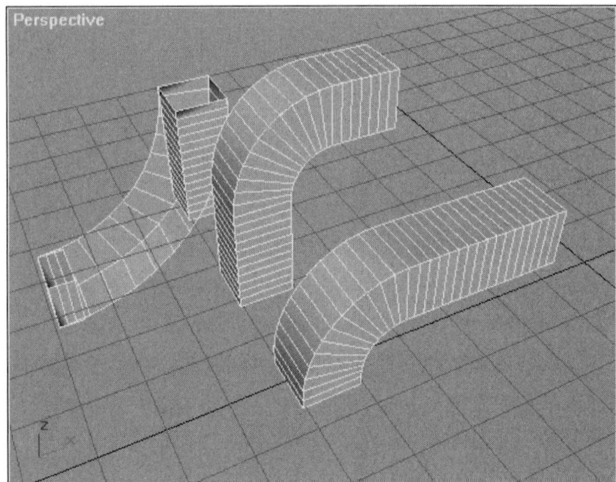

Figure 6.4
From front to back, the first Box has its Upper Limit value set to 20 and its Lower Limit value set to 0. The second Box is the same as the first, but the Gizmo is centered along its height. The third Box's Center is moved in the negative X direction.

Note: *When you're in a subobject mode, only the subobjects of the current objects are selectable—you can't select the other objects in the scene. If you find yourself unable to pick on another scene object, check to see whether the subobject level is active.*

2. The Center subobject, as you would expect, controls the location of the center point from which the bend occurs. Select Center and then move the center point in different directions to see the effects on the Box.

Using Mesh Select to Bend a Mesh's Subobjects

The Mesh Select modifier creates a selection set of an object's subobjects (not to be confused with a modifier's subobjects) and passes them to the modifier just above it in the stack. For example, as an alternate approach in the exercises you've been working on, you can use the Mesh Select modifier to apply the Bend modifier to only a portion of the object, rather than to the object as a whole. Doing so allows multiple bends to occur along the length of one object. Continuing with the Box from the previous exercise, follow these steps:

1. It's important to keep track of the modifiers and what they accomplish. To help do this, you can rename the modifiers in the stack. Select the Bend modifier applied to the Box and right-click on it. In the pop-up menu that appears, select Rename. Type "Bend-initial" in the highlighted field. Turn off the modifier by clicking on the light bulb icon; the Box stands straight, but the orange Gizmo indicator remains in place. Your Modify panel should look like Figure 6.5.

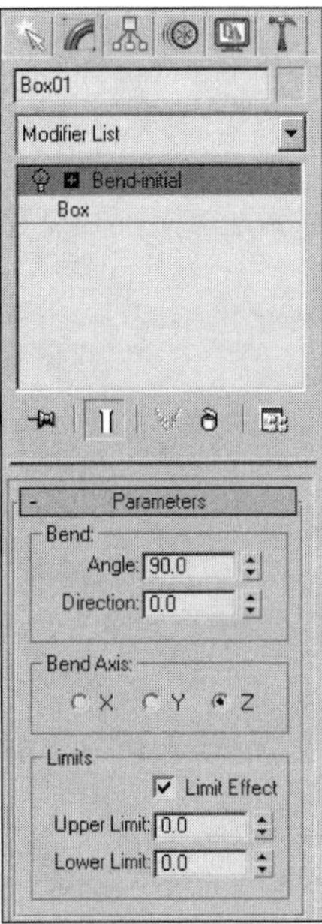

Figure 6.5
The Modify panel with the current Bend settings, after the modifier has been renamed and turned off.

You apply new modifiers just above the currently selected location in the modifier stack. Their results are passed to the next-higher modifier, if one exists. Continue with the exercise:

2. Select the Box level in the stack and apply a Mesh Select modifier from the Modifier List. Mesh Select is now sandwiched between the Box and Bend-initial entries. Expand the modifier and choose Face (or choose Face from the icons in the Mesh Select Parameters rollout).

3. Select the faces that comprise the bottom fourth of the box. (You may need to switch to the Front or Left viewport.) Apply a new Bend modifier to the subobject selection, rename it "Bend-bottom", and enter an Angle value of 90. The result probably isn't what you expect, because the bend starts in the middle of the selection rather than at the top. Fix it by selecting the Bend-bottom Center subobject and moving it up until it is even with the top selected face. Notice the lines that appear on either side of the Mesh Select modifier in the stack; they indicate that the modifier applies to a subobject selection only, not to the entire object.

4. Applying another Bend to the Box at this point would bend the entire object rather than another specific location. To add a second bend without affecting the first, ensure that you are at the Bend-bottom level. Apply another Mesh Select and select the top third of the faces. Apply another Bend modifier, rename it "Bend-top", set the Angle to –90, and move the Center to the bottom of the selected faces. Figure 6.6 shows the Box in various stages of development and the final modifier stack.

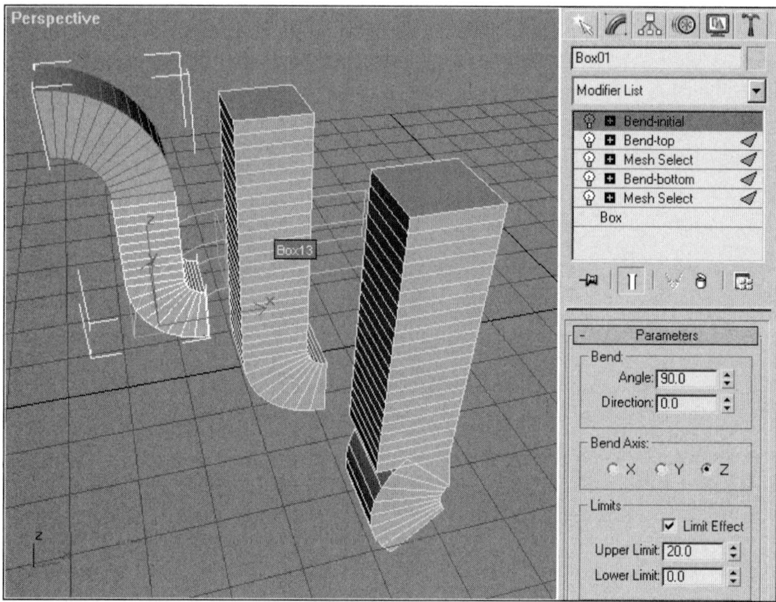

Figure 6.6
From front to back; the first Box has the Bend-bottom modifier applied without moving the Center. The second Box's Center has been moved. The third Box has the second Bend applied, and its Center has been moved. The third Box's Modify panel appears at right.

Taper

To *taper* an object means to shape it so that it has a progressively smaller cross-section along one or more axes. The Taper modifier in MAX has greater control than its name might suggest. The exercises in this section will introduce you to the myriad shapes that Taper can help you create.

Axis and Effect

The default primary axis for the tapering effect is Z, but the effect can run along any axis and can affect one or both of the axes in the plane perpendicular to the tapering axis. Figure 6.7 shows three identical Boxes with, from left to right, the X-, Y-, or Z-axis as the primary axis and the effect applied to both perpendicular axes. Figure 6.8 shows the same Boxes, all with Z as the taper axis, with the effect applied to the XY, X, or Y axis. The Taper modifier always tapers symmetrically along the primary axis, and the Symmetry checkbox constrains the effect axis to be symmetrical, as well.

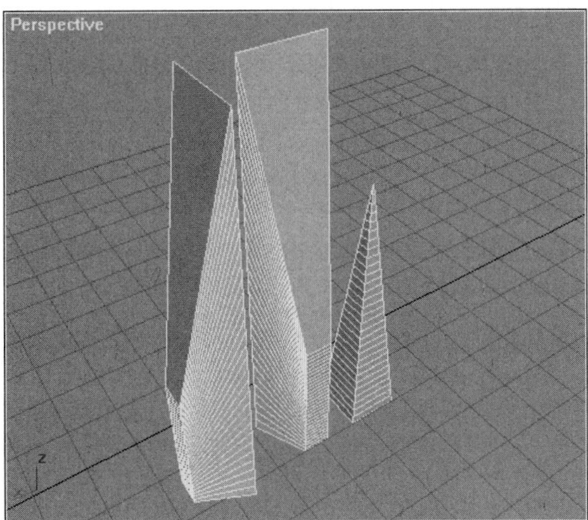

Figure 6.7
From left to right, identical Boxes with X, Y, and Z as the primary axis, respectively, and the effect applied to both perpendicular axes.

To begin working with the Taper modifier, either continue the previous exercise or open the file Chap6 Taper.max from the CD-ROM.

1. Toggle off all the current modifiers applied to the Box by clicking on the light bulb icons in the Stack View window. Your box will again look tall, narrow, and straight.

2. Select the top modifier in the stack to ensure that a new modifier is applied after all the others. Apply a Taper modifier to the Box.

3. Increase and decrease the Amount value to see the effect. Positive numbers cause the Box's cross-section to become larger as the distance from the base increases; negative numbers

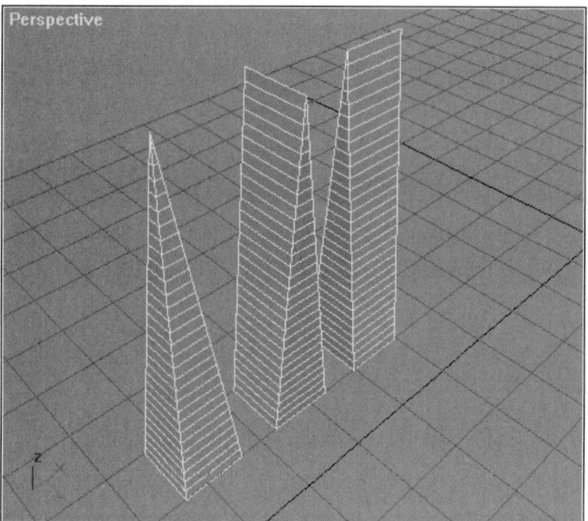

Figure 6.8
From left to right, identical Boxes with Z as the primary axis and the effect applied to both perpendicular axes, then X only, and then Y only.

cause the cross-section to become smaller. An Amount value of –1 will cause the top to come to a point.

The Object's Parameters Matter

The Box's Height parameter determines the direction of the effect of the Taper modifier's Amount value. If the Box has a negative Height value, larger Amount values will cause it to taper to a downward-pointing object—the opposite of the effect a large Amount value would have with a positive Height value.

4. Set Amount to –2, the primary axis to Y, and the effect axis to X. Select the Symmetry checkbox. The Box flattens, although the Taper Gizmo indicates that it should be a diamond shape in the X-axis. Segmentation in that axis is insufficient for the operation to execute successfully.

5. In the Stack View window, go back to the Box level. A warning box will appear, describing a potential error that may occur if you change the Box's parameters. This error can occur because the two applications of the Mesh Select modifier chose specific vertices for their operations; changing or deleting those vertices will have an unknown result up the stack. If you are concerned about the result, click on the Hold/Yes button, which writes a file to your hard drive called Hold.max. If you need to restore the scene to its current state, you can choose Fetch from the Edit menu. In this case, the offending modifiers are toggled off, so click on the Yes button. Slowly increase the number of length segments. Even values create points at the ends, and odd values result in flat spots whose sizes decrease as the number of segments increases. Your Box should look like the one at the far right in Figure 6.9.

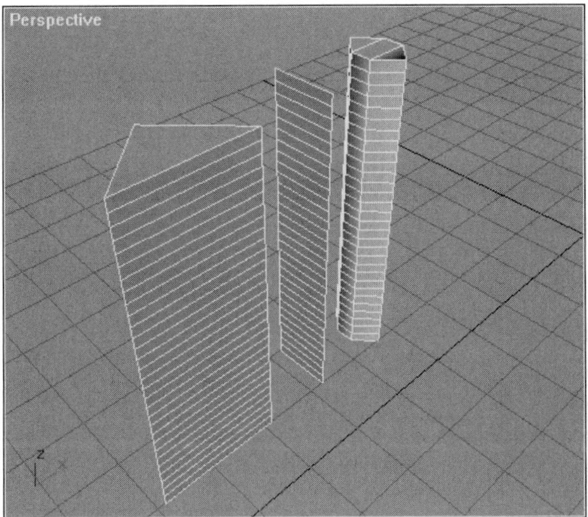

Figure 6.9
Identical Boxes with Y as the primary axis and X as the effect axis. From left to right, the first Box's Symmetry checkbox is deselected, the second Box's Symmetry checkbox is selected, and the third Box's length segments have been increased to 3.

Adding Curvature

To this point, the Taper modifier has done what you would expect: It has created a tapered effect in a linear manner. MAX can also add a curved effect along the taper axis, depending on the Curve value. Negative values create concave curvature, and positive numbers create a convex effect; values between 10 and –10 are valid.

The following exercise illustrates using curved tapers:

1. Continue with the previous exercise or open the file Chap6 Taper2.max. Set the primary axis to Z and the effect axis to XY (producing an offset pyramid look), deselect the Symmetry checkbox, and set the Amount value to –1. The Box should have a square base and taper to a point at the top.

2. Set the Curve value to –2. The taper now applies in two directions, and the Box has a pinch point midway up its height where the cross-section has no area, as shown on the left in Figure 6.10.

3. Just as with the Bend modifier, moving the Taper modifier's Gizmo or Center affects the result of the modifier. Expand the Taper modifier in the Stack View window, select the Gizmo, and experiment with the effect of moving it in the X and Y directions. Place its final location 10 units from the original in the Y direction and –10 in the X direction, similar to the middle example in Figure 6.10.

4. Move the Gizmo up or down along the Z-axis to create a concave or convex ramp that terminates with a point on one end and an edge on the other. Moving the Gizmo in the positive Z direction results in the example at the right in Figure 6.10.

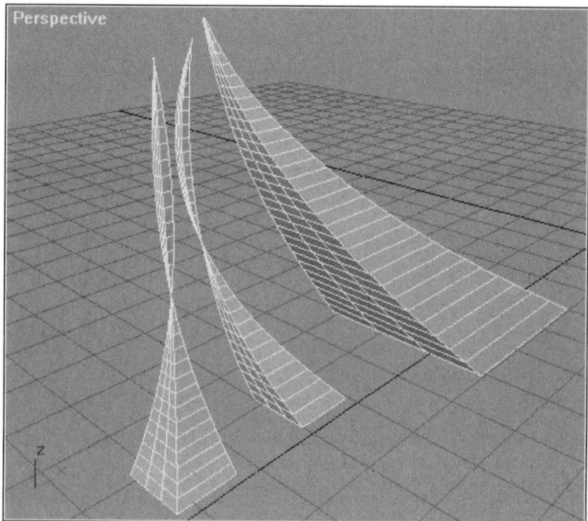

Figure 6.10
Identical Boxes with Z as the primary axis, XY as the effect axis, no symmetry, and the Amount value set to –2. The middle Box's Gizmo has been moved in the positive Y direction, and the right Box's Gizmo has also been moved in both the positive Y and positive Z directions.

Other Taper Implementations

The Taper modifier can also be used to add some fancy touches to your objects, as this exercise shows:

1. Continue with the previous exercise. Turn off the current Taper modifier and resize the Box to 50 units for the Length, Width, and Height, with 10 length and width segments and 30 height segments.

Note: *When an object is deselected and then reselected, or if you leave and then renter the Modify panel, the top modifier in the stack is current. In this exercise, Taper modifiers appear at the top of the stack as well as just above the Box level; therefore, you need to check which level is current each time you reenter the modifier stack.*

2. Apply a new Taper modifier just above the Box level. Give it a small, positive Amount value of about 0.2 and a Curve value of about 1.5. (Precision is not necessary here.) Move the Center subobject to one corner to project the effect in only two directions. The result should look similar to the Box on the right in Figure 6.11.

Using Align with Subobjects

To place a Gizmo, Center, or other subobject precisely, use the Align tool as described in Chapter 5. The only difference is that the Current Object field is grayed out because the subobjects don't have actual dimensions—their center point is used as the reference point.

---

3. The same bulge effect can be applied to a subobject selection, rather than to the entire object, to yield a different result. Turn off the Taper modifier and return to the Box level.

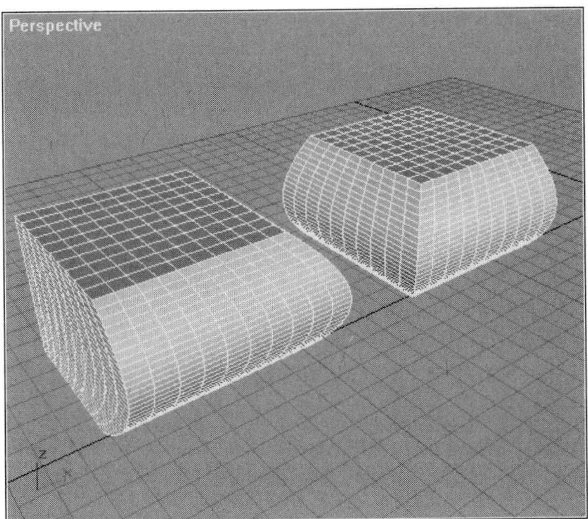

Figure 6.11
The Box on the right, from the exercise in the text, has had its parameters adjusted, resulting in a less tall, thin object. Its Center has been moved to the corner farthest from the viewport. The Taper Amount is set to about 0.2, and the Curve value is about 1.5. On the left, the same Box is mirrored about the X-axis to show the flat side opposite one of the curved sides.

Apply a Mesh Select modifier, choose Vertex as the subobject level, and select the top half of the Box. (You can see the benefit of naming the modifiers in the stack, because you may need to scroll down the list to find the modifier you need.)

4. Ensure that the bottom Mesh Select modifier is highlighted. Apply another Taper modifier and move its Center to the back corner. Increase the Amount and Curve values until the top of the Box resembles the previous look of the Box with the Taper modifier applied to it as a whole. Your Box should look similar to the middle Box in Figure 6.12.

Don't restrict yourself to applying the Taper modifier only as a tool to make rudimentary modifications to symmetrical objects. Figure 6.13 shows the Taper modifier applied to Spheres and a Tube in the front row to create objects with complex curvatures. The objects in the back row are copies of the same Uhg head used in earlier chapters with positive (on the left) and negative (on the right) Amount values.

As you can see, the Taper modifier does more than its simple name implies, and you can use it in a variety of situations. To see the effect of all the combined modifiers applied to the Box, turn them all on in the Stack View window.

Twist

Unlike the Taper modifier, Twist does exactly what its name implies: It incrementally turns the object's vertices along a designated axis. The interface is similar to that of the previous modifiers. You can fine-tune the mesh by applying the right values to the proper spinners.

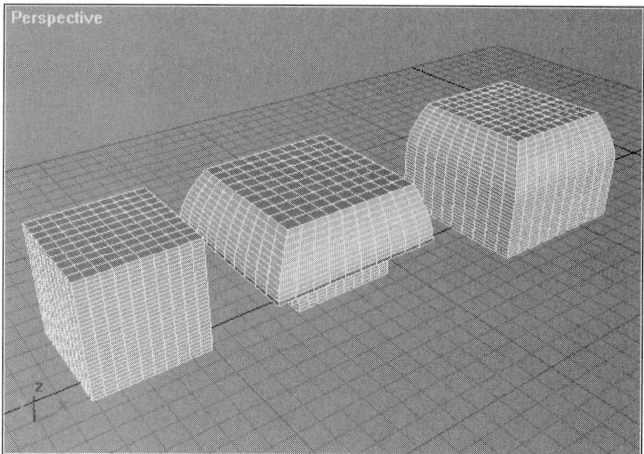

Figure 6.12
Three identical Boxes. The one on the left has no Taper modifier applied, the middle has a Taper modifier applied only to the top half, and the one on the right has a Taper modifier applied to the entire object but limited to the top half.

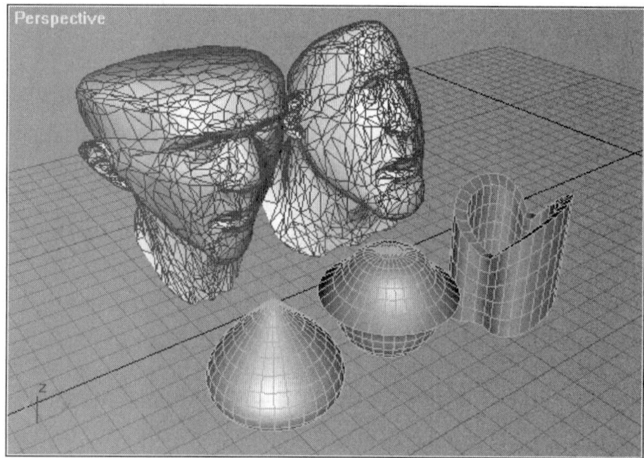

Figure 6.13
A single Taper modifier applied to several different objects. The heads in the back row are the Uhg model used in previous chapters; the one on the left has a positive Amount value and the one on the right has a negative Amount value.

Angle and Segmentation

When you increase and decrease the Twist modifier's Angle value, positive numbers result in a clockwise twist and negative numbers result in a counterclockwise twist. Follow the steps in this exercise to familiarize yourself with the Twist modifier and its possibilities:

1. Create a ChamferBox primitive in the Top viewport, near the origin. Set the Length and Width values to 15, the Height value to 80, and the Fillet value to 1.5. Set all the segmentation values to 1 and deselect the Smooth checkbox.

2. Apply a Twist modifier to the object and set the Angle value to 180. With the default Twist Axis value set to Z, the ChamferBox twists as its elevation above the ground plane increases; however, the twist is not smooth, because the object cannot conform to the Gizmo due to the low level of segmentation.

3. Return to the ChamferBox level and increase the number of height segments until the benefit of more segments becomes less apparent—around 30. Although the height segments are by far the most important to achieving the proper results with the Twist modifier, width and length segments add to the overall smoothness of the twist's transition between vertices. Increase these values to 7 and set the Fillet Segments value to 4 to eliminate the flat area along the edges. Check out the result by clicking on the Quick Render button in the Main toolbar. The result is less than impressive—the ChamferBox looks like it is covered with small, offset triangles of different shades of the same color. Minimize or close the rendered window.

4. MAX works in and renders polygons, and the polygons are further divided into triangles. You're seeing the pairs of triangles that make up each rectangular polygon. MAX's renderer is trying to shift the colors to represent a difference in the angle of each face in relation to the faces around it. With the Smooth checkbox deselected at the ChamferBox level, the program doesn't attempt to represent an even transition from face to face. Return to the ChamferBox level and select the Smooth checkbox. Nothing seems to happen in the viewports, because you must re-render the scene to see the effect of Smooth. Figure 6.14 shows four different stages in creating a ChamferBox.

5. Expand the Twist modifier and select the Center subobject. Moving it up or down along the Z-axis rotates the object so that the faces at the same level as the Center remain constantly perpendicular to the X- and Y-axes. Move the Center away from the ChamferBox and watch in the Top viewport as the object's base (its pivot point) remains fixed while the upper portion wraps around the Center's current location. When you move the Center in both the positive X and positive Y directions, your scene should look similar to Figure 6.15.

Adding Bias

The Bias value shifts the effect of the Twist modifier along the designated twist axis. Positive numbers compress the effect into a decreasingly smaller range at the top of the object, whereas negative numbers drop the effect below the object. Valid Bias values are in the range from 100 to –100.

To see how to use the Bias value, click on the Undo button until the Center returns to its initial location, and then continue with the previous exercise:

1. Increase the Angle value to 360. Increase and decrease the Bias value to see its effect. At its maximum value of 100, Bias can compress the twist to the top 25 percent of the ChamferBox; at the minimum value of –100, the modifier's effect does not reach the object.

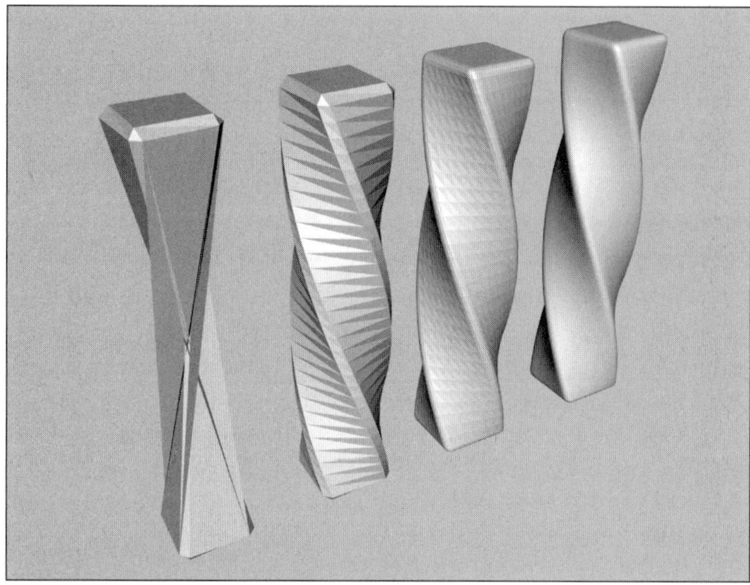

Figure 6.14
A rendering of the same ChamferBox with a 180-degree twist along the Z-axis. The first ChamferBox has no segmentation, the second has segmentation added along the height, and the third has additional segmentation added to the width, length, and fillets. The Smooth checkbox has been selected in the fourth.

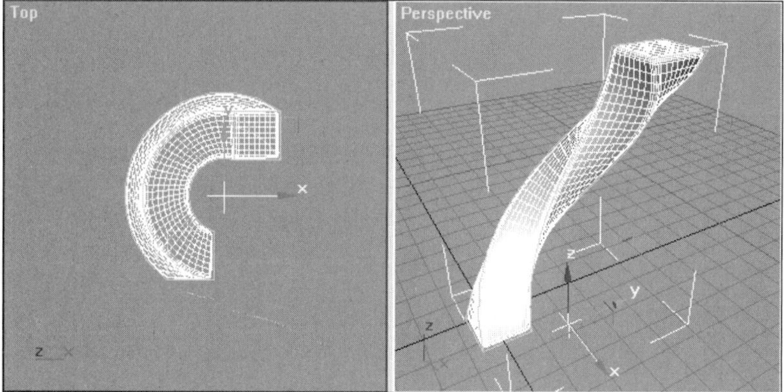

Figure 6.15
When the Twist modifier's Center subobject moves, the object attempts to wrap around the new center point.

2. Set the Bias value to 90 and zoom in to the top of the object. The previously smooth twist is now much rougher, because the effect is concentrated into a smaller area.

As you can see, the primary drawback of adding Bias to a Twist modifier is that more segmentation is needed to maintain smoothness. Figure 6.16 shows the same ChamferBox with different segmentations. The object on the left is rougher, but it has only about 3,500 faces; the object

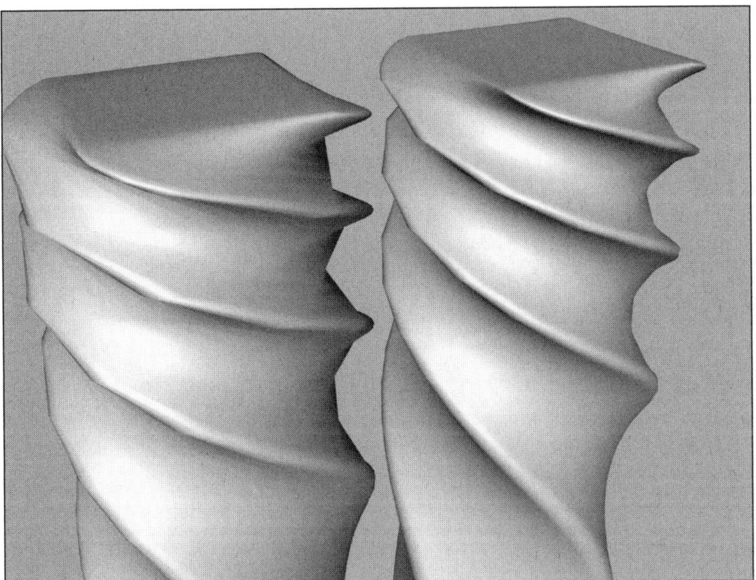

Figure 6.16
The object on the left is rougher, but its facecount is much smaller than that of the smoother object on the right.

on the right is much smoother, but it has about 20,000 faces. You'll constantly encounter this tradeoff when modeling. Later in this chapter, we will cover the methods of reducing the facecount or optimizing the mesh to make the quality-versus-density issue easier to resolve.

Stretch

The Stretch modifier is similar to both the Taper modifier and the Scale transform's Squash option. It increases or decreases an object's cross-section along an axis, with the ability to maintain a constant volume.

The Stretch Axis and Limits groups in the Modify panel should be familiar by now. The Stretch and Amplify parameters define the Stretch modifier. The Stretch value scales the object along the Stretch axis while applying the inverse scale to the two secondary axes, thereby keeping the volume stable. Amplify changes the value of the scale factor applied to the secondary axes and allows the volume to vary from its initial amount. Stretch is often used in animation to give the impression of manipulating or deforming an elastic object. Some of the possibilities of the Stretch modifier are shown in the variety of shapes created from identical Tubes in Figure 6.17.

Squeeze

The Squeeze modifier moves the vertices closest to the pivot point even closer to it in a pinching fashion, always along the object's local Z-axis. You can also apply a bulge along that axis, to emphasize the squeezing effect. The following exercise will show you a few applications of the

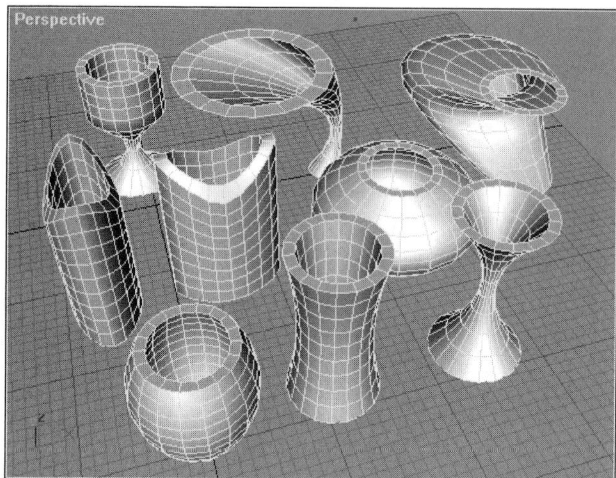

Figure 6.17
Some of the many possibilities you can achieve by using the Stretch modifier and adjusting parameters and the Center location.

Squeeze modifier. (Be aware that two groups in the Parameters rollout have the same spinner names.) Follow these steps:

1. Create a Tube with a height about three times as large as its bigger radius. Set the Height Segments value to 10 and leave the rest of the values at their defaults. Clone the Tube using the Copy option, and then move the clone next to the original Tube.

2. Apply a Squeeze modifier to the original Tube. Then increase and decrease the Amount value in the Radial Squeeze group to see its effect. Set Amount to a value that brings the Tube to a point and causes it to be shaped like a bullet or nose cone, similar to the far-left object in Figure 6.18.

3. Changing the Radial Squeeze Curve value opens the end (lower numbers) or causes the object to cross over itself (higher numbers). Increase the Curve from its default value of 2 to 4 and change the Amount value to compensate, until the Tube is again bullet shaped. The squeeze is concentrated more at the top of the Tube than at the bottom, similar to the second object from the left in Figure 6.18.

4. The Axial Bulge group modifies the object along the Z-axis. Amount elongates or shortens the object, and the Curve value smoothes out the bulging end. To clearly see the effect of the Axial Bulge curve, you may need to open the end of the Tube in the Radial Squeeze group. Apply a small, negative Amount value to shorten the tube and a positive Curve value to flatten the point. The Tube should now look like the third object from the left in Figure 6.18.

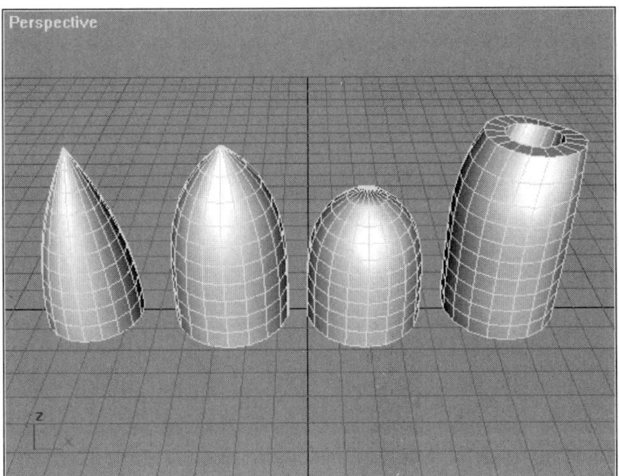

Figure 6.18
Some of the shapes possible by adjusting the parameters or pivot point location when using the Squeeze modifier.

Copying and Pasting Modifiers

When any or all of the modifiers in an object's stack must be replicated for another object, the required portion can be copied and pasted. To do this, select the modifier(s) and right-click on any highlighted one. Select Copy from the resulting pop-up menu. Select the other object, highlight the modifier level above which the new modifier(s) should be inserted, right-click in the Stack View window, and select Paste. The first object's modifier(s) are now inserted into the second object's stack. Note that this technique will not work with the Squeeze modifier, because the identical Gizmos are located in positions relative to each other and nullify the effect of relocating the pivot point. Cutting, copying, and pasting modifiers are covered in more detail later in this chapter.

5. In the Effect Balance group, Bias modifies the effects of the Axis Bulge and Radial Squeeze groups while maintaining a constant volume. The Volume value increases or decreases the effect of both groups simultaneously. Adjust the values of the spinners in this group to see their effects; then return them to their initial values.
6. Changing the location of the pivot point *after* Squeeze is applied has no effect on the result of the modifier. Select the second Tube; move its pivot point to midway up its height and then completely outside it in the positive X and Y directions. Exit any hierarchical tools and apply a Squeeze modifier to the Tube. Adjust its parameters to the same values as for the first Tube. The result is somewhat different, as shown at right in Figure 6.18.

Push

The Push modifier has only one parameter, which adjusts how much it moves an object's vertices outward or inward with respect to the object's center point. Positive or negative values give

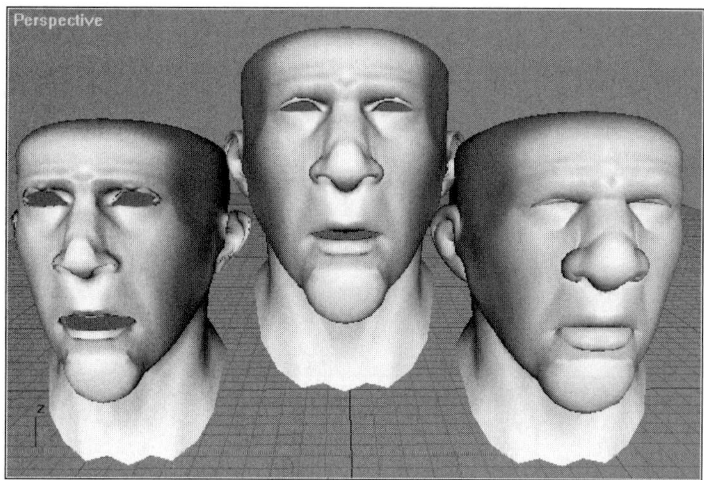

Figure 6.19
The center object is the original. A negative Push modifier value has been applied to the object on the left, and a positive value has been applied to the object on the right.

an inflated or deflated appearance, respectively. Figure 6.19 shows the Push modifier applied to a model using both positive and negative values.

Mirror

Unlike the Mirror transform, the Mirror modifier cannot create a separate clone of the object. You create a primitive and apply the Mirror modifier to it, select the Copy checkbox, and increase the Offset value until the object and its mirror are not touching. Although the scene appears to contain two objects, a check of the Select Objects dialog box reveals that there is really only one object.

The Mirror modifier has an advantage over the Mirror transform: The modifier locks the object and its mirrored twin along the mirror axis or shifts the orientation of the twin by moving or rotating the mirror Center.

Skew

The result of using the Skew modifier is often similar to using Bend with insufficient height segmentation. The modifier moves the end of the object (or subobject) the distance specified in the Amount field of the Skew Axis group. The Direction value rotates the slant application around the skew axis. The sides of the object are then slanted or canted to connect both ends of the object within a straight-sided Gizmo. Figure 6.20 shows two applications of the Skew modifier; the object on the right shows the Gizmo.

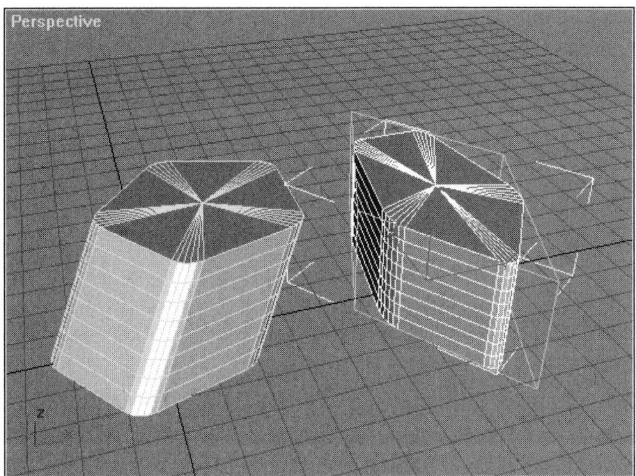

Figure 6.20
Two applications of the Skew modifier. The left object is skewed along the Z-axis with a Direction value of 0; the right object is skewed along the X-axis with a Direction value of 90 degrees.

Noise

In MAX, as well as in the other 3D packages, perfection is easy. It's simple to make a perfectly square box, a perfectly cylindrical post, or a perfectly smooth ball; however, perfection can be detrimental to the quality of a scene. Scenes often need a bit of roughness and attitude to get across the idea of realism and shed the computer-generated shackle inherent to many amateurish attempts.

Noise, in computer graphics terminology, is randomness that can become a central or peripheral part of a scene or graphic image. MAX also uses the concept of noise in the Material Editor to add randomness to the various images you can use to give color and texture to an object. Noise used in a material can give the impression of changes to the surface texture; however, the Noise modifier actually changes the vertices' locations to alter an object's shape.

This section will discuss the application of the Noise modifier to objects and the different effects you can achieve with a little experimentation. (You can add imperfection into a scene several other ways, including using Bump maps and manipulating a mesh at the subobject level; we'll discuss these techniques in Chapters 7 and 12.) The concept of noise can be somewhat intimidating because of the mathematical algorithms used; those algorithms, however, are beyond the scope of this book.

The Noise modifier's Strength values determine the degree to which the vertices will be adjusted within their respective axes' directions. The larger the strength, the further the vertices will move. The Scale value does the opposite of what you may think: It determines the size of the Noise effect, not the strength of the vertex movements. As a result, larger Scale values result in smoother face transitions, and smaller values result in sharper transitions. At extremely low values, no curvature is possible—the mesh is composed of jagged corners. The Seed value is the base number for the Noise algorithm; every whole number, zero or higher, is valid. The results of the Seed numbers do not follow any pattern, and each value produces a different effect.

Noise comes in two flavors, determined by whether the deformation algorithms use the practice of fractal mathematics. The exercises in the following sections will show you how to use both kinds of noise.

Nonfractal Noise

Nonfractal noise creates a smooth transition from one vertex to the next. Follow the steps in this exercise, which concentrates on using the Noise modifier without fractals:

1. Create a cube-shaped Box measuring 100 units on each side. The Noise modifier relies on moving vertices to create texture, so quite a bit of segmentation is needed; set the Length, Width, and Height Segments values to 15. Right-click on the object and choose Properties to open the Object Properties dialog box, and then verify that the object is composed of 2,700 faces—a large number for a simple cube, but necessary for a smooth Noise application.
2. Apply a Noise modifier to the Box. In the Strength group, set the X, Y, and Z values to 25, 50, and 100, respectively. Experiment with the Strength values by increasing and decreasing them to extreme values (including negative numbers). Return the values to 25, 50, and 100.
3. Increase the Scale value to smooth the Box, almost eliminating the Noise effect at about 500 and losing any box-like appearance at about 50. Figure 6.21 shows the different steps to apply nonfractal noise.

Fractal Noise

The theory of fractals describes the use of repeating patterns that increase in scale as they grow distant numerically from the base. Fractals are represented in nature when you look closely at the components of a tree or a river; twigs look like smaller versions of branches or trunks, just as tributaries look like smaller-scale versions of their river parents.

Using fractal noise exaggerates the effect of the Strength values and creates jagged edges at nearly all points of the mesh. The Roughness value determines how jagged the edges become; higher numbers cause greater roughness. All Roughness values between 0 and 1 are valid.

The Iterations value determines the number of times the Fractal value is calculated. An Iterations value of 1 basically eliminates the fractal effect and returns the mesh to its nonfractal counterpart; larger values decrease the smoothness of the facial transitions. With a higher Iterations value, more segmentation may be required to maintain any amount of curvature.

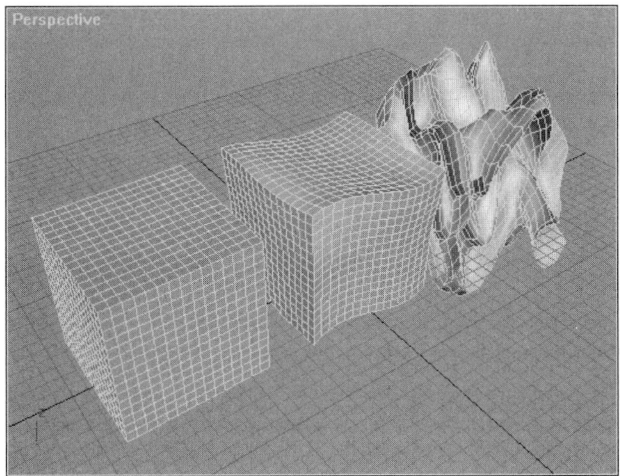

Figure 6.21
Three identical Boxes with the Noise modifier applied. The left Box's Strength values are all set to 0. The middle Box's X, Y, and Z Strength values are set to 25, 50, and 100, respectively. The right Box has the same strengths as the middle Box, but the Scale value is set to 35 and the Seed value is set to 5.

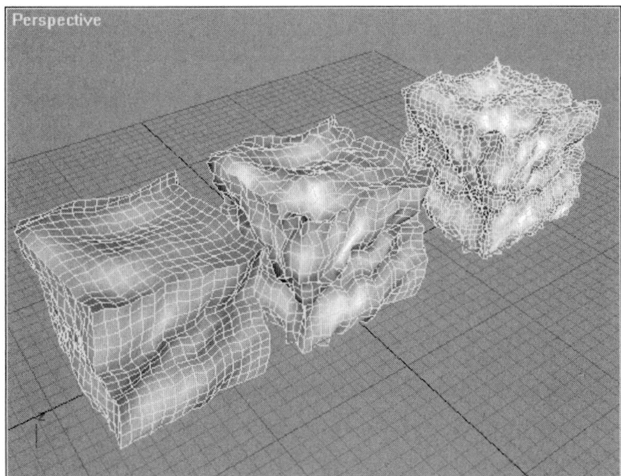

Figure 6.22
Three identical Boxes with the Noise modifier applied and the Fractal checkbox selected. The left Box Strength values are all set to 25. The middle Box is the same, but its Roughness value is set to 0.4 and its Iterations value is set to 10. The right Box has greater segmentation values set at the Box level.

Figure 6.22 shows a few of the possibilities of using the Noise modifier with the Fractal option activated. Figure 6.23 shows rendered close-ups of a fractal-generated Box with different segmentation amounts.

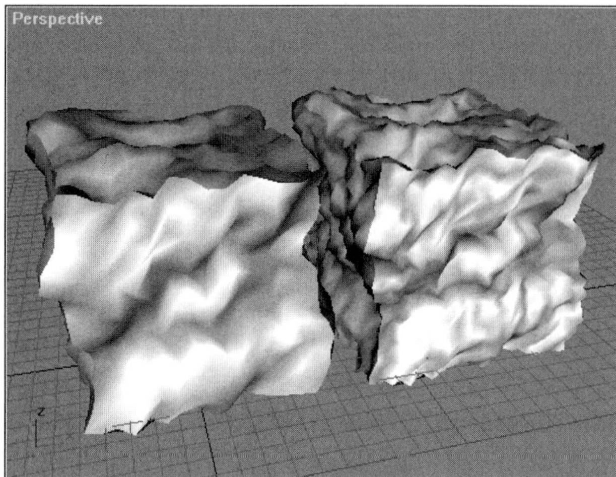

Figure 6.23
A closer rendered view of the middle and right Boxes from Figure 6.22; the right Box has much more segmentation, resulting in a sharper appearance.

You can vary the effect of the Noise modifier—fractal or nonfractal—over time by selecting the Animate Noise checkbox in the Animation group. By default, animation keys are set at the first and last frames of the current animation length to identify the start and end positions for the modifier parameters that can be animated. The Frequency value indicates how quickly the vertices shift positions; very low numbers (0.01 through 0.03) create a slower, flowing effect, and higher numbers result in shakier movement. The Phase value shifts the start and end points of the underlying wave as it is applied to the object.

Let's look at an example of using fractal noise. Continue with the scene from the previous exercise. Before you begin, set all the Strength values to 25 and the Scale value to 100, returning the Box to a state where the distortion is minor along all axes. Now, follow these steps:

1. Select the Fractal checkbox. The impact on the mesh is immediately obvious: All the edges become sharper, and the Box takes on a crumpled look.

Looping the Noise

You may have noticed the jerky movement of the Noise modifier as the current frame moved from the end (100) to the beginning (0). This jerking is caused when the Phase value can't complete a full 360-degree cycle before starting over. Setting animation keys will be explained fully in Chapter 17; for now, we'll briefly summarize the procedure needed to loop the animated noise smoothly. The number of frames must be evenly divisible by 360. The second key is moved to frame 179 and animates half the Phase; the third key is at frame 359 (frame 0 through 359 equals 360 total) and is identical to the first. To see a looping noise animation, open the file Chap6 Noise Loop.max from the CD-ROM and click on the Play button.

2. Set the Roughness value to 0.4 to crumple the mesh even further.
3. Select the Animate Noise checkbox in the Animation group. Set the Frequency value to 0.02 and click on the Play button in the time controls area at the bottom of the MAX window. The Noise modifier changes the shape of the Box from frame to frame.

As you can see, the Noise modifier has many possibilities when it comes to adding randomness to an object. From smashed fenders to drifting asteroids, Noise is quicker and simpler than manipulating the vertices individually.

Relax

The opposite of the Noise modifier is the Relax modifier. Relax smoothes the transitions between non-coplanar faces by relocating the vertices closer to the sharp angled edges. Generally, it results in a slightly smaller mesh. Cubes that are greatly relaxed begin to take on the shape of spheres, and detailed objects lose the characteristics that give them definitive shapes.

As you would expect, positive Relax values cause objects to become smaller and smoother. Negative values cause objects to become larger and more irregular, but not nearly to the extent of the Noise modifier. Iterations multiply the effect of the Relax Value setting. Two checkboxes determine how Relax treats the Gizmo's quadrants and the mesh's open faces, if it has any: Keep Boundary Pts Fixed holds the eight corner points steady as the rest of the vertices are moved; and Save Outer Corners retains the location of the vertices that surround an opening in the mesh, if one exists. Figure 6.24 shows some of the shapes that can be created when the Relax modifier is applied to Boxes with 20 segments along each side and a Relax value of 1.

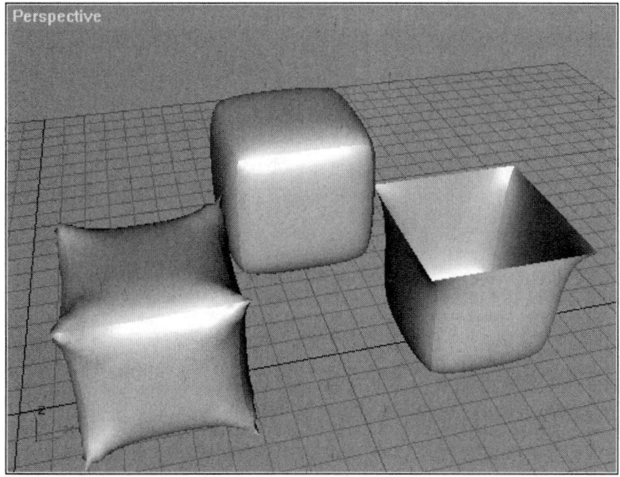

Figure 6.24
The middle Box has a smooth appearance with 30 iterations of the Relax modifier applied. The left Box is identical to the middle box, but the Save Outer Corners checkbox is selected. The right Box's Keep Boundary Pts Fixed checkbox is activated, so its top faces have been removed and its edges stay intact.

Ripple and Wave

The Ripple and Wave modifiers basically accomplish the same task by conforming an object to the shape of a sine wave. Ripple applies the wave distortion in a radial pattern from a center point, and Wave distorts the mesh in a linear pattern. Both modifiers have identical parameters:

- *Amplitude*—The Amplitude settings determine the maximum distance above or below the Plane's base that the modifier will move the vertices. The direction of Amplitude 2 is always 90 degrees apart from that of Amplitude 1.
- *Wave Length*—The Wave Length value is the distance the wave takes to complete one cycle. A cycle begins at the base line, crests at the Amplitude distance above, crosses the base line, crests at the Amplitude distance below, and then returns to the base line.
- *Phase*—The Phase value determines the shift in the Gizmo's crest locations away from the center point. Each whole number represents one complete cycle.
- *Decay*—The Decay parameter reduces the effect of the modifier as the distance from the center increases.

You can set these parameters as shown in the following exercise:

1. Create a Plane primitive in the Top viewport with a length of 150 and a width of 100. Set both Segmentation values to 20.
2. Apply a Ripple modifier to the Plane. Set both Amplitude values to 10.
3. Set the Wave Length to 50. Counting along the Y-axis of the Plane, you will see five upper crests, confirming that the Length value (150) divided by the Wave Length value (50) comes out to an even five cycles. Similarly, you will see that two cycles exist along the Plane's X-axis.
4. Hold down either Phase spinner button and watch as the mesh conforms to the Shifting value. Set the Phase to 0.5.
5. Set the Decay value to 0.025 and hold down either Phase spinner button. Note that the origin of the ripple effect appears as it did previously, but the edges have a substantially reduced amplitude. Reset the Phase to 0.5.
6. The location of the modifier's Center determines the origin of the ripple effect. Select the Center subobject and move it to the middle of one of the Plane's long sides. Figure 6.25 shows the identical parameter settings for the Ripple and Wave modifiers applied to different Planes.

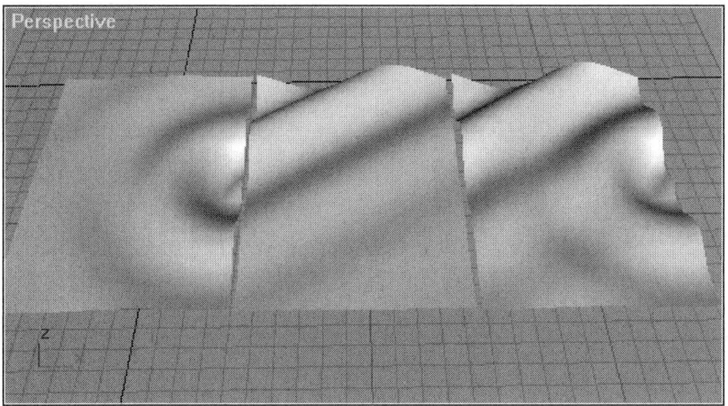

Figure 6.25
The left Plane shows the Ripple modifier applied as described in the exercise. The middle Plane has the Wave modifier applied with the same parameters and the Gizmo moved to a corner and rotated. The right Plane has both modifiers applied: Ripple first and Wave second.

Slice and Cap Holes

The Slice modifier creates a cutting plane that determines the location at which an object's faces become truncated or subdivided. Using Slice properly can show an internal or difficult view of an object or, when animated, give the impression that the object is growing from a base plane. The Slice Type options determine how the mesh is treated where its edges intersect the slice plane. *Refine Mesh* adds a single set of vertices at the intersections to increase the vertex and face density; *Split Mesh* adds a double set of vertices to aid in splitting the mesh into two separate objects. *Remove Top* and *Remove Bottom* truncate the entire mesh at the slice plane.

The *Cap Holes* modifier does exactly what its name implies: It creates faces in meshes to cover any missing areas. The modifiers applied in the book so far have been located in the Parametric Modifiers group in the modifiers drop-down list, but Cap Holes is found in the Mesh Editing group.

To start this exercise, open the file Chap6 Slice.max from the CD-ROM. Then, follow these steps:

1. Apply a Slice modifier to the object. Notice that the center of the Slice Plane is placed at the object's pivot point.
2. Expand the Slice modifier. Select the Slice Plane subobject and move it along the Z-axis until it is about halfway up the straight section.
3. Select the Remove Top option, and everything above the Plane will disappear. The back faces of the object also appear to have been eliminated, but this is the case only because their normal side is facing outward. Use the Arc Rotate tool to see that they are still in place.
4. To cover the open area, apply a Cap Holes modifier at the top of the stack.

Transitioning with Slice

Using the Slice modifier, you can quickly transition from a wireframe to a solid object. First, make a clone of the object at the same location. One object has the desired materials, and the other has a wireframe material applied (wireframe materials are covered in Chapter 11). Apply a Slice modifier to the original object and move the Slice Plane from one end to the other, covering the wireframe object with the standard object. The accompanying figure illustrates this procedure.

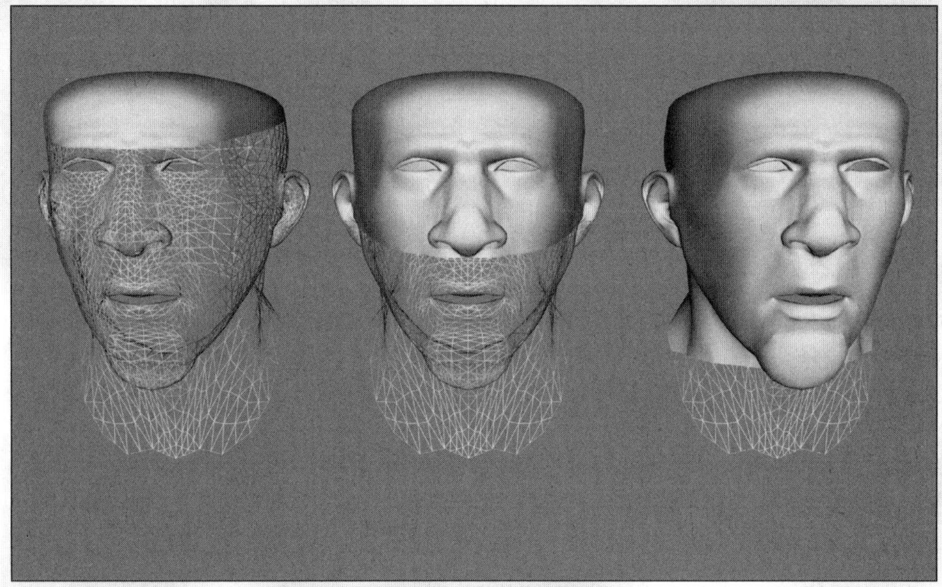

Each head is actually two heads—one with a wireframe material and the other with a solid material and a Slice modifier.

Note: *Because the Cap Holes modifier doesn't distort the mesh but only fills in the gaps, it is often placed at the top of the modifier stack when operations below it have created unwanted openings.*

5. Return to the Slice Plane subobject level and move the Slice Plane subobject further up the Z-axis until it extends across the branching sections; the now-extensive holes continue to be capped.

The Slice modifier has many possibilities, including flattening the top of a rounded object that will act as a pedestal or opening a building or creature so you can see inside. Figure 6.26 shows some of the ways that Slice, in conjunction with Cap Holes, can be used with the object in the exercise.

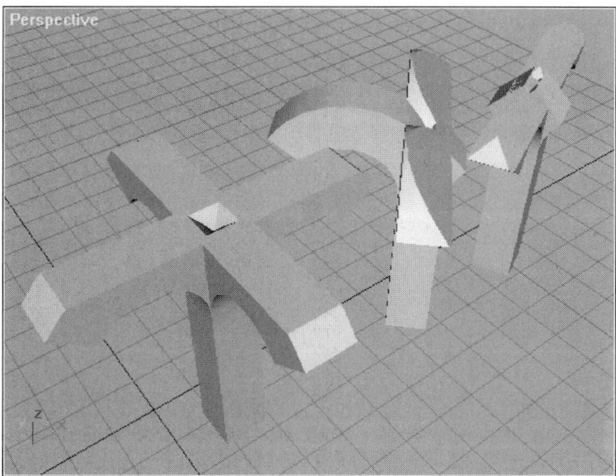

Figure 6.26
The left object shows the results of the exercise. The middle object's Slice Plane has been rotated 45 degrees about its local X-axis. The right object shows the results of using two Slice Planes at right angles to each other.

Spherify and Lattice

The Spherify and Lattice modifiers have specialized purposes that are rarely needed but fun to play with. Spherify acts like the ultimate Relax modifier: All objects to which it is applied attempt to reshape themselves into spheres. A significant amount of segmentation is usually needed to achieve a smooth effect, and the modifier can be applied to multiple objects at one time to restrict all of them to a common center point. Figure 6.27 shows several different objects with the Spherify modifier applied.

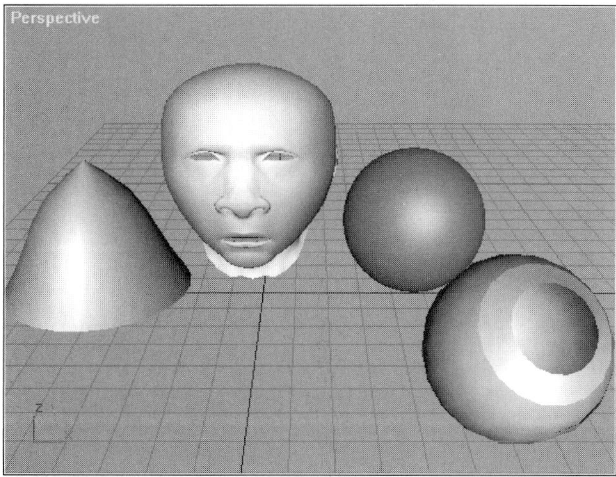

Figure 6.27
From left to right; a Cone, head, Box, and Cylinder with Spherify modifiers applied and different Percent parameters set.

Lattice replaces an object's edges with cylindrical struts and its vertices with faceted or smooth hedra shapes, like a toy building set. Unlike Spherify, Lattice works best with less-dense meshes and has many controls for determining the look you want. Figures 6.28 and 6.29 show the Lattice modifier applied to the objects from Figure 6.27.

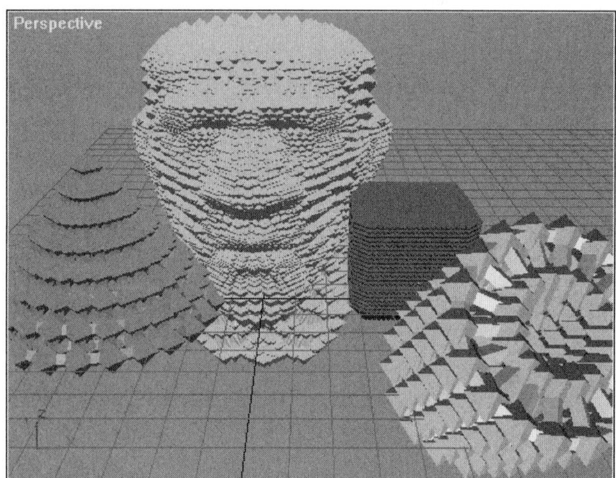

Figure 6.28
The same objects as in Figure 6.27, with the same mesh densities, after the Lattice modifier has been applied.

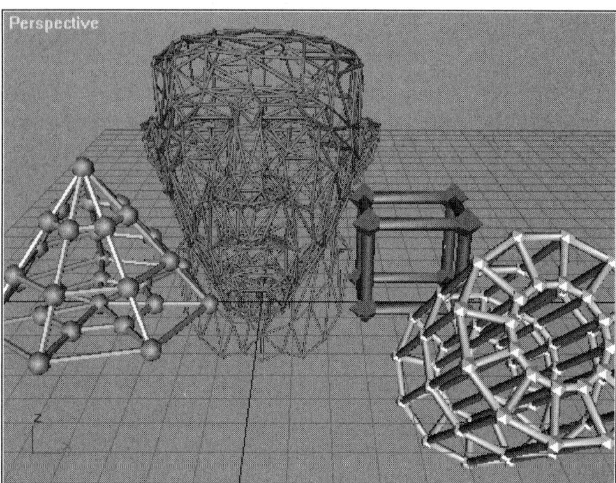

Figure 6.29
The same objects as in Figure 6.27, with much-reduced mesh densities.

Mesh Optimization

The more polygons in your scenes, the slower your system will run. When you refresh the viewports during a Zoom or Pan command or render a viewport, the properties of every subobject on the screen must be calculated—and these operations take time. Even with today's fast computers, video cards, and video games, reducing the polygon count is still a necessary practice. At the high-end cinematic level, dense meshes are often needed to achieve a level of realism; however, an excessively dense mesh offers no additional benefits.

When you're using any of MAX's parametric primitives, you begin the process of mesh optimization in the Parameters rollout. Here, you should enter the lowest required number of segments. But what if an object has a sharp bend with long, straight portions on either side? The density required for a smooth bend is not necessary for the straight areas. And what if your object is not parametric? MAX offers two tools for reducing the polygon count of objects: Optimize and MultiRes.

Using the Optimize Modifier

Although the math behind the Optimize modifier may be cryptic and the interface is somewhat intimidating, the basic concept is easy. The descriptions that follow give a brief overview of this modifier in order to help you understand it and feel less intimidated.

The *Level Of Detail group* allows you to apply two different optimization levels to an object and gives you the option of showing either level in the viewports or a rendered window.

In the *Optimize group*, the Face Threshold value determines which faces are collapsed to reduce the facecount. Higher numbers reduce the count more but provide a less-accurate mesh. The Edge Threshold value determines the treatment of open edges that terminate only one face. When the optimization occurs, it often results in the creation of very skinny triangles (remember that all polygonal faces are actually combinations of triangles). The Bias value helps eliminate these triangles. Lower Bias values produce the smallest and fewest triangles. When faces are collapsed, the edges are extended to accommodate the new face structure. The Maximum Edge Length setting determines how far an edge can be stretched; a value of 0 turns off this option. When Auto Edge is activated, edges that fall below the Face Threshold value are made invisible.

The *Preserve group* determines how to handle situations where either the smoothness or the material of an object spans new faces. Selecting Material Boundaries prevents two faces that have different materials applied from being collapsed into one. Selecting Smooth Boundaries requires faces that are rendered smoothly together to remain so when optimized.

Selecting the Manual Update checkbox lets you update the mesh per the new settings by clicking on the Update button, rather than having the settings update automatically whenever a new value is entered.

To see how to optimize a mesh, open the file Chap6 Polycount.max from the CD-ROM. The file consists of a bent Box primitive and a dense version of the now familiar Uhg model, both of which are collapsed to editable meshes. A quick look at the Summary Info dialog box (File| Summary Info) reveals that the Box consists of 308 faces and the Head consists of 5,688 faces.

Both of these facecounts can be reduced without a significant detrimental effect on the objects. Render the Perspective viewport to get a benchmark image, and then follow these steps:

1. Select the Box and apply the Optimize modifier.
2. Make sure L1 is selected for both Rendered and Viewport options in the Level Of Detail group.
3. In the Optimize group, leave Face Threshold and Edge Threshold at their default values of 4.0 and 1.0, respectively.
4. Increase the Bias amount in 0.1 increments and watch both the screen and the Faces number in the Last Optimize Status group at the bottom of the rollout. A Bias value between 0.3 and 0.4 gives a good-quality mesh with a lower facecount; 0.4 results in a count 50 higher than the result using a value of 0.3. Use a value of 0.35 for the best result.
5. Leave the Maximum Edge Length value set to zero. Leave Auto Edge off or turn it on, at your discretion.
6. Leave both Material Boundaries and Smooth Boundaries deselected.
7. Your Box should now consist of 46 faces, or about 14 percent of the pre-optimization number. In the Level Of Detail group, select the Viewports L2 radio button and change the Face Threshold value to 2.0 and the Bias value to 0.1. Now you have the option of a second, more accurate and denser, but still optimized object. Figure 6.30 shows the various levels of the Box's optimization. Render the scene and compare the new image with the previous one as the latter image is overwritten in the rendering window.

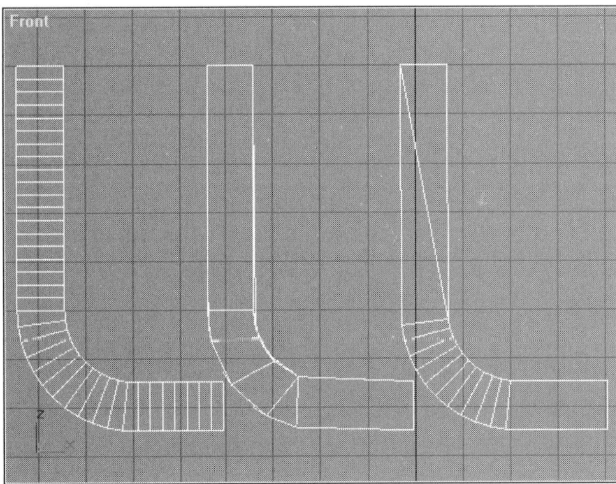

Figure 6.30
The Box on the left is the original, which has 308 faces. In the middle is the L1 example, which has 46 faces; and on the right is the L2 example, which has 100 faces.

Using the MultiRes Modifier

New to 3ds max 4 is the second tool for reducing a mesh's facecount: MultiRes. Formerly a third-party plug-in, MultiRes is a welcome addition to the core package of MAX. It lets you specify an exact number of vertices or the percentage of vertices relative to the original density. With denser meshes, where the tool has more information to work with, MultiRes does a better job of retaining the appearance of the object than the Optimize modifier.

Activating Vertex Merging allows the vertices of different elements (such as two Tori merged into one object, or the four components of a Teapot) to be combined into a single object. Boundary Metric maintains the appearance of faces with materials and material ID numbers as long as possible.

The Multiple Normals Per Vertex checkbox and Crease Angle field determine when MultiRes can assign more than one Normal, or outward-facing, direction to a single vertex. Multiple Normals Per Vertex allows it to happen, giving a more accurate shading result at the expense of a larger file; Crease Angle determines the threshold of the angles between the faces.

This exercise will demonstrate a typical application of the MultiRes modifier. Continue with the previous exercise and follow these steps:

1. Hide the bent Box object. Select and zoom in on the head model and apply the MultiRes modifier to it. Before you make any changes to the parameters, render the viewport.
2. Initially, the Percent and Count fields are grayed out. The Max Vertices and Faces values must be calculated. Start the optimization process by clicking on the Generate button. The cursor will briefly turn into the shape of the letters *MR*, after which the Percent and Count fields will be accessible. Enter "50" in the Percent field to reduce the number of vertices from 2,885 to 1,442. Render the scene again and see if you can tell the difference between the object before and after the vertex reduction.
3. Reduce the Percent value again, this time to 25 percent of the original vertex count; or, enter "721" in the Count field. Render the scene a third time to see that the head has suffered little loss of quality. This kind of reduction, which doesn't produce an inferior model, is sure to please both game and Web developers.

Applying MultiRes to Subobject Selections

To apply MultiRes to a subobject selection, you don't have to pass MultiRes that selection from a Mesh Select modifier. Simply expand the modifier in the Stack View window and choose Vertex; then, highlight the area where the density is to remain stable. Select the Maintain Base Vertices checkbox, click on the Generate button, and reduce the mesh—as shown in this exercise.

4. Leave Vertex Merging and Boundary Metric deselected.
5. Leave Multiple Normals Per Vertex and the Crease Angle field at their default settings.

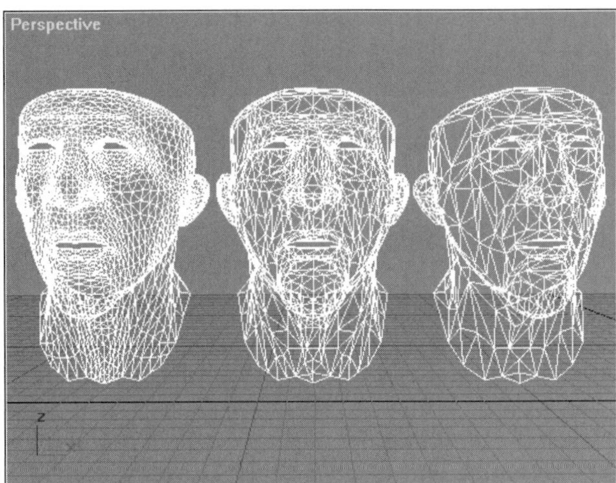

Figure 6.31
Three head models with the original on the left, 50 percent vertex count in the middle, and 25 percent vertex count on the right.

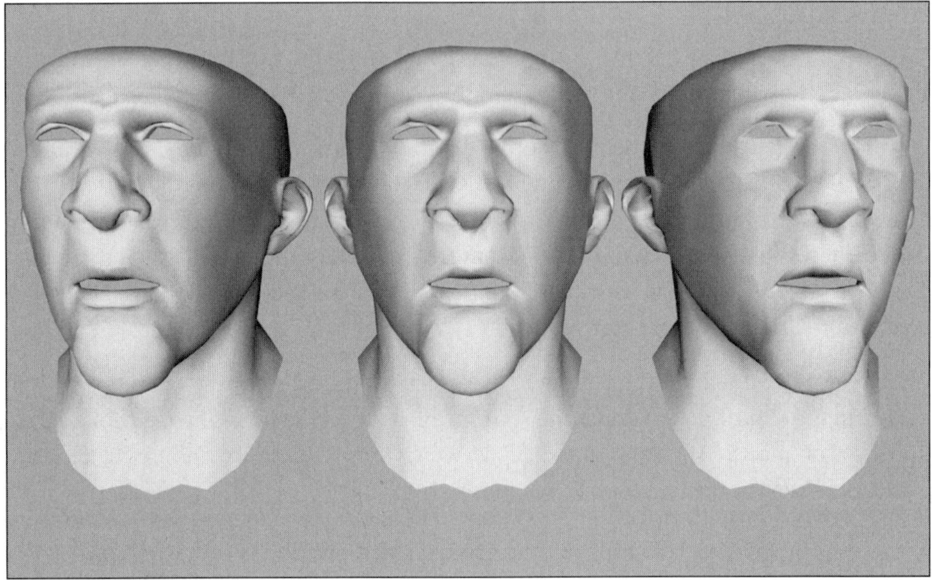

Figure 6.32
The models from Figure 6.31, shown in a rendered window. The most noticeable differences between the original and the 25-percent model are found in the high-density areas of the nose, mouth, and eyes.

Figures 6.31 and 6.32 show the results of using the MultiRes modifier in a viewport and in a rendered window.

The Displace Modifier

Normally, you think of using images in computer graphics to add color or pictures to a scene by placing them onto the surfaces of objects. You can also use images, also called *bitmaps* or simply *maps*, as bump maps to give the appearance of texture to an object, by redefining the image to make it appear to cast shadows on itself. When you're using bump maps, no actual distortion of the geometry occurs.

The Displace modifier, on the other hand, can use an image to move the vertices of an object perpendicular to its surface. This modifier requires very dense meshes to yield a quality result, so it may be prudent to run either the Optimize or MultiRes modifier afterward. The exercises in the following sections will run through the basics of using the Displace modifier.

Displacement without Maps

Although the Displace modifier is intended to work with images, it can also act as a stand-alone displacement tool. The objective of this exercise is to create a spool shape with a bulge in the middle. Follow these steps:

1. Create a Cylinder in the Top viewport with a Radius value of 30 and a Height value of 90. Increase the mesh density by giving it 50 height segments, 1 cap segment, and 30 sides.
2. Apply a Displace modifier. Midway up the Cylinder is an orange rectangle representing the modifier's Gizmo. By default, the type of mapping coordinates used—that is, the information that defines how the map will be applied to the object—is Planar, meaning that MAX will attempt to apply the image flat along the object's Z-axis. In the Map group, change the map type to Cylindrical and leave Cap deselected.
3. The Gizmo is now cylindrical in shape and conforms to the limits of the object. The orange line that is projecting from the top of the Gizmo indicates the location of the top center of the image, if one were applied. Select the Gizmo subobject, change its Height value to 10, and move it in the World Z direction to an absolute elevation of 85 or a relative elevation of 40 to place the top of the Gizmo even with the top of the Cylinder. Your Perspective viewport should look similar to Figure 6.33.

Note: *MAX does not always choose the desired result when two objects are coplanar, as with the top of the Cylinder and the top of the Gizmo. If the tapered effect is not what you expected, nudge the Gizmo upward a little to project it beyond the top of the Cylinder and straighten the sides.*

4. In the Displacement group, set the Strength value to 5 to pull the vertices away from the Cylinder. Doing so produces a flange around the end of the object (a negative value would make a groove in the same location).
5. Apply a second Displace modifier on top of the first. Following a procedure similar to Step 3, create a flange at the other end of the object. Note that the Gizmo is now the size of the object's greatest radius—the upper flange—but this has no bearing on the result of setting the Strength value to 5.

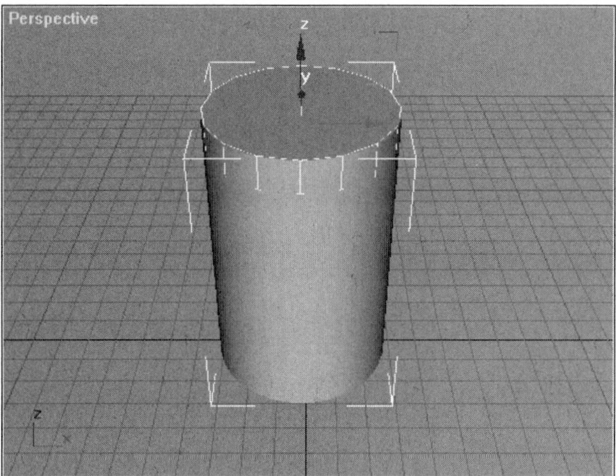

Figure 6.33
The Cylinder with the Displace modifier's Gizmo set at 10 units high and matched to the elevation of the top of the object.

6. Because the spherical mapping type works in all directions simultaneously, you cannot simply apply a second Displace modifier to the middle of the shaft and add strength to bulge the middle; doing so will curve the end caps. Instead, apply a Mesh Select modifier, activate the Vertex subobject, open the Soft Selection rollout, and select the Use Soft Selection checkbox, as shown in Figure 6.34.

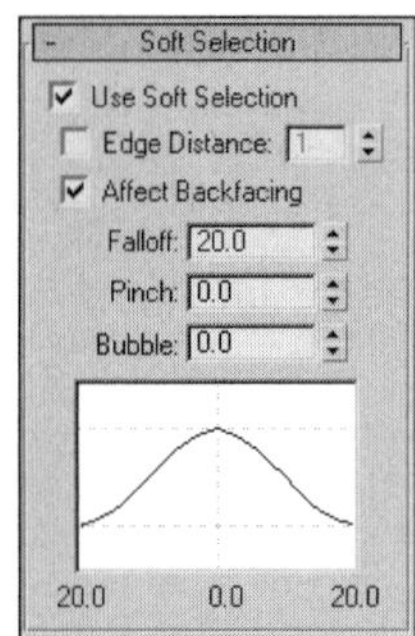

Figure 6.34
The Soft Selection rollout found in many of the selection and editing modifiers.

Note: *The Soft Selection rollout is common among many of the selection and editing modifiers; it lets you specify a region to select and then tapers the modifier's effect to the regions beyond the selection window.*

7. In the Top or Left viewport, select a window of vertices 10 units high across the width of the Cylinder. The selected vertices turn red, and those farther away turn orange, yellow, and then green to signify how much they will adhere to the modifications applied to the selected vertices. Orange vertices will be nearly the same, and green vertices will have very minor changes. Vertices that remain blue are entirely outside the selection envelope and will not be altered. The selection should look similar to Figure 6.35.

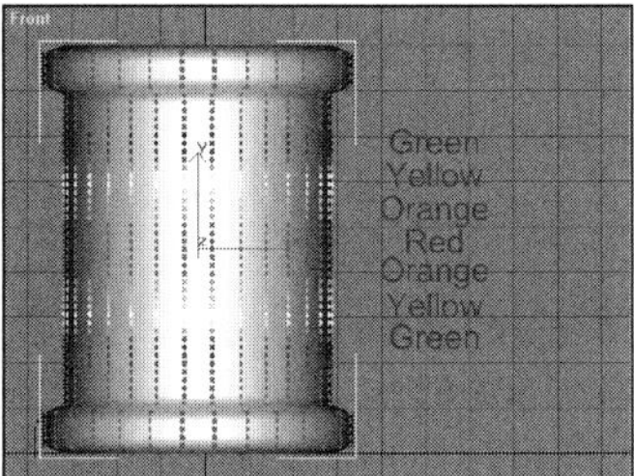

Figure 6.35
Selecting the middle section of vertices while using Soft Selection results in an envelope of vertices of varying adherence to the modifier that will follow.

8. Apply a third Displace modifier on top of the Mesh Select and set the Map type to Spherical. Increase the Strength value to 7, and a bulge will appear around the middle of the Cylinder. The largest radius is at the red vertices; the radius tapers as the radii progress to orange, yellow, and then green.

Even without bitmap images, the Displace modifier can be used to create objects that would be difficult using other methods. The next section shows how to make relief models that are only possible using Displace and maps.

Displacement with Maps

Once you understand the concept of the Displace modifier, its Gizmo, and Soft Selection, obtaining the incredible results of using Displace with image maps will be easy. Before you begin this exercise, hide the displaced Cylinder in the scene from the last exercise. Then, follow these steps:

1. Create a 100×100 Box 2 units high in the Top viewport. Give it 20 length and width segments and only 1 height segment.

2. Apply a Displace modifier and ensure that the Map type is set to Planar.

3. When you assign a bitmap image to be displaced and input a positive Strength value, the image's white areas are moved in a positive direction to its normals. Black areas are not moved, and the gray areas in between are moved according to their variance from black or white. This isn't to say that color maps cannot be used, just that MAX will convert the colors internally to their grayscale equivalents. Click on the Bitmap|None button in the Image group and navigate to the Chap6 Tracks.jpg file from the CD-ROM (the railroad tracks picture from Chapter 4).

4. Increase the Strength value to 3. The impression of the picture will start to form, but the mesh is much too coarse for this type of operation. Go back to the Box level and increase the length and width segments to 200; then, return to the Displace level. The image should look like Figure 6.36.

Figure 6.36
A dense mesh and an image map combine with the Displace modifier to make this relief.

5. The price paid for the model to be this well defined is a Box consisting of more than 161,000 faces. Look at the Box in the Top viewport; it appears that nothing has been done to it, because the vertices have not deflected in the X or Y direction. Use the Arc Rotate tool to see that not only has the top of the Box projected outward, the bottom has projected inward.

Using AVI Files with Displace

For an interesting effect, use an AVI file instead of a static image file. Be sure to set the animation length equal to the length of the AVI, using the Time Configuration button at the bottom of the MAX window. After you click on the Play button, the frames of the AVI will change the displacement of the vertices over time. Because of the mesh density usually required with the Displace modifier, it may not be possible to see the change in the viewports; you'll have to render to an animated file.

---

6. To frame the displaced image with a flat area, change both the Length and Width settings in the Map group to 90. Doing so changes the size of the Gizmo and, in turn, the size of the affected area on the Box.

7. This step is optional and may task all but the most high-end systems—performing an Edit|Hold or saving the file prior to attempting it is highly recommended. At its default

settings, the Optimize modifier reduces the number of faces in the mesh by only about 14 percent. To reduce the facecount further, apply a MultiRes modifier on top of Displace. With a mesh this dense, it may take awhile for the solution to be generated; the tool will indicate its progress and let you know your system is not locked up by slowly turning the MR cursor from gray to white. After the generation is complete, a Percent setting of 30 retains the relief adequately while greatly reducing the mesh density.

8. If you are adventurous, apply the Chap6 Tracks.jpg file to an odd-shaped object, such as a Teapot, or use the Shrink Wrap Map type.

Free Form Deformations

Free Form Deformation (FFD) modifiers, also called Lattice deformers (not to be confused with the Lattice modifier), construct a matrix of control points (CPs) that determine the shape of an object similar to a soft selection approach. This method creates continuous smooth sections between adjusted areas and allows a great amount of flexibility when manipulating surfaces.

FFDs come in two basic shapes: box and cylindrical. You can specify the number of control points for each. Also available are FFD 2×2×2, FFD 3×3×3, and FFD 4×4×4, which are box FFDs with a predetermined and fixed number of CPs.

The following exercise will introduce you to many of the functions available with the FFD modifiers. You'll create a modern art-style loveseat; with practice, this type of modeling can be used to create almost anything. Follow these steps:

1. Create a 36×72×48 Box on the ground plane with 20 segments in each dimension. Apply an FFD(box) modifier.

2. By default, the control point matrix consists of four CPs in each dimension; this setting is not adequate for the task at hand, however. Click on the Set Number Of Points button in the Dimensions group and increase the number of Width points to 8, to allow a larger selection along the Box's long axis.

Using FFD Modifiers with Odd-Shaped Objects

The FFD modifiers are easiest to use with rectilinear, cylindrical, or spherical objects. They are less useful with irregular geometry because the lattice does not conform well to such objects' surfaces. The Set Volume subobject level allows you to move the CPs into new default positions that are closer to the object's shape, prior to deforming the mesh. To compare the new lattice shape to the old, you select and deselect the Source Volume checkbox in the Display group.

The Conform To Shape button in the Control Points group can automatically configure the lattice to follow an object's contours. Although this technique works well in simple operations, such as conforming an FFD(box) to a sphere, more complicated geometry may require a lattice too dense to be feasible.

Note: *When you're selecting control points, be sure that only the CPs you want selected actually are selected. Most of the time, you select control points using a window that selects the CPs you want as well as all CPs beyond them. Therefore, it is imperative that you view the CP selection in at least two viewports to ensure that only the proper ones are selected and to modify the selection as required.*

3. Expand the modifier and choose the Control Points subobject. In the Front viewport, select the six CPs in the middle of the top row (they will turn yellow to identify their selected status). In the Top viewport, press and hold the Alt key and deselect the row furthest to the rear, leaving a total of 18 CPs selected.

4. Without losing the selection, switch back to the Front viewport. Move the selected CPs down to a level just above the next row. Your object should look similar to Figure 6.37.

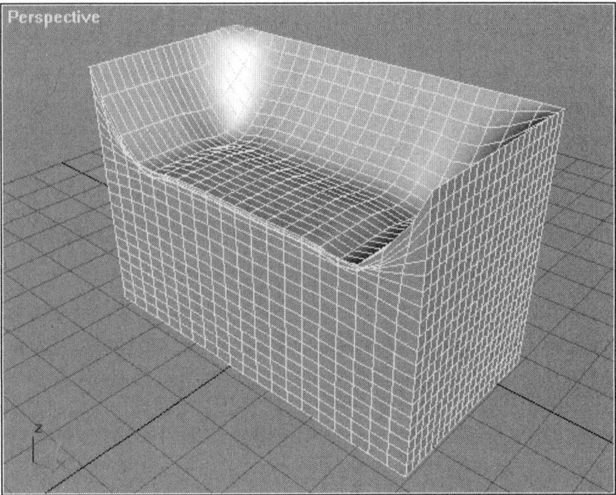

Figure 6.37
The top of the Box has been dropped using an FFD modifier.

5. In the Front viewport, use a window to select the CPs that are currently selected, the CPs in the row directly beneath them, and all CPs behind them. Move them downward to just above the next row. Your object should look similar to Figure 6.38.

6. The loveseat is beginning to take shape, but you need to address a few problems. To soften the sharp edges along the top rim of the object, select the single row of vertices identified by the black circle in Figure 6.39. Move them up, near the top of the object, and then to the left, ensuring that no faces bulge out of the far-left side. Grab both rows of vertices identified by the black triangle in Figure 6.39 and move them to the left to decrease the slope of the sides. Repeat the vertex movements on the right side of the object and perform a similar operation on the back. Clean up any stray faces that are created by moving the necessary control points. Your object should look similar to the one shown in Figure 6.40.

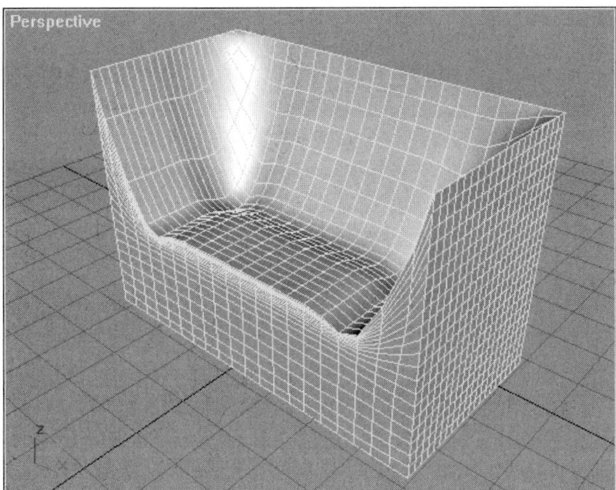

Figure 6.38
The top of the Box has dropped further toward its base.

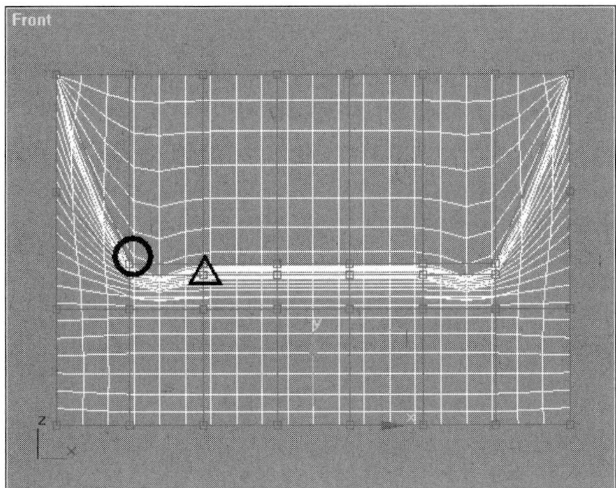

Figure 6.39
A Front view of the object. The rows of vertices (falling in the direction of the user's view) to be used in Step 6 are identified with a circle and a triangle.

7. To create the furniture's feet, move the rows of vertices that are closest to the corners even closer, causing the edge lines along the sides and front to curve toward those corners. From the front and side, select all the CPs along the base, except those at the corners; move them upward, leaving pointed feet aimed at the ground plane. Similar to Figure 6.41, your loveseat should be nearly complete; but it still has a few edges that are a bit too sharp.

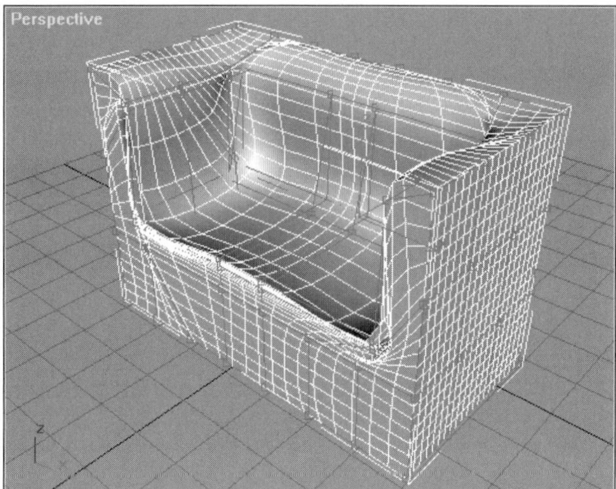

Figure 6.40
The sides and back have been given a smoother appearance by moving their significant vertices upward and toward the outside faces.

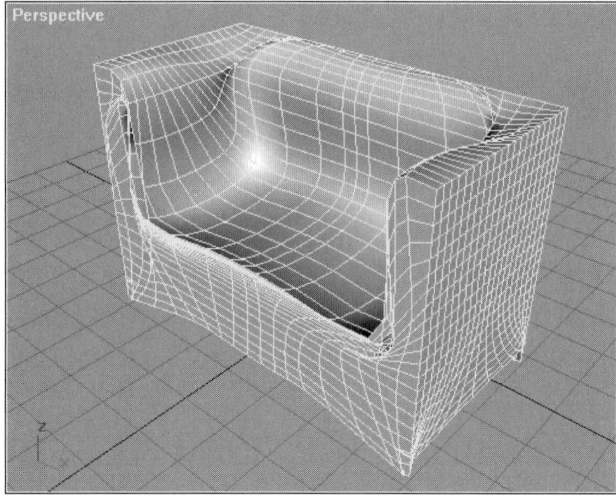

Figure 6.41
Nearly completed, the loveseat still has a few sharp edges that need to be smoothed out.

8. Using the Relax modifier tends to shrink the size of the object, and that result is not desirable in this case. Instead, apply a MeshSmooth modifier (more on this modifier in Chapter 7), found in the Subdivision Surfaces group of the Modifier List pulldown, and set the Iterations value to 1. The final result of this exercise should look similar to Figure 6.42.

As you can see, the FFD modifiers can be used to create nearly any type of object that requires a smooth transition from one area to the next. For some additional experimentation, try using the FFD(cylin) on a Cylinder or Tube and scale all the CPs in a given plane to achieve an hourglass look.

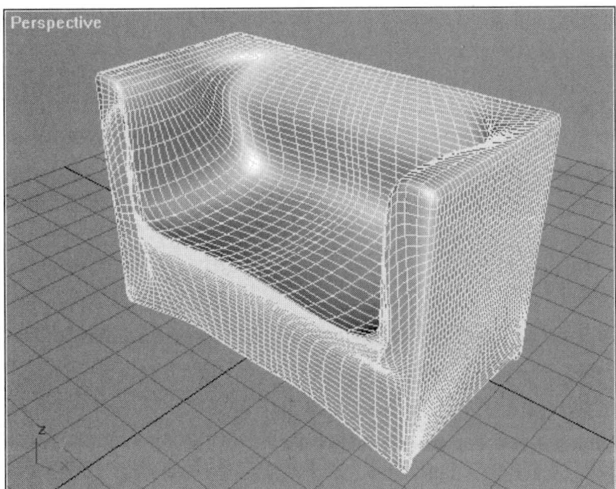

Figure 6.42
The object after the MeshSmooth modifier was used to smooth the edges.

Spline-Based Modifiers

Most of the modifiers discussed in this section create geometry rather than simply modify a spline. Because their implementation is passed through the modifier stack, however, you have the ability to return to the original shape level, edit the spline, and have the new information passed upward to result in a different geometry solution. For example, if a client chooses (at the last moment, of course) to add, delete, or change the wording of an animated ad campaign consisting of extruded text, the original text can be altered and the new data automatically extruded. In this section, we'll discuss the Extrude, Bevel, Lathe, and Fillet/Chamfer modifiers.

Extrude

The Extrude modifier uses a spline as the constant cross-section of an object, projecting it in the direction of its own Z-axis. Any spline, open or closed, can be extruded. By default, the new geometry will have its ends capped; if the original spline object is created from multiple, noncontiguous splines, the end capping will follow a logical altering of the capping to allow capped and uncapped areas.

The Capping group determines if and how the ends of the extruded spline are covered with faces. The default Morph Capping type is almost always preferred over the alternative Grid option. Morph closes the ends with the fewest number of faces, whereas Grid trims the edges of a fine grid to fit the shape of the end cap.

To see the Extrude modifier in action, begin by resetting MAX to start fresh. Then, follow the steps of this exercise:

1. Go to the Create|Shapes tab in the Command panel and drag out a rectangle about 230 units long and 330 units wide. Adjust the Zoom factor so the rectangle fills most of the Top viewport.

2. Apply an Extrude modifier, found in the Mesh Editing section of the Modifier List. Instantly, the rectangle transforms into a planar surface, which is actually an extrusion with a thickness of zero. In the Parameters rollout, set the Amount value high enough to see the effect in the Perspective viewport. Leave the Segments value (the number of cross-section subdivisions) set to 1. You won't be modifying the mesh beyond the extrusion; therefore, extensive mesh density is not required.

3. To appreciate the difference between the Morph and Grid Capping options, with the Morph option selected, use the Quad menu to open the Object Properties dialog box. You'll see that the object has 8 vertices and 12 faces, the minimum number you would expect from a box. Change to the Grid option, and the numbers jump to 890 vertices and 1,776 vertices. These values may be appropriate if a Wave or Ripple modifier is to follow, but not for this exercise. Make sure the Morph option is selected before continuing.

Note: *Because MAX deals in triangles, the 6 sides of the extruded rectangle are each subdivided into 2 triangles, resulting in 12 faces total. To look at the hidden edges created with the two Capping choices, apply an Edit Mesh modifier on top of the Extrude, choose the Edge subobject level, and select the entire object with a window. All hidden edges will be identified with dashed red lines. Remove the modifier before continuing by highlighting it in the Stack View window, right-clicking on it, and choosing Cut from the pop-up menu.*

4. To make the following steps easier to see, temporarily turn off the Extrude modifier. Normally, each time you create a new shape, it is a distinct object that may or may not be parametric, depending on the type chosen. By deselecting the Start New Shape checkbox in the Object Type rollout of the Create|Shapes Command panel, all new shapes will be components of one noncontiguous spline. Deselect the checkbox and then add new spline shapes in and around the rectangle, being as creative as you like. For this exercise, the shapes are configured as shown in Figure 6.43. It's important to understand that the rectangle must be selected prior to adding the new shapes, in order for them to be components of the existing object. (If the rectangle was not selected, the new shapes would all be components of a new spline, separate from the rectangle. You would need to attach them to the rectangle using the Edit Spline modifier.)

5. Go back to the Modify panel. You'll see that the Rectangle entry in the stack is now an editable mesh (because of the additional shapes added to it) and that it is no longer parametric. In addition, the Extrude modifier has been dropped from the stack. Reapply the modifier; it will retain the settings used previously. See how the modifier affects the shapes in and around the original rectangle. The result, using the spline from Figure 6.43, is shown in Figure 6.44.

6. The shapes that are only partially within the rectangle are fully capped and help form the new perimeter. Objects fully within the boundary have not been capped, and their edges project into the extrude direction. The number 4 and the offset circles in the lower-left corner, which have alternating capping, show the logic behind the way nested shapes are treated.

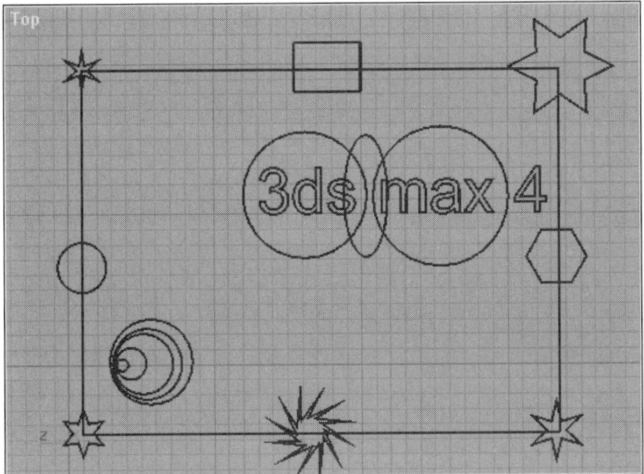

Figure 6.43
The configuration of shapes in one noncontiguous spline used for the Extrude exercise.

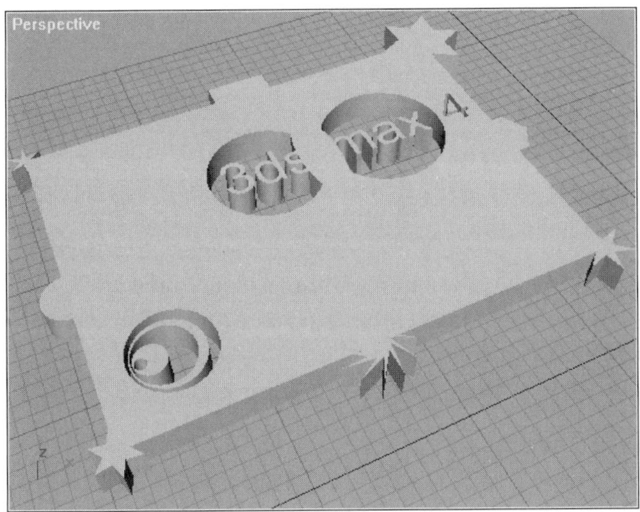

Figure 6.44
The geometry created after applying the Extrude modifier to the complex spline shown in Figure 6.43.

7. Chapter 2 discussed the ways to alter an editable spline; those practices are applicable when you switch to the Editable Spline level of the current object. A new feature in 3ds max 4 is the addition of the Soft Selection rollout, which allows the same type of vertex selection previously available only with mesh objects. Figure 6.45 shows one possibility that can result when several of the Spline and Vertex subobjects are manipulated.

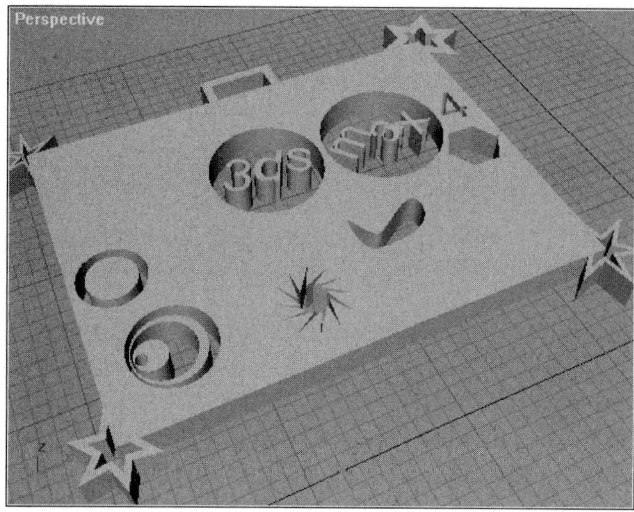

Figure 6.45
By returning to the Editable Spline level in the modifier stack, the spline can be altered and the result passed to the Extrude modifier above.

Bevel

Similar to the Extrude modifier, Bevel creates geometry by extruding the shape. It has the additional ability to change the size of the cross-section at up to four places. Although this modifier is used most often with text, it can be used with virtually any shape.

The Bevel Values rollout contains the settings that determine at what level and how much each segment's cross-section varies. Each value is relative to the level beneath it, and Start Outline is relative to the original spline perimeter. The Start Outline value lets you outline the original text to produce a spline with a perimeter that is larger than the original text.

A positive Level 1 Height value determines the elevation at which the second cross-section resides above the base of the shape. The Outline value determines the distance, beyond the original, that the second perimeter follows.

This exercise will show you the basic application of the Bevel modifier used to extrude a Text primitive with both a curved and flat bevel:

1. Reset the scene from the previous exercise. Create your name as a Text primitive object in the Top viewport. Use the default Size value of 100 and choose a font that does not have many areas where the spline segments are *pinched*, or run too close together; pinched segments may cause problems if the Bevel size gets too large. (Chapter 2 contains more information about choosing fonts.)

2. Apply a Bevel modifier. The Text will gain capped faces similar to the result of applying the Extrude modifier in the previous exercise.

3. Leave the Start Outline value set to 0.

4. Set the Level 1 Height value to 3 and the Outline value to 2. The Left viewport should look similar to Figure 6.46, showing the cross-section tapering to a larger size as the distance from the base increases.

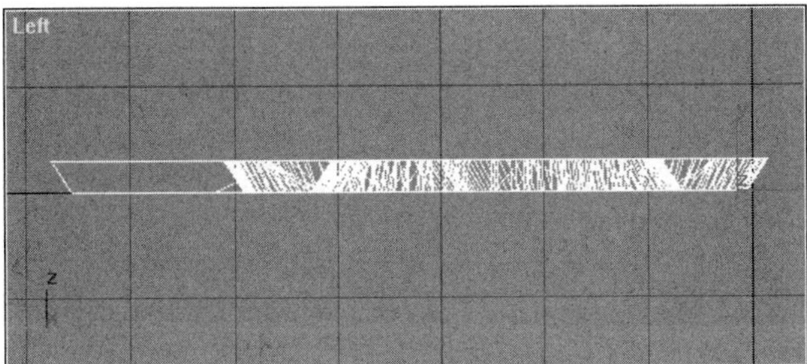

Figure 6.46
The Level 1 settings in the Bevel modifier increase the size of the cross-section relative to the size at the base.

5. Select the Level 2 checkbox. Set the Height value to 3 and the Outline value to 0. These values extend the previous cross-section up three units and leave it the same size as the cross-section at Level 1.

6. Select the Level 3 checkbox. Set the Height and Outline values to 3 and –2, respectively, to make the last cross-section identical to the first. In Figure 6.47, the top letter shows the Bevel as applied in the exercise.

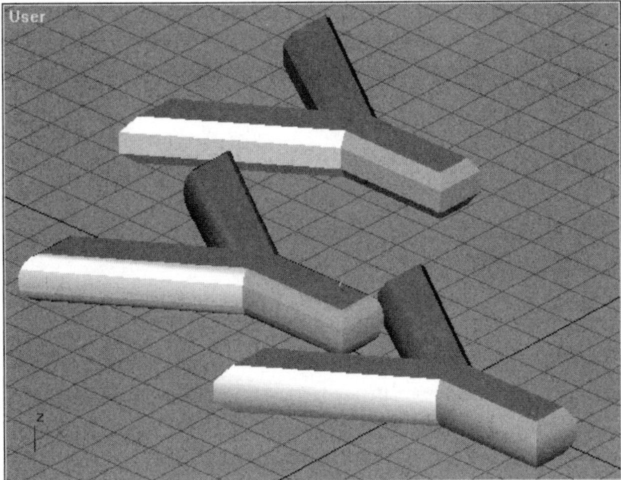

Figure 6.47
The top object has no curvature, the middle object uses the Curved Sides option, and the bottom object uses the Smooth Across Levels option to gain curvature.

Two methods are available for adding curvature to the sides of the beveled shape. In Figure 6.47, the middle object's Curved Sides option is selected in the Surface group and its Segments value is set to 3. These settings curve the beveled areas but leave the vertical section untouched. The bottom letter object's Smooth Across Levels checkbox is selected, adding curvature to the sides but leaving the ends intact.

Lathe and Fillet/Chamfer

The Lathe modifier also creates geometry from a spline. Lathe revolves the spline up to 360 degrees around a moveable axis; the spline's vertices become the edges for the surfaces. This modifier is used to make radial objects with consistent cross-sections that need either curved or straight sides, such as wine glasses, vases, rockets, or planters.

By default, the axis of rotation is located at the center of the shape; however, it can be moved to either extremity by using the Min or Max button in the Align group. The Degrees field determines the extent of the spline's revolution about the axis. When you select a rotation of less than 360 degrees, end caps are placed by default. Use caution when you Lathe an open spline because the normals of the faces will point outward; an object using revolution less than 360 degrees will expose the nonnormal sides, requiring a two-sided material or a two-sided rendering.

The Segments value sets the number of times the cross-section is applied to the revolution. Higher values keep the geometry more accurate but increase the facecount. When inactive, the Smooth checkbox at the bottom of the rollout renders the object in a linear fashion, showing no curvature between edges.

The Fillet/Chamfer modifier is straightforward. In contrast to the Bevel modifier, which adds curved or linear areas to extruded splines, this modifier adds them at a vertex to modify the shape of a spline itself.

This final exercise on spline-based modifiers will examine both Lathe and Fillet/Chamfer:

1. Use the Line tool to create a shape similar to the one shown in Figure 6.48 in the Front viewport. Use the upper-left corner as the start point, turn on the 3D Snap toggle, and snap to the grid points to help keep the straight segments straight. Close the spline when it is completed.

2. Apply a Fillet/Chamfer modifier to the spline. Zoom in on the straight segments (Fillet/Chamfer works only between two linear segments) at the top. Go to the Vertex subobject level. Select the top two vertices, increase the Radius value in the Fillet group until the top of the shape is completely rounded, and click on the Apply button. The vertices are replaced, and the Radius value remains in its field, ready to be applied to more vertices to retain a consistent fillet size.

3. Select the vertex at the upper-right corner of the bottom section of the shape and chamfer it as much as possible. Exit the subobject mode, and your shape should look similar to Figure 6.49.

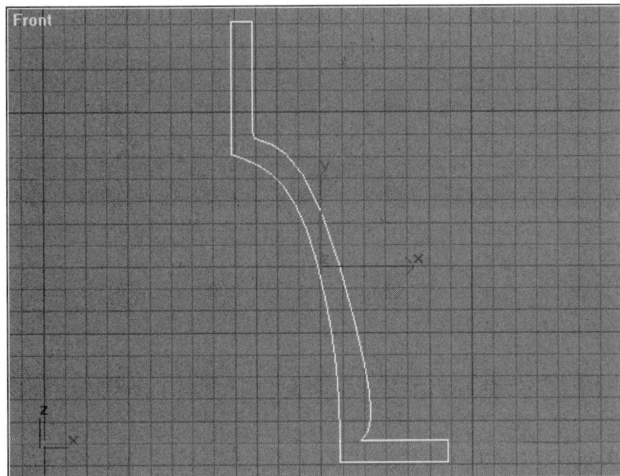

Figure 6.48
The shape to be used in this exercise, created with the Line tool.

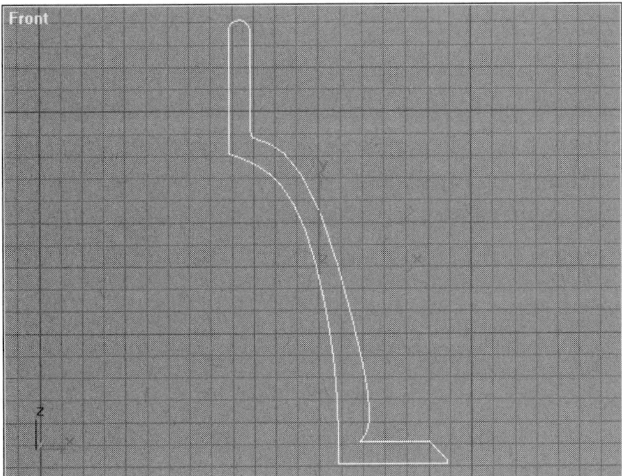

Figure 6.49
The shape looks like this after the top has been filleted and the bottom has been chamfered.

4. Apply a Lathe modifier. To place the axis of rotation with more precision, select the Axis subobject and position it wherever it suits your needs. Figure 6.50 shows some of the possibilities that can be achieved using the Lathe modifier with the shape in this exercise.

Note: *The Lathe modifier works with both splines and the NURBS curves discussed in Chapter 10.*

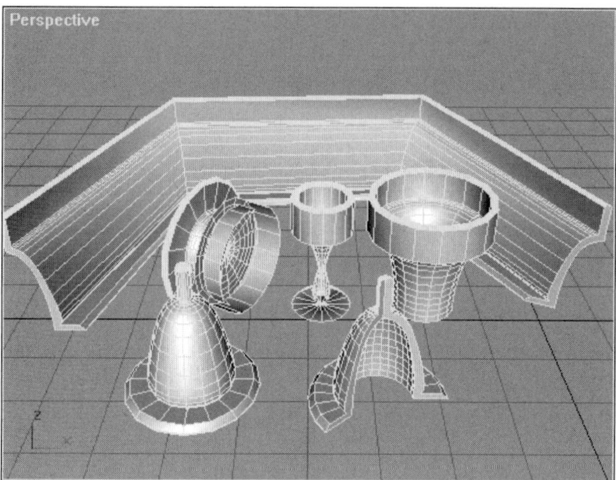

Figure 6.50
Some of the possibilities that can be achieved using the Lathe modifier on the same shape.

Modifying the Stack

As you've seen, the modifier stack can hold several modifiers that apply to a single object. The modifier stack can also be rearranged, unnecessary modifiers can be removed, and modifiers can be copied to new objects. You can also use the stack to remove the connection between instances and references or to collapse objects to their most basic states. The following exercise demonstrates some of these techniques.

Begin the exercise by opening the file Chap6 Stack.max from the CD-ROM. It consists of three Boxes, a four-sided Tube, and a Teapot. Now, follow these steps:

1. The Stack View window lists the modifiers with a different appearance to signify their independence or allegiance to other objects as references or instances. Alternate selecting the left and middle Boxes while watching the Stack View window in the Modify panel. The object type (Box) appears as normal text for the independent Box on the left; it is bold for the middle Box, which is an instance of the Box on the right.

2. Apply a Taper, Twist, and then Bend modifier, in that order, to the left Box, with settings significant enough to see each effect. Apply a Bend, Twist, and Taper modifier, in that order, using the same settings as before, to either of the instanced Boxes. The result is quite different because of the order in which the modifiers were applied and the configuration the geometry was in when passed to the modifier above.

3. To make the right Box independent, select it and click on the Make Unique button in the toolbar under the Stack View window. The object now has a stack of modifiers exclusive to it; the entries are no longer bold.

4. The arrangement of the modifiers in the stack can be altered to suit your needs; for example, you can manipulate the middle Box to resemble the Box on the left. Select the middle Box and drag down the Taper entry in the Stack View window until a blue line appears between the Box and Bend modifiers, signifying where it will reside; release the mouse button. Drag the Bend modifier to the top of the stack and release it to make the middle Box resemble the left Box.
5. Modifiers, singularly or in groups, can be copied or moved to other objects. Highlight the Twist modifier in the Stack View window for the middle Box. Drag and drop it onto the Teapot, which now adheres to the requirements of the Twist modifier that has been copied to its stack. Reselect the middle Box and highlight all of its stack entries. Holding down the Shift key as you drag modifiers moves them from one object to another, whereas holding down the Ctrl key copies them. Hold down the Ctrl key and copy the stack from the middle box to the Tube. Although the objects are of different types, the modifiers are instanced between them. Adjusting the Taper modifier for the middle Box modifies both the Box and the Tube.

If all changes to be made to the Tube are completed, and you're sure you won't need to modify it using any of the currently applied modifiers, you can collapse it, reducing it to a simple editable mesh (or editable spline) with no modification history. This step reduces the MAX file size and dismisses any unnecessary system overhead. To collapse an object, right-click on any modifier entry and choose Collapse All or Collapse To from the pop-up menu. The Collapse All option eliminates all modifiers, and the Collapse To option eliminates all modifiers at or below the highlighted modifier.

Moving On

This chapter dealt with the many modifiers used to alter or create geometry in a scene. The axial deformation modifiers usually have similar rollouts and change objects or subobjects relative to one or more axes, whereas Noise is used to add imperfection to an object. The Displace modifier can be used to introduce surface texture based on user input or an image map, and the spline-based modifiers use the modifier stack concept to create new geometry. The chapter also discussed the ways to manipulate the stack to rearrange modifiers or to copy or cut them to other objects.

The next chapter covers the modeling concepts that surround modeling at the mesh level. It will discuss the Edit Mesh, MeshSmooth, and new HSDS modifiers, among others.

Chapter 7

Mesh-Level Modeling

As you've seen, 3ds max 4 provides many modifiers that were designed to avoid direct mesh-level editing; these tools can never fully replace those that allow you to manipulate the geometry in a hands-on manner, however.

Mesh-level modeling consists of manipulating the basic components (vertices, edges, and faces) of mesh objects. This is done primarily when a modifier or Space Warp is not available or capable of performing the same task. Mesh-level modeling is not an advanced technique, but it may be the most direct way to bring your vision to fruition.

Polygonal Mesh Modeling

3D modeling is generally divided into two categories: polygonal modeling and Non-Uniform Rational B-Spline (NURBS) modeling. This division is a blurry one, however, for a couple of reasons.

First, all models basically are polygonal, because the rendering engine must be passed polygons rather than NURBS surfaces. In this respect, NURBS modeling is just a way to create polygonal models. In NURBS modeling, however, the ultimate mesh—that is, one with no flat faces over curved surfaces—is hidden from you (unless you choose to look at it), so you can work directly with the NURBS curves and the NURBS surfaces that are created from these curves. Thus, NURBS modeling operates at a step above polygonal mesh modeling, and the tools and concepts for working with NURBS surfaces are fundamentally different from those you use when you work directly on the mesh. NURBS will be explained in more detail in Chapter 10.

The second reason for the blurry distinction between polygonal and NURBS modeling is the existence of many non-NURBS spline-modeling tools. MAX used Bezier curves (called *splines* or *shapes* in the MAX interface) before it implemented NURBS, and these Bezier splines are used in most of the same ways as NURBS. Just like NURBS, the Bezier splines can be extruded into 3D geometry, lathed, or lofted along a path.

Now, due in large part to the special powers and subtleties of the NURBS modeling process, NURBS modeling is seen as a field of its own, distinct from other types of modeling. As a result, most modelers tend to distinguish NURBS and polygonal modeling; non-NURBS spline modeling is, somewhat fuzzily, included under the general heading of *polygonal modeling*.

In this chapter, we'll look at manipulating mesh objects at their most basic levels. The apparent curvature in the surfaces is achieved by using the available smoothing tools that subdivide and round out the mesh, and not by the use of splines.

Organic vs. Low-Polygon Modeling

In the modeling field, *organic* generally refers to the smooth, fluid composition of the geometry found in a flower or animal. Many manufactured parts, such as car bodies or art-based architectural elements, require the subtle curvature used in organic modeling techniques. Such models may require a high-density mesh that would be difficult to edit at the mesh level; therefore, the meshes are modeled as simpler, lower-density objects, and the faces are then subdivided and the density increased as required to achieve the desired result. Organic modeling is also useful in some—but not all—3D animation.

3D animation is broken into two types: prerendered animation and realtime animation. Prerendered animations—seen in videos and motion pictures—require that the scene be rendered to sequential images or a video file format, to be viewed at a later time or incorporated into a live-action sequence. Although each frame may take a substantial amount of time to render properly, the final output can be seen at the intended, real-world speed. Organic modeling is perfect for this type of output because its higher density and associated longer rendering time add to—rather than detract from—the quality of the scene.

On the other hand, realtime animation—seen in video games—is rendered as the action occurs and delivered directly to the screen. The frame sequence and content are not predetermined, and the animation must appear on the screen fast enough to give the user a quality gaming experience. To do this, the meshes must be created with the fewest possible faces, using texture mapping to hide the low-quality features of the object. Faster gaming systems, such as the Sony Playstation 2 and the Microsoft Xbox, are able to handle larger polygon counts per scene; in general, however, low-poly characters should consist of about 300 to 500 faces each. For this reason, organic modeling is not appropriate for the interactive portions of today's video games.

Mesh-Editing Tools Overview

Editing an object at the mesh level requires access to the subobjects that compose the mesh itself. You can access the subobjects either by converting the primitive to an editable mesh object and stripping it of any parametric ability and modifier history, or by applying the Edit Mesh modifier to it. The editing toolset is identical regardless of the method chosen.

Edit Mesh Restrictions

When you're working with the Edit Mesh modifier and a parametric object, a unique set of problems arises. The Edit Mesh modifier can be used to move or eliminate vertices, edges, faces, and polygons while the modifier stack retains access to the settings that determine the parameters of the object itself. MAX, understandably, does not know how to handle the situation when a subobject that has been edited is removed or altered at a lower position in the stack.

The following exercise will show you this restriction in action:

1. Create a Box primitive with a value of 2 in all its segmentation fields. Use Arc Rotate to view the front, right, and top sides of the Box simultaneously.
2. Apply an Edit Mesh modifier and go to the Vertex subobject level.
3. Select the vertex at the bottom of the right side and move it in the positive X-direction. The object should look similar to the one in Figure 7.1.

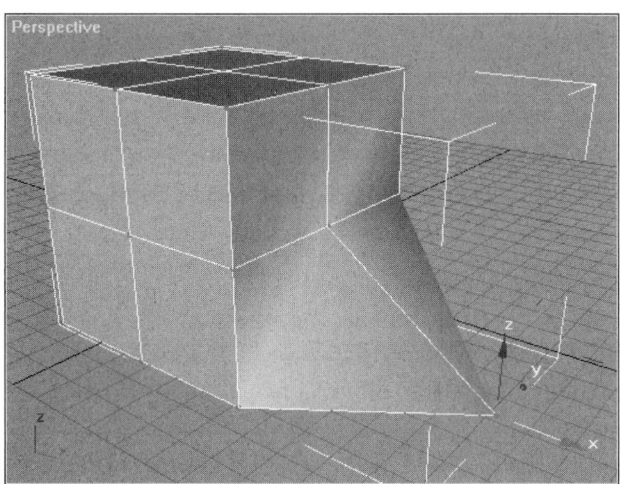

Figure 7.1
The Box primitive with the bottom, side vertex moved using the Edit Mesh modifier.

4. In the modifier stack, return to the Box level (click on Yes in the warning box) and change the Width Segments value to 3. Where did the previously modified vertex go? Switch to a Wireframe view, and you'll see that the vertex has been moved to an interior location on the Box. The edge has been folded back along the base.
5. Step up the Width Segments value to 5 by clicking on the spinner buttons. The vertex reappears outside the Box but it's locked along one side. Continue increasing the Width Segments value, and the vertex will move nearer and nearer to the object.

The warning box in Step 4 warns of this unpredictability. You must be aware of it when you're using the Edit Mesh modifier with a parametric object. The modifier works fine with the primitive objects, and it can always be removed and reapplied—but editing at the object's lowest level may be unwise.

Mesh Subobject Editing

The tools for editing the components of a mesh object (or an object with the Edit Mesh modifier applied) are convenient, logical, and easy to use. The subobject levels can be reached through the buttons at the top of the Selection rollout in the Modify panel, by expanding the modifier in the Stack View window, or by selecting the Sub-Objects option in the Quad menu (the easiest method).

Regardless of the method you use, the available panels will adapt to provide the tools that apply to the selected subobject. To fully appreciate the extent of the tools available for mesh-level editing, activate the Face subobject level, expand all the rollouts, and drag the panel to the left to show multiple columns, as shown in Chapter 4. As you can see, many tools can be used to achieve the look you want when editing at the mesh level.

The Vertex Subobject Level

A *vertex* is the point at which two or more edges meet. The Vertex subobject level permits you to select and edit vertices. Often, you will select vertices at this level in order to move them and change the mesh's shape; but you can also weld vertices together, delete or create new vertices, hide vertices, and assign colors to individual vertices (typically for vertex color rendering). Most of these tools are easy to understand, but some deserve an explanation.

Welding

Welding is the process of combining two or more vertices into one. This process is used both to shape an object and to clean up an object that has generated extraneous or redundant vertices—usually by combining mirrored halves of a mesh. Vertices that are on top of each other or those that are very close should be welded to eliminate errors that may not be evident until the rendering process is complete. A *hole* in an object (created when two side-by-side faces do not share the same vertices) may not be visible in a wireframe or rendered viewport, but it may appear only in a rendered image.

To see how welding works, follow the steps in this exercise:

1. Create a Box primitive in the Perspective viewport, with one segment in each direction. Apply an Edit Mesh modifier.
2. Go to the Vertex subobject level and select the top and bottom vertices along one edge.
3. Clicking on the Selected button in the Weld group probably will result in a box popping up, stating that no vertices are within the weld threshold listed in the field next to the button. Increase the value in this field until clicking on the Selected button combines the two vertices into a single vertex located midway between the two original vertices. The Box should look like the object on the left in Figure 7.2.

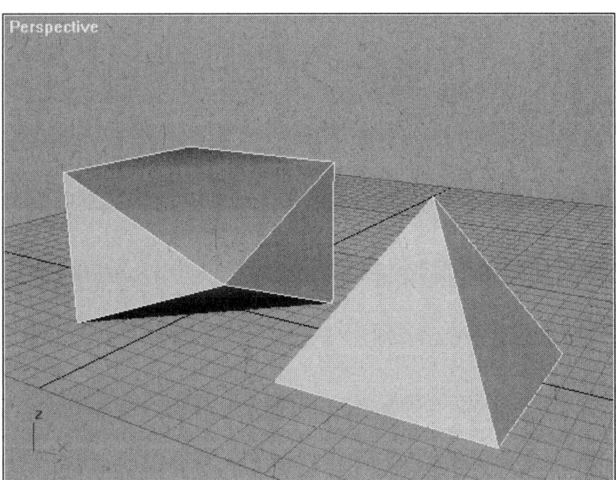

Figure 7.2
The two vertices on the nearest edge of the Box on the left have been welded with the Edit Mesh modifier. The object on the right is a Box whose top vertices have all been welded.

4. Undo the previous step. To combine the vertices at the location of an existing vertex, activate the Target button and drag the edge's top vertex over the lower vertex. The Box should look like the object on the left in Figure 7.3.

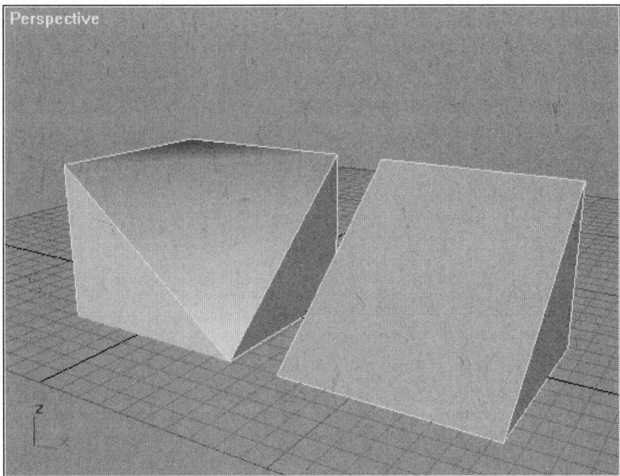

Figure 7.3
The two vertices on the nearest edge of the Box on the left have been welded using the Target option at the location of the lower vertex. The object on the right is a Box whose two top vertices have been welded to the other two to create a wedge shape.

Chamfering

Chamfering is a method of flattening or spreading out a vertex. Unlike welding, this procedure adds vertices and a triangular face to an object. It is used to ease the transition between faces that are at a sharp angle.

To learn how to chamfer, undo the previous exercise until you have the original unedited Box with the modifier applied. Now, follow these steps:

1. Go to the Vertex subobject level and select one of the Box's top corners.
2. Right-click on the vertex to bring up the Quad menu. Choose Chamfer Vertex from the Tools 2 section. Move the cursor over the selected vertex; when the cursor changes shape, click and drag to flatten the corner and create new vertices along the edges. The Box should look like the object on the left in Figure 7.4.

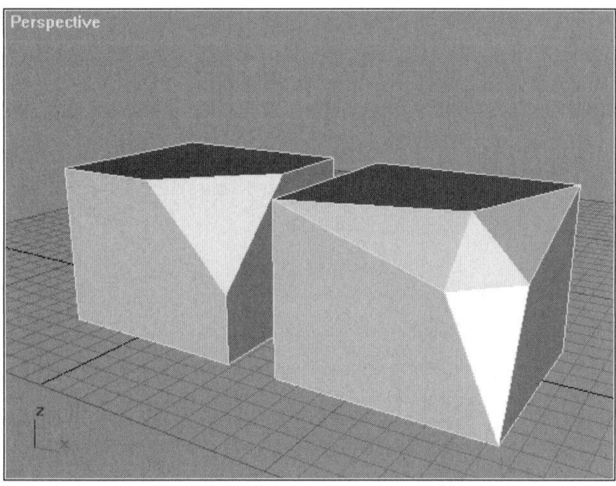

Figure 7.4
The left Box corner vertex has been chamfered once. On the right, the same procedure has been performed a second time on all vertices that remained selected.

3. When you release the mouse button, three vertices are selected instead of just one. Carefully move the cursor over one of these vertices and click and drag until the new vertices extend into the corners. This time, the chamfering is applied to all three vertices at the same time. The Box should look like the object on the right in Figure 7.4.
4. Count the Box's visible vertices: There appear to be 10. Select all the vertices with a window, and the bottom of the Selection rollout shows that 16 are selected—the new vertices are sitting on top of some existing ones. This situation illustrates the need for some of the cleanup mentioned in the "Welding" section. Set the Weld Tolerance value to 0.1 and click on the adjacent Selected button. The collated vertices are combined, and the Selection rollout shows that only 10 vertices are selected.

Soft Selection

Usually, the selection of vertices is specific to those that are explicitly picked. MAX, however, can use soft selection to create an envelope of decreasing adherence to the operation, just as it did in Chapter 6 with the Displace modifier. Soft selection is available for all the subobject types, but it's used most often when you're pulling vertices to shape the mesh. It allows for a smooth transition between the faces of a mesh as they are modified to project from the surface of an object.

In the Soft Selection rollout, the Falloff spinner determines the radius for the envelope effect. The Pinch and Bubble values affect the curvature of the modified object by adjusting the locations of the adherence rings within the falloff area. You can use these values to achieve a pointed or very smooth bulge when the vertices are pulled away from their initial location.

You will see how soft selection works in the following exercise:

1. Create a Box that is 150 units long and wide and 10 units high. Give it 15 length and width segments and 1 height segment.
2. Apply an Edit Mesh modifier. Go to the Vertex subobject level.
3. Drag a rectangle to select nine vertices near the center of the Box. In addition to the vertices on the top surface of the Box, the rectangle selects those on the bottom. Thus 18 vertices are noted in the Selection rollout.
4. Move the vertices in the positive Z-direction to get a feel for how the mesh is shaped without soft selection. Undo the step.
5. Expand the Soft Selection rollout and select the Use Soft Selection checkbox to activate the tool. The red selected vertices are now surrounded by a yellow ring of vertices that are less adhered to the transforms applied to the selected ones.
6. Set the Falloff spinner to 65. The colored vertices now cover most of the top surface of the Box, and the colors range from red (fully adhered) to blue (unaffected).
7. Leave the Pinch and Bubble values at their default settings. Move the selected vertices in the positive Z-direction, as you did before. This time, not only do the selected vertices move, but those within the falloff radius move as well (to a lesser degree as the distance increases). The Box should look similar to the object on the right in Figure 7.5.
8. Move the selected vertices back to their initial location. You would expect this action to reverse the operation and flatten the Box's top surface. Instead, the vertices nearest the selection move the greatest distance, and those farthest from the selection move the least. The result is a raised ring of vertices surrounding the center of the Box along the outer edge.
9. Use the Arc Rotate tool to view the object from below to verify that the vertices from the bottom surface have moved as well.

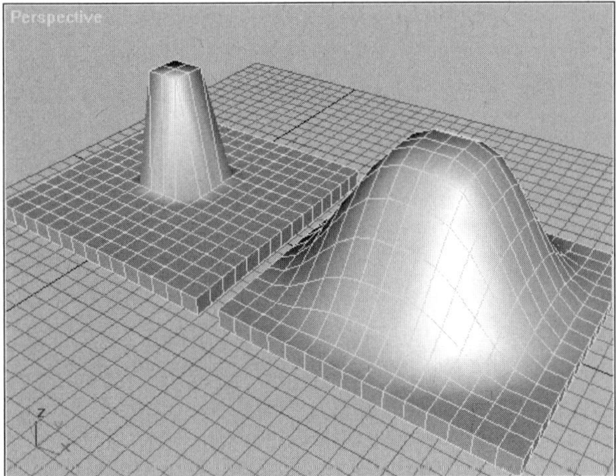

Figure 7.5
On the right, the Box's middle nine vertices (as seen from the top) have been moved in the positive Z-direction with Use Soft Selection active. The same operation was applied on the left without using soft selection.

Face, Polygon, and Element Subobject Levels

It may seem that we should discuss the Edge subobject next, because it appears next on the subobject list. To understand edges, however, you must understand the faces and polygons that they bound.

Selecting Faces, Polygons, and Elements

While working with meshes in MAX, you've been seeing the effect of your actions on the four-sided polygons, or *quadrangles*, that are the default view in the program. All polygons, however, are constructed of two or more triangular faces. Although the word *face* may seem to indicate a coplanar surface, in MAX it refers to the individual components of each polygon that make up the surfaces of a mesh.

Let's see how you can select faces and polygons. To set up this exercise, create an unsegmented Box on the groundplane and convert it to an editable mesh. Now, follow these steps:

1. View the Box in the rendered Perspective viewport with the Edged Faces option selected.
2. Go to the Face subobject level and pick one of the Box's surfaces. The Editable Mesh panel will indicate which face is selected, but it is sometimes difficult to see the face exactly with the default settings in MAX. To change this situation, choose Viewport Configuration from the Customize menu and select the Shade Selected Faces checkbox in the Rendering Method tab. One final step to help the face-editing procedure is to Deselect Backface Cull in the Display tab to show the edges behind the front faces in the nonrendered viewports. Your Box should look similar to the one in Figure 7.6.

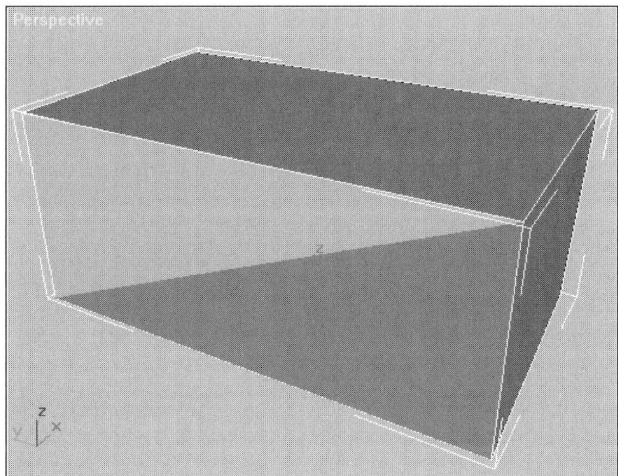

Figure 7.6
A Box with one of its triangular faces selected. The Shade Selected Faces option is activated to help distinguish the selected face from the nonselected faces.

3. Change to the Polygon subobject level and select one of the surfaces of the Box. This time, the entire surface (which is composed of only one polygon) is selected. The Selection rollout shows that both of the polygon's faces are part of the selection set. To see the invisible edges that divide the polygons into triangles, deselect the Edges Only checkbox in the Display tab. Your Box should now look like the one shown in Figure 7.7.

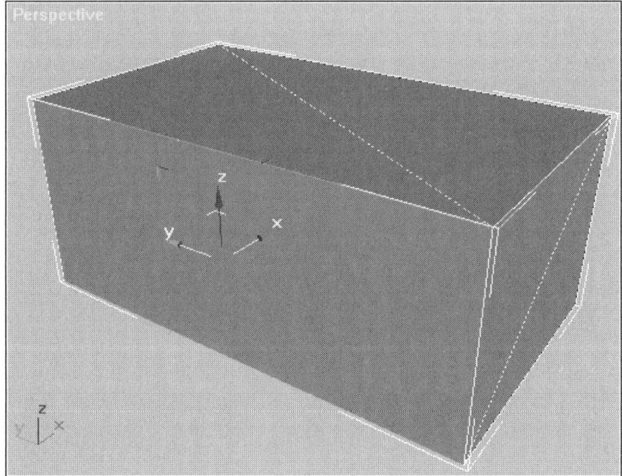

Figure 7.7
The polygon on the front surface is selected. The Edges Only checkbox in the Display tab is deselected to reveal the invisible edges that bound the Box's polygons.

4. When you select a face or polygon subobject in a rendered viewport, it may seem as if nothing has been selected. This happens because MAX cycles through the subobjects that are under the cursor and behind one another when you click the mouse button more than once. To see this behavior in action, change the Perspective viewport to a wireframe mode and click repeatedly in the same location. The selected subobject will rotate through the two or three possible candidates at that location.

5. Change to the Edge subobject level and select one of the vertical edges that border the front face of the Box. When the hidden, diagonal edge appears, select it. Click on the Visible button in the Surface Properties rollout. The edge will remain visible as long as you are at the Edge level. Return to the Polygon level, and the diagonal edge reverts to a dashed line—but when you select the surface, only the triangular face is selected, rather than the entire polygon. One of the rules of MAX is that triangles must be bound by at least one invisible edge. By making the diagonal edge visible, you converted each triangular face into both faces and polygons at the same time.

If you are at the Element subobject level and you select the Box, the entire object is selected. How is selecting an element different from selecting the object at its top level? A mesh object can be made from multiple mesh objects that have been combined for a composite object. To help understand this concept, continue the previous exercise with these steps:

1. Return to the Box's top level. Create a Teapot primitive and convert it to an editable mesh.

2. With the Teapot selected, click on the Attach button in the Edit Geometry rollout. Select the Box. The two objects are combined into one editable mesh. To confirm this action, open the Select Objects dialog box: Only Teapot01 appears in the list.

3. Go to the Element subobject level and select the Box. It becomes highlighted to signify that it is an independent element of the mesh. Select any of the Teapot components (such as the lid or spout), and you will see that each is an element of the combined mesh. Figure 7.8 shows the combined Box and Teapot meshes with the Teapot's Body element selected.

Extruding and Beveling

Extruding and beveling are probably the most frequently conducted operations in mesh-level modeling, because they help define the basic shape of the object. They are used when creating the kind of branching architecture that is typical of organic modeling of plants and animals. In this regard, polygonal modeling still has significant benefits over NURBS modeling. In polygonal modeling, punching out an arm from a torso or a finger from a hand is as simple as extruding the appropriate faces. In NURBS modeling, a branching model must be assembled from separate surfaces to hide the seams between the surfaces—and this is not always an easy task.

When you're using the Extrude and Bevel tools, the faces are projected in the direction of their normals, and additional faces are created to close the gap between the new and existing edges. When two or more adjacent faces or polygons are extruded simultaneously, they will remain connected after the operation.

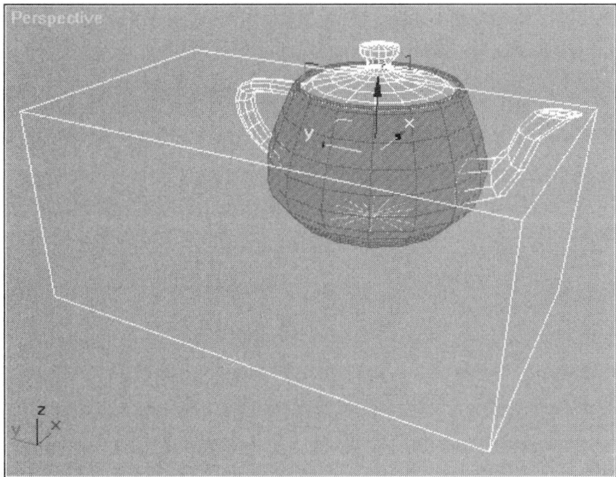

Figure 7.8
The combined Box and Teapot meshes with the Teapot's Body element selected.

To examine the possibilities of the Extrude and Bevel tools, follow the steps of this exercise:

1. Create a Cone near the origin with a Radius 1 value of 60, a Radius 2 value of 20, a Height value of 70, five height segments, two cap segments, and 24 sides.
2. Apply an Edit Mesh modifier and go to the Polygon subobject level.
3. Select five polygons that stretch from the base to the top in a single row. To extrude the faces, bring up the Quad menu and choose Extrude Polygons, or click on Extrude in the Edit Geometry rollout. Either way, the cursor will change when it's over the selected polygons to indicate that you are in Extrude mode. Click and drag upward to pull the polygons away from the existing surface and create new ones to close the gaps between the new face location and the old.
4. Undo the extrusion and then repeat it, this time dragging the mouse downward. With a downward mouse motion, a slot or groove is created in the side of the object. (If you are creating simulations or assemblies of mechanical systems, this may be the ideal way to create keyways in shafts.) Figure 7.9 shows a Cone that has had one section extruded outward and another inward.
5. The Extrude tool can be applied to noncontiguous sets of polygons. Undo the previous step and select every other row of horizontal polygons. The best way to do this is to ensure that the Crossing Selection toggle is active at the bottom of the MAX window; then, press and hold the Ctrl key as you build the selection set from the bottom, middle, and top bands of polygons without adding the faces from the end caps. If the end caps are accidentally selected, switch to a Window Selection and deselect them using the Alt key. The Cone with the selected faces should look like Figure 7.10.

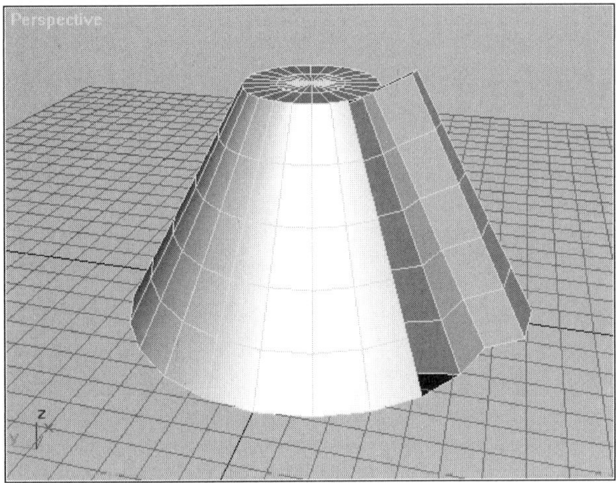

Figure 7.9
The Extrude tool is applied in two different ways. On one section of the Cone, the polygons are extruded outward; on another section, they are extruded inward.

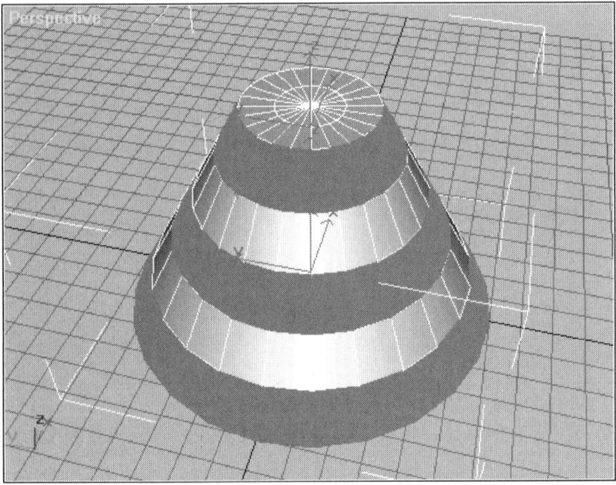

Figure 7.10
The Cone with the top, middle, and bottom bands of polygons selected, but with the end cap polygons unselected.

6. Rather than simply dragging the faces to extrude them with the mouse, you will use the Extrude spinner to place the new face locations precisely. Ensure that the Local radio button is active; it makes the noncontiguous faces move in the direction of their normals rather than away from a centerpoint, as the Group option does. Drag the Extrude spinner to a value of 10. All three bands are extruded perpendicular to the surface of the Cone, as seen in Figure 7.11.

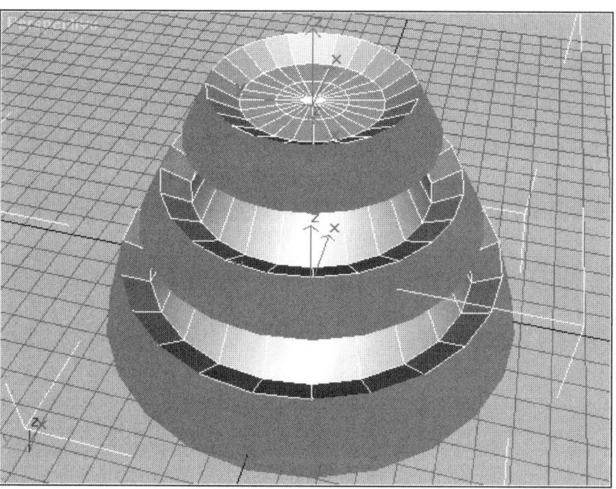

Figure 7.11
The three selected bands of polygons have been extruded using the Normal: Local option.

Note: *You shouldn't continually click on the Extrude spinner buttons to pull out a face selection. The spinner zeros itself after every use, which will cause many unnecessary side and internal faces to be generated. Instead, either click and hold the spinner button and drag it to the desired value, or type the value directly into the spinner field.*

7. The Bevel tool functions like an Extrude tool followed by a localized Scale transform. Select the inner series of faces on the top end cap and activate the Extrude tool. Drag upward to extrude them 10 units and release the mouse. Drag downward and decrease the Bevel spinner value until the top forms a point, similar to the object shown in Figure 7.12.

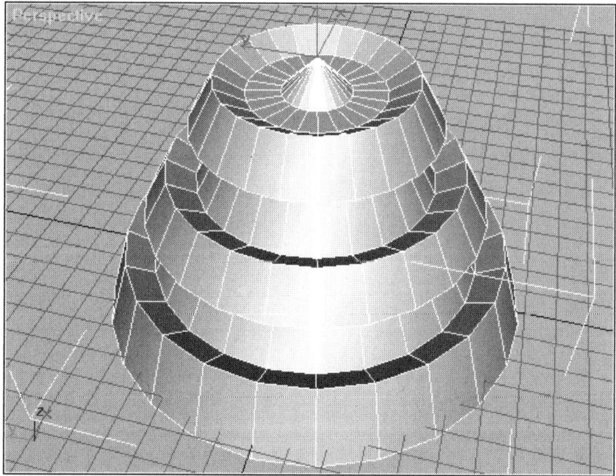

Figure 7.12
The central set of faces in the top end cap have been extruded and then beveled.

As you can see, Extrude and Bevel are powerful tools. You can use them to shape and create the polygons and faces of a mesh to achieve results that would otherwise require you to combine different mesh objects.

Deleting, Detaching, and Creating Faces and Polygons

The ability to delete or create faces is important, because doing so is often the only means of achieving a desired end result. Removing faces, however, has a major drawback, as you will see in this exercise. Follow these steps:

1. Create a short, wide Tube near the origin. Give it a Height Segment value of 1. Apply an Edit Mesh modifier and delete one of the vertical polygons on the object's outer surface, as shown in Figure 7.13. As you can see, once the polygon is deleted, the internal polygons are not visible; MAX displays only the side that faces in the normal or outward direction.

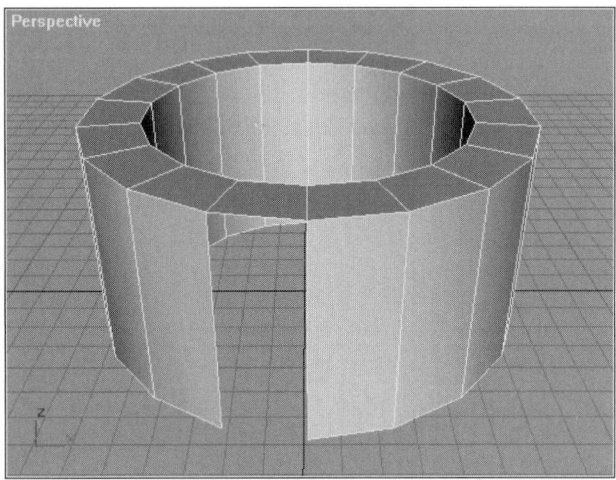

Figure 7.13
An Edit Mesh modifier has been applied to the Tube and one of its polygons has been removed. The nonnormal sides of the interior polygons are facing the viewport.

2. If this is a static shot, where the view will not change to display the bottom, you can fix the situation by flipping the normals on the faces that are now invisible to reverse the direction they are facing. To see the direction of the normals, select the Show Normals checkbox in the Selection rollout. Whenever a face, polygon, or element is selected, blue lines will appear at the center of each face, pointing in the direction of the normal. If the lines are so long that they become confusing, lower the value in the Scale field.

Note: *Objects that come from CAD packages often have normals that face in the wrong direction. Using the Show Normals feature can quickly identify normals that need to be flipped. If the operation is too massive to undertake, it may be prudent to render the scene as 2-Sided or apply a two-sided material to the object. Both of these solutions result in a longer rendering process.*

3. Activate the Flip Normal Mode button in the Surface Properties rollout and pick in the location of an invisible face. It becomes visible, because the normal is now pointing in a direction that the view can see. Continue picking the invisible faces until they are all facing the proper direction and your scene looks similar to Figure 7.14. Turn off Flip Normal Mode.

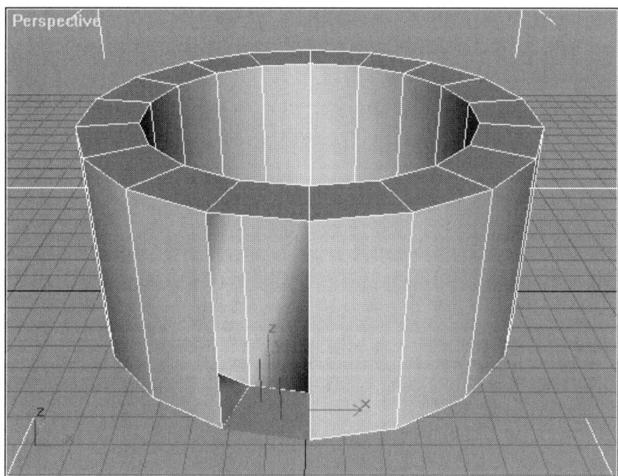

Figure 7.14
The normals have been flipped to show the interior faces of the Tube.

4. To rebuild part of the missing front polygon, open the Grid And Snap Settings dialog box and select the Midpoint option. Close the dialog box. Activate the 3D Snap Toggle. (The Create tool inherently uses an object's vertices, making the Vertex snap option unnecessary.)

5. In the Polygon subobject level, click on the Create button in the Edit Geometry rollout. Pick the vertex in the lower-left corner of the opening (your cursor will change to a white cross to indicate that you are over a valid entity) and click to start the creation process. Move the cursor (now trailed by a rubber-banding dashed line) midway up the left face and into the midpoint snap icon. Click to set the second polygon corner. Cross the gap and click on the midpoint of the opposite polygon on the surface of the object and then the bottom vertex to set the third and fourth corners. To finish the operation, click on the start point. You can now see the normal indicators but no new polygon—the create process must be conducted in a counterclockwise direction to make the normals face outward. However, the polygon you just created has them facing inward.

6. Flip the normals on the polygon that you just created. Make two more polygons, picking in the clockwise direction, to close the two remaining visible gaps, as shown in Figure 7.15.

Rather than deleting faces, it is often preferable to detach them so you can move them to reveal the interior of an object. Detaching actually creates a new mesh object composed of the

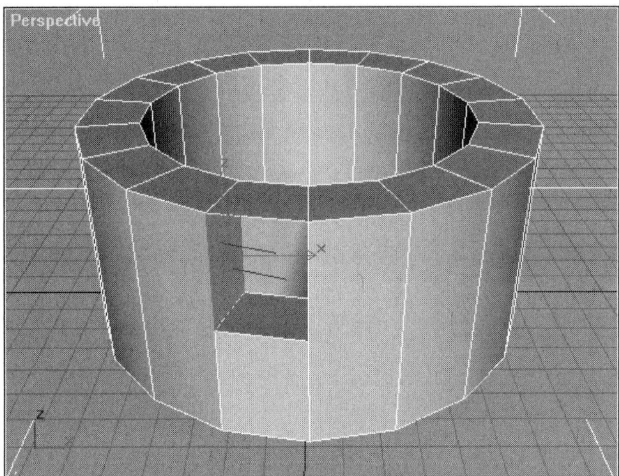

Figure 7.15
A face has been created to cover half of the front opening created when the original polygon was deleted. Two more polygons were then created to close the remaining visible gaps, and the final polygon was selected to reveal the direction of its normals.

detached faces or polygons. To see how detaching works, continue the previous exercise with these steps:

1. Select the polygon that shares edges with only three others and acts like a roof over the opening, as well as the polygon that is the back face of the gap.
2. Click on the Detach option in the Quad menu (or the Modify panel) and, in the subsequent dialog box, give the new object a name. Click on OK. The new object is no longer selectable at the polygon level, because it is no longer a polygon belonging to the current object.
3. Exit the subobject level, select the new object, and move it away from the original. Figure 7.16 shows the original Tube, which now has a slot cut through its front face, along with the new object, which is composed of two of the Tube's original polygons.

Smoothing Groups

The type of smoothing addressed in this section is not related to increasing a mesh's density to decrease the angle between adjacent faces. Instead, this type of smoothing is an instruction to the rendering engine to blend adjacent faces, giving the impression of a smooth, continuous surface rather than the faceted surfaces that actually comprise meshes.

To start this exercise, open the file Chap7_Smoothing.max from the CD-ROM. This is the now-familiar Uhg head model. As you look at the contours of the face, you will notice that no sharp creases appear between any of the adjacent faces. This is the case because all the faces in the model share the same *smoothing group*. Upon its creation, each face is assigned to one of 32 possible smoothing groups. These sequentially numbered groups appear in the Surface

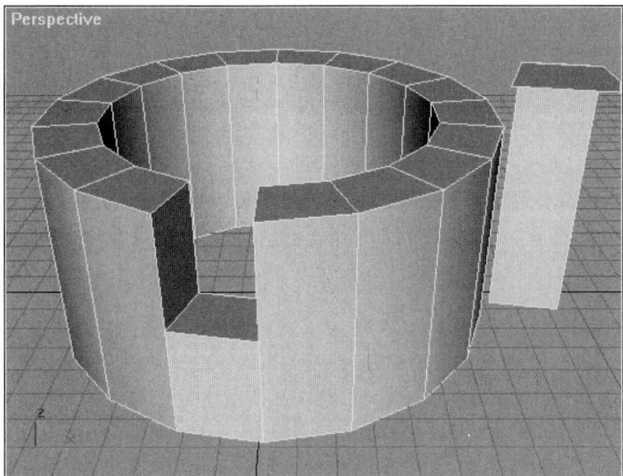

Figure 7.16
The polygons on top of and behind the gap are detached and moved away to help shape the original object into a Tube that has a slot cut through a portion of it.

Properties rollout when the Face, Polygon, or Element subobject is active in an Editable Mesh panel or the Edit Mesh modifier. Whenever two adjacent faces share a smoothing group, the renderer blends across the edge between them. Now, follow these steps:

1. Change the view type to Wireframe and use a window to select all the polygons above the model's eyes. In the Smoothing Groups area, only the number 1 button is active, signifying that all the selected faces belong to Smoothing Group 1. Figure 7.17 shows the selected area as well as the Surface Properties rollout.

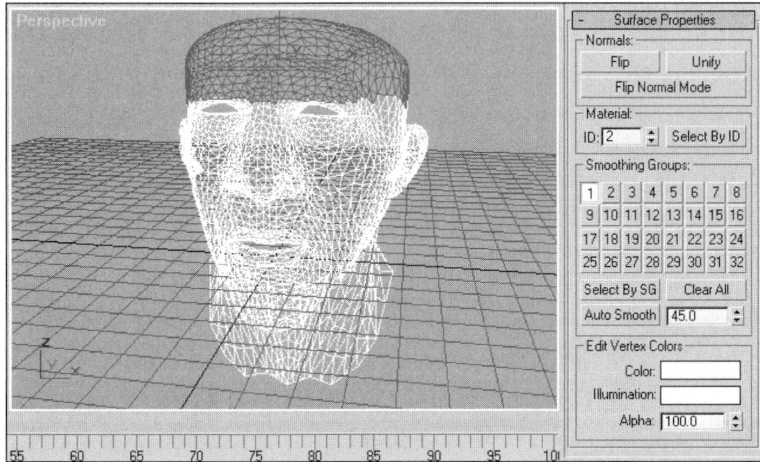

Figure 7.17
The polygons on top of the model's head are selected, and the Smoothing Groups area of the Surface Properties rollout shows that they are all members of Smoothing Group 1.

2. Select a small patch of polygons on the left cheek, picking them individually rather than using a window. Click on 2 in the Smoothing Groups area to activate it, and click on 1 to deactivate it. The cheek now has a section that appears segregated from the rest because of the hard edges surrounding it. Figure 7.18 shows the result of changing the smoothing group for the selected faces. The faces that now belong to Smoothing Group 2 are all blended together. To show each face separately, you would have to assign each its own individual smoothing group.

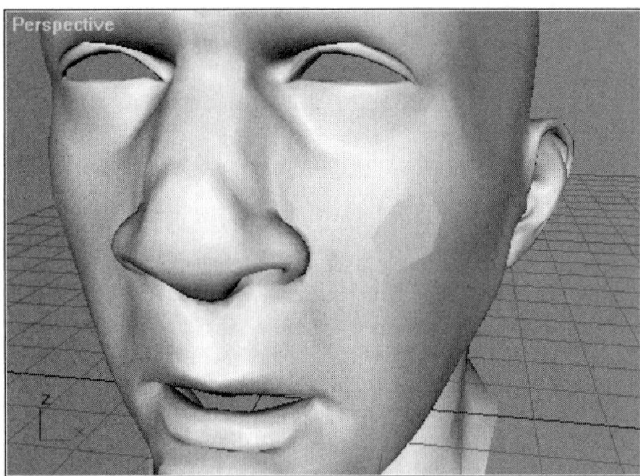

Figure 7.18
Changing the smoothing group for the selected faces creates a visible difference in the contour of the cheek.

3. Hide the head model and unhide the other two objects. Apply an Edit Mesh modifier and attach the 30-sided Cone to the 15-sided Cylinder. Both have the same radius.

4. Two smoothing groups exist: One consists of the base of the Cylinder, the top of the Cone, and the surface that exists between the Cone and the Cylinder, and a second is around the perimeter of both the original objects. Select one of the polygons on the side of the Cone to identify its smoothing group. Select all the faces at the top of the Cone and change them to the same group. The top now appears curved, as seen in Figure 7.19, without you adding any extra segmentation. Under close examination, it's easy to see that the end is actually flat; however, you should use this method whenever the polygon count is critical or when the object is peripheral and should not receive the same scrutiny as the scene's main features.

5. Delete the internal faces that exist between the original Cone and Cylinder and any isolated vertices. Select all the side faces, but none from the end cap areas. You can see from the Modify panel that they all belong to the same smoothing group, but an edge appears where the originals meet. The number of sides differs, so the faces are not adjacent.

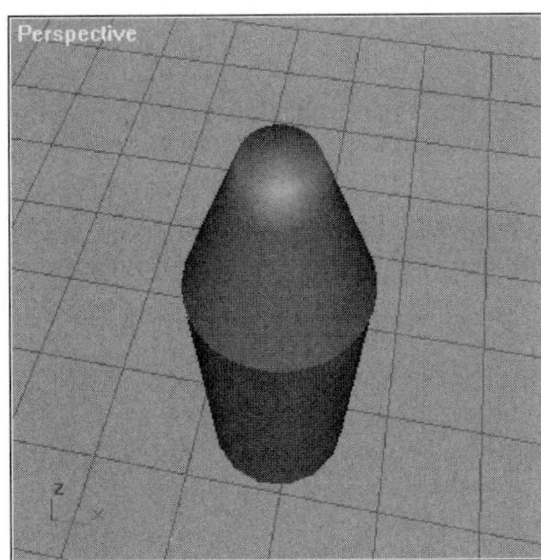

Figure 7.19
By changing the smoothing group for the faces on the end of the Cone to match the group assigned to the sides, the end now appears curved rather than flat.

6. One possible solution is to select all of the vertices between the Cone and Cylinder and weld them together. Instantly, the smoothing becomes apparent in the rendered viewport, but a close examination shows a discrepancy where the odd vertices (vertices from the Cone that are not stacked on top of vertices from the Cylinder) extend beyond the lower object. These vertices must be tied back to the edges they extend beyond. To do this, convert the object to an editable patch (don't convert it to an editable mesh, as you've done previously) and go to the Vertex subobject level. Select one of the odd vertices, as shown in Figure 7.20, and activate the Bind mode from the Quad menu. Click on the vertex, drag it to the edge that it is spanning, watch for the cursor to change to a cross to indicate that

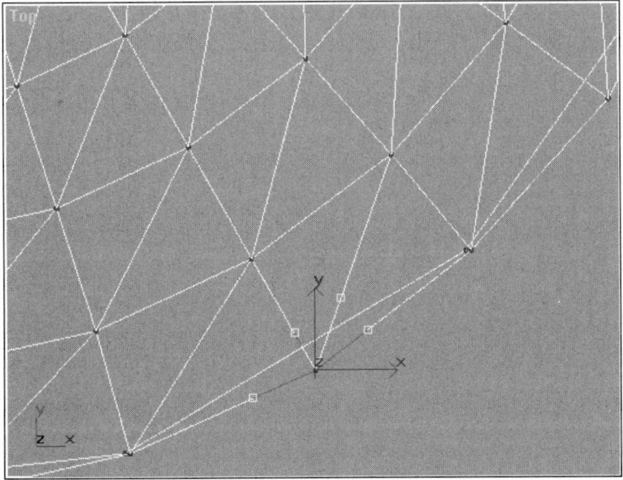

Figure 7.20
A zoomed-in view of one of the odd vertices (selected) that must be bound back to the edge it protrudes beyond.

the operation will succeed, and then release the mouse button. The vertex will snap to the midpoint of that edge and allow for a smooth blend between surfaces. You must conduct the same operation for each odd vertex visible to the person viewing the scene and then convert the object back to an editable mesh.

Editing the smoothing group assignments is surprisingly useful for creating flat spots on tires, flat areas where ID plates may be attached, or any other place where a specific region should not match the curvature of the surrounding area.

Edge Subobject Level

Edges are subobjects that bound faces and terminate at vertices. Editing them properly can yield results such as adding chamfered surfaces and creating new coplanar faces through subdivision. The following exercises will get you accustomed to the most useful features found when editing a mesh's edges.

Chamfering Edges

As mentioned earlier, few surfaces in the real world come together at a sharp angle without even a small transitional face or two. Look at the edges around the face of your computer's monitor, the computer box itself, or the edges of your desk or table, and you will most likely see at least one flat or rounded face sandwiched between the major surfaces. In 3D modeling, it is important to create these chamfered edges to help catch the light and add realism to your scenes. When you're creating low-polygon models, chamfering (used with smoothing groups) can add apparent curvature to objects without adding a large number of faces.

The following exercise demonstrates the procedure for chamfering the edges of an object. Follow these steps:

1. Drag out a Rectangle in the Top viewport. Deselect the Start New Shape checkbox and drag a second Rectangle inside the first. Extrude the shape to about the ratio of a tabletop.

2. When working with edges, you will most often be in the Perspective viewport and need to see all the possible edges. Change the Perspective viewport type to Wireframe. In the Display tab, deselect the Backface Cull checkbox. Your object should look like Figure 7.21.

3. Convert the object to an editable mesh and go the Edge subobject level. Use the Select Object tool without a window to select the four vertical edges of the interior box shape. Use the Chamfer tool to add faces and reshape the interior void to an octagon.

4. Select all the faces around the perimeter of the object and the void (top and bottom) and add just enough chamfer to break the sharp edge. Your object should look similar to Figure 7.22.

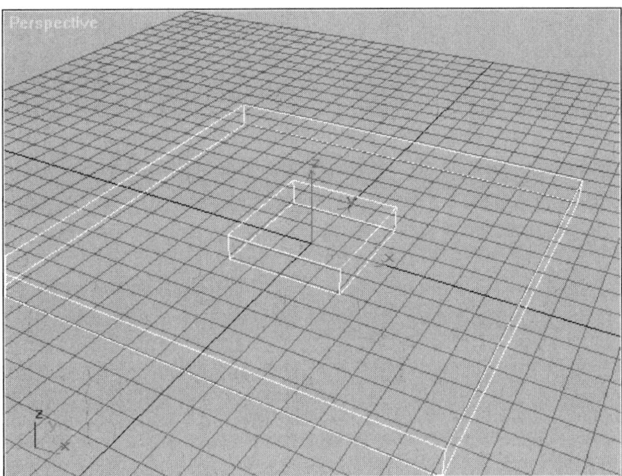

Figure 7.21
The initial shape in a wireframe Perspective viewport with the Backface Cull option deselected in the Display tab.

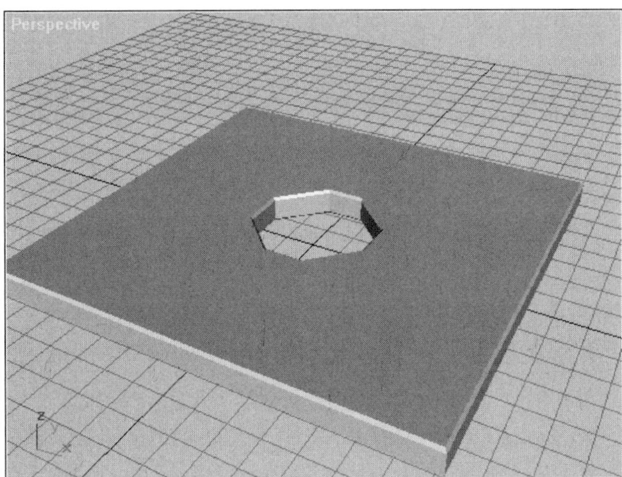

Figure 7.22
The object from Figure 7.21 in a rendered viewport with the vertical sides of the void area chamfered a great deal and the perimeter edges chamfered just a little. Notice how the perimeter chamfer adds a transition color between the top and side faces.

In Figure 7.23, the bottom object is shown as described in Step 4, whereas the upper object has had the same smoothing group assigned to the top, bottom, outside perimeter, and outside chamfer faces. The smoothing groups for the void area are not changed.

Turning and Dividing Edges

Turning an edge simply involves switching corners of the polygon at which its ends terminate and then dividing the edges. This method lets you add edges to cut the mesh into more pieces without adding to its physical size. The techniques for turning and dividing a mesh's edges are

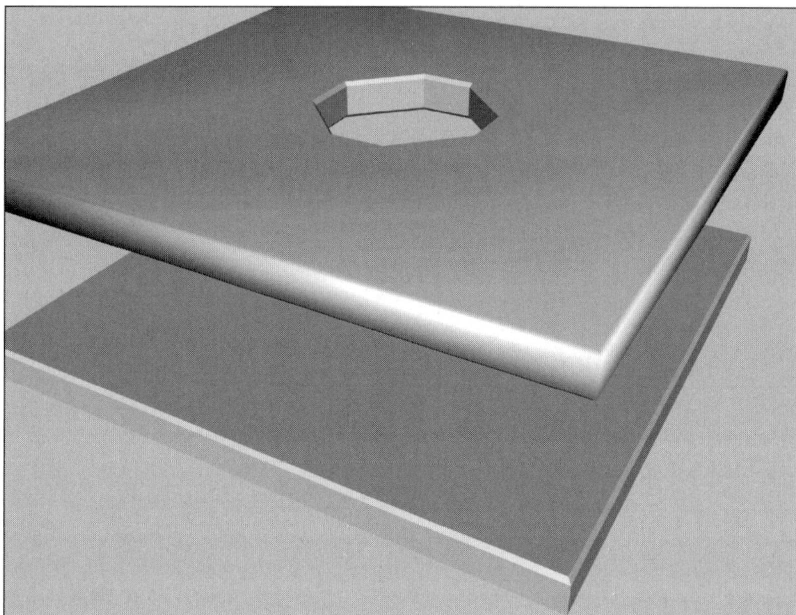

Figure 7.23
By assigning the same smoothing group to the top, side, and chamfered faces, a clean blend is formed, as shown in the upper object.

explained in this next exercise; the goal is to fold in crisply each of a Plane's corners so they're perpendicular to the initial surface. Follow these steps:

1. Reset the scene and create a Plane primitive in the Top viewport with two length and width segments. Convert the Plane to an editable mesh. Select the upper-left face of each polygon, as shown in Figure 7.24. Turn off Edges Only mode by using the keyboard shortcut Ctrl+E.

2. This face configuration will not work for this task, because the edges in the upper-right and lower-left quadrants have the wrong orientation. Switch to the Edge subobject level and select all the edges in the scene. Activate Turn Edges Mode in the Quad menu, or click on the Turn button in the Modify panel, and click on the two incorrect edges to switch their orientation. The invisible edges should form a diamond shape inside the rectangular Plane. Go back to the Face level and select the four triangular faces in the corners of the Plane. Your scene should look similar to Figure 7.25.

3. If you simply move the corner vertices in the positive Z-direction, the midpoint of each side and the center of the object will remain stable and the corners will fold upward but it will appear to smooth the objective. With the corner faces still selected, scroll down to the Smoothing Groups area and assign the faces to a new group. Be sure to deselect their previous group number.

4. Select the four corner vertices, switch to the Perspective viewport, and move them in the positive Z-direction. The corners all rise, and a sharp crease appears between the adjacent

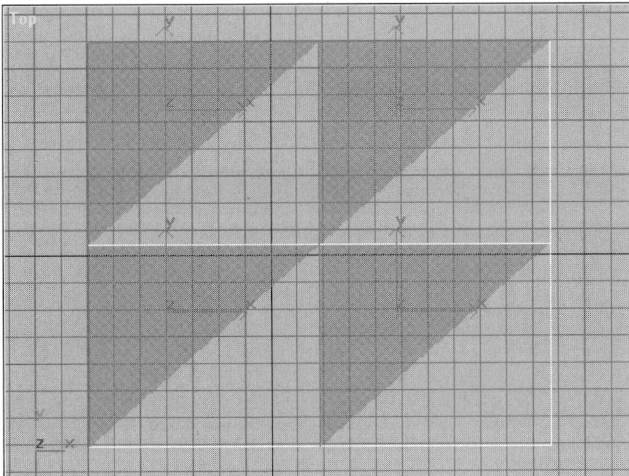

Figure 7.24
The upper-left face of each of the Plane's four polygons is selected.

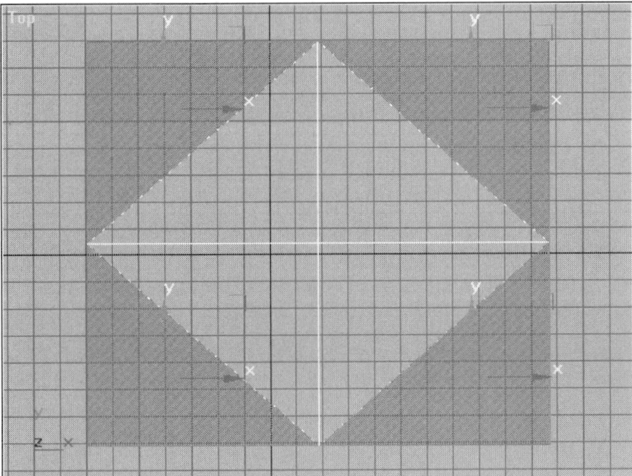

Figure 7.25
With the edges of the upper-right and lower-left polygons turned, the faces that occupy the outside corners can now be selected.

faces. Apply a Scale transform to the vertices to draw them closer to the center of the object and negate some of the stretching that occurred to the faces when the vertices moved. If necessary, flip the normals on the faces that are nearest to the viewport if they seem to have disappeared. Figure 7.26 shows the Plane with the four corners folded inward.

5. To add a second fold, you must make new edges that run parallel to those where the first bend happens. To do so, you divide the edges. Select all of the object's edges by choosing Divide Edges from the Quad menu or Divide from the Divide Edges mode. Activate the Midpoint option of the 3D Snap Toggle. Pick on one of the vertical edges of a face that has been bent to

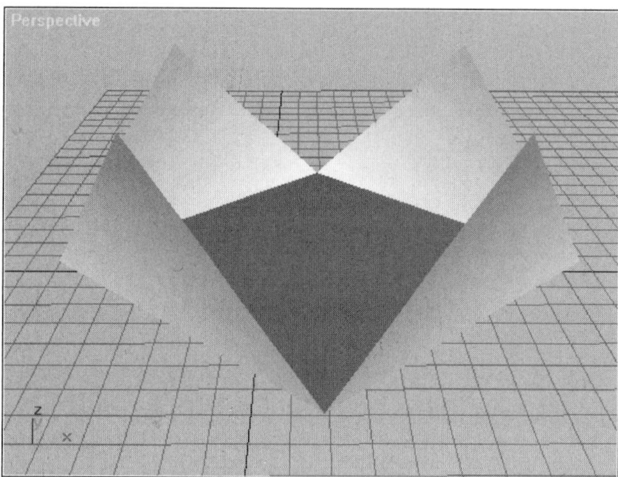

Figure 7.26
The four corner faces are assigned to a new smoothing group, and the corner vertices are moved in the positive Z-direction and scaled inward.

create a new edge from the midpoint of that edge to the opposite corner. Pick on the opposite edge to create an edge from midpoint to midpoint across the vertical face. Where there was only one face, now there are three. Repeat this procedure for the other three bent faces.

6. Assign the new faces to their own smoothing group. Apply a Scale transform to the corner vertices to move them further inward and create a second bend. The final configuration of the Plane should look similar to Figure 7.27.

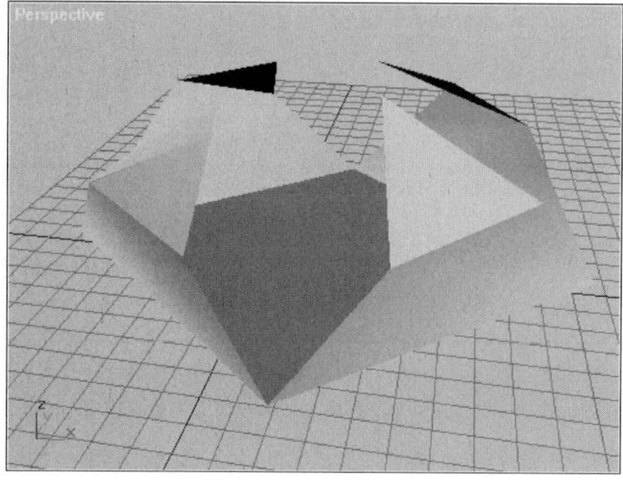

Figure 7.27
The vertical faces have been further subdivided, the new faces assigned to another smoothing group, and the corner vertices scaled inward to create a second bend at each corner.

Putting It Together: A Low-Polygon Head

Several ways exist for building a low-polygon human head. In this exercise, the purpose is to explore the MAX mesh-modeling toolset in a practical context. Each artist must develop a unique approach to achieving artistic goals. The purpose in this section is not to show you how to create the ultimate model, which is an artistic process every creative person handles differently—instead, this book is concerned with you learning to use the tools, so that you can create your own vision. Follow these steps:

1. Begin with an unsegmented cube that is converted to an Editable Mesh object. You will put in all the segmentation yourself.

2. Make a horizontal and a vertical cut all the way through the mesh. Although the Slice modifier and the Slice Plane tool both work, try a new way. Go into the Element subobject level and click on the mesh to select all the faces. Pull down the Modify panel to reveal the Tessellate tool. (*Tessellation* is the process of breaking faces and polygons into smaller units.) Set the spinner value to 0, make sure the Edge radio button is selected, and click on the Tessellate button. Each of the six quadrangles divides into four, with some funny additions of visible edges. Deselect all the faces and choose the Edged Faces option for your Smooth + Highlights view to see things more clearly. Use the Display Floater (Tools| Display Floater), a modeless dialog box with many of the Display tab controls, to deselect the Edges Only checkbox so you can also see the invisible edges. Your mesh should look like Figure 7.28.

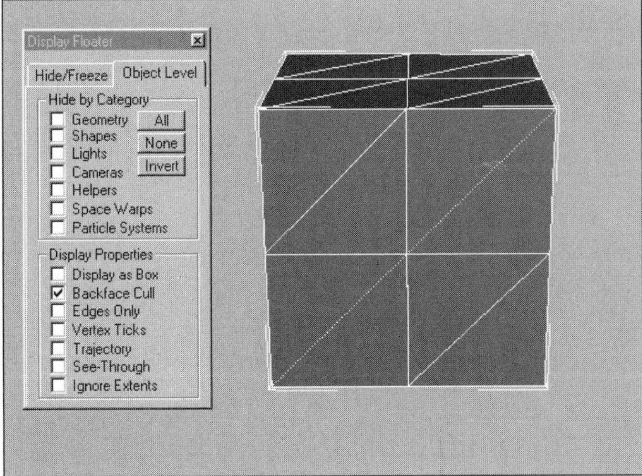

Figure 7.28
An unsegmented editable mesh cube, after subdivision with the Tessellate tool. Reveal the invisible edges by deselecting Edges Only in the Display Floater or by using the Ctrl+E shortcut.

Don't Forget to Merge Vertices

MAX has a remarkable tendency to produce duplicate and unnecessary vertices. Make a habit of periodically selecting all the vertices in a mesh and welding with a small Threshold value (such as 0.1). Check the vertex count before and after, and you may be surprised how many vertices are eliminated. After welding, check the model carefully to make sure it's OK before you continue. Unnecessary vertices give you an incorrect polygon count, so make sure you clean them up before you check your triangle count. The number of triangles in a mesh is found in the Object Properties dialog box, which is available from the right-click menu when you select an object.

3. Turn the edges until the edges of all sides of the cube radiate from the center vertex. This technique creates one of the most basic contour units in low-poly modeling. All sides of your object should look like Figure 7.29.

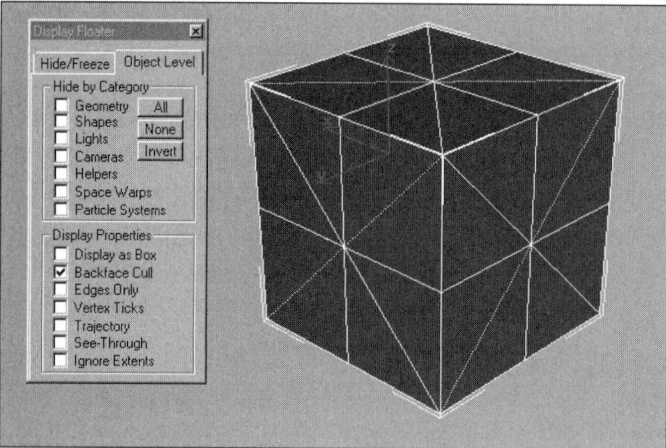

Figure 7.29
The mesh from Figure 7.28, after the edges are turned to create sides composed of eight triangles joined at a central vertex.

4. Make all the diagonal edges invisible for the next few steps. Select the Edges Only checkbox again, so that only the visible edge can be seen. It is now easier to select them and make them invisible in the Edges panel.

5. To create a neck, select the two polygons on the rear bottom of the cube and extrude them down, as shown in Figure 7.30.

6. It's time to move the vertices to get the basic shape. Treat the horizontal row of edges through the head as the brow line. You can select and move vertices individually, but if vertices on the opposite side of the head require symmetry, select both together for movement or nonuniform scaling. Every vertex requires attention to create the proper contours. Take a look at the different views in Figure 7.31 for a possible construction, and take some time to compare this result with yours. It's really quite amazing that you can get from the previous figure to this one by moving only vertices.

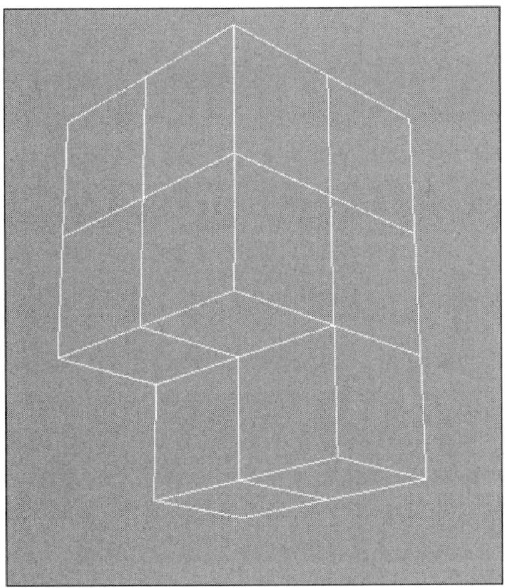

Figure 7.30
With diagonals hidden as invisible edges, two quad polygons are extruded to create a neck.

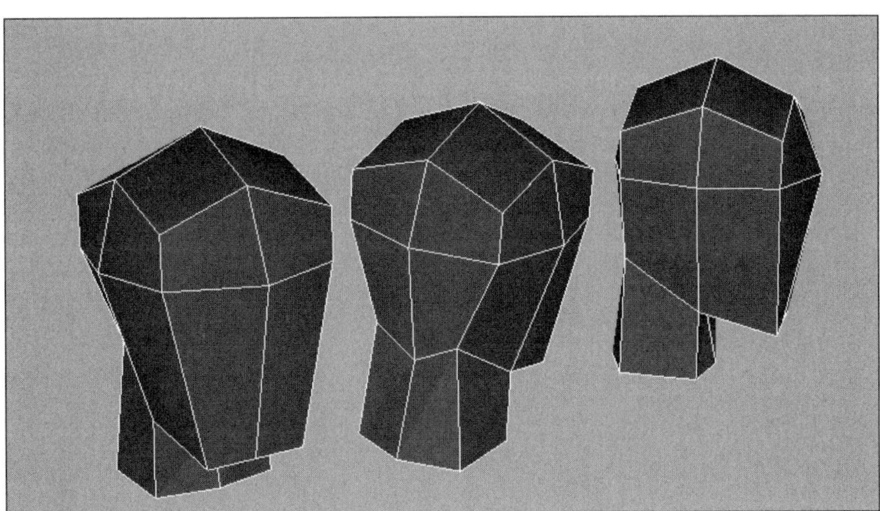

Figure 7.31
The mesh from Figure 7.30 after extensive movements and nonuniform scaling of vertices, seen from three different views.

7. Add another row of edges midway between the chin and the brow line. Go to the Edge subobject level and activate the Cut tool in the Modify panel, which is another method of subdividing faces. Set up some snaps so that the cut lines remain connected as you work around the model. Click on the 3D Snap Toggle to activate it and then right-click on it; you need only the Midpoint and Endpoint options (deselect any other options). The Cut tool now snaps to the ends and center points of edges. Using the Cut tool is always a little tricky, so be

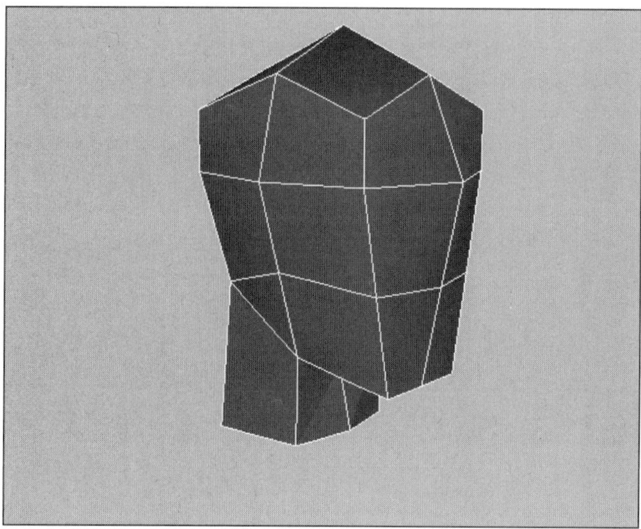

Figure 7.32
The mesh from Figure 7.31, with a new row of edges added by using the Cut tool. Snaps are activated at the endpoints and midpoints of the edges.

prepared for a few Undos. You have to click on each edge to divide it before you can continue to the next edge. When you finish, you've connected a new row of edges around most of the head, beginning and ending where the neck touches the jaw. Use Figure 7.32 as a guide.

8. Straighten out the new vertices so they are roughly level with each other. Select all the edges and make them visible. It's time to turn edges. Turning edges creates contours—it involves individual, creative decision making. It is sometimes helpful to organize the triangles into contour groups by color. You can easily do this by opening the Material Editor in the Main toolbar. Change the Diffuse color in several slots. Select groups of faces to which you want to assign a color and drag from one of the material slots onto your selection. The faces are assigned the color in the slot, which helps to keep you visually organized while modeling and does not prevent you from texturing from scratch when the model is done. After a great deal of edge-turning experimentation, the mesh is divided into contour groups for the brow, the large area beneath it, the top of the head, the back, the two upper sides, the two cheeks, the chin, and the neck. Take some time to consider the organization of edges in Figure 7.33. Consult this book's color section for a reference image.

9. As you turn to the facial features, you will do a lot of detailed work and experimentation; it doesn't make sense to work on both halves of the model. Select the faces of one half and delete them. Rename the remaining model "right side" or "left side," as the case may be. Bring up the Display Floater for the Tools menu, if it's not already up; you will use it constantly from here on. You may now want to deselect the Backface Cull checkbox to see the inside of the model. While you're at it, delete the faces from the bottom of the neck. At this point, your screen should look like Figure 7.34.

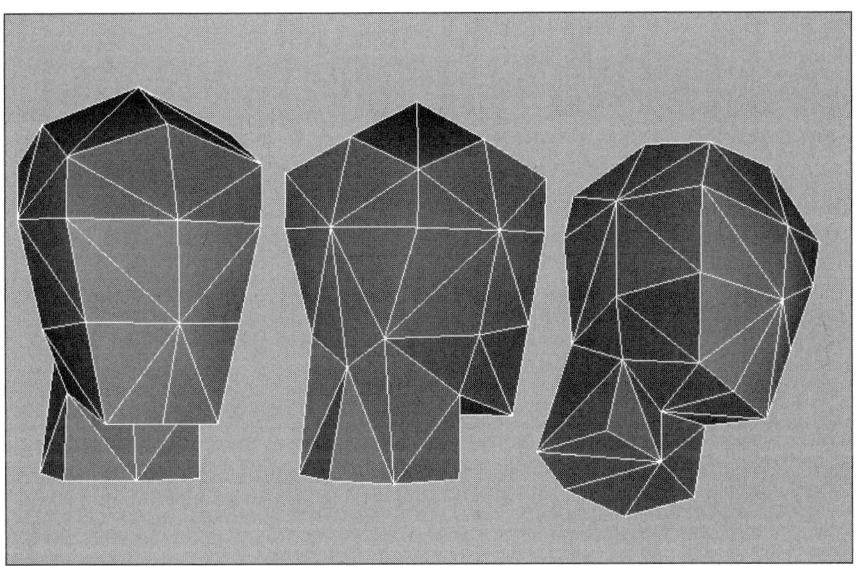

Figure 7.33
The mesh from Figure 7.32, with all edges revealed and organized into contours by turning.

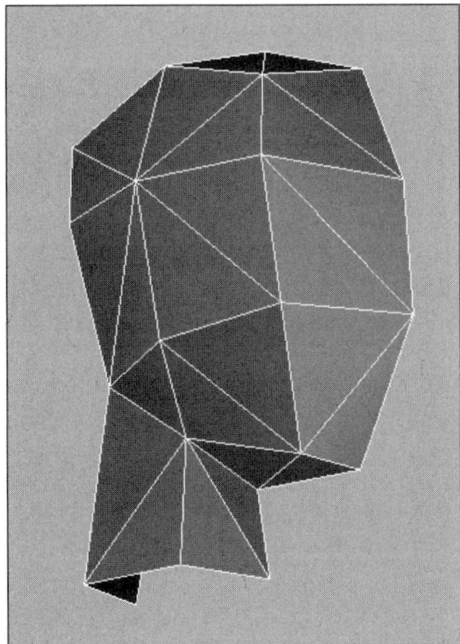

Figure 7.34
The mesh from Figure 7.33, with the faces that constitute the side of the head deleted. The faces at the bottom of the neck are also deleted. The Backface Cull display option is deselected to make visible both sides of the remaining surface.

10. If you wish, you can work on both sides of the head together. Mirror the model by using the Mirror tool and create an instance. Both halves are visible as separate objects. Because they are instances, any edits that you apply to one of the halves automatically apply to the other half. This is an ideal arrangement. For example, with one of the halves selected, move one of the chin vertices inward; watch the opposite vertex follow to keep the screen image symmetrical (as shown in Figure 7.35).

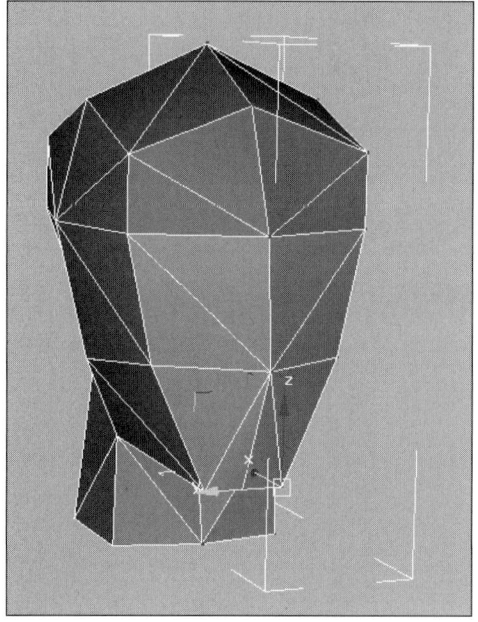

Figure 7.35
The mesh from Figure 7.34, mirrored to create a symmetrical instance across the centerline. Although two models now exist, they act as one. When the selected chin vertex translates inward, the corresponding vertex on the other side also moves in.

11. It may seem like you're spending a lot of time on setup, but these are very important steps. Polygonal modeling (and especially low-poly modeling) is hard work, and it's almost impossible to operate without a good display setup. So, make one further refinement. Because you will work on the character's face from here on, hide all the faces on the back of the object by selecting the faces in the Face subobject level and clicking on the Hide button in the Selection rollout. This action not only makes things easier to see, but it also prevents you from accidentally selecting the vertices on the back of the object. Note the distinction between hiding subobjects (such as faces and polygons) in the Editable Mesh subobject panels, and hiding entire objects in the Display Floater, Display panel, or Quad menu. To hide the back faces, use the former method; to hide and unhide the instanced halves of the head (which are entirely separate objects), use the Display Floater or Quad menu. You have tremendous flexibility in 3ds max 4. Figure 7.36 shows both halves visible, but with

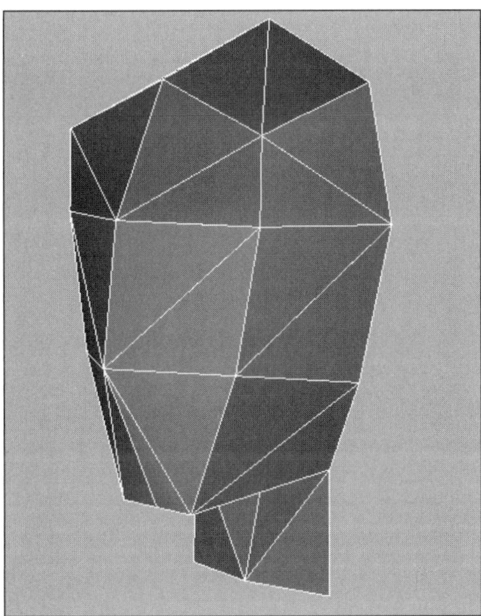

Figure 7.36
The mesh from Figure 7.35, with the face on the rear of the head hidden in the Face subobject panel. This is different from hiding one or both of the instanced halves by using the Display Floater, because these instances are separate objects.

the back faces hidden. Note that the adjoining side faces remain unhidden, even though you work only on the front faces. Many edits that you make on the front faces affect the side faces as well, so you need to see them.

12. Add a brow line. The key to cutting up a mesh, as you've already learned, is the distinction between visible and invisible edges. If an edge is visible, the Cut tool (in the Edge subobject level) divides it. If the edge is invisible, the Cut tool does not divide it—it reorganizes the invisible edges to accommodate the visible edges. At this point, all the edges are visible. (If they are not visible, select them all and click on the Visible button.) Thus, if you make a horizontal cut immediately below the existing brow line, you also cut the diagonal edge. With only half of the model visible for clarity, your screen should look like Figure 7.37. Make sure that the Edges Only checkbox is deselected in the Display Floater to see the new invisible edges added by this cut.

13. Undo the cut. Select the diagonal edge, make it invisible, and try the same cut again. This time, the diagonal is not cut, which eliminates unnecessary cleanup. (Get used to selecting and deselecting the Edges Only display option to understand the organization of the visible and invisible edges.) Select the two vertices at the end of the new edge and move them back to create a sharp brow. Low-poly characters often need exaggerated features. Figure 7.38 shows the result, with the invisible edges hidden by selecting the Edges Only option.

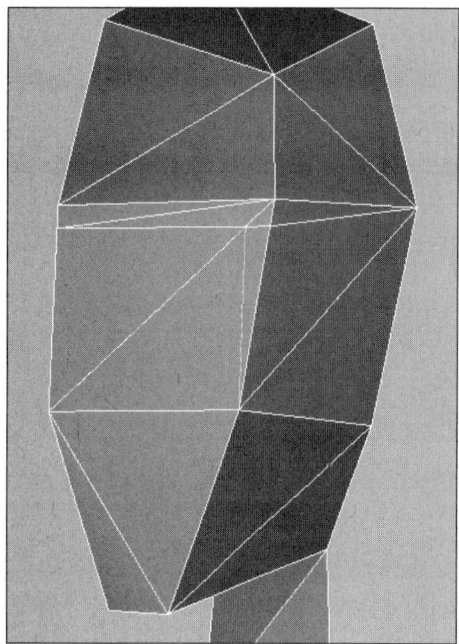

Figure 7.37
A brow line cut added in the Edge subobject level. This action added an undesired cut through the diagonal edge because that edge was visible.

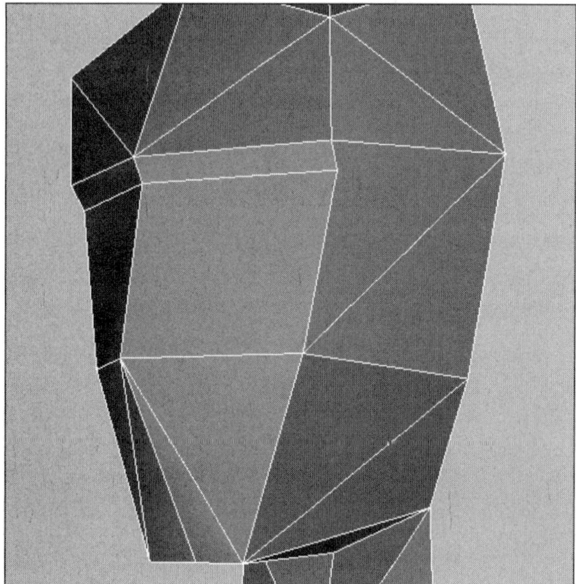

Figure 7.38
The same brow line added, but only after making the diagonal edge invisible. The diagonal edge is no longer divided by the cut, producing a cleaner result. Invisible edges are hidden by selecting the Edges Only display option in the Display Floater.

14. It's time to add the nose. Cut downward from the upper brow edge at an outward slant, through the next two horizontal edges. Your cut should look something like the new one in Figure 7.39.

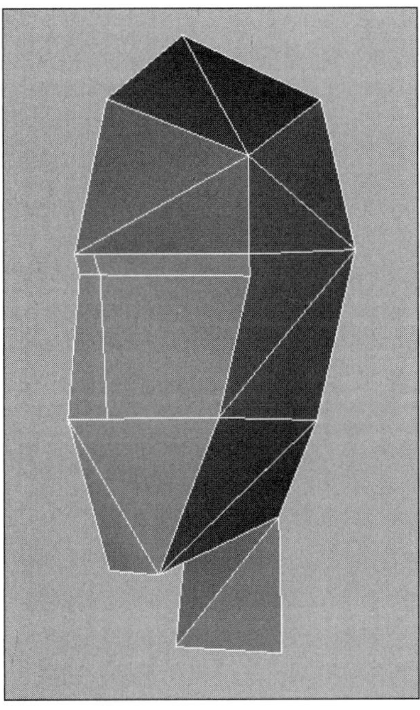

Figure 7.39
The mesh from Figure 7.38, with a vertical cut added to begin to define the nose. The cut divided three edges.

15. To get a sharp shelf under the nose, make a cut to connect the lower corner to a point in the centerline, slightly beneath the tip of the nose. Because it crosses a diagonal, make that diagonal edge invisible before you cut. Turn on the snaps and right-click on the Snaps toggle to set them to snap to vertices. That way, you can start the new cut precisely at the lower corner vertex on the nose. Draw the cut as you see in Figure 7.40.

16. Select the new vertex on the centerline and move it up until there's a distinct ledge in the nostril area. After you are satisfied with the shape, you may want to grab all the vertices at the base of the nose and move them to create better facial proportions, as shown in Figure 7.41.

17. A nose is a pretty complex piece of geometry. Because this is a low-poly version, you have to decide how many triangles to spend on developing it. Right now, the ridge of the nose is a sharp angle. You can improve it with another cut, just inside the previous one. Moving some vertices a bit creates just enough sense of roundness. Take a look at Figure 7.42.

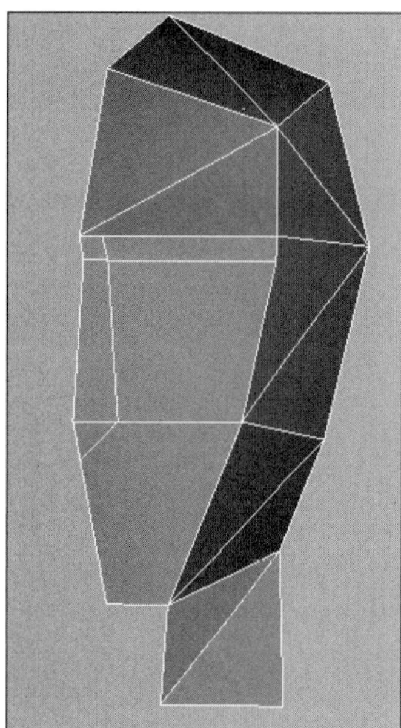

Figure 7.40
A new cut is added from the corner vertex of the nose to a point on the centerline slightly below the tip of the nose. Vertex snapping is used to make sure the cut begins right at the vertex.

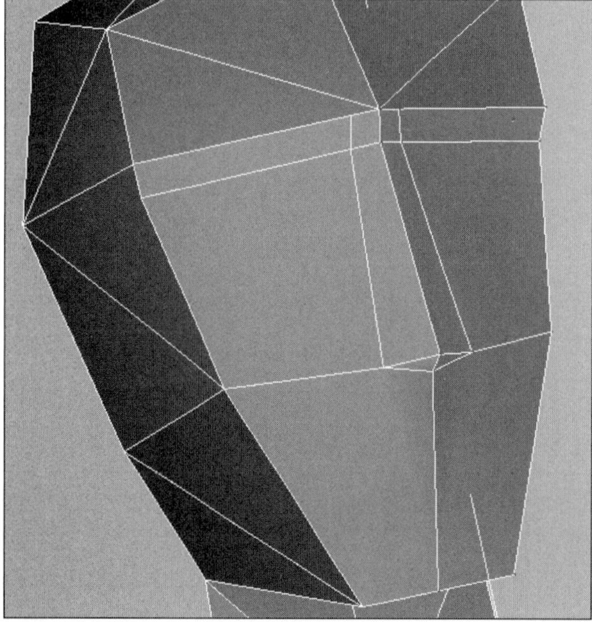

Figure 7.41
The new vertex on the centerline is moved up to create a ledge at the bottom of the nose. All the vertices at the base of the nose are then moved as a group to improve the proportions.

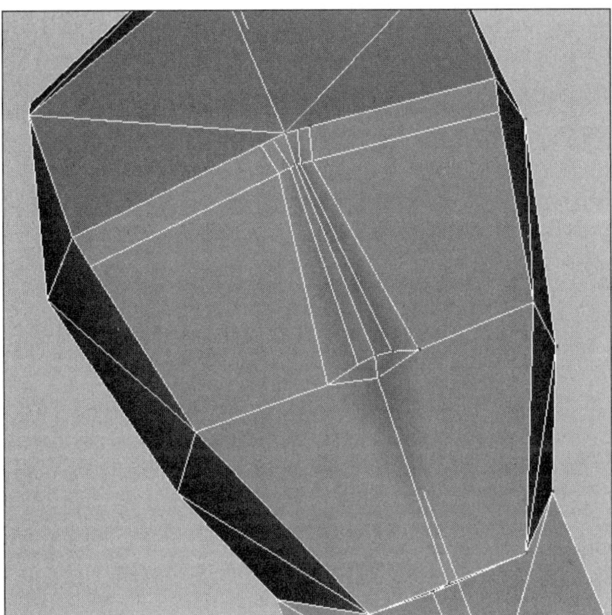

Figure 7.42
To round out the front of the nose, a second cut is added just inside the previous one. Vertices are moved around to create a minimally satisfactory result at both the bridge and the tip of the nose.

18. Move down to create the basis of a jaw (or muzzle) effect. Put a horizontal cut across the jaw, roughly where the mouth should be. As you did before, make a cut that connects the corner of the nose to the outside vertex of the new edge by using vertex snaps. Move this vertex up or in (or both) to create a distinct chin, as shown in Figure 7.43.

Figure 7.43
A cut is added across the mouth, and a second cut connects it to the corner of the nose. Vertices are then moved to create a distinct chin or jaw.

19. To round out the chin, use the Divide tool rather than the Cut tool. Remember that the Divide tool creates invisible edges, so deselect the Edges Only option in the Display Floater to see the invisible edges. Activate the Divide tool in the Edge subobject panel, and click near the center of the chin edge to divide it. Move the new vertex on the chin upward to round out the jaw, as shown in Figure 7.44.

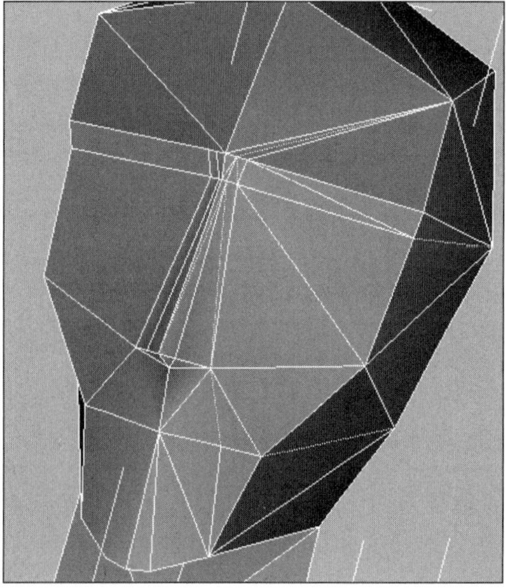

Figure 7.44
By using the Divide tool, a vertex is added to the chin edge and then moved upward to round out the jaw line. The Divide tool (unlike the Cut tool) adds invisible edges, so the Edges Only option in the Display Floater is deselected to show the new edge.

20. By now, you should be getting plenty of ideas of your own, so this exercise will add only one other element before leaving you to the freedom of your imagination. Divide the invisible edge that runs from the top of the nose diagonally to the cheekbone at about the middle of its length. Doing so creates a vertex for the center of the orbits (the holes in the skull where the eyes are positioned). Move this vertex up and back into the head a bit, so it's properly positioned. Figure 7.45 gives you the idea.

From here on, it's up to you. You need to think a great deal about turning edges, once you get the basic contours you need. To create more roundness, you need more edges (if your polygon budget permits it). One way is to create more cuts to the chin, as shown in Figure 7.46, and then move the vertices. Another possibility is to select edges and chamfer them, as we did at the top of the face in Figure 7.46. Both of these methods work, but the chamfer method creates additional structures and ends that might require editing. You may have to delete unnecessary faces by target welding the vertices. Just get in there and divide more edges, make more cuts, turn edges, and move points. Once you have the basics, it's all about practice.

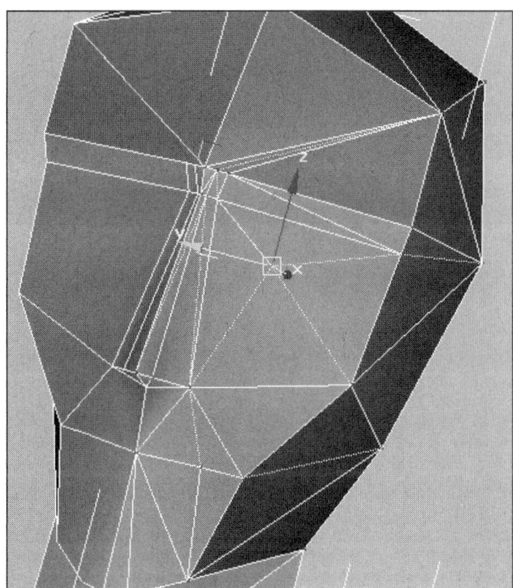

Figure 7.45

The diagonal invisible edge that runs from the top of the nose to the cheekbone is divided, and the resulting vertex moves up and in to create the basis of orbits for the eyes.

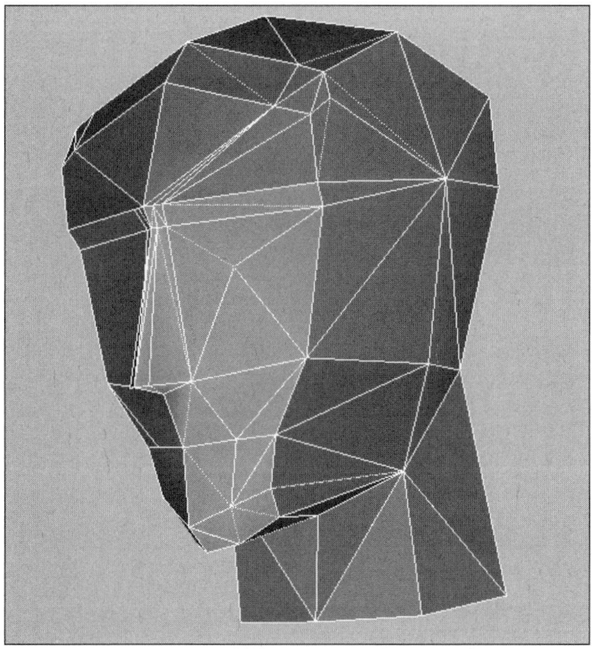

Figure 7.46

The mesh from Figure 7.45, with some additional rounding. A cut across the chin produces vertices that permit a basic reshaping of the jaw. At the top of the face, selected horizontal edges are chamfered to create roundness. The chamfering produces additional geometry at the ends, which requires editing or cleanup.

Using MeshSmooth

MeshSmooth is one of MAX's tools for subdividing many, if not all, of the faces of a mesh to create curvature. Nearly all organic models need a dense mesh to achieve the level of realism necessary in the computer graphics arenas of motion picture special effects, advertising, and high-end computer simulations. Because of the inherently higher facecounts, MeshSmooth is generally avoided when modeling for games or other low-polygon-count situations. To begin building an organic mesh, you must have a sense of how MeshSmooth affects geometry.

Geometric smoothing tools work within two dominating traditions, and both are preserved in the MeshSmooth modifier. The first is the concept of geometric smoothing of polygonal meshes by rounding the sharp edges. Using this approach, a polygonal mesh is essentially completed before the smoothing is applied to clean it up. The other tradition in smoothing is fundamentally different: Smoothing is applied to change rectilinear geometry into an object that tends to be sphere shaped. In this section, we'll examine the methods that incorporate both of these traditions.

Classic Smoothing

In MAX, the edge-rounding method is the Classic option. This option is not the default, so you must select it. Try this exercise to see the result of using this smoothing method:

1. Create a short, thick Tube in the Top viewport, near the origin. Use the default parameter settings, and then convert the Tube into an editable mesh.

2. Make a copy clone of the object and pull it next to the original so you can compare the before and after conditions. Apply the MeshSmooth modifier to the copy. Even before the Iterations value is increased, the object is smoother due to an automatic synchronization of the smoothing groups and the default Strength value of 0.5. Change from the default NURMS (Non-Uniform Rational MeshSmooth) Subdivision Method to the Classic type. With the Iterations value set to 2, your screen should look like Figure 7.47. With Iterations set to 5 (calculating this function may take a short while to complete), it should look like Figure 7.48. The price for the additional smoothness is enormous—the original Tube has 432 faces; the one with two iterations has 6,912 faces; and the one with five iterations has more than 442,000. Take a look at this step through an actual render to appreciate the texture of the second option, although the facecount probably makes the object impractical.

Note: *In a situation where a high-facecount object must be used in a scene, panning or zooming operations may take longer than you want. If this is the case, turn off the modifier (turning it on when it is time to render), use a proxy object as discussed in Chapter 5, or, in the case of MeshSmooth, use the Iterations and Smoothness fields in the Render Values group only and not in the first fields of the Subdivision Amount rollout. This allows the object to appear smoother in a rendering but unsmoothed in the viewports.*

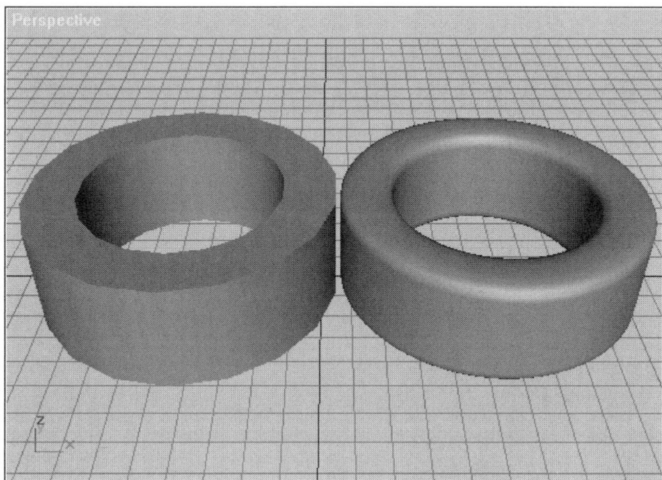

Figure 7.47
The Tube on the left is the starting point. The Tube on the right has the MeshSmooth modifier applied with the default Strength value of 0.5 and the algorithm run through two iterations.

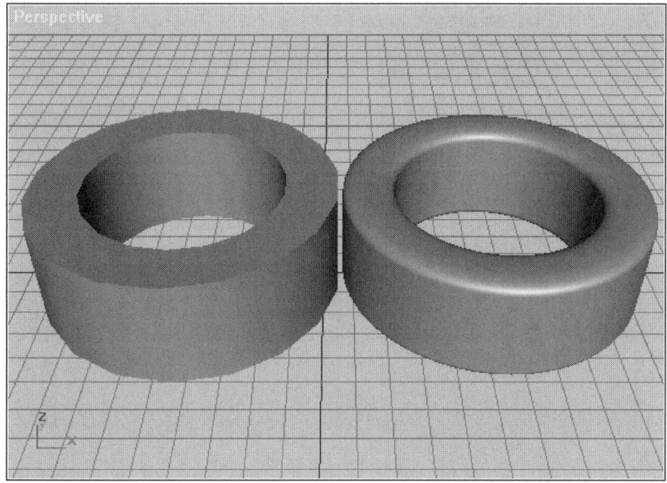

Figure 7.48
The same as Figure 7.47, but the Tube on the right has the MeshSmooth modifier applied with the Iterations value set to 5.

3. Set the Iterations value back to 2. Increase both the Strength and Relax values to their maximum values of 1. The Strength value pulls the edges tighter, and the Relax value spreads out the new edges to get a smoother result. This result is comparable to setting the Iterations value to 5 while using fewer than 2 percent of the faces.

4. Change the Subdivision Method to NURMS. NURMS surfaces have a slightly rounder appearance, closer to the output you would expect from a NURBS surface.

One of the greater strengths of the NURMS option is how it handles open edges. To see this process in action, open the file Chap7_meshsmooth.max from the CD-ROM. It consists of a low-polygon head. Now, follow these steps:

1. Apply a MeshSmooth modifier using the NURMS option and increase the Iterations value to 1. The appearance of the face is greatly improved.
2. Move back and forth among the NURMS, Classic, and Quad Output options, noting how each treats the eye, mouth, and open neck areas. NURMS is clearly the best choice in this instance. Figure 7.49 shows the model before and after applying the MeshSmooth modifier.

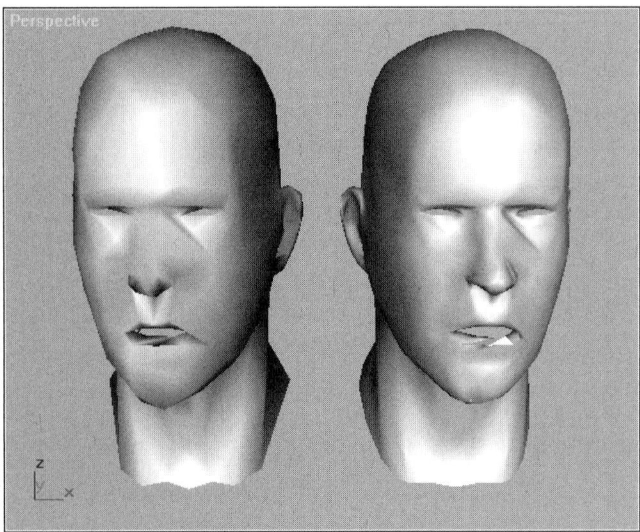

Figure 7.49
With the MeshSmooth modifier applied and using the NURMS option, the head on the right looks much better than the one on the left.

3. To refine the head even further, convert it back to a mesh, select only the polygons that compose the face, and pass them up to the MeshSmooth modifier. Doing so will help you avoid smoothing the top of the head further. You can follow this step with the MultiRes modifier to reduce the facecount in the noncritical areas.

Non-Classic Smoothing

This simple exercise gets you started on organic polygonal modeling with MeshSmooth. You may not think of a car as an organic object, but the typical curvature in today's auto body designs is very fluid and subtle. Follow these steps to design a smooth low-polygon car:

1. Create a Box primitive to serve as the main portion of the car body, without the roof. Create three segments along the side and two across the length. Use Figure 7.50 as a guide.

Figure 7.50
A Box primitive with proper segmentation, converted to an Editable Mesh object.

Convert the object to an editable mesh. Center the pivot point in the object. Center the object to the World space origin by moving it to (0,0,0) with the Transform Type-Ins.

2. Select the two "roof" polygons and extrude them up, as shown in Figure 7.51. Don't try any beveling. You're deliberately starting with a more boxy shape.

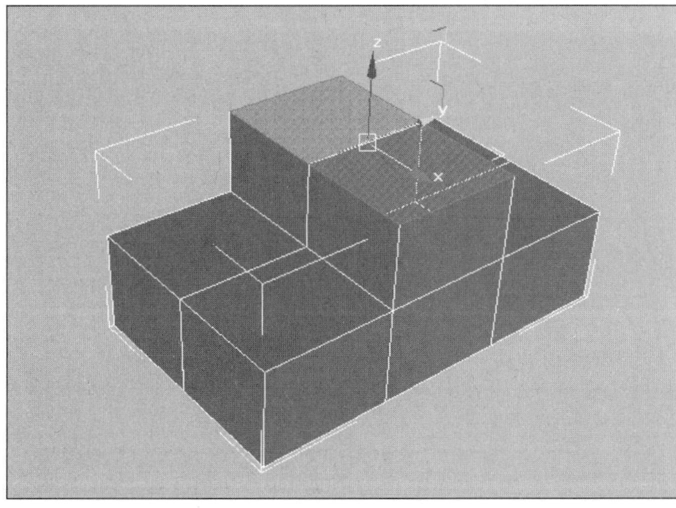

Figure 7.51
The Editable Mesh object from Figure 7.50, with polygons extruded up to make a roof.

3. You need only half the model. Select all the faces on either side of the centerline and delete them. Rename the model "driver's side" or "passenger's side," depending on which half remains. Rotate the model in the Perspective viewport to make sure it's hollow. Sometimes, internal faces are accidentally created when you extrude faces, as you did for the roof. If the mesh is not completely hollow along the centerline, delete any faces until it is.

4. Mirror the half as an instance and name the mirrored object appropriately. Apply a MeshSmooth modifier to either object—it will appear on both. Use the NURMS option with two iterations and make sure the Apply To Whole Mesh checkbox is selected. This option ensures that the entire mesh is smoothed, regardless of whether you select a subobject (such as a vertex) at the Editable Mesh level. Select the checkbox to display the control mesh. At this point, your model should look remarkably like a car, as shown in Figure 7.52.

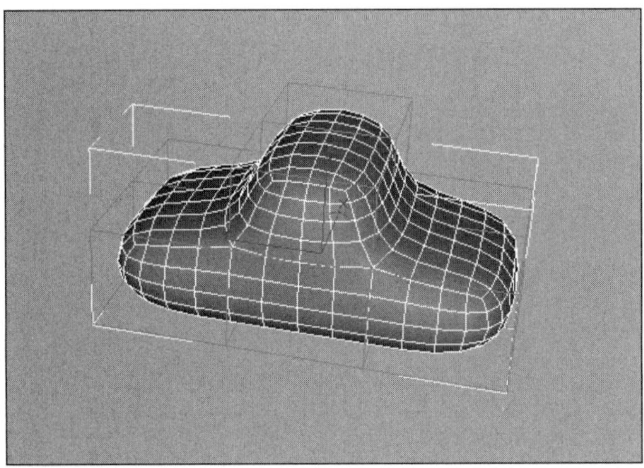

Figure 7.52
The mesh from Figure 7.51, with half of the faces deleted and the remaining faces mirrored as an instance to restore both sides of the car. The MeshSmooth modifier is applied by using NURMS with two iterations, and the control mesh is displayed around the smoothed object.

5. At this point, you can explore three directions: You can return to the Editable Mesh level and move vertices, you can add more segmentation, and you can try the effect of the NURMS weights. Move the vertices first. Go to the Editable Mesh level and make sure you can see the end result by clicking on the Show End Result toggle. Select and move some vertices, and watch the smoothed version of the mesh respond. The front vertices have been pulled out and the rear ones slanted in Figure 7.53.

6. Segmentation has a very important effect on smoothing; tighter segmentation creates sharper curvature. In MAX, you can experiment with this concept in an interactive way. Add a Slice modifier to the stack below the MeshSmooth modifier—it must be below if the effect is to be passed up to MeshSmooth. Make sure you are not in a subobject mode when you add the Slice modifier, or it won't work. If you make this mistake, delete the Slice modifier, get out of the subobject mode, and then reapply the Slice modifier. In the Slice

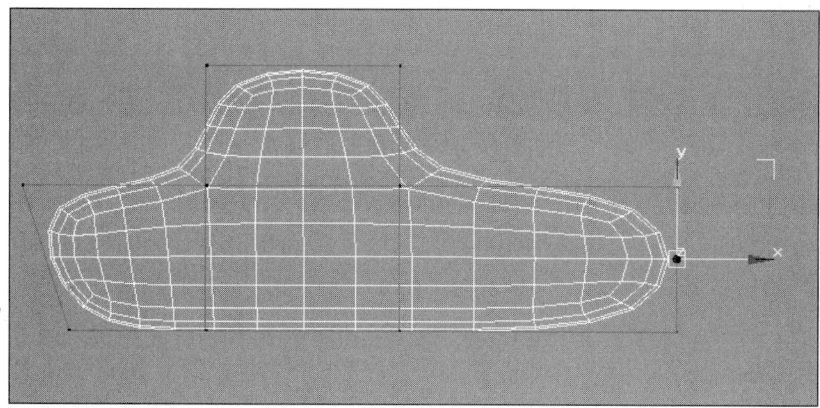

Figure 7.53
The vertices are translated in the underlying Editable Mesh object to shape the smoothed version interactively. The front vertices, shown selected here, were pulled forward.

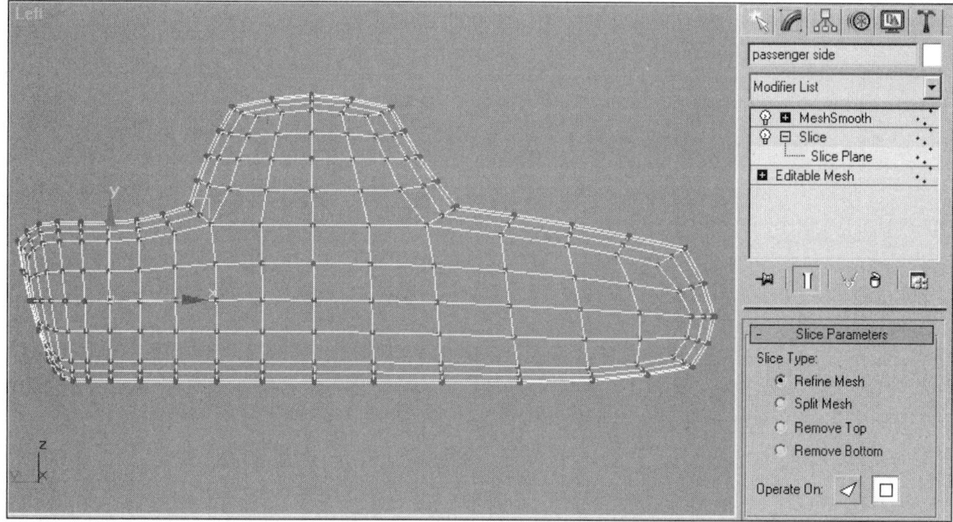

Figure 7.54
A Slice modifier is added beneath the MeshSmooth modifier on the stack and rotated vertically. Passing the new segmentation through the rear of the car sharpens the curvature.

modifier, enter the subobject mode to get the slice plane. Rotate it so it's running vertically through the mesh, and move it back and forth to see what happens. Figure 7.54 shows how placing the new edges close to the rear sharpens that region.

7. Add more slice planes in different directions to better understand the effect of segmentation on smoothing. When you have a result you like, collapse the new segment into the editable mesh. Right-click on the Slice modifier in the Stack View window, and select the Collapse To button to dismiss the Slice modifier but retain its effects in the resulting editable mesh. When you finish,

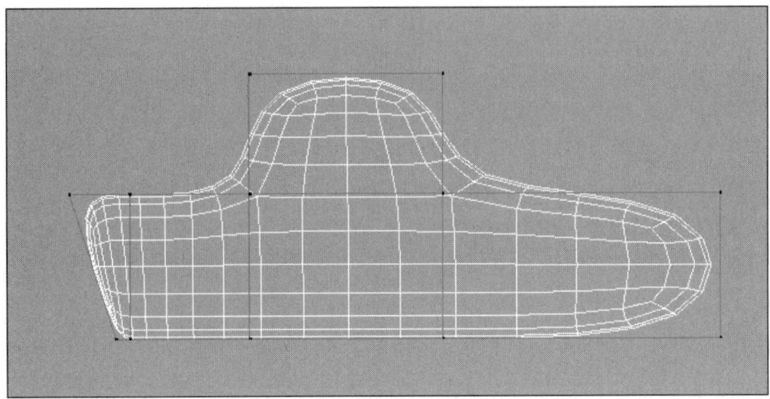

Figure 7.55
The Slice modifier added in Figure 7.54 is collapsed into the editable mesh, creating new vertices for editing.

the new segment is simply part of the mesh, creating new vertices to edit; this is illustrated in Figure 7.55.

8. Try the Weight tools. In the MeshSmooth modifier, enter the Vertex subobject level and select the vertices at the rear of the car. Be aware that the MeshSmooth modifier must be set to use at least one iteration for the Weight tool to be effective. Increase the Weight value at the bottom of the panel to pull the mesh into the corners. You may need to work separately on the top and bottom vertices. The result should look something like Figure 7.56.

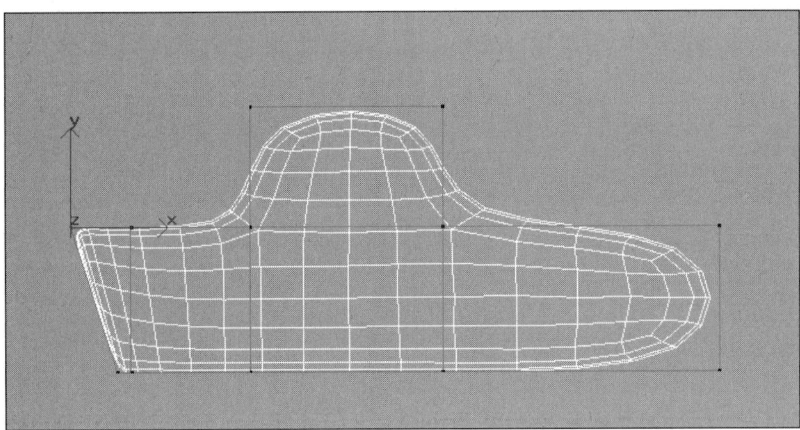

Figure 7.56
The Weight values of the rear vertices increase to pull the mesh in more tightly.

9. After experimenting with all these tools, you will achieve a basic shape you like—but it requires more refinement. Reduce your MeshSmooth Iteration level to 1 and collapse the entire stack to produce a new, more-detailed mesh model for editing, as shown in Figure 7.57. Apply MeshSmooth to this mesh and continue with the process.

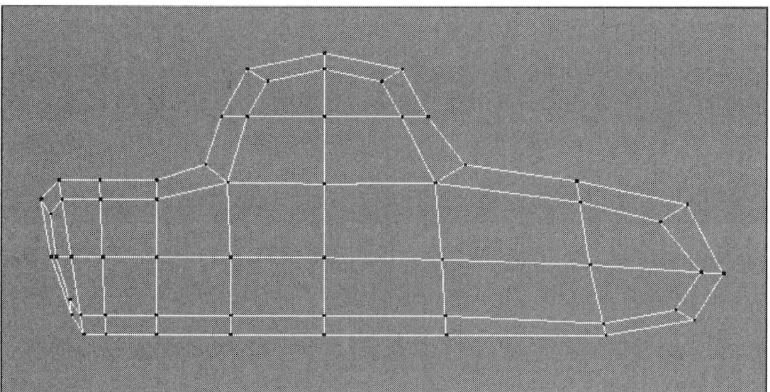

Figure 7.57
The mesh from Figure 7.56, with MeshSmooth reduced to a single iteration and the entire stack collapsed. This more-detailed mesh is ready for more editing and another round of MeshSmooth.

Moving On

This chapter covered the tools that are available to help you edit meshes at their most basic levels. It explained the methods for editing vertices, edges, polygons, and elements—including chamfering, extruding, and beveling, among others.

The next chapter will discuss compound objects such as Lofts, which extrude one shape along another, and Boolean functions, which combine, subtract, or determine the overlapping portions of two objects. The chapter will also discuss Connect (which connects two objects), ShapeMerge (which combines a spline and a mesh), and the other compound objects that use multiple objects to create a single one.

Chapter 8

Compound Objects

A *compound object* is one that requires the use of two or more objects to create a third. By using Boolean functions, meshes (or splines) can be combined, one subtracted from the other, or any overlapping portion retained while the remainder is discarded. A Loft object uses one or more splines as cross-section elements and another as a path they follow. In MAX, the individual elements of compound objects become subobjects themselves; therefore, you can edit them to change the result of the compounding operation.

The Terrain tool creates smooth or faceted landscape meshes, usually based on topography information from other software programs. The Connect tool is used to combine two open-ended meshes into a single, seamless object, and ShapeMerge creates edges on the surface of a mesh based on the information passed from a spline. Scatter can place many instances of an object either randomly in the scene, randomly across the surface of another object, or in a structured pattern on another object's surface.

The Morph object shifts an object's shape between the original configuration and one or more target configurations over time. Although this functionality largely has been replaced with the Morpher modifier, it is still useful for simple morph projects and will be covered here. Often, Morph is used with the Conform tool, which matches the surface of one object with that of another and can be used to make suitable morph targets from different types of objects.

New to 3ds max 4 is the Mesher compound object. Several rules apply when it comes to Space Warps and modifiers; for example, a Bend modifier has no real effect on a particle system, and object Space Warps are always superseded by World Space Warps. Mesher bends these rules by creating an instanced geometry substitute for the original object that can show the result of World Space modifiers and the modifiers that would not normally have an effect on certain objects. For example, a Bend modifier can bend a Mesher substitute for a particle system.

Without the procedures and tools available to create compound objects in 3ds max 4 and discussed in this chapter, achieving your desired final result may be difficult, if not impossible. Starting with the Boolean possibilities, you'll work through exercises that expose the different compound objects.

Boolean Objects

When you're using meshes, a Boolean operation requires two distinct objects. These objects can be joined together (Union); one can be subtracted from another (Subtraction); or, if they overlap, the shared volume can be retained (Intersection). In each case, a new object is created to take the place of the previous two. The original objects are not lost, however; they become the subobjects of the Boolean compound object. These subobjects, called *operands*, can be accessed and edited to change the result of the operation. Also, because the operands have been retained, the Boolean operation itself can be switched between the three types, or the original objects can be extracted.

The Boolean operation is performed on the object selected when the operation is initiated, and this operand's name is retained. This object is called Operand A, and the second object is called Operand B.

In the Create|Compound Objects panel, the Pick Boolean rollout lists four choices for the way Operand B is treated. Move (the default) essentially eliminates the second operand as an object in itself, but retains its information as a subobject of the Boolean compound object. This option is used when the object's sole purpose is to be an operand and not another feature in the scene. Copy, as you would expect, uses a clone of the selected object as the operand and leaves the original intact. Be aware that the original may obstruct your view of the final result until it is moved. The two other choices link changes to the operand with the original object either one way (Reference) or both ways (Instance).

Subtraction is probably the most commonly conducted Boolean operation. Without it, or without an extensive mesh-editing session, you cannot remove one complex shape from another. The Union operation is similar to the Attach tool in the Edit Mesh and Editable Mesh panels, but it has an added strength. When two objects are attached, any faces that are buried within one of the objects remain there and exist as extraneous elements. When two objects are unioned, interior faces are eliminated, resulting in a cleaner model and a lower facecount. Some unique shapes can be created with the Intersection function, which retains overlapping geometry; it is often used to check for an unwanted overlapping condition.

Boolean Stability

Boolean operations have become more stable with each major release of MAX, but they still consist of complex mathematical processes. It's a good practice to use the Edit|Hold command prior to executing a Boolean operation to ensure that you can get back to the scene with the Edit|Fetch command, prior to the Boolean command being issued.

Subtraction

This exercise will introduce you to the Boolean Subtraction function as well as several of the tools and procedures that span the different types of Boolean operations. Having two operands with overlapping, coplanar faces or collinear edges used to be a situation to be avoided when performing a Boolean operation, because you had to rely on MAX to decide how the faces should be treated. In 3ds max 4, this is no longer an issue; in this exercise, however, the text spline is extended beyond the Box in both directions for clarity. Follow these steps:

1. Create a short Box in the Top viewport with one segment in each direction, and a Text spline in the upper-left corner. Use one of the less complex fonts, such as Arial, to reduce the length of time required to calculate the subtraction. Extrude the Text to a height greater than that of the Box. Move it in the negative Z-direction so that it extends past the Box on both sides. Figures 8.1 and 8.2 show the initial layout for this exercise.

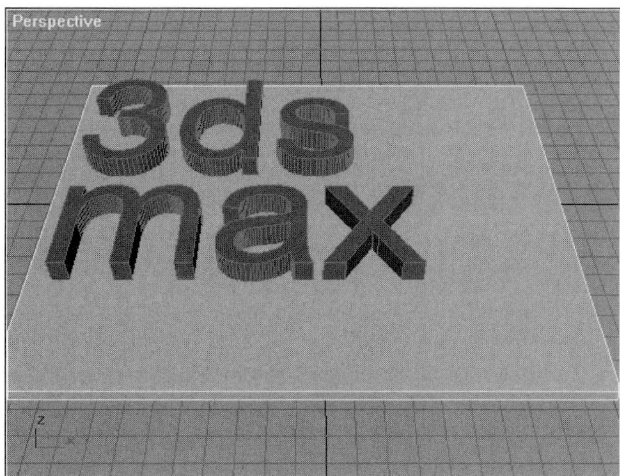

Figure 8.1
A Box primitive with an extruded Text spline in the corner.

2. Select the Box Go To Create|Geometry|Compound Objects and click on the Boolean button.

3. The intent here is to subtract the letters (Operand B) from the Box (Operand A). In the Operands group of the Parameters rollout, Box01 is designated as A, but B is yet to be assigned. Ensure that Subtraction (A-B) is the active option in the Operation group.

4. In the Pick Boolean rollout (discussed earlier), choose the Move option and click on Pick Operand B. Select the extruded text. Figure 8.3 shows one possible result. Because of the mesh-density discrepancy between the two objects, the Boolean algorithm made some choices regarding the vertex locations that caused the top surface of the Box operand to be inconsistent and shadows to appear. A closer face complexity is needed for a better end result.

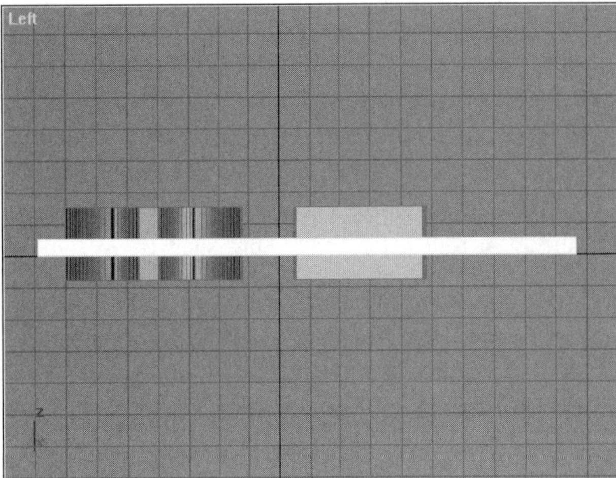

Figure 8.2
The extruded Text is moved in the negative Z-direction so that it extends beyond the Box on both sides.

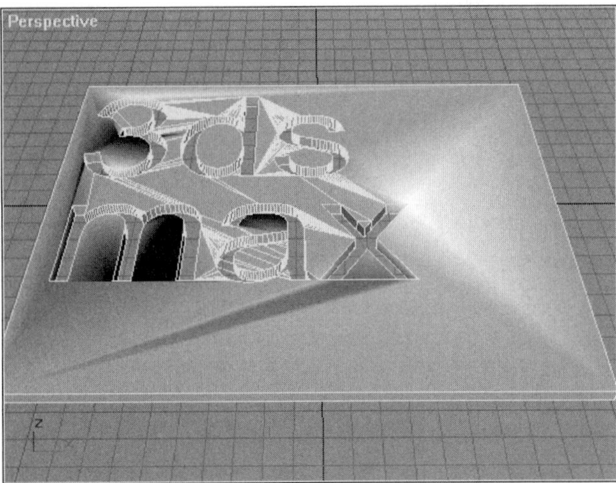

Figure 8.3
Because of the great mesh-density discrepancy, the Boolean operation may yield undesirable results, such as inconsistent surfaces.

5. Undo until before the Boolean operation; two objects should appear in the scene. Increase the Box's segmentation to 30×30×5. Because most of the faces of the final product will be coplanar, an Optimize or MultiRes application will reduce the facecount significantly. Reselect the Text object as Operand B in a Boolean compound object. The result will look similar to Figure 8.4.

6. The operation as it stands is not a fixed outcome. Cycle through the Union, Intersection, and Subtraction (B-A) Operation choices (they may take a few seconds to execute) and see how they affect the operands differently. Return to the Subtraction (A-B) option.

Figure 8.4
With more segmentation in the Box, the end result (shown with Edged Faces turned off) is much better.

The object looks good, but let's change it to make the Text center justified and centered on the Box. To do this, you must edit the operands. Follow these steps:

1. Go to the Modify tab and, in the Display group of the Display/Update rollout, highlight the Operands option. The Text object reappears, similar to the Union operation choice, making it selectable. With the Operand B: Text01 subobject selected in the Parameters rollout, the Stack View window should look like Figure 8.5.

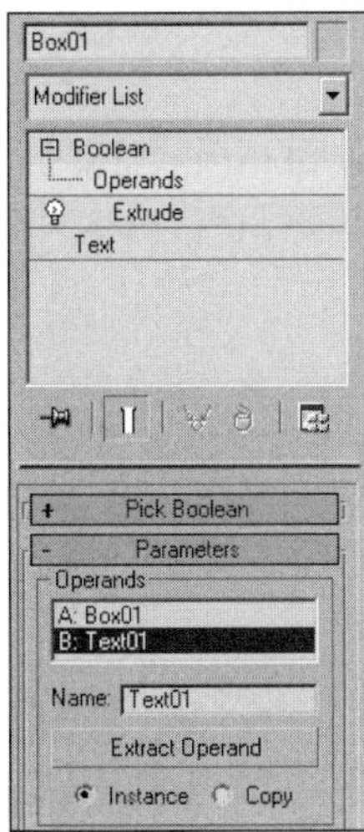

Figure 8.5
With Operand B: Text01 selected in the Parameters rollout, the expanded Stack View window indicates that you are at the Operands subobject level.

2. Go to the Text level in the Stack View window. Center justify the Text and, if you like, change the content itself.

3. Go to the Operands level in the Stack View; you may need to reselect the Operands option in the Display/Update rollout. Use the Align tool to center the Text in the X- and Y-directions on the Box. Go back to the Boolean level and choose the Result + Hidden Ops display option. The object should look similar to the one shown in Figure 8.6.

Figure 8.6
With the Text operand selected, the subobject was moved and justified; then, the Result + Hidden Ops display option was selected.

Extracting and Animating an Operand

If the need arises, you can extract one of the operands into a copy or instance of the one used in the compound object. To see how this process works, follow along with this continuation of the previous exercise:

1. With the Text operand still selected, ensure that the Instance option is selected in the Parameters rollout of the Boolean level. Enter a new name for the extracted object in the Name field—leaving it named the default Text01 may cause it to be confused with the Text01 operand. Click on the Extract Operand button. The new object is created in the same location and configuration as the operand it came from. Move it so you can see the scene objects clearly.

2. Because the new Text object is an instance of the operand, any modifiers applied to one affect the other, as well. Select the extracted Text object and apply a Bend modifier above the Extrude modifier; set the Angle value to 45 and the Bend Axis value to Y. Figure 8.7 shows the new configuration of the Boolean object and the instanced Text.

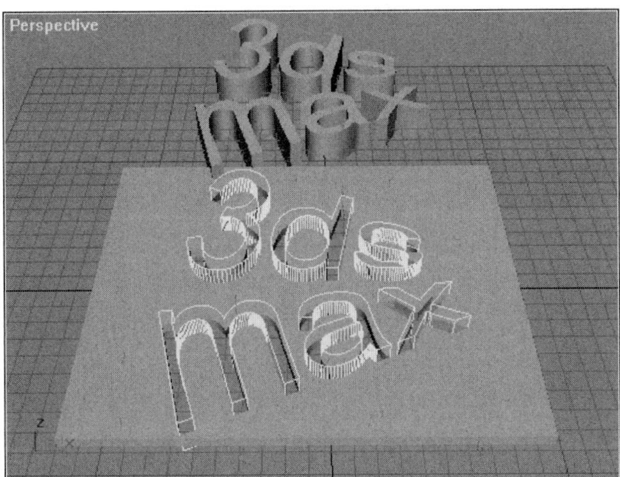

Figure 8.7
The extracted Text is an instance of the Text01 operand, so the Bend modifier applied to the extracted object affects the operand as well.

Like most other things in MAX, you can animate the modifications and locations of the operands. To see the animation in action, you can either view the file named Chap8 Boolean.avi on the CD-ROM using the File|View Image File tool or create your own AVI file by following these steps (rendering will be covered fully in Chapter 15):

1. Move the Time Slider at the bottom of the screen to Frame 100, click on the Animate button, and change the Angle value for the Bend modifier to –45. Turn off the Animate button.

2. Click on the Render Scene button in the Main toolbar, choose the Active Time Segment option in the Common Parameters rollout of the Render Scene dialog box, and click on the Files button in the Render Output group. Enter a file name in the Render Output File dialog box that opens and choose AVI from the Save As Type drop-down list. Click on the Save button.

3. Click on OK in the Video Compression dialog box to accept the default. Back in the Render Scene dialog box, click on the Render button to create the AVI file.

Union and Intersection

To begin the exercise that demonstrates the Boolean Union and Intersection options, create a Box with a Sphere centered on each corner, as shown in Figure 8.8. Leave the Spheres at their default segmentation and segment the Box at 30×30×5. A Boolean operation can consist only of two operands. Therefore, you can use two methods to combine all four Spheres and the Box: Union one Sphere to the Box and then each Sphere to the subsequent object, creating a nested

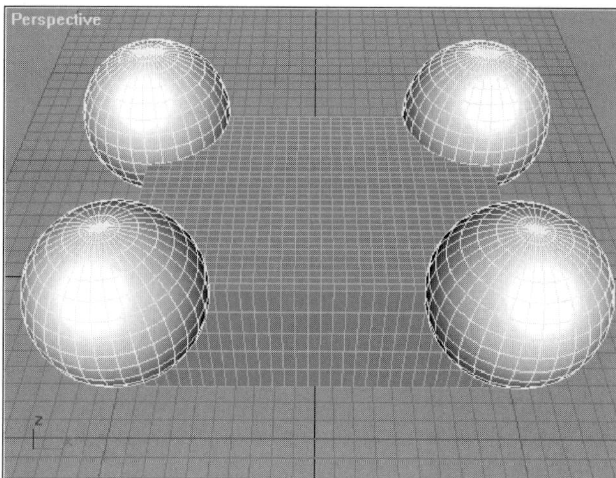

Figure 8.8
A well-segmented Box primitive with a Sphere centered on each corner.

Boolean; or attach the Spheres together to make a single mesh for the second operand. You'll use the second method in this exercise. Follow these steps:

1. Select one of the Spheres and convert it to an editable mesh. Use the Attach tool to combine the other three Spheres with the mesh.

Using Multiple, Editable Operands

Any time two or more objects must be used in a Boolean operation, you must adhere to a strict procedure. Once the first Boolean is created, you cannot simply click on the Pick Operand B button again to select the next object—doing so will replace the first object. You must reenter the Boolean command and use the Boolean compound object as an operand in the next Boolean operation. This technique will allow you to go back several layers deep and edit the operands of the nested Boolean objects.

---

2. Select the Box and, using the Spheres as Operand B, union the two objects together. Figure 8.9 illustrates one of the differences between using the union and attach approaches to combining the objects: The compound object at the top has eliminated the interior faces of the Box that reside inside the Spheres, thereby eliminating approximately 600 faces (which are not visible, anyway).

3. Switch from the Union option to Intersection. What remains is the volume that is shared between the Box and the Spheres, or one-eighth of each sphere.

The Collapse Utility

Under the Utilities tab of the Command Panel is the Collapse tool, which provides much of the functionality of the Boolean tools. Collapse may be quicker to use in some cases, but it does not let you edit the operands and is not an undoable function.

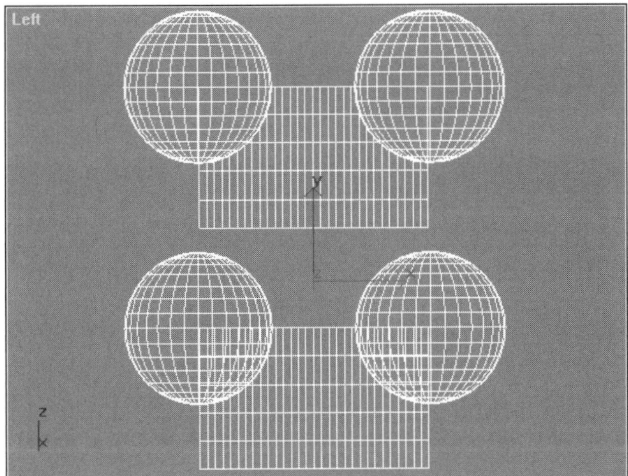

Figure 8.9
The compound object (*top*), using the Union Boolean function, eliminates the Box faces that are buried within the Spheres. The attached objects (*bottom*) retain the buried faces.

Cut

The Cut Boolean function works similarly to the Slice modifier, in that it adds edges and vertices to the operand but does not add or subtract from the total volume. To begin this exercise, open the file Chap8 Cut.max from the CD-ROM; it consists of a Box with a Cylinder near each corner, as shown in Figure 8.10. The Cylinders have been converted to editable meshes and attached together. Follow these steps:

1. Select the Box. Go to Create|Geometry|Compound Objects|Boolean. Choose the Cut and Refine options, click on the Pick Operand B button, and select one of the Cylinders. The

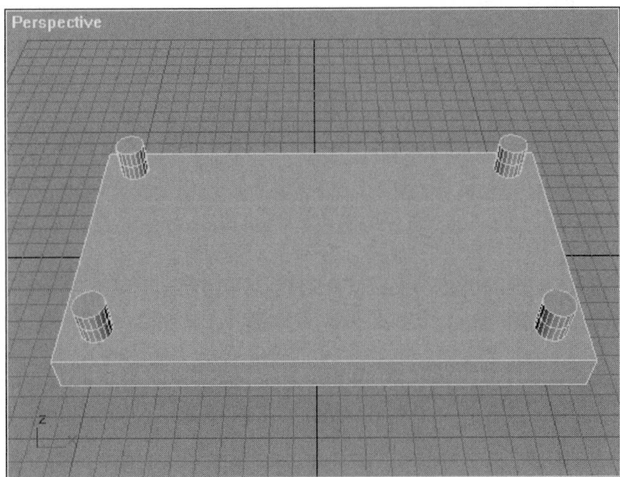

Figure 8.10
The starting point for the Cut exercise, consisting of a Box with a Cylinder near each corner.

Cylinders disappear, and only edges remain around the perimeter where they intersected the Box.

2. The edges and faces that have been created can be extruded, beveled, or subjected to any of the other operations possible using the Edit Mesh modifier.

Spline Booleans

The same Boolean operations that can be performed on meshes (with the exception of Cut) can also be performed on splines. The one notable difference is that whereas mesh Booleans use completely different mesh objects as operands, spline Booleans must use different spline subobjects of the same spline.

This exercise will introduce you to the techniques used to create complex splines using spline Boolean operations:

1. In the Top viewport, draw the spline objects shown in Figure 8.11. Be sure to deselect the Start New Shape checkbox after creating the first spline so that only one object is created, consisting of four noncontiguous spline subobjects.

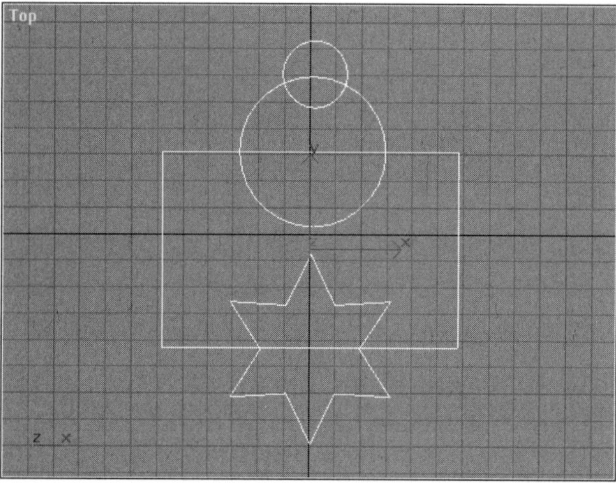

Figure 8.11
A Rectangle, two Circles, and a Star spline subobjects make up the single spline that will be used in this exercise.

2. In the Stack View window, expand the Editable Spline entry and highlight the Spline subobject level. The spline Boolean commands are found and initiated at this level.

3. Select the Rectangle spline. Scroll down to the Geometry rollout and pan upwards until you see the Boolean button and the three options to the right of it. Ensure that the Union option is selected. Click on the Boolean button to activate it.

4. Move your cursor over the splines, and it will change shape to indicate when it is over a valid object. Select the Star and then the large Circle. You will trim both these shapes and the Rectangle to make one contiguous spline subobject with all overlapping segments eliminated.
5. Switch from Union mode to Subtraction mode and select the small Circle to eliminate it and any portion of the large spline object with which it shared a volume. Return to the Editable Spline level. The resulting spline should look similar to the one in Figure 8.12.

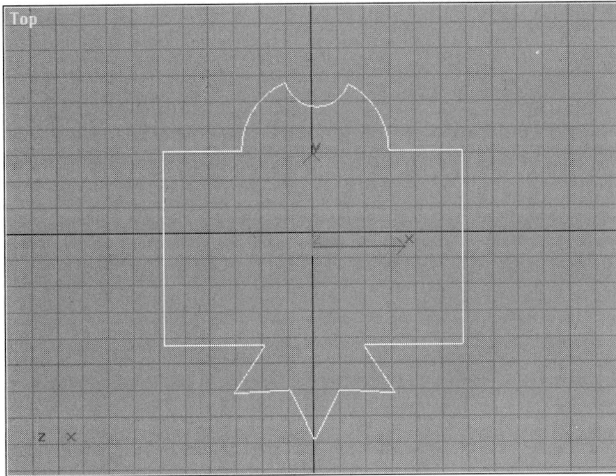

Figure 8.12
The Editable Spline object after performing the Union and Subtraction spline Boolean operations.

Unlike mesh Booleans, you cannot go back into the objects stack and edit the operands for the spline Boolean operations.

Loft Objects

When you use the Extrude modifier, a 2D spline is drawn out into a 3D object perpendicular to itself. Similarly, a Loft compound object also draws out splines into geometry; however, it accomplishes the task by extruding them along a second spline called a *path*. The path may be open or closed, but it must be one contiguous spline; the lofted spline, referred to as the *shape*, can be of any configuration. The shape becomes the cross section at any point along the path.

The Boolean object *absorbs* the components used to make it, whereas a Loft object is created in addition to its components. The two splines still exist in the scene and are readily available to be edited. Because the Loft object is parametric, it maintains a link with its components; therefore, editing them will result in changes to the appearance or configuration of the Loft. If the splines are deleted, the link is broken, and the Loft's shape is fixed relative to its cross sections and path. MAX also lets you control the visibility and segmentation of the Loft, and allows the cross section to change at different locations along its length. Lofts can be used to make anything from fancy, extruded text to roller-coaster rails.

Using a Single Cross-Section Shape

Either spline can be used as the starting point for a Loft object. If the path is the starting point, the shape will be moved to its first vertex and then along the path. If the shape is the starting point, the path will then be moved, and the Loft will initiate from the shape's location. More often than not, it makes sense to draw the spline first, in the location the Loft will reside, and move the shape to it. The following exercise will explain how to create a simple Loft object and the effects of changing the splines:

1. Reset the scene. In the Front viewport, create a short Text spline with a Size value of 50 units. In the Top viewport, draw a straight Line with two segments, with the first vertex near the bottom of the viewport. The layout should look similar to Figure 8.13.

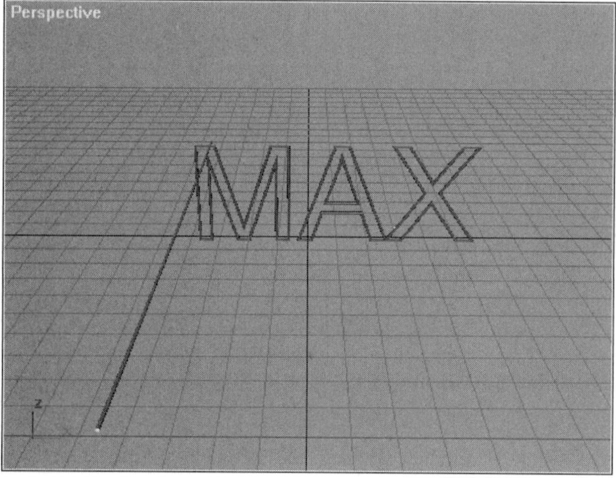

Figure 8.13
The two splines that will compose the Loft. For clarity, the Display Render Mesh option is selected in the splines' Rendering rollouts.

2. Select the Text. Use the Scale Transform Type-Ins to decrease its size by one quarter by entering "75" in the available X field at the bottom of the screen after activating the Uniform Scale transform.

3. Select the Line. Go to Create|Geometry|Compound Objects|Loft. In the Creation Method rollout, both the Get Path and Get Shape buttons are available, which means the line can be either the path or the shape component. If the Text was selected and the Loft command had started, only the Get Path option would be available. Why? Because the Text is not a

valid path (it is made of noncontiguous splines), so it is restricted to being the shape component of the Loft.

4. Click on Get Shape and move the cursor over both objects in the scene. The changing cursor shape indicates that both objects are valid shapes and that the Line can be both the path and the shape. Select the Line first and, in the Left viewport, you'll see that it becomes the cross section of a grid-like object.
5. Undo the previous action. Select the Line again and reenter the Loft command. This time, select the Text as the shape. Your scene should resemble the one shown in Figure 8.14.

Figure 8.14
The Loft object created using the Line as the path and the Text as the shape.

Note: *For a nice end effect, select the Display Render Mesh checkbox in the shape's Render rollout. Doing so generates a rim around the Text that would be difficult to create by any other means.*

Two obvious conditions need to be addressed. First, the Text in the Loft is facing the wrong direction. Although this would not be an issue with a symmetrical shape, in this situation it must be corrected. Simply rotating the Loft would work in this case; if the path was a more complex spline, however, rotating would not be a solution. The shape is turned to face along the path, which is going from near to far in the Perspective viewport.

The second item of concern is the size of the Text, which is larger than the shape used. When MAX applies the transforms, they are the last operations executed before the objects are displayed on the screen. The Text object is a 50-unit-high primitive with a 75 percent Scale transform applied, but the shape being passed to the Loft object is the 50-unit-high Text before the transform.

To remedy these conditions, follow these steps:

1. Use the Select Objects dialog box to see that three objects exist in the scene. Select Line01 and move it so you can see both of its ends. Go to the Vertex subobject level, noting the box around the first vertex of the line, and select the vertex at the opposite end. Click on the Make First button in the Geometry rollout to reverse the Line's orientation and, therefore, the orientation of the lofted Text. Your scene should now look like Figure 8.15. Go back to the top level of the Line object in the Stack View window.

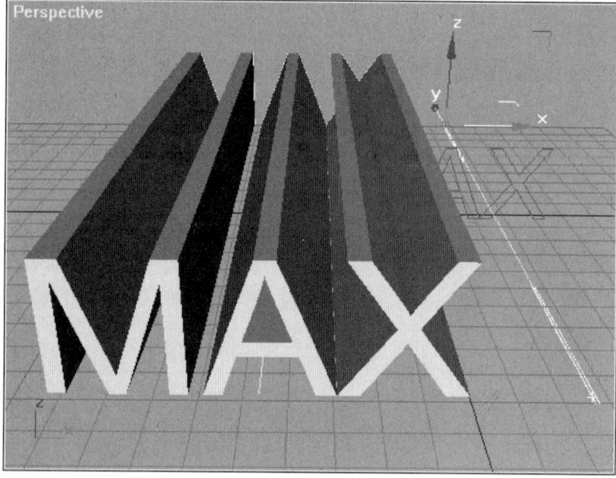

Figure 8.15
With the orientation of the path reversed, the shape now faces in the correct direction to extrude the Text in a readable fashion.

2. To change the Text height, or even the Text content, used in the Loft, edit the spline's Size or Text field.

3. You can also edit the contour of the path spline to change the result of the Loft. Select the path again and go to the Vertex subobject level. Select both vertices and use the Quad menu to change their types to Bezier. One tangent handle is available for each vertex, and they lie in line with the spline itself. Select the handles one at a time and move them slightly in the negative X-direction to add curvature to the Loft, as shown in Figure 8.16.

Display and Resolution

A Loft can be a very dense object, depending on the number of cross sections required to define it properly and the complexity of the shape. MAX provides the controls to adjust the density of the Loft and the way it is displayed in the viewports. As you can see from the angled faces of the letters in the previous example, MAX has smoothed the transition between the faces. The

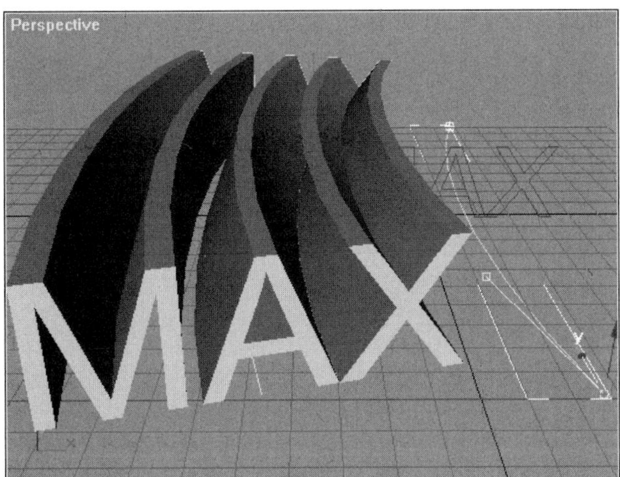

Figure 8.16
By changing the vertices to Bezier types and adding curvature to the path, curvature is also added to the Loft.

segmentation is obvious along the edges at the tops of the Text, however. To make this segmentation less evident, you need to add segmentation along the Loft itself.

In the Loft's Skin Parameters rollout, the two entries at the top of the Options group determine the segmentation of the Loft in relation to its individual components. Shape Steps sets the number of segments that occur between each of the vertices of the cross section, and Path Steps sets the number of steps between each cross section or the last cross section and the end of the Loft. The other settings in the Options group determine how the final output of the Loft command will appear.

In the Display group, two choices are available: Skin and Skin In Shaded. When Skin In Shaded is the only active choice, the faces of the Loft will be visible in shaded or rendered viewports only, whereas only the components (the shape and path) will be visible in the Wireframe viewports. This option can help clean up the Wireframe viewports and make the Pan and Zoom operations quicker. When Skin is selected, Lofts appear in all viewports.

Continuing with the exercise, follow these steps:

1. Select the Loft and open its Skin Parameters rollout. Change the Path Steps value from 5 to 10. The noticeable segmentation along the length of the Loft is reduced.
2. Decrease the number of Shape Steps to zero, and all segments between the vertices of the cross sections become straight. Increasing the value beyond its default should be done only with very complex shapes and can greatly increase the number of faces in an object.

3. Deselect the Skin checkbox. The Loft object appears only in the shaded Perspective viewport. Select Skin but deselect Skin In Shaded, and the reverse is true. Make sure both checkboxes in the Display area are selected before continuing.

Using the Loft Deformation Tools

The Loft deformation tools are available at the bottom of the Modify panel, but not in the Command panel, when a Loft is selected. The Scale, Twist, Teeter, and Bevel options control the treatment of the cross section at any given percentage along the path, and Fit forces the top and sides of the Loft to conform to different spline shapes. The application of the Scale and Twist deformation tools will be demonstrated in the following exercise; Teeter and Bevel effects can be achieved more easily with tools found in other parts of MAX.

Continue the previous exercise with the objects you created, or open the file Chap8 Deform.max from the CD-ROM. Now, follow these steps:

1. Hide the Line and Text objects. Select the Loft. Go to the Modify tab, expand the Deformations rollout, and activate the Scale option. Doing so opens the Scale Deformation dialog box for the Loft object's local X-axis, as shown in Figure 8.17.

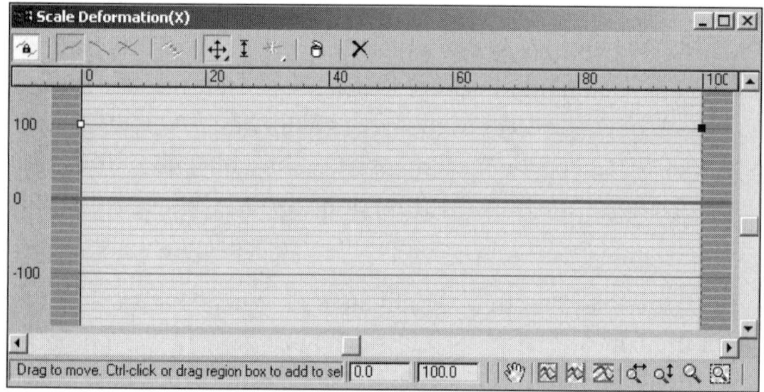

Figure 8.17
The Scale Deformation dialog box in which you change the Loft object's cross-sectional scale along the path.

2. The light gray area, which spans from 0 to 100 along the top ruler bar, represents the total length of the Loft broken into percentages. The red line that spans the gray area is the spline that determines the Loft's scale, in the local X-axis, along its length. This is a straight line at the 100 level, indicating that the scale is at a constant 100 percent of the cross section's size. Click on the Move Control Point button in the dialog box's top toolbar and move the left vertex downward to a value of about 50. (You can also type the exact value into the far-right field at the bottom of the dialog box.) The scale of the cross section changes from 50 percent scale at the first vertex (background) to 100 percent scale at the

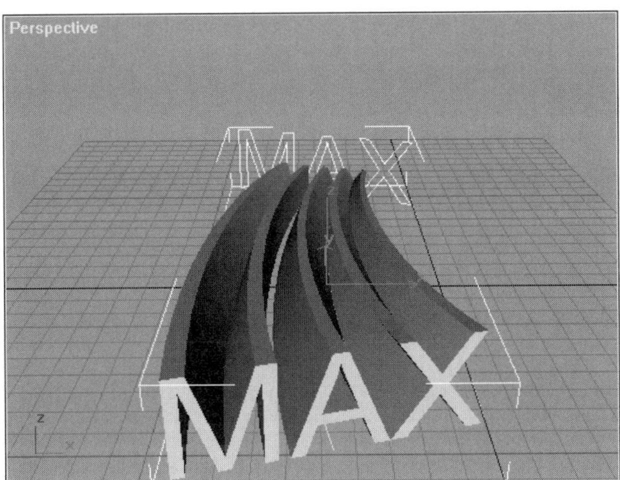

Figure 8.18
The Loft object with the X-axis and (by default) Y-axis scaled from 50 percent to 100 percent along the length of the path.

last vertex (foreground), as shown in Figure 8.18. Notice that both the X and Y dimensions are scaled, because the Make Symmetrical button in the dialog box's upper-left corner is active by default.

3. Deactivate the Make Symmetrical mode and click on the Display Y Axis button. The red X spline is replaced with a green Y spline that follows the same XYZ=RGB color convention used with the Transform Gizmo. Move the left vertex to a value of 10 and the right vertex to 120. These settings modify the Loft so it begins scaling at 10-percent size in the Y-axis and ends at 120 percent, giving it a flat-to-tall appearance.

4. The transitions do not have to be smooth and linear. Click on the Insert Corner Point button and place a new vertex midway along the Y-axis spline. Use the left entry field to place it at 50 percent of the length and the right entry field to place it at a scale value of 65—half the height between the first and last vertices. Right-click on the new vertex and change its type to Bezier-Smooth; this exposes its tangent handles. Use the Move Control Point tool from the Scale Deformation toolbar, and move the right handle down and a bit to the left to add a varying height effect to the Loft along its Y-axis. Click on the Display XY Axes button to show both axes at the same time. Figure 8.19 shows both the Scale-deformed Loft and the Scale Deformation dialog box.

5. Close the dialog box. Turn off the Scale deformation's effect by clicking on the light bulb icon to the right of the Scale button in the Deformations rollout. Activate the Twist deformation, and a similar dialog box will open. The twist is applied to both axes equally, so the axis-related buttons in the Twist Deformation dialog box are grayed out. The ruler bar

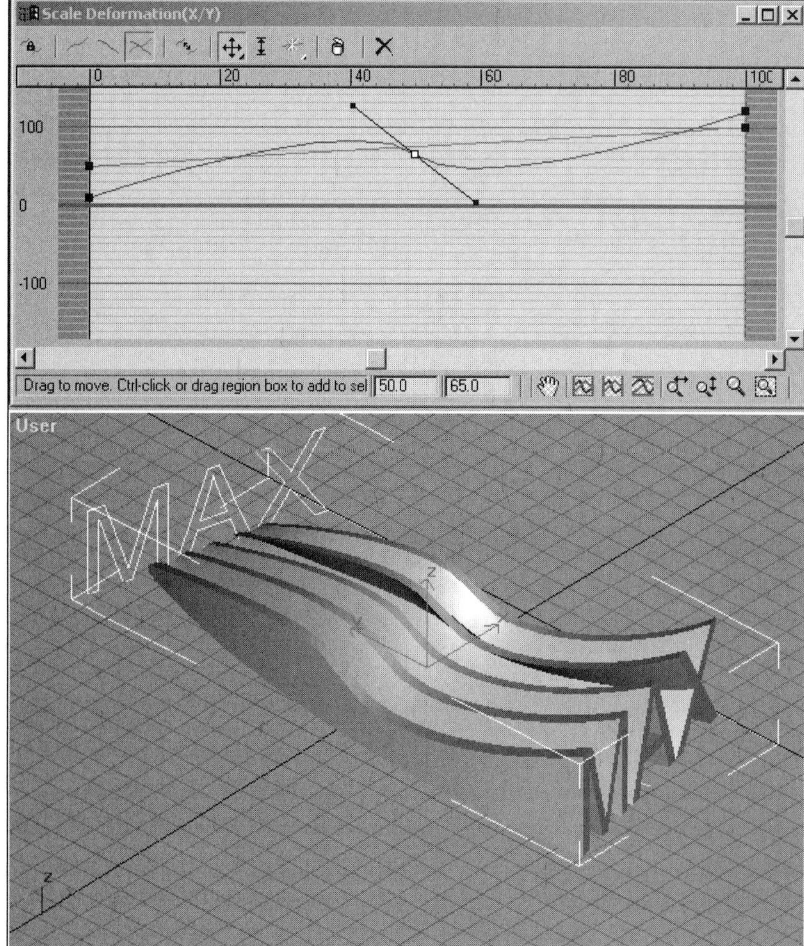

Figure 8.19
The Scale Deformation dialog box showing the changes to both the X- and Y-axes' scales and the deformations that result on the Loft object.

along the top of the dialog box again measures the position along the length of the path, but the vertical scale now measures the twist angle in degrees. Move the left vertex down to a value of –180 to cause a half-revolution twist along the length of the Loft, as illustrated in Figure 8.20.

Lofting Multiple Shapes along a Path

It is often desirable to make a cross section change its shape along a path, rather than just its scale or other deformable parameters. In MAX, the procedure to do this is fairly straightforward. The Path Parameters rollout contains the controls that determine where along the path the shapes are applied. The Path value determines where along the path the next selected

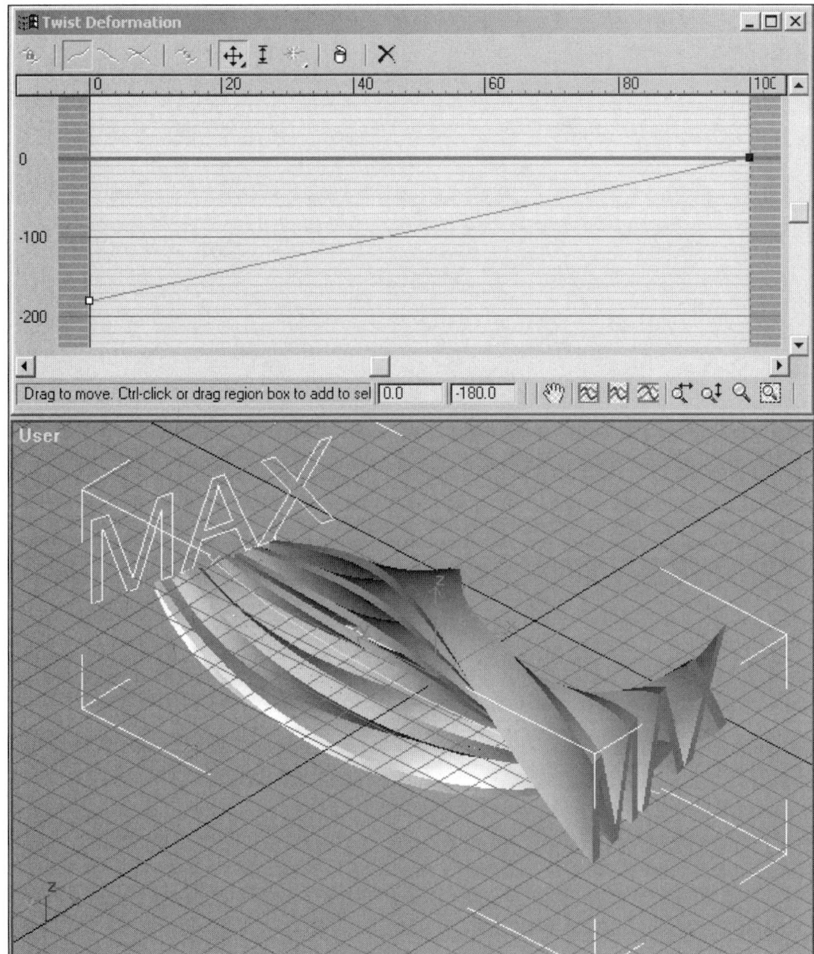

Figure 8.20
The Twist Deformation dialog box shows the change to the twist angle and the deformation that results on the Loft object.

shape will be applied, and the Percentage and Distance radio buttons determine what type of measurement the Path value refers to. In the previous exercises, the Path value has been set at its default value of 0.0, so the shapes applied have started at the first vertex and extend the length of the path.

In this exercise, you'll use four shapes and a path to create the column shown in Figure 8.21. Follow these steps:

1. Open the file Chap8 LoftMultiple.max from the CD-ROM. The scene consists of a Line that will be used as the path, a Rectangle, two Circles of different sizes, and an editable spline

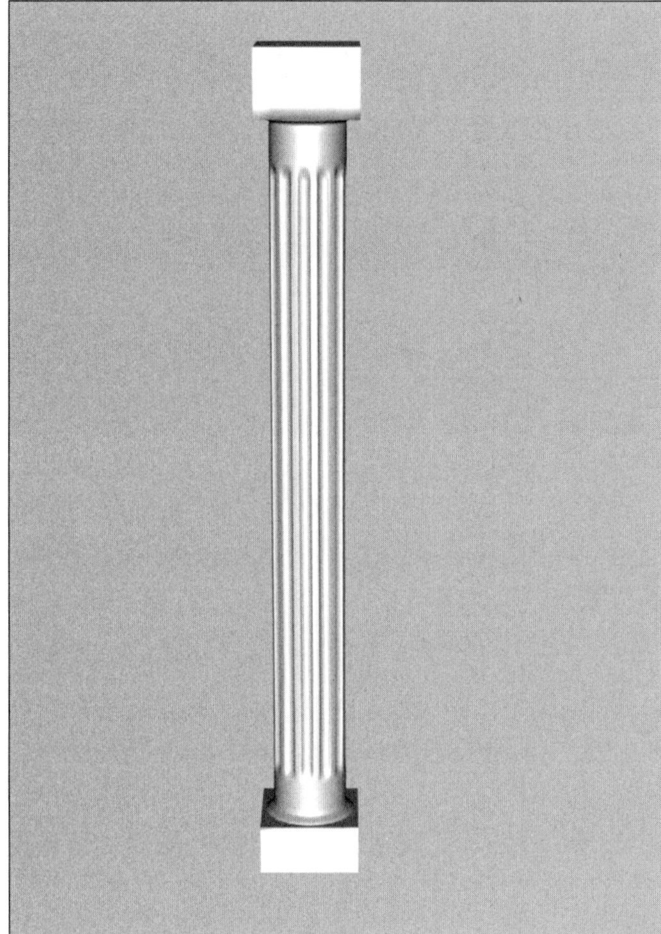

Figure 8.21
The column that is the objective of this exercise.

that will represent the flutes (grooves) along the body of the column. Figure 8.22 shows the initial layout of the scene.

2. Select the Line and, using Get Shape, loft the Rectangle along it so that your object looks like a tall, thin box. For the remainder of this exercise, it is easiest to work in a maximized Perspective viewport with Smooth + Highlights and Edged Faces selected as the viewport options.

3. The path is 96 units long, making the Distance choice easier to work with than Percentage; make Distance the active option in the Path Parameters rollout. Set the Path value to 6, activate Get Shape if necessary, and select the large Circle.

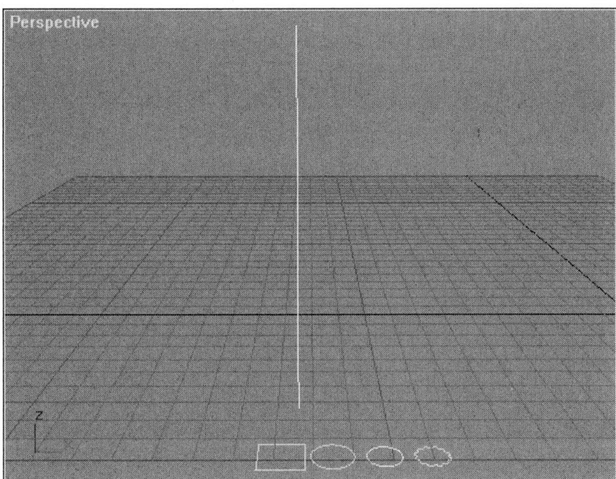

Figure 8.22
The five splines that will be used to create a single Loft object in the shape of a column.

The Rectangle transitions smoothly into the Circle but it twists when doing so; there is no constant rectangular cross section at the base, as shown in Figure 8.21. The twisting effect will be dealt with shortly, but for now, you'll concentrate on the shapes. Wherever along the path a shape is applied, the body of the Loft changes over from the previous cross section to the new one. To maintain a constant cross section before switching, the same shape must be applied to both ends of the unvarying area. Continue with these steps:

4. Change the Distance along the path to 5.95 and select the Rectangle again. Now, the rectangular shape is maintained from 0.0 to 5.95, the shape transitions to a Circle from 5.95 to 6.0, and the cross section remains circular for the remainder of the Loft. The transition is small enough to go unnoticed.

5. To add the small ring around the base of the column's body, set the Path value to 7 (doing this with the Perspective viewport set temporarily to Wireframe will allow you to see the yellow cross that indicated the current location where new shapes will be added) and add the smaller Circle to the Loft. At this point, the base of the column should look like the one in Figure 8.23.

6. Continue with the small circular cross section and then switch to the fluted cross section (created with the spline Boolean functions) by placing the small circle shape at 11 units from the first vertex and the fluted shape at 13. The column should now look like Figure 8.24, with a twisting effect similar to that attained after Step 4.

7. Finish the column by placing the fluted shape 83 units from the first vertex, the small Circle at 85 and 89, the large Circle at 88, and the Rectangle at 90.05. You don't need to

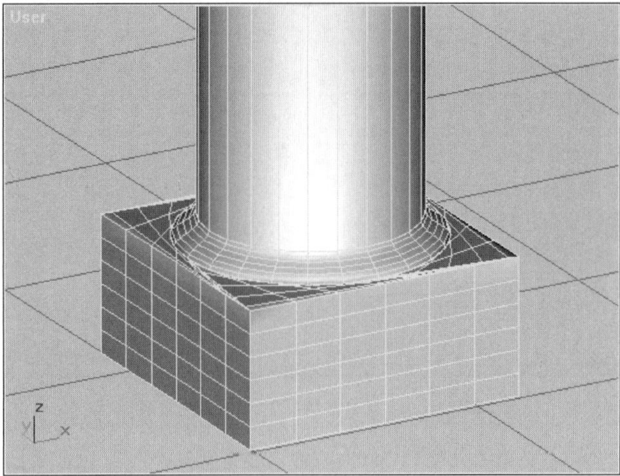

Figure 8.23
The base of the column with a six-units-high straight section, an unnoticeable transition to the large circular cross section, and a one-unit transition to the smaller circular cross section.

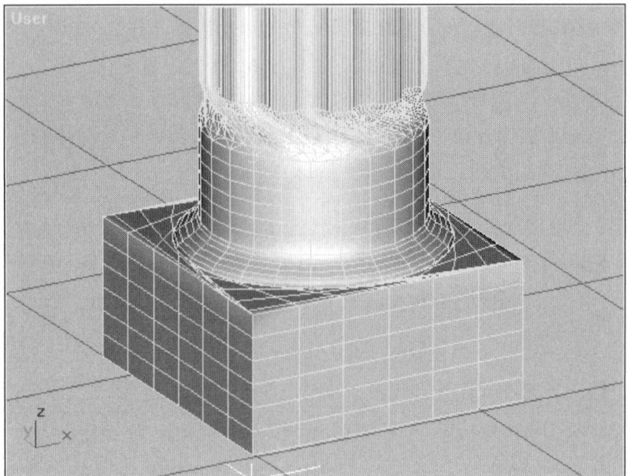

Figure 8.24
The same as Figure 8.23, but with the small circular cross section extending only four units and then transitioning to the fluted cross section over two units. The density of the mesh in the fluted area is due to the number of vertices comprising it and the number of shape steps designated by the Loft's parameters.

place a Rectangle at the end of the line. At this point, you only need to correct the twisting. Your nearly completed column should look like the fully rendered object shown in Figure 8.25.

When shapes are changed along a Loft object's path, MAX tries to keep the segments straight by aligning the first vertices of each shape to each other. This process works fine when the shapes are similar (such as two circles of different sizes) or identical, which is why no twisting occurs

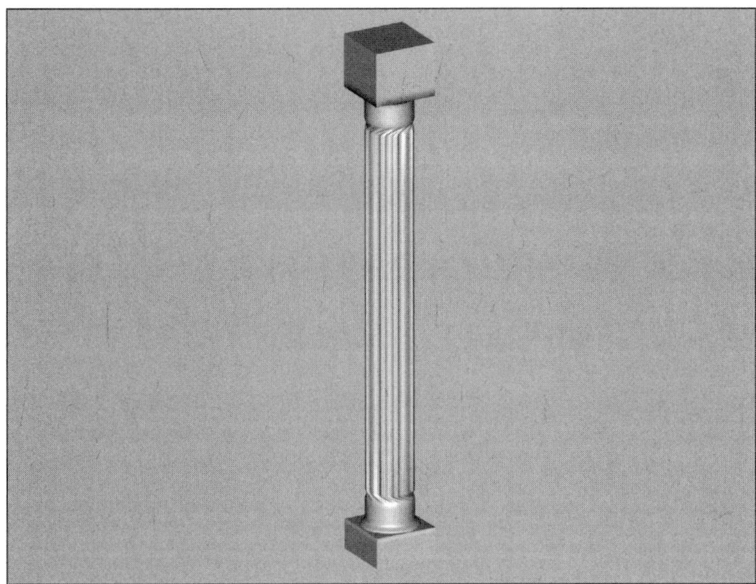

Figure 8.25
A rendering of the column after all the shapes are in place but before the twisting has been corrected.

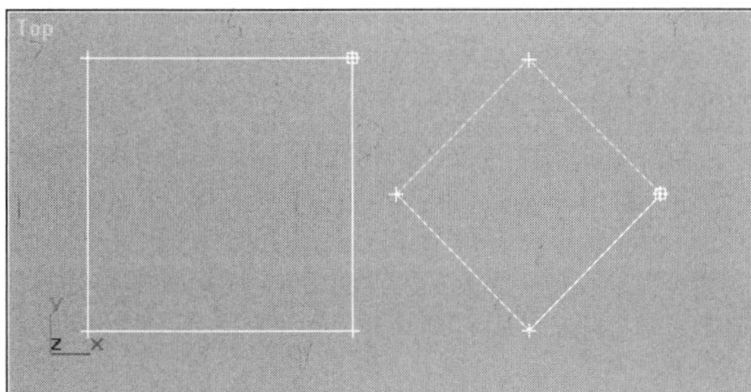

Figure 8.26
The first vertices of the Rectangle and Circle splines are oriented 45 degrees apart.

between two Rectangles or two Circles. Twisting takes place between the Rectangles and the Circles, however, as well as between the Circles and the fluted shapes. Figure 8.26 shows a Rectangle (*left*) and a Circle (*right*) with the Circle's vertices converted to Corner types. As you can see, the Circle's first vertex, which has a white box around it, is rotated –45 degrees from that of the Rectangle. The orientation of the referenced spline is irrelevant—it's the shape's orientation that must be corrected, and MAX provides a utility just for that purpose. Continue with these steps:

8. In the Stack View window, expand the Loft object and choose the Shape subobject level. Click on the Compare button to access the Compare dialog box.

9. Zoom in to the base of the column. In the Compare dialog box, click on the Pick Shape button. Move the cursor over the base of the column and select the second Rectangle shape at

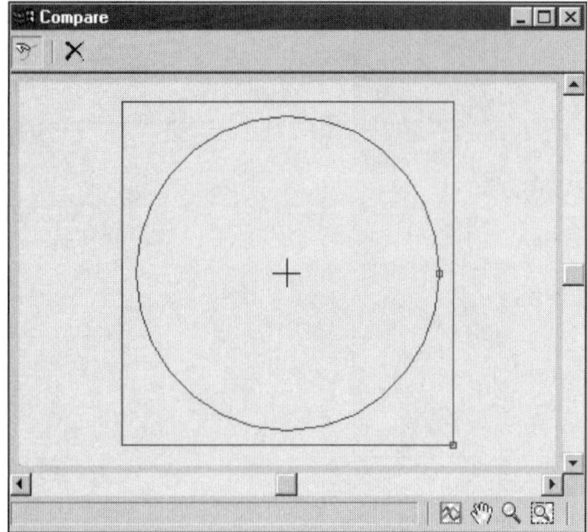

Figure 8.27
The Compare dialog box after picking the top Rectangle shape and the large Circle shape near the base of the column.

the top of the straight section. The shape appears in the Compare field. Select the large Circle shape in the viewport, and the Compare dialog box will look like the one in Figure 8.27.

10. Turn off the Pick Shape mode. Turn on the Angle Snap Toggle button and set the Angle value to 0.5 degrees. This value will allow you to snap to precise values without restricting the precision too much. Switch the viewport to Wireframe mode, select the large Circle shape (in the viewport, not in the Compare dialog box), and activate the Rotate transform. Rotate the shape 45 degrees about its Z-axis, watching the Compare dialog box, until the first vertices line up.

Note: *When the mesh is particularly dense or you use several shapes, making it difficult to discern where the shapes are, you can try deselecting the Skin checkbox in the Display rollout. Doing so will allow you to see the shapes but not the mesh they create.*

11. Click on the Pick Shape button again. Add both small Circle shapes and the fluted shape to the Compare dialog box. Using the same procedure as in Step 10, rotate the shapes near the base, aligning their first vertices with those of the Rectangle and Circle. The base of the column and the Compare window should look like those shown in Figure 8.28.

12. Repeat the aligning process with the shapes at the opposite end of the path. You may notice that the shapes have a greater distance between them at the beginning of the path than at the end (in this particular Loft, the effect is difficult to detect). This happens if the second vertex is a Bezier type rather than a Corner type, causing MAX to misinterpret the location of the shapes. To resolve the situation, select the Line, go to the Vertex subobject level, and change the end vertex type to Corner. Watch as the shapes even out. The column should now look like your goal, shown earlier in Figure 8.21.

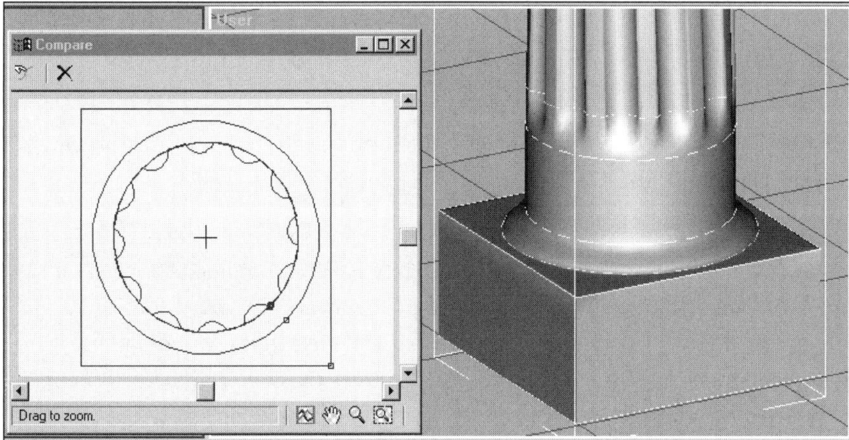

Figure 8.28
Using the Compare window, the first vertices of the shapes at the bottom of the column and the beginning of the path have been aligned to eliminate the twisting that occurred during the creation of the Loft.

As you can see, lofting is a powerful tool that you can use to make complex geometry from relatively simple two-dimensional shapes. The dimensions of the Loft can be twisted or otherwise deformed, and multiple shapes can occur over the length of the path. For added practice, try bulging the center of the fluted area using a Scale deformation.

Terrain

As you would expect, the Terrain compound object creates land surfaces from contour line data that is usually created in a CAD or terrain analysis program. The result is similar to a Loft in that the shapes change with distance between the elevations but no path spline is required. The shapes can transition smoothly or abruptly and switch from single to multiple spline subobjects at each level.

The following exercise will demonstrate the key features of the Terrain compound object and how to implement them. The exercise uses objects imported from AutoCAD. The Import AutoCAD DWG File settings determine the way that the CAD entities are converted to MAX objects. They are, for the most part, self-explanatory; we're primarily concerned with the Derive Objects By group, which establishes whether all the entities on each layer are converted into one object in MAX, all entities assigned the same color become one object, or each entity in the drawing becomes an object. This decision is driven by the convention used when the AutoCAD drawing was created. To import the AutoCAD objects, follow these steps:

1. Reset your scene. Choose File|Import. In the Select File To Import dialog box, change the Files Of Type drop-down list option from 3D Studio Mesh (the original 3D Studio format prior to the first release of 3D Studio) to AutoCAD (*.DWG). Navigate to the Chapter 8 file location on the CD-ROM and import the Chap8_Terrain.dwg file. Accept the default Merge

Objects With Current Scene option in the DWG Import dialog box. (If this file type used a time-length system, the other option would allow its time settings to replace those in the current MAX file.)

2. In the Derive Objects By group, leave the default Layer option selected and click on OK. After a moment, the imported AutoCAD objects will appear.

Note: *When you use the Color option to create the MAX objects, be advised that all entities that obtain their color from the layer to which they are assigned have the color ByLayer in AutoCAD. When imported into MAX, they will be associated with objects that have the same actual color that was assigned explicitly. For example, if Layer 1 is assigned the color red and the entities on that layer are assigned the color ByLayer, they will appear red in AutoCAD. If entities on Layer 2, which may be yellow by default, are assigned a red color, they will appear red in AutoCAD—but, once imported, they will be subobject members of the MAX object containing all red objects.*

The layers in this AutoCAD drawing are named according to their elevation above, below, or at the elevation baseline 0 (zero) and are divided into 20-foot increments. When imported into MAX, these layer names become the objects' names with *.01* appended to them. To begin creating the Terrain compound object, you must move each object in the Z-direction, to its appropriate elevation, with the groundplane corresponding to the 0 elevation. Follow these steps:

1. Open the Select Objects dialog box, select the 20.01 object from the list, and activate the Move transform. Ensure that the Transform Type-Ins are in Absolute mode and enter "20" in the Z field. The splines that form the 20.01 object are moved 20 units above the baseline.

2. Move the remaining splines to their respective locations in the Z-direction in the same manner.

3. With –80.01 (the lowest object) selected, click on the Terrain button in the Create|Geometry|Compound Objects panel. A surface is created, bound by the spline object. The surface is the Terrain object, and the spline (–80.01) is now an operand designated as Op 0 in the Operands group of the Parameters rollout.

4. Activate the Pick Operand button. In order, select the objects from the next lowest to the highest until the object named 100.01 becomes Op 9. The Terrain object now stretches from one elevation to another; the enormous number of vertices in the imported splines, however, causes the side faces to facet terribly, as shown in Figure 8.29. Because you'll apply modifiers on top of the Terrain, take the opportunity now to cycle through the three different types of results achieved by selecting the options in the Form group.

5. The solution that would maintain the most accuracy would be to re-create the Terrain object with a more optimized set of splines. Because this option may not be available, the solution is to minimize the number of vertices inside of MAX. Apply an Edit Mesh modifier to the object, go to the Vertex subobject level, and, in the Top viewport, select all the vertices. The Selection rollout indicates that more than 7,000 vertices are selected.

Figure 8.29
The number of vertices in the imported splines causes the faces that span the different elevations to appear faceted.

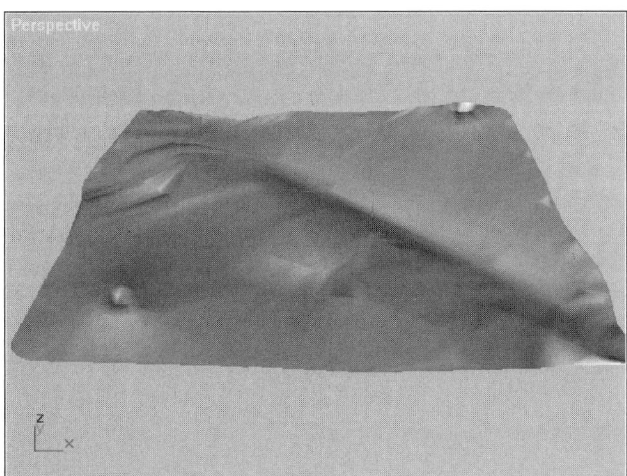

Figure 8.30
Using the Weld feature of the Edit Mesh modifier can reduce the sharp face changes that caused the faceted appearance.

6. Set the Weld threshold (next to the Selected button) to 30. Click on Selected. The number of vertices selected is now just over 900, and the object appears much smoother in the Perspective viewport, as shown in Figure 8.30.

The object can be made even smoother by continuing to edit the vertices and edges that make up the surface, but that step-by-step procedure is outside the scope of this chapter. Revisit the sections on the Edit Mesh modifier and how to work with modifiers to identify the means of reducing the mesh while maintaining its curvature.

Connect

When two mesh objects must be seamlessly connected, the Connect compound object is the key. This feature links the two objects, which become the operands, with a bridge of polygons between the open edges. Connect is a great tool to use when different parts of a model are created by different people and must be combined into one. The following exercise is separated into two short sections that explain the process of connecting meshes; the first exercise is very basic, and the second is more practical.

A Basic Connect Procedure

To try the basic connect procedure, follow these steps:

1. Open the file Chap8 Connect.max from the CD-ROM. Two Spheres and a Cylinder are visible. All of the objects have been converted to editable meshes: Your task is to connect the three objects.

2. Select the left Sphere and attach the right Sphere to it. A Connect operation would have to be nested to connect all three objects. By using the Attach tool, the Spheres are now components of one noncontiguous object that can be used as a single operand.

3. The edges must be exposed to allow the process to occur. Select the Spheres and go to the Face subobject level. Activate the Select Object tool and make sure the Window Selection toggle is active. In the Left viewport, click and drag a rectangular selection region around the end of the Cylinder, selecting all faces that are even partially overlapping the Cylinder. With the faces selected on both sides of both Spheres, your Top viewport should look like Figure 8.31. Only the surfaces that are facing the Cylinder should be open; therefore, hold down the Alt key and then, in the Top viewport, deselect the selected faces on the outside surfaces. Delete the faces and any isolated vertices.

4. Select the Cylinder and delete the faces that compose its end caps. The Perspective viewport should look like Figure 8.32.

5. With the Cylinder selected, but not in a subobject mode, click on the Connect button in the Compound Objects panel. The Cylinder is now Op 0, as shown in the Parameters rollout. Activate the Pick Operand button and select the Spheres. Instantly, faces are created that extend from both perimeters of the open, round edges of the Cylinder to the perimeters of the open, square edges of the Spheres.

6. The Smoothing group in the Parameters rollout determines whether the newly created areas are smoothed. Bridge affects the faces that span the gaps, and Ends affects the transitions between the bridges and the operands. With only Bridge checked, the object should look like the one shown in Figure 8.33.

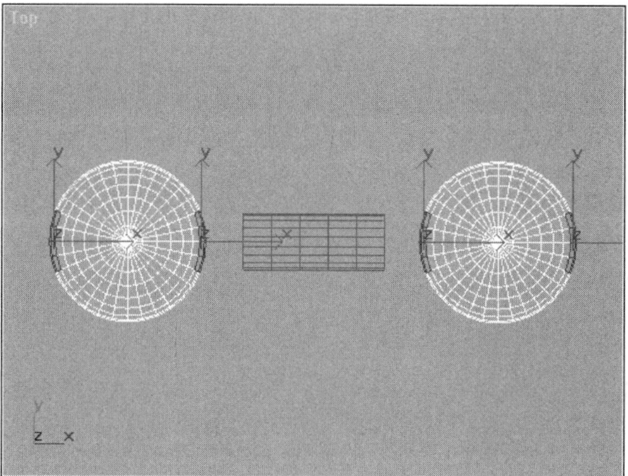

Figure 8.31
Using a region selection selects the faces on both sides of both Spheres that are even with the Cylinder. The selected faces on the outside surfaces must be deselected.

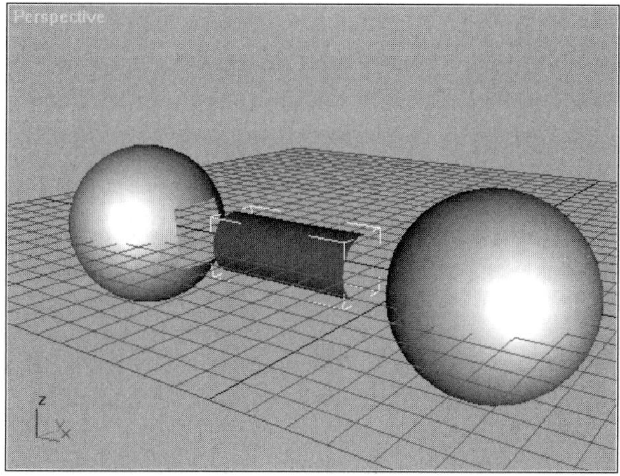

Figure 8.32
The faces of the Spheres that are opposite the Cylinder, as well as those on the Cylinder's end caps, are deleted in preparation for creating a Connect compound object.

A Practical Connect Procedure

Connect is often used to join more practical objects, such as an arm to a shoulder or an instrument panel to the inside of a car or jet. These can be very time-consuming tasks if you're only using the vertex and face manipulation tools found in the Edit Mesh modifier, although these tools may be required for some cleanup work.

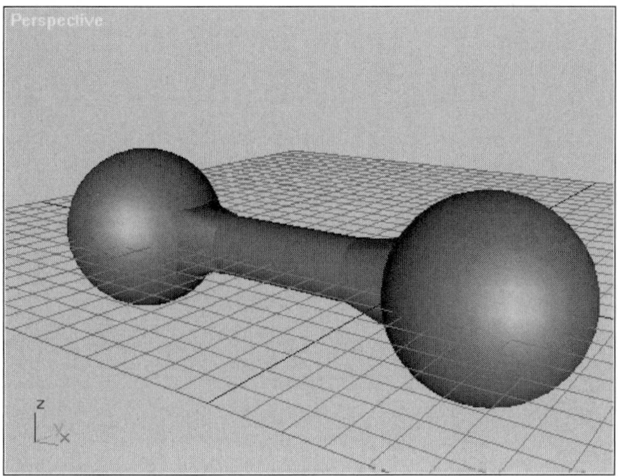

Figure 8.33
With the bridge elements created, the Bridge option in the Smoothing group blends the bridges' faces.

To continue examining how Connect can add to your modeling arsenal, hide the current object from the previous exercise and unhide the New Nose and Head w/Old Nose objects. Your scene should contain a complete head model as well as an unaccompanied nose. The task here is to replace the head model's nose with the new one, which is a situation that would occur when you want to switch body parts among character models and not edit the existing components. Follow these steps:

1. Move the free nose to its new location on the head, as shown in Figure 8.34. In the Front viewport, zoom in to the face, change the viewport type to Smooth + Highlights, and turn on Edged Faces mode.

2. Select the head and go to the Face subobject level. Using a Fence selection region in Crossing Selection mode, select the faces belonging to the head that make up the head's nose and that surround both noses. Deselect the selected faces on the back of the head. Zoom in further to the nose area (maximizing or stretching the viewport will also help) and deselect any faces that are outside the range of either nose. Take your time and do this task well. Delete those faces. When you're finished, delete the selected faces to create a gap in the model's face where the new nose will reside.

Note: *Connect works best if a clear separation exists between objects in the direction of the bridge. You may need to move the nose slightly in front of the head to gain this separation and then move it again once it is an operand of the Connect object.*

3. In the Compound Objects panel, choose Connect. You may see some temporary faces that are generated inside the head, due to the four openings the model already has, but they should disappear once the procedure is executed. If they remain, you can delete them with

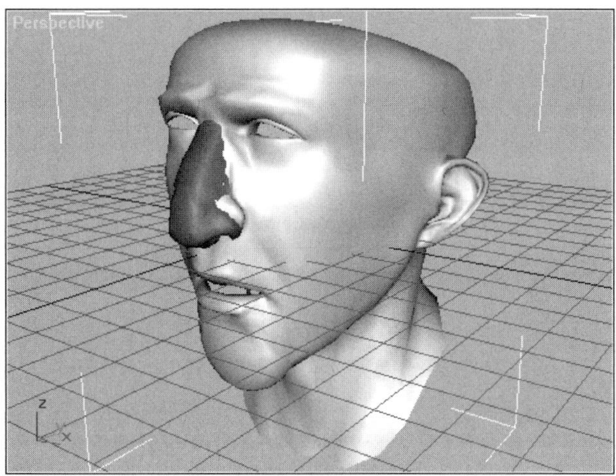

Figure 8.34
The Perspective viewport with the New Nose object in its new location on the face of the head model.

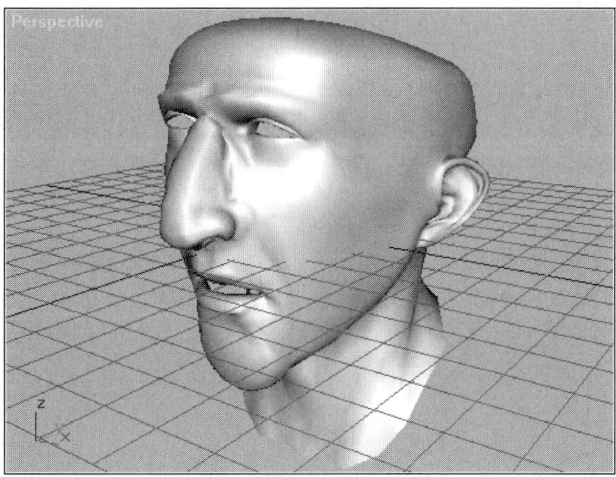

Figure 8.35
After deleting the faces that composed and surrounded the head model's nose, the Connect compound object is created, absorbing the existing objects as operands and spanning the gap with new faces.

Edit Mesh. Click on the Pick Operand button and select the nose to create the faces spanning the gap. Select both Bridge and Ends in the Smoothing group. Your model should look similar to Figure 8.35.

4. If any gaps remain, close them with Edit Mesh or Undo until before the Connect step and make sure that a gap exists between the objects.

ShapeMerge

A ShapeMerge object is a composition of a mesh object and a spline. Once the mesh is created, the spline is projected onto its surface, adding segmentation to the mesh in the shape of the spline. Using this tool, it's possible to pull a logo or other shape from an object rather than using Attach or a Boolean Union function with its inherently large overhead. You can also use Shape-Merge to denote where the cover plate on a machine or robotic character should be bounded.

ShapeMerge performs two types of operation: Cookie Cutter and Merge (the default). Merge simply adds edges, whereas Cookie Cutter removes the faces bounding the shape or, if Invert is selected, removes all faces except those bounding the shape. To familiarize yourself with this next compound object, try the following exercise:

1. Create a Teapot primitive near the origin, give it a Radius value of 50, and accept the default segmentation. In the Front viewport, create a Text entity; use the word *Tea* for this exercise. Set the Size value to 25 and choose a font that is a bit more expressive than the default Arial. Convert the Text to an editable spline and then, in the rollout, change the number of steps to two to reduce the number of faces created.
2. The Text is currently inside the Teapot. Move it forward until it is in front and center it on the body of the Teapot, as shown in Figure 8.36.

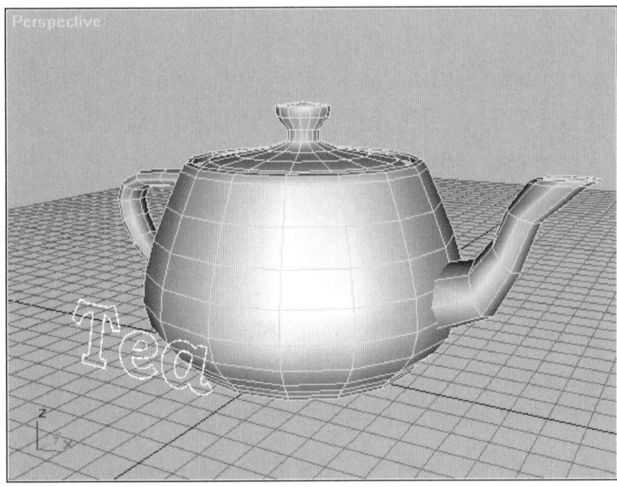

Figure 8.36
The two objects that will make up the ShapeMerge compound object.

3. When the shapes are projected, their influence occurs in their Local negative Z-direction, similar to the way that shapes are projected along a path in Loft objects. With the Text entity as shown in Figure 8.36, the positive Z-direction is to its front and the negative is to

its rear, in the direction of the Teapot. Select the Teapot and then a ShapeMerge. Activate the Pick Shape button and select the Text. After a moment, edges in the shape of the letters *T-e-a* appear on the surface of the mesh. (You may see the effect better in a viewport in Wireframe mode.) Use the Arc Rotate tool to confirm that the edges do not appear on the opposite side. The shape is projected in its negative Z-direction, but it only affects polygons with normals (their positive Z-direction) facing toward the shape.

4. Turn off Pick Shape and hide the Text. Examine the effect of the Cookie Cutter option and then return to the Merge setting.

Note: *The Cookie Cutter option works logically, similar to the Extrude modifier, when working with nested splines by eliminating every other bounded area. For example, notice that when the Cookie Cutter option was selected, the interior sections of the* e *and* a *remained, whereas the faces that made up the letters themselves were removed.*

5. Because the new faces follow the contour of the Teapot, they are not evident in a rendering or a rendered viewport that is not in Edged Faces mode. To make them visible and to add some detail to the mesh, you'll extrude and bevel them. Apply an Edit Mesh modifier and go to the Polygon subobject level. Carefully select the polygons that define the letters, being sure to deselect any that belong to the opposite side. Click on the Bevel button, enter "5" in the Extrude spinner, and specify a small amount of negative bevel, depending on the font you chose. The Teapot with the extruded text shape should look similar to the one in Figure 8.37.

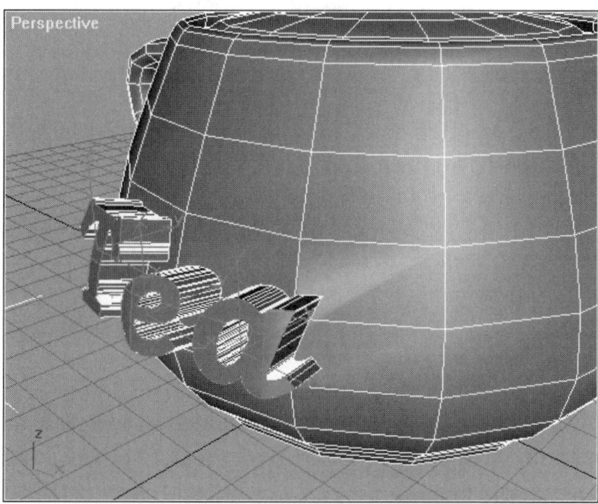

Figure 8.37
The ShapeMerge object with the *Tea* Text shape extruded and beveled.

Making Detachable Labels

Rather than simply using ShapeMerge to add edges and faces to an object, you can use it to create objects with their own purposes. Using this Teapot exercise as an example, suppose you wanted to create a detachable label for the object that must match its curvature. To do this, create the Teapot, clone it in place, and then create the Text. ShapeMerge the Text with one of the Teapots. In the Operation group, choose Cookie Cutter and then Invert, so only the text shape remains. Use Edit Mesh to extrude the label's faces; then, link it to the Teapot. Now, when necessary, the form-fitting label can be removed from the Teapot.

Scatter

The Scatter compound object creates multiple instances of an object either randomly or in a logical pattern. The object being scattered, called the *source object*, can be placed by itself in the scene or on the surface or within the volume of a *distribution object*. Some of the most common uses of Scatter are to distribute objects representing hairs, grass, or trees in a scene; you should use it whenever you need a random array of objects. Many results are possible when using Scatter, as you will see in this section's exercises.

Using Transforms Only

When you use the Use Transforms Only distribution method, the objects are scattered within a range but not relative to another object. To try this technique, follow these steps:

1. In the Top viewport, create a ChamferBox primitive near the origin small enough that you have room to create multiples of it without having to change the viewport's zoom factor.
2. With the object selected, create the Scatter compound object. In the Distribution group of the Scatter Objects rollout, select the Use Transforms Only option. In the Source Object Parameters group of the same rollout, set the number of duplicates to 30. It appears that nothing happens, because all the instances are identical and collocated at the same coordinates.

Note: *The term* translating *is commonly used to denote moving an object, although MAX has generally shifted away from this usage. This term may even be more accurate, because Webster's Ninth New Collegiate Dictionary defines* translation *as: "a transformation of coordinates in which the new axes are parallel to the old ones." This specifies that, wherever the object is relocated to, the orientation is not changed.*

3. Open the Transforms rollout, where the range of the source object's distribution is determined. In the Local Translation group, increase the X, Y, and Z spinners until the duplicates of the ChamferBox are spread out. Your scene should look similar to Figure 8.38. To restrict the range evenly in all directions, set only one of the spinners and select the Use Maximum Range checkbox; doing so synchronizes the three spinners to the value of the highest.
4. Increase the values in the Rotation and Scaling groups. As you can see in Figure 8.39, the duplicates are starting to look more random.

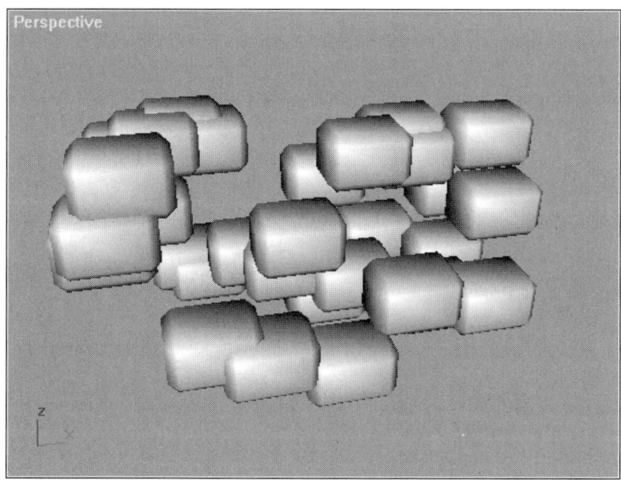

Figure 8.38
With the Use Transforms Only option selected, the source object is duplicated within the range determined by the settings in the Local Translation group.

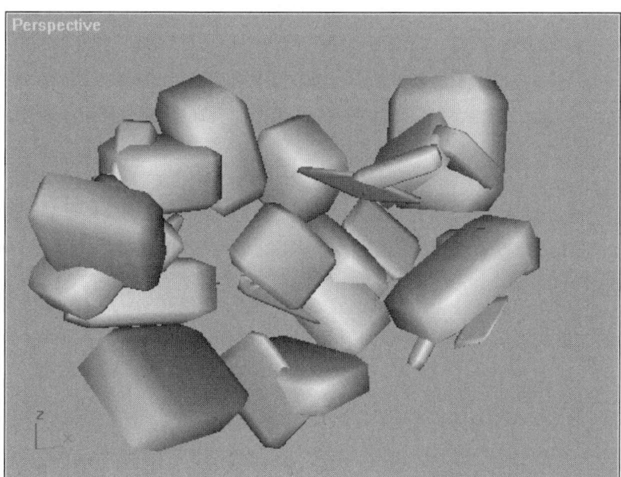

Figure 8.39
The same as Figure 8.38, but with the Rotation and Scaling spinner values increased.

A Scatter object can contain a huge number of duplicates, which could cause your system to slow down to an unacceptable level. The Display value in the Display rollout sets the percentage of duplicates visible in the viewports (all of them are visible when the scene is rendered). The New button in the same rollout sets the Seed Number value randomly to change how the instances are moved (translated), rotated, or scaled within their range.

If you are satisfied with the result of the Scatter settings, you can save them and then apply them to another object, or reapply them to the same object at a later time, using the options in the Load/Save Presets rollout.

Animating with Scatter

You can generate a *spawning* effect by animating the number of duplicates (you can have as few as zero), as well as their transform settings. Doing so will make the duplicates pop into the scene randomly within the animation range.

Using a Distribution Object

The other method of creating Scatter objects restricts the source object over the surface of or within the volume of a distribution object. The following exercise demonstrates this technique:

1. From the CD-ROM, open the Chap8 ScatterD.max file. It consists of the now-familiar Uhg model, which will serve as the distribution object.
2. For the source object, create a small, thin Cylinder with a Radius value of 0.5 and a Height value of 10.
3. Select Use Distribution Object under the Scatter Object rollout. Then, with the Cylinder selected, create a Scatter compound object. Click on the Pick Distribution Object button and select the head. The Cylinder appears on the object's surface.
4. Increase the number of duplicates to 200. The Cylinders appear randomly across the surface of the model, creating a "Pinhead" look, as shown in Figure 8.40. Notice that the pivot points of the Cylinders are placed on the surface of the head; the Cylinders point perpendicular to them and in the direction of the normals. To experiment with other distribution locations, change the Seed value in the Display rollout.

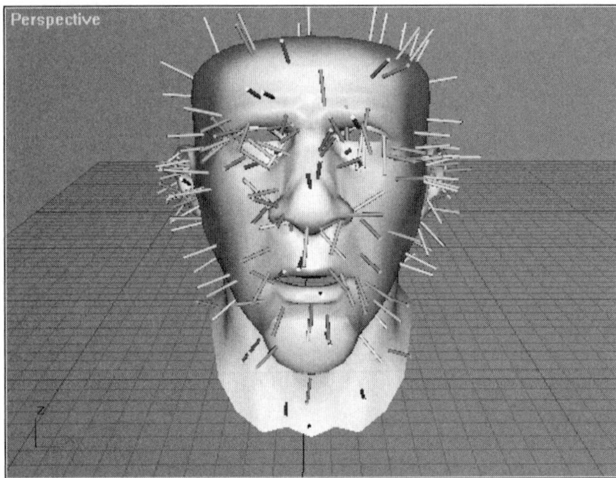

Figure 8.40
Using Scatter with a distribution object; the Cylinder duplicates are placed randomly on the surface of the head model.

5. The Distribution Object Parameters group contains a powerful set of options that determine how the source object is placed relative to the distribution object. Deselecting the Perpendicular checkbox orients the Cylinders in the direction of the original object and not relative to the head's faces. The Distribution Using options determine the relationship between the surface of the distribution object and the location of the source object. The default Even option separates the duplicates by the number of faces between them (this is why more Cylinders are clustered around the dense ear areas than the less dense forehead), and Area separates them by an equal distance. Oddly, the Area option distributes the source objects more evenly than the Even option does. Try the Area option with the model and you will get a more pleasing result, as shown in Figure 8.41.

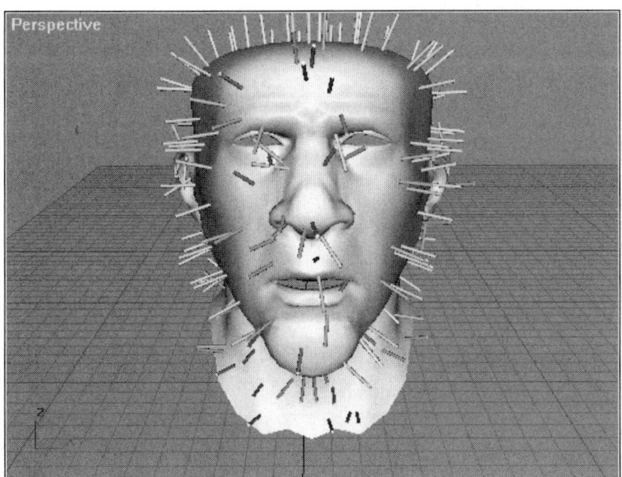

Figure 8.41
The same as Figure 8.40, but with the Distribution Using Area option selected rather than the default Even.

6. Experiment with the other Distribution Using options, keeping in mind that the All Vertices, All Edge Midpoints, and All Face Centers options disregard the number of duplicates assigned and establish a new quantity based on the number of associated subobjects. For example, the All Face Centers option places a source object at the center of every face on the distribution object.

Using Selected Faces Only

Scatter gives you the option of placing the source object on only selected faces of the distribution object. To see how this is done, either Undo to before the Scatter object was created or reopen the scene without saving what you've done. Now, continue with these steps:

1. Create an Instance clone of the head and move it to the side. As you did before, create a Scatter compound object with the Cylinder as the source object and the head as the distribution object. Set the number of duplicates to 200 and use the Area option.

2. Select the clone, go to the Polygon subobject level, and select the polygons at the crown of the head. (If you were using a parametric object, you would need to either convert it to an editable mesh or apply a Mesh Select modifier to it to gain access to the Polygon level.) Go back to the top level of the clone's stack (don't worry about not seeing your polygon selection; it's still there) and reselect the Scatter object. In the Distribution Object parameters group, select the Use Selected Faces Only checkbox. The 200 Cylinders are concentrated on the same faces selected on the clone. After hiding the clone object, your scene should look similar to the one in Figure 8.42.

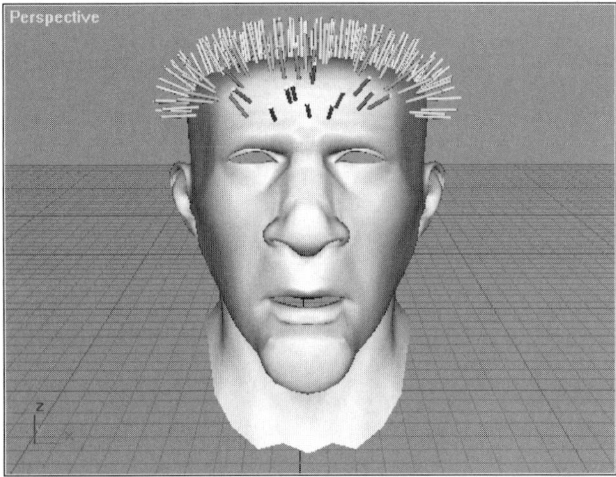

Figure 8.42
Using the Use Selected Faces Only and Area options, the distribution of the duplicates is restricted to the polygons selected on the now-hidden, instanced clone.

As you can see, Scatter is a very useful tool whenever you need to disperse a large quantity of objects over a restricted area.

Morph

As we stated at the beginning of the chapter, the functionality of the Morph compound object is available when you use the Morpher modifier. The Morpher modifier, introduced in 3D Studio MAX 3, gives you greater control of exactly which parts of the object are morphed and to what degree. Still, the Morph compound object is retained as a functional tool whose limited toolset makes for a simpler process when you need simpler morphing; for this reason, we will address it here.

Morphing is the procedure of changing an object's appearance over time. You do so by moving the vertices of the original mesh to match those of one or more target meshes. The original mesh and its targets must possess the same number of vertices in a similar configuration, which is why the morph targets are usually clones of the original with modifications applied. The modifiers and tools that you use cannot change the number of vertices an object has (as Extrude and Bevel do), or the objects will become invalid morph target options.

Reset the scene before starting this exercise. Now, follow these steps:

1. Create a short, wide Tube primitive in the Top viewport and make four clone copies.
2. Select each of the copies individually and change their Radius 1, Radius 2, and Height values. Leave the other settings alone, because modifying them will change the Tubes' vertex counts. Continue altering the Tubes by applying one or more modifiers to each until you are satisfied with their appearances. Figure 8.43 shows the original Tube and the four modified copies.

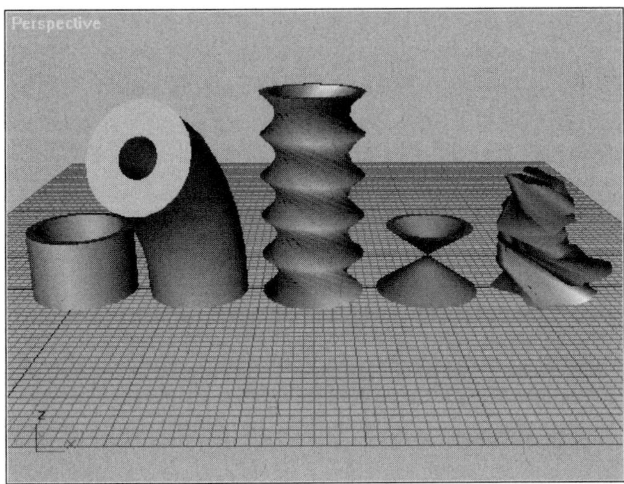

Figure 8.43
The original Tube is at far left. The (1) Bend, (2) Twist, (3) Taper, and (4) Twist, Taper, Bend, and Noise modifiers, respectively, have been applied to the four copies.

3. Select the original Tube and activate the Morph button in the Compound Objects panel. The Tube's name, preceded by *M_*, appears in the Morph Targets field.
4. Move the Time Slider at the bottom of the MAX screen to Frame 20, activate the Pick Target button, and select the first copy. The Morph object (the original Tube) now looks identical to its first target. Move the Time Slider back and forth between Frames 0 and 20 to see the transition the Morph object makes from one state to the next.
5. Move the Time Slider to Frame 40 and pick the second target, to Frame 60 and pick the third target, and to Frame 80 and pick the last morph target. At each step, the Morph assumes the shape of its assigned target, and the target's name is added to the Morph Target list. Deactivate the Pick Target button.

Note: *Did you notice the step that seems to have been omitted when creating this animation? The Animate button was never activated. Because a Morph is an inherently animated object, the animation process is understood—you don't need to click on the Animate button.*

6. Click on the Play Animation button and watch the Morph change from one shape to the next every 20 frames and then hold the last shape for the final 20 frames. To cycle the animation, the state of the object in the final frame should be the same as it is in the first, but you don't have an original Tube to select for the morph target at Frame 100. Just below the Time Slider is the Track Bar, a numbered row showing the animation frames and red squares identifying which frames have animation keys for the selected object. If a key is selected, it will be white rather than red. Select the key at Frame 0, hold down the Shift key, and drag the key to Frame 100. Just as in the viewports, holding down the Shift key creates a copy. Hide the clones and once again play the animation. This time, the Morph cycles through each target and returns seamlessly to its original shape.

Morphing is a common technique used in animation—particularly character animation. We'll revisit this topic when we discuss the Morpher modifier in Chapter 19.

Conform

The Conform compound object is used to match the contours of one object with those of another. The mesh to be conformed, called the *wrapper object*, can be projected directionally onto the mesh it is conforming to, called the *wrap-to object*, or outward if the wrap-to object envelops it. These exercises will show you the functionality of the Conform compound object, much of which is duplicated with the Conform Space Warp. Follow these steps:

1. In the Top viewport, create a flat Box primitive with a well-segmented length and width. Collapse it to an editable mesh, or apply an Edit Mesh modifier, and turn on Use Soft Selection in the Vertex subobject level. Select and pull vertices until your Box looks similar to the bottom object in Figure 8.44. The exact shape is unimportant, as long as you include hills and valleys for the wrapper object to conform to.

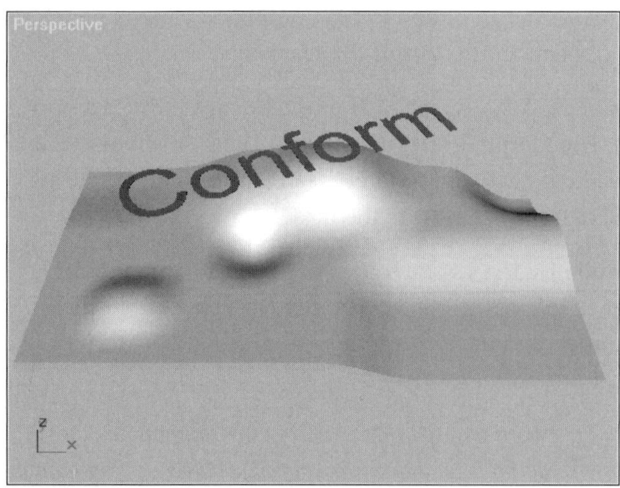

Figure 8.44
The basic setup for this Conform exercise. The extruded Text is placed above a distorted Box primitive.

2. Create a Text shape, extrude it slightly, and move it in the Z-direction so that it hangs above and completely within the boundaries of the Box, as seen in the Top viewport. Use Figure 8.44 as a reference.

3. With the Text still selected, create the Conform compound object. In the Parameters rollout, the Text entity is designated as the wrapper object, but nothing is assigned to be the wrap-to object. Before selecting one, you must determine the type of projection. In the Vertex Projection Direction group are the controls that determine the type of projection used to calculate the Conform direction. Make sure Use Active Viewport is selected. This option projects the wrapper object onto the wrap-to object that is directly behind it in the active viewport when the command is executed. The Top viewport must be active in this situation to project the Text directly onto the Box.

4. Activate the Pick Wrap-To Object button in the rollout of the same name. In the Top viewport, select the Box. After a moment, the Text will conform to the shape of the Box, but this change may be hard to distinguish. In the Update group of the Parameters rollout, select the Hide Wrap-To Object checkbox to view only the wrapper object.

5. To make the wrapper hover above the object to which it is conforming, increase the Standoff Distance value in the Wrapper Parameters group. The rendering shown in Figure 8.45 shows the scene with a shadow-casting light added to emphasize the wrapper object's separation from the wrap-to object below it.

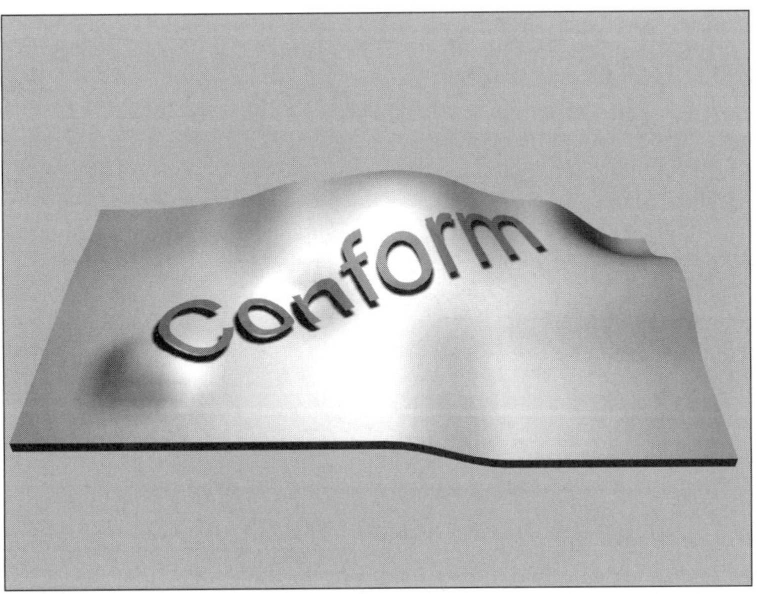

Figure 8.45
After conforming the Text (wrapper) to the Box (wrap-to), the standoff distance was increased to create a gap between the two objects. A shadow-casting light was added, and the scene was rendered for clarity.

Can a ChamferBox primitive be morphed into an OilTank primitive? The answer is no, because the vertex configurations are different. One ChamferBox can be morphed into another ChamferBox that has been conformed to the shape of an OilTank, however, as shown in the continuation of the exercise. Follow these steps:

1. Hide all the objects in the scene. Create a ChamferBox extended primitive. Move/Clone it, using the Copy option, and create an OilTank that is completely within the clone in all axes.
2. With the clone selected, click on the Conform button in the Compound Objects panel. Set the Vertex Projection Direction to Along Vertex Normals to project the ChamferBox inward and essentially collapse it to the shape of the OilTank.
3. Click on Pick Wrap-To Object. Select the OilTank to execute the command. The ChamferBox conforms to the shape of the OilTank. Figure 8.46 shows the three objects. On some occasions, a small amount of mesh-level modeling may be required to clean up any faces that do not conform properly, but this is a much easier task than manipulating all the vertices manually.

Figure 8.46
The ChamferBox (*left*), the conformed ChamferBox (*center*), and the OilTank (*right*).

Mesher

The new Mesher compound object deals with a couple of situations: World Space modifiers and particle systems. These subjects will be explained in depth later in this book, but they are covered here briefly.

The job of the Mesher is to break two of MAX's rules: that modifiers such as Bend or Twist do not affect particle systems, and that object modifiers cannot be placed above World Space Modifier in the modifier stack. The following exercise will demonstrate the Mesher's ability to break the first rule by replacing the particles with instanced geometry on a frame-by-frame basis. Follow these steps:

1. Open the file Chap8 Mesher.max from the CD-ROM. It consists of a simple Spray particle system aimed in the World Z-direction. Move the Time Slider back and forth to see the motion of the particles. Park it at Frame 100.
2. Select the rectangle at the base of the particle system (called the *emitter*) and apply a Bend modifier to it. Increase and decrease the Angle value to see the Gizmo change as the value changes. There is no effect on the particles themselves. Remove the modifier.
3. With the Spray still selected, activate the Mesher compound object button. Drag out a Mesher. It is only a temporary placeholder, so its size doesn't matter.
4. Go to the Modify panel and click on the Pick Object button labeled None. Select the Spray (either the emitter or a particle). The Mesher instantly assumes the shape of the particle system, but it is oriented the wrong way. Rotate the Mesher 180 degrees about the Y-axis in the Perspective viewport.
5. Apply a Bend modifier and then a Twist to the Mesher, giving each substantial Angle settings. The particles conform the modifier's Gizmos just as a geometry object would. It's important to understand that the Mesher's particles are an instance of the Spray's particles; therefore, changing the Spray's parameters also changes those of the Mesher. Figure 8.47 shows the original Spray (which would normally be hidden) to the left and the bent and twisted Mesher to the right.

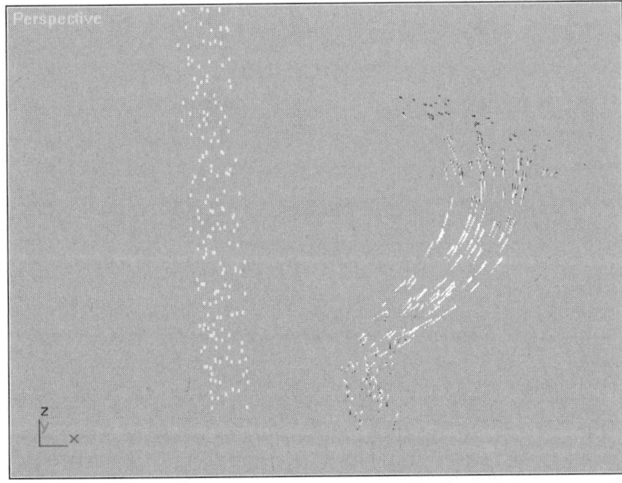

Figure 8.47
The Spray particle system on the left is unaffected by the same Bend and Twist modifiers that distort the instanced particles of the Mesher on the right.

Moving On

This chapter explored the many types of compound objects that exist in 3ds max 4; these use one or more objects to create a third object that may contain any number of individual elements. In most cases, operands are used that can be edited to alter the outcome of the compound object's result. The most commonly used—and, arguably, the most powerful—compound objects are the Boolean and the Loft, which can be used in many different modeling situations.

The next chapter focuses on patch modeling: the use of Bezier patches to create simple and complex surfaces. These three- or four-sided polygons are bound by curves rather than straight line segments. They are the basis of much of the higher-end character modeling used today.

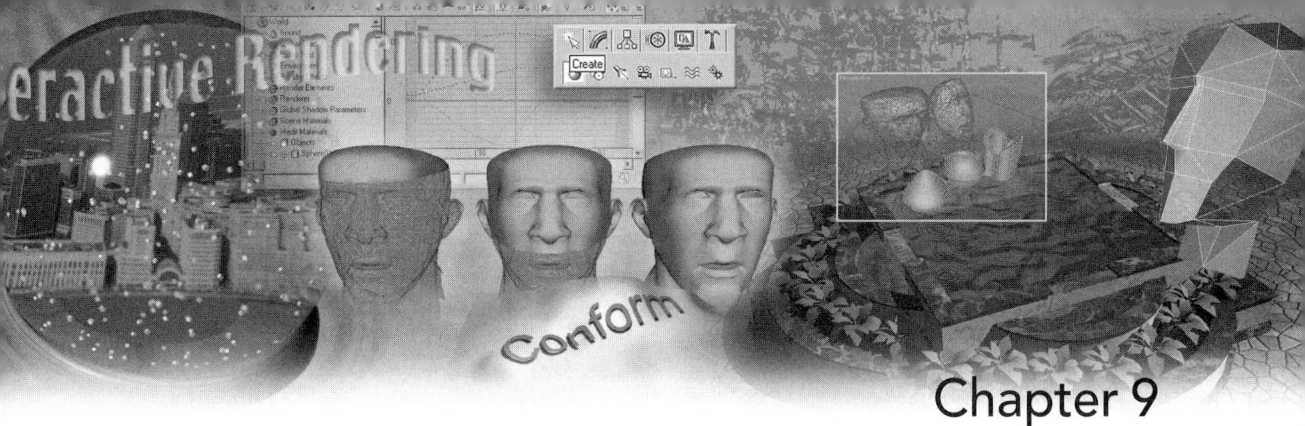

Chapter 9

Patch Modeling

Bezier patches, which appeared in the very first version of MAX, were the program's first essay into true spline modeling. The common attitude was that they were merely a stopgap measure until Kinetix (now Discreet) could implement Non-Uniform Rational B-Spline (NURBS) surface modeling. A great many MAX users never took patch modeling seriously—they might use a Bezier patch to simulate mountainous terrain, but they didn't get around to real organic modeling. Bezier patch modeling was perceived as clumsy, and many thought it certainly would be pushed aside when NURBS arrived.

To the surprise of a great many people, Bezier patch modeling is more alive than ever in 3ds max 4. With new tools and a better interface for patch modeling, Bezier patches are attracting serious attention for organic modeling.

Understanding Bezier Patches

The Bezier patch is a funny creature—a centaur mix of splines and polygons. The easiest way to think of a patch is as a kind of flexible polygon. Imagine a triangle or quadrangle with its vertices connected by Bezier curves instead of straight-line segments, and you have the idea. Just as with regular Bezier curves, the shape of the spline is governed by the length and direction of the tangent handles that are associated with each vertex. The MAX documentation calls the Bezier tangent handles *vector handles* (or just *vectors*), and these words will be used interchangeably. The vector is tangent to the curve at the location of the vertex.

Familiarize yourself with Bezier patches by working through the following introductory exercises.

The Quad Patch

Let's experiment with one type of Bezier patch—the Quad patch:

1. Create a Quad patch in a Front viewport by using Create|Geometry|Patch Grids|Quad Patch. Next, drag out a rectangular shape and adjust the dimensions, if necessary, to make it slightly wider than it is long.

2. Your Quad patch is subdivided into a 6×6 grid. Create another Quad patch next to the first, with similar dimensions, but increase the Length Segments spinner to 2. This grid is now 6×12, and your Front viewport should look like Figure 9.1.

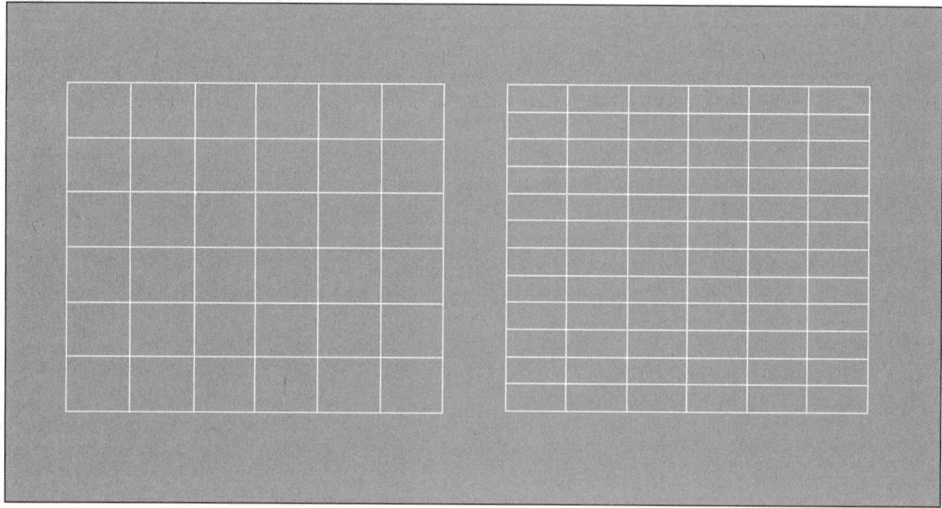

Figure 9.1
Two Quad patches are created in the Front viewport. At left, the default segmentation values produce a 6×6 grid. At right, the Length Segments value is increased from 1 to 2, and the resulting grid is 6×12.

3. Consider these grids in two ways—as Bezier patches and as polygonal meshes. Select each of the grids in turn and use the Quad menu to access the Object Properties dialog box. Check the facecount. The patch on the left is composed of 72 triangular faces, and the one on the right has 144 triangular faces. Because two triangles are in each quadrangle, it's easy to understand that the patch on the left is ultimately a mesh of 36 quad polygons. The one on the right is likewise a mesh of 72 quad polygons. The grid shows you the quad polygon structure of each patch object.

4. To understand the objects from a Bezier patch perspective, convert each of them to editable patch objects by using the Convert To option in the Transform section of the Quad menu. The Modify panel that opens allows you to work in four subobject levels: Vertex, Edge, Patch, and Element. This structure is very similar to that found in the Editable Mesh panel. Go to the Patch subobject for each object and click on the grid to determine how many

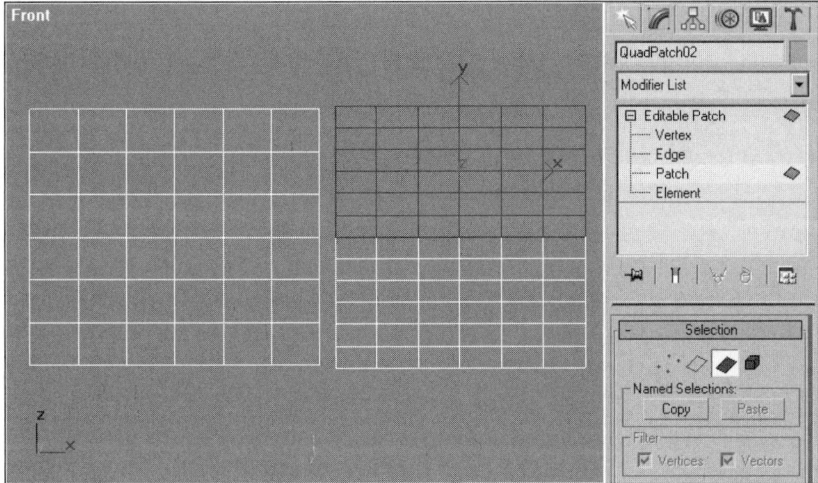

Figure 9.2
The objects from Figure 9.1 are converted to editable patch objects to examine them as Bezier patches. In the Patch subobject level, only the upper of two patches is selected in the object on the right. The object on the left is composed of only one patch.

patches it has. The one on the left is only a single patch, but the grid on the right is composed of two patches, arranged vertically. Figure 9.2 shows the upper patch selected in the object on the right.

5. Note that each of the individual patches is a 6×6 grid of quad polygons. There is only one such grid in the object on the left and two in the one on the right. From all this, you can gather that the Segmentation spinners in the Create panel divide the object into multiple patches, each with a like number of quad polygons.

6. With the upper patch selected, as in Figure 9.2, pull the panel down to the Surface section in the Geometry rollout, where you'll find the Steps spinners. Steps are determined separately for viewport and rendering purposes (an easy thing to forget at render time), and both levels are set to the default of 5. Change the value in the View Steps spinner and watch what happens. The polygonal density of the entire grid changes, and not just within the selected patch. The number of steps is the number of interior lines dividing the grid; it is therefore always one fewer than the number of rows or columns. That is why the default value of 5 steps results in a 6×6 grid for each patch. See Figure 9.3.

7. To understand the steps concept more clearly, deselect the Show Interior Edges checkbox. Only the exterior edges—those bordering each patch—will be visible. Change to the Vertex subobject level and note the vertices at the corners of each patch. Select the bottom-left vertex on the lower patch.

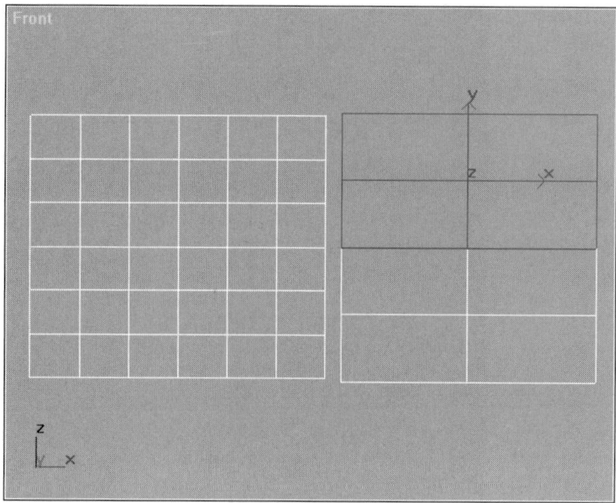

Figure 9.3
The same as Figure 9.2, but with the View Steps value decreased to 1 for the editable patch object on the right. There are two patches in this object, and each is now a 2×2 grid of quad polygons. Note how the Steps value affects the whole object, even though only the upper patch is selected. The object on the left uses the default Steps value of 5, producing a 6×6 grid. The number of steps is always one unit fewer than the number of rows or columns in the grid.

8. Two perpendicular vector (tangent) handles appear. To tilt the one in the lower-left corner upward a bit, activate the Move Transform; the Transform Gizmo appears on top of the selected vertex. It can be difficult to move the vector handles if they are covered by one of the axes of the Transform Gizmo. If necessary, use the – (minus) key to shrink the gizmo and get it out of the way. Move the vector handle up to put some curvature in the bottom edge.

9. It's now evident that the edges are Bezier curves. Change the Step value again to see how it affects the curve resolution. In Figure 9.4, the Steps value is set to 4. This resolution is too low for this much curvature, and the five linear segments in the curve are clearly visible.

The Tri Patch

How does a Tri patch differ from a Quad patch? Let's find out:

1. Use Reset to start over with a fresh screen, if necessary, and draw out a Tri patch in the Front viewport. The creation tools for Tri patches are found in the same place as for Quad patches. Note that Length and Width creation parameters still appear in the panel, but the segmentation parameters are missing. The object you create is a four-sided grid, but there are a couple of obvious differences from the Quad patch. First, the grid is composed of triangles rather than quadrangles. Second, the grid lines look a little sloppy and are not precisely parallel, as can be seen in Figure 9.5.

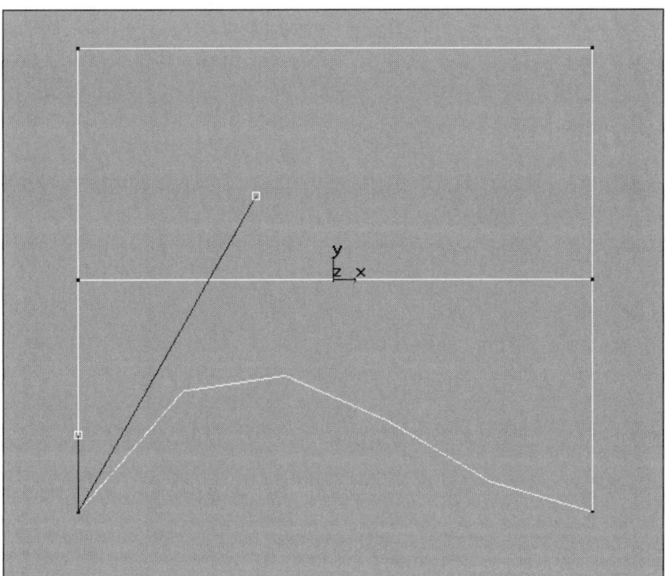

Figure 9.4
The object from the right side of Figure 9.3, with interior edges hidden. Only the edges bordering each patch are visible. The vertex at the bottom-left corner is selected, and the vector handle along the bottom edge is moved up to generate some curvature in the Bezier spline. With a Steps value of only 4, the five linear segments in the spline are clearly distinguishable. This is insufficient resolution for a high-quality render.

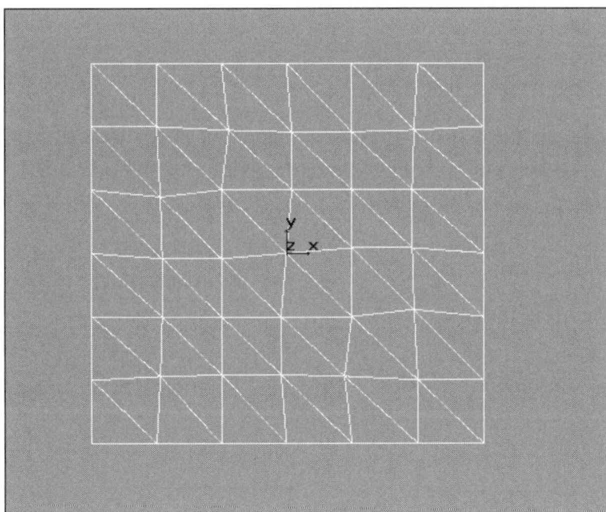

Figure 9.5
A Tri patch created in the Front viewport. This object is four sided, like a Quad patch, but the grid is composed of triangles rather than quadrangles, and the edges of these faces are not precisely parallel.

2. Convert the object to an editable patch. Go to the Patch subobject level and click on the object. It's made of two triangular patches that meet along a central diagonal edge. Delete one of the patches to understand what a single Tri patch looks like. Figure 9.6 shows one of the two triangular patches, which is selected and then deleted.

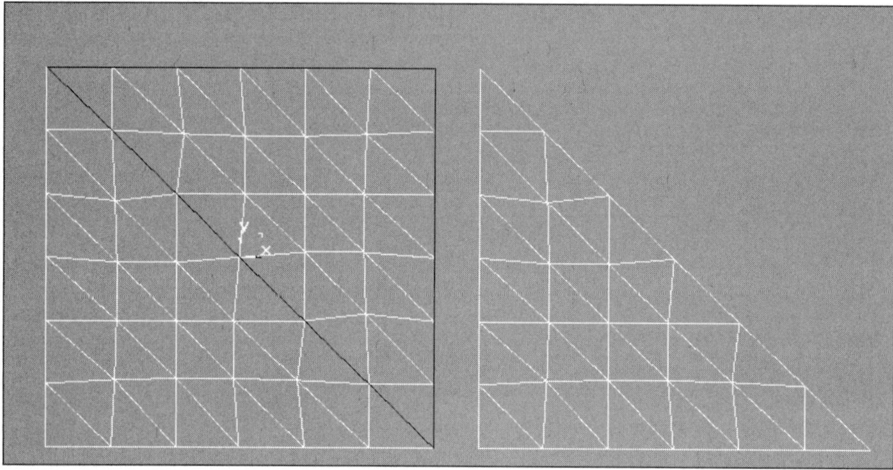

Figure 9.6
The Tri patch object from Figure 9.5 is converted to an editable patch object. Using the Patch subobject level, you see that it's composed of two triangular patches that share a common diagonal edge. The upper-right patch is selected in the object on the left, and it is deleted in the object on the right.

3. Play with the View Steps spinner to see how a Tri patch is tessellated. The concept is the same as with the Quad patch, in that each of the edges (each Bezier curve) is divided into the specified number of equal segments. The resulting polygonal mesh is much harder to read, however, which makes Tri patches generally more difficult to work with than Quad patches. Just as in regular organic polygonal mesh modeling, a quadrangular structure is preferable to triangles, whenever possible. Figure 9.7 shows a Tri patch with a View Steps value of 1 (on the left) and with a value of 9 (on the right). Note the confusing curvature of the interior edges in the more tessellated version.

Building with Patches

Now that you have a sense of what Bezier patches are, you can start working with them in the following exercises.

Adding Patches Together

Follow these steps to add patches:

1. Reset your scene if necessary. Create a Quad patch in the Front viewport and convert it to an editable patch.

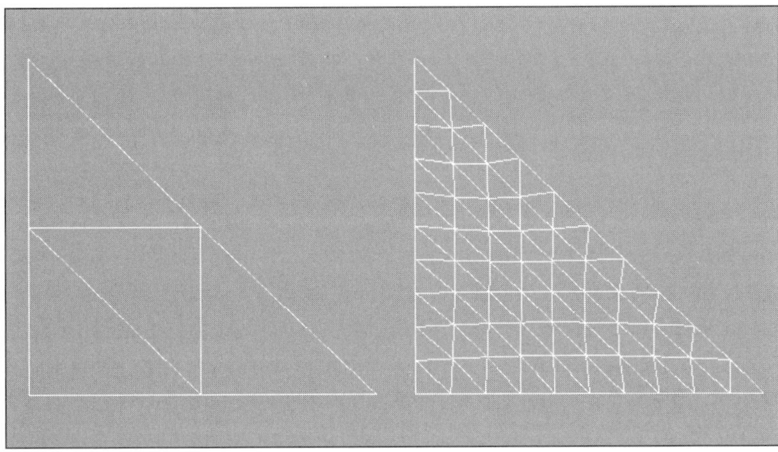

Figure 9.7
A single Tri patch, with different degrees of tessellation. The object on the left uses a View Steps value of 1. Each edge is divided in half, and interior edges connect these vertices. The object on the right illustrates a View Steps value of 9. Note the curvature of the interior edges. Tri patch geometry is more difficult to read than Quad patches.

2. Deselect the Show Interior Edges checkbox so that only the exterior edges are visible. In the Edge subobject level, select the edge on the right. Click on the Shift key and move to the right to create a new patch. Alternately, you can select the edge and then click on the Add Quad button on the Editable Patch panel to add a new Quad patch to the right side of the original one. Your screen should look like Figure 9.8.

Figure 9.8
Adding a Quad patch. A single Quad patch is created and converted to an editable patch object. With the interior edges hidden, the edge on the right side is selected. The Add Quad command on the Editable Patch panel adds an adjoining Quad patch on the right side of the original.

Note: *One of the most attractive features of patch modeling is the power of such a small toolset. Just compare the number of buttons on the Editable Patch panel with the number on the Editable Mesh or (even worse!) NURBS panel, and you'll breathe a sigh of relief. With Bezier patches, you take just a few tools and use them creatively. As a consequence, everything you need fits on the right-click menu, and workflow becomes more intuitive.*

3. Select the two edges on the bottom together and use the Add Quad command on this multiple selection. You now have four patches, arranged in a 2×2 square. Change to the Vertex subobject level and select the vertex in the middle of the bottom row of edges by dragging a small rectangle around it, ensuring that all vertices that occupy the same location are selected. Just above the Soft Selection rollout, the panel indicates that only one vertex is selected—it indicates the number of the selected vertices—but more than one can be selected, as you will see in a moment.

4. Undo to eliminate the lower row of patches and add the lower patches, one at a time. In other words, select one bottom edge and use Add Quad, and then select the other edge and use Add Quad again. Change to the Vertex subobject level and drag a rectangle around the middle vertex on the bottom row of edges. This time, the panel indicates that two vertices are selected. Your screen should look like Figure 9.9.

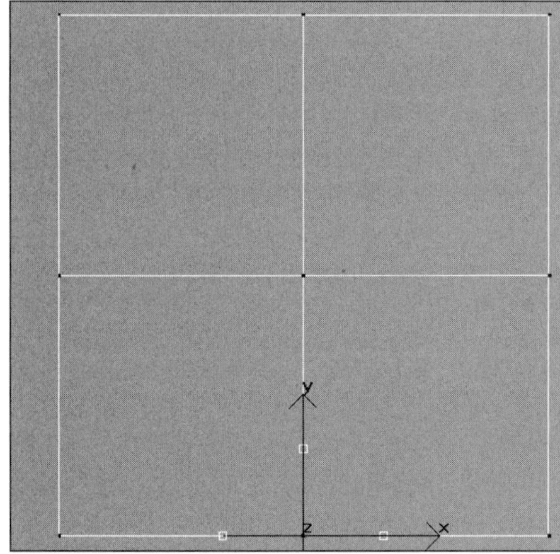

Figure 9.9
The object from Figure 9.8, with two patches added on the bottom. Each patch was added separately, so two separate vertices appear in the middle of the bottom row of edges. If the two patches are added together, by selecting both edges at once when applying the Add Quad command, only a single vertex would exist at that spot.

5. Click on the spot to select only a single vertex. (Check the panel to make sure you have only one.) Move that vertex and, as you'd expect, the two patches rip apart. Undo to put the two vertices back on top of each other. Click on the vertex again to select the other vertex; you'll see the vector handles change direction. Each vertex is associated with only one of the two adjacent patches. Move the upward-pointing vector over to the side. You probably need to shrink the Transform Gizmo (with the minus key) to get it out of the way. As you can see in Figure 9.10, there are two independent edges, and each can have its own curvature.

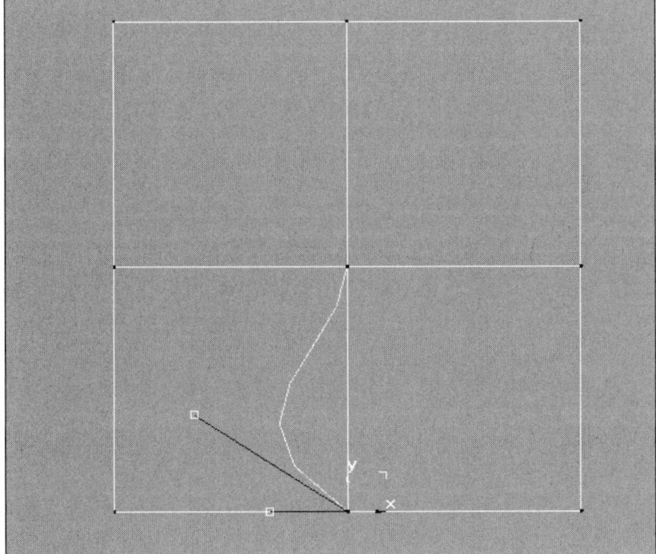

Figure 9.10
The object from Figure 9.9, with only the vertex for the left patch selected. The upward-pointing tangent handle is moved to demonstrate that the two added patches have independent edges. It was necessary to shrink the Transform Gizmo to get it out of the way of the vector handles.

6. To zip up these patches, drag a rectangle to select both vertices; you'll see four distinct vectors—two for each patch. Click on the Selected button in the Weld group of the Modify panel. Now there is only one vertex (with three vectors), and there's only one common edge between the two patches. The object is seamless. Your screen should look something like Figure 9.11.

Using Coplanar and Corner Vertices

When opposing handles for a vertex on a Bezier curve line up in a straight line (that is, when they are *collinear*), the curvature is smooth through that vertex. In the same way, curvature is smooth in all directions when the vector handles of patch vertices are Coplanar. Coplanar

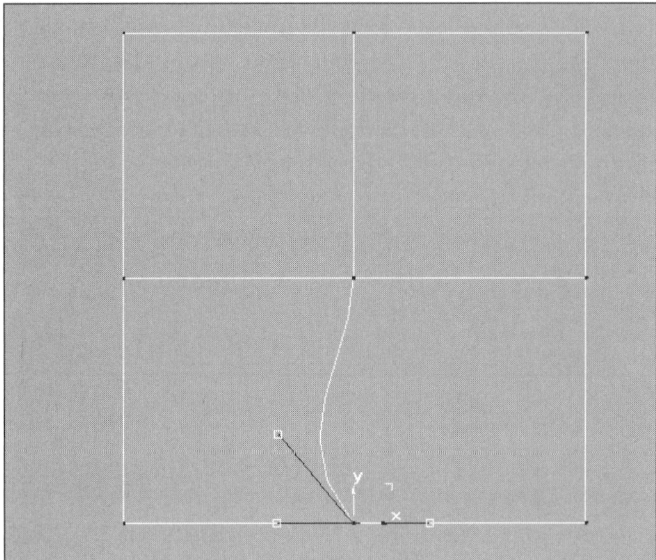

Figure 9.11
The object from Figure 9.10, after welding the two vertices in the center of the bottom row of edges. There is only one vertex (with three vectors), and there's only one common edge between the two patches. The object is now seamless.

vertices are the keys to creating seamless Bezier patch surfaces. Continue the previous exercise by exploring the differences between Coplanar and Corner vertices:

1. Move the center vector so that it's pointing straight up and all four patches are square. Drag a rectangular section around the vertex in the center of the object, at the point where all four patches meet. Confirm that only one vertex is here, and note the four vector handles. With the vertex selected, bring up the Quad menu and note the two types of patch vertices: Coplanar and Corner at the bottom of the upper-right section. Make sure that Coplanar is current. What does this mean?

2. Check the box to display your interior edges again, and activate the Perspective viewport. Move any of the vector handles into or away from the mesh. Note that all four handles remained locked together, so moving any one of them will move them all. All four handles are on a single plane, and they remain so when any one of them is moved. In effect, the handles were rotated as a unit around the vertex. Figure 9.12 illustrates the smooth curvature through the center vertex after the handles are moved.

3. You may notice that the vector handles respond to movement in two different ways. If you move a handle in any direction other than in its own line, all four handles effectively rotate around the vertex. If you move a handle in the direction of its tangent vector, the vector simply becomes longer or shorter, without moving any other handles. These two kinds of control—over both the length and direction of Bezier handles—are the same as for 2D Bezier splines. Figure 9.13 illustrates the effect of pulling out a vector handle.

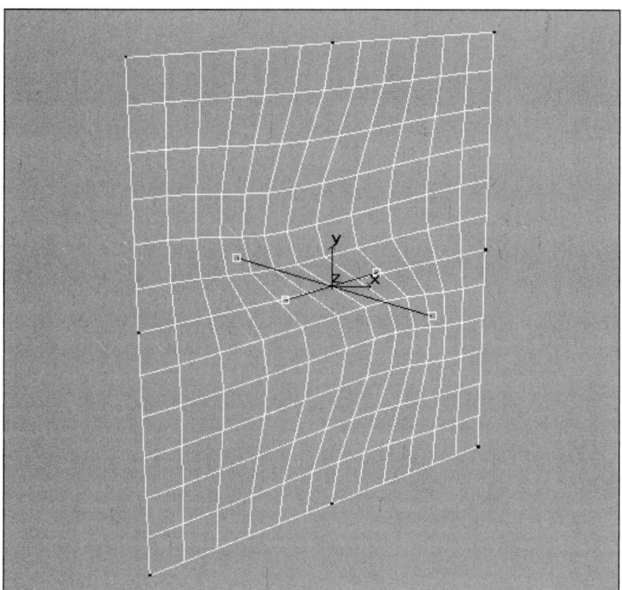

Figure 9.12
The object from Figure 9.11, with its edges straightened and its interior edges revealed. The vertex in the center is selected and its handles are moved. Because this is a Coplanar vertex, all the handles move together so that they stay in a single plane. By keeping the vectors in a common plane, the curvature through the vertex remains unbroken.

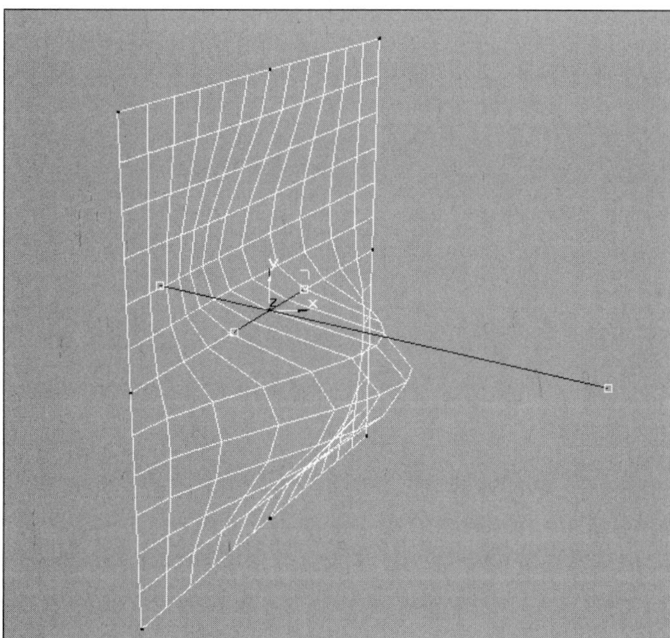

Figure 9.13
The same as Figure 9.12, but with one of the vector handles drawn out in the direction of its own tangent vector. Just as with all Bezier curves, this action increases the effect of the curvature in that direction.

Manipulating Vector Handles Can Be Tough Work

The hardest thing to master in Bezier patch modeling is the manipulation of the vector handles. Bezier handles are great on a 2D plane, but they can be very difficult to control in 3D space. It's hard to figure out which way they are pointed and how long they are without rotating a Perspective viewport.

The Transform Gizmo, which is such a boon when transforming vertices, is a definite interference when moving vector handles. As mentioned before, you often have to shrink it to get it out of the way. Get used to using the keyboard shortcuts to change the directional constraints when moving vectors. F5, F6, and F7 constrain the X, Y, and Z axes, respectively; F8 toggles among XY, YZ, and XZ. Another useful idea is to use the Screen coordinate system in the Perspective viewport. That way, you can stay in the XY constraint and move points parallel to the surface of the screen. Doing so requires rotating your view very often, however.

The Filter group in the Editable Patch panel can be very useful. If both the Vertices and the Vectors checkboxes are selected, you can transform both vertices and vector handles. If only one is selected, the other type of object is not selectable with the mouse cursor. You should often check the Vectors filter to make sure that you don't accidentally move the vertex when you want to move only its handles. Then, when you try to select another vertex, you have to remember to select the Vertices checkbox again.

4. Right-click on the selected vertex and change it to a Corner type. You can move each handle separately; the vectors no longer remain Coplanar. See Figure 9.14.

5. Select the Lock Handles checkbox on the Editable Patch panel. If you move any of the handles, they all move as a rigid unit, even though they are no longer Coplanar.

6. Change the vertex back to the Coplanar type. Watch how all the vector handles jump into a single plane.

Subdividing Patches and Binding Vertices to Edges

As is often the case, the patches must be subdivided in order to give greater definition to the model; vertices are bound to edges to give you greater control over the patch. On a fresh screen, complete the following steps:

1. Create a square Quad patch in the Front viewport, 100 units in length and 100 in width. Convert the object to an editable patch and hide the interior edges.

2. Select all four edges in the Edge subobject level by dragging a rectangle around the patch. Use Add Quad to create a "t" of five patches. Your screen should look like Figure 9.15.

3. Go to the Patch subobject level and select the central patch. Select the Propagate checkbox in the Geometry rollout and click on the Subdivide button. The central patch is divided into four patches, and the new edges continue through the adjacent patches to divide them as well. See Figure 9.16.

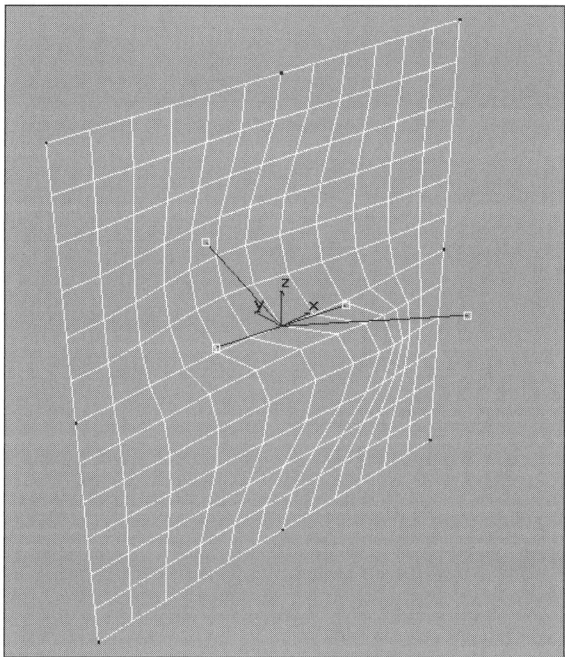

Figure 9.14

The same as Figure 9.13, but with the vertex changed from the Coplanar to the Corner type. One of the handles was moved up, without affecting the others. The handles are no longer constrained to lie on a single plane, allowing sharp changes to the direction.

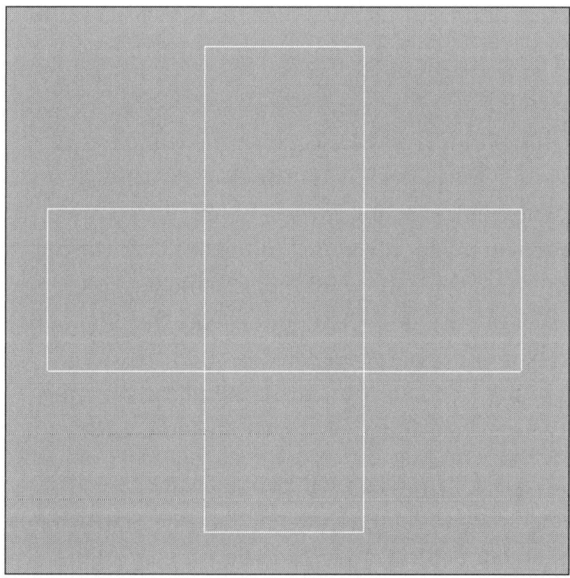

Figure 9.15

A square Quad patch was converted to an editable patch object. All four edges were selected and Add Quad was applied to create four surrounding patches. The interior edges are hidden.

Figure 9.16
The same as Figure 9.15, but with the central patch selected and subdivided. Because the Propagate checkbox is selected, the new edges are continued through the adjacent patches, to divide them as well.

4. Undo back to before the Subdivide step, and try Step 3 again (or use the Quad menu) with the Propagate checkbox deselected. The subdivision is now confined to the selected patch, but it creates discontinuities in the geometry. Go to the Vertex subobject level and select one of the new vertices. There are only three handles, and none extend over the edge into the adjoining patch. Move the vertex you've selected to see the discontinuity. Your screen might look like Figure 9.17.

5. Get ready for something fantastic—something that gives MAX's patch modeling a real *edge*. (The pun will be obvious in a moment.) One of the biggest issues in modeling is how to create local detail in a restricted area, without increasing the resolution of the entire mesh. In this case, for example, you needed an additional vertex in the center of the central patch, but you didn't necessarily want to subdivide the whole object to do it. With vertex binding, you can have it all. Choose bind from the Quad menu, or activate the Bind button, and drag from the new (moved) vertex to the corresponding edge on the adjacent patch. A rubber-band line will stretch from the vertex to your cursor to indicate that the feature is active. The gap in the geometry magically closes, as shown in Figure 9.18.

6. The bound vertex is different from all the others, as you can tell from its black color. First of all, it cannot be moved directly—it moves only when the shape of the edge to which it is bound is changed. Check this out by getting out of Bind mode and selecting one of the vertices on the edge. Move a vector handle to bulge out the curve. The bound vertex stays on the edge. Your screen might look like Figure 9.19.

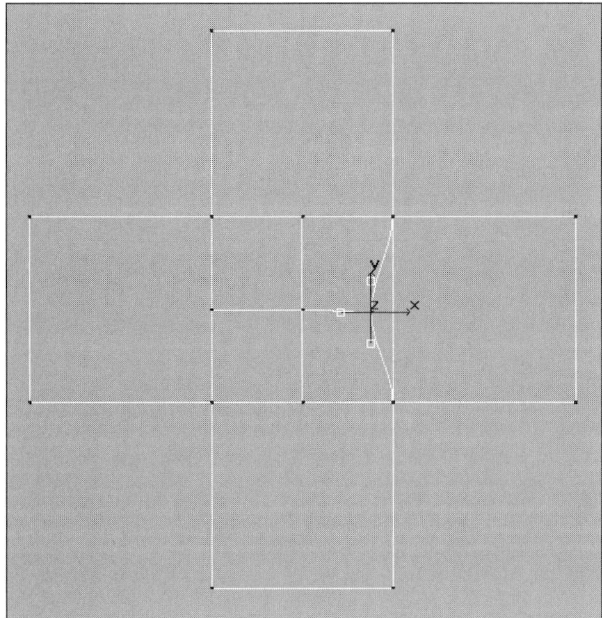

Figure 9.17
By deselecting the Propagate checkbox, the subdivision is confined to the selected patch. This creates discontinuities in the geometry, however, because the adjoining patches do not share the new vertices. Moving one of these vertices reveals that the geometry is no longer seamless.

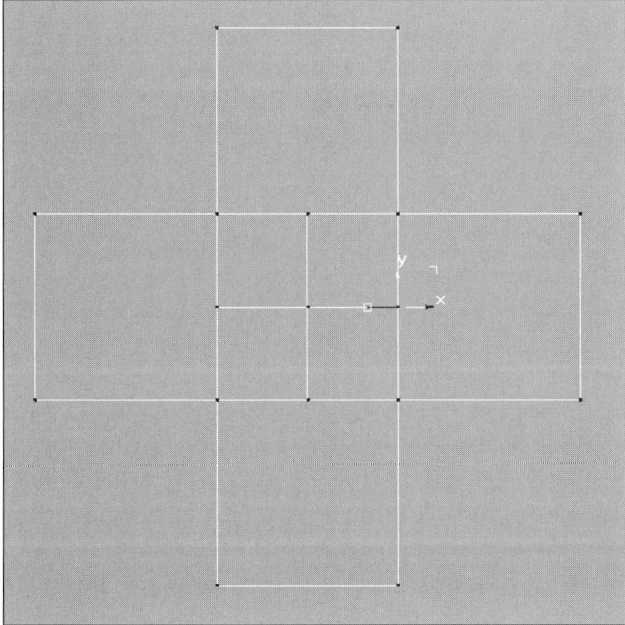

Figure 9.18
The new vertex that was moved in Figure 9.17 is bound to the adjacent edge. The geometry is now seamless.

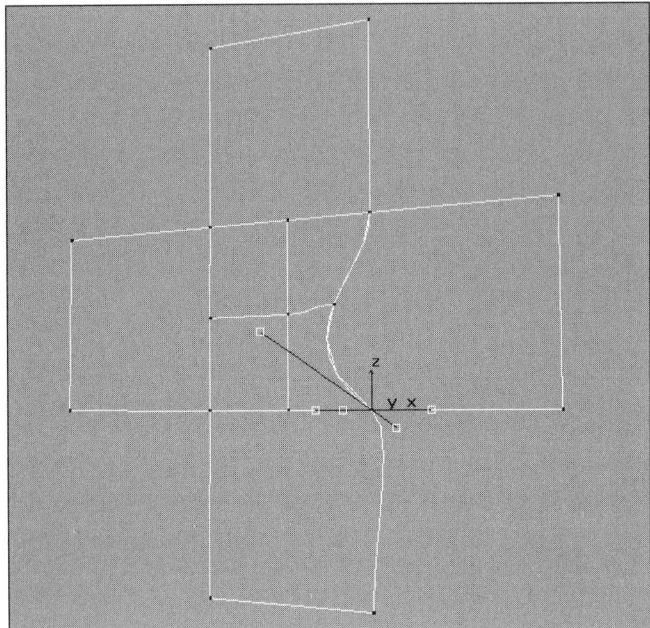

Figure 9.19
The bound vertex from Figure 9.18 is tested. The lower vertex on the edge to which it was bound is selected and its vector handles are translated to put curvature into the edge. The bound vertex sticks to the bulging edge.

7. Zoom in on the bulging edge. The segmentation of the adjoining edges doesn't match up. This makes sense. The whole object, as you've learned, uses a single Steps value. The left side has two patches, so each of its two edges is divided into six segments. The right side has only one patch, so its single edge is divided into six segments. Therefore, the left side has twice as many segments as the right. The close-up view in Figure 9.20 shows the problem.
8. If you render this view, however, the result is seamless. A Wireframe render (use the Force Wireframe option in the Render Scene dialog box) shows how the two edges are merged into a single one. Take a look at Figure 9.21.
9. Try increasing the Render Steps value to get a smoother result. Check it out in a Wireframe render.

It's important to understand the reason for this seamless result. A low-end renderer must input a polygonal mesh; therefore, all spline-based objects are tessellated into polygons before they are handed to the renderer. A high-end renderer, such as that found in MAX, can receive spline-based objects directly, however. It both tessellates and reconstructs the mesh in the rendering process. An important part of the geometry work done by the renderer is to rebuild the edges on adjoining curved surfaces so that they are stitched together into a seamless mesh. This process can work only if the adjoining edges are close enough to each other to begin with. The vertex binding tool keeps the edges together so that the renderer can merge their meshes. This

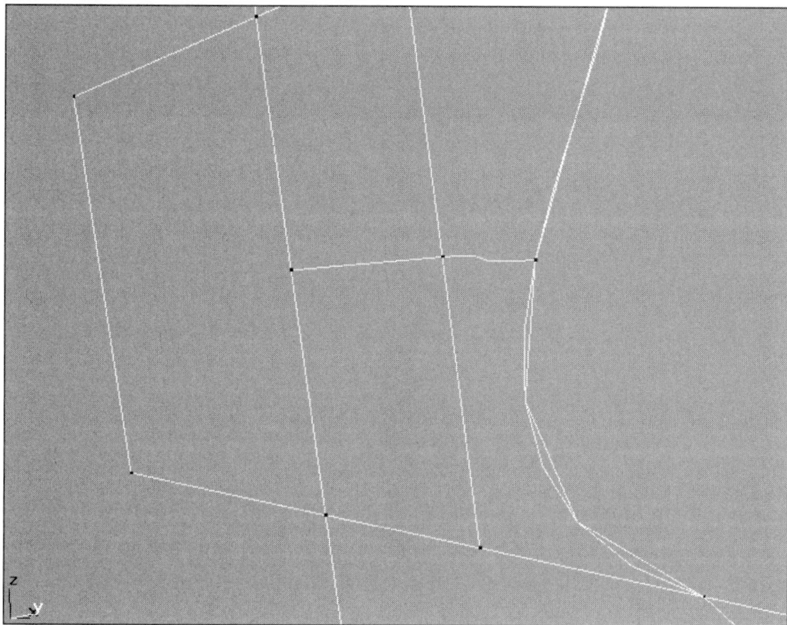

Figure 9.20
A close-up view of the object in Figure 9.19 reveals the different segmentation of the adjoining edges. The two edges on the subdivided patch have twice as many total segments as the single edge to which the vertex was bound.

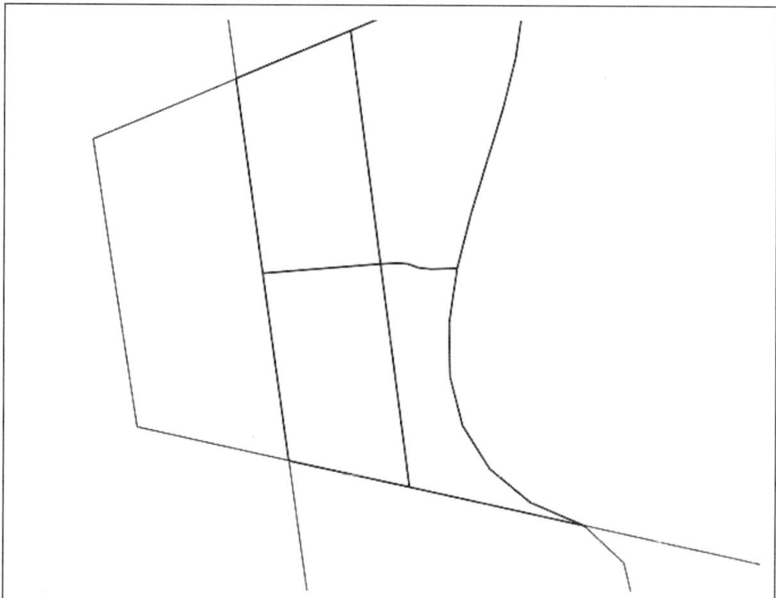

Figure 9.21
The object from Figure 9.20 renders seamlessly. A Wireframe render shows that only a single edge is rendered. In a regular shaded render, the result is smooth and without gaps.

subject of the tessellation of curved surfaces and the merging of edges is especially important in NURBS modeling, and it will be addressed in greater detail in Chapter 10.

Extruding Patches

Patches can be extruded, much like polygons on an editable mesh. The procedures also differ, however, which is attributable to the fact that the edges of patches are Bezier splines. Explore the possibilities by following these steps:

1. Create a square Quad patch in the Front viewport by using a Length value of 100 and a Width value of 100. Set the Length Segs to 3 and the Width Segs to 3 to create a grid of nine patches.

2. Convert the object to an editable patch and hide the interior edges. Your object should look like a tic-tac-toe board.

3. Turn the central patch into a circular one. In the Vertex subobject level, select one of its four vertices. Using the Quad menu, convert the vertex from the Coplanar type to the Corner type. Now, you can tilt the vertex handles to create curved edges. Do this with all four vertices and move the appropriate tangent handles until your object looks like Figure 9.22.

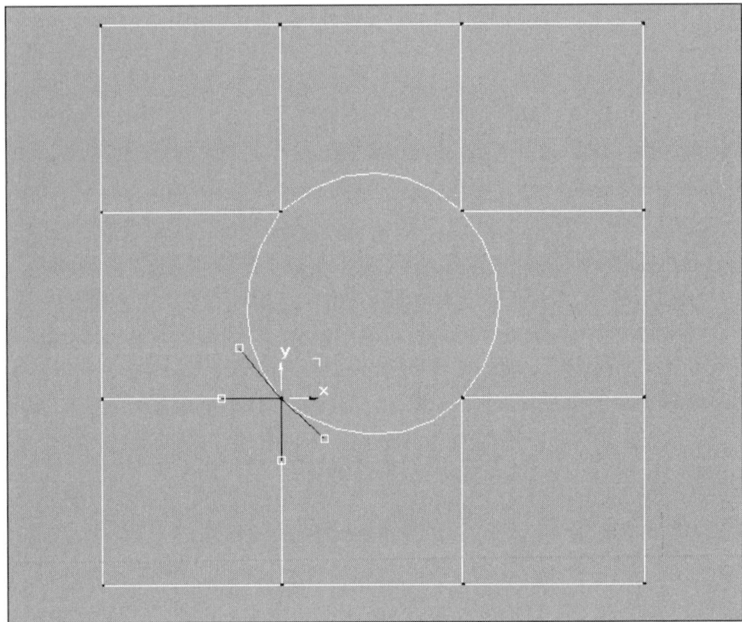

Figure 9.22
An editable patch object, composed of nine Bezier patches. The vertices around the central patch are converted from the Coplanar to the Corner type, and the tangent handles are moved to create curved edges. The central patch is now circular. Note that the tangent handles defining the curve are collinear.

4. Work in the Perspective viewport so that it's easier to see extrusions into 3D space. Hide the Home grid to make things easier to see.

5. Go to the Patch subobject level and select the circular patch. You can extrude either by activating the Extrude Patch or Bevel Patch option in the Quad menu (or the Modify panel) and dragging on the screen, or by using the Extrusion and Outlining spinners. For now, let's get an idea of how the spinners work. Pull the Extrusion spinner up to a value of 50 to extrude out the selected patch. Note that the spinner value returns to 0 when the extrusion is complete.

6. With the extruded patch still selected, drag the Outlining spinner down (into negative values) to scale the patch inward. Note the curvature in the extruded edges. To see the surface better, show your interior edges and increase the View Steps value. Your object should resemble Figure 9.23.

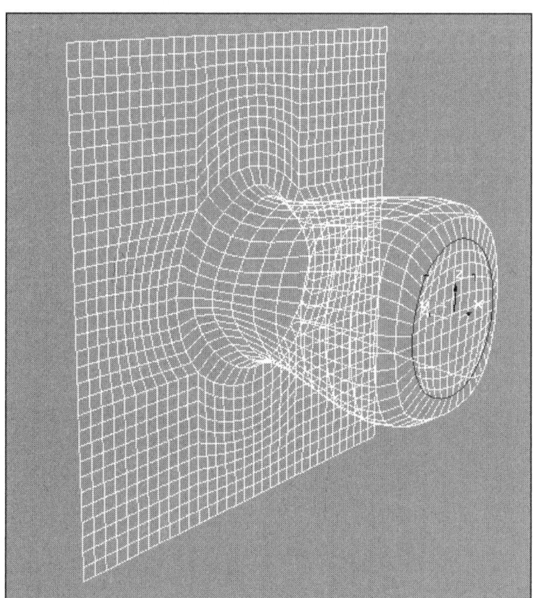

Figure 9.23
The object from Figure 9.22, with the central patch extruded and then scaled inward with the Outlining spinner. The interior faces are made visible and the View Steps value is increased to see the curvature better. The viewport is shown as Wireframe for clarity.

7. The curvature in the sides of the extruded patch is determined by the options in the Bevel Smoothing section of the panel. By default, both the Start and End are set to Smooth. If you're thinking about using this extrusion for an arm, you might get a better result by changing this setting. Undo to before the extrusion operation and change the End option from Smooth to None.

8. This time, work interactively by using Bevel patch from the Quad menu. The Bevel mode permits you to extrude and scale together. Drag on the selected patch to extrude it out as before. After you release the mouse button, you can move the mouse to scale the patch. Scale the extruded patch slightly inward, and then click to complete the process. Notice the difference in curvature between the start of the extrusion and the end. Figure 9.24 shows the result, with the interior edges visible and with a denser mesh resolution.

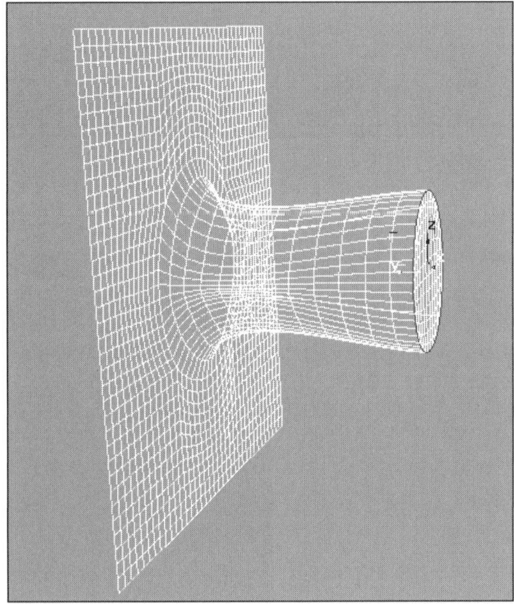

Figure 9.24
Similar to Figure 9.23, but with Bevel Smoothing set to None for the end of the extrusion. This result might be useful for building out a character limb, such as an arm.

The Miracle of Extrusion in Patch Modeling

Anyone with the slightest interest in organic character modeling should take a moment to enjoy the view shown earlier in Figure 9.23. The debate in organic character work today is between smoothed polygonal cages and NURBS. NURBS are naturally smooth, so they are ideal for organic work; by their very nature, however, it's difficult to create branching architecture. You can't just extrude an arm from a torso or a finger from a hand in a NURBS surface the way that you can with polygons. That's why the use of polygonal mesh cages with MeshSmooth remains such an important organic character-modeling method.

With the addition of extrusion to the Bezier patch modeling toolset, a whole new vista opens up. You can build branching architecture with the simplicity of extrusion, yet work directly with seamless curved surfaces. Bezier patches stand just between polygons and NURBS; for many modelers and for many modeling projects, they are the ideal option.

Creating a Torso

Now that we've laid the groundwork, let's explore the Bezier patch toolset in a practical context. Like all areas of modeling, patch modeling cannot be taught using a "paint-by-numbers" approach. There is no single sequence, and each modeler works in a different way. Use this exercise to help you get started and for basic guidance. Then, start doing things your own way. It takes awhile to get comfortable with the process of moving patch vertices and vector handles in 3D space, but the effort is well worth it.

The Basic Architecture

All modeling begins with a conception of the basic architecture of the model. An artist must work from the general to the specific or risk getting stuck in a corner. Throughout this exercise, you'll be concerned with creating a basic shape while the structure is still simple, and you'll add geometry only as necessary:

1. You'll model only one half of the torso and mirror it as you work to see the whole. It makes sense to define the curvature around the side of the torso first. Because you want the torso to face front, create a 100×100 Quad patch in the Left viewport to start the side. Give it one segment in length and three segments in width.

2. Convert the object to an editable patch and hide the interior edges. You should see a grid of three patches across. Start pulling vertices. Go to the Vertex subobject level and, in the Top viewport, drag a rectangle around the column of vertices at one end. Check the panel to make sure that two vertices are selected, and note in the Left viewport that you've selected the vertices at the top and bottom of one side of the object. Hold down the Ctrl key and select the two vertices at the top and bottom of the other side. You should now have the four corners of the object selected.

3. Still in the Top viewport, move the selected vertices in the positive X-direction to create a curved surface around the side of the torso. At this point, your Top viewport should look something like Figure 9.25.

4. It's time to correct the curvature by moving the vector handles. Drag a selection rectangle around the entire object to select all of the vertices. A big part of adjusting vector handles is to keep the Transform Gizmo out of the way. Try the Use Selection Center option to create a single gizmo in the middle of the selected vertices. (This option is the middle of the three drop-down buttons, immediately to the right of the Reference Coordinate System drop-down box in the Main Toolbar.) In a Top viewport, move the handles to create a nice curve. Note that there are two sets of handles to align at each location in a Top viewport. Note also that the handles in both directions from a vertex are locked, because they are Coplanar vertices. Confirm this in the Quad menu. Adjust all the handles until your Top viewport looks close to that shown in Figure 9.26.

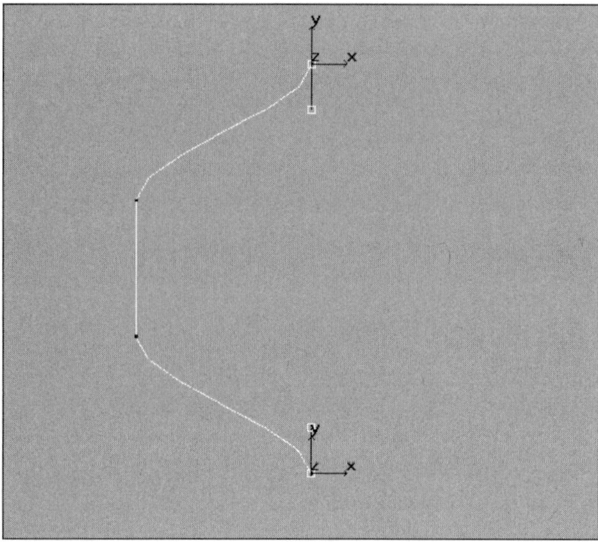

Figure 9.25
A Quad patch is drawn in the Left viewport and divided into three width segments. After conversion to an editable patch object, the four vertices at the corners of the object are selected and moved to create a curved surface for the side of the torso.

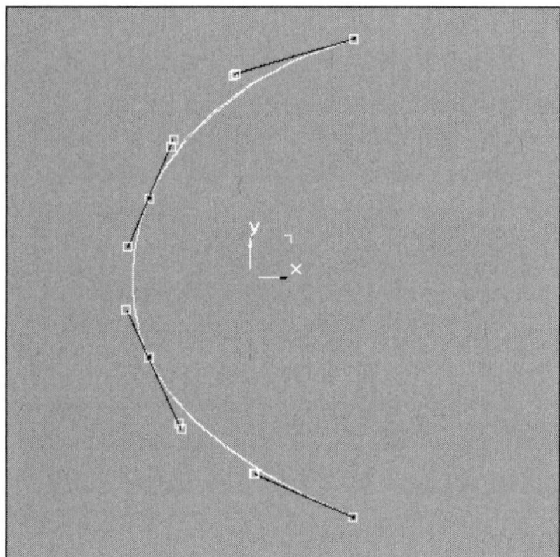

Figure 9.26
The object from Figure 9.25, with all vertices selected and Use Selection Center selected on the Main Toolbar to get the Transform Gizmo out of the way. Vector handles are moved in the Top viewport to create the proper curvature for the side of the torso.

5. The surfaces you've created thus far are the side of the torso beneath the arm. To add the patches for the shoulder area, in the Left viewport go to the Edge subobject level and select all three edges along the top of the object. Shift+drag to extend the surface upwards so that the upper row of patches is about half as tall as the lower row.

6. Select the middle of the three edges along the top and Shift+drag again to create another patch the same size as the one below it. Select all the vertices in the object and check the number indicated in the panel. If this number is greater than 14, you need to look for unwelded vertices and then weld them. Your Left viewport should look like Figure 9.27.

Figure 9.27
The object from Figure 9.26, in the Left viewport. A second row of Quad patches is added above the original row, and the height of the new row is adjusted to about half that of the lower row. Another patch is added at the top center.

7. The top patch is the top of the shoulder. You need to weld each vertex at the top corner of this "flap" to the vertex at the corner of the row of patches below it. When two vertices are welded in the Editable Patch panel, the new single vertex is positioned midway between them. It may make sense to move the vertices on the flap closer to the vertices on the row beneath before you weld. But why not see how things work out with the vertices in their present location? Use the Perspective viewport and select a pair of vertices to be welded. Your screen should look like Figure 9.28.

8. Clicking on the Selected button in the Weld group of the Editable Patch panel probably won't do anything, because the default distance threshold value is very small. Increase the value in the Selected spinner and click on the button until the welding works. Select the pair of vertices on the other side and weld them together as well.

9. It's time to move vertices and vector handles to clean up the result. Jump back and forth between a wireframe view and a shaded view with Edged Faces to understand what you're doing. A great technique is to drag off a clone of the object and make it an instance. Rotate the instance so that you have two views of the same object. You can work on either one, and both

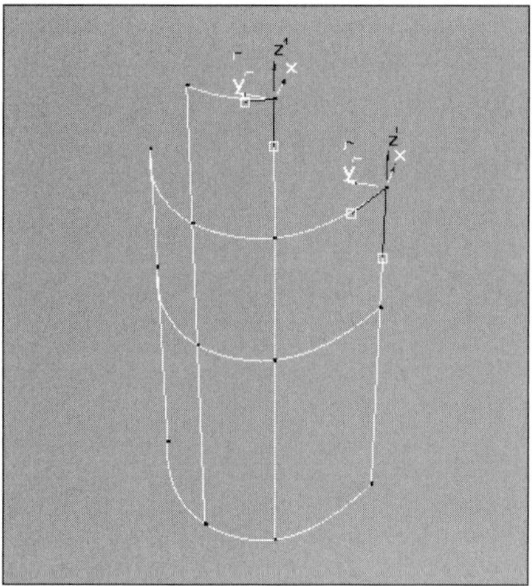

Figure 9.28
A Perspective viewport of the patch object from Figure 9.27, with a pair of vertices selected for welding. The weld will join the two vertices at a point midway between them.

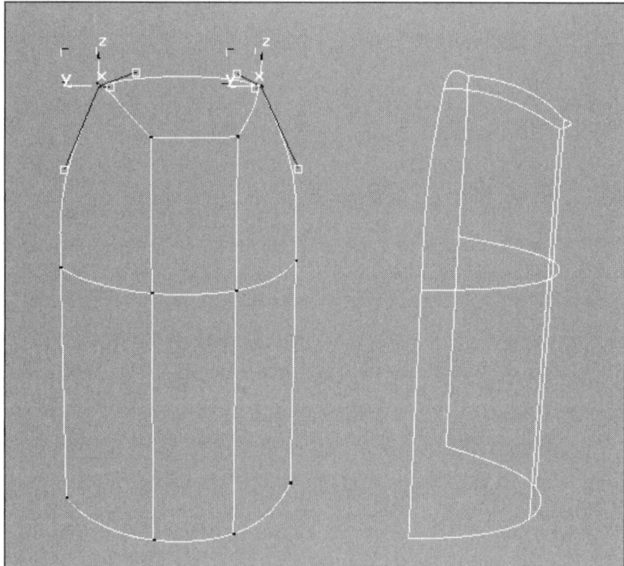

Figure 9.29
After welding both pairs of vertices, the vertices and vector handles around the shoulder area are carefully adjusted to achieve a clean, clear result. An instance of the object is created and rotated to permit two views of the object at once. This technique makes the effect of vertex and vector adjustments much easier to see without having to rotate the view constantly.

objects remain identical. Take some time getting your object to look like the one in Figure 9.29. Remember to use the Vertices and Vectors filters, and to turn the Vertex filter back on when you want to select new vertices. This step should take some time to accomplish well.

Extruding the Arm

Before you build out the arm, adjust your proportions. It's difficult to gauge proportions when using only one-half of the torso, so you'll mirror it:

1. To set up for mirroring, go to the Front viewport and move the object until the centerline is aligned to the World Z-axis. Move the pivot point of the object precisely to the centerline by using the Transform Type-Ins at the bottom of the screen and setting the X value to 0 in the Absolute mode. It doesn't hurt to get all the centerline vertices lined up, as well. In the Vertex subobject level, select all the vertices on the *centerline*, meaning the vertical column where the two mirrored halves will meet at the spine of the character. Use the Align tool to line up the vertices with the Maximum value of the object itself. It's not critical that you achieve all these steps perfectly right now, but give it a try. This scaling technique comes up again and again, so it's worth learning. Your Front viewport should look like Figure 9.30.

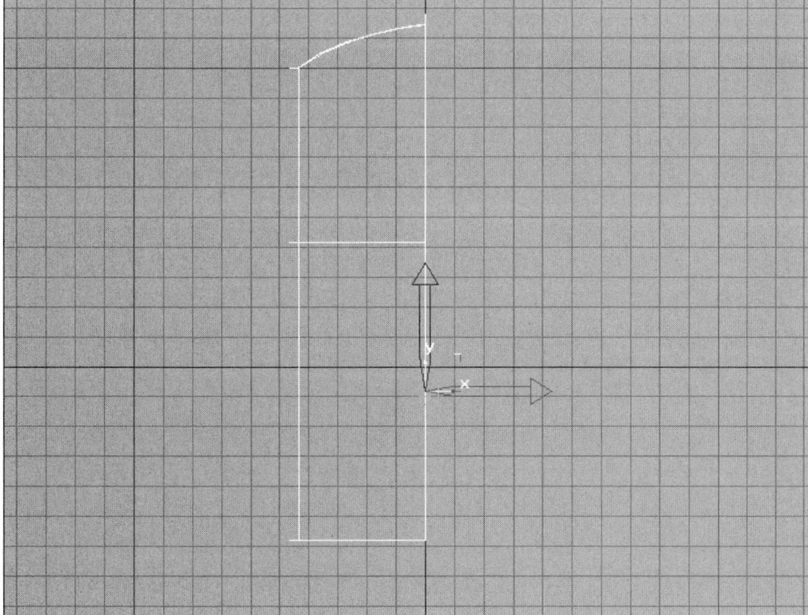

Figure 9.30
The centerline of the object is aligned to the Z-axis in a Front viewport . The pivot point is moved to the centerline and all vertices on the centerline are aligned. This is the ideal setup for mirroring.

2. Make sure that you are not in a subobject mode. In the Front viewport, mirror the object on the X-axis, and make the mirrored clone an instance.

3. Start making adjustments to get this armless trunk into shape. This is going to take a lot of work, so save your file before you start; you can then return to it if necessary. Move and scale vertices and move handles all over the place. You'll quickly notice some of the peculiarity of Bezier surfaces. Moving vertices often creates creases because the tangent vector

directions don't make sense in the new positions. So, you have to move vertices constantly and then adjust their handles. You may have to bounce back and forth between Coplanar and Corner vertex types to manipulate handles properly. Scaling multiple selected vertices as a group is a useful technique, because it tends to keep the surface smooth. If scaling pulls vertices off the centerline, just move them back. It may take a long time to get to something that looks like Figure 9.31, but the skills you're learning are invaluable.

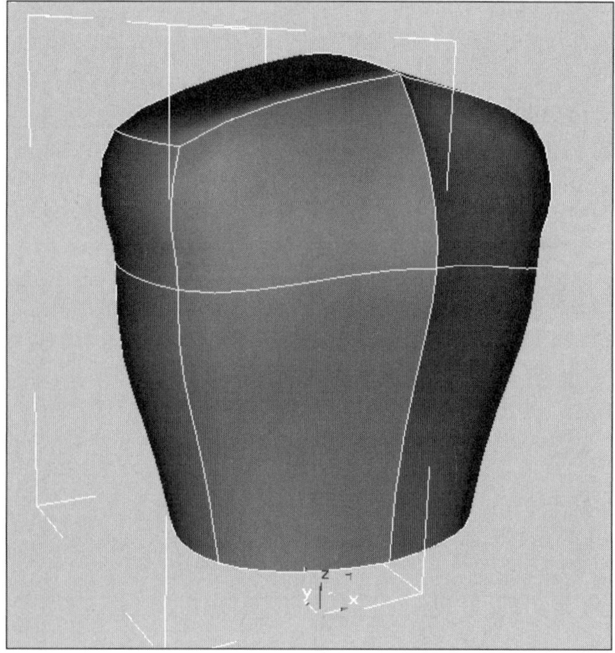

Figure 9.31
After the object in Figure 9.30 is mirrored as an instance, all of the vertices and vector handles are carefully edited to produce a trunk with satisfactory proportions. A shaded view with Edged Faces is invaluable for editing Bezier patch surfaces.

4. Select the four vertices around the patch from which the arm will be extruded and convert them all to the Corner type, if necessary. That way, you can adjust their handles to curve the edges of the patch. Make the patch fairly round and scale it down if the arm hole is too big. After you finish, convert the vertices back to Coplanar and see how the surface smoothes out.

5. Select the circular patch and bevel out a short stump, about halfway to the elbow. Experiment with different options for Bevel Smoothing, but end up with None at both Start and End. Once again, get back in there, and start moving vertices and vector handles to improve the contours. Even though you converted the vertices around the extruded patch to Coplanar, they are returned to the Corner type after the extrusion. When you finish adjusting

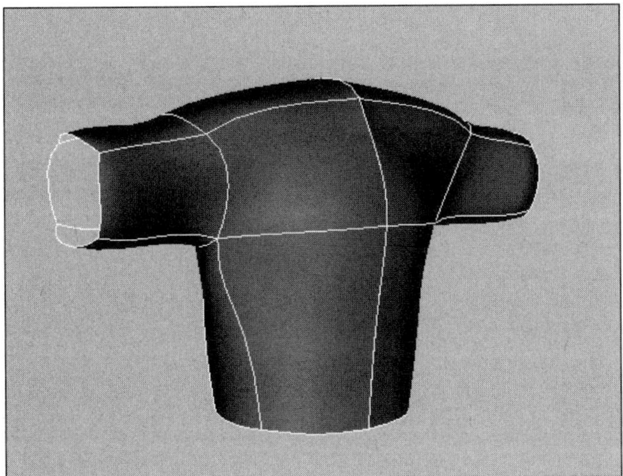

Figure 9.32
After rounding out the edges of the arm patch, the patch is beveled out to about mid-forearm. Bevel Smoothing is set to None for both Start and End. After the extrusions, many vertices and vector handles are edited to improve the contours. The patch at the end of the arm stump is hidden for clarity. Don't delete this patch if you want to make further extrusions.

handles around the base of the arm, convert the vertices back to Coplanar, but leave the vertices at the stump of the arm as Corner type. After some editing, your torso might look like Figure 9.32.

Subdividing for Local Detail

The previous steps are about as far as you can go in this exercise with the edges you have. To add a head, you need a place for the neck to be extruded from:

1. Select the edge on top of the shoulder and click on the Subdivide button. It doesn't matter whether the Propagate checkbox is selected in this case. Two edges are created across the top of each half of the model.
2. The hole for the neck requires continuity between edges on both halves of the model. So, you have to merge both halves into a single unit before you continue. Use the Attach button to attach the instanced half and get out of the Attach mode. In the Vertex subobject level, select all the vertices on the centerline, except the pair on the very top. The panel should tell you that 12 vertices are selected. Perform a weld at a small threshold distance to merge the vertices to a total of six.
3. Scale the two unwelded vertices at the top apart, to open a hole for the neck. Start moving vertices and vector handles around the neck hole to create a clean shape. This is tough work, and you have to jump back and forth quite a bit between Coplanar and Corner vertex types. You need the Corner type to move the vector handles freely, but you have to

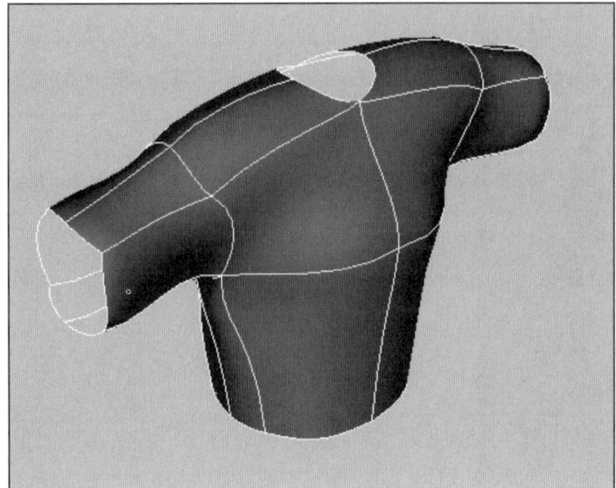

Figure 9.33
A new row of edges is added along the top by selecting the edge across the shoulder and using the Subdivide command. The two instanced halves are attached to create a single patch object, and all of the vertices on the centerline are welded together, except the pair at the top. This pair is scaled outward to open a hole for the neck. Considerable editing of the vertices and vectors around the neck results in a clean opening.

return to the Coplanar type periodically to see the result smoothed out. Take advantage of the new vertices on the shoulder to improve the contours there. After some experimentation, you should be able to produce a result similar to the one in Figure 9.33.

4. Once the neck hole is opened, you can go back to working in halves. In the Element sub-object level, select the patches on half of the torso and delete them. Mirror the object as an instance, as you did before.

5. Now comes the reward of all your efforts. Save the file in this state so that you can return to it, and carefully start to add new vertices by selecting edges and using the Subdivide command. These new vertices allow you to craft more subtle contours. All of your developing skills for transforming vertices and tangent handles come into play here. One technique that really helps is to use the Transform Type-Ins to move and scale selected vertices (this technique doesn't work for vector handles). With one or more vertices selected, call up the required Type-Ins and click on the spinners to transform them easily and precisely. This technique is much better than dragging the vertices on the screen. After a little while, you have a much better looking torso. Use Figure 9.34 as a guide.

Modeling with Spline Networks

When you look at a Bezier patch object in a wireframe view with the interior edges hidden, all you see is a spline cage. A *spline cage* is a network of splines that describes a surface. The vertices on the splines intersect, and the web created by these intersections defines the separate patches. MAX has a set of tools that allow you to create Bezier patch objects from spline cages built from Bezier splines.

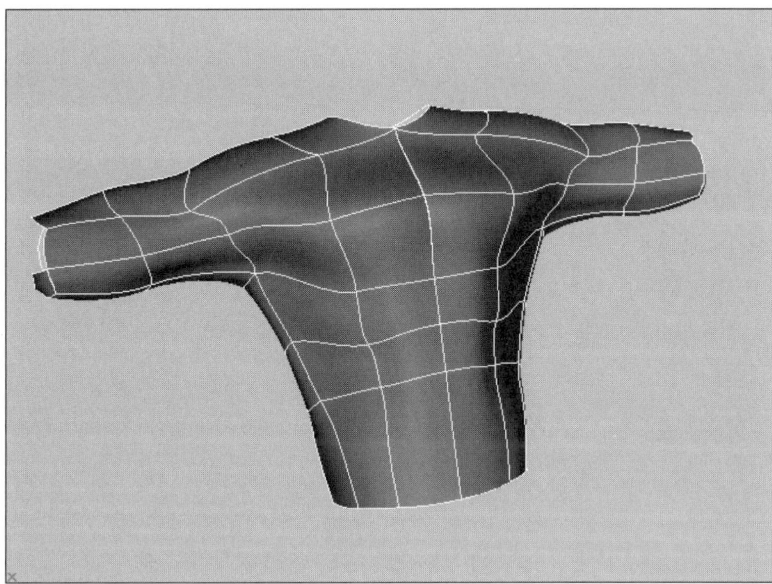

Figure 9.34
By the careful addition of more segmentation, the contours of the model can be defined with much greater precision. The new edges were added by selecting edges and using the Subdivide command. The additional vertices and their tangent handles provide control of localized surface areas.

Introduction to Spline Networks

To create the patches of a spline network, the Surface modifier is placed on top of a spline cage object. Wherever it finds three- or four-sided closed units, it creates a Bezier patch, and it welds coincident vertices between patches. The CrossSection modifier assists in creating spline cages by bridging between splines. Great flexibility undoubtedly is inherent in this approach to patch modeling, but not everyone will find it easy. Building and editing spline cages requires a strong understanding of the Editable Spline (or Edit Spline) toolset. The basic concept is to connect vertices between splines in a single editable spline object. You refine existing splines to add additional vertices and use the snap tools to draw new splines that connect these vertices.

Although this process takes a fair amount of practice and experimentation, its results are difficult to match in any other method. The following exercise will demonstrate the spline network method of creating surfaces:

1. In the Top viewport, create a five-pointed Star and a slightly smaller Circle, both centered near the origin. Move the Circle in the positive Z-direction so that it is above the Star. Your scene should look similar to Figure 9.35.
2. Convert one of the shapes into an editable spline. Attach the other to it. Now only one spline is in the scene, with two spline subobjects.

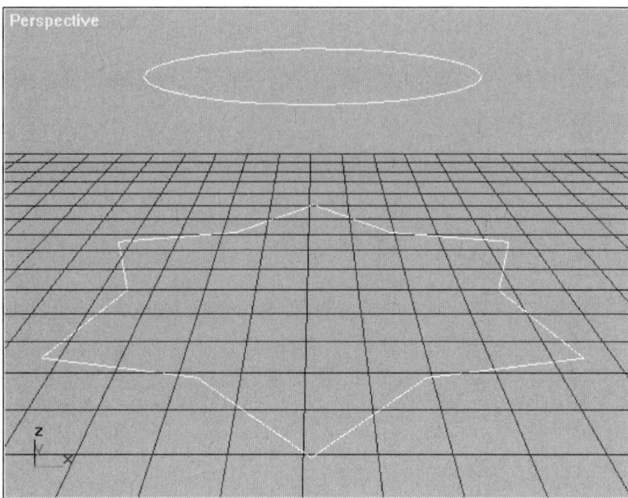

Figure 9.35
A Circle and a Star primitive with the Circle moved in the positive Z-direction.

3. Select the spline and make a reference copy to the side, so that edits at the Spline subobject level can be performed on the original and the result passed to the copy. With the copy selected, apply a Surface modifier to it. The spline disappears except for the surface created spanning the circular shape, as shown in Figure 9.36. The Surface modifier creates a patch between any closed portion of a spline that is bound by three or four segments. MAX circles are formed with four vertices and four segments and, therefore, meet the criteria in this situation.

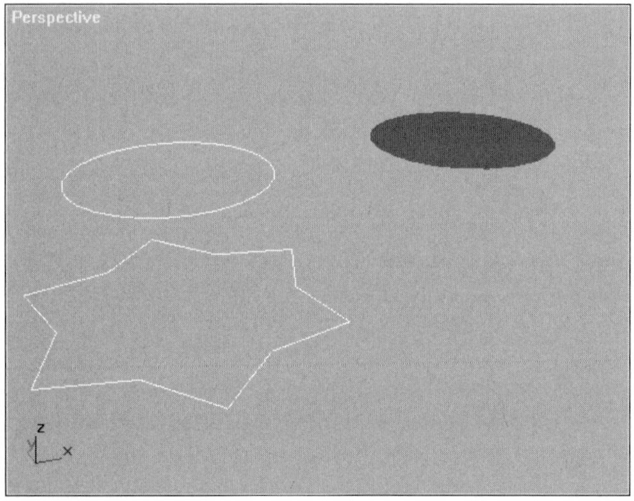

Figure 9.36
The original attached spline, on the left, and the reference copy, on the right, with the Surface modifier applied. This modifier has created a surface spanning the circular spline subobject.

4. The Refine tool, found in the Geometry rollout of an editable spline's Modify panel, adds and relocates new vertices to a spline. Select the original and, at the Vertex level, use the Refine tool to add a new vertex to the Circle. The surface spanning the referenced Circle disappears because it no longer complies with the segment restrictions to create a surface.

5. Activate only the Vertex option, in the Grid And Snap Settings dialog box, and turn on the 3D Snap Toggle. The Create Line mode adds new segments to a spline by connecting existing vertices, and the Vertex snap ensures their proper location. To bring back the circular surface, activate Create Line mode by clicking on the button in the panel or selecting it from the Tools 2 section of the Quad menu. Click on one vertex, then on a vertex immediately to its right, and then on the one to the immediate left of the first. Figure 9.37 shows the result as seen in the Top viewport when the vertex at the 3 o'clock position is selected first. The Circle is only partially surfaced because it is divided into three sections: The left two meet the criteria for surfaces to be created, but the one on the right does not.

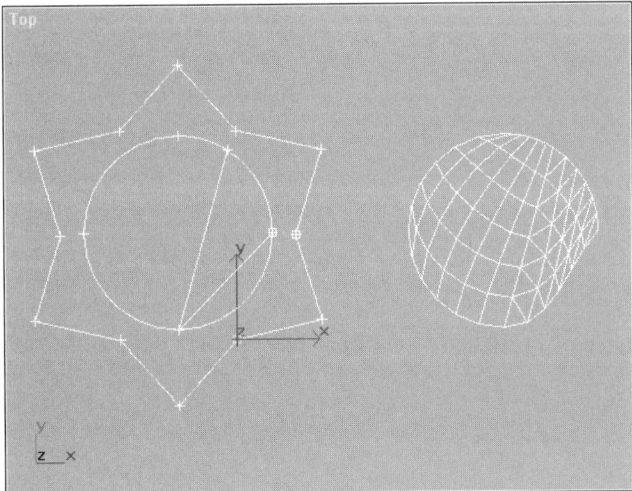

Figure 9.37
The Top viewport after additional lines have been added to the Circle. The circle-shaped spline subobject of the reference copy is only partially covered with surfaces.

6. Undo to before the new lines were added. Create a line from an original vertex to the one directly across from it. This time, the areas on both sides of the new line meet the criteria and are surfaced. When you're adding lines to a spline for the purpose of creating surfaces, always consider the consequences of choosing the vertices and whether the action will assemble or remove surfaces.

7. Create new lines from the peak of one of the Star's points and the intersection at the valleys on either side of it to the corresponding vertex at a quadrant of the Circle. The scene should look similar to Figure 9.38. Continue creating lines and, in turn, surfaces; this will close the gap between the Circle and Star, as shown in Figure 9.39.

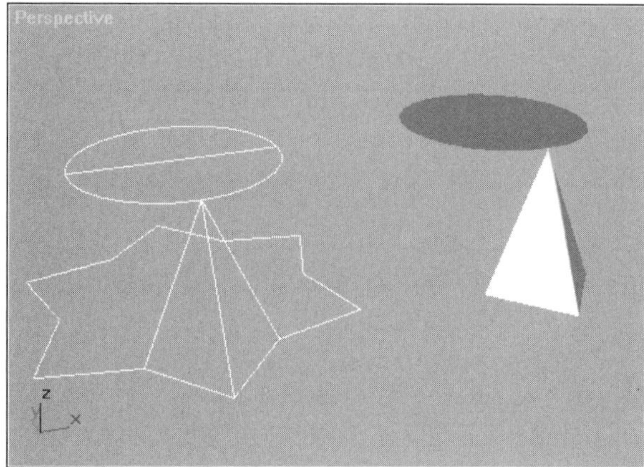

Figure 9.38
In the original, on the left, lines are created to join three vertices on the Star to one on the Circle.

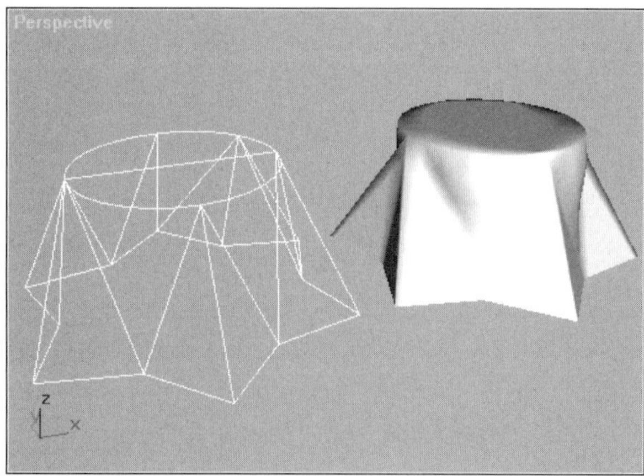

Figure 9.39
The same as Figure 9.38, but with the remaining faces created between the Circle and the Star.

8. You still have control over the vertices of the original shape, and changes to the original are reflected in the referenced copy. To round out the base of the objects, use a window to select all the vertices along the bottom (there should be 24) and change them to the Smooth type. Select both vertices at the tip of one of the Star's peaks and change their type to Bezier. Manipulate the handles that appear to widen the tip, and push the edge into the object, as shown in Figure 9.40.

9. The shape is not restricted to the two splines that currently exist; as many as required can be added and surfaced. Create a Rectangle in the Top viewport, in the general area of the existing spline, and move it in the Z-direction until it is above the Circle. Select the original object and attach the Rectangle to it. Create lines connecting the new spline subobject to the old one. The scene should look similar to the one in Figure 9.41.

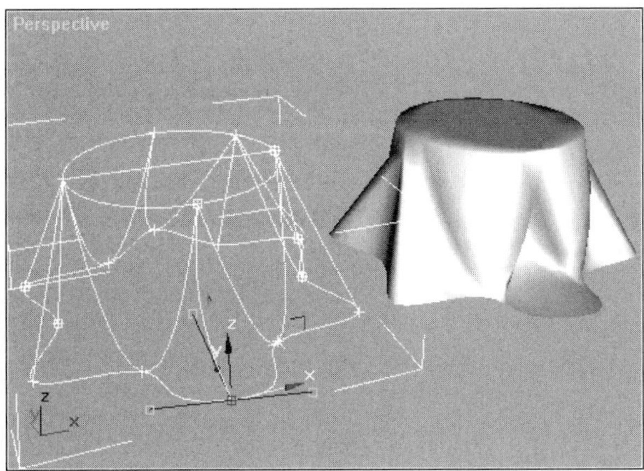

Figure 9.40
The objects shown in Figure 9.39, after the base vertices are converted to the Smooth type and the two vertices at one peak are changed to Bezier and manipulated.

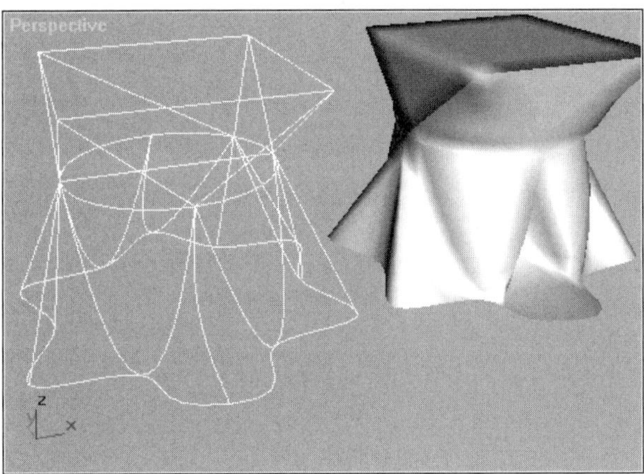

Figure 9.41
After adding and relocating a new spline, it is attached to the existing spline. Lines are added to create surfaces on the reference copy.

As you can see, spline networks are a powerful method of producing smooth, contiguous, and easily editable surfaces. The next section will demonstrate one procedure of using spline networks to create a human head.

Using Spline Networks to Create a Higher Poly Head

Open the file Chap9 Head.max from the CD-ROM. It consists of two Boxes with a front and side sketch of a head applied to them as image maps visible in viewports set to Smooth + Highlights mode. Figure 9.42 shows the Perspective viewport as it should appear in your scene. If the maps (images) do not appear, make sure both the MAX file and the images (Facefront.jpg

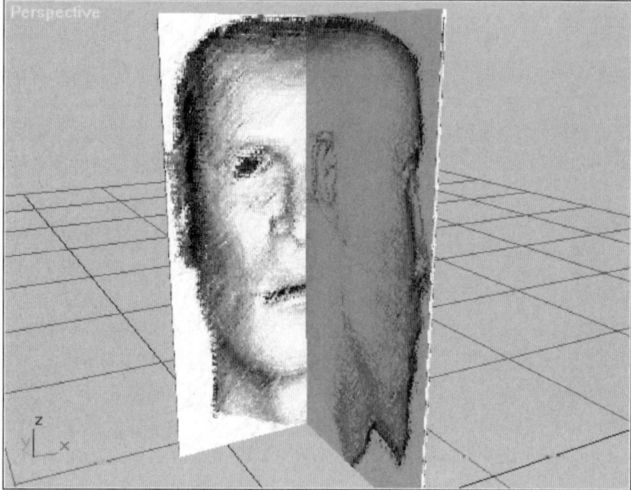

Figure 9.42
The initial state of the Chap9 Head.max file consisting of a sketch of the front and sides of the head to be modeled.

and Faceside.jpg) reside in the same directory; or, add the path to the maps in the Customize|Configure Paths|Bitmaps tab.

The process of creating the head model is as follows:

1. Create a couple of the splines that the patches will span. Attach one to the other.
2. Make a Reference copy of the splines.
3. Apply the Surface modifier to the Reference copy and mirror it, creating an instance copy in the process.
4. Create additional spline elements that divide the original spline into three- or four-sided polygons.
5. Edit the original and view the results on the copies.
6. Collapse the copies and weld their surfaces closed.

This exercise demonstrates, step by step, how to create a human (or nonhuman) head using spline cages. It's not feasible to show every possible editing and creation step, because everyone's models will be different; but the major stages are addressed. The procedures shown here can be extended to complete an entire body, as well as be used to create any type of organic object from a minimum amount of information. This project can take awhile to complete, and you may require even longer to refine the mesh into a presentable project. Follow these steps:

1. The initial layout of the scene is important. Each of the Boxes has been placed just behind the base planes, as seen in the Front and Left viewports, and they have been made very

thin. As a result, splines created in these viewports, and at the base plane, will appear on top of the Boxes rather than behind, inside, or coplanar to them.

2. In the Left viewport, draw a spline around the profile of the head, leaving the bottom of the neck open. The crown and back of the head should have fewer vertices than the face, because of the relative lack of detail in those areas. All the vertices should be Bezier; use their handles to smooth the spline and correct any imperfections. Figure 9.43 shows the spline with Display Render Mesh and Use Viewport settings enabled in the spline's Rendering rollout, for clarity; these settings aren't required for the modeling process.

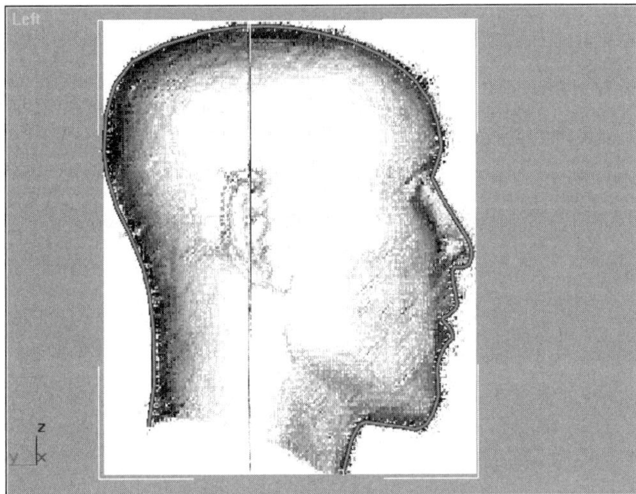

Figure 9.43
In the Left viewport, a spline is drawn around the profile of the head, with the neck area left open.

3. This step requires some visualization on your part. Draw a second spline, inside the first, that follows the contour of the head, about as far away (in the Front viewport) from the first spline as half the width of the nose. Because this is such a close distance, many of the spline segments will fall at or near the first spline drawn; it is a common mistake to draw this spline too far inward. One of the telltale signs of this error is a sharp ridge through the centerline of the head.

4. Switch between the Left and Front viewports, keeping an eye on the Perspective, and move the vertices away from the base plane to their correct location to the left of the original. Figures 9.44 and 9.45 show the proper location and shape of the splines.

5. Select the first spline and, using the command found in the Geometry rollout, attach the second spline to it. With the spline (which now consists of two spline subobjects) selected, Shift/move it and create a Reference copy. Doing so will allow you to apply modifiers to the copy and still see—and easily edit—the original.

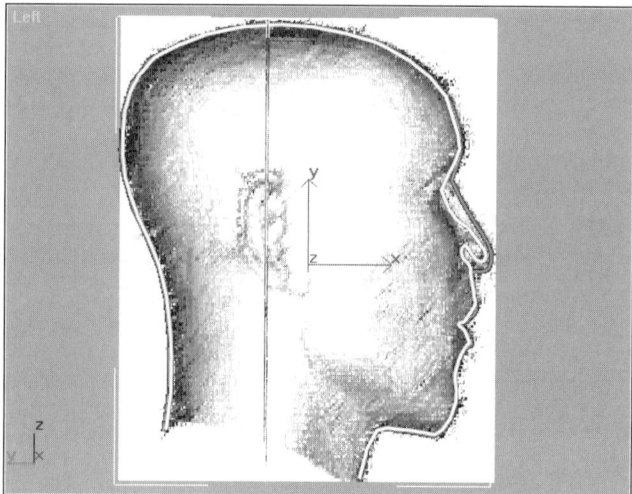

Figure 9.44
The second spline is drawn inside the first, following the contour of the head about the width of half the bridge of the nose away from the first.

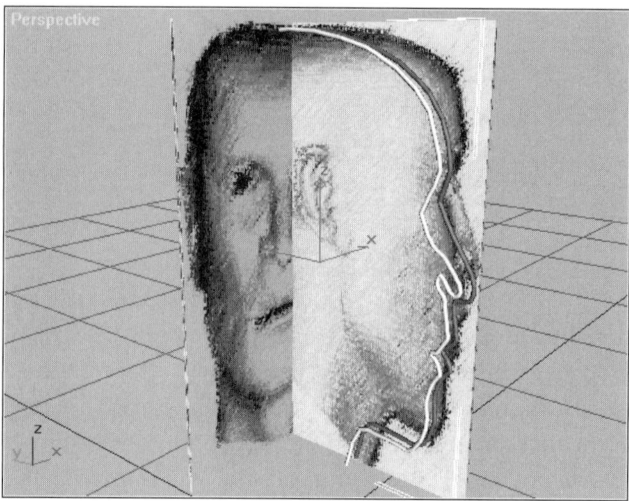

Figure 9.45
The Perspective viewport showing both splines drawn to this point.

6. Apply the Surface modifier to the copy. The copy will disappear, but that is expected: The Surface modifier creates patches when bound by three or four line segments and no bounded shapes exist. The bounded shapes must be created on the original and will be passed to the reference copy.

Note: *If no surfaces appear after you meet the requirements in Step 6, they may be facing inward and, therefore, may not be displayed in the viewports. Selecting the Flip Normals checkbox in the Parameters section to aim the new surfaces outward may be the solution.*

7. Ensure that the 3D Snap Toggle button is active and that only the Vertex option is selected in the Grid And Snap Settings dialog box. Select the original spline (which is now a subobject) and, in the Geometry rollout, activate the Create Line button. Start the new segment by clicking on one of the vertices on the forehead of the first spline segment created and then on a corresponding vertex of the second spline segment. Pick on the next vertex down on the original, and a patch will appear on the reference copy. Continue to zigzag back and forth between the vertices of the splines, watching as the surface grows, as shown in Figure 9.46. It's permissible to connect two or three vertices to one as long as no more than four sides are used to create a polygon. Create five or six polygons at a time; right-click to stop the process, and then restart it to prevent a necessary Undo from undoing too much. Use the Arc Rotate tool as required to adjust the view to snap from vertex to vertex until the entire gap between the spline subobjects is spanned with patches. In the event that too great a distance must be spanned for a single patch, use the Refine tool to add new vertices. Clicking with the Refine tool adds a vertex, whereas clicking and dragging adds and then moves a vertex.

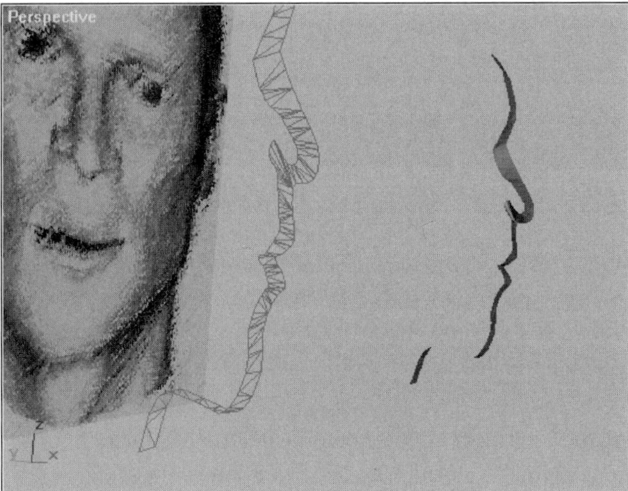

Figure 9.46
The two spline subobjects are offset. Then, the Create Line tool is used to create three- or four-sided polygonal shapes between them. In the background, the reference copy, with the Surface modifier applied, has faces created where the polygons are in the original.

8. The edges between the vertices are straight and need to be adjusted to add curvature to the face, especially in the mouth and nose area. Select the vertices around the specified areas one at a time, and move their handles until the shape looks proper. As necessary, add additional splines to the scene and attach them to the network to add definition.

9. Only half the model need be created manually, but you can see both halves at once. Select the reference copy and mirror it, creating an instance copy in the process. Figure 9.47 shows one of the vertices being edited on the spline network and the completed surfaces between the first two spline subobjects as well as the reference copy mirrored and instanced. The

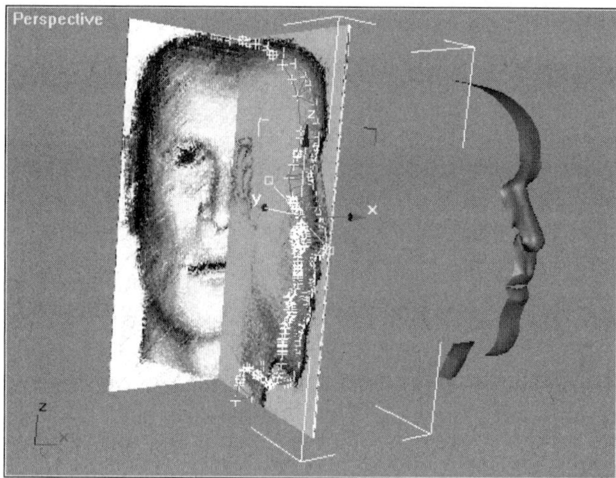

Figure 9.47
The scene with one vertex's Bezier handles adjusted to achieve a smooth nose. By mirroring the reference copy and creating an instance copy in the process, the full head can be seen as it is modeled. The Relax modifier smoothes the surfaces.

surfaces created this way may tend to be a bit faceted, but applying a Relax modifier at the top of the stack will smoothe the model.

Watch the Bounding Box

When picking or moving vertices for the spline network, watch the bounding box for the selection. If it increases greatly in size, the cursor is not near enough to a vertex for the snap to work; it's locating itself on the ground plane beyond the object and increasing the extent of the object's limits. Moving the cursor closer to a vertex will allow it to snap and decrease the size of the bounding box.

---

10. Create a third spline following the profile at a point about even with the eye. Attach it to the existing spline. Repeat the procedure in Step 7 to create patches between the second and third spline subobjects. Around the nose and eye area, you need to incorporate additional splines to contend with the increased definition required. These splines will be added when making modifications later; for now, leave the areas void. Figure 9.48 shows the head after the third and fourth splines have been added and patches created between them and the existing splines. Additional spline subobjects were added around the eye and nostril areas to accommodate the additional definition required.

11. The tough part of the project is completed and, from here out, the steps will be relatively easy. Create the remaining splines required to close off the head and adjust their handles to achieve the desired look. Choose File|Merge to open the Merge File dialog box shown in Figure 9.49. Navigate to the Chapter 9 section of the CD-ROM or the location on your hard drive where those files have been copied, and highlight the file Chap9 Ears.max. A thumbnail image of the last edited view from the file appears in the Thumbnail area.

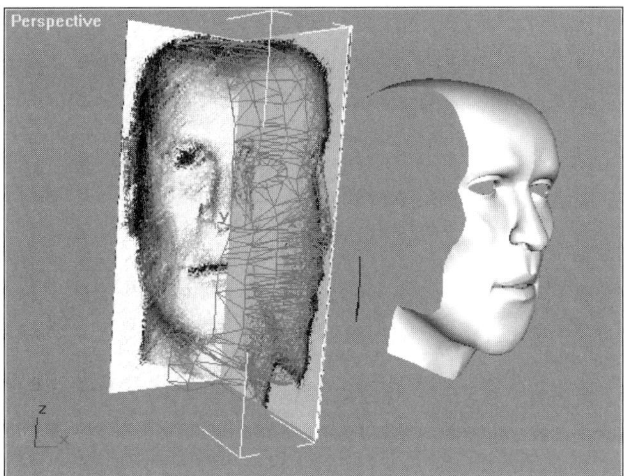

Figure 9.48
After creating and attaching two more splines to the network, additional segments are added between vertices to create surfaces on the reference and instance copies. Additional splines are added to the eye and nose area due to the increased requirement for detail. Nearly all the vertices surrounding the face require adjustment of their Bezier handles.

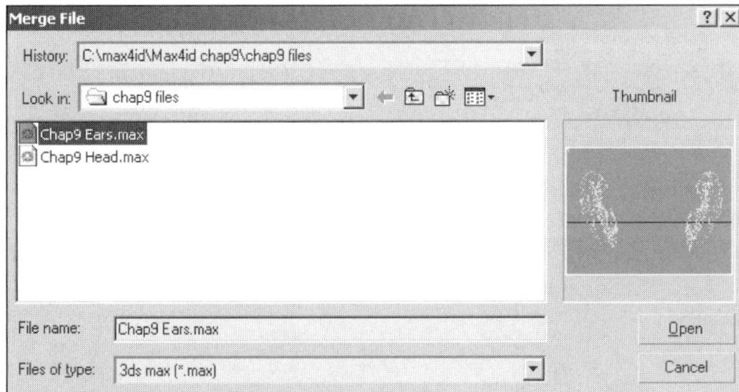

Figure 9.49
The Merge File dialog box, where files can be selected for insertion into the existing scene.

12. When you're merging a file, only specified objects in that file need to be inserted into the existing scene. Click on the Open button to view the contents of the selected file in the Merge – Chap9 Ears.max dialog box shown in Figure 9.50. Select both objects and click on OK to add them to the current scene. Position them as required, near the copies.

13. At this point, it's a good idea to clone/copy both the reference and the instance and both ears and work on the new copies rather than those linked to the spline network. Once they're copied, collapse the right and left sides of the head to editable meshes. Attach one to the other, and then attach the ears to the head.

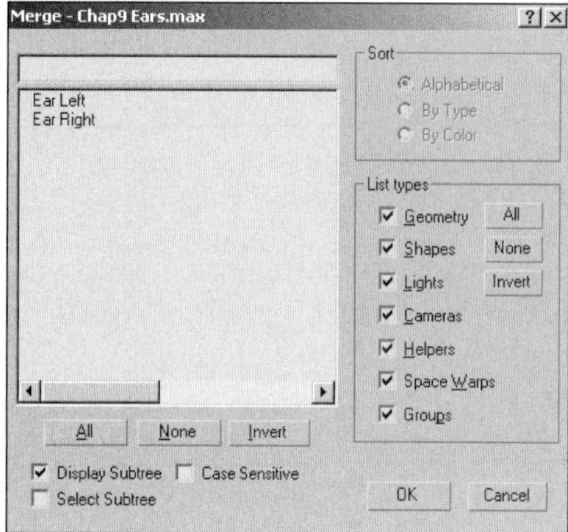

Figure 9.50
The Merge – [*filename.max*] dialog box where the specific objects to be merged are selected.

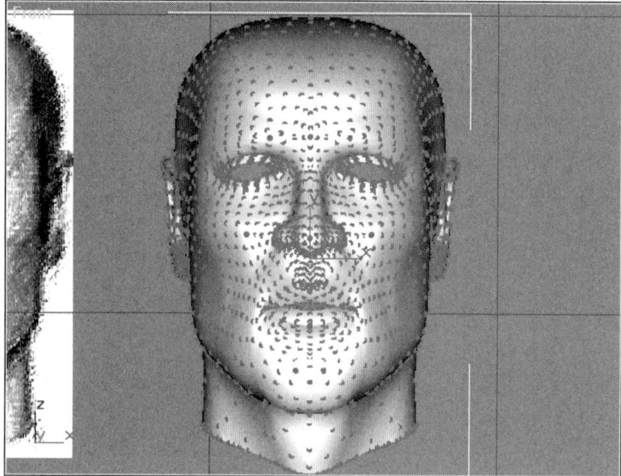

Figure 9.51
After converting the head's sides to editable meshes and attaching them and the ears together, the vertices joining the two halves are selected and welded together.

14. In the Spline subobject level, select the column of vertices at the joint between the two halves, as shown in Figure 9.51, and weld them together. After any required polishing steps, your head model will be complete.

Modeling figures with spline networks can yield unparalleled results, but creating a good model will take a long time. Therefore, be prepared to put forth the effort required to add this technique to your repertoire.

Using the CrossSection Modifier

The CrossSection modifier can connect your splines so you don't have to. It's useful when you are effectively lofting splines, as you might do in NURBS modeling, but it does not give the latitude required for character modeling. For example, the body of an airplane might be modeled by creating a series of cross-section splines, using the CrossSection modifier to bridge them into a spline cage, and then applying the Surface modifier to create the Bezier patches.

Like all lofting or skinning tools, the CrossSection modifier works well only when the cross-sections have the same number of vertices, and those vertices are well aligned. Think of the CrossSection modifier only as a time saver for simple situations. More complex cages need to be connected by hand.

A simple example will give you the idea:

1. Create an Ellipse in a Top viewport and convert it to an editable spline object.
2. Select the spline at the Spline subobject level and drag up a couple of copies so that you have a vertical stack of three identical closed splines.
3. At the Vertex subobject level, edit the splines so that they have somewhat varying shapes. Your stack might look something like Figure 9.52.

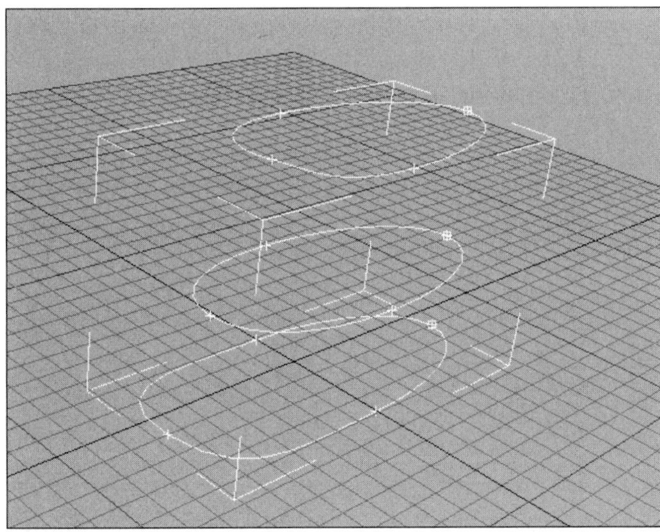

Figure 9.52
Three closed splines in a vertical stack. They are all subobjects of a single editable spline object.

4. Get out of the subobject mode and add a CrossSection modifier to the stack. This modifier connects the vertices to create a spline cage that is suitable for the Surface modifier. See Figure 9.53.

Figure 9.53
The object from Figure 9.52, after the application of the CrossSection modifier. The vertices are connected to create a spline cage that is suitable for the Surface modifier.

5. Add the Surface modifier to the top of the stack and flip the normals, if necessary. The Surface modifier creates an internal patch out of the middle ellipse. Eliminate it by selecting the Remove Interior Patches checkbox.

6. To preserve your stack, you can add an Edit Patch modifier on top of the Surface modifier. Put one on; in the Patch subobject level, select the patches at the top and bottom and hide them. With its interior edges hidden, your object might look like Figure 9.54. You can perform the same kind of patch editing in Edit Patch as you do with an editable patch object. If you collapse this object, it becomes an editable patch.

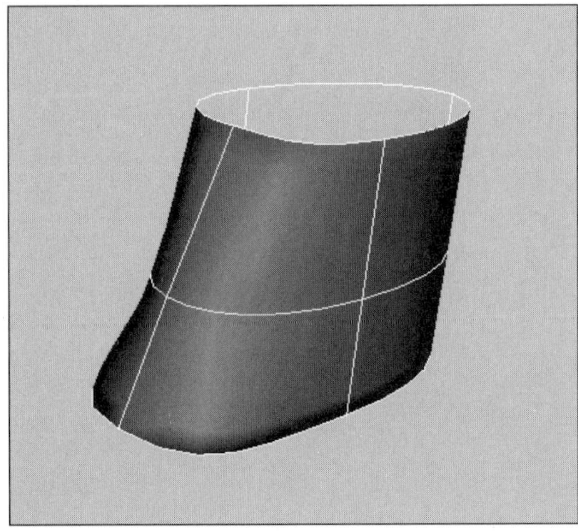

Figure 9.54
The object from Figure 9.53, after the application of the Surface modifier. The patches created at the top and bottom have been hidden.

Moving On

In this chapter, you explored the possibilities of Bezier patch modeling. The Bezier patch modeling toolset is relatively simple when compared with NURBS of polygonal meshes, and it is easy to learn. The challenge is less in learning the toolset than in mastering the act of transforming patch vertices and vector handles in 3D space. It takes many hours of work to become comfortable with the process, but the results can be fabulous.

The new surface tools have augmented the traditional method of building surfaces directly out of patches. The surface tools allow you to build spline cages out of editable spline objects and to rely on the Surface modifier to convert this network into Bezier patch surfaces. This is a new approach that requires a new way of thinking, but serious modelers will begin to integrate it into their repertoires.

The next chapter discusses NURBS modeling. NURBS surfaces are the most sophisticated form of geometry available to the modeler, and the NURBS toolset in 3ds max 4 is both impressive and intimidating. Many consider this to be today's "state-of-the-art" in 3D computer graphics.

Chapter 10
NURBS Modeling

The acronym NURBS stands for Non-Uniform Rational B-Splines, which may mean nothing to you unless you're a mathematician. NURBS are the ultimate form of spline (curve) available to the 3D modeler. NURBS curves are used to build NURBS surfaces, which are essentially networks of NURBS curves. To those just beginning NURBS modeling, these tools may seem a mere extension of the familiar Bezier splines modeling tools, using lathes and lofts. True NURBS modeling is a radical departure from previous techniques, however, and must be approached with a humble and inquisitive spirit. NURBS modeling is used by the serious modeler who wants to be a part of cutting-edge developments in 3D technology.

It would take a book fully as long as this one to teach NURBS modeling, so there are serious limits to what can be achieved in a single chapter. The goal is to give those persons with a genuine interest in this important field the necessary grounding for their own exploration. Even a simple NURBS modeling project typically involves hundreds of steps and uses many special strategy considerations and unique tools to achieve precise and elegant curvature. The figures seen throughout this chapter are at least as important to the interested student as the text, and it is highly recommend that you study these images in detail to sense the feel and workflow of modeling in MAX's NURBS implementation.

NURBS and MAX NURBS

The mathematical nature of NURBS curves and surfaces is a subject above and apart from that of any specific implementation. NURBS were first implemented in the highest-tier 3D applications—Alias Power Animator and Softimage 3D—a decade or so ago, and came to represent the single most important feature that distinguished these more expensive programs from

MAX and the rest of the pack. A certain glamour was associated with NURBS modeling, considered to represent the ultimate high-end modeling technology.

MAX first introduced a NURBS implementation in 3D Studio MAX 2, undoubtedly driven by a marketing push to equate MAX with its top-tier competitors. This implementation and even its improvements in release 2.5 were not technically satisfactory in the view of many users. It was widely believed that MAX NURBS was a promise only to be fully realized in MAX 3 and beyond. This understanding has turned out to be correct. The NURBS implementation is only slightly different from previous versions, but it is immeasurably more reliable. Those who tried their hand at MAX NURBS in the past and who may have been disappointed should be ready to try again now.

We stress the distinction between NURBS in general and a given NURBS implementation for an important reason. Those who want to learn NURBS modeling must learn both. On the one hand, some principles of modeling based on NURBS curves and surfaces stand above any specific implementation. On the other hand, any specific NURBS implementation is bound to be so complex that a great deal of effort is required to understand the toolset and structure of the individual application. In short, you must learn both NURBS and MAX NURBS.

Overview of NURBS Modeling

NURBS modeling is characterized by the interdependence of curves and surfaces. You may already be familiar with the use of Bezier splines in MAX to create surfaces by lofting, lathing, and extruding. NURBS curves can be used to create surfaces in the same way. Splines can be extracted from a NURBS surface, however; therefore, the modeling process is not only from splines to surfaces, but also from surfaces to splines. In this basic concept lies most of the unique power of NURBS modeling.

Extracting Curves from Surfaces

Take a look at Figure 10.1. In the object at left, a NURBS curve was drawn and extruded back to create a NURBS surface. A curve is then extracted from the surface—a curve running perpendicular to the original extruded curve. In the object on the right, the new curve is extruded upward to create a new surface. This kind of thinking, and the modeling practices that flow from it, require a special kind of vision and strategy.

Trimming Surfaces

Trimming plays an essential role in NURBS modeling. A NURBS curve that is on a NURBS surface can be used to trim that surface. After trimming, all geometry on one side of the curve is hidden. Figure 10.2 illustrates the effect of trimming the first surface by the curve that was used to extrude the second surface. This kind of thinking is basic in NURBS modeling.

NURBS Curves and Control Vertices

NURBS curves are built from control vertices (CVs). With NURBS curves, in contrast with Bezier splines, there is no distinction between vertices (which are on the curve) and tangent handles

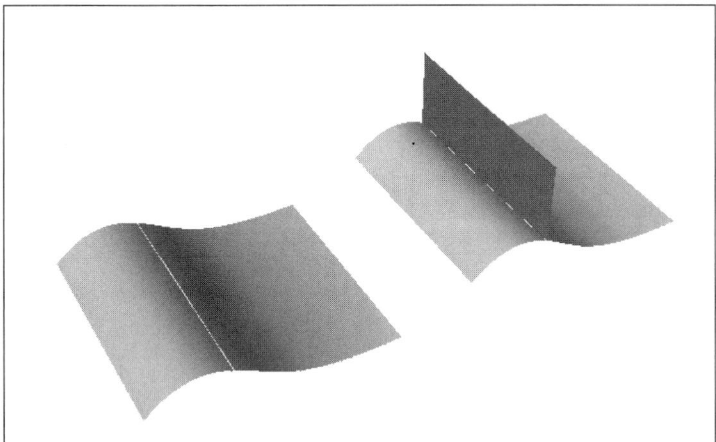

Figure 10.1
The NURBS surface on the left was extruded back from an original NURBS curve. A curve running perpendicular to it (the white line) is extracted from the surface. On the right, the extracted curve is extruded upward to build out a new surface.

Figure 10.2
The curve used to extrude the second surface is used to trim the first surface. The image shows the model before and after the Trim command is applied.

(which are generally not on the curve). Rather, all of the CVs shape the curve, and only the first and last CVs are always on the curve. Figure 10.3 illustrates a NURBS curve. In the upper curve, the CVs are connected by display lines for better comprehension. In the lower copy of the same curve, these lines are hidden.

You can shape the curve by moving the CVs, but you can also adjust the weight of selected CVs. Increased weight pulls the curve closer to the CV and can give the curve a tighter bend. Figure 10.4 illustrates the effect of increasing the weight of the selected CV. The curve is otherwise the same as that in Figure 10.3.

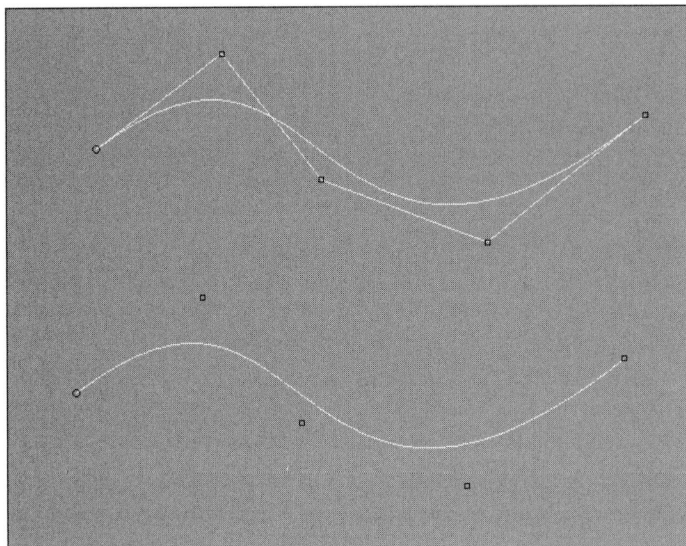

Figure 10.3
A NURBS curve and its control vertices (CVs). In the upper curve, the CVs are connected by display lines for better comprehension.

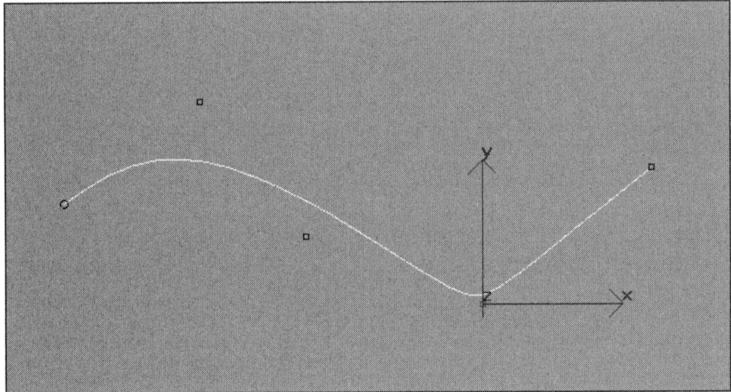

Figure 10.4
The NURBS curve from Figure 10.3, with increased weight applied to the selected control vertex. The weight pulls the curves toward the CV, creating a tight bend and straightening the adjacent regions.

If you delete CVs from a curve, you necessarily change its shape. If you add a single CV, you also change the shape of the curve, although in many cases the change will have a negligible practical effect. To add a CV without changing the shape of the curve, you must adjust the positions of the CVs on either side of the new CV. All NURBS implementations offer this feature; in MAX, it's called *refining the curve*. Figure 10.5 illustrates the process. The original curve is below the refined curve, which is exactly the same shape. To add a CV beneath the dip on the right side, the existing CVs were pushed to either side.

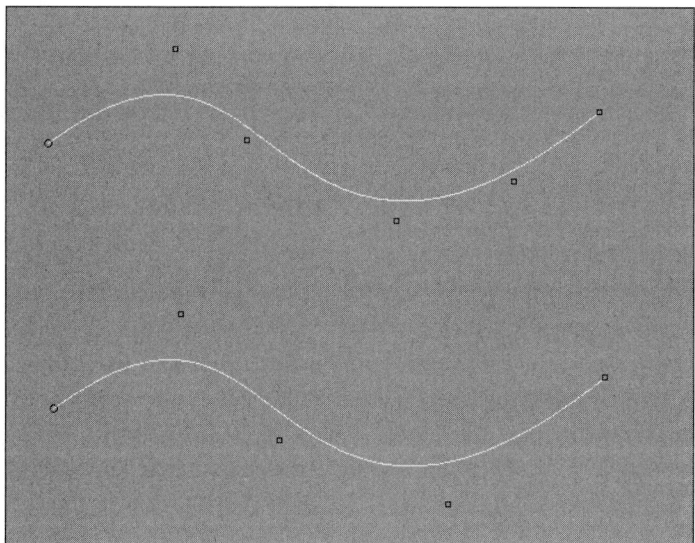

Figure 10.5
Refining a NURBS curve adds CVs without changing the shape of the curve. At bottom is the original curve. Above, a new CV is added beneath the dip on the right. Note that the existing CVs have been pushed to either side to compensate.

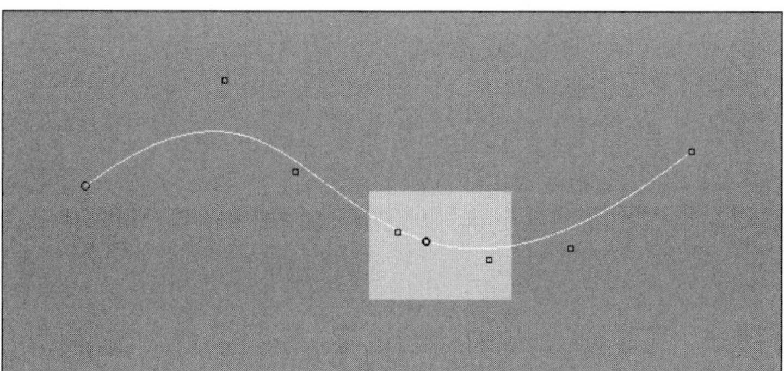

Figure 10.6
The NURBS curve from Figure 10.3 has been cut in two, but the two curves maintain seamless continuity. Note the straight line of CVs in the highlighted region where the two curves meet.

NURBS curves can be cut without changing shape, creating two curves with continuity across their endpoints. Take a close look at Figure 10.6. The NURBS curve from Figure 10.3 has been cut, yet the two new curves are the same shape as the previous single curve. Look at the highlighted box area. The small circle in the middle is where the two curves meet, and there are CVs from both curves at this spot. Note that this circle and the two CVs on either side of it form a straight line. This should remind you precisely of the collinear Bezier tangent handles on a smooth section of a Bezier curve. Continuity between separate NURBS curves (and surfaces) depends on this straight line of CVs. Because NURBS modeling depends so much on connecting lines and curves in a way that appears seamless, this fact is one of the central secrets of NURBS modeling.

Three is the magic number with NURBS curves. Just as three CVs in a line can be used to create continuity between different curves, three CVs in one spot can be used to create a discontinuity in a single curve. In Figure 10.7, two CVs have been added (not refined) and placed on top of a third. When the curve passes the three CVs at one location, continuity is broken and the curve can turn a sharp corner. This is another of the essential secrets of NURBS: MAX allows you to fuse the three CVs together to create a group that can be moved as a unit.

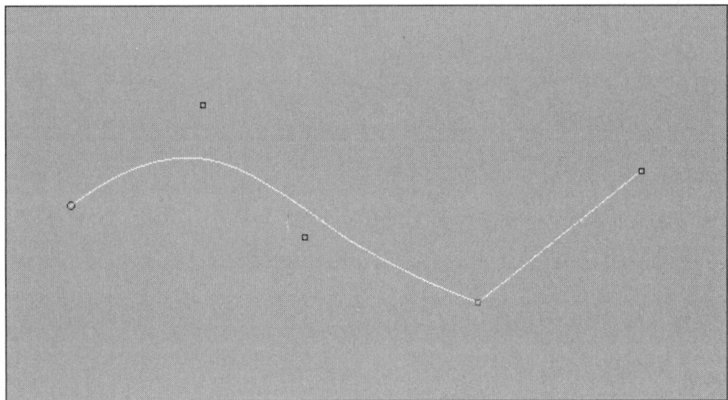

Figure 10.7
Three CVs at a single location break the continuity of the curve, permitting you to turn razor-sharp corners.

Separate NURBS curves can be joined to create a single curve with continuity. The join mechanism closes the gap between the two curves. Figure 10.8 illustrates the join process: The two curves on the left combine to make the single curve on the right. Note the straight line of three CVs create continuity through the join region.

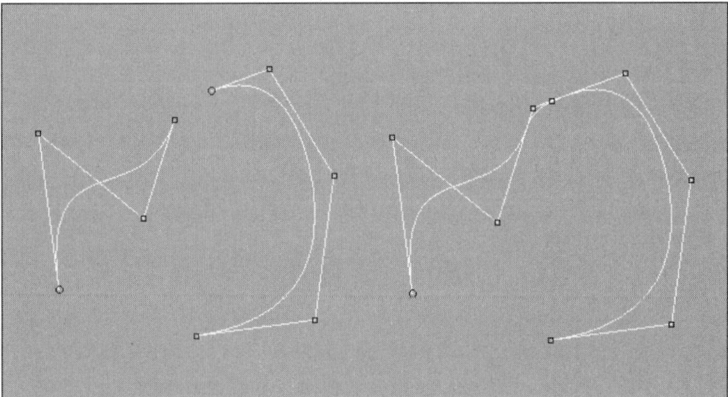

Figure 10.8
Two NURBS curves are joined to make one. The gap between the two curves is bridged so as to create continuity. Note the straight line of three CVs through the bridge.

NURBS Surfaces

NURBS surfaces can be created directly as flat grids, but they are generally created from NURBS curves. However they are created, they are ultimately two-dimensional networks of NURBS curves, with CVs running in both directions. As you will see, many (if not most) NURBS surfaces remain dependent on the curves that were used to create them. As such, they are adjusted or fine-tuned by editing these curves. In this situation, you are not exposed to the true, underlying NURBS surface composed of surface CVs. One way or another, however, the ultimate network of surface CVs is always there and must be understood.

The main point of this section is to stress the similarities between NURBS curves and NURBS surfaces. Figure 10.9 shows a NURBS surface created by extruding the curve from Figure 10.3 (and converted into an independent surface to show its surface CVs). In effect, the surface is a network of curves running in two directions. There are two curves with five CVs, each running in one direction; and five curves with two CVs, each running in the other direction.

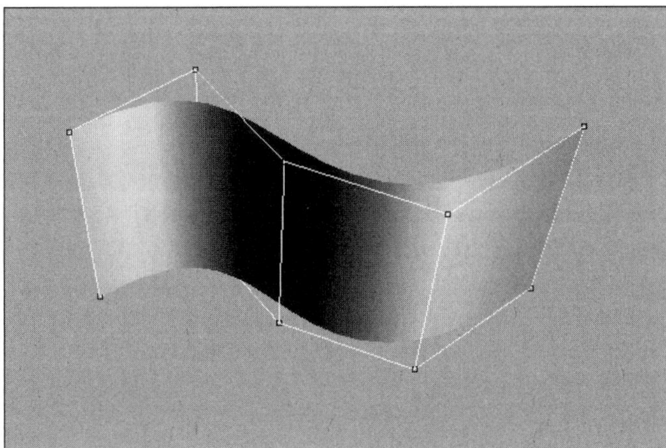

Figure 10.9
A NURBS surface created by extruding the NURBS curve from Figure 10.3. It is a network of CVs composed of two curves with five CVs in one direction and five curves with two CVs running in the perpendicular direction.

Although these are effectively curves, it's easier to think of them in terms of rows and columns of CVs. To add a row or column of CVs without changing the shape of the surface, you use the same refining process that is used with curves. A new row of CVs was added in Figure 10.10. Compare this image with Figure 10.9 to see that the distance between the two adjacent rows of CVs has been adjusted to compensate for the effect of the new row.

Just as with curves, NURBS surfaces can be broken without any loss of continuity. In Figure 10.11, the surface from Figure 10.9 has been broken into two surfaces, but they remain seamless. Note the three rows of CVs that form a straight line over the break. Just as with NURBS curves, this arrangement creates a continuous tangency.

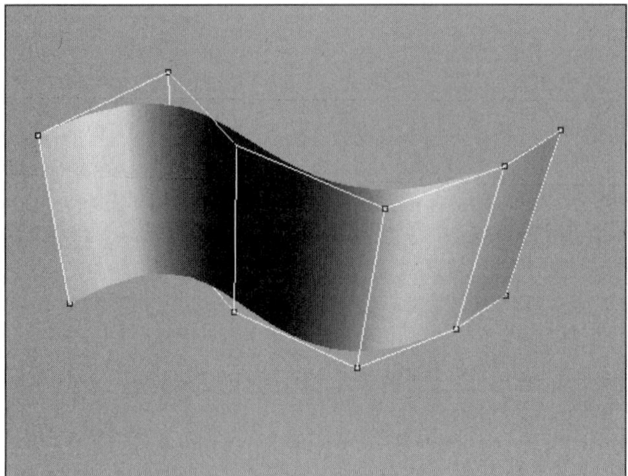

Figure 10.10
A row of CVs is added by refinement to preserve the shape of the surface. Compare with Figure 10.9 to see that distance between the two adjacent rows of existing CVs has been adjusted to compensate.

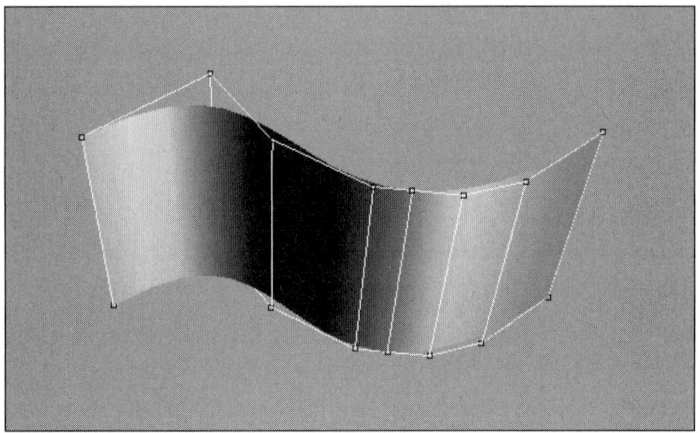

Figure 10.11
Just like a curve, a NURBS surface can be cut in two without loss of continuity. Note the three rows of CVs that form a straight line over the break.

The same principles of discontinuity apply to NURBS surfaces as they do to curves. Three rows of CVs, positioned directly on top of each other, completely break the continuity of the surface, permitting you to fold it as sharply as you wish. And just as with curve CVs, MAX permits you to fuse rows of surface CVs into a functional unit. Take a look at Figure 10.12.

You can adjust the weight of the NURBS surface CVs just as you can with curves. This provides another useful way of tightening up a bend or creating a sharp fold. In Figure 10.13, the weight of a single row of CVs is increased, producing a result that is somewhat similar to that produced with three coincident rows.

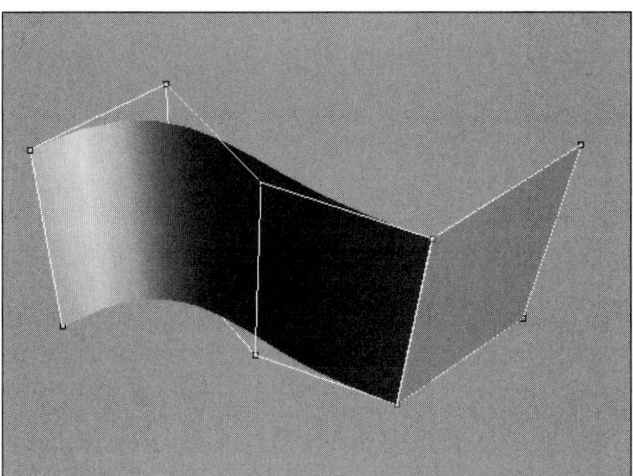

Figure 10.12
Just as with NURBS curves, complete discontinuity is achieved for surfaces by placing three rows of CVs directly on top of each other. You can fold the surface as sharply as you wish.

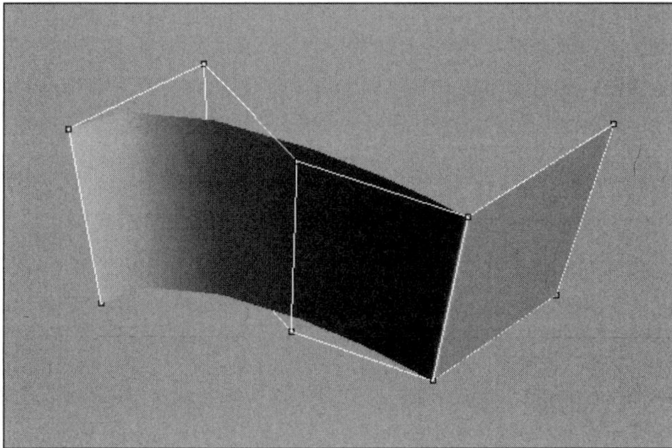

Figure 10.13
NURBS weight is increased for a single row of CVs. This produces a result that is rather similar to that produced by the three coincident rows of CVs shown in Figure 10.12.

Joining separate surfaces into one is an extremely important aspect of NURBS modeling, and, just as with curves, a bridge region must be built between any gaps. Figure 10.14 illustrates the merger of two surfaces. Note that many additional and seemingly unnecessary CVs were created throughout the new surface. It would be wise to clean up this result by deleting many of the excess CVs.

Branching Architecture, Blended Surfaces, and Mesh Tessellation

One of the most important concepts in NURBS modeling—and one of the most difficult to grasp—is the limitations that NURBS surfaces pose on branching architecture. Polygonal models are only as organized as you choose to make them. As long as all the vertices are connected to

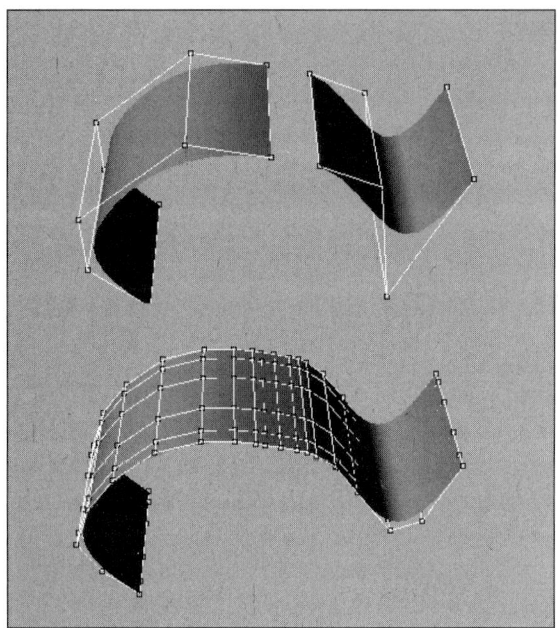

Figure 10.14
Two surfaces are joined by a bridge to make a single continuous surface. Note that many unnecessary CVs were created in this process. It makes sense to carefully delete a number of them.

each other in a mesh, they produce a continuous rendered surface. It's easy to create sharp changes in the direction of a mesh in polygonal models. You can extrude out faces to push out an arm from a torso or a finger from a hand. This kind of branching architecture is typical in character and animal figures, and it is also typical in many organic and inorganic objects.

Figure 10.15 illustrates the classic approach to branching architecture in a polygonal mesh. A quad polygon has been extruded out from the rest of the mesh. After subdivision using MeshSmooth, a smooth and continuous result is obtained. Note the change in the direction of the mesh between the "torso" and the "arm." This is a clear and logical organization that is easy to edit and to bring to a high level of detail.

MAX's Bezier patches can be used in the same way as polygons to produce smooth branching architecture, as discussed in Chapter 9, largely because these patches can be treated as groups of polygons with curvature continuity. NURBS surfaces present a different situation, however. NURBS surfaces have inherent structural limitations that make it difficult or (as is more often the case) impossible to create branching architecture out of a single surface. Much of NURBS modeling is directed at aligning two surfaces in a way that will give the impression, after rendering, of a single continuous surface. Although the word *blending* is used in NURBS modeling in many ways, in the larger sense—and no matter how it is accomplished—it refers to the practice of creating an apparent merger of different surfaces.

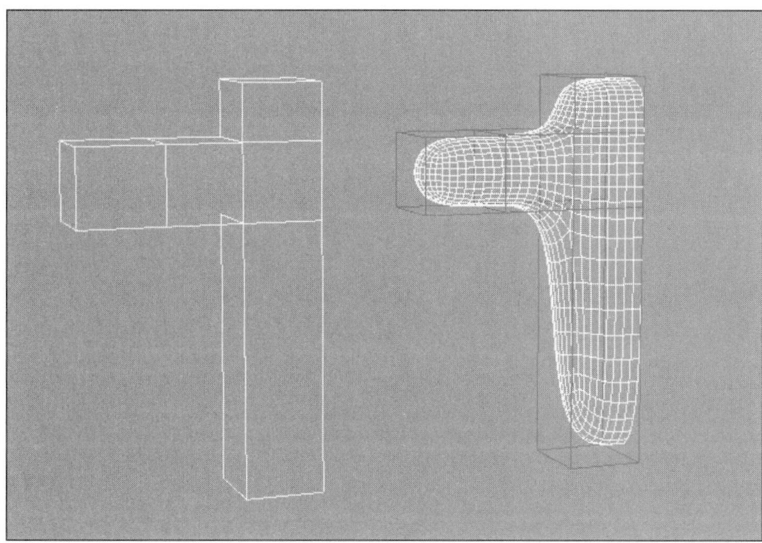

Figure 10.15
Branching architecture with a smoothed polygon mesh. A single quad polygon has been extruded out from the rest of the mesh, and the entire result is subdivided with MeshSmooth. The result is a single, seamless mesh.

Figure 10.16 illustrates a typical NURBS approach to branching architecture. The "arm" and the "torso" are different surfaces. The arm joins the torso at a curve that is on the surface of the torso (and was used to trim out a hole in it). The arm surface picks up the curvature of the torso at this curve, creating a continuous "blended" effect. The image at left shows the basic structure of the two surfaces as networks of curves. The image at right shows the result after tessellation into a polygonal mesh. Compare this tessellated mesh with the tessellated mesh in Figure 10.15.

You have just slipped into one of the most important concepts of NURBS modeling. Although a NURBS surface is an ideal freeform expression of curvature, the rendering engine can understand only a polygonal mesh. Therefore, all NURBS surfaces are tessellated into polygonal meshes to render. This applies just as much to the real-time "render" that you see in a shaded viewport as it does to a true render to create a bitmap for output. Like all digital versions of an analog phenomenon, the tessellated mesh is only an approximation of the ideal, and the greater the tessellation (and the greater the number of faces), the greater the fidelity. Surface approximation tools (as they are called) play a huge role in NURBS modeling because you never render the ideal.

The most impressive aspect of high-end surface approximation tools is the power to bridge small gaps to create a seamless mesh. This power is called *edge merging*, and it is the ultimate reason why blending of NURBS surfaces is possible. Look at Figure 10.17, which is a wireframe render of the blended region from Figure 10.16. Note that the mesh between the two surfaces was carefully and automatically bridged. The object renders as if it were a single seamless

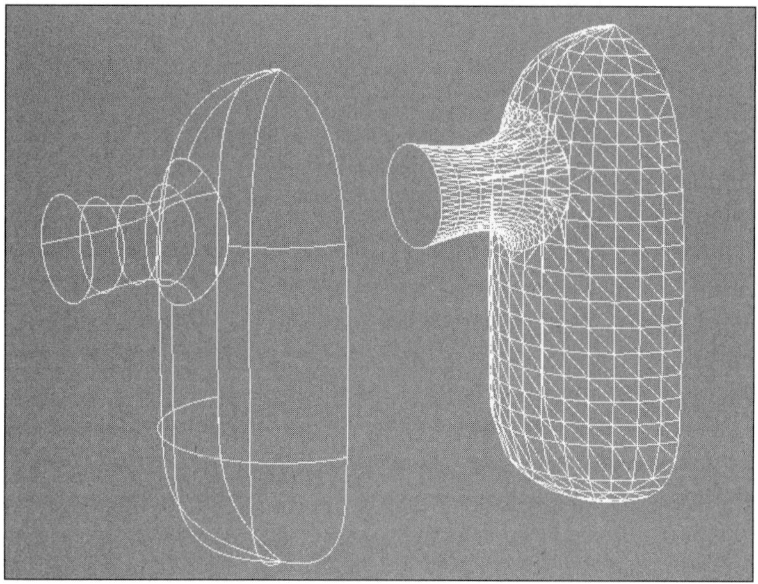

Figure 10.16

Branching architecture with NURBS requires the blending of separate surfaces. The arm surface meets the torso surface at a trim curve on the torso surface and picks up the curvature of the torso. The nature of the blending is seen both in a curves version *(left)* and a tessellated mesh version *(right)* of the same model.

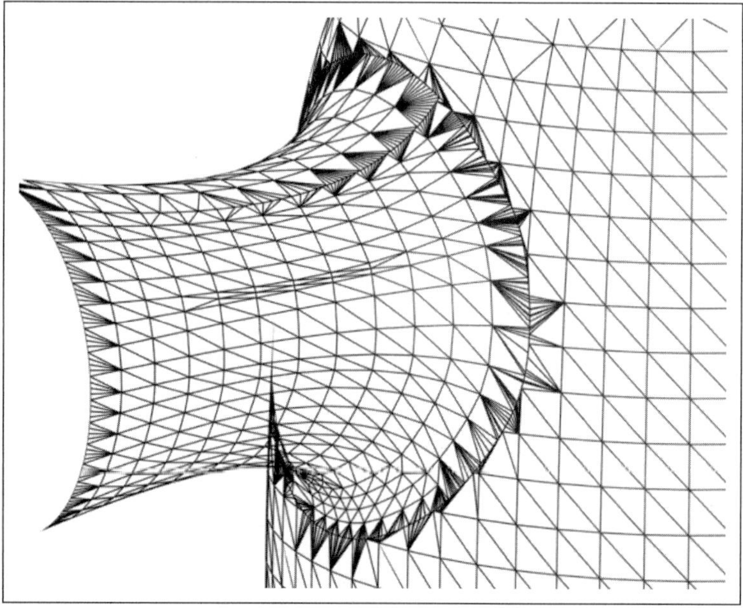

Figure 10.17

A wireframe render shows how, in the tessellation process, the two NURBS surfaces are merged into a single contiguous polygonal mesh. The object renders seamlessly because, after surface approximation and edge merging, it really is seamless.

surface because, after surface approximation and edge merging, it really is a single seamless polygonal mesh. It's impossible to gain real command over NURBS modeling without understanding and having control over the process that converts freeform surfaces to the renderable polygonal mesh. In this way, you can see that NURBS are ultimately vehicles to create a polygonal mesh.

Overview of the 3ds max 4 NURBS Implementation

MAX's NURBS implementation is powerful, unique, complex, and often frustrating. You must understand many basic ideas before you can even begin. You need a lot of patience to master these concepts. The MAX NURBS implementation is based on certain principles that may not be satisfactorily "hacked out" by raw experimentation, no matter how persistent you are.

The Basket Concept

The term *basket* is not a MAX term, but it is the best word for the purpose described in this section. NURBS models are necessarily collections of curves and surfaces, and they often contain a substantial number of both. MAX could have taken the traditional approach (found, for example, in Softimage) of treating each curve and surface as a separate object and giving the user the responsibility of organizing these objects into functional groups by using parent-child hierarchies. MAX did something very different, however, and very typical of MAX—it created a basket object in which the component curves and surfaces are subobjects.

Consider the following material slowly and carefully, because your sanity depends on it. MAX provides two kinds of objects: the NURBS Curve object and the NURBS Surface object. Don't take these names at face value—each of these objects is a basket. A NURBS Surface object can contain any number of NURBS surfaces and NURBS curves as subobjects. In MAX 2.5, a NURBS Curve object could contain only curves, so you had to convert a NURBS Curve object to a NURBS Surface object before you could build any surfaces. With the introduction of version 3, and continued in version 4, MAX now permits you to build and include surfaces in a NURBS Curve object, and thus there is no longer any practical distinction between NURBS Curve objects and NURBS Surface objects. In effect, there is only a single NURBS basket object, under either name, in which curves and surfaces are collected. Thus, you can be faced with such confusing ideas as "There are three NURBS surfaces and six NURBS curves in this NURBS Curve object." You just have to get used to this kind of thinking.

Learn to distinguish between the creation of curves within a NURBS basket object and outside of it. NURBS curves that are created directly by selecting Create|Shapes|NURBS Curves become completely new NURBS Curve objects, being the only objects in the basket. You can then create more curves in this same way, but they will be separate baskets. More commonly, you add more curves to an existing basket by using the curve-creation tools within the basket. New curves thus created become additional subobject curves within the basket. You can bring curves from outside the basket into the basket by using the Attach tools in the top-level NURBS Surface panel, under the General rollout. One way or another, all the curves that will be used together to build or trim surfaces must be in the same basket.

MAX Offers Automatic Attachment

In MAX 2 and 2.5, the Attach tool was the only way to collect curves and surfaces from different baskets together in a single basket. This caused a great deal of confusion for the vast majority of users who didn't understand the basket concept. For example, the novice user would simply create two NURBS curves from the Create panel and then become frustrated by the inability to loft between them to create a surface. To alleviate this frustration, MAX 3 introduced the ability to attach curves from different baskets automatically when you try to loft between them; 3ds max 4 continues with this. The sophisticated user, however, should understand the process better and deliberately collect all necessary curves in a common basket, typically by creating all the curves (except the first) from within the basket itself.

Dependent and Independent Subobjects

Due to the interdependence of NURBS curves and surfaces that characterize the NURBS modeling process, all NURBS implementations offer a *modeling relation* concept by which a subobject curve or surface remains functionally related to the subobjects from which it was created. In MAX, this is achieved by the distinction between dependent and independent objects.

Take this simple example. A NURBS CV curve is created from the Create panel. (Note that only CV curves will be used in this chapter. MAX offers Point curves, which are supposed to be a simplification of CV curves. You should explore their merits only after you are fully grounded in CV curves, which are the true NURBS curves.) The curve is then extruded to create a surface. By default, this surface is a *dependent subobject*. It is dependent on the curve from which it was created; if that curve is edited, the surface will be computed accordingly (see Figure 10.18).

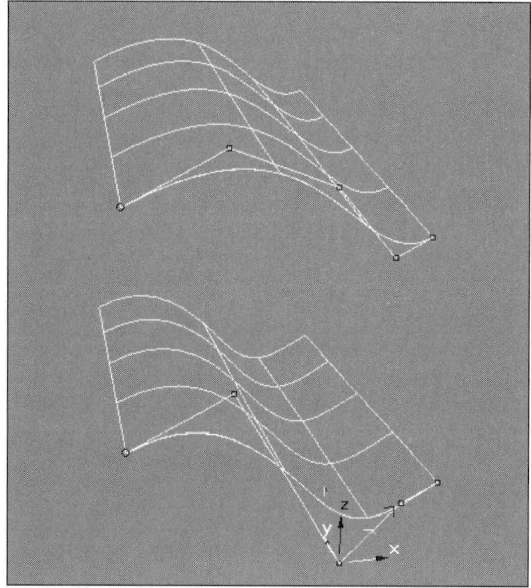

Figure 10.18

An extruded surface remains dependent on the curve from which it was extruded. The surface is effectively re-extruded when the curve is edited by moving the selected point.

Note how the extruded surface updates when the curve is edited by moving the selected curve CV. This may remind you of similar mechanisms elsewhere in MAX. For example, you can change the shape of a lathed object by editing the spline underneath the Lathe modifier. Instancing can also be used in Loft Objects to the same effect. But dependency in NURBS is a much more general and uniform concept that is applied throughout the NURBS toolset.

At this point, the CVs that define the surface definitely exist, but they're unavailable. Because the shape of the surface is dependent entirely upon the shape of the curve, there is no reason to access the surface CVs; therefore, they remain hidden. You can break the dependency, however, by selecting the surface at the Surface Sub-Object level and clicking on the Make Independent button; then, the surface is no longer connected to the curve, and edits to the curve no longer affect the surface. Moreover, the surface CVs for the surface become available and can be edited to change the shape of the surface directly (see Figure 10.19).

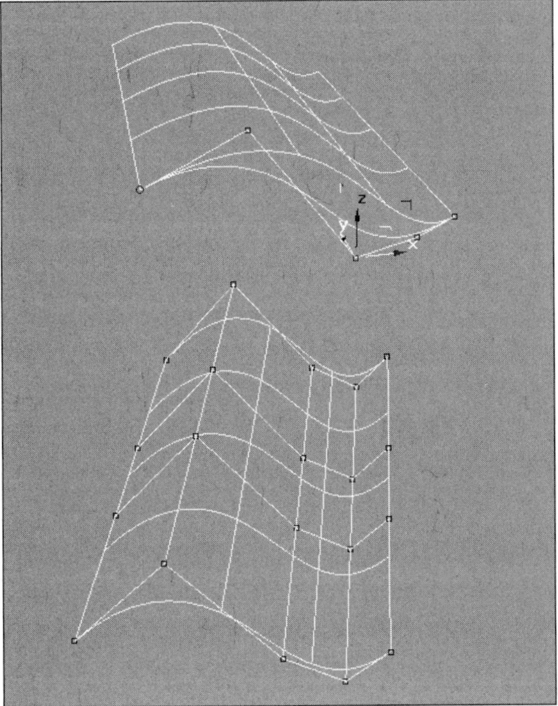

Figure 10.19
After making the extruded surface from Figure 10.18 independent of the curve, edits to the curve no longer affect the surface, as seen at the top. Once independent, the surface's own CV network can be revealed and edited directly to shape the surface, as shown at the bottom.

Be Careful about Breaking Dependencies

Dependencies are an extremely important factor in NURBS modeling. It takes a great deal of experience to determine whether subobjects should be dependent and at what point it is safe to break a dependency. Often, the consequences of a broken dependency appear much later in the modeling process, to your great surprise. You can always break a dependency, but you can't re-create one (except by using the Undo command). Get used to thinking far ahead about the consequences of broken dependencies, and don't break them unless you're forced to do so.

Object and Subobject Levels

The basket concept forces the user to move constantly between the object level (top level) and the various subobject levels. You can do this from the drop-down list at the top of the NURBS Surface panel, from the right-click menu, or by using hotkeys. However you get around, there is a large amount of interface to learn, even in a general way.

Figure 10.20 shows the Modify panel with the subobject list expanded and only the General rollout open. Here, you can attach (and import, which is a variation of attachment) NURBS subobjects from other baskets to add them to the selected basket. The Tools 1 section on the

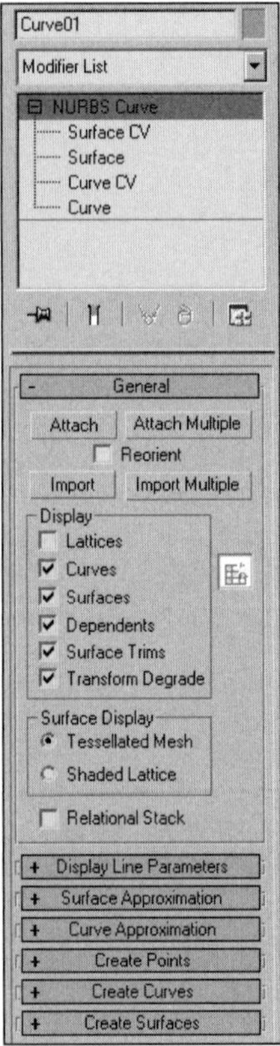

Figure 10.20
The NURBS Modify panel with the subobject list expanded and the General rollout open.

Quad menu contains display options, which are critical; these options are also available from the right-click menu. NURBS models can become an overwhelming mess of curves and surfaces, and you often need a quick way to hide entire classes of subobjects. Note that this is different from hiding selected subobjects from within a given subobject panel.

The Display Line Parameters rollout is used to set the number of curves displayed on a surface in a wireframe view. It's important to understand that these curves are for display purposes only, to help you grasp the contours of a surface. The number and position of the curves do not necessarily indicate the position of the rows and columns of CVs on the surface. The Surface Approximation rollout contains the tools for tessellating NURBS surfaces into polygons. You'll consider this important toolset later; for now, however, note that (because it is at the object level) it applies to all the surfaces in the basket. The three subobject creation rollouts permit you to create subobjects within the basket. All of these tools are generally much more easily reached through the NURBS Toolbox or the right-click menu.

Within each of the subobject levels (Surface CV, Surface, Curve CV, and Curve), the Modify panel provides the tools appropriate for the job. In each case, you will often (but not always) have to select the specific subobjects that you intend to edit. When you have a number of subobjects in a class, this selection process can be tough work. Be sure to name each of your subobjects with a good, descriptive title in the Name field. As is typical throughout MAX, the program generates a generic name when you first create a subobject. Nothing is more frustrating than trying to find a surface or curve in a huge list without the help of a distinctive name. The situation can be especially difficult because the original name assigned by MAX often no longer makes sense after a number of operations (especially after dependencies are broken).

To find subobjects on a list, you need to activate the small button at the bottom center of the MAX window (with the flyout that reads Keyboard Shortcut Override Toggle). If this button is activated, you can click on the H key to bring up the Select Sub-Objects dialog box (rather than the regular Select Objects dialog box).

Hiding subobjects is another task that is essential for sanity and productive workflow. It is especially important due to the necessary consequences of the basket approach to organization. For example, when you move to the Curve CV subobject level to edit a given curve, you see all the curve CVs of every curve in the basket. This display can become impossibly confusing. A typical NURBS model is filled with all kinds of construction curves that you dare not delete, but you don't want cluttering the screen. If you develop strict practices for hiding subobjects, your work will flow much more easily.

The NURBS Creation Toolbox

The centerpiece of MAX's NURBS modeling interface is the NURBS Creation Toolbox. To edit existing NURBS curves and surfaces, you must go to the appropriate subobject level and select from the panel. You can also create curves and surfaces at any time, regardless of your current selection level, by using the NURBS Creation Toolbox.

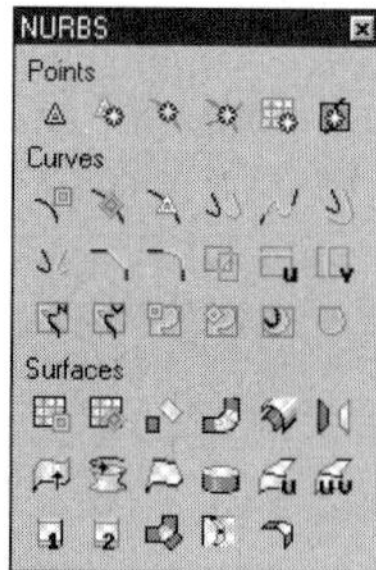

Figure 10.21
The NURBS Creation Toolbox.

The NURBS Creation Toolbox is shown in Figure 10.21. The Toolbox generally appears by default as a floating toolbar on the screen, but it can be toggled on and off through its icon to the right of the Display group, in the object's top level in the Modify panel. The Toolbox is divided into three sections: Points, Curves, and Surfaces. These icons are nothing more than macro buttons that call the subobject creation tools found in the bottom three rollouts of the top-level panels. Creating points independently of curves is a rare occurrence, so let's ignore the point creation tools. Figure 10.22 shows the Create Curves and Create Surfaces rollouts. Although you'll almost always use the Toolbox instead of the rollouts, take a look at the names of the available objects and see how they are organized into groups of independent and dependent objects.

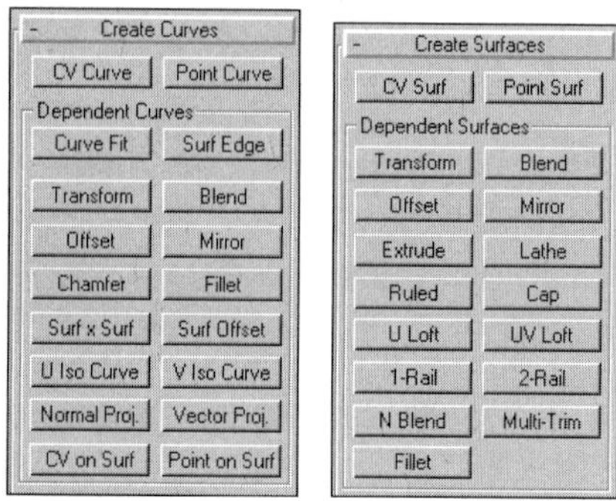

Figure 10.22
The Create Curves and Create Surfaces rollouts from the Modify panel for the NURBS Curve objects and NURBS Surface objects. These tools are found by clicking on the Curve and Surface icons on the NURBS Creation Toolbox.

Some creation tools are much more important than others. Note first that you can create new CV curves within the basket by selecting the tool and drawing. Because the curve is drawn from scratch, it is necessarily an independent object. The dependent curves are all created, in one way or another, from existing curves or surfaces, and are therefore made dependent on those subobjects. You can always break the dependence. A Transform curve is a dependent copy of an existing curve. Because this is considered curve creation, rather than curve copying, you can create a Transform curve without being in the Curve subobject level. By contrast, you can formally copy a curve by selecting it at the Curve subobject level and performing the conventional Shift+drag. After the curve is copied, you can decide whether the copy should be a dependent or independent object.

An Offset curve is also a dependent copy of an existing curve, but one that is automatically scaled as you move it away from the original. Sometimes this process is easier than scaling the curve after copying it, but not often. Mirroring curves is an extremely important way to create bilaterally symmetrical objects in NURBS modeling. The Mirror curve can be a little clumsy to use, however, and it is often easier to use the regular MAX mirror tool to mirror the entire object (basket) and then perform an attachment to merge the baskets.

The most important class of curves that can be created within a basket is that which consists of curves on surfaces. These curves can be used for trimming or building additional surfaces. The Vector Projected curve is a curve that is projected onto a surface in a single direction. The Normal Projected curve, which makes a projection in the direction of the normals of the surface, is much less useful. The other curves are taken directly from the intended surface. The U Iso curve and V Iso curve are extracted anywhere along the surface in either the U- or V-direction. These are *isoparametric curves*, meaning that they represent a constant value in either u or v across the surface, and they reveal the structure of the NURBS surface. A Surface Edge curve is just an easy way of getting the isoparametric curves at the very start or end of the surface in either the U- or V-direction.

Note: *The U- and V- directions referred to here, as well as in Chapter 12, are analogous to the Local X and Y directions. When relocating a curve, it is moved perpendicular to the direction in which it runs, regardless of the orientation of the object or the current coordinate system. The U- and V-directions are consistent regardless of the two factors mentioned.*

So much for the essential curves. You can create new CV grids (called *CV Surfaces*), and you can make dependent copies of surfaces by using the Transform Surface. The most important surface creation tools, however, are those that fashion surfaces out of curves. The Loft Surface is central; it is a surface created by *skinning* (lofting) NURBS curves. It comes in two flavors, permitting you to skin curves in either one or two directions. The Lathe and Extrude Surfaces create surfaces from a single curve and require no explanation to a MAX user who has gotten this far. The Sweeps (1-Rail and 2-Rail) are guided extrusions. Instead of the curve being extruded in a straight line, it is extruded along a path defined by one or two other NURBS curves.

The Blend Surface is used for blending surfaces, as described earlier. The Blend Surface can be created between the edges of two surfaces, between curves on surfaces, or between either of these and a curve off the surface.

When you select a creation tool from the NURBS Creation Toolbox, the appropriate creation rollout appears in the Modify panel. You'll often need to set values on this panel to get the result you want—by picking the direction of an extrusion or the axis of a lathe, for example. When creating all dependent subobjects, the objects available to create the new object turn blue under the cursor. Once a subobject is finally created, its parameters can be changed only by selecting it at the curve or surface subobject level.

NURBS Surface Primitives

Most NURBS modeling involves creating surfaces from curves, but it is often useful to work from NURBS surface primitives. A NURBS CV Surface is simply a flat NURBS grid that can be created by choosing Create|Geometry|NURBS Surfaces. The primary value of this approach, as opposed to extruding a straight NURBS curve, is that you can specify the number of rows and columns of CVs. The same kind of CV Surface can be created with an existing basket from the NURBS Creation Toolbox.

All of the Standard Primitives can be converted from polygons to NURBS by using the Quad menu or Modify panel, including (believe it or not!) the Teapot. The use of a NURBS Sphere primitive is essential in NURBS modeling, but you may have mixed feelings about the other primitives. To some extent, you can save time by converting basic shapes to collections of NURBS surfaces; but for the serious student, this approach takes you off the track of true NURBS modeling strategy and techniques.

Lofting Surfaces

Lofting curves into surfaces is the most essential concept in NURBS modeling. Lofting is often called *skinning* among NURBS modelers, and the terms will be used interchangeably here. MAX sticks with the word *loft*, which at least prevents confusion with the Skin modifier that has nothing to do with skinning curves.

A Loft Surface is dependent on its component curves, at least in the first instance. Any changes made to these curves cause the surface to reloft. You can, of course, convert the lofted surface to an independent CV Surface, after which it will be editable only by its surface CVs. MAX has the unusual power of being able to reloft from any surface, however, and effectively exact curves from the surface and skin them. Let's work through an exercise that will get you started with lofting while introducing a number of general concepts.

Creating a Loft

Start by creating curves and skinning them, as follows:

1. Draw a wavy NURBS curve in a Front viewport, using five CVs. Use Create|Shapes|NURBS Curves|CV Curve. Draw the curve as you would a regular Bezier spline, clicking to lay down CVs and right-clicking to end the process. Pay careful attention to the way the curve takes shape and notice how each additional CV affects the shape of previously drawn sections. It takes a lot of practice to become skilled at drawing with NURBS. Get used to hiding your screen grids if you don't need them, to see things more clearly. Switch to the Modify panel and look at your curve at the Curve CV subobject level. You can select CVs and edit the shape of the curve. Doing so gives you a feeling of how moving CVs affects the curve. When you finish, your Front viewport should look something like Figure 10.23.

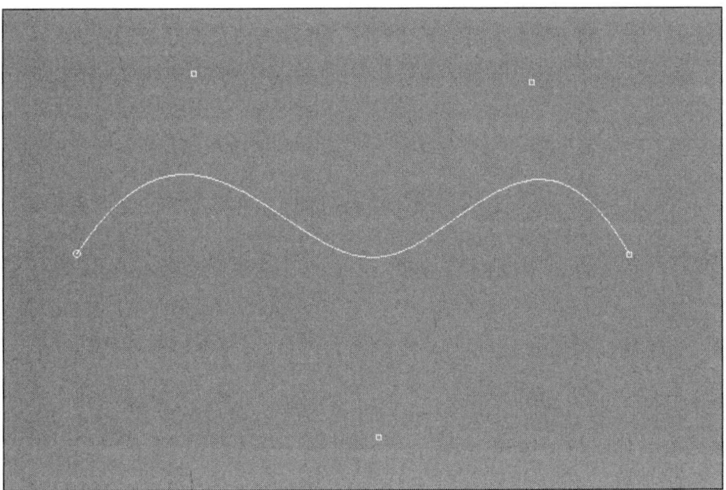

Figure 10.23
A NURBS curve composed of five CVs drawn in a front view and viewed at the Curve CV subobject level. The Display Lattice option is turned off.

2. Make a copy of this curve and skin between both. Do so in a Perspective viewport to get a good feeling of depth. Rotate your Perspective viewport to get an angle on the curve. One way to copy the curve is as a Transform curve. Give this a try by activating the Create Transform Curve button in the NURBS Creation Toolbox. If the Toolbox is hidden, you can unhide it by using the button in the top level of the Modify panel. Place your cursor over the curve; it will turn blue. When you start dragging, however, you'll notice that the Transform Gizmo is not available, making it difficult to position the copy precisely. Right-click to get out of the creation tool and undo to get rid of the Transform curve.

3. Go to the Curve subobject level and select the curve by clicking on it. It turns red and its name (Curve01) appears in the panel. Get into Move mode if you're not already there and note the Transform Gizmo. Hold down the Shift key as you drag off a copy in the World Y-direction. When you release the mouse, you'll see a dialog box. Click on the OK button to accept the default option of an Independent Copy. Your Perspective viewport should now look something like Figure 10.24.

4. Skin the curves. Select the Create U Loft Surface tool from the NURBS Creation Toolbox. Click on one curve, click on the other, and then right-click twice to end the process. If your surface seems to be missing, rotate your Perspective viewport to see whether it's visible from underneath. The surface is visible in only one direction—the direction of its normals. Go to the Surface subobject level, select the surface (its name will appear in the Surface Common rollout), and check the Flip Normals box to reverse the direction, if necessary. Your surface should be facing up. After you know that it's facing in the correct direction, change your display to show both sides of the surface. (You can do this by unchecking the

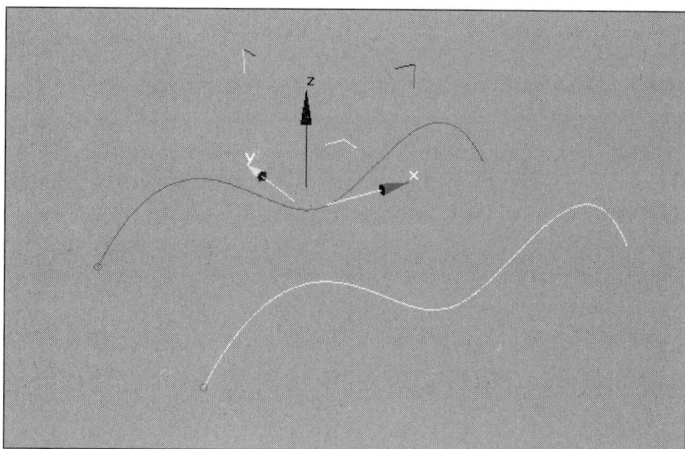

Figure 10.24
The NURBS curve from Figure 10.23 is copied as an independent subobject and moved behind the original.

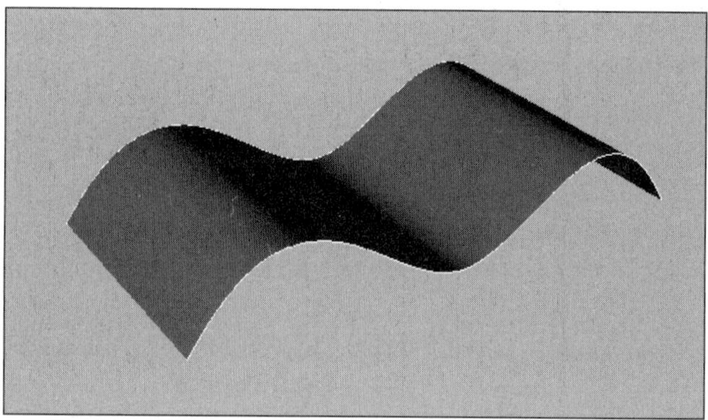

Figure 10.25
The two curves are lofted (skinned) into a surface. After making sure that the surface normals face upward, both sides of the surface are revealed in the viewport for better comprehension.

Backface Cull option in the Display panel, which affects only the selected object.) It's impossible to work with NURBS surfaces when you can't see both sides. Your surface should look like Figure 10.25.

Editing the Loft

You could have created this surface more easily by just extruding the original curve, so you can continue the exercise by making some adjustments that represent the typical modeling process:

1. Switch to the Curve CV subobject level and note that the CVs of both curves are available for editing. Move the middle CV in the back curve straight up. The Loft Surface is dependent on its curves, so the surface is automatically reskinned to reflect the new condition of its curves. Your surface should look something like Figure 10.26.

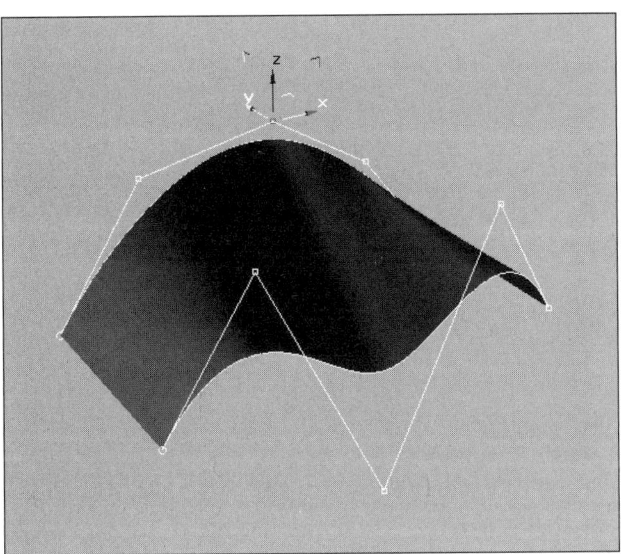

Figure 10.26
The lofted surface is dependent on its component curves. Editing the shape of these curves at the Curve CV subobject level causes the surface to reskin accordingly.

2. You can do only so much with two curves, so let's pull a curve off the surface and add it to the loft. Click on the Create U Iso Curve button in the NURBS Creation Toolbox and pull the cursor over the surface. You can see that the surface can be understood as a continuum of isoparametric curves in the U-direction. When you create a U Loft Surface in MAX, the U-direction is the direction of the loft—the direction connecting the selected curves. Find a curve right in the middle and click on it to accept it. The curve turns green, indicating that it is a dependent subobject. Right-click to get out of the tool (or you'll go on creating Iso curves).

3. The Iso curve is dependent on the surface. You can test this by moving one of the Curve CVs to change the shape of the surface. The Iso curve remains stuck to the surface. Go to the Curve subobject level and select the new Iso curve. Pull the Position spinner in the Iso curve rollout and note that you can move the curve across the surface, effectively creating a different isoparametric curve than the one you began with. You can find this kind of flexibility with dependent objects throughout the toolset.

4. Break the dependency by clicking on the Make Independent button. When this button is gray for a selected subobject, it means that the object is already independent. Go back to the Curve CV level and note that CVs are now available for the Iso curve. The curve has a huge number of CVs, however, which is typical of curves that have been computed to follow a curving surface. Your screen should now look something like Figure 10.27.

5. Add the middle curve to the loft in one of two ways: Simply delete the surface and reloft by using all three curves instead of just the original two, or add curves directly to an existing

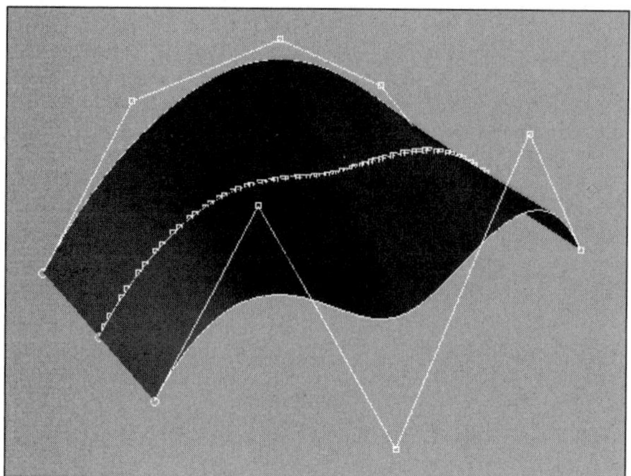

Figure 10.27
An Iso curve is created from the middle of the surface and converted into an independent object. Note the large number of CVs typical of surface curves on curving surfaces.

loft. Let's try the second method by going to the Surface subobject level and selecting the Loft Surface, if necessary. Pull down to the U Loft Surface rollout at the bottom of the panel. The U Curves window lists the component curves in order. To insert the additional curve into the loft, select the second curve on the list and activate the Insert button. Click on the Iso curve, and, after a moment, you'll see it added to the middle of the list.

6. Check to see whether Step 5 worked. If you just go back to the Curve CV level to edit the curve, you'll find that the sheer number of CVs is unworkable. To clean things up, select the middle curve in the Curve Sub-Object level. The curve can now be rebuilt with fewer CVs. Click on the Convert Curve button to bring up the Convert Curve dialog box. Change to the Number option and enter the number 5. If the Preview box is checked, you'll see the curve after it's been resampled down to only five CVs, which is the same number that the other curves in the loft have. The shape of the curve changes, of course, so that it no longer follows the surface; the more points you use, the closer it will remain to its original shape. Click on the OK button to accept the resampled version of the curve. The surface is automatically relofted and interpolates all three curves. Figure 10.28 shows the result. Now, you can move CVs on the middle curve to shape the surface.

7. Actually, there is a much simpler way to add a surface curve to the loft. Go back to the Surface subobject level and click on the Refine button in the U Loft Surface rollout. Pull the cursor over the surface to select an isoparametric curve that is very close to the current middle curve. Click there to see the new curve added to the list. Select the previously added Iso curve from the list and click on the Remove button. The Iso curve disappears from the list, but the curve is still visible on the screen. The curve still exists in the basket, even though it's not in the Loft Object. Go to the Curve subobject level and then select and delete the curve (Iso Curve 01).

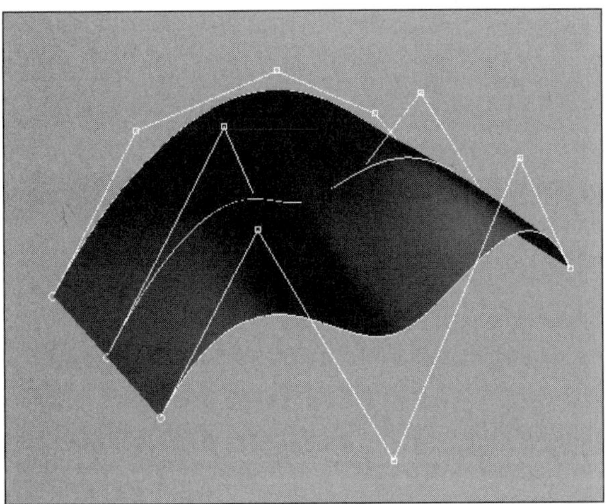

Figure 10.28
The middle curve is resampled down to only five CVs by using the Convert Curve dialog box. After accepting the new curve, the surface is automatically reskinned through the middle curve. The image is seen at the Curve CV level.

8. Go to the Curve CV subobject level again and note the relatively reasonable number of CVs that were created on the refined curve. With only nine or so CVs, the curve manages to follow the original surface very closely. Figure 10.29 illustrates the refined surface. Note that MAX's NURBS implementation is remarkably good at skinning between curves with different numbers of CVs. Often, however, you will need to add or delete CVs from curves in a loft to get a smooth result.

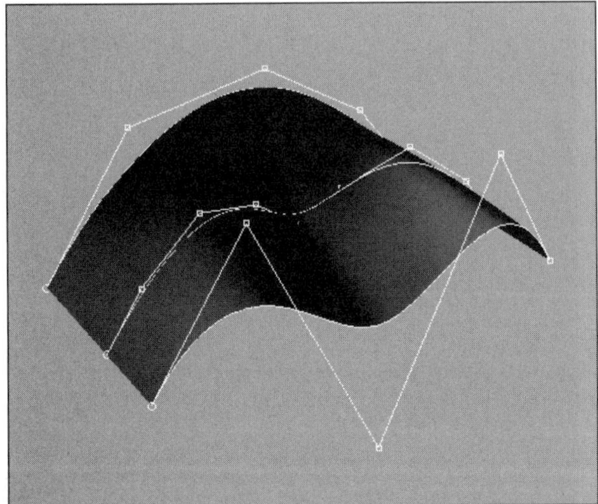

Figure 10.29
A new curve is added to the loft by using the Refine tool, and the inserted curve is removed and deleted. The curve added by refinement has the minimum number of CVs needed to preserve the shape of the surface.

Relofting the Surface

One of the most interesting features of the MAX NURBS toolset is the power to reloft a surface automatically. Typically, you'll use any kind of relofting to change the direction of the lofting curves; but you can also use it to create curves in new positions on the surface that are in the same direction as the original curves. In both cases, the purpose is to position editable Curve CVs in more useful locations as more detail is added to the surface. As we continue our exercise, let's see how relofting works with the surface we've been working with:

1. Select the surface at the Surface subobject level and click on the Make Loft button on the panel. The Make Loft dialog box appears, as illustrated in Figure 10.30. The Make Loft tool samples out isoparametric curves from the surface, in either the U- or V-direction. (It can also sample in both directions to create MAX's unique UV Loft Surface.) Make sure that the Preview box is checked, and then play with different numbers of curves in either direction. By default, the tool provides you with the minimum number of samples that preserve the shape of the surface. As you try numbers below the default, you'll see that the surface loses fidelity to the original contours.

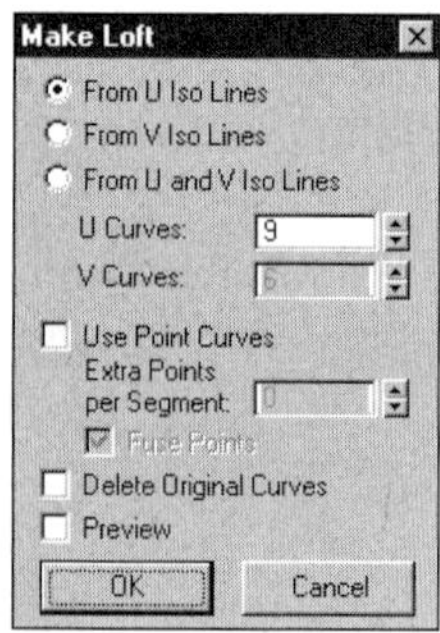

Figure 10.30
The Make Loft dialog box, which allows you to reloft a surface by sampling a given number of curves from the surface in a given direction.

2. Use the default number of samples in the direction opposite to your original curve. Before relofting, you must decide whether you want to delete the curves that currently support the loft. Sometimes, these curves are particularly important and should be preserved, even if they are not used in the loft. In this case, however, it would be easy to use the Make Loft tool again (in the other direction) to recover the edge curves. Check the Delete Original Curves box and click on OK. Take a look at the U Loft Surface rollout to confirm that a new list of curves is supporting the loft.

3. As a general proposition, breaking a dependency is an irrevocable act, but the Make Loft tool also works on independent CV Surfaces. Click on the Make Independent button to

convert the surface to a CV Surface. Go to the Curve subobject level, select all the curves, and delete them—noting in the process that the original curves are already gone. The surface is unaffected because the dependency on the curves is broken. Move on to the Surface CV subobject level and move some surface CVs to change the shape.

4. Convert the surface back into a Loft Surface. With the surface selected in the Surface subobject level, click on the Make Loft button. Once again, an adjustable number of isoparametric curves can be sampled off the surface in a chosen direction. Note that the Delete Original Curves option is grayed out because you're not sampling from an existing Loft Surface. Set a sampling that appeals to you and click on the OK button. You again have a Loft Surface that is edited from the CVs of its component curves.

Surface Curves and Trimming

The whole concept of a curve being confined to a surface is unique to NURBS, and it takes a long time to become accustomed to this idea. The curve is dependent on the surface; therefore, if the surface changes, the curve changes to stay aligned with the surface. In the loft exercise, you saw how isoparametric curves can be sampled from a surface. Isoparametric curves constitute the very structure of a NURBS surface. You can also extract such curves individually as U Iso Curves and V Iso Curves from the NURBS Creation Toolbox.

Isoparametric curves are not often useful for trimming purposes, however. Trimming is a pillar of NURBS modeling. The shape of a surface is defined not only by its structure, but also by surface curves that are not part of that structure. These curves are used to hide portions of the surface or to connect with other surfaces. Trim curves are generally created by projecting a curve onto a surface to create a surface curve. You'll learn the basics in the following exercise.

Projecting a Surface Curve

You project a curve onto a surface in a chosen direction to create a surface curve for trimming. The concept is very similar to that of a Planar projection in texture mapping. Follow these steps:

1. Reset your scene if you're continuing from the previous exercise. Draw a straight, horizontal CV curve in a Front viewport, using five CVs. Switch to the Modify panel and choose the Create Extrude Surface tool from the NURBS Creation Toolbox. Drag down from the curve to extrude a surface. If nothing seems to be happening, try a different Direction option in the Extrude Surface rollout. Note that you can use the spinner in the rollout to set the length of the extrusion. Check in a shaded Perspective viewport to see which way the surface is facing. Flip the surface normals in the rollout, if necessary, to get the surface to face toward you. Right-click, as usual, to end the creation process.

Using an Open Curve

An open curve can be used to trim a surface if it both enters and leaves the surface. Neither endpoint can be on the surface. You'll see how this works with the surface you're working with in this exercise. Continue the exercise from the previous page with these steps:

2. Create a CV curve from the NURBS Creation Toolbox so that the curve is part of the current basket. After activating the icon, draw a curve in a Front viewport so that it begins to the left of the surface and ends to the right of it. Your Front viewport should look something like Figure 10.31.

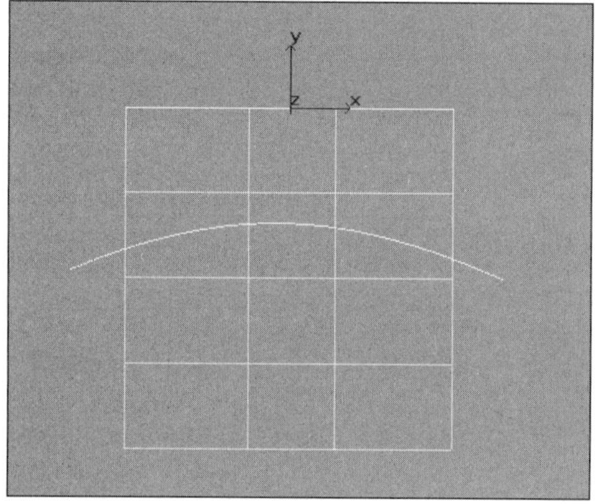

Figure 10.31
A surface is extruded downward from a horizontal curve in a Front viewport. A separate curve is drawn that crosses the surface and extends out on either side.

3. Due to the way you created the curve, it happens to be located precisely on the surface, but it is not a surface curve. To create a surface curve, you need to project the current curve onto the surface. Projection is a strange concept here, because you can "project" the curve even though it is already on top of the surface. To make things more clear, select the curve in the Curve subobject level and move it toward you (in the World Y-direction) in a Perspective viewport. Figure 10.32 shows a rotated Perspective viewport with the curve moved back as directed.

4. Project the curve in the direction that you are looking in the viewport. This is a very important concept that takes a moment to grasp. To get the proper result, you need to perform the projection from a Front viewport. Click on the Create Vector Projected Curve button in the Toolbox and place your cursor over the curve in a Front viewport. When the curve turns blue, click and drag to the extruded surface. When the surface turns blue, release the mouse button. Look at your Perspective viewport to see the Vector Projected curve on the surface, as illustrated in Figure 10.33. Do not right-click yet to end the creation process.

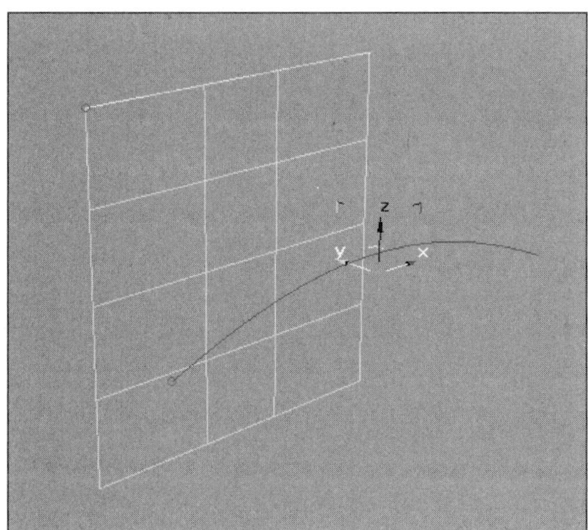

Figure 10.32
A rotated Perspective viewport shows the curve moved back, in the World Y-direction, ready for projection.

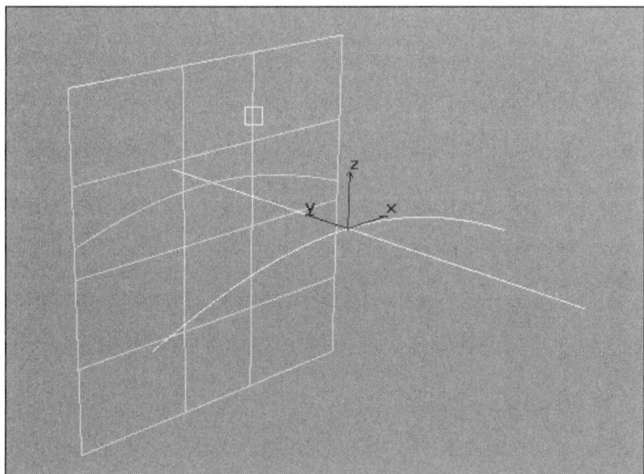

Figure 10.33
After projecting the curve from a Front viewport, a Vector Projected curve is created on the surface. The horizontal line indicates the direction of the projection.

5. Because you didn't right-click to end the creation process, the Vector Projected Curve rollout is visible. (If you did right-click, just undo.) Check the Trim box to hide all of the surface on one side of the projected curve. Check the Flip Trim box to hide the opposite side. End with the top portion of the surface hidden, as shown in Figure 10.34. Right-click out of the creation tool.

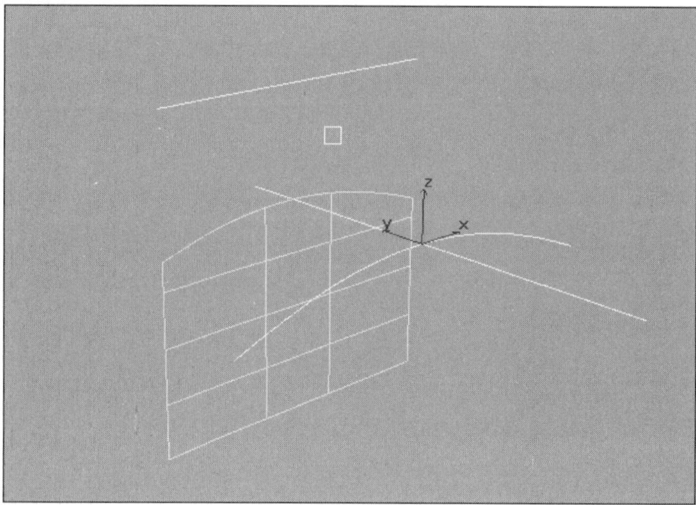

Figure 10.34
The surface curve is used to trim the surface, hiding everything on one side of the surface curve.

6. Multiple dependencies exist here. Although the Vector Projected curve (the surface curve) is dependent on the curve from which it was projected, it is also dependent on the surface. To test this, go to the Curve CV level and change the shape of the projecting curve. Watch both the surface curve and the trim effect update. Then, move the CVs on the curve from which the surface was extruded to put some waves in the surface. The projection is automatically updated. See Figure 10.35.

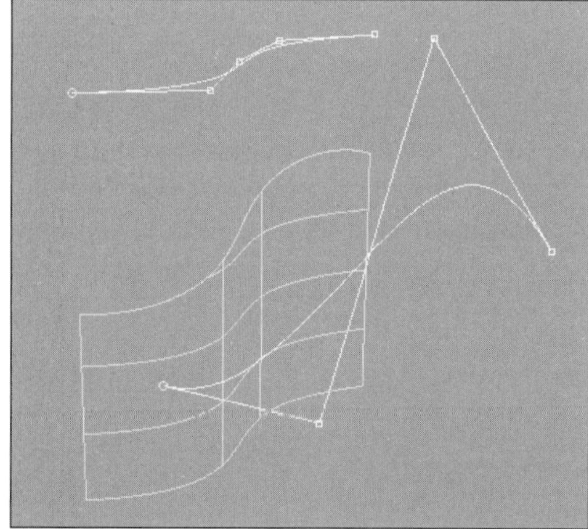

Figure 10.35
Multiple dependencies are tested. The projecting curve is edited, changing the shape of the projected surface curve. The curve from which the extrusion was made is edited, which changes the shape of the surface and therefore the shape of the dependent surface curve.

7. Go back to a Front viewport and move one of the endpoints of the projecting curve so that the curve no longer extends off the end of the surface. Note that the surface turns orange and the trim disappears. This is an error state. Trimming can make sense only if a surface curve divides a surface into two distinct portions—one to be hidden and one to be displayed. If an open curve does not leave the surface at both of its endpoints, it cannot serve as a trimming curve. This is the cause of the vast majority of trim errors.

Cutting Holes with a Closed Curve

You can use a closed curve to cut a hole through two surfaces and create the typical NURBS version of Boolean subtraction. Follow these steps:

1. Create a CV Surface in a Front viewport (Create|Geometry|NURBS Surfaces|CV Surf). Draw it out to make an approximately square grid.

2. Create a Circle object (a Bezier spline) in a Front viewport that fits well inside the NURBS grid. Use the right-click menu to convert it to a NURBS curve in a NURBS basket. When the NURBS panel appears, use the Attach command to add the grid to the current basket.

3. Select the grid (the CV Surface) at the Surface subobject level and, in a Top viewport, move it in the World Y-direction, so that it's a little in front of the Circle. Shift+drag to make an independent copy of the grid behind the Circle, in the World Y-direction. A rotated Perspective viewport should look like Figure 10.36.

Figure 10.36
A circular NURBS curve is sandwiched between two flat NURBS surfaces. They are all subobjects in a single NURBS basket.

4. Project the same curve on both surfaces to cut out a hole. If you used the regular Vector Projected curve method (in a Front viewport), you need to hide one surface to be able to project onto the other without interference. When you use a flat grid, however, it's possible to use the Normal Projected curve method. This method projects in the direction of the surface normals, which is a very confusing idea in any case other than a flat surface. Rotate your Perspective viewport to get an angle that gives cursor access to all three objects. Activate the Create Normal Projected Curve button on the NURBS Creation Toolbar. Click and drag from the Circle to one grid. When the surface curve appears, check the Trim box in the Normal Projected Curve rollout to cut out a hole. Do the same thing for the other surface, and then right-click to get out of the creation tool. Select the curve in the middle in the Curve subobject level and hide it with the Hide button. Your Perspective viewport should look like Figure 10.37.

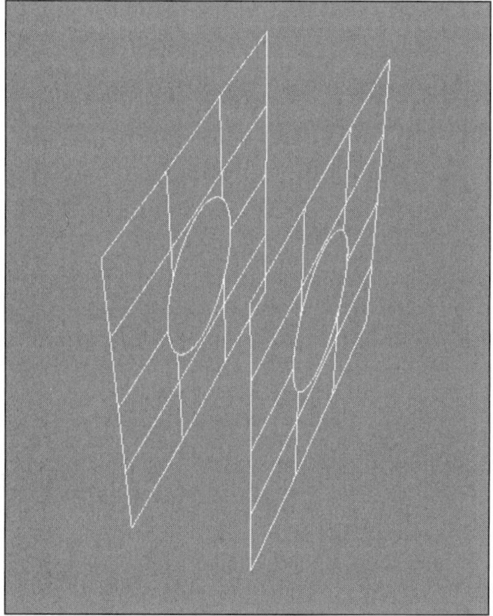

Figure 10.37
The Circle from Figure 10.36 is projected on both surfaces and used to trim out a hole. The Circle is then hidden.

5. To bridge the holes, create a U Loft Surface between the two surface curves. When you finish, you have a tunnel. Figure 10.38 illustrates this in wireframe.

6. Check your model in a shaded Perspective viewport to get the normals right. The back grid may need to have its normals flipped. Whether the loft needs flipping depends on the direction in which you connected the curves.

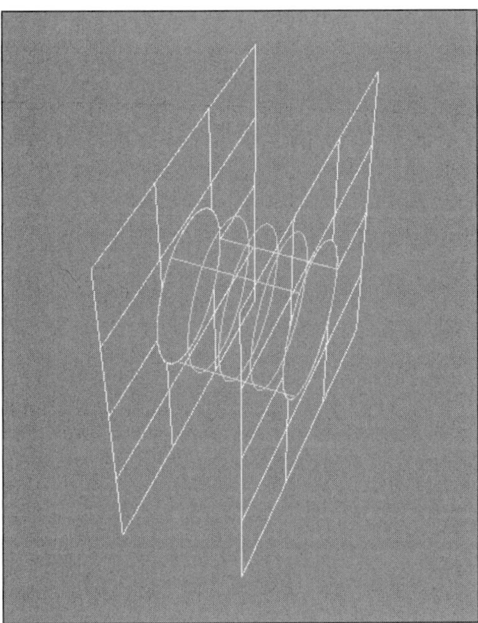

Figure 10.38
The two surface curves are bridged with a U Loft Surface to create a tunnel.

7. The loft created a sharp hole—the one that was drilled out. To create a softer hole, you need a method that maintains some curvature continuity with the flat surfaces. Select the Loft Surface in the Surface subobject level and delete it. Use the NURBS Creation Toolbox to create a Blend Surface between the two surface curves. Drag from one curve to the other, just as with a loft. Right-click when you're done. A wireframe view, as shown in Figure 10.39, reveals the result.

8. Select the Blend Surface and pull down in the panel to see the Blend Surface rollout. You can change the direction of the continuity at either end of the surface by flipping the tangents. Check the Flip Tangents boxes to understand the concept, and then return to the correct result. A Blend Surface is much like a loft; as in all lofts (NURBS and otherwise), the component curves must all be running in the same direction, and their start points must be aligned. The Flip End options allow you to reverse the curves without going back to the Curve subobject level. Select these options to see the effect of reversed curves. In addition, spinners found here align the positions of the start points, which are connected by a dotted blue line in the viewports. These curve-alignments tools are also available for Loft Surfaces.

9. The primary control for Blend Surfaces is Tension, which is set separately for each end. Reducing both values to zero completely eliminates the tangency, producing the same sharp result as the loft approach. Experiment with values, both less and greater than the default of 1.0. The higher the value, the greater the curvature. Figure 10.40 illustrates a Tension value of 2.0 at both ends.

Figure 10.39
The two surface curves are bridged with a Blend Surface to create continuity of curvature and a softer result at the edge of the holes.

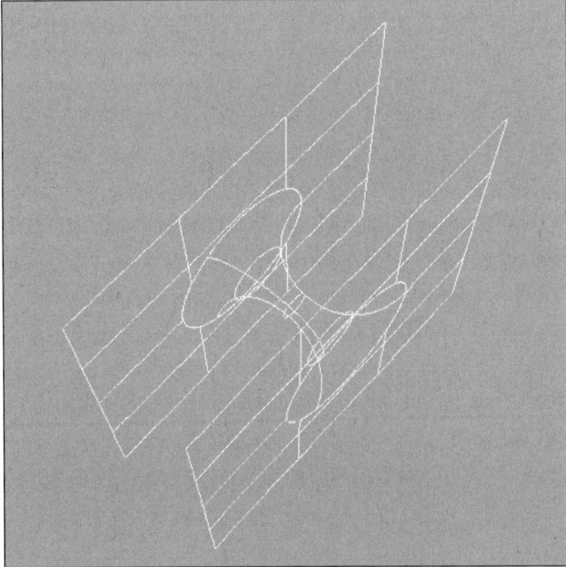

Figure 10.40
The Tension spinner determines the degree of curvature continuity going into the blend. At a value of 2.0, twice the default, the curvature is extreme and organic.

Surface Approximation

It's impossible to stress strongly enough that using NURBS is ultimately a way of generating a polygonal mesh. NURBS surfaces are freeform abstractions that must be reduced to a mesh for rendering. The process of *surface approximation*, as this tessellation is called, is an essential part of the NURBS modeling process. This is not the case merely because NURBS models can generate an excessive number of polygons and slow rendering to a halt. Again and again, you'll discover that NURBS surfaces are not rendering correctly and that the answer to these problems lies in the surface approximation tools.

Surface approximation, like everything in NURBS, is a deep subject, but the serious student must start somewhere. The main Surface Approximation rollout is at the object (basket) level, so it applies to all the surfaces in the basket. You can override these settings with respect to selected surfaces by using the Surface Approximation rollouts at the Surface subobject level, but doing so is rarely necessary.

Figure 10.41 illustrates the Surface Approximation rollout at the object level. The two radio buttons at the top determine whether the present settings are to be applied to the shaded viewports or to the renderer. (Remember that a shaded viewport is a rendering, and therefore requires a polygonal mesh.) In the interest of interactive speed, it obviously makes sense to use a lower degree of tessellation for the viewports than should be used for a finished rendered image. The viewport tessellation is very important, however. You'll often need to use an Edged Faces view to see the tessellated polygonal mesh in the viewports. Even when this tessellation is not as fine as that intended for the final render, it indicates the flow of the mesh and highlights obvious problems of irregularity.

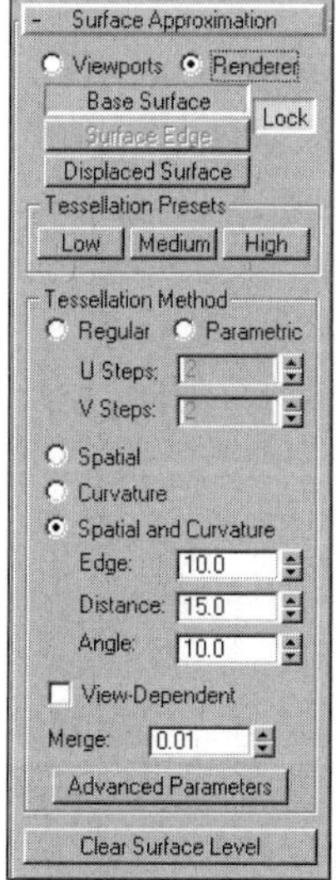

Figure 10.41
The object-level Surface Approximation rollout.

The settings for the renderer require serious consideration. MAX provides three preset values—Low, Medium, and High—that all use the Spatial and Curvature tessellation options. These are adaptive options that generally produce the most intelligent result. The Curvature method uses a maximum angle set by the user. This is effectively the largest possible angle between adjacent polygonal edges after tessellation. The smaller the angle, the finer the mesh must be to meet the test. The Curvature method also uses a Distance measure that determines the maximum distance that the mesh can vary from the ideal NURBS surface being approximated. Once again, the smaller the number, the finer the mesh and the better the approximation. The Spatial method fixes the maximum length of an edge in the resulting polygonal mesh and, again, the smaller the number, the smoother the result. The default Spatial And Curvature method uses both techniques together. The Regular and Parametric methods are nonadaptive and are rarely needed. Make a practice of using wireframe renders (use the Force Wireframe in the Render Scene dialog box) to test your surface approximation results.

The Merge spinner at the bottom of the rollout is one of the most important tools in the entire NURBS implementation. It determines how far the surface approximation tools reach to bridge the mesh between adjacent surfaces. The default value of .01 is often far too small. When your renders display small cracks between surfaces—especially when they meet at surface curves—kick this number up to 1.0 or more.

Moving On

In this chapter, you were exposed to only a small amount of the information needed to use MAX's NURBS implementation. Yet there are weeks of study in these pages alone. NURBS modeling is a subject of such depth and difficulty that it could easily fill an entire book all by itself. This chapter sought to provide only the basic grounding for the serious student.

This chapter first covered some of the essential properties of NURBS curves and surfaces, and then it moved on to the major features of MAX's NURBS implementation. Here, you learned about the basket concept for NURBS objects in MAX, and you saw how the program handles dependencies (modeling relations) between subobject curves and surfaces in a basket. You worked with a basic Loft Surface—building it, editing it, and relofting it from sampled curves. You learned the basics of trimming surfaces with projected surface curves, both open and closed, and saw how a Blend Surface can be used to create continuity between surfaces. Finally, you looked briefly at the important issue of surface approximation.

The next chapter moves on from modeling topics in order to explore Materials and the use of MAX's powerful Material Editor.

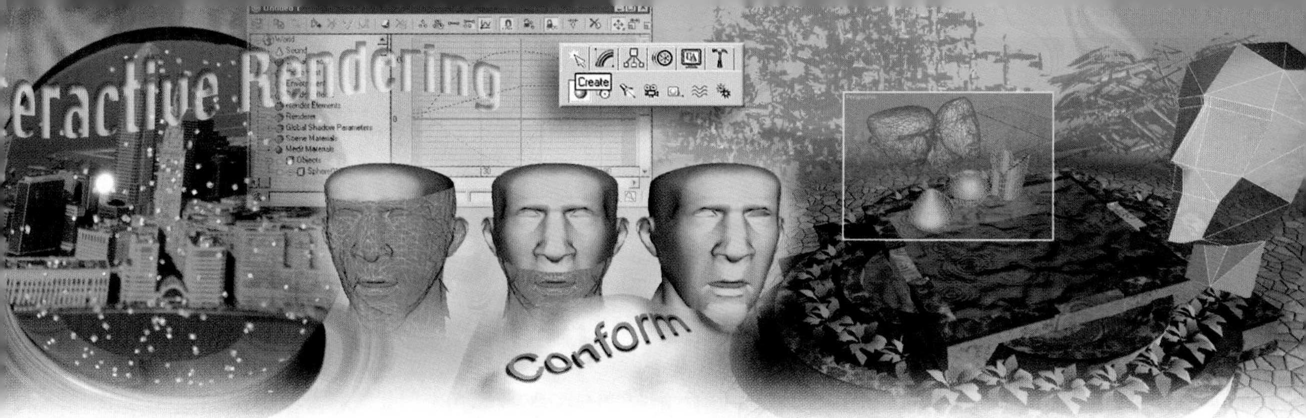

3ds max 4 Color Studio

3ds max 4 provides unparalleled opportunities for creative expression to meet a wide range of professional demands, from entertainment to commercial visualization and beyond. In the following series of color images, you'll see MAX applied in many of these directions.

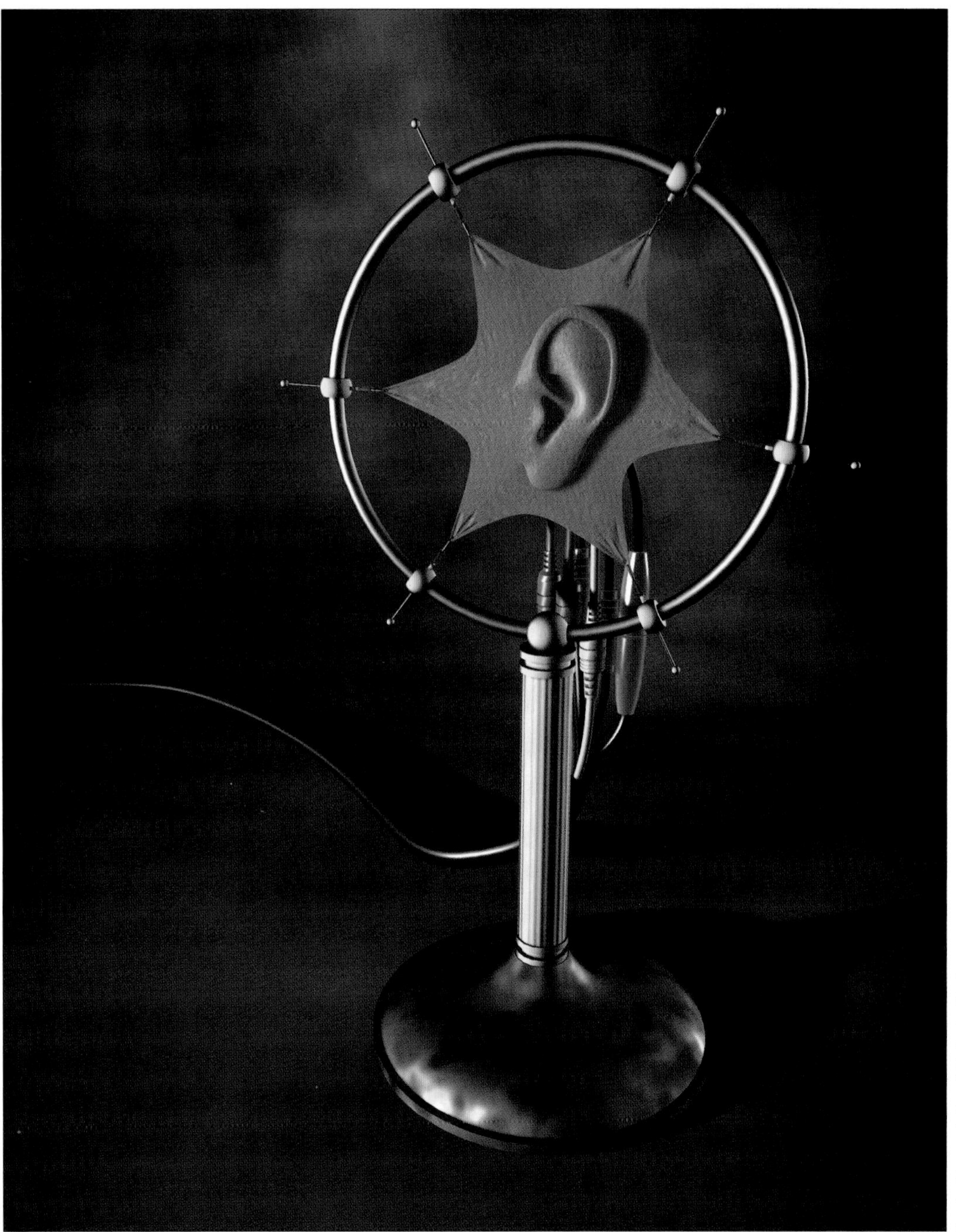

This "Earphone" image, representing an ear used as an old-style microphone with modern connections, was created by Xavier Le Dantec of Ubi Soft Entertainment. It showcases many techniques available to MAX users, including the MeshSmooth modifier used to model the ears and the texture added to the base and background with procedural noise.

"Can anybody hear me?" Once the initial head model was created and the eyes and teeth were added, it was a simple matter of using the Array tool, discussed in Chapter 5, to create this column of heads. This figure is an excellent use of materials, shadows, and camera angles for a dramatic effect.

Is it just us, or does everybody wonder what bonsai trees would look like if they were designed by robots? This is a fun image showing potted plants using only metallic materials and hard shadows.

In this example, the Displace modifier uses the railroad tracks image (*inset*) to create a relief model from a simple Box primitive (see Chapter 6). This technique can be used to add actual texture to a surface when bump mapping (which merely gives the impression of texture) is not effective.

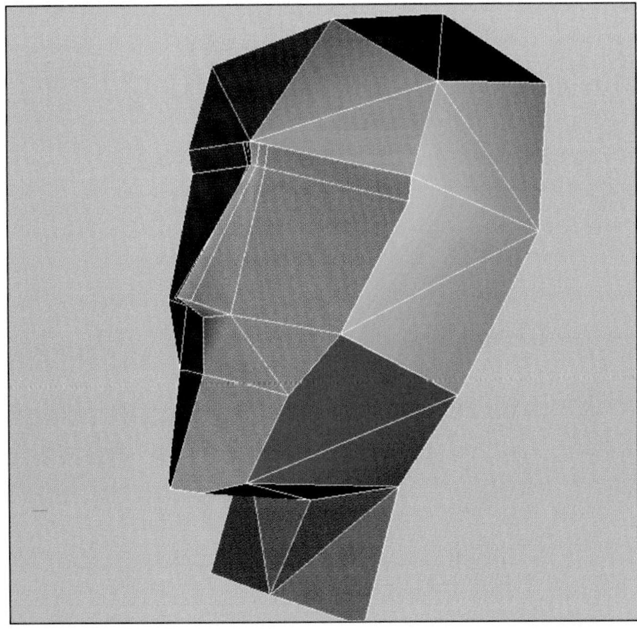

As shown in Chapter 7, low polygon modeling consists of extruding faces, turning edges, and moving vertices. To help distinguish the faces during the mesh-level-modeling process, different faces of a mesh object can be assigned different colors, as illustrated in this figure.

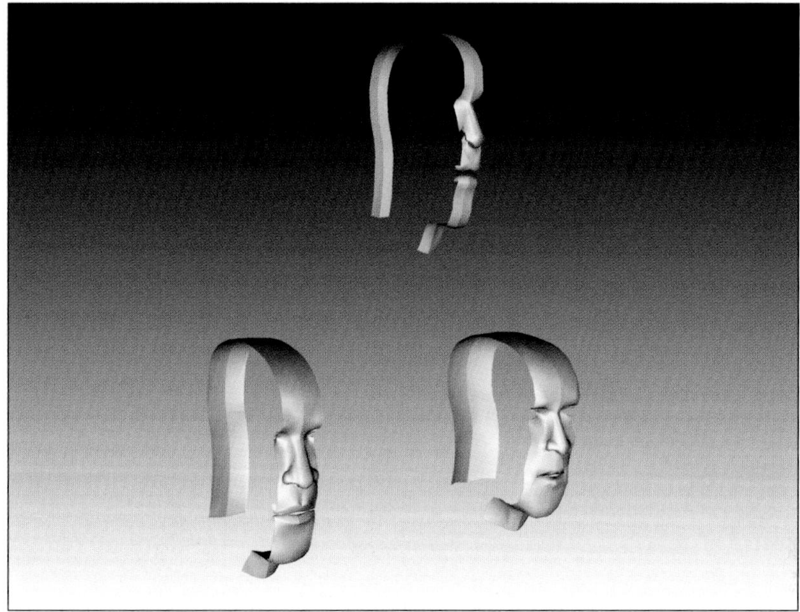

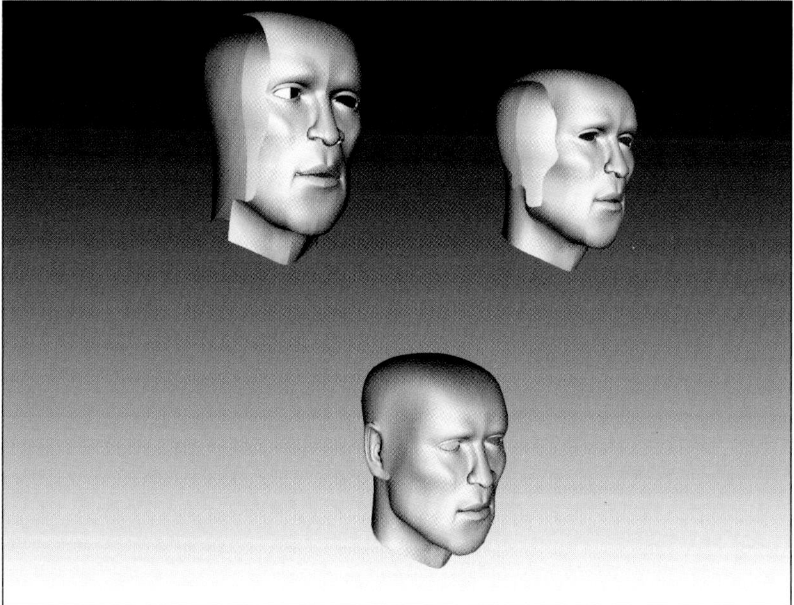

These two figures show the progression of the head created in Chapter 9. The top image shows the head model early in the creation process; the bottom is near completion. Specifically, in these examples, the head model is created by constructing a spline (curved Line object) at the midpoint of the head and then constructing a second spline a short distance away. The splines are combined into one, and surfaces are created between them. The process is repeated, getting further away from the starting point each time one half of the head is completed. Using an instance copy, the opposite side is modeled at the same time.

This violin was created using the NURBS (Non-Uniform Rational B-Splines) techniques discussed in Chapter 10. The curves are nice and smooth, and the surface approximation is clean—resulting in an absence of gaps between adjacent surfaces.

Materials and a particle system add character to this smokestack. Using the Facing option in the Particle Type rollout for Standard Particles (as discussed in Chapter 20), combined with a large number of particles, generates the volume effect. A reflection map on the curved fringe spikes gives the impression of the background being reflected on the metal surface.

Materials are often the key to setting a scene's mood. In this "Head Shop" image, each of the six identical head models takes on a distinct attitude through the application of a unique material. Notice how the use of ray-traced shadows (discussed in Chapter 13) allows the two transparent materials to cast interesting shadows on the wall.

Lighting and texture are two features that can make or break a MAX scene. The quality of this image is much less than that of the one below because the lights are much too bright and wash out the scene, bathing everything in light but robbing it of any warmth. Even the underside of the terrace roof and the exterior brick walls are illuminated by lights located inside the room.

In this image, however, the reflection has been reduced and blurred on the table top, and texture has been added to the sofa and chair to reduce the computer graphics look. Overall, the living room in this image looks warmer and more appealing and inviting than the one above. Lighting is discussed in more detail in Chapter 13.

Multiple applications of the Ripple space warp, in conjunction with the Noise modifier, give life to this multilevel fountain. The rotation and scale transforms applied to several instanced copies of a single plant give variation to the scene without a significant increase in the file size. Overall, this image uses MAX's Material Editor and its lighting capabilities to achieve a high level of realism. See Chapters 6, 12, and 20 for more information.

Ray-traced Materials take into consideration the effect of light traveling through a transparent or translucent object, as well as the reflections off the object's surface, as shown in this image. Notice how the blue figure's color appears in the legs of the clear figure. Ray-traced shadows, as opposed to shadow-mapped shadows, allow for the projection of color onto the surfaces that receive them.

Before

After

Camera matching is a powerful tool for compositing objects that have been created in MAX with photographs that have been scanned or taken with a digital camera. This utility takes image data, combined with helper objects placed in the scene, to match the location and focal length of a MAX camera with those of the camera that took the photograph. Adding an object with an applied Matte/Shadow Material allows you to add accurate shadows to the building, and the Film Grain render effect places a film grain distortion on the objects that matches the film grain of the photo. The before-and-after images shown here (which are also shown in Chapter 14) are photographs of a building without computer graphics, and then with computer graphics added.

Depth-of-Field, which this image shows, can be added as an effect to be applied as an element at render time. New to 3ds max 4 is the ability to use Depth-of-Field and Motion Blur effects in camera viewports while working interactively in a scene; you can learn more about these and other render effects in Chapter 16.

MAX is the top choice for game design, and its complete toolset often makes it the obvious choice for space and science-fiction modeling and animation. This scene uses the Glow render effect (covered in Chapter 16) and Object Motion Blur (covered in Chapter 15) to add some life to the laser and to the thruster and fuselage of the fighters shown here.

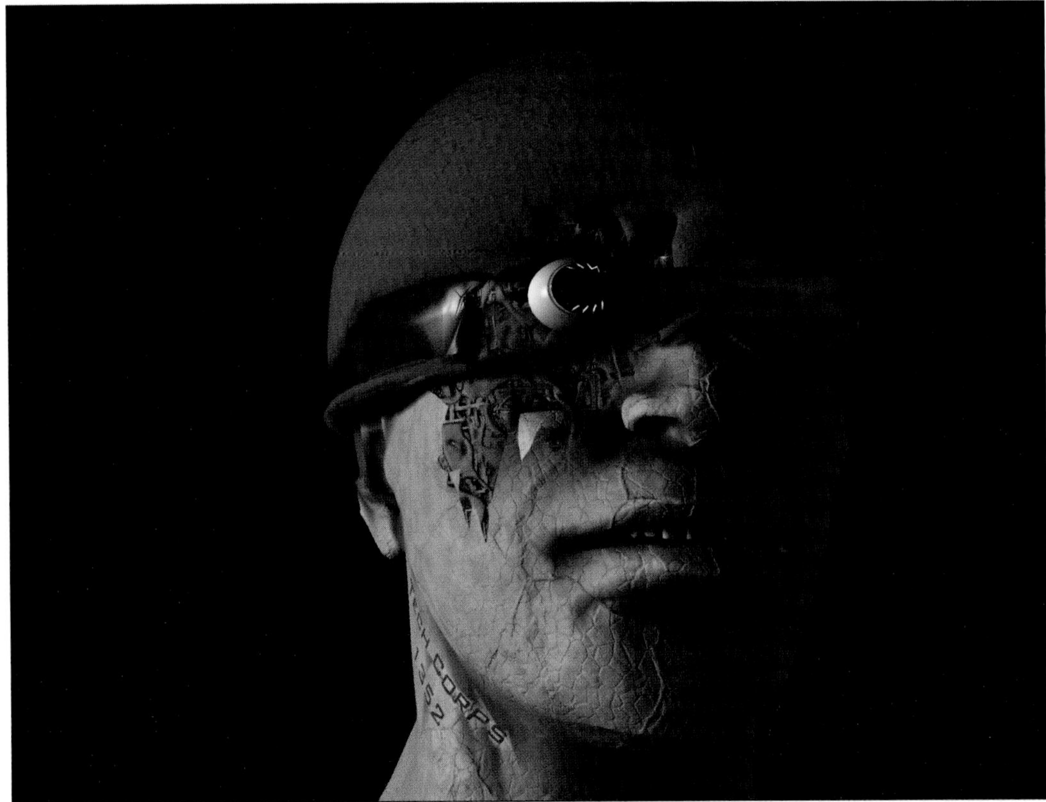

We could not decide whether to name this image "NEVER leave your post" or "I'll keep an eye out for you." The ShapeMerge compound object was used to project a shape onto the model to designate the polygons for the text below the jaw line and the area where the skin was "blown away." These polygons were then assigned material ID numbers different from the skin and each other. A single Multi/Sub-Object material was then applied to the entire head. A Boolean compound object helped to create the damage to the helmet. The main illumination comes from a Directional Light from the left and is augmented with a fill light behind and to the right of the head.

The workflow tools and atmospheric effects found in MAX—such as volumetric lighting—make the creation of animated "flying logos," like this one, a simple project to complete.

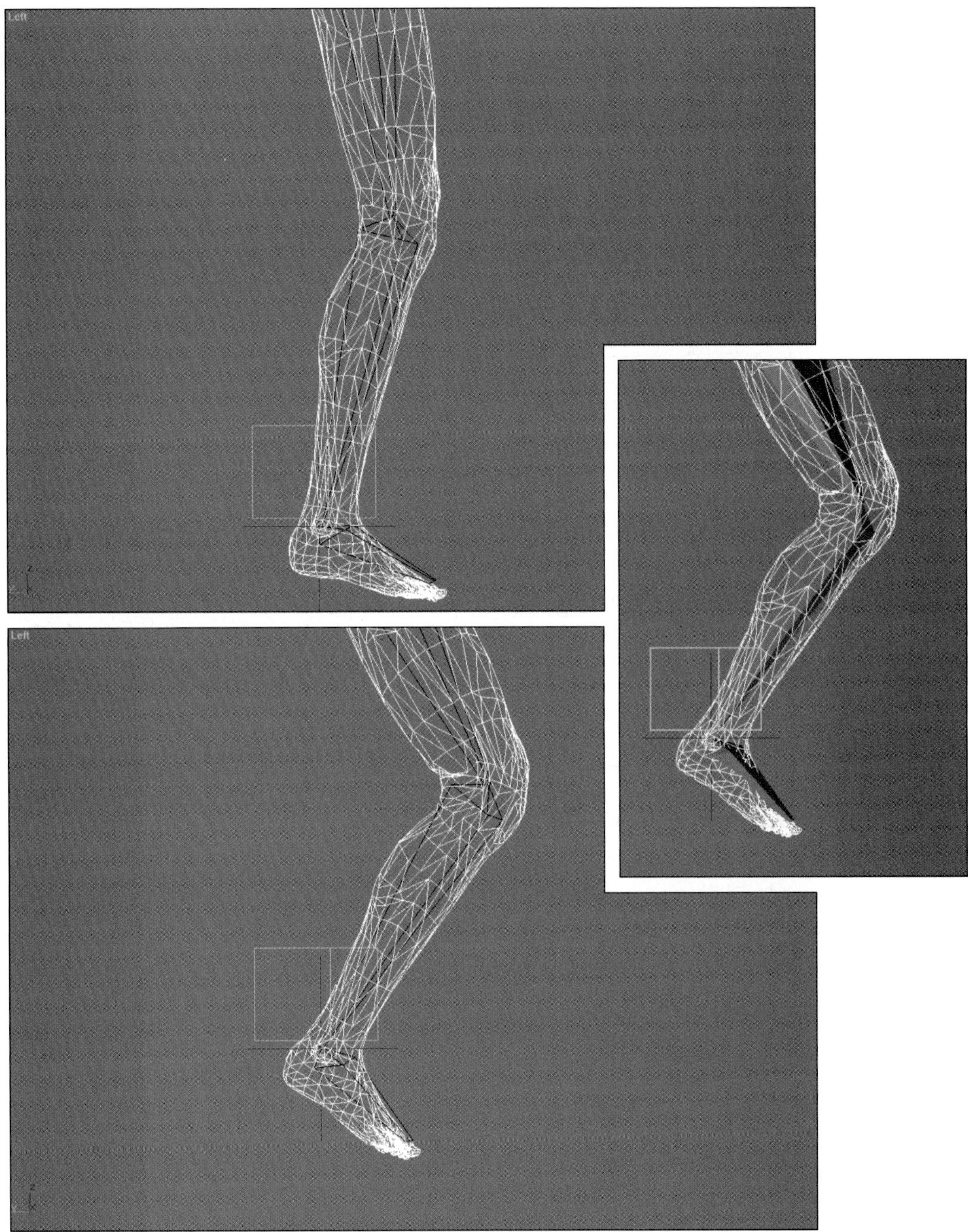

Deforming geometry in character animation is greatly enhanced with the tools discussed in Chapter 19. By moving the Dummy object assigned to the ankle, the knee bends naturally and a Gizmo assigned to the knee causes the back of the upper leg to flex naturally.

3ds max and its sister product, 3ds VIZ, are often used for architectural visualization and marketing, such as with this proposed retail/entertainment facility. In this image, ray-traced shadows help bring out the texture of the brick walkways and the mullions between the windowpanes. The window reflections are muted so as not to be distracting, and the trees and flowers add color to the earth tone–dominated scene. The "mannequins" that are spread out throughout the complex give the image a sense of scale. Altogether, this image shows many of the features (materials, lighting, and depth) of MAX.

3ds max 4 is used for more than simply game design, character animation, or photorealistic scene creation. It can also be used as a hobby or just for enjoyment. This study, which shows contrasts in color and starkness, and in rigidity and fluidity, is an example of the use of MAX in the art realm that would be difficult to re-create in any other medium.

Part IV

Materials and Textures

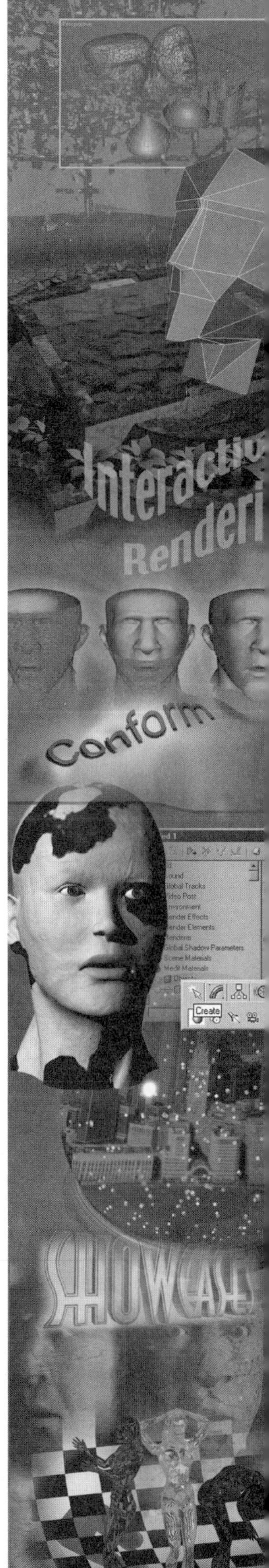

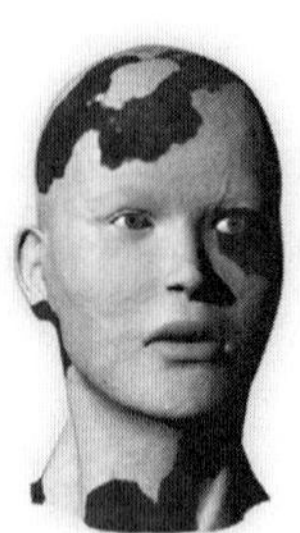

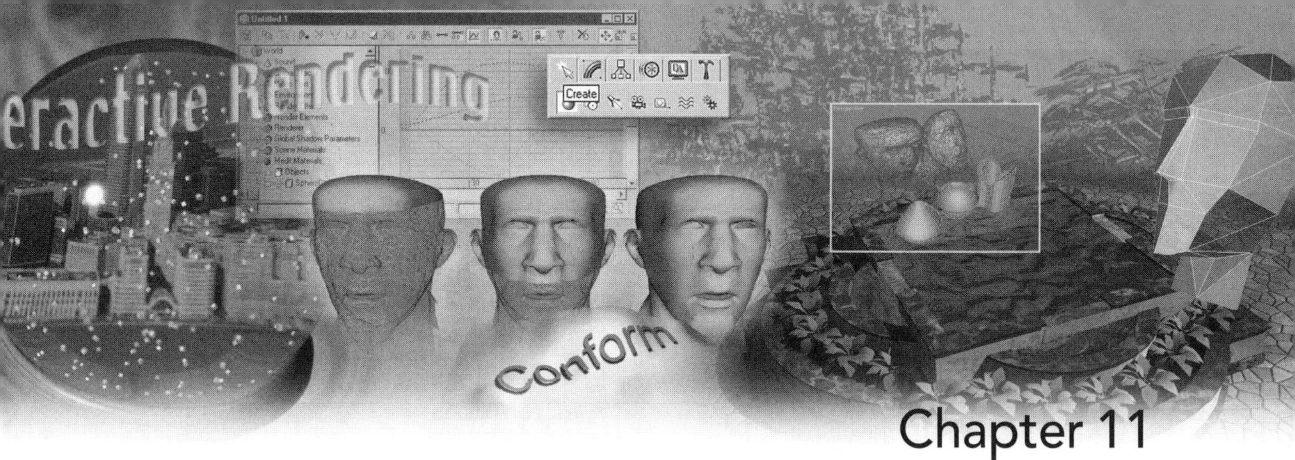

Chapter 11
Materials and the Material Editor

Once you have geometry—the shape or form of your object—you must determine the surface appearance. What colors will render, and what real-world materials should be suggested?

Defining the surface qualities of a 3D model is essentially a question of how it should respond to the lights in the scene. The subject is a mix of quasi-physical principles taken from the real world and practices born out of the peculiar needs of the virtual world.

What Is a Material?

The word *material* is familiar from everyday usage, and this causes confusion to those entering the arcane world of 3D computer graphics. The meaning of the word in computer graphics is technical, and every serious student of 3D graphics must understand this concept. But the word also has a meaning unique to 3ds max 4, which overlaps the general computer graphics (CG) meaning. To keep things clear, the word *Material* will be capitalized to refer to the material object in MAX; *material* will be spelled in lowercase letters when discussing the general concept in computer graphics.

Materials in 3D Computer Graphics

The precise CG meaning of *material* originated in the common meaning of the word. The CG pioneers in the 1970s developed methods for controlling the colors of rendered 3D models to convey the illusion that an object is composed of recognizable substances. For example, a cup-shaped object might be rendered to look like it was made out of glass, ceramic, metal, or plastic. Because the purpose was to create the convincing impression of real-world objects, it was natural to think in terms of simulating real-world materials, and so the word *material* was adopted into the emerging language of computer graphics.

Even from the start, however, the word *material* meant something broader. The features of a physical material that give it characteristic visual qualities can be abstracted into the way it reflects light. In CG, a material is a collection of parameters that determine how the surface of a 3D model responds to the light sources in the scene, and therefore determine the colors of the pixels representing that object in a rendering. These parameters are designed to produce workable results for rendering purposes, and therefore they may not correspond to physical reality. A CG material need not be designed to simulate a real-world substance, however. Any combination of the parameters that determine how a surface responds to the light sources in a CG scene, and, consequently, what pixel colors are produced in a render, is called a *material*.

Material Parameters

Consider the parameters of a given material to be its visual elements. The most important is Diffuse color. This is close to the common meaning of the "color" of an object. When light strikes a physical surface, certain wavelengths of the light are emitted back into space in all directions. This is a base color—the orange in the skin of an orange or the yellow of a lemon. If you look carefully at either of these fruits, however, you notice other colors that the eye and brain interpret to conceive of the surface. White regions are produced by the light source reflecting off the surface. These highlights characterize shiny substances. The brightness of such highlights can vary, as can their spread. A billiard ball is very shiny—with small, tight, and very bright highlights. A waxy crayon has duller highlights that are more spread out.

A close look at the orange or lemon reveals small patterns of darker color that you interpret as the small shadows created by the surface terrain. Thus, variation in the Diffuse color over the surface is likely to be understood as physical texture (relief) rather than as just irregularities in the "true" color of the object.

An orange may be shiny, but not in the same way as a mirror is shiny. A mirror reflects the colors of other objects in the room, and not just the light sources. The shininess of the orange or the billiard ball is called *specularity* (or specular reflection) in CG. The term *reflection* (all by itself) is reserved for mirror-like surfaces, in which the colors of other objects in the scene are visible. This is a great example of the difference between the CG material concept and reality. In physical reality, there is no distinction between specularity and reflection. A reflective surface reflects light from all origins—whether it is the direct light from light sources or the light emitted from objects as Diffuse color. If you look carefully at a shiny billiard ball, you see the highlights caused by the reflection of light from lamps and also the reflection of your own face (Diffuse color). The same is true of a shiny piece of fruit, except that object reflections are much less intense than highlights from light sources and are more likely to be obscured by the Diffuse colors of the fruit itself.

CG distinguishes between highlights (specularity) and reflections for important practical reasons. Highlights can be correctly rendered with only the information relating the direction of the light source to that of the surface. Because this operation is fast enough to perform in realtime, specular highlights are visible in your shaded preview. Reflections require information relating the directions of light paths connecting objects in the scene. This information is most correctly obtained through *ray tracing*—a powerful, but very time-consuming, rendering method. Because object reflections are noticeable only on mirror-like surfaces, it makes sense to ignore them when rendering materials that are intended to reflect only highlights. Highlights are extremely important in conveying a 3D effect. They suggest not only the shininess of the material but also the contours of curved surfaces. Even a small amount of specularity helps communicate the shape of curved geometry.

In Figure 11.1, the ball on the left has no specularity, and its curvature is conveyed only through the gradation of the Diffuse color. The ball in the center has a small degree of specularity. The surface does not look shiny, yet the faint highlights help to communicate the shape. The ball on the right has even more pronounced highlights, but they are spread to avoid a shiny appearance. The curvature of the Sphere is even more apparent with these increased visual clues. Specular highlights also help to tie objects together in a 3D scene, by suggesting their relative positions to the light sources.

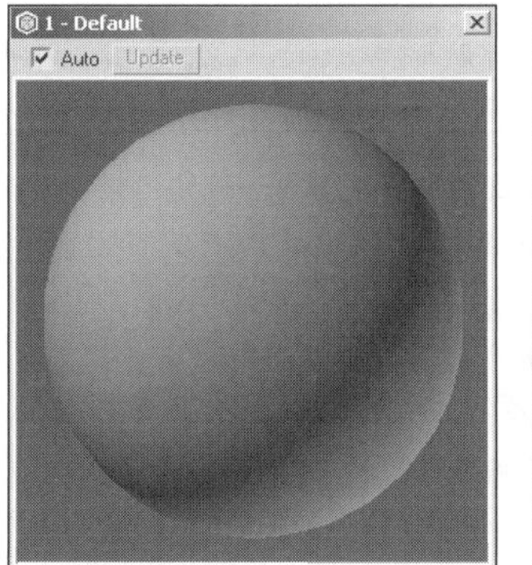

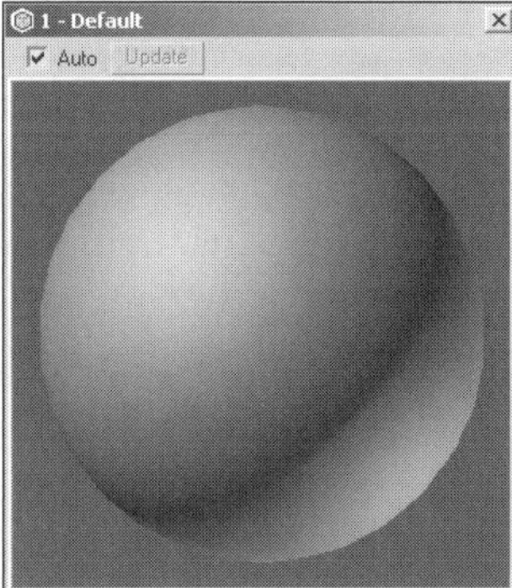

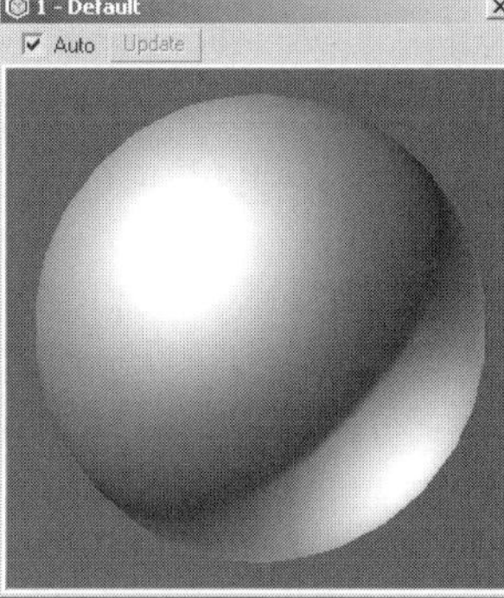

Figure 11.1
Specular highlights contribute visual clues that help the viewer read the curvature in 3D objects. The Sphere on the left is without specularity. Its curvature is revealed only by the gradation of its Diffuse color. Even the small amount of specularity in the middle Sphere does a lot to reveal the contours. In the Sphere on the right, the intensity of the highlight is increased, but the broad spread keeps the object from appearing shiny.

Transparency (or its inverse, *opacity*) is another essential material parameter. If a material is completely transparent, it is invisible. Thus, glasslike surfaces must rely on specular highlights and object reflections to reveal themselves. Transparent objects generally refract light passing through them, so objects appear distorted or shifted as seen through such surfaces. Refraction is therefore a necessary material parameter, but one that is available only if the material contains at least some transparency.

Shaders and Material Parameters

Materials exist within *shading models* (often called *shaders*). A shading model determines what information the Material definition must contain in order to render the surface. The classic Phong or Blinn shaders (discussed later in this chapter) are the most important and contain all the best-known material parameters, such as the following:

- Ambient color
- Diffuse color
- Specular color
- Specular intensity
- Specular spread
- Self-illumination (or luminosity)
- Opacity (or transparency)
- Reflection
- Refraction

Some features of these shading models take a moment to understand. Note the three different kinds of color. The Diffuse color is revealed only to standard light sources in the scene. Ambient light is a kind of general, completely nondirectional lighting that is used to fill out shadow areas. Standard CG lighting does not provide for reflected light. Regions that are shadowed from direct light rays are therefore completely black, without ambient light. In the real world, light reflected off surfaces typically provides a huge percentage of the total illumination, especially indoors. The radiosity rendering technique uses reflected light, and consequently can produce extremely realistic interior scenes. In the absence of radiosity, ambient light is used as a fix to simulate the all-over illumination that results from light bouncing off surfaces. In the Phong and Blinn shaders, the color revealed by the ambient lighting can be different from that revealed by the direct lighting (in the Diffuse color parameter). Once again, this could not occur in the physical world.

Specular color is the color of the specular highlight. Normally, it makes sense to make this color the same as that of the light sources. But colored (or slightly colored) highlights can be used for both realistic and fantasy purposes.

Self-illumination, or luminosity, is a parameter that controls the brightness of Diffuse color independently of the light sources. A surface with a self-luminous material value is visible in a scene without any lights at all. Luminosity is used to make objects such as neon signs appear self-illuminated, but it's also useful simply to add a little brightness to objects that are lit by light sources. The luminosity parameter does not cause the surface to emit light; thus, nearby objects are not affected.

Shading models other than Phong or Blinn differ in their material parameters. Other shading models handle specular highlights in more specific ways than the Phong and Blinn shaders do. And some, such as the Strauss shader, are organized much differently than the Phong and Blinn standards.

Materials Distinguished from Textures

One sure sign of the 3D professional is that he or she knows the difference between materials and textures and doesn't confuse the two. The material is the complete definition of all the parameters required by the shader. Each material parameter, by default, has only a single value. For example, a single Diffuse color applies to the entire material.

By *mapping* a material parameter, you can vary the value of the parameter over the surface. The most important example is the use of a bitmap image to provide the color values for the Diffuse color parameter of a material. Instead of having just one Diffuse color in the material, the colors of all the pixels in the bitmap are used. (The next chapter discusses the way the bitmap is applied to the surface of the model.) The use of a bitmap (or a procedural map) to vary the Diffuse color parameter of a material over a surface is often called *texture mapping*, or *texturing*, because the technique was developed to create the illusion of surface texture, such as the pebbly surface of a basketball. Like the word *material*, however, the term *texture mapping* has a broader meaning than its origin might suggest. To texture map a surface is to map its Diffuse color parameter, regardless of whether the color variations suggest surface relief. The MAX interface does not use the word *texture*, and a texture map in MAX is simply a map that is applied to the Diffuse color parameter of a material. By contrast, a bump map, which always creates the illusion of surface texture, is never called a texture map.

A material is required, but a map is optional. Each parameter of a material has only a single value unless a map is applied. Thus, many maps can be associated with a material—one (or even more than one) for different material parameters.

Materials in MAX

Materials in MAX are a specific implementation of the material concept in 3D computer graphics. A *Material* in MAX is a MAX object. (Remember that the word will be capitalized when referring to the object in MAX, as opposed to the general concept.) A MAX Material is the entire package necessary to define the colors that are rendered to pixels when a surface is rendered.

Think of Materials hierarchically; that is, as a sequence of decisions to be made, from the general to the specific.

Material Types

At the top of the hierarchy is the Material type. The basic Material type is the Standard Material, but Max also includes Raytrace and Matte/Shadow Materials. There are also a number of Compound Materials, which are containers for combining more than one Material on an object. The Compound Materials use the Standard, Raytrace, and Matte/Shadow Materials as Sub-Materials. If a Compound Material is used, each Sub-Material is defined independently.

Shaders

For the Standard and Raytrace Materials, you have a choice of shaders. The number of alternatives is larger for the Standard Material. The Matte/Shadow Material does not have shader choices because its function is to hide a surface rather than to reveal it.

Material Parameters

The choice of shader for a material determines the parameters of the material. The next step is to set these parameter values.

Maps

If a given parameter cannot be satisfied with only a single value for the entire surface, a Map object is applied to that parameter. The Map uses either a bitmap image or a *procedure* (a small program that receives user input) to create the variation in the parameter. The Map object overrides the parameter values entered in the Material Editor.

Using the Material Editor

The only way to understand MAX Materials is to work with them. Fortunately, you can learn a great deal by using only the Material Editor. In this section, you'll get a handle on MAX's powerful but rather complex Material Editor:

1. Create a Sphere object and open the Material Editor through the Main toolbar. The upper, static portion of the Material Editor is illustrated in Figure 11.2.

Figure 11.2
The upper, static portion of the Material Editor with the default six Material slots.

2. By default, 6 slots are visible in the Material Editor, but 24 slots are available. Place your cursor over the space between the slots and, when the cursor changes to a hand shape, drag the window, both horizontally and vertically. You'll see four rows with six slots each.
3. Right-click on any of the slots and note that you can choose to see more, but smaller, samples at one time. Try the 6×4 option. All 24 slots are visible at once, although they are fairly tiny.

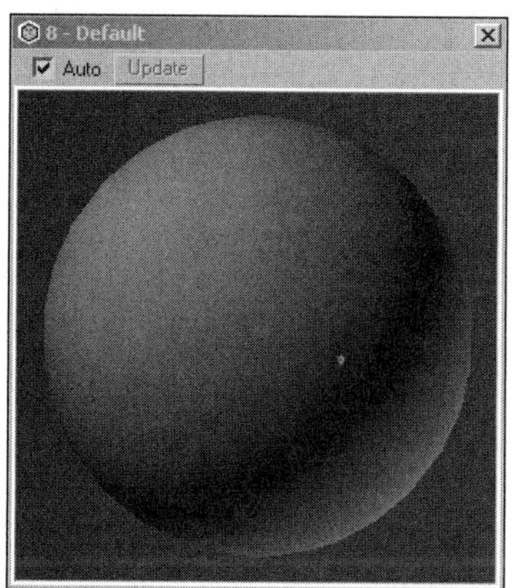

Figure 11.3
The Material Editor, with the display changed to fit all 24 samples in the visible window. The size of each sample is very small, so the selected slot is magnified. The magnified version can be moved around the screen, independently of the Material Editor.

Right-click on any slot again and try the Magnify option. A larger, separate window appears, apart from the Material Editor (see Figure 11.3). The magnified version of a material can also be opened by double-clicking on the Material slot, and resized by dragging its corners.

Moving Materials between Slots and Objects

It's very important to understand the relationship between Materials in the slots in the Material Editor and Materials on objects. When an object is first created, it doesn't have a Material; instead, it has an Object Color. Object Colors are assigned to help distinguish objects on the screen. Let's continue the previous exercise by learning how to move materials between slots and objects:

1. Select your Sphere and go to the Modify Panel. At the top of the panel is the name of the object, and to the right is a color box with the Object Color. Click on that color box and use the Object Color dialog box to change the color. This action does not, however, assign a Material.
2. The Track View tool shows a linear representation of every object in a scene; each has its own entry, or *track*. Scene objects are listed in the left panel and their tracks are shown in the right. Track View is accessed through the button just to the left of the Open Schematic View button in the Main toolbar. Open a Track View window. Expand the Medit Materials (the Material Editor) entry in the left panel and notice that 24 Materials are listed under it, but none under Scene Materials. Put a Material from one of the slots onto the Sphere object. With the Sphere object selected, click on the upper-left slot in the Material Editor. The Material Editor's label bar indicates that 1-Default is selected, and a white border appears around the slot. Beneath the sample slots is a row of icons. The third icon from the right is Assign Material To Selection. Click on this icon and watch your Sphere assume the color of 1-Default.

3. Look at Track View again. A small plus sign has appeared next to the Scene Materials label. Click on this to open the track. Notice that 1-Default is now in two places at once: in a slot in the Material Editor and on an object in the scene. The Material is in a third place, as well. Open the Objects entry and the Sphere within it to find the Material once again. Figure 11.4 shows the current state of the left panel of the Track View window.

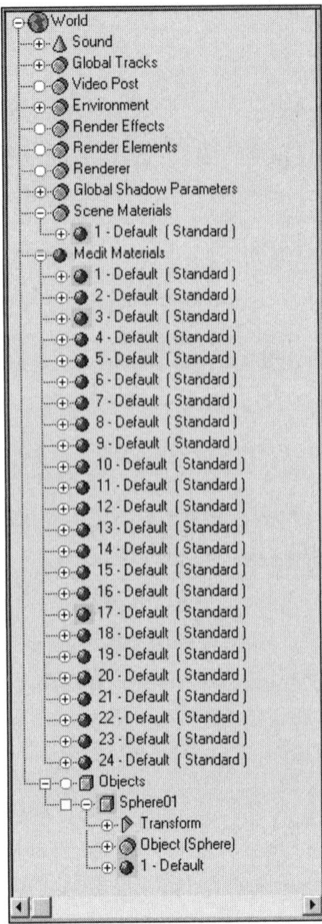

Figure 11.4
After 1-Default (in the first slot of the Material Editor) is assigned to the Sphere, that Material is stored in the MAX file in two separate places: on the object and in the slot. A Track View window shows 1-Default in the Material Editor, in the list of Scene Materials, and on the Sphere object itself.

4. Look at a Wireframe viewport and notice that the Object Color is still used for the wireframe (when the object is unselected), despite the Material assignment. Only a shaded preview shows the color of the Material.

5. Drag 1-Default from its current slot in the Material Editor to the slot next to it. Even though both of these slots now have the same name, only the first slot is connected to the Sphere. Materials in the Material Editor that are assigned to objects in the scene are identified by

the triangles that appear in the corners of their Material slots. With the second slot selected, click on the Diffuse color swatch in the Material Editor. Change the Diffuse color and notice that the change is reflected in the slot sample, but not the object. Go to the first slot and change the Diffuse color there. This time, the Object Color changes along with the slot sample because assigned Materials are dynamic, rather than static, and changes to their parameters are instantly reflected on the object.

The Material/Map Browser

You could continue creating objects and connecting them to slots in the Material Editor, but what happens when you need more than 24 Materials? Even though the Material Editor has room for only 24 Materials, you can include as many Materials in the scene as can be assigned to objects. To do so, you use the Material/Map Browser, shown in Figure 11.5.

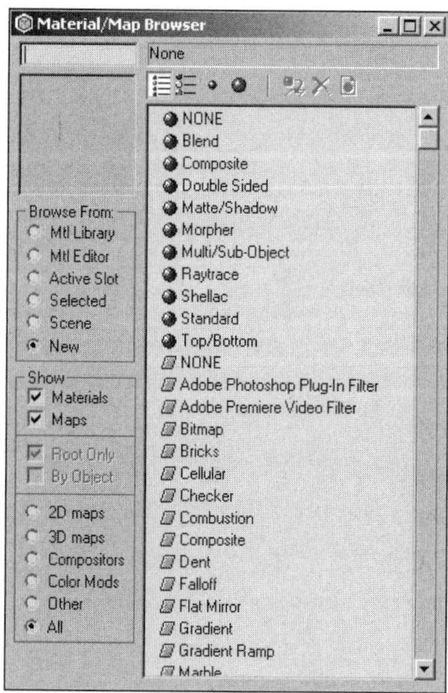

Figure 11.5
The Material/Map Browser.

Take a moment to look over this important dialog box. On the right is a list of all the possible Material and Map objects. The Materials are listed first and are bulleted with a blue ball; the Maps follow with a green parallelogram. The Show section of the dialog box allows you to filter out either category. The dialog box also displays options for new Materials and Maps. The Material Library contains a broad range of stock Materials that are supplied with MAX. If you select one of these with a single click, it will be previewed in the window in the top left corner. If you double-click on a Material choice, it will be loaded into the current slot. The Selected option provides the Material assigned to the selected object (if an object is in fact selected). The other Browse From options are easy to understand.

You'll see how to use the Material/Map Browser as we continue with the previous exercise:

1. To recover the first slot, click on it to select it. Click on the Get Material button—the first one on the left in the row beneath the slots—to open the Material/Map Browser.

2. Page through the options in the Browse From section of the panel to see alternative Materials and Maps. Return to the New option and choose a Standard Material by double-clicking on that item on the list. A new Standard Material appears in the first slot, in the default gray color.

3. You can now use this slot to define a new Material however you wish, and assign it to an object in the scene. But what if you need to edit the Material on the Sphere again? Just pick a slot that you're not using right now and pull the Material off the object. Give it a try. Select the Sphere; then, select a slot and click on the Get Material button. Use the Selected option in the Material/Map Browser and double-click on the only Material that appears in the list (it indicates the name of the selected object). Note that 1-Default is now in the selected slot, ready for editing.

A Couple of Shortcuts

Another way to get a Material off an object is even faster than the process we used in the previous exercise:

1. With the desired slot selected, use the Pick Material From Object tool (with an eyedropper icon) to the left of the Material name to click on the object. The object doesn't have to be selected. Try this in another slot.

2. There's a quicker way to free a slot. Select the slot you just used to pick up the Material from the object. Click on the Make Material Copy button in the middle of the row beneath the sample slots. The Material in the slot does not change, but the white triangles in the corners of the slot disappear. This means that the slot is no longer connected to the object. Change the Diffuse color of the Material in the slot and note that the object remains unaffected.

3. If you wish to put the revised Material back on the object, either select the object and assign the Material in the usual way or just click on the Put Material To Scene button (second from left). This button assigns the Material to the object because the names of the Material in the slot and the Material on the object are still the same.

Using the Material Library

Sometimes, you want to save your Materials. You may have developed a number of variations of a Material, but you don't want to waste valuable space in the Material Editor. Or, you may want to save a useful Material for use in other scenes. Just as you can get a Material from the Material Library, you can save a Material, as well. Let's see how doing so applies to the exercise at hand:

1. Select any slot you want. The current name of the Material is not sufficiently descriptive to be useful in a library. You can change the name in the Material Editor, or you can change

it when you save the Material. Click on the Put To Library icon in the middle of the row beneath the sample slots and change the name if you haven't already.

Creating New Libraries

When you put a Material into a library, it is saved to the current one, which is usually the default 3dsmax.mat file. One of the problems with this process is that, when it comes time to upgrade MAX, the file may be overwritten in the process, and the new Materials may be lost. To prevent accidental deletions, you can create a new library that is then transferred or saved with the new MAX.

Open the Material/Map Browser and select Mtl Library in the Browse From section. The name of the current library is listed in the dialog box's title bar. Select Save As, save the library with a descriptive name, and make it current. In the row of tools at the top of the Material/Map Browser, the last button, Clear Material Library, removes all entries from the library and provides a clean slate for your new or customized Materials. Use the Open button to switch back to the original when necessary.

---

2. To call up the Material from the Material Library, pick a different slot and click on the Get Material button. When the Material/Map Browser appears, use the Material Library option. The name of your Material appears in the list. Check out the viewing options represented by the first four buttons above the list. These options are available regardless of the source of the Materials in the list. The three buttons to the right are available only when you're browsing a Material Library. You can delete a Material from the library, clear the entire library, or update the scene with Materials from the library that have identical names. Double-click on your saved Material to load it into the Material Editor.

The Standard Material Type

The Standard Material type is used in the majority of cases, either by itself or as a Sub-Material in a Compound Material. Indeed, the other two primary Material types, Raytrace and Matte/Shadow, are not really materials in the conventional CG sense. The Standard Material implements the full range of shaders that are available in 3ds max 4. The choice of shading model determines the parameters that must be defined for the Material. As you will see, the primary significance in the choice of shader is in the treatment of specular highlights.

The Phong and Blinn Shaders

The Phong and Blinn shaders are the most important and most suitable for the broadest range of uses. Their parameters are identical; the only difference is the appearance of specular highlights. To try them, follow these steps:

1. Open the Material Editor and select a sample slot. Double-click on the slot to create a magnified window. Right-click and choose Options to call up the Material Editor Options dialog box, as illustrated in Figure 11.6. (This dialog box can also be called from a button in the column to the right of the sample slots.)

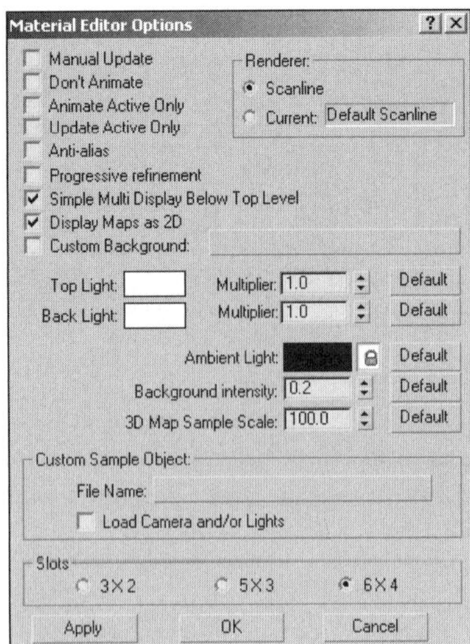

Figure 11.6
The Material Editor Options dialog box, with its default values.

2. Take a moment to look over these options. Note that each sample is rendered by using two lights—one from the top and one from the back. The color and intensity (Multiplier value) can be adjusted in this panel. Increase the Multiplier value for the top light and click on the Apply button. The top light becomes brighter for all the samples in the Material Editor, including the magnified copy. Click on the Default button to return the Multiplier to the default value. Now, increase the setting for Ambient Light intensity by clicking on the color swatch, dragging the Value slider of the resultant Color Selector to the right, and clicking on Apply. All the samples become generally lighter.

Note: *The default value for ambient light is low but significant in the Material Editor. However, the default level of ambient light in a MAX scene is very low. This value can account for a confusing difference between the appearance of a Material in the Material Editor and its appearance on an object in the scene. Ambient light for a MAX scene is set in the Environment dialog box, which is reached through the Rendering menu.*

Specular Highlights

Now, let's continue the previous example by adding specular highlights:

1. Return the Ambient Light intensity setting to its default value and close the Material Editor Options dialog box. Compare the specular highlights in the Blinn and Phong shaders. Drag the Material from the slot in the Material Editor that is being magnified (not the magnified slot itself) into another slot to create an identical copy, and magnify the second slot. Place the two magnified windows side by side for comparison. Both samples will use the Blinn shader because it is the default. Select one of the samples and change it to the Phong shader by using the drop-down list in the Shader Basic Parameters rollout.

2. Increase the Specular Level parameter to 100 for both samples to create a strong highlight. Adjust the Glossiness parameter to see how it changes the spread of the highlight; then, return it to the default value of 10. Leave the Soften parameter at its low default value. Compare the two magnified samples. The top-lit highlight is tighter and a bit softer in the Blinn sample than in the Phong sample. The backlit highlight is much broader in the Phong sample. In both samples, the backlit highlight is glancing, whereas the top-lit highlight is direct. Your samples should look like those shown in Figure 11.7.

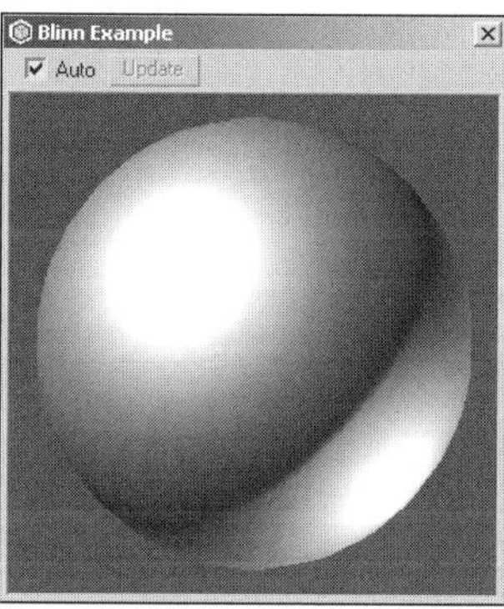

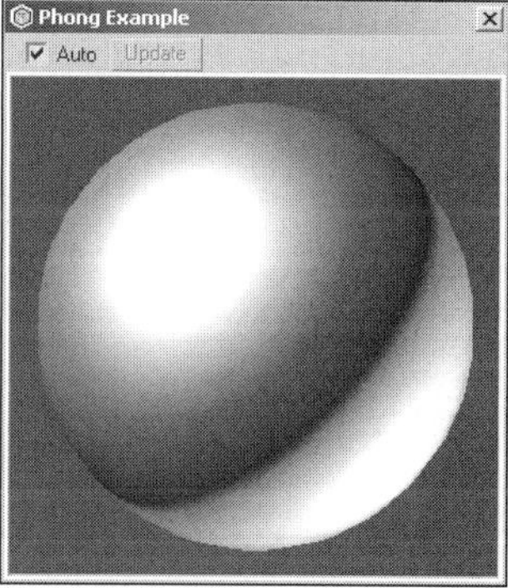

Figure 11.7

Specular highlights in Blinn and Phong shaders, compared in a Standard Material. Both samples use a Specular Level of 100, and Glossiness is set to the default of 10. The top-lit highlight is tighter in the Blinn sample (*left*) than in the Phong sample (*right*). The glancing backlit highlight is much broader in the Phong sample.

3. Increase the Soften parameter to 1.0 (the maximum) for both samples and compare. As you can see in Figure 11.8, softening has a much greater effect on the glancing highlights than it does on the direct highlights. Even so, the Phong highlights remain broader than the Blinn ones.

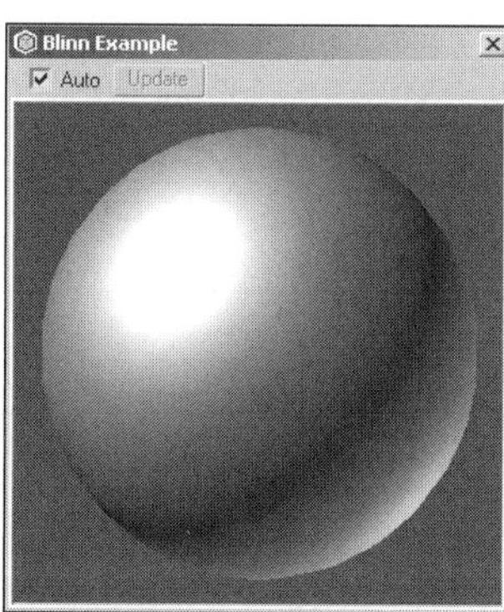

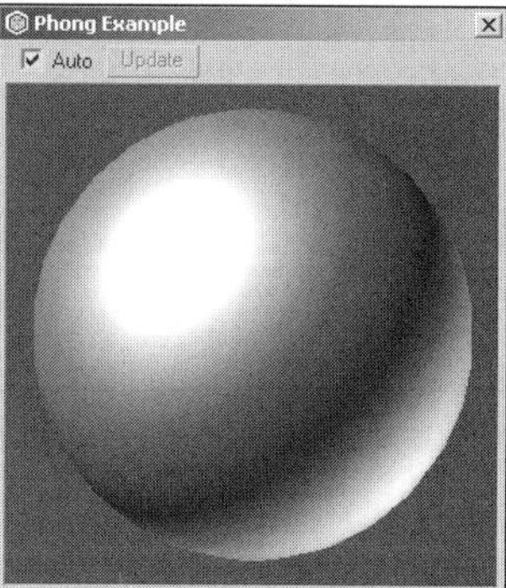

Figure 11.8

The same as Figure 11.7, but with the Soften parameter increased to its maximum value. Softening has a much greater effect on the glancing highlights than on the direct ones, but the Phong highlights (*right*) remain broader than the Blinn highlights (*left*).

4. Note that the default Specular color is white. This effectively means that the highlights will be the color of the light sources that create them, without any tint. Leave the Specular color at its default and change the color of the top light to a strong yellow in the Material Editor Options dialog box. Click on Apply. The top highlight is now yellow because the light is yellow. But the entire Sphere is yellowed, also, because the light affects the Diffuse color response, as well as the specular highlights.

5. Try it the other way. Return the light color to its default white and change the Specular color of the Material to yellow. This time, only the highlights are yellow, and the Diffuse color region is unaffected. Most shiny objects reflect back only the color of the light; therefore, most highlights are white if the light source is white. Some substances (most notably metals) have tinted highlights, however.

Notice that you can lock the Diffuse and Specular colors on the Material Editor. If you lock them, the Specular color always remains the same as the Diffuse, so the color of the highlights is tinted with the Diffuse color of the surface.

Ambient Color

Ambient lighting is a CG shortcut that is not based in physical reality. In the real world, surfaces have only a Diffuse color, which responds equally to direct or indirect light. In CG shading models, an object can use a color in response to indirect (ambient) light that's different from the color that responds to direct light (the Diffuse color). This concept is, admittedly, quite confusing, and it takes awhile to become accustomed to it. Continue your experimentation as follows:

1. In most cases, the Ambient color is a darker shade of the Diffuse color. To maintain this relationship as you change Diffuse color, lock the Ambient and Diffuse values together. Doing so keeps them precisely the same.

2. If you decide that the Ambient color should be darker, open the Color Selector dialog box and lower the Value slider.

The Ambient color is necessarily most noticeable in areas that are not exposed to direct light. The rendered color is the result of the color of the ambient light in the scene and the Ambient color of the material. Unlike most direct light sources, the ambient light is often a color other than white, because Ambient color is used to approximate the effect of light bouncing off surfaces in a room. This indirect light takes on a mix of the colors of the surfaces. Unfortunately, the Material Editor is not capable of applying colored ambient light in the slots, and thus any real testing must be done by rendering MAX scenes.

Opacity and Advanced Transparency

Opacity and transparency are inverses of each other. A surface that is 0 percent opaque is 100 percent transparent. MAX uses both terms in the Material Editor. The overall value is set in the Basic Parameters rollout as Opacity, and the Extended Parameters rollout contains Advanced Transparency controls. All of these parameters are identical in both the Blinn and Phong shaders. Let's continue our exercise by seeing how opacity and advanced transparency work:

1. Select a fresh sample slot and click on the checkerboard icon to the right of the samples to get a colored background image in the slot. Adjust the Opacity spinner to see the effect.

2. Open the Extended Parameters rollout to look at the Extended Transparency controls. Note the three Type options. The default of Filter allows you to tint or intensify the color of the transparent object to simulate the effect of light passing through colored glass. To test it, change the Diffuse color of the Material to a bright yellow and set the Opacity spinner to 40 percent. The effect is merely washed out. Set the Filter color to the same yellow and notice how the sample brightens up.

3. The Falloff controls are also very useful. Set the Opacity of your sample back to 100 percent. Choose the In option for Falloff and increase the Amount spinner to 100. The sample Sphere is now 100 percent transparent in the center and opaque around the edges. These settings are excellent for simulating the walls of glass vessels. Flip to the Out option, and the effect reverses. The increasing transparency toward the edges is just right for smoke and clouds. To see these effects better, toggle off the background pattern. Open the Material Editor Options dialog box and increase the Background intensity to 1.0, which makes the background white. Select the Anti-alias checkbox. Anti-aliasing increases the refresh time for the samples, but displays much sharper edges. See Figure 11.9.

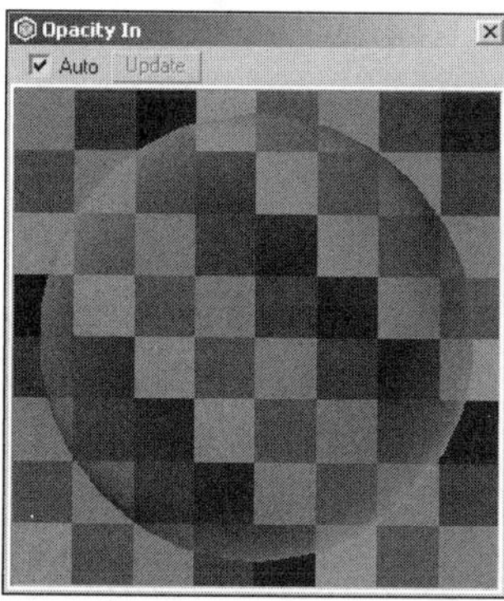

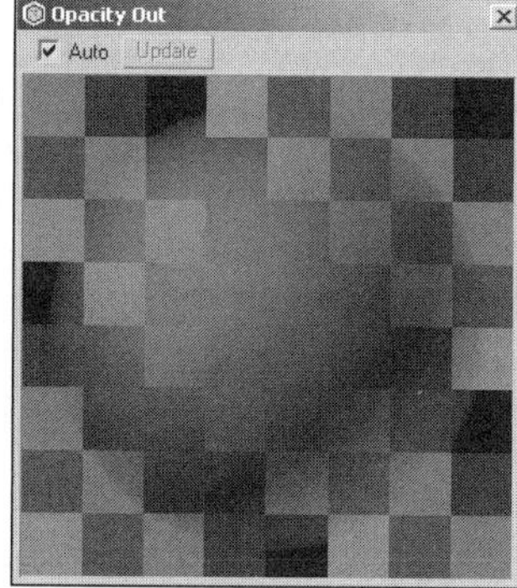

Figure 11.9
Falloff transparency options are compared. In the sample on the left, the In option causes transparency to increase toward the center of an object, leaving the opaque edges typical of glass vessels. The sample on the right used the Out option, and its transparency increases toward the edges.

Metal Shader

The Metal shader generates its Specular color from the Diffuse and Ambient colors. The distinguishing characteristic of metals is that they reflect mostly specular highlights. Take a gold ring into the shade and it's very dull—only in direct light does it reveals its characteristic color. Let's try out the Metal shader:

1. Select a slot in the Material Editor and change to the Metal shader. Notice that there is no Specular color parameter. Magnify the sample.

2. Set the Diffuse color to a brownish yellow. The Diffuse and Ambient colors are locked by default and can be toggled between locked and unlocked states with the button to the left and centered on both labels. With the two colors the same, unlock them and reduce the Value slider for the Ambient color until it is a very dark version of the Diffuse color. Note the effect of moving the slider in your sample.

3. Set the Glossiness parameter to 60 to create a fairly tight highlight that will be evident in a moment. Increase the Specular Level value. Note that increasing this value increases the contrast between the specular region and the diffuse region of the surface. The area within the highlight grows brighter using the Diffuse color of the surface. The remaining area grows darker. At high Specular Level values (above 100), the area outside the highlights is black. In Figure 11.10, the Specular Level values are 50, 100, and 200 from left to right, respectively.

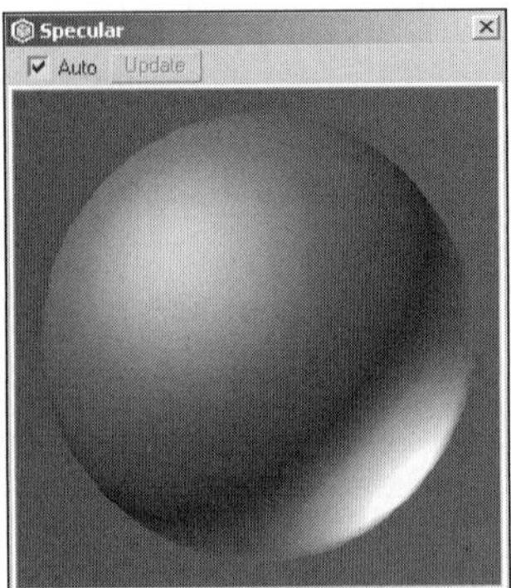

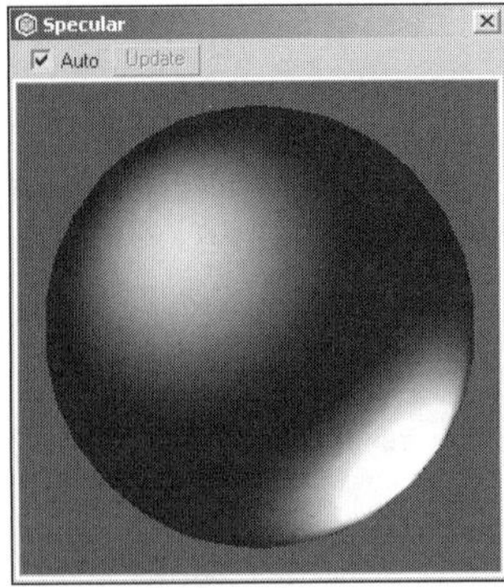

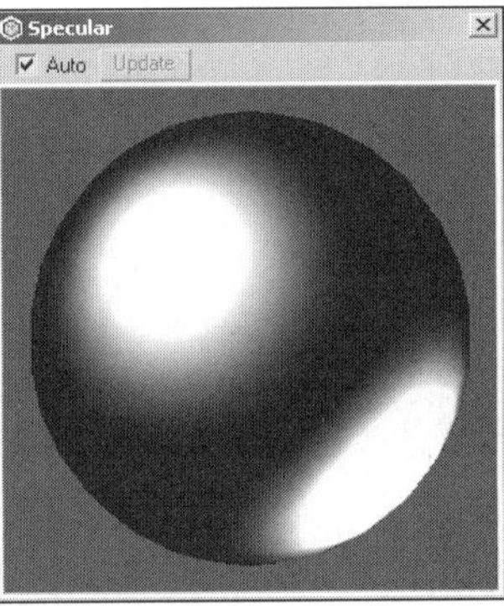

Figure 11.10
The Metal shader produces increased contrast between the highlights and the nonspecular areas of the surface as the Specular Level value is increased. All three samples shown here use a Glossiness value of 60, but the Specular Level values are, from left to right, 50, 100, and 200.

4. Return to the Ambient color and experiment a bit. Increase the value of the color until it's closer to the Diffuse color. Then, try different hues. The impact of Ambient color is much stronger when the Specular Level values are lower. Tinting the material with a contrasting Ambient color can produce a very exciting effect.

Note that all the other parameters in the Metal shader are identical to those found in the Blinn and Phong shaders.

Anisotropic Shader

The Anisotropic shader differs from the Blinn and Phong shaders in that it is able to create the elliptical highlights that are characteristic of glass and brushed metal surfaces. To use the Anisotropic shader, follow these steps:

1. Select a slot in the Material Editor and change to the Anisotropic shader. (You may want to use the Reset Map/Material To Default Settings button [with the X icon] to restore default parameters before you do.) Increase the Specular Level parameter to a high value, such as 75, to get a strong highlight.

2. Play with the Anisotropy spinner. At a value of 0, the specular region is circular, like a regular Blinn highlight. As you increase the value, it narrows in one dimension and becomes elliptical. You can see the effect both in the sample slot and in the clever 3D graph on the panel. Change the Orientation value to rotate the highlight. Figure 11.11 illustrates this effect. On the left, the Anisotropy value is 0. In the center, the value is increased to 50. On the right, the highlight is rotated.

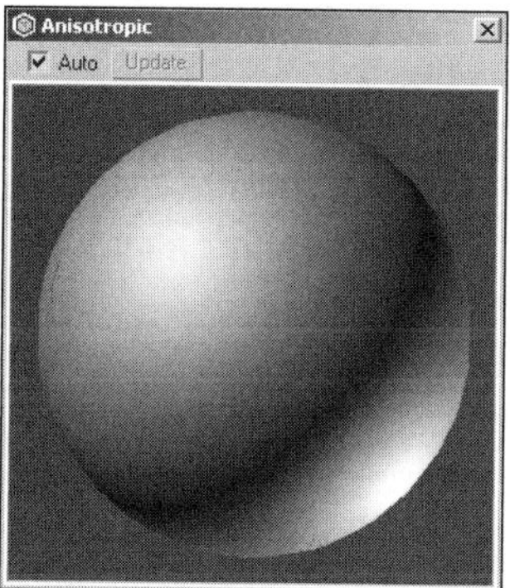

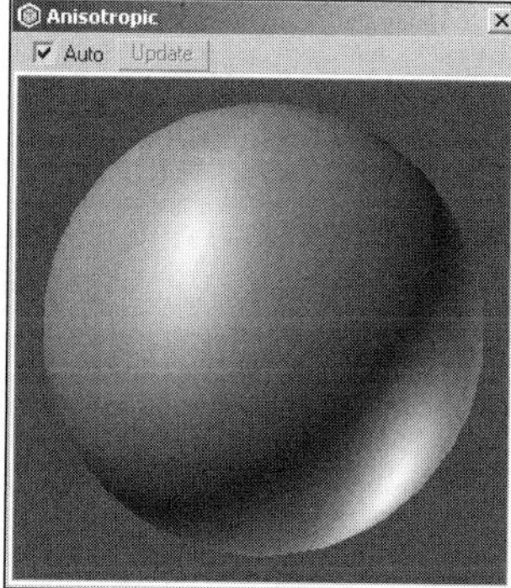

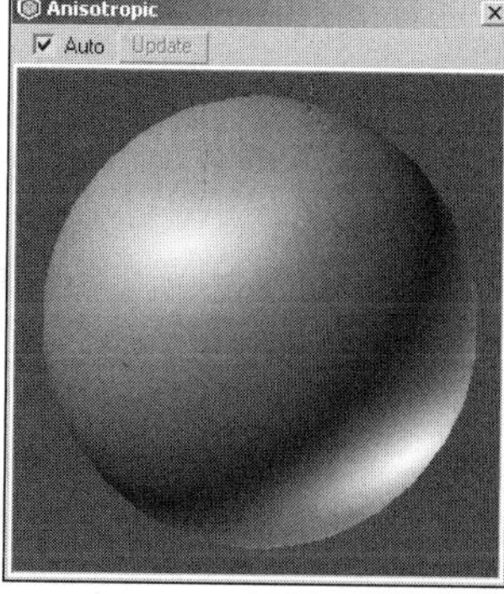

Figure 11.11
The Anisotropic shaders permit elliptical highlights that are characteristic of many shiny materials. On the left, an Anisotropy value of 0 produces the same circular highlight as the Blinn or Phong shader. In the middle, a value of 50 creates an elliptical highlight. On the right, the elliptical highlight is rotated using the Orientation parameter.

All other parameters of the Anisotropic shader are the same as those found in the Blinn and Phong shaders, except for Diffuse Level. Reducing the Diffuse Level from its default value of 100 reduces the value of the Diffuse color—in short, it darkens it. The same result can be achieved by reducing the value of the Diffuse color with the Color Selector dialog box, but the separate Diffuse Level is mappable. This parameter makes it easy to create grayscale maps to vary a single Diffuse color, or even to vary a color texture map.

Other Shaders

The Multi-Layer shader is identical to the Anisotropic shader, but it permits you to superimpose two layers of specular highlights on a surface, each with its own values. The Oren-Nayar-Blinn shader is a Blinn shader with additional diffuse parameters. One is the Diffuse Level parameter found in the Anisotropic shader (and discussed previously). The other parameter, Roughness, is unique to the Oren-Nayar-Blinn shader. Increasing Roughness narrows the range of Diffuse color values over a surface, producing a matte effect. The word *roughness* should not be understood to suggest a textured surface. Rather, the physical cause of a matte appearance is a very fine surface roughness (just as specularity is ultimately attributable to surface smoothness). Run your finger over the surface of a terra cotta pot, and you'll feel the very fine texture that breaks up reflected light.

The Strauss shader is a simpler alternative to the Metal shader. It has only a single Color parameter, and therefore it makes no distinction between Ambient and Diffuse color. The Specular Level and Glossiness parameters of the other shaders are merged into a single Glossiness parameter. When a high specularity is added to a surface using this parameter, the Metalness parameter darkens the contrasting Diffuse color to give the characteristic metal effect.

Other Material Types

The MAX Materials, other than Standard Material, fall into two classes. The Raytrace and Matte/Shadow Materials can be used as alternatives to the Standard Material. The various Compound Materials are combinations built from two or more Standard or Raytrace Materials as Sub-Materials. Although theoretically possible, it is not likely that a Matte/Shadow Material would be used as a Sub-Material in a Compound Material. The most important Compound Material is the Multi/Sub-Object Material, which is used to assign different Materials to different regions of an object.

Raytrace and Matte/Shadow Materials

Ray tracing is a rendering method for producing accurate shadows, reflections, and refractive effects through transparent and translucent objects. MAX implements ray tracing in a rather unique way. MAX has always offered raytraced shadows as an option available for lights. The ray tracing of reflections and refractions appeared first in 3d Studio Max 2, and it is offered as an option for the specific surfaces that are intended to be reflective or refractive. Ray tracing is not a material in the CG sense; if you want a surface to render with raytraced reflections or refractions, however, you can assign it a Raytrace Material. You can also use a Standard Material and assign a Raytrace Map to the Reflection or Refraction Map channel. Ray tracing is no more a map than it is a Material, but this is the way the MAX interface allows you to instruct the renderer to ray trace a surface. The Raytrace Material, together with the Raytrace Map types, will be discussed in Chapter 12.

The Matte/Shadow Material is used for compositing. A surface that is assigned a Matte/Shadow Material becomes invisible but also blocks any geometry behind it, revealing only the background image (if there is one) or color. The Matte/Shadow is typically used on flat silhouette objects that are used to mask out geometry. In the most common example, a scene contains a background image of buildings or trees. A 3D object is added to the scene, but it must appear as if it is behind the background "objects." Masking surfaces are modeled and placed in front of the 3D object. If a Matte/Shadow Material is assigned to a masking object, the region of the 3D object directly behind it disappears, revealing the background. The effect is as if the 3D object is partially obscured by the background "objects" and is therefore behind them. A *matte* is a background image, in motion picture parlance, so the Material effectively turns a masking object into a part of the background. Objects with Matte/Shadow Materials can both cast and receive shadows.

To understand the concept of a Matte/Shadow Material, follow the steps in this exercise:

1. Open the file Chap11 Matte.max from the CD-ROM, which consists of a shadow-casting light fixed on an extruded Text entity and a Box. The image used as a background image in both the viewport and renderings is LAKE_MT.jpg, from the \Maps\Backgrounds folder (which ships with 3ds max 4). Its path must be listed in the Customize|Configure Paths|Bitmaps tab.
2. Render the scene. The Text's shadows are visible on the Box, as shown in Figure 11.12.

Figure 11.12
The shadow-casting light projects the Text's shadows onto the Box.

3. No materials have been assigned to the objects yet. Select a material slot, change the Diffuse color to a bright yellow, and assign it to the Text. Select a second slot and change its Material type from Standard to Matte/Shadow. Select the Receive Shadows checkbox and assign the Material to the Box.
4. Render the scene again. This time the Box is not visible, but its surface holds the shadows from the Text, as shown in Figure 11.13.

Figure 11.13
The same as Figure 11.12, but with a yellow Standard Material assigned to the Text and a Matte/Shadow Material assigned to the Box to catch the shadows.

5. Switch the Material assignments so that the Matte/Shadow Material is assigned to the Text and the Standard Material is assigned to the Box. Re-render the scene. These settings result in an interesting scene in which the text allows you to see through to the background, but its shadows are received by the Box; see Figure 11.14.

Multi/Sub-Object Material

The Multi/Sub-Object Material is an absolutely essential tool that every MAX user must understand completely. Every application has its own approach to assigning different Materials to different regions of a single object. In MAX, the entire object is assigned a Multi/Sub-Object Material that contains two or more Sub-Materials. Each Sub-Material (which is often a Standard Material) is assigned to regions of the objects on the basis of Material IDs. Thus, the process is divided into two steps:

1. Divide the object into the appropriate Material IDs.
2. Define the Material for each Material ID as a Sub-Material in a Multi/Sub-Object Material.

Assigning Material IDs is accomplished differently for different objects. For polygonal mesh objects, Material IDs are assigned to faces; for Patch objects, they are assigned to patches; for Non-Uniform Rational B-Spline (NURBS) Surface objects, they are assigned to surfaces. Thus, you may have to divide NURBS and Patch surfaces to create regions to be assigned separate Materials.

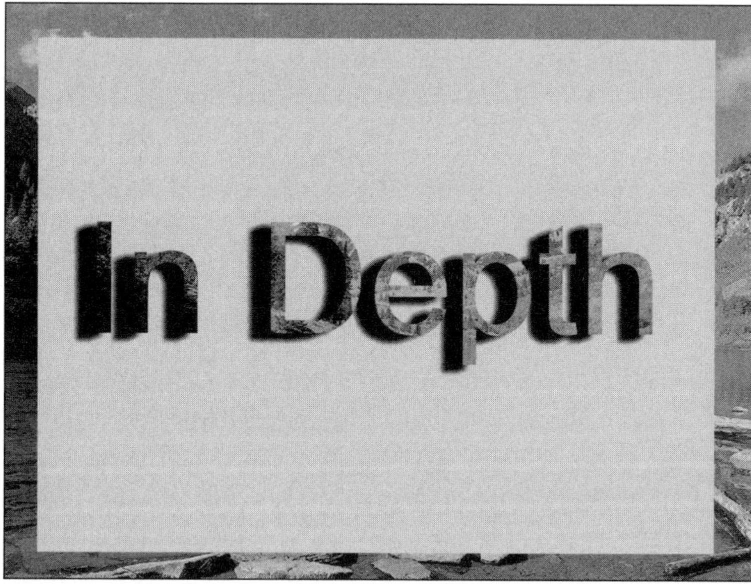

Figure 11.14
The same as Figure 11.13, but with the Material assignments reversed.

This exercise uses an editable mesh. You can assign Material IDs in the Edit Mesh Modify panel on a parametric object, but it sometimes makes more sense to convert to an Editable Mesh object before you start assigning and defining Materials.

The Traditional Method

To assign and define Materials using the traditional method, follow these steps:

1. Create a Box object of any size and convert it to an editable mesh or apply an Edit Mesh modifier to it. In the Face subobject level, pull the panel down to the tiny section titled Material in the Surface Properties rollout.

2. When you create the primitive object, MAX typically has already divided the surface into Material IDs, which can be convenient. Most objects have Material ID 1 assigned to all faces, but the Box is an exception; a different ID is assigned to each of its sides. To see which Material IDs are already assigned, click on the Select By ID button. If you page through the numbers 1 through 6 in the Select By Material ID dialog box, you find that all six quad sides of the mesh have been assigned different Material IDs.

3. Assigning your own Material IDs is a subtractive process. You start by assigning all the faces to one ID, and then pull faces from the group to assign to other IDs. Use Select All in the Edit menu to select all the faces. Enter the number 1 in the ID spinner on the Editable Mesh panel and press Enter. Click on the screen to clear your selection.

4. Test to see whether the assignment was successful. Bring up the Select By Material ID dialog box and try the number 1. All the faces should be selected. Try some other numbers and note that these are now clear.

5. Create three Material IDs, as follows: Select the faces on the top and bottom of the mesh. (Changing from the Face to the Polygon subobject level makes this easier.) Enter the number 2 in the ID spinner and press Enter. Select the front and back of the mesh and assign them Material ID 3. Use the Select By Material ID dialog box to confirm that the assignments worked. Don't be surprised if they didn't—this can be a tricky task. Keep trying until you get it right.

6. Now that the Material IDs are assigned, line them up with a Multi/Sub-Object Material. Open the Material Editor and pick a sample slot. Change the Material Type from Standard to Multi/Sub-Object. (Click on the Type button that reads "Standard" and select Multi/Sub-Object from the Material/Map Browser.)

7. You are asked whether to include the current Material as a Sub-Material, or whether to start with all default Materials. The choice does not matter for your present purposes. When you complete these steps, you see a list of Standard Sub-Materials. You need only three Materials, so set that number at the top of the panel.

8. Enter each of the three Standard Sub-Materials and give them different Diffuse colors. You can navigate between the Sub-Materials in a couple of ways. Use the Go To Parent button (the up arrow) to return to the Multi/Sub-Object level, and then select another Sub-Material from the list. Or, move directly from one Sub-Material to another using the Go Forward To Sibling button (the right-pointing arrow). A very direct way to assign only Diffuse colors is to click on the color box next to each entry on the Sub-Materials list. Note that the sample Sphere displays all three Sub-Materials.

9. The moment of truth: Exit any subobject level, so the editable mesh is selected at the object level. Assign the Multi/Sub-Object Material to the selected object. If everything works, the mesh is appropriately divided into three different Materials. Render the scene to see the result.

A Faster Method for Editable Meshes

Now that you know how to define Materials the hard way, try a streamlined method that works with subobjects:

1. As before, create a Box object and convert it to an editable mesh. In the Polygon subobject level, select all the faces and assign them to Material ID 1. Use the Select By Material ID dialog box to confirm that this assignment worked.

2. With all the faces selected (and assigned to Material ID 1), drag from a slot in the Material Editor that contains a simple Standard Material onto the mesh. Make sure two of the Material slots contain Materials other than the default gray. All the faces will adopt this Standard Material. Select the faces on the top and bottom and drag from a second slot onto them. Repeat this process with the front and back. In the end, you should have three different Materials on the mesh, each in a separate slot.

3. Even though you created this collection from separate slots in the Material Editor, MAX already created a Multi/Sub-Object Material for you. Pick a new slot and use Get Material to grab the Material off the selected object. A Multi/Sub-Object Material is ready to go, with all the Material IDs assigned for you.

NURBS and Bezier Patches

NURBS Surface objects can be composed of multiple Surface subobjects. Material IDs can be assigned to a selected Surface subobject in its Material Properties rollout. For Bezier Patch objects, selected Patch subobjects are assigned their Material IDs in the Surface Properties rollout in the Edit Patch or Editable Patch panel.

Composite, Blend, and Shellac Materials

The Composite, Blend, and Shellac Materials are used to layer different Materials on top of each other. The Blend Material is limited to two Sub-Materials. The Mix Amount spinner determines their combination. At 0, only the first Sub-Material is visible; at 100, the second Sub-Material completely takes over. A Map object can be used as a mask between the Materials.

The Composite Material has no masking but can layer up to 10 materials. Using such a Material can be a superior alternative to nesting Blend Materials inside each other. The Shellac Material is, once again, limited to two Materials, but it performs a distinctive color-blending effect that is more sophisticated than simple color compositing.

Top/Bottom Material and Double-Sided Materials

The Top/Bottom Material and Double-Sided Materials position Materials on opposing sides of an object. The Top/Bottom Material can save a lot of the effort that would be spent selecting faces to assign Material IDs. The Double-Sided Material places different Materials on opposite sides of a single surface, which can be achieved no other way. The obvious application is pages in a book. A translucency feature allows the two Materials to blend together.

Morpher Material

The Morpher Material works in sync with the Morpher modifier. The Morpher modifier has 100 channels to assign different morphing effects to an object. The Morpher Material also has 100 channels that correspond to the modifier's channels. In this way, when the Morpher modifier bulges a character's face to indicate effort, the Morpher Material can change its colors correspondingly.

Moving On

In this chapter, you explored both the basic principles of materials in computer graphics and their particular implementations in MAX. You saw that MAX relies primarily on a Standard Material type, but that type is available in many different shaders. The choice of shader determines the parameters that must be defined to create the Material. You also examined the various Compound Materials that are used to combine multiple materials on a single object or surface. The most important of these is the Multi/Sub-Object type, which relies on Material IDs to assign different Materials to different regions of an object.

The next chapter covers maps and mapping. As this chapter explained, each Material parameter can be mapped so that its values can vary over the surface of the object. Mapping is essential for creating subtle and realistic Material effects.

Chapter 12
Maps and Mapping

Simple Material definitions are often insufficient for creating rich and convincing surfaces. Bitmaps and procedural textures provide the necessary detail and realism. Mapping is perhaps MAX's greatest strength. No application has as complete and powerful a toolset for applying bitmap images to surfaces, and this is one of the reasons for MAX's high status in the games-development world. Where the geometry must be simple, texture mapping becomes critical; but mapping is also important in high-end work. MAX offers an outstanding collection of procedural textures that are often more useful than bitmaps. This is a big subject, so let's get started.

Mapping Material Parameters

For most of the parameters within a selected Material type, you choose between using a single overall value or using a map type that varies the values over the affected surface. The most obvious and important example is when the pixel colors of a bitmap image are used in place of a single color in the diffuse color parameter. This is the technique called (rather confusingly) *texture mapping*, although the color pattern need not necessarily suggest a surface texture. The concept is much more general, however. Any time different values are to be distributed over a surface for a given Material channel, a MAX Map object is used.

Mapping is the process of determining what values are assigned to what regions of the surface. Think of real-world maps. If you have a map of the United States set before you, you know that each point on the map corresponds to a spot on the Earth. There may be issues of scale and distortion, but you can at least be certain that the locations that are next to each other on the map are also next to each other on the surface of the Earth. You are accustomed to starting with real-world terrain and then drawing a mapped representation—going from the real world to a 2D (or even 3D) representation. In computer graphics, however, you generally go in the other direction—placing colors or other values from the representation onto the virtual 3D object. For example, you map from a bitmap image to the surface of the 3D model. It takes awhile to get used to thinking this way.

The Map channels are available in the Maps rollout in the Material Editor. Figure 12.1 shows the Map channels available for the Blinn and Phong shaders in a Standard Material. This is the list you'll work with most of the time.

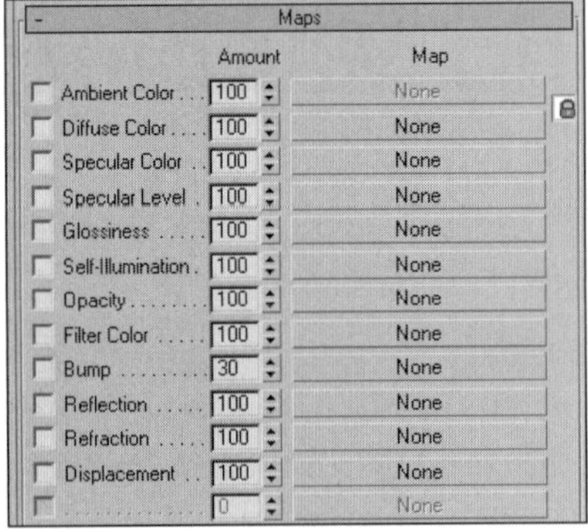

Figure 12.1
The Maps rollout of the Material Editor for a Standard Material, using the Blinn or Phong shader.

Maps for Standard Material Parameters

Take a moment to compare this incomplete list of Map channels with the elements found in the Material's Parameters rollout. The channels listed are the same as parameters in the Material:

- Ambient Color
- Diffuse Color
- Specular Color
- Specular Level
- Glossiness
- Self-Illumination
- Opacity
- Filter Color (Extended Parameters rollout)

This relationship is confirmed by the little gray squares next to each of the parameters in the Material Editor. These squares can be used to assign a Map object to the parameter, just as you can do in the Maps rollout. If a map is assigned, an *M* appears in the box. Figure 12.2 shows the Basic and Extended Parameters rollouts for a Blinn Material in the Material Editor. The

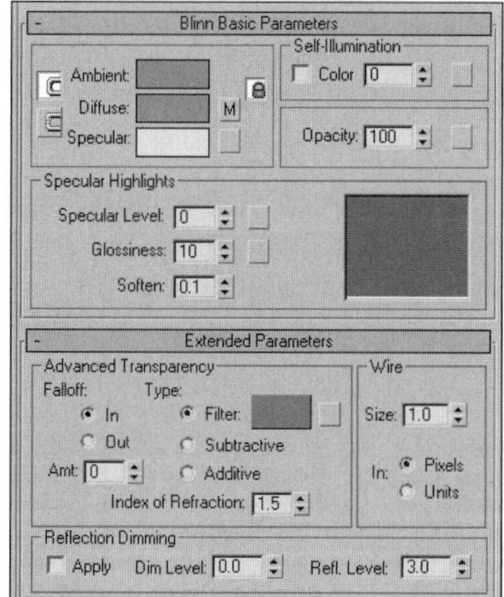

Figure 12.2
The Basic and Extended Parameters rollouts for the Standard Material using the Blinn shader. Small gray boxes on the right of certain parameters indicate that they can be mapped. The *M* next to the Diffuse Color parameter means that a Map object has been assigned to that parameter.

gray squares are to the right of each of the parameters listed previously. A map was assigned to the Diffuse Color parameter.

The Ambient Color mapping is locked to the Diffuse Color mapping, by default. This setting almost always is desirable; if you wish to change it, however, you can deactivate the lock icon in either the Basic Parameters rollout or the Maps rollout. After you do so, a Map channel becomes available for Ambient Color, which allows a map to be applied to an object's ambient components.

Mapping the Diffuse Color channel to create the traditional texture map is basic. This is the primary way to create convincing real-world surfaces, but mapping is also useful for the Specular Level. On the human face, the nose and forehead are much shinier than the cheeks, and the lips are often very specular. A Specular Level map is necessary to create these variations. Opacity mapping is useful for suggesting the small irregularities in the transparency of glass objects.

Other Map Channels

This leaves four Map channels that do not correspond with the Material Parameters:

- Bump
- Reflection
- Refraction
- Displacement

We'll discuss these channels in the following sections.

Bump and Displacement Mapping

Bump mapping is a tool for creating the illusion of texture. The illumination of a point on the surface of a model is determined by the angle between the surface normal at that point and the direction of the light. (The *normal* is a vector pointing in a direction perpendicular to the surface.) Think about this concept for a moment. At noon, the rays of the sun are directly perpendicular to the surface of the ground. To put it another way, they are aligned with the normal vector of the surface of the ground. Under these circumstances, the illumination of the ground is at its maximum.

A few hours later, the sun is setting, and an angle opens between the rays of sunlight and the normal vector of the ground. Illumination intensity decreases until, when the angle is 90 degrees at sunset, the surface is no longer illuminated.

The eye interprets the surface relief (texture) in two ways. If the relief is great enough or if you are very close, you actually see the surface geometry that causes the relief. But even when your vision cannot resolve the actual surface geometry, you interpret fine-dappled lighting patterns on the surface as shadows cast by the surface relief. Bump mapping creates these patterns, which are interpreted as shadows (and therefore as relief) without changing the surface geometry. It does so by jogging the normals used to compute the illumination at rendered points. Instead of the normals pointing perpendicular to the surface, they point at various angles. These create illumination patterns that the viewer sees as shadows.

To get the idea, try this exercise:

1. Pick a slot in the Material Editor and open the Maps rollout.

2. Click on the None button to the right of the Diffuse Color channel to get the Material/Map Browser. Look for the Map type called *Marble*. If you don't see it on the list, make sure that either All or 3D Maps is selected as the filter. Double-click on the Marble type to put a Marble Map object in the Diffuse Color channel.

3. The default settings for this map type produce a pattern in dark brown and tan, as you can see in the sample slot. After assigning the map, MAX automatically brings you into the panel for the map. You don't need to make any changes, so return to the Material level by using the Go To Parent button (with the up arrow), immediately above the word *Marble* in the Type box.

4. Back in the Maps rollout of the Material Editor, you see the Marble map applied to the Diffuse Color channel. Drag the Marble map down to the Bump channel to clone it. Choose the Instance option from the dialog box that appears. This option ensures that any changes made to the Map object in either channel are reflected in both. Look at your sample slot and notice the Bump effect. Sharp differences in relief occur between the areas that are mapped with darker and lighter colors. Increase the Amount from the default of 30 to about 50 and notice the suggestion of illumination and shadow at the edges of the color regions. To see this effect clearly, drag your sample into an adjacent slot and turn off the

Bump channel for the copy by deselecting the checkbox to the left of the word *Bump* in the Maps rollout. (To delete a map from the Material, rather than turn it off, you drag and drop one of the None buttons over the map's slot.) Figure 12.3 shows two magnified samples, with the Bump channel turned off for the one on the left. Notice that the Bump channel is deselected in the Maps rollout for the current slot, on the left. The current slot in the Material Editor is identified with a white border.

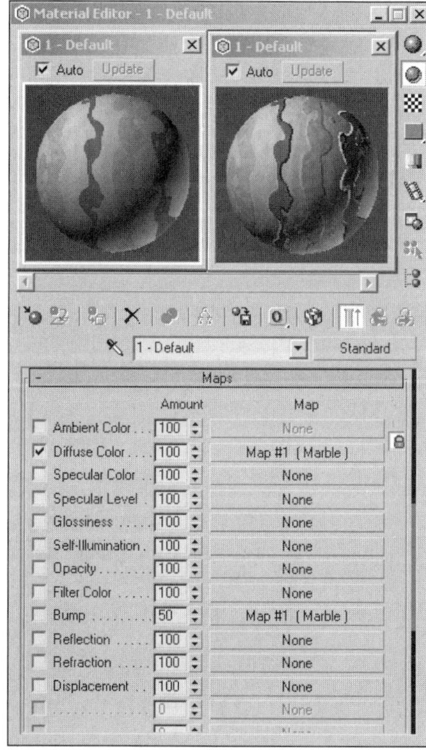

Figure 12.3
Compare magnified samples with and without bump mapping. Both samples share the same default Marble map in both the Diffuse Color and Bump channels, but in the version on the left the Bump channel is disabled. Note the illumination and shadow effects on the borders of the color change in the version on the right.

Note: *This is a good time to reflect on the term* texture map. *Both samples share the same texture map (meaning the Diffuse Color map). But this "texture" map does not suggest surface texture at all. Rather, it's the bump mapping that creates the impression of surface relief.*

5. Using the same texture map and bump map is often desirable, but it's not necessary. Disable the Diffuse Color channel in the original version by deselecting it to see the effect of the bump map alone. Increase the amount of the Bump to very high levels and note that the effect degenerates. Bump mapping is an illusion created by illumination patterns. At high levels of relief, the viewer begins to expect to see the contours of the actual geometry. This effect requires displacement mapping.

6. Drag a copy of your Material to another slot. Using the copied sample, drag the Marble map from the Bump slot to the Displacement slot, and use the Instance option to clone it. Adjust the value of the Amount spinner for the Displacement slot. Note that the actual geometry is affected because the surface is displaced in and out, based on the color values in the map. Disable the Bump channel to see the displacement effect alone.

Samples in the Material Editor cannot give an accurate impression of the way that displacement mapping works on a real model. In a high-quality render, the displacement mapping resolves the terrain very accurately. In Figure 12.4, the sample on the right uses bump mapping alone. Note that the sample ball is round. In the middle sample, because the same Map was used for displacement mapping as well, the geometric contours are affected. On the left, the bump mapping is disabled to show only the displacement; however, the sample does not convey the accuracy of a true render, which would resolve the details quite closely. Displacement mapping is ultimately a method of modeling surfaces with maps and was more fully discussed in Chapter 6.

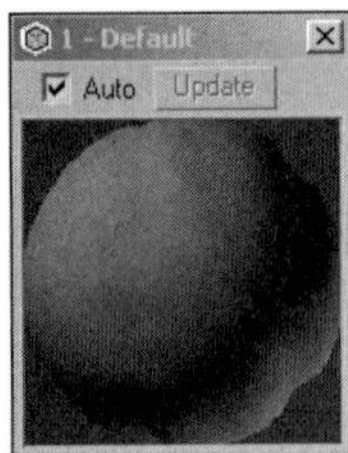

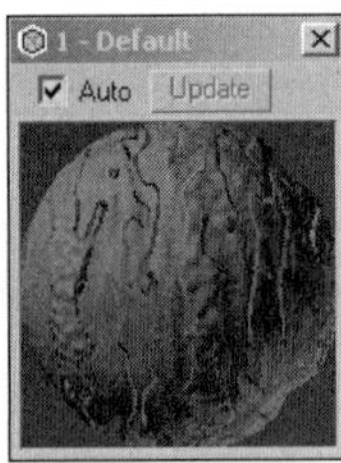

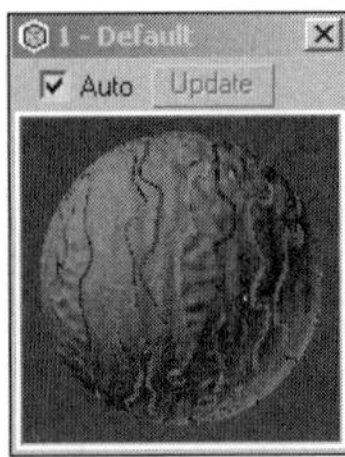

Figure 12.4
Bump mapping and displacement mapping are compared using Material Editor samples. On the right, bump mapping alone does not affect the geometry; the ball is still round. In the center, displacement mapping is added by using the same Marble map, and the contours are visibly affected. On the left, the bump mapping is disabled to reveal only the displacement effect.

Note: *It should be clear now why the Bump and Displacement channels do not correspond to any Material parameters. Bump and displacement effects require variation over the surface, so any single value for the entire Material would not make sense. The variations are based on the grayscale values of a map. If a color map is used, as in our exercise, the color values are converted to their grayscale equivalents.*

Reflection and Refraction

MAX is unique among 3D packages in handling reflection and refraction effects through Map objects. This subject can be very confusing and is based in the history of the program. See the "Reflections, Refractions, and Ray Tracing" section later in this chapter for more information.

Using Bitmaps

Bitmap images are the primary vehicles for mapping Material parameters. When most people use the term *texture map*, they mean a diffuse color map achieved by applying a bitmap to the surface. But how do you get a flat bitmap image to wrap correctly around a 3D surface? This is a very big and often difficult subject that requires an understanding of both mapping coordinates generally and MAX's specific tools for creating them. The mapping of bitmap images will always remain a mystery to those who are unwilling to master some rather subtle concepts. This chapter will try to make the subject as simple as possible.

Creating Mapping Coordinates

If you look at a text version of a MAX scene and find a polygonal model to which a bitmap has been applied as a texture, you see mapping coordinates (also called *texture coordinates*) for each vertex. The mapping coordinate tells the application which location on the bitmap corresponds to that vertex. The color at that spot on the bitmap becomes the color of the object at the vertex when it is rendered. Understanding how flat images correspond to 3D geometry is an important concept to master.

Texture Space in UV Coordinates

You need to become accustomed to the concept of *texture space*. A 3D object is in 3D Cartesian space, and each point in that space is designated by the coordinates X, Y, and Z. The texture space of a bitmap is only 2D, however; rather than using the coordinates X and Y, however, you use the coordinates U and V to designate locations in that space. (The use of U and V as coordinates on a surface should be familiar to those accustomed to Non-Uniform Rational B-Splines [NURBS] modeling, and this correspondence gives NURBS special mapping advantages, as you'll see.)

The values of UV texture space are always between 0 and 1 in each dimension. The positive U-direction is horizontal, from left to right of the map, regardless of its orientation. The positive V-direction is vertical, from bottom to top of the map. The four corners are therefore at the coordinates (0,0), (0,1), (1,1), and (1,0). The point (.5,.5) is exactly in the center of the rectangle (U = .5 and V = .5). Take a look at Figure 12.5 to get the idea.

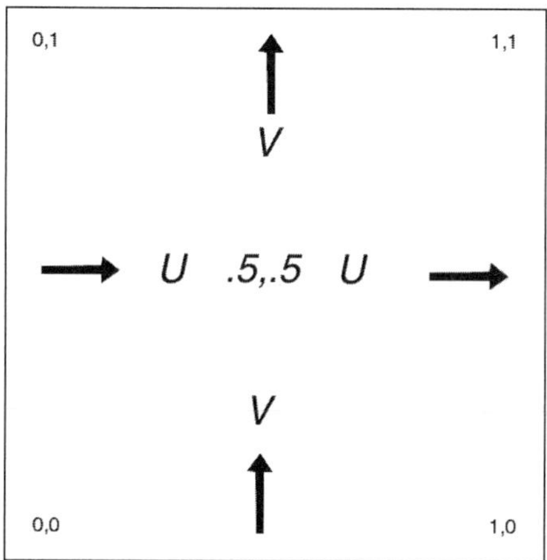

Figure 12.5

Texture space in UV coordinates. The origin (U = 0, V = 0) is in the lower-left corner. The positive U-direction is horizontal, and the positive V-direction is vertical. The U and V coordinates are always in the range from 0 to 1. Thus, the four corners are at (0,0), (0,1), (1,1), and (1,0). (.5,.5) is in the center.

The texture space must be rectangular, but it need not be square. If the U- and V-dimensions are unequal in length, they are still measured between 0 and 1. Think of mapping coordinates as percentages of the distance across the texture space, not as fixed units of measurement. Figure 12.6 illustrates a texture space that is not square. The corners are still at (0,0), (0,1), (1,1), and (1,0); (.5,.5) is still in the center of the rectangle.

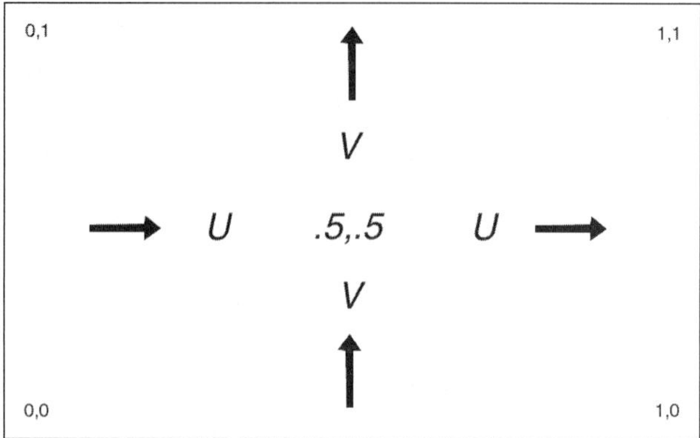

Figure 12.6
The texture space must be a rectangle, but it need not be square. The UV coordinates measure the percentage of the distance across the map in the horizontal and vertical directions. Thus, the upper-right corner is still at (1,1).

When mapping coordinates are assigned to a 3D model, each vertex on the model is given a corresponding UV location in texture space. A triangular face on the model therefore corresponds to a triangular region in the UV texture space. Take a good long look at Figure 12.7 to understand this most basic concept. A triangular face on the mesh is highlighted in white. Its three vertices are numbered 1, 2, and 3. Each of these vertices is assigned a corresponding point in the texture space, creating a triangle in texture space (shown in black). Thus, the black triangular region of the texture space will be applied to the white face on the mesh. Note that the shapes of the two triangles need not be the same—the region on the map will be squeezed or stretched to fit the face. The texture vertex labeled 1 is roughly at (.15,.2) in UV coordinates. These UV coordinates will be assigned to vertex 1 on the mesh as its mapping or texture coordinates. Whatever way it's achieved, the mapping process produces these assignments for every vertex that requires mapping.

Note that you haven't begun to deal with an image yet. Imagine the 2D texture space as empty. If you slide a picture into the space, the mapping assigns specific pixel colors at the UV coordinates to the textured object. But the mapping process does not necessarily require an image—mapping coordinates can be generated before any specific image is applied, and the image can be changed without changing the mapping coordinates. This process will become clearer as we go along.

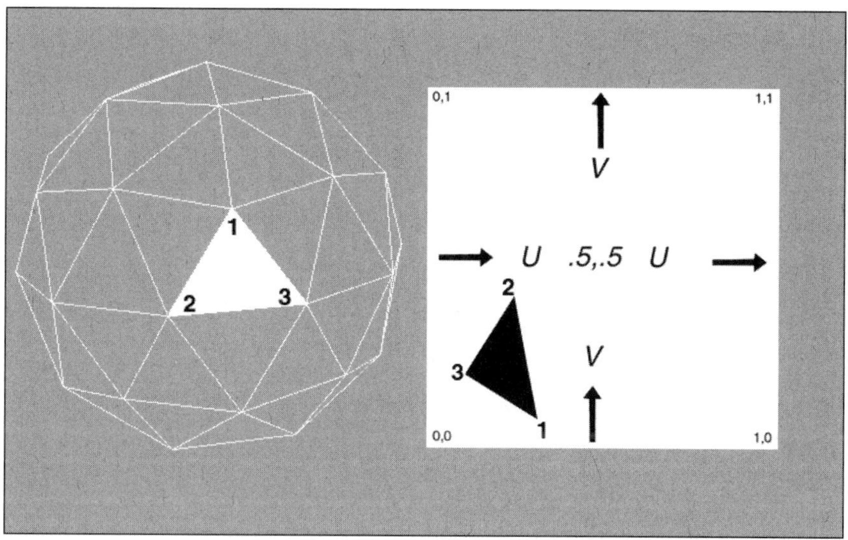

Figure 12.7
The meaning of mapping coordinates. A triangular face on the mesh object is highlighted and its vertices are numbered 1, 2, and 3. In the mapping process, a triangular region of the UV texture space (in black) is assigned to the face. The UV coordinates of the corners of the triangle in texture space are specifically assigned to the corresponding vertex on the mesh.

Projecting Mapping Coordinates: The UVW Mapping Modifier

So, now that you know what it means to generate mapping coordinates for a model, how do you do it? When you're working with primitive objects, MAX automatically assigns mapping coordinates when mapped Materials are applied. These default mapping coordinates can be overridden, or augmented with the UVW Mapping modifier, using the same approach used to apply them to nonprimitive objects.

Two fundamentally different approaches exist. One uses the inherent topology of the object to create mapping coordinates automatically. Where this is possible, it will generally be the preferred method, because the mapping follows the surface in a logical way. In most applications, only NURBS surfaces can be mapped in this way, but MAX offers this method for a surprisingly wide array of geometry. You'll learn this mapping approach in a bit.

The other method of generating mapping coordinates is by *projection*. Imagine shining a slide projector on a white object. You turn off the projector, turn on the lights, and discover that the image is burned into the surface of the object, just as if it were photosensitive. Although this description gives you the general idea of projecting mapping coordinates, the only way to understand the process is by hands-on experience; therefore, let's get started with an exercise:

1. Create a Box object. The dimensions are not particularly important. Open the Material Editor and pick a slot. Assign the Material to the selected object.

2. You will generate mapping coordinates before you apply a map. Put a UVW Mapping modifier on your object. Oddly, this modifier is listed as UVW Map in the modifier list, but it appears as UVW Mapping in the Stack View window. Why is it called UVW instead of just UV? Unlike any other application, MAX provides a third dimension for texture space. You can comfortably ignore the W-dimension in the overwhelming majority of situations.

3. The default projection is the Planar type. In a Planar projection, the image is mapped to a face of the bounding box of the geometry. Because you're using a Box object, the model is the same shape as its bounding box. The projection goes right through the object. Cycle through the X, Y, and Z alignment options and watch as the Gizmo reorients itself but does not alter its size. For each of these options, use the Fit button to snap the size of the Projection Gizmo to the dimensions of the bounding box. Use the Length and Width spinners to adjust the dimensions of the Gizmo, and then use Fit to snap back to the natural defaults. In the vast majority of situations, you will use Fit this way.

4. Look at the results with a test bitmap. Use the image shown earlier in Figure 12.5, because it will help you understand the mapping process. Select your Material in the Material Editor. In the Maps rollout, click on the None button in the Diffuse Color channel. When the Material/Map Browser appears, double-click on the Bitmap type. (If you don't see it, make sure that the 2D Map types are visible.)

5. The Select Bitmap Image File dialog box appears. Find the bitmap image named uvtest.tif in the Chapter 12 directory on this book's companion CD-ROM. After opening the image, you'll see it in the sample slot. To see it on the object, click on the Show Map In Viewport button with the blue and white checkered box in the row beneath the sample slots. Depending on the dimensions of your Box and the direction of your projection, your screen should look something like Figure 12.8.

6. Rotate the object to see the projection on the opposite side. The other sides of the object are white. To understand the situation better, increase the Length and Width parameters of the Gizmo until the arrows and letters fall over the side, as shown in Figure 12.9. A sliver of the map is dragged over other faces because they are perpendicular to the direction of the projection. A tiny fraction of UV texture space is being applied to large areas, creating extreme distortion. A Planar projection therefore makes sense only where surfaces are relatively flat. That often means dividing an object into many regions and applying separate Planar projections to each. You'll learn about this shortly.

7. Hide or delete your Box and make a Cylinder object. Put a UVW Mapping modifier on it and project a Planar projection along the length of the object by changing the alignment to Y. Use Fit to align the Projection Gizmo to the bounding box of the Cylinder. Unlike the Box object, the Cylinder is distinct from its bounding box, and it's therefore easier to see a natural relationship between a Planar projection and a bounding box. In the Material Editor, put the Material you used before onto the new object, and make sure the bitmap is

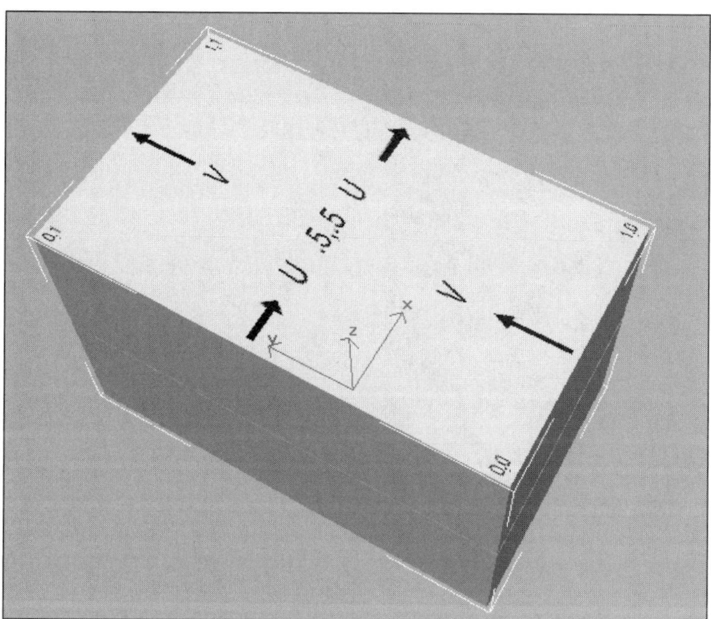

Figure 12.8
A Planar projection is made on a Box object, fitted to the dimensions of the object's bounding box. The bitmap image from Figure 12.5 is used to help you understand the projection. In this basic type of projection, the corners of the texture space map to the corners of the face of the bounding box.

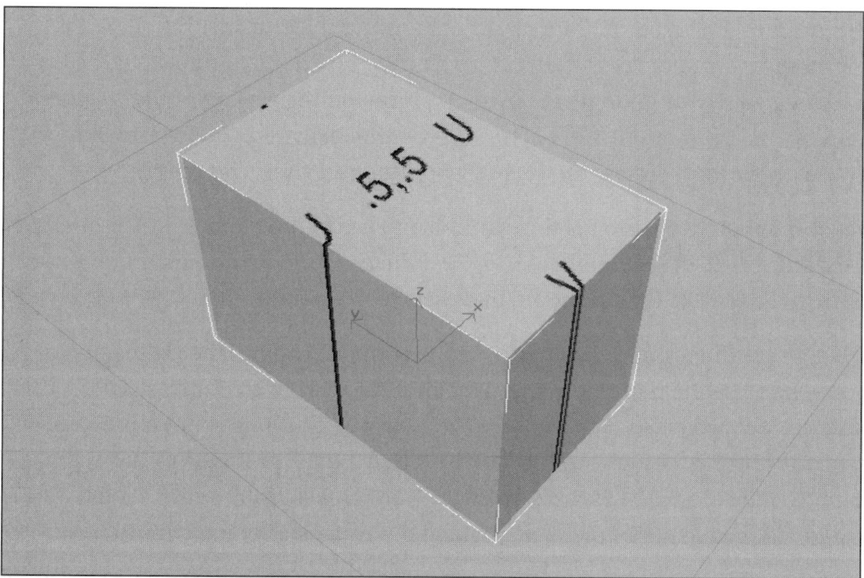

Figure 12.9
Increasing the size of the Planar Projection Gizmo brings some of the black areas of the bitmap over the edge of the object's bounding box. Because the projection is perpendicular to the sides of the Box object, only a sliver of texture space is mapped to these faces. This kind of distortion is a major issue when you use Planar projections.

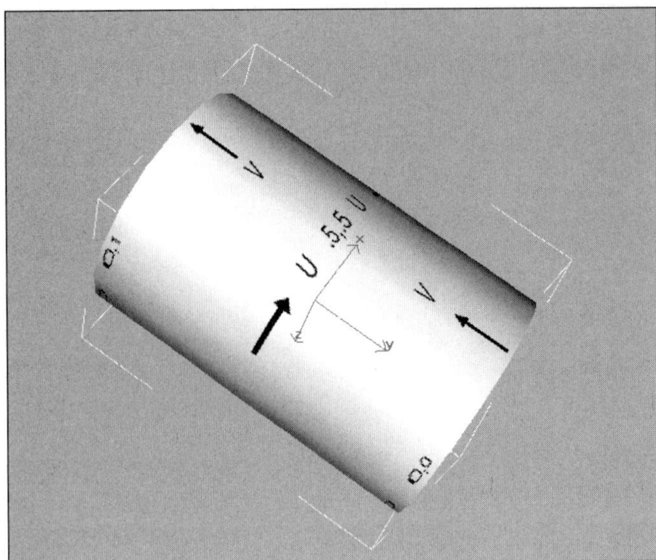

Figure 12.10
A Planar projection on a Cylinder shows mild distortion in the center and more extreme stretching at the ends. A Cylinder is typical of the gently curving surfaces on the faces and bodies of character figures, where Planar mapping is very often used. The bounding box of the object is now distinct, and it's easy to see how the Planar projection is fitted to a face of the bounding box.

visible on the surface. Rotate the view if necessary to see the result. As you can see in Figure 12.10, a general distortion of the map occurs—minor in the center but more extreme toward the edges—where the cylinder turns sharply away. The numbers at the corners are quite stretched. Try to imagine the bitmap placed on the surface of the bounding box and then projected onto the curved object. This example gives a good sense of the way Planar projections work (and distort) on the body and faces of character figures.

8. A second kind of mapping projection is the cylindrical type. In the Mapping UVW modifier panel, select Cylindrical in the Mapping group. Find the appropriate alignment and use Fit. The Cylindrical Projection Gizmo should fit closely to the object.

9. Rotate the object to see the result. The bitmap is now wrapped around the Cylinder. No distortion occurs, because the projection and the object are exactly the same shape. A line must appear where the two edges of the map meet, however. This line is not a problem with the image you're using, because both edges are white. But if the image included a pattern, and the pattern did not coincide at both edges, you'd see a visible seam. Figure 12.11 shows the Cylindrical projection in the region where the two edges of the bitmap meet.

10. To see the effect of a nontileable map applied to an object, create a second Material and choose Background.jpg from MAX's Maps\Backgrounds directory as the Diffuse Color map. Make sure the map is visible in the viewport. Rotate the object in the scene to see the seam

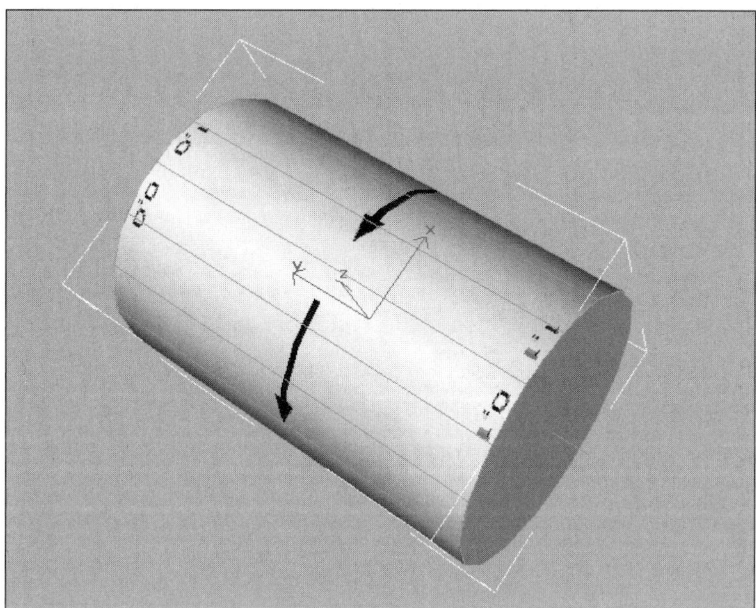

Figure 12.11
A Cylindrical projection is applied to the Cylinder object. The Cylindrical Projection Gizmo shows an exact fit to the geometry of the object, and thus no distortion occurs. The two edges of the bitmap meet in a line, as if a piece of paper were wrapped around the surface. If this were a patterned bitmap, and the pattern was not the same at both edges, a troubling seam would be visible.

where the bitmap edges meet. Click on the Bitmap button in the Bitmap Parameters rollout, which now shows the current map's name and path. Change the map to Brkrun.jpg from the Maps\Brick directory and rotate the object again. This time, no seam is visible, because the image file was manipulated and the image was made tileable.

11. It makes a great deal of difference when you project mapping coordinates in the modeling process. Although you'll often deal with a finished editable mesh object, whose stack (if any) was collapsed before the entire texturing and materials process began, it pays to think ahead. Put a Bend modifier on top of your stack and give your stack some bend. Because the Cylindrical projection was applied before the object was bent, the mapping follows the deformation correctly. In the Stack View window, click and drag the Bend modifier until a blue line appears between the Cylinder and UVW Mapping entries. Release the mouse button to move the Bend modifier to before UVW Mapping and swap their order in the stack. Bend the Cylinder again. The result does not make sense, because the Cylindrical projection is applied after the object is no longer really cylindrical. See Figure 12.12. This issue comes up very often. For example, when you're texture mapping a curved surface, it may make sense to start with a flat surface that can be easily mapped with a Planar projection. Apply the UVW Mapping modifier and then deform the surface. The mapping correctly follows the surface.

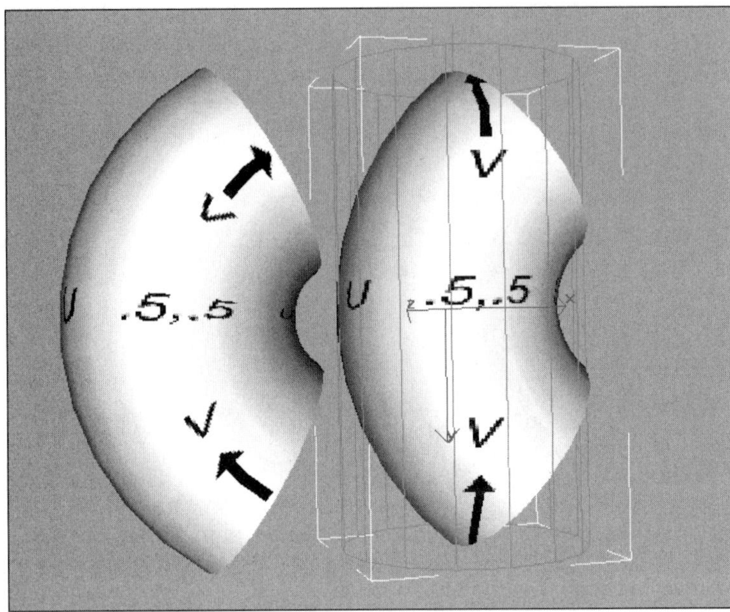

Figure 12.12
Establishing mapping coordinates, before and after deformation. At left, Cylindrical projection is used to establish texture coordinates before the object is bent. The map sticks to the surface as it deforms, because the vertices were already assigned their UV coordinates. At right, Cylindrical projection is applied after the object is bent. The mapping no longer makes sense, because the shape of the object is no longer cylindrical. Note that the Cylindrical Projection Gizmo was fitted to the bounding box of the object.

12. The other mapping projections are used less often. Create a Sphere and use the uvtest.tif bitmap to get the basic idea. The Planar and Cylindrical projections do not distort the image if the surface being mapped is flat or cylindrical. There's no way to wrap a flat rectangle (the bitmap) around a Sphere without some distortion, however. The Spherical projection wraps around the object in the horizontal (U) direction but closes up at the vertical (V) poles. The Shrink Wrap projection creates intense distortion by pulling all four corners of the map to a single point. This projection is very rarely useful. The Box projection option is simply six Planar projections from the six perpendicular directions. This is sometimes a better alternative than a Spherical projection for getting a finely patterned bitmap wrapped all around an object. The mapping doesn't close up at the poles; however, because there are multiple projections, seams are likely to be visible where the separate Planar projections meet. The Spherical, Shrink Wrap, and Box projections are illustrated in Figure 12.13.

13. Try the Face mapping option, which projects the same map separately to every polygon. This option sometimes make sense with fine texture patterns. The XYZ To UVW option applies to 3D procedural maps, as you'll see later in this chapter.

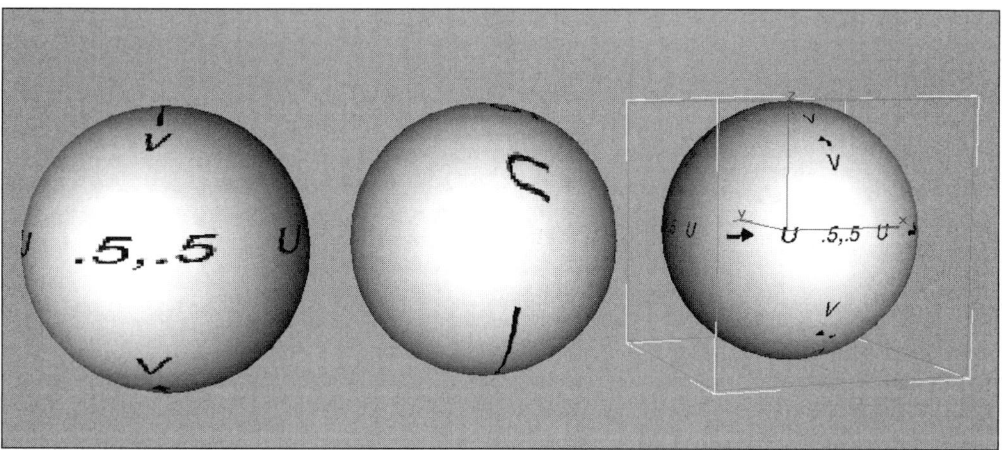

Figure 12.13
A Sphere object using the Spherical, Shrink Wrap, and Box projection options. The Spherical projection on the left wraps around the object in the horizontal (U) direction, just like the Cylindrical projection. Unlike the Cylindrical projection, however, it closes up at the vertical (V) poles. In the center, the rarely used Shrink Wrap option pulls all four corners of the bitmap to a single point, at the cost of considerable distortion. On the right, the Box projection simply consists of six perpendicular Planar projections.

Editing Mapping Coordinates: The Unwrap UVW Modifier

For many texturing jobs, a simple projection isn't good enough. The Unwrap UVW modifier is an extremely powerful tool for editing mapping coordinates that were obtained in the first instance by projection with the UVW Mapping modifier. If nothing else, a little experimentation with this modifier will greatly clarify the very meaning of mapping coordinates. This basic exercise will get you started:

1. Create a Rectangle in the Front viewport and convert it to an editable mesh. In the Edge subobject level, select the invisible diagonal edge by dragging a rectangular selection region (using the Crossing Selection option) inside the Rectangle. Convert to a visible diagonal edge in the Surface Properties rollout, as described in Chapter 7. Doing so creates two separate triangles for purposes of selection in the Unwrap UVW modifier. Get out of the subobject level.

2. Apply a UVW Mapping modifier and fit a Planar projection to it. In the Material Editor, pick a slot and assign a bitmap to the Diffuse Color slot. Use the uvtest.tif file from this book's companion CD-ROM and put the Material onto the object. Make sure the bitmap is visible in the Front shaded viewport. Your screen should resemble Figure 12.14.

3. Put an Unwrap UVW modifier on top of the stack. Click on the Edit button in the Parameters rollout to get the editing interface. This is a direct look at your UV texture space. To see it better, hide the bitmap with the blue-and-white checkered Show Map button at the top of the Edit UVWs dialog box. As you may expect, your projection mapped the four vertices of the mesh object to the four corners of texture space, as you can see by the white

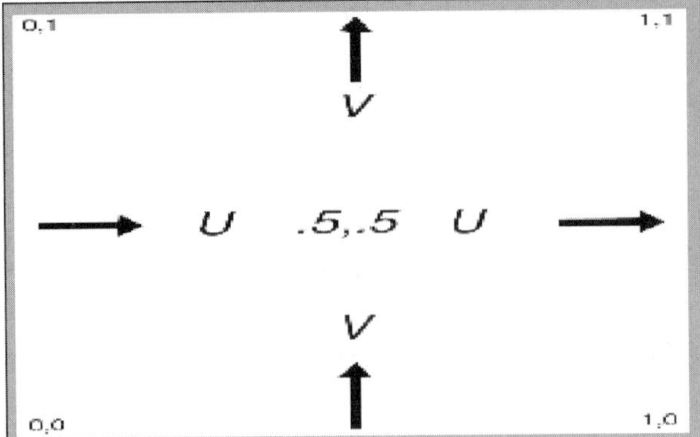

Figure 12.14
A Rectangle spline is converted to an editable mesh object and mapped with Planar projection.

boxes at the corners. Move these vertices in the dialog box so that they enclose only the lower-left quarter. Use the type-in spinners at the bottom to set the U and V coordinates for each vertex exactly: (0,0), (0,.5), (.5,.5), and (.5,0). Leave the W value alone. Look back at your Front viewport to see the new mapping. As you can see in Figure 12.15, the object is now mapped with only a quarter of the bitmap.

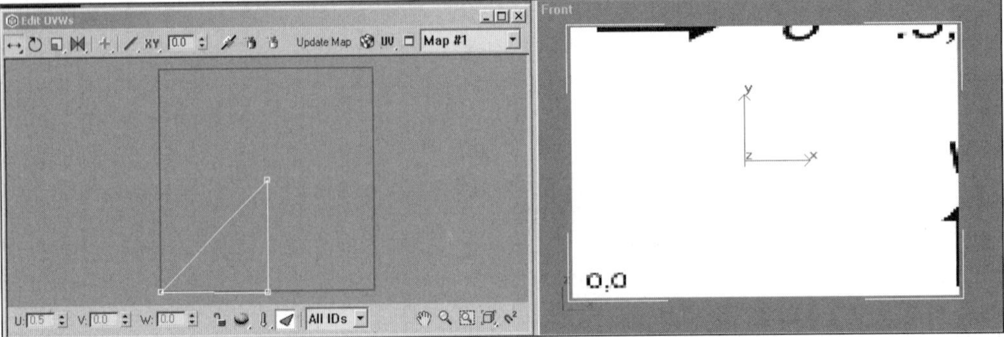

Figure 12.15
The Unwrap UVW modifier is used to move the vertices of the editable mesh object in texture space. The four corners of the mesh are assigned the texture coordinates of (0,0), (0,.5), (.5,.5), and (.5,0). Thus, only the lower-right quarter of the bitmap is mapped to the surface.

4. Your mesh object has only two triangles and four vertices, so it's obvious which vertices in the Edit UVWs dialog box correspond to the specific vertices on the object. But with any reasonably complex mesh, things can get quite confusing. In the Stack View window, expand the Unwrap UVW modifier and enter the Select Face subobject level. Click on a corner of your object in a viewport to select one of the two triangular faces. You may want to glance at a wireframe view to confirm this selection. Things won't look any different in the Edit UVWs dialog box until you click on the triangle icon (Filter Selected Faces) at the

bottom. Once you do, only the single selected triangle for the mesh will be visible in the texture space.

5. To edit the texture space of the triangle, you want to see the bitmap image. Make it visible. You can't see the lines and vertices because they are white against the white bitmap. Click on the Unwrap Options button at the top of the dialog box and change the Line Color swatch to a dark blue. Click on OK, and the selected triangle is clearly visible in texture space. Move the vertices to define a region within the triangle and note that the same portion of the map appears in the corresponding triangle on the mesh object. See Figure 12.16.

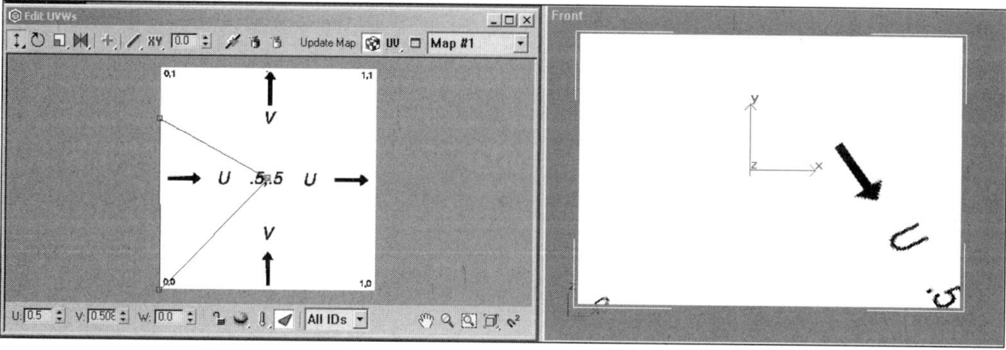

Figure 12.16
The Select Face subobject level is used to isolate the lower-right triangle on the editable mesh object for editing in texture space. Note that the region of the map inside this triangle in the Edit UVWs dialog box appears on the corresponding triangle on the mesh object.

6. Put this exercise to some practical use by straightening out a Planar projection on a curved surface. Create a short and rather fat Cylinder object. Make it half a Cylinder by using the Slice parameter and setting Slice To at 180 degrees. Convert the object to an editable mesh and delete the faces on the top, bottom, and back. This leaves only the curved surface.

7. Put a UVW Mapping modifier in the stack and fit a Planar projection to the object from the front. Assign the object a Material in the Material Editor and put the uvtest.tif bitmap in the Diffuse Color map channel.

8. As you saw earlier in the chapter, this projection stretches the map around the edges. Add an Unwrap UVW modifier and open the Edit UVWs dialog box to understand why. (Change the Line Color, if necessary, to see the lines against the white bitmap.) All the faces on the mesh are exactly the same size, but they are not assigned equal amounts of texture space. Due to the direction of the projection, the faces at the edge of the object have only a sliver of the texture space. Figure 12.17 illustrates the problem. Note the stretching of the numbers at the edges of the mesh.

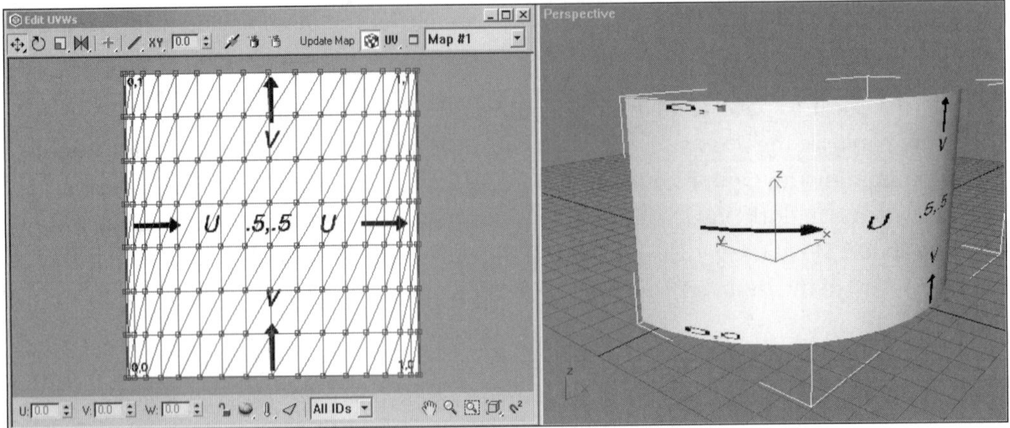

Figure 12.17
A Planar projection is fitted to the front of a curved editable mesh made from half a Cylinder object. The Edit UVWs dialog box shows that the faces, although equal in size, have been allocated unequal amounts of the texture space. The faces near the receding edges are allocated only a sliver of the map. This allocation accounts for the stretching of the numbers on the bitmap.

9. You can fix the problem by moving the columns of vertices in the U-direction (horizontally) in texture space until they are fairly even. Select all the vertices in a column by carefully dragging a rectangle around them; then, use the U-direction spinner at the bottom to move them. Figure 12.18 shows half the vertices corrected. Note that the distortion has been eliminated.

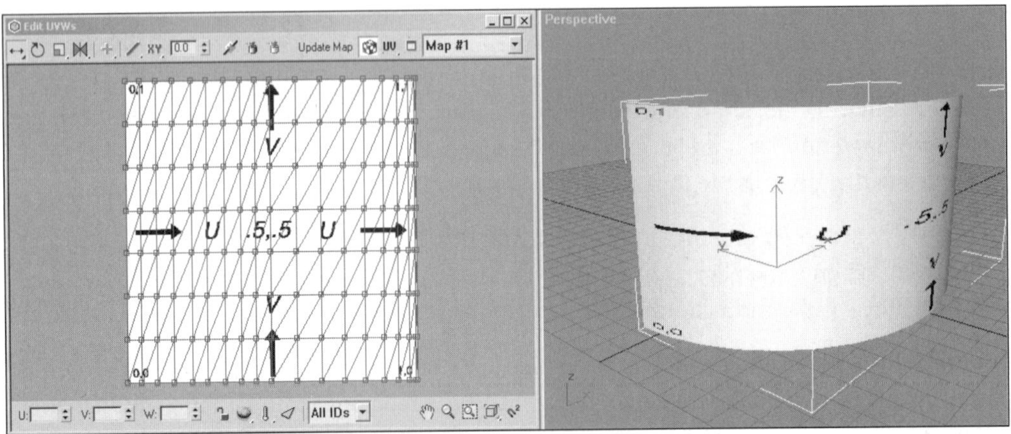

Figure 12.18
The same as Figure 12.17, but with half the columns of vertices moved in texture space to even out the distribution of the map over the mesh. Note that the distortion has been eliminated.

Mapping Multiple Surfaces

Maps often must be applied separately to different regions of the same mesh. The process can be tedious, but if you don't work carefully and systematically you'll make a mess of things. The following exercise demonstrates a reliable method for this kind of work:

1. Create a longish Box object and convert it to an editable mesh. Move a couple of edges and scale some pairs of vertices to create angles. Your object might look something like Figure 12.19.

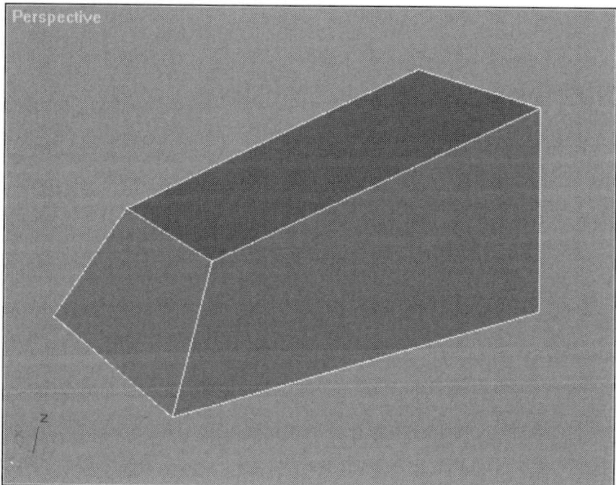

Figure 12.19
A Box object is converted to an editable mesh, which is then edited to create angular surfaces.

2. You will apply a texture map of an aluminum surface to all sides of this object, which requires dividing the object into six different Material IDs for use in a Multi/Sub-Object Material. This subject was covered (without maps) in Chapter 11, so refer there, if necessary. MAX automatically created six Material IDs for the Box, but it's good practice to assign them yourself. Start by entering the Polygon subobject level, selecting all the Polygons, and assigning them to Material ID #1. Test with the Select By ID button to make sure that the entire mesh is assigned to a single ID.

3. Leave only one of the quad Polygons as Material ID #1 and assign all the others to IDs #2 through #6. This can be frustrating work unless you've had a lot of practice. Select a Polygon and enter a number in the Material ID spinner (or click on the spinner). Test after each assignment using the Select By ID button. Make sure that all sides have been properly assigned before you go on.

4. You need a separate projection for each surface; you'll create them by using the Mesh Select modifier to select the affected faces and then applying a UVW Mapping modifier for each group of faces. Add a Mesh Select to the modifier stack and add a UVW Mapping modifier. Repeat this process until you have six pairs of these modifiers. Look at the stack

in the Stack View window; use the right-click menu to rename each pair to add an identifying number that corresponds with the Material ID number (Mesh Select 1, UVW Mapping 1; Mesh Select 2, UVW Mapping 2; and so on). This step is critical to your sanity, so don't omit it. Your Stack View window should look like Figure 12.20.

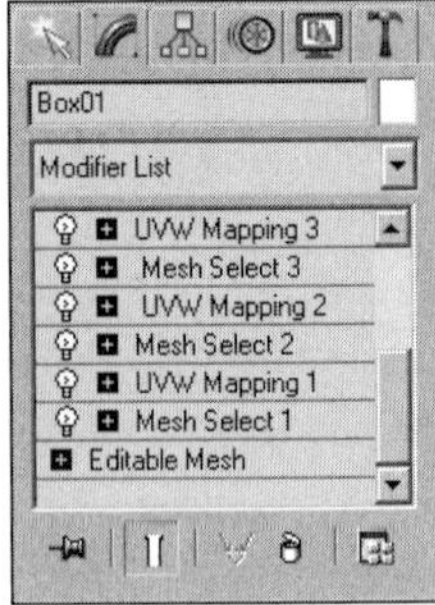

Figure 12.20
After assigning a different Material ID to each side of the object, a stack is built of pairs of Mesh Select and UVW Mapping modifiers. The Stack View window is used to add an identifying number to each pair.

5. Create a separate mapping projection for each of the Material IDs. At the bottom of the stack, enter Mesh Select 1. (Click on the Yes button to dismiss the warning box.) Go into the Faces or Polygon subobject level and find the Select By Material ID section. Enter "1" in the spinner and click on the Select button. The quad (two triangular faces) that you selected should now be assigned to Material ID #1. Only these faces will be passed up to the first UVW Mapping modifier.

6. Don't leave the subobject level of Mesh Select before moving up to UVW Mapping 1. Get the Planar Projection Gizmo aligned in the direction for the chosen side. If that side is slanted, align the Gizmo by activating the Normal Align button. As you drag across the sides of the object, notice how the Gizmo aligns to the surfaces. When you're aligned to the appropriate surface, choose Fit to get the proportions right. Figure 12.21 shows the Planar Projection Gizmo aligned to the Polygon designated as Material ID #1. Note that the projection is fitted to the bounding box only for the selected faces, not for the bounding box as a whole.

7. Repeat this process for the five other sides, working very carefully. Use the Mesh Select modifier to select the faces within the designated Material ID, and then use the corresponding UVW Mapping modifier to align and fit the Planar Projection Gizmo to the surface. When you're finished, get out of any subobject level.

8. All the mapping coordinates are established, so it's time to try a bitmap. Pick a slot in the Material Editor and change it from a Standard Material type to Multi/Sub-Object Material. Click on OK in the Replace Material dialog box. Apply the Material to the selected object. Use the Set number and the resulting Set Number Of Materials dialog box to set the

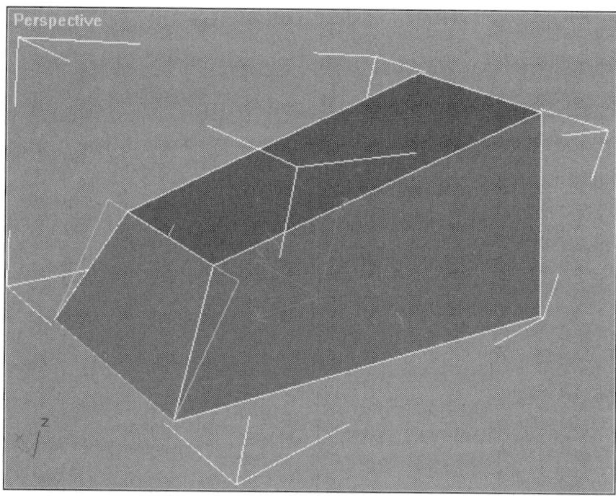

Figure 12.21
The faces in Material ID #1 are selected in the Mesh Select 1 modifier and sent up the stack to the UVW Mapping 1 modifier. The Normal Align tool is used to align the Planar Projection Gizmo to the slanted surface, and Fit is then used to constrain its dimensions to the bounding box of the selected faces (not the entire object). Texture coordinates have now been established for only the single surface.

number of Sub-Materials to 6. Enter the first one (which will be assigned to the faces with Material ID #1) and enter a Bitmap Map type in the Diffuse Color channel of the Maps rollout. For the bitmap itself, choose Aluminm3.gif from Max's Maps/Space directory. Use the Show Map In Viewport button to make the bitmap visible on the surface; notice that it's properly mapped to the faces that you designated as Material ID #1. Your screen might look like Figure 12.22.

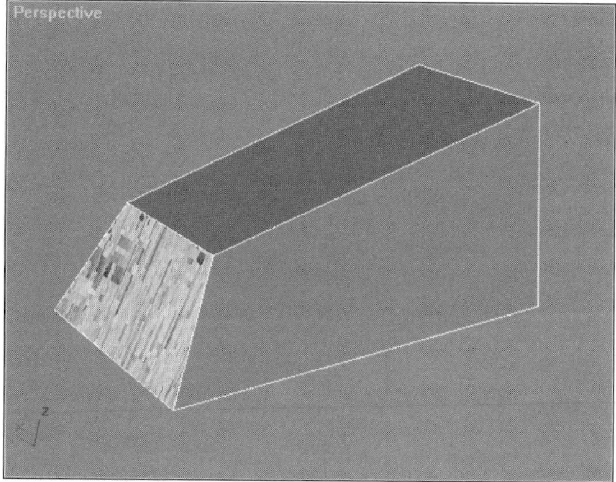

Figure 12.22
A Multi/Sub-Object Material is created and assigned to the object and is given six Sub-Materials. The Sub-Material assigned to Material ID #1 is given a bitmap in the Diffuse Color channel. The pattern is now visible on the affected faces.

9. Back in the list of Sub-Materials, drag a copy of the first Material into each of the other slots (use either Copy or Instance) and watch how the bitmap appears on all the surfaces. There's a problem, however: The pattern is uneven, because the same bitmap was mapped to surfaces of different sizes. To correct this unevenness, go to the UVW Mapping modifier for one of the small faces and use the Length and Width spinners to scale the Planar Projection Gizmo larger. At some point, the pattern will match the scale of the larger faces. See Figure 12.23.

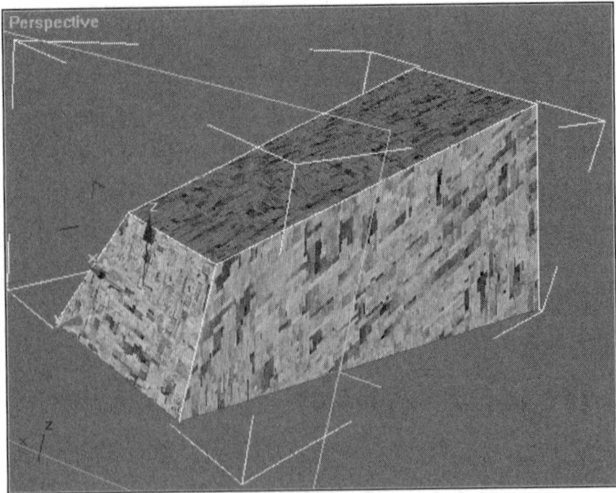

Figure 12.23
After the Material with the bitmap is copied to all the other Sub-Materials, the mapping alignments are corrected, but the scales are wrong. The pattern is much denser on the smaller sides, and the longer sections may appear stretched. To equal things out, the Length and Width spinners for each UVW Mapping modifier are used to adjust the dimensions of the Projection Gizmos. In this example, the pattern on the small region in the front is stretched to better resemble the rest of the object, and the Gizmo is rotated 90 degrees.

Using Drag and Drop to Create Materials

Once Material IDs are assigned, or if the default IDs are acceptable, you can quickly create Multi/Sub-Object Materials by dragging Materials from the Material Editor to the object. The following exercise explains this:

1. Open the Material Editor. Click on the Get Material button, choose Material Library in the Browse From area, and select a Material identified with a blue sphere. Repeat this process in five more slots.
2. Create a Box primitive near the origin and convert it to an editable mesh.
3. In the Polygon subobject level, select the polygon on the top surface of the Box. Drag the Material from one slot in the Material Editor and drop it onto the selected polygon. The selected polygon now contains the Material from that slot.

4. Using the same procedure, select the remaining five polygons and assign a unique Material to each of them.

5. Click on the Get Material button. Activate Selected or Scene in the Browse From area and double-click on the Material to place the newly created Multi/Sub-Object in the current slot of the Material Editor.

Map Channels

Map channels are very sophisticated, but it's so important that you must have at least some basic understanding of the subject. Until now, we've assumed that an object can have only a single set of mapping coordinates. After an object is mapped, each affected vertex is assigned a UV coordinate in texture space that tells it where to get its color (or other) values from a map. But what if a vertex could have more than one such number? If multiple maps were used on a single surface, each map could be applied using different mapping coordinates. Multiple maps might apply where different bitmaps were used for different parameters. For example, a Diffuse Color map might be different from a Bump map or a Specular Level map. This is not the most important use of multiple mapping coordinates, however.

The most important use of multiple texture coordinates is when maps of the same type are layered on top of each other to create complex texture effects—and, above all, to hide seams. Consider this fundamental problem: You're texturing a character figure that necessarily requires an assemblage of different maps. If each is assigned to a different Material ID, obvious seams will appear where the borders meet. Although careful work on the edges of both images in a program such as Photoshop may help soften the effect, a better alternative is to allow maps to overlap lightly and to use a transparency effect to disguise the overlap. Try this simple (yet challenging) exercise:

1. Create the same kind of half-cylindrical editable mesh that you made earlier in this chapter (in the "Editing Mapping Coordinates: The Unwrap UVW Modifier" section) and fit a Planar projection to the front. Refer back to Figure 12.17; your object should look like the one in that figure. Note that the Map Channel in your UVW Mapping modifier panel is set to the default of 1.

2. Add a second UVW Mapping modifier directly on top. Set this Channel to 2. Use the Normal Align tool in the alignment area to align the Planar Gizmo with the Polygons about halfway around the side. Go into the Gizmo subobject level and move the Gizmo outside the surface so that the sense of the projection is evident; in addition, size and position the object so that the map projects only to approximately halfway around the object before it starts to tile. This Channel 2 projection should look like Figure 12.24.

3. Before you go on, rename your modifiers UVW Mapping Ch 1 and UVW Mapping Ch 2 in the Stack View window. It is best that you not skip this step, or you may experience frustration later.

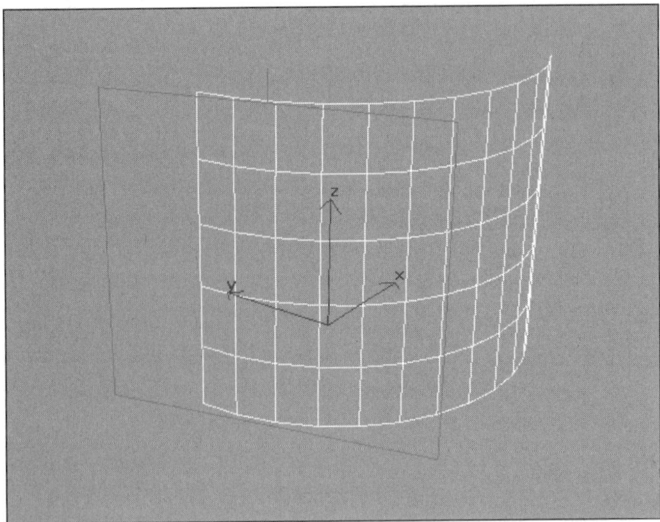

Figure 12.24
A second Planar projection for a single surface is aligned with the sides of the object. This is Channel 2. An earlier Planar projection (Channel 1) was made directly from the front.

4. To put two overlapping bitmaps to a single surface, you need to use the Composite Map type. Pick a slot in the Material Editor and assign the Material to the object. In the Diffuse Color channel, choose Composite from the Material/Map Browser. (This is not the same thing as a Composite Material.) Doing so gives you two slots in which to put Bitmap Map types. Put a Bitmap type in the Map 1 slot and select uvtest.tif from this book's companion CD-ROM. Make sure that it's the Map 1 slot, because the first slot is the lowest layer on the blending stack. Also be sure that the image will be visible on your surface. Note in the Material Editor that Map Channel 1 is specified by default as the Explicit Map Channel. This means that the map uses the projection coordinates established with the first UVW Mapping modifier.

5. Try the second channel. Navigate up though the Material Editor (using the Go To Parent button to get to the two Composite channels). Drag the bitmap in the Map 1 slot down to Map 2 to create a copy. Click on the Map 2 button to get to the Map 2 panel and change the Map Channel number from 1 to 2 in the Coordinates rollout. Click on the blue-and-white checkered box to refresh your screen; after doing so, you'll notice the new projection on your object. The preview can support only one map at a time.

6. This step involves some sophisticated stuff, so take your time and use the Chap12_Composite.max file from this book's companion CD-ROM (which is designed to be used only after you've worked through the exercise yourself). The Composite Map type will completely hide Map 1 with Map 2, because both maps were assigned to the entire surface (although in different directions). Do a Quick Render (from the Main toolbar), and you'll

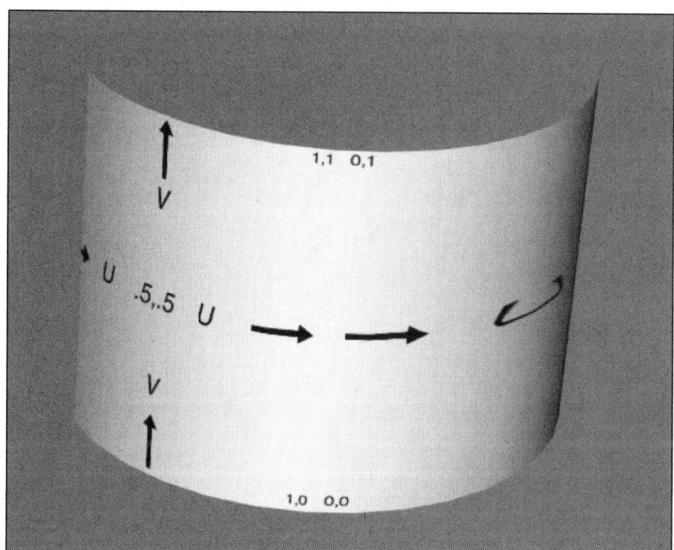

Figure 12.25
A render shows that only the Channel 2 projection is visible, because Map 1 is completely covered. Most of this mapping is distorted because the projection was only aligned to the side.

see the Channel 2 projection duplicated around the surface, as shown in Figure 12.25. The projection is obviously distorted in the region for which it was not intended.

Note: *Remember that the maps assigned to the files on the CD-ROM contain paths that reference their creators' map locations. The maps must be colocated with the file—or in one of the designated map paths on your system—for MAX to find them automatically. If not, you must reassign the map with the correct path on your system.*

7. To let Map 1 (with Channel 1 coordinates) show through, go into the Material Editor panel for Map 2, where you'll see Map Channel 2 designated in the spinner. Deselect the Tile checkbox in the U-direction. The map is no longer repeated beyond the range of its projection. Render again: Map 1 is now revealed, but a visible seam appears where the Channel 2 projection ends. Take a look at Figure 12.26.

8. To eliminate the seam, you need an Alpha (transparency) channel in the bitmap. Back in Photoshop, a thin masking strip was added along the right edge of the bitmap and saved as an Alpha channel. The new file is named uvtest_alpha.tif (it appears on this book's companion CD-ROM). Take a look at Figure 12.27.

9. To replace the bitmap in Map 2 with the updated version, go down into the Bitmap level for this map in the Material Editor and click on the long button with the name of the current map. A dialog box opens; use it to select uvtest_alpha.tif from the CD-ROM. Render again with the new bitmap, and the seam is gone. Your result should look like Figure 12.28.

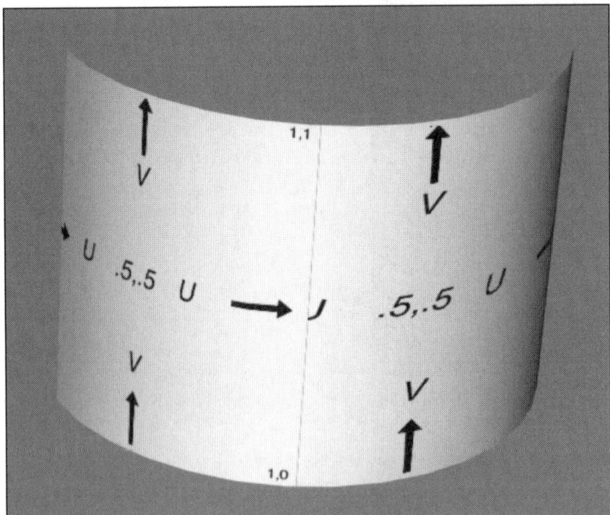

Figure 12.26
Tiling is turned off for Map 2 (using the Channel 1 projection) so it doesn't cover areas beyond its projection. Map 1 is now visible, but there is a troubling seam.

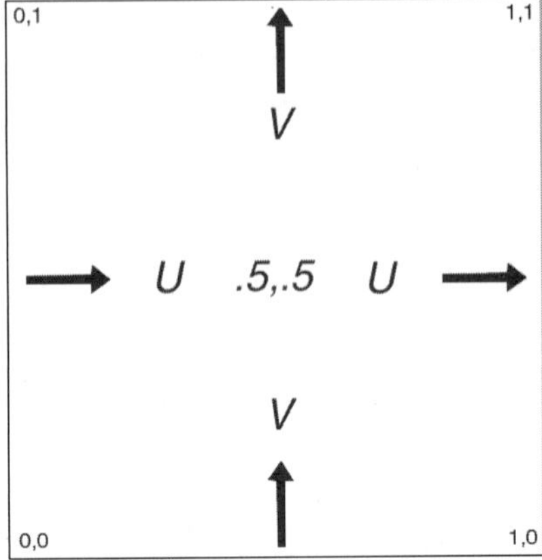

Figure 12.27
The uvtest_alpha.tif file from the CD-ROM.

Note: *For most purposes, you'll use a gradient rather than a solid mask in the Alpha channel so that the upper image fades gently into the adjoining lower one. Sophisticated mapping techniques, such as the one addressed here, are often difficult to master and take a great deal of practice. Most of all, they demand a firm understanding of principles. Two maps could overlap because the affected vertices could be assigned more than a single set of texture coordinates. Understanding these subtle ideas does not always come easily.*

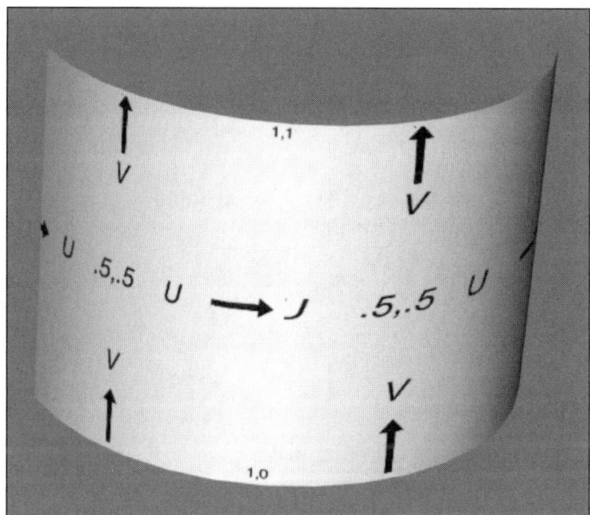

Figure 12.28
The same as Figure 12.26, but using the revised bitmap with the transparency (Alpha) channel along the edge. The seam at the overlap between the maps is now eliminated.

Using Implicit Mapping Coordinates

Earlier in this chapter, we noted that you can use two methods to establish mapping coordinates on a surface. We've just covered one of them—using the UVW Mapping modifier to project texture coordinates onto vertices. The other method is very important and, where possible, is often preferable.

A NURBS surface is inherently defined in its own two-dimensional UV space. In other words, every location on a NURBS surface can be specified by a (U,V) pair of values. These can then be used directly for the texture space. One of the strongest arguments for NURBS modeling is in this direct correspondence between surface and texture coordinates. Maps, therefore, naturally follow a curved NURBS surface without the distortion inherent in most projection techniques. Take a look at some of the possibilities with NURBS surfaces and then touch on the use of implicit coordinates in non-NURBS surfaces; you can experiment with the Chap12_Implicit.max file on the CD-ROM.

Figure 12.29 shows a gently curving NURBS surface with the uvtest.tif bitmap applied. No UVW Mapping modifier is necessary, because the surface's inherent UV coordinate space is used for mapping coordinates. The image follows the surface perfectly, although it is uniformly stretched because the surface does not have the same dimensions as the bitmap.

Because of the connection between the coordinates on the geometry and the mapping coordinates, changes to the geometry change the mapping. For example, if the surface is relofted in the opposite direction—so that the former U-direction is now the V-direction—the mapping reflects the new direction. Figure 12.30 shows the same surface after relofting.

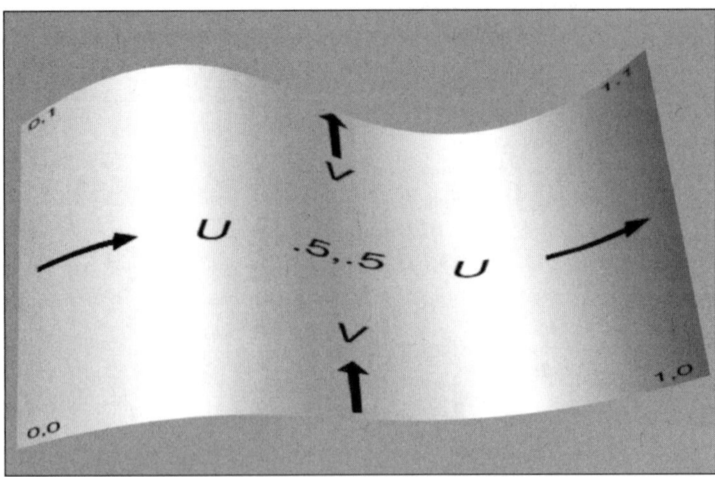

Figure 12.29
The uvtest.tif bitmap is applied to a curved NURBS surface using the inherent UV coordinates as the mapping coordinates. The map follows the curvature perfectly.

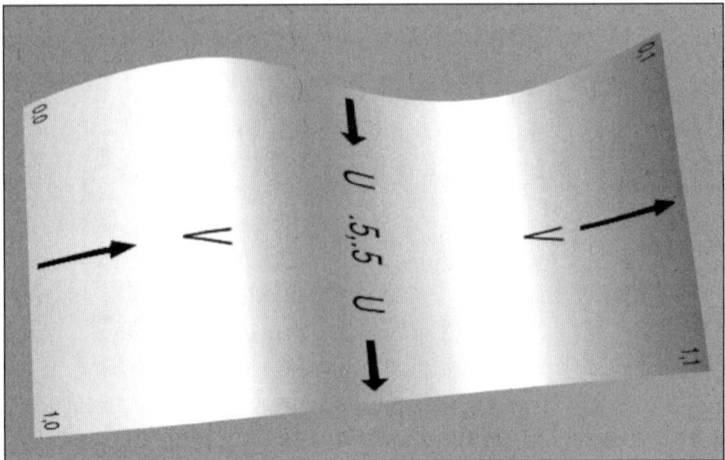

Figure 12.30
The NURBS surface from Figure 12.29 is relofted in the opposite direction, so that the U- and V-directions are reversed. The mapping coordinates reflect this change in the underlying geometry.

This reversal of directions could be a problem, but MAX has a complete set of tools for adjusting the mapping coordinates with respect to the surface coordinates. These tools are all found in the Material Properties rollout for the selected Surface subobject in the NURBS Surface object. To turn the map back around without changing the underlying surface coordinates again, you can set the Rotation Angle to 90 degrees. To apply only a portion of the map to the surface, you can choose each of the four corners of the surface and change the corresponding texture coordinates. In Figure 12.31, the corners are set to (.5,0), (1,0), (.5,1), and (1,1). As a result, only the right half of the map (from U = .5 to U = 1) is mapped to the surface.

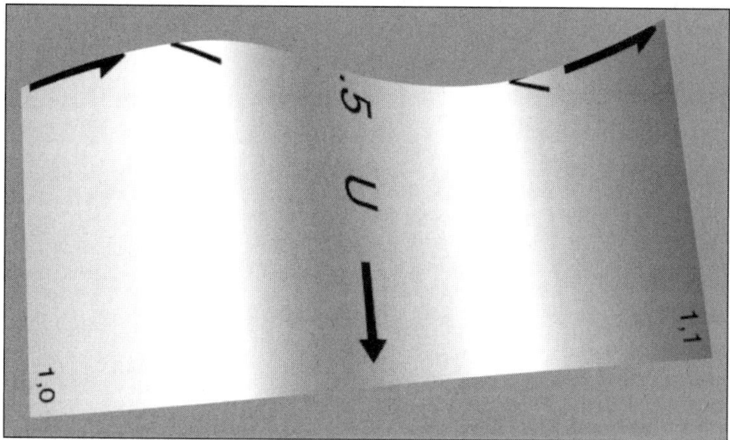

Figure 12.31
The NURBS surface from Figure 12.30, with the corners of the surface assigned to (.5,0), (1,0), (.5,1), and (1,1) in texture space. Thus, only the right half of the bitmap is mapped to the surface.

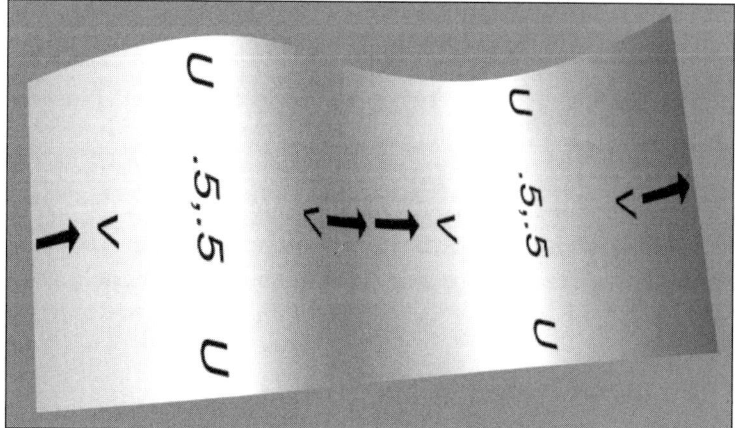

Figure 12.32
The same as Figure 12.31, but with an offset applied to center the image in the U-direction. Tiling is applied in the V-direction to fit two vertical units on the surface.

The mapping can be offset and tiled on the NURBS surface. In Figure 12.32, the mapping is offset in one direction to center the image, and then it is tiled in the other direction.

Detailed editing of NURBS surface mapping is easier and more powerful than using the Unwrap UVW modifier. A Texture Surface is slipped between the true texture space and the geometry of the object. You can access this Texture Surface by selecting the User Defined option in the Material Properties rollout of a NURBS surface's Surface subobject. Once you have done so, you can edit the Texture Surface directly by using a dialog box that is very similar to that used in the Unwrap UVW modifier. Or, you can edit Texture Points directly on the object's surface.

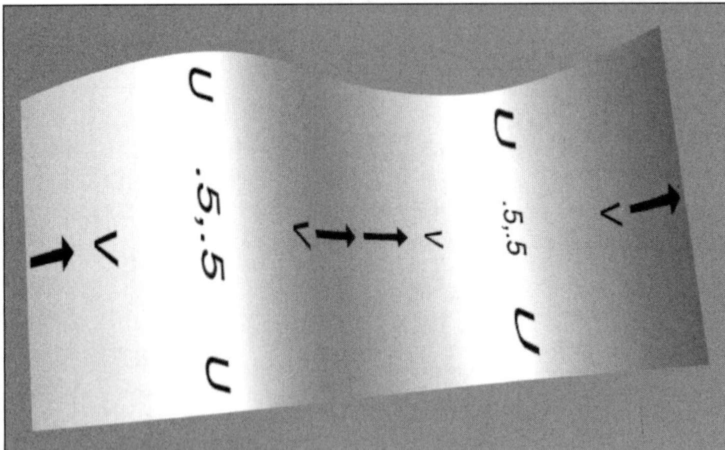

Figure 12.33
The same as Figure 12.32, but with the Texture Surface edited slightly on the right side of the NURBS surface.

Both of these methods give you extremely refined control over mapping. In Figure 12.33, the Texture Surface was edited on the right side of the surface.

This kind of mapping makes perfect sense for NURBS surfaces, because they necessarily have their own 2D coordinate spaces. However, MAX is unique among 3D applications because it has analogous tools for a wide range of other objects. Primitives automatically assign mapping coordinates, consistent with their structure. Loft objects can generate mapping coordinates that automatically follow the surface without need for projections. If you think ahead, the correct approach to modeling automatically produces the mapping coordinates that you need. Every time you see the Generate Mapping Coordinates checkbox, take note and think of how that object might serve in the mapping process.

For example, suppose you want to wrap an image continuously around a sharp corner. With most modeling methods, you must use projections to get the image properly aligned, and the result might never look perfect. If the surface is generated from an extruded spline, however, the Extrude modifier has a Generate Mapping Coordinates checkbox. When mapping coordinates are established this way, rather than with a UVW Mapping projection, the mapping follows the polygonal surface in a manner similar to what you just saw with NURBS. See Figure 12.34.

The Bitmap Panel

When a Bitmap Map type is assigned to a mapping channel, the Material Editor makes available a wide range of controls. The Coordinates rollout is shown in Figure 12.35.

The primary controls are for offset and tiling of the bitmap. As a rule, you should do your tiling here rather than in the similar tiling spinners in the UVW Mapping modifier. Tiling makes sense only with bitmaps designed to line up seamlessly. The Mirror option is a way of making

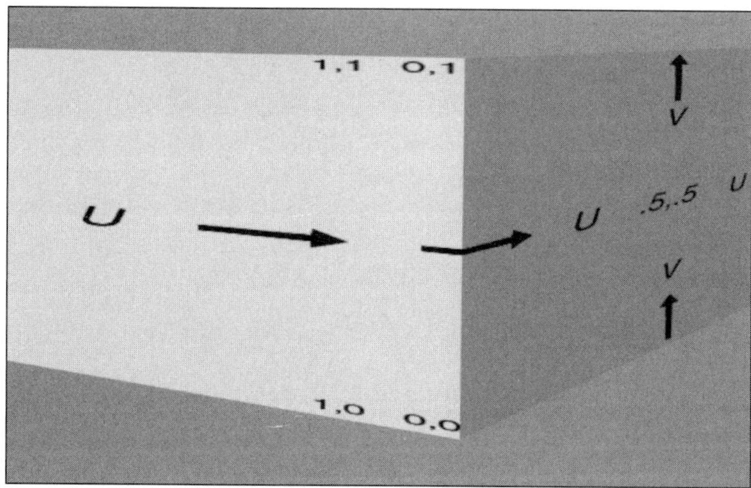

Figure 12.34
A polygonal surface is created with a spline to which an Extrude modifier is applied. By selecting the Generate Mapping Coordinates checkbox in the Extrude modifier, texture coordinates are created that follow the surface. Note how the image flows perfectly around the corner.

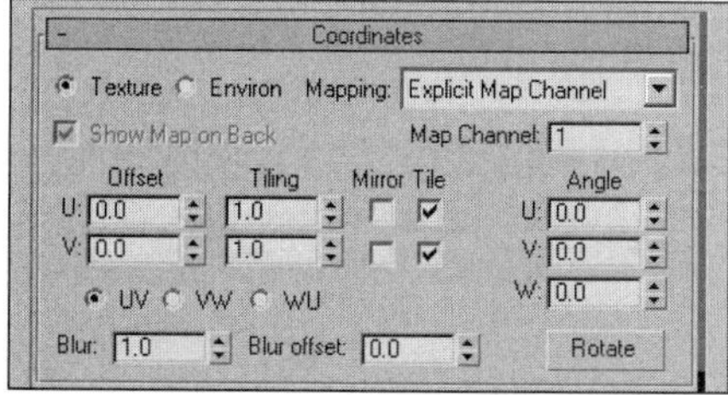

Figure 12.35
The Coordinates rollout in the Material Editor for a Bitmap Map type.

tiling less noticeable with images that do not have perfectly tileable edges. Figure 12.36 illustrates the effect of mirroring in both directions. When you're using a bitmap with a fine pattern, the repeating pattern of edges is slightly less noticeable.

Now, you can finally consider the meaning of the W-dimension. If U and V are the directions on the 2D plane of texture space, W is perpendicular to that plane. By dragging the W spinner above the Rotate button, the plane is rotated like a wheel on an axle. This is sometimes a valuable adjustment. Figure 12.37 shows the previous image rotated in W.

In the Bitmap Parameters rollout, the Crop option allows you to use only a portion of a bitmap without having to go into a separate bitmap-editing application to redefine the image. The Place option allows you to scale down the bitmap to fit over only a portion of the affected surface. The remaining region reveals the underlying Material in a render. Both of these tools are set up with the Specify Cropping/Placement dialog box, which you access by clicking on the View Image button.

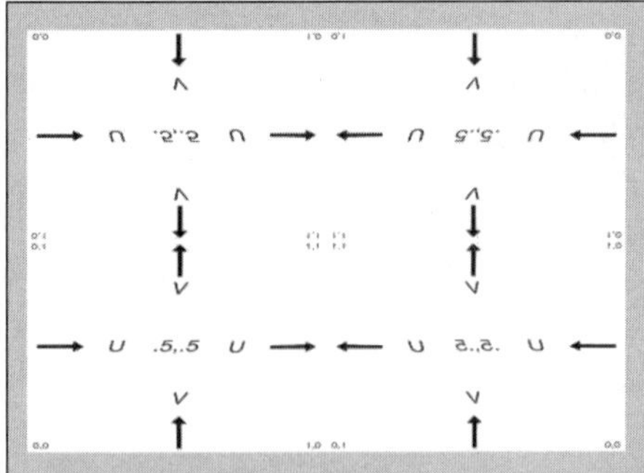

Figure 12.36
Mirroring a bitmap in both directions. With a fine image pattern, this arrangement makes tiling slightly less noticeable.

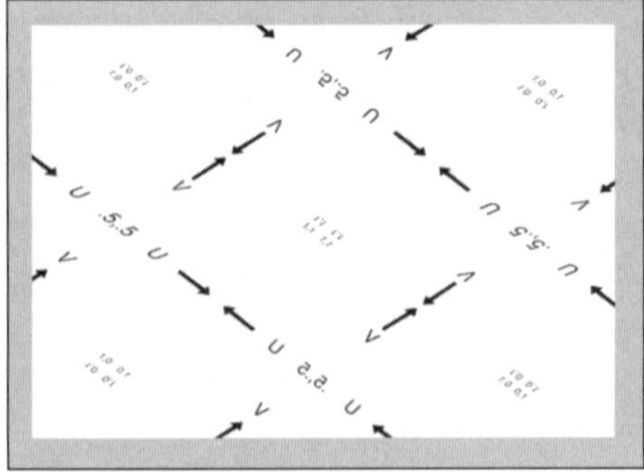

Figure 12.37
The same as Figure 12.36, but with the image rotated about its W axis.

If a bitmap contains an Alpha channel, this channel is used to determine the transparent areas of the image. By default, Image Alpha is selected as the Alpha Source when an Alpha channel is present. By changing to None, the Alpha channel in the image is disregarded. Using an Alpha mask is one of the ways you can put "decals" on surfaces. In the image on the right in Figure 12.38, the bitmap appears with the Alpha channel as an overlay. Everything covered by the mask is made transparent. When applied to the object and rendered, the underlying Material shows through where the Alpha channel masked out the image (see the image on the left in Figure 12.38). You may want to try the image named uvtest_alpha2.tif on this book's companion CD-ROM to duplicate the result in this figure.

Procedural Maps

A *procedural map* (also called a *procedural texture* or *procedural shader*) is a small program. By setting the parameters of the procedure, you change the color, pattern, and general appearance of the output. You used a Marble procedure earlier in this chapter (in the "Bump and Displacement Mapping" section) to create a pattern without resorting to a bitmap image.

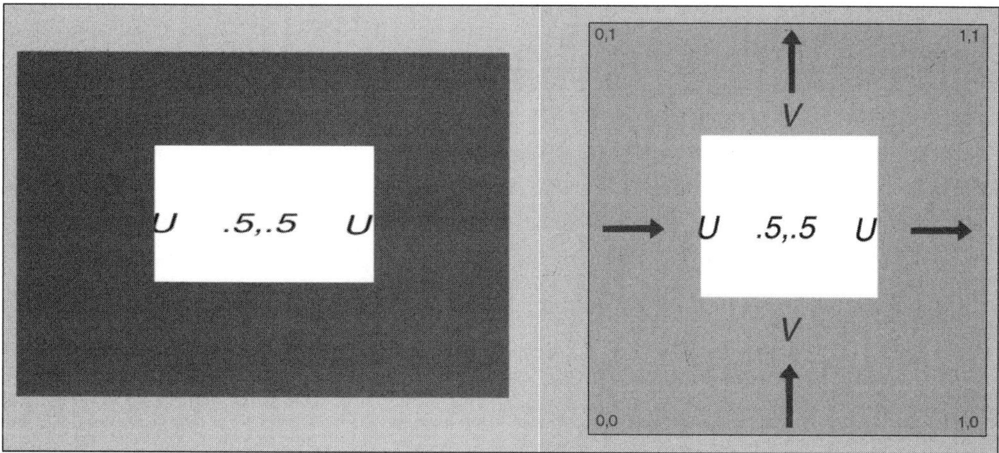

Figure 12.38
Using an Alpha channel. On the right is the bitmap image, with the masked area in the Alpha channel indicated. The effect on the rendered surface is on the left. The masked region is made transparent, revealing the underlying Material.

It's hard to talk about procedural mapping in general terms because each procedure is a different program. MAX's procedures are especially sophisticated, with a wide range of input parameters for each. The only way to learn what you can do with procedural textures is to experiment with them, making numerous tests with different parameter values. The interaction of the various parameters can make results hard to predict.

Procedural mapping is extremely important, however, and it is becoming more significant as shaders improve. The most important procedures are 3D, but MAX has a small range of 2D procedures that are very handy.

Don't Judge a Procedure by its Name

The range of possibilities hiding under a name like Wood or Marble is simply astounding. Most procedural shaders are given a name that reflects their primary purpose, but vast new possibilities open up once you start playing with the parameters. You simply can't understand what a shader is capable of without a lot of experimentation.

2D Maps

Figure 12.39 shows the Material/Map Browser filtered to show only 2D Map types. Not all of these map types are procedures. The Bitmap type is the opposite of a procedure, and it is what you've been using to map bitmap images to surfaces. The two Adobe filter types are tools for applying third-party Photoshop and Premiere filters. The Combustion map type is an interface that connects Discreet Logic's combustion* painting and compositing program with MAX. Only Bricks, Checker, Gradient, Gradient Ramp, and Swirl are procedures, as the term is used here.

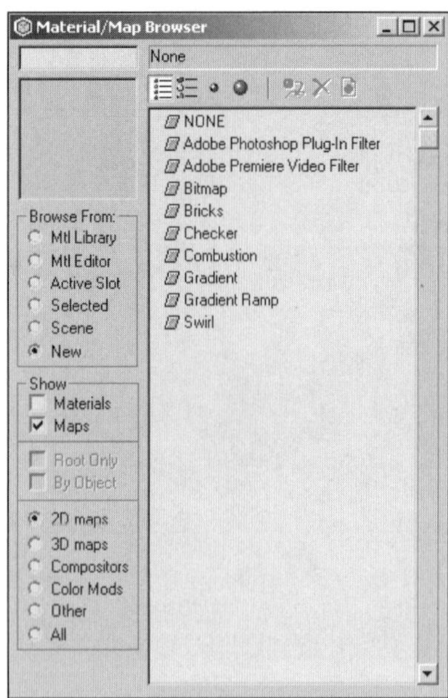

Figure 12.39
The Material/Map Browser, filtered to show only the 2D Map types.

The 2D procedures are simply ways to create bitmap images directly within MAX. This can be a great convenience. Why go into Photoshop to create a checkered pattern or a color gradient if you can do it in MAX? Remember, though, that you are creating a bitmap, so you'll face all the same mapping issues as when you use a bitmap from outside the program. To understand your 2D procedural output as a bitmap, change the Sample Type in the Material Editor slots that you're using from a sphere to a cube, using the Sample Type button in the vertical row of buttons to the right of the sample slots. Remember that procedural maps should be assigned to the map channels of a Material and not to the Material itself, as accessed from the Get Material button. Each face of the cube will display a copy of the bitmap.

The Gradient Ramp Map type is a particularly valuable tool. The color gradient can be adjusted to any degree of complexity and then projected in a variety of ways. Noise can be added for greater subtlety or for a fractal look. Figure 12.40 shows six possibilities for a single color gradient.

3D Maps

3D maps are the most important kind of procedural shader. Like the 2D versions, they permit you to define the characteristics of the map by setting parameter values. Unlike the 2D versions, however, these procedures do not create bitmaps—they create patterns in 3D space. The mapped object picks up these patterns as its surfaces intersect this 3D texture space. This behavior has two very important consequences. First, you don't need to trouble with mapping coordinates. You are not wrapping a flat image around a 3D surface, so you don't need to use the UVW Mapping modifier to project anything. There's no image to project. There's no question of unwanted seams at the edges of bitmaps.

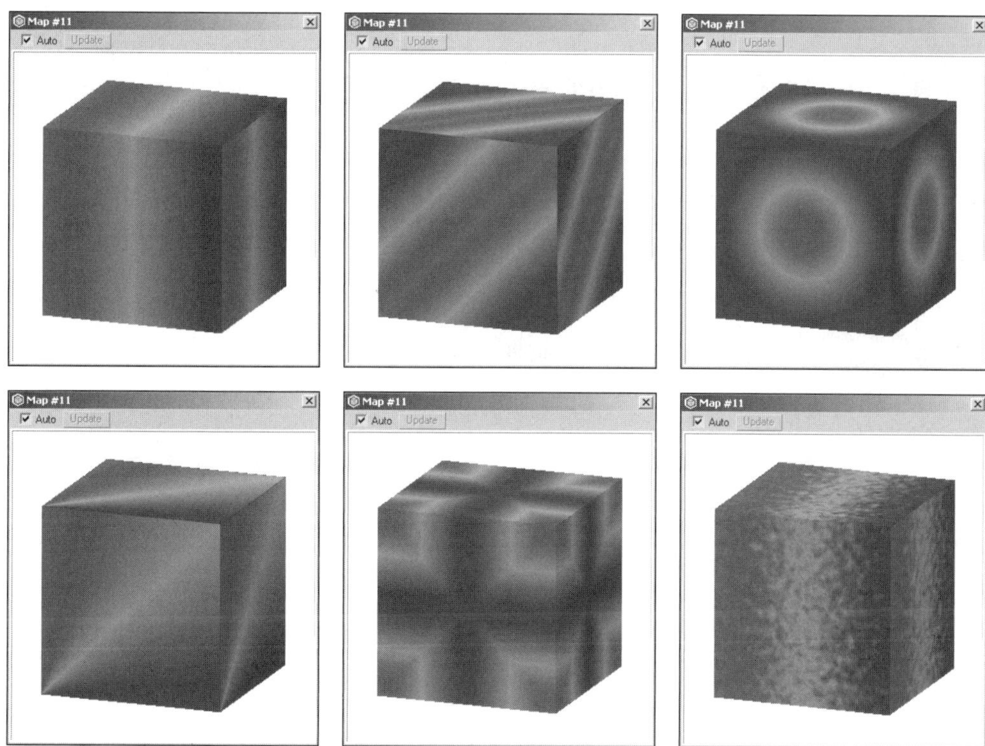

Figure 12.40
Six variations of a single color gradient, using the Gradient Ramp Map type. The Linear, Diagonal, Radial, Sweep, and Tartan gradient types are shown, followed by an example of noise applied to the Linear sample.

The second consequence is that patterns can flow through the 3D space of an object in a natural way. The patterns that you see on the surface of a wood or marble object are just the intersection of patterns that run in all directions through the substance. Figure 12.41 shows a Wood procedural map and a Perlin Marble procedural map applied to a Cylinder. They look as if they were cut out of a single larger piece of material. It is nearly impossible to create bitmaps for the sides and top to produce this effect of internal continuity.

Note: *3D maps are not visible in the shaded viewports. Use the sample slots in the Material Editor to get some rough bearings, and then make test renders to see the result on your geometry.*

3D maps are applied, by default, in the Local space of the object. That way, the map stays in place as the object is transformed. The map isn't actually stuck to the vertices on the geometry, however, which can be a problem when vertices are deformed in animation. For example, if a Noise map is used on the surface of a character that is being deformed with bones, you need to be sure that the pattern stays with the surface in the same way that a bitmap would. To create hard texture coordinates on vertices for 3D maps, use the UVW Mapping modifier with the XYZ To UVW option. Then, make sure that your 3D map is using the Explicit Map Channel option in the Material Editor. See Figure 12.42. On the left is a Cylinder with a Noise map applied. In

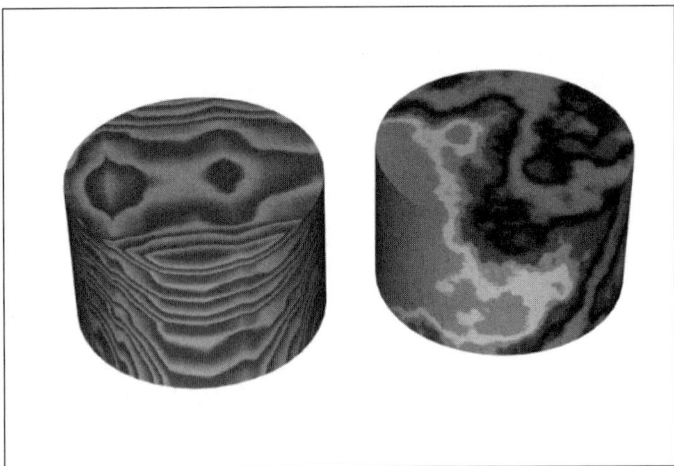

Figure 12.41
Wood and Perlin Marble 3D procedural shaders are applied to a Cylinder. Note the continuity of the pattern over the edge from the top and down the sides. This effect of an internal pattern running through material is nearly impossible to achieve with bitmaps.

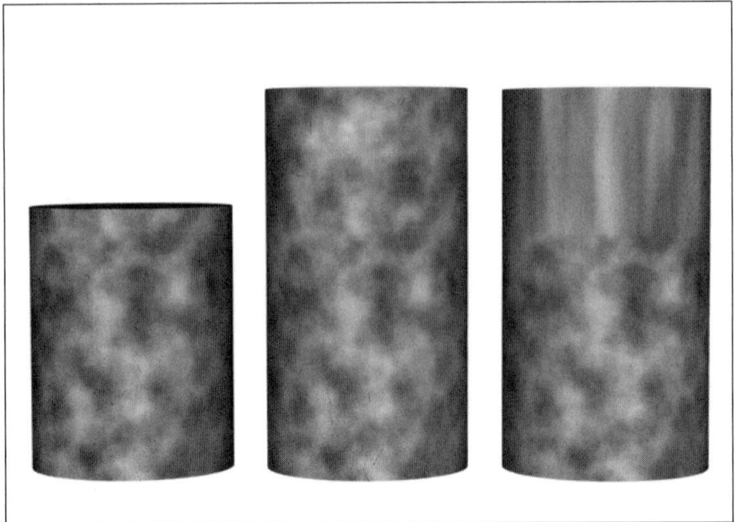

Figure 12.42
Using the UVW Mapping modifier to create hard texture coordinates for a 3D map. On the left is a cylinder with a Noise map applied. In the center, the top row of vertices extends the object into a new region of the 3D texture space. On the right, the UVW Mapping modifier is used to pin the map to the vertices. The map now stretches as the top row of vertices is moved upward.

the center, the top row of vertices was moved upward, but the object simply expanded into a new region of the 3D texture space. At right, the UVW Mapping modifier is used to create mapping coordinates on the vertices before the vertices are moved in an Edit Mesh modifier. Now, the top of the map stretches to follow the moved vertices.

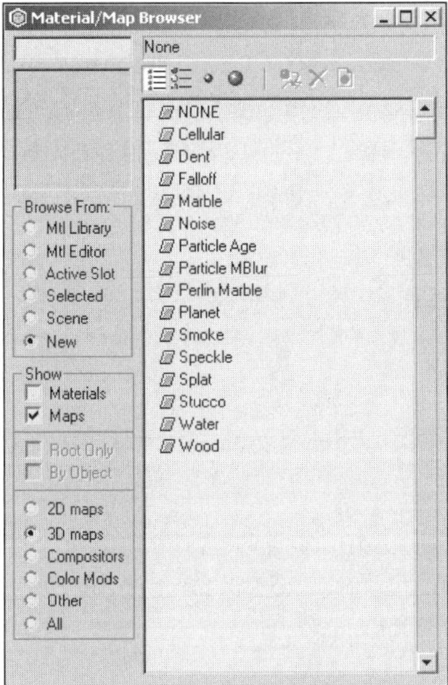

Figure 12.43
MAX's 3D maps listed in the Material/Map Browser.

Figure 12.43 shows the list of 3D maps from the Material/Map Browser.

Reflections, Refractions, and Ray Tracing

A reflective Material reveals other objects in the scene on its surface. If a Material is completely or partially transparent, it reveals other objects through it. Most transparent Materials are at least somewhat refractive—that is, they bend the light passing through them, distorting objects seen from behind.

True Object Reflections and Refractions

The most important method of creating accurate reflection and refraction effects is ray tracing. *Ray tracing* is a rendering technique that follows a ray of light through the scene, bouncing from one reflective object to another or passing through transparent objects to find objects behind them. MAX has always offered ray tracing for shadows, but it did not offer ray-traced reflections and refractions until 3D Studio MAX 2. The older program filled the gap with some makeshift alternatives in the Map channels for reflection and refraction. Some of these options are still useful, because they can produce a satisfactory result without the enormous rendering times that ray tracing often requires.

When MAX introduced ray tracing for reflections and refractions, it did so in a very confusing way. You can apply ray tracing at the Material level by using a Raytrace Material. Or, you can use the Raytrace Map type in the reflection or refraction Map channels. The Raytrace Material offers some more advanced parameters, but the panels for both the Map and Material types are extremely complex and intimidating. Nothing about ray tracing should require so many parameters for the general user. Fortunately, the default settings are almost always satisfactory for anyone who is not a professional rendering specialist. Make sure that Antialiasing is selected in the Raytracer Options dialog box (available from the Options button in the Raytracer Controls rollout).

An alternative to ray tracing, the Flat Mirror map, can be applied to coplanar surfaces by means of the Reflection channel and the faces' Material ID number. This method yields excellent results, as seen in the following exercise:

1. Open the file Chap12_Mirror.max, which consists of a head model, a pedestal, and an editable mesh floor entity.
2. Pick a slot in the Material Editor and, in the Diffuse Color channel, assign the image BURLOAK.JPG from the \Maps\Wood directory. Apply the Material to the floor entity and render the scene to get an idea of how the wood Material looks.
3. Select the floor object and, using the Modify panel, confirm that its top face bears Material ID #1 and that this is unique among the other faces. Flat Mirror reflections work only if they are assigned to coplanar faces.
4. In the Maps rollout of the Material Editor, click on the None button for the Reflection channel. In the Material/Map Browser, ensure that New is active in the Browse From area and that all maps and Materials are displayed. Choose Flat Mirror.
5. In the Flat Mirror Parameters rollout of the Material Editor, select the Apply To Faces With ID checkbox and make sure "1" appears in the number field to its right.

Note: *An alternate method of assigning a Flat Mirror reflection is to apply it as a map contained in a Multi/Sub-Object Material. Using this method, the Sub-Material is assigned to the faces containing the proper Material ID number. With either method, if all the faces assigned the map are not coplanar, the reflection will simply not work without any type of warning.*

6. Render the scene again. This time, the model is accurately reflected in the top face of the floor, as shown in Figure 12.44. It is often a good idea to raise the Blur value and lower the Amount value in the Reflection slot in the Maps rollout to make the reflection less sharp and the object appear less polished. To finish the scene, use the Mesh Select and UVW Mapping modifiers to correct the distortion of the map on the narrow side faces.

Reflection Maps

Often, you don't need to produce reflections of true geometry in the scene. For example, a reflective surface may be blurry enough that the reflections are not identifiable, and all you need are vague reflected patterns. In other cases, you need reflections of discernible objects, but

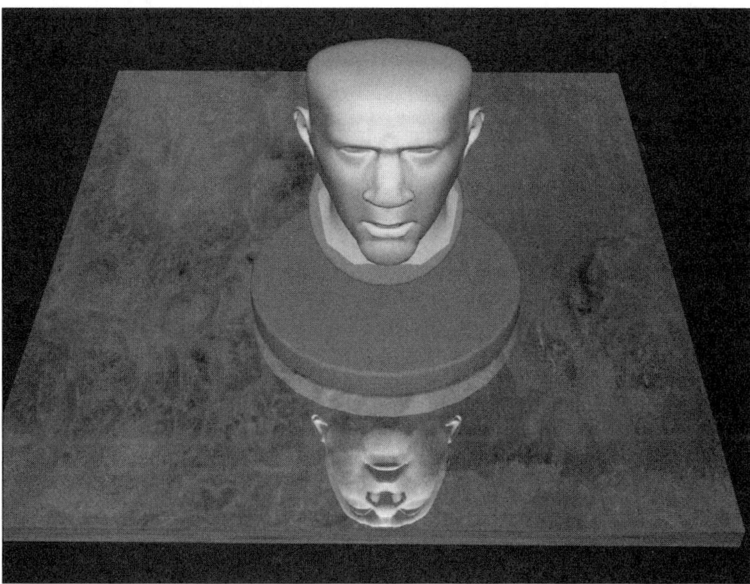

Figure 12.44
Using a Flat Mirror, in the base object's Reflection map channel, creates an accurate reflection of the objects above it.

you don't need (or want) to model them directly. In either case, you can use bitmaps or procedural textures to get a satisfactory effect. Putting such a map in the Reflection map channel creates a Spherical Environment map that is reflected off the surface of the object. A Spherical Environment map is a map projected on the inside of an infinite sphere enclosing the scene. Using a reflection map of a cloudy sky (such as sky.jpg in MAX's\Maps\Skies directory) is a very standard practice. The final project for this exercise can be found on the CD-ROM as Chap12_Mirror_Final.max.

Moving On

In this chapter, you learned that mapping is the process by which a Material parameter (such as Diffuse Color) can be made to vary over a surface. You learned how bitmap images are used for mapping, and particularly how texture coordinates are established on a surface, either by projection or through the use of a surface's intrinsic coordinates. You explored the vast possibilities of MAX's procedural mapping tools, which permit you to create patterns without the use of bitmaps. And you looked briefly at object reflections and the use of ray tracing.

The next chapter turns to lighting in 3ds max 4. You'll learn the important ways in which lighting in computer graphics differs from real-world lighting, and you'll explore the full scope of MAX's lighting toolset.

Part V

Lights, Camera, Render!

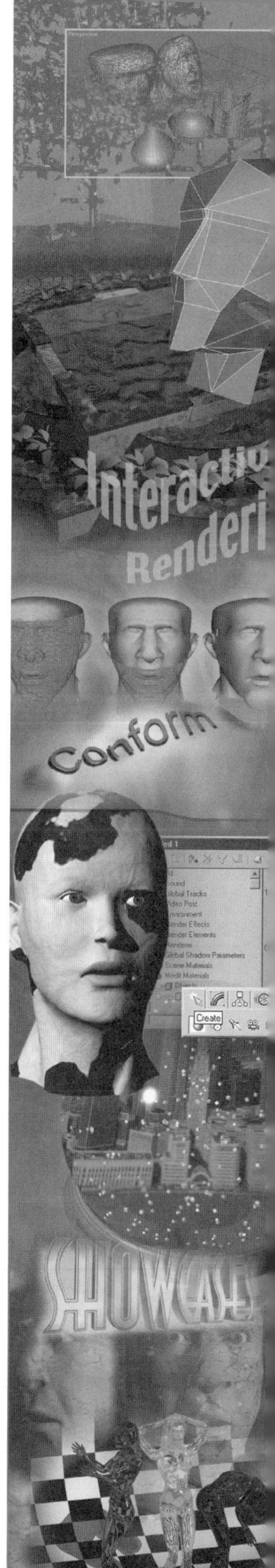

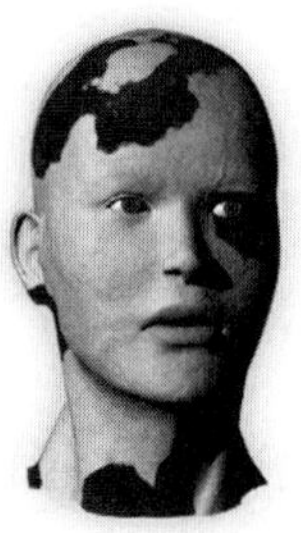

Chapter 13
Lights

In 3D graphics, lighting is often treated as an afterthought; little time is spent on thinking about how to illuminate a scene properly. This lack of attention is a mistake, because poor lighting can greatly reduce the overall quality of a scene, regardless of the quality of the modeling.

The process of creating a scene in MAX is similar to that of creating a scene for a feature film. Objects are constructed and placed in the appropriate locations; lights illuminate the scene; and the action is recorded to a physical medium through the lens of a camera. In MAX, though, the objects, lights, and cameras are virtual rather than physical, and therefore they do not follow the rules to which you may be accustomed.

The rules that deviate the most from physical reality apply to lighting. This chapter will explain the concepts of lighting in computer graphics, as well as the lighting tools found in MAX.

Lighting in Computer Graphics

On the surface, lighting in computer graphics (CG) appears to mimic lighting in the real world: A light is created and aimed at an object, and the object becomes illuminated. Understanding the way the light is emitted and what it does when it hits its target are paramount to understanding how to light your scenes.

Diffuse Reflection

Look around at the workspace you're in now. If it is set up like most, light comes from fixtures overhead, and sunlight comes in from a nearby window. The top and side surfaces of the objects may be in the direct path of the light, but all surfaces (including the ceiling and under the desk) are also illuminated—just to a lesser degree. This is the case because the light bounces off all surfaces with which it comes in contact until all its energy is dissipated. The sunlight may be reflected off nearby buildings, vehicles, or the ground. Some surfaces, such as carpet and clothing, absorb more light than other surfaces, such as walls or metal fixtures. *Diffuse reflection* is the term used to describe the illumination of objects through the occurrence of bounced light. MAX does not calculate bounced light, but understanding it is necessary in order to be able to replicate it in your CG scenes.

When you see something, you are seeing the light that has bounced off it and into your eye. When the light bounces off an object, it changes frequency based on that object's properties; that change in frequency is what we refer to as *color*. Not all light bouncing off an object will result in the same color. Figure 13.1 shows a series of identical red Spheres, each of which has either a red, white, or blue light trained on it. Although the red light (RGB value 255,0,0) returns a highlighted area that is difficult to distinguish from its surroundings, the white light (255,255,255) yields a more defined highlight. The blue light (0,0,255) reflects a highlight almost the same size as the red one, but not nearly as intense. The white highlight is the brightest because it returns the sum of the red, green, and blue portions of the white light. This scene can be found on the CD-ROM in the file Chap13 RWB.max. When setting up the lighting in your scene, you must consider the colors that exist in the scene and how the light bouncing off them would change color in the real world.

The absence of automatic diffuse reflection is one of the biggest issues that an animator or artist will have to deal with in MAX. By default, anything that is not directly in the uninterrupted

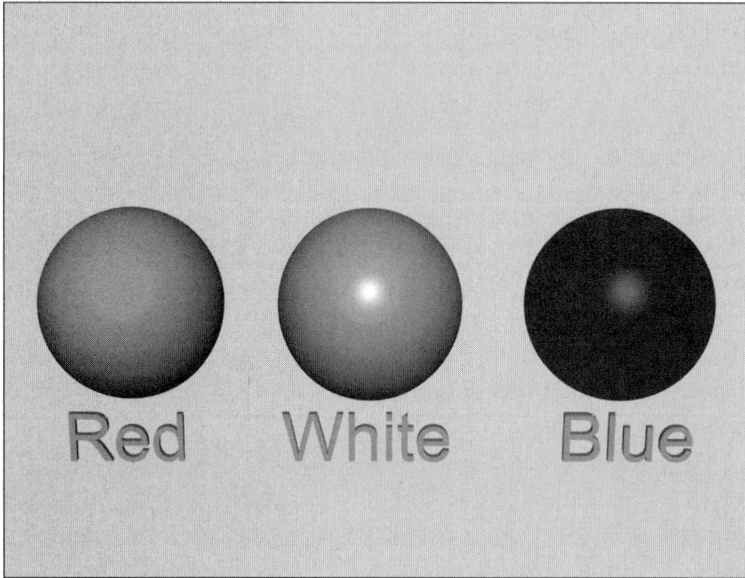

Figure 13.1
Red, white, or blue lights yield different results when trained on identical red Spheres. The white light yields the greatest highlight, whereas the blue light yields almost none.

path of emitted light will appear very dark, with little or no contrast. Using the capabilities of MAX to overcome this problem is a task that takes patience and practice. A good rule of thumb is to expect to spend about 20 to 25 percent of your production time illuminating an indoor scene and 5 to 7 percent illuminating an outdoor scene.

Figure 13.2 illustrates this problem. The scene is illuminated with one Directional Light that is parallel to the wall to the left, providing it with no illumination. The front of the bottle is seen clearly until its background becomes the dark wall and the contrast between the two is lost. The back of the bottle is not in the path of the light and is also dark. The back wall is over-lit and washed out, and it shows little of its texture. Although the shadow falls nicely between the floor and back wall, in a real-world situation the back wall and floor would reflect light to illuminate the back of the bottle and side wall.

Figure 13.2
The absence of diffuse reflection causes the scene to look unrealistic. The single Directional Light illuminates the front of the bottle, the back wall, and, to a smaller degree, the floor. In a real-world situation, the darker areas would be illuminated with reflected light.

Using Radiosity for Global Illumination

The radiosity rendering technique produces outstanding results by calculating and using diffuse reflection. The surfaces in the scene transmit the light they receive back onto other surfaces in a way that closely resembles real-world illumination. The results can be startlingly realistic and are essential for visualization projects in architecture and interior design. The premier product in this area is Lightscape from Discreet. Lightscape can work as a standalone product or seamlessly with MAX. You model objects or scenes in MAX, create the radiosity solution in Lightscape, and then import the solution back into MAX for rendering. Radiosity rendering takes some study, but the results are unparalleled.

Ambient Light

The Ambient light setting in MAX is used to create the illusion of global illumination. The ambient light does not exist in your scenes as an actual light, however; it is the calculated self-illumination of an object's surfaces based on the object's material or color and the Ambient setting. Having ambient light present gives the impression of an overall light source and helps define objects that have escaped illumination. Ambient lighting is often called an *ambient factor* to suggest that it is more of an adjustment to the existing illumination than a source of illumination itself.

In MAX, the default Ambient light level is very low (11,11,11). You should increase the factor sparingly, because increased ambient light washes out contrast between the faces of objects. More often than not, you will leave the Ambient level alone or even reduce it to 0, relying instead on the properties of the placed lights to illuminate the scene fully.

Another way to change the global appearance of the light in a scene is to change the hue of the Tint setting. A red tint could be used for a cheap hotel room or the back room of a bar. Yellow ambient light can be used when the scene appears to be lit by torches or a campfire. The Ambient and Tint settings are found in the Global Lighting section of the Environment dialog box (see Figure 13.3), which is reached through the Rendering drop-down menu. The color swatches for both settings bring up the MAX standard Color Selector.

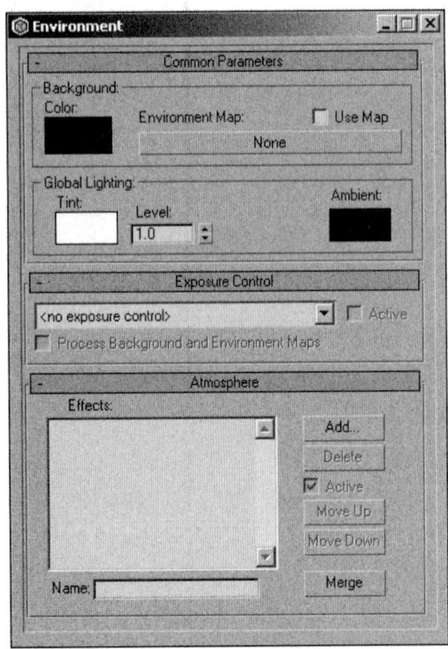

Figure 13.3
The Ambient and Tint settings can be found in the Global Lighting section of the Environment dialog box.

Figure 13.4
The same as Figure 13.2, but with the scene's Ambient setting increased.

Figure 13.4 shows the scene from Figure 13.2 with the Ambient setting increased. The back wall is even more washed out, and the floor has lost some of its definition. Even worse, the bottle has lost its rounded appearance and looks flat with a misshapen label.

Figure 13.5 shows the same scene with the Ambient setting back at its default and a better lighting scheme. A backlight is in place to illuminate the label and create highlights along the back of the bottle's base and neck. An attenuated light (covered later in the chapter) is used to light the side wall, and attenuation has been turned on for the original Directional Light.

Shadow Casting

In the real world, all lights produce shadows if their paths are blocked by surfaces. In computer graphics, however, shadow casting is optional. You can decide whether a light will cast shadows generally, and you can also decide whether a particular object in the path of a light will cast shadows on other objects. You can further dictate whether an object will receive shadows from other objects. These options are available in the Modify panel for the selected light or in the Object Properties dialog box for the selected object.

These shadow-casting options are important for optimizing rendering time, but they also give the 3D artist a kind of flexibility that is unknown to the photographer without the use of post-production editing. Undesirable shadows can be eliminated without moving the lights. More important, however, lighting can be designed so that certain lights cast shadows and others serve only to illuminate the scene. Shadows are extremely important to establish depth and

Figure 13.5
The same scene with a better lighting scheme applied. Notice how the highlights that now appear at the back of the bottle help maintain its appearance as a rounded object.

substance in a 3D image. Shadow placement can be handled with great independence of overall illumination by using a combination of shadow-casting and non–shadow-casting lights.

Figure 13.6 demonstrates the concept in an extreme that is the opposite of realism. The specular highlights show the direction of the main source of illumination, but the only shadow in the scene is cast by a light in the opposite direction.

This extreme example is used only to make a point. If you eliminate the specular component from the front Directional Light, as in Figure 13.7, the troubling highlight disappears. The light thus serves only to fill out what would otherwise be the dark areas of the Sphere and generally to even the illumination of the scene.

Inclusion and Exclusion of Objects

Another striking difference between real-world and CG lighting is the power to exclude specific objects from the illumination of specific lights. In Figure 13.8, the scene from Figure 13.7 is altered to exclude the head and other objects from illumination by the front Directional Light. That light still illuminates the floor (Box) object. Simply turning off the light would cause the scene to lose its illumination of the floor.

MAX provides an Exclude/Include dialog box for every type of light. Figure 13.9 shows this dialog box, as used in the current scene. The left side begins with a list of all objects in the scene. Selected objects can be moved to the panel on the right side; these objects are excluded or included in the illumination of the light, depending on the choice made at the top right.

Figure 13.6
Different lights are used for general illumination and for shadow casting. The specular highlight shows the direction of one Directional Light. The shadow is cast only by a second Directional Light from behind—the opposite of realism.

Figure 13.7
With the specular highlights removed, the improper lighting is less evident.

Figure 13.8
The same as Figure 13.7, but with the head and platform components excluded from illumination by the front Directional Light. The floor (Box) object remains lit by that light.

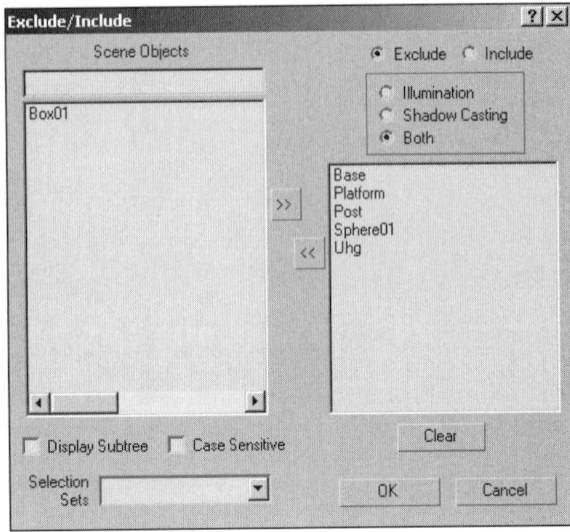

Figure 13.9
The Exclude/Include dialog box for the front light in the scene rendered in Figure 13.8. The head and related objects were moved from the left panel to the right panel for exclusion.

Sometimes it's easier to organize the objects you wish to include in the illumination than to list those that you wish to exclude, so that future objects are not included in the scene's lighting. Generally, you'll exclude objects from both illumination and shadow casting, but this dialog box can also be used as a method for sorting out your shadow-casting decisions alone.

Light Types and their Parameters

MAX offers the three standard light types that are common to all 3D graphics applications: Directional, Omni, and Spot. A Directional Light is best conceived of as a plane that generates light rays perpendicular to that plane and parallel to each other. In the real world, this type most closely simulates sunlight. Of course, the rays of sunlight received on Earth are not exactly parallel, but our distance from the Sun is so great that they may be treated as parallel, for all practical purposes. MAX offers the Sunlight System, a system feature that uses a Directional Light and provides information about time and location to get a correct angle for sunlight on the scene. This kind of precision is typically necessary only in scientific or commercial visualizations. The Sunlight System is available from Create|Systems in the Command Panel. MAX's Directional Lights can use either an infinite plane of rays or some defined region of a plane, either rectangular or circular.

An Omni Light is sometimes called a *bulb light* or a *point light* in other applications. The Omni Light is located at a single point in World space and generates light rays in all directions, radiating out like a sphere. This effect simulates the way light is distributed from a conventional light bulb and is therefore extremely useful in enclosed spaces.

The Spot Light is like a conic region of an Omni Light. Like the Omni Light, the Spot Light generates light from a single point, but the distribution is limited to a cone. The effect is similar to a flashlight or a car's headlights.

Don't Trust Your Shaded Preview

When working with lights, the rule is, "render, render, render!" The realtime shaded previews in your viewports are often very different from your rendered results. Even the rough effects of light placement and basic parameter changes cannot be assessed without rendering. And, of course, the preview can't show you your shadows. The new ActiveShade feature, discussed in Chapter 15, yields much better results, but it is not a replacement for actual renderings.

Creating Lights

Lights are created by selecting Create|Lights in the Command panel. Both the Directional Light and the Spot Light have Free and Target options. Because these lights must be pointed in some appropriate direction, it generally makes sense to use a Target object. When you create a Target Direct or Target Spot Light and drag on the screen, you create both the light and the Target object (a nonrendering null object). The light is given a LookAt controller that keeps it directed at the Target object. Moving the Target object in the scene rotates the light; to point a light at a renderable object, you simply align the Target with the object. If you create a Free Direct or Free Spot Light, no Target object is created. The lights are redirected with the Rotate transform, usually using the Local coordinate system. When you're rotating a Free Light, use the Views menu in the right-click viewport menu to assign a viewport to look directly at the light. When the light's viewport is active, the view tools, in the lower-right corner of the MAX window, are customized specifically to adjust lights; they can also be used to orient the light correctly.

An Omni Light is completely nondirectional, so there is no need to rotate it. No Free or Direct choice is offered. You create the light by simply clicking on a location in a viewport and moving the light, as necessary. When lights are created, you remain in the Create mode until another action is performed; as a result, a new light is created every time you click in the viewport.

Setting General Parameters

After a light is created, its parameters are freely adjustable in the Modify panel. In fact, you can even change the light to another type from the Type drop-down list. If you do this, remember to change the name of the light to reflect the new type. Figure 13.10 shows the General Parameters rollout from the Modify panel. Although the selected light is a Target Spot type, this rollout is the same for all light types.

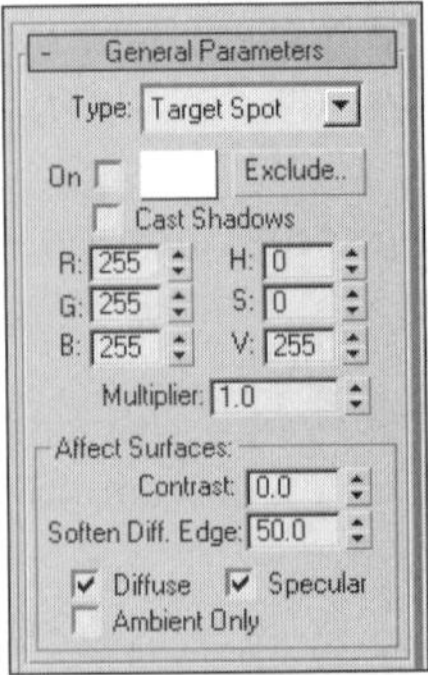

Figure 13.10
The General Parameters rollout for a Target Spot Light. This rollout is the same for all light types.

Using the Default Lights

MAX always starts a scene with one of two kinds of Default Lighting. The "default" Default Lighting is a single Directional Light that remains aligned with your view, so that objects remain illuminated at every viewing angle. However, you can change from this 1 Light option to a 2 Lights option in the Viewport Configuration dialog box (under the Customize menu). The 2 Lights option uses two Omni Lights. A Key light is positioned above-front-left, and a Fill light is positioned diagonally opposite—below-rear-right. You can easily compare the two Default Lighting options by creating a Sphere in the center of World space and flipping between them.

The default lights are unselectable and uneditable. To make them into true lights that may be transformed and otherwise edited, use the Add Default Lights To Scene command in the Views menu. This command applies only to the 2 Lights option, and you can choose to convert either one or both of them.

The On checkbox toggles the light on and off. The rectangular color swatch to the right of this checkbox indicates the color of the light, and clicking on it brings up the Color Selector dialog box. If you change the color in the Color Selector dialog box, the values in the RGB (Red, Green, Blue) and HSV (Hue, Saturation, Value) spinners in the General Parameters rollout change accordingly. You can also work in the opposite direction, changing the values in the spinners and seeing the effect in the Color Selector and the color swatch.

The Exclude button brings up the Exclude/Include dialog box, discussed earlier in this chapter, for limiting the illumination of the light only to specified objects. The Multiplier spinner adjusts the intensity of the light. It's a common mistake to overlight a scene by increasing a light's intensity too much.

The options in the Affect Surfaces section of the rollout are for specialized purposes. By default, a light generates both diffuse and specular illumination. In other words, a light illuminates the Diffuse color of the object and generates highlights if the object's material is defined to include specularity. On the other hand, the light should have no impact on the ambient illumination. You can disable the diffuse or specular elements for a light, so that a light either does not produce highlights or produces only highlights. By selecting the Ambient Only option, the light is used to illuminate only the Ambient color of the material.

The Contrast spinner increases the contrast between the diffuse and ambient regions of a surface. In Figure 13.11, a Sphere is lit from above with only a single Directional Light. A small but significant ambient factor was added to fill out the bottom half of the object. (The ambient factor, as explained earlier, is a combination of the ambient color of the material and the color of the ambient light set for the scene.) The render on the left side uses the default Contrast values. The render on the right uses a high Contrast value of 60. Note that the area lit by the light (the diffuse illumination region) is relatively brighter and the ambient region below is relatively darker.

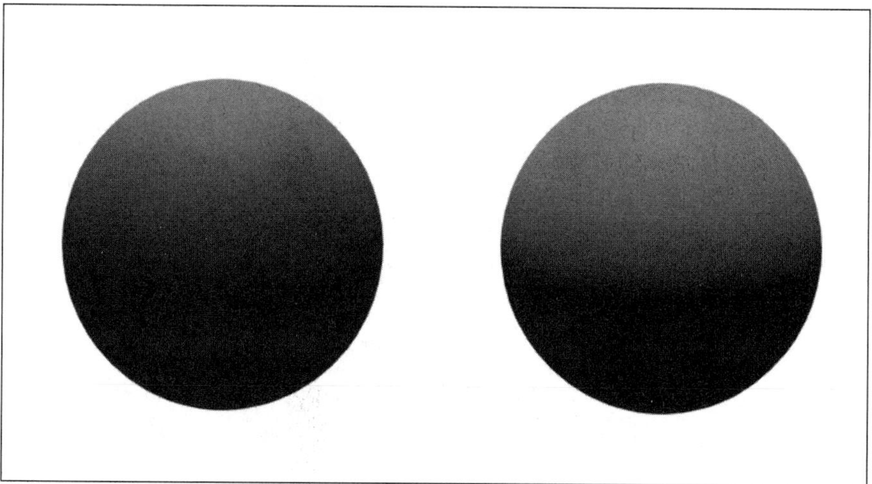

Figure 13.11
The Contrast spinner increases the contrast between diffuse and ambient regions. The Sphere is lit only with a single Directional Light from above, and the bottom of the object is filled out with an ambient factor. The render on the left uses the default Contrast value, and the render on the right uses a high value of 60.

The Directional Lights and Spot Lights have special rollouts to set additional parameters. The Directional Parameters rollout for a Directional Light determines whether the light extends in an infinite plane or whether it is limited to a defined region. By limiting the light to a defined region, the light becomes a kind of cylindrical or rectangular spotlight—something that doesn't exist in the real world. The Overshoot checkbox is deselected by default, but this may not be the most frequently desired choice. The vast majority of uses for Directional Lights require an infinite plane, and MAX users are often confused when they add a Directional Light that appears to do little or nothing. If you do not intend to use a Directional Light as a sort of spotlight, make sure that the Overshoot checkbox is selected.

The whole idea of *overshoot* assumes some defined region to which the light is restricted, and which is optionally ignored (or *overshot*). This defined region is either cylindrical or rectangular. The Circle option creates the cylindrical region. Figure 13.12 illustrates the effect of a cylindrical Directional Light. A Plane object is illuminated by only a single Directional Light, pointing down on the surface. On the left is a top Wireframe view. Two concentric circles represent the Directional Light. The outer circle is the limit of the cylinder of light and is controlled by the Falloff spinner in the rollout. The inner circle is the area of constant maximum intensity; it is controlled by the Hot Spot spinner. As you can see in the rendered image on the right, the light intensity falls off between the inner and the outer circles. The new Manipulate transform has a special link to light that is found elsewhere only when you're working with Inverse Kinematics. When you activate the transform, the Hot Spot and Falloff values of Spot Lights can be adjusted manually by clicking and dragging their representative circles directly. This technique eliminates the step of opening their rollouts or creating wiring schemes to adjust the lights easily.

The Spotlight Parameters rollout for Spot Lights provides precisely the same functions that the Directional Parameters rollout does for Directional Lights. Both these rollouts permit you to use

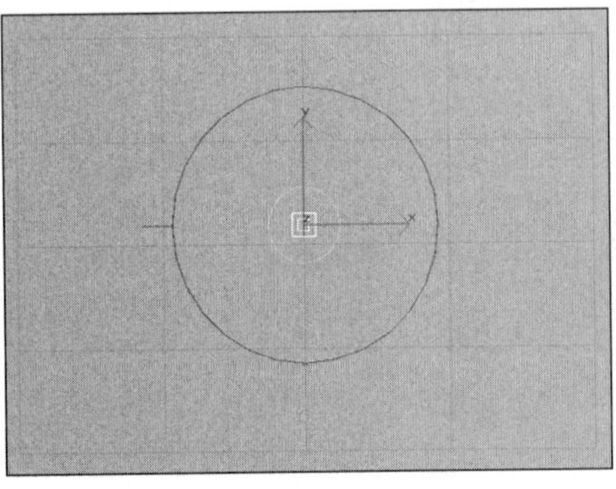

Figure 13.12
Using the Directional Light to create a cylindrical spotlight. A single Directional Light is pointing down on a flat surface. In the top Wireframe view, on the left, the outer concentric circle defines the limits of the cylinder of light. The inner circle defines the region of maximum intensity. The render on the right shows how the light intensity falls off between the inner and outer circles.

Figure 13.13
The scene from Figure 13.8 with an image projected from a shadow-casting Directional Light.

the light to project a Map. Figure 13.13 shows the scene from Figure 13.8, with the Clouds2.jpg file projected through a Directional Light and onto the scene. Oddly enough, an Omni Light can also be used as a projector, but this function is in a separate rollout.

Using the Attenuation Parameters Rollout

Lights in computer graphics differ from real-world lights because a CG light continues for an infinite distance, unless you instruct it otherwise. Objects that are far away from the light source are illuminated with the same intensity as those close by. The tools in the Attenuation Parameters rollout cause light intensity to decrease over distance. Figure 13.14 shows the Attenuation Parameters rollout with some values set.

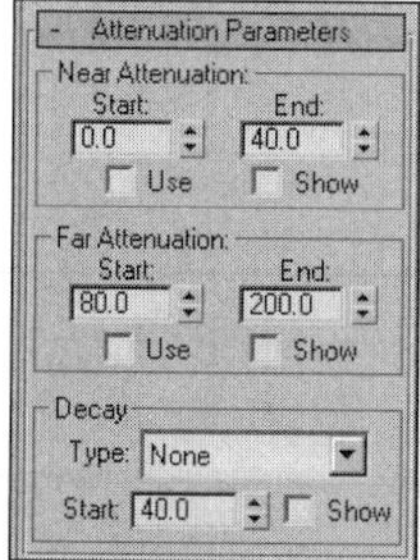

Figure 13.14
The Attenuation Parameters rollout, with some values set for use.

You can use two approaches to the problem. First, the Near and Far Attenuation sections of the rollout give you precise control. Everyone is confused at first by these controls because the whole idea of Near Attenuation seems peculiar. If Near Attenuation is used, the light actually increases in intensity as it leaves the light source. Far Attenuation is what you would naturally understand as light attenuation. The viewports display the Start and End limits that you set by using the spinners in the rollout, in a form appropriate to the type of light. Attenuation begins at the Start distance, meaning that the light begins to fall off. At the End distance, the light is completely attenuated.

Figure 13.15 illustrates a Far Attenuation setup. A top Wireframe view shows five objects, arranged in a diagonal line. A single Directional Light is placed in front, at the base of the arrow icon, and the scene contains no ambient illumination. The first line perpendicular to the light's direction is the Start distance and the second is the End distance. Thus, the light is at full intensity prior to the Start line and then falls off to the End line. A perspective render in Figure 13.16 shows the result. The first object is at full intensity, and the attenuation at the second object is not significant. The third, fourth, and fifth objects have diminishing amounts of illumination, with the last having almost none at all. The Chap13 Atten.max file used in Figures 13.15 and 13.16 is available on the CD-ROM.

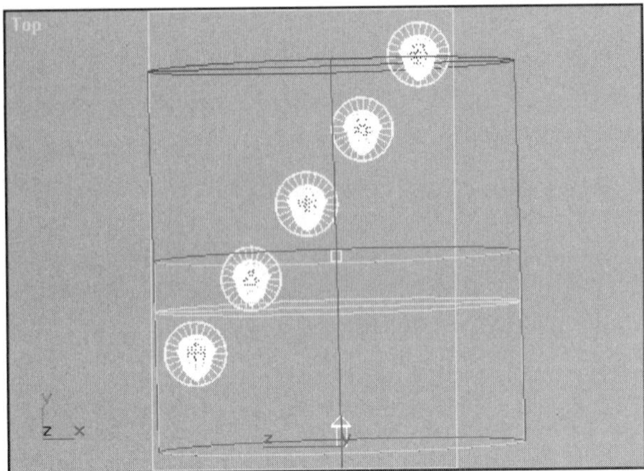

Figure 13.15
A Far Attenuation setup seen in a top Wireframe view. Five objects are arranged in a diagonal line and a single Directional Light is placed in front. The first line is the Start distance and the second is the End distance. Thus, the light will lose intensity beginning at the Start line and will fade out entirely by the End line.

Understanding Inverse Square Attenuation

Inverse square attenuation is based on the intensity of the illumination rapidly decreasing relative to the increase in distance. At one unit away from the light source, no illumination is lost. At two units away, only one-fourth (the inverse square of two) of the illumination is applied to an object. At four units distance, one-sixteenth of the illumination is applied; at eight units, one-sixty-fourth; and so forth.

Figure 13.16
A perspective render of the setup in Figure 13.15. The first two objects are fully, or nearly fully, illuminated. The attenuation decreases the illumination on the remaining objects until the farthest one is almost completely unilluminated.

An easier and more physically correct way to obtain attenuation is with the Decay tools at the bottom of the Attenuation Parameters rollout. By default, the Decay Type is set to None, and there is no attenuation. The Inverse option causes the light to fall off gradually (the inverse of the distance), and the Inverse Square option is a more accelerated decay. The Start spinner controls where the Decay begins. Use the Show option to see the Start distance in the viewports.

Shadows

It's important to understand that shadows are not the absence of light, but areas where light has been blocked. This may sound obvious, but it's very easy to forget. Computer graphics always refers to *shadow-casting*, whether with respect to lights or objects, and this term makes it sound like the shadow is being projected as a dark region. Rather, the light is being projected, and the shadows occur where the light is occluded. You don't create shadows—you create light and then obstruct its path in the scene. If a surface is already highly illuminated, a shadow cast on it is barely visible. Shadows don't make surfaces darker—they prevent them from becoming lighter than they would be otherwise.

As discussed earlier in this chapter, MAX has controls for determining whether a light casts shadows and whether each individual object casts or receives shadows. You can turn off shadows for the entire scene in the Render Scene dialog box, which speeds up the renders made to test elements other than shadows.

Basic Shadow Parameters

The toolset for shadows is not very complex. For the selected light in the Modify panel, the Shadow Parameters rollout allows you to choose between Shadow Map and Ray Traced Shadows. If the Shadow Map type is used, a Shadow Map Params rollout appears below, providing specialized parameters. If the Ray Traced Shadows option is used, a Ray Traced Shadow Params rollout appears. Figure 13.17 shows the rollouts for both shadow types, with shadows off and the default values.

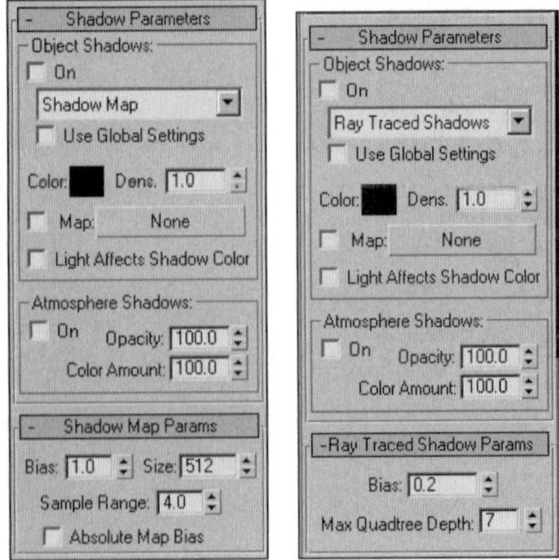

Figure 13.17
The rollouts for Shadow Map (*left*) and Ray Traced Shadows (*right*), with shadows off and the default values.

The Use Global Settings option is a kind of instancing. Every light in the scene for which this checkbox is selected shares some of the same settings, and changing any of these settings for any one of the lights changes it for all of them. This arrangement can be a great convenience when there are many lights in the scene. All the lights that share Global Settings share the same type (Shadow Map or Ray Traced Shadows), and they will share all the values in the Shadow Map or Ray Traced Shadows rollouts. For example, they will all share the same Bias value. They will not share parameters in the Shadow Parameters rollout (except for the shadow type), and thus they can have different settings for color and density. When you deselect the Use Global Settings checkbox, independent control of the light returns for all parameters.

Overshoot Doesn't Affect Shadows

Spot Lights and Directional Lights are confined to their Falloff region, unless the Overshoot checkbox is selected. Overshoot turns a Directional Light into an infinite plane of light and turns a Spot Light into the equivalent of an Omni Light. The same is not true for shadows, however. Even if the Overshoot checkbox is selected, shadows are not cast for regions outside the Falloff. This lack of shadows can be very confusing, especially for Directional Lights. You often have to expand the Falloff to cast the necessary shadows, even if Overshoot is selected.

The color of a shadow should nearly always be black, but you can change it for special effects. The color of the light can also be used to influence the color of the shadow. The Density control is extremely important. When the value is at the default of 1.0, the light is completely occluded. Lesser values make the shadow more transparent, softening its effect. A separate section of the rollout provides for shadows to be cast by atmospheric effects, such as fog.

Choosing between Shadow Maps and Ray Traced Shadows

Ray tracing produces extremely accurate shadows that have very sharp edges. Shadow maps can produce shadows with much softer edges, but they can also yield undesirable artifacts. In interior scenes, the large amount of global illumination reflecting off the wall softens shadows. In outdoor scenes, the Sun is usually the only light source, and reflected illumination that might soften shadows is typically absent (unless the scene represents a cloudy day). Thus, as a general rule, the Ray Traced Shadows type is used for outdoor scenes, and the Shadow Map type is used for indoor scenes.

Shadow Map Parameters

Working with shadow maps can be frustrating. It may seem that every time you try to correct one thing, something else goes wrong. The logic of the situation runs like this: A shadow map is computed at a certain resolution. The default map size is 512×512 pixels, as you can see in the Size spinner. Increasing the size of the map increases its resolution. The main purpose of a shadow map is to create soft shadows, however, and increasing the resolution makes the map sharper. A low-resolution map is softer, but it can generate flaws. A higher-resolution map reduces these artifacts, but it may make the shadow too sharp. The Sample Range affects the softness of the shadows, but increasing this value can produce artifacts in the same way as an insufficient map size.

Let's walk through a series of images to demonstrate the kind of balancing act that is typical when you use shadow maps. The scene consists of a room with a Sphere and a tall, thin Cylinder. A single Directional Light is used. Figure 13.18 shows the results of using the Shadow Map default values. Thin, dark lines appear where the walls meet—lines that did not exist before the shadow map was turned on. The shadow cast by the Sphere is soft, but not soft enough for the environment. The shadow cast by the Cylinder is unrealistically hard and does not meet the base of the object on the floor.

Increasing the Sample Range from 4 to 10 softens the shadow from the ball quite well, but the shadows where the walls meet grow far worse. The shadow from the Cylinder broadens without blurring, producing an even worse result than the previous version. Figure 13.19 illustrates this poor result.

To get rid of those horrible artifacts on the walls, the floor polygons were detached from the rest of the room to create a separate object. That way, the walls (but not the floor) could be turned off to shadows by using the Object Properties dialog box. Adjusting the Bias value to 0 brings the shadow from the Cylinder back in contact with the object itself. Take a look at Figure 13.20.

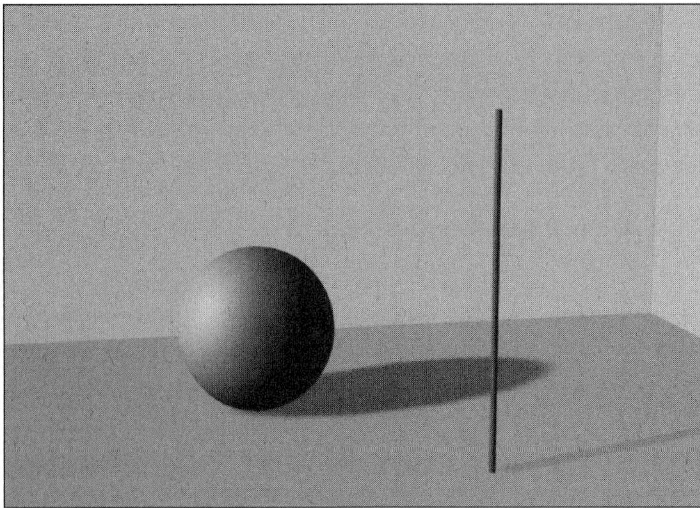

Figure 13.18
An interior scene, with a single Directional Light using the default Shadow Map parameters. Thin, dark shadow lines appear where the walls meet. The shadow cast by the ball is not soft enough for the environment. The shadow cast by the Cylinder is unrealistically hard, and it does not touch the base of the object on the floor.

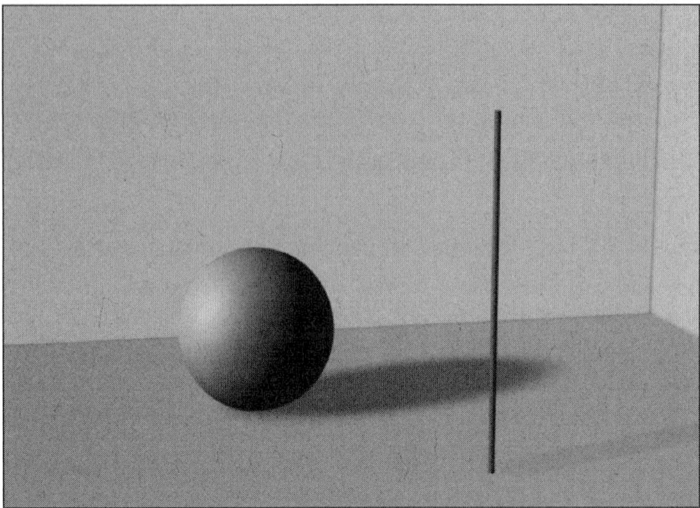

Figure 13.19
The same as Figure 13.18, but with the Sample Range increased from 4 to 10. The shadow cast by the Sphere is pleasingly softer, but the shadow lines where the walls meet have grown much darker and more noticeable. The shadow from the Cylinder broadens without blurring.

In Figure 13.21, the Map Size is increased from 512 to 1024. The increased resolution essentially offsets the softening quality that is achieved by increasing the Sample Range. The result is better for the Cylinder, because even a sharper shadow is preferable to the unrealistically broad one.

Figure 13.20
The same as Figure 13.19, but with the walls separated from the floor at the object level to eliminate shadows from the walls alone. This step eliminates the shadow artifacts at the edges. The Bias is adjusted to bring the shadow of the Cylinder into contact with the object on the floor.

Figure 13.21
The same as Figure 13.20, but with the Map Size increased from 512 to 1024. The increased resolution effectively cancels out the softening achieved by increasing the Sample Range, but the shadow from the Cylinder is more acceptable.

Figure 13.22
The same as Figure 13.21, but with the shadow Density decreased from 1.0 to 0.7. The paler shadows feel softer and the flaws are less noticeable.

A possible compromise might be to decrease the Density of the shadows from 1.0 to 0.7. The paler shadow seems softer and the flaws are less noticeable. Figure 13.22 shows the result.

Ray Tracing Parameters

You have a lot of room to play with ray-traced shadows. Increasing the Max Quadtree Depth above the default value of 7 produces greater accuracy (and longer render times), but you'll rarely need to do this. On the other hand, you'll often have to play with the Bias spinner. Bias is typically used as it was earlier in this chapter—to move the shadow into alignment with the shadow-casting object—but Bias adjustment also solves some other problems.

Figure 13.23 shows the scene you've been seeing, but with the Ray Traced Shadows type used instead of Shadow Map. The shadows are very precise. They are much too sharp for most indoor illumination, and this is especially noticeable with the ball. The ray tracing generated some small artifacts where the walls meet. They are not as extreme as in the Shadow Map versions, but they are still noticeable.

Adjusting the Bias up to 0.5 eliminates these artifacts, as you can see in Figure 13.24. Fortunately, this increase in Bias is not large enough to pull the shadows away from the objects on the floor.

Using Shadows with Translucent Materials

When you're using Shadow Map shadows, the point at which the light rays are interrupted is calculated; everything beyond that point ceases to be illuminated, regardless of the type of material used. For example: If a stained glass window is in a scene, and a light shines through it, the shadow on the ground will not retain any of the color contained in the glass. Ray Traced Shadows, on the other hand, calculate and retain the glass's colors and project them onto other surfaces.

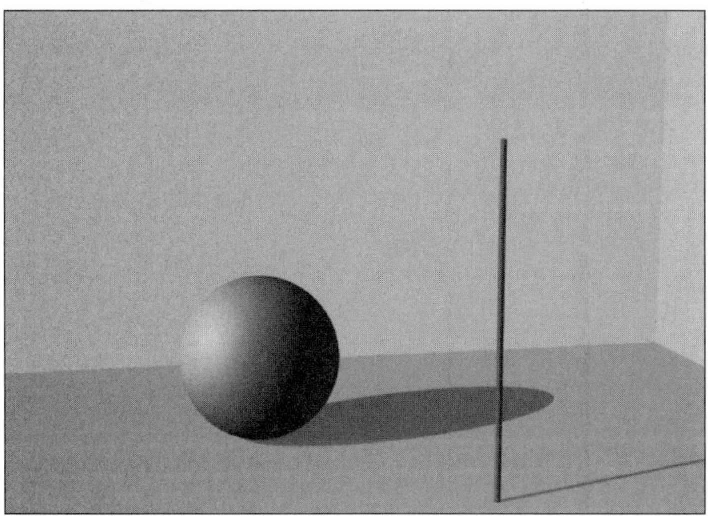

Figure 13.23
Using the Ray Traced Shadows type produces very sharp and accurate shadows—much too sharp for this indoor scene. Note the small artifacts where the walls meet. These are not nearly as extreme as in the Shadow Map example, but they are still irritating.

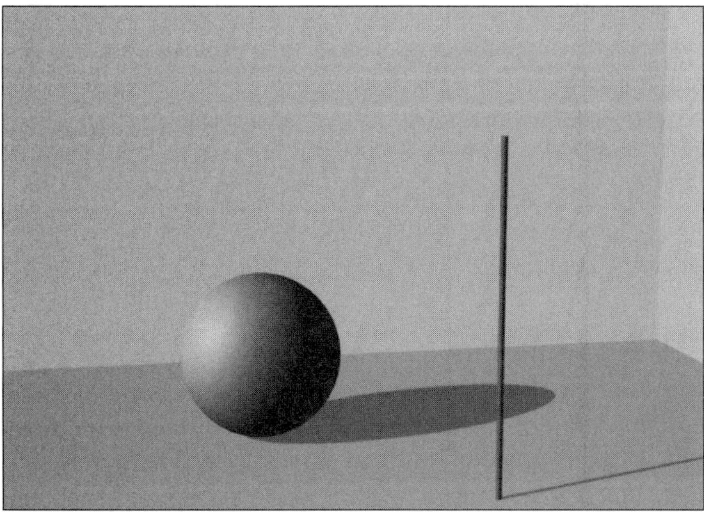

Figure 13.24
The same as Figure 13.23, but with Bias increased to 0.5 to eliminate the artifacts. This adjustment is not enough to pull the shadows away from the objects on the floor.

Using the Light Lister

If you have more than a couple of lights in a scene, managing the lighting can become a nightmare. 3ds max 4 has revamped the interface of the Light Lister dialog box, which is available from the Tools drop-down menu. Figure 13.25 shows the dialog box, with both rollouts expanded, for a scene containing four lights.

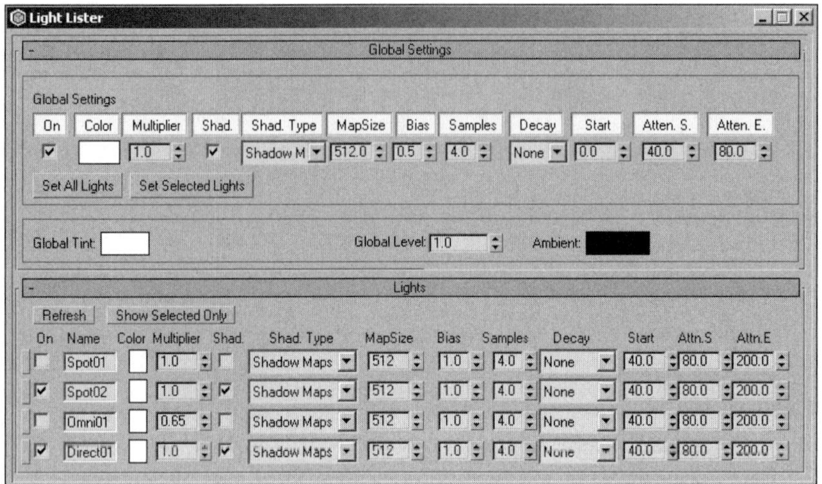

Figure 13.25
The Light Lister dialog box for a scene with four lights.

The Lights rollout lists all the lights and permits you to change the most important parameters without using the Modify panel. The checkbox for each light turns it on and off. Clicking on the gray box to the left selects the light and brings it up in the Modify panel. The Global Settings rollout is divided into two sections. The upper section allows you to define parameters to apply to all the lights in the scene. Once they are set, you use the Set All Lights or Set Selected Lights button to transfer the values to the individual lights. The lower section is of much more general value. You can apply a color tint and a level to all the lights in the scene. This action does not replace the existing values; it is a separate adjustment layer. You can also set the ambient light for the scene in this section. These three controls are also available in the Environment dialog box from the Rendering menu.

Using the Sunlight System

3ds max 4 provides a system for creating a Directional Light that represents the Sun and that maintains control based on the assigned time of day and location. The following exercise will demonstrate how to use and modify a light created with the Sunlight system. Follow these steps:

1. Create a large, flat Box in the Top viewport that will represent the ground.
2. From the Create|Systems menu, choose Sunlight. Click and drag to place and size the Compass Rose, which is also the target of the Free Directional Light representing the Sun. Drag a second time to set the distance from the Rose to the light. Figure 13.26 shows a typical Sunlight system setup.
3. Use the Rotate transform to orient the North arrow of the Compass Rose to the North direction in your scene. The Sun moves correspondingly.

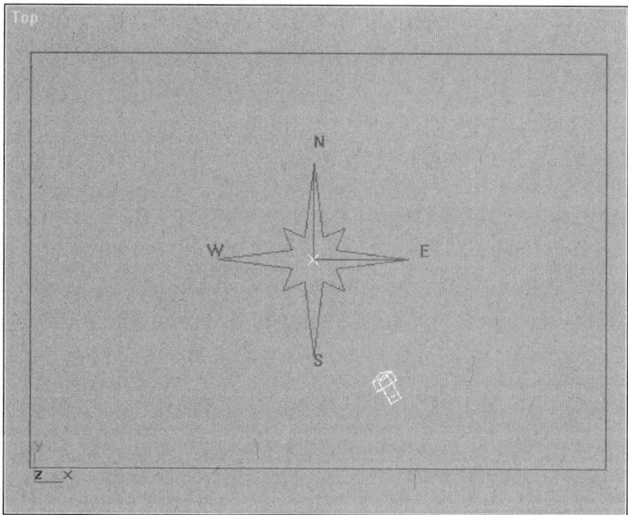

Figure 13.26.
A typical Sunlight system arrangement with the Compass Rose determining the orientation of the Free Directional Light.

4. To set the time of day and location, select the light and then click on the Motion tab of the Command Panel. In the Time group, you set the time and date the scene represents. In the Location group, click on the Get Location button to open the Geographic Location dialog box shown in Figure 13.27. Select a map from the Map drop-down list and a city from the list to the left. A magenta cross appears over the location selected in the map image. Click on the OK button to apply the parameters and orient the light to the location of the sun at the specified date and time for the location selected.

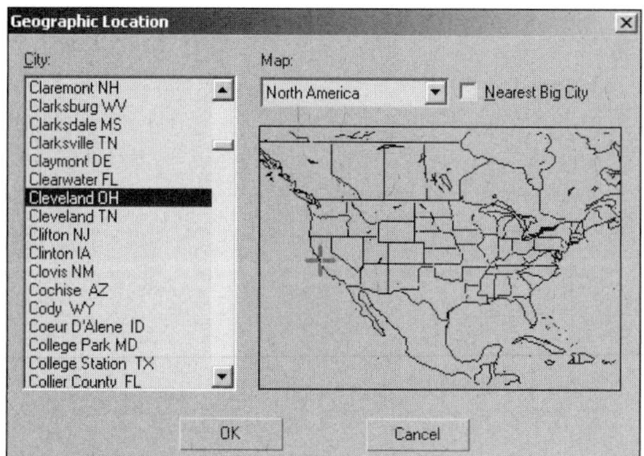

Figure 13.27
The Geographic Location dialog box, where you set the location of the scene.

The Sunlight system is an invaluable tool for accurate architectural visualization and studies of shadow patterns. Used in an animated scene, it can show the time-lapse effect of the Sun on the scene's objects.

Moving On

In this chapter, you learned about lighting in computer graphics and about MAX's particular lighting toolset. Lighting in 3D applications such as MAX differs fundamentally from real-world lighting. Most important is the lack of global illumination. Illumination in MAX is not reflected off walls and other surfaces, so it is necessary to work creatively to create the illusion of such reflected light.

You learned about the three light types in MAX and their specific parameters. You also learned about shadows, particularly about the choice between shadow mapping and ray tracing of shadows.

The next chapter turns to cameras and compares the two types of cameras—Free Cameras and Target Cameras (similar to Free and Target Spot Lights)—and their parameters. You'll work through exercises that will teach you how to manipulate cameras, either by transforming them directly or by using special camera-navigation tools.

Chapter 14
Cameras

If the viewpoint is to be animated, you need to create a *camera*. And if you wish to work with multiple viewpoints in the scene, in order to cut from one to another you need more than one camera. Even where you don't absolutely need a camera, it can be useful. For example, you can set up camera locations, and then use a Perspective window (or another camera) to navigate freely through the scene.

3ds max 4 uses two kinds of camera: Free Cameras and Target Cameras. Just as with lights, a Target Camera automatically comes with a nonrendering Target object that is used to aim the camera. The Target Camera is given a LookAt controller (controllers are covered in Chapter 18) that keeps it pointed toward the Target object, and thus you rotate the camera by moving the Target. In contrast, a Free Camera comes without a Target object and is rotated using the Rotate transform, usually with the Local coordinate system active. In the vast majority of cases, it's much easier to manage a Target Camera, which has the additional feature of a Target object that you can animate separately.

When you create a camera, it becomes available as a viewport option. When you activate a camera viewport, special navigation options replace the standard options at the bottom-right corner of the MAX screen. A collection of parameters for each camera also appear in the Modify panel. As you'll see in this chapter, some overlap exists between these parameters and the camera navigation tools.

The best way to understand the MAX camera toolset is to walk though an exercise. You'll work on the same example throughout most of this chapter.

Creating and Transforming Target Cameras

Begin the exercise as follows:

1. Create a Sphere object near the origin. Begin to create a Target Camera by choosing Create| Cameras in the Command panel; then, in the Top viewport, click and drag to create and direct the camera. Click in front of the object to place the camera, and then drag toward the Sphere and release to lay down the Target object right in the middle of the Sphere. With the camera selected, switch to the Local coordinate system. Your Top viewport should look something like Figure 14.1.

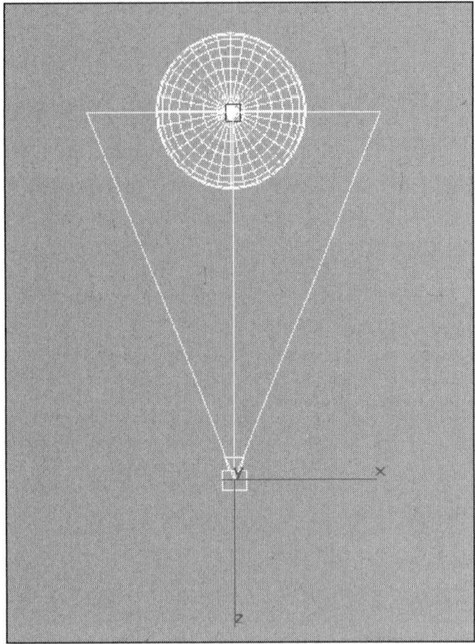

Figure 14.1
A top view showing a Sphere and a Target Camera pointing at it. The camera is created and directed by clicking to establish the location of the camera and then dragging to establish the location of the Target. The Target Camera is selected and is using the Local coordinate system. Note that it is pointing in its Local negative Z-direction.

2. Take a moment to examine your scene or the scene in Figure 14.1. The small square in the middle of the Sphere is the Target. The line connecting the Target to the Target Camera is called the *Target Line*, and the angular structure defining the field of view is called the *Camera Cone*. With the Target Camera selected and using Local coordinates, you can see that the Target Camera is looking down its Local negative Z-axis.

3. Move the Target Camera to understand the LookAt concept. No matter where you move it, the Local Z-axis is always in line with the Target object. In effect, moving the Target Camera causes it to orbit the Target, although you can also move the Target Camera closer to (or farther away from) the Target. Figure 14.2 shows the Target Camera moved around the Target and closer to it.

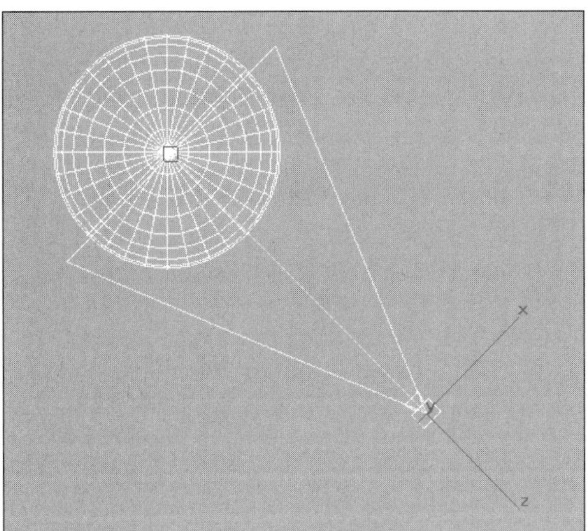

Figure 14.2
The same as Figure 14.1, but with the Target Camera moved around the Target and closer to it. Note how the Local Z-axis remains oriented to the Target object.

4. Select the Target object and move it to rotate the Target Camera away from the Sphere. You'll probably need to use the Select Objects dialog box (press the H key) to select the Target. Notice that the distance of the Target object from the Target Camera is irrelevant—only the direction of the Target matters. Your Top viewport should look something like Figure 14.3.

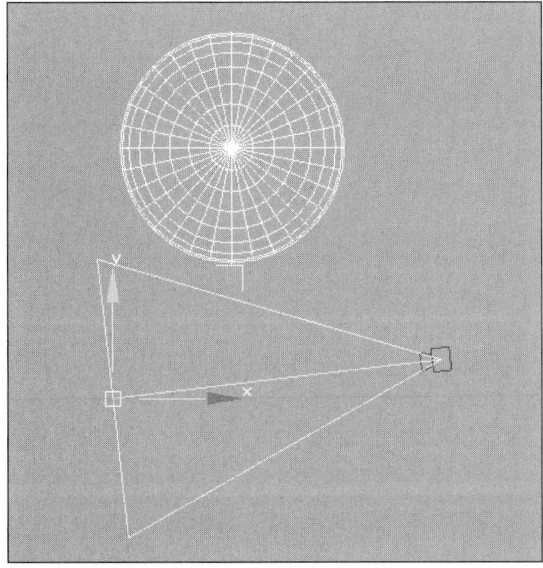

Figure 14.3
The same as Figure 14.2, but with the Target object moved to rotate the Target Camera off the Sphere. The distance between the Target and the Target Camera doesn't matter.

Note: *Like any other objects in MAX, cameras and Targets should have descriptive names so they can be selected quickly. Changing a camera's name will automatically change the name of its associated Target to the same name with .Target appended to it. Changing the name of the Target object, however, has no effect on the camera's name.*

5. With the Target still selected, use the Ctrl key to add the Target Camera to the selection. (A quick method of selecting both the Target and the camera is to pick directly on the Target Line.) Notice how the camera and Target have different Local coordinate systems. This is one time when the View or World coordinate system is preferable and when it yields the most predictable results. Then switch to the View coordinate system. Moving the Target Camera and its Target together translates the Target Camera without affecting its rotation. Move the two objects so that the Sphere is back within the Camera Cone, as in Figure 14.4.

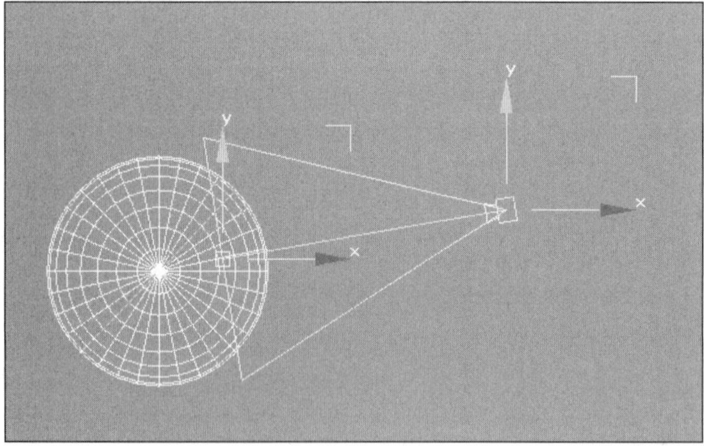

Figure 14.4
Moving the Target Camera and its Target as a single unit moves the camera without rotating it. This figure shows the Target Camera and the Target from Figure 14.3 moved together until the Sphere is back within the Camera Cone.

Creating and Transforming Free Cameras

You can add a Free Camera to the scene and compare it to the Target Camera. A Free Camera is not only harder to transform, it's also harder to position and direct in the first place. Rotating a Free Camera is like moving the Target with a Target Camera, but it can be more difficult because you typically are trying to point the camera at an object. By aligning a Target to an object, you automatically cause a Target Camera to rotate correctly.

Free Cameras are used most often when the camera is animated and the view is not linked to a specific object. A typical scene might be an architectural fly-through, the view from a cockpit, or a camera weaving through a serpentine tunnel. In these situations, moving both the camera and the Target in a synchronized fashion to get a smooth result would be very difficult.

Just like the Target Camera, the Free Camera points down its Local Z-axis. It uses no Target object or Target Line, however. (The Target Line is a great help in seeing where a camera is pointed, especially in a complex scene.) The Camera Cone remains, however, to indicate the field of view.

To continue the exercise, follow these steps:

1. Hide the Target Camera and Target objects in your scene and click on the Free Camera button. Before you click in a viewport to place the Free Camera in the scene, take a moment to think. The Free Camera's Local Z-axis will point in the direction of the viewport in which you click. This orientation can be confusing, so try to position the Free Camera just as you did the Target Camera—in front of the Sphere and pointing toward the origin. If you use the Top viewport and click on the right location, the Free Camera is pointing downward, in the negative Z-direction in World space. That means you have to rotate it. On the other hand, if you click in the Front viewport, the Free Camera is pointed in the correct direction, but it is located in the wrong place. It's generally easier to move an object than to rotate it, so this second choice is preferable. Figure 14.5 shows a Top viewport of a Free Camera created in the Front viewport and then moved to the desired location.

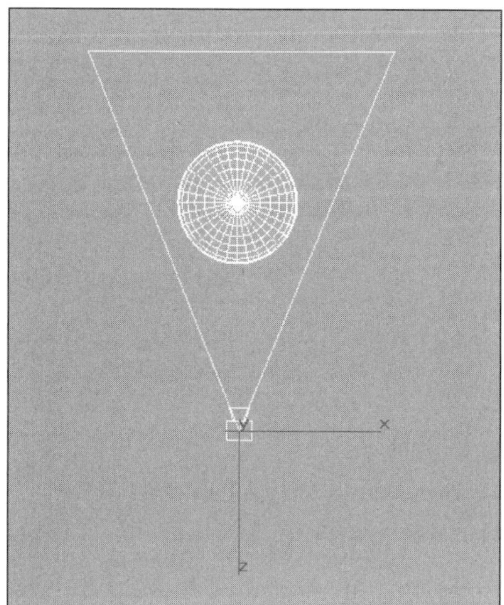

Figure 14.5
A Top viewport showing a Free Camera pointed toward a Sphere. The selected Free Camera is shown using its Local coordinate system, so you can see that (like the Target Camera) it points in its Local negative Z-direction. The view contains no Target object or Target Line, but there still is a Camera Cone.

2. Orbiting the Free Camera around the object takes two steps: First you move it, and then you rotate it. You may find it hard to do so in a way that keeps the focus on a constant point. Give it a try. When you finish, your Top viewport might look like Figure 14.6. As you can see, rotating was much easier with the Target Camera.

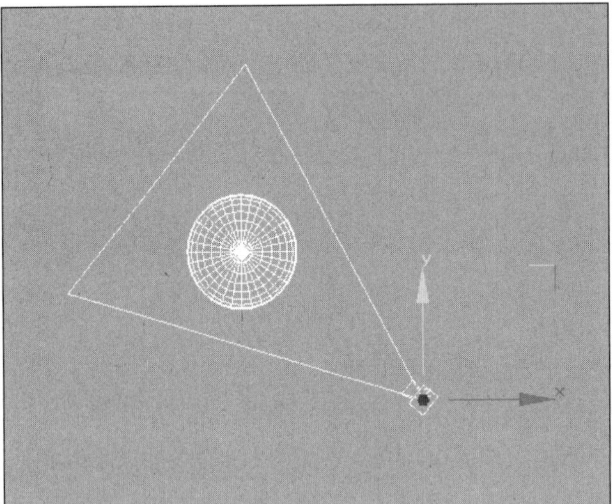

Figure 14.6
The same as Figure 14.5, but the Free Camera is orbited around the Sphere. This technique requires separate move-and-rotate steps, which can be difficult to do precisely. With a Target Camera, this result is achieved easily in a single intuitive step by simply moving the camera.

3. Move the Free Camera without rotating it, and you get the same result as when you move a Target Camera along with its Target. This is the only technique that's easier to do with a Free Camera than with a Target Camera.

Camera Parameters

You can set camera parameters when you create a camera, but you'll generally work in the Modify panel with the camera selected. Figure 14.7 shows the parameters for the Free Camera that was shown in Figure 14.6.

Converting between Camera Types

Note the Target Distance spinner at the bottom of the Parameters rollout in Figure 14.7. To figure out what this setting means, let's pick up the exercise where we left off:

1. Change the value of the Target Distance spinner and watch the Camera Cone expand outward or contract inward.

2. Adjust the value so that the line marking the end of the Camera Cone cuts right through the center of the Sphere.

3. Convert the Free Camera to a Target Camera by changing the option in the Type drop-down list.

You now have a Target Camera with the Target at the distance you set in the Target Distance spinner—meaning at the end of the Camera Cone. These settings are a fantastic convenience. Of course, you can always change a Target Camera to a Free Camera as well.

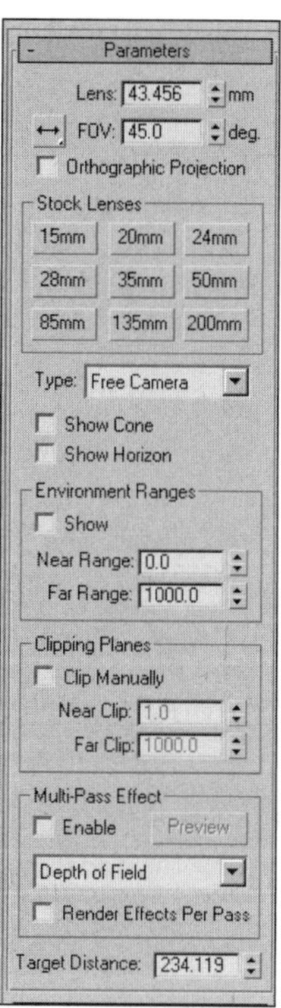

Figure 14.7
The Parameters rollout for the Free Camera shown in Figure 14.6 (from the Modify panel).

Adjusting Field-of-View

All of the parameters on the Parameters rollout above the Type choice affect a single thing. With a real camera, the length of the lens (measured in millimeters) determines the angle constituting the field-of-view (FOV). Shorter lenses produce wider fields, and longer lenses produce narrower fields. In the Modify panel, you can change the length of the lens and watch the FOV spinner change value, or you can change the FOV value and watch the Lens spinner change—they're interdependent. The buttons allow you to grab common stock lens lengths without bothering with the spinners.

To see how these settings work in the ongoing exercise, experiment with the Lens and FOV parameters. As you change values, the angle of the Camera Cone changes on the screen. Figure 14.8 shows the Free Camera from Figure 14.6 (converted to a Target Camera) using the stock 24mm lens. This lens corresponds to a 73.74–degree horizontal angle for the field-of-view.

Clipping Planes

Clipping planes define the depth for which the camera is active. In most cases, you want the camera to capture everything in its field-of-view, no matter how close or far away. Sometimes, however, it makes sense to narrow the clipping region—typically, when you don't want the renderer to waste time with distant objects that are too small to be seen. The Environment

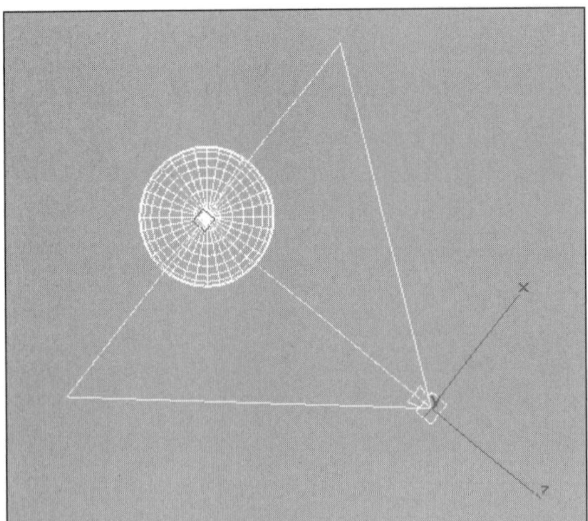

Figure 14.8
The Free Camera from Figure 14.6 is converted into a Target Camera and assigned a 24mm lens. This lens creates a very wide field-of-view angle, as can be seen from the shape of the Camera Cone.

Ranges controls in the Modify panel are just like the Clipping Planes controls, but they apply to atmospheric effects rather than to geometry.

Continuing with the exercise will show you how to adjust the camera's clipping planes. In the Parameters rollout, select the Clip Manually checkbox and adjust the spinners for the clipping planes. The planes are visible in the viewports. Set them so that the Near Clip plane is just in front of the Sphere and the Far Clip plane is just behind it. A Top viewport should look like Figure 14.9.

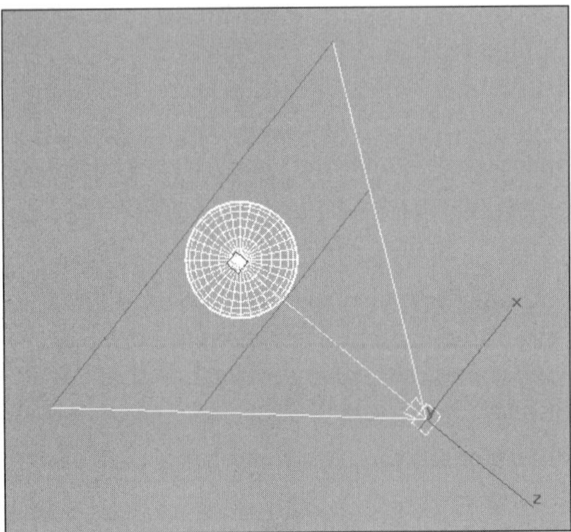

Figure 14.9
Similar to Figure 14.8, but with clipping planes set just before and behind the Sphere. In a view through this camera, objects created in front of or behind the Sphere are not visible.

In a view through this camera, any objects created in front of or behind the Sphere would not be visible. Deselect the Clip Manually checkbox before you continue this exercise.

Camera Viewports and Navigation

Now, let's look through the camera for which you've been creating settings:

1. Pick a viewport and right-click on its name to get to the Views menu. The cameras in the scene are listed. Make sure that you pick the correct one. If you have followed this exercise and created two cameras (one hidden), the visible one is named Camera02. Pick this camera for the viewport.

2. When the camera viewport is active, you'll notice some new navigation tools in the bottom-right corner of the MAX screen. Sometimes, it's easier to adjust a camera from a viewport in which you can see the camera object, and sometimes it's easier to work while looking directly through the camera. You've already explored the former approach, so try navigating through camera view. Make sure that you have a Top viewport next to your camera viewport for easy comparison. Also make sure that the Show Cone checkbox is selected in the camera's Modify panel; that way, the cone remains visible if you lose the selection of the camera.

Dollying the Camera

In filmmaking, moving a camera toward the object on which it's focused is called *dollying* the camera. Using the MAX Dolly Camera tool, you can dolly only the Target, or dolly both the camera and the Target. If you use a Free Camera instead of a Target Camera, you have only the Dolly Camera option. Because a Free Camera has no Target, the Dolly Camera tool moves the Free Camera along its Local Z-axis.

To see the effect of using the dollying feature in MAX, continue the exercise with these steps:

1. Make sure that you're in the camera viewport. The navigation icon with the up and down arrows is the Dolly Camera button. Click on this button to activate it, and drag in the camera viewport. The object grows bigger or smaller, and you can see the camera moving in the Top viewport. Take a look at Figure 14.10.

2. Click on the Dolly Camera button again to see the other options, as specified earlier.

Using the Field-Of-View Tool

The Field-Of-View tool does the same thing for the camera viewport that it does for a Perspective viewport. To see how it applies to the current exercise, activate the Field-Of-View button (the angle icon) and drag in the camera viewport to narrow the field-of-view quite a bit. You see the Camera Cone contract in the Top viewport, and, if the camera is selected, you can see the Lens and FOV values change in the Modify panel. Your screen should look something like Figure 14.11. This is the true zoom, as opposed to the dolly.

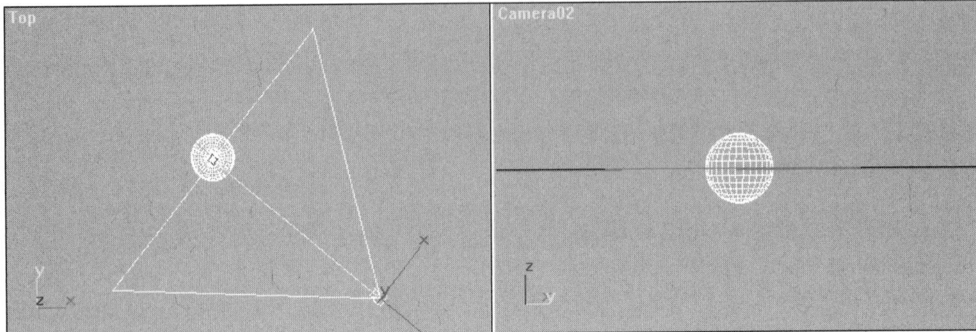

Figure 14.10
The same as Figure 14.9, but with the Clip Manually checkbox deselected and the camera moved away from the object using the Dolly Camera tool, which is available when a camera viewport is active. The Top viewport shows the new position of the camera, and the Camera02 viewport shows the result.

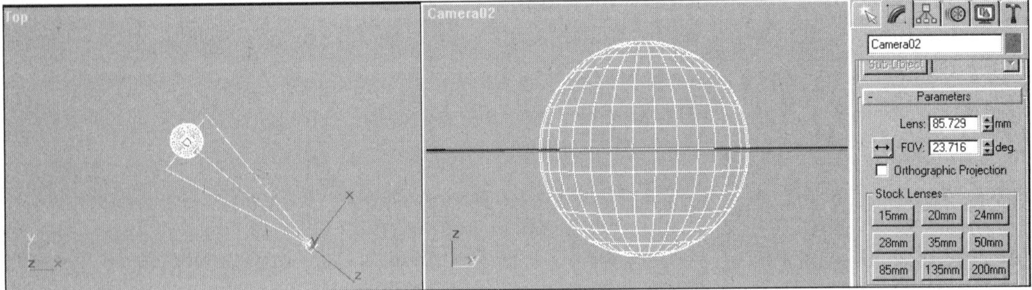

Figure 14.11
The same as Figure 14.10, but with the FOV angle decreased to zoom in on the object. Compare the Camera Cone in the Top viewport with the image through the Camera02 viewport. The values in the Modify panel indicate that you have the equivalent of about an 85mm lens. This is a true zoom, as opposed to dollying the camera.

Using the Perspective Tool

Dollying the camera and zooming a lens (changing the field-of-view angle) have very different effects on perspective. A wide field-of view creates a strong perspective distortion, called *perspective flare*. A fish-eye lens provides the most extreme example. The narrow angle associated with a telephoto lens has minimal distortion. In order to correct (or sometimes increase) perspective flare, you often have to change your field-of-view angle and then dolly the camera to compensate while maintaining your scene composition. The Perspective tool performs these steps automatically.

Continuing the exercise, activate the Perspective tool (the distorted box icon). As you drag in the Camera02 viewport, look at the Top viewport and at the values in the Modify panel. Notice that the camera is being dollied and the field-of view angle is changing at the same time. Back in the Camera02 viewport, notice that the Sphere isn't getting any bigger or smaller. As you drag with the Perspective tool, watch the lines on the Sphere surface carefully. Figure 14.12

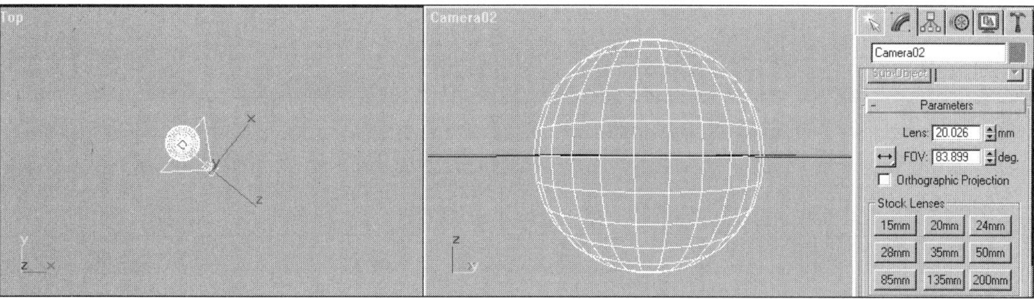

Figure 14.12

The same as Figure 14.11, but with the Perspective tool used to increase perspective flare. The field-of-view angle is greatly increased, but the camera is automatically dollied in to compensate. The result in the camera view is a change in the amount of perspective distortion without changing the composition of the frame.

illustrates a change in perspective using this tool. The camera is moved much closer to the Sphere, but the field-of-view angle is correspondingly increased. The Sphere takes up the same amount of space in the camera view, but the perspective flare is very strong.

Rolling the Camera

The Roll Camera tool is immediately to the right of the Perspective icon. Dragging in the camera viewport rotates the camera around its Local Z-axis. Rolling a camera generally makes sense only if the camera is animated; the same effect is more commonly achieved by banking the camera as it follows a curved animation path.

Let's try the Roll Camera tool, as well as the Dolly and Roll spinners, on your Sphere:

1. Adjust the perspective to something less distorted than what you saw in Figure 14.12. Activate the Roll Camera tool and drag in the camera viewport. Take a look at Figure 14.13. The rotation of the viewing axis results in a slanted horizon line in the camera viewport and is evident from the Camera Cone seen in a Front viewport.

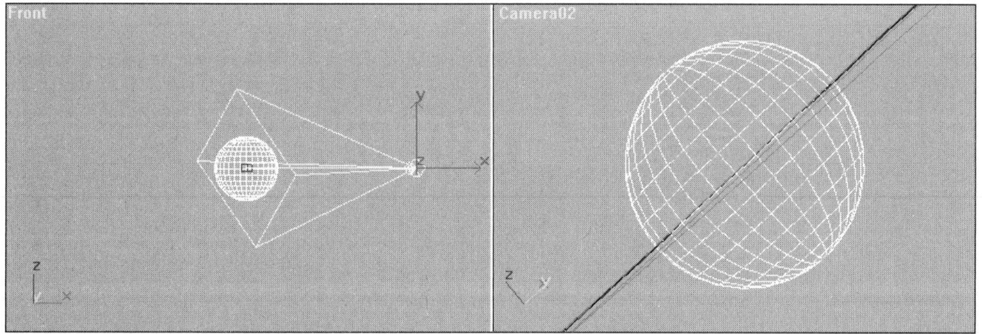

Figure 14.13

Rolling the camera causes it to rotate around its Local Z-axis. The rotation of the viewing axis results in a slanted horizon line in the Camera02 viewport at right. The Front viewport at left shows the rotation of the Camera Cone.

2. To eliminate the roll, take a moment to check out a precision alternative to dragging in the viewport. In the Main toolbar (and with the Target Camera selected), activate the Rotate transform, and right-click on that button to bring up the Rotate Transform Type-In dialog box. Notice that Dolly and Roll spinners are added to the dialog box. Experiment with these spinners to see how easy they are to use, and then set the Roll value to 0. The Dolly and Roll controls are available from the Move and Scale Transform Type-In dialog boxes, as well.

Trucking the Camera

The button with the hand icon is called the Pan tool when used with any viewport other than a camera viewport. With a camera viewport active, this same button becomes the Truck Camera tool, which performs the same function as the Pan tool in a regular Perspective viewport. *Trucking* means moving a camera in its Local XY plane. Dragging vertically in the camera viewport trucks in the camera's Local Y-direction, and dragging horizontally trucks in the Local X-direction. With a Target Camera, trucking moves the Target Camera and the Target object together. With a Free Camera, the Truck Camera tool moves the camera alone in the plane perpendicular to its Local Z-axis (the Local XY plane).

To experiment with trucking the camera in the current exercise, make sure the camera viewport is active so you can access the camera navigation tools. Figure 14.14 shows the result of a truck operation that moved the Target away from the Sphere and moved the Target Camera along a parallel path. Compare the Camera02 viewport with the Top viewport at left. As you truck the camera, notice how it moves in the direction parallel to the endline of the Camera Cone.

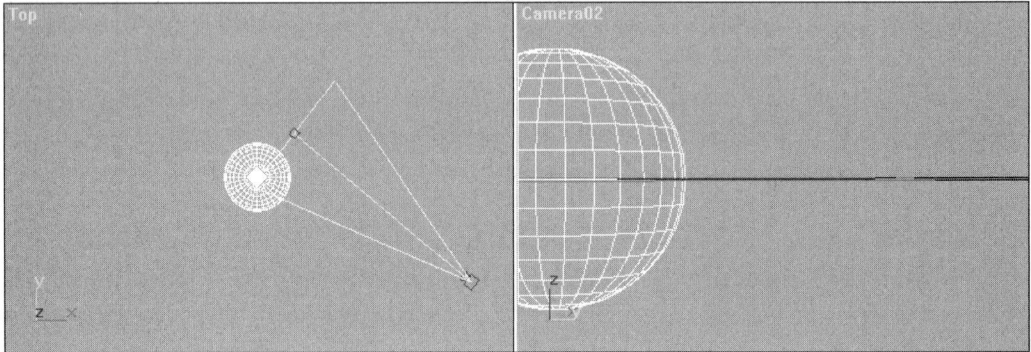

Figure 14.14
Trucking a camera moves it in its Local XY plane—the plane perpendicular to its viewing axis. In this figure, trucking the Target Camera moves both the Target Camera and its Target object along parallel paths. The Target object is no longer in the center of the Sphere, as you can see in the Top viewport at left, producing the same result.

Experiment with all these concepts before moving on. Mastering this kind of thinking brings you closer to the mentality and practice of conventional filmmaking.

Orbiting the Camera

The final pair of camera navigation tools is found in the button to the right of the Truck Camera tool. The default icon looks like a tiny version of the planet Saturn: This is the Orbit Camera tool. With a Target Camera, the camera orbits its Target object while remaining pointed toward it. The Orbit Camera tool works the same way with a Free Camera. Doesn't the Orbit Camera necessarily require a Target object to orbit the camera around? Yes, it does. But a Free Camera has an implicit Target object, which is why you can convert freely between the two camera types. This implicit Target is located where the Local Z-axis of the camera intersects the endline of the Camera Cone, and it is the location used at the center of rotation when orbiting the Free Camera.

Let's experiment with this tool in the ongoing exercise:

1. Truck the Target Camera back until the Target object is in the center of the Sphere. Activate the Orbit Camera tool and drag in the camera viewport. Keep an eye on the other viewport to see what the camera is doing. The Target Camera moves, and the Target object stays fixed. Note that the Target Distance (the distance between the Target Camera and the Target object) at the bottom of the camera panel remains constant. Figure 14.15 shows the scene with the Target Camera orbited so that it points downward on the Sphere and from the opposite direction. The Perspective viewport at left helps in understanding the new location and orientation of the Target Camera.

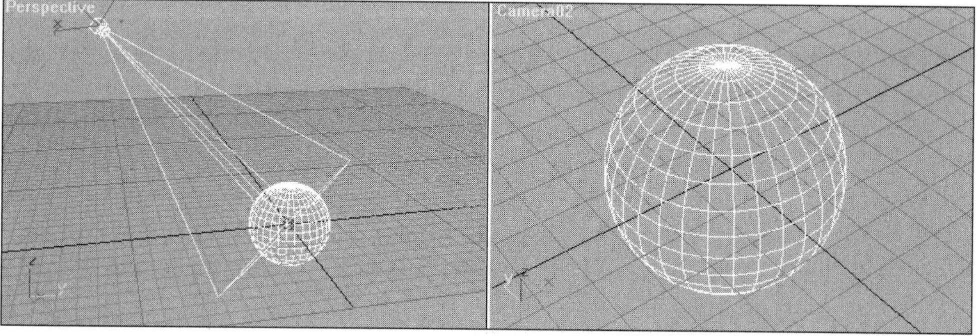

Figure 14.15
Orbiting a Target Camera moves it around its Target object while maintaining a fixed distance. The Target object does not move. The Target Camera is now orbited so that it points at the Target (and therefore the Sphere) from above and from the opposite direction. The Perspective viewport at left helps to visualize the new location and orientation of the Target Camera.

2. Orbit to get the Target Camera back straight in front of the Sphere and level with the groundplane. You should be looking at the Sphere dead-on from the front. Click and hold the Orbit Camera button to select the alternative choice: the Pan Camera tool (discussed in the next section).

Panning the Camera

The hand icon is the Pan Camera tool—a completely different creature from the Pan tool used in noncamera viewports. The Pan Camera tool is closer to what a filmmaker means by *panning*—rotating the camera from a fixed position. Specifically, the Pan Camera tool rotates a camera around its Local X- and Y-axes. (The Roll tool, as you have seen, rotates the camera around its Local Z-axis.) Let's try the Pan Camera tool on the Sphere:

1. Drag in the camera viewport and keep an eye on the other viewports for reference. The Target Camera stays in its place, but the Target orbits the Target Camera. This action causes the Target Camera to rotate, much as when a person stands in one spot and turns his or her head to look around. Figure 14.16 shows the Target Camera panned horizontally a bit from a straight-on front view. Note in the Top viewport, on the left, that the Target object is not in the center of the Sphere.

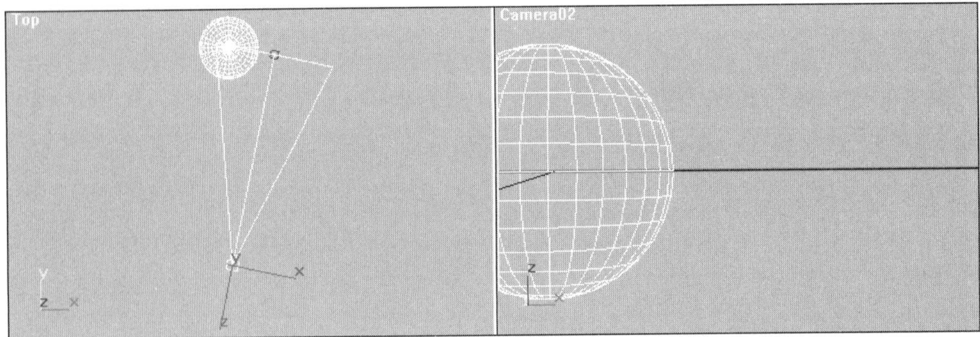

Figure 14.16
Panning a camera rotates it without moving it. In this figure, the Target Camera was originally directed straight at the center of the Sphere. By panning horizontally a bit, the Target object orbits the Target Camera, causing the Target Camera to rotate.

2. Convert your Target Camera into a Free Camera. The Pan Camera tool works the same way it did before, except that there is no Target object to orbit. The Free Camera simply rotates around its Local X- and Y-axes.

Adding Multi-Pass Effects

New to 3ds max 4 are added capabilities that let you incorporate effects into cameras that were previously found only in the realm of Render Effects, Video Post, or Object Properties. It is now possible to assign depth-of-field parameters that focus the camera at a specific distance, rather than being limited to the infinite focus that is standard for MAX's cameras. You can also assign *motion blur*—a distortion effect caused by movements faster than a camera or the human eye can isolate—to specific cameras. The remaining steps in this very long exercise will center on these new features.

Depth Of Field

Adding a depth-of-field effect to a scene can help direct a viewer's attention to a specific object or area and can project the idea that the scene is being viewed through a traditional camera. To try this effect, follow these steps:

1. Create two more Spheres directly behind the existing one and hide any visible cameras. Create a new Target Camera in the Top viewport, with its Target object centered on the middle Sphere. Activate Show Cone. The scene should look similar to the one shown in Figure 14.17.

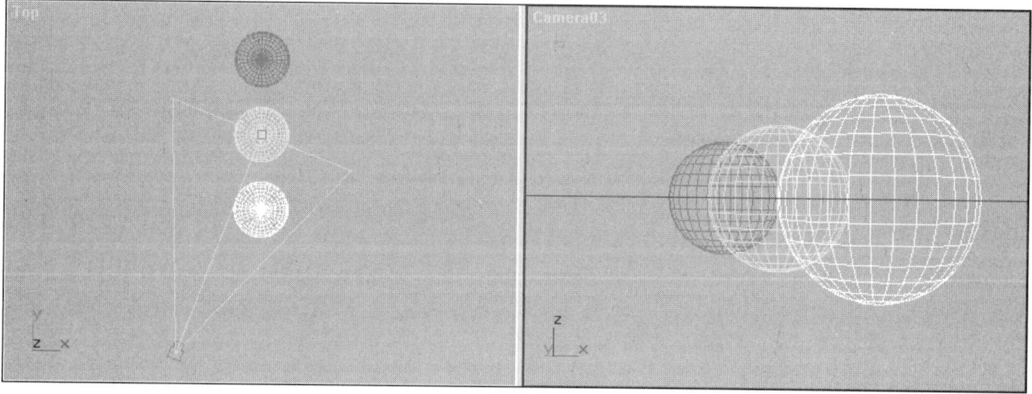

Figure 14.17
To set up the scene for the multi-pass effects, two more Spheres are added behind the first and a new Target Camera is created, with its Target object centered on the middle Sphere.

2. Switch one of the viewports to be able to view through the new camera; then change its mode to Smooth + Highlights. In the Multi-Pass Effect group of the camera's Modify panel, select the Enable checkbox and ensure that the Depth Of Field option is selected in the drop-down list. Click on the Preview button. As you watch the Camera03 viewport, it will appear that the Spheres move a little. This movement occurs when MAX calculates the maximum volume that the objects in the scene will occupy with blur applied to them. When it is finished, the near and far objects appear blurry in the viewport, whereas the middle object appears sharper.

3. In the Depth Of Field Parameters rollout, the Use Target Distance checkbox in the Focal Depth group is selected. This setting indicates that the objects nearest to the camera's Target (or implied Target for Free Cameras) will be in focus, whereas objects nearer or farther from the Target will be out of focus. Deselect the Use Target Distance checkbox and increase or decrease the Focal Depth value, clicking on the Preview button after each adjustment, until the nearest Sphere is in focus and the other two are not.

4. Click on the Quick Render button in the Main toolbar to see an actual render of the scene. Rather than a single rendering pass, the renderer runs through 12 passes, each adding a

little to the scene. To adjust the number of passes and, in turn, the accuracy of the Depth-Of-Field effect, change the value in the Total Passes field, keeping in mind that having more passes translates to longer rendering times. To increase or decrease the amount of out-of-focus blur, adjust the Sample Radius value.

Motion Blur

The Motion Blur effect can give the impression of speed and movement in a scene by adding small, offset rendering passes to the objects that are being transformed. Follow these steps:

1. Switch the Multi-Pass effect from Depth Of Field to Motion Blur and ensure that it is enabled.

2. Select the middle Sphere, change its Segments value to 5, and deselect its Smooth checkbox. The Sphere should now look like a nonsymmetrical diamond, as shown in Figure 14.18. Move the Time Slider to Frame 100, turn on the Animate button, and rotate the middle Sphere 360 degrees about its Y-axis. Turn off the Animate button.

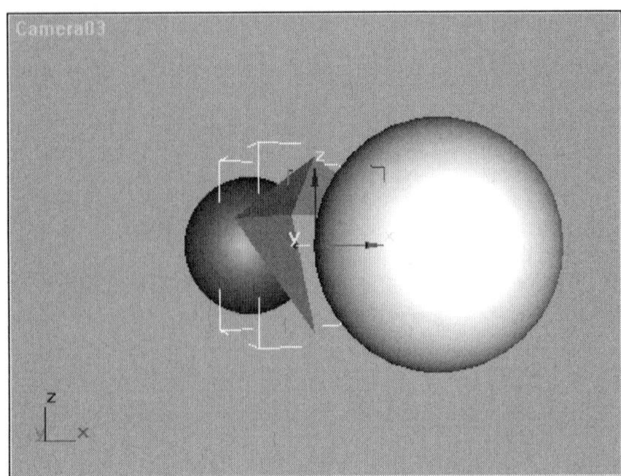

Figure 14.18
The middle Sphere's parameters are changed to sharpen its appearance.

3. Play the animation to test it. Stop the animation at around Frame 50. Select the camera again and, in the Motion Blur Parameters rollout, change the Duration (frames) value to 6. This option sets the number of frames that will occupy the blur effect for the moving object. Click on the Preview button to see the effect in the viewport; then, perform an actual render to see a shaper view of the Motion Blur effect. Figure 14.19 shows the Motion Blur effect as viewed through Camera03 and rendered.

Camera Matching

It is often the case, especially in filmmaking and architectural visualization, that computer graphics (CG) elements must be incorporated into an image of a real-world scene. To do so, the virtual camera must match the location and focal length of the actual camera, or the scene

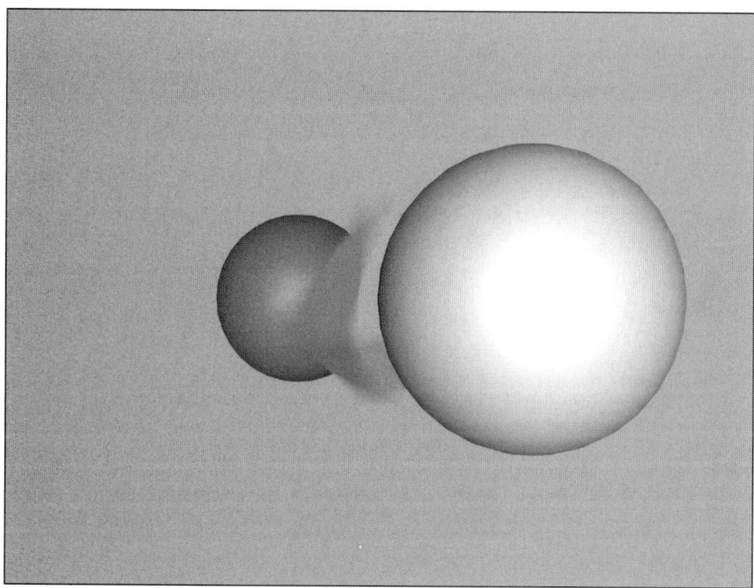

Figure 14.19
A rendering of the view, as seen from Camera03, with a Motion Blur effect highlighting the movement of the middle Sphere.

will not mesh properly. The Camera Match utility aids this task immeasurably, but you must provide actual dimensions for features that appear in the image. To use the utility, a minimum of six reference points must appear in a scene, and they must reside in more than one plane. The more reference points you use, the more accurate the camera solution will be.

Reset the scene to begin a new—and final—exercise that will cover the procedure used to match a virtual camera to an actual one:

1. Reset MAX. Assign the file Chap14 CamMatch.jpg, from the CD-ROM, as the background image in the Perspective viewport. Hide the grid. Figure 14.20 shows the background image as well as the dimensions necessary to complete this exercise.

2. Identify the origin (0,0,0) in the scene and the orientation of the X-, Y-, and Z-axes. In this scene, the origin will be at the bottom corner of the building, where it meets the sidewalk, with the shadow falling on one side of it. Positive Z will point straight up, positive Y will point down the road to the left, and positive X will point down the road in the same direction the photographer is facing.

3. You need to add nonrendering helper objects to the scene in their physical locations; they will match physical locations to actual locations. From the Create|Helpers panel, change the drop-down list option to Camera Match and click on the CamPoint button. In the Top viewport, click once to create a CamPoint helper object; rename it "Origin". Activate the Move transform and use the Transform Type-Ins to move the helper object to the origin (0,0,0). This CamPoint will represent the bottom corner of the building.

Figure 14.20
The Perspective viewport with the Chap14 CamMatch.jpg image as the background. The dimensions and CamPoint locations displayed here are informational and will not appear in your scene.

4. Create a second CamPoint object that's even with the right edge of the lower window, to the left of the building's corner, and at the ground level. Rename it "Window Edge Lower Ground" to indicate the area it corresponds to with respect to the lower window. Move it 78 units in the positive Y-direction, away from the origin (0,78,0).

5. Clone the last CamPoint object, name it "Window Edge Lower Canopy", and move it in the positive Z-direction 197 units (0,78,197); it will match with the top-right corner of the canopy over the window. Clone the last CamPoint, name it "Window Edge Upper Top" to match the top corner of the upper window, and move it up an additional 169 units (0,78,366).

6. Currently, you have only four CamPoints, and they are all in the YZ plane. To meet the camera-matching criteria, you need to add CamPoints that correspond with features on the front face of the building. This face, however, is not at a right angle to the Y-direction, but at a 45-degree angle to it, requiring the use of another helper: the Tape object. Go to the Standard list of objects under Create|Helpers and click on Tape. Select Specify Length and enter "90.5" in the Length field. Click at the origin to set the Tape's location and drag the Target object until the To X Axis field reads 135 and the To Y Axis field reads 45 in the World Space Angles group. The end of the Tape indicator line is now at a 45-degree angle to the origin and 90.5 units away from it; this point corresponds to the left edge of the window, on the short face of the building, even with the ground.

7. Create another CamPoint, name it "Window Edge Right Ground", and move it to the end of the Tape line.

Note: *No snap option is available to snap an object to the end of the Tape line. To accomplish this task, zoom in on the endpoint and move the CamPoint close to it visually.*

8. Reselect the Tape object and change its Length value to 361. Create a new CamPoint, name it "Window Edge Far Right Ground", and place it at the end of the Tape line.
9. To create the last CamPoint helper object, extend the Tape Length to 451.5 and place a CamPoint named Building Edge Right Ground at the end of it. For this exercise, seven CamPoints will be sufficient. Figure 14.21 shows the layout of the CamPoints as seen in the Top viewport.

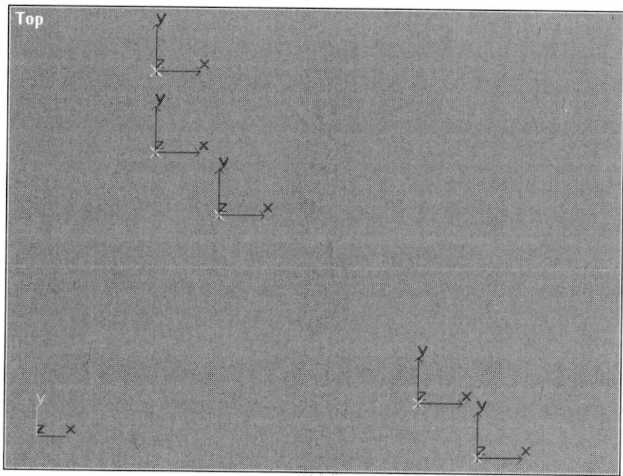

Figure 14.21
The layout of the CamPoints as seen in the Top viewport.

10. You need to indicate for MAX which features in the image the CamPoints relate to. Maximize the Perspective viewport and hide or delete the Tape and Tape Target objects. From the Utilities tab in the Command panel, click on the Camera Match button to expose the rollouts shown in Figure 14.22.
11. Select Building Edge Right Ground from the list in the CamPoint Info rollout and click on the Assign Position button. Click on the point where the right corner of the building's short face meets the ground. A person is standing in that location; therefore, you must estimate the location. If a warning box appears asking if MAX should set the background image aspect ratio, click on Yes.
12. Select the Origin option from the list and assign its position to the point where the left edge of the building's short side meets the ground. Click on the remaining list items and assign them to their positions in the image.
13. Click on the Create Camera button. MAX will attempt to create a Free Camera that matches the criteria that have been passed to it through the assignments in the Camera

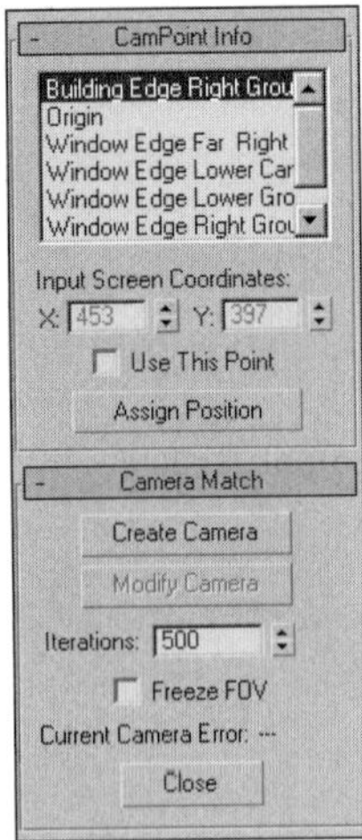

Figure 14.22
The rollouts found under the Camera Match utility.

Match utility. If the camera can be created, any error will be expressed just above the Close button. An error of less than 5 percent is desirable; you can improve the error value by reassigning or moving the CamPoints as necessary. If the camera cannot be created, a warning box will appear and give possible causes.

14. Change the Perspective viewport to show the view from the new camera. Create a tall Box primitive and move it so that the top-right corner, as seen in the Top viewport, is at the origin. In the newly created camera viewport, the Box will appear in the shadowed area and match the perspective of the camera.

Camera Match is a fantastic utility that you will use whenever you need to match a virtual camera to an actual one. With a little practice, you can use Camera Match to quickly add realism and accuracy to your 3ds max 4 scenes.

Moving On

In this chapter, you learned about the two camera types in MAX and how easily you can convert between them. You saw how to create and transform cameras in your scene by operating on them directly. You examined the important camera parameters, including the Field-Of-View and Clipping Plane controls. You also learned to use the camera navigation tools to manipulate a camera when working in a camera viewport and how to apply and preview the new multi-pass effects to cameras. Finally, we explained the procedure to match a virtual camera in MAX to the actual camera that took a photograph.

The next chapter turns to MAX's rendering toolset to show how a scene or animation can be output to different types of bitmap images or video. It will also look into rendering only portions of a scene and the methods of adding and specifying anti-aliasing and motion blur.

Chapter 15

Rendering Tools

The results of all your labors are images, either single or in sequences to be run as animations. The only thing your audience sees are pictures, so they'd better be good.

Although you may think of rendering 3D scenes into bitmapped images as just the last thing you do, in fact you're always rendering, at every stage of the process, to test the current state of your efforts. Many aspects of your work cannot be judged adequately, or at all, without rendering. In any case, rendering takes time—often an enormous amount of time. You need a good command of the rendering toolset to work efficiently and with minimum time lost to errors.

Rendering Essentials

The following exercises will make you comfortable with all the essentials for rendering in 3ds max 4.

Production and Draft Rendering Configurations

In this exercise, you'll explore the relationship between Production and Draft renders:

1. Create a Box object in the center of the groundplane. Pull the Main toolbar over to the left, if necessary, to make sure that the render tools (the four buttons with the teapot icons) are visible.

2. The second teapot button from the left is the Quick Render tool. Don't let this name confuse you—there's no difference between a Quick Render and a render made using the Render Scene dialog box (which will be covered shortly). The only thing that's quicker about a Quick Render is that you don't have to open the dialog box to make it. Quick Render uses the set-

tings from the last rendering and applies them to the active viewport. Rest your cursor over the Quick Render icon to bring up the label. Note that it says *Quick Render (Production)*.

3. Click on the Quick Render button to render the scene. Note that you are rendering the active viewport. If the Perspective viewport is active, you render a perspective view. If a Top viewport is active, you render a top view (in an orthographic projection). The Virtual Frame Buffer screen appears, with the rendered image in it. Unless you've changed from the defaults, your image will be at a resolution of 640×480 pixels.
4. Hold down the Quick Render button to reveal your options. The upper icon is the same blue teapot that you just used to create a Production render. The gray teapot below it is the Draft Render option. The bottom, red teapot button is for the new ActiveShade feature that will be discussed later in the "ActiveShade" section. Drag to the gray teapot button and release it to perform a Draft render. You see that the Virtual Frame Buffer is redrawn, but with exactly the same image. What gives?
5. MAX permits you to keep two rendering configurations active at once. By default, the Production configuration and the Draft configuration are exactly the same. That's why you saw no difference when you moved from one to the other. Change the settings for the Draft configuration so that you can understand how this system works. Click on the Render Scene button immediately to the left of the Quick Render button. Doing so brings up the Render Scene dialog box, as seen in Figure 15.1. You can also access this dialog box from the Rendering menu.
6. At the very bottom of the panel, you see radio button options for Production, Draft, and ActiveShade configurations. Click on the ActiveShade option and notice that many of the dialog box options are grayed out. The ActiveShade option applies to the ActiveShade window only; the image cannot be saved, and sequential images cannot be shown. Click back and forth between the Production and Draft choices, and notice that none of the settings in the panel change. The main purpose for providing two alternative configurations is to allow you to jump back and forth between a faster Draft mode and a slower (but finished quality) Production mode. Try this out. Go into the Draft mode and change the output size from 640×480 pixels to 320×240 pixels by clicking on the button for this option in the Output Size area. The values in the Width and Height spinners change accordingly. Flip back and forth between the Draft and Production configurations to make sure that they now have different resolution settings. Click on the Render button at the bottom of the dialog box for each of these configurations. When you render with the Draft option selected, the image in the Virtual Frame Buffer is now 320×240 pixels, and the Production render is still at 640×480 pixels.
7. Notice that the Render Scene dialog box, being modeless, persists on the screen. It might get hidden behind the Virtual Frame Buffer, but it's still there. Close the dialog box by clicking on the Close button. The Virtual Frame Buffer remains on screen.

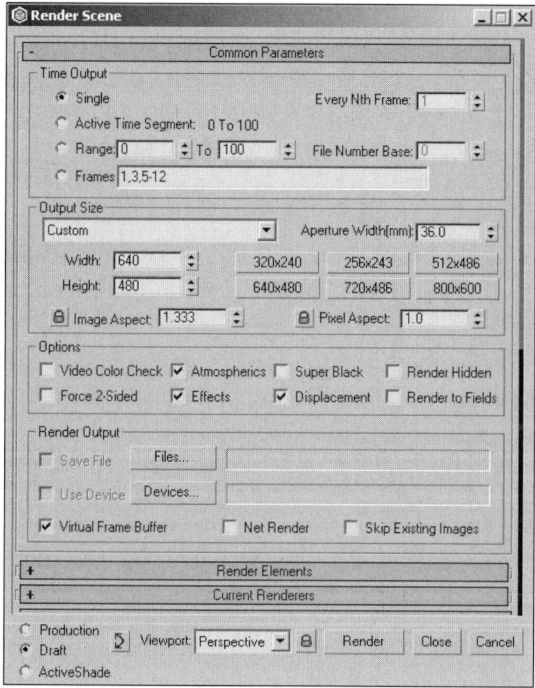

Figure 15.1
The Render Scene dialog box, available from the Main toolbar and Rendering menu.

Configuring Resolution Presets

MAX assigns six commonly used image resolutions to the buttons in the Output Size area of the Render Scene dialog box. Custom values can be typed directly into the Width and Height fields to the left of these buttons. If you find that you often use resolutions other than those assigned, the buttons can be customized to your requirements. To do so, right-click on the button that is to be customized to open the Configure Preset dialog box. Type in the desired values; then, click on the OK button. The button in the Render Scene dialog box now shows the new values.

---

8. Go back to the Quick Render button on the Main Toolbar and render by using the Production and Draft options (the blue and gray teapot icons). You get the same results as rendering from the Render Scene dialog box.

Using the Virtual Frame Buffer

This is a good moment to consider the Virtual Frame Buffer. The renderer produces a bitmap, which it can output to different places. The main purpose of a renderer, of course, is to create saved bitmap files to be used (and viewed) outside MAX. Thus, rendered images can be saved to disk in standard image and video file formats. Rendered images can also be sent directly to external devices, such as a video recorder. Prior to rendering your final output, however, you'll typically need to see the current test renderings of single images from within MAX. The Virtual

Frame Buffer displays rendered images that are stored temporarily in RAM. You'll become familiar with the Virtual Frame Buffer in this exercise:

1. Create a Box object on the center of the groundplane, or continue with the existing Box, and render the Perspective viewport. The Virtual Frame Buffer appears with the rendered image, reflecting the current Draft or Production settings. It may seem strange to think of the Virtual Frame Buffer as receiving output from the renderer, so open the Render Scene dialog box and look at the Render Output section of the Common Parameters rollout. This section is obviously intended to direct render output to files for disk storage or to external devices. The Virtual Frame Buffer is also shown as an output option, however. It is active by default, so deselect the checkbox and render again. Although the Rendering panel appears and the action along its progress bar indicates that rendering is occurring, the output of the renderer has no place to be stored, even in RAM. Select the Virtual Frame Buffer checkbox again to output to RAM.

Note: *A frame buffer is a region in memory that holds pixel data for screen display. The entire image that you see on your computer monitor is a reflection of the frame buffer of the display at that moment. High-end video cards have high-speed memory on the card dedicated for use as a frame buffer. This buffer makes for faster display update speed than is possible by using system RAM on the motherboard.*

2. Render your scene again. Your Virtual Frame Buffer should look like Figure 15.2.

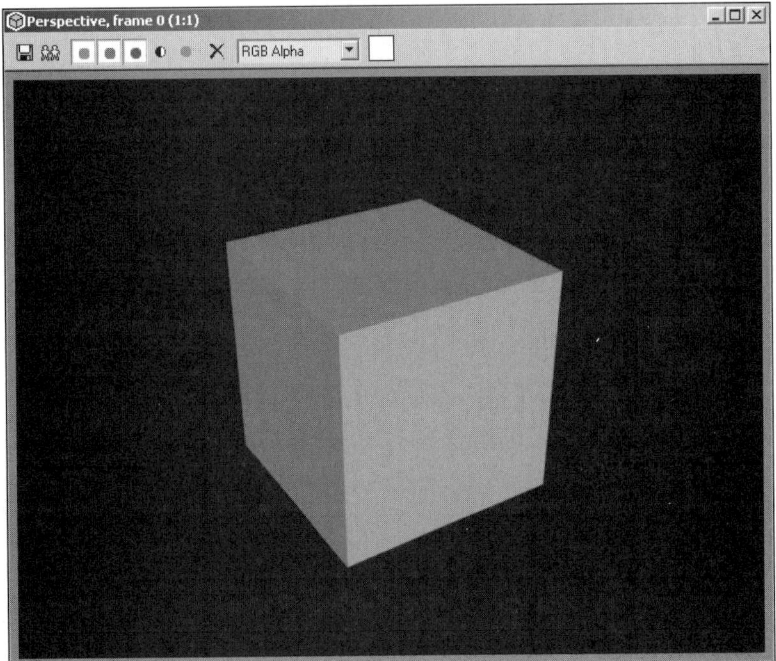

Figure 15.2
The Virtual Frame Buffer displaying the render of a Box object.

3. The Virtual Frame Buffer is not just a picture; it also contains a lot of important functionality. Click on the Save Bitmap button, the leftmost button with the disk icon, to see the options for saving the rendered image to disk. In the dialog box that appears, check out the wide range of file types from the Save As Type drop-down list. It's often easier to render to the Virtual Frame Buffer and save the image than it is to set up the file-saving parameters in the Render Scene dialog box.

4. Next to the Save Bitmap button is an icon with twins, which permits you to clone the Virtual Frame Buffer. This is a critical tool. Click on the button to produce a copy of the Virtual Frame Buffer that you can minimize if you want. Move the Box in your scene a bit and re-render. Note that the original Virtual Frame Buffer is overwritten with the new image, but the clone is unaffected. This way, you can compare different render results (reflecting changes in lights, materials, and so on) side by side.

5. The rendered bitmap is a 32-bit image, meaning that the image has separate 8-bit (1-byte) channels for red, green, blue, and alpha. You'll rarely need to isolate the separate color channels, as the panel lets you do, but it's great to be able to see (and even save) the alpha channel. Click on the Display Alpha Channel button (to the right of the red, green, and blue buttons). As you can see in Figure 15.3, MAX generates an Alpha channel for rendered

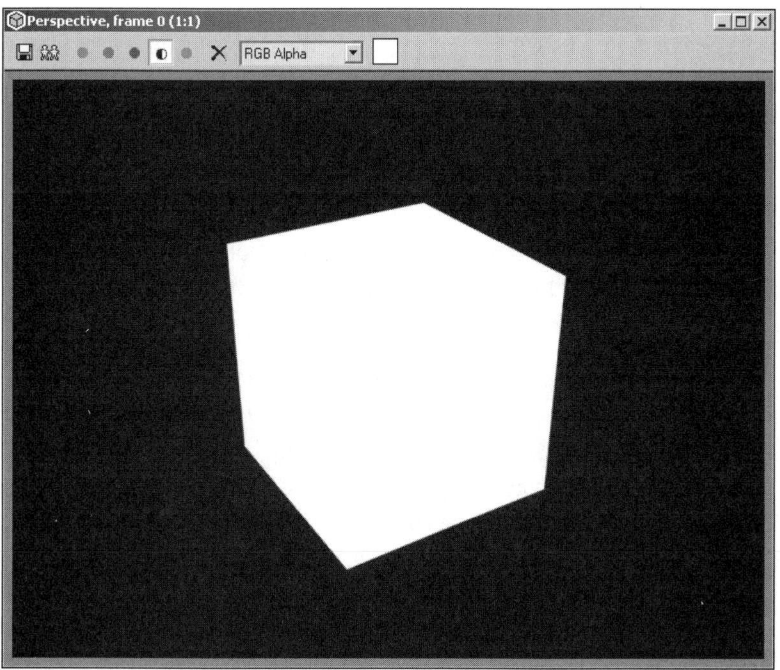

Figure 15.3
The Virtual Frame Buffer from Figure 15.2, showing only the Alpha channel. The pixels for the opaque Box object are white and the background is black. This bitmap can be used as a mask when compositing with other images, so that the region outside the Box is treated as transparent.

images, in which opaque objects receive white pixels and the background is black. This channel allows rendered images to be used in compositing, because the background is masked (treated as transparent) when layered with other images. If the Box were made semi-transparent, its pixels in the Alpha channel would be gray.

Outputting to Disk

To send an image (or sequence of images) directly from the renderer to a file on disk, open the Render Scene dialog box and go to the Render Output section. Click on the Files button, and you'll see a dialog box that asks you to name or choose a file for saving. A complete list of file formats is available. Generally, the Targa (.tga) format is the most universally useful for individual bitmaps or bitmap sequences, but a good argument can be made for TIFF (.tif) files, as well. For animation files intended to be run only on a computer, the PC standard AVI (.avi) and Apple's QuickTime (.mov) formats are the obvious options. You have to think about your needs. If you need to preserve the Alpha channel of the rendered images, you must use a 32-bit (4-channel) format like Targa or TIFF. If image-file size is an important issue (as for Web graphics), JPEG (.jpg) images may be the best. The new PNG (.png) format has great compression and an Alpha channel, as well. Whatever format you pick, you'll be given the options (typically, compression options) that are appropriate to that format. Note that 3ds max 4 does not output to the GIF (.gif) file format.

Figure 15.4 shows the Render Scene dialog box set up to save only the current frame as a single image. Note the Single option chosen at the top. The rendered frame will be saved in JPEG format under the name mytest.jpg. Even after the file name is entered, saving can be disabled by deselecting the Save File checkbox.

Rendering Animation

When you render out animation, you are saving a sequence of bitmap images for consecutive frames, either as separate images or collected into a single video file. Create a simple animation, as follows:

1. On a fresh screen, place a Sphere object near the left side of the Perspective viewport, as seen from the front. Drag the Time Slider to Frame 100 and turn on the Animate button at the bottom of the MAX screen. Move the Sphere in the World X-direction to the right edge of the viewport. Turn off the Animate button and pull the Time Slider back and forth. You should have a simple animation of the Sphere moving across the screen. Click on the Play Animation button to watch the animation run, if you wish.

2. To save this animation, open the Render Scene dialog box. Change from Production to Draft mode at the bottom of this dialog box and choose the 320×240 resolution option to make the render proceed more quickly. Click on the Render button; you get a render of only the single current frame. Move the Time Slider and render again. The image in the Virtual Frame Buffer is replaced with a render of the new current frame.

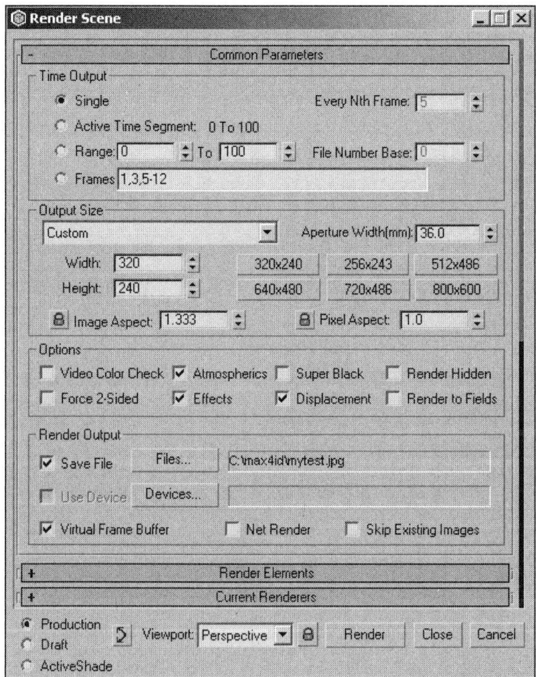

Figure 15.4

The Render Scene dialog box set up to save only the current frame as a single image. The rendered frame will be saved in JPEG format under the name mytest.jpg. Saving can be disabled at any time by deselecting the Save File checkbox.

To save a sequence, rather than a single frame, you need to change the settings at the top of the panel. The Active Time Segment option is the most commonly used. It renders the range of frames set in the Time Configuration dialog box, which can be reached from a button on the bottom-right of the MAX screen. By default, the Active Time Segment is from Frame 0 to Frame 100—the current range of the animation. The other options permit you to select a specific range of frames or even specific individual frames. Continue the exercise with these steps:

1. Choose the Active Time Segment option and note how the Every Nth Frame spinner becomes active.
2. At the default value of 1, every frame from 0 to 100 is rendered. You don't need such smooth animation for your current purposes, so save time by rendering only every fifth frame: Change the spinner value to 5.

Now, you have to save the animation. With single images, you can render to the Virtual Frame Buffer if you want and then save to disk from there. With an animation, however, you have to save directly from the renderer. Click on the Files button and look at the different format options in the drop-down menu. Many options appear, but the basic choice is between saving as a bitmap sequence or as a video file.

Saving as a Bitmap Sequence

Saving to bitmap sequences is the safest method for saving finished production-rendered animation. When you choose any of the bitmap files formats (such as Targa, TIFF, or JPEG), the render outputs a sequence of numbered files—each one a still image of a rendered frame. This kind of output has important advantages. It can be loaded into any digital video-editing environment for finishing and output to tape. And each frame can be separately loaded into a bitmap editor (such as Photoshop) for retouching and correction. It's also easy to divide a rendering job over time or on different machines.

Using the moving-ball animation file from the last section, follow these steps:

1. Choose the Targa format and name the file "ball". When you click on the Save button, you are presented with the Targa Image Control dialog box, in which you can add personalized information to the file. Accept the defaults.

2. Click on the Render button to render the sequence. You see each frame rendered, one after another, in the Virtual Frame Buffer. Note that the frame numbers increment in units of 5. When the animation finishes, only the final frame (100) is visible in the Virtual Frame Buffer.

3. Open the View File dialog box from the File drop-down menu. Go to the directory in which you saved the sequence; you should find a list of 21 Targa files from ball0000.tga to ball0100.tga. MAX has added a four-digit extension to the name you chose, which allows you to save sequences as long as 10,000 frames.

4. Click on a number of different file names and watch the image appear in the Preview box. Open any one of the files. The image will appear, full size, in a window that resembles the Virtual Frame Buffer. Click on the right and left arrows to move forward and backward through the bitmap sequence. Of course, you can also view these files in Photoshop or any other application that can read Targa files.

You may have noticed the Rendering panel, which is displayed during the rendering process. The render was completed so quickly that you probably didn't have a good chance to look it over, but you can examine it (with interest and a bit of impatience) during longer renders. Figure 15.5 shows the panel as it stood when Frame 25 was being rendered during the previous exercise. The upper progress bar (for Total Animation) indicates that a quarter of the job is rendered, and the lower progress bar (for Current Task: Rendering Image) indicates that most of the current frame is rendered. In the Rendering Progress section, you can see that the previous frame took only 3 seconds to render and the rendering process has gone on for only 19 seconds. This panel shows you the settings you selected (or accepted by default) in the Render Scene dialog box, and it also provides information about the scene.

The buttons at the top of the Rendering panel permit you to pause or cancel a render. Canceling a render simply cancels it; pausing a render stops it, which gives you the option to

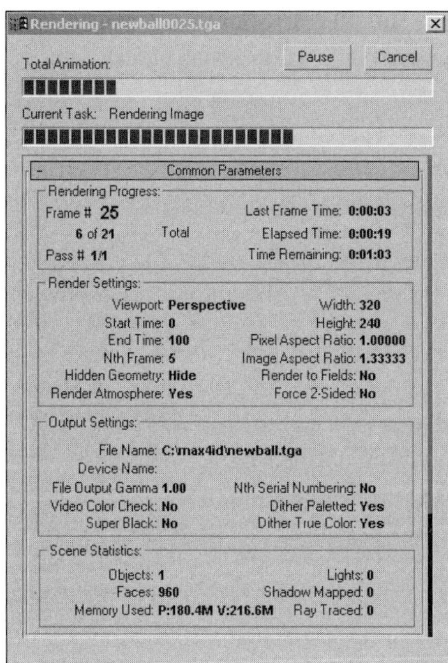

Figure 15.5
The Rendering panel, as it stood when Frame 25 was being rendered. The progress bars indicate progress through the entire animation and through the current frame.

resume from where you left off or to cancel it for good. To experiment, continue with the previous exercise:

1. In the Render Scene dialog box, click on the Files button to save the animation again under a new file name: "newball.tga". Before you click on the Render button, prepare to click on the Cancel button in the Rendering panel when Frame 20 (the fifth frame) is about half-rendered. Go ahead and render, and then cancel when you are in Frame 20.

2. Open the View File dialog box and note that there are only four Targa files, beginning with newball. Frame 20 was not saved, because it was not finished. Clicking on the Render button again will render the entire sequence, overwriting the existing files. To complete the job without rerendering what you already finished, select the Skip Existing Images box in the Render Scene dialog box. Click on the Render button again and notice that the rendering starts at Frame 20.

Use the RAM Player to Run a Bitmap Sequence

The RAM Player in MAX is available from the Rendering drop-down menu. This fantastic tool permits you to run bitmap sequences at true frame rate, although you're necessarily limited by the amount of your system RAM. The results are far superior to AVI video files that run in the Windows Media Player.

Saving a Video File

To play an animation on a computer, you need to package it in a video file format. Unlike a bitmap sequence, a video file is a single file that contains all of the images in order. Video files generally require compression to keep their size manageable. Everyone prefers different values for compression options, which are called *codecs* (meaning compression-decompression algorithms). The Cinepak codec at a Compression Quality value between 90 and 100 is a safe place to start.

The QuickTime MOV format is very important (it was even available during the installation of 3ds max 4), but stick to the AVI format for this exercise because it's universal on all Windows systems. Follow these steps:

1. Use the moving-ball animation file from the previous exercise, and this time save it under the name "ball" using the AVI format. You'll get a dialog box with a drop-down menu of compression options. The Full Frames option at the bottom of the list is completely uncompressed, giving you the same quality as the uncompressed Targa files you created earlier. Go ahead and render with the codec of your choice or use Full Frames.

Codecs

To compress an image sequence, codecs save only the pixels that change from one image to the next. For example: If an area of the frame is solid black from frame to frame, that area's data need only be stored for the first frame and then shown for all the following frames that do not change. This method reduces the amount of data needed to compose the entire file.

2. After rendering, bring up the View File dialog box from the File menu on the MAX menu bar. Select the file named ball.avi. The animation will run in the Windows Media Player—it will probably run fairly well, because this is a tiny file. (AVI playback is often slow and disappointing even on today's most powerful systems, if they do not have special video hardware, but the quality is constantly improving even as the cost of computer technology drops.)

3. In the Render Scene dialog box, change the file name to "ball2.avi"; then, after starting the render, cancel it after a few frames. Run the file from the Media Player and note that it stops where you canceled. If you want to start it again, do you have to re-render from the very beginning? Make sure that the Skip Existing Images checkbox is selected in the Render Scene dialog box and render again. Note that, unlike the case with the Targa sequence, rendering starts over again from Frame 0, regardless of the instruction to Skip Existing Images.

Planning for Render Shutdowns

Rendering animations of any significant size or complexity may take a large amount of time, depending on the hardware setup at your disposal. A possibility always exists that your render will terminate before it's complete, either intentionally or by accident. Rendering to bitmap sequences rather than video files ensures that you'll never lose whatever is already rendered. Any standard video-editing package, such as Adobe Premiere, permits you to save a bitmap sequence as a video file. In fact, you can do it in MAX's own Video Post by inputting the bitmap sequence and outputting to an AVI or MOV file.

Output Size and Other Options

One of the most important decisions that you must make in the rendering process concerns the resolution and aspect ratio of the image. These words have overlapping meanings. *Resolution* is simply the total number of pixels in the image. More pixels mean higher resolution, and thus greater detail (but also longer rendering time). A resolution of 640×480 is a total of 307,200 pixels. A resolution of 320×240 is 76,800 pixels—exactly one-quarter as many. Note that the resolution of an image is always defined in terms of the number of pixels in width, multiplied by the number of pixels in height. Thus, the resolution necessarily defines the relative dimensions in the width and height. This relative dimension is called the *aspect ratio*. A 640×480 image and a 320×240 image have different resolutions, but the same aspect ratio. The aspect ratio is determined by dividing the width by the height. In both cases, the aspect ratio is 4/3, or 1.333. In other words, both images are one-third wider than they are high.

Open the Render Scene dialog box and (using the default Custom Output Size option) click on any of the resolution choice buttons. Notice that the 1.333 value in the Image Aspect spinner does not change, because all the resolution choices share the same standard aspect ratio. If you pull the Height or Width spinners, however, the Image Aspect ratio changes. You can lock the aspect ratio by pressing the lock icon, after which both spinners move together to maintain a constant ratio.

Pixel Aspect ratios are something different. On a computer monitor, the pixels are square. Because the width and height are equal, the aspect ratio of each pixel is 1/1, or 1.00. Some display devices—namely, standard video monitors meeting National Television Standards Committee (NTSC) or Phase Alternating Line (PAL) standards—do not have square pixels, however. If you select either of the NTSC options from the Output Size drop-down menu, you see that the Pixel Aspect ratio is 0.90000, meaning that the pixels are slightly taller than they are wide. Also notice that the Width and Height values from the NTSC D-1 (video) option maintain an Image Aspect ratio of 1.333. The NTSC DV (video) has slightly different values that change the Image Aspect ratio to 1.35, but the Pixel Aspect remains the same. Let's examine this situation by comparing NTSC D-1 (video) with the standard 640×480 resolution. Because the NTSC pixels are taller than they are wide, you need more pixels in the horizontal direction to preserve the 4/3 aspect ratio. If you render an image for NTSC video in 720×486

NTSC and PAL

NTSC is the standard output resolution and frame rate (30 frames per second) for televisions in North America, Japan, and most of Central and South America.

PAL is the standard output resolution and frame rate (28 frames per second) for televisions in Europe.

Each standard allows for each of the frames to be split into two fields, and MAX can output these fields. Each field contains either the odd or even horizontal line of resolution; using fields generally yields smoother animations. To render to fields, select the Render To Fields checkbox in the Options area of the Render Scene dialog box. Rendering to fields is not a valid option when you're creating an AVI file.

with the .9 Pixel Aspect value, it appears a little squashed on your square pixel computer monitor; it looks correct on a screen with NTSC pixels, however.

The checkbox options in the Common Parameters Rollout of the Render Scene dialog box are straightforward. Atmospheric effects, render effects, and displacement mapping are all enabled by default. Because these are all time-consuming processes, however, it's helpful to be able to disable them when making test renders. The Video Color Check and Super Black options are for video output purposes. The Force 2-Sided option results in rendering both sides of all faces in the scene, rather than only the sides in the direction of the normals. Don't use this option rashly—if you really need to render both sides of a surface (with a flag, for example), it makes more sense to define the Material for that surface as 2-Sided in the Material Editor.

Rendering Portions of the Scene

Test renderings are essential, but they can be very time consuming. It's important to be able to render only a portion of a frame to speed things up. The following exercise demonstrates the options:

1. Create a Box and a Sphere on the groundplane. Make sure that you can see the rendering tools at the right end of the Main toolbar. The Render Type drop-down box shows the default View option, which means that the entire active viewport will be rendered.

2. Open the Render Scene dialog box and make sure that the Single frame option is selected and that any file saving is disabled. Close the dialog box. Select the Box object and change the Render Type to Selected. Click on the Quick Render button. Only the Box renders. That makes sense, and it's obviously very useful to be able to render only a single object, if necessary.

3. Select the Sphere and render again. Although you may be surprised to see that the Box remains while the Sphere is rendered, this result is also useful. By keeping the existing image in the Virtual Frame Buffer and rewriting only the pixels for the selected object, you don't have to re-render everything when only the selected objects change.

4. To clear the Virtual Frame Buffer, click on the X (Clear) button on its toolbar. Try rendering the selected Sphere again; note that it appears all by itself.

5. To get a close-up render of the selected Sphere, change to the Box Selected option. This option renders only within the region defined by the bounding box of the selected object. When you render, you get the Render Bounding Box/Selected dialog box that permits you to adjust the dimensions of the image. Set the size you want and continue with the render. Note an important difference between this option and the previous one—the Selected option renders only the selected object. The Box Selected option renders the region of the viewport bordered by the bounding box. Objects in front of or behind the selected object are rendered with this option if they intersect this region.

6. Another way to render a region is with the Blowup option. Switch to this option and click on the Quick Render button. You see a cropping frame appear in the active window. You can move this window and size it, but you can't change its aspect ratio, because it keeps the same aspect ratio as your full-size image. When you have it where you want it, click on the OK button that appears in the corner of your active viewport. The defined region is blown up to fill the entire image space. Figure 15.6 shows the cropping frame and the resulting enlarged render of the selected region.

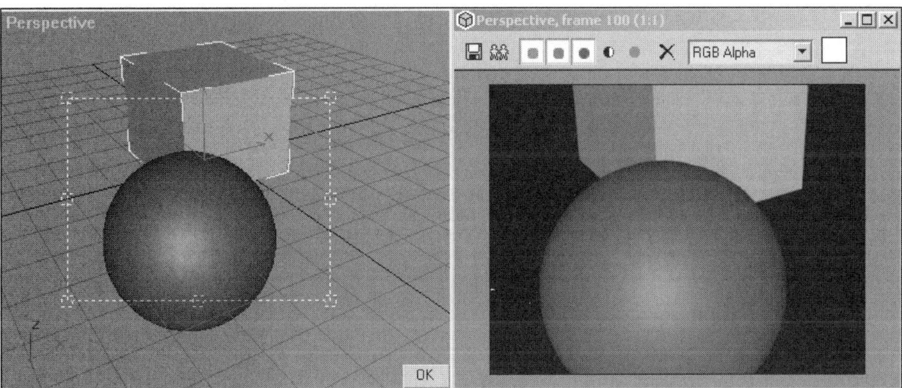

Figure 15.6
A Blowup render that shows the region within the cropping frame (*left*) and the rendered result (*right*).

7. In contrast, the Crop option does not change the resolution of the selected region. Select the Crop option and click on the Quick Render button. Once again, you get a cropping frame in the active viewport, but this time you can adjust its dimensions however you want. Click on the OK button to see the result. As illustrated in Figure 15.7, the defined region is isolated in its own image.

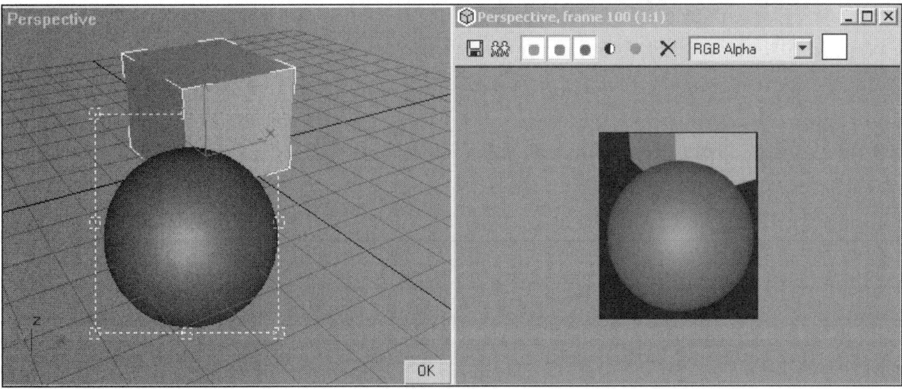

Figure 15.7
A Crop render that shows the region within the cropping frame (*left*) and the rendered result (*right*). Unlike the Blowup render in Figure 15.6, the resolution of the selected region is not changed.

8. Switch to the Region option and render the same defined region. This time, you see the entire frame space, with the selected region rendered in its proper place. Figure 15.8 gives you the idea. This approach has the same value as the Selected option—if you first render the entire scene (using the View option), you can rerender selected regions without losing the other pixels already in the Virtual Frame Buffer.

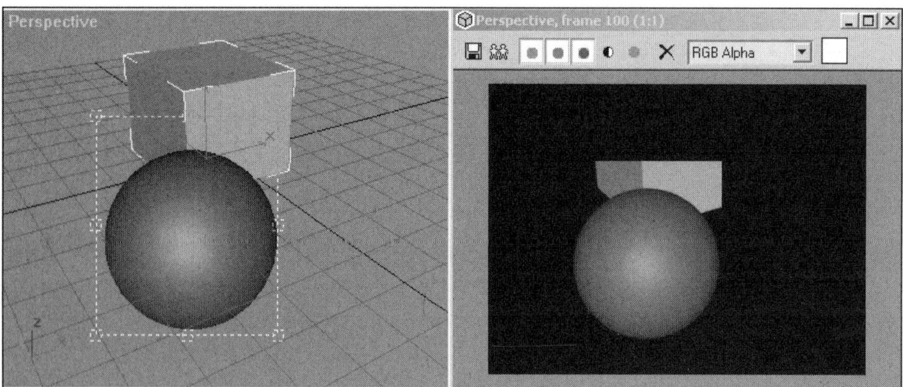

Figure 15.8
A Region render that shows the region within the cropping frame (*left*) and the rendered result (*right*). Unlike the Crop render, the entire frame space is preserved with the selected region in its place. If the entire viewport were rendered to the Virtual Frame Buffer first, the selected region could be updated without losing the rest of the image.

Two new Render Type options in 3ds max 4 are Region Selected and Crop Selected. Region Selected renders all objects within the selected object's bounding box, but it leaves the remainder of the Virtual Frame Buffer unchanged. Crop Selected, on the other hand, renders all objects within the selected objects bounding box and crops the Virtual Frame Buffer to fit the cropped area.

MAX Scanline Rendering Options

Thus far, you've paid attention only to the upper rollout in the Render Scene dialog box—the one named Common Parameters. It's called this because the included parameters are the kind that would be the same, regardless of the renderer used. MAX is not wedded to a single renderer, however. The standard MAX package comes with two renderers: the Default Scanline Renderer and the VUE File Renderer.

You probably only need to know about the Default Scanline Renderer; it's the renderer you've been using all along, unless you took the trouble to change it. The VUE File Renderer outputs an ASCII-rendering script that can be edited before rendering to pixels from the command line. It's safe to say that very few people need the VUE File Renderer, but you can replace the Default Scanline Renderer in the Current Renderers rollout of the Render Scene dialog box. You can add other renderers as plug-ins; the most common plug-ins are the Mental Ray and Ray Gun renderers.

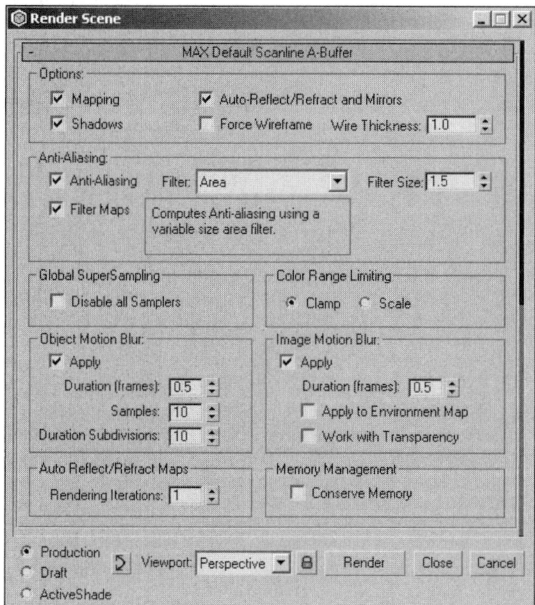

Figure 15.9
The MAX Default Scanline A-Buffer rollout in the Render Scene dialog box.

All the parameters for the Default Scanline Renderer are in the lowest rollout in the Render Scene dialog box. Pull down to reach this rollout, which is shown in Figure 15.9. We'll discuss these options, and how they affect the rendered output, in the following sections.

Motion Blur

Motion blur is essential for creating convincing animation. Although the virtual camera in a 3D animation package records each frame at a mathematical instant in time, a real camera has its shutter open for some duration of time, however short. Objects necessarily blur as they move across the field of view during that duration. A faster shutter speed (a shorter duration) can decrease the blur to the point that it is unnoticeable, but the blur is always there. Nor is the blur always attributable to the movement of the objects in the scene. If the camera is moving during the exposure, all objects in the scene are inherently blurred.

Blur is not just a flaw or limitation to be tolerated or minimized. Human vision operates much faster than a camera, but high-speed objects like a propeller are blurred to human sight. You can sense their speed from the extent of the smear.

Motion blur in MAX can be a little confusing. In addition to the motion blur applied through a camera, two methods are available for applying it in the renderer: Object Motion Blur creates copies of the object during the rendering process, and Image Motion Blur produces a generally superior result by smearing the image after rendering is complete. You need to use two different dialog boxes when using either type of blur: The blur must be turned on for the selected objects in the Object Properties dialog box; then, the blur parameters are adjusted in the Render Scene dialog box.

Object Motion Blur

You'll test motion blur effects by rendering single frames. Follow these steps to see how Object Motion Blur works:

1. Place a Sphere object near the left side of the Perspective viewport, as seen from the front. Drag the Time Slider to Frame 100 and turn on the Animate button at the bottom of the MAX screen. Move the Sphere in the World X-direction to the right edge of the viewport. Turn off the Animate button and pull the Time Slider back and forth to see the Sphere moving across the screen.

2. Pull the Time Slider to Frame 50, right in the middle of the animation. To make the motion blur effect clearer, open the Environment dialog box (from the Rendering menu) and change the Background Color from the default black to white. Close the Environment dialog box when you're done.

3. Select and then right-click on the Sphere object and open the Object Properties dialog box. The Motion Blur section is to the left. Figure 15.10 shows the Object Properties dialog box in its default state.

4. The choice between Object and Image is obvious enough, but why do we need both a None option and an Enabled checkbox? The Enabled checkbox can be animated to turn blurring on and off, as necessary. You definitely don't want to waste rendering time computing motion blur when you don't need it. For now, just leave the Enabled checkbox selected, and choose the Object option.

5. Object Motion Blur is now enabled for the Sphere. The next step is to adjust the parameters in the Render Scene dialog box. Click on OK to accept the changes and then close the Object Properties dialog box. Open the Render Scene dialog box and drag down to the MAX

Motion Blur and Rotations

Motion blur is especially critical for animated rotations. NTSC Video runs at 30 frames per second, and film runs at 24 frames per second. These speeds are not nearly fast enough to capture enough samples of quickly rotating objects. For example, assume that a wheel or propeller is rotating 15 times per second. At 30 frames per second, you have only two samples (frames) for each rotation. This is far too few to convey continuous rotation—as a result, the viewer sees only a kind of random strobing or a movement that seems to alternate back and forth. In early motion pictures, directors struggled with the same problem when wagon wheels appeared to suddenly rotate backward.

Animating the rotation of propellers and rapidly turning wheels depends almost entirely on motion blur. Typically, the rotation is animated just fast enough to give a satisfactory number of samples for each rotation, even though this is far slower than the rotation should be. The effect is then "accelerated" with motion blur.

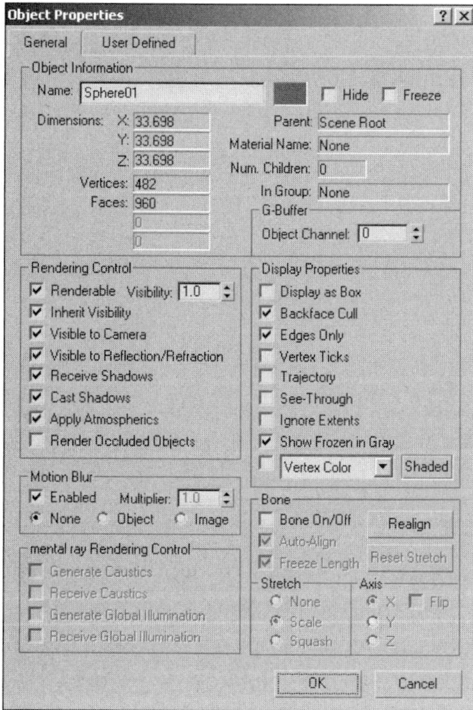

Figure 15.10
The Object Properties dialog box for the selected object, with default settings. The Motion Blur section is to the left. Just beneath the Motion Blur section is an area that would become selectable if the Mental Ray plug-in were installed.

Default Scanline A-Buffer rollout. If you refer back to Figure 15.9, you will see that both Object and Image Motion Blur are enabled by default. This two-layer structure allows you to turn off either (or both) for the entire scene, even if they are enabled for individual objects—a valuable option when making test renders.

6. The basic parameter for both kinds of motion blur is Duration. By default, the blur is computed on the basis of the "shutter" being open half the time (0.5) between successive frames. The longer the Duration, the greater the blur. Try a test render with the default settings. The result will be only slightly blurred.

7. To increase the blur, increase the Duration value to a much larger number, such as 10, and render again. With this extreme value, 10 copies of the Sphere are rendered over the distance the object would cover in 10 frames. This does not look much like true motion blur in a still image, but the effect is much more satisfactory when run in an animation. Your render should look similar to Figure 15.11.

8. Adjust the Samples and Duration Subdivision spinners, and you'll notice something peculiar: Both values top out at 16. The Samples value can be less than or equal to the Duration

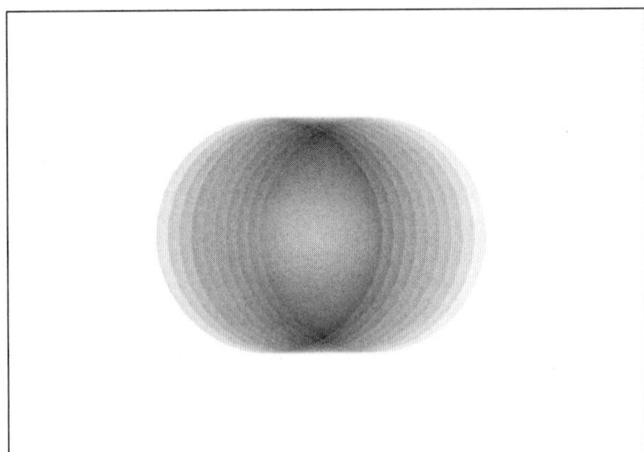

Figure 15.11
Object Motion Blur on an animated Sphere, using an extremely long Duration setting and the default value of 10 for both the Samples and Duration Subdivision spinners. Ten overlapping copies of the Sphere are rendered.

Subdivision value, but not more. The Duration Subdivision is the number of copies rendered in each frame. If the number of Samples is the same as the Duration Subdivision, you get the clean copies similar to Figure 15.11. If the number of Samples is lower than the Duration Subdivision value, however, you'll get a grainy smear in which the separate copies are less discernible. Try a render by using a Duration Subdivision value of 16 but a Samples value of 8. This effect will sometimes produce a more convincing result.

9. Turn off the blur for part of the animation. Bring the Time Slider to Frame 51 and turn on the Animate button. Right-click on the Sphere to open the Object Properties dialog box. Deselect the Enabled checkbox and click on OK. Before you do anything else, turn off the Animate button. Notice that a red block appears in the Track Bar, immediately beneath the Time Slider. Move the Time Slider back to Frame 50 and bring up the Object Properties dialog box for the Sphere. Note that the Enabled checkbox is selected. Move the Time Slider past Frame 51 and look again. The Enabled checkbox is deselected. Enter "47" and "53" in the Range fields in the Time Output area to render the frames just before and after Frame 51 and see the difference.

Although the term *Object Motion Blur* might suggest that the blur doesn't work if the camera—and not the object—is animated, it actually works in either case. To test this behavior, follow these steps:

1. Delete your Sphere and create another in the center of the groundplane.
2. Create a camera that points toward the new Sphere and use the Animate button to move the camera so that the sphere passes across its field of view.
3. Select the Sphere and enable Object Motion Blur in the Object Properties dialog box. Change a viewport to a camera view and render a frame. The result looks the same as when the object, and not the camera, was animated.

Remember something important, however: Even though the camera is animated, the blur is applied only to objects for which the blur was enabled. If you put another object in the scene and don't give it motion blur, it will look oddly sharp. When you animate a camera, you usually need to turn on motion blur for all the objects in the scene. This can be easily accomplished by selecting all the objects together and using the Object Properties dialog box for the multiple selection.

Image Motion Blur

In most cases, Image Motion Blur produces a much better result than Object Motion Blur. Object Motion Blur is typically preferable only where the quality is good enough and the rendering time is much faster than with Image Motion Blur. Object Motion Blur renders multiple copies of the same object and is therefore fastest when the geometry is simple. Image Motion Blur smears pixels after the object is rendered and is therefore independent of geometry.

Image Motion Blur also has the important advantage of having an animatable Multiplier parameter. (The Multiplier spinner applies only to Image Motion Blur.) To get a spinning wheel or propeller to look like it's speeding up or slowing down, you need to be able to animate the amount of blur. And, just as with Object Motion Blur, animating the camera will blur any objects for which Image Motion Blur has been enabled. Unlike Object Motion Blur, Image Motion Blur also can blur an environment map, like a starry sky. To test Image Motion Blur, follow these steps:

1. Use either the animated camera or the animated Sphere scene from the previous exercise. Select the Sphere and use the Object Properties dialog box to enable Image Motion Blur. Note the default Multiplier value of 1.0.

2. Open the Render Scene dialog box and find the Image Motion Blur section. The parameters are few and simple to understand. The Duration spinner performs the same function as with Object Motion Blur: The longer the Duration, the greater the blur. Render a frame using the default values. Note that the object is completely rendered before the blur passes are applied to smear the pixels.

3. The blur is rather small, but go back and animate the Multiplier instead of increasing the Duration value. Drag the Time Slider to Frame 100 and click on the Animate button. Select the Sphere and bring up the Object Properties dialog box. Enter "10.0" in the Multiplier spinner and turn off the Animate button. Move the Time Slider to different frames and look back at the Multiplier values; note that they increase between Frame 0 and Frame 100. Render different frames to see the result. Figure 15.12 shows the Sphere with a moderate amount of blur. Note how much more realistic this render looks than the render with Object Motion Blur in Figure 15.11.

Anti-Aliasing

Anti-aliasing is the process that reduces or eliminates contrasts between adjacent pixels. Without good anti-aliasing, objects appear to have rough edges, and the image looks obviously (and crudely) digital.

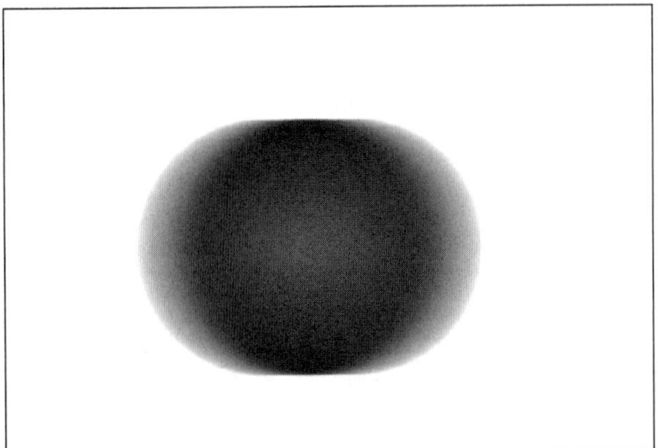

Figure 15.12
Image Motion Blur generally produces a more realistic blur than Object Motion Blur. Compare this image with Figure 15.11.

Anti-aliasing in MAX is always on by default, so you may take it for granted. To understand it, you have to turn it off. Figure 15.13 shows a portion of a Sphere rendered with the Anti-Aliasing option disabled in the Render Scene dialog box. The roughness around the edges is due to the fact the digital images have limited resolution—that is, they are divided into just so many pixels. Pixel color typically changes very suddenly at the edges of rendered objects, and this contrast tends to make the pixel network visible.

Figure 15.13
A portion of a Sphere rendered with the Anti-Aliasing option disabled. The color contrast at the edge of the object makes the pixel network visible.

The answer to this problem is a process that tests the color of each pixel against the color of its adjacent pixels. If the color contrast is above a certain threshold, the pixel probably represents an edge. The colors of adjacent pixels are then blended to smooth the transition of the edge. As you can see in Figure 15.14, anti-aliasing eliminates the roughness very effectively.

Figure 15.14
The same as Figure 15.13, but with MAX's default Anti-Aliasing option turned back on. The colors of the pixels along the edge are blended for a smooth transition.

3ds max 4 has a large range of anti-aliasing options. It includes a long list of filters, shown in Figure 15.15, many of which have adjustable parameters. They may strike you as needless overkill at first, or perhaps as just another complex feature to learn, but they are actually very important. Experiment with these options whenever you render—you'll discover that different choices result in striking differences in render quality. As a general rule, you trade sharpness for smoothness, because anti-aliasing is inherently a blurring technique. The right choice of filter and settings keeps your image sharp while blending only the edges. You can also use the anti-aliasing options to soften an image. Note that the Filter Size option refers to the range of adjacent pixels used in the process. The wider the range (the wider the pixel area considered), the softer or blurrier the result is likely to be.

Render Previews

To test only the motion and composition of an animation, it often makes sense to render out a preview. This is a render only in the strict technical sense, because previews are nothing more than a sequence of screenshots. In other words, they store frames only in the display formats in which they are available in the viewports (Wireframe, Smooth + Highlight, and so on). Because they are prerendered and stored in a video file, they run faster than when you simply use the Play button. They can also be saved for reference and later viewing.

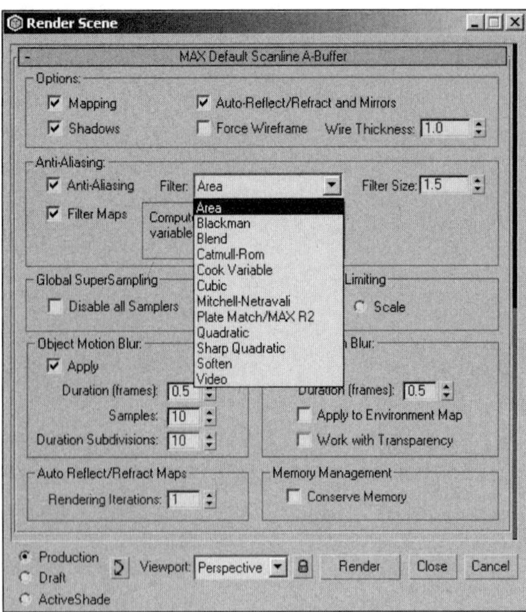

Figure 15.15
The list of anti-aliasing filters available in 3ds max 4. Many of them have adjustable parameters. The correct choice of anti-aliasing options can make a great deal of difference in render quality. MAX's default settings are rarely the best choice.

The Make Preview dialog box, shown in Figure 15.16, is available from the Rendering menu. The controls are self-explanatory. After you make a preview in the default AVI video format, the Windows Media Player immediately appears and runs the preview. If the preview looks unacceptably rough, you can change the codec (compression) settings.

The preview is saved in the Previews directory in your MAX folder. Use the View Preview command on the Rendering menu to review the current preview. You can also rename the current preview so that it won't be overwritten when a new preview is made.

Render Elements

When a scene is rendered, many elements are considered as MAX calculates the output for the final image. These elements include the Alpha channel, the background image, the objects' self-illumination, and more. Another feature new to 3ds max 4 is the ability to render out these elements to separate files that can be used when compositing the scene in a video editing program. The following exercise will show you how to render the scene's elements separately:

1. Create a few primitive objects on top of a Box used as a base. Place a Spot Light in the scene, train it on the objects, and turn on Cast Shadows. In the Environment dialog box, change the background color to a light gray. Render the scene. It should look similar to Figure 15.17.

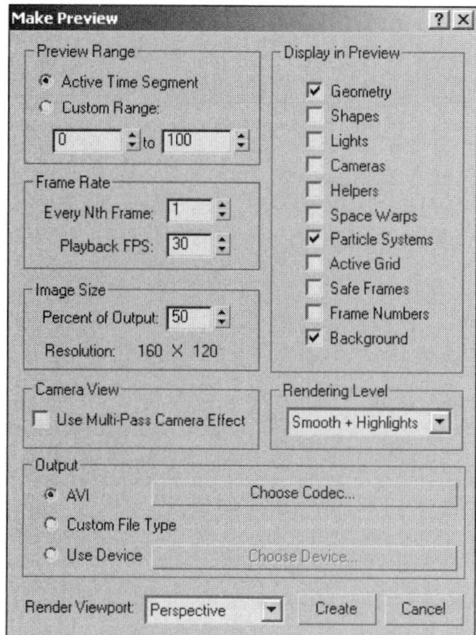

Figure 15.16
The Make Preview dialog box, which is available from the Rendering menu.

Figure 15.17
A simple scene consisting of primitive objects and a shadow-casting Spot Light.

2. Expand the Render Elements rollout in the Render Scene dialog box. Click on the Add button and choose Alpha from the list that appears. Click on the Files button and assign the pathname and file name for the image consisting of the scene's Alpha channel.

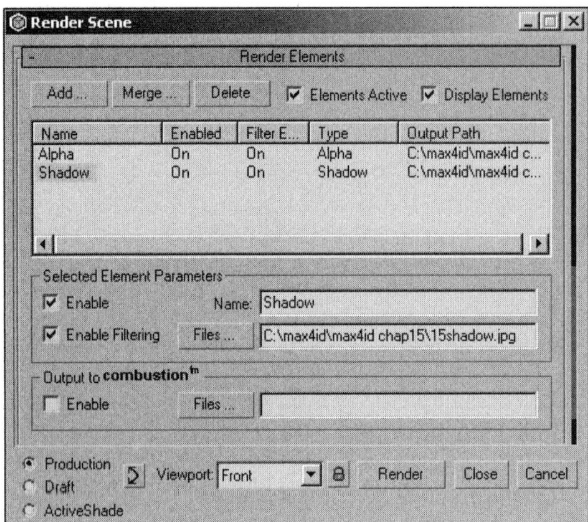

Figure 15.18
The Render Elements rollout set to render the Alpha channel and shadows to separate files.

3. Click on Add again, add the Shadow element to the list, and give it a file name and path. The Render Elements rollout should look similar to Figure 15.18.

4. Render the scene. The Virtual Frame Buffer renders as you would expect. Then, two similar windows, named Alpha and Shadow, open. They contain the elements that you specified should be rendered separately. Click on the Display Alpha Channel button in the Shadow window to see the areas where the shadows fell. Figure 15.19 shows the two elements as they appear in their respective windows.

5. Choose View Image File from the File menu to see the individual files that were written to the hard drive.

ActiveShade

A viewport in Smooth + Highlights can provide you with a good idea of the composition and lighting in a scene. If Show Map In Viewport is active for a particular map, the viewport can also display the maps; this option may often show quite a bit of distortion in the map, however.

The new ActiveShade tool allows a rendered window to contain lighting, shadows, and materials. To make this window occupy a viewport, you right-click on the viewport name and choose ActiveShade from the Views menu. ActiveShade can also be in a separate window called the *ActiveShade floater*, as the following exercise will show:

1. Use the scene from the previous exercise. Make sure the Perspective viewport is active and, from the Main toolbar, click on the far-right button labeled ActiveShade Floater. A new window opens. After a moment, the rendered scene appears.

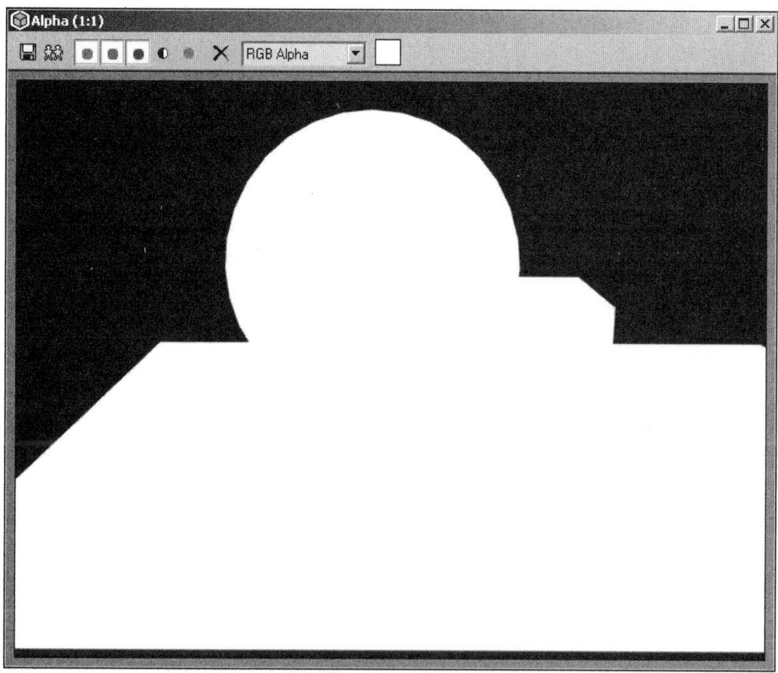

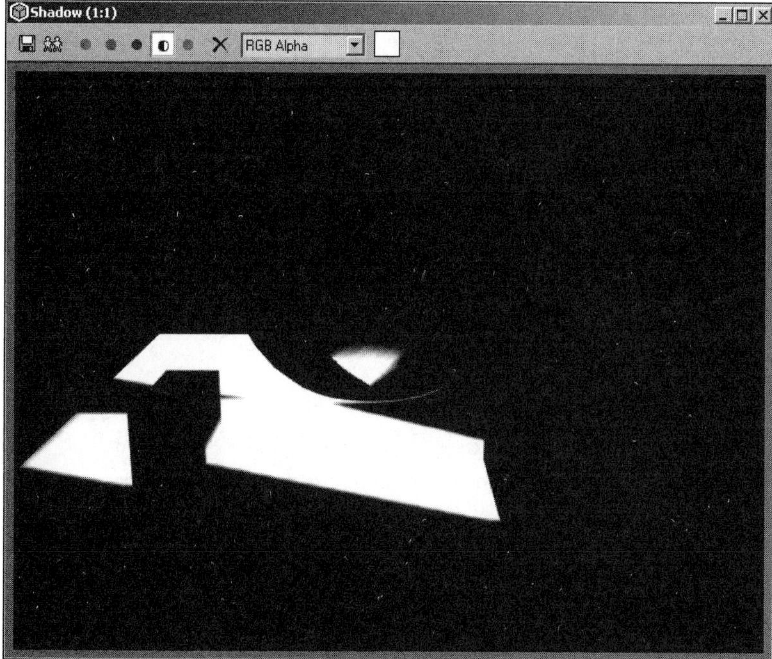

Figure 15.19
The image on the top is the separately rendered Alpha channel element; the image on the bottom shows where the scene's shadows fall. The Display Alpha Channel button was clicked on in the window on the bottom.

2. In the Material Editor, get several mapped Materials from the material library and assign them to the objects in the scene. As each is assigned, it appears in the ActiveShade floater. Notice that, in addition to the Diffuse Color map channel, any Bump-map features are also shown in the ActiveShade window.
3. Move the light. The ActiveShade window updates to reflect the new scene configuration. Notice the yellow line that drops along the right edge of the image to indicate progress as the ActiveShade refreshes itself. Figure 15.20 shows the ActiveShade floater displaying the current scene with Materials applied to the objects in the scene.

Figure 15.20
The ActiveShade floater displaying the current scene, which includes Materials applied to the objects and a shadow-casting light.

Moving On

In this chapter, you learned about all the essential tools for rendering MAX scenes into bitmapped images. You learned how to use the Production and Draft rendering modes, how to save single images and animations, and how to use the Virtual Frame Buffer. You learned about the methods for controlling your output and how to render only fractions of a frame. You explored the main features of MAX's Default Scanline Renderer, compared Object Motion Blur and Image Motion Blur, and learned the importance of anti-aliasing. You looked at the process of creating animation previews and, finally, you explored the new Render Elements and ActiveShade rendering capabilities.

The next chapter will cover MAX's powerful environment and render effects. You'll see how the new Render Effects toolset permits you to develop post-processing effects interactively, such as glows and contrast adjustments, within the regular render process. You'll also learn about environment maps and the various atmospheric effects, such as fog and volumetric lights.

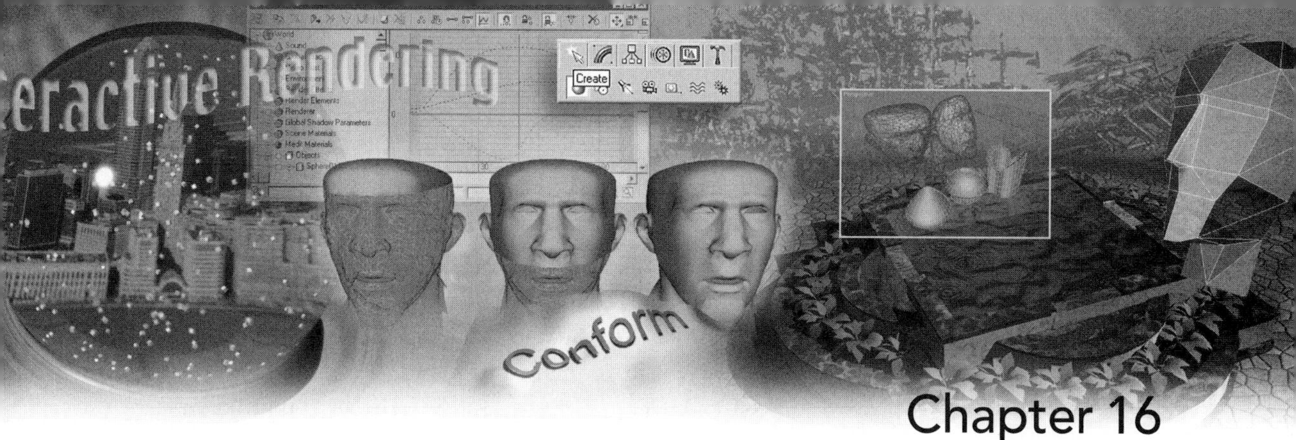

Chapter 16

Environment and Render Effects

The term *visual phenomena* has recently become popular in 3D computer graphics. It suggests that the artist is creating imagery in the most general sense, not just rendering models. Indeed, geometry is hardly the only means for creating visual elements in your scene. Atmospheric effects—such as fog, water, clouds, and fire—are not produced from geometry. These are all created as environment effects in MAX. Because most of them are confined to a defined volume, however, they are often called *volumetric effects*. The volume is defined by a nonrendering geometric object or, in the case of the volume lights, by the light cone.

Another aspect of a MAX environment is the background. Although not a geometric object, it can hold a color or an image that is placed behind all the rendered objects in the scene. An environment map can be projected as if on an infinite sphere or cylinder surrounding the scene.

After rendering is complete, the finished bitmap can be subjected to a wide range of post-processing tools known as *render effects*. Render effects are added immediately after rendering, but without the need of Video Post, as will be discussed in Chapter 21. This makes it much easier to experiment with them in the regular course of workflow. Render effects include the lens effects to create visual "objects" such as glows and flares, and the standard image-adjustment tools for blurs and contrast adjustments.

Render Effects

The subject of render effects is narrow but very deep. Many people make little or no use of any post-processing tools in their work; others use render effects very extensively and become experts in this niche. This chapter doesn't attempt to cover the full scope of this fascinating field, but you'll still get a good general sense of the toolset.

MAX packages two distinct classes of tools under the name "Render Effects." One is the collection of Lens Effects, which are creative tools for producing visual effects such as glows and flares. The other class consists of correction or adjustment tools, which are not designed to produce visual objects, but rather to balance color or blur the image, among other things. These correction tools generally perform the kinds of functions that you can perform in Photoshop with your rendered images, but it's obviously a great convenience to be able to do these tasks in MAX. In any case, all of the render effects are post-processing effects: You fully render the image to pixels before you apply the render effects. Render effects operate on pixels in a bitmap, rather than on objects in the underlying 3D scene.

The Rendering Effects dialog box seems confusing at first; once you learn your way, however, you'll find it's fun to experiment with. Experimentation is at the very heart of using render effects—particularly the Lens Effects group. The more trials and comparisons you can make, the better your result is likely to be. And until you experiment extensively with the toolset, you may not understand its remarkable range of possibilities.

When you bring up the Rendering Effects dialog box (from the Rendering pull-down menu), the list of effects in the Effects rollout is empty. To add effects to the scene, click on the Add button; doing so brings up the Add Effect dialog box, with a list of all the available effects. Figure 16.1 shows the Effects rollout and the Add Effect dialog box. In this example, two effects have been added to the list.

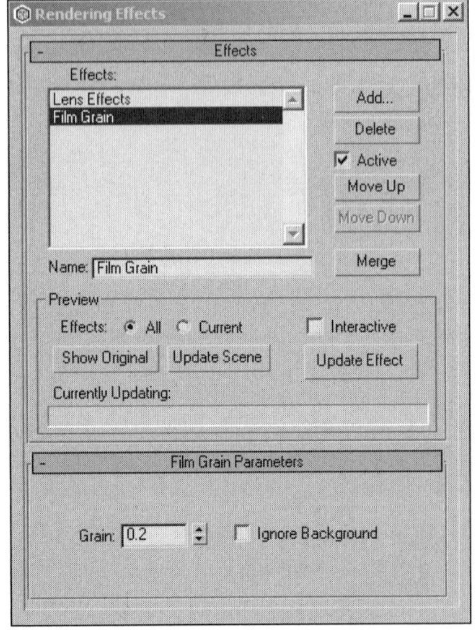

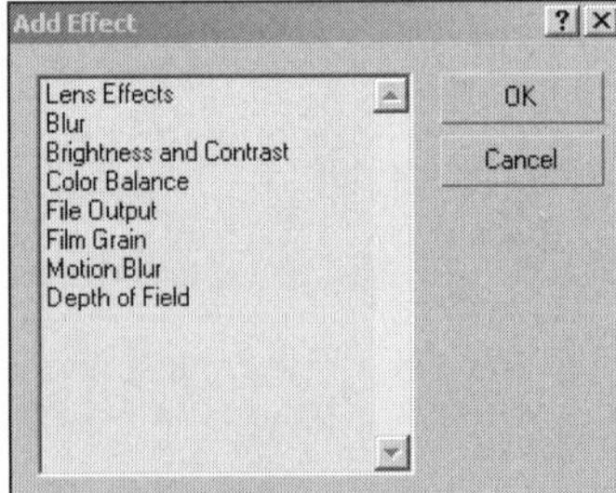

Figure 16.1
The Effects rollout and Parameters rollout for the selected effect of the Rendering Effects dialog box and the Add Effect dialog box. Two effects have already been added to the list.

You can have multiple instances of the same effect. If you do, use the Name field to rename the effect with a distinguishing title. You can delete effects in the scene or simply disable them by deselecting the Active checkbox. You can even incorporate effects from other scenes.

The Preview section of the Effects rollout is the key to the most powerful feature in the toolset. You'll often have to make render after render after render when experimenting with how to construct render effects. Instead of rendering in the usual way, however, you can make your test renders directly from the Preview group. Any objects in the scene are rendered first to the Virtual Frame Buffer. Then, the render effects are applied as post-processing. When you change a render effect and click on the Update Effect button, only the post-processing is updated; this generally saves a considerable amount of time. If the Interactive checkbox is selected, the effect updates automatically every time a parameter is changed. You can always refresh the underlying render by clicking on the Update Scene button. You'll use these tools extensively in the following sections.

Lens Effects

Lens Effects, unlike all the other effects, are a collection rather than a single effect. When you add a Lens Effects package to the scene, you must choose one or more effects within the package to use. The logic of this system makes sense, but it definitely takes some getting used to. Each effect within a Lens Effects package is called a parameter in one of the rollouts and an element in another rollout. The name *parameter* is terribly confusing, because each of these "parameters" has numerous adjustable parameters (like everything else in MAX). To keep this discussion as clear as possible, the collection of Lens Effects will be referred to as *elements*.

Figure 16.2 shows the Rendering Effects dialog box with a Lens Effects package added and selected at the top of the panel. In the Lens Effects Parameters rollout, the list on the left contains all the available effects. The box on the right contains the elements from that list that are being applied in the current Lens Effects package. In this case, Glow and Star elements are being used. The left and right arrows are used to add and remove elements.

Lens Effects are applied to specific objects and lights in the scene. For this reason, you need to be able to have multiple instances of each element. For example, you might need three glowing objects, each with its own Glow parameters. This means adding three separate Glow elements to the list, each directed to a different object. But you can also have multiple elements directed to a single object, and the same elements for multiple objects.

The exercise in the following section introduces you to most of the elements in the Lens Effects package.

Glow

Glow is the most important and generally useful element in the Lens Effects package. Its inclusion in the Lens Effects group is not entirely logical, because all the other elements in the group are related to or derived from the effects that occur when using a lens on a real camera.

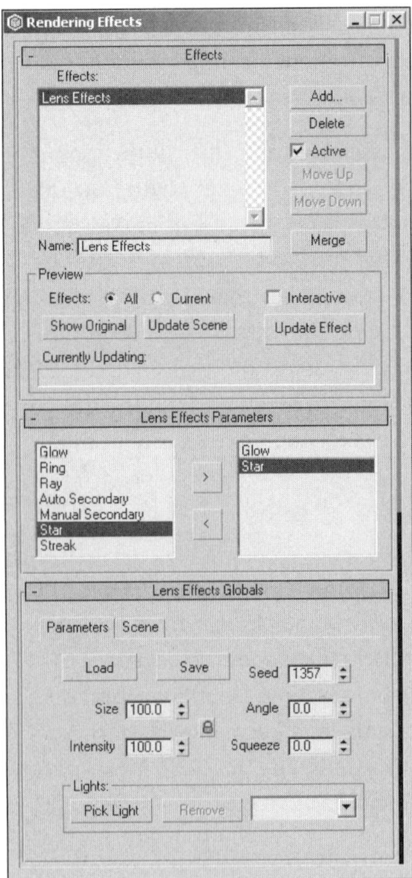

Figure 16.2
The Rendering Effects dialog box with a single Lens Effects package added and selected at the top of the panel. In the Lens Effects Parameters rollout, Glow and Star have been selected from the list of available elements for the current Lens Effects package.

Although these elements are used for a broad range of visual purposes, they are essentially variations of the basic lens flare that appears when a lens looks directly into a light source. On the other hand, a Glow is simply a region of colored pixels around an object that creates the sensation that the object is self-illuminated. As such, a Glow can be applied to the entire surface of an object. The other elements can emanate only from a point.

You add a Glow element in the Lens Effects Parameters rollout of the Rendering Effects dialog box. This dialog box's Lens Glow Element rollout is the meat of the business. The rollout is divided into two tabs: The Parameters tab provides all the parameters that control the appearance of the Glow, and the Options tab determines where the Glow will be applied in the scene. Take a moment to examine these controls. Both tabs are illustrated in Figure 16.3.

Start with the Options tab. A Glow can be applied to a light or to geometry. If it is applied to geometry, it can be applied to the surface of the object or it can simply radiate from a point in

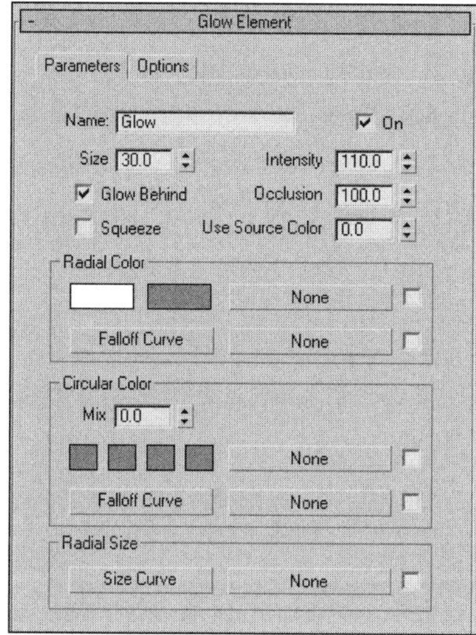

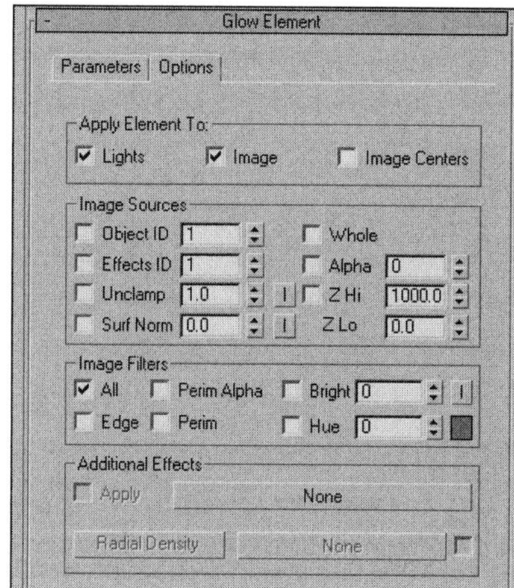

Figure 16.3
The two tabs in the Glow Element rollout. The Parameters tab (*left*) provides all the parameters that control the appearance of the Glow. The Options tab (*right*) determines where the Glow will be applied in the scene.

the center of the object. In the Apply Element To section, the Lights and Image options are active, by default. No lights appear in the scene—the default lights do not count for this purpose. The Image option uses the pixels attributable to specified objects. You can make this assignment. If the entire surface of the object is to be used for the Glow, you can use the Object ID. If the Glow is to be applied only to specified regions of the surface, you can use the Effects ID. One object can have only a single Object ID, although multiple objects can share one Object ID. An Effects ID is assigned to a material in the Material Editor (by using the Material Effects Channel button). Any portion of an object (or multiple objects) with that material will receive the Glow.

The size of a Glow is a function of both the Global Size for the entire Lens Effects package and the Size parameter for the single Glow element. Like all of the lens effects, a Glow can use three different color effects: Source Color, Radial Color, and Circular Color.

Let's experiment with applying a Glow:

1. Create a Cylinder in the middle of the groundplane with a Radius value of 10 and a Height value of 30, and zoom in on it in the Perspective viewport. You can adjust its size as you go along.

2. Open the Material Editor and assign the Cylinder a Material. Give the Material a bright yellow Diffuse Color value. This will be the Source Color of the object when you apply render effects.

3. Open the Rendering Effects dialog box from the Rendering menu and add a Lens Effects package to the scene. Use the arrow buttons in the Lens Effects Parameters rollout to add a single Glow element to the empty package.

4. As you scroll down through the rest of this long dialog box, you'll come to the Lens Effects Globals rollout. The Parameters and Scene tabs in this rollout provide parameters that affect all components in the Lens Effects package together. Because you are using only a single element (Glow), you can ignore this panel for now.

5. Use the Object ID approach to assign the pixels the application should use when it generates the Glow. Select and right-click on the Cylinder and bring up the Object Properties dialog box from the Quad menu. Look for the G-Buffer section and change the Object Channel number to 1. (A G-Buffer stores information for each pixel in a rendered image that designates the object in the scene that generated the pixel.) Click on the OK button to close the Object Properties dialog box and return to the Glow Element panel. Activate the Object ID option and make sure that the value is set to 1. The application now knows to use the pixels rendered from the Cylinder when generating the Glow. Note that the All checkbox is selected in the Image Filters section; as a result, all the pixels from the Cylinder will be used.

6. Scroll to the top of the Rendering Effects dialog box and click on the Update Effect button. The scene will render in the Virtual Frame Buffer, as usual; after a short while, the Glow will be applied. The Cylinder is surrounded with a tapering white glow and its center is burned out. What happened?

7. First, you need to get the size under control. Reduce the Size value drastically in the Parameters tab of the Glow Element rollout, from the default of 30 to 3 or 4. Click on the Update Effect button again to recompute the Glow without rerendering the scene. You may need to adjust your Perspective viewport to center the object; if you do, use the Update Scene button to rerender everything. Figure 16.4 shows the result of using a Size value of 3.

8. It still looks like a white burn spot rather than a glow. You can start experimenting to get a softer effect, and the Intensity spinner is a good place to start. The default value is 110. You can try lowering it drastically, even below 1.0, but this will not make much difference. The problem is the color. By default, the Use Source Color parameter is set to 0, and thus it is not a factor in your current glow. The Circular Color Mix value is also set to 0. Therefore, only the Radial Color is being used. The default white color is much too hot. Click on the white color box for Radial Color and bring the color down to a medium gray. Make test after test, changing the Intensity and the Size values until you can clearly see the Cylinder through a soft white glow. Be prepared to be surprised by the interaction of all these parameters. Figure 16.5 shows an acceptable result.

9. You have probably realized the biggest single problem with Glows—it's very easy to make them too hot. You can use the Source Color of the object rather than the Radial Color—increase the Use Source Color value to 100 percent and start experimenting. You'll soon discover that decreasing Intensity alone is not enough. Just as with the Radial Color, you'll probably need to darken the yellow Diffuse Color of the Material in the Material Editor.

Figure 16.4
An upright Cylinder with a Glow effect applied to all of its pixels. Except for Size, all of the parameters are at their defaults.

After you do, remember to use Update Scene to rerender from scratch, because the Glow must start with the color of the pixels in the rendered image. After a lot of experimenting with Size and Intensity values, you'll probably get something that looks okay—but the Glow on the surface of the object will remain uneven. Why is that?

10. Remember that you are using the rendered pixel colors, not the Diffuse Color of the Material. Even though the Material is a single hue, the color of the pixels on the object varies due to shading. In particular, the caps of the Cylinder are probably darker than the front of the object. To even out the color of the pixels, significantly increase the Self-Illumination factor for the Material in the Material Editor (deselect the Color checkbox first). Use Update Scene to rerender from scratch. This time, the Glow is more evenly distributed over the Cylinder, which finally looks like a glowing yellow tube. A black-and-white picture is not really adequate, but Figure 16.6 should give you the general idea.
11. Return to the Options tab of the Glow Element rollout. You've been using the All option in the Image Filters section to generate the Glow from all the pixels in the Cylinder. Some-

Figure 16.5
The same as Figure 16.4, but with the Radial Color darkened from white to gray to reduce intensity. The Size and Intensity values have been adjusted so you can see the illuminated Cylinder from within the Glow.

times, it makes sense to restrict the Glow to the region outside the object. To make the effect clearer, go back to the Material Editor and remove the Self-Illumination factor. Then, try the Perimeter Alpha option in the Image Filters section. You changed the underlying color of the object, so remember to rerender from scratch. Play with other parameters, as needed, to get a good result. As you can see from Figure 16.7, the object no longer appears to be glowing itself; instead, it is highlighted by a background glow.

Next, let's take a look at using Glow with lights. You can apply a Glow to any type of light, but the effect is always the same: The Glow radiates out spherically from the location of the light. Delete your Cylinder and create an Omni Light in the center of World space. In the Rendering Effects dialog box, reset all the options for the Glow element to their default values. Use the two parts of Figure 16.3 for reference. Now, follow these steps:

1. Before anything can happen, you have to include the light in the Lens Effects. In the Parameters tab of the Lens Effects Globals rollout, click on the Pick Light button, and then click on your light in a viewport. The name of the light will appear in the panel.

Figure 16.6
The same as Figure 16.5, but with the Use Source Color option used and parameters adjusted. To get the even glow that suggests a self-illuminated object, the Material was given self-illumination. This creates a more consistent color for the pixels rendered from the object; the consistent color is then passed on to the Glow.

2. Click on the Update Scene button to render. An empty scene renders first, and then the Glow is applied in post-processing. Unlike the situation in which you rendered the Cylinder, your initial Glow trial should look pretty good—something like Figure 16.8. Be sure you're in a Perspective (or camera) viewport.

3. If you look carefully at your own image (not at the black-and-white figure), you'll notice a slight reddening around the perimeter of the glow. This is the second of the two radial colors. Click on the Falloff Curve button in the Radial Color section to bring up the graph in the Radial Falloff dialog box. The default curve tails off swiftly toward a zero value, which is why the red color is so faint. Drag the last point on this curve up to 1.0 and use its Bezier handle to create a straight line, if necessary. Click on the Update Effect button. This time, the red color remains at full intensity all the way to the end of the glow. The result is like a solid sphere—white at the center and changing to red toward the edges. Your result should look like Figure 16.9.

Figure 16.7
Using the Perimeter Alpha option in the Image Filters section restricts the glow to only the region surrounding the object. The Cylinder no longer appears to be self-illuminated but is highlighted by a background glow.

4. To get a Glow that falls off at a constant rate, adjust the curve in the Radial Falloff dialog box so that it falls from 1 to 0 in a straight line. Play with different radial colors to see what's possible. Change other parameters, such as Size and Intensity. The possibilities are endless.

5. Although you can mix in the source color of the light, let's look at the Circular Color option. The default Mix value for Circular Color is 0. Increase it to the maximum of 100 and update. Your Glow turns completely red.

6. The four color boxes are currently red. Change them to four different colors and update. The Glow is now a circular color gradient, passing through all four colors. Click on the Falloff Curve button in the Circular Color section to get a graph like the one you just used for radial color. By default, it's a constant value of 1. Play with different curves to see the result. Decreasing values along the graph decreases the intensity of the glow. Figure 16.10 shows the effect of Circular Fallout. In contrast, the Radial Size graph decreases the size of the glow as it circles the light.

Figure 16.8
A Glow is applied to a single Omni Light, using default settings.

Figure 16.9
The same as Figure 16.8, but with the falloff eliminated. The Glow remains at constant intensity all the way to the perimeter. Without the falloff, the color gradient from white to red is clearly evident, even in this black-and-white image. The apparent gray in the image is actually bright red.

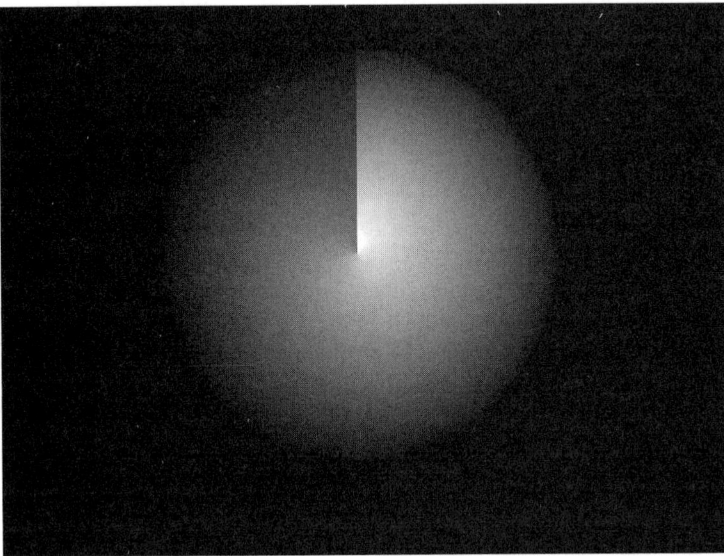

Figure 16.10
Illustration of Circular Falloff for a Glow around an Omni Light.

Other Lens Effects

Once you have the Glow element pretty well figured out, the other Lens Effects elements are easy—they have similar parameters for Size, Intensity, and the color options. The primary difference between Glow and the other Lens Effects elements (as mentioned previously) is that whereas Glow can be applied across the surface of an object, the other elements necessarily radiate from a single point. You can apply them to any light, but if applied to a geometric object, they operate only from a point in the center of the object.

Take a quick run through these elements, and add them on top of each other:

1. Reset your scene, if necessary, to start fresh. Create a Box primitive in the center of the groundplane.

2. Open the Rendering Effects dialog box and add a Lens Effects package. In the Lens Effects Parameters rollout, bring a Ring element over to the right side. Just as with Glow, the Ring Element rollout has Parameters and Options tabs. In the Options tab, note that the Image checkbox is grayed out. Select the Image Centers option.

3. To let the application know what object you want the Ring applied to, select the Object ID option. Bring up the Object Properties dialog box for the Box and set its G-Buffer Object Channel to 1. Try a render from the Render Effects panel. The Box renders first, and then the Ring is applied. But the Ring knows nothing about the size of the Box. It's just centered on the Box, and therefore can look like it was pasted on it, as shown in Figure 16.11, or it can surround the Box with a relatively huge radius.

Figure 16.11
A Ring element is applied to the image center of a Box. The Ring has no relationship to the size of the Box and looks like it was pasted on top.

Of course, you can adjust the Size of the Ring, but all the Lens Effects elements (other than Glow) are more typically applied to lights. That's because they create reflection-like effects that are derived from the basic lens flare that occurs when intense light reflects off the surface of a lens (as when light rings appear in photographs). For example, follow these steps:

1. Delete the Box and create an Omni Light in the center of World space. By default, all Lens Effects apply to lights, but you have to use the Pick Light tool in the Lens Effects Globals rollout to include the specific lights. Once you set up the lights, remember to click on Update Scene to rerender in a Perspective viewport from the ground up.

2. You now have a very satisfactory Ring that uses the white and red default Radial Colors. To adjust the size of the Ring, try changing the Size value in the Lens Effects Globals rollout. Your render should resemble Figure 16.12.

3. Add a Ray element to the package in the Lens Effects Parameters and update your render. The Ray sends out streaks radially around the light (see Figure 16.13). The number of Ray elements is set in the Parameters tab of the Ray Element rollout, along with all the other standard parameters, such as Size and Intensity. Change the Size value in the Lens Effects Globals rollout and update. Note that the Ring and the Ray elements are scaled together.

4. Remove the Ray element with the arrow buttons and add a Star element in its place. Update again (or select the Interactive checkbox for automatic updates) and you'll see that the Star is very similar to the Ray. Unlike the Ray, the Star pattern is regular and the tapering of its rays can be adjusted. Increase the Intensity of the Star alone (not globally) to make it stand out against the ring. Figure 16.14 shows a Star element with its Taper value adjusted.

Figure 16.12
A Ring element applied to an Omni Light. Because the light is not volumetric, you cannot see it specifically—only the assigned ring effect.

Figure 16.13
The same as Figure 16.12, but with a Ray element added, using the default parameters.

5. You don't need to remove an element to disable it. Deselect the On checkbox in the Star Element rollout's Parameters panel. Now, add a Streak element and update. The Streak is quite tiny, by default. Its intended function is to simulate scratches on the surface of a lens. In Figure 16.15, the Width of the Streak has been increased to its maximum of 20.

Figure 16.14
The same as Figure 16.13, but with a Star element in place of the Ray. The Star's rays have been tapered outward and its Intensity value has been increased to make it stand out against the Ring.

Figure 16.15
The same as Figure 16.14, but with a Streak element added and the Star element disabled. The Streak is seen at its maximum Width value of 20.

Other Render Effects

As we've already discussed, all the render effects other than Lens Effects provide batch image processing of rendered images. These effects include Blur, Brightness and Contrast, Color Balance, File Output, Film Grain, Motion Blur, and Depth of Field.

Blur

You can go crazy with the possibilities available in the Blur Parameters rollout, but the settings will be simple most of the time. Generally, you'll want a uniform blur, but you can create a directional or even a radial blur. You can blur the entire image or only a portion, such as the background or a selection defined by luminance or with a mask.

Blurring shows up in so many places in MAX that you may never need this tool. Try using the new selection of anti-aliasing filters in the Render Scene dialog box to create blurring during, rather than after, the render process.

Brightness and Contrast

Nothing could be simpler than the controls in the Brightness And Contrast Parameters rollout. You can adjust the Brightness and Contrast values of your frames as they are output from the renderer, which can be much easier than adjusting the lighting in the scene.

Color Balance

Like Brightness and Contrast, the Color Balance tool is right out of programs like Photoshop. You can shift hues from red to cyan (green-blue), from green to magenta (red-blue), and from blue to yellow (red-green). Anyone familiar with basic bitmap-editing techniques may already understand this tool.

File Output

File Output is a way of saving a frame before some or all of the render effects are applied. The placement of the File Output effect on the list determines the stage at which saving occurs.

Film Grain

Film Grain applies a look that you can get in Photoshop or any bitmap editor with Gaussian Noise. A grainy look is an interesting touch in itself, but the main purpose of this tool is to blend a MAX scene nicely with background images that were scanned from photographs. A checkbox allows you to exclude the background image from the Film Grain effect.

Motion Blur

The Motion Blur effect yields the same result as using the Multi-Pass Effect option of the same name (in a Camera's Modify panel). Additionally, the Motion Blur effect has an option that allows objects located behind transparent objects to be omitted from the blur operation. Omitting these objects decreases render time.

Depth of Field

Depth of Field is an important effect. A real-life camera has a range of focus in depth. If a large aperture setting is used on the lens, objects in front of and behind the object being focused on will be out of focus. As the aperture closes down, the depth of field increases, and foreground and background objects remain in focus. Limiting the depth of field is an essential tool in photography and filmmaking, because it focuses viewer attention on an object or character. Computer graphics uses an ideal pinhole camera, in which everything is in focus—an effect that strikes many viewers as unrealistic.

The simplest way to use the Depth of Field effect is to pick an object as the Focal Node. This object will be the center of the range of focus. The Focal Range spinner controls the distance that will remain in focus both in front of and behind this point. The Focal Limit value defines the depth over which the blurring will reach its maximum. The maximum degree of blur is defined in the Horizontal and Vertical Focal Loss spinners. Because these last two values should generally be the same, a spinner lock is available to keep them identical.

Environment

Three separate toolsets are grouped under the Environment heading. Figure 16.16 shows the Environment dialog box with its default settings; you can reach this dialog box via the Rendering menu.

The Common Parameters rollout contains two of the three Environment toolsets. The Global Lighting section sets the ambient light for the scene and lets you globally adjust the tint and

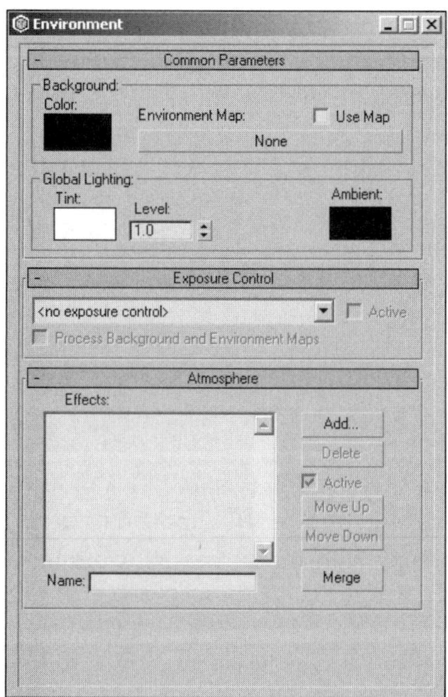

Figure 16.16
The Environment dialog box, with its default settings.

intensity of all the light sources in the scene. It's a great convenience to be able to adjust all the lights together. These same controls also appear in the Light Lister, but (unlike the Light Lister) they operate even on the default lighting.

The Background section of the Common Parameters rollout allows you to choose the background color and to apply an environment map. The background color is the color of all pixels that are not attributable to rendered objects. The background color is completely independent of the lighting in the scene. If you raise or lower the intensity of the lights (or change their colors), the background color does not change at all—it can therefore look very artificial, unless you adjust it carefully. Sometimes, it makes sense to enclose your scene in a large sphere or to put a flat plane in the rear of the scene, in order to get a background that responds to scene lighting. The Environment Map option allows you to replace the background color with a map.

When the Automatic Exposure Control option is selected in the Exposure Control rollout, an additional Parameters rollout becomes available. This rollout gives you control over the dynamic range of the brightness of a scene. Automatic Exposure Control can help adjust the brightness of attenuated lights to simulate the greater range that the human eye can see into the limited range that a monitor can display.

The Atmosphere rollout provides MAX's atmospheric effects. Like the render effects, these are post-processing effects that are applied to a bitmap after the frame is rendered. These effects include Fog, Volume Fog, Volume Light, and Fire Effect.

***Note:** Fire Effect is the renamed feature formerly called Combustion. Because 3ds max 4 is now part of Discreet's product line, this effect's name was changed so it wouldn't be confused with one of Discreet's other products, called "combustion*".*

Environment Maps

You can apply maps to your background for greater realism or a stronger visual effect than is possible with a single color. These environment maps can be applied in a number of ways. The following exercise will get you up to speed.

The Basic Screen Projection

Let's see how to work with a Screen projection:

1. Start a new scene without any objects. Open the Environment dialog box and click on the Environment Map button (labeled None). The Material/Map Browser will appear. Choose the Bitmap map type. A dialog box will appear, enabling you to choose a specific bitmap.
2. To understand the process, use the same uvtest.tif bitmap you used in Chapter 12. (You can find it on the CD-ROM.) It is a square bitmap, illustrating UV coordinate space. The U-direction is horizontal, and the V-direction is vertical. The bottom-left corner is at 0,0 in UV coordinates, and the top-right corner is at 1,1. Figure 16.17 illustrates this bitmap. Make sure you understand this image before you go on.

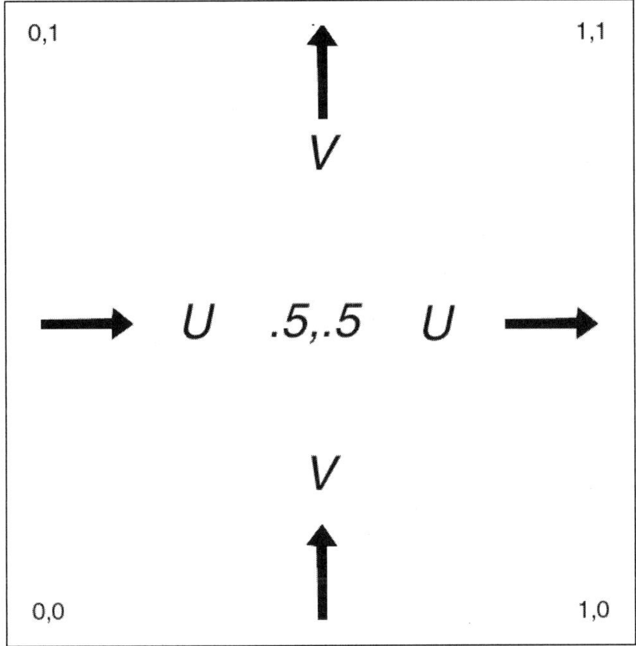

Figure 16.17
The uvtest.tif bitmap from the CD, illustrating UV coordinate space. The U-direction is horizontal and the V-direction is vertical. The bottom-left corner is at 0,0 in UV coordinates, and the top-right corner is at 1,1.

3. Render from a Perspective viewport. By default, the environment map is applied as a screen projection, meaning that it's fitted to the screen. Because the default render output uses a 1.333 aspect ratio, the screen is wider than it is tall. The bitmap is stretched horizontally to fit, as you can see in Figure 16.18. Generally, you need a bitmap with the same aspect ratio as your rendered output to use a Screen projection.

4. Open the Material Editor and pick a slot. Click on the Get Material button to bring up the Material/Map Browser. You want to get the current environment map into the slot, so choose Scene from the Browse From list. Double-click on the environment map when it appears. The environment map should now be assigned to the slot.

5. Take a look at the Coordinates rollout in the Material Editor. Note that the current Mapping projection is Screen. You can try some other options in a moment. Experiment with Offset and Tiling values to see what they do. As a rule, a map that was designed for a screen projection will not tile or offset correctly. Play with the Blur offset spinner. Sometimes, an image mapped directly to the background will be distractingly sharp. A little blur applied only to the environment map can help. Reset the parameters to their defaults before you go on (Offset = 0, Tiling = 1).

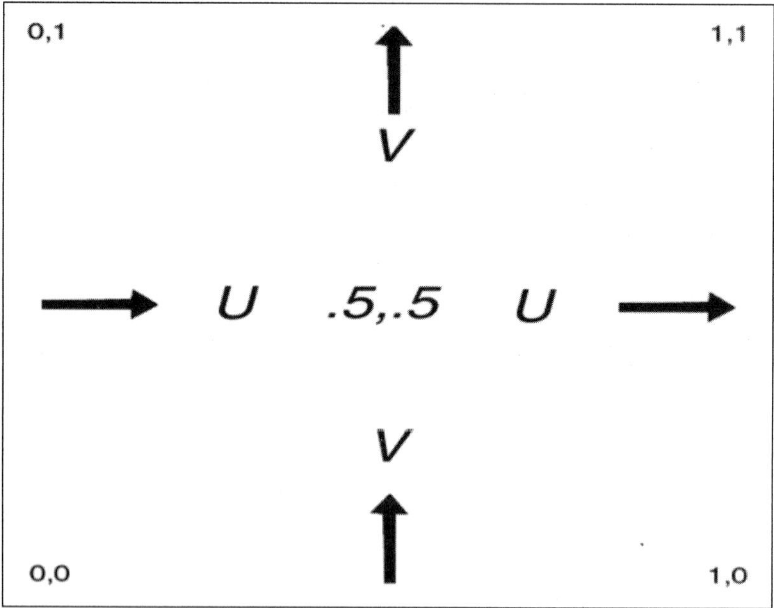

Figure 16.18
The bitmap shown in Figure 16.17 is applied as an environment map in an empty scene and rendered. The default Screen projection fits the image to the dimensions of the screen. Because the default output aspect ratio is 1.333, the environment map has been stretched horizontally.

Using an Animated Background

You can use a video file instead of a still image. The subject of compositing live-action backgrounds into MAX scenes is an extremely important professional technique. You will find, however, that it often makes sense to composite MAX animations together. For example, you might want to render out an animated sky background with moving clouds. You can then use this animation as an environment map (using Screen projection) behind an animated model of a fighter plane. The tools for using animated maps are found in the Time rollout in the Material Editor.

---

6. Unless you are using an animated map, a Screen projection doesn't make sense if the camera will be animated. And a Screen projection seems sometimes unconvincingly flat, in any event. Change from Screen projection to Spherical Environment projection in the Mapping drop-down list. This projection maps the image to the inside of an infinitely large virtual sphere surrounding your scene. This process is generally preferable to creating your own giant sphere, because it adds no geometry to clutter your scene. Render the Perspective viewport again. Only a tiny fraction of the image is blown up to fill the screen, because your field of view is only a tiny fraction of the circumference of the sphere.
7. The background image is necessarily very grainy, even using a fairly large bitmap. Very few background bitmaps can be designed to be tilable. A starry sky is the only example that

comes to mind of a pattern that can be seamlessly repeated without attracting attention—and even this image is tough. For the most part, you need to be able to tile and offset the image so that a single tile fits within the frame (or covers the entire range of camera angles). This is not an easy task, so take some time here to give it a try. You'll need to try many renders to make it work, so reduce your image size to 320×240 to speed up the process. Adjust the Offset and Tiling values incrementally in both U and V until you have a single instance of the image to fit within a frame, with the corners of the bitmap over the edge to leave room for a little camera movement. Be prepared for some frustration. When you finish, a rendered image should look something like Figure 16.19.

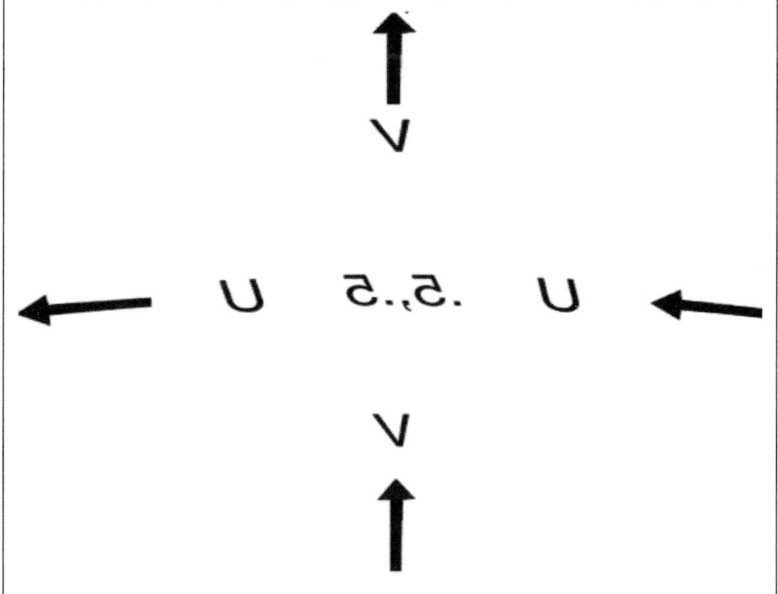

Figure 16.19
The same as Figure 16.18, but using a Spherical Environment projection. The image has been mapped to the inside of an infinite sphere. After a great deal of experimentation with Offset and Tiling values, only a single instance of the bitmap fills the frame (with the edges hanging over to leave room for a little camera rotation). The image is backward in the horizontal direction.

8. A Cylindrical Environment projection differs from a spherical one in that it doesn't curve in the vertical direction. Such a projection is sometimes easier to use if the camera does not point very much above or below the horizon. Change to a Cylindrical Environment projection, and once again try to get a single instance of the image to fill the screen. This is a tough job, and the primary reason for addressing the problem here is to stress the difficulty of working with Spherical and Cylindrical Environment projections. The Shrink-Wrap option is even more difficult to use and is only rarely useful.

Atmospheric Effects

Atmospheric effects are used to give substance to space. Even on a relatively clear day, mist or particulate matter in the air causes objects to become blurrier with distance from the viewer. And many scenes require fog, smoke, or even the sense that they are under water. MAX provides Fog as an atmosphere that pervades the entire scene. In contrast, Volume Fog is confined to defined volumes and is therefore useful for clouds and similar effects. Volume Lights likewise confine the atmospheric haze to the volume of a light cone, to create the effect that is typical of theatrical and outdoor spotlights. Fire Effect is a completely different kind of end product. To create the impression of fire and explosions, bright but ragged volumetric atmospheres can be animated. You can add any number of atmospheric effects together in a single scene. The following sections discuss these atmospheric effects—Fog, Volume Fog, Fire Effect, and Volume Light.

Fog

The standard MAX Fog environment effect is not confined to a precise volume, and it is therefore appropriate for large-scale atmospheres, whether of airborne mist or under water. Fog is available in two flavors: Standard and Layered. The default is Standard Fog. Unlike Layered Fog, Standard Fog fills the entire scene. The following exercise covers all the basics for both Standard and Layered Fog:

1. With a fresh scene, create a Box in the center of the groundplane. Make it 30 units wide and long and 60 units high. Make sure that the Box is a strongly saturated color to test its visibility through fog. Open the Environment dialog box and use the Add button in the Atmosphere rollout to add a Fog to the list of effects. Carefully examine the Fog Parameters rollout that appears below it. The panel is shown in Figure 16.20.

2. Render your perspective view to take your first look at Standard Fog. The entire background should be bright white, and the Box should be softened by a white haze.

3. Deselect the Fog Background checkbox and render again. This time, the background is solid black, although the Box is still hazed. Note that black is the default background color at the top of the Environment panel. When the Fog Background checkbox is selected, the fog color is used for the background. When it is not selected, the background color is used. There's no middle ground, but this is generally okay. In most scenes, the fog color naturally consumes the far distance. Select the Fog Background checkbox again before continuing.

4. The Near and Far percentages are easy to understand. By default, the Near percentage is 0, and the Far percentage is 100. These values mean that the fog density is 0 immediately in front of the viewer, and it reaches full density at a long distance away. This point will be clarified in a moment. Increase the Near value to 100 percent and rerender. The scene is completely white, because the fog density is 100 percent immediately in front of the viewer. Return the Near value to 0 and reduce the Far value to 50 percent. Render again. The background is now gray, because the white fog has only 50-percent density when applied

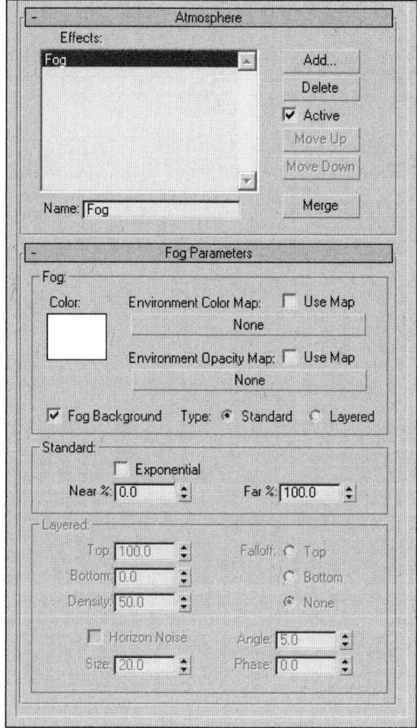

Figure 16.20
The Atmosphere and Fog Parameters rollouts in the Environment dialog box. A Fog effect has been added to the list of effects at top. Any number of effects can be included in a single scene.

to the black background color. The Box is also brighter because the density is less at every point in depth. Reset your Far percentage value to 100 before continuing.

Because you have not created a Camera and are rendering from a Perspective viewpoint, you do not have control over the environment range. The environment range defines the near and far distances from a Camera over which the fog will be applied. Create a Camera (either a Free or Target type) with a view of your scene that is similar to the one in your Perspective viewport and assign the Camera to a viewport. Adjust your Top viewport so that you have a good view of the camera cone. Now, follow these steps:

1. In the Modify panel for the Camera, find the Environment Ranges section. Note that, by default, the Near Range is 0 and the Far Range is 1,000. As a result (as when rendering from a Perspective viewport), the fog begins immediately in front of the Camera and reaches its maximum intensity at 1,000 units. Select the Show checkbox to see these ranges in the Camera Cone. This feature works the same as the clipping planes. Change the Near and Far Range spinner values and watch the indicator lines move back and forth. You'll probably have to type in the Far value with a much lower number, because a distance of 1,000 units is very far away from the Camera to begin with.

2. To test the environment ranges, copy your Box object twice and arrange the three Boxes in increasing depths from the Camera. Adjust the Near and Far Range values until the Near Range begins after the nearest Box and the Far Range ends before the farthest Box. Your Top viewport should look something like Figure 16.21.

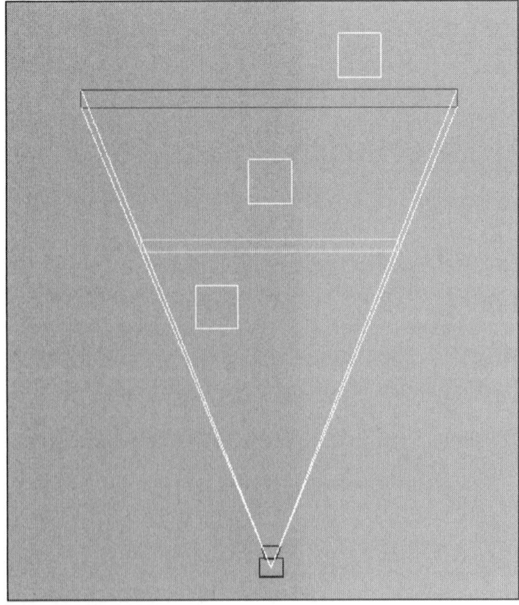

Figure 16.21
A Top viewport showing environment ranges set for a Camera. The Camera faces three Box objects at increasing distances. The Near Range value is set between the first and second Boxes, and the Far Range value is set between the second and third Boxes. Fog will be applied only within these limits.

3. Activate your Camera viewport, and then render. As you can see in Figure 16.22, the closest Box is completely unobscured by the fog. The middle Box is partially obscured, because it's in the middle of the environment range. The most distant Box disappeared because, like the background, it is completely obscured by the fog color.

4. By default, fog density increases linearly at a constant rate from the Near to Far values. Select the Exponential checkbox in the Fog Parameters rollout to make the density increase much more quickly across the environment range. When you render again, notice how much denser the fog becomes on the Box within the environment range. Take a look at Figure 16.23.

Now that you understand the basics of Standard Fog, let's move on to Layered Fog. Switch your Fog Type from Standard to Layered and note that the Layered section of the Fog Parameters rollout becomes active. Take a good look at the parameters, illustrated in Figure 16.24. Standard fog operates in a range of depth from the Camera. In contrast, Layered Fog operates verti-

Figure 16.22
A render through the Camera from Figure 16.21. As discussed in the text, the closest Box is completely unobscured by the fog, the middle Box is partially obscured, and the most distant Box disappeared because it is completely obscured by the fog color.

Figure 16.23
The same as Figure 16.22, but with the Exponential checkbox selected. The fog density increases much more quickly from near to far across the environment range, causing the Box in the center to be more obscured by fog than in the previous figure. The Box at left is outside the environment range, and therefore it is unaffected.

cally in World space. The basic parameters are therefore Top and Bottom instead of Near and Far. By default, the Layered Fog starts on the groundplane (Z = 0) and continues until Z = 100. Fog density is set to 50 percent.

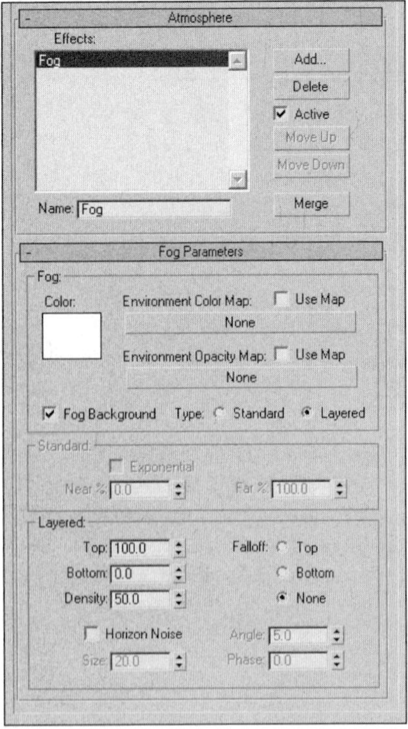

Figure 16.24
The Environment dialog box, showing a Layered Fog effect with default values. A vertical layer of fog begins at the groundplane (Z = 0) and ends at Z = 100. Fog Density is set to 50 percent.

Layered Fog sounds easy in principle, but it can be confusing to use. You should know that it makes a great deal of difference whether the Camera itself is in the fog layer. Assuming the default settings, the Camera will be in the fog if its position is between 0 and 100 in the World Z-dimension. If the Camera is located above the plane where Z = 100, it will be above the fog and looking down on it. Right now, your Boxes stand 60 units high on the groundplane. To work with Layered Fog, follow these steps:

1. Set the Top value of the fog to 30 so that the fog layer is limited to only the bottom half of the Boxes. Then, position your Camera vertically at Z = 20 in World coordinates. Make sure you're in the World coordinate system for the rest of this exercise.

2. Point the Camera in a straight horizontal line toward the Boxes. If you're using a Free Camera, just rotate it. If you're using a Target Camera, move the Target object. Figure 16.25 shows a Left viewport of this setup and the resulting view through the Camera. Because the fog is between 0 and 30, the Camera is in the fog. Environment ranges (in depth) have no significance for layered fog, so hide them by deselecting the Show checkbox in the Parameters rollout of the Camera panel.

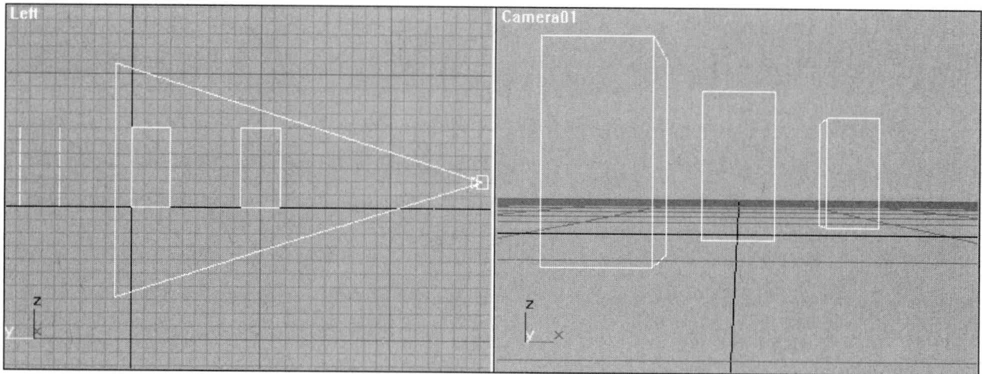

Figure 16.25
The Camera is 20 units above the groundplane and pointing horizontally at the Boxes, as seen in the Left viewport. The resulting view is seen through a camera viewport. Because the fog's Top value has been set to 30, the Camera itself is in the fog.

Figure 16.26
A rendering of the scene from Figure 16.25. The defined layer of fog from the bottom to the middle of the Boxes is evident. But the region above the upper fog line is nonetheless seen through the fog, because the Camera itself is in the fog. The region below (and in front of) the Boxes is also seen through the fog, producing a similar gradient.

3. Activate your camera viewport, and then render. (It's easy to forget to activate the camera viewport after adjusting the Camera in an Orthographic viewport.) Your result should look much like Figure 16.26. The fog density is greatest in the band constituting the lower half of the Boxes: This is the defined layer. But the regions above and below show a fog gradient,

from white to dark gray. Think this through. The region above the upper fog line is nonetheless seen through the fog, because the Camera is in the fog. As you move higher in the frame, the camera view necessarily intersects a smaller region of fog. Below the lower fog line is much the same—the Camera is looking through the fog and through a decreasing amount of it as you move lower in the frame. This concept definitely takes a moment to grasp. But note the same idea at work, even in the fog layer. The more distant Boxes are more obscured because you're looking through more fog.

4. Move your Camera up above the fog line to Z = 50. In the Camera panel, select the Show Horizon checkbox. Notice the line in your camera viewport that cuts across the scene at Z = 50. (It passes through the tops of the Boxes.) This line in the distance is even with the height of the Camera itself. Now, render again from your camera viewport—you should get a result similar to Figure 16.27. The view is now from above the fog. The Boxes are completely unobscured above Z = 30, and the fog extends all the way to the horizon line. This makes sense, but the horizon line is much too sharp.

Figure 16.27
The same as Figure 16.26, but the Camera has been moved above the fog, to Z = 50. Because the Camera is no longer looking through the fog, the Boxes are completely unobscured above the fog layer. The fog is applied to the background as high as the horizon. The horizon is defined by the plane Z = 50, the vertical position of the Camera.

5. Select the Horizon Noise checkbox in the Fog Parameters rollout and render again by using the existing values. As you can see in Figure 16.28, this creates a noisy region of fog at the horizon. The Size spinner does not affect the size of the region, but it affects the size of the Noise effect. The Angle parameter determines the size of the region. For example, reducing the Angle value to 1 degree results in a very narrow band of horizon noise.

Figure 16.28
The same as Figure 16.27, but with the default values for Horizon Noise applied. The Angle parameter determines the width of the horizon noise band.

6. By default, the fog layer is computed at a constant density. The Falloff option is set to None. By changing it to Top, the fog density decreases exponentially from bottom to top. The Bottom option does the reverse. Choose the Top option and rerender. As you can see in Figure 16.29, the fog layer fades out as it rises toward the plane where Z = 30.

Volume Fog

Volume Fog produces a cloud or smokelike effect within a defined volume. The volume is defined by an Atmospheric Apparatus that comes in three different shapes: the BoxGizmo, the SphereGizmo, and the CylGizmo. You must create one of these gizmos first, and then assign a Volume Fog effect to it. The Volume Fog then renders only within the space of the gizmo. If you create a Volume Fog without the restriction of an Atmospheric Apparatus, it will fill the entire scene.

Volume Fog is a highly animatable effect. For example, you can animate the position of the gizmo to move a cloud through a scene. You can also animate the shape or form of the effect by using various parameters to produce the characteristic evolutions of a cloud or smoke.

Like most volumetric effects, applying Volume Fog can be a science. The panel contains a large number of parameters with cryptic names, which can be rather intimidating to someone seeking to create only a simple effect. Even worse, many of the parameters are interdependent in many ways, so that the significance of one value depends on the other values.

Figure 16.29
The same as Figure 16.28, but with the Top Falloff option used. The fog density decreases exponentially as it rises toward Z = 30.

This book is not able to address all aspects of this powerful feature, but let's work through the following exercise to get you started:

1. To create a gizmo that will contain the volume fog, go to Create|Helpers in the Command panel. In the drop-down list, change from Standard to Atmospheric Apparatus. Three gizmo choices appear. Create a BoxGizmo on the groundplane that is big enough to take up a significant portion of the Perspective viewport. Your Perspective viewport should look something like Figure 16.30.

2. You can bind a Volume Fog to the BoxGizmo two ways. With the BoxGizmo still selected, change to the Modify panel. Go to the Atmosphere rollout and click on the Add button. You can create a Volume Fog effect by selecting it from the list—but don't do it now. Open the Environment dialog box and add the Volume Fog in the Atmosphere rollout.

3. Had you added the Volume Fog to the gizmo from the Modify panel, you would have both created the Volume Fog and bound it to the gizmo. Because you created the Volume Fog in the Environment dialog box, you must bind it to the gizmo in a separate step. Activate the Pick Gizmo button and click on the BoxGizmo in a viewport. The name of the BoxGizmo appears on the panel. The lower portion of your Environment dialog box should now look like Figure 16.31.

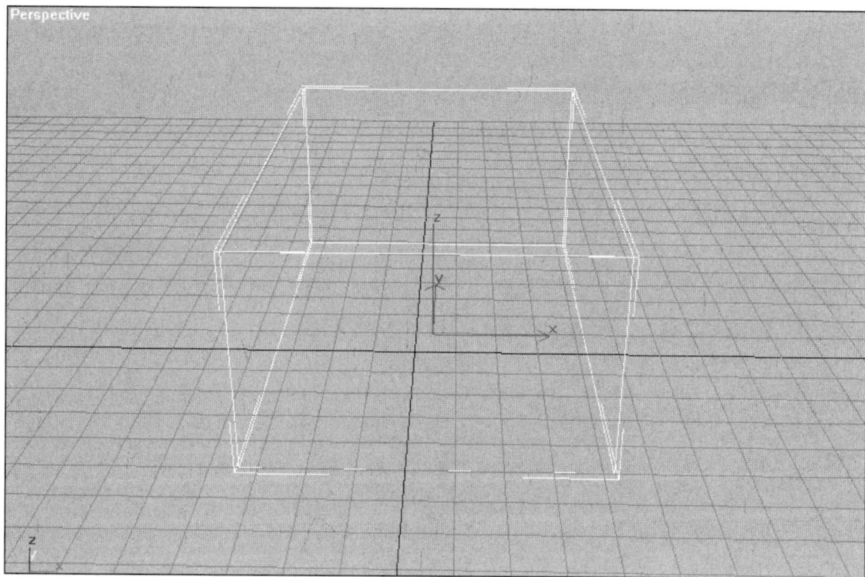

Figure 16.30
A BoxGizmo created to hold a Volume Fog effect.

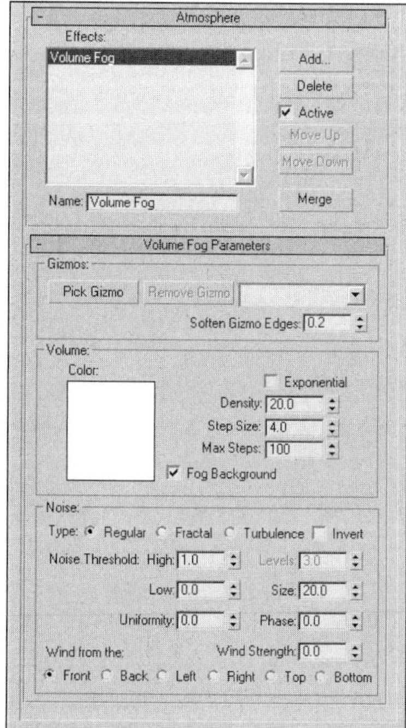

Figure 16.31
The Atmosphere and Volume Fog Parameters rollouts of the Environment dialog box. A Volume Fog is created and bound to a BoxGizmo. All other settings are at their default values.

4. Rendering time for volumetric effects can be astronomical, and many of the decisions you make are less about appearance than about rendering speed. Render your Perspective viewport at the default 640×480 size. Unless you have a very fast system, you're likely to be surprised by how long it takes to render this scene with only a single object and the default lighting. To speed things up during this exercise, you may want to change your output size to 320×240. In any case, your render should look something like Figure 16.32.

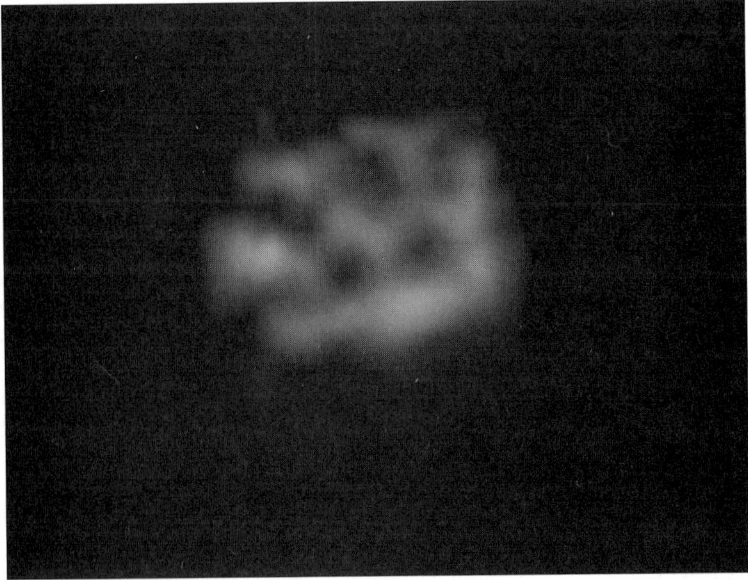

Figure 16.32
A render of the perspective view from Figure 16.30, using the default settings seen in Figure 16.31.

5. The fog looks like a cloud because, unlike regular fog, Volume Fog necessarily contains noise. Switch from Regular to Fractal noise, and then rerender. It takes a little longer, but the result is better, as you can see in Figure 16.33. The Fractal noise produces a crisper, more intricate result. When you changed from Regular to Fractal noise, the Levels spinner became active. Like all fractal effects in MAX, you can control the number of iterations. A higher Levels value produces a more detailed result, but at the cost of increased rendering time.

6. Switch to the Turbulence option, and then render again. Turbulence typically produces very high-contrast results that are better suited to a starry nebula or a galaxy than a cloud. Take a look at Figure 16.34.

7. Because render times are so long, perhaps the most important parameter on the panel is Max Steps. This option requires is a fairly straightforward trade-off between render speed and quality. Change back to fractal noise and render at the default Max Steps value of 100. While rendering, take a look at the Rendering Progress section on the Rendering

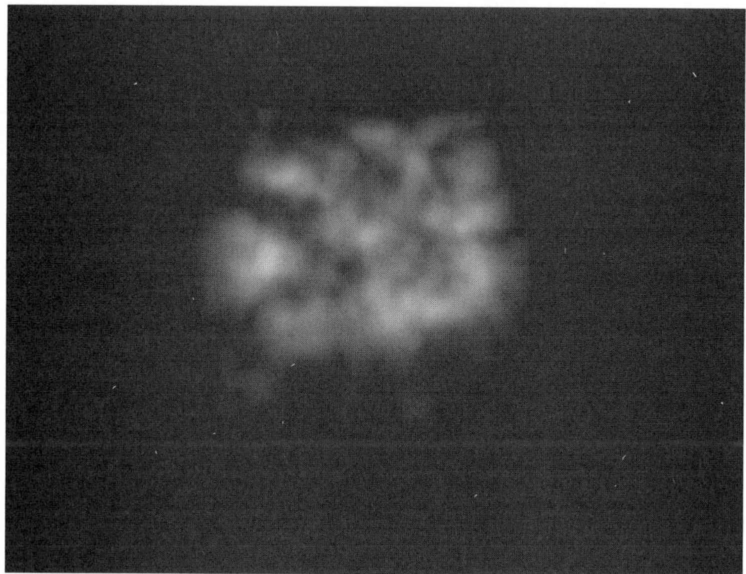

Figure 16.33
The same as Figure 16.32, but with Fractal noise instead of the default Regular noise. The result is much more detailed and cloudlike, but the render time is longer.

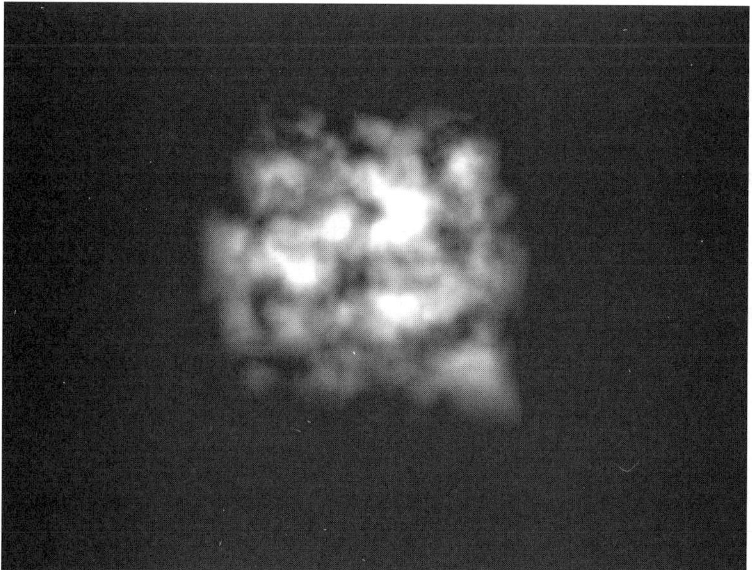

Figure 16.34
The same as Figure 16.33, but with the Turbulence option selected instead of the Fractal option in the Noise group. This high-contrast result looks more like a starry nebula than a cloud.

panel; note that it informs you of the time consumed rendering the last frame. Clone the Virtual Frame Buffer. Lower the Max Steps value to 75, render again, and write down the render time of the previous render. Continue in this way, cloning the Virtual Frame Buffer and lowering the Max Steps value, and then compare the quality of your results against render time. You'll probably find that you can cut your render time substantially before you see a noticeable degradation in results.

8. Experiment with some animation possibilities. Animate the gizmo's size or move it through space. To make the cloud churn in place, animate Phase by going to Frame 100 and activating the Animate button, and then change the Phase value to something like 100. Make test renders at different frames and note how the cloud changes shape. As you pull the Time Slider, you'll see the Phase value change in the spinner. Render out an animation to see the result.

Fire Effect

The Fire Effect can be thought of as a type of Volume Fog, using multiple colors and other specialized parameters that are designed to create the impression of flames and explosions. Fire Effects generally look much better when animated than they do in individual frames, because the movement of the flames sells the effect.

Use the Online Help for Fire Effect

MAX's Online Help is an excellent resource at any time, but particularly when using Fire Effects. The Fire Effect page contains many color examples of different parameter settings that provide an invaluable reference.

Let's take a brief look at Fire Effect with an exercise:

1. Just as with Volume Fog, a Fire Effect must be bound to an Atmospheric Apparatus that defines its volume and location. Use Create|Helpers|Atmospheric Apparatus to create a CylGizmo on the groundplane. Make the CylGizmo 60 units high with a 30-unit radius.

2. For reference, create a small Box (not a BoxGizmo), about 10 units high, at the bottom of the CylGizmo. This Box represents the fuel at the base of the fire—symbolic logs, if you will.

3. Select the CylGizmo again and go to the Atmosphere rollout in the Modify panel. Add a Fire Effect right here. You could do this in the Environment dialog box as well, but this method is faster. At this point, your screen should look something like Figure 16.35.

4. With Fire Effect selected in the Atmosphere rollout, click on the Setup button; the Environment dialog box appears with the Fire Effect Parameters rollout open, as seen in Figure 16.36. Take a good look at this panel. The Colors section provides for Inner, Outer, and Smoke Colors. The Smoke Color applies only if an Explosion is used. The other sections are Shape, Characteristics, Motion, and Explosion. Motion and Explosion apply only to animation.

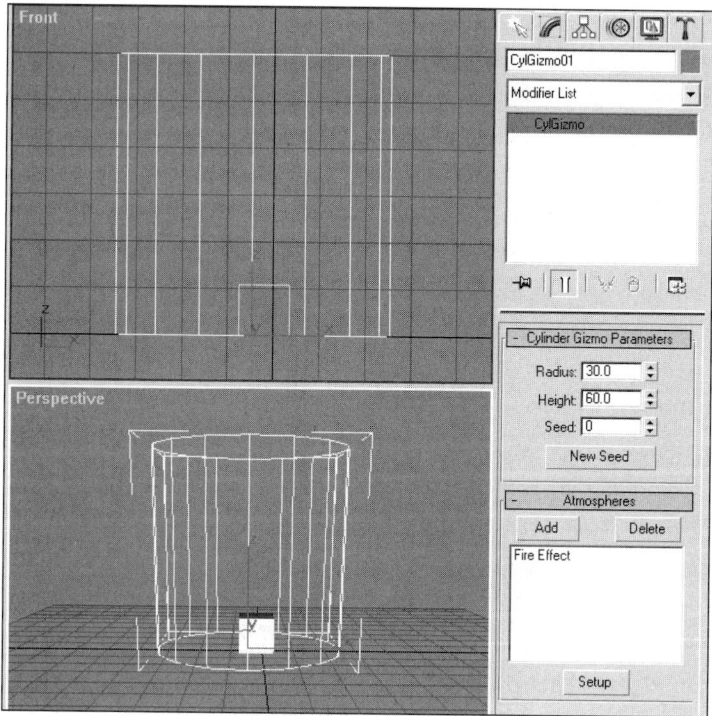

Figure 16.35
A CylGizmo with a Fire Effect added in the Modify panel. A Box object is placed at the bottom of the gizmo in place of fuel for the fire.

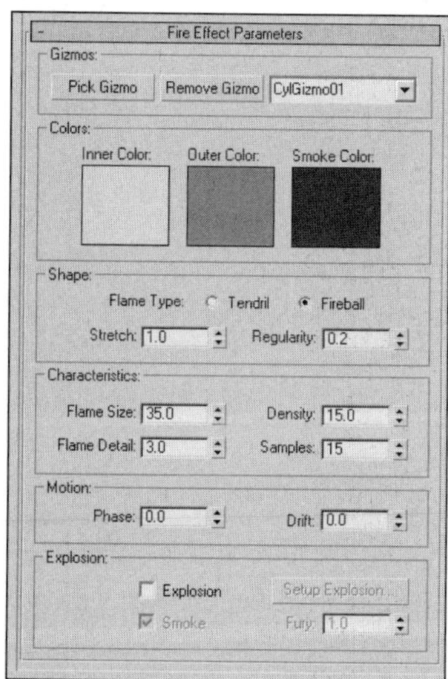

Figure 16.36
The Fire Effect Parameters rollout in the Environment dialog box, with default values.

5. The default Flame Type is Fireball, which is good for explosions. Because you are creating a burning fire, switch to the Tendril type. Render your Perspective viewport. The result is probably much different from what you might have expected. A small reddish cloud is floating well above your "log." You can change this image two ways: within the Fire Effect Parameters or by changing the shape of the CylGizmo (see Steps 6 and 7).

6. Within the Fire Effect Parameters, your first instinct might be to increase the Stretch value; doing so, however, only makes the flames more vertical in shape without increasing the volume. You need the Regularity parameter. Regularity determines the amount of the gizmo volume that is used for the effect. At the default level of 0.2, only the middle fifth of the CylGizmo is being used. Try increasing this value closer to 1.0, and then render. You probably won't be too happy with the result, however, because the effect will begin to look too cylindrical.

7. To keep the result diffuse, return to the 0.2 value for Regularity and change the shape of the CylGizmo. Make it twice as high, either by doubling the Height parameter or by using a nonuniform scale in the Z-dimension (you can ignore the warning box). Either way, you have to move the gizmo down until it's roughly centered on the log. Render again to see your result, and continue to adjust the gizmo to get the correct size and position.

8. It's time to improve the look of your flames. Try reducing the Regularity value to 0.1 or below for a more diffuse look. Increase the Stretch value to 2.0 for more vertical tendrils. Move down to the Characteristics section and reduce the Flame Size for more delicate tendrils. Reduce or increase the Density value to adjust the transparency of the fire. You may have to experiment with many parameters to get the result you want.

9. To animate your fire, you need to set keyframes for Phase. Activate the Animate button and move the Time Slider to Frame 100. Set the Phase value to 100 and turn off the Animate button. Pull the Time Slider and watch the Phase value change in the panel. Render out at different frames to see the result, or render out an animation at 320×240 size. Because the Phase is changing at a constant rate, the fire churns at a constant rate. (To produce more intensified burning, you can change the slope of the curve in Track View so it's not linear—as discussed in Chapter 1. Track View will also be covered in depth in Chapter 17.) Try animating the height of the gizmo to make the flames scale up and down.

Let's see what else Fire Effect can do by trying a quick explosion:

1. Reset your scene and create a SphereGizmo; then assign the Fire Effect to it. Select the Explosion checkbox near the bottom of the panel. When the Explosion checkbox is selected, the animation of Phase produces a specific result. Between the values of 0 and 100, the explosion builds from nothing to full intensity. From 100 to 200, the explosion burns and turns to smoke (using the smoke color) if the Smoke checkbox is selected. From 200 to 300, the explosion clears. You can create your own explosion Phase curve in Track View, but you can also produce a default one automatically. Click on the Setup Explosion button and accept the defaults, to generate a curve from Frame 0 to Frame 100.

2. To find the curve, open Track View, find the Fire Effect under the Environment heading, and click on the Phase parameter. To see the curve, click on the Function Curves button in the Track View. Click on the Zoom Horizontal Extents and Zoom Value Extents buttons in the bottom toolbar to size the curve to the available space. Examine the curve on your screen or in Figure 16.37. Note that Phase value reaches 100 by Frame 18, about half a second at video frame rate (30 fps). This is the height of the explosion. It burns until Frame 44 (Phase = 200) and then dies out over the remaining frames.

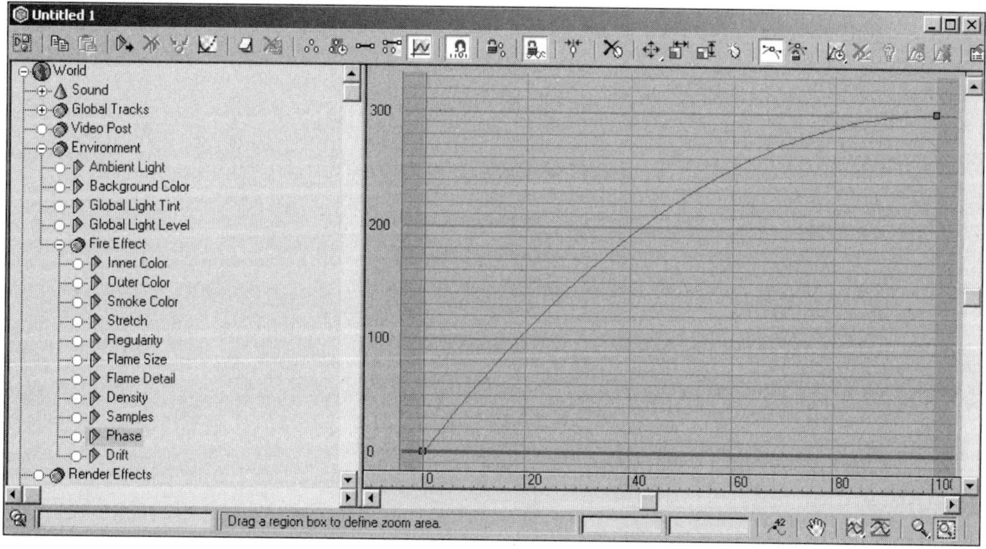

Figure 16.37

The Phase curve for a default explosion, as seen in Track View. The explosion grows from 0 to its maximum in the first 18 frames (from Phase = 0 to Phase = 100). It burns and turns to smoke until Phase = 200 is reached at Frame 44. The effect then dissipates until it completely terminates at Phase = 300.

3. It's hard to see the dark smoke against a black background, so change the background color to white at the top of the Environment dialog box. Use a 320×240 output size for faster rendering. Keep your eye on the current frame number as you watch the rendering. Note how quickly the explosion builds, how it turns completely to smoke by Frame 44, and how long it takes for the smoke to dissipate. If you saved this animation to a file, you can run it from View Image File in the File menu, as discussed in Chapter 15.

Volume Lights

Volume Lights create a volumetric glow within a region defined by a light. You can create a glowing cylinder with a Direct Light or a glowing sphere around an Omni Light, but the most common use is to illuminate the cone of a Spot Light. Try the following exercise:

1. Start by opening the file Chap16_Volume Light.max from the CD-ROM. It consists of a head model and a Target Spot Light trained on it. Your Front viewport should resemble Figure 16.38.

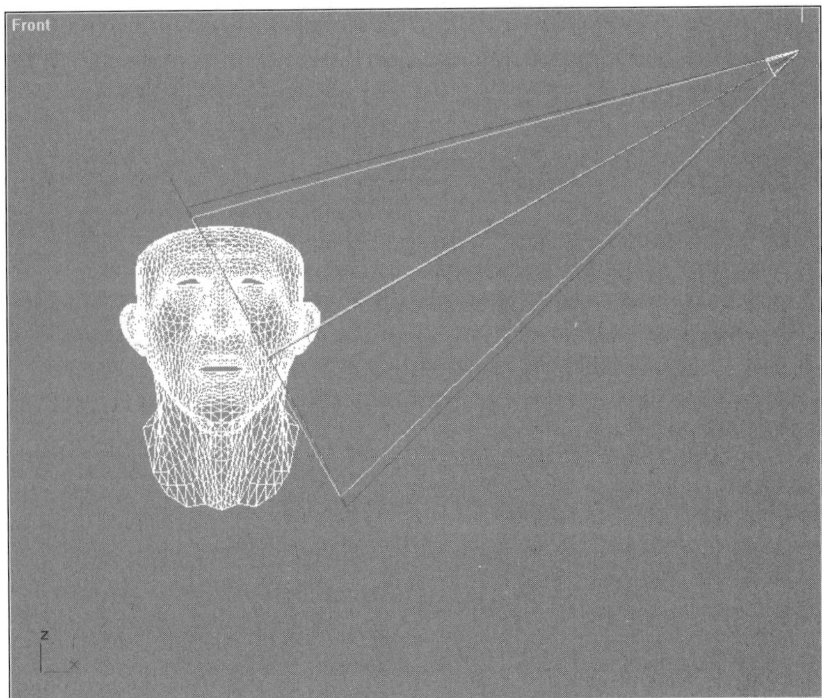

Figure 16.38
Setup for testing a Volume Light. A Target Spot Light is pointed at a head model.

2. With the light selected, go to the Atmospheres & Effects rollout at the bottom of the Modify panel. Add a Volume Light effect here, and use the Setup button to open the Environment dialog box with the Volume Light Parameters rollout displayed. Figure 16.39 shows this panel with its default settings.

3. As with other volumetric effects, rendering can be very slow. Use a 320×240 output size and render your Perspective viewport against a black background. It should look something like Figure 16.40. Note that the light becomes unrealistically hot past a certain point, because the cone is getting wider and the effect is being multiplied. To correct this flaw, reduce the Max Light % value from 90 to about 50. This setting ensures that the glow will never get brighter than 50 percent of the Fog Color parameter (the default is white). Render again to see the result.

Note: *Volume Light effects are visible only when rendered through Perspective or camera viewports.*

4. The image is not realistic, because the head should cut the light with a volumetric shadow. Adding a Shadow Map shadow to the light itself corrects the scene. With the light selected, turn on Cast Shadows in the Modify panel. Render again. Your result should now look like Figure 16.41.

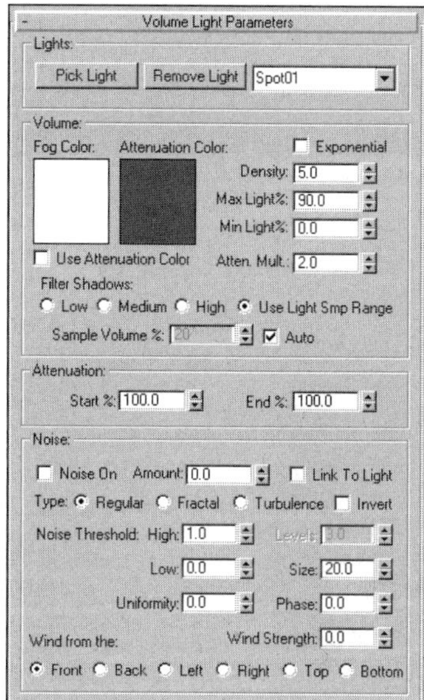

Figure 16.39
The Volume Light Parameters rollout in the Environment dialog box, with default settings.

Figure 16.40
Render of a Perspective viewport of the scene in Figure 16.38, using the default settings in Figure 16.39. The glow gets too hot past the head. Reducing the Max Light % value prevents this situation.

Figure 16.41
The same as Figure 16.40, but with Cast Shadows turned on for the Spot Light. The head now cuts a volumetric shadow through the light cone.

5. Set some attenuation so that the glow falls off with distance. With the light selected, turn on Far Attenuation in the Attenuation Parameters rollout in the Modify panel by selecting the Use checkbox. Adjust the Start and End spinners so that attenuation begins a little before the model and ends a little after it. Select the Show checkbox so that the ranges remain visible, even when the light is not selected. Your Front viewport should look something like Figure 16.42.

6. Render your Perspective viewport again. As you can see in Figure 16.43, the glow tails off by the end of the attenuation range.

7. The Fog Color is the color of the volumetric glow. Actually, the glow is a combination of the Fog Color and the color of the light itself, but it generally makes sense to make these two colors the same. You can add another color to the attenuation range only. The Attenuation Color is blue by default; if you select the Use Attenuation Color checkbox, you might expect to see this color. But the default value for the Atten. Mult. (Attenuation Multiplier) spinner is too low. Change it to a much higher value, such as 30, and render again. This time, you'll see a bright blue color in the attenuation range. The Attenuation Multiplier controls the impact of the Attenuation Color, and not the effect of attenuation generally.

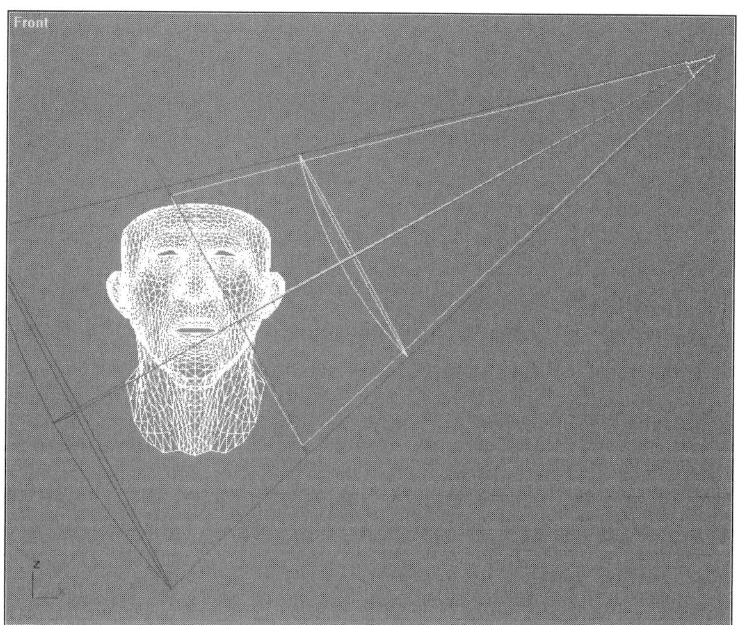

Figure 16.42
Adding far attenuation. The light begins to decay at the line in front of the head, and it is completely attenuated after it passes beyond it.

Figure 16.43
A render of the scene from Figure 16.42, showing the attenuation of the volume glow.

The Noise parameters are essentially identical to those found with Volume Fog. Remember that the glow in a Volume Light is typically intended to convey the effect of illuminating airborne mist or particulate matter. In an animation, the viewer expects this material to be moving, and even a small amount of animated noise is convincing.

Moving On

In this chapter, you learned about the tools used to create visual phenomena by means other than the rendering of geometry. You saw how the Render Effects toolset permits you to add post-processing in the normal workflow. You explored the possibilities of the various Lens Effects and experimented with the image-adjustment post-processing tools. You then learned about how to map an image to the background by using an environment map. Finally, you investigated the broad range of atmospheric effects, including Fog, Volume Fog, Fire Effect, and Volume Light.

The next chapter discusses essential techniques used with MAX's animation toolset. Much attention will be focused on the powerful Track View tool and its ability to adjust and even create animation parameters. In addition, the chapter will discuss the treatment of repetitive animation tasks and how to add sound and visibility tracks.

Part VI

Animation

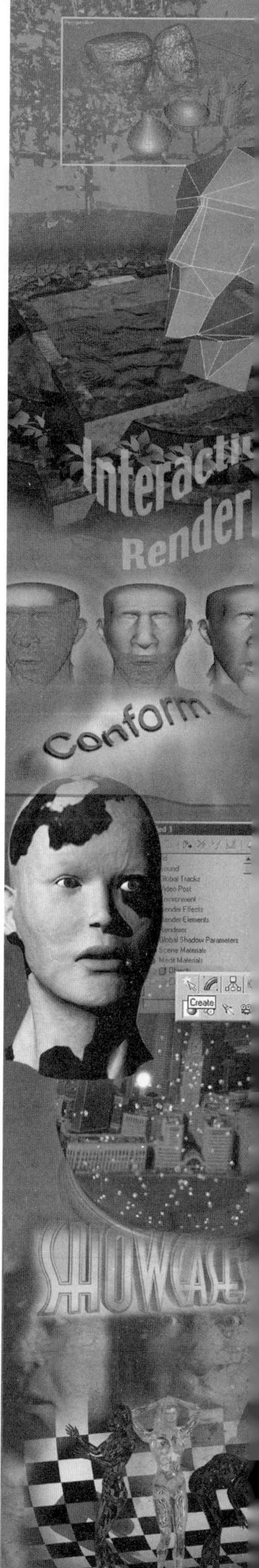

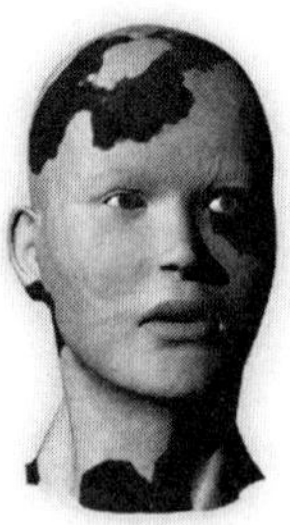

Chapter 17

Animation Essentials

In the opinion of many people, MAX's strongest suit is animation. Its animation toolset is unrivaled for strength and versatility. And nearly everything in MAX can be animated.

You need to learn and understand a lot before you can make use of MAX's strong animation toolset. Animation is a challenging subject in any case, and the very size and power of MAX's toolset can be rather intimidating. In this chapter, you'll become well grounded in the fundamentals. Although we call them fundamentals, this material isn't simple—you have to be willing to think deeply and explore the possibilities at every step. We're always returning to these fundamentals, and we're always learning new things about them.

What Is Animation in 3ds max 4?

To ask "What is animation?" is not a naïve question, and it deserves a precise answer: *Animation* is the variation of one or more parameter values in a scene over time. The next sections discuss this central idea.

You are probably already familiar with the term *parameter*. In computer programming, a parameter is an input value sent to a function that determines the output of that function. Every object in MAX (not just geometric objects) can be understood as a function that receives input parameters and outputs some result. A Sphere object has a Radius parameter, a Material has a Diffuse Color parameter, and a Bend modifier has an Angle parameter. The Environment has a Background Color parameter. A light has a Multiplier parameter. All objects that have locations in a scene have transform parameters for Position, Rotation, and Scale. The list is nearly endless.

Each of these parameters is assigned a specific value. When that value is made to change over time, the parameter is said to be *animated.* Although not all parameters can be varied over time, MAX is remarkable among 3D applications for the number of its parameters that can be animated. All features that can be animated have their own track in the Track View panel, and these tracks can be viewed as keyframes or as function curves that define the animation.

How Do I Know whether a Parameter Can Be Animated?

Every animatable parameter in your scene is given an animation track in Track View. To determine whether a parameter can be animated, open Track View and find the desired parameter within its object. A green arrow indicates that a parameter can receive an animation controller and can therefore be animated.

Understanding Function Curves

The idea of function curves is basic to computer animation. A *function curve* describes the way a parameter changes over time. It's not an overstatement to say that a function curve *is* the animation.

In traditional 2D cel animation, the extremes of motion are drawn first as *keyframes.* Then, the intermediate frames are filled during a process called *inbetweening.* This approach is essential to cel animation. When many people begin working in 3D computer animation, they adopt the 2D approach instinctively. They pose a character or adjust other scene parameters at keyframes, and then they allow the application to do the inbetweening. It's very important not to be limited to this approach.

3D computer animation allows you to understand animation as continuous change, not just as the linking together of still poses. The animation is the function curve that describes the changing parameters. The keys are used only to create the curve. (Note that the term *keys* is used to designate the fixed values set directly on the curve in 3D animation. In contrast, the term *keyframes* is used to designate the primary frames drawn in 2D cel animation. These ideas are closely connected but ultimately different, as you shall see.)

To understand this idea, take a look at a couple of function curves from Track View. It doesn't matter which parameters are involved right now. In Figure 17.1, an animation is achieved with five keys. The parameter values at Frames 0, 50, and 100 are all set to 0. At Frame 25, the value decreases to a minimum of –20; at Frame 75, it rises to a maximum of 20. The keys were used to define the curve, but it is the curve, not the keys themselves, that define the animation. Imagine the flow of this animation just from looking at the curve. If this curve were applied to a position transform in the World Z-direction, an object would be moving up and down. If applied in the World X-direction, the object would be shifting back and forth. The serious 3D animator can read function curves the way a musician can read music. Function curves are the language of computer animation.

The same animation can be created with a different number of keys if you change the interpolation, however. In Figure 17.2, keys appear only at 0, 50, and 100. MAX's function curves are

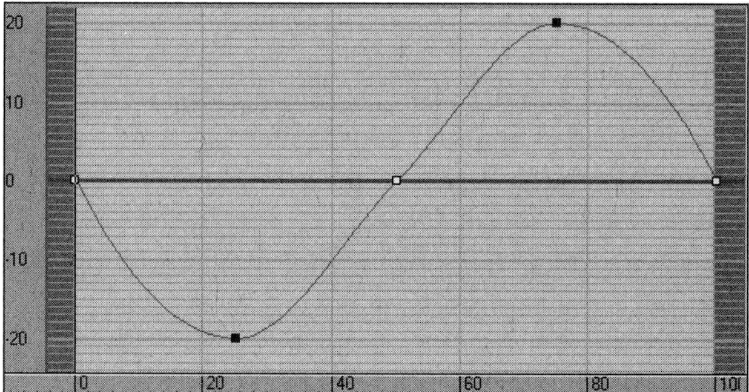

Figure 17.1
A simple function (a curve) is created from five keys at Frames 0, 25, 50, 75, and 100. The interpolation between these keys determines the shape of the curve and therefore determines the value of the parameter at every frame.

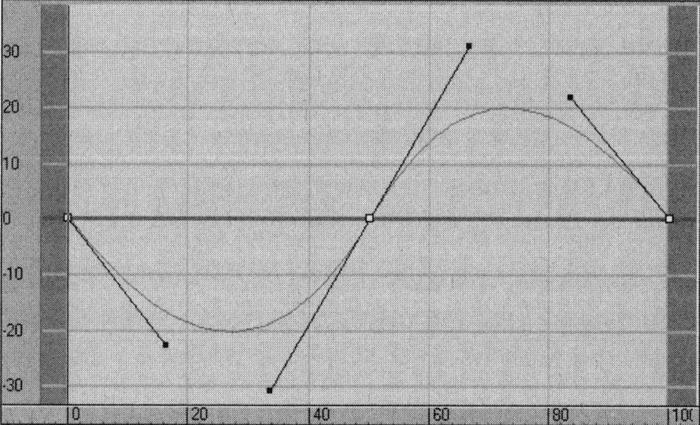

Figure 17.2
A function curve nearly identical to Figure 17.1 is created with fewer keys by adjusting the interpolation between them with tangent handles. MAX's function curves are the same Bezier splines found in the rest of the program, and the keys amount to the same thing as spline vertices. The curve appears slightly different from the one in Figure 17.1 due to the vertical stretching of the display, but its values at any given frame are very close to those found in Figure 17.1.

the same Bezier splines found in the rest of the program. By adjusting the tangent handles for these keys (which amount to the same thing as vertices on a regular spline), you can create the same curve shape as in Figure 17.1. If it looks a bit different to you, examine it carefully. The display in Figure 17.2 is vertically stretched compared to Figure 17.1, but the curves are nearly identical in terms of their value at any given frame.

This comparison can be used to make two points. One is that keys need not represent extremes of motion the way keyframes do in 2D cel animation. In cel animation, keyframes would have been drawn at 0, 25, 75, and 100 (but not necessarily at 50), because these are the frames at the extremes of motion (values of 0, –20, and 20), and they define the limits of the inbetweening. The curve in Figure 17.1 adopts this approach, although it uses a key at Frame 50 to help shape the interpolation between the extremes. The curve in Figure 17.2 has all three keys at a single value (0), and there are no keys at the extremes. The shape of the curve, and therefore the progress of the animation, is defined by the interpolation tools.

Why would you prefer one curve over another? The answer should be familiar to the experienced 3D modeler. Curves with fewer keys (vertices) are generally easier to edit than curves with many keys. And, it will often make more sense to edit a curve by using Bezier handles than by adding and positioning more keys.

Working with Keys

You should now understand how keys are used to create the function curves that actually define the animation of a parameter. MAX has three approaches to creating keys. The Animate button can be used to create keys interactively by transforming objects or changing parameters; in addition, all key-related operations can be handled in Track View, including creation, deletion, and editing. The third way is to use Track Bar beneath the Time Slider and the key-creation tools that are available from the Time Slider itself. You can create, delete, and move keys by using these important tools.

Experienced MAX animators develop their own work styles, incorporating all the various tools. The serious student must learn to master Track View from the very start, however. Beginners often think of Track View as an advanced feature that they need not address until they have developed skills using the Animate button. At most, they think that Track View is something to use in editing, but not creating, an animation. This mindset can be an impediment to the development of serious animation skills. Track View is a fantastic tool—probably the strongest competitive feature in MAX. Every animation tool is available here, and nearly every animation question can be answered by reference to it. And, most important, a student animator needs constant exposure to function curves to develop a feel for the control of timing and movement.

To understand the integration of all the available tools for key creation and management, let's work through a series of instructional exercises.

Managing Keys in Track View

We'll start right off with Track View, the control center for animation in 3ds max 4:

1. One of the more useful screen configurations for animation uses only two viewports extending the width of the screen. This setup allows the full length of Track View to be visible above a scene viewport that is big enough to see motion. To get this configuration, right-click on any of the viewport labels and choose Configure from the menu. Choose the Layout tab from the Viewport Configuration dialog box that appears and select the fourth option on the top row, as shown in Figure 17.3.

2. Open Track View from the Graph Editors menu or from the Main toolbar, and position it over the upper viewport. Depending on the size and resolution of your monitor, you may want to allow it to extend over the lower viewport (which is a Front viewport, by default).

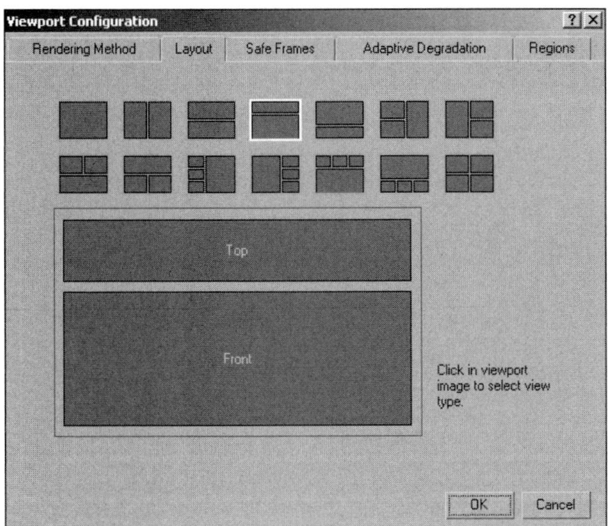

Figure 17.3
The Layout tab of the Viewport Configuration dialog box, with a useful layout option selected for animation work. The upper viewport can hold Track View and the lower one provides a large view of the scene. The reverse layout option immediately to the right is just as suitable.

3. Create a Box in the middle of the Front viewport. Because you don't have multiple viewports to see it, use the Parameters rollout to set the size of the Box to 50 units in all three dimensions. Use the Move Transform Type-In to place it precisely at the World origin (0,0,0). In Track View, expand the Object's track by clicking on the plus sign next to its title. Expand all the tracks under the Box01 entry and the Object (Box) entry. If necessary, move the cursor to a blank area to the right of the listed objects and click and drag to pan the list upward. Adjust the view so that you can see all the tracks together. Your Track View panel should look like Figure 17.4. The three transforms are obviously all animatable, but note that all of the underlying parameters of the primitive object can be animated, as well. The small green triangle to the left of each parameter name indicates that it is animatable. No keys exist in any of the tracks yet, but the current static value of each parameter is displayed.

Before you set a single key, you have to know what *controllers* you are working with. The concept of controllers is powerful and unique to MAX. Each animatable track is assigned one; many different types are available for each track, and each one determines how the function curve is created and what it means to the affected object. Controllers are covered in depth in Chapter 18, but you must understand at least the basics right from the start. Unfortunately, Track View does not show you your controller names by default. To determine what controllers are currently being used, click on the Filters button at the far left end of the Track View toolbar. The Filters dialog box will appear, as shown in Figure 17.5.

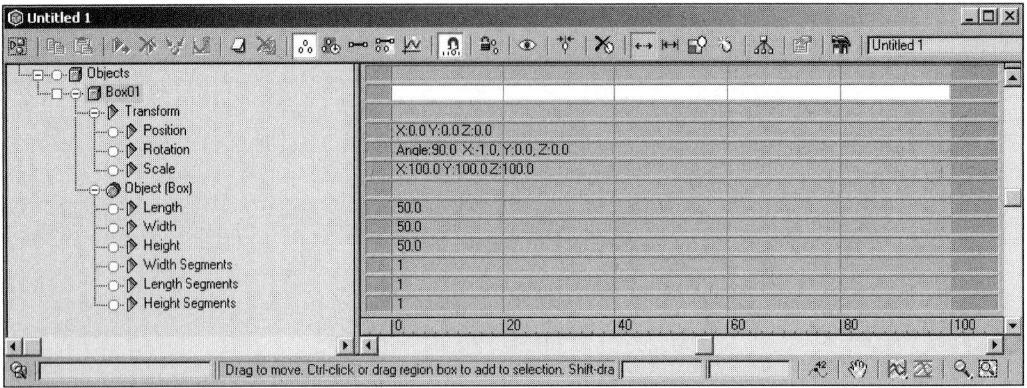

Figure 17.4
The Track View panel for an unanimated Box object, with all tracks expanded. The three transforms are all animatable parameters, and all the underlying parameters of the Box object are also animatable. The small green triangle to the left of each parameter name indicates that it is animatable. No keys appear in any of the tracks, but the current static value of each parameter is displayed.

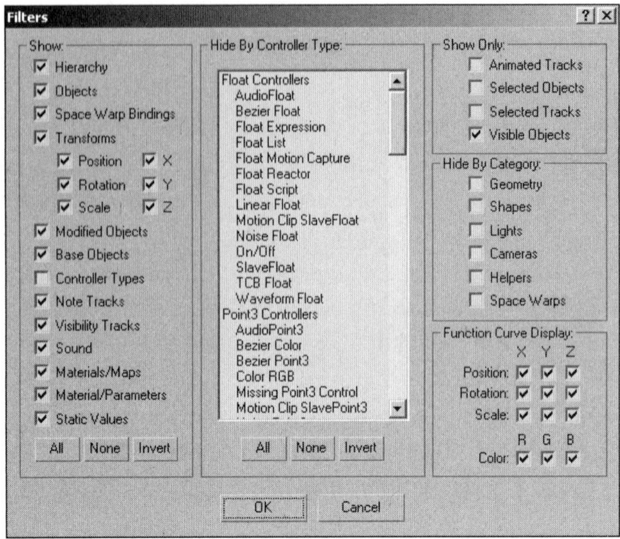

Figure 17.5
The Filters dialog box is critical to the effective use of Track View because a complex scene will contain much data. Filters are used to hide unnecessary tracks and information. Note the long list (only partially displayed) of controller types.

The Filters dialog box is critical to the effective use of Track View. Track View's great value is in the fact that it is comprehensive—it contains everything in one place. The downside is that it can be quite complicated. With a scene of any complexity, you need to be able to hide unnecessary tracks and information, and the Filters dialog box allows you to do this.

The large list of controller types in the center section is divided into Float Controllers, Point3 Controllers, Position Controllers, Rotation Controllers, Scale Controllers, and Transform Controllers. Keep this organization in mind. When you change an animatable parameter from one controller type to another, the available choices will depend on the nature of the parameter.

Continue the exercise as follows:

1. Click on the Filters button. Considering all the information that is displayed in the Filters dialog box by default, it's difficult to understand why you need to ask to see your all-important controller types. In the Show section of the dialog box, select the Controller Types checkbox.

2. Close the Filters dialog box and look again at your Track View panel. The controller types are now visible for each track.

Note that Position is animated by default using a Bezier Position controller. This kind of controller has two distinguishing features. First, the values defined by its function curves are the positions of the object in X, Y, Z coordinates. Thus, the Bezier Position controller generates a separate curve for each of the three dimensions. Second, the function curves are Bezier splines. The keys are effectively Bezier spline vertices, and the interpolation between them can be controlled, if desired, by Bezier tangent handles. When you create keys using a Bezier Position controller, you are fixing a location in space at the specified frame. Then, you can interpolate between different locations using Bezier-type controls.

Let's start creating keys. Continue the exercise with these steps:

1. Click on the Add Keys button on the Track View toolbar to activate it. Click in the Box's Position track to set a key. The key is selected (white) and its current frame location is indicated in a box in the status bar at the bottom of Track View. Type "0" in the box to move the key precisely to Frame 0. Create a second key at Frame 100. Get out of Add Keys mode by right-clicking anywhere in the right panel, or you'll create more keys every time you click in that panel. Close the Object level tracks to simplify the display. At this point, your Track View should look like Figure 17.6.

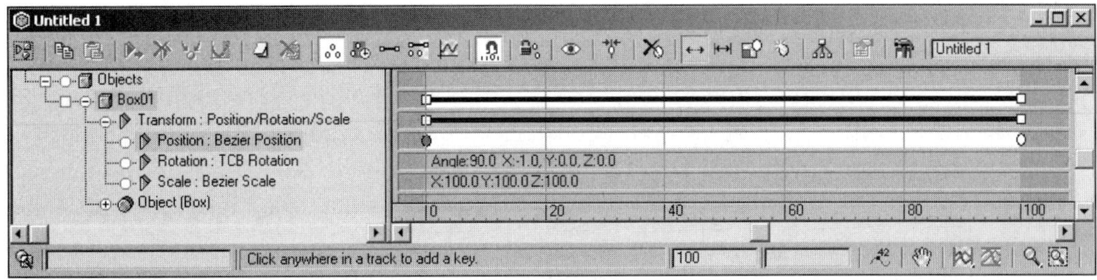

Figure 17.6
Keys have been created directly in Track View in the Position track at Frames 0 and 100. The controller type is Bezier Position. This is an Edit Keys view, showing the location of the keys and the range of the animation, but not the actual function curves.

2. Right now, you are looking at the tracks in Edit Keys mode. You see only the location of the keys and the range of the animation. The range is an important idea. By default, the range extends from the first key in a track to the last key. Select either of your keys and move it to a different frame. Notice how the ranges expand and contract accordingly. Reset back to 0 and 100, and use the Add Keys button to create a third key at 50. Right-click to get out of Add Keys mode. Try moving the endpoints of the range bars above the animated track. Note how doing so shortens or lengthens the animation by scaling the distance between the keys. This is just one of many fantastic features of Track View, and the results are echoed in the Track Bar at the bottom of the MAX screen.

3. You've set three keys, but what do they mean? Because the track uses the Bezier Position controller, each key contains a location in X, Y, Z coordinates. Click on the key at Frame 0 to select it. It turns white. Right-click on the same key to bring up a small dialog box. As you can see in Figure 17.7, the dialog box tells you a number of important things about the key. The title *Box01\Position* indicates that the parameter being keyed is the Position transform of the object Box01. The number 1 at the top means that this is the first key in the track. The Time field indicates that this key is currently at Frame 0. The X, Y, and Z Value fields tell you that, at this key, the Box is located at (0,0,0) in World space. Use the small arrows at the top to page through all three keys. (This method is an easier way to select them than by clicking on the keys themselves.)

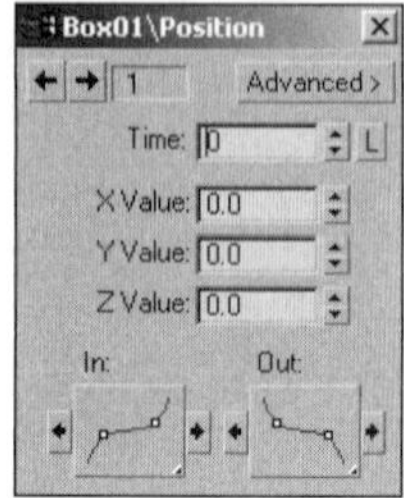

Figure 17.7
The dialog box for the first key in the track illustrated in Figure 17.6. The dialog box indicates the object and its affected parameter (Box01\Position), the number of the key in the track (1), and the time at which the key is set (Frame 0). It also tells you the value of the parameter at this key—a location of (0,0,0) in World space.

4. All three keys have precisely the same values. *Values* refers specifically to the information stored in the key, not information about the key. The information stored in the key—its value—is the position in X, Y, Z coordinates. This idea will become clearer when you look at the function curves. All three keys have the position values (0,0,0). Animation is the variation in the value of a parameter. Therefore, right now there is no animation, even though there are keys. Pull the Time Slider back and forth to confirm that nothing is moving. Switch to a Function Curve view in Track View by clicking on the Function Curves button (the curve icon) on the Track View toolbar. Use the scrollbar on the right side of the Track View window to show the 0 value. You'll see a straight line running through three

keys (now squares instead of circles). The straight line means that the Box is maintaining a position of (0,0,0) throughout the 100-frame range.

5. To animate the scene, select the second key, at Frame 50, either by using the arrows in the dialog box or by clicking on the key on the function curve. Move the Time Slider to Frame 50. Increase the Z value in the Box01\Position dialog box to 50. Two things happen at once: The key moves up in the window, creating a rounded blue curve; because the Time Slider is at Frame 50, you can see the new position of the Box in the viewport at this frame. Pull the Time Slider back and forth to see the animation, and watch the time line move across the function curve in the Track View panel. Your screen should look like Figure 17.8 when the Time Slider is at Frame 50.

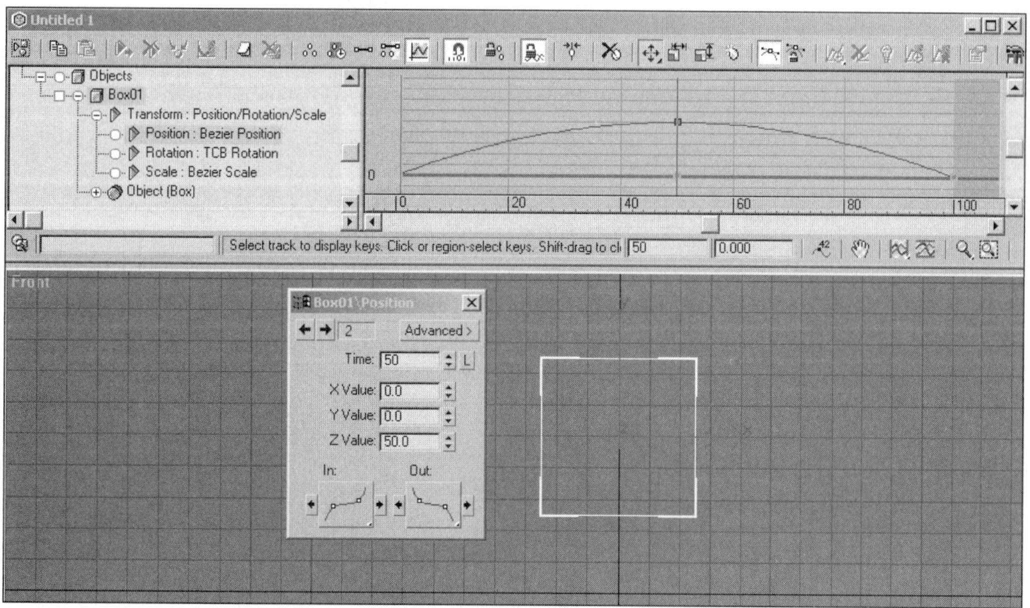

Figure 17.8
The Z value for key #2, which is currently at Frame 50, has been increased to 50 in the dialog box. This setting creates a rounded function curve in which the Z value increases from 0 to 50 and decreases again over a range of 100 frames. Because the Time Slider (not seen) is currently at Frame 50, the Box is located at Z=50 in the Front viewport.

Some controllers produce only one curve, and some produce three. Bezier Position produces three curves: for X, Y, and Z. In most applications, curves affecting the X-dimension or axis are displayed in red, curves for Y are green, and curves for Z are blue. It's easy to remember the same "XYZ—RGB" convention that's used to determine the axis colors. Only the blue curve is animated, and the two others can still be seen as straight lines. It can be difficult to work with the multiple curves in a single controller. The best approach is often to use the value spinners in the dialog box to make sure that only a single curve is affected at a time. Another approach is to filter out all but a single curve. You can use a filter to animate the movement in the X-direction. Follow these steps:

1. Open the Filters dialog box and find the section titled Function Curve Display. By default, all three dimensions are selected for all three transforms. Deselect the Y and Z options for Position. After you click on the OK button, only the red X curve will be visible in Track View.

2. Pull the Time Slider to Frame 100. Select the third key in Track View, at Frame 100. Increase the X value of this key until the Box has moved some significant distance to the right of the screen. You can do this in a number of ways. One method is to drag the key upward in Track View, although you'll probably have to zoom or pan the window to give yourself enough room. Another way is to increase the X value in the spinner in the dialog box, just as you did before. Yet another way is to type a value directly into the second field in the Track View status bar. Experiment with all these methods, but finally set the X value to 100.

3. Use the Zoom Value Extents button, at the bottom of the Track View panel, to get a good view of the curve, which should now look like Figure 17.9.

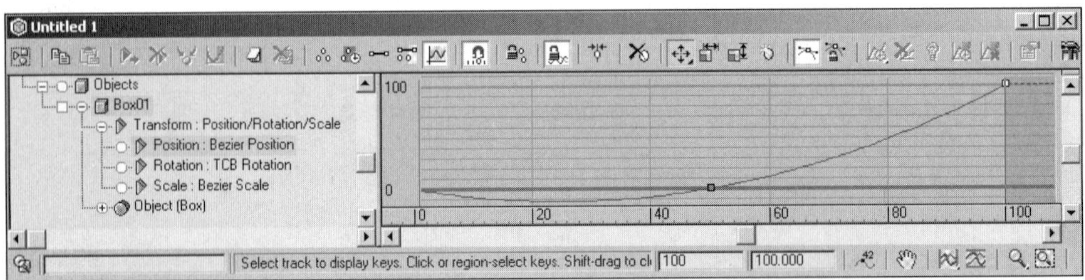

Figure 17.9
The Y and Z curves have been filtered out, leaving only the (red) X curve. The value of the key at Frame 100 has been increased from 0 to 100. Note how the interpolation dips the curve below 0 between the first two keys.

Take a good look at the X curve on your screen or in Figure 17.9, because we have come to something very important. You have three successive keys with X values of 0, 0, and 100, respectively. Without a view of the function curves, you might expect that the Box would remain still between Frames 0 and 50, and then move 100 units in the X-direction during the remaining 50 frames. But this is not what happens. By default, the interpolation between keys is spline interpolation, not linear interpolation. That means the keys are treated as the vertices of Bezier splines. If you create Smooth vertices (the default) when drawing Bezier splines in MAX's regular viewports, you expect to see them connected by curving lines. It's just the same with the function curves that are used to control animation. Due to spline interpolation, MAX fits a smooth curve between the keys. As a result, two things are noticeable: The curve dips below 0 between the first two keys, and the function curve is not a straight line between the second two keys. Rather, it's a curve whose slope increases as it approaches Frame 100. Thus the motion accelerates between Frames 50 and 100.

Now, continue with these steps:

1. Unhide the Z curve by using the Filters dialog box to see both curves. Use the Play Animation button at the bottom-right of the MAX screen to run the animation. Watch very carefully and compare the motion you see to the curve in Track View, both for position and speed. Note that the Box drifts backward in the X-direction at the start, and that it accelerates in the Z-direction toward the end. Click on the Play Animation button again to stop the animation when you finish.

2. If you set your keys outside of Track View without looking at the curves, you probably would be very surprised at the animated result. Suppose that what you want is for the X value to remain constant for the first 51 frames (remember that Frame 0 is included). To make things as simple as possible, eliminate the Z animation to isolate only the X animation. Select the Frame 50 key on the Z curve and set the value to 0. The Z (blue) curve becomes a straight line again. Filter out the Z curve to get it out of the way and pull the Time Slider to confirm that the only animation is back and forth in the X-direction.

3. Select the Frame 50 key (#2) on the X curve and right-click, if necessary, to bring up its dialog box. At the bottom of the dialog box are buttons under the headings In and Out. These buttons control the spline interpolation in and out of the selected key. Click and hold down the In button to see your choices, as shown in Figure 17.10. Select the bottom-most option to make your Bezier tangent handles visible. Notice that the handles appear on both sides (In and Out), even though you used only the In button. The new icons for both In and Out on the dialog box confirm this change. Note also that the shape of the curve is completely unaffected. The handles are locked together to keep them collinear. As you know from MAX's regular Bezier splines, collinear handles keep the curve smooth through

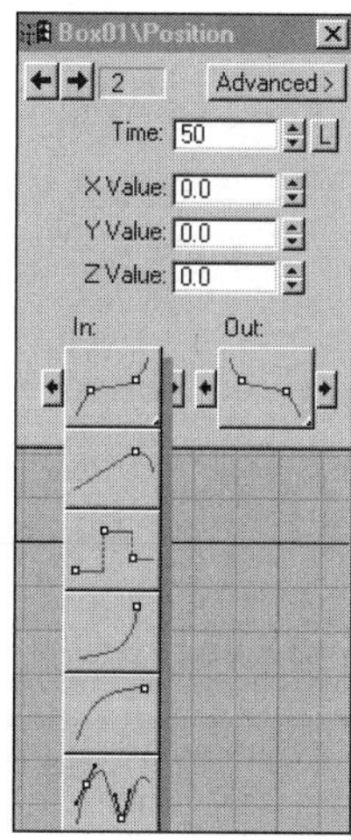

Figure 17.10
The spline-interpolation options for a curve heading into the selected key. The same options are available heading out of the same key.

the selected vertex. Move either of the handles to test this behavior. But you need a sharp change—a discontinuity. Click on the Advanced button in the dialog box for the selected key to reveal additional parameters. Click on the small lock icon for the X-dimension to unlock the handles. Now, you can move each handle separately.

4. Move to key #1 and display its Bezier handle. Because this is the start point of the function curve, it has only a single handle. Use the Move Keys button to adjust the outgoing handle of key #1 and the incoming handle of key #2 to point at each other in a straight line. If you prefer, hold down the Move Keys button to reveal alternate choices that constrain the handle's movements to the vertical and horizontal directions, relative to the dialog box. Your curve should look like Figure 17.11. The straight linear segment between the first two keys means that the Box's X coordinate will maintain a constant value between Frames 0 and 50. Play the animation to confirm that you have eliminated the backward drift.

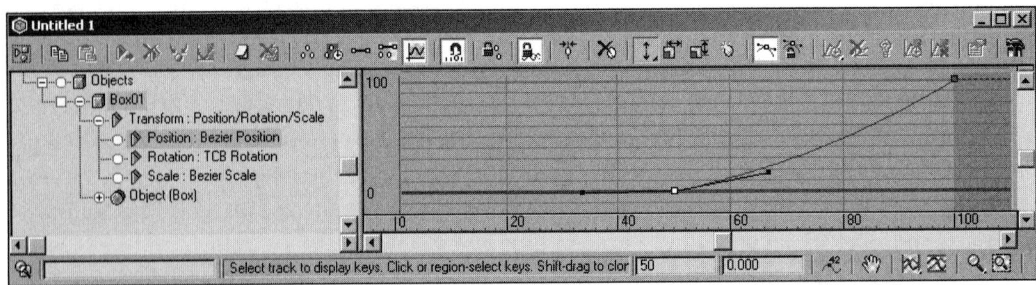

Figure 17.11
The function curve from Figure 17.9, with the Bezier handles of the first two keys revealed. By adjusting the outgoing handle from the first key into a straight line with the incoming handle for the second key, the value remains constant for the first 50 frames. This change eliminates the backward drift at the start of the animation.

Turn to the second 50 frames. Right now, the Box accelerates constantly until it reaches Frame 100, where it comes to a sudden stop. For most objects, this behavior is not realistic or pleasing. Physical objects have inertia—it takes energy to speed them up and slow them down. In the language of traditional animation, you usually need to *ease in* to motion and *ease out* of it. In other words, there should be acceleration at the start and a deceleration at the end.

Acceleration or deceleration is achieved by changes in the slope of the curve. If the slope is changing so that it grows more vertical with time, the rate of speed is increasing. If the slope is changing so that the curve grows flatter with time, the rate of speed is decreasing. These concepts, right out of high-school physics, are the meat and potatoes of 3D computer animation. You already have a constant acceleration, so you need to add a deceleration at the end. You could do this with a Bezier handle, but let's try another way. Follow these steps:

1. Select the third key and look at the interpolation options in the dialog box for In. Select the one just above the Bezier handle option (with the flattening curve icon). This option creates an automatic ease-in.

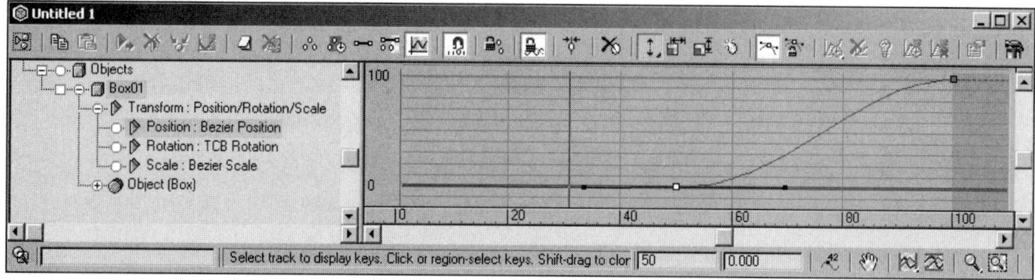

Figure 17.12

The function curve from Figure 17.11, with an ease-out applied to the end and the outgoing Bezier handle for the second key adjusted to provide a matching ease-in. These settings create a slight acceleration into the motion (from a dead stop) and a slight deceleration out of the motion.

2. Go back to key #2 and adjust its outgoing handle downward to create an ease-out that mirrors the ease-in. Your curve should look like Figure 17.12. Play the animation to see the result.

Using the Animate Button

Now that you understand how keys are used to create function curves, you are in a position to understand the Animate button.

The Animate button simply places a key defining the current state of any objects that have been altered from the previous key. Because of its simplicity, it is often used for very simple operations or as a starting point for an animation sequence. You may find yourself always working in Track View to set keys, because you'll want to see and edit your function curves at every stage. The Animate button may also be a bit confusing. In many other animation applications, the user transforms the selected object at a given frame and then creates a key if he or she wants to. In MAX, however, you turn the Animate button on before you change anything, and any change you then make to an object automatically creates a key at the current frame. This behavior requires that you constantly test and adjust the keys.

The two most common mistakes animators make when working with the Animate button are forgetting to turn it on when you want to create keys and forgetting to turn it off when you don't. If you leave it on, you create keys unintentionally every time you make a modification. If you forget to turn it on, you change an object's state without this change being animated.

Many animators work exclusively with the Animate button and are not used to any other approach. The Animate button also makes special sense when you're animating rotations with MAX's default TCB Rotation controller, because it uses no function curves, in any case.

The following exercise shows you how using the Animate button ties into the larger picture:

1. Set up a scene, as in the first few steps in the previous exercise. If you completed the previous exercise, you can simply eliminate the animation by changing to an Edit Keys view in

Track View (click on the Edit Keys button in the Track View toolbar), selecting the three keys by dragging a rectangle around them, and clicking on the Delete Keys button on the Track View toolbar or the Delete key on your keyboard. Click on the Yes button in the resulting Delete Keys dialog box to acknowledge that you want to delete the keys. But be careful what frame you are on when you do this—when you delete all the keys in a track, the new static value is taken from the curve at the current frame. Put the Time Slider at Frame 0 (or at least between Frames 0 and 50) to position the unanimated Box at the center of World space. Make sure that Track View stays open.

2. Click on the Animate button to activate it. Drag the Time Slider to Frame 100. Select the Box and move it 100 units in the positive World X-direction. Turn off the Animate button and take a look at Track View. A key was created in the Position track at Frame 100, but another one was also created at Frame 0. Switch to a Function Curve view in Track View to see the curve shown in Figure 17.13. Note the linear curve between a value of 0 at Frame 0 and a value of 100 at Frame 100. Before you run the animation, you should be able to determine that the Box will move at a constant rate in the X-direction, without any acceleration or deceleration.

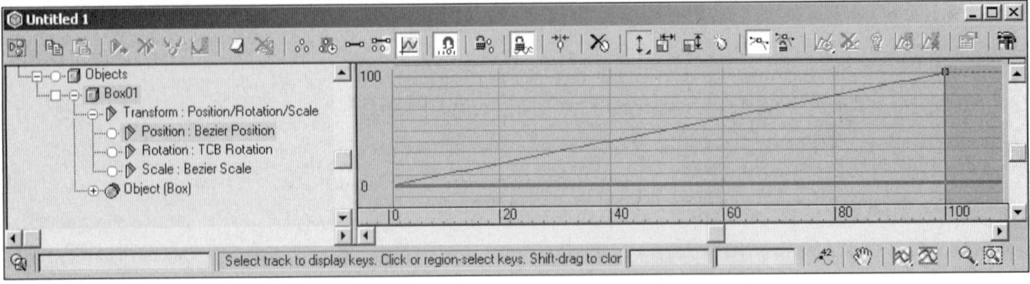

Figure 17.13
The function curve created from keys set by using the Animate button. The unanimated Box was located at (0,0,0) in World space. The Animate button was turned on, and the Time Slider was set at Frame 100. Moving the box to (100,0,0) created keys at Frame 0 and Frame 100 to produce an animation.

3. Now that you have a very simple animation, what would happen if you moved the object with the Animate button off? Put the Time Slider at any frame you want and move the object forward in the X-direction. What happens to the curve in Track View? As you can see in Figure 17.14, moving the object with the Animate button off moves the entire animation so that it starts and ends farther forward in the X-direction. Pull the Time Slider to confirm this result in the viewport. Try moving the Box again with the Time Slider on a different frame. As you'll see, the result is the same no matter which frame you are on—this is an important feature of MAX animation that comes up in many contexts.

4. Any animation can be rigidly moved or rotated in a scene as a single unit. This step clarifies exactly what the Animate button does. When the Animate button is on, only the value at the current frame is affected by any change. When it is off, all existing keys are

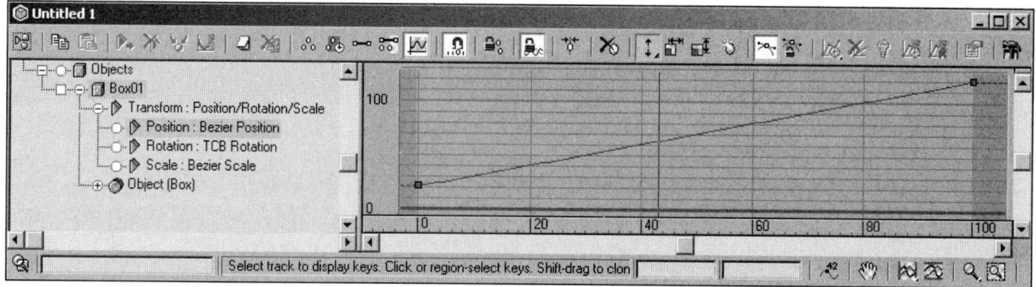

Figure 17.14

The function curve from Figure 17.13, after the object has been moved farther in the X-direction with the Animate button off. This action moves the entire animation as a rigid unit to a new position in space.

affected together. Test this idea by moving the Time Slider to Frame 100. With the Animate button still off, move the Box up in the World Z-direction. If it is not being filtered out, the blue linear curve in Track View rises as a rigid unit, with both of its keys moving in parallel. Undo to return to Z=0. Turn on the Animate button and move the Box up in the Z-direction. Notice that only a single key moves up in the function curve. Because a key already existed at this point, turning on the Animate button permits you to change its value by moving the object. The same result can be achieved in the opposite way by editing the key in Track View and watching the object move in the viewport.

Using the Track Bar

The Animate button may be too simple and general a tool for much of your animation work, but Track View can sometimes present too complex an interface for basic key creation and editing. 3ds max 4 has some important tools that provide a happy medium. You can now create keys by using a dialog box available from the Time Slider, and you can edit keys with the Track Bar located immediately beneath the Time Slider. The following exercise explains this toolset.

Using the Create Key Dialog Box

Let's start the exercise by experimenting with the Create Key dialog box:

1. Create an animation of a Box using the settings shown in Figure 17.13. You can create the keys using the Animate button or, preferably, directly in Track View. The Box is animated only in its X Position transform, moving from the World origin to (100,0,0) over 101 frames from Frame 0 to Frame 100. Make sure that Track View is open and displaying the function curve.

2. Drag the Time Slider to Frame 50 and make sure that the Box is selected. It's probably a good idea to lock your selection (by using the spacebar) to make sure you don't lose it. When you create and edit keys in Track View, it doesn't matter whether the affected object is selected, but it does matter when you're using the Track Bar or Time Slider tools. Right-click on the Time Slider to bring up the Create Key dialog box. As you can see in Figure 17.15,

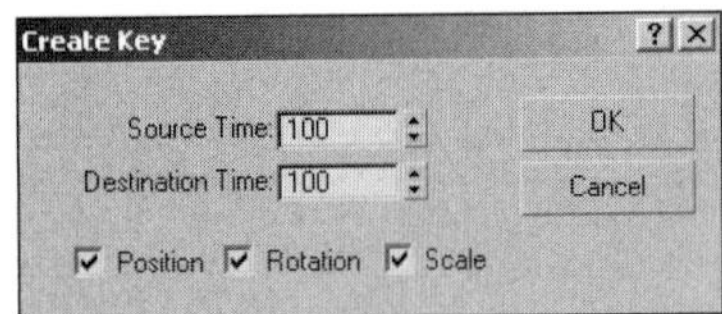

Figure 17.15
The Create Key dialog box, reached by right-clicking on the Time Slider. The Source Time and Destination Time spinners both display the current frame. All three of the transforms are selected by default.

the Source Time and Destination Time spinners both display the current frame. By default, all three of the transforms are selected (Position, Rotation, and Scale).

3. As you can deduce from the three checkboxes, you can set keys only for transforms—not for any other parameters—from this dialog box. You want to create keys only for the Position transform, so deselect the Rotation and Scale boxes. Click on the OK button and take a look at your function curve in Track View. It should now look like Figure 17.16.

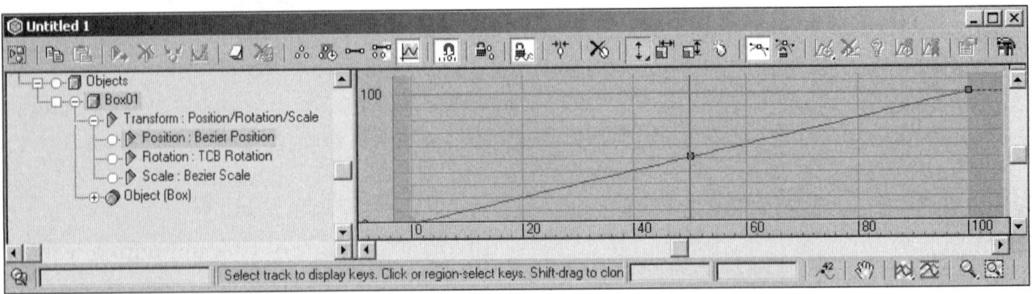

Figure 17.16
The function curve from Figure 17.13, with a Position key added using the Source Time and Destination Time settings from the Create Key dialog box. The key is placed at Frame 50 because that is its Destination Time. It is placed exactly on the existing curve because it uses the value of its Source Time (also Frame 50).

4. As you can see from Figure 17.16, a key was added at Frame 50 by using a value of X=50. This new key did not change the shape of the curve at all. Make sure that you understand exactly what happened. The new key was placed at Frame 50 because the Destination Time was set to 50. The value of the new key is determined from the Source Time, which was also set to 50. Prior to the addition of the key, the value of the parameter at Frame 50 was X=50. Therefore, this value is used for the new key. Select the new key in Track View and delete it to try something different.

5. With only the two original keys remaining, bring up the Create Key dialog box. This time, use 0 as your Source Time and 60 as your Destination Time. Click on OK and look at the function curve in Track View, as shown in Figure 17.17. You have created a new key at Frame 60 (the Destination Time). The value of that key was taken from Frame 0 (the Source Time). As a result, the new key at Frame 60 has a value of X=0. Note the spline

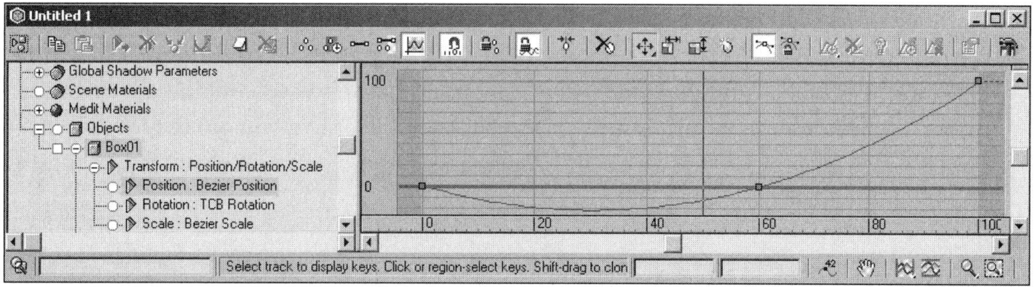

Figure 17.17
The function curve from Figure 17.13, with a Position key added using a Source Time of 0 and Destination Time of 60. The new key at Frame 60 uses the value of the parameter at Frame 0, effectively copying it to a new location on the graph. Note the spline interpolation that dips the curve below 0.

interpolation that brings the curve below 0, causing the Box to move backward before it moves forward. You learned how to correct this behavior with Bezier handles earlier in this chapter, but don't bother to do so here.

Editing from the Track Bar

The horizontal window immediately beneath the Time Slider is the Track Bar. You see the same square key symbols that you'd find in a Function Curves view in Track View, and they are used in much the same way. Let's continue our exercise by moving on to explore the possibilities of the Track Bar:

1. Currently, keys exist at 0, 60, and 100. Select the second key in the Track Bar and move it from Frame 60 to Frame 50. See the result on your function curve in Track View.

2. Right-click on the second key in the Track Bar to bring up a small, modeless menu. At the top is the name of the animated parameter—Box 01: Position. If you don't get this option, be sure to right-click exactly on the key. Click on this option to bring up the same key-editing dialog box that you get when you right-click on a key in Track View. You can use it to change the values for the keys, or their interpolation options, in the standard way.

3. Several options exist for deleting keys. Make sure that the second key is selected and right-click in the Track Bar, although not on a key. You'll get a similar version of the menu. Try the Delete Selected Keys option to delete the second key. This is a good way to delete many keys at once.

4. With only two keys remaining, right-click directly on the key at Frame 100 without selecting it first. This time, the menu allows you to delete the specific key by selecting Box01: Position from the Delete Key option. Delete the key to see that this method works, and then undo to get the key back.

5. Right-click anywhere in the Track Bar to bring up the menu and look at the Filter options. Here, you determine what keys are visible in the Track Bar. The options are All Keys, All

Transform Keys, Current Transform, Object, and Material. Experiment with these filters. Your present Position keys will always remain visible when you use All Keys and All Transform Keys, and they will always be hidden when you use Object and Material. If you use the Current Transform option, the Position keys will be visible only if you are in Move mode. The Object filter displays keys set for the underlying parameters of an object or the parameters of its modifiers.

Ranges and Out-of-Range Types

The *range* is a central and extremely useful concept in MAX animation. The animation of any parameter extends over a time range, which is generally specified in frames. For example, all the animations you have been working with in this chapter occupy a range of 101 frames, from Frame 0 to Frame 100. The ranges are displayed as black bars in Track View and are adjustable so as to scale the animation or to move them.

Ranges are hierarchical. They exist for each animated parameter and for the parents of related parameters. This setup permits you to scale or move related ranges as a unit by adjusting their common parent. But ranges are independent of the Active Time Segment, which is the unit of frames available to the Time Slider. As a result, the Active Time Segment can be longer than the ranges within it. At first, this idea may seem rather confusing, but it is very important. The animation may be made to continue outside of its ranges using some very powerful controls.

The following exercise introduces all these tools and concepts.

Using Child and Parent Ranges

Let's begin the exercise by becoming familiar with different types of ranges:

1. If you used the spacebar to lock the Box as a selection, unlock it at this time. Use the same viewport layout you've been using all along, with Track View above and the Front viewport below. Create a Box and position it at the World origin. Using any method you want, create Position keys at Frames 0 and 50. The value at Frame 0 should be (0,0,0), and the value at Frame 50 should be (50,0,0). Thus, the Box should move 50 units in the World X-direction over 50 frames.

2. Look at the ranges in Track View using an Edit Keys view, as illustrated in Figure 17.18. The Edit Keys view shows only parent ranges. Black range bars appear at the Box level and at the Transform level. These are composite ranges of all the ranges beneath them. In this case, there is only one animated track, Position, with keys at 0 and 50. Thus, both of the parent range bars extend from 0 to 50.

3. To understand the concept of parent ranges, create keys in the Scale track at Frames 0 and 70. Set the X value of the key at 70 to 200, so that the Box both moves and "grows." As you can see in Figure 17.19, the parent ranges now extend from Frame 0 to Frame 70. In other words, they cover the full extent of any of their child ranges. The value of this system is obvious if you

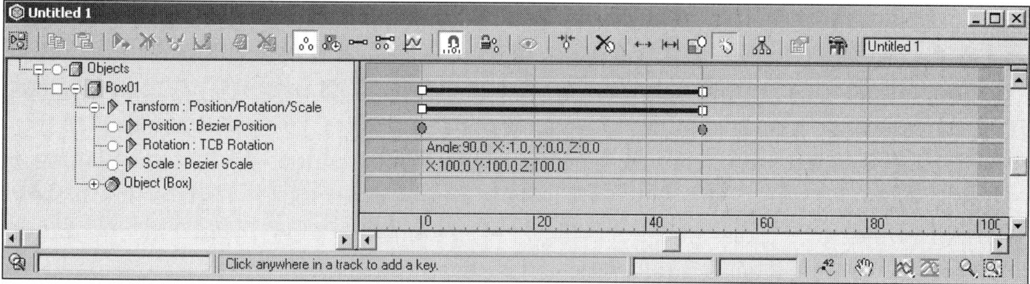

Figure 17.18

An Edit Keys view of an animation created with two keys in the Position track. Only the parent ranges are shown as range bars.

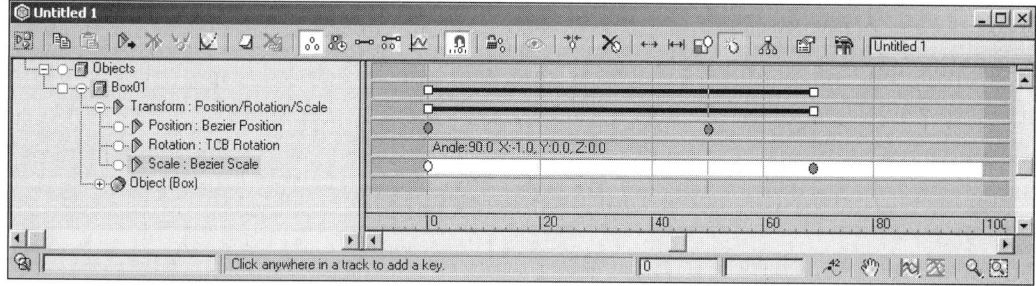

Figure 17.19

Keys are added to the Scale track at Frames 0 and 70. The parent ranges expand to include the full extent of their child ranges.

move the end of either of the parent range bars. Notice how all the keys in the child ranges scale together, allowing you to slow down or speed up animated tracks as a unit.

4. What if you want to scale only the Scale track? Switch to an Edit Ranges view on the Track View toolbar. All of the keys disappear, and all the child tracks display their range bars. Drag the end of the Scale range back to Frame 50 so that both animated tracks have identical ranges. The parent ranges will contract, as well. See Figure 17.20.

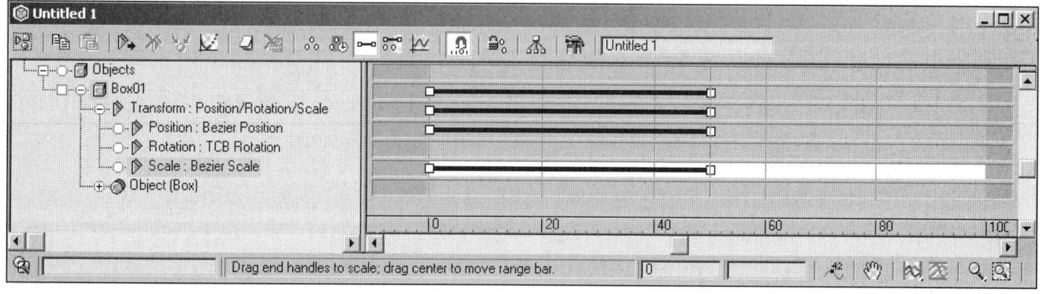

Figure 17.20

Using an Edit Ranges view allows you to see all of the child ranges, instead of their keys. Here, the Scale range is adjusted to end at 50, the same as the Position range. Note that the parent ranges also contracted.

5. To get the full picture of the relationship between child and parent ranges, go back to an Edit Keys view and open the Object (Box) tracks. Create keys at Frames 0 and 80 for the Width parameter. Change back to an Edit Ranges view. Your Track View panel should look like Figure 17.21. Begin adjusting the lengths of the ranges. Adjusting the length of the Box range at the top of the hierarchy scales all of its child ranges. Adjusting the Transform range scales its children, the Position and Scale ranges. Adjusting the Object range scales only its child, the Width range. Adjusting a keyed range—Position, Scale, or Width—affects only its parents if doing so changes the end of those ranges.

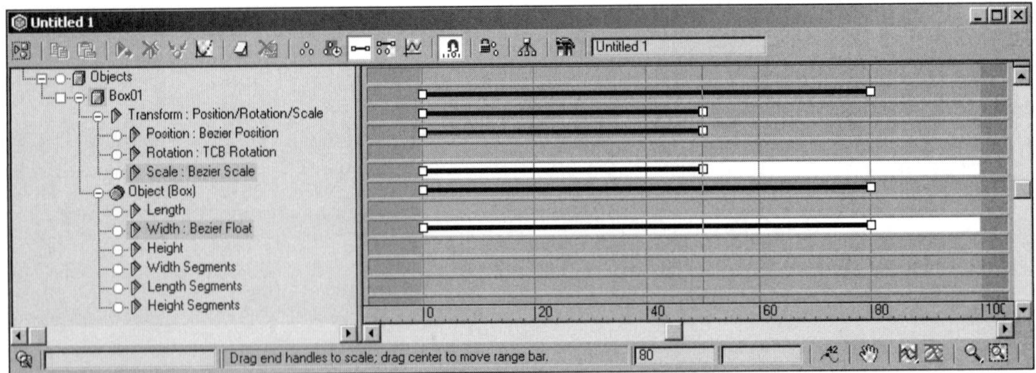

Figure 17.21
The same as Figure 17.20, but with a range created for the Width parameter at the Object level using keys at Frames 0 and 80. Adjusting the Box range scales all of the child ranges together. Adjusting the Transform range or the Object range scales only its respective child ranges.

It takes awhile to get used to these tools, but their flexibility is one of the reasons why Track View is so highly respected.

Working with Out-of-Range Parameters

Let's continue the exercise by working with out-of-range parameters:

1. In an Edit Keys view, delete the keys in the Width and Scale tracks, leaving only the Position track with an animated range. You can do this in the standard MAX way by dragging a rectangle around the desired keys to select them all at once and then using the Delete Keys button on the Track View toolbar. Your panel should again look as it did in Figure 17.18. Note that the keys extend only to Frame 50, but the light-gray region of the panel extends between Frames 0 and 100. This region is the Active Time Segment.

2. Open the Time Configuration dialog box using the Time Configuration button in the bottom-right corner of the MAX screen. As you can see in Figure 17.22, this panel permits you to set the frame rate of the animation and the time units used for display. It also determines playback speeds used when running animation in the viewports. The Real Time option drops frames, if necessary, to keep the display speed at frame rate. Focus, however,

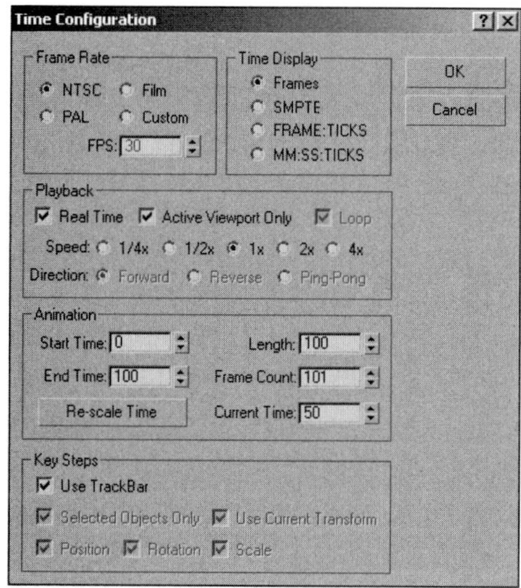

Figure 17.22
The Time Configuration dialog box. The Start Time and End Time parameters determine the Active Time Segment.

on the Animation section. The Active Time Segment is the unit of time beginning at the Start Time and ending with the End Time. Change these values and note the corresponding changes in the light-gray region in Track View. Note also how the Active Time Segment is indicated on the Time Slider. Once you have the idea, cancel out or otherwise return to an Active Time Segment of 0 to 100.

3. The Position range ends at 50. What happens after that? Switch to a Function Curves view to see, or look at Figure 17.23. The curve is a solid color during its range, from Frame 0 to Frame 50. After Frame 50, the curve continues as a dotted line, indicating that this is beyond the end of range of the keys. However, the out-of-range portion is every bit as important as the in-range portion. Pull the Time Slider or play the animation to see that the Box remains still from Frame 50 to Frame 100.

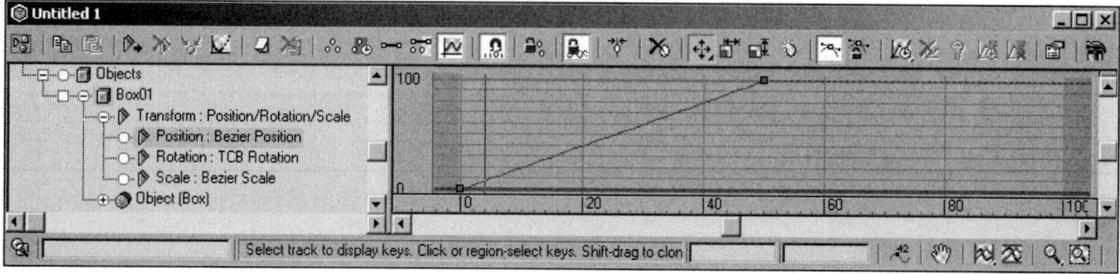

Figure 17.23
A Function Curve view of Figure 17.18. The region within the range (from 0 to 50) is displayed as a solid color with its keys. Beyond the end of the range, it becomes a dotted line.

4. This behavior is no big surprise, of course, but why did it happen? Click on the Parameter Curve Out-Of-Range Types button on the Track View toolbar to open the dialog box seen in Figure 17.24. These important options determine what happens when the animation extends outside of a range. Each option has two arrows: The left arrow applies the option to the frames prior to the beginning of a range, and the right arrow applies the option to the frames after the end of the range. For the most part, you'll rarely create ranges that don't begin at the start of the animation, so consider only the right arrow for now.

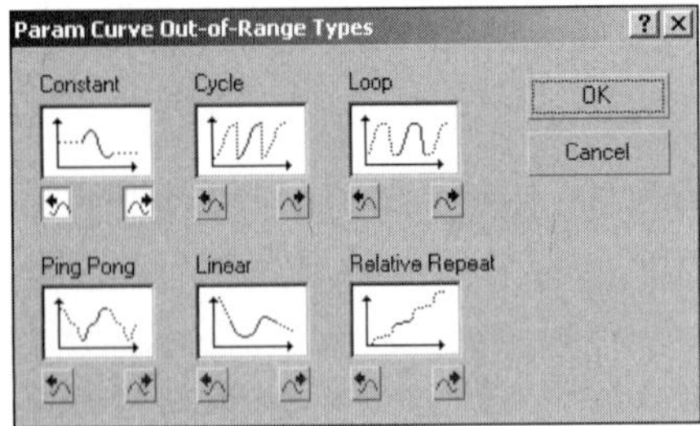

Figure 17.24
The Param Curve Out-Of-Range Types dialog box. These options control the shape of the function curve before and after the keyed range. The default out-of-range type is Constant.

5. Note that the Constant out-of-range type is currently active. This means that the final value in the range is simply continued unchanged. Click on the right arrow under Loop and click on the OK button. The function curve now shows the animation in the range being repeated after the end of the range, as illustrated in Figure 17.25. Run the animation to test this behavior. Then, select the second key on the curve and move it. Notice how the repeating pattern in the out-of-range region adjusts accordingly.

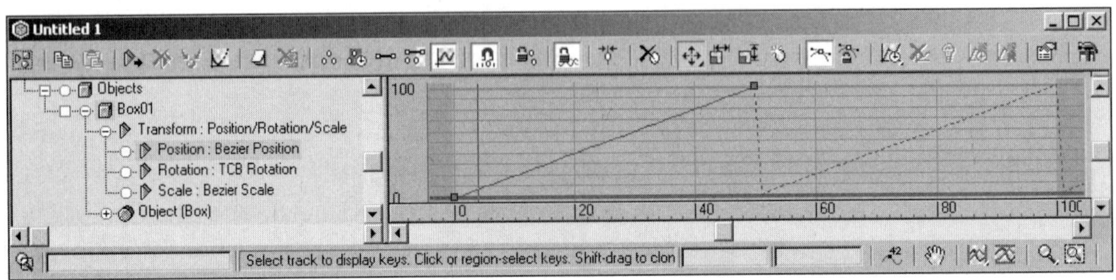

Figure 17.25
The function curve from Figure 17.23, with the outgoing out-of-range type changed from Constant to Loop. The animation in the range repeats in the region beyond the end of the range.

6. Experiment with all the other out-of-range types, particularly the Relative Repeat. A Loop repeats the exact animation in the range, always jumping back to the beginning. By contrast, Relative Repeat adjusts the repeat to begin where the previous unit left off. In our example, this means only that the Box keeps going in the same direction. This is not a

particularly valuable use, but Relative Repeat can be used to keep a character walking forward or climbing steps.

Visibility and Sound Tracks

You may want to have an object "fade in" or "fade out" of your scene. In addition, the impact of an animation is greatly enhanced with the addition of a sound track. 3ds max 4 has the ability to control the visibility of objects in a scene as well as assign audio files to be played when a scene is rendered. The exercises in this section will demonstrate how to add Visibility tracks to objects and how to assign audio files to your scenes.

Adding a Visibility Track

The following exercise will introduce you to the basics of adding a Visibility track to an object in MAX:

1. Create two objects so that one is in front of the other, as seen in the Perspective viewport. The specifics of the objects are irrelevant as long as they are either geometry or renderable splines. This exercise uses a Sphere in the foreground and a Box in the background.
2. Select the foreground object and open Track View.
3. Make sure that you're in an Edit Keys mode and that the highest level of the object in Track View (such as Sphere01 or Box01) is highlighted. In the Track View toolbar, click on the Add Visibility Track button (the eye icon). Between the Object name and Transform entries, in the Track View's left panel, a Visibility track is now present.
4. Create keys in the Visibility track at Frames 0, 50, and 100. The extreme values for the visibility keys are 0 and 1: 0 makes the object completely invisible, and 1 makes it completely opaque. Select the key at Frame 50 and set its value to 0. Your Track View window should look like Figure 17.26.

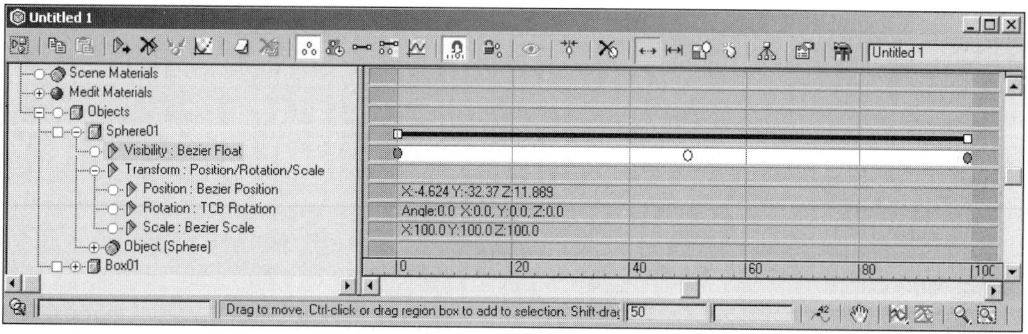

Figure 17.26
A Visibility track is added to the Sphere01 object in Track View and keys are placed at Frames 0, 50, and 100.

5. Play the animation and watch the effect of the Visibility track in the Perspective viewport. The foreground object begins opaque at Frame 0, becomes completely invisible by Frame 50, and is opaque again by Frame 100. Figure 17.27 shows a scene with the same setup at Frame 15. Render the scene to an AVI file and view it to get a clearer example of the effects of a Visibility track.

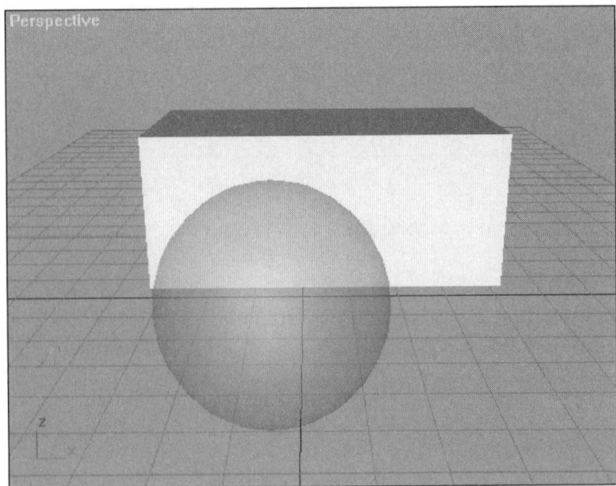

Figure 17.27
The keys in the Sphere's Visibility track dictate that by Frame 15 (shown) it is nearly one-third invisible.

Adding a Sound Track

Admittedly, audio is not one of the strongest features available in MAX. The Metronome feature produces a timed series of beats to assist in the rhythm of the scene, and you can assign an audio file, in WAV format, to be played in sync with the animation. No audio-editing features are inherent to the core package. The following steps will show you how to add an audio file to a MAX scene:

1. Open a Track View window. At the top of the left panel, just under World, open the Sound track to reveal a single Metronome track. This is where audio files are assigned.

2. Four hash marks define the times where the metronome beeps are heard when the option is active. Right-click on the Metronome track (or, if you are in a Function Curves mode, right-click on the word "Metronome" and choose Properties) to bring up the Sound Options dialog box shown in Figure 17.28. In the Metronome area, you can adjust the Beats Per Minute and Beats Per Measure values to change the pace of the beeps it produces. Select the Active checkbox and close the dialog box. Play the animation, and you'll hear the beeps through your computer's speakers.

3. Open the Sound Option dialog box again and deactivate the metronome. In the Audio section, click on the Choose Sound button to access the Open Sound dialog box shown in

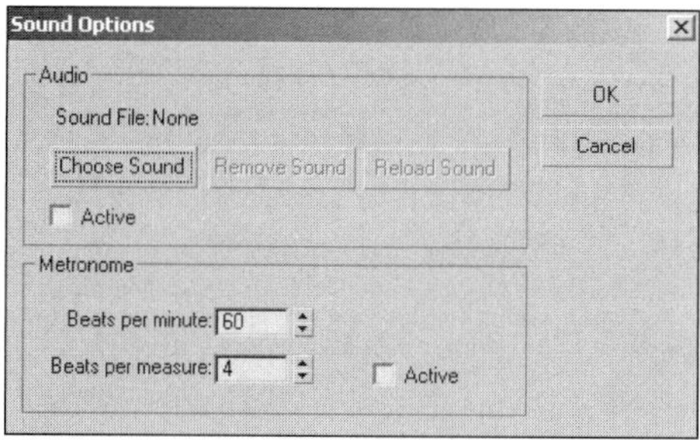

Figure 17.28
The Sound Options dialog box, accessed by right-clicking on the Metronome track. This track is used to assign audio tracks and to activate the Metronome feature.

Figure 17.29
The Open Sound dialog box where WAV files are assigned to the MAX scene. Clicking once on a file name brings up the preview controls.

Figure 17.29. Click once on one of the WAV files that MAX provides, or navigate to another file on your system. After a brief pause, controls appear that allow you to preview the sound before assigning it.

4. Choose a sound and close the Open Sound dialog box. In the Sound Options dialog box, the sound file is shown at the top, the Active button is selected, but the Reload button will remain grayed out until you close and then reopen the dialog box. (You can use the Reload button when editing and saving the WAV file in another package, to assign the edited version quickly.) Close the dialog box. Figure 17.30 shows the Track View with the NotGoingAnywhere.wav file assigned. The blue and red waveforms show the intensity of the sound's left and right stereo channels. Play the animation to hear the sound and watch the Track View to see how the waveforms relate to the sound.

Note: *Real Time, the option in the Playback section of the Time Configuration dialog box, controls whether a scene is played at its actual speed or at the maximum speed it can be played at while showing all objects. This option must be selected to hear the assigned sound file.*

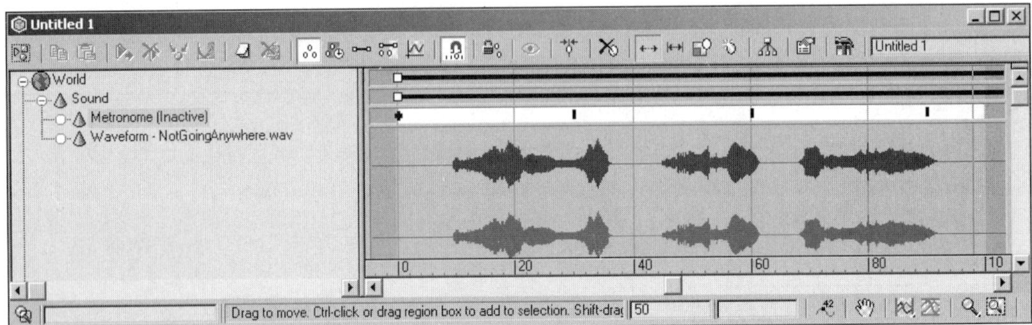

Figure 17.30
The Track View windows shows the stereo waveforms for the assigned WAV file.

5. A new feature in 3ds max 4 is the ability to view the sound's waveforms in the Track Bar. Right-click on the Track Bar and choose Configure; then, choose Show Sound Track. The Track Bar is enlarged to accommodate the waveforms.

Moving On

In this chapter, you learned the essential tools of MAX animation—the features on which all your animation work will rest. You learned that animation is the variation of parameters over time and how such variation is both described and controlled by function curves in Track View. You explored the basic toolsets for creating and editing keys, including Track View, the Animate button, and the Track Bar. You learned about the use of ranges, and how animation can be made to continue beyond the limits of its ranges. Finally, we addressed adding a Visibility track and assigning audio files.

The next chapter looks into the animation of the transforms—movement, rotation, scale, and manipulation. You'll learn how the different animation controllers are used for each of these transforms, and you'll look at the special powers of inverse kinematics.

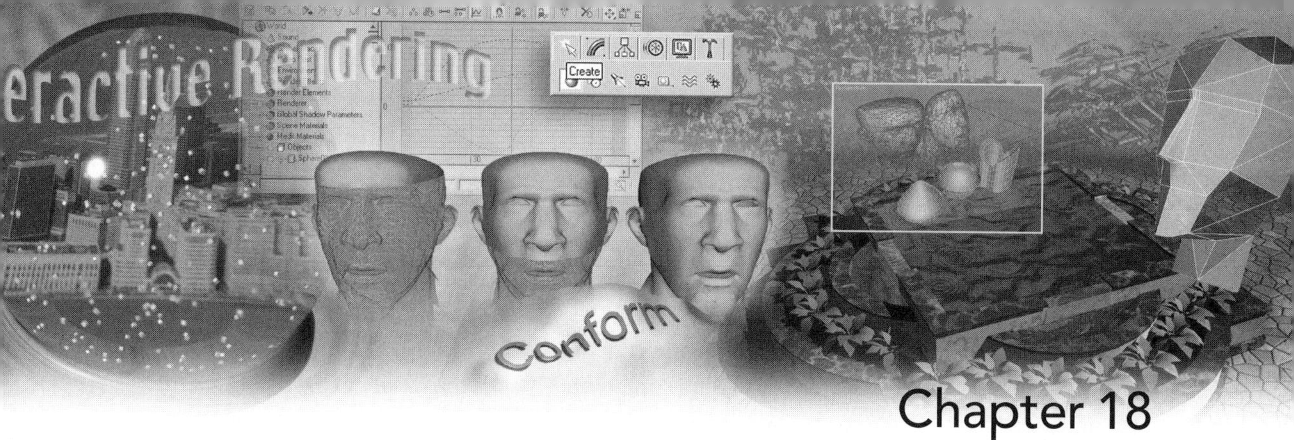

Chapter 18

Animating the Transforms

3D animation can be divided into two aspects. The first is the animation of an object's transforms. You move and rotate objects in space, but you do not change their shape. This is the topic of this chapter. The second aspect of animation is the deformation of an object's geometry so that it changes shape during animation. The two subjects overlap in many important ways, and the animation of scale (although clearly a transform) could be understood as a kind of deformation. Deformation is covered in Chapter 19.

Transforms, Controllers, and Constraints

Controllers and constraints are pure MAX. Like modifiers and space warps, they implement concepts that are both central and unique to this powerful application. Controllers and constraints are MAX's way of organizing the varied possibilities for animation. When you first begin animating, you may not be aware of the importance of choosing the right controller or constraint, but this choice is always critical.

Constraints are new to 3ds max 4 and perform the same task as controllers; therefore, this text will often refer to both constraints and controllers under the general term *controller*. The main difference between controllers and constraints is that constraints require a second object to reference for their task to be completed. Several controllers from the program's previous version have been categorized as constraints in 3ds max 4.

Controllers and constraints apply to all animated parameters, not just to transforms. For other animated parameters, you'll typically stick with whatever default controller MAX offers. Not so with the transforms, or rather with position and rotation, because the animation of scale is a minor issue. The differences between the possible controller choices are drastic. For rotations in particular, the choice may mean the difference between having editable function curve control of your motion and not having it. Nor can you simply trust the defaults until you run into a problem. It's not always easy to change controllers in midstream without adverse ramifications to existing animation.

People who work in building trades live by the rule that calls for the "right tool for the job." You can't drive a nail with a screwdriver or plane a board with a saw. So it is with MAX's animation controllers and constraints—but it's impossible to understand the relative strengths and weaknesses of the competing controllers without a good general exposure to all of them. Some animation problems absolutely demand a given controller. In other situations, the choice of controllers depends on personal preferences and work styles. In all cases, however, understanding the animation process means understanding the underlying tools, and the most important animation tools are the controllers and constraints.

Animating Position

When animating movements, you have many controller or constraint choices—perhaps too many—but some are far more important than others. The default Bezier Position controller and the Position XYZ controller are basically the same, because they set positional values in space for selected moments in time and then interpolate between these positions. In contrast, the Path constraint puts an object on a path defined by a previously created spline. You can control an object's speed and direction along the spline and control the amount it varies from that spline with a second spline.

The Bezier Position and Position XYZ Controllers

The Bezier Position controller is poorly named. Although the name correctly suggests that this controller uses Bezier splines as function curves to describe changes in position over time, this controller might be better called an "explicit XYZ" controller because its function curves store changing values in space (in X,Y,Z coordinates). When you create a key with the Bezier Position controller, you are storing the X,Y,Z location of the object at the indicated frame, and you are therefore shaping the function curve.

The Position XYZ controller does precisely the same thing, so its name is more apt. The difference between the two controllers is in their tracks. The Bezier Position controller has only a single track, which contains all three function curves. As a result, whenever you set a key, it appears on all three graphs—which can produce a lot of meaningless keys. Take a look at the function curves in Figure 18.1. The object was animated only in the Z-dimension. The X and Y values remain constant. Keys were automatically created on the X and Y tracks, however.

Unnecessary keys can become very confusing when you edit the curves, but a bigger problem arises when you animate a different curve. Take a look at Figure 18.2. When one of the keys is adjusted upward in value, all the existing keys on the graph create all kinds of complications. The curve is pinned at undesired frames; instead of a single soft bend, you get wavy interpolations.

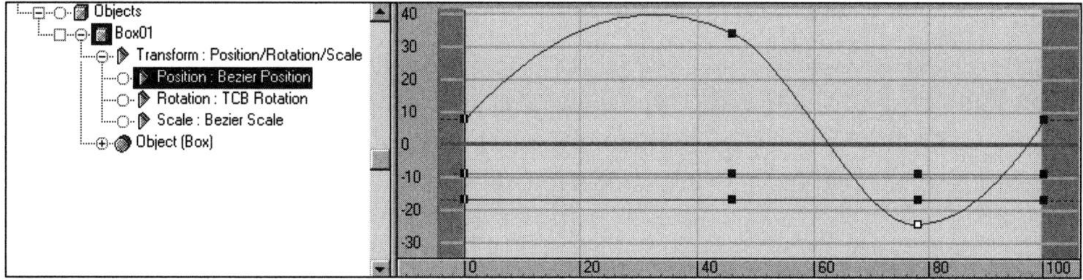

Figure 18.1
The function curves of an animated movement, using the Bezier Position controller. All the curves (X, Y, and Z) are included in a single track, and all three curves are keyed together. The object is animated only in the Z-dimension, but unnecessary keys were automatically created on the nonanimated curves. The filtering of the controller types has been turned off in the Filters dialog box.

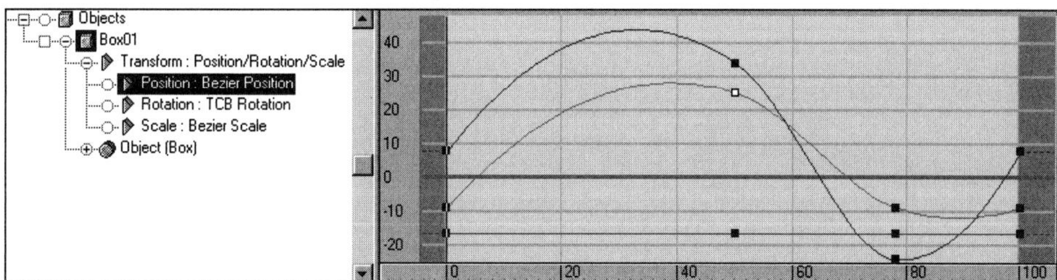

Figure 18.2
The curves from Figure 18.1, with a key added for the purpose of animating a second dimension (X). Any adjustments to the X graph are complicated by the presence of the other keys, which necessarily pin the graph to values. Instead of a single soft bend, the interpolation among all the keys produces a complex wave.

The answer here is editing. By adding a key and adjusting the values of a couple of existing keys, a curve can be created that follows the simple, intended path. The curve is unnecessarily complex, but at least it is shaped correctly; see Figure 18.3. Another minor nightmare is moving keys in time. If you move a key to a new frame on any one graph, all three keys move together.

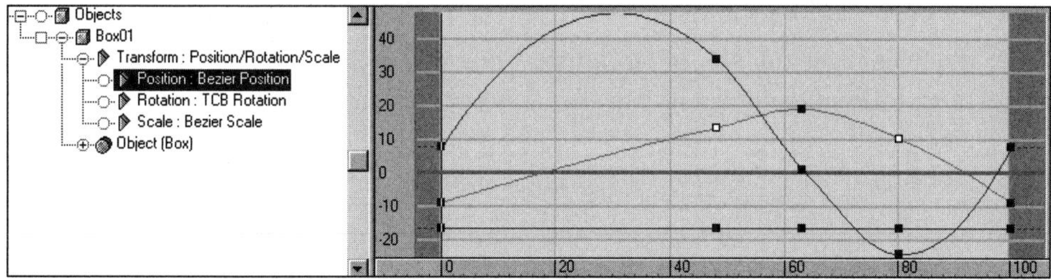

Figure 18.3
The curves from Figure 18.2, with a key added and the shape of the X curve adjusted. The resulting curve is the simple back-and-forth movement originally intended.

The single-track approach has other problems. With all three curves occupying the screen at once, it's often necessary to use the Filters dialog box to hide the ones you don't need to see. All the hiding and unhiding can quickly become tedious and can impact your productivity. Key selection can be difficult, especially when different curves lie right on top of each other. It's very easy to select unintended keys on multiple curves together.

The Position XYZ controller, by contrast to the Bezier Position controller, arranges the three curves on independent tracks. If you place a key on the X curve, it does not also appear on Y and Z curves. If you move a key in time, it changes only in a single dimension. Figure 18.4 shows the same animation as Figure 18.1, but using the Position XYZ controller instead of Bezier Position. Note that the Position XYZ track is the parent to three separate tracks: X Position, Y Position, and Z Position. In Figure 18.4, the Position XYZ (parent) track is selected, and all three curves are displayed together as dotted lines. This display is for information only. No keys are shown, and the curves cannot be edited in this track.

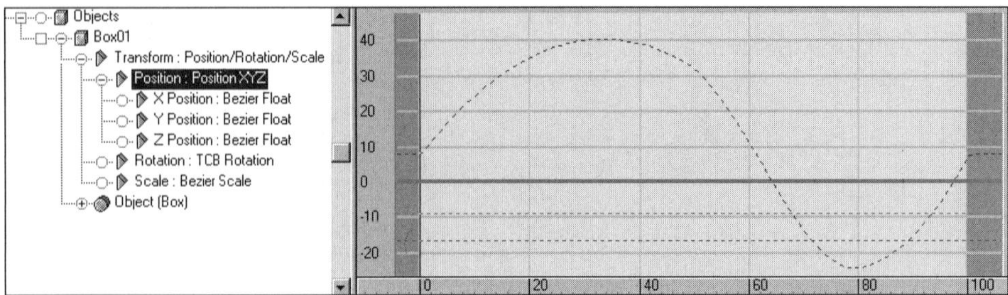

Figure 18.4
The animation from Figure 18.1, implemented by using the Position XYZ controller instead of Bezier Position. The Position XYZ track is the parent to three separate tracks: X Position, Y Position, and Z Position. The parent track is selected, and all three child curves are displayed together as dotted lines without keys.

The three individual tracks have their own controllers. Each one is of the Bezier Float type. In mathematics and computer programming, a *float* is a floating-point number—it is expressed in mathematical notation as a number multiplied by a power of 10 (for example, $203=2.03\times10^2$ or $32,725=3.2725\times10^4$. In contrast, an integer is a number without a decimal point—a whole number, such as 598,825 or –3. Floating-point values are obviously essential for continuous motion. If your animation tools could only jump rigidly between whole number values, they wouldn't be very useful. Thus, the Bezier Float controller generates a single continuous Bezier spline.

Figure 18.5 shows the Z Position track with its keyframed function curve. These keys are associated with this track alone, and any edits made to this track—adding or deleting keys, moving keys in time, or changing their values—have no impact on the other dimensions. If you looked at the other two tracks, you'd find no keys at all.

The downside of the Position XYZ controller is essentially the same as the upside. The independence of the tracks necessarily means jumping between them during editing. You can't see all three curves at once (with their keys) as you can with Bezier Position. In short, the Position XYZ

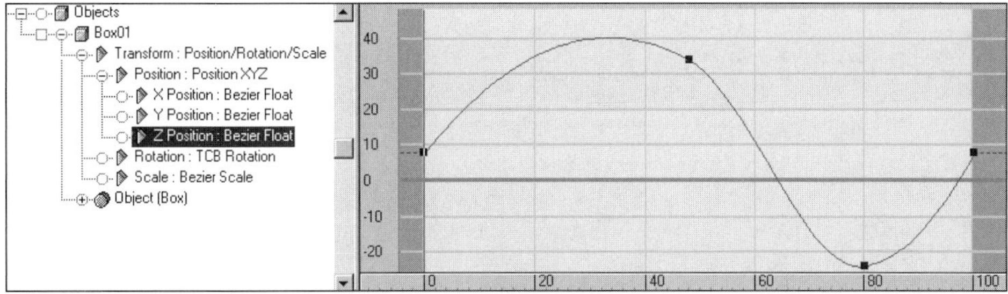

Figure 18.5
The Z Position track from Figure 18.4 is selected. Only a single function curve is displayed, and all keys in this track are completely independent of any keys placed in the X Position or Y Position track.

controller can be more difficult to use than Bezier Position, where an object is being moved three dimensions at once, typically as the result of arbitrary movement from location to location. Many animation tasks tend to involve movements that can be easily isolated into separate dimensions, however. A much stronger argument for the Bezier Position controller is that it permits you to use Trajectory keys, a process that you'll explore shortly. In the end, the decision to use one controller rather than the other turns on personal predilections as much as anything else.

Converting Existing Animation between Controller Types

You can convert one controller to another, even after keys have been set. For example, you may have started with the default Bezier Position controller and then discovered that your work would be much easier with the separate tracks available in the Position XYZ controller. Conversion between such closely related controllers works reliably. Not all conversions work well, and many don't work at all because the nature of the two controllers or constraints may be fundamentally different.

Getting Started

The tools for animating explicit positions with either of the two controllers are remarkably powerful and flexible—you'll never stop discovering new possibilities. Once you develop a sense of how well integrated they are, you will be in a good position to establish your own working style.

The following exercise introduces you to most of the tools available in the Bezier Position and Position XYZ controllers. You'll start with the Position XYZ controller for clarity, and then move to the Bezier Position controller along the way:

1. Configure your viewports as you did in the Chapter 17, as follows: Open the Viewport Configuration Panel from the Customize menu and go to the Layout tab. Select the option in the middle of the top row of icons, with a smaller viewport above and a larger one below. Create a Sphere in the lower viewport (it doesn't matter where you put it for now). Open a Track View panel and fit it over the upper viewport. Open the tracks for the object and center them in the visible portion of the panel. Your viewports should resemble Figure 18.6.

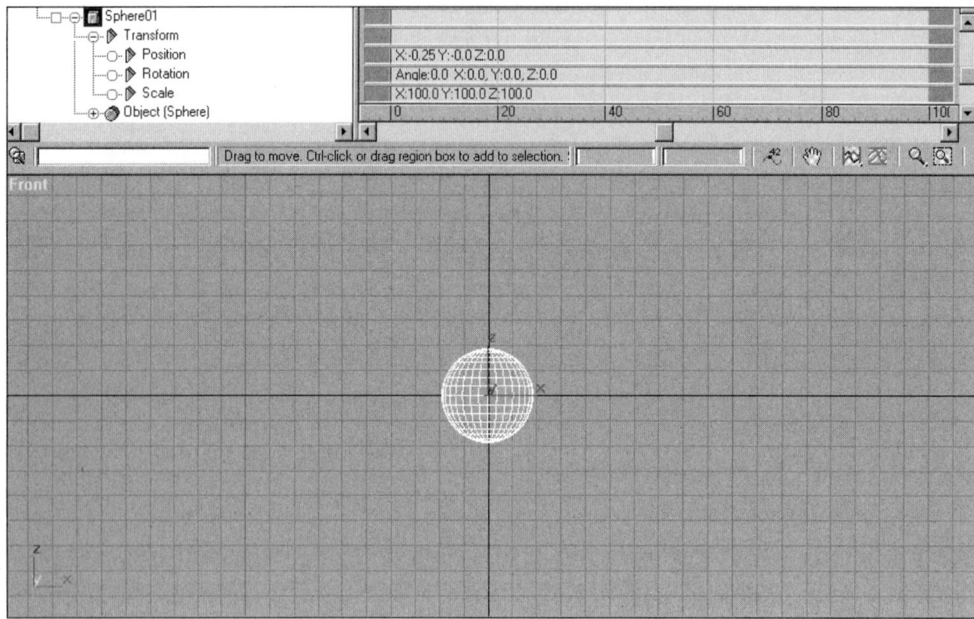

Figure 18.6
A Front viewport and Track View, set up to begin the exercise.

2. You will animate the position of the Sphere. Before you set a single key, ask two questions: What controller is currently being used? And what controller or constraint is the best choice? As we mentioned in Chapter 17, MAX doesn't show you your controller types in Track View unless you ask it to in the Filters dialog box. Always choose to see your controller types. When you do, you'll see that the Bezier Position controller was applied by default. That answers the first question. You've already decided the answer to the second question for the purposes of this exercise—to change from the Bezier Position controller to the Position XYZ controller, highlight the Position entry, and then click on the Assign Controller button on the Track View toolbar. The Assign Position Controller dialog box appears, as shown in Figure 18.7.

3. The dialog box contains a list of all the controller and constraint types available for animating the Move transform. Bezier Position is indicated as the current controller and also as the default controller. Select Position XYZ from the list. The Make Default button activates, allowing you to make this the default controller. Ignore this button and click on OK to change the controller.

Using the Motion Panel

You're all ready to animate with the new controller. Rather than using Track View or the Animate button to create keys, however, let's try a completely different approach by using the tools in the Motion panel. This panel can get lost in the shuffle of animation tools. To some extent, it duplicates tools that are available elsewhere in the MAX interface, but these are well organized in a single panel to the right of the viewport, in a way that often makes them more convenient. Other tools are found only in the Motion panel, and these will be our focus here.

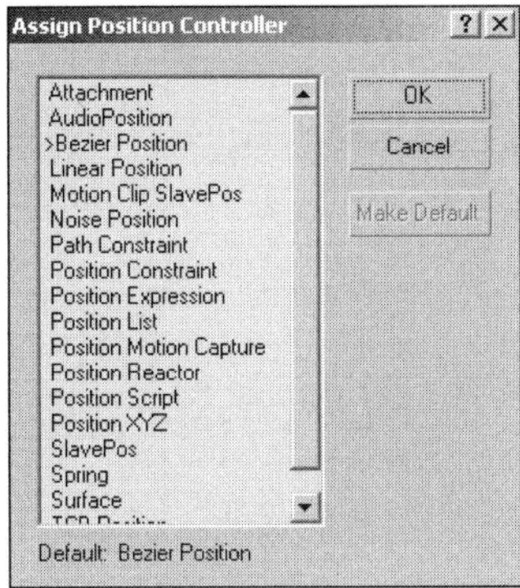

Figure 18.7
The Assign Position Controller dialog box with its list of available controller and constraint types. The small right-pointing arrow indicates that Bezier Position is the current controller. Bezier Position is also the default position controller.

With the Sphere selected from the previous exercise, click on the Motion tab on the Command panel (it has a wheel on it). The Motion panel is divided into the Parameters and Trajectories subpanels. When you open the Motion panel, you'll be in the long Parameters subpanel. The topmost rollout is called the Assign Controller. Just as in Track View, you select a track in the window and use the Assign Controller button to access the Assign Controller dialog box. The PRS Parameters rollout immediately below contains tools for creating and deleting keys at the current frame in the Time Slider for Position, Rotation, and Scale. These tools work very much like the Track Bar tools discussed in Chapter 17. The Position XYZ Parameters rollout determines the track whose information is displayed in the next two rollouts. The final two rollouts provide the same controls for individual keys that are found in the expanded dialog box that appears when you right-click on a key in Track View or the Track Bar. In short, the Parameters subpanel provides an alternative route to existing tools. Figure 18.8 shows this long subpanel in two parts, side by side.

Creating Trajectories from Splines

Your real business is the Trajectories subpanel of the Motion panel. Before you open it, let's think about a different approach to animating movement that doesn't involve setting your own keyframes, at least to start. It often makes sense to draw a curve to represent the motion path of an object and then cause the object to follow that path. True path animation using the Path constraint will be discussed later in this chapter and will be contrasted with what you're doing here. Right now, you are concerned with continuing the exercise by simply setting Position XYZ keys, using a spline as a guide:

1. Draw a straight Line object across the length of your Front viewport, below your Sphere. Use only two vertices and make sure that the Line is precisely level by setting both vertices to the same World Z value. (Or, use Grid Snaps when drawing it.) Your Front viewport should look something like Figure 18.9.

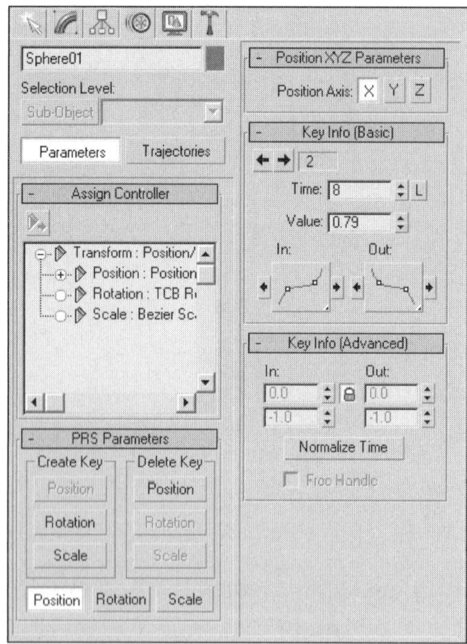

Figure 18.8
The Parameters subpanel of the Motion panel, seen in two parts, side by side.

Figure 18.9
Preparing to create a straight Trajectory from a spline. A straight Line object (Bezier spline) is drawn in the Front viewport below the Sphere from Figure 18.6.

2. Select the Sphere, go to the Motion panel, and click on the Trajectories button. Stop and look at the object name at the top of the panel. It should be the name of the Sphere and not the name of the Line object. We stress this action because it's easy to create a Trajectory for the wrong object. If you have the correct object, begin looking over this important subpanel, which is shown in Figure 18.10.

3. Two buttons—Convert To and Convert From—permit you to convert from a spline to a Trajectory and from a Trajectory to a spline. You'll use the Convert From button, because

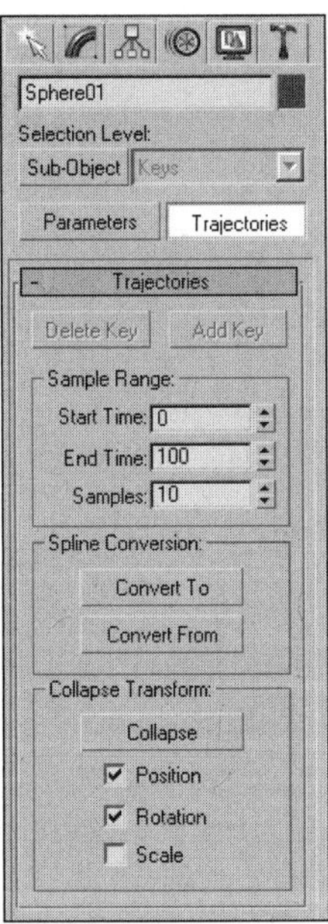

Figure 18.10
The Trajectories subpanel of the Motion panel for the selected Sphere.

you want to convert the existing spline object into a Trajectory for the Sphere. This conversion is accomplished by sampling along the curve—that is, by picking points along the spline and using them as the locations for keyframes. Look at the Sample Range section of the panel. Here, you determine when you want the animation to start and end. Leave these values at Frames 0 and 100. Then, you must determine how many keys will be sampled along the curve. Use the default of 10. Click on the Convert From button and then click on the Line. The Sphere should have jumped onto the Line, and a red line, with white dashes to represent the individual frames, indicates that an animated Trajectory has been created. Ten keys appear across the Track Bar. Your screen should resemble Figure 18.11. To see the Trajectory clearly, select your Line object and move it out of the way. Reselect the Sphere and notice that the Trajectory stays where it is. The spline was used only to create the keys. Once they are created, the spline has no continuing relation with the Sphere or its Trajectory.

4. Save your scene as it is now, so that you can easily return to it as necessary. To figure out exactly what you have, go to an Edit Keys view in Track View and look at the keys in the three position tracks. Click on each key to determine what frame it is on. You might have expected that, by using 10 samples over 100 frames, keys would have been created at 10-frame intervals. But because the keys must begin on the first frame and end on the last, the frames are placed at 11-frame intervals. The last frame is automatically rounded up from 99 to 100.

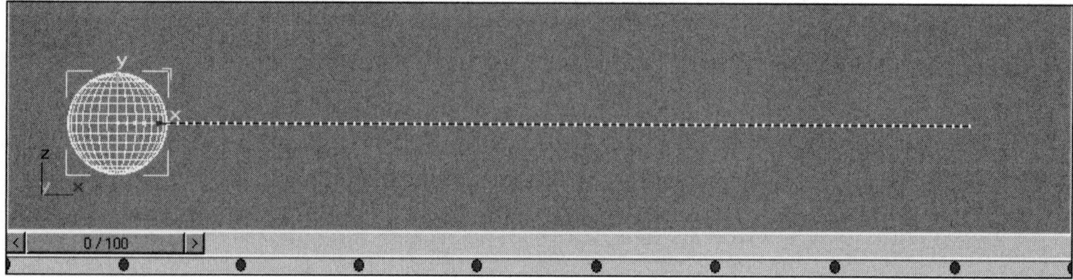

Figure 18.11
The result of creating a Trajectory from the spline in Figure 18.9, using the default parameters. The Sphere jumped down to the Line object, and a red line with white dashes indicates its animated Trajectory. The Track Bar immediately below indicates 10 keys, set at equal time intervals.

5. The spline-conversion method places keys in all three dimensions, because the motion path might need to move in all three. In this case, the object is moving only in the X-direction. Should you delete the unnecessary keys? That depends on where you want to go from here. As we discussed earlier, if you're going to animate only in one dimension or need the freedom to manage each dimension separately, you may want to delete the unnecessary keys. To delete, drag a selection rectangle around all the Y Position and Z Position keys in Track View; click on the Delete Keys button in the Track View toolbar or press the Delete key on your keyboard. Switch to a Function Curves view and look at each curve. Only the X Position curve should have keys.

Now that you know how to delete these keys, let's back up and try to work with them. Undo (or reload the saved scene) to get back the keys on all three tracks.

Adding an Acceleration

The essence of the skilled animator is the ability to control timing and acceleration. An *acceleration* is described by a curve with a constantly increasing slope. Although in the current exercise you really don't need 10 keys to make the Sphere move in a straight line (2 keys are enough), you can use these keys to cause the object to accelerate along the path. Look at a Function Curves view of your X Position track, as shown in Figure 18.12. Unlike an Edit Keys view (or the Track Bar), the curve directly illustrates both the time location of the keys and their values in the X-dimension. You already know that the keys are equally spaced in time, and the graph shows that they are equally spaced in distance. In other words, between every two adjacent keys, the Sphere moves the same distance in the same amount of time. The curve is a straight line, and the Sphere moves at a constant speed from start to finish. You can confirm this by playing the animation.

To make the Sphere move more quickly, you could bunch the keys closer together so they move the prescribed distance in a shorter amount of time. Before you start moving anything, however, think about the keys for the Y and Z Position tracks. The situation can get confusing if

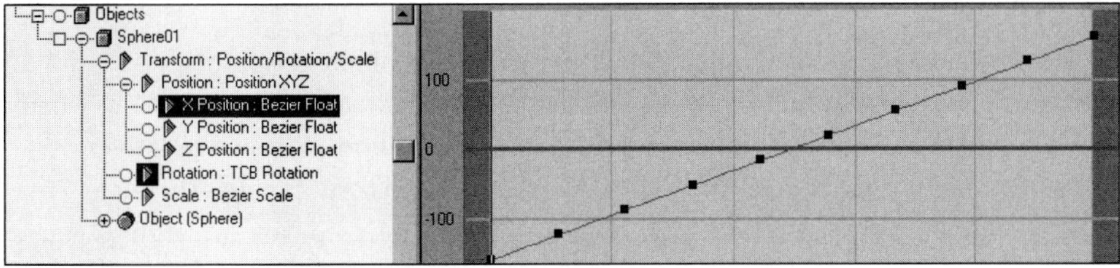

Figure 18.12
The X Position curve directly illustrates both the time location of the keys and their X-dimension values. The object moves an equal distance in space for each equal distance in time. It moves at a constant speed, and its function curve is a straight line.

these keys do not remain aligned with the X Position keys. One way to make sure that they all move together is to switch to an Edit Keys view and select a column of three keys together when moving. A more powerful way to do so uses the new Track Bar.

Each key you see on your Track Bar is actually all the keys located at that frame. As you drag a key, all three move together as a grouped unit. (To move only one of the three, right-click on the key and select the track you want from the menu.) In the current example, move all these keys until they bunch increasingly together toward the end of the animation; this movement takes some practice to get right. Use the function curve as a guide. When you finish, your screen should look something like Figure 18.13. Note how the Trajectory indicates the distance covered between frames. The distances get longer toward the right. This is a fantastic way to read the timing without running the animation.

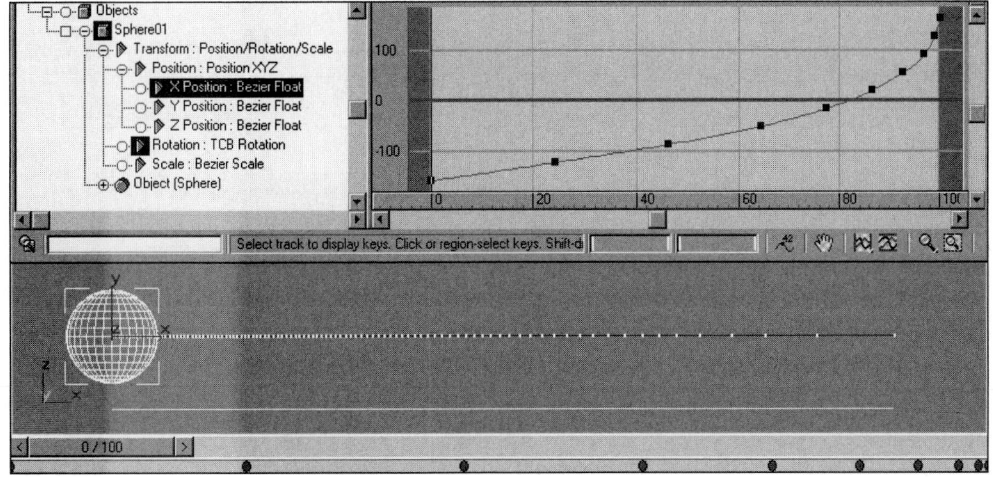

Figure 18.13
The keys are dragged in the Track Bar to create an acceleration. Because the distance values between the keys are constant, bunching them closer in time causes the object to move faster. The function curve now has a constantly increasing slope. Note how the Trajectory indicates the distance covered between frames. The distances grow longer toward the right.

Using Trajectory Keys

You just accelerated the animation by moving the keys in time. A different approach is to move the keys in space. MAX allows you to view and edit the keys directly on the Trajectory, but where are these keys? Trajectory keys don't make sense if you use the Position XYZ controller, because each key must represent a complete position in X-, Y-, and Z-dimensions at once. Therefore, Trajectory keys are available only when the Bezier Position controller is used. You can change controllers from the Assign Controller buttons in Track View or the Motion Panel, but you can also use the Collapse Transform section at the end of the Trajectories subpanel. To see how Trajectory keys let you edit the animation directly on the motion path, continue our exercise as follows:

1. Reload the saved scene to return to the original, unaccelerated animation. In the Collapse Transform section at the end of the Trajectories subpanel, select only the Position checkbox and click on the Collapse button. The controller changes to Bezier Position, and the keys on the Trajectory appear, as shown in Figure 18.14.

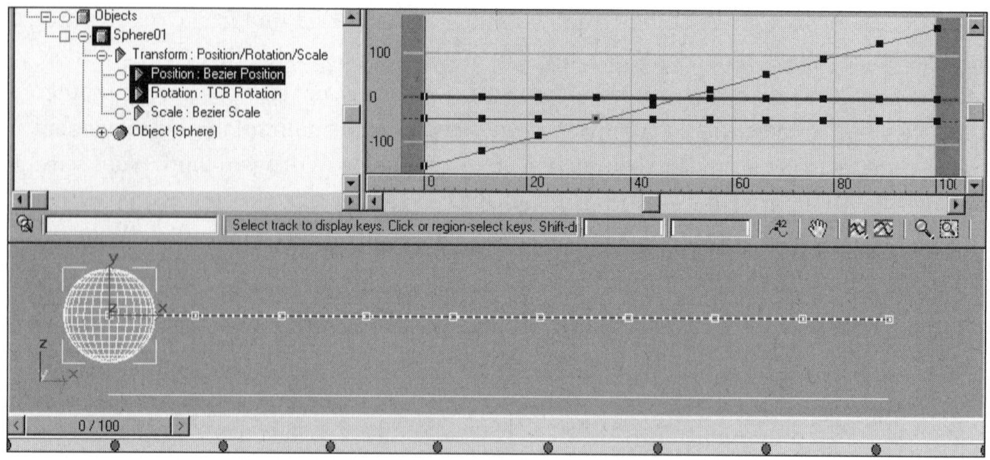

Figure 18.14
After the controller is converted from Position XYZ to Bezier Position, Trajectory keys appear.

2. Save this scene so that you can return to it, as necessary. You can now try to achieve the same acceleration as before, but by moving the keys in space (the viewport) rather than in time (the Track Bar). Click on the Sub-Object button in the Motion panel to get access to the Trajectory keys. As you click on a key on the Trajectory, notice that the corresponding key is highlighted in Track View and in the Track Bar. As you move the keys in the X-direction (along the path), the corresponding keys in the Track Bar do not move. You are changing their values in the X-dimension without changing their positions in time. This idea definitely takes some getting used to. In which direction should the keys be bunched? Think about it. They remain at equal intervals in time, and the Sphere moves faster if it covers more distance within a given time interval. Thus, the Trajectory keys must be spread farther apart as the Sphere moves along the path. Adjust the Trajectory keys to get a smooth acceleration.

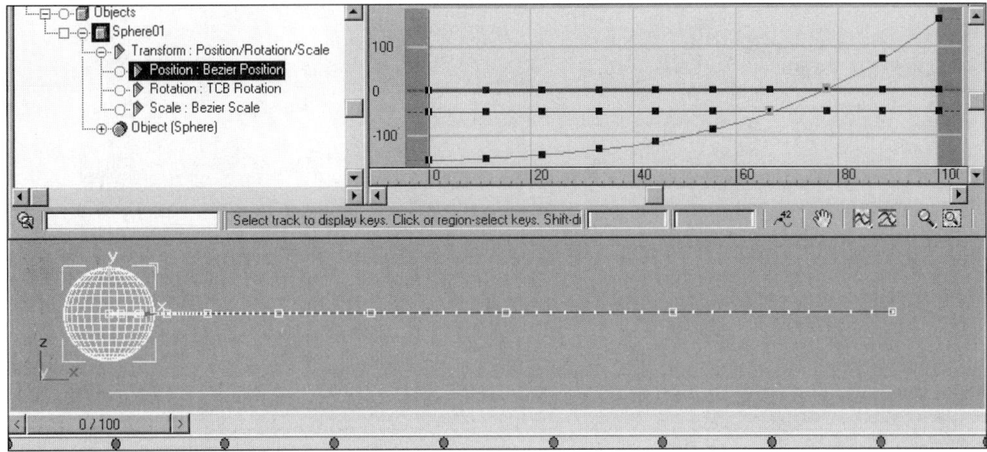

Figure 18.15

To create an acceleration, the Trajectory keys are positioned so that the distances between keys increase toward the right. As you can see in the Track Bar, the keys remain at equal distances in time, and the Sphere accelerates as it covers more ground between keys. Note the accelerated shape of the X-dimension function curve in Track View.

Use the shape of the X-dimension function curve as a guide. Note how moving the Trajectory keys stretches out or compresses the frames, as displayed on the Trajectory itself. When you finish, your screen will look something like Figure 18.15.

Creating a Bouncing Ball

You are now in a position to put a lot of concepts together. The idea is to learn to see the interdependence of all the tools, so that you can develop a style that is suited to your own inclinations. As you continue this exercise to create a bouncing ball, take time to explore for yourself:

1. You can start with the accelerated Sphere or reload the unaccelerated one. Although you can just begin moving the Trajectory keys to create peaks and valleys, make the task easier by deleting most of the keys first. Do this by selecting them on the Trajectory (or the Track View or Track Bar) and pressing the Delete key on your keyboard. Delete all but the first three keys and the final one at Frame 100. The first key on the Z curve is the highest point of the path, the second key is at the ground, and the third is back up, although slightly lower than the first. Your screen should look like Figure 18.16.

2. Take a good, long look at your screen or at Figure 18.16 to see what's right and what's wrong with it. A couple of things are obviously wrong. The Trajectory continues upward in a long arc after the third key, to finally arrive at the last one. This behavior is inherent in the default spline interpolation between keys that was already discussed. You can see the same problem in the shape of the Z function curve in the Track View panel. Also wrong is the rounded path around the second key, where the ball hits the ground; this is also due to spline interpolation (on the other hand, that same rounding is perfect for the top of the

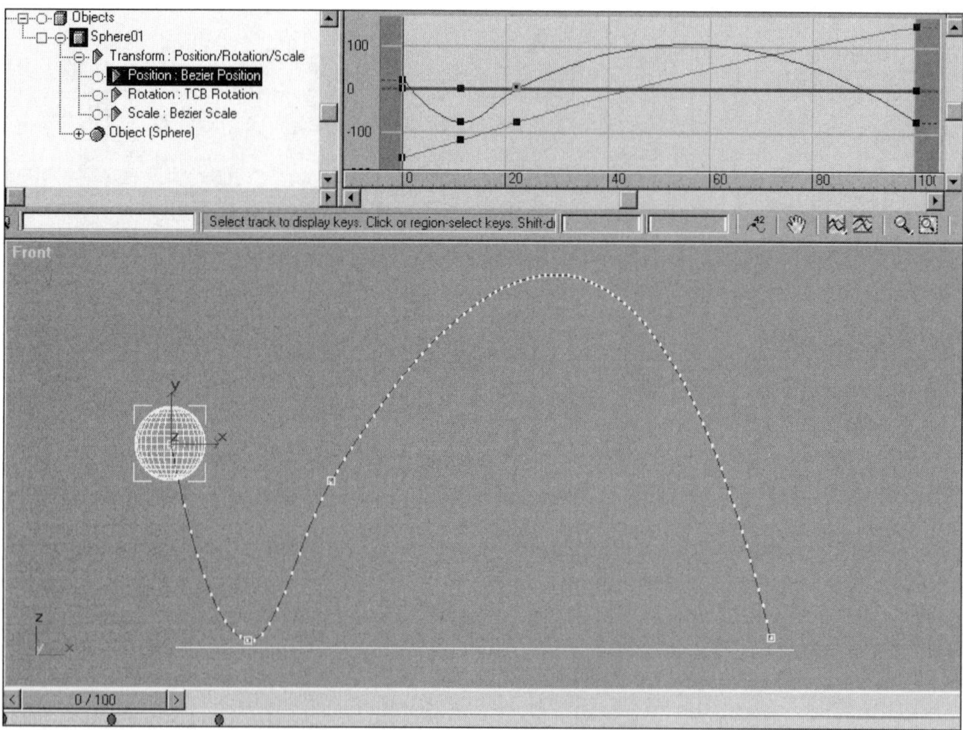

Figure 18.16
After deleting all but the first three keys and the last one, a single bounce is created by moving the Trajectory keys into position. Note the rounded path through all the keys, and the accelerations and decelerations indicated by the compression of the frame ticks on the Trajectory.

bounce). And take a good look at the timing. Notice how the ball decelerates into a curve and accelerates as its path straightens out. You can see this in the relative compression of the frame ticks in the Trajectory. They are much closer together around a curve and are wider apart elsewhere. Play the animation to check the accelerations and decelerations, and try to see how they correspond to the shape of the Z function curve and to the spacing of the frame ticks on the Trajectory. These are the basic skills of the MAX animator, which take considerable effort and innumerable hours to polish.

3. Correct the actual bounce first. When a ball falls toward the ground, it accelerates until impact, and then it immediately changes direction. To create this discontinuity, you must break the spline interpolation. Select all the keys in the animation in Track View and right-click. The dialog box for the multiple key selection is blank, but click on the In or Out button at the bottom and choose the Bezier handle option at the bottom of the menu. Although you need Bezier handles for all of these keys, you also need to unlock the handles for the keys at the floor level. Choose the second key. Bring up its dialog box and use the Advanced button to unlock the handles for the Z curve, as you learned to do in Chapter 17. Clean up your Track View by hiding the X and Y curves with the Filters dialog box.

4. Adjust the handles for the first two keys on the Z curve to get the correct shape and timing. Notice that the shape of the Trajectory changes as you change the shape of the function curve. You need a sharp v-shaped discontinuity through the second key and a nice clean drop from the first key. Move the Bezier handles until you get the correct acceleration. The ball should speed up as it approaches the ground. Use the frame ticks on the Trajectory to assess this action—they should spread out as the ball moves downward. On the other side of the second key, do your best to duplicate the same path and acceleration, only in reverse. You can only go so far, because the interpolation through the remainder of the spline interferes. Take time to develop a feel for the way the function curves control the shape and timing of the Trajectory. When you finish, your animation should look similar to Figure 18.17.

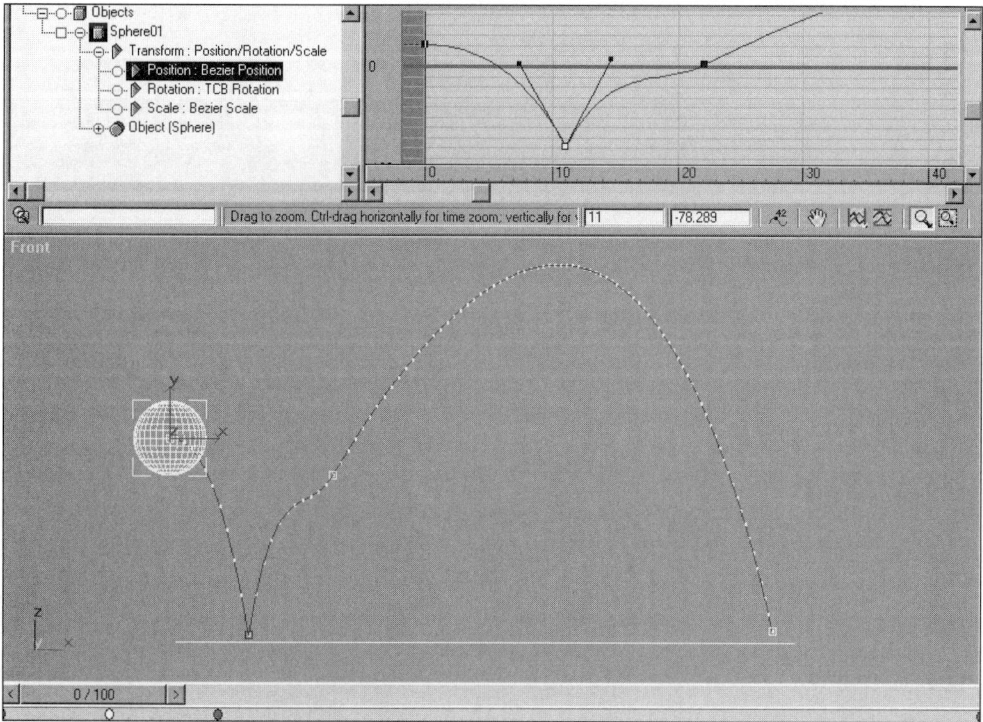

Figure 18.17
Editing the start of the Z function curve with Bezier handles changes the shape and timing of the Trajectory. The Bezier handles on the second key were unlocked to create a sudden discontinuity in the Trajectory where the ball hits the floor. Adjustment of the shape of the function curves also produces an acceleration as the ball falls toward the floor and a deceleration as it rises after the bounce. The shape of the curve between the second and third keys is complicated by the interpolation of the remainder of the spline.

5. Add more keys directly to the Trajectory. Make sure that you're in Sub-Object mode in the Motion panel. Click on the Add Key button to activate it and then click on the Trajectory just past the third key. Add another key somewhat further on, and then deactivate the Add Key button by clicking on it again.

6. Move these keys into position to describe a second bounce. The curve will probably behave wildly because of the spline interpolation, but you can tame it quickly. Level out the locked Bezier handles on the third key. Adjust the outgoing handle on the previous key to create a clean, rounded path between the two keys. Move on to the fourth key. Display its Bezier handles and unlock them as you did previously. Adjust the handles to fashion a sharp bounce. The next key is OK as is; there's no need to display its Bezier handles. Set the Z values for the two keys at the "floor" to the same amount. Your screen should now look something like Figure 18.18.

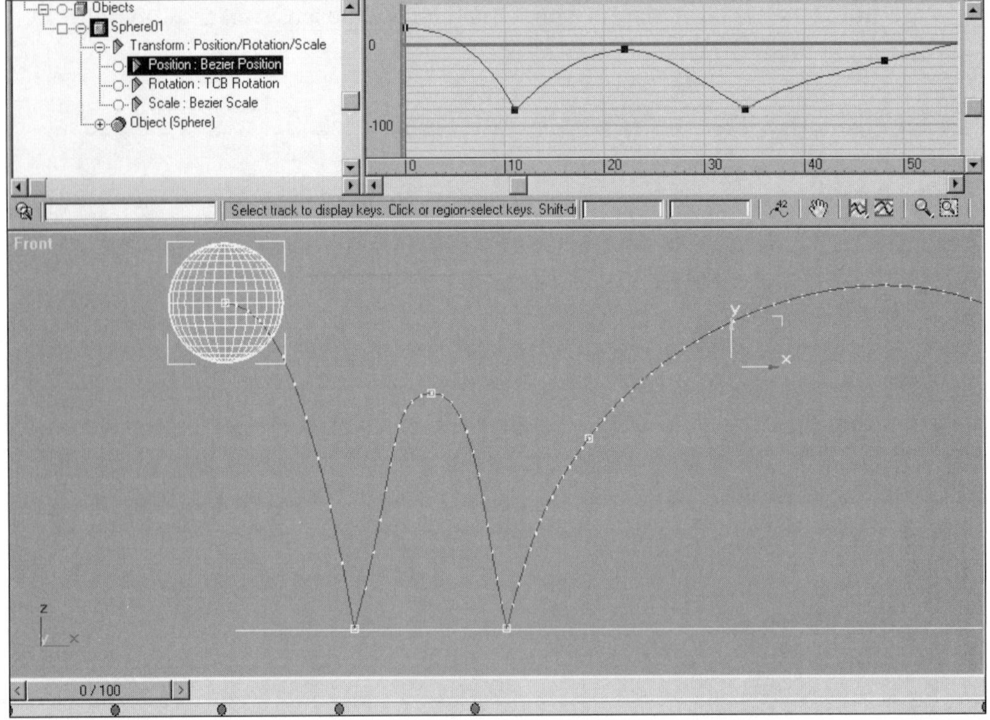

Figure 18.18

Two more keys are added to the animation from Figure 18.17 and adjusted to fashion the second bounce. The locked Bezier handles at the third key are positioned horizontally to create a smooth and equal interpolation into and out of the key. The fourth key's Bezier handles are unlocked and adjusted similarly to those for the second key to create a sharp discontinuity.

7. Add some more keys further down the Trajectory and make all the adjustments you've learned thus far. Display and unlock the Bezier handles on the "floor" keys and adjust them. You also need to display the handles on the keys at the top of the arc. See how making these handles horizontal keeps the key at the very top of the interpolation curve. You'll generally need to level these handles out before you can work effectively with the "floor" vertices.

8. Pay attention to the X distance between bounces. Just as each successive bounce should be smaller in Z, each bounce should also cover a shorter horizontal distance—the ball loses energy as it bounces. As you position the keys in the X-dimension, you'll no doubt need to rework your spline interpolation using the Bezier handles. Take some time with this process. Your screen should end up looking something like Figure 18.19.

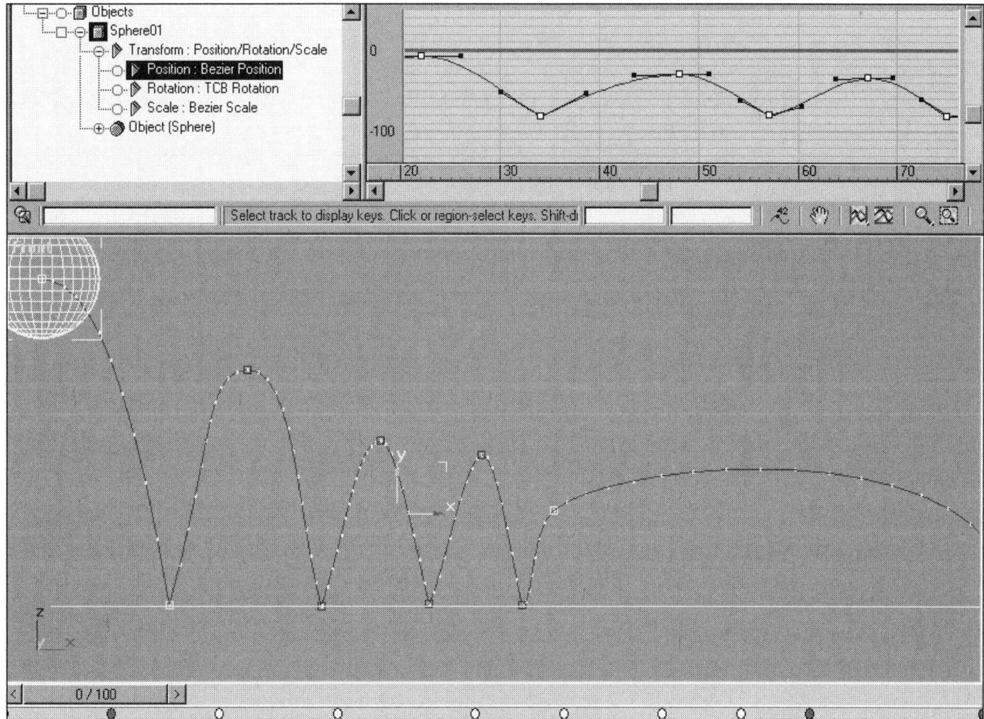

Figure 18.19
More keys are added and positioned for additional smaller bounces. Locked Bezier handles on the upper keys are made horizontal to position the keys at the very top of the arcs. Unlocked handles on the lower vertices are used to create sudden changes of direction (discontinuity). The horizontal (X) distance between successive bounces is decreased, reflecting the loss of energy as the ball bounces.

9. You have a lot of serious balancing to do. Add as many further keys as you wish to finish the remaining bounces. Timing now becomes an important issue. For one thing, you should have about the same number of frames on each side of the key at the top of each arc. If there are seven frames going up, there should be about seven going down. You need to move the keys in time. The most effective way to adjust the key location is with the Time Spinner in any of the dialog boxes that provide key information. As you increment or decrement the frame number, watch the number of frame ticks change on the adjacent segments of the Trajectory. This is a fantastic way of getting precise timing. Play the animation often to test the timing. You need to make a lot of Bezier handle adjustments at all

stages. A special consideration is getting your X-direction movement correct. Unhide the X function curve and try to get this curve into a fairly straight line by adjusting values and Bezier tangent handles. Take your time and learn, because there's a lot going on here, even with such a "simple" project. Try to get your result to look close to (or even better than) Figure 18.20. The purpose is not to make the perfect bouncing ball; it is to learn the complex interaction of function curves, Trajectories, and keys.

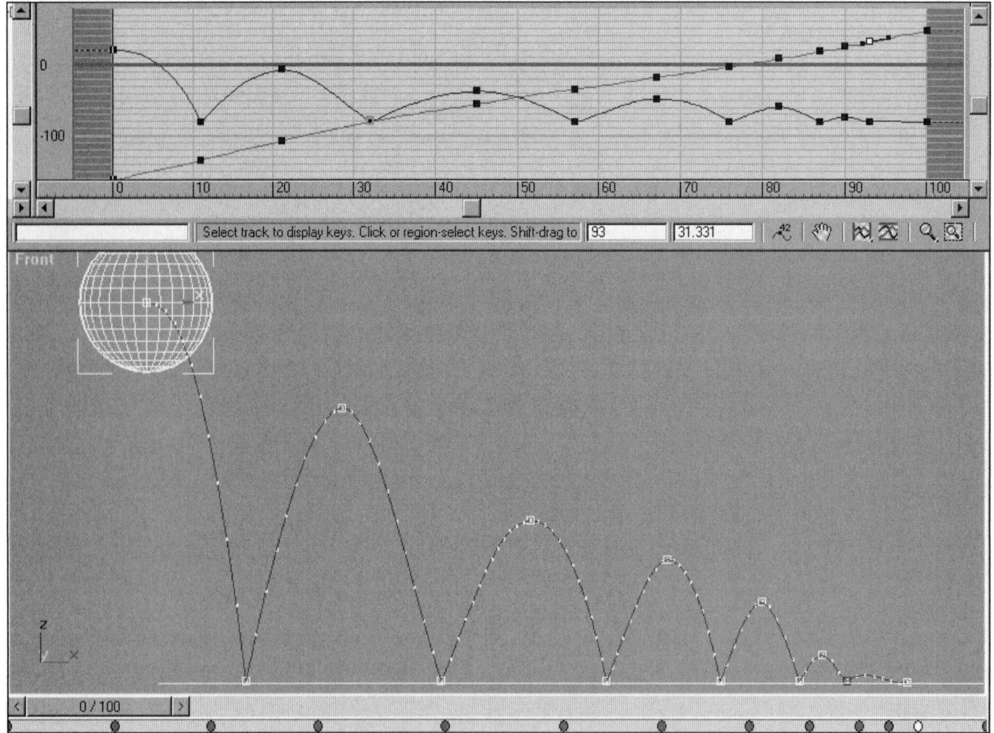

Figure 18.20
The finished bounce Trajectory requires a great deal of careful balancing. Note that the timing of the bounces is equalized—the number of frames on each side of an apex is the same or close to it. The X-dimension function curve is adjusted into a fairly straight line.

The Path Constraint

The Path constraint implements what is generally called *path animation* in computer graphics. The path in space that an object will follow is defined first, with a spline. Then, the object is put to the path and follows it over the course of the animation. Any changes made to the underlying spline are automatically reflected in the path animation. Path animation is extremely important because an animation is often most easily understood as a motion path. A jet fighter in flight and a racing car moving around a track are only the most obvious examples. A camera is often best animated by putting it to a predefined path.

The 3D animator is often faced with the choice between explicit XYZ animation (using the Bezier Position or Position XYZ controller) and path animation (using the Path constraint). The choice can be difficult, so it's important to understand the differences between these two approaches. When using the Bezier Position or Position XYZ controller, you create function curves that determine the locations of objects in 3D space over a period of time. The keys that you set designate values in X, Y, and Z. In contrast, when you use a Path constraint, you create a function curve that defines the motion of an object along a previously defined path. The shape of the function curve controls the speed and direction of the object along the path; in setting a key, you fix the object's percentage distance along the path at the specified frame. Using a second spline, you can vary the assigned object from the path, although its primary motion control is along the path.

Someone once called the Path constraint a "gas pedal," and this is a good metaphor. With the Path constraint, you can speed up or slow down with ease. The metaphor, however, must be expanded to include the brakes and the forward and reverse gears, because you can both stop and go backward on the path, if desired. As a general proposition, the Path constraint is preferable to an explicit XYZ controller when the motion path of an object can be defined in advance and control or speed and timing is more important than control over location. For example, the Path constraint would make no sense in the bouncing ball exercise in the previous section, because you need to edit the location of the object constantly over the course of the animation.

The following exercise introduces you to most of the important aspects of the Path constraint.

Putting an Object onto a Path

You'll start this exercise with the basics: drawing a spline path and putting an object onto it:

1. From the CD-ROM, open the file Chap18 Plane.max. It consists of a simple, box-modeled plane; the viewports are configured as they were in the previous exercise. A plane object is good for understanding Path animation because it has a directional "nose."

2. Draw an Ellipse object in your Front viewport. This will be the motion path, so make it large enough to fill much of the viewport. At this point, your viewports should look like Figure 18.21.

3. Open Track View to cover the upper viewport and open the Transform tracks for the plane. Use the Filters dialog box to display your controller types. You see that your current controller in the Position track is not Path (it's almost certainly Bezier Position), so you're ready to change it by using the Assign Controller button. This method will work, but let's do it in the Motion panel instead, for practice. Make sure that the plane (and not the Ellipse) is selected when you open the Motion panel.

4. Open the Assign Controller rollout at the top of the Motion panel and select the text of the Position track—selecting the green arrow does not highlight the option. Click on the button with the green triangle and select Path Constraint from the list in the Assign Position

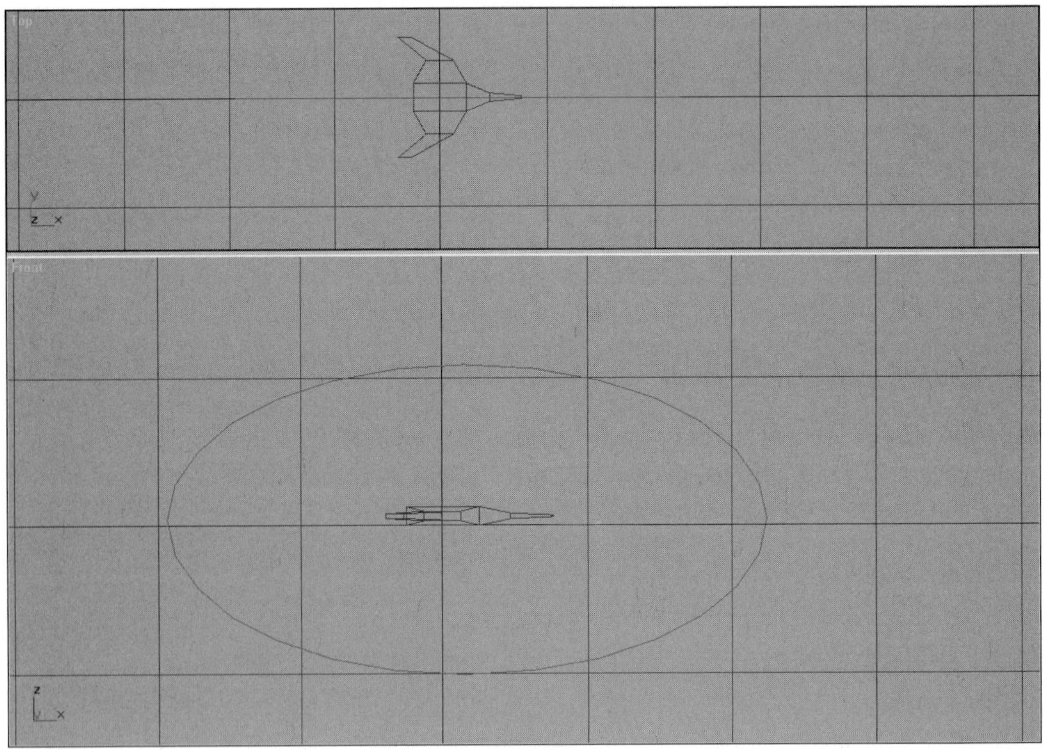

Figure 18.21
Setting up for the Path constraint exercise. An Ellipse (Bezier spline) is drawn as a motion path around the plane.

Controller dialog box. Click on OK to confirm and note that the words *Path Constraint* appear in the Position tracks in Track View and the Motion panel. But notice something striking: An animation range has suddenly appeared in Track View. Expand the Position track in Track View, and you'll see that keys were created in the Percent track at Frames 0 and 100.

5. Nothing has changed in the viewports; if you pull the Time Slider, you'll see that nothing has been animated. The function curve for the Percent parameter shows the value increasing from 0 percent at the start to 100 percent at the end. The curve is a straight line, meaning that the parameter is increasing at a constant rate. The Percent parameter is the percentage of the distance along the path. Because you have not yet put the object to a path, this percentage has no meaning. To put the object to the path, look at the Path Parameters rollout that now appears in the Motion panel. Click on the Add Path button to activate it and then click on the Ellipse in the viewport. The plane will jump to a point on the Ellipse. Click on the Add Path button again to deactivate it.

6. The plane still points to the right, just as it did before you put it to the path. Play the animation or pull the Time Slider to see the motion. The pivot point of the object follows the path, and the plane does not rotate at all. If you needed to change the location of the object where it attaches to the path, you would simply change the location of the pivot point, as discussed in Chapter 3. Figure 18.22 uses the Snapshot tool in the MAX Main toolbar to illustrate the plane at a number of positions on the path.

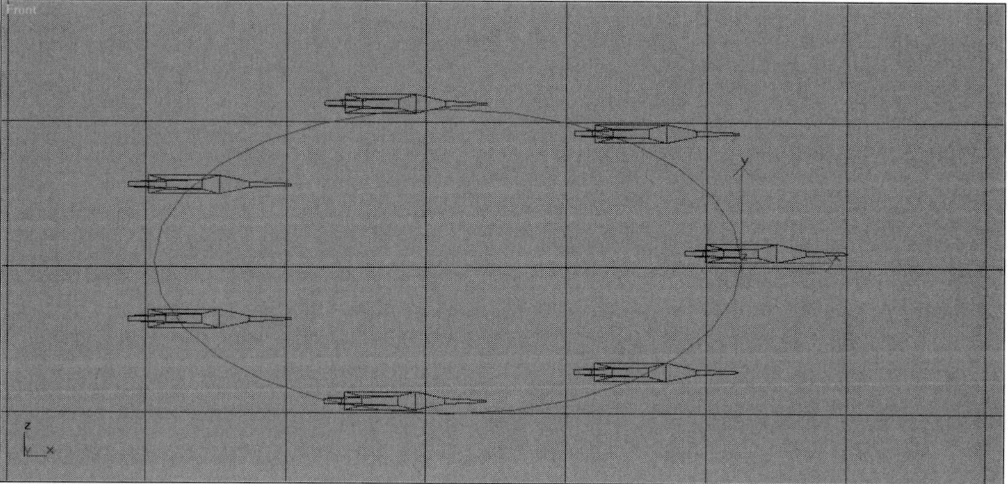

Figure 18.22
After the plane is put to the path, it follows a circuit around the Ellipse. The pivot point of the object is placed directly on the path. The plane was not rotated from its original orientation when it was put to the path, and it does not rotate as it follows the path.

Returning to the Spline

The plane jumped to the spot it did because that point was the start point (first vertex) of the Ellipse. Remember that the Ellipse is just a Bezier spline and can be edited in the same way as a spline drawn using the Line object. See what happens when you edit the Ellipse, as you continue the previous exercise:

1. To edit the Ellipse, select it and go to the Modify panel. You can simply convert the object to an editable spline using the Quad menu; in this case, however, place an Edit Spline modifier on the stack, instead. Go to the Vertex subobject level and select one of the vertices on the spline other than the present first vertex (where the animation began). The first vertex is distinguished from the others by a tiny square icon. After another vertex is selected, click on the Make First button in the Geometry rollout. The animation now begins at the new location.

Note: *The first vertex position is only an issue with closed splines. When an open spline is used, the end points are obviously a given. The Make First button can then be used only to switch the first vertex (the start point) from one end to the other, which is the same thing as reversing the spline at the Spline subobject level. If you do this, the path animation proceeds in the opposite direction.*

2. Undo or otherwise change the first vertex back to its original location. Edit a vertex or two to change the shape of the spline. For example, tilt some Bezier handles. Pull the Time Slider to see how the animation follows the revised path. Undo back to the original shape and delete the Edit Spline modifier. Move and rotate the Ellipse, noting how the plane moves with it. It doesn't change its orientation with the spline, however, as you can see in Figure 18.23.

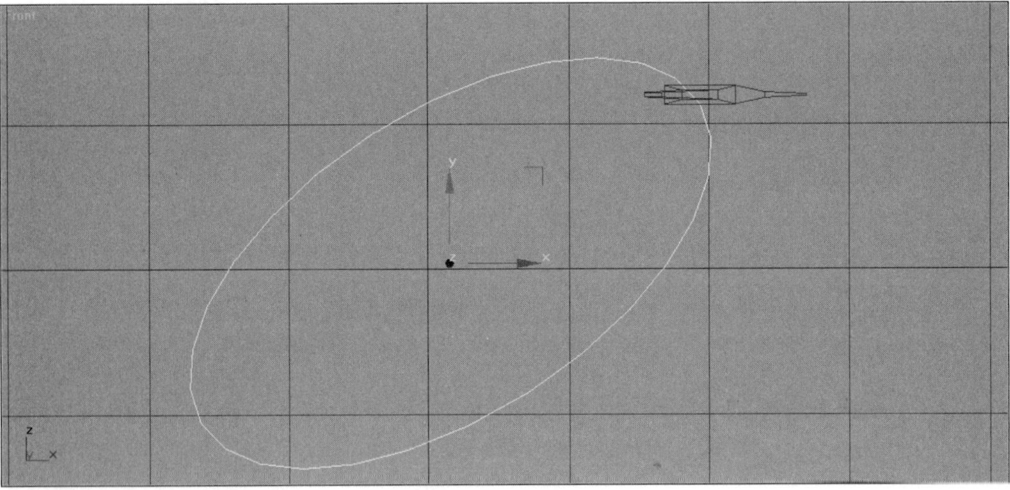

Figure 18.23
If the spline is moved or rotated, the plane moves to stay on the path, but it doesn't change its orientation with the spline.

Aligning Rotations to the Path

Most objects that are put to a path need to rotate as they move. Your plane looks odd because it doesn't appear to be following its nose around the path. To align an object's rotation to a curved path means keeping a Local coordinate axis of the object constantly aligned with the changing tangent to the curve. MAX permits such alignment using the Follow checkbox in the Motion panel. Apply this tool to your plane as follows:

1. Undo from the last step in this exercise to eliminate any movement or rotation of the Ellipse. Select the plane and change to its Local coordinate system in the Main toolbar. The Local X-axis should be pointing though the length of the plane, from nose to tail. This axis is the one to be aligned with the path.

2. Look in the Path Parameters rollout in the Motion panel for the Follow checkbox. Select this box. The default alignment axis is X, which is correct for the plane. If you needed to align another axis to the path, you would set it in the Axis section at the bottom of the rollout. (Note the Flip checkbox, which reverses the direction of the selected axis.) Pull the Time Slider to see that the plane now rotates to remain aligned to the path. But there's something wrong. As you can see in Figure 18.24, the plane flips over midway along the path.

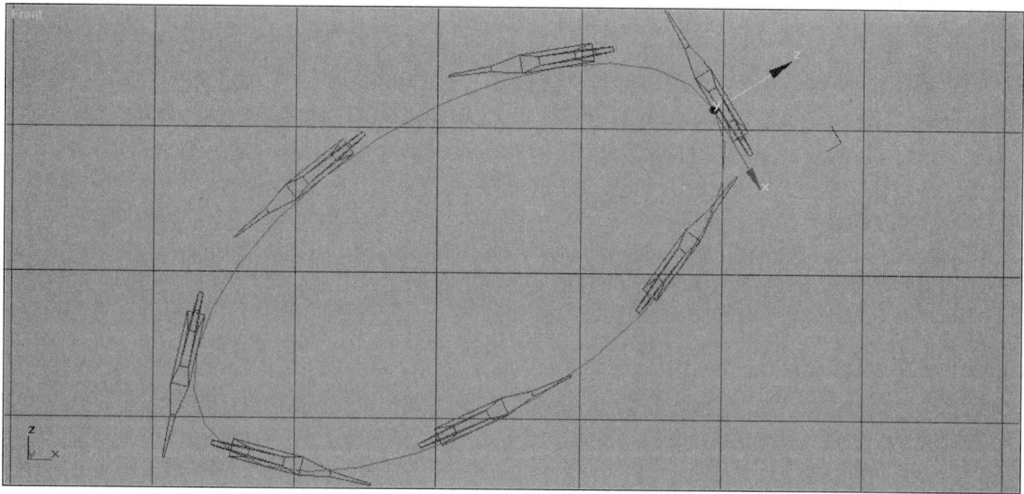

Figure 18.24
The Local X-axis of the plane is aligned to the path by using the Follow checkbox in the Motion panel, but the plane flips over midway along the path. This is a Snapshot view of the animation.

3. To correct this behavior, select the Allow Upside Down checkbox. The plane will follow the path without changing its orientation. Unfortunately, the plane is now upside down throughout the motion. Select the plane and rotate it 180 degrees about its Local X-axis. As you can see in Figure 18.25, the plane is now properly aligned to the path.

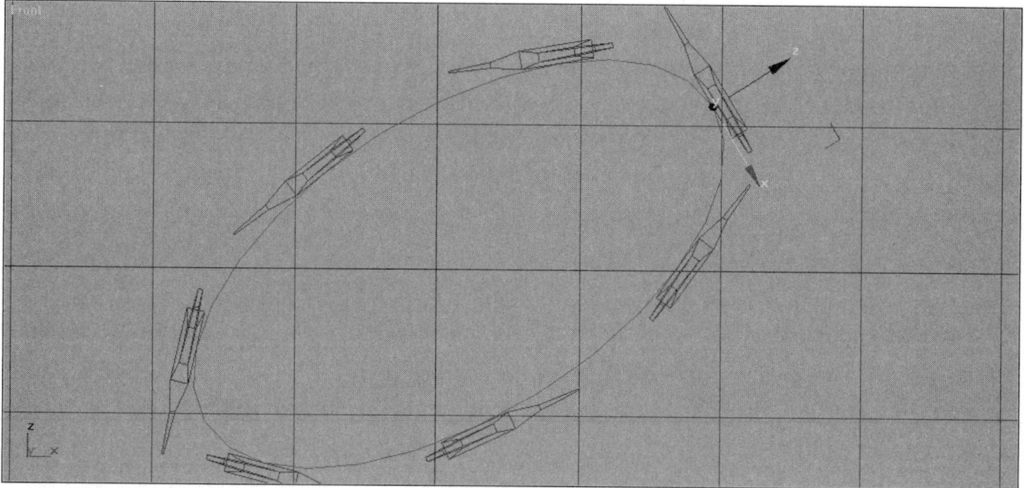

Figure 18.25
The same as Figure 18.24, but with the Allow Upside Down checkbox selected and the plane rotated 180 degrees about its Local X-axis. The plane is now properly aligned to the path.

Alignment to a Motion Path Is Not Limited to the Path Constraint

You can do the kind of rotational alignment you do with the Follow command in the Path constraint with a motion path that was created using the Bezier Position or Position XYZ controller. Find the Follow/Bank utility under the Utilities tab in the Command panel (you'll need to use the More button). Unlike the Path constraint, however, this tool creates explicit keys in rotation tracks. You must determine how many samples along the motion path you'll need to set a reasonable number of keys. Winding paths will need more samples to capture all the rotations. Many users assume that they must use a Path constraint if they need rotational alignments, but this is not so. It's unclear why such an important tool has been buried so deeply in the interface.

Adjusting Rotations

Rotations are covered in the "Animating Rotations" section later in this chapter, but let's look now at their effect on path animation. A quick glance at Track View confirms that there is no animation range in the Rotation track. The plane in our example is constantly rotating, however, which means that the basic alignment rotation for the Path constraint is applied beneath any direct rotations. The alignment rotation becomes a baseline against any direct rotations. To see how rotations can be applied to cause the plane to tail out as it moves into a tight bend, continue with the exercise:

1. Before you can add rotations, you have to consider your controller. As you can see in Track View or the Motion panel, the current rotation controller is TCB Rotation. As you will see later in this chapter, this controller does not display a function curve. Although it could be used for your simple purposes here, it's important to work with function curves wherever possible; therefore, change the rotation controller to Euler XYZ.

2. Select the plane, if it's not already selected. In Local coordinates (or in World coordinates, for that matter) you can see that the Y-axis is the right one for creating a tail-out rotation. Expand the Euler XYZ track in Track View and create two keys in the Y Rotation track—one at Frame 0 and one at Frame 100—to bookend the animation. Switch to a Function Curves view, if you're not already using it. The function curve is a straight line with a constant value of zero.

3. Think carefully about where the keys belong in time. You need three more of them: at the moment where the tail-out rotation begins, where it reaches its maximum, and where it ends. Drag the Time Slider to identify these three points around the bend opposite the start point and create keys for them on the function curve. They will be located where the plane begins to enter the bend, at the apex of the bend, and where it leaves the bend. The exact positions are not important.

4. Place the Time Slider at the point where the plane goes through the apex of the bend. Drag the key that was placed at this frame up to a value of about 20 degrees. Watch how the plane rotates to create the tail-out effect. But look at the graph—spline interpolation has animated the rotation all along the curve. Take a look at Figure 18.26.

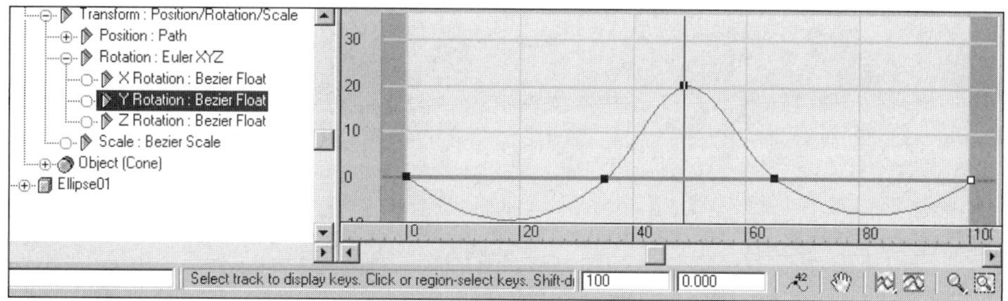

Figure 18.26
The key set at the apex of the bend is adjusted to a value of 20 degrees. The tail-out rotation in the viewport looks fine, but spline interpolation has caused the function curve to bend outside the intended region.

5. Before you correct the interpolation, take a look at another problem. Pull the Time Slider slowly around the bend, moving frame by frame if necessary. Notice that the plane does not maintain a consistent orientation along the path outside the tail-out effect.

6. To fix this problem, you need to set the interpolation out of the first key and into the last as a linear value. Select the first key and change its interpolation by using the right-click dialog box (plane/Y Rotation). Go to the Out interpolation options and, in the drop-down list of icons, choose the third one from the top—the option with square interpolation lines. This option, which keeps an interpolation at a constant value until the next key is reached, is used for sudden changes in value. Check your graph to see that the interpolation problem is fixed and run the animation to see whether the plane is now rotating properly. If it is, use the same interpolation option on the key at Frame 100 (In). This is a great way to create linear segments between keys with identical values, without having to deal with Bezier handles.

Controlling Speed

You have the plane rotating nicely along its path, but there's still the issue of its velocity. Let's continue this exercise by exploring the ways in which the object's speed can be modified:

1. You should be able to see the object slowing down into the bends from playing the animation. To understand this behavior, select the plane, if necessary, and click on the Trajectories button in the Motion panel. You can now see the frame ticks, as shown in Figure 18.27. (You'll probably want to hide the Ellipse to see the Trajectory better.) Note that the frames get compressed through the bends, which slows down the velocity. You already saw the same thing earlier in this chapter in the bouncing ball exercise, using the Bezier Position controller. But it's rather strange here, if you think about it. It's as if MAX uses an elastic ruler to measure percentage. The distance covered by increments of 1 percent of the path differs, depending where you are on the path.

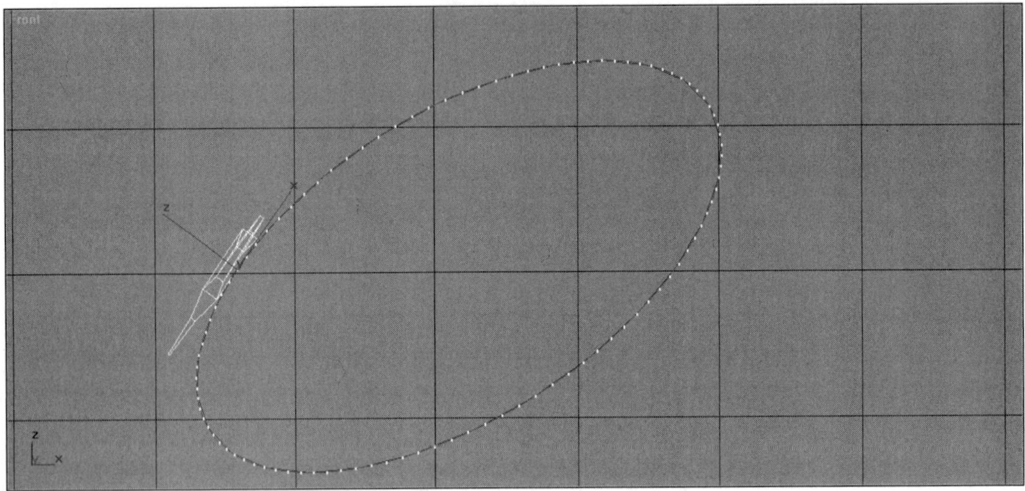

Figure 18.27
A Trajectory view shows how the plane's velocity slows down into the bends and speeds up out of them. The frame ticks are compressed through the bends.

2. Switch back to the Parameters subpanel in the Motion panel and select the Constant Velocity checkbox in the Path Parameters rollout (if the last transform adjustment made was for the rotation, you may need to click on the Position button in the PRS Parameters rollout to see this checkbox). Go back to Trajectories to see the frame ticks. As you can see in Figure 18.28, the frames are now spaced evenly in distance. Try playing the animation and jump back and forth between the default acceleration and Constant Velocity. Can you see the difference? It takes a lot of practice to read motion from a computer monitor. The default acceleration is clearly more appropriate, so deselect the Constant Velocity checkbox before continuing.

3. The most important control over velocity (and direction) is the Percent function curve in the Path constraint. Open this function curve in Track View and add a key at Frame 30, right on the curve. Add a second one at Frame 40. You will make the plane slow to a stop at Frame 30, stay still for 10 frames, and then accelerate away. Change the value of the key at Frame 40 to 30 percent. This is the same distance along the path as at Frame 30. The function curve should look pretty good. It rises and then flattens out through Frame 30. After Frame 40, it accelerates again; if you move the Time Slider slowly, however, you'll see some small irritating wavering during the time that the plane should be stopped. This is a tiny amount of spline interpolation that may be too small to be visible on the graph. Change the interpolation between the keys as you did in Step 6 in the previous section to get a perfectly linear segment. Check the animation again. It should be completely still during the linear segment. Your function curve should look like Figure 18.29.

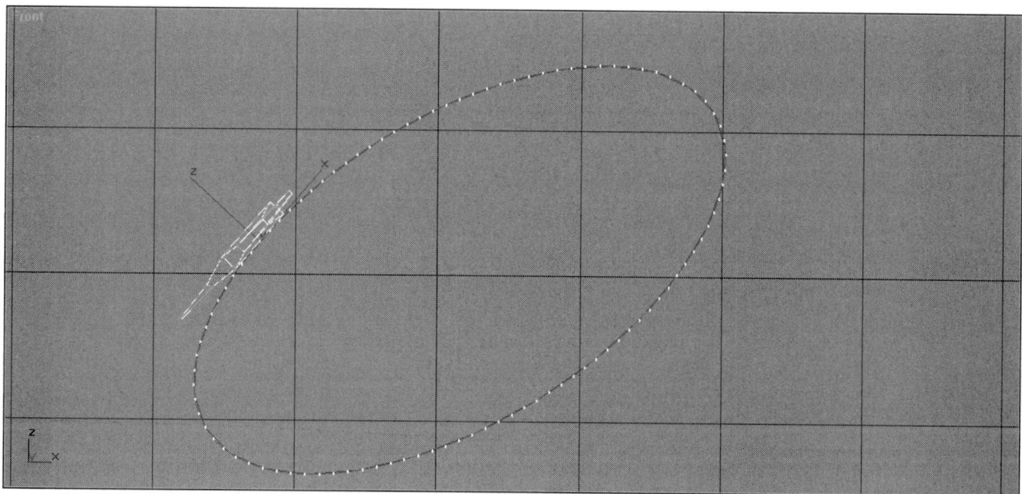

Figure 18.28
The same as Figure 18.27, but with the Constant Velocity option used in place of the default acceleration. The distance covered between frames is equal, and the plane does not accelerate and decelerate around bends.

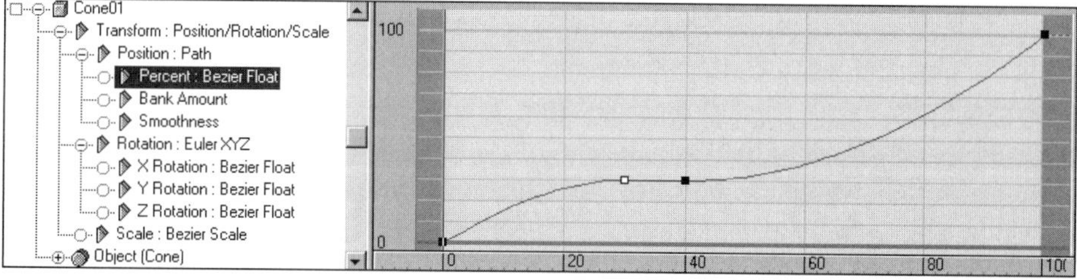

Figure 18.29
The plane is made to slow down, stop for 10 frames, and accelerate again. The interpolation during the stopped segment is made perfectly linear to eliminate a slight wavering.

4. If you examine the scene carefully, you'll find new problems. The rotations that you set for the tail-out are now incorrect, and the object is no longer going through the bend at the same frames it was before. This problem is easy to fix in Track View. Pull the Time Slider to find the frame that is now at the apex of the curve. In the Y Rotation track in Track View, select the four keys that comprise the rotation and move them so that the second key in this group is set directly on the current frame. Use Figure 18.30 as a guide. Run the animation to see that it's working.

5. Try adjusting the Percent function curve to bend downward and make the plane move backward, either by moving keys or by adjusting Bezier handles. Doing so helps you to understand the meaning of this function curve as it controls both velocity and direction. Any changes you make here require another adjustment of the tail-out rotation, as you did in the previous step. Figure 18.31 shows a simple adjustment to make the plane drift back and forth, instead of stopping.

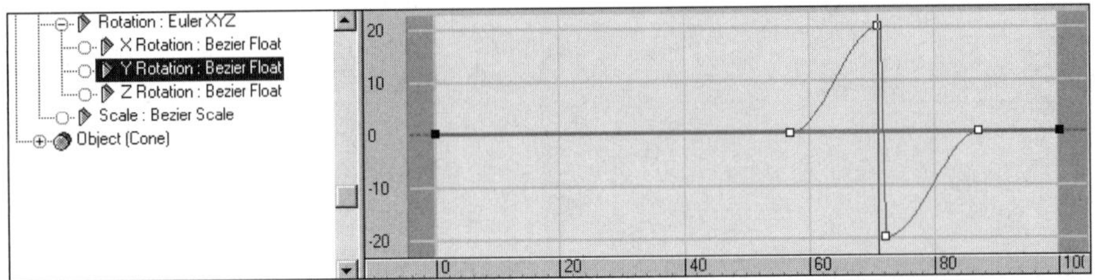

Figure 18.30
The tail-out rotation is moved to its proper location. The stop that was added in Figure 18.29 changed the time at which the plane passed through the bend. Compare this with the graph in Figure 18.26.

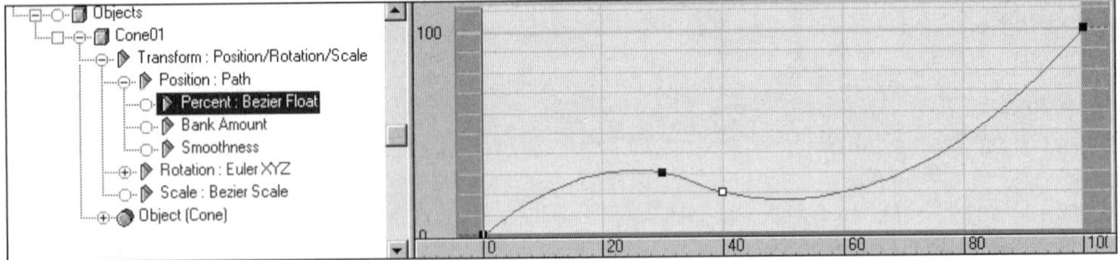

Figure 18.31
The Percent curve is adjusted to cause the plane to drift backward and forward on the path.

Adding a Second Path

The object assigned to a path using the Path constraint is not locked to the path as it would have been using the Path controller in previous versions of the program. An object's location can be influenced by the presence of other splines. Let's finish this Path constraint exercise by following these steps:

1. Draw a Line similar to the one shown in Figure 18.32.
2. Select the plane and, in the Motion panel, click on the Add Path button. Select the new spline and then deactivate the Add Path button. Move the Time Slider to see that the motion of the plane is different than it was. Its motion is now based on the average distance between the splines. Also note that the plane does not completely follow the path, so a cyclical motion can be shown. Having multiple splines assigned to one object works best when the splines are open rather than closed.
3. In the Path Parameters rollout, choose Ellipse01 from the list and set its Weight value to 100. Select Line01 and set it to 0. Play the animation and you'll see that the second path has no influence on the plane. Reverse the values and the plane follows only the second path. Set the values to 100 and 10, as shown in Figure 18.33, and move the Time Slider to see the plane generally follow the path but get pulled somewhat to the right.

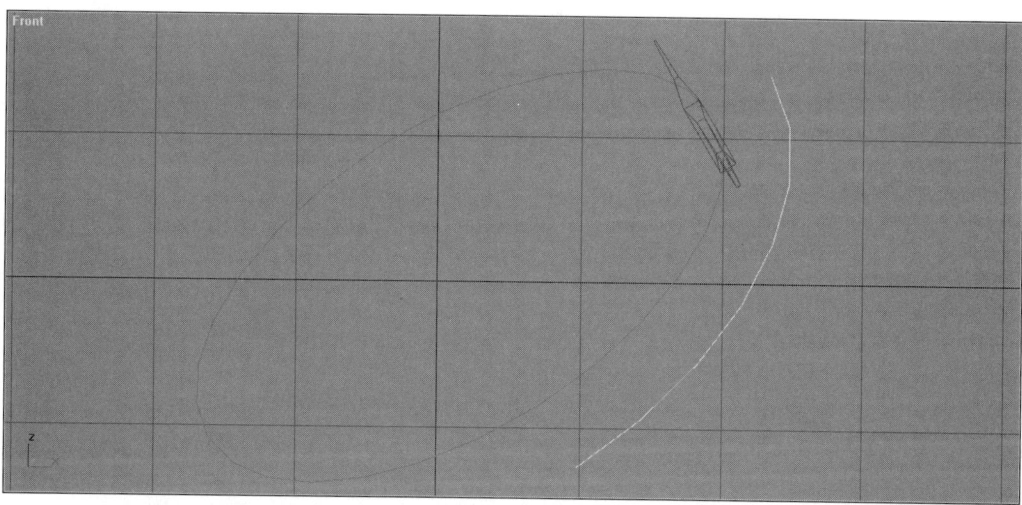

Figure 18.32
A second spline is added to the scene to influence the plane's motion.

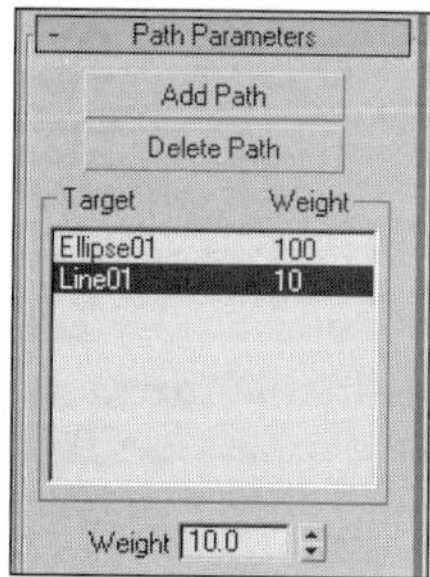

Figure 18.33
The top portion of the Path Parameters rollout with the settings that will pull the plane off the elliptical path due to the influence of the second path.

Other Position Controllers and Constraints

The remaining position controllers and constraints are much less important in everyday use than Bezier Position, Position XYZ, and Path. Some are more significant than others, however, and deserve a brief introduction.

Position Expression and Position Script

Much sophisticated animation is not created by using keys to shape a function curve. A considerable range of motion can be more accurately and flexibly specified in programming code. *Expressions* are relatively simple units of code that can be constructed by people with no prior programming experience. Expressions are used in Expression controllers; of these, Position Expression is dedicated to position animation. MAXScript is a much more complex coding language than that used in expressions, and it is much more powerful. The use of expressions to control animations will be discussed in Chapter 20.

Position List and Noise Position

The List controller is available in Position, Rotation, and Scale versions. It allows you to group multiple controllers together. Extremely sophisticated results are possible in this manner, but the most common use of List controllers is to add noise to an existing transform with a Noise controller.

The Noise controller need not be an element of a List controller, but it is rarely used by itself. Instead, you'll typically have an object on a motion path that requires periodic rattling or vibration. When you assign a Position List controller to a position track, it automatically includes whatever Position controller was already there. For example, if you've already created keys in a Bezier Position controller, you won't lose them. The Bezier Position controller with all of its keys intact becomes the first item in the list, as illustrated in Figure 18.34.

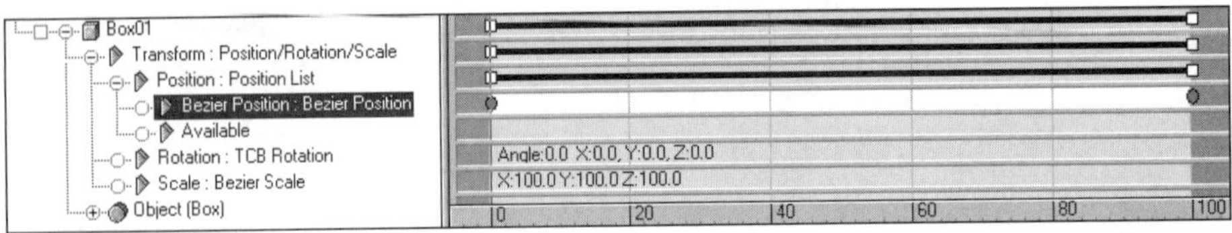

Figure 18.34
A motion path was already created using the Bezier Position controller. To add noise, the controller is converted to a Position List controller. The Bezier Position track is included as the first item in the list—its keys are unaffected.

The Available track can now be assigned a Noise Position controller. A new Available track then appears to add other controllers to the list, if desired. The Noise Position controller is keyed in its Noise Strength track. This track uses a Bezier Point3 controller, meaning that it contains X,Y,Z function curves in a single track, just like the Bezier Position controller. By default, all three curves have a constant value of 50. That means the object will move randomly in all three dimensions to a maximum of 50 units. You can apply noise differently in different dimensions if you want. For example, Figure 18.35 shows noise added only in the Z-dimension. The Noise Strength function curve for Z rises quickly from 0 to 100 units and then tails off. The Bezier nature of the function curves, for the Z axis, causes the curve to rise above the key at Frame 100; meanwhile, the X and Y curves hold a constant value of zero.

The effect of the Noise Strength function curve is seen in a Function Curve view when its parent track, Noise Position, is selected; see Figure 18.36. The erratic curve is positional movement in the Z-dimension only. Note that the amplitude of the curve tracks the shape of the Noise Strength function curve. If noise were animated in all three dimensions, three such curves would be visible.

The composite picture of all the animation in the List controller can be seen in Track View as well, as shown in Figure 18.37. With the Position List track selected, the function curve shows the object moving at a constant rate in the X-direction while it rattles up and down in the Z-dimension.

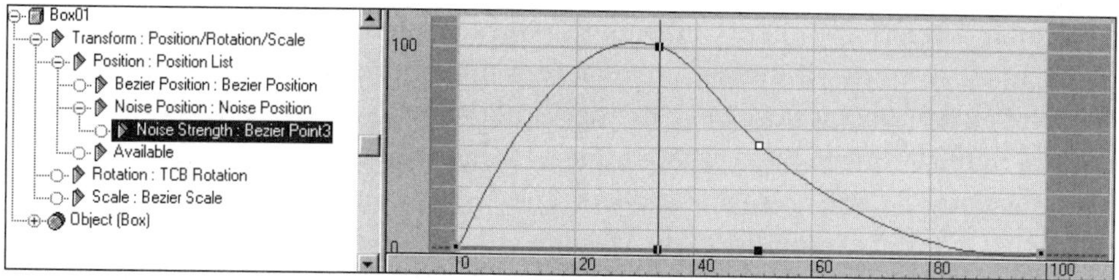

Figure 18.35

The Available track in Figure 18.34 has been assigned a Noise Position controller. Noise Strength is animated only in the Z-direction. The X and Y function curves maintain a constant level of zero.

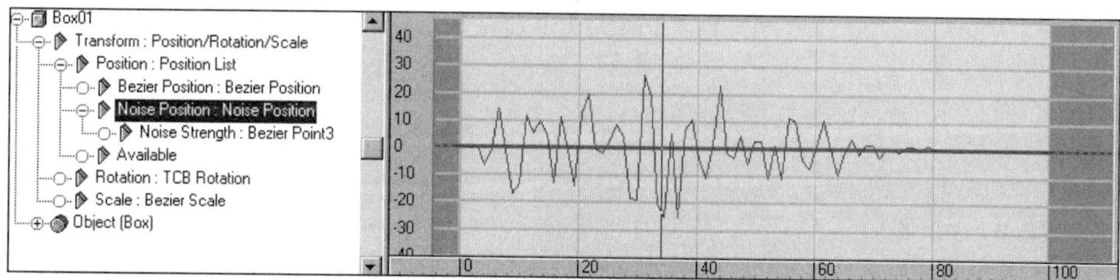

Figure 18.36

The function curve for the Noise Position track (the parent of Noise Strength) shows the positional animation of the object. The amplitude of this erratic curve tracks the shape of the Noise Strength curve in Figure 18.35.

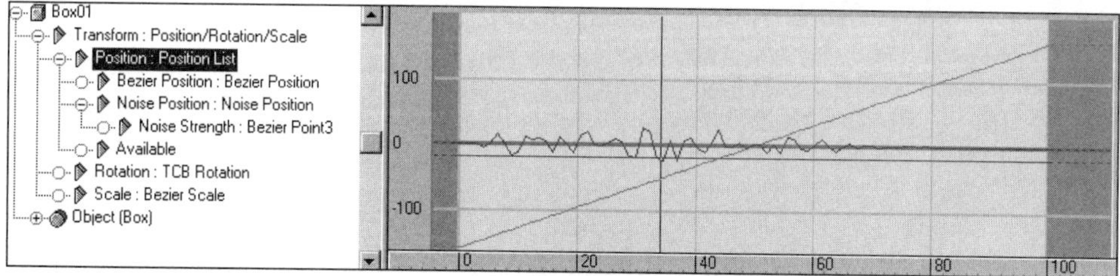

Figure 18.37

With the Position List track selected, the composite result of both controllers is visible. The object is moving at a constant rate in the X-direction, as set in the Bezier Position controller. But it's also rattling up and down in the Z-direction, due to the Noise Position controller.

Attachment and Surface Constraints

Although Attachment and Surface are not explicitly called constraints in the Assign Position Controller dialog box, they fall under this category. The Attachment and Surface constraints align an object to the surface of another object. The Attachment constraint is used where the surface to be aligned with is a polygonal mesh. You take the object to be attached to the mesh surface and assign it an Attachment constraint in the Position track. The controls in the Motion panel allow you to choose the surface object and even to create keys at different locations on the surface, but this kind of animation across the surface of an object is clumsy and unreliable with polygonal meshes. A better use of the Attachment constraint is to keep an object stuck to a surface that is being deformed.

Unlike polygonal meshes, Non-Uniform Rational B-Splines (NURBS) surfaces are inherently parameterized. In other words, NURBS surfaces can be continuously measured in two dimensions. Every point on a NURBS surface has an exact location in the UV coordinate system of the surface. This characteristic makes NURBS surfaces far more appropriate for animations in which objects must travel along geometric surfaces. The Surface controller allows you to do just this. After applying a Surface controller to the Position track of the object to be animated, you choose a NURBS surface. The object can then be positioned and keyed in the UV coordinates of the surface using spinners. Figure 18.38 illustrates such an animation (using the Snapshot tool to record multiple frames). Keys were set for the Box object for positions at the top and bottom of the sloping NURBS surface. The Box follows the surface continuously between the two keyed positions. If the surface itself is deformed in animation, the Box remains aligned to it.

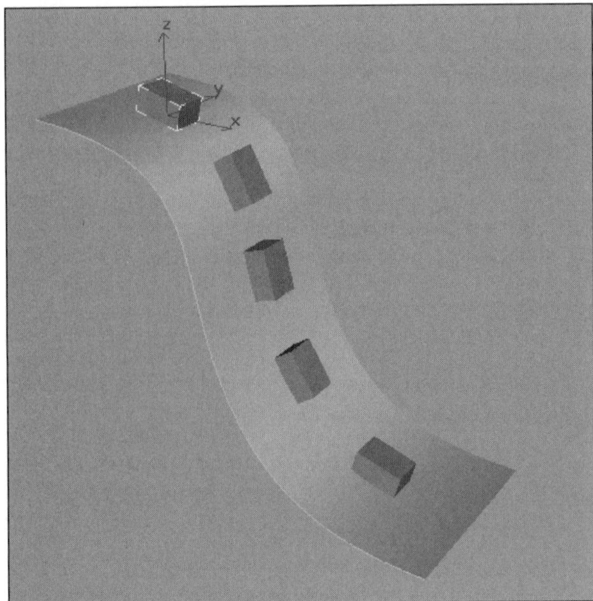

Figure 18.38
The Surface controller is used to animate a Box object along a NURBS surface. This Snapshot view of the animation shows the Box following the surface between its keyed positions at the top and bottom of the slope.

Spring and Position Reactor Controllers

The Spring controller adds secondary motion to an object. Follow these steps to see its effects on an object:

1. Animate a Box moving from Frame 0 to Frame 60 and play the animation. The Box moves smoothly and then stops from Frame 60 until the end of the active time segment.
2. Change the Position controller to Spring. Like the Position List controller, the original Bezier Position controller remains intact as a track beneath Spring. Leave the defaults in the

Spring Properties dialog box that opens. Play the animation again, and you may notice small pauses in the Box's linear movement and around Frame 60.

3. In the Spring Properties dialog box, increase the Mass value to 1500 and the Drag value to 0.1. Play the animation again. This time, the pauses in the linear motion are more pronounced, as is the jitter at the end. These pauses give the impression of friction between the Box and a floor element and make it seem that the Box's movement is not constant. Look at the Track View in a Function Curve view to see the complex position track.

The Position Reactor controller can influence the position of an object based on its proximity to another object. For example, an airplane may have a linear motion, but its Z value will increase when it approaches and passes over a building, or vary to one side when passing another aircraft. Reactor controllers are great for adding animation based on other elements in a scene.

Animating Rotations

Animating rotations is sometimes difficult, and many people think it's the single most difficult aspect of animation in MAX or any other program. The problem is largely rooted in the mathematics of rotations. The order in which the three axial rotations (around X, around Y, and around Z) are performed makes a considerable difference in the result. At an extreme, the order of rotations can produce the phenomenon known as *gimbal lock*, in which rotations around two different axes become identical.

MAX's approach to rotations is highly controversial, and much of this section will be devoted to making clear the problems with this special approach and the need to turn to a more conventional one in the vast majority of cases. This opinion is not shared by everyone, however. Each practitioner must make up his or her own mind on this central issue, but the decision must be made through careful investigation and experience.

The conventional method applies three rotations in a prescribed order around the three coordinate axes. As we already mentioned, this method creates occasional problems due to the order of rotations. These problems can almost always be resolved by parenting (linking) a null object (a Point or Dummy in MAX) to the misbehaving object. The null object can be rotated to rotate the child object. By dividing the rotations around the three axes between the two objects, you can control the order of the rotations, because the parent's rotations are necessarily applied first.

The designers of MAX decided, however, to avoid the entire problem of order of rotations by implementing a radically different approach. This approach uses quaternion mathematics—hardly intuitive to the vast majority of users. The main problem with this implementation is that it does not produce an editable function curve, which may be a fatal compromise. To offer this approach as an optional controller would have been unobjectionable, but MAX's designers decided to make it the default in the TCB Rotation controller. Most people who learn MAX naturally work with the default controllers until they learn the other options. It's very important to understand the larger picture: The purpose is not to learn to use MAX for its own sake, but rather to learn 3D graphics and animation using MAX. As a result, the following material introduces you to the TCB Rotation controller primarily to help you understand its nature and limitations. You then quickly move on to MAX's Euler controllers, which implement the conventional approach to rotations.

The TCB Rotation Controller

The TCB Rotation controller (like the Bezier Position controller discussed at the beginning of this chapter) is poorly named. TCB stands for Tension, Continuity, and Bias—three parameters used to control the interpolation between vertices on a cardinal spline. The *cardinal spline*, sometimes called the *natural spline*, does not use Bezier-type tangent handles for interpolation, and TCB controls are the only way to shape spline segments between vertices. MAX doesn't use natural splines in its modeling interface, so you may not be familiar with them if you haven't used them with other applications.

Thus, the TCB element in the controller name tells us two important things: Spline interpolation is implemented, and this interpolation is controlled by Tension, Continuity, and Bias parameters. By itself, this would be only a relatively minor change from the regular Bezier splines used in function curves. What the name *TCB Rotation* doesn't tell you, however, is the most important aspect of the controller: It implements a quaternion approach to rotations.

Now, let's start an exercise to get some hands-on experience with the TCB Rotation controller:

1. Reset the scene so you are now using a fresh screen, and then switch to the two-viewport layout that you've been using throughout this chapter; you should have a narrow Top viewport above and a large Front viewport below. Create a small Box object in the Top viewport. You can always adjust its size later. Be sure that you create it in the Top viewport so it's built on the groundplane. Doing so ensures that the Box will have a Local coordinate system aligned to World space. In other words, the Local Z-direction will point up in a Front viewport, Y will extend toward the back, and X will run to the right. Confirm that this is so by switching back and forth between Local and World coordinate systems. The pivot point (or Transform Gizmo) should remain unchanged as you do so.

2. Note that the pivot point is currently at the base of the Box. You want the Box to rotate around a point in the center. Center the pivot point in the object, and move the Box precisely to the center of World space by using the Move Transform Type-In dialog box. At this point, your screen should look like Figure 18.39.

3. Open a Track View panel to cover the upper viewport, and find the Box's Rotation track. Show your controller types by using the Filters dialog box, and you'll see that you have a TCB Rotation controller. Stay in the Edit Keys view in Track View and create a key at Frame 0. Right-click on the key to bring up the key information dialog box. Then, with the Box selected, activate the Rotate tool on the Main toolbar. Get into the Local coordinate system, if you're not there already, and open the Rotate Transform Type-In dialog box. Your screen should look like Figure 18.40.

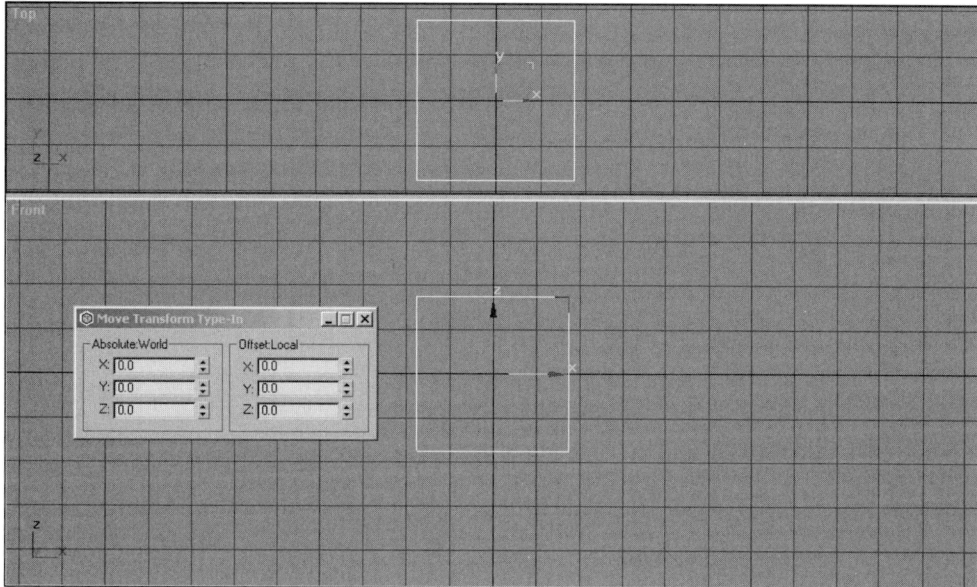

Figure 18.39
Setting up for the TCB Rotation exercise. A Box object is created in the Top viewport to align its Local coordinate system with World space. The pivot point is centered, and the object is moved to the origin (0,0,0). This view is in Local coordinates.

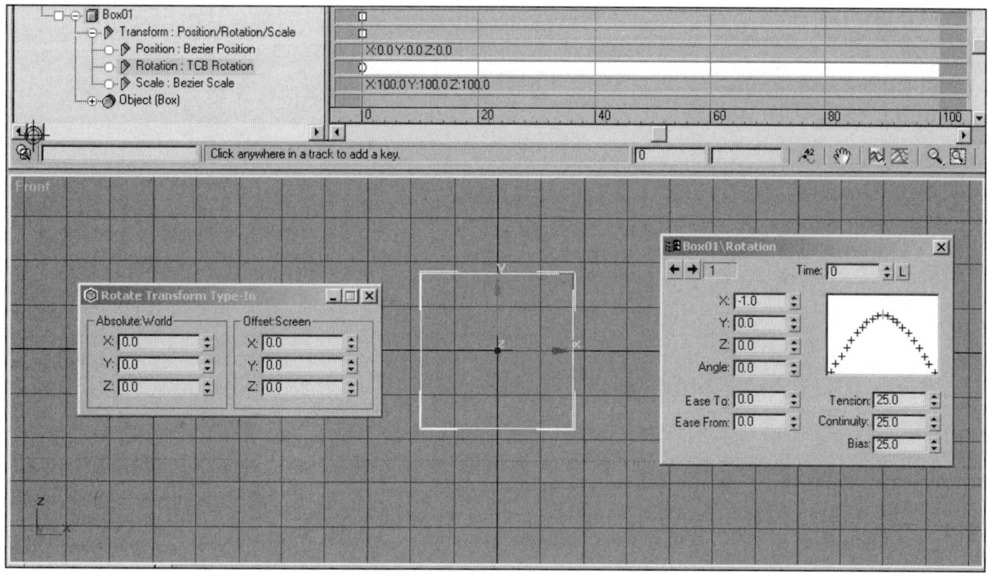

Figure 18.40
In the Rotation track, and using the default TCB Rotation controller, a key is created at Frame 0. The informational dialog box for that key is displayed. The Rotate Transform Type-In dialog box is also displayed.

4. You're looking at two approaches to rotation at the same time. The World X, Y, and Z values on both sides of the Rotate Transform Type-In dialog box reflect the conventional approach: They rotate the object around each of the three axes independently. The key information uses the quaternion approach: The X, Y, and Z values are used to point a vector in an arbitrary direction from the pivot point, and the Angle value represents a rotation around that vector. The X, Y, and Z values vary between 0 and 1, because they are angular measures using trigonometric functions. You can play with the values in both dialog boxes, if you're so inclined. If you do, you'll certainly notice that rotation values that are easy to understand in the Rotate Transform Type-In dialog box are incomprehensible as quaternions, unless they are around only a single axis.

5. Animate a rotation around the Local Y-axis. Set the quaternion values to X=0, Y=1, and Z=0. These settings align the axis of rotation with the Y-axis. Experiment with the Angle value to confirm that the Box is rotating around the Local Y-axis, and then reset the Angle value to 0. Create a second key at Frame 50. Give this key the same values as the first one, but change the Angle value to 45. Pull the Time Slider to make sure the Box is rotating 45 degrees. See Figure 18.41.

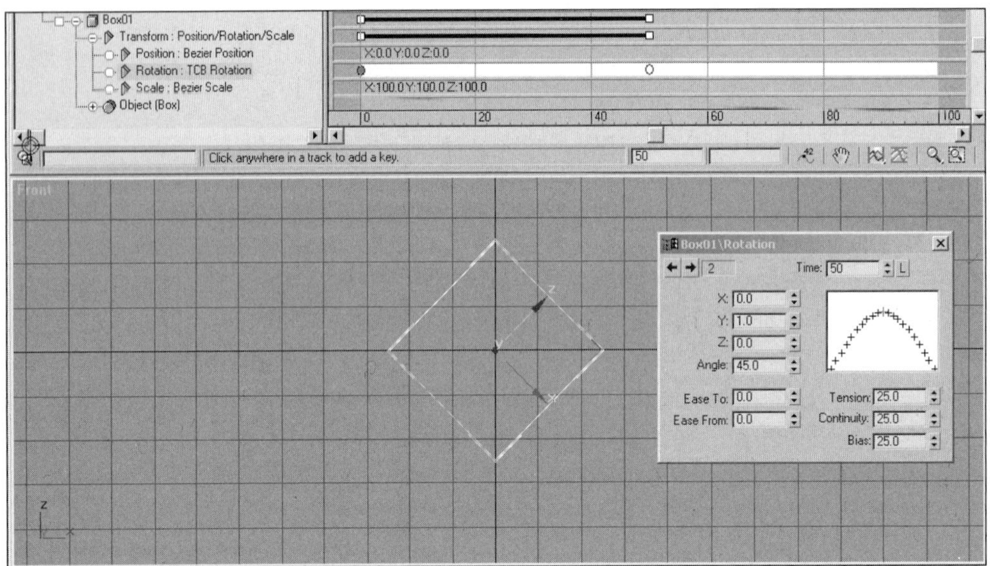

Figure 18.41
An animation, rotating the Box 45 degrees around the Y-axis. Note the Y quaternion value of 1, which aligns the axis of rotation with the Y-axis. The Angle value rotates the object around the axis of rotation.

6. So far, the animation is understandable, at least if you rotate around only a single axis. Create a third key at Frame 100, and give it the same values as the second key. Before you pull the Time Slider to check the results, think about what should happen. Your three keys have Angle values of 0, 45, and 45, respectively. Thus, you might likely conclude that the

Box will rotate 45 degrees between Frames 0 and 50, and then remain still through Frame 100. This is not what happens, however. Pull the Time Slider and see that the Box rotates 45 degrees and then a second 45 degrees, ending up with a 90-degree rotation. In other words, the Angle values are not absolute but only relative to the previous key. That fact makes it very difficult to understand an animated parameter directly from its data.

7. Switch to the Function Curves view in Track View. No curve appears. Function curves can make sense only with absolute values. This fact is the root of the single biggest problem with the TCB controller.

8. Just because you don't have function curves doesn't mean you don't need to control interpolations. To get the result that you originally intended, change the Angle value of the third key to 0. The Box should therefore not rotate after Frame 50. If you pull the Time Slider you'll see the Box wiggle, however, due to the interpolation of a spline that you cannot see or directly edit. To edit the interpolation, change the Continuity setting of the second key to 0. The display indicates a linear interpolation. Test to see whether the waver is gone. A lot can be done with these TCB tools, but they are extremely unintuitive compared with Bezier handles on splines you can see.

Is the TCB Rotation Controller Ever Preferable?

The TCB Rotation controller can make sense in special situations in which an object is tumbling in an arbitrary manner (such as down a flight of stairs). Very complex rotations like these are sometimes too difficult to understand as function curves, and the quaternion approach prevents complications due to order-of-rotation problems. The obvious purpose of this controller is to allow you to set keys interactively with the Animate button, rotating your object freely as you go, without worrying about problems due to order of rotations. This approach makes it easy to do simple character animation, for example. But the loss of function curve control is a high price to pay, unless order-of-rotation problems become unmanageable.

The Euler XYZ Controller

MAX has always offered a conventional rotational controller, named Euler XYZ. (Leonhard Euler was a famous Swiss mathematician who lived in the eighteenth century.) The operation of this controller is easy to understand. It contains three child tracks for X Rotation, Y Rotation, and Z Rotation, and thus should remind you of the Position XYZ controller. Each of these tracks can be keyed separately, and each has an editable function curve. If you create a key in the parent track in Track View, all three child tracks will receive keys together.

The Euler XYZ controller sets X,Y,Z rotation values in the parent coordinate space of the object. If an object has no parent, the World coordinate system is used. MAX 3 added a Local Euler XYZ controller that used the Local coordinate system of the object. This short-lived feature has been retired, but scenes containing this controller still allow its parameters to be adjusted. Local Euler XYZ controllers cannot be added to new scenes. The two controllers are otherwise identical, however.

As mentioned previously, the disadvantage of the conventional rotational approach used in the Euler controllers is in the peculiarities introduced by the order in which the three rotations are applied. You can change this order in the Motion panel. When you click on the Rotation button in the PRS Parameters rollout, a drop-down list appears containing all possible arrangements (XYZ, YXZ, XZY, and so on for a total of nine possibilities). But few people can think this way. It makes more sense to deal with order-of-rotation problems by linking an object to a Point or Dummy and moving one of the rotations to the null object. This technique was demonstrated on an animated rotation at the end of Chapter 3 (in the section "Linking Objects").

Another problem with the Euler controllers is a lack of correspondence between the named rotation tracks and the object's pivot point. Sometimes, you adjust the Y Rotation function curve, only to see that object rotate around. Rather than sweat the complex reasons for this when it happens, just find the track that works.

Because you already know how to set keys in Track View and adjust function curves, the following introductory exercise is short:

1. Create the same Box and viewport layout as you did in the first two steps of the previous exercise. Your screen should look like Figure 18.39. If you're continuing from the previous exercise, you can just select your keys in Track View and delete them.
2. Make sure that your controller type names are showing in Track View. Change the Rotation controller to Euler XYZ. In the Y Rotation track, create keys at Frames 0 and 100. Set the value of the second key to 720 degrees. Run the animation to confirm that the Box makes two complete rotations at a constant speed. Your Y Position function curve should look like Figure 18.42.

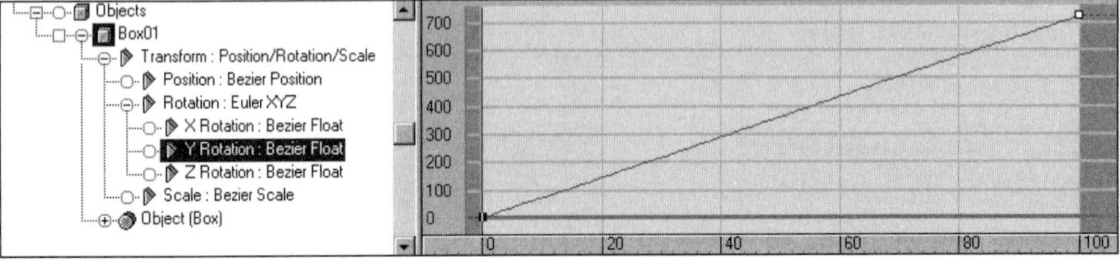

Figure 18.42
The function curve for rotation around the Y-axis. The rotation runs at a constant speed, turning 720 degrees (two complete rotations) over the course of the animation.

3. Bring up the Bezier handles for both keys and adjust them to get a nice ease in and ease out. Run the animation to see how much more convincing it is with these small accelerations and decelerations; they suggest that your Box has physical mass. Your function curve should look like Figure 18.43.

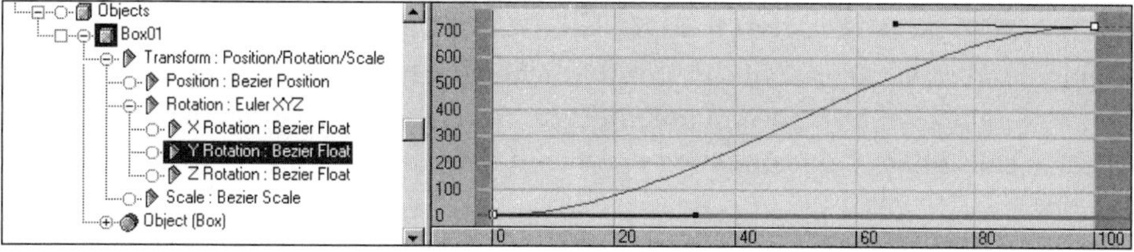

Figure 18.43
The same as Figure 18.42, but with Bezier handles used to create an ease in and ease out. These small accelerations and decelerations suggest that the object has physical mass.

4. Try making the Box spin back and forth. Bring the key at Frame 100 down to a value of 0 degrees and add a new key at Frame 50. Set the value of the new key to 360 degrees. Your function curve should look like the one in Figure 18.44. Run the animation; you might be surprised to see how pleasing and convincing such simple movement can be.

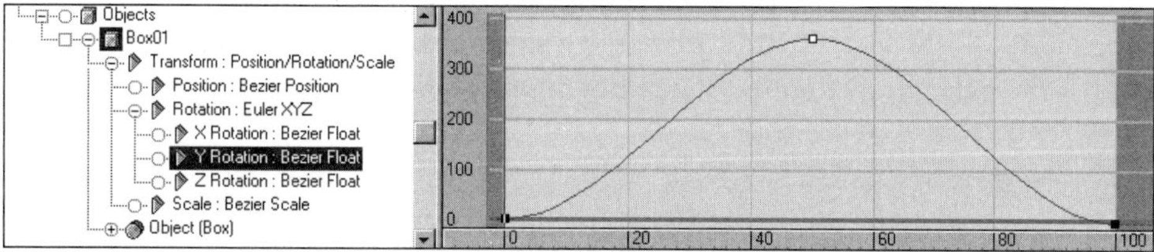

Figure 18.44
The Box spins forward 360 degrees and then backward the same amount. The curve shows a flowing change in direction.

5. For a final touch, cause the Box to stop for 10 frames. Move the second key to Frame 45 and create a new key at Frame 55. Set the new key to 360 degrees, the same value as the previous one. The curve will look pretty good, but there will be a slight spline interpolation problem. Pull the Time Slider and note the slight drifting in the object when it's supposed to be stopped. Make the interpolation between the two keys linear, as you have been doing throughout this chapter, and the problem will be solved. Your function curve should look like Figure 18.45.

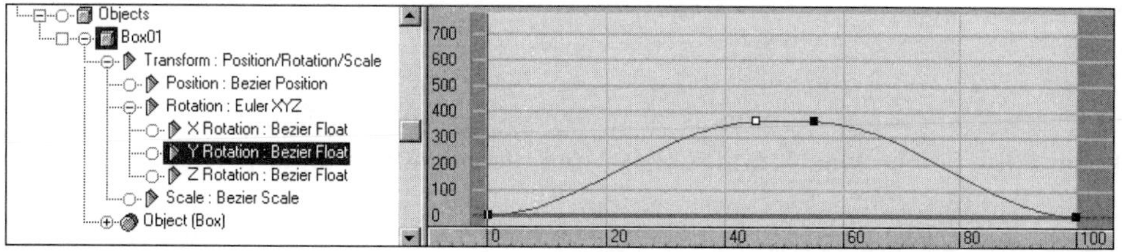

Figure 18.45
The same as Figure 18.44, but the Box comes to a stop for 10 frames before it begins turning forward.

Other Rotation Controllers and Constraints

The remaining rotation controllers and constraints are much less important in everyday use than TCB Rotation and Euler XYZ. Several are rotation "flavors" of their counterparts as position controllers or constraints. Some are more significant than others, however, and deserve a brief introduction.

Orientation and LookAt Constraints

Both the Orientation constraint and LookAt constraint control the orientation of one object based on another. The Orientation constraint is similar to the functions of the Path constraint. One object's orientation can be influenced by its weighted average with the orientation of one or more other objects.

The LookAt constraint orients one object so that it always follows another. This behavior is excellent when an object such as a gun turret must remain locked on a target. The following exercise will introduce you to the functions of the LookAt constraint:

1. In the Top viewport, create a tall, thin Tube and a small Sphere, as shown in Figure 18.46. The Sphere will be the target that the Tube must remain trained on.

Figure 18.46
The Front viewport showing the Tube and Sphere created in the Top viewport.

2. Select the Tube and change its rotation controller to the LookAt constraint. In the LookAt Constraint rollout of the Modify panel, click on the Target button and then select the Sphere. Turn off the Add LookAt Target button.

3. Move the Sphere in the Top viewport and watch the Tube change orientation to match the Sphere's current location. It's working properly, but the goal is to make the Tube face the Sphere and have the Tube's new orientation follow the Sphere. Select Z in the Select LookAt Axis section of the LookAt Constraint rollout, and the Tube reorients itself to follow the Sphere along its Z-axis.

Inverse Kinematics

When objects are organized into parent-child hierarchies, child objects share their parents' transforms. This characteristic is exceedingly useful in animation because it allows you to mimic real-world hierarchical structures, such as the human body. If you rotate your right upper arm, you expect the forearm and hand to rotate as well. However, rotating your hand at the wrist should not, in itself, move the bones back up the chain.

This behavior leads naturally to a certain approach to animating hierarchical chains, and particularly the character figure. For example, consider a character leg assembled from a thigh, a calf, and a foot, all properly parented in a chain, and with the pivot points located at the location of the joints (hip, knee, and heel). To animate a step, you have to start at the top of the chain and rotate the thigh, which rotates the entire unit. Then, you continue down to the calf and rotate it at the knee to give it a bend. Finally, you may wish to continue to the foot to rotate it a little at the heel. You have to work from top to bottom. This method is often called *forward kinematics*, suggesting movement down the parent-child chain. It is always the default.

Forward kinematics can be very tedious and is somewhat unintuitive. Especially in character animation, it is useful to have a method in which transforms move backward up the chain. The most important example is the step just discussed. Using *inverse kinematics* (IK), you can simply lift the foot (at the heel), and the thigh and calf will rotate accordingly. IK is not limited to character animation—interactive mechanical parts often require this method. Character animation is, by far, the most important application for IK, however.

Inverse Kinematics in MAX

Inverse kinematics in MAX can be intimidating. New users are often baffled by it, and users migrating from other applications are surprised at the complexity of the implementation. The irony is that MAX's IK is really quite workable and reliable—it's just buried in the most confusing and frustrating array of options and parameters. Only a few words are spent on background here; then you'll proceed to a hands-on practical use of IK that will put you on the road to confidence.

MAX uses three kinds of IK: IK solvers, interactive IK, and applied IK. When you assign an IK solver (a specialized controller) in the Rendering menu, the IK solutions are calculated. The IK panel under the Hierarchy tab in the Command panel contains a startling array of options and parameters that affect interactive and applied IK. In the Sliding Joints rollout, you can constrain rotations to specific axes and to specific angular ranges. And in the Object Parameters rollout, you can designate an object in a chain as a *Terminator*, meaning that it does not respond to IK that is generated further down the chain—for example, a hip object should not rotate when a foot is lifted.

Many long-time MAX animators are used to working with interactive IK and have figured out its many peculiarities. The main disadvantage of this method in animation is that it produces separate keys for every rotated object in the chain, making editing difficult.

Applied IK is a method apparently designed to provide more reliable results than interactive IK could produce, at least in the earlier versions of MAX. It involves binding the object at the end of the chain to another object, animating this second object, and then generating a result. This clumsy approach is of little interest today.

The only IK method that we will address in any detail uses Bones and the IK solvers. This method is very similar to that used in other major applications. In the early versions of MAX, Bones were only display tools; with MAX 2, however, they became a vehicle for inverse kinematics through the IK solver. The new IK solvers in 3ds max 4—History Independent (HI) IK solver and IK Limb solver—give animators even more power to control their animations. Bones can be used by themselves to create a skeleton to deform a mesh in Character Studio or by using the Skin modifier. They can also be applied directly to a hierarchy of objects, such as the segments of a robot, by using the Auto Boning tools when the Bones system is created.

In order to give you a practical perspective, the rest of this section is devoted to an exercise in which you use a Bones system to create a stepping motion.

Animating a Step with Bones

The walk or stepping action is the most basic unit in character animation. You'll work with only a single leg unit and use IK to take a single step forward. This unit can be repeated to create further steps and applied in reverse for another leg. The purpose here is to get you into the very challenging workflow of character animation:

1. Set up a two-viewport layout as you've been doing throughout this chapter, with a narrow Top viewport above and a large Front viewport below. Go to Create|Systems in the Command panel and activate the Bones button to draw Bones. Before you draw, look at the panel, shown in Figure 18.47. The IK solver section contains two checkboxes. Assign To Children applies the IK controller to all the Bones in the system except the first one, which is the *root*. Select this checkbox. Assign To Root applies the IK controller to the root Bone, as well. Select this checkbox, because you want your first bone (the hip) to be part of the IK chain.

2. Before drawing the Bones, pan your Front viewport down until the dark groundplane line (Z=0) is close to the bottom. Use this line as a reference. The Bones should be drawn so the foot is on or very near this line. At the left side of your Front viewport, activate the Bones button and draw three Bones vertically (top to bottom) to create the thigh and calf. This may sound peculiar, but the Bones are actually the joints—not what are normally called *bones*. Thus, you create three Bones at the hip, the knee, and the heel to effectively create the thigh and calf. This kind of thinking takes some getting used to. Click three times to create the Bones, and then right-click to stop creating them. Draw your Bones with a slight bend at the knee. Doing so helps IK to know the proper direction of rotation and is a huge help later on. Your Front viewport should look like Figure 18.48. Note the End Effector (the cross) at the end of the chain.

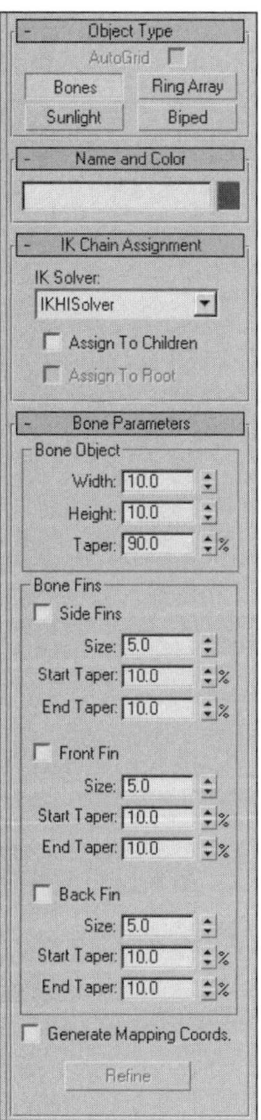

Figure 18.47

The Bones creation panel with default settings. The Assign To Children and Assign To Root checkboxes should be selected in your exercise to make the root Bone in the chain—the thigh—part of the IK system.

3. Rename Bones 01, 02, and 03 as hip, thigh, and calf, respectively. It's very important to name Bones correctly, or you may become confused. Press the H key to bring up the Select Objects dialog box, and select the Display Subtree checkbox to show the hierarchy. The Bones should be arranged in a parent-child hierarchy—hip, thigh, and calf.

4. Select the calf Bone (the last one) and try to move it up and down. You're not able to. Select the End Effector, which is connected to the Bone by a kind of string, and move it vertically; you'll see IK in action, bending the knee. However, if you open the Select Objects dialog box, you won't find the End Effector. To improve your setup, link the End Effector to a Dummy object. Create a Dummy and name it *Heel Dummy*. In the Pivot Panel of the Hierarchy tab, select Affect Pivot Only and then Align To World to align the Dummy's pivot point to that of the Bones. Link the End Effector to the Dummy and move the Dummy to test the link. See Figure 18.49.

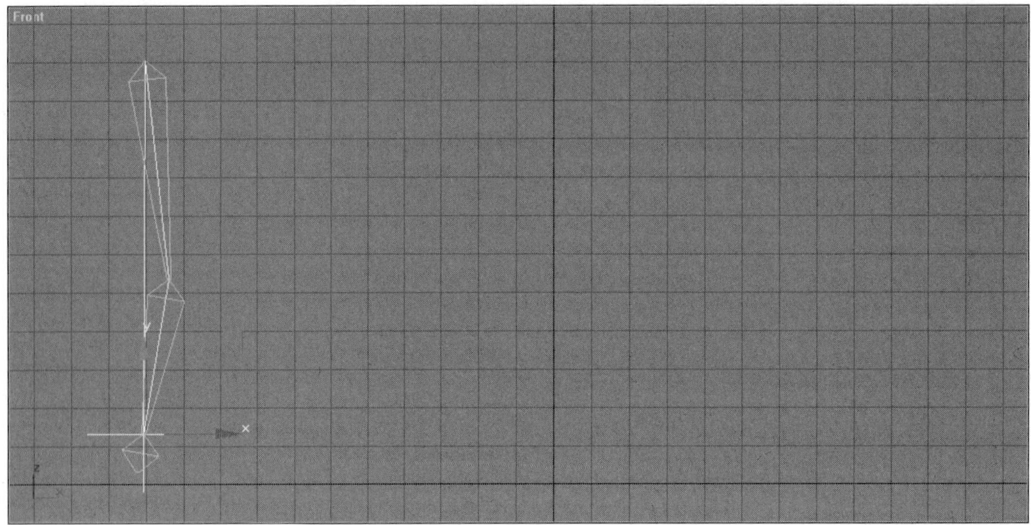

Figure 18.48
The three Bones are created at the hip, knee, and heel to effectively create a thigh and calf. A slight angle at the knee helps IK understand the proper direction to bend. Note the End Effector (the cross) at the end of the chain.

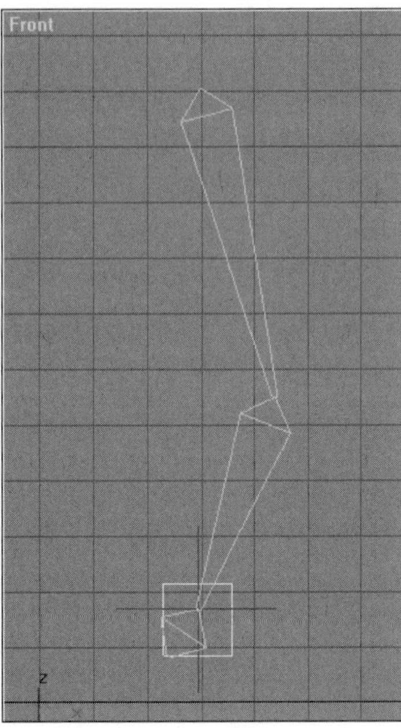

Figure 18.49
The End Effector is linked to a Dummy object. Animating the Dummy now animates the End Effector.

5. Add a foot Bone by clicking on the heel and clicking again some distance to the right. Right-click to stop creating Bones. Press the H key to bring up the Select Objects dialog box, and notice two things. First, two new Bones appear; and second, the Bones have automatically been added to the hierarchical chain as the children of the calf Bone.

6. Select the Heel Dummy and move it around. Due to the End Effector at the end of the foot Bone, that Bone remains pointing at the ground. This behavior can be useful for a sophisticated setup with a flexible foot, but it will create too many problems in this simple setup. With the foot End Effector selected, click on the Delete button. The End Effector disappears. Try moving the Heel Dummy again. The foot stays rigid, maintaining a constant angle with the calf, as shown in Figure 18.50.

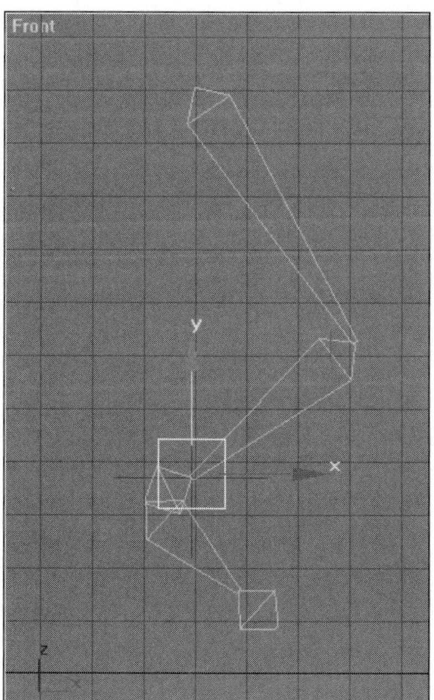

Figure 18.50
A foot Bone is added to the end of the chain, but its End Effector is eliminated. The foot follows the rest of the chain but stays rigid, maintaining a constant angle with the calf.

7. IK is not just a one-way street: It's used not only to rotate from the end of the chain, but also to keep the end fixed when the start of the chain is moved. For example, when you squat from the waist, your knees bend and your feet stay on the ground. Select the hip Bone and move it down to create a squat. Everything works except the foot—it stays rigid, because you made it so in Step 6. Therefore, it rotates into the floor. To correct this behavior, select the foot Bone and from the Animation menu of the Main toolbar, choose IK Solvers|HI Solver. Drag the rubberbanding line from the foot Bone to the calf Bone and release. The foot Bone's rotations are now controlled by the calf Bone's End Effector. This

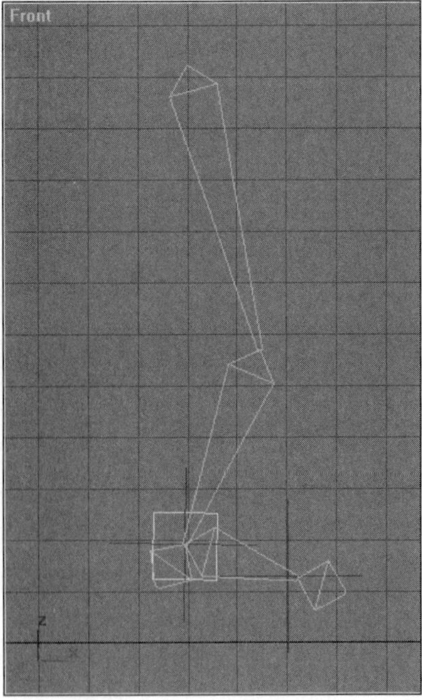

Figure 18.51
The same as Figure 18.50, but with a Rotation End Effector created for the calf Bone. This End Effector locks the foot Bone's rotation to the orientation of the calf Bone, and therefore to the Heel Dummy. One consequence is that the foot does not rotate when the knees bend in a squat.

End Effector is in turn controlled by the Heel Dummy. This arrangement means two things. First, you can bend the knee by moving the hip, and the foot will remain flat on the ground, as shown in Figure 18.51. And second, you can rotate the foot up and down by rotating the Heel Dummy. Play around a bit with these possibilities before continuing.

8. You can create all the necessary poses with just the Heel Dummy and the hip. For a cleaner setup, create a second Dummy to control the hip. Create a small Dummy object on top of the hip Bone and, as you did with the Heel Dummy, align its pivot point to World space. Change its name to *Hip Dummy* and link the hip Bone to the Hip Dummy. Doing so makes the Hip Dummy the root object of the entire hierarchy, as you can see in the Select Objects dialog box. Note that this is conventional linking, unlike the special linking of the End Effector.

9. A step is composed of three poses, as shown in Figure 18.52. From left to right, the leg first extends behind the hip. Then, the foot moves forward until it is about even with the hip. The foot lifts, bending the knee, and rotates to dip the toe towards the floor. Finally, the foot is planted on the floor in front of the hip. Practice making these poses before starting to animate, by moving and rotating the Heel Dummy alone. You'll move the Hip Dummy when you animate.

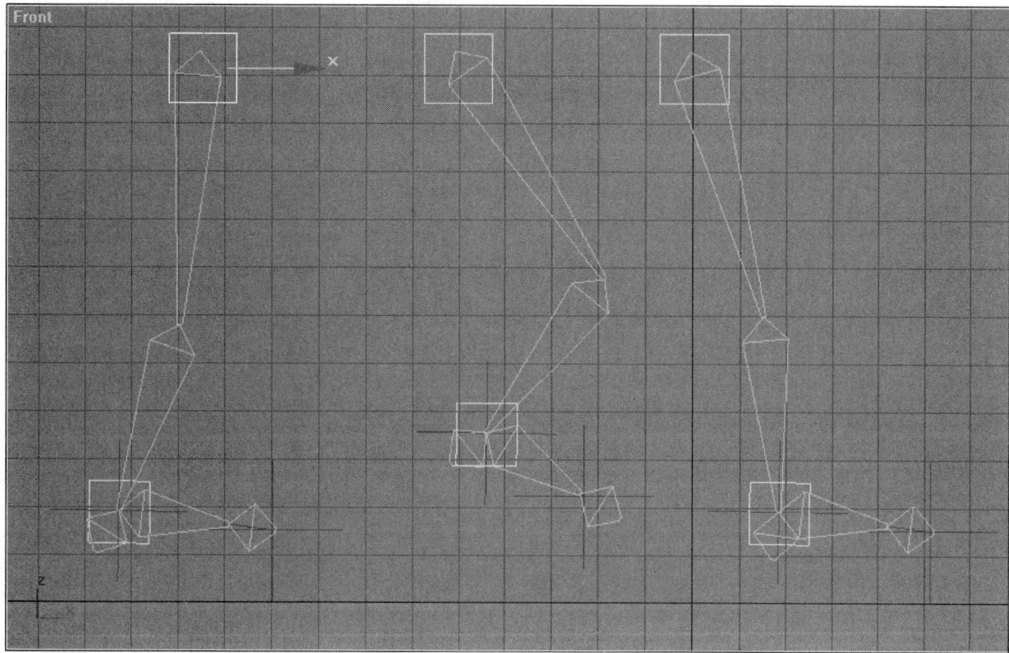

Figure 18.52
The step begins with the leg extended behind the hip. The foot moves forward until it is about even with the hip. The foot is lifted, bending the knee, and rotated to dip the toe. Finally, the foot is planted on the floor in front of the hip.

10. It's time to animate. Open Track View to cover the Top viewport and make sure your controller type names are displayed. All of the animation will be achieved by using only the Heel Dummy and the Hip Dummy. The Hip Dummy will be moved using the default Bezier Position controller. The Heel Dummy will be both moved and rotated. The Bezier Position controller will be fine here, but convert the TCB Rotation controller to Euler XYZ. Because you don't need to expand the tracks below the Hip Dummy, your Track View should look like Figure 18.53.

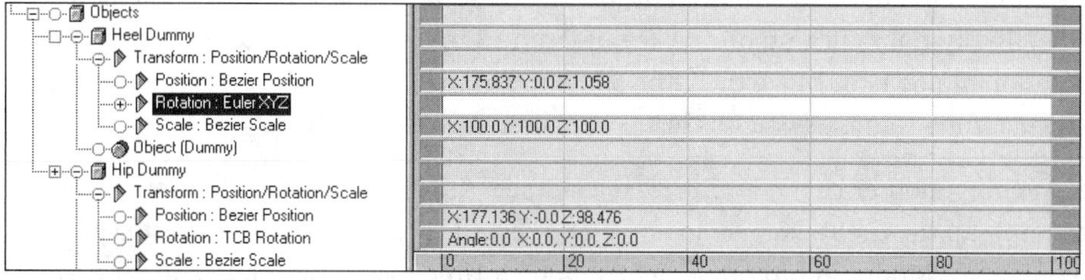

Figure 18.53
Track View ready for animating the Hip Dummy and Heel Dummy. Both objects will be moved using the default Bezier Position controller. The Heel Dummy will also be rotated by using the Euler XYZ controller. No need exists for expanding the tracks below the Hip Dummy.

11. Think through the process carefully. You begin with the foot at its extreme rear position and bring it to its forward position. Half a second is a reasonable time for this action, so it will occur over 15 frames when using the standard 30 frames per second (fps) video frame rate. The complete cycle will bring the foot back to where it began, behind the hip. You don't slide your feet backward when you walk. The forward foot becomes the rear foot, because the hips move forward while the front foot remains planted—the other foot is stepping forward to accomplish this movement. Thus, your leg animation will step from back to front from Frame 0 to Frame 15. This range actually consists of 16 frames, but the extra frame can be ignored here. The Heel Dummy will remain planted while the Hip Dummy moves forward to its final position at Frame 30. Make sure you understand these ideas by taking some steps with your own body. Move the Heel Dummy into position to create the pose on the left in Figure 18.52.

12. Turn on the Animate button and move to Frame 8, halfway through the step. With the Heel Dummy selected, go to the Motion panel and click on the Trajectories button. You can see the motion path as you build it. Move the Heel Dummy into the lifted position in the center of Figure 18.52. Be sure to rotate the Heel Dummy as well, to get the proper dip in the toe. Drag the Time Slider to Frame 15 and create the forward pose in Figure 18.52 by moving and rotating. Turn off the Animate button. Pull the Time Slider to check the animation, and take a look at the keys in Track View. Note that the Animate button creates rotation keys in all three dimensions, even though they are only needed in Y. These extra keys are not a major problem. Also, note that the Trajectory allows you to see the motion path with key placement. Your screen should look like Figure 18.54 when in Local coordinates.

13. You can edit the shape of the step with the Trajectory keys. Click on the Sub-Object button in the Motion panel and move the keys. For example, lower the height of the step on the second key and move it forward a bit. Run the animation to test your results as you edit. Pay attention to the frame ticks in the Trajectory. Note in Figure 18.55 that they indicate a slowing down as the foot is planted. (A much better step can be created by rotating to place the toe down before the heel, but we'll leave this refinement to the more ambitious reader.) You need to adjust the rotation at the top of the step to accommodate the new height. Do this by right-clicking on the key at Frame 8 in the Track Bar and bringing up the Y Rotation dialog box. Move the Time Slider to Frame 8 and adjust the Value spinner. Watch the Dummy rotate as you do this.

14. You need to add another key at Frame 30 to complete the cycle. Right-click on the Time Slider to bring up the Create Key dialog box. Deselect the Scale checkbox so that keys are created only for position and rotation. Set the Source Time to 15 and the Destination Time to 30, to create keys at Frame 30 with the same values they have at Frame 15. After you finish, you'll see a new key symbol appear at Frame 30 in the Track Bar. You'll also see a funny tail appear at the end of the Trajectory. Pull the Time Slider to see the drifting effect of spline interpolation between Frames 15 and 30.

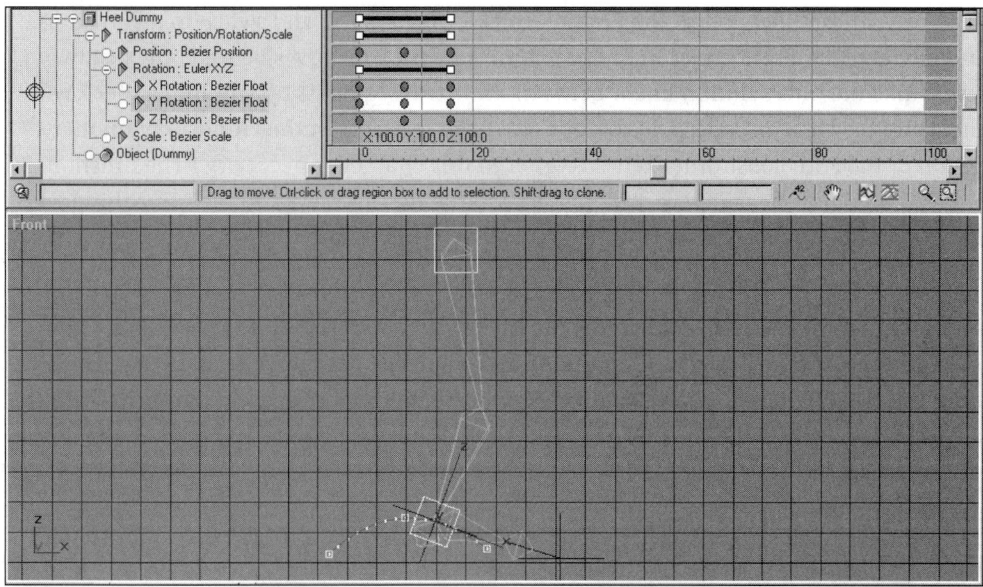

Figure 18.54
Keys are created for the Heel Dummy with the Animate button to define the step. The Trajectory shows the motion path. Note that rotation keys were automatically created in all three dimensions, even though they are needed only in Y.

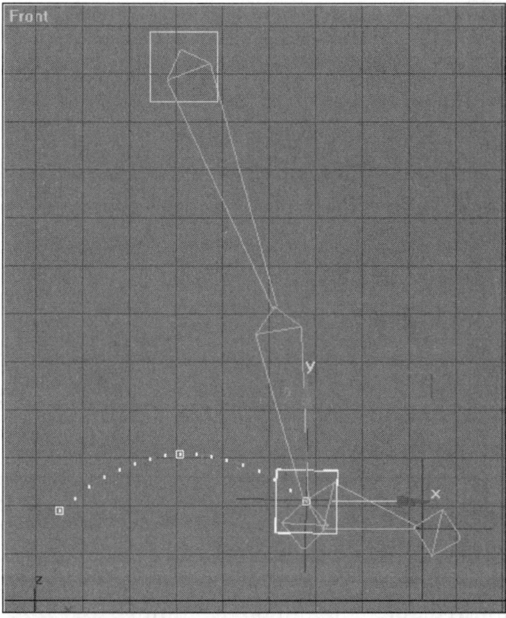

Figure 18.55
The step is adjusted by using Trajectory keys to reduce the height. Note from the frame ticks that the animation slows down as the foot is planted.

15. To correct this problem, select the Position track in Track View and switch to a Function Curves view. You'll see a bend in both the X and Z function curves between the last two keys. Make the interpolation linear between these two segments by selecting either key and using the constant interpolation option. (Refer to Step 5 in the "Adjusting Rotations" section of the Path constraint exercise earlier in this chapter, if necessary.) The function curves should now be perfectly straight between the two last keys. Do the same thing with the Y Rotation function curve. Test the animation to make sure that it's completely still between Frames 15 and 30.

16. Add the hip movement. In mid-stride, the hips move forward at a fairly constant rate. Select the Hip Dummy and turn on the Animate Button. Set the Time Slider to Frame 30. Move the Hip Dummy forward until you duplicate the original pose at Frame 0, with the foot extended behind the hips. Your screen should look like Figure 18.56 when the Trajectory is visible.

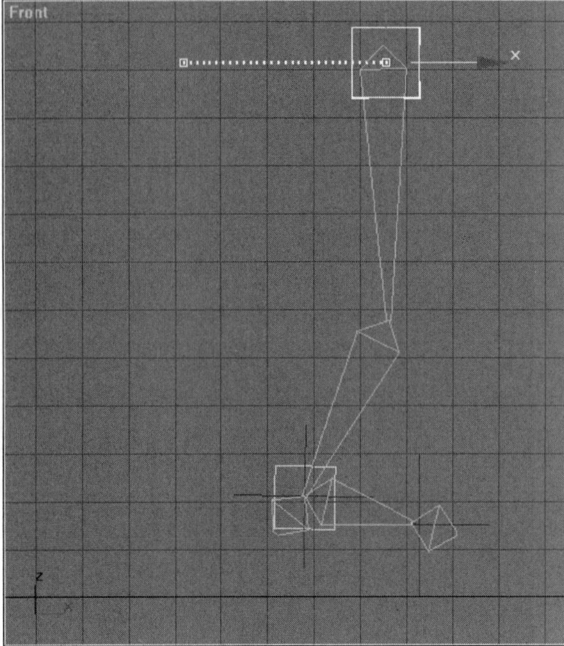

Figure 18.56
The Hip Dummy is animated to move forward between Frame 0 and Frame 30. At Frame 30 (pictured here), it's positioned in front of the foot to duplicate the original pose at Frame 0.

17. Further adjustments are possible, to create a better walk cycle, and you can work on them if you wish. For one thing, the Hip Dummy is now in a different position at Frames 8 and 15 than it was when you posed the Heel Dummy. Try repositioning the Heel Dummy at these frames to accommodate this position. If you do, you'll need to rekey Frame 30, as well.

Create a second leg chain and parent its hip Bone to the Hip Dummy. Create the opposing step. You have to keep the second foot (the front one) on the ground until Frame 16 or so, after the back foot is planted.

Animating Scale

Animating scale raises no significant issues, nor does it come up very often in animation projects. Most of the time, when an object is changing size, it's also changing shape, and is therefore animated by using the morphing techniques discussed in Chapter 19. The default scale controller is Bezier Scale. Like Bezier Position, all three function curves (X, Y, and Z) are included in a single track and keyed together. The Scale XYZ controller corresponds to Position XYZ in that the three dimensions are placed on separate tracks and can be keyed separately. A List and a Noise controller are available for scale, as is an Expression controller.

Moving On

In this chapter, you took on the exciting challenge of animating object transforms. You learned the central role that MAX's animation controllers and constraints play in this kind of work. You compared the most important controllers and constraints for animating position—Bezier Position, Position XYZ, and Path—to assess their relative strengths. You also learned how the choice between the two most important types of rotation controllers, TCB Rotation and Euler XYZ, determines your access to function curves. You finished with a look at how inverse kinematics can be used to create a character-stepping motion.

The next chapter discusses the animation tools that deform object geometry. Those tools that are most central to basic character animation—skeletal deformation and morphing—will be emphasized.

Chapter 19

Deforming the Geometry

Although inorganic or manufactured objects transform rigidly, living things change shape as they move. To animate living things, you need to be able to deform the geometry of your objects. In the final analysis, this amounts to the movement of the individual vertices of the polygonal mesh over time. MAX provides many powerful tools for deforming object geometry, which make this challenging task workable and even fun.

Introduction to 3D Character Animation

Character animation is, without question, the most difficult and demanding application of 3D computer graphics. 3D tools are easily suited to animating rigid objects in space, but the animation of subtle deformations in organic objects pushes existing toolsets to their extremes. The situation is complicated by the standards for character animation that have long been established in Disney-tradition cel animation. The viewing public expects high production values for this kind of entertainment.

Note: *Cel animation was, for a long time, the cornerstone of motion picture cartoon animations. It consisted of drawing the animated events on sheets of clear celluloid (hence the name), showing the static background through the nonpainted areas.*

Character animation is not just a visual art—it is, even more, a dramatic art. Character animation is animation in the service of storytelling and moviemaking, and its ultimate skills are in the refinement of timing in character movement and facial expression. Unlike in cel animation, however, 3D animators cannot simply draw a smile or a character pose directly. Rather, they must obtain subtle control of the shape of the mesh—control powerful enough to permit continuous animation of the surfaces. Character animation in 3D computer graphics is a subject that requires a book fully as long as this one, and thus the goals of this chapter are very narrow. Character animation rests on the power to control mesh deformation. Only after you understand the available tools and have mastered them in the simplest situations can you begin to think about their creative application in character animation. This chapter lays the groundwork for those who are interested in moving further.

A clarifying point is in order here. Not all mesh deformation is character animation. Many inorganic objects are flexible or fluid in motion, water being the most obvious example. In this chapter, however, you'll focus almost exclusively on the application of mesh deformation in the character animation context because this is such an important direction for 3D animators. In 3ds max 4, Discreet has increased the power of the deformation toolset even further to give those seeking employment in the character animation world the best tools ever. Character animation is where much of the paying work in 3D graphics is found.

Mesh deformation in all 3D packages can be divided into two basic approaches: skeletal deformation and morphing. These concepts are covered next.

Skeletal Deformation

Skeletal deformation involves the creation of a hierarchy of nonrendering objects called *Bones*, as discussed in Chapter 18. The Bones (generally a complete character skeleton) are positioned inside the character model and are then attached to the mesh. Transforming the bones causes the mesh to deform, because the vertices on the model are rigidly associated with specific Bones. Although the concept is similar to the way in which real bones are attached to muscles, the similarity is very thin. There are no "muscles" in the character model, which is simply a hollow shell. It takes an enormous amount of practice to create skeletal deformations that suggest solid flesh. Note that skeletal deformation is mesh deformation, not object transformation. The Bones (as objects) are moved and rotated, but the character model is deformed by these transforms. It takes awhile to grasp this concept clearly.

MAX 3 introduced new skeletal-deformation tools that greatly changed the status of the package as a character-animation environment. 3ds max 4 enhances those tools to make the workflow faster and more precise.

Note: *One of the best approaches to character animation is Character Studio, an add-on package for 3ds max 4. Character Studio allows for footstep-driven animation that literally consists of footsteps being placed in a scene and the associated bipod character following them. Once the motion is in place, any number of bipods—and the geometry that is skinned, or associated, to them—can be assigned to the steps. Motions from one object can be save and assigned to another. The latest version, CS3, has the ability to control the ebb and flow of crowds without editing each individual character. If character animation is your goal, Character Studio may be the tool you are looking for.*

Morphing

Skeletal deformation is the preferred approach to bending limbs and extremities. It's used to make a character walk, move its arms and hands, and rotate the torso and head. Muscles in the arms and legs bulge as they are flexed, and these changes can be represented in MAX. Bones are unsuitable for a large range of mesh deformations, however. For example, a character breathes by moving the chest in and out; more important, the face (and especially the mouth) changes shape while speaking or shifting emotion. These kinds of deformations require morphing.

Morphing is a big word in 3D computer graphics. In the broadest sense, it includes all geometric deformations by whatever means, including Bones. It's generally used, however, to refer to a specific method in which various versions of a single model (called *targets*) are interpolated in the course of animation. This method is called *target morphing*, and it is implemented in MAX with the Morpher modifier (which effectively replaced the older Morph compound object discussed in Chapter 8). As with all implementations, you must generally create all of your morph targets from a single model. For example, a face model is created with the mouth in a neutral position. Then, copying the original model and editing the vertices creates a smiling version. You can then morph between the two targets in time by setting keys. Morphing moves the vertices from their positions in one target to their positions in the next target. Each vertex has a motion path. That's why you have to work with copies of a single model. If your targets have different numbers of vertices or if the vertices are not in the same order in the model file, it's impossible to specify the motion of each vertex.

Because morphing amounts to animating vertices, it can be achieved by other means than interpolating between complete versions of the mesh. At an extreme, you can animate individual vertices or control vertices (CVs) on an editable mesh object by using the Animate button. Once they've been animated to any degree, they'll appear as tracks in Track View for further editing. This method is more workable, however, if some refinements are made. For example, you can animate vertices on a low-poly cage object, which is then subdivided with MeshSmooth. That way, you work with a more manageable number of vertices, and the deformations are smoother because they are applied before subdivision. Non-Uniform Rational B-Splines (NURBS) surfaces provide an analogous approach: You can select and animate NURBS control vertices and get a smooth result.

This brings us to the concept generally known as *cluster animation*, in which a selection of vertices or CVs is animated as a named unit with its own pivot point. MAX achieves this result with the XForm modifier. Multiple vertices or CVs can be passed to an XForm modifier, and that modifier's gizmo can then be animated. This process keeps animated objects or subobjects organized, and it is especially suited to the control of facial features, such as eyebrows. A Linked XForm modifier goes further, allowing you to control the selected vertices by transforming a Dummy or other independent object.

Modifiers and Space Warps

Thus far, you've seen techniques that are common to most 3D packages in one form or another, but MAX has some unique powers attributable to its modifier stack concept. Most of MAX's modifiers deform geometry and can be used in modeling, but the parameters of these modifiers are typically animatable. You can animate the amount of a bend produced by a

Bend modifier or the degree of twist applied by a Twist modifier. When MAX was first introduced, these tools were touted as replacements for "old-fashioned" morph targeting. The problem with using modifiers, however, is that the results tend not to look "organic" enough. The modifiers implement mathematical principles that are often too perfect to be convincing in the character animation context. Use them with caution.

The FFD (Free Form Deformation) modifier, however, stands apart from the other deformation modifiers. As a lattice-deformation tool, it's a flexible interface for animating vertices fluidly, and is well suited to localized morphing. For example, it can be fitted around an upper arm to animate a muscle bulge.

Space warps are the flip side of modifiers. If a modifier can deform an object directly, space warps do so indirectly. Strictly speaking, space warps deform the space, which is then reflected in the deformation of the object. The geometry is deformed as it moves through the affected space. Although they are very useful, it's safe to say that space warps are peripheral to most character animation work. They are more applicable to the geometric deformation of inorganic surfaces—for example, to animate waves or ripples in water. We'll look at space warps in Chapter 20.

The Skin Modifier

The Skin modifier is a wonderful tool. So much in MAX can be complex, and many of its powerful tools are difficult and frustrating for creative people to master. Character animators, in particular, need to worry about their art and not about their tools. The Skin modifier, however, is remarkably intuitive. It offers a lot of power if you care to explore it, but you can also go an enormous distance with only a basic understanding. This tool is actually fun to use.

Let's cover the basics in an exercise.

Getting Started

The Skin modifier requires a mesh to be deformed and objects to control the deformation. The latter can be any kind of objects, such as Boxes. They can even be splines, in which case the mesh deforms to the curvature of the spline. The most important objects to control deformation are Bones, however, because they are easily assembled into a skeletal hierarchy, do not render, and implement inverse kinematics. You can deform a mesh with Bones by following these steps:

1. Open the file Chap19 Leg.max from the CD-ROM. It is a model of a human right leg that is a dense-enough mesh for deformation.

2. To draw the Bones, activate the Bones button in the Create|Systems panel. Before drawing, make sure that the Assign To Root checkbox is selected in the IK Chain Assignment rollout. This setting ensures that the entire Bones chain will be subject to inverse kinematics. To create the Bones, click three times in a vertical line—at the hip, the knee, and the ankle.

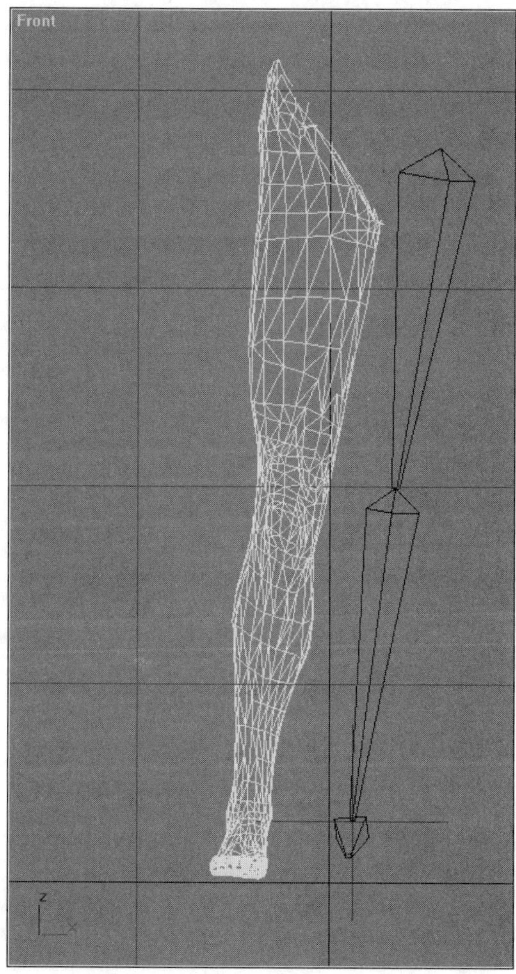

Figure 19.1
A leg with Bones running down the center in preparation for skeletal deformation, as seen from a Front viewport. The Bones have been moved outside the leg for clarity.

Right-click to stop creating Bones. In the Modify panel, adjust the parameters in the Bone Object section to scale the size of the Bones appropriately to the size of the object. At this point, your Front viewport should look like Figure 19.1. Check in multiple viewports to make sure that the Bones are running through the middle of the leg and to the ends of the toes. If they are not, move, rotate, or nonuniform scale them until they are.

Note: *3ds max 4 has introduced fins to Bone objects to help define the volume of the Bone. If you like, add and size the fins in the Modify panel.*

3. Note the End Effector at the end of the Bone chain. Make it a rule always to link the End Effector to a Dummy object. Doing so will make your life much easier, because the End

Effector is not as easy to select. Create a small Dummy and position it over the End Effector. Select the last Bone in the chain (Bone03) and link it to the Dummy.

4. Move the Dummy to test the inverse kinematics (IK). The IK should rotate the Bones correctly, but nothing happens to the leg. Your Front viewport should look like Figure 19.2.

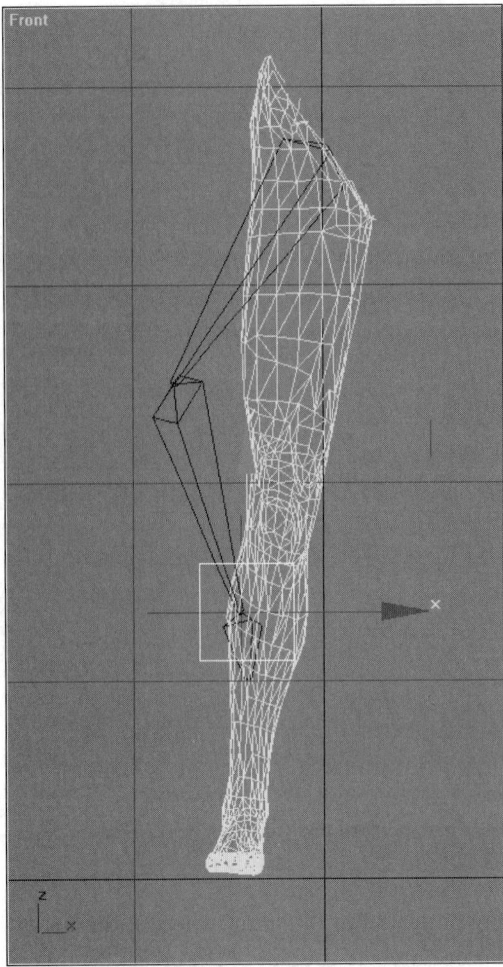

Figure 19.2
A Dummy object is created to be a parent of the End Effector of the Bones chain. Moving the Dummy moves the End Effector, thereby rotating the Bones in the chain. The leg object is as yet unaffected, however.

5. Undo the last step or make your Bone chain straight again before continuing. A skeleton must always be in its default position when you attach it to an object. To attach the Bones to the leg, select the leg and put a Skin modifier on its stack. Click on the Add Bone button beneath the empty window. A dialog box appears, containing all the objects that can be used to deform the mesh. Pick the three available Bones from the list and click on the Select button to close the dialog box.

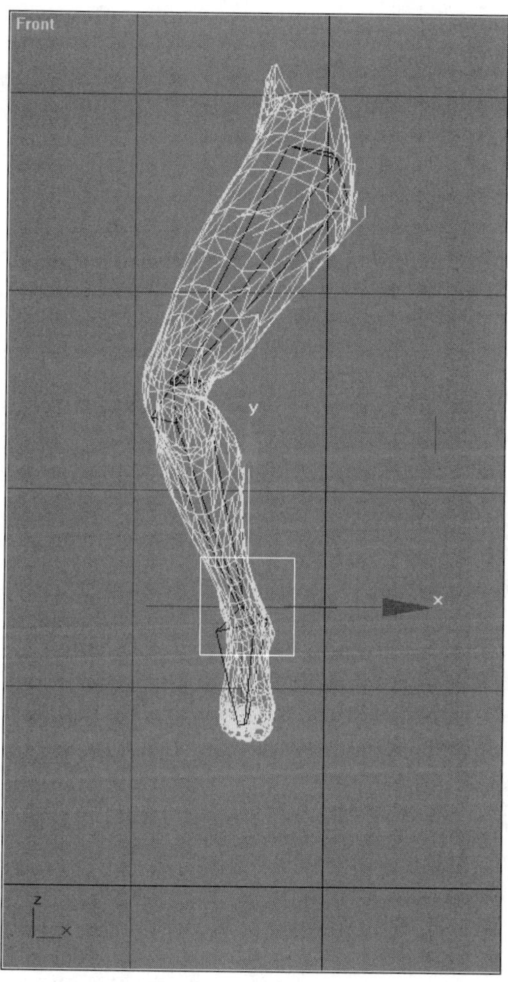

Figure 19.3
A Skin modifier is applied to the leg object and the Bones are added to the modifier. Now, the rotations of the Bones deform the mesh.

6. Go back and select the Dummy object. Move it to flex the skeleton, and watch the mesh deform. Pretty cool, huh? Your screen should look like Figure 19.3.

Vertex Weighting

It's important to have a good basic understanding of the way skeletal deformation operates. When you attach Bones to a mesh (or vice versa—both ways of speaking are correct), each individual vertex in the mesh becomes associated with one or more Bones. Each such vertex is said to be *weighted* with respect to each Bone. The weighting is always between 0 and 100 percent. If a vertex has a zero weight, it is completely unaffected by a Bone. If it has a 100 percent weight, it moves rigidly along with the Bone as the Bone is rotated or moved. Values between 0 and 100 cause a vertex to move only proportionally to the transformation of a Bone. For example, a vertex weighted 50 percent to a Bone moves only half the distance it would move if the weight were 100 percent. The concept is very similar to that found in the Soft Selection tools in MAX.

Dividing vertex weights between two Bones is the key to effective deformation at joints. Vertices at a knee or elbow region may be weighted 50 percent to the upper Bone and 50 percent to the lower one. This overlapping influence of two Bones on the same vertices is called *joint blending*.

The controls that pertain to vertex weighting are available only in the Envelope subobject level. An *envelope* is a region around a Bone that is used to determine vertex weighting. As a general proposition and starting point, only vertices within a Bone's envelope can be attached to that Bone.

The ultimate issue is always the weight of the vertices, and envelopes are only a convenient way of assigning weights. The color of a vertex tick within the envelope indicates the weight of the vertex with respect to the selected Bone. Using the same color convention as the Soft Selection option found in several modifiers' subobject levels, a red tick means that the weight is 100 percent. A blue tick is close to zero percent. Let's continue with the previous exercise to explore how vertex weighting is controlled:

1. Straighten out your Bones again to make them vertical. Select the leg object. Expand the Skin modifier and select Envelope to get into the Envelope subobject level. You'll see an envelope appear around whichever of the Bones is highlighted in the panel. You'll also see colored tick marks at all the vertices that are weighted more than zero for that Bone. Black-and-white images are not really adequate here; with the upper Bone selected, however, your screen should look like Figure 19.4. Look at the object in a shaded viewport, and the vertex colors extend to the shaded faces.

2. To test the vertex weights, and to see that vertex weight can be set independently of envelopes, select the Vertices checkbox in the Filters section. This setting allows you to select individual vertices for weighting. MAX allows you to "paint" the vertices to be affected by the selected Bone. Click on the Paint Weights button in the Weight Properties section and move your cursor over the object to see the size of the brush. Adjust the Radius value until the brush is a manageable size; then, click-drag-release in short strokes to add weighted vertices to the selected Bone's envelope. This action should give you a good sense of the meaning of the colored ticks within the envelope. Those at the very top, in red, are completely controlled by the upper Bone. Those by the knee are only partially influenced by that Bone, and those near the bottom of the envelope receive little or no control from the upper Bone. Turn off Paint Weights and use the Reset Selected Vertices button in the Advance Params rollout to return the vertices to their original states. Deselect the Vertices checkbox in the Filters section.

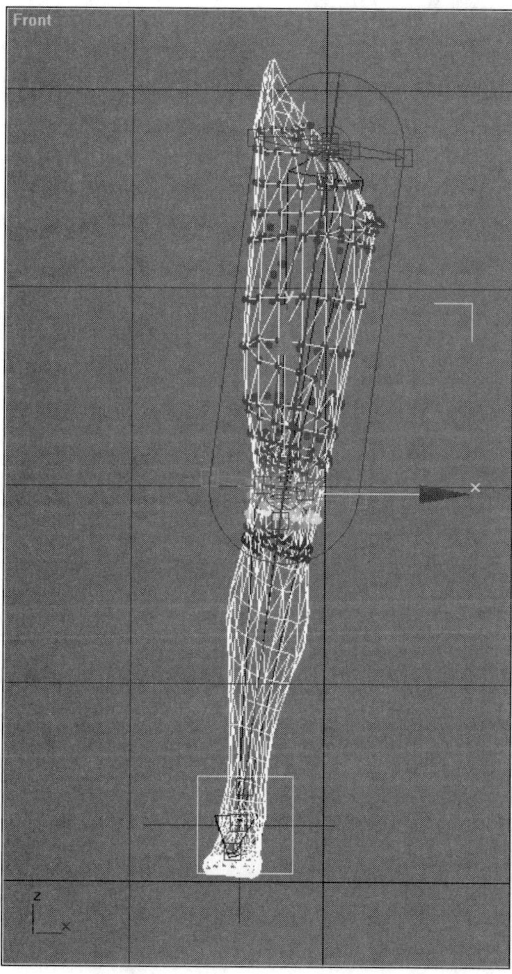

Figure 19.4
In the Envelope subobject level, the envelope for the upper Bone is displayed. Note the inner and outer bounding regions. Note also the tick marks for vertices that are weighted to the Bone. These vertex ticks are color-coded in a spectrum from red to blue to indicate weight percentages. In this black-and-white image, the yellow and light green ticks clustered around the knee cannot be seen, but they are nonetheless present.

3. Click on the lower Bone (Bone03) in the selection window to see its envelope and vertex weighting effect. The situation is the exact reverse of that for the upper Bone. The red vertices with full weight are at the toes, and weighting decreases as you go toward the ankle. This distribution makes perfect sense. At the very top and bottom of the mesh, the vertices should be controlled only by a single Bone. Toward the middle, however, vertices should be influenced by both Bones, and their weights should be divided between them. This division of weights is achieved by the overlapping of envelopes. Select the Draw All Envelopes checkbox in the Display rollout to see both envelopes together, although only the vertex weights for the selected Bone are visible. Your screen should look like Figure 19.5.

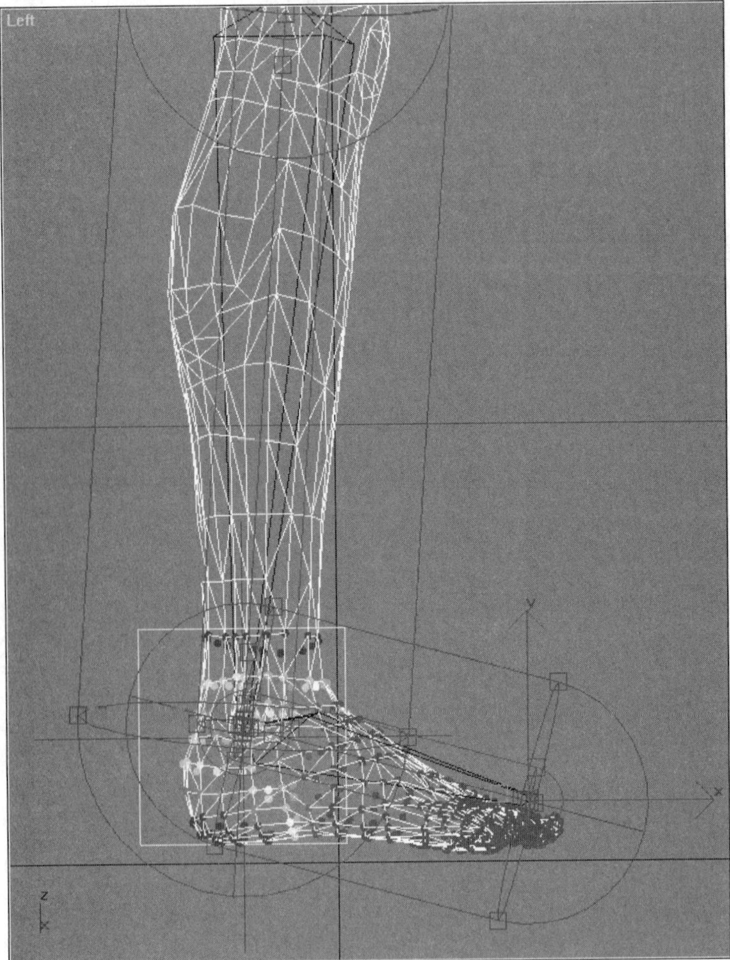

Figure 19.5
The Left viewport, showing a zoomed-in view of the lower leg. With the lower Bone selected, the vertex tick colors are reversed from those of the upper Bone. The fully weighted (red) vertices are at the very bottom, and their weights decrease as they go up. The vertices in the middle of the object are about equally weighted to each Bone to create a smooth blend. By showing the upper envelope at the same time, you can see how this blending is attributable to the overlap of the upper and lower envelopes.

Adjusting the Joint Bulges

The great thing about the Skin modifier is that you can work interactively to adjust your envelopes (and therefore your vertex weights), seeing the result as you work. After a short time, the envelopes begin to make good practical sense. In the previous version of MAX, bulge control was primarily determined by scaling and adjusting the envelopes themselves. As you'll see in the continuation of this exercise, the new Gizmos make this job much easier. Follow these steps:

1. Get out of the subobject mode and select the Dummy object. Move it to create a bend in the knee like the one in Figure 19.3. This deformation is not very convincing. Due to the symmetrical weighting of the vertices, it looks more like an elastic object than human flesh.

2. Go back to the leg object at the Editable Mesh level and select the vertices at the back of the knee. Go to the Envelope subobject level. In the Gizmos rollout, select Bulge Angle Deformer from the drop-down list and click on the Add Gizmo button to add a Bulge Angle Deformer Gizmo around the selected vertices, as shown in Figure 19.6.

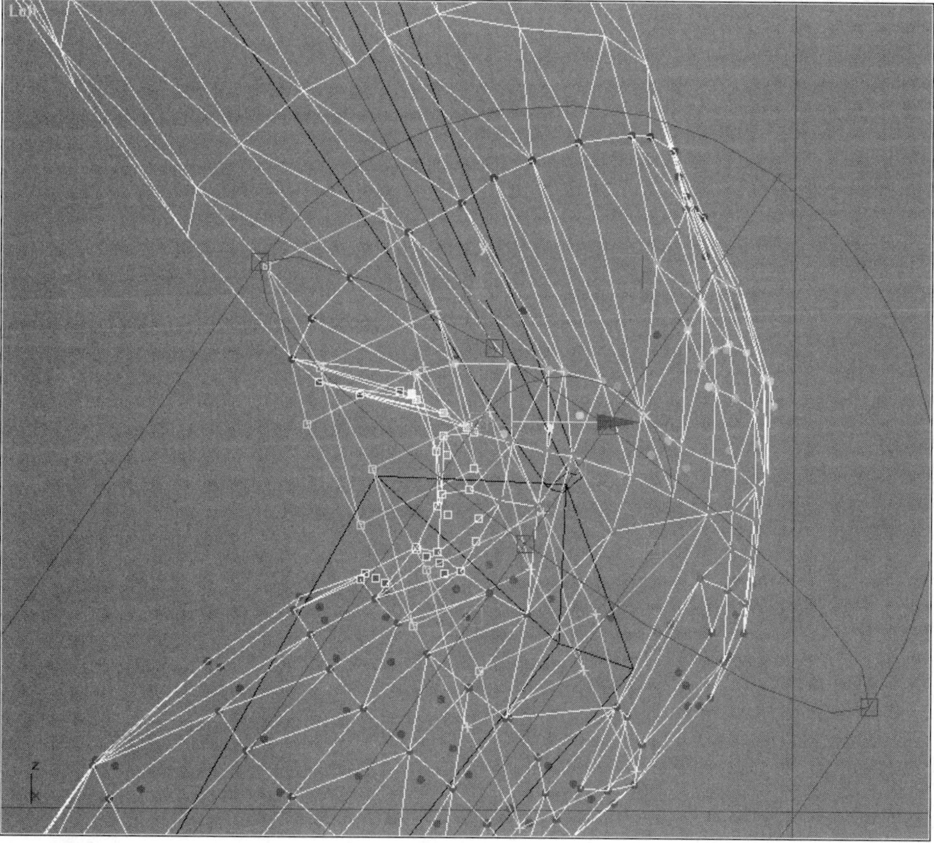

Figure 19.6
The Left viewport showing the knee joint with a Bulge Angle Deformer Gizmo assigned to the vertices at the back of the knee.

3. The Gizmo is a lattice that is similar in function to the Free Form Deformation Gizmo. Check the Use Bounding Volume in the Deformer Parameters and click on the Edit Lattice button. In the viewport, manipulate the CVs to bulge the back of the knee as it would if bent naturally. Your screen should look like Figure 19.7.

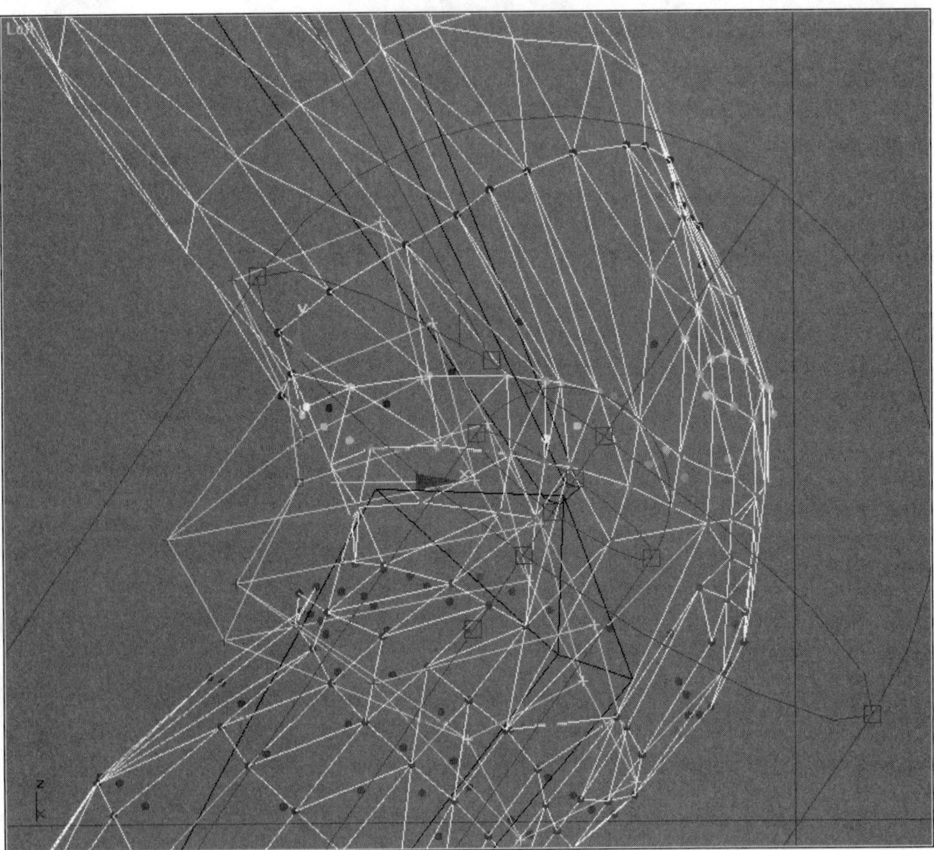

Figure 19.7
By manipulating the CVs of the Bulge Angle Deformer Gizmo, the curvature at the back of the knee is made more natural.

4. Move the Dummy up and down again and notice that the bend at the back of the knee maintains a natural bulge from the extended position to the point where you applied the Gizmo.

5. Look at the movement of the leg in the Perspective viewport as you move the Dummy up and down. It may tend to bend outward rather than straight forward. At the top of the Bone chain (at the hip), MAX has placed a Plane Angle Manipulator to control the swivel of the bones. Select the top Bone and click on the Manipulate button in the Main toolbar to expose the Manipulator, as shown in Figure 19.8. Moving the Manipulator causes a readout to appear that describes the current angle. Click on the Manipulate button to hide the Manipulator before continuing.

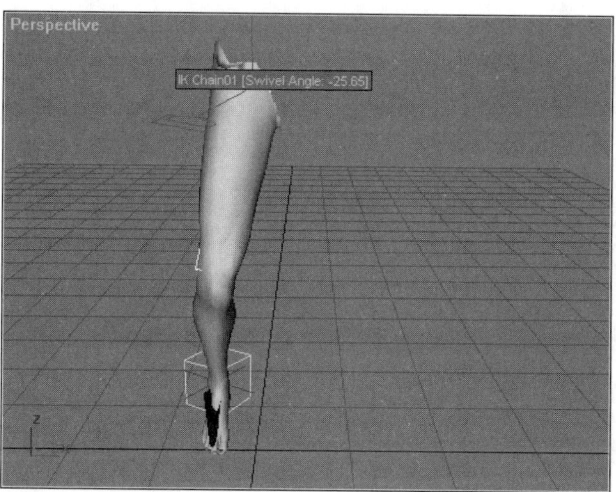

Figure 19.8
A Plane Angle Manipulator is found at the top of the Bone chain and used to adjust the angle of the Bones and, therefore, the leg. The readout shows the angle as the Manipulator is being adjusted.

Adding a Second Leg

All of the objects, Bones, and Gizmos are in place and functioning for a single leg. It's a simple task to add and set up a second leg in the scene; just follow these steps:

1. Select all the objects in the scene and mirror them, using the Copy option, with an offset appropriate for a human stance, as shown is Figure 19.9. Move the new Dummy up and down, and you'll notice that it is linked to the new Bones on the right; however, the Bones are not skinned to the leg. In fact, the new leg is skinned to the old Bones, but much of it is probably outside the Bones' envelopes. Lift the Dummy on the left. Some movement may occur in the right leg near the crotch area, if it falls within the envelope of the upper-left Bone.

2. Make any adjustments necessary to fit the new Bones within the leg on the right. Select the leg on the right. In the Parameters rollout of the Modify panel, select each of the Bones in the window and click on the Remove Bone button. When the list is clear, click on the Add Bone button. Select Bones 04, 05, and 06 and add them to the list. Moving the Dummy on the right up and down now moves the leg, as well.

The Morpher Modifier

Morphing between morph targets is possible through the Morph compound object, as covered in Chapter 8. A Morph compound object contains all the morph targets associated with a single object, and you can morph between these targets by setting keyframes associated with individual targets. This tool is simple and workable, but it is far less powerful than those offered by the most important competing packages. For true morphing power, you'll want to

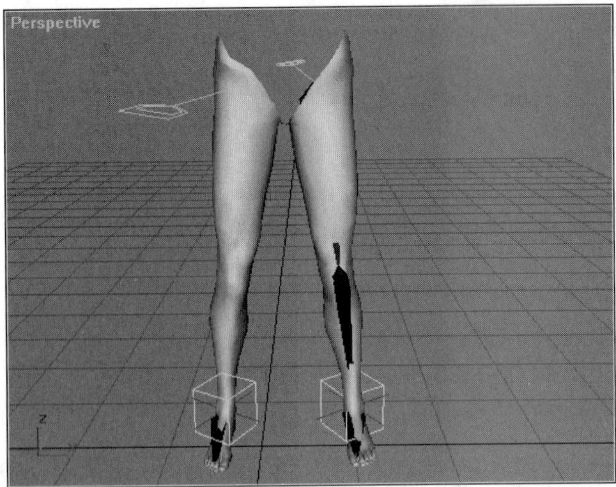

Figure 19.9
The leg and Bones on the left are mirrored to create the leg and Bones on the right. The leg on the right, however, is still skinned to the Bones on the left.

employ the Morpher modifier. This tool is fantastic—a remarkable combination of power and ease of use. The Morph compound object is still included in 3ds max 4, for purposes of forward compatibility and for very simple morph applications. It has been functionally replaced by the Morpher modifier, however, so only this new toolset is discussed here.

The best way to understand the Morpher modifier is to work with it. The exercise in this section will introduce you to all of the basics.

Creating Morph Targets

Morphing requires morph targets. As we explained earlier in this chapter, all morph targets for a single model must be created by editing the original geometry. This requirement means that you start with a base version of the model (often called an *anchor object* in 3D animation parlance) and move vertices or CVs to create the various targets. On some occasions, this process will be too difficult because the intended morph target is very different from the anchor object (for example, a Box morphing into a Sphere). MAX's Conform compound object provides a method by which a mesh can be "shrink-wrapped" to fit another object. This method can be used to create multiple morph targets from a single mesh without editing vertices. But the shrink-wrap method is only rarely useful, and the results are not always good. In this exercise, you stick to the basic method, which is at the very heart of the character animator's skill set:

1. In the Top viewport, create a Sphere object on the groundplane. Convert the object to an editable mesh and copy it a couple of times to the right to create three identical models along the World X-axis.

2. Maximize your Front viewport to get a good view of the three objects in a line. Leave the one on the left as the base or anchor object. This is the default version that will be morphed by its targets. Select the middle Sphere and rename it *up target*. Select some rows of vertices on the top of this object and move them sharply upward. Go to the rightmost object and rename it *down target*. Move some rows on the bottom of the object downward. When you're done, your Front viewport should look like Figure 19.10.

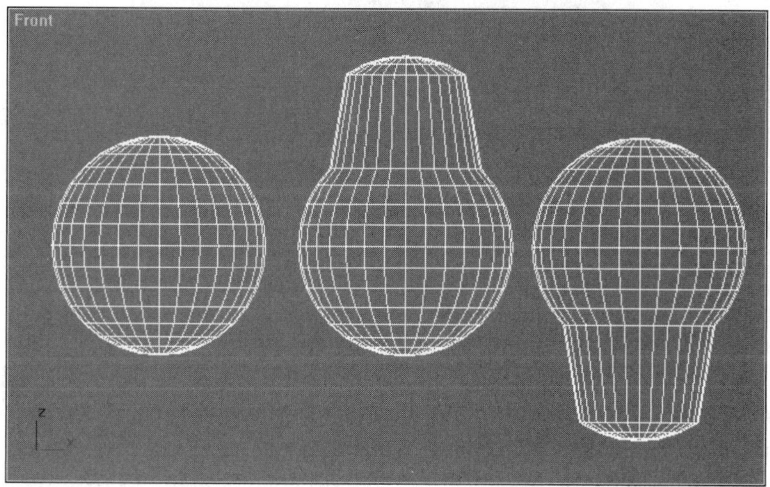

Figure 19.10
The base (or anchor) object at left is the original editable mesh that will be morphed. The two targets at center and right are created by selecting and moving vertices.

Applying the Morpher Modifier

Once the morph targets are created, you're ready to morph by applying the Morpher modifier to the base object and selecting the targets. Continue the previous exercise with these steps:

1. Select the base object (Sphere01) and apply a Morpher modifier to its stack. The Morpher panel appears. The Channel List rollout indicates all the current morph targets. Because you haven't selected any yet, the channels all read *-empty-*.

2. Pull down to the Channel Parameters rollout and open it, if necessary. Channel 1 is currently selected. Click on the Pick Object From Scene button and then click on the up target object in the viewport. Test the result by dragging the Channel 1 spinner in the Channel List. As you increase the value between 0 and 100, the anchor object morphs into the up target. Figure 19.11 illustrates the Channel List with a value of 50 percent.

3. Click on the second channel in the Channel List to activate it; apply the down target object to this channel. Manipulate the spinners of both channels to see how both morphs are added together. Because the edited vertices in each target are different, both targets can be

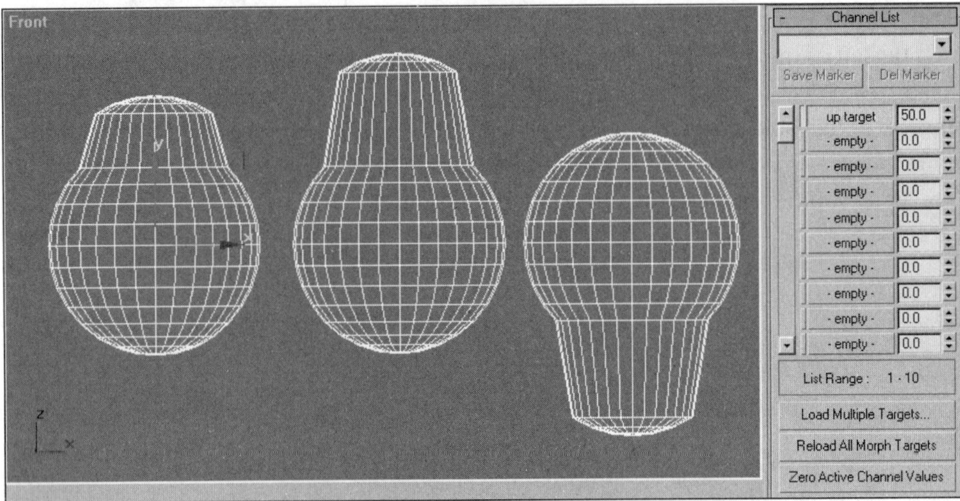

Figure 19.11
The up target model (*center*) has been used as a morph target for the anchor object in Channel 1. With the value in the Channel 1 spinner set to 50 percent, the anchor object is morphed halfway into the target.

used together. Imagine the first target as controlling the shape of the eyebrows on a head and the second as controlling the mouth. The power to add together morph targets permits you to create specialized targets affecting only narrow areas and blend them together in animation. Figure 19.12 illustrates both targets applied together.

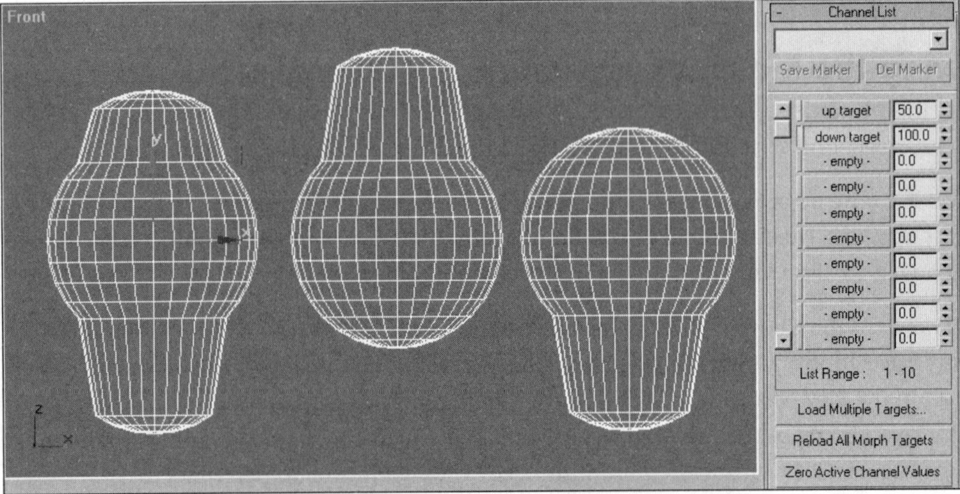

Figure 19.12
The down target model is added to the Channel List in the second channel. Because the edited regions of the two targets are different, they can be used together to create an additive result.

4. After you create an additive result, it may make sense to save it as an independent morph target of its own so that you can grab it whenever you need it. Adjust your channels to produce some combination of both targets, as shown in Figure 19.12. Activate the empty Channel 3. In the Channel Parameters rollout, click on the Capture Current State button. In the Name Captured Object dialog box that appears, name the new target *both* and click on the Accept button. The new target appears in the third channel. To test it, reduce the first two channels to 0 and then increase the third channel to 100. Your result should look the same as when you created the new target. See Figure 19.13.

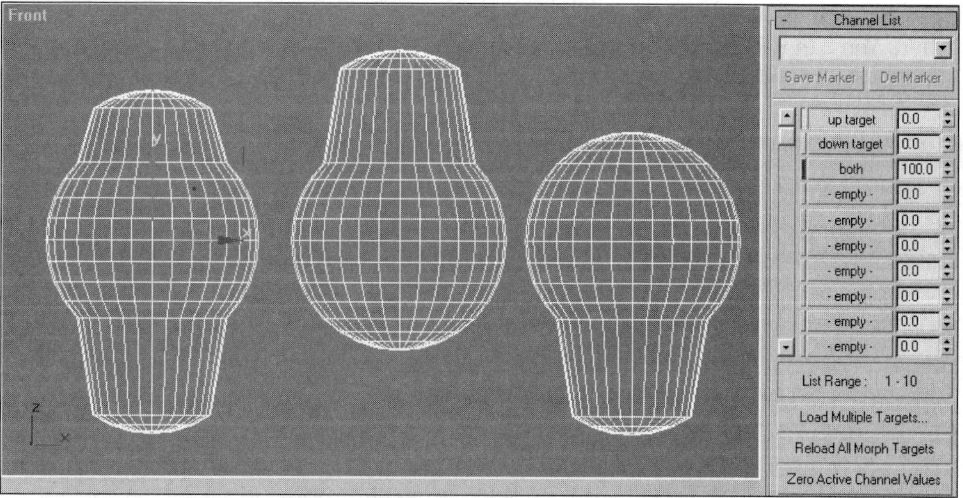

Figure 19.13
The blended result in Figure 19.12 was made into a new morph target in the third channel under the name *both*. With this channel set to 100 percent and the others set to 0, the result is the same as when the first two channels were blended.

5. Some excellent tools are available for managing the Channel List. Delete the first two channels by right-clicking on each and selecting Delete Channel from the pop-up menu. Now there's empty space above the third channel. Open the Advanced Parameters rollout and click on the Compact Channel List button. Note how this action moves the third channel to the top of the list.

6. Delete the first channel to create an empty list. This time, load both targets at once. Click on the Load Multiple Targets button and select the two target models from the list. When you finish, down target and up target will be loaded into the first two channels.

Making the Most of Targets

Once your targets have been loaded into channels, you have more flexibility with them than you might first imagine. Let's continue our exercise:

1. Open the Global Parameters rollout and note the spinner that limits the range of percentage values. By default, you are confined to values between 0 and 100 percent. Deselect the Use Limits checkbox and set a value for the down target channel that is greater than 100 percent. Note how this setting extrapolates the target beyond its original limits, saving you the trouble of having to re-edit your morph targets on many occasions. Set the up target channel to a negative value and watch how the morph is extrapolated in the opposite direction. You can use this action to turn a smile into a frown. Your screen should look something like Figure 19.14.

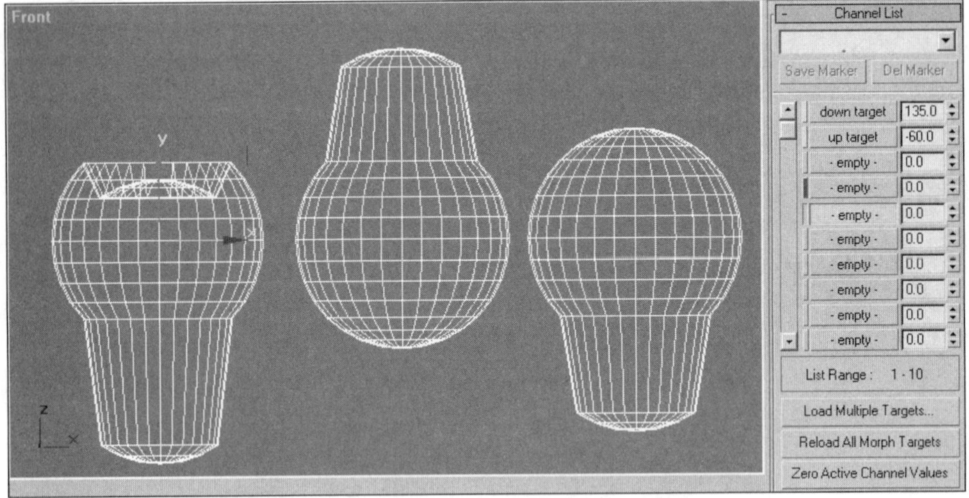

Figure 19.14
With the percentage limits off, you can morph to values greater than 100 percent and less than 0 (producing a negative morph).

2. Click on the Zero Active Channel Values button to return all the channels to a zero value. Try editing the morph targets. Select the up target object (the editable mesh, not the channel in the Morpher modifier). Move the previously edited vertices over to the right to create a slanted top. Return to the base object and increase the up target channel. The object will morph as it did before. To use the newly edited version, right-click on the channel and select Reload Target. The morph will use the slanted version, as illustrated in Figure 19.15. Note that if the Automatically Reload Targets checkbox at the bottom of the Channel List rollout is selected, you don't need to reload after editing a target.

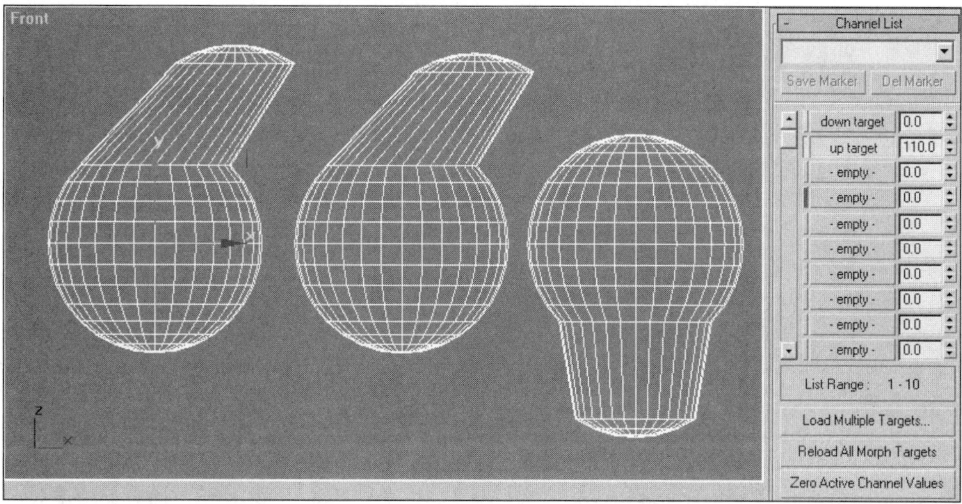

Figure 19.15
The up target model has been re-edited to create a slanted top. After reloading the target into its channel, the morph incorporates the new version.

Animating the Morphs

Now that you know how to set up morph targets, let's continue our exercise by animating with them. The plan is to pull out the top in the first 26 frames and then pull out the bottom in the next 25 frames. Follow these steps:

1. Reset all channel values to zero and then turn on the Animate button. Pull the Time Slider to Frame 25 and set the up target value to 100 percent. Note that keys appear in the Track Bar at Frames 0 and 25. Pull the Time Slider to confirm that the top of the object morphs up over these 26 frames.

2. Move to Frame 50 and set the down target value to 100 (leaving the up target also at 100). Turn off the Animate button and drag the Time Slider to see the result. It is not what you want—the bottom starts morphing at Frame 0, not at Frame 25, as you might have expected. Confirm this action by watching the down target spinner values as you pull the Time Slider.

3. To understand this problem, open Track View and pan your Front viewport down so that you can see everything at once. In Track View, open the tracks for the base object (Sphere01) until you find the tracks for the morph targets under the Morpher modifier. Select the down target track and change to a function curve view. As you can see in Figure 19.16, the down target track is changing values continuously between Frame 0 and Frame 50. The key you set at Frame 25 did not affect this track.

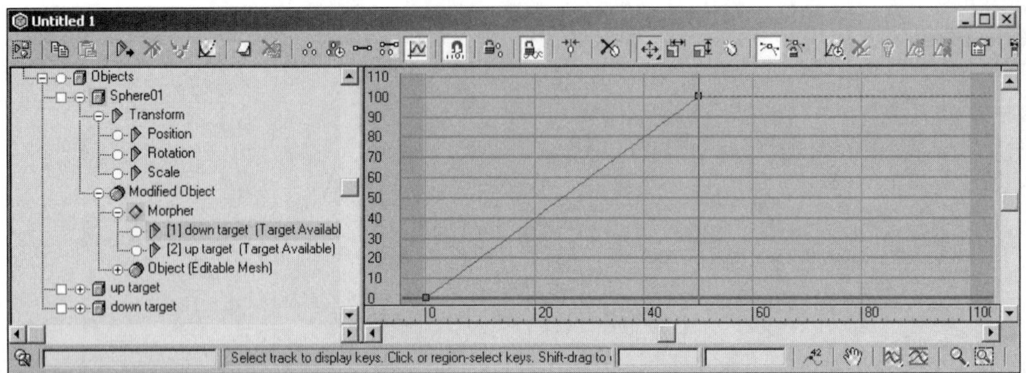

Figure 19.16
The function curve for the down target track shows the morph building continuously between Frames 0 and 50.

4. To fix this situation, create a key at Frame 25 and set it to a zero value. The default spline interpolation will create an extreme curve, so correct the interpolation to get a straight line between the first two keys and a smooth, rising curve between the second and third keys. (Methods for adjusting interpolation are discussed in Chapter 17.) When you finish, your function curve should look like Figure 19.17.

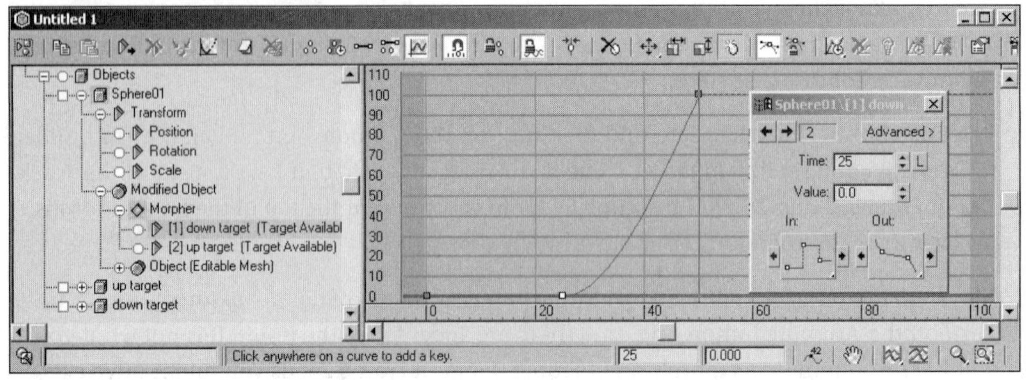

Figure 19.17
The function curve shown in Figure 19.16 is corrected by the addition of a key at Frame 25. After adjusting the interpolation, the morph holds a constant zero value until Frame 25; only then does it begin to build.

5. Pull the Time Slider to confirm that the animation is now working as intended. As a final step, try moving the keys in the Track Bar to change the timing of the two morphs. Note that the second key contains both tracks at once, so that if you move it forward, the first morph slows down and the second speeds up. It takes quite awhile to master the animation of additive (overlapping) morphs. Take some time to explore this subject.

Morphing Materials

Morphing geometry is often associated with animated Materials. For example, a character's cheeks might change color when the face morphs into an angry scowl. MAX has a Material type that automatically ties Material definitions to morph targets. You can try it out on the animation we've been working with:

1. Change to a Smooth + Highlight view. Open the Global Parameters rollout in the Morpher panel and click on the Assign New Material button. You'll see your base object assume the default gray Material.

2. Open the Material Editor and pick a slot. Click on the Get Material button to bring up the Material/Map Browser. Use the Selected option to find the Material on the selected object and double-click on its name to load it into the slot. When this is accomplished, the panel for the Morpher Material type will appear in the Material Editor, as shown in Figure 19.18.

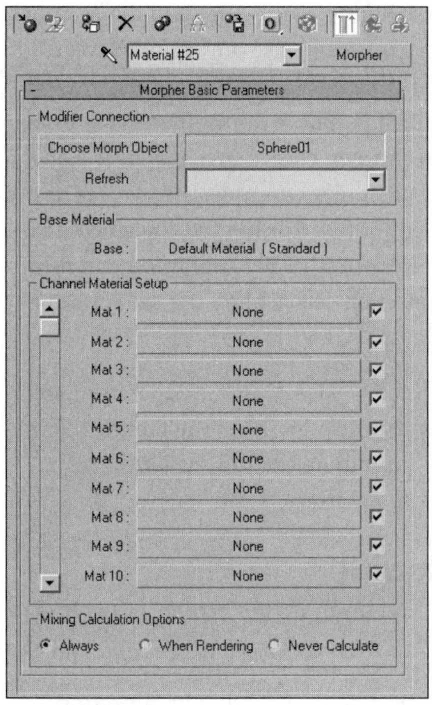

Figure 19.18
The panel for the Morpher Material type in the Material Editor. The numbered Material slots correspond to the channels in the Morpher modifier.

3. Open the Base Material by clicking on the Default Material button. Set its Diffuse Color parameter to red. Return to the top level for the Morpher Material by clicking on the Go To Parent button; then, click on the Mat 1 slot and assign it a Standard Material. Set the Diffuse Color of this Material to green. Put a Standard Material in Mat 2 and make its Diffuse Color blue. Pull the Time Slider and watch your viewports. If nothing happens, don't be surprised. Check the bottom of the Morpher Material panel to make sure that the Always radio button is selected under Mixing Calculation Options. In theory, this feature should show the color morphing in a shaded viewport, but the functionality may be dependent on your system's video card.

4. Render Frames 0 through 50 and watch the transformation in the Virtual Frame Buffer, or output the frames to an AVI file.

The XForm and Linked XForm Modifiers

The XForm modifier is used to bring the transforms (Move, Rotate, and Scale) into the modifier stack, overriding the general operation of MAX, in which transforms are only applied to objects after they have emerged from the end of the modifier pipeline. The XForm modifier is of considerable general importance in MAX, but one of its most valuable applications is to implement cluster animation. As was mentioned earlier in this chapter, *cluster animation* is the animation of groups of vertices or control vertices as defined units. For example, the vertices at the corners of a mouth can be defined as a cluster and then animated. Raising the cluster causes the character to smile and lowering the cluster causes it to frown. Cluster animation can be a useful alternative to morphing, because moving vertex selection sets is often a more intuitive concept than interpolating between morph targets.

You can animate the XForm Gizmo that contains the selected vertices, but a cleaner approach involves linking that Gizmo to another object, typically a Dummy, by using the Linked XForm modifier. That way, you can transform the XForm Gizmo (and therefore the cluster) by transforming the object. A short exercise will be enough to get you started.

Cluster Animation Using an HSDS Modifier

In the following exercise, you will make a simple mouth and animate the corners of the lips with the XForm modifier:

1. Create a Box object in the Front viewport to serve as the mouth. It should be short and wide, and divided into three segments across. Use Figure 19.19 as a guide.

2. Collapse the Box to an editable mesh. Put a Mesh Select modifier on the stack and use it to select all the vertices at the right and left ends of the object. The panel indicates that eight vertices have been selected.

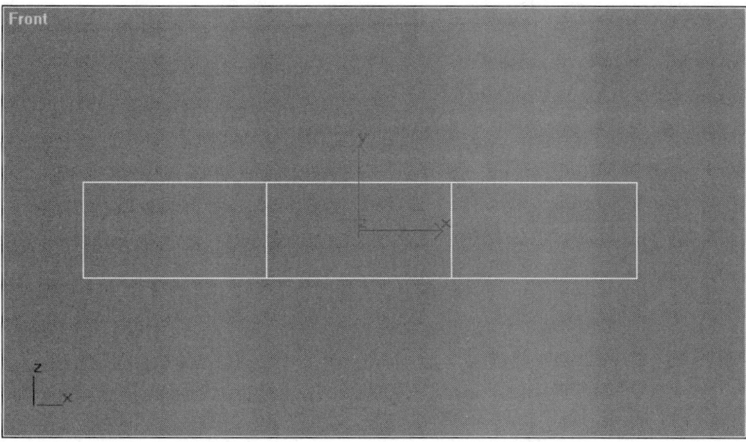

Figure 19.19
A Box object in the Front viewport to serve as an animated mouth.

3. Add an XForm modifier on top of the Mesh Select. The XForm will be passed only the selected vertices, which are now under the control of the XForm Gizmo. Move the XForm Gizmo upward to raise the cluster. Your Front viewport should look like Figure 19.20.

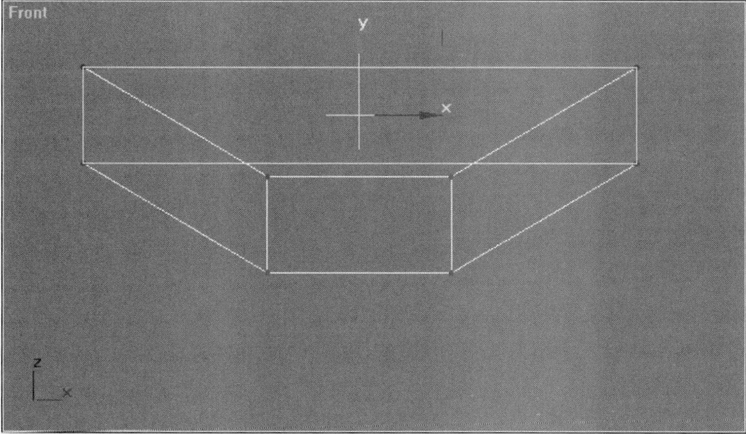

Figure 19.20
The vertices at the ends of the mouth are selected in a Mesh Select modifier and then passed to an XForm modifier. Moving the XForm Gizmo moves the cluster.

4. This doesn't look much like a mouth, so give it some organic subdivision. Place a Hierarchical SubDivision Surfaces (HSDS) modifier at the top of the stack. Similar to the MeshSmooth modifier, the new HSDS modifier adds definition and curvature to a surface by increasing the polygon count in selected areas. Go to the Vertex subobject level, select all the vertices in the mouth, and click on the Subdivide button. Select all the vertices again and subdivide the

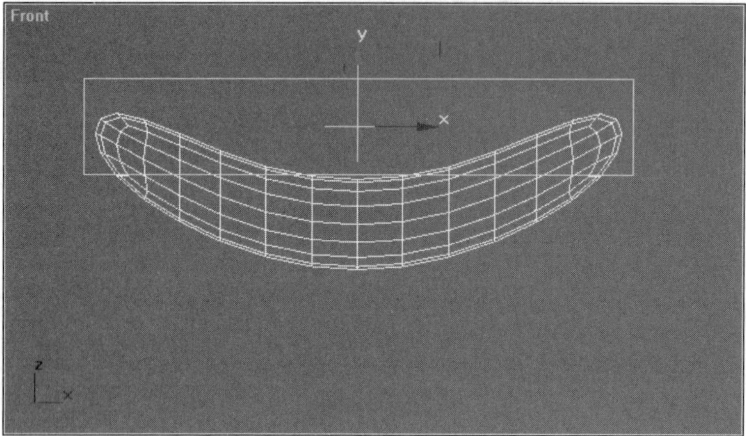

Figure 19.21
The same as Figure 19.20, but with an HSDS modifier applied above the XForm.

surfaces a second time. The Level Of Detail spinner should read 2, and your mouth should now look like Figure 19.21. Go back to the XForm modifier and move it up and down to test the result. You can always increase the Level Of Detail value in HSDS or apply it to only a portion of the vertices to achieve a smoother end product and the result you desire.

Using a Finished Mesh

To get a smooth result, you used XForm on a cage and applied HSDS at the top of the stack. What happens if you start with a finished mesh? Let's continue our exercise to find out:

1. Delete the Mesh Select and XForm modifiers from the stack. Subdivide all the vertices in the object once more and collapse that modifier into the editable mesh. This results in a dense editable mesh object without any modifiers in its stack.

2. Put a Mesh Select modifier on the stack and use it to select only the single vertices at the very ends of the mouth. You have to zoom in a bit to get them. The panel should indicate that only two vertices are selected.

3. Go to the Soft Selection rollout at the bottom of the Mesh Select panel and select the Use Soft Selection checkbox. You'll see a gradient of colored vertices that extend inward from the selected ones. You are creating, in effect, a "soft cluster."

4. Place an XForm modifier on the stack and move its Gizmo up to create a smile. You may not be happy with the shape of the mouth right now, so go back down to the Mesh Select modifier and make sure that you can see all the way up the stack (use the Show End Result On/Off Toggle button in the toolbar above the rollouts in the Modify panel). Adjust the spinners in the Soft Selection rollout to get a pleasing result, as shown in Figure 19.22. You have a remarkable amount of flexibility, especially when you consider that the Soft Selection parameters can be animated to produce subtle changes in expression.

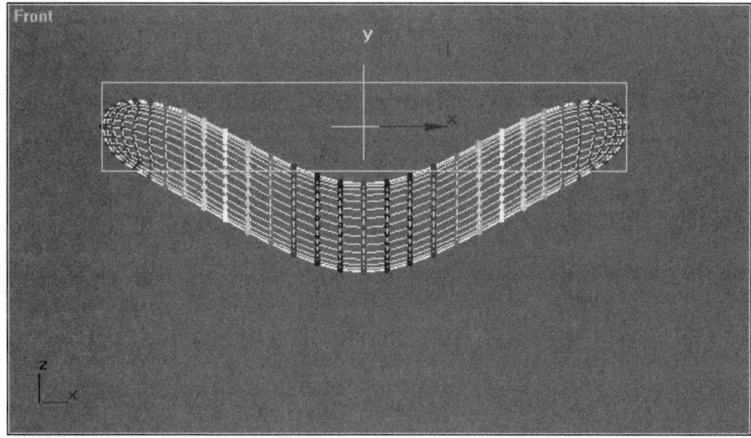

Figure 19.22
A high-density finished mesh is deformed smoothly by using a Soft Selection, which passes selection set information to an XForm modifier. This process produces a kind of "soft cluster."

Animating the Cluster with Linked XForm

Now that you can deform the mouth, you can animate the deformations by keyframing the XForm Gizmo in different positions. Grabbing the Gizmo means having to enter the modifier stack of the object. In a full character, it generally makes more sense to link the Gizmo to a Dummy object using Linked XForm. Finish the exercise by creating this kind of setup:

1. Create a Dummy object some distance above the mouth. This will be the controller that "pulls the strings" of the selected cluster. Check from different views to make sure the Dummy is in the same vertical plane as the mouth and is above the very center of that object. Use the Align tool if necessary.

2. Cut the XForm modifier from the stack of the mouth object and replace it with a Linked XForm modifier. Click on the Pick Control Object button and then click on the Dummy.

3. Select the Dummy and move it up and down to move the cluster. Your screen should look like Figure 19.23 when it's been moved down to create a frown.

4. Turn on the Animate button and try setting some keyframes by moving the Dummy. After you do, you can adjust the timing by moving the keys in the Track Bar. On a real model, you could name the Dummy *mouth cluster* and edit its function curves in Track View.

Other Deformation Tools

Skeletal deformation, morphing, and cluster animation are, by far, the most important tools in character animation. But the character animator must also be aware of some other tools for animating deformations that MAX offers.

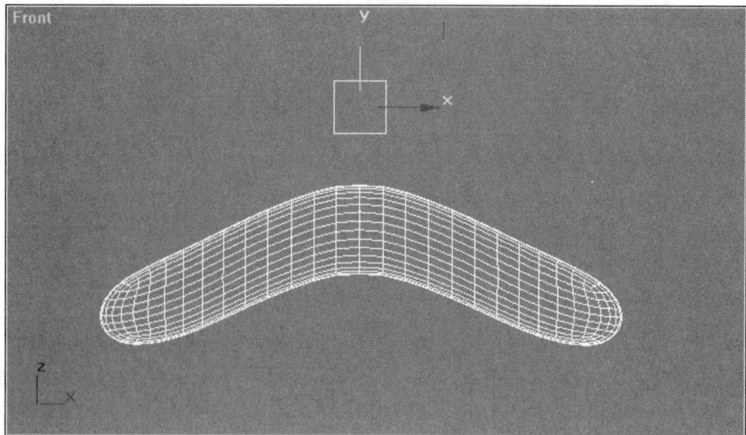

Figure 19.23
A Dummy object positioned above the mouth is used to control the cluster by way of a Linked XForm modifier.

Path and Surface Deformation

Path and surface deformation are often the only ways to get the result you want in 3D animation. *Path deformation* deforms an object along a spline path (either Bezier splines or NURBS curves). The object assumes the shape of the path as it moves along it; thus, a long cylinder will slither like a snake if animated along a wavy deformation path. *Surface deformation* conforms the shape of an object to a surface. The classic example is a tear dripping down a cheek, but the possibilities are endless. Some fantastic results are possible with surface deformation when the deforming surface is hidden and therefore invisible in the final render.

In MAX, path deformation is handled through two PathDeform modifiers. Surface deformation is divided between the SurfDeform modifiers and the PatchDeform modifiers. The SurfDeform modifiers are used when the deforming surface is a NURBS surface, and the PatchDeform versions are used when the deforming surface is a Bezier patch. All three types of modifiers come in two "flavors": Object Space modifier and World Space modifier (WSM). Without getting into the confusing details, it's enough to say that the World Space versions are superior for most applications because they bring the deformed object to the deforming object, rather than vice versa.

Figure 19.24 illustrates the use of PathDeform. A NURBS curve was drawn as a path (although it could be a Bezier spline). An extruded text object was given a PathDeform(WSM) modifier and then put to the path. It's necessary both to select the path and to instruct the object to move to that path. Once on the path, you need to select the correct Local axis of the deformed object and rotate the object around that axis, as necessary. You can then move the object along the path (as a percentage distance) and set keyframes to animate this movement. The image shows a small amount of stretch applied to the deformation.

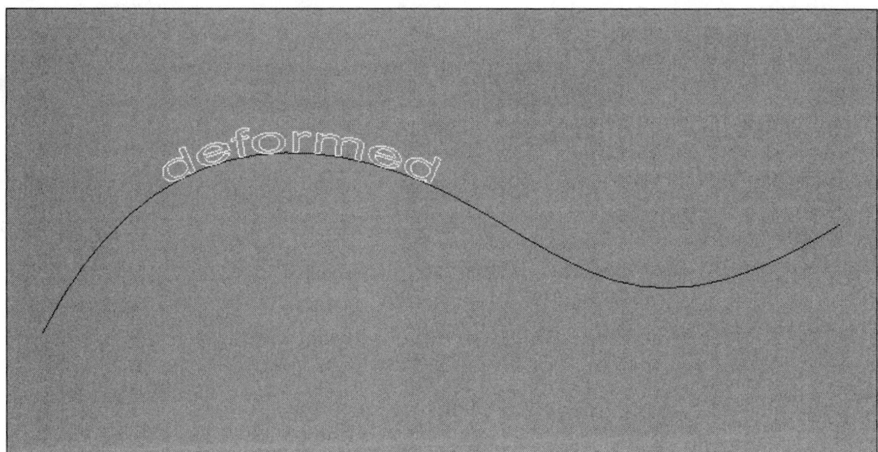

Figure 19.24
An extruded text object with a PathDeform(WSM) modifier applied. The object is positioned midway along the path, and a small amount of stretch has been applied.

Figure 19.25
The extruded text object is deformed by a NURBS sphere using the SurfDeform(WSM) modifier. The object has been moved a bit off the surface for greater impact.

Figure 19.25 illustrates surface deformation using the SurfDeform(WSM) modifier. The text object is deformed by a NURBS sphere. The parameters and methods are essentially the same as those of the PathDeform modifier, except that they are applied in two dimensions instead of one. Moving the deformed object moves it away from (or closer to) the surface.

Flex

The Flex modifier adds elasticity to objects. It's very easy to use. Once a Flex modifier is added to the stack, an animated object deforms in a flexible, springlike way. The object stretches as if resisting the motion and then swings back into position after the motion stops. Three parameters—Flex, Strength, and Sway—control the character of the effect, essentially controlling the elasticity of the object.

The axis of the flex is determined by the position of the subobject center. This point remains rigid and follows the underlying motion exactly. Color-coded vertices, similar to those found in the Skin modifier or the Soft Selection tools, indicate the flexibility gradient across the object. The weighting of these vertices can be edited to get precise results. You can also apply space warps, such as gravity and wind, to a Flex modifier, causing it to behave elastically under these forces.

This short exercise should familiarize you with the powerful Flex modifier:

1. Open the file Chap19 Flex.max from the CD-ROM. It consists of the Uhg head as a Scatter compound object, as created in Chapter 8. A number of hairs have been added for this exercise.

2. Apply a Flex modifier to the top of the stack.

3. Pan the Left viewport so that the head is to the far left side. Move the Time Slider to Frame 50 and turn on the Animate button. Move the object to the right side of the viewport and turn off the Animate button.

4. It may be difficult to see the effect of the Flex modifier in a static viewport, and viewing it in motion may task your system beyond its video capabilities. Render the Left viewport for the entire active time segment and view the AVI file. An initial drag occurs, and then a bounce at the far end of the animation.

5. Increase the Flex value to 5 and rerender the animation. This time, more flexing takes place, but it is applied to the entire head, giving an unrealistic look. This result may be appropriate for a more comical look, but not for what you are trying to achieve here.

6. The Flex modifier allows its impact to apply only to certain parts of a model. Those parts to be impacted the most are determined by vertex painting, similar to the method used to determine the influence of Bones on a mesh. Expand the Flex modifier and go to the Weights & Springs subobject level. Click on the Paint button in the Weights And Painting rollout. Change the Strength value to 1, Radius to 5, and Feather to 0. "Paint" across the hair to turn the vertices blue. Blue vertices are the most flexible.

7. Rerender the scene. This time, only the hair flexes noticeably.

From the CD-ROM, open the Chap 19 flex.avi file to see a wireframe rendering of the scene. This file shows the final result of using the Flex modifier, as discussed in this section.

Moving On

In this chapter, you learned about the tools used to deform geometry, primarily for the purposes of organic character animation. You explored the process of skeletal deformation with the Skin modifier, learning how envelopes are used to control vertex weighting. You then examined target morphing with the Morpher modifier. You moved on to learn about how the cluster animation of vertices is achieved with the XForm and Linked XForm modifiers. Finally, you looked briefly at the path and surface deformation and the Flex modifier.

The next chapter explores some specialized animation toolsets found in MAX. These include space warps for deforming geometry and expressions for controlling animation. Also discussed are the implementation of particle systems and the creation of dynamics simulations to achieve animation results based on an object's physical properties.

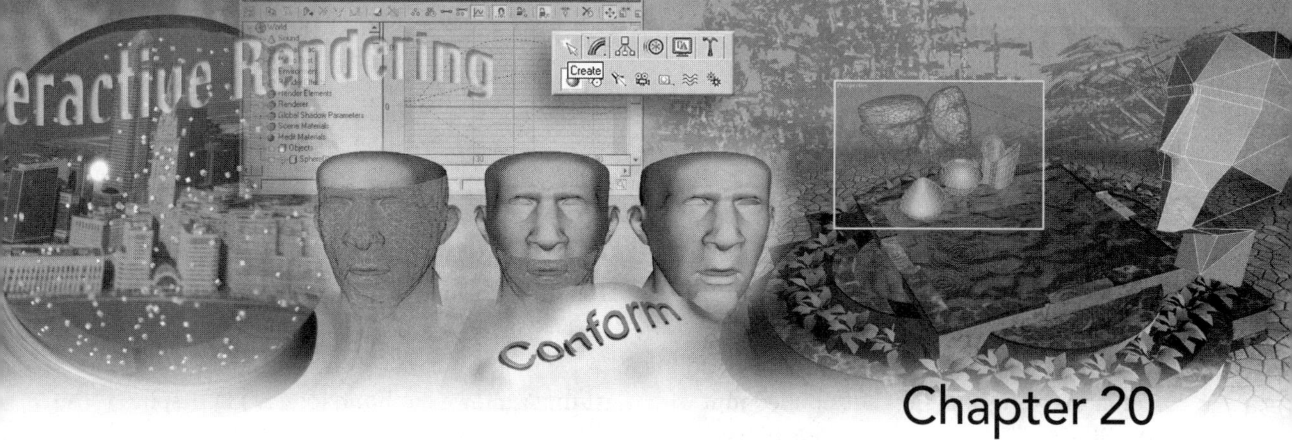

Chapter 20

Special Animation Topics

This chapter touches on some special animation tools that every MAX animator must understand in at least a basic way. *Space warps* are like modifiers that operate in World space, rather than in the Local space of individual objects. Thus, objects with binding to space warps change shape as they move through space. Space warps also provide the motive forces for dynamic simulations, which are animations that are computed by applying physical principles to objects and forces.

Particle systems are used to manage the animation of large numbers of objects that share a common behavior or that are meant to be perceived as fluids. Falling snow and water fountains are characteristic uses of particle systems.

Expressions are simple units of programming code used in expression controllers to precisely define animated movement. They are often used to create interdependent systems in which the animation of one object automatically controls the animation of other objects. Expressions are the basis of the wiring tools discussed in Chapter 5.

Space Warps

It's hard to characterize space warps, because a number of related but distinct ideas are clustered under this title. The term *space warps* implies the curved space of relativistic physics. Albert Einstein introduced the notion that the motion of objects in the universe could be better understood as expressing a curvature of the space in which they moved. This is undoubtedly a very subtle idea that is comfortable only for physicists and mathematicians, but it takes on practical meaning in MAX.

Visualize MAX's World space system as a 3D network of points connected by lines. In a pure Cartesian system (such as the default World space), all the points are at equal distances from their neighbors, and the lines connecting them are rectilinear. Now, imagine this network of points and connecting lines being subjected to heat so that it begins to melt and sag. The points are no longer at equal intervals (measured in the conventional way), and the network of connecting lines is no longer strictly rectilinear. (A similar idea can be visualized in 2D by comparing a fishing net that's pulled taut with a net that's allowed to hang loosely.) If, despite the distortion, the points continue to be used for measurement of other objects, the objects subject to such "measurement" will appear deformed in comparison to those defined by the metric of a purely rectilinear space.

Space warps in MAX are created and then bound to specific objects. If you create a space warp and fail to bind it to any objects, it will have no effect. If you bind it to some objects and not others, only those that are bound will show the effects of the space warp. Thus, unlike Einstein's space warps, which affect all matter and energy, MAX's space warps are selective.

Space warps can be used for modeling purposes, but they play a much more significant role in animation. In some cases, the space warp provides the "force" that generates or shapes a motion path. In others, a space warp is used to deform an object as it moves through the deformed space generated by the space warp. Space warps are not tools that all artists pick up readily, nor are their creative applications always obvious. But the MAX practitioner must have a good basic grasp of their organization and potential.

Two Classes of Space Warps

To best understand the organization of the space warps, take a look at the drop-down list in Create|Space Warps from the Command panel shown in Figure 20.1.

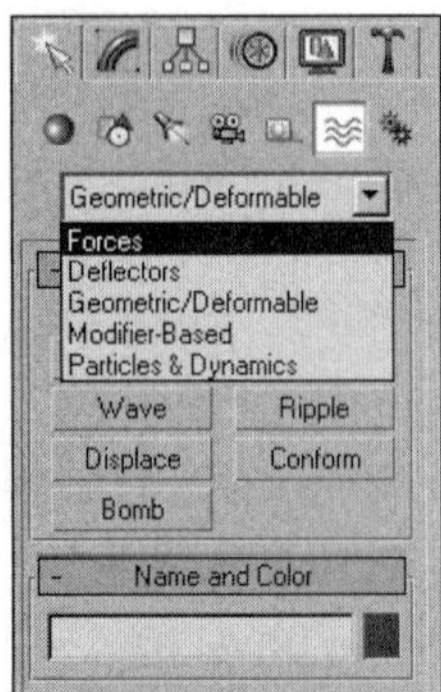

Figure 20.1
The drop-down list of space warps under the Create tab of the Command panel.

The space warps can be generally divided into two classes. The first class can be used to deform the geometry of standard objects as these are moved though the deformed space. These kinds of space warps are included under the Geometric/Deformable and Modifier-Based headings:

- Geometric/Deformable
  - FFD(Box)
  - FFD(Cyl)
  - Wave
  - Ripple
  - Displace
  - Conform
  - Bomb
- Modifier-Based
  - Bend
  - Noise
  - Skew
  - Taper
  - Twist
  - Stretch

The names of all these space warps may already be familiar to you from other parts of MAX. There is a Conform compound object, and all the other names (except Bomb) are those of modifiers. Only the Bomb is completely unique to space warps. Thus, in almost every case, these space warps are World space deformation versions of other tools that operate only in the Local space of the model.

The space warps in the first class apply to objects that are not necessarily animated. Of course, they almost certainly are animated, but the space warp does not depend on existing animation. The space warps in the second class apply to certain objects that are necessarily animated, and the purpose of the space warp is to influence or control their motion paths. These objects are either particle systems or objects that are included in a dynamic simulation. In the case of dynamic simulations, space warps provide the forces (such as gravity) that drive the simulation. Dynamic simulations can be created using any kinds of objects. Particle systems are inherently animated by the action of their particle emitters, and space warps are used to shape the path of the animated particles. Thus, the second class of space warps includes those that can be used on either particle systems or dynamic simulations:

- Forces
  - Motor
  - Push
  - Vortex
  - Drag
  - Path Follow
  - Pbomb
  - Displace
  - Gravity
  - Wind
- Deflectors
  - PDynaFlect
  - POmniFlect
  - SDynaFlect
  - SOmniFlect
  - UDynaflect
  - UOmniFlect
  - SDeflector
  - UDeflector
  - Deflector
- Particles & Dynamics
  - Vector Field (if you've installed Character Studio 3 or the trial version from the 3ds max 4 installation CD-ROM)

The second class of space warps will be considered later in this chapter, in the context of dynamics and particle systems. For the present, let's look at the space warps of the first class.

Space Warps for Geometric Deformation

The grouping of the space warps in the first class under two headings is not especially helpful. All the options in the Modifier-Based group are space warp (World space) versions of regular modifiers, but the same is true of almost all the space warps in the Geometric/Deformable group. In any case, all of them deform object geometry as it moves through the deformed space created by the space warp.

An Example

Let's try a simple example that demonstrates the difference between modifiers and space warps, as follows:

1. Create a tall, thin Box object near the origin, and give it enough segmentation so that it is capable of bending smoothly. Drag a copy of the Box a little way to either side. Place a Bend modifier on one of the two Boxes and give the object a noticeable bend.
2. Create a Bend space warp on the groundplane, about the same size as the Box (choose Create|Space Warps|Modifier-Based in the Command panel). Bend the space warp and note that it has no effect on either object. A Front viewport should look something like Figure 20.2.

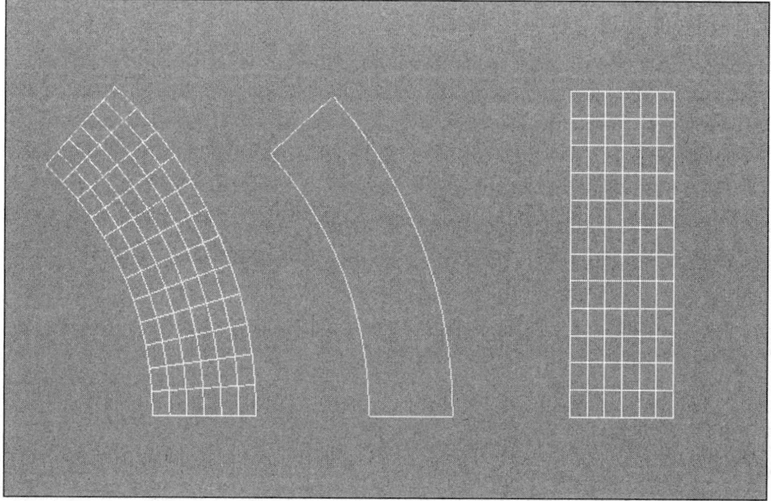

Figure 20.2
Setting up for a space warp. At left, a segmented Box object with the Bend modifier applied. At right, a copy of the same Box without any modifier. At center, a Bend space warp that has not yet been bound to an object.

3. To give the space warp effect, you must bind it to the object. Click on the Bind To Space Warp button on the Main toolbar to activate it. Now, click on the unmodified Box and drag it to the space warp. When you release the button, the Space Warp Gizmo should briefly light up, indicating that the binding has occurred. A second later, the Box will

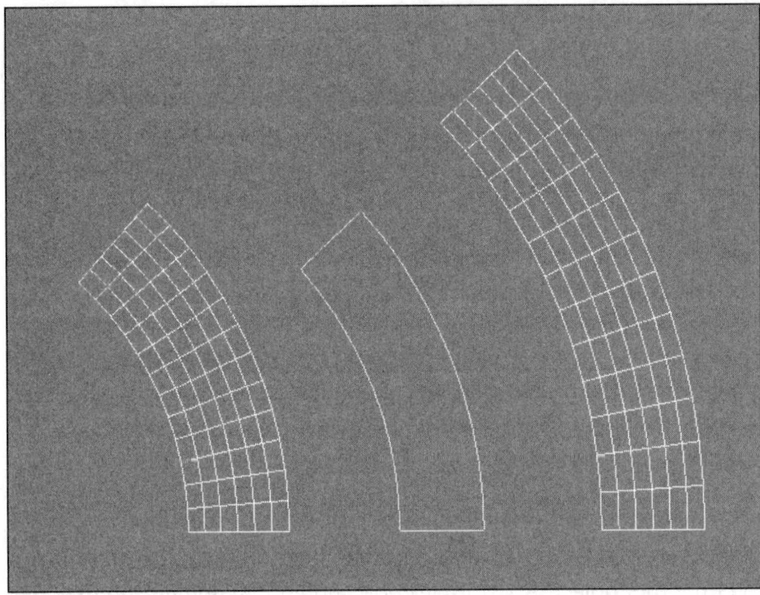

Figure 20.3
After binding the space warp to the Box on the right, that object assumes the bend of the Space Warp Gizmo. Note that this bend is a projection of the bend in the gizmo.

assume the bend. Check the Stack View for this Box to confirm that a Bend Binding is placed on the stack. Your screen should now look like Figure 20.3.

4. Click on the Select Object button on the Main toolbar to get out of the Binding mode (this step is easy to forget). Move the two Boxes in different directions, leaving the Space Warp Gizmo in place, and notice the difference between the modifier bend and the space warp bend. The modifier bend is local to the object and moves with it. Moving the object doesn't change the bend. This is a reflection of a basic fact about MAX—that transforms are applied after the object is output from the modifier stack. In contrast, the space warp version changes shape as you move it. It's as if the Space Warp Gizmo is being used to deform the entire World space for any object bound to it. Your screen should look something like Figure 20.4. For this system to work, space warps must be applied after objects' transforms. Open Track View and expand the tracks to see that a Space Warps track appears above the Transform track for the affected box.

5. Using the Animate button, cause the space-warped Box to move between Frames 0 and 100. Note the effect of the space warp on the animated object. When you're done, delete the Bend Binding from the modifier stack. The Box is no longer deformed by the space warp.

Some Useful Space Warps

The Wave and Ripple space warps have modifier versions; they often make more sense as space warps in animation, however, because you move the object through the space warp

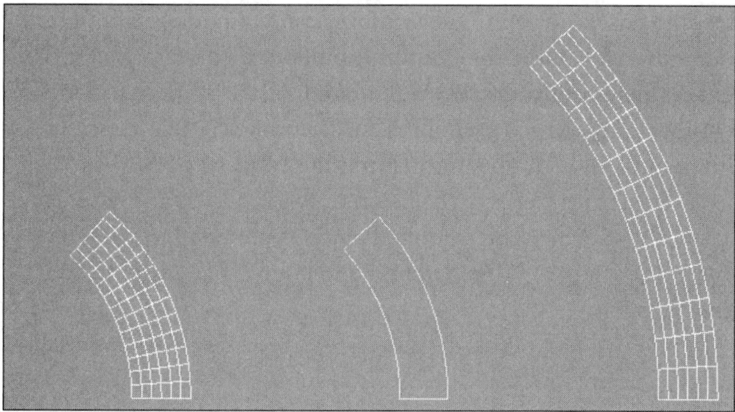

Figure 20.4
Moving the Box on the left with the Bend modifier does not affect its shape, because transforms are applied after modifiers. In contrast, moving the Box with the space warp binding changes its shape, because space warps are applied after object transforms. The position of the Box in the deformed space determines its shape.

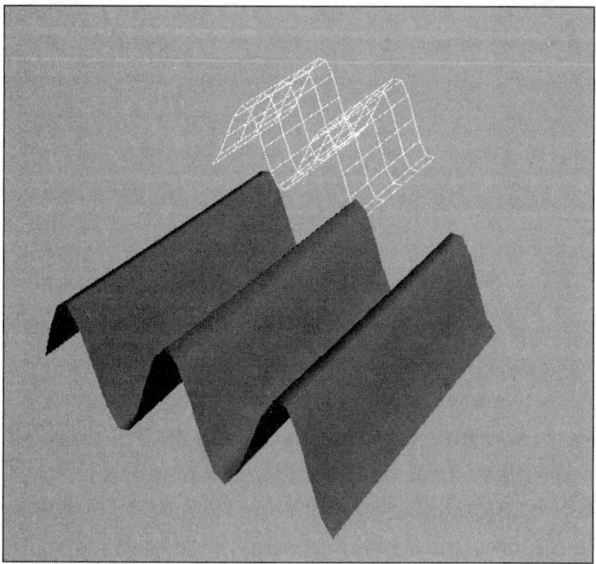

Figure 20.5
A Wave space warp is used to deform a polygonal grid. The pattern established by the Space Warp Gizmo extrapolates out into World space in all directions, invisibly repeating the same deformation pattern.

rather than the modifier gizmo through the object. Figure 20.5 shows a Wave space warp bound to a polygonal grid. Note that the pattern established by the Space Warp Gizmo extrapolates out into World space in all directions, invisibly repeating the same pattern. The gizmo shows only two wave crests, but the longer grid contains three. This is a great illustration of the way space warps deform all of World space.

The Conform space warp shares the basic concept of the Conform compound object in that it "shrink-wraps" one surface to another. Although the Conform compound object is used primarily to create morph target models, the Conform space warp is best used to animate surfaces to follow other surfaces. This technique may remind you of the SurfDeform(WSM) discussed in Chapter 19, but important differences exist. For one, the deforming surface need not be a Non-Uniform Rational B-Splines (NURBS) surface. Second, the deformation in the Conform space warp uses a kind of "gravity" concept, in which the deformed object is projected in a linear direction on the deforming object. In Figure 20.6, a polygonal grid bound to a Conform space warp is projected onto a Cylinder object.

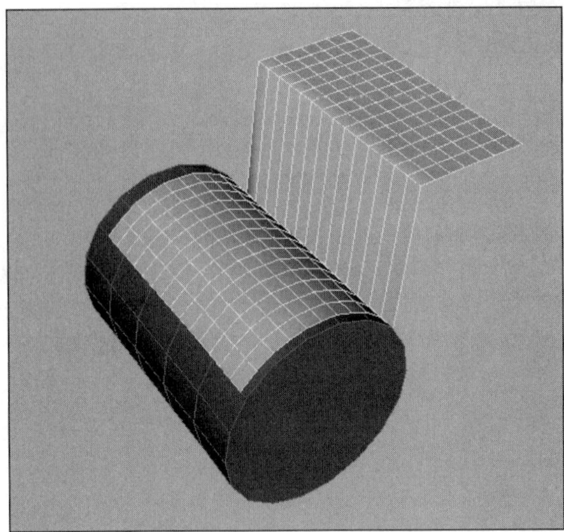

Figure 20.6
A polygonal grid, bound to a Conform space warp, is projected onto a Cylinder object.

The Bomb space warp is unlike any of the others in that it has no parallel modifier or compound object elsewhere in the program. It also differs because it creates its own animation, somewhat analogous to the explosion in a Fire Effect render effect. In any case, the explosion involves breaking the object into its individual faces and scattering them. The minimum and maximum number of faces in each fragment can be set with spinners. Note that the Bomb is called the MeshBomb in its Modify panel, presumably to distinguish it from the PBomb for particle systems.

The location of the Bomb Gizmo determines the center of the explosion. Figure 20.7 illustrates an exploding Sphere with the gizmo placed in the center of the object. Small Spin and Chaos values in the Bomb Parameters rollout give the result a more random look that helps disguise the obvious regularity of the fragment sizes. The detonation can be set to occur at any desired frame. The Gravity parameter causes the fragments to settle down to earth.

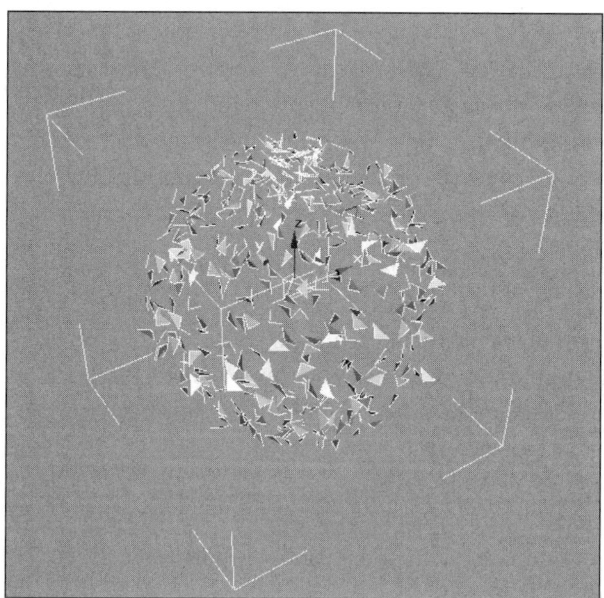

Figure 20.7
A Sphere is exploded by a Bomb space warp placed in the center of the object. Small Spin and Chaos values in the parameters create a more random look that helps to disguise the regularity of the fragments.

Dynamic Simulations

A *dynamic simulation* is an animation created entirely by the application. The user provides all the necessary physical information about the objects and the forces acting on them, and the computer figures out the consequences. The results are function curves that can be used as is or edited.

Dynamic simulations tend to be useful in three instances:

- In scientific, commercial, and forensic visualizations in which the user relies on the physical accuracy of the animation
- In entertainment contexts in which a realistic behavior of an object might be hard to imagine
- In any case in which multiple objects interact with each other (such as balls on a billiard table)

Dynamic simulations in MAX always involve space warps, because space warps are used to provide the motive forces. The Gravity space warp applies a constant acceleration in a specified direction. The Wind space warp is similar to Gravity, but it introduces an element of turbulence. The Push space warp creates a directional force at a specified point. The Motor space warp applies a rotating force to the objects in the dynamic simulation.

A Basic Simulation

Dynamic simulations can be very complex and can consume extraordinary amounts of processing power. MAX also provides extremely sophisticated tools for specifying the physical parameters of the objects involved in the simulation. In this book, you'll be introduced to the toolset, but any serious use of the full power of dynamic simulations requires considerable experimentation and a firm grounding in physical principles.

A dynamic simulation consists of objects and forces. The objects can be either standard geometric objects or particles systems. Although this chapter sticks to standard geometric objects, note that the DynaFlect series of space warps allows particle streams to "push" an object in a dynamic simulation. To create a dynamic simulation, you must determine which objects in the scene are included in a given simulation and assign forces (called *effects*) to these objects. You must also determine the physical properties of the objects.

The following exercise gets you started:

1. Create a small Sphere object on the groundplane. Pan your Front viewport vertically so you have room to watch the object fall downward.
2. In the Top viewport, create a Gravity space warp (choose Create|Space Warps|Forces). It doesn't matter where you create it as long as you do so in the Top viewport. Check the other viewports to confirm that the arrow in the Gravity space warp icon is pointing down (in the World Z-direction).
3. To create the simulation, go to the Utilities tab in the Command panel and click on the Dynamics button. This utility panel consists of two rollouts: Dynamics and Timing & Simulation. Because no current simulation exists, almost all of the controls are grayed out. Click on the New button to create a simulation with the default title Dynamics00.
4. To put objects into the simulation, click on the Edit Object List button. The Edit Object List dialog box appears, as shown in Figure 20.8. The left window contains all the objects that are available for inclusion in the simulation. Select Sphere01 in the left window and use the right arrow key to move it to the right window. The object is now included in the simulation. Click on the OK button to accept the setting and close the dialog box.
5. To assign the space warp as an effect in the simulation, click on the Edit Object button to bring up the Edit Object dialog box. As you can see in Figure 20.9, this is a complex panel. The Sphere01 object is specified in the OBJECT drop-down list in the upper-left corner. If more objects were in the simulation, they could be chosen from the drop-down list. Note that the density of the object is assigned a value of 1g/cc (one gram per cubic centimeter), which necessarily determines the object's mass in grams. Because the acceleration of objects under gravity is independent of mass, the mass or density of the object does not matter in this simple simulation. (Think of the story of Galileo dropping balls from the Leaning Tower of Pisa, when balls of different masses fell at the same rate.)

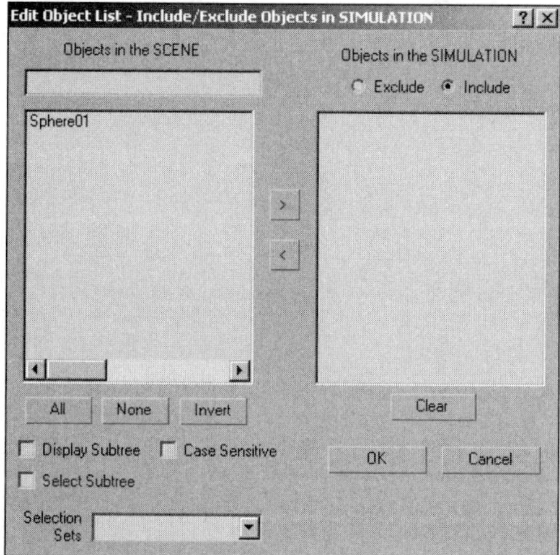

Figure 20.8
The Edit Object List dialog box. In the left window are all the objects available for inclusion in the simulation. Moving the Sphere01 object to the right window causes it to be included in the simulation.

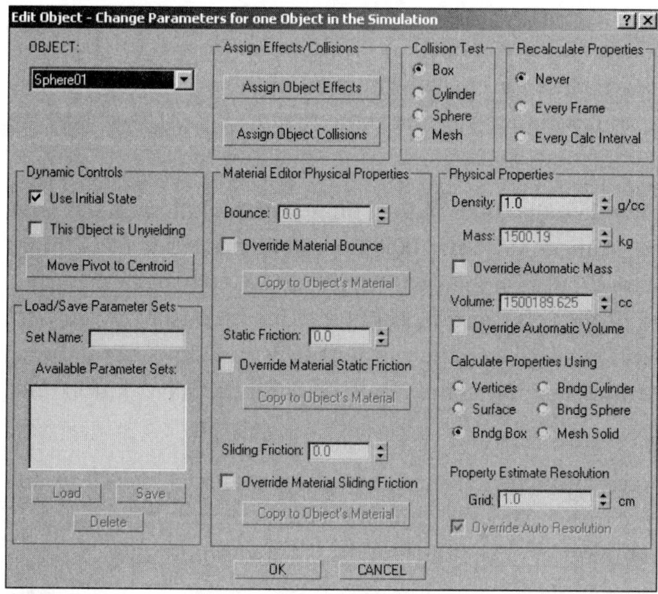

Figure 20.9
The Edit Object dialog box, showing the parameters for Sphere01. The density of the object is assigned a default value of 1.0 gram per cubic centimeter, which produces a mass in grams, based on the volume of the Sphere. The mass or density is irrelevant to the acceleration of an object falling due to gravity.

6. You can assign effects globally to all objects in a simulation, or you can assign effects individually to objects. Note that Effects By Object is the default in the Effects section of the Dynamics rollout. Click on the Assign Object Effects button at the top of the Edit Object

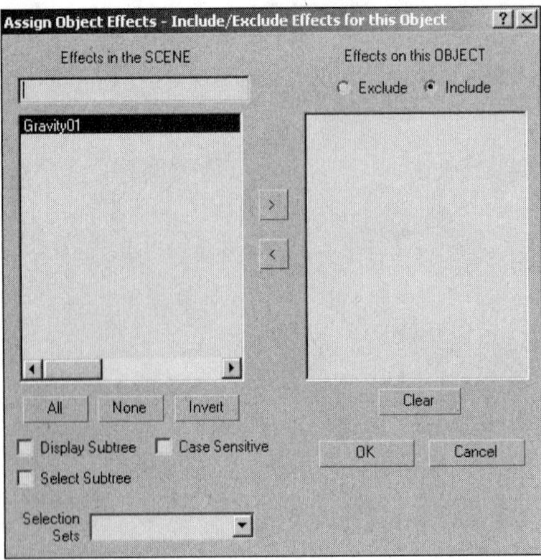

Figure 20.10
The Assign Object Effects dialog box for the Sphere object in the simulation. All available effects (the space warps) are listed in the left window. Moving the Gravity effect to the right window causes it to be applied to the Sphere in the simulation.

dialog box. The Assign Object Effects dialog box appears, as shown in Figure 20.10. All available effects (the space warps) are listed in the left window. Use the right arrow button to move the Gravity effect to the right window. Close both the Assign Object Effects and the Edit Object dialog boxes.

7. To solve the simulation, consult the default values in the Timing & Simulation rollout. The simulation will be computed from Frame 0 to Frame 100. Keys will be created at every single frame. There will be no air resistance, because the Density spinner is at 0 percent. Return to the Dynamics rollout and look at the Solve section. Select the Update Display w/ Solve checkbox in order to see your solution develop in the viewport. This step slows down the process quite a bit and is useful only for simple simulations. Click on the Solve button and watch what happens.

8. The Sphere moves downward, accelerating as it goes. If the Sphere is selected, you'll see the Track Bar fill up with keys at every frame. Play the animation to see the result. You may have to zoom out for the entire animation to be visible in the Front viewport.

9. To figure out what happened, open Track View and expand all the Transform tracks for the Sphere object. Make the controller types visible by using the Filters dialog box. As you can see in Figure 20.11, the Position and Rotation tracks have been automatically assigned a Dynamics Position Controller and a Dynamics Rotation Controller. Each of these is the parent of two children. The first child controller contains the keys set by the simulation, using the controller types already in place (Bezier Position and TCB Rotation, if you have not changed the defaults). The second child contains the animation (if any) prior to solving

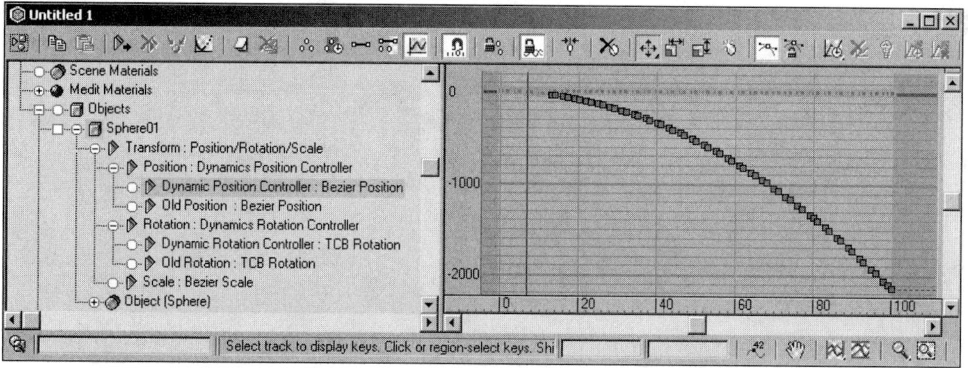

Figure 20.11
The position function curves generated by the simulation are *raw* curves with keys at every frame. The Z-function curve is bending downward at a constantly accelerating rate.

the simulation. Select the first child controller for Position and change to a Function Curves view. You see a pretty crowded picture, as shown in Figure 20.11. A function curve with keys on every frame is called a *raw function curve*, and it is the typical result of input from simulations or motion capture. Even so, you can see that the Z-function curve is bending downward at a constantly accelerating rate.

10. This function curve is editable, but editing it could be hard work because it has so many keys. One approach is to resolve the simulation with the Keys Every N Frames spinner, in the Timing & Simulation rollout, set to a higher value than 1. For example, at a value of 5, keys are created only at every fifth frame. Although this is fine for such a simple animation, a safer practice is to compute a solution with the maximum number of samples (one per frame) and then optimize the resulting function curve in Track View. To do this, enter the Edit Time mode in Track View and select the complete time segment by dragging across the position track with the 101 keys. With all frames from 0 to 100 selected, click on the Reduce Keys button on the right side of the Track View toolbar. The Reduce Keys dialog box appears. Accept the default Threshold value of 0.5 and click on OK. You'll see almost all the keys disappear. Switch to a Function Curves view to see the result. As shown in Figure 20.12, almost all the keys have been eliminated, but the shape of the curve is nearly unchanged. This is now a highly editable function curve.

11. The parent-child controller structure preserves any animation you had before solving the simulation. To restore the original animation, you copy and paste the Old Position and Old Rotation controllers. Your scene was unanimated, but let's use the same technique to restore the state of the scene prior to the simulation. In Track View, click on the Old Position controller to select it, and then click on the Copy Controller button on the left side of the Track View toolbar. Select the parent position controller and click on the Paste Controller button. Accept the default Copy option and note that you're back to your default Bezier Position controller. Do the same thing with the rotation controllers.

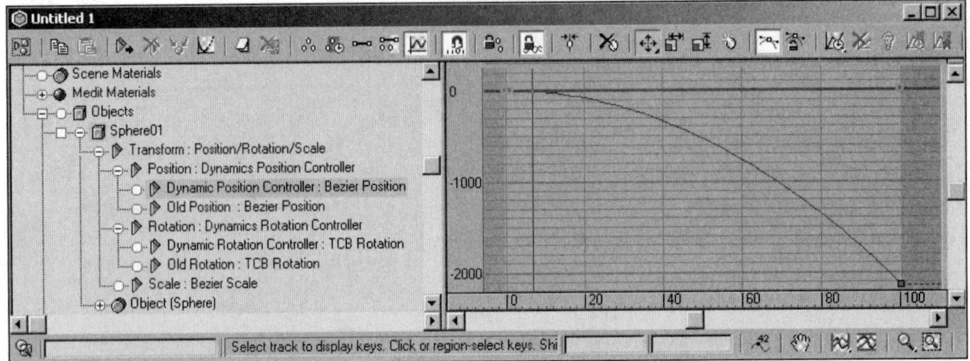

Figure 20.12
The raw function curve from Figure 20.11, after optimization by using the Reduce Keys tool. The shape of the curve is essentially unchanged, but it is now highly readable and editable.

Adding Collisions in Dynamic Simulations

The real power of dynamic simulations is in collisions; at this point, however, the subject becomes extremely complex. The following is a simple exercise to introduce you to the basic concepts and methods (this is a mere beginning to any serious exploration). In this example, a Sphere will fall under the influence of gravity and bounce when it collides with a Box. The Box, on the other hand, will remain fixed and rigid throughout the entire simulation. Follow these steps:

1. Reset the scene. Create a Sphere with a Radius value of 10 and position of 100 units above the origin, at (0,0,100) in World coordinates.

2. Create a thin Box object on the groundplane directly beneath the Sphere. Make it about 100 units in width and length, and only 1 or 2 units high. You may wonder why you are not creating a flat 2D surface, such as a plane object. The collision-detection tools do not produce reliable results with such surfaces, so it's advisable to stick with 3D objects in dynamic simulations.

3. Create a Gravity space warp in the Top viewport to create a downward force on the Sphere.

4. Everything is now in position. Open the Dynamics utility and create a new simulation. Open the Edit Object List dialog box and move both objects (the Box and the Sphere) into the simulation.

5. The next steps require a bit more thought. Open the Edit Object dialog box and select the Sphere from the OBJECT drop-down list, if it's not already selected. Click on the Assign Object Effects button and assign the Gravity effect to the Sphere. This effect causes it to fall, as it did in the previous exercise.

6. Click on the Assign Object Collisions button. You see the Assign Object Collisions dialog box, shown in Figure 20.13. Its purpose is to determine which objects should be tested for

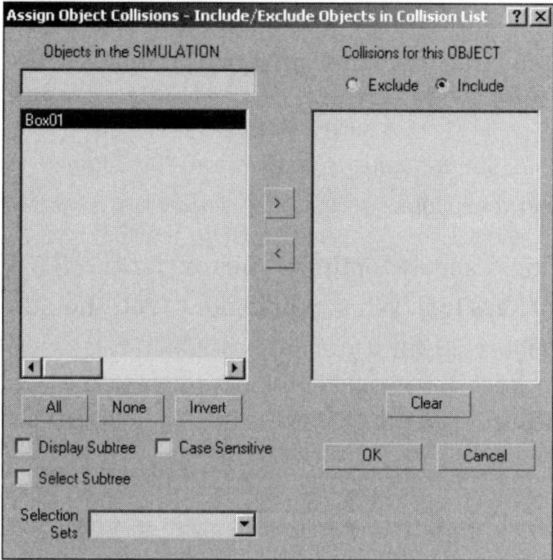

Figure 20.13
The Assign Object Collisions dialog box for the currently selected (Sphere) object. After the Box object is moved to the right window, the simulation tests for collisions between the Sphere and the Box.

collisions against the currently selected object. Move the Box object to the right window so that the Sphere recognizes collisions with the Box. Click on OK to close the Assign Object Collisions dialog box.

7. The Collision Test section of the Edit Object dialog box is very important. Collision testing between objects is extremely processor intensive. The Mesh option provides the most accurate test, but its computations can be unreasonably time consuming. Whenever possible, you should use a simplification of the geometry. Because your current object is already a Sphere, it makes sense to use a Sphere for collision testing. Choose the Sphere option in the Collision Test section.

8. Select the Box in the OBJECT drop-down list. The Box does not move and thus it is not assigned any effect. Moreover, the Box should remain rigid upon collision with the Sphere. In the Dynamic Controls section of the dialog box, select the This Object Is Unyielding checkbox. Note that most of the other parameters in the dialog box are now grayed out. The Collision Test section is still active, so make sure that the Box option is set there. It's unnecessary to add the Sphere to the Box's collision list. Click on OK to close the dialog box.

9. Click on the Solve button to compute the solution. The solution should compute quickly. Play the animation. The Sphere should bounce convincingly, except that it bounces back to the level where it started. It's as if no energy were being expended at the point of the bounce—a physically impossible occurrence.

10. To add some degradation to the bounce, open the Edit Object dialog box and make sure the Box is selected in the OBJECT drop-down list. In the Material Editor Physical Properties section, select the Override Material Bounce checkbox. Enter "0.8" in the Bounce field to

simulate 80 percent of the Sphere's energy being used to propel it upwards. Close the Edit Object dialog box and solve the simulation again. This time, the Sphere has a more realistic bounce: Its return height is lower with each cycle.

Note: *When a Material is assigned to a collision object, its Bounce value is passed from the Bounce Coefficient value in the Material Editor's Dynamics Properties rollout.*

11. Go into Track View and, as you did in the previous exercise, optimize the raw function curves in the position track by using the Reduce Keys tool. When you're done, you should have a nice clean function curve, as shown in Figure 20.14.

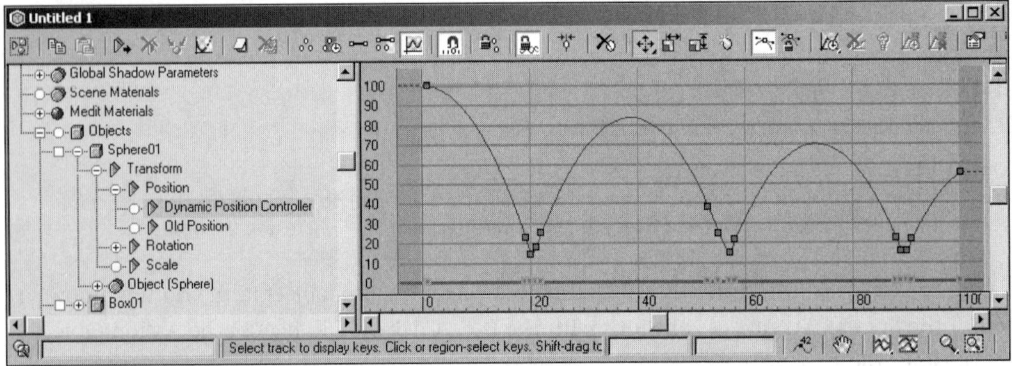

Figure 20.14
After applying the Reduce Keys tool in Track View, the function curve describes a nice, clean bounce.

Particle Systems

Water, fire, snow, and smoke are all examples of phenomena that are often best simulated by the coordinated animation of a large number of small particles. In all these cases (and many others), the individual particles respond to common forces and thus have many of the qualities of a single object. For example, a school of fish is composed of individual creatures, yet the school behaves largely as a single unit.

MAX particle systems are inherently animated. Particles are emitted from a source and flow in a regular path. More sophisticated control of particle behavior is possible through the use of space warps. Indeed, these phenomena are cases in which space warps make the most obvious sense, and a number of space warps are especially directed at the control of particle streams.

Choosing a Particle System

Six types of particle systems are available when you choose Create|Geometry|Particle Systems:

- Spray
- Snow
- Blizzard

- PArray
- PCloud
- Super Spray

Spray and Snow are two of the original MAX particle systems. Although they are part of 3ds max 4, they are rudimentary and their parameters are extremely limited. Although these particle systems are easy to use, Super Spray and Blizzard have effectively superseded them.

The other particle systems, however sophisticated, are not difficult to master, primarily because their members share most of the same parameters. You'll quickly notice that the panels for Blizzard, PArray, PCloud, and Super Spray differ only in their respective Basic Parameters and Particle Generation rollouts. The Particle Type, Rotation And Collision, Object Motion Inheritance, Bubble Motion (not available for Blizzard), Particle Spawn, and Load/Save Presets rollouts are identical for all four of these particle systems. Thus, most of the skills you obtain with respect to any of these particle systems can be applied to all of them.

These last four particle systems differ in the manner in which they emit particles, as we'll discuss in the following sections.

Super Spray

Super Spray is the classic particle emitter—something of a fountain. Particles are generated from a single point. Figure 20.15 shows the Super Spray icon emitting particles at default values. The stream is a single line of particles flowing in the direction of the axis indicated by the arrow.

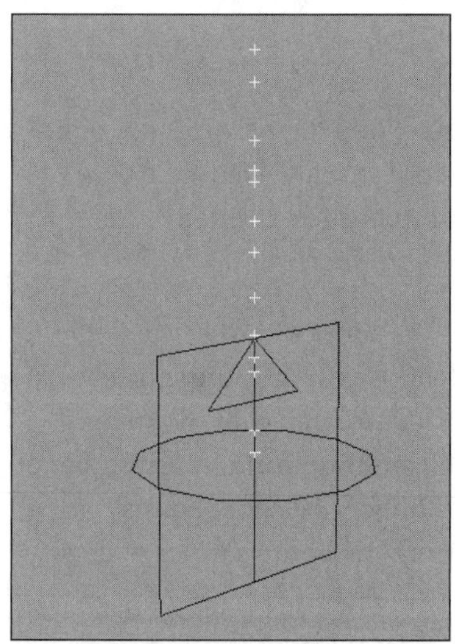

Figure 20.15
A Super Spray particle system, using default values. The stream is a single line of particles flowing in the direction of the axis indicated by the arrow.

Figure 20.16
The Super Spray emitter from Figure 20.15 is adjusted to spread out the particle stream into the standard particle fountain.

This spray can be fanned out along the indicated plane and on either side of the plane by altering the Spread values in the Basic Parameters rollout to produce the standard particle fountain. This result is illustrated in Figure 20.16. One example of the effects that can be achieved using the Super Spray particle system is shown in the smoke stack image in this book's color section.

Blizzard

The Blizzard particle emitter is simple—the emitter icon is a plane, and the particles are emitted randomly from the surface, in a direction perpendicular to that surface. This emitter is perfect for falling rain or snow. Figure 20.17 illustrates the Blizzard particle emitter.

PArray

The PArray (Particle Array) particle system emits particles from the surface of a selected object. The emitter object can be visible or hidden. The PArray is created (like all the other particle systems) by drawing out an icon. The size and location of the icon are irrelevant, however. After the PArray is created, you must pick an object to use as the emitting surface. A number of emission options are available, including emission from a set number of distinct points and emission from selected faces. Figure 20.18 illustrates emission from the entire surface of a selected Sphere. The PArray icon is visible on the left.

PCloud

The PCloud (Particle Cloud) particle system is a little confusing. It can be used much like the PArray system to emit particles from a volume, and it has the advantage of being able to create Box, Sphere, and cylindrical emitters as icon choices. The PCloud can also be used to confine particles

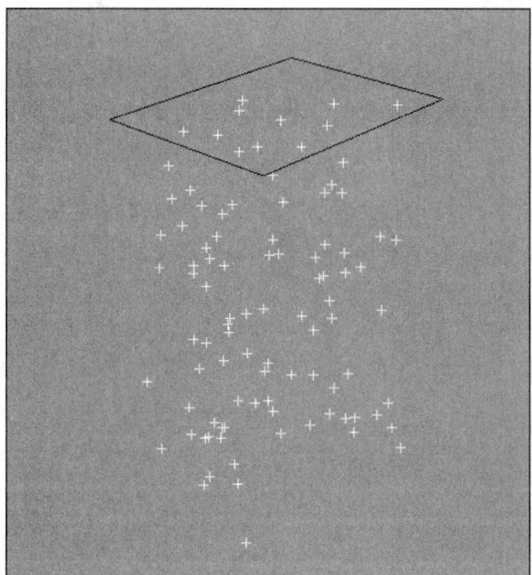

Figure 20.17
The Blizzard particle emitter releases particles randomly from a plane icon, in a direction perpendicular to the plane.

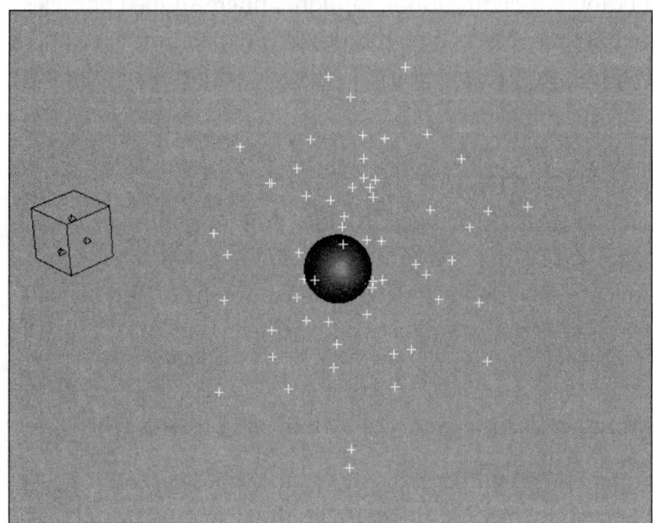

Figure 20.18
The PArray particle system is used to emit particles from the surface of a selected Sphere. The PArray icon is visible on the left.

randomly (typically, instanced objects) inside a volume. In this use, the particles are not animated, although the icon may be animated as a means of moving all the particles together as a group. In order to keep the particles confined to the volume, the Speed parameter in the Particle Generation rollout must be kept at 0. At values greater than 0, the PCloud emits the particles.

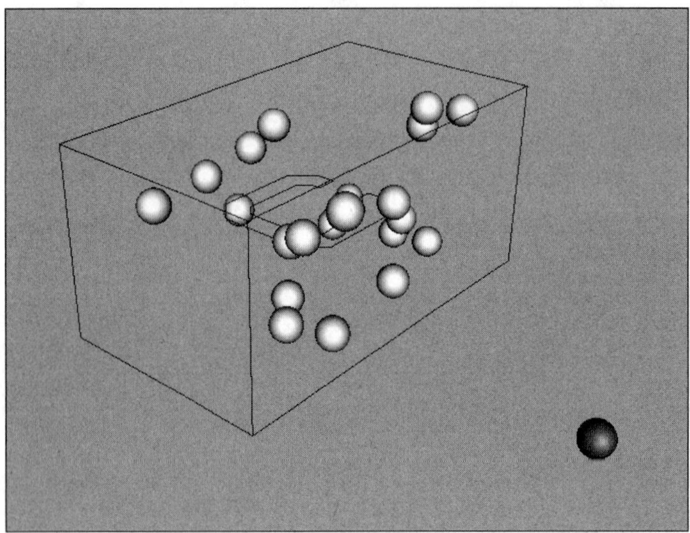

Figure 20.19
The PCloud is used to confine random Sphere-shaped particles inside a box-shaped volume.

Figure 20.19 illustrates a box-shaped PCloud, used to confine random Sphere-shaped particles (assigned in the Standard Particles area of the Particle Type rollout) inside a volume. The particles' sizes were greatly increased by raising the Size value in the Particle Size area of the Particle Generation rollout.

Particle Generation and Rendering

The Particle Generation rollouts for each of the particle systems differ only in minor ways. In the case of the latter four, parameters govern Particle Quantity, Particle Motion, Particle Timing, and Particle Size. After these factors are set, you must determine what type of particle will render. A short exercise using the Super Spray emitter will get you oriented.

Speed and Timing

First, get control over the speed and timing of particle emission by following these steps:

1. In the Top viewport, drag out a Super Spray emitter near the origin (choose Create|Geometry|Particle Systems|Super Spray). By default, the particles are displayed as ticks. Pull the Time Slider and watch the particle stream flow in a straight line. Note that new particles cease to be emitted after Frame 30.

2. Increase the two Spread parameters in the Basic Parameters rollout to 30 degrees. Pull the slider to see a fountain effect. By default, only 10 percent of the true (renderable) number of particles is made visible in the viewports. Increase this percentage, if you wish, in the Percentage Of Particles field of the Basic Parameters rollout.

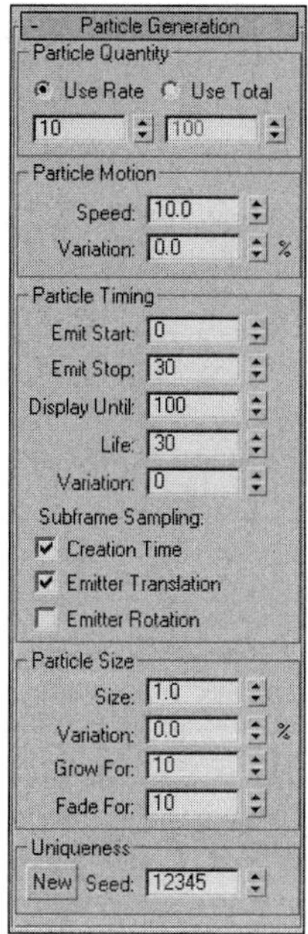

Figure 20.20
The Particle Generation rollout for the Super Spray emitter. The parameters are extremely similar to those found in Blizzard, PArray, and PCloud.

3. Open the Particle Generation rollout, shown in Figure 20.20. The default Use Rate option for Particle Quantity determines the rate of particle emission in particles per frame. By default, 10 new particles are emitted every second. Experiment with this spinner to get the idea, and then return to the default value.

4. The Particle Timing parameters inform you that particles are being emitted between Frames 0 and 30, and that each particle has a life of 30 frames. It follows that all particles should disappear after Frame 60. Pull the Time Slider to confirm this. Particle speed is measured in units per frame. Increase the Speed parameter in the Particle Motion section to 20 and pull the Time Slider. The particles travel twice the distance over their lives.

Rendering Particles

The particles that actually render can be Standard Particles, MetaParticles, or instances of selected geometry. You can try all three on your particle stream by continuing the exercise as follows:

1. Open the Particle Type rollout, shown in Figure 20.21. The default settings will render your particles as triangles, one of the Standard Particles options. Move your Time Slider to Frame 25 and adjust your Perspective viewport to get a good view of the particle stream. Before you render, set the background color to white in the Environment dialog box. Now, render. Depending on your view, the triangles may be very small. Go back to the Particle Generation rollout and increase the Size parameter in the Particle Size section. Render again to see the difference.

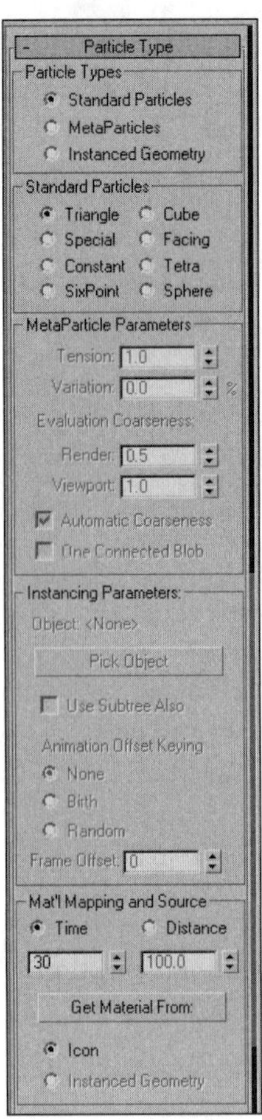

Figure 20.21
The Particle Type rollout for the Super Spray emitter. The default settings cause the particles to render as triangles.

2. In the Particle Type rollout, switch from the Triangle to the Facing option and render again. Notice that the particles are much denser. The Facing option creates squares that always face the camera. By texture mapping these particles and using an opacity map to create transparent edges, you can create convincing leaves and snowflakes.

3. Change your particle type to MetaParticles. MetaParticles are a species of the common metaball technology that merges adjacent objects into larger units to create organic and fluid forms. At its best, the MetaParticles type can produce excellent simulations of liquids and viscous fluids, but the process is extremely taxing on anything but the most powerful systems. The Tension parameter controls the tendency of particles to blend. Set it to a low value such as .1, and render. After a little while, and after an adjustment to the Size parameter as required, you get a result like Figure 20.22.

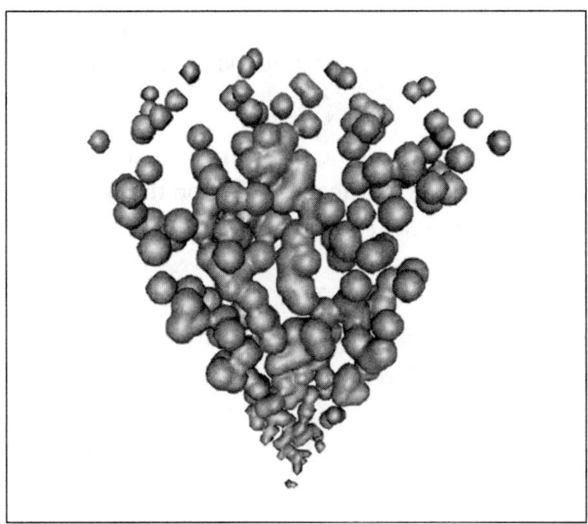

Figure 20.22
MetaParticles applied to a Super Spray particle stream. A Tension value of .1 was used to increase the blending of the particles.

4. Create a small Teapot object somewhere in your scene, to be instanced as particles. With the Super Spray object selected again, go to the Particle Type rollout in the Modify panel. Switch to the Instanced Geometry type. In the Instancing Parameters section, click on the Pick Object button to activate it. Select the Teapot in your viewport. Go back to the Particle Generation rollout and set the Size parameter to 1 if you changed it earlier. Now, render. You should see a fountain of Teapots, as illustrated in Figure 20.23.

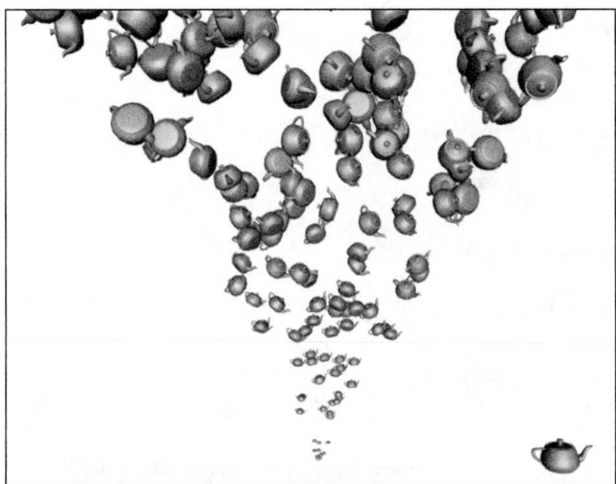

Figure 20.23
A small Teapot (seen apart at bottom right) is used as instanced geometry in the Super Spray particle system.

5. Go back to the Particle Size section of the Particle Generation rollout and set the Variation parameter to 50 percent. When you rerender, notice that the Teapots are now in varying sizes.

6. Assign a Material to the original Teapot. In the Mat'l Mapping And Source area of the Particle Type rollout, make sure Instanced Geometry is selected and click on the Get Material From button. Render the scene again; the instanced Teapots bear the same Material as the original.

Controlling Particle Streams with Space Warps

Space warps are ideal tools for shaping particle streams in useful ways. The following exercises explore some of the possibilities.

Experimenting with Wind and Gravity

Let's experiment with the Wind and Gravity space warps:

1. In the Top viewport, create a Super Spray emitter near the origin and set its two Spread parameters to 40 degrees. Doing so creates a simple fountain.

2. Create a Wind space warp in the Left viewport and bind the Super Spray to it. Pull the Time Slider and note that the particles are now being pushed in the direction the Wind icon's arrow is pointing, as in Figure 20.24.

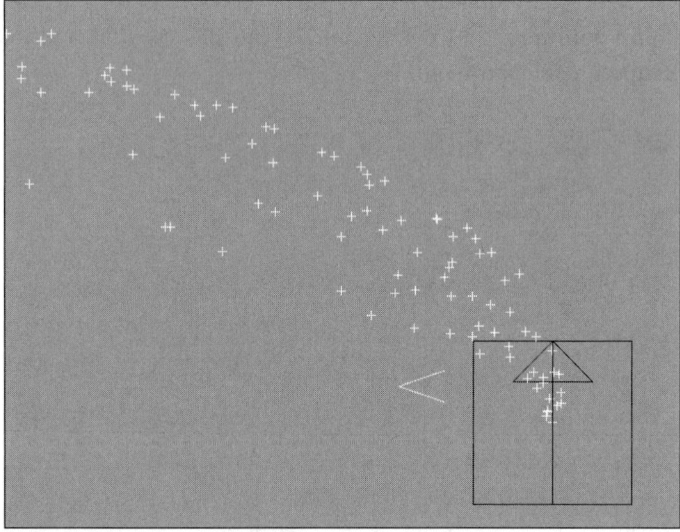

Figure 20.24
A Super Spray particle system is bound to a Wind space warp. The particle stream is being turned in the direction of the Wind arrow icon.

3. Add a Gravity space warp in the Top viewport so that its arrow is pointing down; bind the Super Spray to it. The particle stream is dragged down by gravity in addition to being pushed by the wind. Change the values of the Force parameters for both the Wind and Gravity space warps to adjust the effect. Try adding some turbulence to the wind.

Gravity Strength Values and Force Types

Using the default Planar option in a Gravity space warp's Parameters rollout causes a linear application of the gravity effect in the direction of the icon's arrow. The Spherical option, on the other hand, pulls the particles toward the icon. In either case, negative Strength values reverse the effect.

Deflecting Particle Streams

In the Create panel, you'll find a class of space warps named Deflectors (choose Create|Space Warps|Deflectors). The Deflector, SDeflector, and UDeflector space warps can generally be ignored, because they have been replaced by the superior OmniFlect versions. These space warps deflect a particle stream off a surface: The POmniFlect deflects off a plane, and the SOmniFlect deflects off a Sphere. These warps can be aligned with renderable objects in the scene. The UOmniFlect uses the mesh of a renderable object directly. Continue the previous exercise as follows:

1. Create a POmniFlect space warp and position it so that it intersects the particle stream. Bind the Super Spray to the POmniFlect and pull the Time Slider.

2. If the Wind space warp makes it difficult to control the stream, lower its strength, turn it off in the Stack View, or remove it from the stack. The particle stream will bounce off the plane.

Using a Spline Path

Let's continue the exercise by creating a spline path:

1. Delete all three of the space warps and set the two Spread parameters of your Super Spray to 5 degrees. This setting generates a fairly narrow vertical spray.

2. In the Front viewport, draw a curving Bezier spline (a Line object) to direct the flow of the particles. Place the first vertex near the tip of the emitter. Your screen should look something like Figure 20.25.

3. Create a Path Follow space warp (from the Forces group) by dragging out an icon anywhere in your scene. Click on the Pick Shape Object button and then click on your spline. Bind the warp to the Super Spray.

Note: *Notice that binding an object to a space warp and binding a space warp to an object yield the same result: The binding appears in the object's stack.*

4. Pull the Time Slider to see how the particle stream follows the path. In the space warp's Modify panel, compare the two Particle Motion options: Along Offset Splines and Along Parallel Splines. Figure 20.26 illustrates the Along Offset Splines option.

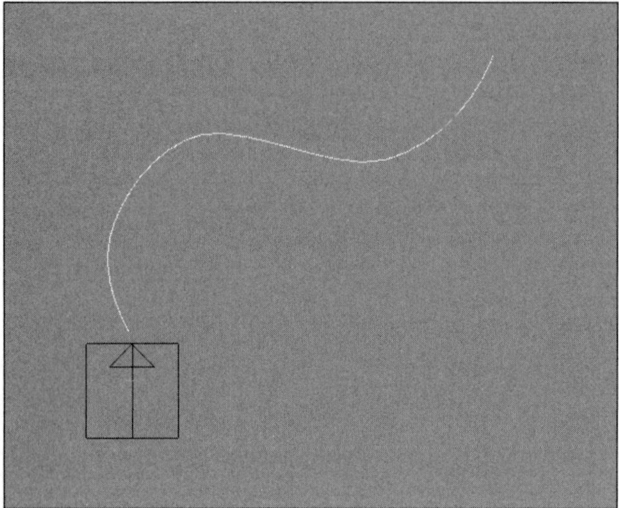

Figure 20.25
A spline path is drawn to shape the flow of the particle stream from a Super Spray emitter.

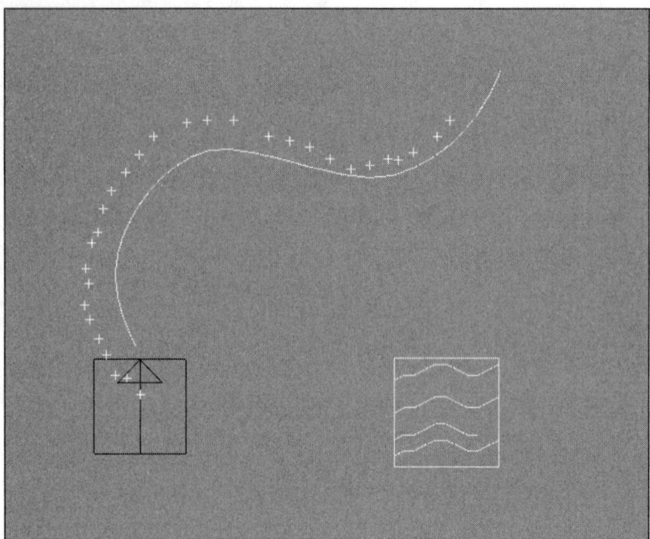

Figure 20.26
The same as Figure 20.25, but with a Path Follow space warp added and bound to the Super Spray. The Path Follow icon is at bottom right. The spline was assigned to the Path Follow space warp, causing the particle stream to follow the spline. The Along Offset Splines option for particle motion was used in this image.

Animating with Expressions

Expressions are small units of programming code that define animatable parameters by referencing them to the other parameters or to the current time in the scene. At each frame, the expression is evaluated to produce a new value. Wiring has largely made the use of expressions easier by streamlining the interface, but a firm understanding of the underlying concepts makes the wiring decisions easier to understand.

Most people who are just beginning to use 3D graphics have little or no programming experience and readily conclude that expressions are something they don't need to understand. This view could not be more incorrect. Anyone capable of handling the enormous technical complexities of 3ds max 4 has the ability to write and understand simple expressions. Once 3D artists understand how powerful expressions can be, they quickly learn to love them.

MAX actually has two ways of producing "programmed" animation. Expressions are relatively simple and can be mastered by nearly anyone. In contrast, MAXScript, the scripting program inside MAX, is a full-strength object-oriented scripting language that can be used to write instructions of almost infinite complexity. Every animatable parameter has both an expression controller and a script controller. Although the expression "language" is easy enough for any serious user to master, MAXScript requires considerable effort to learn and is most useful to those who are familiar with object-oriented programming languages. We cannot do it justice in the scope of this book, and we'll stick to expressions here.

Expressions for Interdependent Animation

The most important use of expressions is to create interdependent animation, in which the animation of one object or parameter automatically controls the animation of another object or parameter. The range of applications for this concept is unlimited. For example, you can write an expression that rotates the wheels of a car the correct amount for the distance the car travels down the road. You can cause the front wheels to rotate as the steering wheel is turned. You can even create a character setup in which the hips move as the feet are moved. Expression controllers can be combined with regular keyframe controllers under a List controller, so that you can always tweak the results of the expression.

In the following exercise, you'll create a network of turning gears. As you animate the first gear, all the others will rotate along, producing a virtual machine.

Modeling the Gears

To correctly model a network of interlocking gears, you must make the number of teeth proportional to the radius of the gear. If one gear is twice as big as another, it must have twice as many teeth. The size of the teeth must be the same for all the gears, however, or they won't mesh together properly. Follow these steps:

1. Create a Cylinder in the Front viewport with a radius of 20 and a height of –10. Set the Height Segments value to 1 and the number of sides to 20. Convert this object to an editable mesh.

2. Select every other quad polygon around the rim of the object (a total of 10) and extrude them out 5 units. Use a slight negative bevel to slant them in. Your result should look like Figure 20.27.

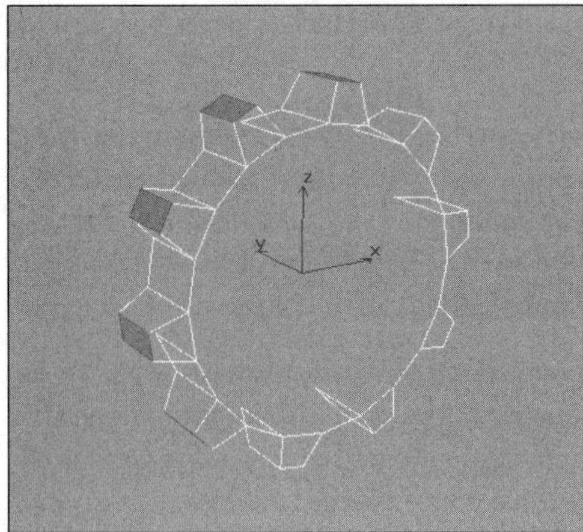

Figure 20.27
A gear with 10 teeth is modeled from a Cylinder object that has been converted to an editable mesh. Alternate quad polygons were selected and then extruded and slightly beveled.

3. Create a second gear in the same way, but use a radius of 30 and give it 30 sides. Extrude out the 15 alternate quads five units and bevel them as before. Position the second gear so that it meshes with the first, as shown in Figure 20.28. Do not rotate the second gear when aligning it.

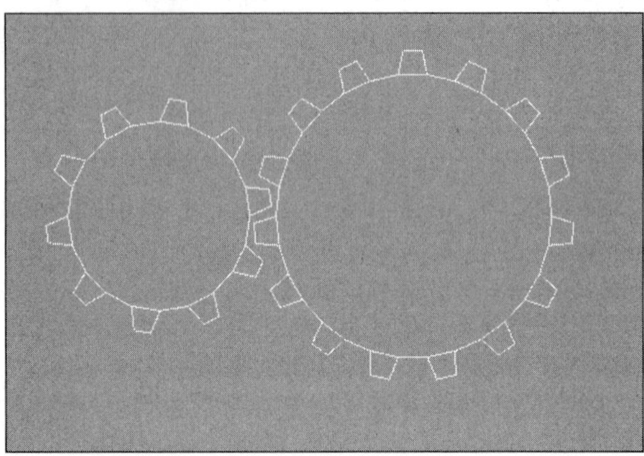

Figure 20.28
A second gear is added that is 50 percent larger than the first, with 50 percent more teeth. The second gear is positioned to mesh with the first gear.

4. Create a third, much smaller gear with a radius of 10 and 10 sides. Extrude out the five alternate teeth, and bevel as in the previous steps. Rotate this gear 90 degrees so that it's parallel to the groundplane. Align it carefully to mesh with the bottom of the second gear. Doing so will almost certainly require some rotation of the gear around its own axis. When you're done, your finished gear system should look like Figure 20.29 in the Perspective viewport.

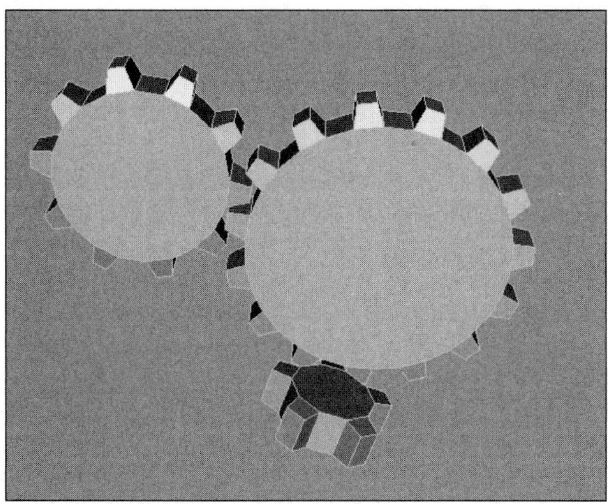

Figure 20.29
A third, much smaller gear is added and rotated to mesh at a right angle with the second gear.

Setting Up the Expressions

As you continue this exercise, the first gear will be animated in the conventional way, and the other two gears will be assigned expressions to cause them to rotate in coordination with the first gear. Follow these steps:

1. To set up the rotation controller for the first gear, open Track View and use the Filters dialog box to show your controller types. Open the tracks for the Cylinder01 object and change the rotation controller to Euler XYZ (if you have not already made this the default rotation controller).

2. Open the tracks for the second gear, Cylinder02, and once again change the rotation controller to Euler XYZ. This gear will rotate around the World Y-direction, so open the Y Rotation track and change the controller from Bezier Float to Float Expression. This track will now use an expression to produce an animated value.

3. Changing to an expression-based controller automatically opens the Expression Controller dialog box shown in Figure 20.30. This dialog box can also be opened by right-clicking on the name of the controller and choosing Properties from the pop-up menu.

Take a good look at this panel. The expression that is evaluated at every frame is written in the Expression window. The simplest possible expression is just a literal value. If you typed a number in the box, it would set the Y-rotation value for the object. This is not a useful approach, however. To produce an animated result, in which the value of the expression can change from frame to frame, you need to create a variable in the expression. As the value of the variable changes, the value of the expression changes accordingly.

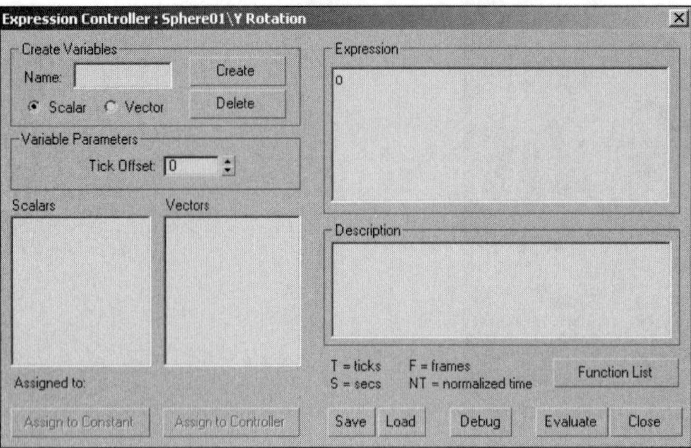

Figure 20.30

The Expression Controller dialog box. The expression that is evaluated at every frame is written in the Expression window. Variables are created on the left side of the panel.

The variable you need is the current Y-rotation value of the first gear. As this value changes, the expression governing the Y-rotation of the second gear will change as well. To create and use a variable, continue with these steps:

1. Type the name "yrot" (for Y-rotation) in the variable Name field in the Create Variables area. Before you click on the Create button to confirm this name, you must decide whether the variable is to be a vector or a scalar. A vector is a three-coordinate value; a scalar is a single number. Because the Y-rotation is a single number, choose the Scalar option. If you were creating a position variable from a Bezier Position controller, which uses an (X,Y,Z) value, you would use the Vector option. Click on the Create button to create the variable; note that its name appears in the list of scalar variables.

2. At this point, you have a named variable, but it doesn't know where to get its value. To connect it to the Y-rotation value of the first gear, click on the Assign To Controller button. The Track View Pick dialog box appears, which is like a miniature version of Track View. Open the tracks for Cylinder01 and select its Y Rotation track. Click on the OK button. When you're done, the Expression Controller dialog box will indicate that the **yrot** variable has been assigned to Cylinder01/Y Rotation. Take a look at Figure 20.31.

3. To use the variable in the expression, type the word "yrot" in the Expression window (overwrite the zero if it is present). The Y-rotation value of the second gear is now determined by the Y-rotation value of the first gear. Click on the Close button to close the dialog box.

4. Test this expression by animating the first gear. Open the Y Rotation track for Cylinder01 in Track View and create two keys, one at Frame 0 and the other at Frame 100. The value of the first key should remain at 0, but change the value of the second key to 360 degrees. This setting causes the first gear to make one full rotation.

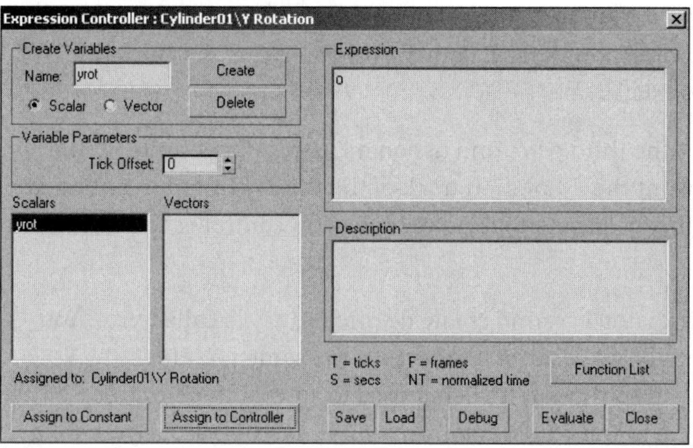

Figure 20.31
A scalar variable named **yrot** is created and assigned to the Y-rotation controller for the first gear (Cylinder01). This variable now contains the current Y-rotation value of the first gear.

5. Pull the Time Slider to see the result. The first gear rotates correctly, but the second gear rotates incorrectly. For one thing, it's rotating in the same direction as the first gear, when it should be rotating in the opposite direction. Second, it's rotating at the same speed as the first gear. Because the second gear is 50 percent larger than the first, it must rotate proportionately slower. Specifically, it should rotate two-thirds of a turn for every full rotation of the first gear. Open the Expression Controller dialog box and change the expression to read "–.666*yrot". Doing so tells the controller to multiply the current value of **yrot** by negative two-thirds. The result therefore rotates more slowly and in the opposite direction. Your dialog box should look like Figure 20.32. Close the dialog box and pull the Time Slider again. The gears now mesh correctly as they turn.

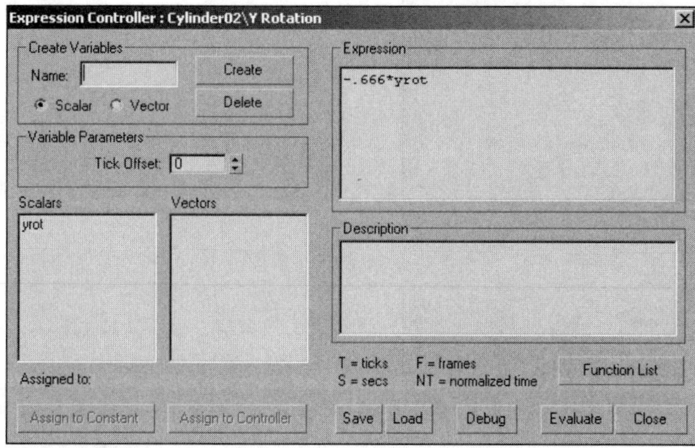

Figure 20.32
The expression for the second gear must account for the fact that the second gear is 50 percent larger than the first gear, so it rotates only two-thirds as fast. Using a negative multiplier causes the second gear to rotate in the opposite direction.

Adding the Third Gear

The third gear rotates in a different direction than the other two; otherwise, the concepts remain the same. Continue with these steps:

1. Open the tracks for Cylinder03, the third gear, and assign a Euler XYZ controller to the rotation track. This time, you want the Z Rotation track of the third gear to be controlled by the Y Rotation track of the first gear. Assign a Float Expression controller to the Z Rotation track of Cylinder03.

2. Open the Expression Controller dialog box and create a scalar variable called **yrot**. You use the same name you did previously because it's precisely the same variable—the Y-rotation value of the first gear—even though it's being used to control the Z-rotation of the affected gear. Assign the variable to the Y Rotation track of Cylinder01, just as you did with the second gear.

3. It's time to write the expression. If you rotate this gear around the World Z-direction to position it in the first place, you'll see a peculiar number already in the Expression window. This is the current angle value, but expressed in radians rather than degrees. A *radian*, which equals approximately 57 degrees, is a basic and useful unit of measure in trigonometry. The expression controller often uses radians instead of degrees, so you sometimes have to use one of the built-in functions from the Function List to convert from one unit of measurement to the other. Type the expression "(–2*yrot)+" in front of whatever rotation value is already present. For example, in this case, the current rotation value in the Expression window is 0.628319 radians. Therefore, the expression is **(–2*yrot)+0.628319**, as illustrated in Figure 20.33. This expression tells the controller to multiply the Y-rotation value of the first gear by two (because the third gear is half the size of the first gear) and to

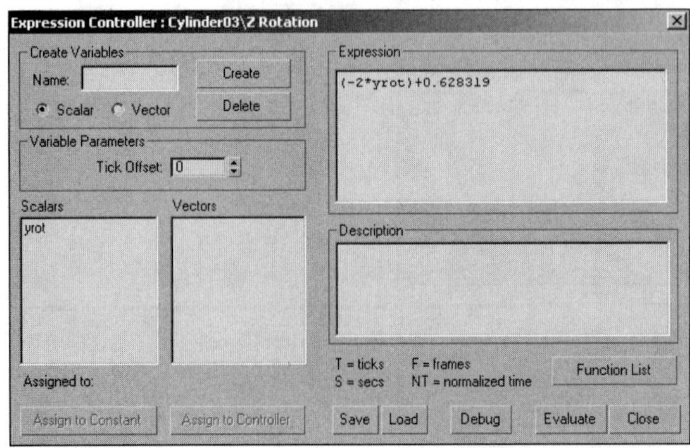

Figure 20.33
The expression for the third gear also uses the Y-rotation value of the first gear as its primary input. The rotation amount is multiplied by two because the third gear is half the size of the first one. The original rotational adjustment that is required to make the gears mesh is added to the expression. This number is in radians, and it is equivalent to about 36 degrees.

rotate in the opposite direction. Then, the expression adds the rotational adjustment to it so the gears remain in the same alignment as in the original setup.

4. Close the dialog box and pull the Time Slider to test the result. Everything should be working. What's great is that this is a working machine. Go back to the Y Rotation track for the first gear. Look at the function curve and edit it. Add keys and make the gear turn forward and backward. When you run the animation, all the other gears follow automatically.

The completed files for this and the next exercise (Chap 20 expressions1.max and Chap 20 expressions2.max) are located on the CD-ROM for reference.

Expressions Based on Time

Expressions produce animated results because the input value of a variable in the expression can change with each frame. The most important type of variable is one that tracks the current value of another animated parameter, as you saw in the previous exercise. But the current time, typically expressed as a frame number, can also be used as a variable.

In the simplest example, an object is assigned a Position Expression controller with the expression **[0,0,F]**. **F** is a built-in variable that inputs the current frame number. Using this expression, the object will move from (0,0,0) to (0,0,100) in World space as the Time Slider moves between Frame 0 and Frame 100.

Things can get a lot more interesting (and useful) when trigonometric functions are involved. The expression **[0,0, 100*sin(4*F)]** causes the object to rise from 0 to 100 in the World Z-direction, fall to –100, and return to 0—all over 90 frames. If you remember your high-school trigonometry, you will be able to figure out why. A sine function rises from 0 at 0 degrees to 1 at 90 degrees. It falls back to 0 at 180 degrees and falls further to –1 at 270, before circling back to 0 at 360 degrees. The multiplier of 4 causes the **F** value to increase from 0 to 360 over 90 frames. The sine value therefore follows the sine wave, multiplied by 100, over the course of the animation. The resulting function curve is illustrated in Figure 20.34.

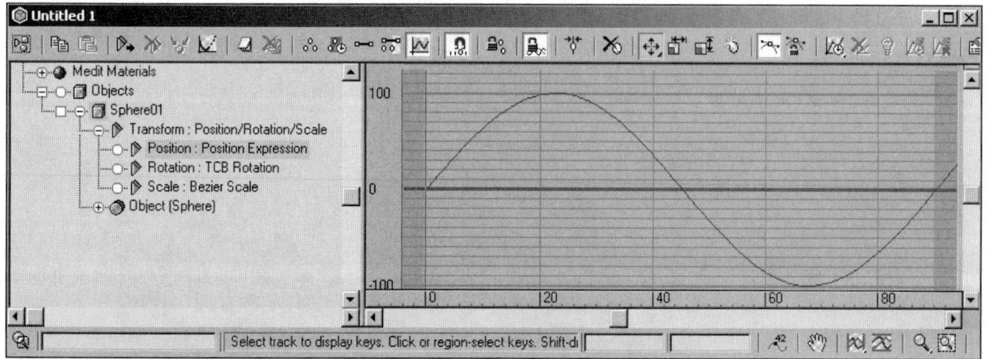

Figure 20.34
The Z-position function curve for an object using the Position Expression **[0,0, 100*sin(4*F)]**. A sine function is applied to the current frame number, resulting in a sine wave.

Moving On

In this chapter, you looked briefly at some of the important, but specialized, animation tools that may not be a part of your everyday work. You examined how space warps can be used to deform geometry in World space, so that the object's shape changes as its position is animated. You worked through some basic dynamic simulations to understand how MAX can create animation, based on physical forces and principles. You learned the essentials of MAX's particle systems and how space warps can be used to control the behavior of a particle stream. Finally, you learned how expressions can be used to create systems of interdependent animation, in which the animation of one object automatically controls the animation of another.

The next, and final, chapter discusses Video Post, MAX's powerful internal utility that can be used for video editing, compositing, and post-processing effects.

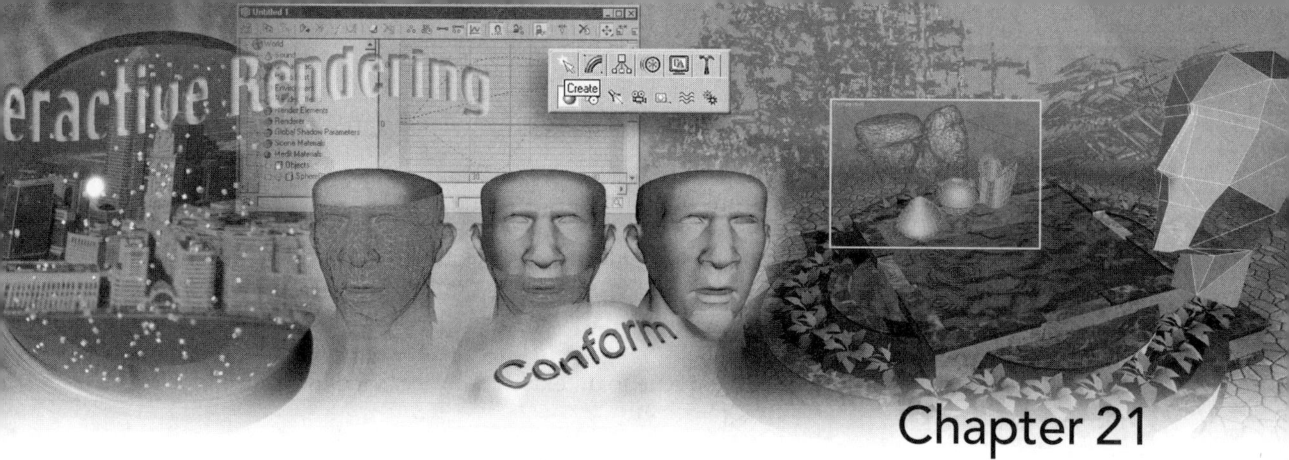

Chapter 21

Using Video Post

Video Post is a remarkably powerful tool for performing video editing, compositing, and post-processing within 3ds max. It's much simpler to use than it looks; you can use it to edit together different rendered video sequences, or you can combine such sequences with your current scene. Video Post is not a replacement for a true nonlinear video editing or compositing package, but it's handy and effective for many simple, routine tasks.

The Video Post Queue

The Video Post process entails setting up a *Queue* (list) of events to be processed in order. You must decide what events are in the Queue and in what sequence they are to be executed. *Events* is a general, nondescript term. The best way to understand an event is as a step in the Video Post process.

Video Post Events

You can place seven types of Events in the Queue:

- *Scene Event*—Inputs the rendering of the current MAX scene to the Queue from a specified camera or viewport. By using multiple Scene Events, you can use Video Post to cut or transition between different cameras or viewports in the course of your video.
- *Image Input Event*—Inputs bitmap images, whether single or in sequence, rather than images from the current scene.
- *Image Filter Event*—Applies image processing to the image it receives from events above it in the Queue.

- *Image Layer Event*—Composites or transitions between two images.
- *Image Output Event*—Sends the output of the Video Post queue to a file. Without an Image Output Event, the results are displayed in the Virtual Frame Buffer frame by frame, but they are not saved.
- *External Event*—Sends the output of the queue to an external device, such as a video tape recorder (VTR).
- *Loop Event*—Generates repeated frame sequences.

The Video Post Panel

The Video Post interface is reached from the Rendering pull-down menu. Strictly speaking, it's a modeless dialog box, but it more closely resembles Track View with its adjustable range bars. Most people call it the *Video Post panel,* and that term will be used here. Figure 21.1 shows the Video Post panel with an empty Queue, just as you see it when you first bring it up in a scene.

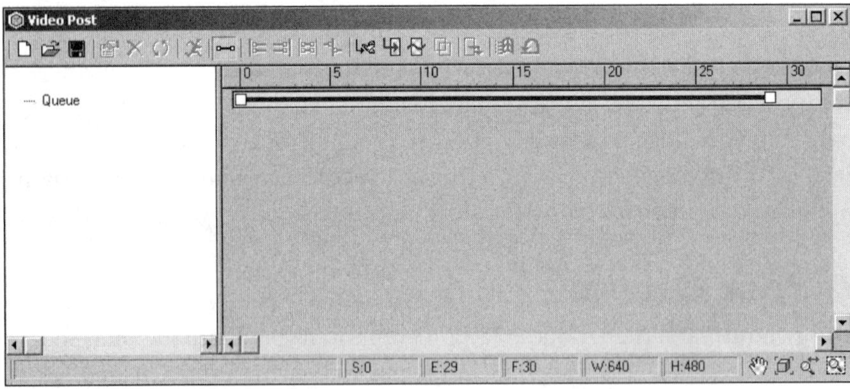

Figure 21.1
The Video Post panel with default settings.

Across the bottom of the panel (from left to right) are a prompt line, a status bar with information about frame ranges for the selected track, and navigation tools. The start frame (S) is 0 and the end frame (E) is 29, for a total of 30 frames (F). This is the range of the Queue because there are as yet no other tracks. The current output is set at 640×480. Clicking on the hand icon pans the range window, and other buttons control the window's zoom factor. (These tools are easy to figure out.)

The top of the panel is also rather simple. The first three buttons create a new sequence by deleting the current Queue, opening (load) a saved sequence, and saving the current sequence. The Video Post Queue is always saved with your scene file, but you can save it independently as a VPX file to be loaded into another scene.

The next three buttons are currently grayed out because they apply to events, and there are as yet no events in the Queue. The first button allows you to edit the parameters for the selected event. The second button deletes the selected event, and the third swaps the positions in the Queue of two events that are selected together.

The next button, a running-man icon, is also grayed out. Clicking on this button executes the Video Post Queue, once you have one to run. The following five buttons are used to edit the range bars. Only the first button, the Edit Range Bar button, is active right now, because the others are used to align multiple range bars for different events.

The final seven buttons are used to create the various event types. Only the Add Scene Event, Add Image Input Event, and Add Image Filter Event options are available at this point, because the other event types are dependent on the existence of these events.

Video Post Essentials

Not many MAX users use Video Post, for a couple of reasons. First, it can be somewhat confusing and intimidating. Although it's rather simple once you understand it, Video Post can be daunting at first exposure.

A second reason is more important, however. When MAX first appeared, access to video editing and compositing software was not nearly as common as it is today. The professional-level packages were quite expensive and were often far too sophisticated for people seeking to accomplish only basic editing tasks. But the situation is much different today. Adobe Premiere and After Effects packages have grown into serious professional-level tools for video editing and finishing, and Discreet, the creators of 3ds max 4, produce a wide range of video compositing and editing packages. These packages are affordable and have become ubiquitous among serious professional 3D animators, and they are sure to meet the needs of any level of video production. Anyone who needs a video-editing toolset for use with MAX is better advised to buy and learn a true nonlinear editing program instead of making do with Video Post. Like Photoshop, these products are essential auxiliary tools for the 3D artist.

Formerly, all of MAX's post-processing functions could be accomplished only through Video Post. For example, render effects such as glows and flares were available only if you set up a Video Post Queue. This requirement made post-processing effects difficult to access and use. As discussed in Chapter 16, 3ds max 4 has a wide range of important post-processing tools under the Render Effects interface. This interface lets you use them without recourse to Video Post and allows you to experiment with them easily.

For all these reasons, the discussion of Video Post in this book will be limited to the basic and routine tasks for which it makes the most sense. The following exercises introduce you to the workings of the Video Post Queue and leave you with the most important skills in this area of MAX. These exercises are cumulative, building directly from each other using a single file.

First Steps in Video Post

Let's begin by setting up the simplest possible queue. To create the Scene Event, follow these steps:

1. Open a fresh scene and create any kind of very simple animation. For example, cause a Sphere to move diagonally across the Perspective viewport over 100 frames. The nature of the animation doesn't really matter here, and you can change it later if you want. Don't render it out, but save the scene.
2. Open the Video Post panel from the Rendering menu. (Refer back to Figure 21.1.) Note that the range bar in the Video Post panel extends from Frame 0 to Frame 29, and that the end frame is 29 at the bottom of the panel. However, the Active Time Segment of your scene runs from Frame 0 to Frame 100.
3. Click on the Teapot icon on the Video Post toolbar to create a Scene Event. Doing so adds the current scene to the Video Post Queue. The Add Scene Event dialog box will appear, as seen in Figure 21.2.

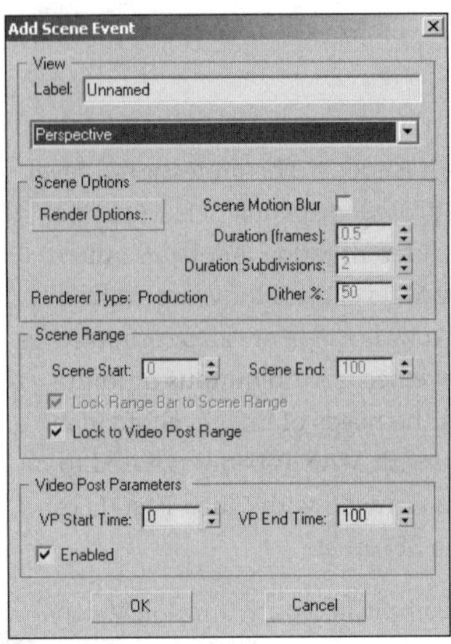

Figure 21.2
The Add Scene Event dialog box appears when you add a Scene Event to the Video Post Queue.

In the Add Scene Event dialog box, the Perspective viewport option is chosen by default. If you have not created any cameras, your only choices are the currently available viewports.

Clicking on the Render Options button brings up a Render Options dialog box, which looks like the Render Scene dialog box without the output options. Anything you change here changes in the Render Scene dialog box as well, and it will therefore affect the result if you render in the usual way (outside of Video Post). Output options, including both time and resolution, are set independently within Video Post. (Before proceeding, close the Render Options dialog box by clicking on the Cancel button.)

Scene Motion Blur is the third form of motion blur in MAX. Object and Image Motion Blur, discussed in Chapter 15, are more commonly used because they do not require the use of Video Post. It's usually not wise to add Scene Motion Blur to a scene that is already using another kind of motion blur. You may want to try Scene Motion Blur in Video Post, however, if you are not satisfied with the results from the other kinds. As usual, increasing the Duration value of the virtual shutter increases the blur, and the Duration Subdivisions option determines the number of samples used. The greater the number, the better the result; a longer processing time is required, however. Scene Motion Blur necessarily applies to the entire frame, rather than to selected objects.

Continue with these steps:

1. Leave the default Perspective option. You will be adding a render of the current scene through your Perspective viewport to the Video Post Queue.
2. Select the Scene Motion Blur checkbox, and the parameters will activate.
3. Accept the remaining defaults, which lock the Scene Range values to the Video Post Range values. Click on the OK button and take a look at your Video Post panel. As you can see in Figure 21.3, the Scene Event name Perspective was added as the first (and only) event in the Video Post Queue.

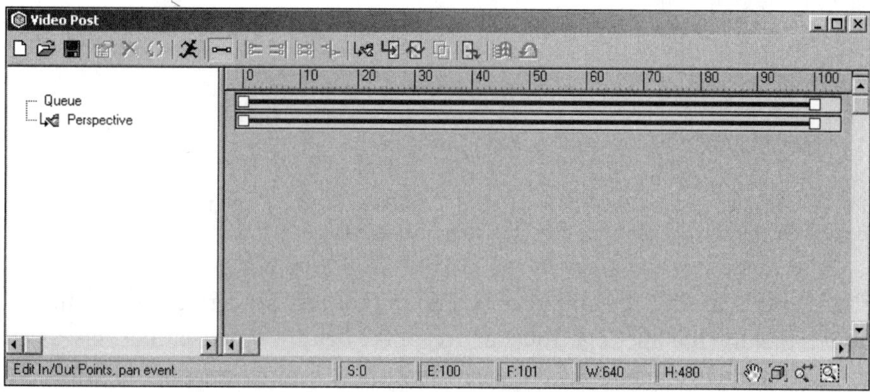

Figure 21.3
The Video Post panel from Figure 21.1 after a Scene Event has been added using the parameters in Figure 21.2. The Scene Event is named Perspective, because it renders the scene from the Perspective viewport.

To edit the parameters of your new event, you select it by clicking on its name or on its range bar, and then click on the Edit Current Event button on the toolbar. The resulting Edit Scene Event dialog box is exactly the same as the Add Scene Event dialog box you've already explored.

Currently, the only thing in the Video Post Queue is the Perspective viewport of the current scene. Clicking on the Execute button renders out the frame sequence, but this rendered frame sequence isn't saved anywhere. To save it to a file, you need to create an Image Output Event at the bottom of the Queue. (This procedure is not as odd as it may first appear. You have to name an output file when rendering outside of Video Post, or you'll lose your render.) Follow these steps to create the Image Output Event and then render:

1. Click in some empty space in the panel to deselect the Perspective Scene Event. (If the Scene Event is selected when you add the Image Output Event, the Image Output Event is added as a child of the Scene Event, rather than simply at the bottom of the Queue.) Add the Image Output Event from the toolbar. The Add Image Output Event dialog box appears, as shown in Figure 21.4. The same parameters are available if you edit the event after creating it.

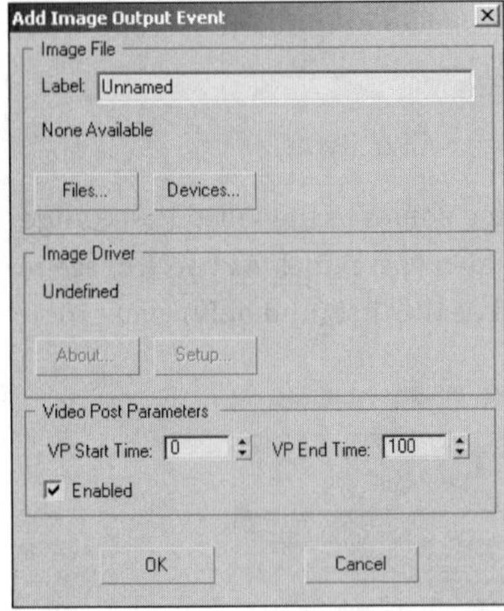

Figure 21.4
The Add Image Output Event dialog box appears when you add an Image Output Event to the Video Post Queue. The same parameters remain available for editing after you create the event.

2. Click on the Files button to save the output as you do in ordinary rendering. Choose the AVI format and name the file test1.avi. You can accept the default codec settings (discussed in Chapter 15) or change to something you like better—these settings are not important for your present purposes. After closing the Add Image Output Event dialog box, your Video Post Queue will contain two events: the Perspective Scene Event and the test1.avi Image Output Event. Take a look at Figure 21.5.

3. Click on the Execute Sequence button on the Video Post toolbar (the running man) to open the Execute Video Post dialog box seen in Figure 21.6. This dialog box contains the same output options you're familiar with from the top of the Render Scene dialog box, except that these options are used only for outputting from Video Post. To speed things up, render only every fourth frame and use a 320×240 output size.

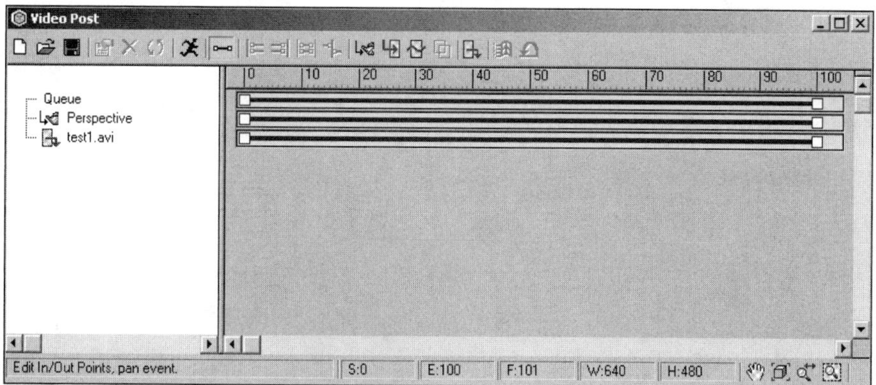

Figure 21.5
The Video Post Panel from Figure 21.3 with an Image Output Event added. The Image Output Event is named test1.avi—the name of the output file.

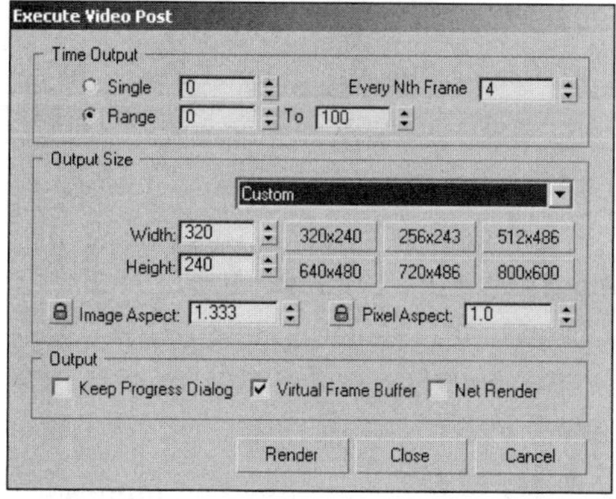

Figure 21.6
The Execute Video Post dialog box contains the same output options as the Render Scene dialog box, but the options apply only to output from Video Post.

4. Click on the Render button. In this simplest setup, the scene renders exactly as it would the usual way, outside of Video Post. Choose the View Image File option from the File menu to view your animation in the Windows Media Player.

Adding a Fade

Thus far, you haven't done anything differently than you would in a regular render. Let's make things more interesting by adding an Image Filter Event to fade out the scene. Fading to black is a very important method for closing an animated sequence, either at the end of an entire piece or as a transition. Follow these steps to add a fade to your scene:

1. Before adding the fade, make sure that no events in your queue are currently selected. Click on the Add Image Filter Event button, and the Add Image Filter Event dialog box appears. Open the drop-down list and look at the long list of options; note that the Lens

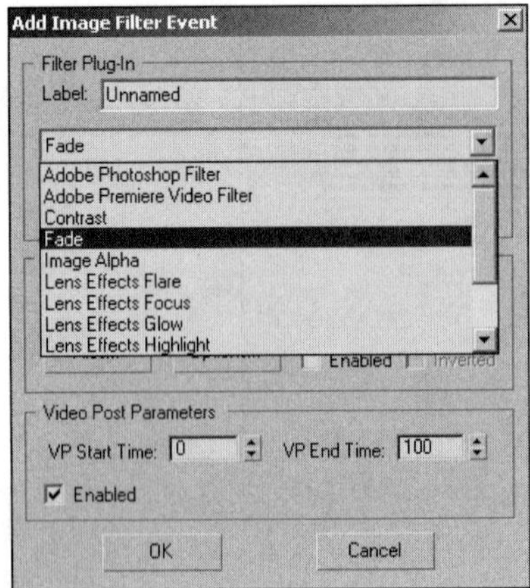

Figure 21.7
The Add Image Filter Event dialog box, with most of the options displayed in the open drop-down list. The Fade option is selected.

Effects are available for this kind of event. Figure 21.7 shows the Add Image Filter Event dialog box with most of the options displayed in the open drop-down list. Select the Fade option and close the dialog box.

2. The Fade Image Filter Event will appear at the very bottom of the Queue. This placement won't work, because the fade must be applied before the Image Output Event; drag the Fade Event up above the test1.avi Image Output Event in the sequence. Another way to do this is to select both of the last two events (by using the Shift key) and use the Swap Events button on the Video Post toolbar to reverse their positions.

3. With only Fade selected, drag the start point of its range from 0 to 50. Use the S number in the status bar at the bottom of the panel to confirm the change. This action creates a fade that begins halfway through the animation and finishes at the very end. Click on the Zoom Extents button at the bottom of the Video Post panel; your Video Post panel should now look like Figure 21.8.

4. Before executing the sequence, select the fade and click on the Edit Current Event button on the Video Post toolbar. Once again, you see a dialog box offering the same parameters you saw when the event was first created. You can change Fade to any one of the other Image Filter Event types, if you wish. Close the dialog box without changing anything.

5. A fade dissolves the entire frame to black. This effect is less than clear if you start with a black background, so open the Environment dialog box and change the background color to white.

6. Execute the Video Post Queue, using the same output parameters as before (320×420 and every fourth frame). Keep a close eye on the rendering process, particularly when the fade begins. For every frame, the image is rendered with two subsamplings, and then a fade is

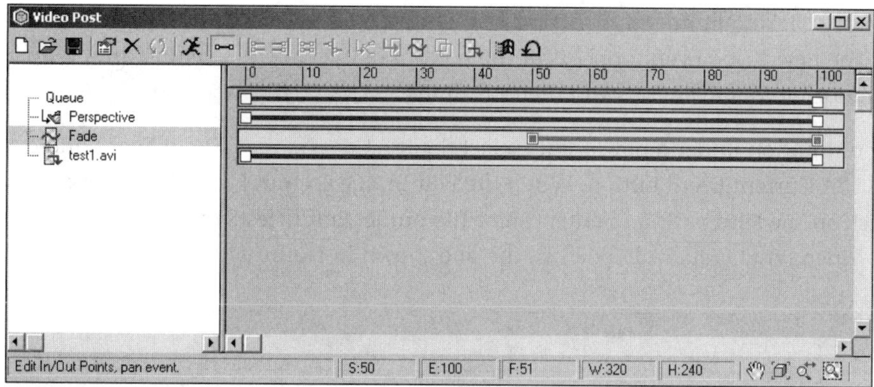

Figure 21.8
The Video Post panel from Figure 21.5 with Fade (an Image Filter Event) added beneath the Perspective Scene Event. The fade range has been set to begin at Frame 50 and end at Frame 100.

applied as a post-process effect. Two obvious, distinct steps correspond to the two events (Perspective and Fade) in the Video Post Queue.

7. Take a look at your finished AVI file by using the Windows Media Player, and confirm the Fade Image Filter Event.

Cutting between Views or Cameras

The most valuable use of Video Post is probably to switch views within the course of an animation. You'll rarely render from an orthographic window, so you'll either use multiple cameras or a combination of one or more cameras with the Perspective viewport. Without Video Post, you'd either have to animate a single camera to jump sharply between frames or render out separate sequences to be edited together outside of MAX.

Continue your exercise by creating a couple of cameras and making a straight cut between them:

1. Select the Fade Image Filter Event in the Video Post Queue and delete it using the Delete Current Event button on the Video Post toolbar. Your Queue should now contain only the Scene Event (Perspective) and the Image Output Event (test1.avi).

2. Create a couple of cameras to view your simple animation from different directions. For example, make Camera01 look down from above and set up Camera02 for a front view. Create viewports for each of these cameras, and pull the Time Slider to see how the animation is framed in both cameras. Adjust your camera views to get something that pleases you.

3. Select the Perspective Scene Event in the Video Post Queue and click on the Edit Current Event button. Choose Camera01 from the drop-down menu and close the dialog box. The Scene Event on your Video Post Queue should now be named Camera01 instead of Perspective.

4. While the Camera01 Event is still selected, notice that the button for Add Scene Event is grayed out. To create a Scene Event for the other camera, you must first deselect any Events

in the Queue by clicking in an empty region. Add another Scene Event and assign it to Camera02. The new Scene Event appears at the bottom of the Queue, so either drag it up above the Image Output Event or swap their positions.

5. To save this animation under a new name, select the test1.avi Image Output Event and click on the Edit Current Event button. When the Edit Image Output Event dialog box appears, click on the Files button to enter a new file name. Enter "test2.avi". When you finish, your Video Post Queue will look like the one shown in Figure 21.9.

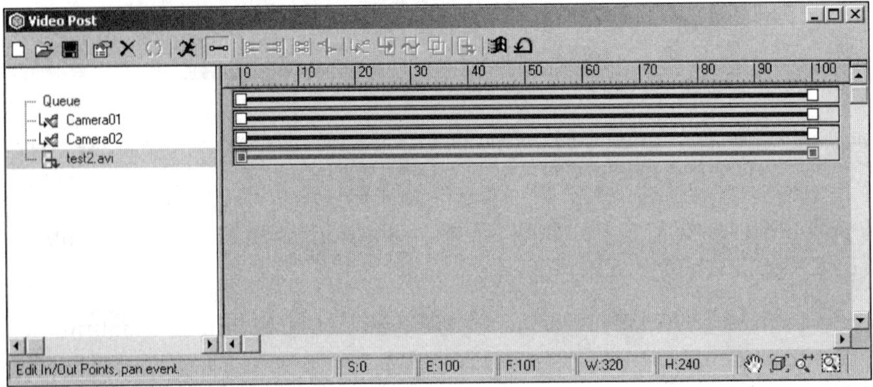

Figure 21.9
The Video Post panel with two Scene Events for two cameras and an Image Output Event (test2.avi). The range bars for both of the Scene Events (Camera01 and Camera02) extend the entire length of the Video Post range.

6. At this point, both Scene Events (Camera01 and Camera02) have range bars that extend the entire length of the Queue range—from Frame 0 to Frame 100. Before rendering, guess what's likely to happen. Then, click on the Execute Sequence button and use the same output settings you've been using all along. Watch the frames as they render to see the process.

7. For each frame, the Camera01 view renders first, and then the Camera02 view renders right on top of it, completely overwriting the Camera01 image. This is the Video Post Queue concept in action: For each frame, each Event is executed in order from top to bottom. In this case, it means that the second Scene Event completely obscures the first before being sent to the Image Output Event. Run the animation test2.avi in the Windows Media player to confirm that only the Camera02 view survived in the output.

8. Select the range bar for Camera02 and drag its start to Frame 50. The range bars of the two Scene Events now overlap only between Frame 50 and Frame 100. From Frame 0 to Frame 49, Camera01 is not obscured. Your Video Post panel should look like Figure 21.10.

9. Execute this sequence and watch the process. (If you get a warning box about the output file, make sure that the Windows Media Player is closed before you execute again.) For the first half of the range, only the Camera01 view renders. During the second half, Camera01

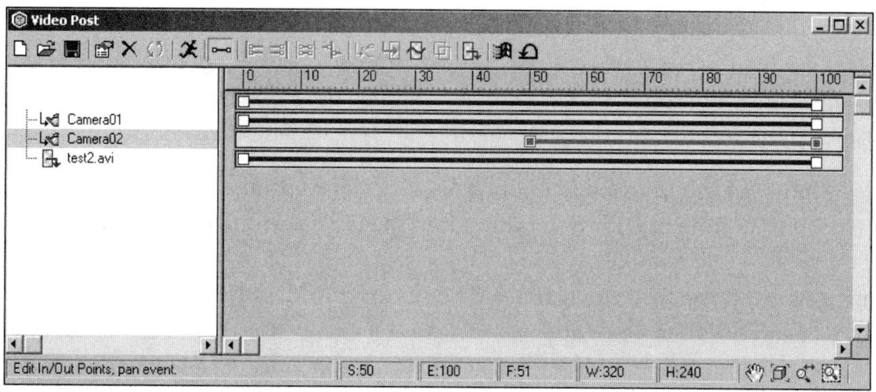

Figure 21.10
The Video Post panel from Figure 21.9, with the range bar for Camera02 adjusted to extend only between frame 50 and frame 100. The two Scene Events overlap between these frames, but Camera01 is unobscured for the first 50 frames in the Video Post range.

renders first, but it is then overwritten by the rendering of the Camera02 view. Look at the result in the Windows Media Player to confirm a cut from Camera01 to Camera02, halfway through the sequence.

10. This method works to create a jump cut between cameras, but the Video Post Queue is not as clear is it might be. With such a simple setup, it hardly matters; if you're working with multiple cuts or more than two cameras, however, the arrangement of the range bars must be readable. Move the end of the Camera01 range bar to Frame 49. As you can see in Figure 21.11, it is much more evident where one Scene Event ends and the next one begins.

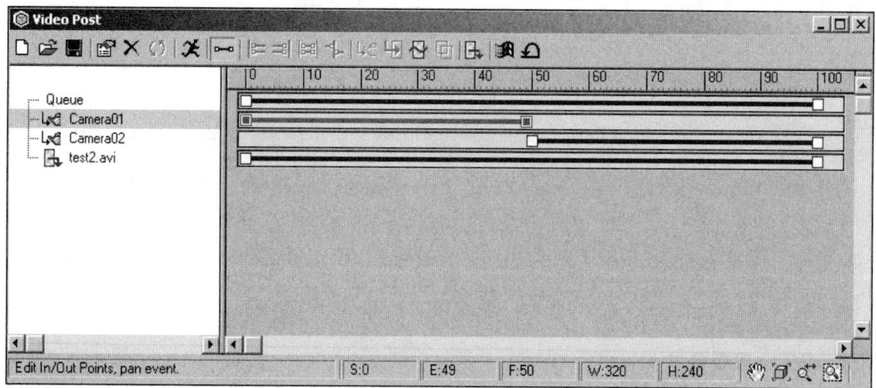

Figure 21.11
The Video Post panel from Figure 21.10, with the range bar for Camera01 adjusted to extend only between frames 0 and 49. Without the overlap, it's much clearer that a straight cut was created between the two cameras at Frame 50 and the needless rendering of the Camera01 view has been eliminated.

11. Execute again and watch the process. This time, only Camera02 renders from frame 50 to frame 100, eliminating the needless rendering from Camera01. The process speeds up quite a bit—with a complex scene, such a change would be absolutely essential. As you can see by viewing the AVI file, however, the final result is no different.

12. To cut back to Camera01, you must add another Scene Event for that camera. Add a new Scene Event, assign it to Camera01, and position it in the Queue immediately beneath the Camera02 Event. In a more complex scene, it might make sense to give this event a distinctive name, because it amounts to a camera shot in an editing sequence. To try this, open the Edit Scene Event dialog box and enter the name Camera01_Shot B in the Label box. After closing the dialog box, this name will appear in the Video Post Queue.

13. Adjust the range bars so that Camera01 extends from Frame 0 to Frame 40, Camera02 extends from Frame 41 to Frame 69, and Camera01_Shot B extends from Frame 70 to Frame 100. Use the display at the bottom of the panel to confirm these ranges. When you finish, your Video Post panel should look like Figure 21.12.

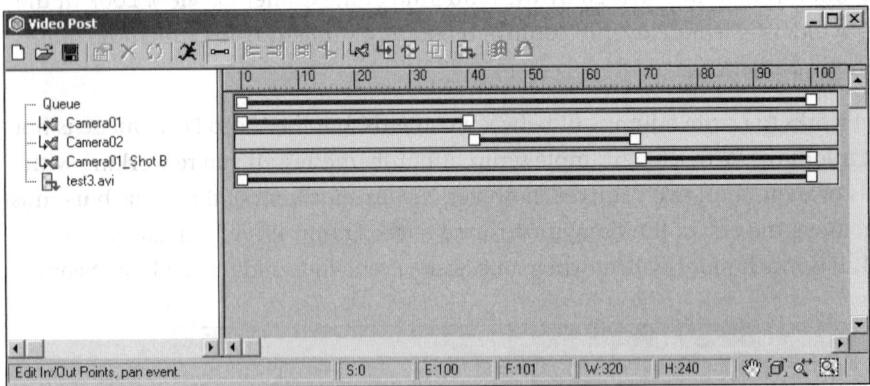

Figure 21.12
The Video Post panel from Figure 21.11 with a third Scene Event added. The new Scene Event renders Camera01 again, so it has been given a distinguishing name. The range bars for all three events have been adjusted to cut from Camera01 to Camera02 at Frame 40, and then back to Camera01 at Frame 70.

14. Execute the Video Post sequence and watch the process. There should be no overlapping, and the final animation should cut back and forth between the two cameras.

Adding a Cross Fade

Thus far, you've learned how to dissolve to black by using a fade—an Image Filter Event. You've also learned how to cut between cameras. A cross-dissolve between sequences is an essential film- and video-editing technique that fades one sequence out as it fades another in. Now, add a cross fade to your scene by following these steps:

1. Adjust the range bar for the Camera02 Event so that it extends from Frame 41 to Frame 80. Adjust the range bar for the Camera01_Shot B Event so that it extends from Frame 60

to Frame 100. Thus, these two events will overlap from Frame 60 to Frame 80. Select the Image Output Event and change the output file name to test3.avi.

2. If you execute the Video Post Queue now, the Camera01_Shot B Event overwrites the Camera02 Event where their ranges overlap. This action effectively creates a cut from Camera02 to Camera01_Shot B at Frame 60. To create a cross-dissolve, select both of these events together, using the Shift key. Look at the Video Post toolbar and notice that all the Add Event buttons are disabled, except the Add Image Layer Event button.

3. Click on the Add Image Layer Event button to bring up the Add Image Layer Event dialog box. Look at the list of options in the drop-down list, as illustrated in Figure 21.13. As you can see, an Image Layer Event provides tools for simple compositing and transitions between image sequences. Select the Cross Fade Transition option and close the dialog box.

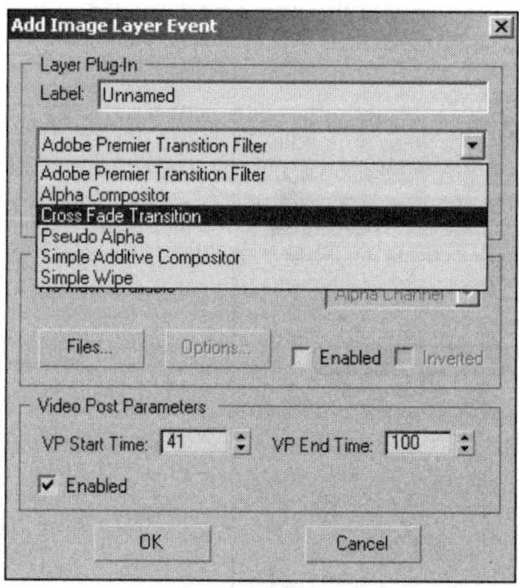

Figure 21.13
The Add Image Layer Event dialog box with the drop-down list revealed. All of these options provide simple compositing and transitioning between image sequences.

4. Your Video Post panel should now look like Figure 21.14. Note how the two Scene Events have become hierarchical children of the Image Layer Event (Cross Fade Transition). Take a look at the default range of the cross fade transition: It extends from the beginning of the Camera02 range to the end of the Camera01_Shot B range. If you execute the sequence right now, you'll get an undesired result. The Camera02 view will begin to dissolve to black at Frame 40, well before the Camera01_Shot B Event begins. On the other side, Camera01_Shot B will fade in from Frame 60 all the way to Frame 100.

5. Adjust the range of the cross fade transition so that it covers only the overlapping ranges of the Scene Events (Frame 60 to Frame 80). Your Video Post panel should look like Figure 21.15.

6. You're interested only in the cross fade, so there's no need to render out the whole scene. After clicking on the Execute Sequence button, set the range to operate from Frame 55 to

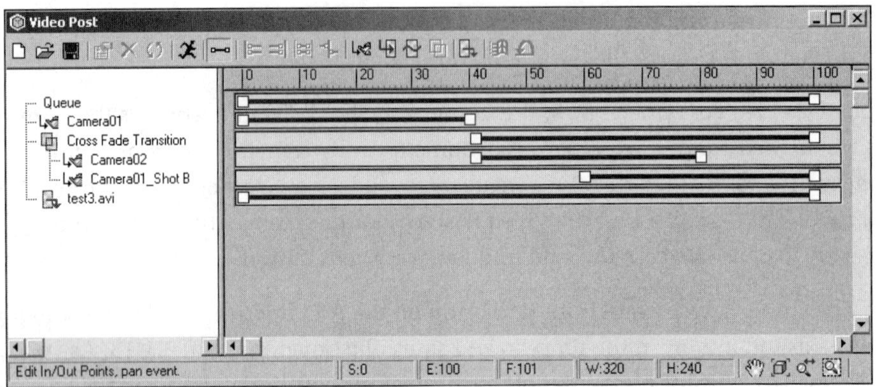

Figure 21.14
The Video Post panel from Figure 21.12 with an Image Layer Event (Cross Fade Transition) added as a parent to two overlapping Scene Events. The default range of the cross fade transition covers the combined ranges of the two Events, rather than just where they overlap.

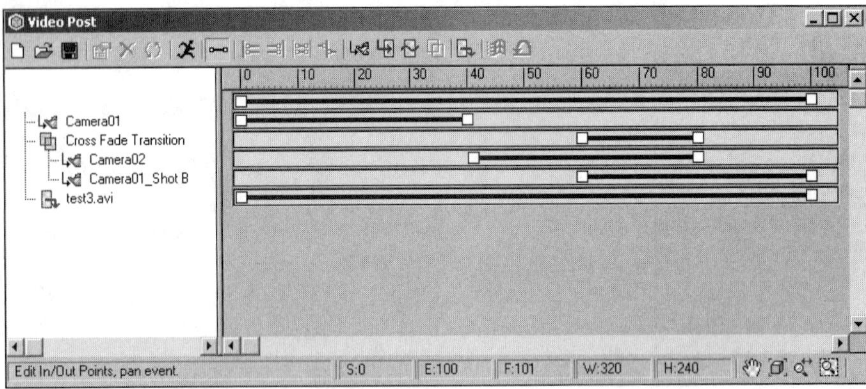

Figure 21.15
The Video Post panel from Figure 21.14 with the Image Layer Event (Cross Fade Transition) range adjusted to cover only the overlapping region of its children Scene Events.

Frame 85 and bring the frame interval back to 1 (from 4) so that each frame will render. Click on the Render button and watch the process. You should get a nice cross-dissolve between the two camera views.

Using Prerendered Sequences

Video Post is a valuable tool for the quick editing and compositing of image sequences that you've already rendered out—either by themselves or in combination with the current scene, as you'll see in this exercise. If you want to save the existing Queue, click on the Save Sequence button. Then, follow these steps:

1. In your current scene, create a fresh Video Post Queue by clicking on the New Sequence button. Add a Scene Event for one of your cameras. Use the Add Image Input Event button

to add one of the test.avi animations you made in this chapter. Click on the Files button in the Add Image Input Event dialog box to find the file. Unless you rendered out the full 101 frames for the AVI file, it should be much shorter than the 100-frame Scene Event. Adjust the Scene Event to begin one frame after the Image Input Event ends. Your Video Post panel should look something like Figure 21.16.

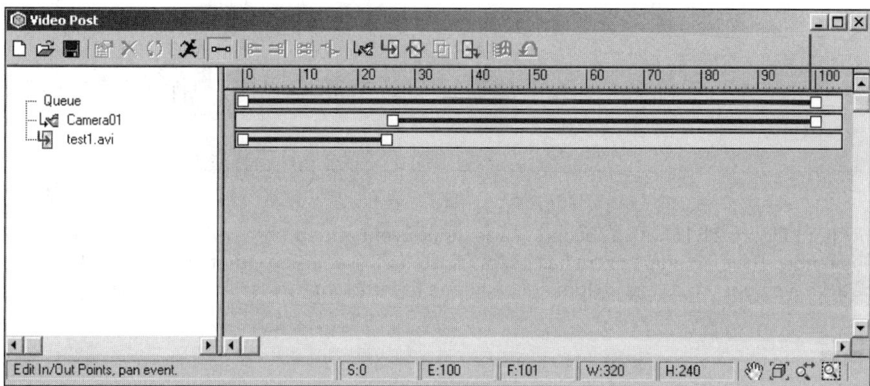

Figure 21.16
The Video Post panel with a Scene Event (Camera01) and an Image Input Event (test1.avi). The Image Input Event is a 26-frame AVI file rendered out earlier in this exercise. The range of the Scene Event has been set to start one frame after the Image Input Event ends.

2. Add another Image Input Event to the bottom of the Queue, using another test animation. Click on its range bar (not on the ends) and drag it until it ends at Frame 100. (Dragging in this way keeps the length of the range constant as you move it.) Adjust the end of the Scene Event back from Frame 100 so that it overlaps some, but not all, of the new Image Input Event.

3. Create a cross fade where the Scene Event and the second Image Input Event overlap by selecting both of the overlapping Events, clicking on the Add Image Layer Event button, and choosing the Cross Fade Transition option. Notice how the order of the Queue is rearranged to group the two child Events together. Adjust the length of the Cross Fade Transition range bar to cover only the overlapping region of its children. Add an Image Output Event at the bottom of the Queue to save the output to a file named test4.avi. Your Video Post panel should look like Figure 21.17.

4. The Queue shown in Figure 21.17 should work as follows: First, the prerendered test1.avi sequence will be copied into test4.avi. Then, the current scene renders from Frame 26, using the view from Camera01. Between Frame 75 and 85, a cross fade will occur between the current scene and the prerendered sequence in test2.avi. The files will finish at Frame 100 with test2.avi alone. Your own example should be very similar. Execute the sequence and see how it works out. You already have cuts and fades in the prerendered sequences, so don't be confused by them. Compare the prerendered sequences with the final result in Media Player to confirm that everything worked as planned.

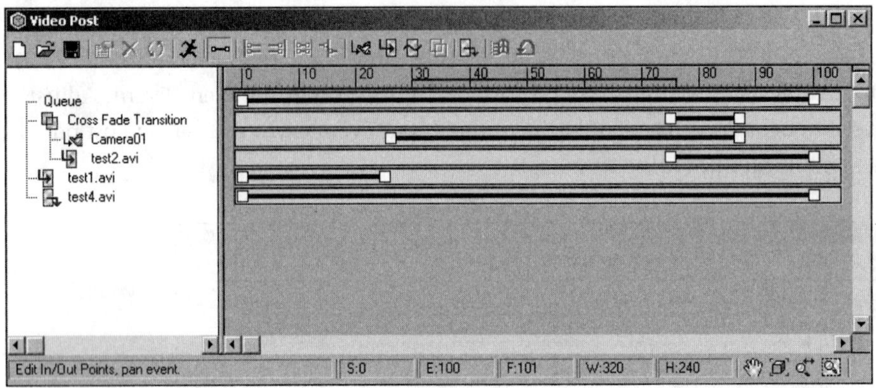

Figure 21.17
The Video Post panel from Figure 21.16 with a second Image Input Event added (test2.avi) and moved to the end of the Queue range. The Camera01 event has been adjusted to overlap only part of test2.avi. Both Camera01 and test2.avi have been made the children of an Image Layer Event (Cross Fade Transition).

Conclusion

In this final chapter, you looked at the essential skills needed to use MAX's Video Post utility for its most common functions. You began by learning simply to render a scene through Video Post by setting up a Queue involving only a Scene Event and Image Output Event. You learned how to dissolve the scene by using an Image Filter Event—the fade. You then learned how to include multiple camera views in your animation, first by simply cutting between them, and then by using an Image Layer Event to create a cross fade transition. Finally, you learned how prerendered sequences can be used in place of, and in addition to, the rendering of the current scene in the Video Post Queue.

We hope you've enjoyed reading this book and working through the exercises as much as we've enjoyed writing those exercises. 3ds max 4 is an expansive program with many features you can use to create world-class animations and still shots. It will, however, take time, patience, and practice to achieve the necessary skills to bring your ideas to fruition. This book has provided you with a firm foundation that you can build upon to create and animate the worlds in your mind. Until *3ds max 5 In Depth*, enjoy.

Appendix
Keyboard Shortcuts

Main User Interface Shortcuts

User Interface Function	Keyboard Shortcut
Adaptive Degradation Toggle	O (the letter o)
Adaptive Perspective Grid Toggle	Shift+Ctrl+A
Align	Alt+A
Angle Snap Toggle	A
Animate Mode Toggle	N
Back View	K
Background Lock Toggle	Alt+Ctrl+B
Backup Time One Unit	, (comma)
Bottom View	B
Camera View	C
Cycle Selection Method	Ctrl+F
Default Lighting Toggle	Ctrl+L
Delete Objects	Delete
Disable Viewport	D
Display Edges Only Toggle	Ctrl+E
Display First Tab	Alt+1
Expert Mode Toggle	Ctrl+X
Fetch	Alt+Ctrl+F
Forward Time One Unit	. (period)
Freeze Selection	6
Front View	F
Go to End Frame	End
Go to Start Frame	Home

(continued)

Main User Interface Shortcuts *(continued)*

User Interface Function	Keyboard Shortcut
Hide Cameras Toggle	Shift+C
Hide Geometry Toggle	Shift+O (the letter o)
Hide Grids Toggle	G
Hide Helpers Toggle	Shift+H
Hide Lights Toggle	Shift+L
Hide Particle Systems Toggle	Shift+P
Hide Space Warps Toggle	Shift+W
Hold	Alt+Ctrl+H
Isometric User View	U
Lock User Interface Toggle	Alt+0 (zero)
Match Camera to View	Ctrl+C
Material Editor	M
Maximize Viewport Toggle	W
MAXScript Listener	F11
New Scene	Ctrl+N
Normal Align	Alt+N
Nudge Grid Down	Minus Sign (numeric keypad)
Nudge Grid Up	Plus Sign (numeric keypad)
NURBS Shaded Lattice Toggle	Alt+L, Ctrl+4
NURBS Tessellation Preset 1	Ctrl+1
NURBS Tessellation Preset 2	Ctrl+2
NURBS Tessellation Preset 3	Ctrl+3
Offset Snap	Alt+Ctrl+Spacebar
Open File	Ctrl+O (the letter o)
Pan View	Ctrl+P
Pan Viewport	I (the letter i)
Perspective User View	P
Place Highlight	Ctrl+H
Play Animation	/ (forward slash)
Quick Render	Shift+Q
Redo Scene Operation	Ctrl+A
Redo Viewport Operation	Shift+A
Redraw All Views	1 (one)
Render Last	Shift+E, F9
Render Scene	Shift+R, F10
Restrict Plane Cycle	F8
Restrict to X	F5
Restrict to Y	F6
Restrict to Z	F7
Right View	R
Rotate View Mode	Ctrl+R, V
Save File	Ctrl+S
See-Through Display Toggle	Alt+X

(continued)

Main User Interface Shortcuts *(continued)*

User Interface Function	Keyboard Shortcut
Select Ancestor	Page Up
Select Child	Page Down
Select by Name Dialog	H
Selection Lock Toggle	Spacebar
Shade Selected Faces Toggle	F2
Show All Grids Toggle	Shift+G
Show Command Panel Toggle	3,Q
Show Floating Toolbars Toggle	4
Show Last Rendering	Ctrl+I (the letter i)
Show Main Toolbar Toggle	Alt+6
Show Safeframes Toggle	Shift+F
Show Tab Panel Toggle	2,Y
Snap Percent Toggle	Shift+Ctrl+P
Snap Toggle	S
Snaps Cycle	Alt+Spacebar
Sound Toggle	\ (backslash)
Spacing Tool	Shift+I (the letter i)
Spot/Directional Light View	Shift+4
Sub-Object Level Cycle	Insert
Sub-Object Selection Toggle	Ctrl+B
Texture Correction	Ctrl+T
Top View	T
Track View Viewport	E
Transform Gizmo Size Down	= (equals sign)
Transform Gizmo Size Up	- (minus sign)
Transform Gizmo Toggle	X
Transform Type-In Dialog	F12
Undo Scene Operation	Ctrl+Z
Undo Viewport Operation	Shift+Z
Unfreeze All	7
Unhide by Name	5
Update Background Image	Alt+Shift+Ctrl+B
View Edged Faces Toggle	F4
Viewport Background	Alt+B
Viewport Box Mode Toggle	Shift+B
Virtual Viewport Pan Down	2 (numeric keypad)
Virtual Viewport Pan Left	4 (numeric keypad)
Virtual Viewport Pan Right	6 (numeric keypad)
Virtual Viewport Pan Up	8 (numeric keypad)
Virtual Viewport Toggle (must be activated for the other Virtual Viewport shortcuts to work)	1 (numeric keypad)
Virtual Viewport Zoom In	7 (numeric keypad)
Virtual Viewport Zoom Out	9 (numeric keypad)

(continued)

Main User Interface Shortcuts *(continued)*

User Interface Function	Keyboard Shortcut
Wireframe / Smooth+Highlights Toggle	F3
Zoom Extents	Alt+Ctrl+Z
Zoom Extents All	Shift+Ctrl+Z
Zoom In 2X	Shift+Plus Sign (numeric keypad)
Zoom Mode	Z
Zoom Out 2X	Shift+Minus Sign (numeric keypad)
Zoom Region Mode	Ctrl+W
Zoom Viewport In	[(open square bracket)
Zoom Viewport Out	] (closed square bracket)

Track View Shortcuts

Track View Function	Keyboard Shortcut
Add Keys	A
Backup Time One Unit	, (comma)
Edit Keys Mode	E
Edit Ranges Mode	F3
Edit Time Mode	F2
Expand Object Toggle	O (the letter o)
Forward Time One Unit	. (period)
Function Curves Mode	F5, F
Lock Selection	Spacebar
Move Highlight Down	Down Arrow
Move Highlight Up	Up Arrow
Nudge Keys Left	Left Arrow
Nudge Keys Right	Right Arrow
Position Ranges Mode	F4
Redo Scene Operation	Ctrl+A
Render Last	F9
Render Scene	F10
Scroll Down	Ctrl+Down Arrow
Scroll Up	Ctrl+Up Arrow
Undo Scene Operation	Ctrl+Z

Material Editor Shortcuts

Material Editor Function	Keyboard Shortcut
Render Last	F9
Render Scene	F10
Undo Scene Operation	Ctrl+Z

Schematic View Shortcuts

Schematic View Function	Keyboard Shortcut
Backup Time One Unit	, (comma)
Forward Time One Unit	. (period)
Redo Scene Operation	Ctrl+A
Undo Scene Operation	Ctrl+Z

ActiveShade Shortcuts

ActiveShade Function	Keyboard Shortcut
Draw Region	D
Initialize	P
Render	R
Toggle Toolbar (Docked)	Spacebar

Video Post Shortcuts

Video Post Function	Keyboard Shortcut
Add Image Filter Event	Ctrl+F
Add Image Input Event	Ctrl+I (the letter i)
Add Image Layer Event	Ctrl+L
Add Image Output Event	Ctrl+O (the letter o)
Add New Event	Ctrl+A
Add Scene Event	Ctrl+S
Edit Current Event	Ctrl+E
Execute Sequence	Ctrl+R
New Sequence	Ctrl+N
Undo Scene Operation	Ctrl+Z

Free-Form Deformation (FFD) Shortcuts

Free-Form Deformation Function	Keyboard Shortcut
Switch to Control Point Level	Alt+Shift+C
Switch to Lattice Level	Alt+Shift+L
Switch to Set Volume Level	Alt+Shift+S
Switch to Top Level	Alt+Shift+T

Reactor Controller Shortcuts

Reactor Controller Function	Keyboard Shortcut
Create Reaction	Alt+Ctrl+C
Delete Reaction	Alt+Ctrl+D
Edit State Toggle	Alt+Ctrl+S
Set Max Influence	Ctrl+I (the letter i)
Set Min Influence	Alt+I (the letter i)
Set Reaction Value	Alt+Ctrl+V

NURBS Shortcuts

Noncustomizable Keyboard Shortcut Function for NURBS	Keyboard Shortcut
Cycle Sub-Object Level	Insert
Delete Sub-Object	Delete

Customizable Keyboard Shortcut Function for NURBS	Keyboard Shortcut
CV Constrained Normal Move	Alt+N
CV Constrained U Move	Alt+U
CV Constrained V Move	Alt+V
Display Curves	Shift+Ctrl+C
Display Dependents	Ctrl+D
Display Lattices	Ctrl+L
Display Shaded Lattice	Alt+L
Display Surfaces	Shift+Ctrl+S
Display Toolbox	Ctrl+T
Display Trims	Shift+Ctrl+T
Local Select Sub-Object by Name (beneath mouse)	Ctrl+H
Lock 2D Selection	Spacebar
Select Next in U	Ctrl+Right Arrow
Select Next in V	Ctrl+Up Arrow
Select Previous in U	Ctrl+Left Arrow
Select Previous in V	Ctrl+Down Arrow
Select Sub-Object by Name	H
Set Custom Tessellation	Alt+4
Set Tessellation Preset 1	Alt+1
Set Tessellation Preset 2	Alt+2
Set Tessellation Preset 3	Alt+3
Soft Selection	Ctrl+S
Switch to Curve CV Level	Alt+Shift+Z
Switch to Curve Level	Alt+Shift+C
Switch to Imports Level	Alt+Shift+I
Switch to Point Level	Alt+Shift+P
Switch to Surface CV Level	Alt+Shift+V
Switch to Surface Level	Alt+Shift+S
Switch to Top (Object) Level	Alt+Shift+T
Transform Degrade	Ctrl+X

Unwrap UVW Shortcuts

Unwrap UVW Function	Keyboard Shortcuts
Break Selected Vertices	Ctrl+B
Detach Edge Vertices	Ctrl+D
Edit UVWs	Ctrl+E
Filter Selected Faces	Ctrl+Spacebar
Flip Horizontal	Alt+Shift+Ctrl+B
Flip Vertical	Alt+Shift+Ctrl+V
Freeze Selected	Ctrl+F
Get Face Selection from Stack	Alt+Shift+Ctrl+F
Hide Selected	Ctrl+H
Load UVW	Alt+Shift+Ctrl+L
Lock Selected Vertices	Spacebar
Mirror Horizontal	Alt+Shift+Ctrl+N
Mirror Vertical	Alt+Shift+Ctrl+M
Move Horizontal	Alt+Shift+Ctrl+J
Move Vertical	Alt+Shift+Ctrl+K
Pan	Ctrl+P
Pixel Snap	S
Planar Map Faces/Patches	| (vertical bar)
Reset UVWs	Alt+Shift+Ctrl+R
Save UVW	Alt+Shift+Ctrl+S
Scale Horizontal	Alt+Shift+Ctrl+I (the letter i)
Scale Vertical	Alt+Shift+Ctrl+O (the letter o)
Texture Vertex Contract Selection	- (minus sign)
Texture Vertex Expand Selection	+ (plus sign)
Texture Vertex Move Mode	Q
Texture Vertex Rotate Mode	W
Texture Vertex Scale Mode	E
Texture Vertex Weld Selected	Alt+Ctrl+W
Texture Vertex Target Weld	Ctrl+W
Unfreeze All	Alt+F
Unhide All	Alt+H
Unwrap Options	Ctrl+O (the letter o)
Update Map	Alt+Shift+Ctrl+M
Zoom	Z
Zoom Extents	Alt+Ctrl+Z
Zoom Region	Ctrl+Z
Zoom Selected Elements	Alt+Shift+Ctrl+Z
Zoom to Gizmo	Shift+Spacebar

Index

A

B

D

E

F

G

H

I

N

O

T

U

What's on the CD-ROM

The companion CD-ROM for *3ds max 4 In Depth* contains elements specifically selected to enhance the usefulness of this book, including:

- All of the MAX files required to complete the exercises in the book, covering the entire 3ds max 4 toolset.
- Supporting files required to augment the exercises in the book.
- Several examples of completed exercises for the reader to compare to his or her work.

Note: The following software (not included on this CD) is required to complete the exercises and tutorials.

- 3ds max 4.

System Requirements

Software

- Windows 98, Windows NT 4.0 SP5, or Windows 2000 (SP1 recommended).
- Internet Explorer 5 (or greater) to access the 3ds max 4 online help files.

Hardware

- An Intel compatible processor running at 300 MHz or better. Under Windows NT or 2000, 3ds max will take advantage of a second processor if present.
- 125 MB RAM minimum. More RAM may be required for complex scenes.
- A minimal amount of hard drive space is required to complete the exercises in the book.
- CD-ROM drive to access the files.
- Microsoft compatible pointing device (Microsoft Intellimouse recommended).
- Sound card and speakers.